BUTTERWORTHS LANDLORD AND TENANT HANDBOOK

SECOND EDITION

Edited by
BUTTERWORTHS EDITORIAL STAFF

Consulting editor
JAMES BOWMAN, LLB
Solicitor

LONDON
BUTTERWORTHS
1987

United Kingdom	Butterworth & Co (Publishers) Ltd, 88 Kingsway, LONDON WC2B 6AB and 61A North Castle Street, EDINBURGH EH2 3LJ
Australia	Butterworths Pty Ltd, SYDNEY, MELBOURNE, BRISBANE, ADELAIDE, PERTH, CANBERRA and HOBART
Canada	Butterworths. A division of Reed Inc, TORONTO and VANCOUVER
New Zealand	Butterworths of New Zealand Ltd, WELLINGTON and AUCKLAND
Singapore	Butterworth & Co (Asia) Pte Ltd, SINGAPORE
South Africa	Butterworth Publishers (Pty) Ltd, DURBAN and PRETORIA
USA	Butterworths Legal Publishers, ST PAUL, Minnesota, SEATTLE, Washington, BOSTON, Massachusetts, AUSTIN, Texas and D & S Publishers, CLEARWATER, Florida

ISBN 0 406 25371 4

Typeset, printed and bound in Great Britain by
William Clowes Limited, Beccles and London

PREFACE

The aim of this book is to make available in a convenient form the statutory texts relating to one of the major fields of practice. It contains both statutes and statutory instruments relating to Landlord and Tenant in their up-to-date form.

The book is divided into two parts: Part I, the Acts, set out in chronological order, and Part II, Statutory Instruments, also in chronological order.

The texts are set out in their current form, with amendments incorporated in the appropriate places, repealed provisions deleted and prospective amendments and repeals indicated. If the sole effect of a section is to amend earlier legislation, the text of that section is not reproduced (the amendments having been incorporated in the earlier legislation). If, however, the amendment is not entirely straightforward or if it is a modification rather than a textual amendment, the text of the amending section is reproduced.

The notes at the end of each section indicate the authority for any amendment of the text. The notes also indicate the date on which each section came into force, except in the case of provisions which were in force before 1 January 1970. Where relevant, the numbers of the commencement orders which apply to the section are given. If a commencement order simply appoints one date, the text of the order is not reproduced: if its effect is partial or transitional, the full text is set out in Part II of the book.

The second edition of the Handbook has been necessitated by the following major legislative changes since 1982: the Rent (Amendment) Act 1985, the consolidation of the Secure Tenancies provisions of the Housing Act 1980 in the Housing Act 1985, Pt IV, the consolidation of the Landlord and Tenant Act 1962 in the Landlord and Tenant Act 1985, the Landlord and Tenant Act 1987, and associated subordinate legislation.

Butterworth & Co
October 1987

CONTENTS

Preface iii

PART I STATUTES

	Para
Common Law Procedure Act 1852	[1]
Statement of Rates Act 1919	[10]
Law of Property Act 1922 (s 145, Sch 15)	[14]
Law of Property Act 1925 (ss 1, 5–6, 8, 40, 44, 48, 52, 54–56, 76–79, 84, 139–154, 196, 205, Sch 2)	[16]
Settled Land Act 1925 (ss 41–48)	[60]
Landlord and Tenant Act 1927	[68]
Leasehold Property (Repairs) Act 1938	[92]
Accommodation Agencies Act 1953	[99]
Landlord and Tenant Act 1954	[101]
Costs of Leases Act 1958	[181]
Leasehold Reform Act 1967	[184]
Defective Premises Act 1972 (ss 4, 6)	[234]
Housing Act 1974 (ss 118, 131, Sch 8)	[236]
Rent (Agriculture) Act 1976	[239]
Rent Act 1977	[289]
Protection from Eviction Act 1977	[434]
Leasehold Reform Act 1979	[448]
Housing Act 1980	[480]
Supreme Court Act 1981 (s 38)	[534]
County Courts Act 1984 (ss 138–140)	[535]
Rent (Amendment) Act 1985	[538]
Housing Act 1985 (ss 79–117, 612–625, Schs 1–3A)	[541]
Landlord and Tenant Act 1985	[605]
Landlord and Tenant Act 1987	[651]

PART II STATUTORY INSTRUMENTS

Renewable Leaseholds Regulations 1925, SR & O 1925/857	[719]
Filing of Leases Rules 1925, SR & O 1925/1128	[721]
Landlord and Tenant (Determination of Rateable Value Procedure) Rules 1954, SI 1954/1255	[734]
Landlord and Tenant (Notices) Regulations 1957, SI 1957/1157	[743]
Leasehold Reform (Notices) Regulations 1967, SI 1967/1768	[763]
Leasehold Reform (Enfranchisement and Extension) Regulations 1967, SI 1967/1879	[775]
Rent (County Court Proceedings) Rules 1970, SI 1970/1851	[781]
Rent Assessment Committees (England and Wales) Regulations 1971, SI 1971/1065	[814]

Secure Tenancies (Designated Courses) Regulations 1980, SI 1980/1407 . . . [826]
Notices to Quit (Prescribed Information) Regulations 1980, SI 1980/1624 . . . [828]
Assured Tenancies (Approved Body) (No 1) Order 1980, SI 1980/1694 . . . [831]
Rent Act 1977 (Forms etc) Regulations 1980, SI 1980/1697 . . . [833]
Rent Regulation (Cancellation of Registration of Rent) Regulations 1980, SI 1980/1698 . . . [860]
Rent Assessment Committees (England and Wales) (Rent Tribunal) Regulations 1980, SI 1980/1700 . . . [865]
Rent Act (County Court Proceedings for Possession) Rules 1981, SI 1981/139 . . . [874]
Rent Assessment Committee (England and Wales) (Leasehold Valuation Tribunal) Regulations 1981, SI 1981/271 . . . [883]
Assured Tenancies (Approved Body) (No 1) Order 1981, SI 1981/590 . . . [897]
Assured Tenancies (Notice to Tenant) Regulations 1981, SI 1981/591 . . . [899]
Assured Tenancies (Approved Body) (No 2) Order 1981, SI 1981/1009 . . . [902]
Rent Assessment Committees (England and Wales) (Amendment) Regulations 1981, SI 1981/1783 . . . [904]
Housing (Exclusion of Shared Ownership Tenancies from the Leasehold Reform Act 1967) Regulations 1982, SI 1982/62 . . . [907]
Assured Tenancies (Approved Bodies) (No 1) Order 1982, SI 1982/582 . . . [910]
Assured Tenancies (Approved Body) (No 2) Order 1982, SI 1982/850 . . . [913]
Rent Regulation (Local Authority Applications) Regulations 1982, SI 1982/1015 . . . [915]
Assured Tenancies (Approved Bodies) (No 3) Order 1982, SI 1982/1016 . . . [934]
Assured Tenancies (Approved Bodies) (No 4) Order 1982, SI 1982/1229 . . . [937]
Rent Book (Forms of Notice) Regulations 1982, SI 1982/1474 . . . [940]
Assured Tenancies (Approved Bodies) (No 5) Order 1982, SI 1982/1481 . . . [947]
Assured Tenancies (Approved Bodies) (No 6) Order 1982, SI 1982/1551 . . . [950]
Assured Tenancies (Approved Bodies) (No 7) Order 1982, SI 1982/1638 . . . [953]
Assured Tenancies (Approved Bodies) (No 8) Order 1982, SI 1982/1815 . . . [956]
Assured Tenancies (Approved Bodies) (No 1) Order 1983, SI 1983/19 . . . [959]
Assured Tenancies (Approved Bodies) (No 2) Order 1983, SI 1983/88 . . . [962]
Landlord and Tenant Act 1954, Part II (Notices) Regulations 1983, SI 1983/133 . . . [965]

Assured Tenancies (Approved Bodies) (No 3) Order 1983, SI 1983/364 . . . [989]
Assured Tenancies (Approved Bodies) (No 4) Order 1983, SI 1983/511 . . . [992]
Assured Tenancies (Approved Bodies) (No 5) Order 1983, SI 1983/840 . . . [995]
Assured Tenancies (Approved Bodies) (No 6) Order 1983, SI 1983/1079 . . . [998]
Assured Tenancies (Approved Bodies) (No 7) Order 1983, SI 1983/1375 . . . [1001]
Assured Tenancies (Approved Bodies) (No 8) Order 1983, SI 1983/1537 . . . [1004]
Assured Tenancies (Approved Bodies) (No 9) Order 1983, SI 1983/1856 . . . [1007]
Assured Tenancies (Approved Bodies) (No 1) Order 1984, SI 1984/276 . . . [1010]
Assured Tenancies (Approved Bodies) (No 2) Order 1984, SI 1984/638 . . . [1013]
Assured Tenancies (Approved Bodies) (No 3) Order 1984, SI 1984/1312 . . . [1016]
Assured Tenancies (Approved Bodies) (No 4) Order 1984, SI 1984/1827 . . . [1019]
Landlord and Tenant (Appropriate Multiplier) Order 1984, SI 1984/1932 . . . [1022]
Assured Tenancies (Approved Bodies) (No 1) Order 1985, SI 1985/812 . . . [1025]
Assured Tenancies (Approved Bodies) (No 2) Order 1985, SI 1985/1312 . . . [1028]
Secure Tenancies (Right to Repair Scheme) Regulations 1985, SI 1985/1493 . . . [1031]
Protected Tenancies (Exceptions) Regulations 1986, SI 1986/541 . [1043]
Assured Tenancies (Approved Bodies) (No 1) Order 1986, SI 1986/866 . . . [1048]
Assured Tenancies (Approved Bodies) (No 2) Order 1986, SI 1986/1209 . . . [1051]
Assured Tenancies (Approved Bodies) (No 3) Order 1986, SI 1986/1729 . . . [1054]
Landlord and Tenant Act 1954, Part II (Assured Tenancies) (Notices) Regulations 1986, SI 1986/2181 . . . [1057]
Assured Tenancies (Approved Bodies) (No 4) Order 1986, SI 1986/2240 . . . [1064]
Assured Tenancies (Prescribed Amount) Order 1987, SI 1987/122 . [1067]
Rent (Relief from Phasing) Order 1987, SI 1987/264 . . . [1070]
Protected Shorthold Tenancies (Rent Registration) Order 1987, SI 1987/265 . . . [1075]
Rent Act 1977 (Forms etc) (Amendment) Regulations 1987, SI 1987/266 . . . [1078]
Protected Shorthold Tenancies (Notice to Tenant) Regulations 1987, SI 1987/267 . . . [1081]

Assured Tenancies (Approved Bodies) (No 1) Order 1987, SI 1987/737 . . . . [1085]
Secure Tenancies (Notices) Regulations 1987, SI 1987/755 . . [1088]
Assured Tenancies (Approved Bodies) (No 2) Order 1987, SI 1987/822 . . . . [1092]
Assured Tenancies (Approved Bodies) (No 3) Order 1987, SI 1987/1164 . . . . [1095]
Assured Tenancies (Approved Bodies) (No 4) Order 1987, SI 1987/1525 . . . . [1098]

Index

PART I
STATUTES

COMMON LAW PROCEDURE ACT 1852
(c 76)

ARRANGEMENT OF SECTIONS

EJECTMENT

Section		Para
210	Proceedings in ejectment by landlord for non-payment of rent	[1]
211	Lessee proceeding in equity not to have injunction or relief without payment of rent and costs	[2]
212	Tenant paying all rent, with costs, proceedings to cease	[3]
214	On trial of any ejectment between landlord and tenant, juries to give damages for mesne profits down to the verdict, or to a day specified therein	[4]
218	Saving of former remedies	[5]
221	Jurisdiction of courts and judges	[6]
227	Interpretation of terms	[7]
235	Short title of Act	[8]
236	Act not to extend to Ireland or Scotland	[9]

An Act to amend the Process, Practice, and Mode of Pleading in the Superior Courts of Common Law at Westminster, and in the Superior Courts of the Counties Palatine of Lancaster and Durham [30 June 1852]

EJECTMENT

210. Proceedings in ejectment by landlord for non-payment of rent

In all cases between landlord and tenant, as often as it shall happen that one half year's rent shall be in arrear, and the landlord or lessor, to whom the same is due, hath right by law to re-enter for the non-payment thereof, such landlord or lessor shall and may, without any formal demand or re-entry, serve a writ in ejectment for the recovery of the demised premises, . . . which service . . . shall stand in the place and stead of a demand and re-entry; and in case of judgment against the defendant for nonappearance, if it shall be made appear to the court where the said action is depending, by affidavit, or be proved upon the trial in case the defendant appears, that half a year's rent was due before the said writ was served, and that no sufficient distress was to be found on the demised premises, countervailing the arrears then due, and that the lessor had power to re-enter, then and in every such case the lessor shall recover judgment and execution, in the same manner as if the rent in arrear had been legally demanded, and a re-entry made; and in case the lessee or his assignee, or other person claiming or deriving under the said lease, shall permit and suffer judgment to be had and recovered on such trial in ejectment, and execution to be executed thereon, without paying the rent and arrears, together with full costs, and without proceeding for relief in equity within six months after such execution executed, then and in such case the said lessee, his assignee, and all other persons claiming and deriving under the said lease, shall be barred and foreclosed from all relief or remedy in law or equity, other than by bringing error for reversal of such judgment, in case the same shall be erroneous, and the said landlord or lessor shall from thenceforth hold the said demised premises discharged from such lease; . . . provided that nothing herein contained shall extend to bar the right of any mortgagee of such lease, or any part thereof, who shall not be in possession, so as such mortgagee shall and do, within six months after such judgment obtained and execution executed pay all rent in arrear, and all costs and damages sustained by such lessor or person entitled to the remainder or reversion as aforesaid, and perform all the covenants and agreements which, on the part and behalf of the first lessee, are and ought to be performed. **[1]**

NOTES

Words omitted repealed with savings by the Statute Law Revision Act 1892.

211. Lessee proceeding in equity not to have injunction or relief without payment of rent and costs

In case the said lessee, his assignee, or other person claiming any right, title, or interest, in law or equity, of, in, or to the said lease, shall, within the time aforesaid, proceed for relief in any court of equity, such person shall not have or continue any injunction against the proceedings at law on such ejectment, unless he does or shall, within forty days next after a full and perfect answer shall be made by the claimant in such ejectment, bring into court, and lodge with the proper officer such sum and sums of money as the lessor or landlord shall in his answer swear to be due and in arrear over and above all just allowances, and also the costs taxed in the said suit, there to remain till the hearing of the cause, or to be paid out to the lessor or landlord on good security, subject to the decree of the court; and in case such proceedings for relief in equity shall be taken within the time aforesaid, and after execution is executed, the lessor or landlord shall be accountable only for so much and no more as he shall really and bona fide, without fraud, deceit, or wilful neglect, make of the demised premises from the time of his entering into the actual possession thereof; and if what shall be so made by the lessor or landlord happen to be less than the rent reserved on the said lease, then the said lessee or his assignee, before he shall be restored to his possession, shall pay such lessor or landlord, what the money so by him made fell short of the reserved rent for the time such lessor or landlord held the said lands. **[2]**

212. Tenant paying all rent, with costs, proceedings to cease

If the tenant or his assignee do or shall, at any time before the trial in such ejectment, pay or tender to the lessor or landlord, his executors or administrators, or his or their attorney in that cause, or pay into the court where the same cause is depending, all the rent and arrears, together with the costs, then and in such case all further proceedings on the said ejectment shall cease and be discontinued; and if such lessee, his executors, administrators, or assigns, shall, upon such proceedings as aforesaid, be relieved in equity, he and they shall have, hold, and enjoy the demised lands, according to the lease thereof made, without any new lease. **[3]**

214. On trial of any ejectment between landlord and tenant, juries to give damages for mesne profits down to the verdict, or to a day specified therein

Wherever it shall appear on the trial of any ejectment, at the suit of a landlord against a tenant, that such tenant or his attorney hath been served with due notice of trial, the judge before whom such cause shall come on to be tried shall, whether the defendant shall appear upon such trial or not, permit the claimant on the trial, after proof of his right to recover possession of the whole or of any part of the premises mentioned in the writ in ejectment, to go into evidence of the mesne profits thereof which shall or might have accrued from the day of the expiration or determination of the tenant's interest in the same down to the time of the verdict given in the cause, or to some preceding day to be specially mentioned therein; and the jury on the trial finding for the claimant shall in such case give their verdict upon the whole matter, both as to the recovery of the whole or any part of the premises, and also as to the amount of the damages to be paid for such mesne profits; and in such case the landlord shall have judgment within the time herein-before provided, not only for the recovery of possession and costs, but also for the mesne profits found by the jury: Provided always, that nothing herein-before contained shall be construed to bar any such landlord from bringing any action for the mesne profits which shall accrue from the verdict, or the day so specified therein down to the day of the delivery of possession of the premises recovered in the ejectment. **[4]**

218. Saving of former remedies

Nothing herein contained shall be construed to prejudice or affect any other right of action or remedy which landlords may possess in any of the cases herein-before provided for, otherwise than herein-before expressly enacted. **[5]**

221. Jurisdiction of courts and judges

The several courts and the judges thereof respectively shall and may exercise over the proceedings the like jurisdiction as heretofore exercised in the action of ejectment, so as to ensure a trial of the title, and of actual ouster, when necessary, only, and for all other purposes for which such jurisdiction may at present be exercised; and the provisions of all statutes not inconsistent with the provisions of this Act, and which may be applicable to the altered mode of proceeding, shall remain in force and be applied thereto. **[6]**

NOTES

Repealed with savings by the Statute Law Revision and Civil Procedure Act 1883, s 3, Schedule.

227. Interpretation of terms

In the construction of this Act the word "court" shall be understood to mean any one of the Superior Courts of Common Law at Westminster in which any action is brought; and the word "judge" shall be understood to mean a judge or baron of any of the said courts; and the word "master" shall be understood to mean a master of any of the said courts; and the word "action" shall be understood to mean any personal action brought by writ of summons in any of the said courts; and no part of the United Kingdom of Great Britain and Ireland, nor the Islands of Man, Guernsey, Jersey, Alderney, or Sark, nor any Islands adjacent to any of them, being part of the Dominions of Her Majesty, shall be deemed to be "beyond the seas" within the meaning of this Act: And wherever in this Act, in describing or referring to any person or party, matter or thing, any word importing the singular number or masculine gender is used, the same shall be understood to include and shall be applicable to several persons and parties as well as one person or party, and females as well as males, and bodies corporate as well as individuals, and several matters and things as well as one matter or thing, unless it otherwise be provided, or there be something in the subject or context repugnant to such construction. **[7]**

NOTES

Repealed with savings by the Statute Law Revision and Civil Procedure Act 1883, s 3, Schedule.

235. Short title of Act

In citing this Act in any instrument, document, or proceeding, it shall be sufficient to use the expression "The Common Law Procedure Act 1852." **[8]**

236. Act not to extend to Ireland or Scotland

Nothing in this Act shall extend to Ireland or Scotland . . . **[9]**

NOTES
Words omitted repealed by the Statute Law Revision Act 1892.

STATEMENT OF RATES ACT 1919

(c 31)

ARRANGEMENT OF SECTIONS

Section		Para
1	Provisions with respect to demands and receipts for rent in which any sum for rates is included	[10]
2	Definition	[11]
3	Penalty	[12]
4	Short title, commencement and extent	[13]

An Act to provide for the information to occupiers of the amount of the rates payable for the houses which they occupy [22 July 1919]

1. Provisions with respect to demands and receipts for rent in which any sum for rates is included

(1) . . . every document containing a demand for rent or receipt for rent, which includes any sum for rates paid or payable under any statutory enactment by the owner instead of the occupier, shall state either the annual, half yearly, quarterly, monthly, or weekly amount of such rates paid or payable in accordance with the last demands received by the owner from the rating authorities at the time of making his demand or giving his receipt in respect of the hereditament in question: Provided that, where such a statement as is required by this section has been furnished in connection with a demand for rent or receipt for rent in respect of a particular period, it shall not be necessary to furnish the statement upon any subsequent demand for rent or receipt for rent in respect of that period.

(2) This Act shall not apply to weekly lettings at inclusive rentals in any market established under or controlled by statute. **[10]**

NOTES
Words omitted repealed by the Statute Law Revision Act 1927.

2. Definition

The expressions "demand for rent" and "receipt for rent" shall include a rent-book, rent-card and any document used for the notification or collection of rent due or for the acknowledgment of the receipt of the same. **[11]**

3. Penalty

If any person makes a demand for rent or gives a receipt for rent in contravention of this Act, he shall, in respect of each offence, be liable on summary conviction to a fine of not exceeding [level 1 on the standard scale]. **[12]**

NOTES
Maximum fine increased by the Criminal Law Act 1977, s 31(6), and converted to a level on the standard scale by the Criminal Justice Act 1982, ss 37, 46.

4. Short title, commencement and extent

(1) This Act may be cited as the Statement of Rates Act 1919.

(2) . . .

(3) This Act shall not extend to Scotland or Ireland. **[13]**

NOTES
Sub-s (2): repealed by the Statute Law Revision Act 1927.

LAW OF PROPERTY ACT 1922
(c 16)

An Act to assimilate and amend the law of Real and Personal Estate, to abolish copyhold and other special tenures, to amend the law relating to commonable lands and of intestacy, and to amend the Wills Act 1837, the Settled Land Acts 1882 to 1890, the Conveyancing Acts 1881 to 1911, the Trustee Act 1893, and the Land Transfer Acts 1875 and 1897 [29 June 1922]

PART VII

PROVISIONS RESPECTING LEASEHOLDS

Conversion of Perpetually Renewable Leaseholds into Long Terms

145. Conversion of perpetually renewable leaseholds

For the purpose of converting perpetually renewable leases and underleases (not being an interest in perpetually renewable copyhold land enfranchised by Part V of this Act, but including a perpetually renewable underlease derived out of an interest in perpetually renewable copyhold land) into long terms, for preventing the creation of perpetually renewable leasehold interests and for providing for the interests of the persons affected, the provisions contained in the Fifteenth Schedule to this Act shall have effect. **[14]**

SCHEDULES

SCHEDULE 15

Section 145

PROVISIONS RELATING TO PERPETUALLY RENEWABLE LEASES AND UNDERLEASES

Conversion of perpetually renewable leases into long terms

(1) Land comprised in a perpetually renewable lease which was subsisting at the commencement of this Act shall, by virtue of this Act, vest in the person who at such commencement was entitled to such lease, for a term of two thousand years, to be calculated from the date at which the existing term or interest commenced, at the rent and subject to the lessees' covenants and conditions (if any) which under the lease would have been payable or enforceable during the subsistence of such term or interest.

(2) The rent, covenants and conditions (if any) shall (subject to the express provisions of this Act to the contrary) be payable and enforceable during the subsistence of the term created by this Act; and that term shall take effect in substitution for the term or interest created by the lease, and be subject to the like power of re-entry (if any) and other provisions which affected the term or interest created by the lease, but without any right of renewal. **[15]**

LAW OF PROPERTY ACT 1925
(c 20)

ARRANGEMENT OF SECTIONS

PART I
GENERAL PRINCIPLES AS TO LEGAL ESTATES, EQUITABLE INTERESTS AND POWERS

Section		Para
1	Legal estates and equitable interests	[16]
5	Satisfied terms, whether created out of freehold or leasehold land to cease	[17]
6	Saving of lessors' and lessees' covenants	[18]
8	Saving of certain legal powers to lease	[19]

PART II
CONTRACTS, CONVEYANCES AND OTHER INSTRUMENTS

Contracts

40	Contracts for sale, etc, of land to be in writing	[20]
44	Statutory commencements of title	[21]
48	Stipulations preventing a purchaser, lessee, or underlessee from employing his own solicitor to be void	[22]

Conveyances and other Instruments

52	Conveyances to be by deed	[23]
54	Creation of interests in land by parol	[24]
55	Savings in regard to last two sections	[25]
56	Persons taking who are not parties and as to indentures	[26]

Covenants

76	Covenants for title	[27]
77	Implied covenants in conveyance subject to rents	[28]
78	Benefit of covenants relating to land	[29]
79	Burden of covenants relating to land	[30]
84	Power to discharge or modify restrictive covenants affecting land	[31]

PART V
LEASES AND TENANCIES

139	Effect of extinguishment of reversion	[32]
140	Apportionment of conditions on severance	[33]
141	Rent and benefit of lessee's covenants to run with the reversion	[34]
142	Obligation of lessor's covenants to run with reversion	[35]
143	Effect of licences granted to lessees	[36]
144	No fine to be exacted for licence to assign	[37]
145	Lessee to give notice of ejectment to lessor	[38]
146	Restrictions on and relief against forfeiture of leases and underleases	[39]
147	Relief against notice to effect decorative repairs	[40]
148	Waiver of a covenant in a lease	[41]
149	Abolition of interesse termini, and as to reversionary leases and leases for lives	[42]
150	Surrender of a lease, without prejudice to underleases with a view to the grant of a new lease	[43]
151	Provision as to attornments by tenants	[44]
152	Leases invalidated by reason of non-compliance with terms of powers under which they are granted	[45]
153	Enlargement of residue of long terms into fee simple estates	[46]
154	Application of Part V to existing leases	[47]

Section Para

PART XI

MISCELLANEOUS

Notices

196 Regulations respecting notices .. .. [48]

PART XII

CONSTRUCTION, JURISDICTION, AND GENERAL PROVISIONS

205 General definitions .. .. [49]

SCHEDULES

Second Schedule—*Implied Covenants* .. ..

Part I—Covenant implied in a Conveyance for valuable Consideration, other than a Mortgage, by a Person who Conveys and is expressed to Convey as Beneficial Owner .. .. [50]

Part II—Further Covenant Implied in a Conveyance of Leasehold Property for valuable Consideration, other than a Mortgage, by a person who Conveys and is expressed to Convey as Beneficial Owner .. .. [51]

Part III—Covenant Implied in a Conveyance by way of Mortgage by a Person who Conveys and is expressed to Convey as Beneficial Owner .. [52]

Part IV—Covenant implied in a Conveyance by way of Mortgage of Freehold Property subject to a Rent or of Leasehold Property by a Person who Conveys and is expressed to Convey as Beneficial Owner .. .. [53]

Part V—Covenant implied in a Conveyance by way of Settlement, by a Person who Conveys and is expressed to Convey as Settlor .. .. .. [54]

Part VI—Covenant implied in any Conveyance, by every person who Conveys and is expressed to Convey as Trustee or Mortgagee, or as Personal Representative of a Deceased Person, ... or under an Order of the Court .. .. [55]

Part VII—Covenant Implied in a Conveyance for valuable consideration, other than a Mortgage, of the Entirety of Land affected by a Rentcharge .. [56]

Part VIII—Covenants implied in a Conveyance for valuable Consideration, other than a Mortgage, or Part of Land affected by a Rentcharge, subject to a Part (not legally apportioned) of that Rentcharge .. [57]

Part IX—Covenant in a Conveyance for valuable Consideration, other than a Mortgage, of the Entirety of the Land comprised in a Lease for the Residue of the Term or Interest created by the Lease .. .. .. [58]

Part X—Covenants implied in a Conveyance for Valuable Consideration, other than a Mortgage, of Part of the Land comprised in a Lease, for the Residue of the Term or Interest created by the Lease, subject to a Part (not legally apportioned) of that Rent .. .. [59]

An Act to consolidate the enactments relating to Conveyancing and the Law of Property in England and Wales [9 April 1925]

PART I

GENERAL PRINCIPLES AS TO LEGAL ESTATES, EQUITABLE INTERESTS AND POWERS

1. Legal estates and equitable interests

(1) The only estates in land which are capable of subsisting or of being conveyed or created at law are—

(*a*) An estate in fee simple absolute in possession;
(*b*) A term of years absolute.

(2) The only interests or charges in or over land which are capable of subsisting or of being conveyed or created at law are—

(*a*) An easement, right, or privilege in or over land for an interest equivalent to an estate in fee simple absolute in possession or a term of years absolute;
(*b*) A rentcharge in possession issuing out of or charged on land being either perpetual or for a term of years absolute;
(*c*) A charge by way of legal mortgage;
(*d*) . . . and any other similar charge on land which is not created by an instrument;
(*e*) Rights of entry exercisable over or in respect of a legal term of years absolute, or annexed, for any purpose, to a legal rentcharge.

(3) All other estates, interests, and charges in or over land take effect as equitable interests.

(4) The estates, interests, and charges which under this section are authorised to subsist or to be conveyed or created at law are (when subsisting or conveyed or created at law) in this Act referred to as "legal estates," and have the same incidents as legal estates subsisting at the commencement of this Act; and the owner of a legal estate is referred to as "an estate owner" and his legal estate is referred to as his estate.

(5) A legal estate may subsist concurrently with or subject to any other legal estate in the same land in like manner as it could have done before the commencement of this Act.

(6) A legal estate is not capable of subsisting or of being created in an undivided share in land or of being held by an infant.

(7) Every power of appointment over, or power to convey or charge land or any interest therein, whether created by a statute or other instrument or implied by law, and whether created before or after the commencement of this Act (not being a power vested in a legal mortgagee or an estate owner in right of his estate and exercisable by him or by another person in his name and on his behalf), operates only in equity.

(8) Estates, interests, and charges in or over land which are not legal estates are in this Act referred to as "equitable interests", and powers which by this Act are to operate in equity only are in this Act referred to as "equitable powers."

(9) The provisions in any statute or other instrument requiring land to be conveyed to uses shall take effect as directions that the land shall (subject to creating or reserving thereout any legal estate authorised by this Act which may be required) be conveyed to a person of full age upon the requisite trusts.

(10) The repeal of the Statute of Uses (as amended) does not affect the operation thereof in regard to dealings taking effect before the commencement of this Act. **[16]**

NOTES
Sub-s (2): words omitted repealed by the Finance Act 1963, s 73(8)(*b*), Sch 14 and the Tithe Act 1936, s 48(3), Sch 9.

5. Satisfied terms, whether created out of freehold or leasehold land to cease

(1) Where the purposes of a term of years created or limited at any time out of freehold land, become satisfied either before or after the commencement of this Act (whether or not that term either by express declaration or by construction

of law becomes attendant upon the freehold reversion) it shall merge in the reversion expectant thereon and shall cease accordingly.

(2) Where the purposes of a term of years created or limited, at any time, out of leasehold land, become satisfied after the commencement of this Act, that term shall merge in the reversion expectant thereon and shall cease accordingly.

(3) Where the purposes are satisfied only as respects part of the land comprised in a term, this section shall have effect as if a separate term had been created in regard to that part of the land. **[17]**

6. Saving of lessors' and lessees' covenants

(1) Nothing in this Part of this Act affects prejudicially the right to enforce any lessor's or lessee's covenants, agreements or conditions (including a valid option to purchase or right of pre-emption over the reversion), contained in any such instrument as is in this section mentioned, the benefit or burden of which runs with the reversion or the term.

(2) This section applies where the covenant, agreement or condition is contained in any instrument—

(*a*) creating a term of years absolute, or
(*b*) varying the rights of the lessor or lessee under the instrument creating the term. **[18]**

8. Saving of certain legal powers to lease

(1) All leases or tenancies at a rent for a term of years absolute authorised to be granted by a mortgagor or mortgagee or by the Settled Land Act 1925, or any other statute (whether or not extended by any instrument) may be granted in the name and on behalf of the estate owner by the person empowered to grant the same, whether being an estate owner or not, with the same effect and priority as if this Part of this Act had not been passed; but this section does not (except as respects the usual qualified covenant for quiet enjoyment) authorise any person granting a lease in the name of an estate owner to impose any personal liability on him.

(2) Where a rentcharge is held for a legal estate, the owner thereof may under the statutory power or under any corresponding power, create a legal term of years absolute for securing or compelling payment of the same; but in other cases terms created under any such power shall, unless and until the estate owner of the land charged gives legal effect to the transaction, take effect only as equitable interests. **[19]**

Part II

Contracts, Conveyances and other Instruments

Contracts

40. Contracts for sale, etc, of land to be in writing

(1) No action may be brought upon any contract for the sale or other disposition of land or any interest in land, unless the agreement upon which such action is brought, or some memorandum or note thereof, is in writing, and signed by the party to be charged or by some other person thereunto by him lawfully authorised.

(2) This section applies to contracts whether made before or after the commencement of this Act and does not affect the law relating to part performance, or sales by the court. **[20]**

44. Statutory commencements of title

(1) After the commencement of this Act [fifteen years] shall be substituted for forty years as the period of commencement of title which a purchaser of land may require; nevertheless earlier title than [fifteen years] may be required in cases similar to those in which earlier title than forty years might immediately before the commencement of this Act be required.

(2) Under a contract to grant or assign a term of years, whether derived or to be derived out of freehold or leasehold land, the intended lessee or assign shall not be entitled to call for the title to the freehold.

(3) Under a contract to sell and assign a term of years derived out of a leasehold interest in land, the intended assign shall not have the right to call for the title to the leasehold reversion.

(4) On a contract to grant a lease for a term of years to be derived out of a leasehold interest, with a leasehold reversion, the intended lessee shall not have the right to call for the title to that reversion.

(5) Where by reason of any of the three last preceding subsections, an intending lessee or assign is not entitled to call for the title to the freehold or to a leasehold reversion, as the case may be, he shall not, where the contract is made after the commencement of this Act, be deemed to be affected with notice of any matter or thing of which, if he had contracted that such title should be furnished, he might have had notice.

(6) Where land of copyhold or customary tenure has been converted into freehold by enfranchisement, then, under a contract to sell and convey the freehold, the purchaser shall not have the right to call for the title to make the enfranchisement.

(7) Where the manorial incidents formerly affecting any land have been extinguished, then, under a contract to sell and convey the freehold, the purchaser shall not have the right to call for the title of the person entering into any compensation agreement or giving a receipt for the compensation money to enter into such agreement or to give such receipt, and shall not be deemed to be affected with notice of any matter or thing of which, if he had contracted that such title should be furnished, he might have had notice.

(8) A purchaser shall not be deemed to be or ever to have been affected with notice of any matter or thing of which, if he had investigated the title or made enquiries in regard to matters prior to the period of commencement of title fixed by this Act, or by any other statute, or by any rule of law, he might have had notice, unless he actually makes such investigation or enquiries.

(9) Where a lease whether made before or after the commencement of this Act, is made under a power contained in a settlement, will, Act of Parliament, or other instrument, any preliminary contract for or relating to the lease shall not, for the purpose of the deduction of title to an intended assign, form part of the title, or evidence of the title, to the lease.

(10) This section, save where otherwise expressly provided, applies to contracts for sale whether made before or after the commencement of this Act, and applies to contracts for exchange in like manner as to contracts for sale,

save that it applies only to contracts for exchange made after such commencement.

(11) This section applies only if and so far as a contrary intention is not expressed in the contract. **[21]**

NOTES

Sub-s (1): amended by the Law of Property Act 1969, s 23 in relation to contracts made after 1 January 1970.

48. Stipulations preventing a purchaser, lessee, or underlessee from employing his own solicitor to be void

(1) Any stipulation made on the sale of any interest in land after the commencement of this Act to the effect that the conveyance to, or the registration of the title of, the purchaser shall be prepared or carried out at the expense of the purchaser by a solicitor appointed by or acting for the vendor, and any stipulation which might restrict a purchaser in the selection of a solicitor to act on his behalf in relation to any interest in land agreed to be purchased, shall be void; and, if a sale is effected by demise or subdemise, then, for the purposes of this subsection, the instrument required for giving effect to the transaction shall be deemed to be a conveyance:

Provided that nothing in this subsection shall affect any right reserved to a vendor to furnish a form of conveyance to a purchaser from which the draft can be prepared, or to charge a reasonable fee therefor, or, where a perpetual rentcharge is to be reserved as the only consideration in money or money's worth, the right of a vendor to stipulate that the draft conveyance is to be prepared by his solicitor at the expense of the purchaser.

(2) Any covenant or stipulation contained in, or entered into with reference to any lease or underlease made before or after the commencement of this Act—

(*a*) whereby the right of preparing, at the expense of a purchaser, any conveyance of the estate or interest of the lessee or underlessee in the demised premises or in any part thereof, or of otherwise carrying out, at the expense of the purchaser, any dealing with such estate or interest, is expressed to be reserved to or vested in the lessor or underlessor or his solicitor; or

(*b*) which in any way restricts the right of the purchaser to have such conveyance carried out on his behalf by a solicitor appointed by him;

shall be void:

Provided that, where any covenant or stipulation is rendered void by this subsection, there shall be implied in lieu thereof a covenant or stipulation that the lessee or underlessee shall register with the lessor or his solicitor within six months from the date thereof, or as soon after the expiration of that period as may be practicable, all conveyances and devolutions (including probates or letters of administration) affecting the lease or underlease and pay a fee of one guinea in respect of each registration, and the power of entry (if any) on breach of any covenant contained in the lease or underlease shall apply and extend to the breach of any covenant so to be implied.

(3) Save where a sale is effected by demise or subdemise, this section does not affect the law relating to the preparation of a lease or underlease or the draft thereof.

(4) In this section "lease" and "underlease" include any agreement therefor or other tenancy, and "lessee" and "underlessee" and "lessor" and "underlessor" have corresponding meanings. **[22]**

NOTES
Modified by the Building Societies Act 1986, s 124, Sch 21, paras 9, 12.
See further: Administration of Justice Act 1985, ss 9, 34(2), Sch 2, para 37.

Conveyances and other Instruments

52. Conveyances to be by deed

(1) All conveyances of land or of any interest therein are void for the purpose of conveying or creating a legal estate unless made by deed.

(2) This section does not apply to—
(*a*) assents by a personal representative;
(*b*) disclaimers made in accordance with [sections 178 to 180 or sections 315 to 319 of the Insolvency Act 1986] or not required to be evidenced in writing;
(*c*) surrenders by operation of law, including surrenders which may, by law, be effected without writing;
(*d*) leases or tenancies or other assurances not required by law to be made in writing;
(*e*) receipts not required by law to be under seal;
(*f*) vesting orders of the court or other competent authority;
(*g*) conveyances taking effect by operation of law. **[23]**

NOTES
Words in italics repealed with savings by the Insolvency Act 1985, s 235, Sch 8, para 4 and the Insolvency Act 1986, s 437, Sch 11; amendment in square brackets made by the Insolvency Act 1986, s 439(2), Sch 14.

54. Creation of interests in land by parol

(1) All interests in land created by parol and not put in writing and signed by the persons so creating the same, or by their agents thereunto lawfully authorised in writing, have, notwithstanding any consideration having been given for the same, the force and effect of interests at will only.

(2) Nothing in the foregoing provisions of this Part of this Act shall affect the creation by parol of leases taking effect in possession for a term not exceeding three years (whether or not the lessee is given power to extend the term) at the best rent which can be reasonably obtained without taking a fine. **[24]**

55. Savings in regard to last two sections

Nothing in the last two foregoing sections shall—
(*a*) invalidate dispositions by will; or
(*b*) affect any interest validly created before the commencement of this Act; or
(*c*) affect the right to acquire an interest in land by virtue of taking possession; or
(*d*) affect the operation of the law relating to part performance. **[25]**

56. Persons taking who are not parties and as to indentures

(1) A person may take an immediate or other interest in land or other property, or the benefit of any condition, right of entry, covenant or agreement over or

respecting land or other property, although he may not be named as a party to the conveyance or other instrument.

(2) A deed between parties, to effect its objects, has the effect of an indenture though not indented or expressed to be an indenture. **[26]**

Covenants

76. Covenants for title

(1) In a conveyance there shall, in the several cases in this section mentioned, be deemed to be included, and there shall in those several cases, by virtue of this Act, be implied, a covenant to the effect in this section stated, by the person or by each person who conveys, as far as regards the subject-matter or share of subject-matter expressed to be conveyed by him, with the person, if one, to whom the conveyance is made, or with the persons jointly, if more than one, to whom the conveyance is made as joint tenants, or with each of the persons, if more than one, to whom the conveyance is (when the law permits) made as tenants in common, that is to say:

(A) In a conveyance for valuable consideration, other than a mortgage, a covenant by a person who conveys and is expressed to convey as beneficial owner in the terms set out in Part I of the Second Schedule to this Act;

(B) In a conveyance of leasehold property for valuable consideration, other than a mortgage, a further covenant by a person who conveys and is expressed to convey as beneficial owner in the terms set out in Part II of the Second Schedule to this Act;

(C) In a conveyance by way of mortgage (including a charge) a covenant by a person who conveys or charges and is expressed to convey or charge as beneficial owner in the terms set out in Part III of the Second Schedule to this Act;

(D) In a conveyance by way of mortgage (including a charge) of freehold property subject to a rent or of leasehold property, a further covenant by a person who conveys or charges and is expressed to convey or charge as beneficial owner in the terms set out in Part IV of the Second Schedule to this Act;

(E) In a conveyance by way of settlement, a covenant by a person who conveys and is expressed to convey as settlor in the terms set out in Part V of the Second Schedule to this Act;

(F) In any conveyance, a covenant by every person who conveys and is expressed to convey as trustee or mortgagee, or as personal representative of a deceased person, . . . or under an order of the court, in the terms set out in Part VI of the Second Schedule to this Act, which covenant shall be deemed to extend to every such person's own acts only, and may be implied in an assent by a personal representative in like manner as in a conveyance by deed.

(2) Where in a conveyance it is expressed that by direction of a person expressed to direct as beneficial owner another person conveys, then, for the purposes of this section, the person giving the direction, whether he conveys and is expressed to convey as beneficial owner or not, shall be deemed to convey and to be expressed to convey as beneficial owner the subject-matter so conveyed by his direction; and a covenant on his part shall be implied accordingly.

(3) Where a wife conveys and is expressed to convey as beneficial owner, and the husband also conveys and is expressed to convey as beneficial owner,

then, for the purposes of this section, the wife shall be deemed to convey and to be expressed to convey by direction of the husband, as beneficial owner; and, in addition to the covenant implied on the part of the wife, there shall also be implied, first, a covenant on the part of the husband as the person giving that direction, and secondly, a covenant on the part of the husband in the same terms as the covenant implied on the part of the wife.

(4) Where in a conveyance a person conveying is not expressed to convey as beneficial owner, or as settlor, or as trustee, or as mortgagee, or as personal representative of a deceased person, . . . or under an order of the court, or by direction of a person as beneficial owner, no covenant on the part of the person conveying shall be, by virtue of this section, implied in the conveyance.

(5) In this section a conveyance does not include a demise by way of lease at a rent, but does include a charge and "convey" has a corresponding meaning.

(6) The benefit of a covenant implied as aforesaid shall be annexed and incident to, and shall go with, the estate or interest of the implied covenantee, and shall be capable of being enforced by every person in whom that estate or interest is, for the whole or any part thereof, from time to time vested.

(7) A covenant implied as aforesaid may be varied or extended by a deed or an assent, and, as so varied or extended, shall, as far as may be, operate in the like manner, and with all the like incidents, effects, and consequences, as if such variations or extensions were directed in this section to be implied.

(8) This section applies to conveyances made after the thirty-first day of December, eighteen hundred and eighty-one, but only to assents by a personal representative made after the commencement of this Act. **[27]**

NOTES

Sub-ss (1), (4): words omitted repealed by the Mental Health Act 1959, s 149(2), Sch 8, Part I.

77. Implied covenants in conveyance subject to rents

(1) In addition to the covenants implied under the last preceding section, there shall in the several cases in this section mentioned, be deemed to be included and implied, a covenant to the effect in this section stated, by and with such persons as are hereinafter mentioned, that is to say:—

(A) In a conveyance for valuable consideration, other than a mortgage, of the entirety of the land affected by a rentcharge, a covenant by the grantee or joint and several covenants by the grantees, if more than one, with the conveying parties and with each of them, if more than one, in the terms set out in Part VII of the Second Schedule to this Act. Where a rentcharge has been apportioned in respect of any land, with the consent of the owner of the rentcharge, the covenants in this paragraph shall be implied in the conveyance of that land in like manner as if the apportioned rentcharge were the rentcharge referred to, and the document creating the rentcharge related solely to that land:

(B) In a conveyance for valuable consideration, other than a mortgage, of part of land affected by a rentcharge, subject to a part of that rentcharge which has been or is by that conveyance apportioned (but in either case without the consent of the owner of the rentcharge) in respect of the land conveyed:—

(i) A covenant by the grantee of the land or joint and several covenants by the grantees, if more than one, with the conveying parties and with each of them, if more than one, in the terms set out in paragraph (i) of Part VIII of the Second Schedule to this Act;

(ii) A covenant by a person who conveys or is expressed to convey as beneficial owner, or joint and several covenants by the persons who so convey or are expressed to so convey, if at the date of the conveyance any part of the land affected by such rentcharge is retained, with the grantees of the land and with each of them (if more than one) in the terms set out in paragraph (ii) of Part VIII of the Second Schedule to this Act:

(C) In a conveyance for valuable consideration, other than a mortgage, of the entirety of the land comprised in a lease, for the residue of the term or interest created by the lease, a covenant by the assignee or joint and several covenants by the assignees (if more than one) with the conveying parties and with each of them (if more than one) in the terms set out in Part IX of the Second Schedule to this Act. Where a rent has been apportioned in respect of any land, with the consent of the lessor, the covenants in this paragraph shall be implied in the conveyance of that land in like manner as if the apportioned rent were the original rent reserved, and the lease related solely to that land:

(D) In a conveyance for valuable consideration, other than a mortgage, of part of the land comprised in a lease, for the residue of the term or interest created by the lease, subject to a part of the rent which has been or is by the conveyance apportioned (but in either case without the consent of the lessor) in respect of the land conveyed:—

(i) A covenant by the assignee of the land, or joint and several covenants by the assignees, if more than one, with the conveying parties and with each of them, if more than one, in the terms set out in paragraph (i) of Part X of the Second Schedule to this Act;

(ii) A covenant by a person who conveys or is expressed to convey as beneficial owner, or joint and several covenants by the persons who so convey or are expressed to so convey, if at the date of the conveyance any part of the land comprised in the lease is retained, with the assignees of the land and with each of them (if more than one) in the terms set out in paragraph (ii) of Part X of the Second Schedule to this Act.

(2) Where in a conveyance for valuable consideration, other than a mortgage, part of land affected by a rentcharge, or part of land comprised in a lease is, without the consent of the owner of the rentcharge or of the lessor, as the case may be, expressed to be conveyed—

(i) subject to or charged with the entire rent—

then paragraph (B) (ii) or (D) (i) of the last subsection, as the case may require shall have effect as if the entire rent were the apportioned rent; or

(ii) discharged or exonerated from the entire rent—

then paragraph (B) (ii) or (D) (ii) of the last subsection, as the case may require, shall have effect as if the entire rent were the balance of the rent, and the words "other than the covenant to pay the entire rent" had been omitted.

(3) In this section "conveyance" does not include a demise by way of lease at a rent.

(4) Any covenant which would be implied under this section by reason of a person conveying or being expressed to convey as beneficial owner may, by

express reference to this section, be implied, with or without variation, in a conveyance, whether or not for valuable consideration, by a person who conveys or is expressed to convey as settlor, or as trustee, or as mortgagee, or as personal representative of a deceased person, . . . or under an order of the court.

(5) The benefit of a covenant implied as aforesaid shall be annexed and incident to, and shall go with, the estate or interest of the implied covenantee, and shall be capable of being enforced by every person in whom that estate or interest is, for the whole or any part thereof, from time to time vested.

(6) A covenant implied as aforesaid may be varied or extended by deed, and, as so varied or extended, shall, as far as may be, operate in the like manner, and with all the like incidents, effects and consequences, as if such variations or extensions were directed in this section to be implied.

(7) In particular any covenant implied under this section may be extended by providing that—

(*a*) the land conveyed; or
(*b*) the part of the land affected by the rentcharge which remains vested in the covenantor; or
(*c*) the part of the land demised which remains vested in the covenantor;

shall, as the case may require, stand charged with the payment of all money which may become payable under the implied covenant.

(8) This section applies only to conveyances made after the commencement of this Act. **[28]**

NOTES

Sub-s (4): words omitted repealed by the Mental Health Act 1959, s 149(2), Sch 8, Part I.

78. Benefit of covenants relating to land

(1) A covenant relating to any land of the covenantee shall be deemed to be made with the covenantee and his successors in title and the persons deriving title under him or them, and shall have effect as if such successors and other persons were expressed.

For the purposes of this subsection in connexion with covenants restrictive of the user of land "successors in title" shall be deemed to include the owners and occupiers for the time being of the land of the covenantee intended to be benefited.

(2) This section applies to covenants made after the commencement of this Act, but the repeal of section fifty-eight of the Conveyancing Act 1881 does not affect the operation of covenants to which that section applied. **[29]**

79. Burden of covenants relating to land

(1) A covenant relating to any land of a covenantor or capable of being bound by him, shall, unless a contrary intention is expressed, be deemed to be made by the covenantor on behalf of himself his successors in title and the persons deriving title under him or them, and, subject as aforesaid, shall have effect as if such successors and other persons were expressed.

This subsection extends to a covenant to do some act relating to the land, notwithstanding that the subject-matter may not be in existence when the covenant is made.

(2) For the purposes of this section in connexion with covenants restrictive

of the user of land "successors in title" shall be deemed to include the owners and occupiers for the time being of such land.

(3) This section applies only to covenants made after the commencement of this Act. **[30]**

[84. Power to discharge or modify restrictive covenants affecting land

(1) The Lands Tribunal shall (without prejudice to any concurrent jurisdiction of the court) have power from time to time, on the application of any person interested in any freehold land affected by any restriction arising under covenant or otherwise as to the user thereof or the building thereon, by order wholly or partially to discharge or modify any such restriction on being satisfied—

(*a*) that by reason of changes in the character of the property or the neighbourhood or other circumstances of the case which the Lands Tribunal may deem material, the restriction ought to be deemed obsolete; or

(*aa*) that (in a case falling within subsection (1A) below) the continued existence thereof would impede some reasonable user of the land for public or private purposes or, as the case may be, would unless modified so impede such user; or

(*b*) that the persons of full age and capacity for the time being or from time to time entitled to the benefit of the restriction, whether in respect of estates in fee simple or any lesser estates or interests in the property to which the benefit of the restriction is annexed, have agreed, either expressly or by implication, by their acts or omissions, to the same being discharged or modified; or

(*c*) that the proposed discharge or modification will not injure the persons entitled to the benefit of the restriction;

and an order discharging or modifying a restriction under this subsection may direct the applicant to pay to any person entitled to the benefit of the restriction such sum by way of consideration as the Tribunal may think it just to award under one, but not both, of the following heads, that is to say, either—

(i) a sum to make up for any loss or disadvantage suffered by that person in consequence of the discharge or modification; or

(ii) a sum to make up for any effect which the restriction had, at the time when it was imposed, in reducing the consideration then received for the land affected by it.

(1A) Subsection (1)(*aa*) above authorises the discharge or modification of a restriction by reference to its impeding some reasonable user of land in any case in which the Lands Tribunal is satisfied that the restriction, in impeding that user, either—

(*a*) does not secure to persons entitled to the benefit of it any practical benefits of substantial value or advantage to them; or

(*b*) is contrary to the public interest;

and that money will be an adequate compensation for the loss or disadvantage (if any) which any such person will suffer from the discharge or modification.

(1B) In determining whether a case is one falling within subsection (1A) above, and in determining whether (in any such case or otherwise) a restriction ought to be discharged or modified, the Lands Tribunal shall take into account the development plan and any declared or ascertainable pattern for the grant or refusal of planning permissions in the relevant areas, as well as the period at which and context in which the restriction was created or imposed and any other material circumstances.

(1C) It is hereby declared that the power conferred by this section to modify a restriction includes power to add such further provisions restricting the user of or the building on the land affected as appear to the Lands Tribunal to be reasonable in view of the relaxation of the existing provisions, and as may be accepted by the applicant; and the Lands Tribunal may accordingly refuse to modify a restriction without some such addition.

(2) The court shall have power on the application of any person interested—

(*a*) to declare whether or not in any particular case any freehold land is, or would in any given event be, affected by a restriction imposed by any instrument; or

(*b*) to declare what, upon the true construction of any instrument purporting to impose a restriction, is the nature and extent of the restriction thereby imposed and whether the same is, or would in any given event be, enforceable and if so by whom.

Neither subsections (7) and (11) of this section nor, unless the contrary is expressed, any later enactment providing for this section not to apply to any restrictions shall affect the operation of this subsection or the operation for purposes of this subsection of any other provisions of this section.

(3) The Lands Tribunal shall, before making any order under this section, direct such enquiries, if any, to be made of any government department or local authority, and such notices, if any, whether by way of advertisement or otherwise, to be given to such of the persons who appear to be entitled to the benefit of the restriction intended to be discharged, modified, or dealt with as, having regard to any enquiries, notices or other proceedings previously made, given or taken, the Lands Tribunal may think fit.

(3A) On an application to the Lands Tribunal under this section the Lands Tribunal shall give any necessary directions as to the persons who are or are not to be admitted (as appearing to be entitled to the benefit of the restriction) to oppose the application, and no appeal shall lie against any such direction; but rules under the Lands Tribunal Act 1949 shall make provision whereby, in cases in which there arises on such an application (whether or not in connection with the admission of persons to oppose) any such question as is referred to in subsection (2)(*a*) or (*b*) of this section, the proceedings on the application can and, if the rules so provide, shall be suspended to enable the decision of the court to be obtained on that question by an application under that subsection, or by means of a case stated by the Lands Tribunal, or otherwise, as may be provided by those rules or by rules of court.

(5) Any order made under this section shall be binding on all persons, whether ascertained or of full age or capacity or not, then entitled or thereafter capable of becoming entitled to the benefit of any restriction, which is thereby discharged, modified or dealt with, and whether such persons are parties to the proceedings or have been served with notice or not.

(6) An order may be made under this section notwithstanding that any instrument which is alleged to impose the restriction intended to be discharged, modified, or dealt with, may not have been produced to the court or the Lands Tribunal, and the court or the Lands Tribunal may act on such evidence of that instrument as it may think sufficient.

(7) This section applies to restrictions whether subsisting at the commence-

ment of this Act or imposed thereafter, but this section does not apply where the restriction was imposed on the occasion of a disposition made gratuitously or for a nominal consideration for public purposes.

(8) This section applies whether the land affected by the restrictions is registered or not, but, in the case of registered land, the Land Registrar shall give effect on the register to any order under this section in accordance with the Land Registration Act 1925.

(9) Where any proceedings by action or otherwise are taken to enforce a restrictive covenant, any person against whom the proceedings are taken, may in such proceedings apply to the court for an order giving leave to apply to the Lands Tribunal under this section, and staying the proceedings in the meantime.

(11) This section does not apply to restrictions imposed by the Commissioners of Works under any statutory power for the protection of any Royal Park or Garden or to restrictions of a like character imposed upon the occasion of any enfranchisement effected before the commencement of this Act in any manor vested in His Majesty in right of the Crown or the Duchy of Lancaster, nor (subject to subsection (11A) below) to restrictions created or imposed—

(*a*) for naval, military or air force purposes,
[(*b*) for civil aviation purposes under the powers of the Air Navigation Act 1920, of section 19 or 23 of the Civil Aviation Act 1949 or of section 30 or 41 of the Civil Aviation Act 1982.]

(11A) Subsection (11) of this section—

(*a*) shall exclude the application of this section to a restriction falling within subsection (11)(*a*), and not created or imposed in connection with the use of any land as an aerodrome, only so long as the restriction is enforceable by or on behalf of the Crown; and
(*b*) shall exclude the application of this section to a restriction falling within subsection (11)(*b*), or created or imposed in connection with the use of any land as an aerodrome, only so long as the restriction is enforceable by or on behalf of the Crown or any public or international authority.

(12) Where a term of more than forty years is created in land (whether before or after the commencement of this Act) this section shall, after the expiration of twenty-five years of the term, apply to restrictions, affecting such leasehold land in like manner as it would have applied had the land been freehold:

Provided that this subsection shall not apply to mining leases.] **[31]**

NOTES

Set out as reprinted with amendments in the Law of Property Act 1969, s 28(1), Sch 3.
Sub-s 11: amended by the Civil Aviation Act 1982, s 109, Sch 15, para 1.

PART V

LEASES AND TENANCIES

139. Effect of extinguishment of reversion

(1) Where a reversion expectant on a lease of land is surrendered or merged, the estate or interest which as against the lessee for the time being confers the next vested right to the land, shall be deemed the reversion for the purpose of

preserving the same incidents and obligations as would have affected the original reversion had there been no surrender or merger thereof.

(2) This section applies to surrenders or mergers effected after the first day of October, eighteen hundred and forty-five. **[32]**

140. Apportionment of conditions on severance

(1) Notwithstanding the severance by conveyance, surrender, or otherwise of the reversionary estate in any land comprised in a lease, and notwithstanding the avoidance or cesser in any other manner of the term granted by a lease as to part only of the land comprised therein, every condition or right of re-entry, and every other condition contained in the lease, shall be apportioned, and shall remain annexed to the severed parts of the reversionary estate as severed, and shall be in force with respect to the term whereon each severed part is reversionary, or the term in the part of the land as to which the term has not been surrendered, or has not been avoided or has not otherwise ceased, in like manner as if the land comprised in each severed part, or the land as to which the term remains subsisting, as the case may be, had alone originally been comprised in the lease.

(2) In this section "right of re-entry" includes a right to determine the lease by notice to quit or otherwise; but where the notice is served by a person entitled to a severed part of the reversion so that it extends to part only of the land demised, the lessee may within one month determine the lease in regard to the rest of the land by giving to the owner of the reversionary estate therein a counter notice expiring at the same time as the original notice . . .

(3) This section applies to leases made before or after the commencement of this Act and whether the severance of the reversionary estate or the partial avoidance or cesser of the term was effected before or after such commencement:

Provided that, where the lease was made before the first day of January eighteen hundred and eighty-two nothing in this section shall affect the operation of a severance of the reversionary estate or partial avoidance or cesser of the term which was effected before the commencement of this Act. **[33]**

NOTES

Sub-s (2): words omitted repealed with savings by the Agricultural Holdings Act 1948, ss 98, 100(1), Sch 8.

Applied by the Agricultural Holdings Act 1986, s 74.

141. Rent and benefit of lessee's covenants to run with the reversion

(1) Rent reserved by a lease, and the benefit of every covenant or provision therein contained, having reference to the subject-matter thereof, and on the lessee's part to be observed or performed, and every condition of re-entry and other condition therein contained, shall be annexed and incident to and shall go with the reversionary estate in the land, or in any part thereof, immediately expectant on the term granted by the lease, notwithstanding severance of that reversionary estate, and without prejudice to any liability affecting a covenantor or his estate.

(2) Any such rent, covenant or provision shall be capable of being recovered, received, enforced, and taken advantage of, by the person from time to time entitled, subject to the term, to the income of the whole or any part, as the case may require, of the land leased

(3) Where that person becomes entitled by conveyance or otherwise, such

rent, covenant or provision may be recovered, received, enforced or taken advantage of by him notwithstanding that he becomes so entitled after the condition of re-entry or forfeiture has become enforceable, but this subsection does not render enforceable any condition of re-entry or other condition waived or released before such person becomes entitled as aforesaid.

(4) This section applies to leases made before or after the commencement of this Act, but does not affect the operation of—

(*a*) any severance of the reversionary estate; or
(*b*) any acquisition by conveyance or otherwise of the right to receive or enforce any rent covenant or provision;

effected before the commencement of this Act. **[34]**

142. Obligation of lessor's covenants to run with reversion

(1) The obligation under a condition or of a covenant entered into by a lessor with reference to the subject-matter of the lease shall, if and as far as the lessor has power to bind the reversionary estate immediately expectant on the term granted by the lease, be annexed and incident to and shall go with that reversionary estate, or the several parts thereof, notwithstanding severance of that reversionary estate, and may be taken advantage of and enforced by the person in whom the term is from time to time vested by conveyance, devolution in law, or otherwise; and, if and as far as the lessor has power to bind the person from time to time entitled to that reversionary estate, the obligation aforesaid may be taken advantage of and entered against any person so entitled.

(2) This section applies to leases made before or after the commencement of this Act, whether the severance of the reversionary estate was effected before or after such commencement:

Provided that, where the lease was made before the first day of January eighteen hundred and eighty-two, nothing in this section shall affect the operation of any severance of the reversionary estate effected before such commencement.

This section takes effect without prejudice to any liability affecting a covenantor or his estate. **[35]**

143. Effect of licences granted to lessees

(1) Where a licence is granted to a lessee to do any act, the licence, unless otherwise expressed, extends only—

(*a*) to the permission actually given; or
(*b*) to the specific breach of any provision or covenant referred to; or
(*c*) to any other matter thereby specifically authorised to be done;

and the licence does not prevent any proceeding for any subsequent breach unless otherwise specified in the licence.

(2) Notwithstanding any such licence—

(*a*) All rights under covenants and powers of re-entry contained in the lease remain in full force and are available as against any subsequent breach of covenant, condition or other matter not specifically authorised or waived, in the same manner as if no licence had been granted; and (*b*) The condition or right of entry remains in force in all respects as if the licence had not been granted, save in respect of the particular matter authorised to be done.

(3) Where in any lease there is a power or condition of re-entry on the lessee assigning, subletting or doing any other specified act without a licence, and a licence is granted—

(*a*) to any one of two or more lessees to do any act, or to deal with his equitable share or interest; or

(*b*) to any lessee, or to any one of two or more lessees to assign or underlet part only of the property, or to do any act in respect of part only of the property;

the licence does not operate to extinguish the right of entry in case of any breach of covenant or condition by the co-lessees of the other shares or interests in the property, or by the lessee or lessees of the rest of the property (as the case may be) in respect of such shares or interests or remaining property, but the right of entry remains in force in respect of the shares, interests or property not the subject of the licence.

This subsection does not authorise the grant after the commencement of this Act of a licence to create an undivided share in a legal estate.

(4) This section applies to licences granted after the thirteenth day of August, eighteen hundred and fifty-nine. **[36]**

144. No fine to be exacted for licence to assign

In all leases containing a covenant, condition, or agreement against assigning, underletting, or parting with the possession, or disposing of the land or property leased without licence or consent, such covenant, condition, or agreement shall, unless the lease contains an express provision to the contrary, be deemed to be subject to a proviso to the effect that no fine or sum of money in the nature of a fine shall be payable for or in respect of such licence or consent; but this proviso does not preclude the right to require the payment of a reasonable sum in respect of any legal or other expense incurred in relation to such licence or consent. **[37]**

145. Lessee to give notice of ejectment to lessor

Every lessee to whom there is delivered any writ for the recovery of premises demised to or held by him, or to whose knowledge any such writ comes, shall forthwith give notice thereof to his lessor or his bailiff or receiver, and, if he fails so to do, he shall be liable to forfeit to the person of whom he holds the premises an amount equal to the value of three years' improved or rack rent of the premises, to be recovered by action in any court having jurisdiction in respect of claims for such an amount. **[38]**

146. Restrictions on and relief against forfeiture of leases and underleases

(1) A right of re-entry or forfeiture under any proviso or stipulation in a lease for a breach of any covenant or condition in the lease shall not be enforceable, by action or otherwise, unless and until the lessor serves on the lessee a notice—

(*a*) specifying the particular breach complained of; and

(*b*) if the breach is capable of remedy, requiring the lessee to remedy the breach; and

(*c*) in any case, requiring the lessee to make compensation in money for the breach;

and the lessee fails, within a reasonable time thereafter, to remedy the breach, if it is capable of remedy, and to make reasonable compensation in money, to the satisfaction of the lessor, for the breach.

(2) Where a lessor is proceeding, by action or otherwise, to enforce such a right of re-entry or forfeiture, the lessee may, in the lessor's action, if any, or in any action brought by himself, apply to the court for relief; and the court may grant or refuse relief, as the court, having regard to the proceedings and conduct of the parties under the foregoing provisions of this section, and to all the other circumstances, thinks fit; and in case of relief may grant it on such terms, if any, as to costs, expenses, damages, compensation, penalty, or otherwise, including the granting of an injunction to restrain any like breach in the future, as the court, in the circumstances of each case, thinks fit.

(3) A lessor shall be entitled to recover as a debt due to him from a lessee, and in addition to damages (if any), all reasonable costs and expenses properly incurred by the lessor in the employment of a solicitor and surveyor or valuer, or otherwise, in reference to any breach giving rise to a right of re-entry or forfeiture which, at the request of the lessee, is waived by the lessor, or from which the lessee is relieved, under the provisions of this Act.

(4) Where a lessor is proceeding by action or otherwise to enforce a right of re-entry or forfeiture under any covenant, proviso, or stipulation in a lease, or for non-payment of rent, the court may, on application by any person claiming as under-lessee any estate or interest in the property comprised in the lease or any part thereof, either in the lessor's action (if any) or in any action brought by such person for that purpose, make an order vesting, for the whole term of the lease or any less term, the property comprised in the lease or any part thereof in any person entitled as under-lessee to any estate or interest in such property upon such conditions as to execution of any deed or other document, payment of rent, costs, expenses, damages, compensation, giving security, or otherwise, as the court in the circumstances of each case may think fit, but in no case shall any such under-lessee be entitled to require a lease to be granted to him for any longer term than he had under his original sub-lease.

(5) For the purposes of this section—

(*a*) "Lease" includes an original or derivative under-lease; also an agreement for a lease where the lessee has become entitled to have his lease granted; also a grant at a fee farm rent, or securing a rent by condition;

(*b*) "Lessee" includes an original or derivative under-lessee, and the persons deriving title under a lessee; also a grantee under any such grant as aforesaid and the persons deriving title under him;

(*c*) "Lessor" includes an original or derivative under-lessor, and the persons deriving title under a lessor; also a person making such grant as aforesaid and the persons deriving title under him;

(*d*) "Under-lease" includes an agreement for an underlease where the underlessee has become entitled to have his underlease granted;

(*e*) "Underlessee" includes any person deriving title under an underlessee.

(6) This section applies although the proviso or stipulation under which the right of re-entry or forfeiture accrues is inserted in the lease in pursuance of the directions of any Act of Parliament.

(7) For the purposes of this section a lease limited to continue as long only as the lessee abstains from committing a breach of covenant shall be and take

effect as a lease to continue for any longer term for which it could subsist, but determinable by a proviso for re-entry on such a breach.

(8) This section does not extend—

(i) To a covenant or condition against assigning, underletting, parting with the possession, or disposing of the land leased where the breach occurred before the commencement of this Act; or

(ii) In the case of a mining lease, to a covenant or condition for allowing the lessor to have access to or inspect books, accounts, records, weighing machines or other things, or to enter or inspect the mine or the workings thereof.

(9) This section does not apply to a condition for forfeiture on the bankruptcy of the lessee or on taking in execution of the lessee's interest if contained in a lease of—

(*a*) Agricultural or pastoral land;

(*b*) Mines or minerals;

(*c*) A house used or intended to be used as a public-house or beershop;

(*d*) A house let as a dwelling-house, with the use of any furniture, books, works of art, or other chattels not being in the nature of fixtures;

(*e*) Any property with respect to which the personal qualifications of the tenant are of importance for the preservation of the value or character of the property, or on the ground of neighbourhood to the lessor, or to any person holding under him.

(10) Where a condition of forfeiture on the bankruptcy of the lessee or on taking in execution of the lessee's interest is contained in any lease, other than a lease of any of the classes mentioned in the last subsection, then—

(*a*) if the lessee's interest is sold within one year from the bankruptcy or taking in execution, this section applies to the forfeiture condition aforesaid;

(*b*) if the lessee's interest is not sold before the expiration of that year, this section only applies to the forfeiture condition aforesaid during the first year from the date of the bankruptcy or taking in execution.

(11) This section does not, save as otherwise mentioned, affect the law relating to re-entry or forfeiture or relief in case of non-payment of rent.

(12) This section has effect notwithstanding any stipulation to the contrary.

[(13) The county court has jurisdiction under this section—

(*a*) in any case where the lessor is proceeding by action in court to enforce the right of entry or forfeiture; and

(*b*) where the lessor is proceeding to enforce the said right otherwise than by action, in a case where the net annual value for rating of the property comprised in the lease does not exceed the county court limit.] **[39]**

NOTES

Commencement: 1 August 1984 (sub-s (13)); before 1 January 1970 (remainder).

Sub-s (13): added by the County Courts Act 1984, s 148(1), Sch 2, para 5.

147. Relief against notice to effect decorative repairs

(1) After a notice is served on a lessee relating to the internal decorative repairs to a house or other building, he may apply to the court for relief, and if, having regard to all the circumstances of the case (including in particular the length of

the lessee's term or interest remaining unexpired), the court is satisfied that the notice is unreasonable, it may, by order, wholly or partially relieve the lessee from liability for such repairs.

(2) This section does not apply:—

(i) where the liability arises under an express covenant or agreement to put the property in a decorative state of repair and the covenant or agreement has never been performed;

(ii) to any matter necessary or proper—

(*a*) for putting or keeping the property in a sanitary condition, or

(*b*) for the maintenance or preservation of the structure;

(iii) to any statutory liability to keep a house in all respects reasonably fit for human habitation;

(iv) to any covenant or stipulation to yield up the house or other building in a specified state of repair at the end of the term.

(3) In this section "lease" includes an underlease and an agreement for a lease, and "lessee" has a corresponding meaning and includes any person liable to effect the repairs.

(4) This section applies whether the notice is served before or after the commencement of this Act, and has effect notwithstanding any stipulation to the contrary.

[(5) The county court has jurisdiction under this section where the net annual value for rating of the house or other building does not exceed the county court limit.] **[40]**

NOTES

Commencement: 1 August 1984 (sub-s (5)); before 1 January 1970 (remainder).

Sub-s (5): added by the County Courts Act 1984, s 148(1), Sch 2, para 6.

148. Waiver of a covenant in a lease

(1) Where any actual waiver by a lessor or the persons deriving title under him of the benefit of any covenant or condition in any lease is proved to have taken place in any particular instance, such waiver shall not be deemed to extend to any instance, or to any breach of covenant or condition save that to which such waiver specially relates, nor operate as a general waiver of the benefit of any such covenant or condition.

(2) This section applies unless a contrary intention appears and extends to waivers effected after the twenty-third day of July, eighteen hundred and sixty. **[41]**

149. Abolition of interesse termini, and as to reversionary leases and leases for lives

(1) The doctrine of interesse termini is hereby abolished.

(2) As from the commencement of this Act all terms of years absolute shall, whether the interest is created before or after such commencement, be capable of taking effect at law or in equity, according to the estate interest or powers of the grantor, from the date fixed for commencement of the term, without actual entry.

(3) A term, at a rent or granted in consideration of a fine, limited after the commencement of this Act to take effect more than twenty-one years from the

date of the instrument purporting to create it, shall be void, and any contract made after such commencement to create such a term shall likewise be void; but this subsection does not apply to any term taking effect in equity under a settlement, or created out of an equitable interest under a settlement, or under an equitable power for mortgage, indemnity or other like purposes.

(4) Nothing in subsections (1) and (2) of this section prejudicially affects the right of any person to recover any rent or to enforce or take advantage of any covenants or conditions or, as respects terms or interests created before the commencement of this Act, operates to vary any statutory or other obligations imposed in respect of such terms or interests.

(5) Nothing in this Act affects the rule of law that a legal term, whether or not being a mortgage term, may be created to take effect in reversion expectant on a longer term, which rule is hereby confirmed.

(6) Any lease or underlease, at a rent, or in consideration of a fine, for life or lives or for any term of years determinable with life or lives, or on the marriage of the lessee, or any contract therefor, made before or after the commencement of this Act, or created by virtue of Part V of the Law of Property Act 1922, shall take effect as a lease, underlease or contract therefor, for a term of ninety years determinable after the death or marriage (as the case may be) of the original lessee, or of the survivor of the original lessees, by at least one month's notice in writing given to determine the same on one of the quarter days applicable to the tenancy, either by the lessor or the persons deriving title under him, to the person entitled to the leasehold interest, or if no such person is in existence by affixing the same to the premises, or by the lessee or other persons in whom the leasehold interest is vested to the lessor or the persons deriving title under him:

Provided that—

(*a*) this subsection shall not apply to any term taking effect in equity under a settlement or created out of an equitable interest under a settlement for mortgage, indemnity, or other like purposes;

(*b*) the person in whom the leasehold interest is vested by virtue of Part V of the Law of Property Act 1922, shall, for the purposes of this subsection, be deemed an original lessee;

(*c*) if the lease, underlease, or contract therefor is made determinable on the dropping of the lives of persons other than or besides the lessees, then the notice shall be capable of being served after the death of any person or of the survivor of any persons (whether or not including the lessees) on the cesser of whose life or lives the lease, underlease, or contract is made determinable, instead of after the death of the original lessee or of the survivor of the original lessees;

(*d*) if there are no quarter days specially applicable to the tenancy, notice may be given to determine the tenancy on one of the usual quarter days. **[42]**

150. Surrender of a lease, without prejudice to underleases with a view to the grant of a new lease

(1) A lease may be surrendered with a view to the acceptance of a new lease in place thereof, without a surrender of any under-lease derived thereout.

(2) A new lease may be granted and accepted, in place of any lease so surrendered, without any such surrender of an under-lease as aforesaid, and the

new lease operates as if all under-leases derived out of the surrendered lease had been surrendered before the surrender of that lease was effected.

(3) The lessee under the new lease and any person deriving title under him is entitled to the same rights and remedies in respect of the rent reserved by and the covenants, agreements and conditions contained in any under-lease as if the original lease had not been surrendered but was or remained vested in him.

(4) Each under-lessee and any person deriving title under him is entitled to hold and enjoy the land comprised in his under-lease (subject to the payment of any rent reserved by and to the observance of the covenants agreements and conditions contained in the under-lease) as if the lease out of which the under-lease was derived had not been surrendered.

(5) The lessor granting the new lease and any person deriving title under him is entitled to the same remedies, by distress or entry in and upon the land comprised in any such under-lease for rent reserved by or for breach of any covenant, agreement or condition contained in the new lease (so far only as the rents reserved by or the covenants, agreements or conditions contained in the new lease do not exceed or impose greater burdens than those reserved by or contained in the original lease out of which the under-lease is derived) as he would have had—

(*a*) If the original lease had remained on foot; or
(*b*) If a new under-lease derived out of the new lease had been granted to the under-lessee or a person deriving title under him;

as the case may require.

(6) This section does not affect the powers of the court to give relief against forfeiture. **[43]**

NOTES
Commencement: Before 1 January 1970.

151. Provision as to attornments by tenants

(1) Where land is subject to a lease—

(*a*) the conveyance of a reversion in the land expectant on the determination of the lease; or
(*b*) the creation or conveyance of a rentcharge to issue or issuing out of the land;

shall be valid without any attornment of the lessee:

Nothing in this subsection—

(i) affects the validity of any payment of rent by the lessee to the person making the conveyance or grant before notice of the conveyance or grant is given to him by the person entitled thereunder; or
(ii) renders the lessee liable for any breach of covenant to pay rent, on account of his failure to pay rent to the person entitled under the conveyance or grant before such notice is given to the lessee.

(2) An attornment by the lessee in respect of any land to a person claiming to be entitled to the interest in the land of the lessor, if made without the consent of the lessor, shall be void.

This subsection does not apply to an attornment—

(*a*) made pursuant to a judgment of a court of competent jurisdiction; or (*b*) to a mortgagee, by a lessee holding under a lease from the mortgagor where the right of redemption is barred; or

(*c*) to any other person rightfully deriving title under the lessor. **[44]**

152. Leases invalidated by reason of non-compliance with terms of powers under which they are granted

(1) Where in the intended exercise of any power of leasing, whether conferred by an Act of Parliament or any other instrument, a lease (in this section referred to as an invalid lease) is granted, which by reason of any failure to comply with the terms of the power is invalid, then—

(*a*) as against the person entitled after the determination of the interest of the grantor to the reversion; or

(*b*) as against any other person who, subject to any lease properly granted under the power, would have been entitled to the land comprised in the lease;

the lease, if it was made in good faith, and the lessee has entered thereunder, shall take effect in equity as a contract for the grant, at the request of the lessee, of a valid lease under the power, of like effect as the invalid lease, subject to such variations as may be necessary in order to comply with the terms of the power:

Provided that a lessee under an invalid lease shall not, by virtue of any such implied contract, be entitled to obtain a variation of the lease if the other persons who would have been bound by the contract are willing and able to confirm the lease without variation.

(2) Where a lease granted in the intended exercise of such a power is invalid by reason of the grantor not having power to grant the lease at the date thereof, but the grantor's interest in the land comprised therein continues after the time when he might, in the exercise of the power, have properly granted a lease in the like terms, the lease shall take effect as a valid lease in like manner as if it had been granted at that time.

(3) Where during the continuance of the possession taken under an invalid lease the person for the time being entitled, subject to such possession, to the land comprised therein or to the rents and profits thereof, is able to confirm the lease without variation, the lessee, or other person who would have been bound by the lease had it been valid, shall, at the request of the person so able to confirm the lease, be bound to accept a confirmation thereof, and thereupon the lease shall have effect and be deemed to have had effect as a valid lease from the grant thereof.

Confirmation under this subsection may be by a memorandum in writing signed by or on behalf of the persons respectively confirming and accepting the confirmation of the lease.

(4) Where a receipt or a memorandum in writing confirming an invalid lease is, upon or before the acceptance of rent thereunder, signed by or on behalf of the person accepting the rent, that acceptance shall, as against that person, be deemed to be a confirmation of the lease.

(5) The foregoing provisions of this section do not affect prejudicially—

(*a*) any right of action or other right or remedy to which, but for those provisions or any enactment replaced by those provisions, the lessee named in an invalid lease would or might have been entitled under any covenant on the part of the grantor for title or quiet enjoyment contained therein or implied thereby; or

(*b*) any right of re-entry or other right or remedy to which, but for those provisions or any enactment replaced thereby, the grantor or other person for the time being entitled to the reversion expectant on the termination of the lease, would or might have been entitled by reason of any breach of the covenants, conditions or provisions contained in the lease and binding on the lessee.

(6) Where a valid power of leasing is vested in or may be exercised by a person who grants a lease which, by reason of the determination of the interest of the grantor or otherwise, cannot have effect and continuance according to the terms thereof independently of the power, the lease shall for the purposes of this section be deemed to have been granted in the intended exercise of the power although the power is not referred to in the lease.

(7) This section does not apply to a lease of land held on charitable, ecclesiastical or public trusts.

(8) This section takes effect without prejudice to the provision in this Act for the grant of leases in the name and on behalf of the estate owner of the land affected. **[45]**

153. Enlargement of residue of long terms into fee simple estates

(1) Where a residue unexpired of not less than two hundred years of a term, which, as originally created, was for not less than three hundred years, is subsisting in land, whether being the whole land originally comprised in the term, or part only thereof,—

(*a*) without any trust or right of redemption affecting the term in favour of the freeholder, or other person entitled in reversion expectant on the term; and

(*b*) without any rent, or with merely a peppercorn rent or other rent having no money value, incident to the reversion, or having had a rent, not being merely a peppercorn rent or other rent having no money value, originally so incident, which subsequently has been released or has become barred by lapse of time, or has in any other way ceased to be payable;

the term may be enlarged into a fee simple in the manner, and subject to the restrictions in this section provided.

(2) This section applies to and includes every such term as aforesaid whenever created, whether or not having the freehold as the immediate reversion thereon; but does not apply to—

(i) Any term liable to be determined by re-entry for condition broken; or

(ii) Any term created by subdemise out of a superior term, itself incapable of being enlarged into fee simple.

(3) This section extends to mortgage terms, where the right of redemption is barred.

(4) A rent not exceeding the yearly sum of one pound which has not been collected or paid for a continuous period of twenty years or upwards shall, for the purposes of this section, be deemed to have ceased to be payable:

Provided that, of the said period, at least five years must have elapsed after the commencement of this Act.

(5) Where a rent incident to a reversion expectant on a term to which this section applies is deemed to have ceased to be payable for the purposes aforesaid, no claim for such rent or for any arrears thereof shall be capable of being enforced.

(6) Each of the following persons, namely—

(i) Any person beneficially entitled in right of the term, whether subject to any incumbrance or not, to possession of any land comprised in the term, and, in the case of a married woman without the concurrence of her husband, whether or not she is entitled for her separate use or as her separate property, . . . ;

(ii) Any person being in receipt of income as trustee, in right of the term, or having the term vested in him in trust for sale, whether subject to any incumbrance or not;

(iii) Any person in whom, as personal representative of any deceased person, the term is vested, whether subject to any incumbrance or not;

shall, so far as regards the land to which he is entitled, or in which he is interested in right of the term, in any such character as aforesaid, have power by deed to declare to the effect that, from and after the execution of the deed, the term shall be enlarged into a fee simple.

(7) Thereupon, by virtue of the deed and of this Act, the term shall become and be enlarged accordingly, and the person in whom the term was previously vested shall acquire and have in the land a fee simple instead of the term.

(8) The estate in fee simple so acquired by enlargement shall be subject to all the same trusts, powers, executory limitations over, rights and equities, and to all the same covenants and provisions relating to user and enjoyment, and to all the same obligations of every kind, as the term would have been subject to if it had not been so enlarged.

(9) But where—

(*a*) any land so held for the residue of a term has been settled in trust by reference to other land, being freehold land, so as to go along with that other land, or, in the case of settlements coming into operation before the commencement of this Act, so as to go along with that other land as far as the law permits; and

(*b*) at the time of enlargement, the ultimate beneficial interest in the term, whether subject to any subsisting particular estate or not, has not become absolutely and indefeasibly vested in any person, free from charges or powers of charging created by a settlement;

the estate in fee simple acquired as aforesaid shall, without prejudice to any conveyance for value previously made by a person having a contingent or defeasible interest in the term, be liable to be, and shall be, conveyed by means of a subsidiary vesting instrument and settled in like manner as the other land, being freehold land, aforesaid, and until so conveyed and settled shall devolve beneficially as if it had been so conveyed and settled.

(10) The estate in fee simple so acquired shall, whether the term was originally created without impeachment of waste or not, include the fee simple in all mines and minerals which at the time of enlargement have not been severed in right or in fact, or have not been severed or reserved by an inclosure Act or award. **[46]**

NOTES

Sub-s (6): words omitted repealed by the Married Women (Restraint upon Anticipation) Act 1949, s 1, Sch 2.

154. Application of Part V to existing leases

This part of this Act, except where otherwise expressly provided, applies to leases created before or after the commencement of this Act, and "lease" includes an under-lease or other tenancy. **[47]**

PART XI

MISCELLANEOUS

Notices

196. Regulations respecting notices

(1) Any notice required or authorised to be served or given by this Act shall be in writing.

(2) Any notice required or authorised by this Act to be served on a lessee or mortgagor shall be sufficient, although only addressed to the lessee or mortgagor by that designation, without his name, or generally to the persons interested, without any name, and notwithstanding that any person to be affected by the notice is absent, under disability, unborn, or unascertained.

(3) Any notice required or authorised by this Act to be served shall be sufficiently served if it is left at the last-known place of abode or business in the United Kingdom of the lessee, lessor, mortgagee, mortgagor, or other person to be served, or, in case of a notice required or authorised to be served on a lessee or mortgagor, is affixed or left for him on the land or any house or building comprised in the lease or mortgage, or, in case of a mining lease, is left for the lessee at the office or counting-house of the mine.

(4) Any notice required or authorised by this Act to be served shall also be sufficiently served, if it is sent by post in a registered letter addressed to the lessee, lessor, mortgagee, mortgagor, or other person to be served, by name, at the aforesaid place of abode or business, office, or counting-house, and if that letter is not returned through the post-office undelivered; and that service shall be deemed to be made at the time at which the registered letter would in the ordinary course be delivered.

(5) The provisions of this section shall extend to notices required to be served by any instrument affecting property executed or coming into operation after the commencement of this Act unless a contrary intention appears.

(6) This section does not apply to notices served in proceedings in the court. **[48]**

NOTES

See further the Landlord and Tenant Act 1987, s 49.

PART XII

CONSTRUCTION, JURISDICTION, AND GENERAL PROVISIONS

205. General definitions

(1) In this Act unless the context otherwise requires, the following expressions have the meanings hereby assigned to them respectively, that is to say:—

(i) "Bankruptcy" includes liquidation by arrangement; also in relation to a corporation means the winding up thereof;

(ii) "Conveyance" includes a mortgage, charge, lease, assent, vesting declaration, vesting instrument, disclaimer, release and every other assurance of property or of an interest therein by any instrument, except a will; "convey" has a corresponding meaning; and "disposition" includes a conveyance and also a devise, bequest, or an appointment of property contained in a will; and "dispose of" has a corresponding meaning;

(iii) "Building purposes" include the erecting and improving of, and the adding to, and the repairing of buildings; and a "building lease" is a lease for building purposes or purposes connected therewith;

[(iiiA) "the county court limit", in relation to any enactment contained in this Act, means the amount for the time being specified by an Order in Council under section 145 of the County Courts Act 1984 as the county court limit for the purposes of that enactment (or, where no such Order in Council has been made, the corresponding limit specified by Order in Council under section 192 of the County Courts Act 1959);]

(iv) "Death duty" means estate duty, . . . and every other duty leviable or payable on a death;

(v) "Estate owner" means the owner of a legal estate, but an infant is not capable of being an estate owner;

(vi) "Gazette" means the London Gazette;

(vii) "Incumbrance" includes a legal or equitable mortgage and a trust for securing money, and a lien, and a charge of a portion, annuity, or other capital or annual sum; and "incumbrancer" has a meaning corresponding with that of incumbrance, and includes every person entitled to the benefit of an incumbrance, or to require payment or discharge thereof;

(viii) "Instrument" does not include a statute, unless the statute creates a settlement;

(ix) "Land" includes land of any tenure, and mines and minerals, whether or not held apart from the surface, buildings or parts of buildings (whether the division is horizontal, vertical or made in any other way) and other corporeal hereditaments; also a manor, an advowson, and a rent and other incorporeal hereditaments, and an easement, right, privilege, or benefit in, over, or derived from land; but not an undivided share in land; and "mines and minerals" include any strata or seam of minerals or substances in or under any land, and powers of working and getting the same but not an undivided share thereof; and "manor" includes a lordship, and reputed manor or lordship; and "hereditament" means any real property which on an intestacy occurring before the commencement of this Act might have devolved upon an heir;

(x) "Legal estates" mean the estates, interests and charges, in or over land (subsisting or created at law) which are by this Act authorised to subsist or to be created as legal estates; "equitable interests" mean all the other interests and charges in or over land or in the proceeds of sale thereof; an equitable interest "capable of subsisting as a legal estate" means such as could validly subsist or be created as a legal estate under this Act;

(xi) "Legal powers" include the powers vested in a chargee by way of legal mortgage or in an estate owner under which a legal estate can be transferred or created; and "equitable powers" mean all the powers in or over land under which equitable interests or powers only can be transferred or created;

(xii) "Limitation Acts" means the Real Property Limitation Acts 1833, 1837 and 1874, and "limitation" includes a trust;

[(xiii) "Mental disorder" has the meaning assigned to it by [section 1 of the Mental Health Act 1983] and "receiver" in relation to a person suffering from mental disorder, means a receiver appointed for that person under [Part VIII of the Mental Health Act 1959 or Part VII of the said Act of 1983].]

(xiv) a "mining lease" means a lease for mining purposes, that is, the searching for, winning, working, getting, making merchantable, carrying away, or disposing of mines and minerals, or purposes connected therewith, and includes a grant or licence for mining purposes;

(xv) "Minister" means [the Minister of Agriculture, Fisheries and Food];

(xvi) "Mortgage" includes any charge or lien on any property for securing money or money's worth; "legal mortgage" means a mortgage by demise or subdemise or a charge by way of legal mortgage and "legal mortgagee" has a corresponding meaning; "mortgage money" means money or money's worth secured by a mortgage; "mortgagor" includes any person from time to time deriving title under the original mortgagor or entitled to redeem a mortgage according to his estate interest or right in the mortgaged property; "mortgagee" includes a chargee by way of legal mortgage and any person from time to time deriving title under the original mortgagee; and "mortgagee in possession" is, for the purposes of this Act, a mortgagee who, in right of the mortgage, has entered into and is in possession of the mortgaged property; and "right of redemption" includes an option to repurchase only if the option in effect creates a right of redemption;

(xvii) "Notice" includes constructive notice;

(xviii) "Personal representative" means the executor, original or by representation, or administrator for the time being of a deceased person, and as regards any liability for the payment of death duties includes any person who takes possession of or intermeddles with the property of a deceased person without the authority of the personal representatives or the court;

(xix) "Possession" includes receipt of rents and profits or the right to receive the same, if any; and "income" includes rents and profits;

(xx) "Property" includes any thing in action, and any interest in real or personal property;

(xxi) "Purchaser" means a purchaser in good faith for valuable consideration and includes a lessee, mortgagee or other person who for valuable consideration acquires an interest in property except that in Part I of this Act and elsewhere where so expressly provided "purchaser" only means a person who acquires an interest in or charge on property for money or money's worth; and in reference to a legal estate includes a chargee by way of legal mortgage; and where the context so requires "purchaser" includes an intending purchaser; "purchase" has a meaning corresponding with that of "purchaser"; and "valuable consideration" includes marriage but does not include a nominal consideration in money;

(xxii) "Registered land" has the same meaning as in the Land Registration Act 1925, and "Land Registrar" means the Chief Land Registrar under that Act;

(xxiii) "Rent" includes a rent service or a rentcharge, or other rent, toll, duty, royalty, or annual or periodical payment in money or money's worth, reserved or issuing out of or charged upon land, but does not include mortgage interest; "rentcharge" includes a fee farm rent; "fine" includes a premium or foregift and any payment, consideration, or benefit in the nature of a fine, premium or foregift; "lessor" includes an underlessor and a person deriving title under a lessor or underlessor; and "lessee" includes an underlessee and a person deriving title under a lessee or underlessee, and "lease" includes an underlease or other tenancy;

(xxiv) "Sale" includes an extinguishment of manorial incidents, but in other respects means a sale properly so called;

(xxv) "Securities" include stocks, funds and shares;

(xxvi) "Tenant for life", "statutory owner", "settled land", "settlement", "vesting deed", "subsidiary vesting deed", "vesting order", "vesting instrument", "trust instrument", "capital money" and "trustees of the settlement" have the same meanings as in the Settled Land Act 1925;

(xxvii) "Term of years absolute" means a term of years (taking effect either in possession or in reversion whether or not at a rent) with or without impeachment for waste, subject or not to another legal estate, and either certain or liable to determination by notice, re-entry, operation of law, or by a provision for cesser on redemption, or in any other event (other than the dropping of a life, or the determination of a determinable life interest); but does not include any term of years determinable with life or lives or with the cesser of a determinable life interest, nor, if created after the commencement of this Act, a term of years which is not expressed to take effect in possession within twenty-one years after the creation thereof where required by this Act to take effect within that period; and in this definition the expression "term of years" includes a term for less than a year, or for a year or years and a fraction of a year or from year to year;

(xxviii) "Trust Corporation" means the Public Trustee or a corporation either appointed by the court in any particular case to be a trustee or entitled by rules made under subsection (3) of section four of the Public Trustee Act 1906 to act as custodian trustee;

(xxix) "Trust for sale", in relation to land, means an immediate binding trust for sale, whether or not exercisable at the request or with the consent of any person, and with or without a power at discretion to postpone the sale; "trustees for sale" mean the persons (including a personal representative) holding land on trust for sale; and "power to postpone a sale" means power to postpone in the exercise of a discretion;

(xxx) "United Kingdom" means Great Britain and Northern Ireland;

(xxxi) "Will" includes codicil.

[(1A) Any reference in this Act to money being paid into court shall be construed as referring to the money being paid into the Supreme Court or any other court that has jurisdiction, and any reference in this Act to the court, in a context referring to the investment or application of money paid into court, shall be construed, in the case of money paid into the Supreme Court, as referring to the High Court, and in the case of money paid into another court, as referring to that other court.]

(2) Where an equitable interest in or power over property arises by statute or operation of law, references to the creation of an interest or power include references to any interest or power so arising.

(3) References to registration under the Land Charges Act 1925, apply to any registration made under any other statute which is by the Land Charges Act 1925, to have effect as if the registration had been made under that Act.

[49]

NOTES

Sub-s (1): para (iiiA) added by the County Courts Act 1984, s 148(1), Sch 2, para 10; in para (iv) words omitted repealed by the Finance Act 1949, s 52(9), (10), Sch 11, Part IV; para (xiii) substituted by the Mental Health Act 1959, s 149(1), Sch 7, Part I, amended by the Mental Health Act 1983, s 148, Sch 4, para 5; para (xv) amended by the Transfer of Functions (Ministry of Food) Order 1955, SI 1955 No 554.

Sub-s (1A): added by the Administration of Justice Act 1965, ss 17, 18, Sch 1.

SCHEDULES

SECOND SCHEDULE

Sections 76, 77

Implied Covenants

Part I

Covenant implied in a Conveyance for valuable Consideration, other than a Mortgage, by a Person who Conveys and is expressed to Convey as Beneficial Owner

That, notwithstanding anything by the person who so conveys or any one through whom he derives title otherwise than by purchase for value, made, done, executed, or omitted, or knowingly suffered, the person who so conveys has, with the concurrence of every other person, if any, conveying by his direction, full power to convey the subject-matter expressed to and be conveyed, subject as, if so expressed, and in the manner in which, it is expressed to be conveyed, and that, notwithstanding anything as aforesaid, that subject-matter shall remain to and be quietly entered upon, received, and held, occupied, enjoyed, and taken by the person to whom the conveyance is expressed to be made, and any person deriving title under him, and the benefit thereof shall be received and taken accordingly, without any lawful interruption or disturbance by the person who so conveys or any person conveying by his direction, or rightfully claiming or to claim by, through, under, or in trust for the person who so conveys or any person conveying by his direction, or by, through, or under any one (not being a person claiming in respect of an estate or interest subject whereto the conveyance is expressly made), through whom the person who so conveys, derives title, otherwise than by purchase for value:

And that, freed and discharged from, or otherwise by the person who so conveys sufficiently indemnified against, all such estates, incumbrances, claims, and demands, other than those subject to which the conveyance is expressly made, as, either before or after the date of the conveyance, have been or shall be made, occasioned, or suffered by that person or by any person conveying by his direction, or by any person rightfully claiming by, through, under, or in trust for the person who so conveys, or by, through, or under any person conveying by his direction, by, through, or under any one through whom the person who so conveys derives title, otherwise than by purchase for value:

And further, that the person who so conveys, and any person conveying by his direction, and every other person having or rightfully claiming any estate or interest in the subject-matter of conveyance, other than an estate or interest subject whereto the conveyance is expressly made, by, through, under, or in trust for the person who so conveys, or by, through, or under any person conveying by his direction, or by, through, or under any one through whom the person who so conveys derives title, otherwise than by purchase for value, will, from time to time and at all times after the date of the conveyance, on the request and at the cost of any person to whom the conveyance is expressed to be made, or of any person deriving title under him, execute and do all such lawful assurances and things for further or more perfectly assuring the subject-matter of the conveyance to the person to whom the conveyance is made, and to those deriving title under him, subject as, if so expressed, and in the manner in which the conveyance is expressed to be made, as by him or them or any of them shall be reasonably required.

In the above covenant a purchase for value shall not be deemed to include a conveyance in consideration of marriage. **[50]**

PART II

FURTHER COVENANT IMPLIED IN A CONVEYANCE OF LEASEHOLD PROPERTY FOR VALUABLE CONSIDERATION, OTHER THAN A MORTGAGE, BY A PERSON WHO CONVEYS AND IS EXPRESSED TO CONVEY AS BENEFICIAL OWNER

That, notwithstanding anything by the person who so conveys, or any one through whom he derives title, otherwise than by purchase for value, made, done, executed, or omitted, or knowingly suffered, the lease or grant creating the term or estate for which the land is conveyed is, at the time of conveyance, a good, valid, and effectual lease or grant of the property conveyed, and is in full force, unforfeited, unsurrendered, and has in nowise become void or voidable, and that, notwithstanding anything as aforesaid, all the rents reserved by, and all the covenants, conditions, and agreements contained in, the lease or grant, and on the part of the lessee or grantee and the persons deriving title under him to be paid, observed, and performed, have been paid, observed, and performed up to the time of conveyance.

In the above covenant a purchase for value shall not be deemed to include a conveyance in consideration of marriage. **[51]**

PART III

COVENANT IMPLIED IN A CONVEYANCE BY WAY OF MORTGAGE BY A PERSON WHO CONVEYS AND IS EXPRESSED TO CONVEY AS BENEFICIAL OWNER

That the person who so conveys, has, with the concurrence of every other person, if any, conveying by his direction, full power to convey the subject-matter expressed to be conveyed by him, subject as, if so expressed, and in the manner in which it is expressed to be conveyed.

And also that, if default is made in payment of the money intended to be secured by the conveyance, or any interest thereon, or any part of that money or interest, contrary to any provision in the conveyance, it shall be lawful for the person to whom the conveyance is expressed to be made, and the persons deriving title under him, to enter into and upon, or receive, and thenceforth quietly hold, occupy, and enjoy or take and have, the subject-matter expressed to be conveyed, or any part thereof, without any lawful interruption or disturbance by the person who so conveys, or any person conveying by his direction, or any other person (not being a person claiming in respect of an estate or interest subject whereto the conveyance is expressly made):

And that, freed and discharged from, or otherwise by the person who so conveys sufficiently indemnified against, all estates, incumbrances, claims, and demands whatever, other than those subject whereto the conveyance is expressly made:

And further, that the person who so conveys and every person conveying by his direction, and every person deriving title under any of them, and every other person having or rightfully claiming any estate or interest in the subject-matter of conveyance, or any part thereof, other than an estate or interest subject whereto the conveyance is expressly made, will from time to time and at all times, on the request of any person to whom the conveyance is expressed to be made, or of any person deriving title under him, but as long as any right of redemption exists under the conveyance, at the cost of the person so conveying, or of those deriving title under him, and afterwards at the cost of the person making the request, execute and do all such lawful assurances and things for further or more perfectly assuring the subject-matter of conveyance and every part thereof to the person to whom the conveyance is made, and to those deriving title under him, subject as, if so expressed, and in the manner in which the conveyance is expressed to be made, as by him or them or any of them shall be reasonably required.

The above covenant in the case of a charge shall have effect as if for references to "conveys", "conveyed" and "conveyance" there were substituted respectively references to "charges", "charged" and "charge". **[52]**

PART IV

COVENANT IMPLIED IN A CONVEYANCE BY WAY OF MORTGAGE OF FREEHOLD PROPERTY SUBJECT TO A RENT OR OF LEASEHOLD PROPERTY BY A PERSON WHO CONVEYS AND IS EXPRESSED TO CONVEY AS BENEFICIAL OWNER

That the lease or grant creating the term or estate for which the land is held is, at the time of conveyance a good, valid, and effectual lease or grant of the land conveyed and is in full force, unforfeited, and unsurrendered and has in nowise become void or voidable, and that all the rents reserved by, and all the covenants, conditions, and agreements contained in, the lease or grant, and on the part of the lessee or grantee and the persons deriving title under him to be paid, observed, and performed, have been paid, observed, and performed up to the time of conveyance:

And also that the person so conveying, or the persons deriving title under him, will at all times, as long as any money remains owing on the security of the conveyance, pay, observe, and perform, or cause to be paid, observed, and performed all the rents reserved by, and all the covenants conditions and agreements contained in, the lease or grant, and on the part of the lessee or grantee and the persons deriving title under him to be paid, observed, and performed, and will keep the person to whom the conveyance is made, and those deriving title under him, indemnified against all actions, proceedings, costs, charges, damages, claims and demands, if any, to be incurred or sustained by him or them by reason of the non-payment of such rent or the non-observance or non-performance of such covenants, conditions, and agreements, or any of them.

The above convenant in the case of a charge shall have effect as if for references to "conveys", "conveyed" and "conveyance" there were substituted respectively references to "charges", "charged" and "charge". **[53]**

PART V

COVENANT IMPLIED IN A CONVEYANCE BY WAY OF SETTLEMENT, BY A PERSON WHO CONVEYS AND IS EXPRESSED TO CONVEY AS SETTLOR

That the person so conveying, and every person deriving title under him by deed or act or operation of law in his lifetime subsequent to that conveyance, or by testamentary disposition or devolution in law, on his death, will, from time to time, and at all times, after the date of that conveyance, at the request and cost of any person deriving title thereunder, execute and do all such lawful assurances and things for further or more perfectly assuring the subject-matter of the conveyance to the persons to whom the conveyance is made and those deriving title under them, as by them or any of them shall be reasonably required, subject as, if so expressed, and in the manner in which the conveyance is expressed to be made. **[54]**

PART VI

COVENANT IMPLIED IN ANY CONVEYANCE, BY EVERY PERSON WHO CONVEYS AND IS EXPRESSED TO CONVEY AS TRUSTEE OR MORTGAGEE, OR AS PERSONAL REPRESENTATIVE OF A DECEASED PERSON, ... OR UNDER AN ORDER OF THE COURT

That the person so conveying has not executed or done, or knowingly suffered, or been party or privy to, any deed or thing, whereby or by means whereof the subject-matter of the conveyance, or any part thereof, is or may be impeached, charged, affected, or incumbered in title, estate, or otherwise, or whereby or by means whereof the person who so conveys is in anywise hindered from conveying the subject-matter of the conveyance, or any part thereof, in the manner in which it is expressed to be conveyed.

The foregoing covenant may be implied in an assent in like manner as in a conveyance by deed. **[55]**

NOTES

Words omitted from heading repealed by the Mental Health Act 1959, s 149(2), Sch 8, Part I.

PART VII

COVENANT IMPLIED IN A CONVEYANCE FOR VALUABLE CONSIDERATION, OTHER THAN A MORTGAGE, OF THE ENTIRETY OF LAND AFFECTED BY A RENTCHARGE

That the grantees or the persons deriving title under them will at all times, from the date of the conveyance or other date therein stated, duly pay the said rentcharge and observe and perform all the covenants, agreements and conditions contained in the deed or other document creating the rentcharge, and thenceforth on the part of the owner of the land to be observed and performed:

And also will at all times, from the date aforesaid, save harmless and keep indemnified the conveying parties and their respective estates and effects, from and against all proceedings, costs, claims and expenses on account of any omission to pay the said rentcharge or any part thereof, or any breach of any of the said covenants, agreements and conditions. **[56]**

PART VIII

COVENANTS IMPLIED IN A CONVEYANCE FOR VALUABLE CONSIDERATION, OTHER THAN A MORTGAGE, OF PART OF LAND AFFECTED BY A RENTCHARGE, SUBJECT TO A PART (NOT LEGALLY APPORTIONED) OF THAT RENTCHARGE

(i) That the grantees, or the persons deriving title under them, will at all times, from the date of the conveyance or other date therein stated, pay the apportioned rent and observe and perform all the covenants (other than the covenant to pay the entire rent) and conditions contained in the deed or other document creating the rentcharge, so far as the same relate to the land conveyed:

And also will at all times, from the date aforesaid, save harmless and keep indemnified the conveying parties and their respective estates and effects, from and against all proceedings, costs, claims and expenses on account of any omission to pay the said apportioned rent, or any breach of any of the said covenants and conditions, so far as the same relate as aforesaid.

(ii) That the conveying parties, or the persons deriving title under them, will at all times, from the date of the conveyance or other date therein stated, pay the balance of the rentcharge (after deducting the apportioned rent aforesaid, and any other rents similarly apportioned in respect of land not retained), and observe and perform all the covenants, other than the covenant to pay the entire rent, and conditions contained in the deed or other document creating the rentcharge, so far as the same relate to the land not included in the conveyance and remaining vested in the covenantors:

And also will at all times, from the date aforesaid, save harmless and keep indemnified the grantees and their estates and effects, from and against all proceedings, costs, claims and expenses on account of any omission to pay the aforesaid balance of the rentcharge, or any breach of any of the said covenants and conditions so far as they relate aforesaid. **[57]**

PART IX

COVENANT IN A CONVEYANCE FOR VALUABLE CONSIDERATION, OTHER THAN A MORTGAGE, OF THE ENTIRETY OF THE LAND COMPRISED IN A LEASE FOR THE RESIDUE OF THE TERM OR INTEREST CREATED BY THE LEASE

That the assignees, or the persons deriving title under them, will at all times, from the date of the conveyance or other date therein stated, duly pay all rent becoming due under the lease creating the term or interest for which the land is conveyed, and observe and perform all the covenants, agreements and conditions therein contained and thenceforth on the part of the lessees to be observed and performed:

And also will at all times, from the date aforesaid, save harmless and keep indemnified the conveying parties and their estates and effects, from and against all proceedings, costs, claims and expenses on account of any omission to pay the said rent or any breach of any of the said covenants, agreements and conditions. **[58]**

PART X

COVENANTS IMPLIED IN A CONVEYANCE FOR VALUABLE CONSIDERATION, OTHER THAN A MORTGAGE, OF PART OF THE LAND COMPRISED IN A LEASE, FOR THE RESIDUE OF THE TERM OR INTEREST CREATED BY THE LEASE, SUBJECT TO A PART (NOT LEGALLY APPORTIONED) OF THAT RENT

(i) That the assignees, or the persons deriving title under them, will at all times, from the date of the conveyance or other date therein stated, pay the apportioned rent and observe and perform all the covenants, other than the covenant to pay the entire rent, agreements and conditions contained in the lease creating the term or interest for which the land is conveyed, and thenceforth on the part of the lessees to be observed and performed, so far as the same relate to the land conveyed:

And also will at all times from the date aforesaid save harmless and keep indemnified, the conveying parties and their respective estates and effects, from and against all proceedings, costs, claims and expenses on account of any omission to pay the said apportioned rent or any breach of any of the said covenants, agreements and conditions, so far as the same relate as aforesaid.

(ii) That the conveying parties, or the persons deriving title under them, will at all times, from the date of the conveyance, or other date therein stated, pay the balance of the rent (after deducting the apportioned rent aforesaid and any other rents similarly apportioned in respect of land not retained) and observe and perform all the covenants, other than the covenant to pay the entire rent, agreements and conditions contained in the lease and on the part of the lessees to be observed and performed so far as the same relate to the land demised (other than the land comprised in the conveyance) and remaining vested in the covenantors:

And also will at all times, from the date aforesaid, save harmless and keep indemnified, the assignees and their estates and effects, from and against all proceedings, costs, claims and expenses on account of any omission to pay the aforesaid balance of the rent or any breach of any of the said covenants, agreements and conditions so far as they relate as aforesaid. **[59]**

SETTLED LAND ACT 1925

(c 18)

ARRANGEMENT OF SECTIONS

PART II

POWERS OF A TENANT FOR LIFE

Leasing Powers

Section		Para
41	Power to lease for ordinary or building or mining or forestry purposes	[60]
42	Regulations respecting leases generally	[61]
43	Leasing powers for special objects	[62]

Provisions as to building, mining and forestry leases

44	Regulations respecting building leases	[63]
45	Regulations respecting mining leases	[64]

Section		Para
46	Variation of building or mining lease according to circumstances of district	[65]
47	Capitalisation of part of mining rent	[66]
48	Regulations respecting forestry leases	[67]

An Act to consolidate the enactments relating to Settled Land in England and Wales. [9 April 1925]

PART II

POWERS OF A TENANT FOR LIFE

Leasing Powers

41. Power to lease for ordinary or building or mining or forestry purposes

A tenant for life may lease the settled land, or any part thereof, or any easement, right, or privilege of any kind over or in relation to the land, for any purpose whatever, whether involving waste or not, for any term not exceeding—

(i) In case of a building lease, nine hundred and ninety-nine years;
(ii) In case of a mining lease, one hundred years;
(iii) In case of a forestry lease, nine hundred and ninety-nine years;
(iv) In case of any other lease, fifty years. **[60]**

(1) Save as hereinafter provided, every lease—

42. Regulations respecting leases generally

(i) shall be by deed, and be made to take effect in possession not later than twelve months after its date, or in reversion after an existing lease having not more than seven years to run at the date of the new lease;
(ii) shall reserve the best rent that can reasonably be obtained, regard being had to any fine taken, and to any money laid out or to be laid out for the benefit of the settled land, and generally to the circumstances of the case;
(iii) shall contain a covenant by the lessee for payment of the rent, and a condition of re-entry on the rent not being paid within a time therein specified not exceeding thirty days.

(2) A counterpart of every lease shall be executed by the lessee and delivered to the tenant for life or statutory owner, of which execution and delivery the execution of the lease by the tenant for life or statutory owner shall be sufficient evidence.

(3) A statement, contained in a lease or in an indorsement thereon, signed by the tenant for life or statutory owner, respecting any matter of fact or of calculation under this Act in relation to the lease, shall, in favour of the lessee and of those claiming under him, be sufficient evidence of the matter stated.

(4) A fine received on the grant of a lease under any power conferred by this Act shall be deemed to be capital money arising under this Act.

(5) A lease at the best rent that can be reasonably obtained without fine, and whereby the lessee is not exempted from punishment for waste, may be made—

(i) Where the term does not exceed twenty-one years—

(*a*) without any notice of an intention to make the lease having been given under this Act; and (*b*) notwithstanding that there are no trustees of the settlement; and

(ii) Where the term does not extend beyond three years from the date of the writing, by any writing under hand only containing an agreement instead of a covenant by the lessee for payment of rent. **[61]**

43. Leasing powers for special objects

The leasing power of a tenant for life extends to the making of—

(i) a lease for giving effect (in such manner and so far as the law permits) to a covenant of renewal, performance whereof could be enforced against the owner for the time being of the settled land; and

(ii) a lease for confirming, as far as may be, a previous lease being void or voidable, but so that every lease, as and when confirmed, shall be such a lease as might at the date of the original lease have been lawfully granted under this Act or otherwise, as the case may require. **[62]**

Provisions as to building, mining and forestry leases

44. Regulations respecting building leases

(1) Every building lease shall be made partly in consideration of the lessee, or some person by whose direction the lease is granted, or some other person, having erected or agreeing to erect buildings, new or additional, or having improved or repaired or agreeing to improve or repair buildings, or having executed or agreeing to execute on the land leased, an improvement authorised by this Act for or in connexion with building purposes.

(2) A peppercorn rent or a nominal or other rent less than the rent ultimately payable, may be made payable for the first five years or any less part of the term.

(3) Where the land is contracted to be leased in lots, the entire amount of rent to be ultimately payable may be apportioned among the lots in any manner:

Provided that—

(i) the annual rent reserved by any lease shall not be less than [50p]; and

(ii) the total amount of the rents reserved on all leases for the time being granted shall not be less than the total amount of the rents which, in order that the leases may be in conformity with this Act, ought to be reserved in respect of the whole land for the time being leased; and

(iii) the rent reserved by any lease shall not exceed one-fifth part of the full annual value of the land comprised in that lease with the buildings thereon when completed. **[63]**

NOTES

Amended by the Decimal Currency Act 1969, s 10(1).

45. Regulations respecting mining leases

(1) In a mining lease—

(i) the rent may be made to be ascertainable by or to vary according to the acreage worked, or by or according to the quantities of any mineral or substance gotten, made merchantable, converted, carried away, or disposed of, in or from the settled land, or any other land, or by or according to any facilities given in that behalf; and

(ii) the rent may also be made to vary according to the price of the minerals or substances gotten, or any of them, and such price may be the saleable value, or the price or value appearing in any trade or market or other price list or return from time to time, or may be the marketable value as ascertained in any manner prescribed by the lease (including a reference to arbitration), or may be an average of any such prices or values taken during a specified period; and

(iii) a fixed or minimum rent may be made payable, with or without power for the lessees, in case the rent, according to acreage or quantity or otherwise, in any specified period does not produce an amount equal to the fixed or minimum rent, to make up the deficiency in any subsequent specified period, free of rent other than the fixed or minimum rent.

(2) A lease may be made partly in consideration of the lessee having executed, or agreeing to execute, on the land leased an improvement authorised by this Act, for or in connexion with mining purposes. **[64]**

46. Variation of building or mining lease according to circumstances of district

(1) Where it is shown to the court with respect to the district in which any settled land is situate, either—

(i) that it is the custom for land therein to be leased for building or mining purposes for a longer term or on other conditions than the term or conditions specified in that behalf in this Act; or

(ii) that it is difficult to make leases for building or mining purposes of land therein, except for a longer term or on other conditions than the term and conditions specified in that behalf in this Act;

the court may, if it thinks fit, authorise generally the tenant for life or statutory owner to make from time to time leases of or affecting the settled land in that district, or parts thereof for any term or on any conditions as in the order of the court expressed, or may, if it thinks fit, authorise the tenant for life or statutory owner to make any such lease in any particular case.

(2) Thereupon the tenant for life or statutory owner, and, subject to any direction in the order of the court to the contrary, each of his successors in title being a tenant for life or statutory owner, may make in any case, or in the particular case, a lease of the settled land, or part thereof, in conformity with the order. **[65]**

47. Capitalisation of part of mining rent

Under a mining lease, whether the mines or minerals leased are already opened or in work or not, unless a contrary intention is expressed in the settlement there shall be from time to time set aside, as capital money arising under this Act, part of the rent as follows, namely—where the tenant for life or statutory owner is impeachable for waste in respect of minerals, three fourth parts of the rent, and otherwise one fourth part thereof, and in every such case the residue of the rent shall go as rents and profits. **[66]**

48. Regulations respecting forestry leases

(1) In the case of a forestry lease—

(i) a peppercorn rent or a nominal or other rent less than the rent ultimately payable, may be made payable for the first ten years or any less part of the term;

(ii) the rent may be made to be ascertainable by, or to vary according to the value of the timber on the land comprised in the lease, or the produce thereof, which may during any year be cut, converted carried away, or otherwise disposed of;

(iii) a fixed or minimum rent may be made payable, with or without power for the lessee, in case the rent according to value in any specified period does not produce an amount equal to the fixed or minimum rent, to make up the deficiency in any subsequent specified period, free of rent other than the fixed or minimum rent; and

(iv) any other provisions may be made for the sharing of the proceeds or profits of the user of the land between the reversioner and the Forestry Commissioners.

(2) In this expression "timber" includes all forest products. **[67]**

LANDLORD AND TENANT ACT 1927

(c 36)

ARRANGEMENT OF SECTIONS

PART I

COMPENSATION FOR IMPROVEMENTS AND GOODWILL ON THE TERMINATION OF TENANCIES OF BUSINESS PREMISES

Section		Para
1	Tenant's right to compensation for improvements	[68]
2	Limitation on tenant's right to compensation in certain cases	[69]
3	Landlord's right to object	[70]
8	Rights of mesne landlords	[71]
9	Restriction on contracting out	[72]
10	Right of entry	[73]
11	Right to make deductions	[74]
12	Application of 13 and 14 Geo 5 c 9, s 20	[75]
13	Power to apply and raise capital money	[76]
14	Power to sell or grant leases notwithstanding restrictions	[77]
15	Provisions as to reversionary leases	[78]
16	Landlord's right to reimbursement of increased taxes, rates or insurance premiums	[79]
17	Holdings to which Part I applies	[80]

PART II

GENERAL AMENDMENTS OF THE LAW OF LANDLORD AND TENANT

18	Provisions as to covenants to repair	[81]
19	Provisions as to covenants not to assign, etc, without licence or consent	[82]
20	Apportionment of rents	[83]

Section Para

PART III

GENERAL

21 The tribunal .. [84]
23 Service of notices .. [85]
24 Application to Crown, Duchy, ecclesiastical and charity lands .. [86]
25 Interpretation .. [87]
26 Short title, commencement and extent .. [88]

SCHEDULES

First Schedule—*Provisions as to Charges* .. [89]
Second Schedule ..
Part I—Application to Crown and Duchy Land .. [90]
Part II—Application to Ecclesiastical and Charity Land .. [91]

An Act to provide for the payment of compensation for improvements and goodwill to tenants of premises used for business purposes, or the grant of a new lease in lieu thereof; and to amend the law of landlord and tenant

[22 December 1927]

PART I

COMPENSATION FOR IMPROVEMENTS AND GOODWILL ON THE TERMINATION OF TENANCIES OF BUSINESS PREMISES

1. Tenant's right to compensation for improvements

(1) Subject to the provisions of this Part of this Act, a tenant of a holding to which this Part of this Act applies shall, if a claim for the purpose is made in the prescribed manner [and within the time limited by section forty-seven of the Landlord and Tenant Act 1954] be entitled, at the termination of the tenancy, on quitting his holding, to be paid by his landlord compensation in respect of any improvement (including the erection of any building) on his holding made by him or his predecessors in title, not being a trade or other fixture which the tenant is by law entitled to remove, which at the termination of the tenancy adds to the letting value of the holding:

Provided that the sum to be paid as compensation for any improvement shall not exceed—

(*a*) the net addition to the value of the holding as a whole which may be determined to be the direct result of the improvement; or

(*b*) the reasonable cost of carrying out the improvement at the termination of the tenancy, subject to a deduction of an amount equal to the cost (if any) of putting the works constituting the improvement into a reasonable state of repair, except so far as such cost is covered by the liability of the tenant under any covenant or agreement as to the repair of the premises.

(2) In determining the amount of such net addition as aforesaid, regard shall be had to the purposes for which it is intended that the premises shall be used after the termination of the tenancy, and if it is shown that it is intended to demolish or to make structural alterations in the premises or any part thereof or to use the premises for a different purpose, regard shall be had to the effect of such demolition, alteration or change of user on the additional value attributable

to the improvement, and to the length of time likely to elapse between the termination of the tenancy and the demolition, alteration or change of user.

(3) In the absence of agreement between the parties, all questions as to the right to compensation under this section, or as to the amount thereof, shall be determined by the tribunal hereinafter mentioned, and if the tribunal determines that, on account of the intention to demolish or alter or to change the user of the premises, no compensation or a reduced amount of compensation shall be paid, the tribunal may authorise a further application for compensation to be made by the tenant if effect is not given to the intention within such time as may be fixed by the tribunal. **[68]**

NOTES
Amended by the Landlord and Tenant Act 1954, s 47(5).

2. Limitation on tenant's right to compensation in certain cases

(1) A tenant shall not be entitled to compensation under this Part of this Act—

(*a*) in respect of any improvement made before the commencement of this Act; or

(*b*) in respect of any improvement made in pursuance of a statutory obligation, or of any improvement which the tenant or his predecessors in title were under an obligation to make in pursuance of a contract entered into, whether before or after the passing of this Act, for valuable consideration, including a building lease; or

(*c*) in respect of any improvement made less than three years before the termination of the tenancy; or

(*d*) if within two months after the making of the claim under section one, subsection (1), of this Act the landlord serves on the tenant notice that he is willing and able to grant to the tenant, or obtain the grant to him of, a renewal of the tenancy at such rent and for such term as, failing agreement, the tribunal may consider reasonable; and, where such a notice is so served and the tenant does not within one month from the service of the notice send to the landlord an acceptance in writing of the offer, the tenant shall be deemed to have declined the offer.

(2) Where an offer of the renewal of a tenancy by the landlord under this section is accepted by the tenant, the rent fixed by the tribunal shall be the rent which in the opinion of the tribunal a willing lessee other than the tenant would agree to give and a willing lessor would agree to accept for the premises, having regard to the terms of the lease, but irrespective of the value attributable to the improvement in respect of which compensation would have been payable.

(3) The tribunal in determining the compensation for an improvement shall in reduction of the tenant's claim take into consideration any benefits which the tenant or his predecessors in title may have received from the landlord or his predecessors in title in consideration expressly or impliedly of the improvement. **[69]**

3. Landlord's right to object

(1) Where a tenant of a holding to which this Part of this Act applies proposes to make an improvement on his holding, he shall serve on his landlord notice of his intention to make such improvement, together with a specification and plan showing the proposed improvement and the part of the existing premises affected thereby, and if the landlord, within three months after the service of the notice, serves on the tenant notice of objection, the tenant may, in the

prescribed manner, apply to the tribunal, and the tribunal may, after ascertaining that notice of such intention has been served upon any superior landlords interested and after giving such persons an opportunity of being heard, if satisfied that the improvement—

(*a*) is of such a nature as to be calculated to add to the letting value of the holding at the termination of the tenancy; and

(*b*) is reasonable and suitable to the character thereof; and

(*c*) will not diminish the value of any other property belonging to the same landlord, or to any superior landlord from whom the immediate landlord of the tenant directly or indirectly holds;

and after making such modifications (if any) in the specification or plan as the tribunal thinks fit, or imposing such other conditions as the tribunal may think reasonable, certify in the prescribed manner that the improvement is a proper improvement:

Provided that, if the landlord proves that he has offered to execute the improvement himself in consideration of a reasonable increase of rent, or of such increase of rent as the tribunal may determine, the tribunal shall not give a certificate under this section unless it is subsequently shown to the satisfaction of the tribunal that the landlord has failed to carry out his undertaking.

(2) In considering whether the improvement is reasonable and suitable to the character of the holding, the tribunal shall have regard to any evidence brought before it by the landlord or any superior landlord (but not any other person) that the improvement is calculated to injure the amenity or convenience of the neighbourhood.

(3) The tenant shall, at the request of any superior landlord or at the request of the tribunal, supply such copies of the plans and specifications of the proposed improvement as may be required.

(4) Where no such notice of objection as aforesaid to a proposed improvement has been served within the time allowed by this section, or where the tribunal has certified an improvement to be a proper improvement, it shall be lawful for the tenant as against the immediate and any superior landlord to execute the improvement according to the plan and specification served on the landlord, or according to such plan and specification as modified by the tribunal or by agreement between the tenant and the landlord or landlords affected, anything in any lease of the premises to the contrary notwithstanding:

Provided that nothing in this subsection shall authorise a tenant to execute an improvement in contravention of any restriction created or imposed—

(*a*) for naval, military or air force purposes;

(*b*) for civil aviation purposes under the powers of the Air Navigation Act 1920;

(*c*) for securing any rights of the public over the foreshore or bed of the sea.

(5) A tenant shall not be entitled to claim compensation under this Part of this Act in respect of any improvement unless he has, or his predecessors in title have, served notice of the proposal to make the improvement under this section, and (in case the landlord has served notice of objection thereto) the improvement has been certified by the tribunal to be a proper improvement and the tenant has complied with the conditions, if any, imposed by the tribunal, nor unless the improvement is completed within such time after the service on the landlord of the notice of the proposed improvement as may be agreed between the tenant

and the landlord or may be fixed by the tribunal, and where proceedings have been taken before the tribunal, the tribunal may defer making any order as to costs until the expiration of the time so fixed for the completion of the improvement.

(6) Where a tenant has executed an improvement of which he has served notice in accordance with this section and with respect to which either no notice of objection has been served by the landlord or a certificate that it is a proper improvement has been obtained from the tribunal, the tenant may require the landlord to furnish to him a certificate that the improvement has been duly executed; and if the landlord refuses or fails within one month after the service of the requisition to do so, the tenant may apply to the tribunal who, if satisfied that the improvement has been duly executed, shall give a certificate to that effect.

Where the landlord furnishes such a certificate, the tenant shall be liable to pay any reasonable expenses incurred for the purpose by the landlord, and if any question arises as to the reasonableness of such expenses, it shall be determined by the tribunal. **[70]**

NOTES

Air Navigation Act 1920: see now Civil Aviation Act 1949.

8. Rights of mesne landlords

(1) Where, in the case of any holding, there are several persons standing in the relation to each other of lessor and lessee, the following provisions shall apply:—

Any mesne landlord who has paid or is liable to pay compensation under this Part of this Act shall, at the end of his term, be entitled to compensation from his immediate landlord in like manner and on the same conditions as if he had himself made the improvement . . . in question, except that it shall be sufficient if the claim for compensation is made at least two months before the expiration of his term:

A mesne landlord shall not be entitled to make a claim under this section unless he has, within the time and in the manner prescribed, served on his immediate superior landlord copies of all documents relating to proposed improvements and claims which have been sent to him in pursuance of this Part of this Act:

Where such copies are so served, the said superior landlord shall have, in addition to the mesne landlord, the powers conferred by or in pursuance of this Part of this Act in like manner as if he were the immediate landlord of the occupying tenant, and shall, in the manner and to the extent prescribed, be at liberty to appear before the tribunal and shall be bound by the proceedings:

. . .

(2) In this section, references to a landlord shall include references to his predecessors in title. **[71]**

NOTES

Words omitted repealed by the Landlord and Tenant Act 1954, ss 45, 68(1), Sch 7.

9. Restriction on contracting out

This Part of this Act shall apply notwithstanding any contract to the contrary, being a contract made at any time after the eighth day of February, nineteen hundred and twenty-seven:

. . . **[72]**

NOTES
Words omitted repealed by the Landlord and Tenant Act 1954, s 49.

10. Right of entry

The landlord of a holding to which this Part of this Act applies, or any person authorised by him may at all reasonable times enter on the holding or any part of it, for the purpose of executing any improvement he has undertaken to execute and of making any inspection of the premises which may reasonably be required for the purposes of this Part of this Act. **[73]**

11. Right to make deductions

(1) Out of any money payable to a tenant by way of compensation under this Part of this Act, the landlord shall be entitled to deduct any sum due to him from the tenant under or in respect of the tenancy.

(2) Out of any money due to the landlord from the tenant under or in respect of the tenancy, the tenant shall be entitled to deduct any sum payable to him by the landlord by way of compensation under this Part of this Act. **[74]**

12. Application of 13 and 14 Geo 5 c 9, s 20

Section twenty of the Agricultural Holdings Act 1923 (which relates to charges in respect of money paid for compensation), as set out and modified in the First Schedule to this Act, shall apply to the case of money paid for compensation under this Part of this Act, including any proper costs, charges, or expenses incurred by a landlord in opposing any proposal by a tenant to execute an improvement, or in contesting a claim for compensation, and to money expended by a landlord in executing an improvement the notice of a proposal to execute which has been served on him by a tenant under this Part of this Act. **[75]**

13. Power to apply and raise capital money

(1) Capital money arising under the Settled Land Act 1925 (either as originally enacted or as applied in relation to trusts for sale by section twenty-eight of the Law of Property Act 1925), or under the University and College Estates Act 1925, may be applied—

(*a*) in payment as for an improvement authorised by the Act of any money expended and costs incurred by a landlord under or in pursuance of this Part of this Act in or about the execution of any improvement;

(*b*) in payment of any sum due to a tenant under this Part of this Act in respect of compensation for an improvement . . . and any costs, charges, and expenses incidental thereto;

(*c*) in payment of the costs, charges, and expenses of opposing any proposal by a tenant to execute an improvement.

(2) The satisfaction of a claim for such compensation as aforesaid shall be included amongst the purposes for which a tenant for life, statutory owner, trustee for sale, or personal representative may raise money under section seventy-one of the Settled Land Act 1925.

(3) Where the landlord liable to pay compensation for an improvement . . . is a tenant for life or in a fiduciary position, he may require the sum payable as

compensation and any costs, charges, and expenses incidental thereto, to be paid out of any capital money held on the same trusts as the settled land.

In this subsection "capital money" includes any personal estate held on the same trusts as the land, and "settled land" includes land held on trust for sale or vested in a personal representative. **[76]**

NOTES

Words omitted repealed by the Landlord and Tenant Act 1954, s 45, Sch 7, Part I.

14. Power to sell or grant leases notwithstanding restrictions

Where the powers of a landlord to sell or grant leases are subject to any statutory or other restrictions, he shall, notwithstanding any such restrictions or any rule of law to the contrary, be entitled to offer to sell or grant any such reversion or lease as would under this Part of this Act relieve him from liability to pay compensation thereunder, and to convey and grant the same, and to execute any lease which he may be ordered to grant under this Part of this Act. **[77]**

15. Provisions as to reversionary leases

(1) Where the amount which a landlord is liable to pay as compensation for an improvement under this Part of this Act has been determined by agreement or by an award of the tribunal, and the landlord had before the passing of this Act granted or agreed to grant a reversionary lease commencing on or after the termination of the then existing tenancy, the rent payable under the reversionary lease shall, if the tribunal so directs, be increased by such amount as, failing agreement, may be determined by the tribunal having regard to the addition to the letting value of the holding attributable to the improvement:

Provided that no such increase shall be permissible unless the landlord has served or caused to be served on the reversionary lessee copies of all documents relating to the improvement when proposed which were sent to the landlord in pursuance of this Part of this Act.

(2) The reversionary lessee shall have the same right of objection to the proposed improvement and of appearing and being heard at any proceedings before the tribunal relative to the proposed improvement as if he were a superior landlord, and if the amount of compensation for the improvement is determined by the tribunal, any question as to the increase of rent under the reversionary lease shall, where practicable, be settled in the course of the same proceedings.

(3) . . . **[78]**

NOTES

Sub-s (3): repealed by the Landlord and Tenant Act 1954, s 45, Sch 7, Part I.

16. Landlord's right to reimbursement of increased taxes, rates or insurance premiums

Where the landlord is liable to pay any . . . rates (including water rate) in respect of any premises comprised in a holding, or has undertaken to pay the premiums on any fire insurance policy on any such premises, and in consequence of any improvement executed by the tenant on the premises under this Act the assessment of the premises or the rate of premium on the policy is increased, the tenant shall be liable to pay to the landlord sums equal to the amount by which—

(*a*) the . . . rates payable by the landlord are increased by reason of the increase of such assessment;

(*b*) the fire premium payable by the landlord is increased by reason of the increase in the rate of premium;

and the sums so payable by the tenant shall be deemed to be in the nature of rent and shall be recoverable as such from the tenant, [. . .] **[79]**

NOTES

First and second words omitted repealed by the Finance Act 1963, s 73(7), Sch 13, Part IV; third words omitted repealed by the Housing Act 1980, s 152, Sch 26.

17. Holdings to which Part I applies

(1) The holdings to which this Part of this Act applies are any premises held under a lease, other than a mining lease, made whether before or after the commencement of this Act, and used wholly or partly for carrying on thereat any trade or business, and not being agricultural holdings within the meaning of the *Agricultural Holdings Act 1923* [Agricultural Holdings Act 1986].

(2) This Part of this Act shall not apply to any holding let to a tenant as the holder of any office, appointment or employment, from the landlord, and continuing so long as the tenant holds such office, appointment or employment, but in the case of a tenancy created after the commencement of this Act, only if the contract is in writing and expresses the purpose for which the tenancy is created.

(3) For the purposes of this section, premises shall not be deemed to be premises used for carrying on thereat a trade or business—

(*a*) by reason of their being used for the purpose of carrying on thereat any profession;

(*b*) by reason that the tenant thereof carries on the business of subletting the premises as residential flats, whether or not the provision of meals or any other service for the occupants of the flats is undertaken by the tenant:

Provided that, so far as this Part of this Act relates to improvements, premises regularly used for carrying on a profession shall be deemed to be premises used for carrying on a trade or business.

(4) In the case of premises used partly for purposes of a trade or business and partly for other purposes, this Part of this Act shall apply to improvements only if and so far as they are improvements in relation to the trade or business. **[80]**

NOTES

Sub-s (1): words in italics repealed with savings and words in square brackets substituted with savings by the Agricultural Holdings Act 1986, ss 99, 100, Sch 13, para 3, Sch 14, para 14.

Agricultural Holdings Act 1923: see now Agricultural Holdings Act 1948.

PART II

GENERAL AMENDMENTS OF THE LAW OF LANDLORD AND TENANT

18. Provisions as to covenants to repair

(1) Damages for a breach of a covenant or agreement to keep or put premises in repair during the currency of a lease, or to leave or put premises in repair at the termination of a lease, whether such covenant or agreement is expressed or

implied, and whether general or specific, shall in no case exceed the amount (if any) by which the value of the reversion (whether immediate or not) in the premises is diminished owing to the breach of such covenant or agreement as aforesaid; and in particular no damage shall be recovered for a breach of any such covenant or agreement to leave or put premises in repair at the termination of a lease, if it is shown that the premises, in whatever state of repair they might be, would at or shortly after the termination of the tenancy have been or be pulled down, or such structural alterations made therein as would render valueless the repairs covered by the covenant or agreement.

(2) A right of re-entry or forfeiture for a breach of any such covenant or agreement as aforesaid shall not be enforceable, by action or otherwise, unless the lessor proves that the fact that such a notice as is required by section one hundred and forty-six of the Law of Property Act 1925, had been served on the lessee was known either—

(*a*) to the lessee; or
(*b*) to an under-lessee holding under an under-lease which reserved a nominal reversion only to the lessee; or
(*c*) to the person who last paid the rent due under the lease either on his own behalf or as agent for the lessee or under-lessee;

and that a time reasonably sufficient to enable the repairs to be executed had elapsed since the time when the fact of the service of the notice came to the knowledge of any such person.

Where a notice has been sent by registered post addressed to a person at his last known place of abode in the United Kingdom, then, for the purposes of this subsection, that person shall be deemed, unless the contrary is proved, to have had knowledge of the fact that the notice had been served as from the time at which the letter would have been delivered in the ordinary course of post.

This subsection shall be construed as one with section one hundred and forty-six of the Law of Property Act 1925.

(3) This section applies whether the lease was created before or after the commencement of this Act. **[81]**

19. Provisions as to covenants not to assign, etc, without licence or consent

(1) In all leases whether made before or after the commencement of this Act containing a covenant condition or agreement against assigning, under-letting, charging or parting with the possession of demised premises or any part thereof without licence or consent, such covenant condition or agreement shall, notwithstanding any express provision to the contrary, be deemed to be subject—

(*a*) to a proviso to the effect that such licence or consent is not to be unreasonably withheld, but this proviso does not preclude the right of the landlord to require payment of a reasonable sum in respect of any legal or other expenses incurred in connection with such licence or consent; and
(*b*) (if the lease is for more than forty years, and is made in consideration wholly or partially of the erection, or the substantial improvement, addition or alteration of buildings, and the lessor is not a Government department or local or public authority, or a statutory or public utility company) to a proviso to the effect that in the case of any assignment, under-letting, charging or parting with the possession (whether by the holders of the lease or any under-tenant whether immediate or not)

effected more than seven years before the end of the term no consent or licence shall be required, if notice in writing of the transaction is given to the lessor within six months after the transaction is effected.

(2) In all leases whether made before or after the commencement of this Act containing a covenant condition or agreement against the making of improvements without licence or consent, such covenant condition or agreement shall be deemed, notwithstanding any express provision to the contrary, to be subject to a proviso that such licence or consent is not to be unreasonably withheld; but this proviso does not preclude the right to require as a condition of such licence or consent the payment of a reasonable sum in respect of any damage to or diminution in the value of the premises or any neighbouring premises belonging to the landlord, and of any legal or other expenses properly incurred in connection with such licence or consent nor, in the case of an improvement which does not add to the letting value of the holding, does it preclude the right to require as a condition of such licence or consent, where such a requirement would be reasonable, an undertaking on the part of the tenant to reinstate the premises in the condition in which they were before the improvement was executed.

(3) In all leases whether made before or after the commencement of this Act containing a covenant condition or agreement against the alteration of the user of the demised premises, without licence or consent, such covenant condition or agreement shall, if the alteration does not involve any structural alteration of the premises, be deemed, notwithstanding any express provision to the contrary, to be subject to a proviso that no fine or sum of money in the nature of a fine, whether by way of increase of rent or otherwise, shall be payable for or in respect of such licence or consent; but this proviso does not preclude the right of the landlord to require payment of a reasonable sum in respect of any damage to or diminution in the value of the premises or any neighbouring premises belonging to him and of any legal or other expenses incurred in connection with such licence or consent.

Where a dispute as to the reasonableness of any such sum has been determined by a court of competent jurisdiction, the landlord shall be bound to grant the licence or consent on payment of the sum so determined to be reasonable.

(4) This section shall not apply to leases of agricultural holdings within the meaning of the *Agricultural Holdings Act 1923* [Agricultural Holdings Act 1986], and paragraph (*b*) of subsection (1), subsection (2) and subsection (3) of this section shall not apply to mining leases. **[82]**

NOTES

Sub-s (4): words in italics repealed with savings and words in square brackets substituted with savings by the Agricultural Holdings Act 1986, ss 99, 100, Sch 13, para 3, Sch 14, para 15.

Agricultural Holdings Act 1923: see now Agricultural Holdings Act 1948.

20. Apportionment of rents

(1) An order of apportionment of a rent reserved by a lease or any such other rent or payment as is mentioned in section ten of the Inclosure Act 1854, may be made by the [Secretary of State] under sections ten to fourteen of that Act, on the application of any person interested in the rent or payment, or any part thereof, or in the land in respect of which such rent or payment is payable, without the concurrence of any other person:

Provided that the Minister may in any such case, on the application of any person entitled to the rent or payment or any part thereof, require as a condition of making the order that any apportioned part of the rent or payment which does not exceed the yearly sum of [£5] shall be redeemed forthwith [in accordance with sections 8 to 10 of the Rentcharges Act 1977 (which, for the purposes of this section, shall have effect with the necessary modifications)].

[(1A) An order of apportionment under sections 10 to 14 of the said Act of 1854 may provide for the amount apportioned to any part of the land in respect of which the rent or payment is payable to be nil.]

(2) Where the reason for the application was due to any action taken by a person other than the applicant, the Minister shall, notwithstanding anything in section fourteen of the Inclosure Act 1854, have power to direct by whom and in what manner the expenses of the application or any part thereof are to be paid. **[83]**

NOTES

Commencement: Before 1 January 1970 (sub-ss (1), (2)); 3 October 1980 (sub-s (1A)).

Commencement order: SI 1980 No 1406.

Sub-s (1): first amendment made by SI 1955 No 554, SI 1965 No 143, SI 1967 No 156, SI 1970 No 1681; second amendment made by the Housing Act 1980, s 143; third amendment made by the Rentcharges Act 1977, s 17(1), Sch 1.

Sub-s (1A): added by the Housing Act 1980, s 143.

PART III

GENERAL

[21. The tribunal

The tribunal for the purposes of Part I of this Act shall be the court exercising jurisdiction in accordance with the provisions of section sixty-three of the Landlord and Tenant Act 1954.] **[84]**

NOTES

Substituted by the Landlord and Tenant Act 1954, s 63(10).

23. Service of notices

(1) Any notice, request, demand or other instrument under this Act shall be in writing and may be served on the person on whom it is to be served either personally, or by leaving it for him at his last known place of abode in England or Wales, or by sending it through the post in a registered letter addressed to him there, or, in the case of a local or public authority or a statutory or a public utility company, to the secretary or other proper officer at the principal office of such authority or company, and in the case of a notice to a landlord, the person on whom it is to be served shall include any agent of the landlord duly authorised in that behalf.

(2) Unless or until a tenant of a holding shall have received notice that the person theretofore entitled to the rents and profits of the holding (hereinafter referred to as "the original landlord") has ceased to be so entitled, and also notice of the name and address of the person who has become entitled to such rents and profits, any claim, notice, request, demand, or other instrument, which the tenant shall serve upon or deliver to the original landlord shall be deemed to have been served upon or delivered to the landlord of such holding. **[85]**

24. Application to Crown, Duchy, ecclesiastical and charity lands

(1) This Act shall apply to land belonging to His Majesty in right of the Crown or the Duchy of Lancaster and to land belonging to the Duchy of Cornwall, and to land belonging to any Government department, and for that purpose the provisions of the Agricultural Holdings Act 1923, relating to Crown and Duchy Lands, as set out and adapted in Part I of the Second Schedule to this Act, shall have effect.

(2) The provisions of the Agricultural Holdings Act 1923, with respect to the application of that Act to ecclesiastical and charity lands, as set out and adapted in Part II of the Second Schedule to this Act, shall apply for the purposes of this Act.

(3) . . .

(4) Where any land is vested in the [official custodian for charities] in trust for any charity, the trustees of the charity and not the [custodian] shall be deemed to be the landlord for the purposes of this Act. **[86]**

NOTES

Sub-s (3): repealed by the Endowments and Glebe Measure 1976, s 47(4), Sch 8.
Sub-s (4): amended by the Charities Act 1960, s 48(1), Sch 6.
Agricultural Holdings Act 1923: see now Agricultural Holdings Act 1948.

25. Interpretation

(1) For the purposes of this Act, unless the context otherwise requires—

The expression "tenant" means any person entitled in possession to the holding under any contract of tenancy, whether the interest of such tenant was acquired by original contract, assignment, operation of law or otherwise;

The expression "landlord" means any person who under a lease is, as between himself and the tenant or other lessee, for the time being entitled to the rents and profits of the demised premises payable under the lease;

The expression "predecessor in title" in relation to a tenant or landlord means any person through whom the tenant or landlord has derived title, whether by assignment, by will, by intestacy, or by operation of law;

The expression "lease" means a lease, under-lease or other tenancy, assignment operating as a lease or under-lease, or an agreement for such lease, under-lease tenancy, or assignment;

The expression "mining lease" means a lease for any mining purpose or purposes connected therewith, and "mining purposes" include the sinking and searching for, winning, working, getting, making merchantable, smelting or otherwise converting or working for the purposes of any manufacture, carrying away, and disposing of mines and minerals, in or under land, and the erection of buildings, and the execution of engineering and other works suitable for those purposes;

The expression "term of years absolute" has the same meaning as in the Law of Property Act 1925;

The expression "statutory company" means any company constituted by or under an Act of Parliament to construct, work or carry on any . . . water, electricity, tramway, hydraulic power, dock, canal or railway undertaking; and the expression "public utility company" means any company within the meaning of the Companies (Consolidation) Act 1908, or a society registered under the Industrial and Provident Societies Acts 1893 to 1913, carrying on any such undertaking;

The expression "prescribed" means prescribed by County Court Rules, except that in relation to proceedings before the High Court, it means prescribed by rules of the Supreme Court.

(2) The designation of landlord and tenant shall continue to apply to the parties until the conclusion of any proceedings taken under or in pursuance of this Act in respect of compensation. **[87]**

NOTES

Sub-s (1): word omitted from definition "statutory company" repealed by the Gas Act 1986, s 67(4), Sch 9, Part I.

26. Short title, commencement and extent

(1) This Act may be cited as the Landlord and Tenant Act 1927.

(2) . . .

(3) This Act shall extend to England and Wales only. **[88]**

NOTES

Sub-s (2): repealed by the Statute Law Revision Act 1950.

SCHEDULES

FIRST SCHEDULE

Section 12

PROVISIONS AS TO CHARGES

(1) A landlord, on paying to the tenant the amount due to him under Part I of this Act, in respect of compensation for an improvement . . . under that Part, or on expending after notice given in accordance with that Part such amount as may be necessary to execute an improvement, shall be entitled to obtain from the Minister of Agriculture and Fisheries (hereinafter referred to as the Minister) an order in favour of himself and the persons deriving title under him charging the holding, or any part thereof, with repayment of the amount paid or expended, including any proper costs, charges or expenses incurred by a landlord in opposing any proposal by a tenant to execute an improvement or in contesting a claim for compensation, and of all costs properly incurred by him in obtaining the charge, with such interest, and by such instalments, and with such directions for giving effect to the charge, as the Minister thinks fit.

(2) Where the landlord obtaining the charge is not an absolute owner of the holding for his own benefit, no instalment or interest shall be made payable after the time when the improvement . . . in respect whereof compensation is paid will, in the opinion of the Minister, have become exhausted.

(3) Where the estate or interest of a landlord is determinable or liable to forfeiture by reason of his creating or suffering any charge thereon, that estate or interest shall not be determined or forfeited by reason of his obtaining such a charge, anything in any deed, will or other instrument to the contrary thereof notwithstanding.

(4) The sum charged shall be a charge on the holding, or the part thereof charged, for the landlord's interest therein and for interests in the reversion immediately expectant on the termination of the lease; but so that, in any case where the landlord's interest is an interest in a leasehold, the charge shall not extend beyond that leasehold interest.

(5) Any company now or hereafter incorporated by Parliament, and having power to advance money for the improvement of land, may take an assignment of any charge made under this Schedule, upon such terms and conditions as may be agreed upon between the company and the person entitled to the charge, and may assign any charge so acquired by them.

(6) Where a charge may be made under this Schedule for compensation due under an award, the tribunal making the award shall, at the request and cost of the person

entitled to obtain the charge, certify the amount to be charged and the term for which the charge may properly be made, having regard to the time at which each improvement . . . in respect of which compensation is awarded is to be deemed to be exhausted.

(7) A charge under this Schedule may be registered under section ten of the Land Charges Act 1925, as a land charge of Class A. **[89]**

NOTES
Words omitted repealed by the Landlord and Tenant Act 1954, s 45, Sch 7, Part I; words "Minister of Agriculture and Fisheries" substituted for "Minister of Agriculture, Fisheries and Food" by the Transfer of Functions (Ministry of Food) Order 1955, SI 1955 No 554.

SECOND SCHEDULE

Section 24

PART I

APPLICATION TO CROWN AND DUCHY LAND

1.—(*a*) With respect to any land belonging to His Majesty in right of the Crown, or to a Government department, for the purposes of this Act, the Commissioners of Crown Lands, or other the proper officer or body having charge of the land for the time being, or, in case there is no such officer or body, then such person as His Majesty may appoint in writing under the Royal Sign Manual, shall represent His Majesty, and shall be deemed to be the landlord.

(*b*) . . .

2.—(*a*) With respect to land belonging to His Majesty in right of the Duchy of Lancaster, for the purposes of this Act, the Chancellor of the Duchy shall represent His Majesty, and shall be deemed to be the landlord.

(*b*) The amount of any compensation under Part I of this Act payable by the Chancellor of the Duchy shall be raised and paid as an expense incurred in improvement of land belonging to His Majesty in right of the Duchy within section twenty-five of the Act of the fifty-seventh year of King George the Third, chapter ninety-seven.

3.—(*a*) With respect to land belonging to the Duchy of Cornwall, for the purposes of this Act, such person as the Duke of Cornwall, or the possessor for the time being of the Duchy of Cornwall appoints, shall represent the Duke of Cornwall or other the possessor aforesaid, and be deemed to be the landlord, and may do any act or thing under this Act which a landlord is authorised or required to do thereunder.

(*b*) Any compensation under Part I of this Act payable by the Duke of Cornwall, or other the possessor aforesaid, shall be paid, and advances therefor made, in the manner and subject to the provisions of section eight of the Duchy of Cornwall Management Act 1863, with respect to improvements of land mentioned in that section. **[90]**

NOTES
Para 1: words omitted repealed by the Crown Estate Act 1961, s 9(4), Sch 3, Part II.

PART II

APPLICATION TO ECCLESIASTICAL AND CHARITY LAND

1. (*a*) Where lands are assigned or secured as the endowment of a see, the powers by this Act conferred on a landlord in respect of charging land shall not be exercised by the bishop in respect of those lands, except with the previous approval in writing of the Estates Committee of the Ecclesiastical Commissioners.

(*b*) . . .

(*c*) The Ecclesiastical Commissioners may, if they think fit, on behalf of an ecclesiastical corporation, out of any money in their hands, pay to the tenant the amount of compensation due to him under Part I of this Act, and thereupon they may, instead of the corporation obtain from the minister a charge on the holding in respect thereof in favour of themselves, . . .

2. The powers by this Act conferred on a landlord in respect of charging land shall not be exercised by trustees for ecclesiastical or charitable purposes, except with the approval in writing of the Charity Commissioners or the Board of Education, as the case may require. **[91]**

NOTES

Para 1: words omitted repealed by the Endowments and Glebe Measure 1976, s 47(4), Sch 8.

LEASEHOLD PROPERTY (REPAIRS) ACT 1938

(c 34)

ARRANGEMENT OF SECTIONS

Section		Para
1	Restriction on enforcement of repairing covenants in long leases of small houses	[92]
2	Restriction on right to recover expenses of survey, etc	[93]
3	Saving for obligation to repair on taking possession	[94]
5	Application to past breaches	[95]
6	Court having jurisdiction under this Act	[96]
7	Application of certain provisions of 15 and 16 Geo 5 c 20	[97]
8	Short title and extent	[98]

An Act to amend the law as to the enforcement by landlords of obligations to repair and similar obligations arising under leases [23 June 1938]

1. Restriction on enforcement of repairing covenants in long leases of small houses

(1) Where a lessor serves on a lessee under subsection (1) of section one hundred and forty-six of the Law of Property Act 1925, a notice that relates to a breach of a covenant or agreement to keep or put in repair during the currency of the lease [all or any of the property comprised in the lease], and at the date of the service of the notice [three] years or more of the term of the lease remain unexpired, the lessee may within twenty-eight days from that date serve on the lessor a counter-notice to the effect that he claims the benefit of this Act.

(2) A right to damages for a breach of such a covenant as aforesaid shall not be enforceable by action commenced at any time at which [three] years or more of the term of the lease remain unexpired unless the lessor has served on the lessee not less than one month before the commencement of the action such a notice as is specified in subsection (1) of section one hundred and forty-six of the Law of Property Act 1925, and where a notice is served under this subsection, the lessee may, within twenty-eight days from the date of the service thereof, serve on the lessor a counter-notice to the effect that he claims the benefit of this Act.

(3) Where a counter-notice is served by a lessee under this section, then, notwithstanding anything in any enactment or rule of law, no proceedings, by action or otherwise, shall be taken by the lessor for the enforcement of any right of re-entry or forfeiture under any proviso or stipulation in the lease for breach of the covenant or agreement in question, or for damages for breach thereof, otherwise than with the leave of the court.

(4) A notice served under subsection (1) of section one hundred and forty-six of the Law of Property Act 1925, in the circumstances specified in subsection

(1) of this section, and a notice served under subsection (2) of this section shall not be valid unless it contains a statement, in characters not less conspicuous than those used in any other part of the notice, to the effect that the lessee is entitled under this Act to serve on the lessor a counter-notice claiming the benefit of this Act, and a statement in the like characters specifying the time within which, and the manner in which, under this Act a counter-notice may be served and specifying the name and address for service of the lessor.

(5) Leave for the purposes of this section shall not be given unless the lessor proves—

(*a*) that the immediate remedying of the breach in question is requisite for preventing substantial diminution in the value of his reversion, or that the value thereof has been substantially diminished by the breach;

(*b*) that the immediate remedying of the breach is required for giving effect in relation to the [premises] to the purposes of any enactment, or of any byelaw or other provision having effect under an enactment, [or for giving effect to any order of a court or requirement of any authority under any enactment or any such byelaw or other provision as aforesaid];

(*c*) in a case in which the lessee is not in occupation of the whole of the [premises as respects which the covenant or agreement is proposed to be enforced], that the immediate remedying of the breach is required in the interests of the occupier of [those premises] or of part thereof;

(*d*) that the breach can be immediately remedied at an expense that is relatively small in comparison with the much greater expense that would probably be occasioned by postponement of the necessary work; or

(*e*) special circumstances which in the opinion of the court, render it just and equitable that leave should be given.

(6) The court may, in granting or in refusing leave for the purposes of this section, impose such terms and conditions on the lessor or on the lessee as it may think fit. **[92]**

NOTES

Amended by the Landlord and Tenant Act 1954, s 51(2), (5).

2. Restriction on right to recover expenses of survey, etc

A lessor on whom a counter-notice is served under the preceding section shall not be entitled to the benefit of subsection (3) of section one hundred and forty-six of the Law of Property Act 1925, (which relates to costs and expenses incurred by a lessor in reference to breaches of covenant), so far as regards any costs or expenses incurred in reference to the breach in question, unless he makes an application for leave for the purposes of the preceding section, and on such an application the court shall have power to direct whether and to what extent the lessor is to be entitled to the benefit thereof. **[93]**

3. Saving for obligation to repair on taking possession

This Act shall not apply to a breach of a covenant or agreement in so far as it imposes on the lessee an obligation to put [premises] in repair that is to be performed upon the lessee taking possession of the premises or within a reasonable time thereafter. **[94]**

NOTES
Amended by the Landlord and Tenant Act 1954, s 51(2).

5. Application to past breaches

This Act applies to leases created, and to breaches occurring, before or after the commencement of this Act. **[95]**

6. Court having jurisdiction under this Act

(1) In this Act the expression "the court" means the county court, except in a case in which any proceedings by action for which leave may be given would have to be taken in a court other than the county court, and means in the said excepted case that other court.

(2) . . . **[96]**

NOTES
Sub-s (2): repealed by the County Courts Act 1959, s 204, Sch 3.

7. Application of certain provisions of 15 and 16 Geo 5 c 20

(1) In this Act the expressions "lessor", "lessee" and "lease" have the meanings assigned to them respectively by sections one hundred and forty-six and one hundred and fifty-four of the Law of Property Act 1925, except that they do not include any reference to such a grant as is mentioned in the said section one hundred and forty-six, or to the person making, or to the grantee under such a grant, or to persons deriving title under such a person; and "lease" means a lease for a term of [seven years or more, not being a lease of an agricultural holding within the meaning of the *Agricultural Holdings Act 1948* [Agricultural Holdings Act 1986]].

(2) The provisions of section one hundred and ninety-six of the said Act (which relate to the service of notices) shall extend to notices and counter-notices required or authorised by this Act. **[97]**

NOTES
First amendment in square brackets made by the Landlord and Tenant Act 1954, s 51(2); words in italics repealed with savings and subsequent words in square brackets substituted with savings by the Agricultural Holdings Act 1986, ss 99, 100, Sch 13, para 3, Sch 14, para 17.

8. Short title and extent

(1) This Act may be cited as the Leasehold Property (Repairs) Act 1938.

(2) This Act shall not extend to Scotland or to Northern Ireland. **[98]**

ACCOMMODATION AGENCIES ACT 1953

(c 23)

An Act to prohibit the taking of certain commissions in dealings with persons seeking houses or flats to let and the unauthorised advertisement for letting of houses and flats [14 July 1953]

1. Illegal commissions and advertisements

(1) Subject to the provisions of this section, any person who, . . . —

(*a*) demands or accepts payment of any sum of money in consideration of registering, or undertaking to register, the name or requirements of any person seeking the tenancy of a house;

(*b*) demands or accepts payment of any sum of money in consideration of supplying, or undertaking to supply, to any person addresses or other particulars of houses to let; or

(*c*) issues any advertisement, list or other document describing any house as being to let without the authority of the owner of the house or his agent,

shall be guilty of an offence.

(2) A person shall not be guilty of an offence under this section by reason of his demanding or accepting payment from the owner of a house of any remuneration payable to him as agent for the said owner.

(3) A person being a solicitor shall not be guilty of an offence under this section by reason of his demanding or accepting payment of any remuneration in respect of business done by him as such.

(4) A person shall not be guilty of an offence under this section by reason of his demanding or accepting any payment in consideration of the display in a shop, or of the publication in a newspaper, of any advertisement or notice, or by reason of the display or publication as aforesaid of an advertisement or notice received for the purpose in the ordinary course of business.

(5) Any person guilty of an offence under this section shall be liable on summary conviction to a fine not exceeding [level 3 on the standard scale] or to imprisonment for a term not exceeding three months, or to both such fine and imprisonment.

(6) In this section the following expressions have the meanings hereby assigned to them that is to say:—

"house" includes any part of a building which is occupied or intended to be occupied as a dwelling;

"newspaper" includes any periodical or magazine;

"owner", in relation to a house, means the person having power to grant a lease of the house. **[99]**

NOTES

Sub-s (1): words omitted repealed by the Expiring Laws Act 1969, s 1.

Sub-s (5): maximum fine increased and converted to a level on the standard scale by the Criminal Justice Act 1982, ss 37, 38, 46.

2. Short title, extent, commencement and duration

(1) This Act may be cited as the Accommodation Agencies Act 1953.

(2) This Act shall not extend to Northern Ireland.

(3) This Act shall come into operation one month after the date on which it is passed.

(4) . . . **[100]**

NOTES

Sub-s (4): repealed by the Expiring Laws Act 1969, s 1.

LANDLORD AND TENANT ACT 1954

(c 56)

ARRANGEMENT OF SECTIONS

PART I

SECURITY OF TENURE FOR RESIDENTIAL TENANTS

Security of tenure for tenants under ground leases, etc

Section		Para
1	Protection of residential tenants on termination of long tenancies at low rents	[101]
2	Tenancies to which s 1 applies	[102]

Continuation and termination of tenancies to which s 1 applies

3	Continuation of tenancies to which s 1 applies	[103]
4	Termination of tenancy by the landlord	[104]
5	Termination of tenancy by the tenant	[105]

Statutory tenancies arising under Part I

6	Application of Rent Acts where tenant retains possession	[106]
7	Settlement of terms of statutory tenancy	[107]
8	Provisions as to repairs during period of statutory tenancy	[108]
9	Principles to be observed in determining terms of statutory tenancy as to repairs and rent	[109]
10	Provisions as to liabilities under tenant's covenants in former lease	[110]

Provisions as to possession on termination of long tenancy

12	Grounds for resumption of possession by landlord	[111]
13	Landlord's application for possession	[112]
14	Provisions where tenant not ordered to give up possession	[113]

General and supplementary provisions

16	Relief for tenant where landlord proceeding to enforce covenants	[114]
17	Prohibition of agreements excluding Part I	[115]
18	Duty of tenants of residential property to give information to landlords or superior landlords	[116]
19	Application of Part I to tenancies granted in continuation of long tenancies	[117]
20	Assumptions on which court to determine future questions	[118]
21	Meaning of "the landlord" in Part I and provisions as to mesne landlords, etc	[119]
22	Interpretation of Part I	[120]

PART II

SECURITY OF TENURE FOR BUSINESS, PROFESSIONAL AND OTHER TENANTS

Tenancies to which Part II applies

23	Tenancies to which Part II applies	[121]

Continuation and renewal of tenancies

24	Continuation of tenancies to which Part II applies and grant of new tenancies	[122]
24A	Rent while tenancy continues by virtue of s 24	[123]
25	Termination of tenancy by the landlord	[124]
26	Tenant's request for a new tenancy	[125]
27	Termination by tenant of tenancy for fixed term	[126]
28	Renewal of tenancies by agreement	[127]

Application to court for new tenancies

29	Order by court for grant of a new tenancy	[128]
30	Opposition by landlord to application for a new tenancy	[129]

Section		Para
31	Dismissal of application for new tenancy where landlord successfully opposes	[130]
31A	Grant of new tenancy in some cases where section 30(1)(*f*) applies	[131]
32	Property to be comprised in new tenancy	[132]
33	Duration of new tenancy	[133]
34	Rent under new tenancy	[134]
35	Other terms of new tenancy	[135]
36	Carrying out of order for new tenancy	[136]
37	Compensation where order for new tenancy precluded on certain grounds	[137]
38	Restriction on agreements exluding provisions of Part II	[138]

General and supplementary provisions

39	Saving for compulsory acquisitions	[139]
40	Duty of tenants and landlords of business premises to give information to each other	[140]
41	Trusts	[141]
41A	Partnerships	[142]
42	Groups of companies	[143]
43	Tenancies excluded from Part II	[144]
43A	Jurisdiction of county court to make declaration	[145]
44	Meaning of "the landlord" in Part II, and provisions as to mesne landlords, etc	[146]
46	Interpretation of Part II	[147]

PART III

COMPENSATION FOR IMPROVEMENTS

47	Time for making claims for compensation for improvements	[148]
48	Amendments as to limitations on tenant's right to compensation	[149]
50	Interpretation of Part III	[150]

PART IV

MISCELLANEOUS AND SUPPLEMENTARY

51	Extension of Leasehold Property (Repairs) Act 1938	[151]
53	Jurisdiction of county court where lessor refuses licence or consent	[152]
54	Determination of tenancies of derelict land	[153]
55	Compensation for possession obtained by misrepresentation	[154]
56	Application to Crown	[155]
57	Modification on grounds of public interest of rights under Part II	[156]
58	Termination on special grounds of tenancies to which Part II applies	[157]
59	Compensation for exercise of powers under ss 57 and 58	[158]
60	Special provisions as to premises provided under Distribution of Industry Acts 1945 and 1950, etc	[159]
60A	Welsh Development Agency premises	[160]
60B	Development Board for Rural Wales premises	[161]
63	Jurisdiction of court for purposes of Parts I and II and of Part I of Landlord and Tenant Act 1927	[162]
64	Interim continuation of tenancies pending determination by court	[163]
65	Provisions as to reversions	[164]
66	Provisions as to notices	[165]
67	Provisions as to mortgagees in possession	[166]
68	Repeal of enactments and transitional provisions	[167]
69	Interpretation	[168]
70	Short title and citation, commencement and extent	[169]

SCHEDULES

Schedule 1—*Supplementary Provisions as to Payments for Accrued Tenant's Repairs*	
Part I—Provisions as to making of payment in lump sum	[170]
Part II—Provisions as to making of payment by instalments	[171]
Part III—Variation of agreement or determination as to time for making payment	[172]
Part IV—Supplementary	[173]
Schedule 2—*Further Provisions as to Repair where Tenant retains Possession*	[174]
Schedule 3—*Grounds for Possession on Termination of Tenancy*	[175]
Schedule 4—*Modifications of Part I in relation to Periodical Tenancies*	[176]

Section Para
Schedule 5—*Provisions for purposes of Part I where Immediate Landlord is not the Freeholder* .. .. [177]
Schedule 6—*Provisions for purposes of Part II where Immediate Landlord is not the Freeholder* .. .. [178]
Schedule 8—*Application of Part II to land belonging to Crown and Duchies of Lancaster and Cornwall* .. .. [179]
Schedule 9—*Transitional provisions* .. .. [180]

An Act to provide security of tenure for occupying tenants under certain leases of residential property at low rents and for occupying sub-tenants of tenants under such leases; to enable tenants occupying property for business, professional or certain other purposes to obtain new tenancies in certain cases; to amend and extend the Landlord and Tenant Act 1927, the Leasehold Property (Repairs) Act 1938; and section eighty-four of the Law of Property Act 1925; to confer jurisdiction on the County Court in certain disputes between landlords and tenants; to make provision for the termination of tenancies of derelict land; and for purposes connected with the matters aforesaid. [30 July 1954]

PART I

SECURITY OF TENURE FOR RESIDENTIAL TENANTS

Security of tenure for tenants under ground leases, etc

1. Protection of residential tenants on termination of long tenancies at low rents

On the termination in accordance with the provisions of this Part of this Act of a tenancy to which this section applies the tenant shall be entitled to the protection of the [Rent Act] subject to and in accordance with those provisions.
[101]

NOTES
Amended by the Rent Act 1968, s 117(2), Sch 15.
The Rent Act: Rent Act 1977.

2. Tenancies to which s 1 applies

(1) The foregoing section applies to any long tenancy at a low rent, being a tenancy as respects which for the time being the following condition (hereinafter referred to as "the qualifying condition") is fulfilled, that is to say that the circumstances (as respects the property comprised in the tenancy, the use of that property, and all other relevant matters) are such that on the coming to an end of the tenancy at that time the tenant would, if the tenancy had not been one at a low rent, be entitled by virtue of the [Rent Act] to retain possession of the whole or part of the property comprised in the tenancy.

(2) At any time before, but not more than twelve months before, the term date application may be made to the court as respects any long tenancy at a low rent, not being at the time of the application a tenancy as respects which the qualifying condition is fulfilled, for an order declaring that the tenancy is not to be treated for the purposes of this Part of this Act as a tenancy to which the foregoing section applies; and where such an application is made—

(*a*) the court, if satisfied that the tenancy is not likely, immediately before the term date, to be a tenancy to which the foregoing section applies, but not otherwise, shall make the order;

(*b*) if the court makes the order, then notwithstanding anything in subsection (1) of this section the tenancy shall not thereafter be treated as a tenancy to which the foregoing section applies.

(3) Anything authorised or required to be done under the following provisions of this Part of this Act in relation to tenancies to which the foregoing section applies shall, if done before the term date in relation to a long tenancy at a low rent, not be treated as invalid by reason only that at the time at which it was done the qualifying condition was not fulfilled as respects the tenancy.

(4) In this Part of this Act the expression "long tenancy" means a tenancy granted for a term of years certain exceeding twenty-one years, whether or not subsequently extended by act of the parties or by any enactment.

(5) In this Part of this Act the expression "tenancy at a low rent" means a tenancy the rent payable in respect whereof (or where that rent is a progressive rent, the maximum rent payable in respect whereof) is less than two-thirds of the rateable value of the property comprised in the tenancy; and [for the purposes of this subsection the rateable value of the property is that which would be taken as its rateable value for the purposes of section 5 of the Rent Act 1977].

(6) In this Part of this Act the expression "term date", in relation to a tenancy granted for a term of years certain, means the date of expiry of the term.

[(7) In determining whether a long tenancy is, or at any time was, a tenancy at a low rent there shall be disregarded such part (if any) of the sums payable by the tenant as is expressed (in whatever terms) to be payable in respect of rates, services, repairs, maintenance, or insurance, unless it could not have been regarded by the parties as a part so payable.

In this section "long tenancy" does not include a tenancy which is, or may become, terminable before the end of the term by notice given to the tenant.]

[102]

NOTES

Commencement: Before 1 January 1970 (sub-ss (1)-(6)); 29 August 1977 (sub-s (7)).
Sub-s (1): amended by the Rent Act 1968, s 117(2), Sch 15.
Sub-s (5): amended by the Rent Act 1977, s 155, Sch 23, para 12.
Sub-s (7): added by the Rent Act 1977, s 155, Sch 23, para 13.
The Rent Act: Rent Act 1977.

Continuation and termination of tenancies to which s 1 applies

3. Continuation of tenancies to which s 1 applies

(1) A tenancy which is current immediately before the term date and is then a tenancy to which section one of this Act applies shall not come to an end on that date except by being terminated under the provisions of this Part of this Act, and if not then so terminated shall subject to those provisions continue until so terminated and shall, while continuing by virtue of this section, be deemed (notwithstanding any change in circumstances) to be a tenancy to which section one of this Act applies.

(2) Where by virtue of the last foregoing subsection a tenancy is continued after the term date, then—

(*a*) if the premises qualifying for protection are the whole of the property comprised in the tenancy, the tenancy shall continue at the same rent and in other respects on the same terms as before the term date;

(*b*) if the premises qualifying for protection are only part of the property comprised in the tenancy, the tenancy while continuing after the term date shall have effect as a tenancy of those premises to the exclusion of the remainder of the property, and at a rent to be ascertained by apportioning the rent payable before the term date as between those premises and the remainder of the property, and in other respects on the same terms (subject to any necessary modifications) as before the term date.

(3) In this Part of this Act the expression "the premises qualifying for protection" means the aggregate of the premises of which, if the tenancy in question were not one at a low rent, the tenant would be entitled to retain possession by virtue of the [Rent Act] after the coming to an end of the tenancy at the term date.

(4) Any question arising under paragraph (*b*) of subsection (2) of this section as to the premises comprised in a tenancy continuing as mentioned in that paragraph, as to the rent payable in respect of a tenancy so continuing, or as to any of the terms of such a tenancy, shall be determined by agreement between the landlord and the tenant or, on the application of either of them, by the court. **[103]**

NOTES

Sub-s (3): amended by the Rent Act 1968, s 117(2), Sch 15.

The Rent Act: Rent Act 1977.

4. Termination of tenancy by the landlord

(1) The landlord may terminate a tenancy to which section one of this Act applies by notice given to the tenant in the prescribed form specifying the date at which the tenancy is to come to an end (hereinafter referred to as "the date of termination"), being either the term date of the tenancy or a later date:

Provided that this subsection has effect subject to the provisions of this Part of this Act as to the annulment of notices in certain cases and subject to the provisions of Part IV of this Act as to the interim continuation of tenancies pending the disposal of applications to the court.

(2) A notice under the last foregoing subsection shall not have effect unless it is given not more than twelve nor less than six months before the date of termination specified therein.

(3) A notice under subsection (1) of this section shall not have effect unless it specifies the premises which the landlord believes to be, or to be likely to be, the premises qualifying for protection and either—

(*a*) it contains proposals for a statutory tenancy, as defined by subsection (3) of section seven of this Act, or

(*b*) it contains notice that, if the tenant is not willing to give up possession at the date of termination of the tenancy, of all the property then comprised in the tenancy, the landlord proposes to apply to the court, on one or more of the grounds mentioned in section twelve of this Act, for possession of the property comprised in the tenancy, and states the ground or grounds on which he proposes to apply.

(4) A notice under subsection (1) of this section shall invite the tenant,

within two months after the giving of the notice, to notify the landlord in writing whether he is willing to give up possession as mentioned in paragraph (*b*) of the last foregoing subsection.

(5) A notice under subsection (1) of this section containing proposals such as are mentioned in paragraph (*a*) of subsection (3) of this section is hereinafter referred to as a "landlord's notice proposing a statutory tenancy", and a notice under subsection (1) of this section not containing such proposals is hereinafter referred to as a "landlord's notice to resume possession".

(6) References in this Part of this Act to an election by the tenant to retain possession are references to his notifying the landlord, in accordance with subsection (4) of this section, that he will not be willing to give up possession. **[104]**

5. Termination of tenancy by the tenant

(1) A tenancy to which section one of this Act applies may be brought to an end at the term date thereof by not less than one month's notice in writing given by the tenant to the immediate landlord.

(2) A tenancy continuing after the term date thereof by virtue of section three of this Act may be brought to an end at any time by not less than one month's notice in writing given by the tenant to the immediate landlord, whether the notice is given after or before the term date of the tenancy.

(3) The fact that the landlord has given a notice under subsection (1) of the last foregoing section, or that the tenant has elected to retain possession, shall not prevent the tenant from giving a notice terminating the tenancy at a date earlier than the date of termination specified in the landlord's notice. **[105]**

Statutory tenancies arising under Part I

6. Application of Rent Acts where tenant retains possession

(1) Where a tenancy is terminated by a landlord's notice proposing a statutory tenancy [the Rent Act shall apply], subject as hereinafter provided, as if the tenancy (hereinafter referred to as "the former tenancy")—

(*a*) had been a tenancy of the dwelling-house, as hereinafter defined, and
[(*b*) had not been a tenancy at a low rent and, except as regards the duration of the tenancy and the amount of the rent, had been a tenancy on the terms agreed or determined in accordance with the next following section and no other terms].

(2) The [Rent Act] shall not apply as aforesaid, if at the end of the period of two months after the service of the landlord's notice the qualifying condition was not fulfilled as respects the tenancy, unless the tenant has elected to retain possession.

(3) In this Part of this Act the expression "the dwelling-house" means the premises agreed between the landlord and the tenant or determined by the court,—

(*a*) if the agreement or determination is made on or after the term date of the former tenancy, to be the premises which as respects that tenancy are the premises qualifying for protection,
(*b*) if the agreement or determination is made before the term date of the former tenancy, to be the premises which are likely to be the premises qualifying for protection.

(4), (5) . . . **[106]**

NOTES

Sub-s (1): first amendment made by the Rent Act 1968, s 117(2), Sch 15; second amendment made by the Leasehold Reform Act 1967, s 39(2), Sch 5, para 3(1).

Sub-s (2): amended by the Rent Act 1968, s 117(2), Sch 15.

Sub-s (4): repealed by the Leasehold Reform Act 1967, s 41(2), Sch 7, Part I.

Sub-s (5): repealed by the Rent Act 1957, s 26(3), Sch 8, Part I.

The Rent Act: Rent Act 1977.

7. Settlement of terms of statutory tenancy

(1) The . . . terms on which the tenant and any successor to his statutory tenancy may retain possession of the dwelling-house during that period [other than the amount of the rent] shall be such as may be agreed between the landlord and the tenant or determined by the court . . .

(2) A landlord's notice proposing a statutory tenancy and anything done in pursuance thereof shall cease to have effect if by the beginning of the period of two months ending with the date of termination specified in the notice any of the following matters, that is to say,—

(*a*) what premises are to constitute the dwelling-house;

(*b*) [as regards the rent] of the dwelling-house during the period of the statutory tenancy, the intervals at which instalments of that rent are to be payable, and whether they are to be payable in advance or in arrear;

(*c*) whether any, and if so what, initial repairs (as defined in the next following section) are to be carried out on the dwelling-house;

(*d*) whether initial repairs to be so carried out are to be carried out by the landlord or by the tenant, or which of them are to be carried out by the landlord and which by the tenant; and

(*e*) the matters required by the next following section to be agreed or determined in relation to repairs before the beginning of the period of the statutory tenancy,

has not been agreed between the landlord and the tenant and no application has been made by the beginning of the said period of two months for the determination by the court of such of those matters as have not been agreed:

Provided that this subsection shall not have effect if at the end of the period of two months after the service of the landlord's notice the qualifying condition was not fulfilled as respects the tenancy unless the tenant has elected to retain possession.

(3) In paragraph (*a*) of subsection (3) of section four of this Act, the expression "proposals for a statutory tenancy" means [proposals as to the rent of the dwelling-house during the period of the statutory tenancy] proposals as to the matters specified in paragraphs (*b*) to (*e*) of the last foregoing subsection, and such other proposals (if any) as to the terms mentioned in subsection (1) of this section as the landlord may include in his notice.

(4) Any such proposals—

(*a*) shall be made, and be expressed to be made, on the assumption that the dwelling-house will be the premises specified in the landlord's notice in accordance with subsection (3) of section four of this Act;

(*b*) shall not be treated as failing to satisfy the requirements of the said subsection (3) by reason only of a difference between the premises to which the proposals relate and the premises subsequently agreed or determined to be the dwelling-house,

and in the event of any such difference the landlord shall not be bound by his proposals notwithstanding that they may have been accepted by the tenant.

(5) An application for securing a determination by the court in accordance with the foregoing provisions of this section shall be made by the landlord, and—

(*a*) shall be made during the currency of the landlord's notice proposing a statutory tenancy and not earlier than two months after the giving thereof, so however that if the tenant has elected to retain possession it may be made at a time not earlier than one month after the giving of the notice;

(*b*) subject to the provisions of the last foregoing subsection, shall not be made for the determination of any matter as to which agreement has already been reached between the landlord and the tenant.

(6) In this Part of this Act the expression "the period of the statutory tenancy" means the period beginning with the coming to an end of the former tenancy and ending with the earliest date by which the tenant, and any successor to his statutory tenancy, have ceased to retain possession of the dwelling-house by virtue of the [Rent Act]. **[107]**

NOTES

Sub-s (1): words omitted repealed by the Rent Act 1957, s 26(3), Sch 8, Part I; amendment in square brackets made by the Leasehold Reform Act 1967, s 39(2), Sch 5, para 3(1).

Sub-ss (2), (3): amended by the Leasehold Reform Act 1967, s 39(2), Sch 5, para 3(1).

Sub-s (6): amended by the Rent Act 1968, s 117(2), Sch 15.

The Rent Act: Rent Act 1977.

8. Provisions as to repairs during period of statutory tenancy

(1) Where it is agreed between the landlord and the tenant, or determined by the court, that the terms mentioned in subsection (1) of the last foregoing section shall include the carrying out of specified repairs (hereinafter referred to as "initial repairs"), and any of the initial repairs are required in consequence of failure by the tenant to fulfil his obligations under the former tenancy, the landlord shall be entitled to a payment (hereinafter referred to as a "payment for accrued tenant's repairs"), of an amount equal to the cost reasonably incurred by the landlord in ascertaining what repairs are required as aforesaid and in carrying out such of the initial repairs as are so required and as respects which it has been agreed or determined as aforesaid that they are to be carried out by the landlord, excluding any part of that cost which is recoverable by the landlord otherwise than from the tenant or his predecessor in title.

(2) A payment for accrued tenant's repairs may be made either by instalments or otherwise, as may be agreed or determined as aforesaid; and the provisions of the First Schedule to this Act shall have effect as to the time for, and method of, recovery of such payments, the persons from whom they are to be recoverable, and otherwise in relation thereto.

(3) The obligations of the landlord and the tenant as respects the repair of the dwelling-house during the period of the statutory tenancy shall, subject to the foregoing provisions of this section, be such as may be agreed between them or as may be determined by the court.

(4) The matters referred to in paragraph (*e*) of subsection (2) of the last foregoing section are:

(*a*) which of the initial repairs (if any) are required in consequence of failure by the tenant to fulfil his obligations under the former tenancy and, where there are any initial repairs so required, the amount to be included in the payment for accrued tenant's repairs in respect of the cost incurred by the landlord in ascertaining what initial repairs are so required;

(*b*) the estimated cost of the repairs so required, in so far as they are to be carried out by the landlord;

(*c*) whether any payment for accrued tenant's repairs is to be payable by instalments or otherwise, and if by instalments the amount of each instalment (subject to any necessary reduction of the last), the time at which the first is to be payable and the frequency of the instalments;

(*d*) whether there are to be any, and if so what, obligations as respects the repair of the dwelling-house during the period of the statutory tenancy, other than the execution of initial repairs.

(5) The provisions of the Second Schedule to this Act shall have effect as respects cases where the landlord or the tenant fails to carry out initial repairs, as to the cost of carrying out such repairs in certain cases and as to the making of a record, where required by the landlord or by the tenant, of the state of repair of the dwelling-house. **[108]**

9. Principles to be observed in determining terms of statutory tenancy as to repairs and rent

(1) Where it falls to the court to determine what initial repairs (if any) should be carried out by the landlord, the court shall not, except with the consent of the landlord and the tenant, require the carrying out of initial repairs in excess of what is required to bring the dwelling-house into good repair or the carrying out of any repairs not specified by the landlord in his application as repairs which he is willing to carry out.

(2) In the last foregoing subsection the expression "good repair" means good repair as respects both structure and decoration, having regard to the age, character and locality of the dwelling-house.

(3) Notwithstanding anything in subsection (1) of section seven of this Act, the court shall not have power to determine that any initial repairs shall be carried out by the tenant except with his consent.

(4) Any obligations imposed by the court under this Part of this Act as to keeping the dwelling-house in repair during the period of the statutory tenancy shall not be such as to require the dwelling-house to be kept in a better state of repair than the state which may be expected to subsist after the completion of any initial repairs to be carried out or, in the absence of any agreement or determination requiring the carrying out of initial repairs, in a better state of repair than the state subsisting at the time of the court's determination of what obligations are to be imposed.

(5) . . . **[109]**

NOTES

Sub-s (5): repealed by the Leasehold Reform Act 1967, s 41(2), Sch 7, Part I.

10. Provisions as to liabilities under tenant's covenants in former lease

(1) If on the termination of the former tenancy the tenant retains possession of the dwelling-house by virtue of section six of this Act, any liability, whether of

the tenant or of any predecessor in title of his, arising under the terms of the former tenancy shall be extinguished:

Provided that this subsection shall not affect any liability—

(*a*) for failure to pay rent or rates or to insure or keep insured, or

(*b*) in respect of the use of any premises for immoral or illegal purposes,

or any liability under the terms of the former tenancy in so far as those terms related to property other than the dwelling-house.

(2) During the period of the statutory tenancy no order shall be made for the recovery of possession of the dwelling-house from the tenant [in any of the circumstances specified in Cases 1 to 3 in [Schedule 15] to the Rent Act] (which relate to the recovery of possession where an obligation of the tenancy has been broken or where certain specified acts or defaults have been committed) by reason only of any act or default which occurred before the date of termination of the former tenancy. **[110]**

NOTES

Sub-s (2): amended by the Rent Act 1968, s 117(2), Sch 8; further amended by the Rent Act 1977, s 155, Sch 23, para 14.

Provisions as to possession on termination of long tenancy

12. Grounds for resumption of possession by landlord

(1) The grounds on which a landlord may apply to the court for possession of the property comprised in a tenancy to which section one of this Act applies are the following:—

(*a*) that for purposes of redevelopment after the termination of the tenancy the landlord proposes to demolish or reconstruct the whole or a substantial part of the relevant premises;

(*b*) the grounds specified in the Third Schedule to this Act (which correspond, subject to the necessary modifications, to the [[Cases 1 to 9 in Schedule 15] to the Rent Act which specify circumstances in which a court may make an order for possession under that Act)].

(2) In this section the expression "the relevant premises" means—

(*a*) as respects any time after the term date, the premises of which, if the tenancy were not one at a low rent, the tenant would have been entitled to retain possession by virtue of the [Rent Act] after the coming to an end of the tenancy at the term date;

(*b*) as respects any time before the term date, the premises agreed between the landlord and the tenant or determined by the court to be likely to be the premises of which, if the tenancy were not one at a low rent, the tenant would be entitled to retain possession as aforesaid. **[111]**

NOTES

Sub-s (1): first amendment made by the Rent Act 1977, s 155, Sch 23, para 15; second amendment made by the Rent Act 1968, s 117(2), Sch 15.

Sub-s (2): amended by the Rent Act 1968, s 117(2), Sch 15.

The Rent Act: Rent Act 1977.

13. Landlord's application for possession

(1) Where a landlord's notice to resume possession has been served and either—

(*a*) the tenant elects to retain possession, or

(*b*) at the end of the period of two months after the service of the landlord's notice the qualifying condition is fulfilled as respects the tenancy,

the landlord may apply to the court for an order under this section on such of the grounds mentioned in the last foregoing section as may be specified in the notice:

Provided that the application shall not be made later than two months after the tenant elects to retain possession, or, if he has not elected to retain possession, later than four months after the service of the notice.

(2) Where the ground or one of the grounds for claiming possession specified in the landlord's notice was that mentioned in paragraph (*a*) of subsection (1) of the last foregoing section, then if on such an application the court is satisfied that the landlord has established that ground as respects premises specified in the application, and is further satisfied,—

(*a*) that on the said ground possession of the specified premises will be required by the landlord on the termination of the tenancy; and

(*b*) that the landlord has made such preparations (including the obtaining, or, if that is not reasonably practicable in the circumstances preparations relating to the obtaining, of any requisite permission or consent, whether from any authority whose permission or consent is required under any enactment or from the owner of any interest in any property) for proceeding with the redevelopment as are reasonable in the circumstances,

the court shall order that the tenant shall, on the termination of the tenancy, give up possession of all the property then comprised in the tenancy.

(3) Where in a case falling within the last foregoing subsection the court is not satisfied as therein mentioned, but would be satisfied if the date of termination of the tenancy had been such date (in this subsection referred to as "the postponed date") as the court may determine, being a date later, but not more than one year later, than the date of termination specified in the landlord's notice, the court shall, if the landlord so requires, make an order specifying the postponed date and otherwise to the following effect, that is to say:—

(*a*) that the tenancy shall not come to an end on the date of termination specified in the landlord's notice but shall continue thereafter, as respects the whole of the property comprised therein, at the same rent and in other respects on the same terms as before that date;

(*b*) that unless the tenancy comes to an end before the postponed date; the tenant shall on that date give up possession of all the property then comprised in the tenancy.

(4) Where the ground or one of the grounds for claiming possession specified in the landlord's notice was one mentioned in the Third Schedule to this Act, then if on an application made in accordance with subsection (1) of this section the court is satisfied that the landlord has established that ground and that it is reasonable that the landlord should be granted possession, the court shall order that the tenant shall, on the termination of the tenancy, give up possession of all the property then comprised in the tenancy.

(5) Nothing in the foregoing provisions of this section shall prejudice any power of the tenant under section five of this Act to terminate the tenancy; and subsection (2) of that section shall apply where the tenancy is continued by an order under subsection (3) of this section as it applies where the tenancy is continued by virtue of section three of this Act. **[112]**

14. Provisions where tenant not ordered to give up possession

(1) The provisions of this section shall have effect where in a case falling within paragraph (*a*) or (*b*) of subsection (1) of the last foregoing section the landlord does not obtain an order under the last foregoing section.

(2) If at the expiration of the period within which an application under the last foregoing section may be made the landlord has not made such an application, the landlord's notice, and anything done in pursuance thereof, shall thereupon cease to have effect.

(3) If before the expiration of the said period the landlord has made an application under the last foregoing section, but the result of the application, at the time when it is finally disposed of, is that no order is made, the landlord's notice shall cease to have effect; but if within one month after the application to the court is finally disposed of the landlord gives a landlord's notice proposing a statutory tenancy, the earliest date which may be specified therein as the date of termination shall, notwithstanding anything in subsection (2) of section four of this Act, be the expiration of three months from the giving of the subsequent notice.

(4) The reference in the last foregoing subsection to the time at which an application is finally disposed of shall be construed as a reference to the earliest time at which the proceedings on the application (including any proceedings on or in consequence of an appeal) have been determined and any time for appealing or further appealing has expired, except that if the application is withdrawn or any appeal is abandoned the reference shall be construed as a reference to the time of withdrawal or abandonment.

(5) A landlord's notice to resume possession may be withdrawn at any time by notice in writing served on the tenant (without prejudice, however, to the power of the court to make an order as to costs if the notice is withdrawn after the landlord has made an application under the last foregoing section); and if within one month of the withdrawal of a landlord's notice to resume possession the landlord gives a landlord's notice proposing a statutory tenancy, the earliest date which may be specified therein as the date of termination shall, notwithstanding anything in subsection (2) of section four of this Act, be the expiration of three months from the giving of the subsequent notice or six months from the giving of the withdrawn notice, whichever is the later.

(6) Where by virtue of subsection (3) or (5) of this section the landlord gives a landlord's notice proposing a statutory tenancy which specifies as the date of termination a date earlier than six months after the giving of the notice, subsection (2) of section seven of this Act shall apply in relation to the notice with the substitution, for references to the period of two months ending with the date of termination specified in the notice and the beginning of that period, of references to the period of three months beginning with the giving of the notice and the end of that period. **[113]**

General and supplementary provisions

16. Relief for tenant where landlord proceeding to enforce covenants

(1) The provisions of the next following subsection shall have effect where, in the case of a tenancy to which section one of this Act applies,—

(*a*) the immediate landlord has brought proceedings to enforce a right of re-entry or forfeiture or a right to damages in respect of a failure to comply with any terms of the tenancy,
(*b*) the tenant has made application in the proceedings for relief under this section, and
(*c*) the court makes an order for the recovery from the tenant of possession of the property comprised in the tenancy or for the payment by the tenant of such damages as aforesaid, and the order is made at a time earlier than seven months before the term date of the tenancy.

(2) The operation of the order shall be suspended for a period of fourteen days from the making thereof, and if before the end of that period the tenant gives notice in writing to the immediate landlord that he desires that the provisions of the two following paragraphs shall have effect, and lodges a copy of the notice in the court,—

(*a*) the order shall not have effect except if and in so far as it provides for the payment of costs, and
(*b*) the tenancy shall thereafter have effect, and this Part of this Act shall have effect in relation thereto, as if it had been granted for a term expiring at the expiration of seven months from the making of the order.

(3) In any case falling within paragraphs (*a*) and (*b*) of subsection (1) of this section, the court shall not make any such order as is mentioned in paragraph (*c*) thereof unless the time of the making of the order falls earlier than seven months before the term date of the tenancy:

Provided that (without prejudice to section ten of this Act) this subsection shall not prevent the making of an order for the payment of damages in respect of a failure, as respects any premises, to comply with the terms of a tenancy if, at the time when the order is made, the tenancy has come to an end as respects those premises.

(4) The foregoing provisions of this section shall not have effect in relation to a failure to comply with—

(*a*) any term of a tenancy as to payment of rent or rates or as to insuring or keeping insured any premises, or
(*b*) any term restricting the use of any premises for immoral or illegal purposes.

(5) References in this section to proceedings to enforce a right to damages in respect of a failure to comply with any terms of a tenancy shall be construed as including references to proceedings for recovery from the tenant of expenditure incurred by or recovered from the immediate landlord in consequence of such a failure on the part of the tenant.

(6) Nothing in the foregoing provisions of this section shall prejudice any right to apply for relief under any other enactment.

(7) Subsection (3) of section two of this Act shall not have effect in relation to this section. **[114]**

17. Prohibition of agreements excluding Part I

The provisions of this Part of this Act shall have effect notwithstanding any agreement to the contrary:

Provided that nothing in this Part of this Act shall be construed as preventing the surrender of a tenancy. **[115]**

18. Duty of tenants of residential property to give information to landlords or superior landlords

(1) Where the property comprised in a long tenancy at a low rent is or includes residential premises, then at any time during the last two years of the term of the tenancy, or (if the tenancy is being continued after the term date by subsection (1) of section three of this Act) at any time while the tenancy is being so continued, the immediate landlord or any superior landlord may give to the tenant or any sub-tenant of premises comprised in the long tenancy a notice in the prescribed form requiring him to notify the landlord or superior landlord, as the case may be,—

(*a*) whether the interest of the person to whom the notice is given has effect subject to any sub-tenancy on which that interest is immediately expectant and, if so,

(*b*) what premises are comprised in the sub-tenancy, for what term it has effect (or, if it is terminable by notice, by what notice it can be terminated), what is the rent payable thereunder, who is the sub-tenant and (to the best of the knowledge and belief of the person to whom the notice is given) whether the sub-tenant is in occupation of the premises comprised in the sub-tenancy or any part of those premises and, if not, what is the sub-tenant's address,

and it shall be the duty of the person to whom such a notice is given to comply therewith within one month of the giving of the notice.

(2) In this section the expression "residential premises" means premises normally used, or adapted for use, as one or more dwellings, the expression "sub-tenant" in relation to a long tenancy means the owner of a tenancy created (whether immediately or derivatively) out of the long tenancy and includes a person retaining possession of any premises by virtue of the [Rent Act] after the coming to an end of a sub-tenancy, and the expression "sub-tenancy" includes a right so to retain possession. **[116]**

NOTES
Amended by the Rent Act 1968, s 117(2), Sch 15.
The Rent Act: Rent Act 1977.

19. Application of Part I to tenancies granted in continuation of long tenancies

(1) Where on the coming to an end of a tenancy at a low rent the person who was tenant thereunder immediately before the coming to an end thereof becomes (whether by grant or by implication of law) tenant of the whole or any part of the property comprised therein under another tenancy at a low rent, then if the first tenancy was a long tenancy or is deemed by virtue of this subsection to have been a long tenancy the second tenancy shall be deemed for the purposes of this Part of this Act to be a long tenancy irrespective of its terms.

(2) In relation to a tenancy from year to year or other tenancy not granted for a term of years certain, being a tenancy which by virtue of the last foregoing subsection is to be deemed to be a long tenancy, this Part of this Act shall have effect subject to the modifications set out in the Fourth Schedule to this Act. **[117]**

20. Assumptions on which court to determine future questions

Where under this Part of this Act any question falls to be determined by the court by reference to the circumstances at a future date, the court shall have regard to all rights, interests and obligations under or relating to the tenancy as they subsist at the time of the determination and to all relevant circumstances as they then subsist and shall assume, except in so far as the contrary is shown, that those rights, interests, obligations and circumstances will continue to subsist unchanged until the said future date. **[118]**

21. Meaning of "the landlord" in Part I and provisions as to mesne landlords, etc

(1) Subject to the provisions of this section, in this Part of this Act the expression "the landlord", in relation to a tenancy (in this section referred to as "the relevant tenancy"), means the person (whether or not he is the immediate landlord) who is the owner of that interest in the property comprised in the relevant tenancy which for the time being fulfils the following conditions, that is to say—

(*a*) that it is an interest in reversion expectant (whether immediately or not) on the termination of the relevant tenancy, and
(*b*) that it is either the fee simple or a tenancy the duration of which is at least five years longer than that of the relevant tenancy,

and is not itself in reversion expectant (whether immediately or not) on an interest which fulfils those conditions.

(2) References in this Part of this Act to a notice to quit given by the landlord are references to a notice to quit given by the immediate landlord.

(3) For the purposes of subsection (1) of this section the question whether a tenancy (hereinafter referred to as "the superior tenancy") is to be treated as having a duration at least five years longer than that of the relevant tenancy shall be determined as follows:—

(*a*) if the term date of the relevant tenancy has not passed, the superior tenancy shall be so treated unless it is due to expire at a time earlier than five years after the term date or can be brought to an end at such a time by notice to quit given by the landlord;
(*b*) if the term date of the relevant tenancy has passed, the superior tenancy shall be so treated unless it is due to expire within five years or can be brought to an end within five years by notice to quit given by the landlord.

(4) In relation to the premises constituting the dwelling-house where the [Rent Act applies] by virtue of subsection (1) of section six of this Act, the expression "the landlord", as respects any time falling within the period of the statutory tenancy, means the person who as respects those premises is the landlord of the tenant for the purposes of the [Rent Act]:

Provided that in relation to the carrying out of initial repairs, and to any payment for accrued tenant's repairs, the said expression, as respects any time falling within that period, means the person whose interest in the dwelling-house fulfils the following conditions, that is to say:—

(*a*) that it is not due to expire within five years and is not capable of being brought to an end within five years by notice to quit given by the landlord, and
(*b*) that it is not itself in reversion expectant on an interest which is not due to expire or capable of being brought to an end as aforesaid.

(5) The provisions of the Fifth Schedule to this Act shall have effect for the application of this Part of this Act to cases where the immediate landlord of the tenant is not the owner of the fee simple in respect of the premises in question.

(6) Notwithstanding anything in subsection (1) of this section, if at any time the interest which apart from this subsection would be the interest of the landlord is an interest not bound by this Part of this Act and is not the interest of the immediate landlord, then as respects that time the expression "the landlord" means in this Part of this Act (subject to the provisions of subsection (2) of this section) the person (whether or not he is the immediate landlord) who has the interest in the property comprised in the relevant tenancy immediately derived out of the interest not bound by this Part of this Act.

[In this subsection "interest not bound by this Part of this Act" means an interest which belongs to Her Majesty in right of the Crown and is not under the management of the Crown Estate Commissioners or an interest belonging to a government department or held on behalf of Her Majesty for the purposes of a government department.] **[119]**

NOTES
Sub-s (4): amended by the Rent Act 1968, s 117(2), Sch 15.
Sub-s (6): amended by the Housing Act 1980, s 73(4).
The Rent Act: Rent Act 1977.

22. Interpretation of Part I

(1) In this Part of this Act:—

. . .

"date of termination" has the meaning assigned to it by subsection (1) of section four of this Act;

"the dwelling-house" has the meaning assigned to it by subsection (3) of section six of this Act;

"election to retain possession" has the meaning assigned to it by subsection (6) of section four of this Act;

"former tenancy" has the meaning assigned to it by subsection (1) of section six of this Act;

"initial repairs" has the meaning assigned to it by subsection (1) of section eight of this Act;

"the landlord" has the meaning assigned to it by the last foregoing section;

"landlord's notice proposing a statutory tenancy" and "landlord's notice to resume possession" have the meanings assigned to them respectively by subsection (5) of section four of this Act;

"long tenancy" has the meaning assigned to it by subsection (4) of section two of this Act;

"order" includes judgment;

"payment for accrued tenant's repairs" has the meaning assigned to it by subsection (1) of section eight of this Act;

"the period of the statutory tenancy" has the meaning assigned to it by subsection (6) of section seven of this Act;

"premises qualifying for protection" has the meaning assigned to it by subsection (3) of section three of this Act;

"qualifying condition" has the meaning assigned to it by subsection (1) of section two of this Act;

["the Rent Act" means [the Rent Act 1977] as it applies to regulated tenancies but exclusive of [Parts II to V] thereof;]

"tenancy at a low rent" has the meaning assigned to it by subsection (5) of section two of this Act;

"term date" has the meaning assigned to it by subsection (6) of section two of this Act.

(2) In relation to the premises constituting the dwelling-house the expression "the tenant" in this Part of this Act means the tenant under the former tenancy and, except as respects any payment for accrued tenant's repairs not payable by instalments, includes any successor to his statutory tenancy, and the expression "successor to his statutory tenancy", in relation to that tenant, means a person who after that tenant's death retains possession of the dwelling-house by virtue of the [Rent Act].

(3) In determining, for the purposes of any provision of this Part of this Act, whether the property comprised in a tenancy or any part of that property was let as a separate dwelling, the nature of the property or part at the time of the creation of the tenancy shall be deemed to have been the same as its nature at the time in relation to which the question arises, and the purpose for which it was let under the tenancy shall be deemed to have been the same as the purpose for which it is or was used at the last-mentioned time. **[120]**

NOTES

Sub-s (1): words omitted repealed by the Rent Act 1977, s 155, Sch 25; definition "the Rent Act"substituted by the Rent Act 1968, s 117(2), Sch 15, amended by the Rent Act 1977, s 155, Sch 23, para 16.

Sub-s (2): amended by the Rent Act 1968, s 117(2), Sch 15.

PART II

SECURITY OF TENURE FOR BUSINESS, PROFESSIONAL AND OTHER TENANTS

Tenancies to which Part II applies

23. Tenancies to which Part II applies

(1) Subject to the provisions of this Act, this Part of this Act applies to any tenancy where the property comprised in the tenancy is or includes premises which are occupied by the tenant and are so occupied for the purposes of a business carried on by him or for those and other purposes.

(2) In this Part of this Act the expression "business" includes a trade, profession or employment and includes any activity carried on by a body of persons, whether corporate or unincorporate.

(3) In the following provisions of this Part of this Act the expression "the holding", in relation to a tenancy to which this Part of this Act applies, means the property comprised in the tenancy, there being excluded any part thereof which is occupied neither by the tenant nor by a person employed by the tenant and so employed for the purposes of a business by reason of which the tenancy is one to which this Part of this Act applies.

(4) Where the tenant is carrying on a business, in all or any part of the property comprised in a tenancy, in breach of a prohibition (however expressed) of use for business purposes which subsists under the terms of the tenancy and extends to the whole of that property, this Part of this Act shall not apply to the tenancy unless the immediate landlord or his predecessor in title has consented to the breach or the immediate landlord has acquiesced therein.

In this subsection the reference to a prohibition of use for business purposes does not include a prohibition of use for the purposes of a specified business, or of use for purposes of any but a specified business, but save as aforesaid includes a prohibition of use for the purposes of some one or more only of the classes of business specified in the definition of that expression in subsection (2) of this section. **[121]**

NOTES
Disapplied for certain purposes by the Dockyard Services Act 1986, s 3.

Continuation and renewal of tenancies

24. Continuation of tenancies to which Part II applies and grant of new tenancies

(1) A tenancy to which this Part of this Act applies shall not come to an end unless terminated in accordance with the provisions of this Part of this Act; and, subject to the provisions of section twenty-nine of this Act, the tenant under such a tenancy may apply to the court for a new tenancy—

(*a*) if the landlord has given notice under [section 25 of this Act] to terminate the tenancy, or

(*b*) if the tenant has made a request for a new tenancy in accordance with section twenty-six of this Act.

(2) The last foregoing subsection shall not prevent the coming to an end of a tenancy by notice to quit given by the tenant, by surrender or forfeiture, or by the forfeiture of a superior tenancy [unless—

(*a*) in the case of a notice to quit, the notice was given before the tenant had been in occupation in right of the tenancy for one month; or

(*b*) in the case of an instrument of surrender, the instrument was executed before, or was executed in pursuance of an agreement made before, the tenant had been in occupation in right of the tenancy for one month.]

(3) Notwithstanding anything in subsection (1) of this section,—

(*a*) where a tenancy to which this Part of this Act applies ceases to be such a tenancy, it shall not come to an end by reason only of the cesser, but if it was granted for a term of years certain and has been continued by subsection (1) of this section then (without prejudice to the termination thereof in accordance with any terms of the tenancy) it may be terminated by not less than three nor more than six months' notice in writing given by the landlord to the tenant;

(*b*) where, at a time when a tenancy is not one to which this Part of this Act applies, the landlord gives notice to quit, the operation of the notice shall not be affected by reason that the tenancy becomes one to which this Part of this Act applies after the giving of the notice. **[122]**

NOTES
Sub-ss (1), (2): amended by the Law of Property Act 1969, ss 3(2), 4(1).
Disapplied for certain purposes by the Dockyard Services Act 1986, s 3.

[24A. Rent while tenancy continues by virtue of s 24

(1) The landlord of a tenancy to which this Part of this Act applies may,—

(*a*) if he has given notice under section 25 of this Act to terminate the tenancy; or

(*b*) if the tenant has made a request for a new tenancy in accordance with section 26 of this Act;

apply to the court to determine a rent which it would be reasonable for the tenant to pay while the tenancy continues by virtue of section 24 of this Act, and the court may determine a rent accordingly.

(2) A rent determined in proceedings under this section shall be deemed to be the rent payable under the tenancy from the date on which the proceedings were commenced or the date specified in the landlord's notice or the tenant's request, whichever is the later.

(3) In determining a rent under this section the court shall have regard to the rent payable under the terms of the tenancy, but otherwise subsections (1) and (2) of section 34 of this Act shall apply to the determination as they would apply to the determiation of a rent under that section if a new tenancy from year to year of the whole of the property comprised in the tenancy were granted to the tenant by order of the court.] **[123]**

NOTES
Commencement: 1 January 1970.
Added by the Law of Property Act 1969, s 3(1).
Disapplied for certain purposes by the Dockyard Services Act 1986, s 3.

25. Termination of tenancy by the landlord

(1) The landlord may terminate a tenancy to which this Part of this Act applies by a notice given to the tenant in the prescribed form specifying the date at which the tenancy is to come to an end (hereinafter referred to as "the date of termination"):

Provided that this subsection has effect subject to the provisions of Part IV of this Act as to the interim continuation of tenancies pending the disposal of applications to the court.

(2) Subject to the provisions of the next following subsection, a notice under this section shall not have effect unless it is given not more than twelve nor less than six months before the date of termination specified therein.

(3) In the case of a tenancy which apart from this Act could have been brought to an end by notice to quit given by the landlord—

(*a*) the date of termination specified in a notice under this section shall not be earlier than the earliest date on which apart from this Part of this Act the tenancy could have been brought to an end by notice to quit given by the landlord on the date of the giving of the notice under this section; and

(*b*) where apart from this Part of this Act more than six months' notice to quit would have been required to bring the tenancy to an end, the last foregoing subsection shall have effect with the substitution for twelve months of a period six months longer than the length of notice to quit which would have been required as aforesaid.

(4) In the case of any other tenancy, a notice under this section shall not specify a date of termination earlier than the date on which apart from this Part of this Act the tenancy would have come to an end by effluxion of time.

(5) A notice under this section shall not have effect unless it requires the tenant, within two months after the giving of the notice, to notify the landlord in writing whether or not, at the date of termination, the tenant will be willing to give up possession of the property comprised in the tenancy.

(6) A notice under this section shall not have effect unless it states whether

the landlord would oppose an application to the court under this Part of this Act for the grant of a new tenancy and, if so, also states on which of the grounds mentioned in section thirty of this Act he would do so. **[124]**

NOTES
Disapplied for certain purposes by the Dockyard Services Act 1986, s 3.

26. Tenant's request for a new tenancy

(1) A tenant's request for a new tenancy may be made where the tenancy under which he holds for the time being (hereinafter referred to as "the current tenancy") is a tenancy granted for a term of years certain exceeding one year, whether or not continued by section twenty-four of this Act, or granted for a term of years certain and thereafter from year to year.

(2) A tenant's request for a new tenancy shall be for a tenancy beginning with such date, not more than twelve nor less than six months after the making of the request, as may be specified therein:

Provided that the said date shall not be earlier than the date on which apart from this Act the current tenancy would come to an end by effluxion of time or could be brought to an end by notice to quit given by the tenant.

(3) A tenant's request for a new tenancy shall not have effect unless it is made by notice in the prescribed form given to the landlord and sets out the tenant's proposals as to the property to be comprised in the new tenancy (being either the whole or part of the property comprised in the current tenancy), as to the rent to be payable under the new tenancy and as to the other terms of the new tenancy.

(4) A tenant's request for a new tenancy shall not be made if the landlord has already given notice under the last foregoing section to terminate the current tenancy, or if the tenant has already given notice to quit or notice under the next following section; and no such notice shall be given by the landlord or the tenant after the making by the tenant of a request for a new tenancy.

(5) Where the tenant makes a request for a new tenancy in accordance with the foregoing provisions of this section, the current tenancy shall, subject to the provisions of subsection (2) of section thirty-six of this Act and the provisions of Part IV of this Act as to the interim continuation of tenancies, terminate immediately before the date specified in the request for the beginning of the new tenancy.

(6) Within two months of the making of a tenant's request for a new tenancy the landlord may give notice to the tenant that he will oppose an application to the court for the grant of a new tenancy, and any such notice shall state on which of the grounds mentioned in section thirty of this Act the landlord will oppose the application. **[125]**

NOTES
Disapplied for certain purposes by the Dockyard Services Act 1986, s 3.

27. Termination by tenant of tenancy for fixed term

(1) Where the tenant under a tenancy to which this Part of this Act applies, being a tenancy granted for a term of years certain, gives to the immediate landlord, not later than three months before the date on which apart from this Act the tenancy would come to an end by effluxion of time, a notice in writing that the tenant does not desire the tenancy to be continued, section twenty-four

of this Act shall not have effect in relation to the tenancy [unless the notice is given before the tenant has been in occupation in right of the tenancy for one month].

(2) A tenancy granted for a term of years certain which is continuing by virtue of section twenty-four of this Act may be brought to an end on any quarter day by not less than three months' notice in writing given by the tenant to the immediate landlord, whether the notice is given . . . after the date on which apart from this Act the tenancy would have come to an end [or before that date, but not before the tenant has been in occupation in right of the tenancy for one month]. **[126]**

NOTES
Amended by the Law of Property Act 1969, s 4(2).
Disapplied for certain purposes by the Dockyard Services Act 1986, s 3.

28. Renewal of tenancies by agreement

Where the landlord and tenant agree for the grant to the tenant of a future tenancy of the holding, or of the holding with other land, on terms and from a date specified in the agreement, the current tenancy shall continue until that date but no longer, and shall not be a tenancy to which this Part of this Act applies. **[127]**

NOTES
Disapplied for certain purposes by the Dockyard Services Act 1986, s 3.

Application to court for new tenancies

29. Order by court for grant of a new tenancy

(1) Subject to the provisions of this Act, on an application under subsection (1) of section twenty-four of this Act for a new tenancy the court shall make an order for the grant of a tenancy comprising such property, at such rent and on such other terms, as are hereinafter provided.

(2) Where such an application is made in consequence of a notice given by the landlord under section twenty-five of this Act, it shall not be entertained unless the tenant has duly notified the landlord that he will not be willing at the date of termination to give up possession of the property comprised in the tenancy.

(3) No application under subsection (1) of section twenty-four of this Act shall be entertained unless it is made not less than two nor more than four months after the giving of the landlord's notice under section twenty-five of this Act or, as the case may be, after the making of the tenant's request for a new tenancy. **[128]**

NOTES
Disapplied for certain purposes by the Dockyard Services Act 1986, s 3.

30. Opposition by landlord to application for a new tenancy

(1) The grounds on which a landlord may oppose an application under subsection (1) of section twenty-four of this Act are such of the following grounds as may be stated in the landlord's notice under section twenty-five of this Act or, as the case may be, under subsection (6) of section twenty-six thereof, that is to say:—

(*a*) where under the current tenancy the tenant has any obligations as respects the repair and maintenance of the holding, that the tenant ought not to be granted a new tenancy in view of the state of repair of the holding, being a state resulting from the tenant's failure to comply with the said obligations;

(*b*) that the tenant ought not to be granted a new tenancy in view of his persistent delay in paying rent which has become due;

(*c*) that the tenant ought not to be granted a new tenancy in view of other substantial breaches by him of his obligations under the current tenancy, or for any other reason connected with the tenant's use or management of the holding;

(*d*) that the landlord has offered and is willing to provide or secure the provision of alternative accommodation for the tenant, that the terms on which the alternative accommodation is available are reasonable having regard to the terms of the current tenancy and to all other relevant circumstances, and that the accommodation and the time at which it will be available are suitable for the tenant's requirements (including the requirement to preserve goodwill) having regard to the nature and class of his business and to the situation and extent of, and facilities afforded by, the holding;

(*e*) where the current tenancy was created by the sub-letting of part only of the property comprised in a superior tenancy and the landlord is the owner of an interest in reversion expectant on the termination of that superior tenancy, that the aggregate of the rents reasonably obtainable on separate lettings of the holding and the remainder of that property would be substantially less than the rent reasonably obtainable on a letting of that property as a whole, that on the termination of the current tenancy the landlord requires possession of the holding for the purpose of letting or otherwise disposing of the said property as a whole, and that in view thereof the tenant ought not to be granted a new tenancy;

(*f*) that on the termination of the current tenancy the landlord intends to demolish or reconstruct the premises comprised in the holding or a substantial part of those premises or to carry out substantial work of construction on the holding or part thereof and that he could not reasonably do so without obtaining possession of the holding;

(*g*) subject as hereinafter provided, that on the termination of the current tenancy the landlord intends to occupy the holding for the purposes, or partly for the purposes, of a business to be carried on by him therein, or as his residence.

(2) The landlord shall not be entitled to oppose an application on the ground specified in paragraph (*g*) of the last foregoing subsection if the interest of the landlord, or an interest which has merged in that interest and but for the merger would be the interest of the landlord, was purchased or created after the beginning of the period of five years which ends with the termination of the current tenancy, and at all times since the purchase or creation thereof the holding has been comprised in a tenancy or successive tenancies of the description specified in subsection (1) of section twenty-three of this Act.

[(3) Where the landlord has a controlling interest in a company any business to be carried on by the company shall be treated for the purposes of subsection (1)(*g*) of this section as a business to be carried on by him.

For the purposes of this subsection, a person has a controlling interest in a company if and only if either—

(*a*) he is a member of it and able, without the consent of any other person, to appoint or remove the holders of at least a majority of the directorships; or

(*b*) he holds more than one-half of its equity share capital, there being disregarded any shares held by him in a fiduciary capacity or as nominee for another person;

and in this subsection "company" and "share" have the meanings assigned to them by section 455(1) of the Companies Act 1948 and "equity share capital" the meaning assigned to it by section 154(5) of that Act.] **[129]**

NOTES

Commencement: Before 1 January 1970 (sub-ss (1), (2)); 1 January 1970 (sub-s (3)).
Sub-s (3): added by the Law of Property Act 1969, s 6.
Disapplied for certain purposes by the Dockyard Services Act 1986, s 3.

31. Dismissal of application for new tenancy where landlord successfully opposes

(1) If the landlord opposes an application under subsection (1) of section twenty-four of this Act on grounds on which he is entitled to oppose it in accordance with the last foregoing section and establishes any of those grounds to the satisfaction of the court, the court shall not make an order for the grant of a new tenancy.

(2) Where in a case not falling within the last foregoing subsection the landlord opposes an application under the said subsection (1) on one or more of the grounds specified in paragraphs (*d*), (*e*) and (*f*) of subsection (1) of the last foregoing section but establishes none of those grounds to the satisfaction of the court, then if the court would have been satisfied of any of those grounds if the date of termination specified in the landlord's notice or, as the case may be, the date specified in the tenant's request for a new tenancy as the date from which the new tenancy is to begin, had been such later date as the court may determine, being a date not more than one year later than the date so specified,—

(*a*) the court shall make a declaration to that effect, stating of which of the said grounds the court would have been satisfied as aforesaid and specifying the date determined by the court as aforesaid, but shall not make an order for the grant of a new tenancy;

(*b*) if, within fourteen days after the making of the declaration, the tenant so requires the court shall make an order substituting the said date for the date specified in the said landlord's notice or tenant's request, and thereupon that notice or request shall have effect accordingly. **[130]**

NOTES

Disapplied for certain purposes by the Dockyard Services Act 1986, s 3.

[31A. Grant of new tenancy in some cases where section 30(1)(f) applies

[(1) Where the landlord opposes an application under section 24(1) of this Act on the ground specified in paragraph (*f*) of section 30(1) of this Act the court shall not hold that the landlord could not reasonably carry out the demolition, reconstruction or work of construction intended without obtaining possession of the holding if—

(*a*) the tenant agrees to the inclusion in the terms of the new tenancy of terms giving the landlord access and other facilities for carrying out the work intended and, given that access and those facilities, the landlord could reasonably carry out the work without obtaining possession of the holding and without interfering to a substantial extent or for a substantial time with the use of the holding for the purposes of the business carried on by the tenant; or

(*b*) the tenant is willing to accept a tenancy of an economically separable part of the holding and either paragraph (*a*) of this section is satisfied with respect to that part or possession of the remainder of the holding would be reasonably sufficient to enable the landlord to carry out the intended work.

(2) For the purposes of subsection (1)(*b*) of this section a part of a holding shall be deemed to be an economically separable part if, and only if, the aggregate of the rents which, after the completion of the intended work, would be reasonably obtainable on separate lettings of that part and the remainder of the premises affected by or resulting from the work would not be substantially less than the rent which would then be reasonably obtainable on a letting of those premises as a whole.] **[131]**

NOTES
Commencement: 1 January 1970.
Added by the Law of Property Act 1969, s 7(1).
Disapplied for certain purposes by the Dockyard Services Act 1986, s 3.

32. Property to be comprised in new tenancy

(1) [Subject to the following provisions of this section], an order under section twenty-nine of this Act for the grant of a new tenancy shall be an order for the grant of a new tenancy of the holding; and in the absence of agreement between the landlord and the tenant as to the property which constitutes the holding the court shall in the order designate that property by reference to the circumstances existing at the date of the order.

[(1A) Where the court, by virtue of paragraph (*b*) of section 31A(1) of this Act, makes an order under section 29 of this Act for the grant of a new tenancy in a case where the tenant is willing to accept a tenancy of part of the holding, the order shall be an order for the grant of a new tenancy of that part only.]

(2) The foregoing provisions of this section shall not apply in a case where the property comprised in the current tenancy includes other property besides the holding and the landlord requires any new tenancy ordered to be granted under section twenty-nine of this Act to be a tenancy of the whole of the property comprised in the current tenancy; but in any such case—

(*a*) any order under the said section twenty-nine for the grant of a new tenancy shall be an order for the grant of a new tenancy of the whole of the property comprised in the current tenancy, and

(*b*) references in the following provisions of this Part of this Act to the holding shall be construed as references to the whole of that property.

(3) Where the current tenancy includes rights enjoyed by the tenant in connection with the holding, those rights shall be included in a tenancy ordered to be granted under section twenty-nine of this Act [except as otherwise agreed between the landlord and the tenant or, in default of such agreement, determined by the court]. **[132]**

NOTES
Commencement: Before 1 January 1970 (sub-ss (1), (2), (3)); 1 January 1970 (sub-s (1A)).
Amended by the Law of Property Act 1969, ss 7(2), 8.
Disapplied for certain purposes by the Dockyard Services Act 1986, s 3.

33. Duration of new tenancy

Where on an application under this Part of this Act the court makes an order for the grant of a new tenancy, the new tenancy shall be such tenancy as may be agreed between the landlord and the tenant, or, in default of such an agreement, shall be such a tenancy as may be determined by the court to be reasonable in all the circumstances, being, if it is a tenancy for a term of years certain, a tenancy for a term not exceeding fourteen years, and shall begin on the coming to an end of the current tenancy. **[133]**

NOTES

Disapplied for certain purposes by the Dockyard Services Act 1986, s 3.

34. Rent under new tenancy

[(1)] The rent payable under a tenancy granted by order of the court under this Part of this Act shall be such as may be agreed between the landlord and the tenant or as, in default of such agreement, may be determined by the court to be that at which, having regard to the terms of the tenancy (other than those relating to rent), the holding might reasonably be expected to be let in the open market by a willing lessor, there being disregarded—

(*a*) any effect on rent of the fact that the tenant has or his predecessors in title have been in occupation of the holding,

(*b*) any goodwill attached to the holding by reason of the carrying on thereat of the business of the tenant (whether by him or by a predecessor of his in that business),

[(*c*) any effect on rent of an improvement to which this paragraph applies],

(*d*) in the case of a holding comprising licensed premises, any addition to its value attributable to the licence, if it appears to the court that having regard to the terms of the current tenancy and any other relevant circumstances the benefit of the licence belongs to the tenant.

[(2) Paragraph (*c*) of the foregoing subsection applies to any improvement carried out by a person who at the time it was carried out was the tenant, but only if it was carried out otherwise than in pursuance of an obligation to his immediate landlord, and either it was carried out during the current tenancy or the following conditions are satisfied, that is to say,—

(*a*) that it was completed not more than twenty-one years before the application for the new tenancy was made; and

(*b*) that the holding or any part of it affected by the improvement has at all times since the completion of the improvement been comprised in tenancies of the description specified in section 23(1) of this Act; and

(*c*) that at the termination of each of those tenancies the tenant did not quit.]

[(3) Where the rent is determined by the court the court may, if it thinks fit, further determine that the terms of the tenancy shall include such provision for varying the rent as may be specified in the determination.] **[134]**

NOTES

Commencement: Before 1 January 1970 (sub-s (1)); 1 January 1970 (remainder).
Amended by the Law of Property Act 1969, ss 1(1), 2.
Disapplied for certain purposes by the Dockyard Services Act 1986, s 3.

35. Other terms of new tenancy

The terms of a tenancy granted by order of the court under this Part of this Act (other than terms as to the duration thereof and as to the rent payable thereunder) shall be such as may be agreed between the landlord and the tenant or as, in default of such agreement, may be determined by the court; and in determining those terms the court shall have regard to the terms of the current tenancy and to all relevant circumstances. **[135]**

NOTES
Disapplied for certain purposes by the Dockyard Services Act 1986, s 3.

36. Carrying out of order for new tenancy

(1) Where under this Part of this Act the court makes an order for the grant of a new tenancy, then, unless the order is revoked under the next following subsection or the landlord and the tenant agree not to act upon the order, the landlord shall be bound to execute or make in favour of the tenant, and the tenant shall be bound to accept, a lease or agreement for a tenancy of the holding embodying the terms agreed between the landlord and the tenant or determined by the court in accordance with the foregoing provisions of this Part of this Act; and where the landlord executes or makes such a lease or agreement the tenant shall be bound, if so required by the landlord, to execute a counterpart or duplicate thereof.

(2) If the tenant, within fourteen days after the making of an order under this Part of this Act for the grant of a new tenancy, applies to the court for the revocation of the order the court shall revoke the order; and where the order is so revoked, then, if it is so agreed between the landlord and the tenant or determined by the court, the current tenancy shall continue, beyond the date at which it would have come to an end apart from this subsection, for such period as may be so agreed or determined to be necessary to afford to the landlord a reasonable opportunity for reletting or otherwise disposing of the premises which would have been comprised in the new tenancy; and while the current tenancy continues by virtue of this subsection it shall not be a tenancy to which this Part of this Act applies.

(3) Where an order is revoked under the last foregoing subsection any provision thereof as to payment of costs shall not cease to have effect by reason only of the revocation; but the court may, if it thinks fit, revoke or vary any such provision or, where no costs have been awarded in the proceedings for the revoked order, award such costs.

(4) A lease executed or agreement made under this section, in a case where the interest of the lessor is subject to a mortgage, shall be deemed to be one authorised by section ninety-nine of the Law of Property Act 1925 (which confers certain powers of leasing on mortgagors in possession), and subsection (13) of that section (which allows those powers to be restricted or excluded by agreement) shall not have effect in relation to such a lease or agreement. **[136]**

NOTES
Disapplied for certain purposes by the Dockyard Services Act 1986, s 3.

37. Compensation where order for new tenancy precluded on certain grounds

(1) Where on the making of an application under section twenty-four of this Act the court is precluded (whether by subsection (1) or subsection (2) of section thirty-one of this Act) from making an order for the grant of a new tenancy by reason of any of the grounds specified in paragraphs (*e*), (*f*) and (*g*) of subsection (1) of section thirty of this Act and not of any grounds specified in any other paragraph of that subsection [or where no other ground is specified in the landlord's notice under section 25 of this Act or, as the case may be, under

section 26(6) thereof, than those specified in the said paragraphs (*e*), (*f*) and (*g*) and either no application under the said section 24 is made or such an application is withdrawn], then, subject to the provisions of this Act, the tenant shall be entitled on quitting the holding to recover from the landlord by way of compensation an amount determined in accordance with the following provisions of this section.

(2) The said amount shall be as follows, that is to say,—

(*a*) where the conditions specified in the next following subsection are satisfied it shall be [the product of the appropriate multiplier and] twice the rateable value of the holding,

(*b*) in any other case it shall be [the product of the appropriate multiplier and] the rateable value of the holding.

(3) The said conditions are—

(*a*) that, during the whole of the fourteen years immediately preceding the termination of the current tenancy, premises being or comprised in the holding have been occupied for the purposes of a business carried on by the occupier or for those and other purposes;

(*b*) that, if during those fourteen years there was a change in the occupier of the premises, the person who was the occupier immediately after the change was the successor to the business carried on by the person who was the occupier immediately before the change.

(4) Where the court is precluded from making an order for the grant of a new tenancy under this Part of this Act in the circumstances mentioned in subsection (1) of this section, the court shall on the application of the tenant certify that fact.

(5) For the purposes of subsection (2) of this section the rateable value of the holding shall be determined as follows:—

(*a*) where in the valuation list in force at the date on which the landlord's notice under section twenty-five or, as the case may be, subsection (6) of section twenty-six of this Act is given a value is then shown as the annual value (as hereinafter defined) of the holding, the rateable value of the holding shall be taken to be that value;

(*b*) where no such value is so shown with respect to the holding but such a value or such values is or are so shown with respect to premises comprised in or comprising the holding or part of it, the rateable value of the holding shall be taken to be such value as is found by a proper apportionment or aggregation of the value or values so shown;

(*c*) where the rateable value of the holding cannot be ascertained in accordance with the foregoing paragraphs of this subsection, it shall be taken to be the value which, apart from any exemption from assessment to rates, would on a proper assessment be the value to be entered in the said valuation list as the annual value of the holding;

and any dispute arising, whether in proceedings before the court or otherwise, as to the determination for those purposes of the rateable value of the holding shall be referred to the Commissioners of Inland Revenue for decision by a valuation officer.

An appeal shall lie to the Lands Tribunal from any decision of a valuation officer under this subsection, but subject thereto any such decision shall be final.

(6) The Commissioners of Inland Revenue may by statutory instrument

make rules prescribing the procedure in connection with references under this section.

(7) In this section—

the reference to the termination of the current tenancy is a reference to the date of termination specified in the landlord's notice under section twenty-five of this Act or, as the case may be, the date specified in the tenant's request for a new tenancy as the date from which the new tenancy is to begin;

the expression "annual value" means rateable value except that where the rateable value differs from the net annual value the said expression means net annual value;

the expression "valuation officer" means any officer of the Commissioners of Inland Revenue for the time being authorised by a certificate of the Commissioners to act in relation to a valuation list.

[(8) In subsection (2) of this section "the appropriate multiplier" means such multiplier as the Secretary of State may by order made by statutory instrument prescribe.

(9) A statutory instrument containing an order under subsection (8) of this section shall be subject to annulment in pursuance of a resolution of either House of Parliament.] **[137]**

NOTES

Commencement: Before 1 January 1970 (sub-ss (1)-(7)); 25 March 1981 (remainder).
Sub-s (1): amended by the Law of Property Act 1969, s 11.
Sub-s (2): amended by the Local Government, Planning and Land Act 1980, s 193, Sch 33.
Sub-ss (8), (9): added by the Local Government, Planning and Land Act 1980, s 193, Sch 33.
Disapplied for certain purposes by the Dockyard Services Act 1986, s 3.

38. Restriction on agreements excluding provisions of Part II

(1) Any agreement relating to a tenancy to which this Part of this Act applies (whether contained in the instrument creating the tenancy or not) shall be void [(except as provided by subsection (4) of this section)] in so far as it purports to preclude the tenant from making an application or request under this Part of this Act or provides for the termination or the surrender of the tenancy in the event of his making such an application or request or for the imposition of any penalty or disability on the tenant in that event.

(2) Where—

(*a*) during the whole of the five years immediately preceding the date on which the tenant under a tenancy to which this Part of this Act applies is to quit the holding, premises being or comprised in the holding have been occupied for the purposes of a business carried on by the occupier or for those and other purposes, and

(*b*) if during those five years there was a change in the occupier of the premises, the person who was the occupier immediately after the change was the successor to the business carried on by the person who was the occupier immediately before the change,

any agreement (whether contained in the instrument creating the tenancy or not and whether made before or after the termination of that tenancy) which purports to exclude or reduce compensation under the last foregoing section shall to that extent be void, so however that this subsection shall not affect any agreement as to the amount of any such compensation which is made after the right to compensation has accrued.

(3) In a case not falling within the last foregoing subsection the right to compensation conferred by the last foregoing section may be excluded or modified by agreement.

[(4) The court may—

(*a*) on the joint application of the persons who will be the landlord and the tenant in relation to a tenancy to be granted for a term of years certain which will be a tenancy to which this Part of this Act applies, authorise an agreement excluding in relation to that tenancy the provisions of sections 24 to 28 of this Act; and

(*b*) on the joint application of the persons who are the landlord and the tenant in relation to a tenancy to which this Part of this Act applies, authorise an agreement for the surrender of the tenancy on such date or in such circumstances as may be specified in the agreement and on such terms (if any) as may be so specified;

if the agreement is contained in or endorsed on the instrument creating the tenancy or such other instrument as the court may specify; and an agreement contained in or endorsed on an instrument in pursuance of an authorisation given under the subsection shall be valid notwithstanding anything in the preceding provisions of this section.] **[138]**

NOTES

Commencement: Before 1 January 1970 (sub-ss (1)-(3)); 1 January 1970 (sub-s (4)).
Amended by the Law of Property Act 1969, s 5.
Disapplied for certain purposes by the Dockyard Services Act 1986, s 3.

General and supplementary provisions

39. Saving for compulsory acquisitions

(1) . . .

(2) If the amount of the compensation which would have been payable under section thirty-seven of this Act if the tenancy had come to an end in circumstances giving rise to compensation under that section and the date at which the acquiring authority obtained possession had been the termination of the current tenancy exceeds the amount of [the compensation payable under section 121 of the Lands Clauses Consolidation Act 1845 or section 20 of the Compulsory Purchase Act 1965 in the case of a tenancy to which this Part of this Act applies], that compensation shall be increased by the amount of the excess.

(3) Nothing in section twenty-four of this Act shall affect the operation of the said section one hundred and twenty-one. **[139]**

NOTES

Amended by the Land Compensation Act 1973, ss 47, 86, Sch 3.
Disapplied for certain purposes by the Dockyard Services Act 1986, s 3.

40. Duty of tenants and landlords of business premises to give information to each other

(1) Where any person having an interest in any business premises, being an interest in reversion expectant (whether immediately or not) on a tenancy of those premises, serves on the tenant a notice in the prescribed form requiring him to do so, it shall be the duty of the tenant to notify that person in writing within one month of the service of the notice—

(*a*) whether he occupies the premises or any part thereof wholly or partly for the purposes of a business carried on by him, and

(*b*) whether his tenancy has effect subject to any sub-tenancy on which his tenancy is immediately expectant and, if so, what premises are comprised in the sub-tenancy, for what term it has effect (or, if it is terminable by notice, by what notice it can be terminated), what is the rent payable thereunder, who is the sub-tenant, and (to the best of his knowledge and belief) whether the sub-tenant is in occupation of the premises or of part of the premises comprised in the sub-tenancy and, if not, what is the sub-tenant's address.

(2) Where the tenant of any business premises, being a tenant under such a tenancy as is mentioned in subsection (1) of section twenty-six of this Act, serves on any of the persons mentioned in the next following subsection a notice in the prescribed form requiring him to do so, it shall be the duty of that person to notify the tenant in writing within one month after the service of the notice—

(*a*) whether he is the owner of the fee simple in respect of those premises or any part thereof or the mortgagee in possession of such an owner and, if not,

(*b*) (to the best of his knowledge and belief) the name and address of the person who is his or, as the case may be, his mortgagor's immediate landlord in respect of those premises or of the part in respect of which he or his mortgagor is not the owner in fee simple, for what term his or his mortgagor's tenancy thereof has effect and what is the earliest date (if any) at which that tenancy is terminable by notice to quit given by the landlord.

(3) The persons referred to in the last foregoing subsection are, in relation to the tenant of any business premises,—

(*a*) any person having an interest in the premises, being an interest in reversion expectant (whether immediately or not) on the tenant's, and

(*b*) any person being a mortgagee in possession in respect of such an interest in reversion as is mentioned in paragraph (*a*) of this subsection;

and the information which any such person as is mentioned in paragraph (*a*) of this subsection is required to give under the last foregoing subsection shall include information whether there is a mortgagee in possession of his interest in the premises and, if so, what is the name and address of the mortgagee.

(4) The foregoing provisions of this section shall not apply to a notice served by or on the tenant more than two years before the date on which apart from this Act his tenancy would come to an end by effluxion of time or could be brought to an end by notice to quit given by the landlord.

(5) In this section—

the expression "business premises" means premises used wholly or partly for the purposes of a business;

the expression "mortgagee in possession" includes a receiver appointed by the mortgagee or by the court who is in receipt of the rents and profits, and the expression "his mortgagor" shall be construed accordingly;

the expression "sub-tenant" includes a person retaining possession of any premises by virtue of [the Rent Act 1977] after the coming to an end of a sub-tenancy, and the expression "sub-tenancy" includes a right so to retain possession. **[140]**

NOTES
Sub-s (5): amended by the Rent Act 1977, s 155, Sch 23, para 17.
Disapplied for certain purposes by the Dockyard Services Act 1986, s 3.

41. Trusts

(1) Where a tenancy is held on trust, occupation by all or any of the beneficiaries under the trust, and the carrying on of a business by all or any of the beneficiaries, shall be treated for the purposes of section twenty-three of this Act as equivalent to occupation or the carrying on of a business by the tenant; and in relation to a tenancy to which this Part of this Act applies by virtue of the foregoing provisions of this subsection—

(*a*) references (however expressed) in this Part of this Act and in the Ninth Schedule to this Act to the business of, or to carrying on of business, use, occupation or enjoyment by, the tenant shall be construed as including references to the business of, or to carrying on of business, use, occupation or enjoyment by, the beneficiaries or beneficiary;
(*b*) the reference in paragraph (*d*) of [subsection (1) of] section thirty-four of this Act to the tenant shall be construed as including the beneficiaries or beneficiary; and
(*c*) a change in the persons of the trustees shall not be treated as a change in the person of the tenant.

(2) Where the landlord's interest is held on trust the references in paragraph (*g*) of subsection (1) of section thirty of this Act to the landlord shall be construed as including references to the beneficiaries under the trust or any of them; but, except in the case of a trust arising under a will or on the intestacy of any person, the reference in subsection (2) of that section to the creation of the interest therein mentioned shall be construed as including the creation of the trust. **[141]**

NOTES
Amended by the Law of Property Act 1969, s 1(2).
Disapplied for certain purposes by the Dockyard Services Act 1986, s 3.

[41A. Partnerships

(1) The following provisions of this section shall apply where—

(*a*) a tenancy is held jointly by two or more persons (in this section referred to as the joint tenants); and
(*b*) the property comprised in the tenancy is or includes premises occupied for the purposes of a business; and
(*c*) the business (or some other business) was at some time during the existence of the tenancy carried on in partnership by all the persons who were then the joint tenants or by those and other persons and the joint tenants' interest in the premises was then partnership property; and
(*d*) the business is carried on (whether alone or in partnership with other persons) by one or some only of the joint tenants and no part of the property comprised in the tenancy is occupied, in right of the tenancy, for the purposes of a business carried on (whether alone or in partnership with other persons) by the other or others.

(2) In the following provisions of this section those of the joint tenants who for the time being carry on the business are referred to as the business tenants and the others as the other joint tenants.

(3) Any notice given by the business tenants which, had it been given by all the joint tenants, would have been—

(*a*) a tenant's request for a new tenancy made in accordance with section 26 of this Act; or

(*b*) a notice under subsection (1) or subsection (2) of section 27 of this Act;

shall be treated as such if it states that it is given by virtue of this section and sets out the facts by virtue of which the persons giving it are the business tenants; and references in those sections and in section 24A of this Act to the tenant shall be construed accordingly.

(4) A notice given by the landlord to the business tenants which, had it been given to all the joint tenants, would have been a notice under section 25 of this Act shall be treated as such a notice, and references in that section to the tenant shall be construed accordingly.

(5) An application under section 24(1) of this Act for a new tenancy may, instead of being made by all the joint tenants, be made by the business tenants alone; and where it is so made—

(*a*) this Part of this Act shall have effect, in relation to it, as if the references therein to the tenant included references to the business tenants alone; and

(*b*) the business tenants shall be liable, to the exclusion of the other joint tenants, for the payment of rent and the discharge of any other obligation under the current tenancy for any rental period beginning after the date specified in the landlord's notice under section 25 of this Act or, as the case may be, beginning on or after the date specified in their request for a new tenancy.

(6) Where the court makes an order under section 29(1) of this Act for the grant of a new tenancy on an application made by the business tenants it may order the grant to be made to them or to them jointly with the persons carrying on the business in partnership with them, and may order the grant to be made subject to the satisfaction, within a time specified by the order, of such conditions as to guarantors, sureties or otherwise as appear to the court equitable, having regard to the omission of the other joint tenants from the persons who will be the tenant under the new tenancy.

(7) The business tenants shall be entitled to recover any amount payable by way of compensation under section 37 or section 59 of this Act.] **[142]**

NOTES

Commencement: 1 January 1970.
Added by the Law of Property Act 1969, s 9.
Disapplied for certain purposes by the Dockyard Services Act 1986, s 3.

42. Groups of companies

(1) For the purposes of this section two bodies corporate shall be taken to be members of a group if and only if one is a subsidiary of the other or both are subsidiaries of a third body corporate.

In this subsection "subsidiary" has the same meaning as is assigned to it for the purposes of the [Companies Act 1985 by section 736 of that Act].

(2) Where a tenancy is held by a member of a group, occupation by another member of the group, and the carrying on of a business by another member of

the group, shall be treated for the purposes of section twenty-three of this Act as equivalent to occupation or the carrying on of a business by the member of the group holding the tenancy; and in relation to a tenancy to which this Part of this Act applies by virtue of the foregoing provisions of this subsection—

(*a*) references (however expressed) in this Part of this Act and in the Ninth Schedule to this Act to the business of or to use occupation or enjoyment by the tenant shall be construed as including references to the business of or to use occupation or enjoyment by the said other member;

(*b*) the reference in paragraph (*d*) of [subsection (1) of] section thirty-four of this Act to the tenant shall be construed as including the said other member; and

(*c*) an assignment of the tenancy from one member of the group to another shall not be treated as a change in the person of the tenant.

[(3) Where the landlord's interest is held by a member of a group—

(*a*) the reference in paragraph (*g*) of subsection (1) of section 30 of this Act to intended occupation by the landlord for the purposes of a business to be carried on by him shall be construed as including intended occupation by any member of the group for the purposes of a business to be carried on by that member; and

(*b*) the reference in subsection (2) of that section to the purchase or creation of any interest shall be construed as a reference to a purchase from or creation by a person other than a member of the group.] **[143]**

NOTES

Commencement: 1 January 1970 (sub-s (3)); before 1 January 1970 (sub-ss (1), (2)).

Sub-s (1): amended by the Companies Consolidation (Consequential Provisions) Act 1985, s 30, Sch 2.

Sub-s (3): added by the Law of Property Act 1969, ss 1(2), 10.

Disapplied for certain purposes by the Dockyard Services Act 1986, s 3.

43. Tenancies excluded from Part II

(1) This Part of this Act does not apply—

(*a*) to a tenancy of an agricultural holding [or a tenancy which would be a tenancy of an agricultural holding if *the proviso to subsection (1) of section two of the Agricultural Holdings Act 1948, did not have effect or, in a case where the approval of the Minister of Agriculture, Fisheries and Food was given as mentioned in the said subsection (1)* [subsection (3) of section 2 of the Agricultural Holdings Act 1986 did not have effect or, in a case where approval was given under subsection (1) of that section], if that approval had not been given];

(*b*) to a tenancy created by a mining lease;

(*c*) . . .

[(*d*) to a tenancy of premises licensed for the sale of intoxicating liquor for consumption on the premises, other than—

(i) premises which are structurally adapted to be used, and are bona fide used, for a business which comprises one or both of the following, namely, the reception of guests and travellers desiring to sleep on the premises and the carrying on of a restaurant, being a business a substantial proportion of which consists of transactions other than the sale of intoxicating liquor;

(ii) premises adapted to be used, and bona fide used, only for one or more of the following purposes, namely, for judicial or public administrative purposes, or as a theatre or place of public or private entertainment, or as public gardens or picture galleries, or for exhibitions, or for any similar purpose to which the holding of the licence is merely ancillary;

(iii) premises adapted to be used, and bona fide used, as refreshment rooms at a railway station.]

(2) This Part of this Act does not apply to a tenancy granted by reason that the tenant was the holder of an office, appointment or employment from the grantor thereof and continuing only so long as the tenant holds the office, appointment or employment, or terminable by the grantor on the tenant's ceasing to hold it, or coming to an end at a time fixed by reference to the time at which the tenant ceases to hold it:

Provided that this subsection shall not have effect in relation to a tenancy granted after the commencement of this Act unless the tenancy was granted by an instrument in writing which expressed the purpose for which the tenancy was granted.

(3) This Part of this Act does not apply to a tenancy granted for a term certain not exceeding [six months] unless—

(*a*) the tenancy contains provision for renewing the term or for extending it beyond [six months] from its beginning; or

(*b*) the tenant has been in occupation for a period which, together with any period during which any predecessor in the carrying on of the business carried on by the tenant was in occupation, exceeds [twelve months]. **[144]**

NOTES

Sub-s (1): para (*a*) first amendment in square brackets made by the Agriculture Act 1958, s 8(1), Sch 1, Part I, para 29, words in italics repealed with savings and subsequent words in square brackets substituted with savings by the Agricultural Holdings Act 1986, ss 99, 100, Sch 13, para 3, Sch 14, para 21; para (*c*) repealed by the Housing Act 1980, s 152, Sch 26; para (*d*) substituted by the Finance Act 1959, s 2(6), Sch 2, para 5.

Sub-s (3): amended by the Law of Property Act 1969, s 12.

Disapplied for certain purposes by the Dockyard Services Act 1986, s 3.

[43A. Jurisdiction of county court to make declaration

Where the rateable value of the holding is such that the jurisdiction conferred on the court by any other provision of this Part of this Act is, by virtue of section 63 of this Act, exercisable by the county court, the county court shall have jurisdiction (but without prejudice to the jurisdiction of the High Court) to make any declaration as to any matter arising under this Part of this Act, whether or not any other relief is sought in the proceedings.] **[145]**

NOTES

Commencement: 1 January 1970.

Added by the Law of Property Act 1969, s 13.

Disapplied for certain purposes by the Dockyard Services Act 1986, s 3.

44. Meaning of "the landlord" in Part II, and provisions as to mesne landlords, etc

(1) Subject to the next following subsection, in this Part of this Act the expression "the landlord", in relation to a tenancy (in this section referred to as "the relevant tenancy"), means the person (whether or not he is the immediate landlord) who is the owner of that interest in the property comprised in the relevant tenancy which for the time being fulfils the following conditions, that is to say—

(*a*) that it is an interest in reversion expectant (whether immediately or not) on the termination of the relevant tenancy, and

[(*b*) that it is either the fee simple or a tenancy which will not come to an end within fourteen months by effluxion of time and, if it is such a tenancy, that no notice has been given by virtue of which it will come to an end within fourteen months or any further time by which it may be continued under section 36(2) or section 64 of this Act],

and is not itself in reversion expectant (whether immediately or not) on an interest which fulfils those conditions.

(2) References in this Part of this Act to a notice to quit given by the landlord are references to a notice to quit given by the immediate landlord.

(3) The provisions of the Sixth Schedule to this Act shall have effect for the application of this Part of this Act to cases where the immediate landlord of the tenant is not the owner of the fee simple in respect of the holding. **[146]**

NOTES

Sub-s (1): amended by the Law of Property Act 1969, s 14(1).
Disapplied for certain purposes by the Dockyard Services Act 1986, s 3.

46. Interpretation of Part II

In this Part of this Act:—

"business" has the meaning assigned to it by subsection (2) of section twenty-three of this Act;

"current tenancy" has the meaning assigned to it by subsection (1) of section twenty-six of this Act;

"date of termination" has the meaning assigned to it by subsection (1) of section twenty-five of this Act;

subject to the provisions of section thirty-two of this Act, "the holding" has the meaning assigned to it by subsection (3) of section twenty-three of this Act;

"mining lease" has the same meaning as in the Landlord and Tenant Act 1927. **[147]**

NOTES

Disapplied for certain purposes by the Dockyard Services Act 1986, s 3.

PART III

COMPENSATION FOR IMPROVEMENTS

47. Time for making claims for compensation for improvements

(1) Where a tenancy is terminated by notice to quit, whether given by the landlord or by the tenant, or by a notice given by any person under Part I or Part II of this Act, the time for making a claim for compensation at the termination of the tenancy shall be a time falling within the period of three months beginning on the date on which the notice is given:

Provided that where the tenancy is terminated by a tenant's request for a new tenancy under section twenty-six of this Act, the said time shall be a time falling within the period of three months beginning on the date on which the landlord gives notice, or (if he has not given such a notice) the latest date on which he could have given notice, under subsection (6) of the said section twenty-six or, as the case may be, paragraph (*a*) of subsection (4) of section fifty-seven or paragraph (*b*) of subsection (1) of section fifty-eight of this Act.

(2) Where a tenancy comes to an end by effluxion of time, the time for making such a claim shall be a time not earlier than six nor later than three months before the coming to an end of the tenancy.

(3) Where a tenancy is terminated by forfeiture or re-entry, the time for making such a claim shall be a time falling within the period of three months beginning with the effective date of the order of the court for the recovery of possession of the land comprised in the tenancy or, if the tenancy is terminated by re-entry without such an order, the period of three months beginning with the date of the re-entry.

(4) In the last foregoing subsection the reference to the effective date of an order is a reference to the date on which the order is to take effect according to the terms thereof or the date on which it ceases to be subject to appeal, whichever is the later.

(5) . . . **[148]**

NOTES
Sub-s (5): amends the Landlord and Tenant Act 1927, s 1(1).

48. Amendments as to limitations on tenant's right to compensation

(1) So much of paragraph (*b*) of subsection (1) of section two of the Act of 1927 as provides that a tenant shall not be entitled to compensation in respect of any improvement made in pursuance of a statutory obligation shall not apply to any improvement begun after the commencement of this Act, but section three of the Act of 1927 (which enables a landlord to object to a proposed improvement) shall not have effect in relation to an improvement made in pursuance of a statutory obligation except so much thereof as—

(*a*) requires the tenant to serve on the landlord notice of his intention to make the improvement together with such a plan and specification as are mentioned in that section and to supply copies of the plan and specification at the request of any superior landlord; and

(*b*) enables the tenant to obtain at his expense a certificate from the landlord or the tribunal that the improvement has been duly executed.

(2) Paragraph (*c*) of the said subsection (1) (which provides that a tenant shall not be entitled to compensation in respect of any improvement made less than three years before the termination of the tenancy) shall not apply to any improvement begun after the commencement of this Act.

(3) No notice shall be served after the commencement of this Act under paragraph (*d*) of the said subsection (1) (which excludes rights to compensation where the landlord serves on the tenant notice offering a renewal of the tenancy on reasonable terms). **[149]**

50. Interpretation of Part III

In this Part of this Act the expression "Act of 1927" means the Landlord and Tenant Act 1927, the expression "compensation" means compensation under Part I of that Act in respect of an improvement, and other expressions used in this Part of this Act and in the Act of 1927 have the same meanings in this Part of this Act as in that Act. **[150]**

Part IV

Miscellaneous and Supplementary

51. Extension of Leasehold Property (Repairs) Act 1938

(1) The Leasehold Property (Repairs) Act 1938 (which restricts the enforcement of repairing covenants in long leases of small houses) shall extend to every tenancy (whether of a house or of other property, and without regard to rateable value) where the following conditions are fulfilled, that is to say,—

(*a*) that the tenancy was granted for a term of years certain of not less than seven years;

(*b*) that three years or more of the term remain unexpired at the date of the service of the notice of dilapidations or, as the case may be, at the date of commencement of the action for damages; and

(*c*) that the property comprised in the tenancy is not an agricultural holding.

(2) . . .

(3) The said Act of 1938 shall apply where there is an interest belonging to Her Majesty in right of the Crown or to a Government department, or held on behalf of Her Majesty for the purposes of a Government department, in like manner as if that interest were an interest not so belonging or held.

(4) Subsection (2) of section twenty-three of the Landlord and Tenant Act 1927 (which authorises a tenant to serve documents on the person to whom he has been paying rent) shall apply in relation to any counter-notice to be served under the said Act of 1938.

(5) This section shall apply to tenancies granted, and to breaches occurring, before or after the commencement of this Act, except that it shall not apply where the notice of dilapidations was served, or the action for damages begun, before the commencement of this Act.

(6) In this section the expression "notice of dilapidations" means a notice under subsection (1) of section one hundred and forty-six of the Law of Property Act 1925. **[151]**

NOTES

Sub-s (2): amends the Leasehold Property (Repairs) Act 1938, ss 1(1), (2), (5), 3, 7(1).

53. Jurisdiction of county court where lessor refuses licence or consent

(1) Where a landlord withholds his licence or consent—

(*a*) to an assignment of the tenancy or a sub-letting, charging or parting with the possession of the demised property or any part thereof, or

(*b*) to the making of an improvement on the demised property or any part thereof, or

(*c*) to a change in the use of the demised property or any part thereof, or to the making of a specified use of that property,

and the High Court has jurisdiction to make a declaration that the licence or consent was unreasonably withheld, then without prejudice to the jurisdiction of the High Court the county court shall have [the like jurisdiction whatever the net annual value for rating of the demised property is to be taken to be for the purposes of the County Courts Act 1984] and notwithstanding that the tenant does not seek any relief other than the declaration.

(2) Where on the making of an application to the county court for such a declaration the court is satisfied that the licence or consent was unreasonably withheld, the court shall make a declaration accordingly.

(3) The foregoing provisions of this section shall have effect whether the tenancy in question was created before or after the commencement of this Act and whether the refusal of the licence or consent occurred before or after the commencement of this Act.

(4) Nothing in this section shall be construed as conferring jurisdiction on the county court to grant any relief other than such a declaration as aforesaid. **[152]**

NOTES

Sub-s (1): amended by the County Courts Act 1984, s 148(1), Sch 2, para 23.

54. Determination of tenancies of derelict land

Where a landlord, having power to serve a notice to quit, on an application to the county court satisfies the court—

(*a*) that he has taken all reasonable steps to communicate with the person last known to him to be the tenant, and has failed to do so,

(*b*) that during the period of six months ending with the date of the application neither the tenant nor any person claiming under him has been in occupation of the property comprised in the tenancy or any part thereof, and

(*c*) that during the said period either no rent was payable by the tenant or the rent payable has not been paid,

the court may if it thinks fit by order determine the tenancy as from the date of the order. **[153]**

55. Compensation for possession obtained by misrepresentation

(1) Where under Part I of this Act an order is made for possession of the property comprised in a tenancy, or under Part II of this Act the court refuses an order for the grant of a new tenancy, and it is subsequently made to appear to the court that the order was obtained, or the court induced to refuse the grant, by misrepresentation or the concealment of material facts, the court may order the landlord to pay to the tenant such sum as appears sufficient as compensation for damage or loss sustained by the tenant as the result of the order or refusal.

(2) In this section the expression "the landlord" means the person applying for possession or opposing an application for the grant of a new tenancy, and the expression "the tenant" means the person against whom the order for possession was made or to whom the grant of a new tenancy was refused. **[154]**

56. Application to Crown

(1) Subject to the provisions of this and the four next following sections, Part II of this Act shall apply where there is an interest belonging to Her Majesty in right of the Crown or the Duchy of Lancaster or belonging to the Duchy of Cornwall, or belonging to a Government department or held on behalf of Her Majesty for the purposes of a Government department, in like manner as if that interest were an interest not so belonging or held.

(2) The provisions of the Eighth Schedule to this Act shall have effect as respects the application of Part II of this Act to cases where the interest of the

landlord belongs to Her Majesty in right of the Crown or the Duchy of Lancaster or to the Duchy of Cornwall.

(3) Where a tenancy is held by or on behalf of a Government department and the property comprised therein is or includes premises occupied for any purposes of a Government department, the tenancy shall be one to which Part II of this Act applies; and for the purposes of any provision of the said Part II or the Ninth Schedule to this Act which is applicable only if either or both of the following conditions are satisfied, that is to say—

(*a*) that any premises have during any period been occupied for the purposes of the tenant's business;

(*b*) that on any change of occupier of any premises the new occupier succeeded to the business of the former occupier,

the said conditions shall be deemed to be satisfied respectively, in relation to such a tenancy, if during that period or, as the case may be, immediately before and immediately after the change, the premises were occupied for the purposes of a Government department.

(4) The last foregoing subsection shall apply in relation to any premises provided by a Government department without any rent being payable to the department therefor as if the premises were occupied for the purposes of a Government department.

(5) The provisions of Parts III and IV of this Act amending any other enactment which binds the Crown or applies to land belonging to Her Majesty in right of the Crown or the Duchy of Lancaster, or land belonging to the Duchy of Cornwall, or to land belonging to any Government department, shall bind the Crown or apply to such land.

(6) Sections fifty-three and fifty-four of this Act shall apply where the interest of the landlord, or any other interest in the land in question, belongs to Her Majesty in right of the Crown or the Duchy of Lancaster or to the Duchy of Cornwall, or belongs to a Government department or is held on behalf of Her Majesty for the purposes of a Government department, in like manner as if that interest were an interest not so belonging or held.

[(7) Part I of this Act shall apply where—

(*a*) there is an interest belonging to Her Majesty in right of the Crown and that interest is under the management of the Crown Estate Commissioners; or

(*b*) there is an interest belonging to Her Majesty in right of the Duchy of Lancaster or belonging to the Duchy of Cornwall;

as if it were an interest not so belonging.] **[155]**

NOTES

Commencement: Before 1 January 1970 (sub-ss (1)-(6)); 28 November 1980 (sub-s (7)).
Commencement order: SI 1980 No 1706.
Sub-s (7): added by the Housing Act 1980, s 73(4).

57. Modification on grounds of public interest of rights under Part II

(1) Where the interest of the landlord or any superior landlord in the property comprised in any tenancy belongs to or is held for the purposes of a Government department or is held by a local authority, statutory undertakers or a development corporation, the Minister or Board in charge of any Government department may certify that it is requisite for the purposes of the first-mentioned department, or, as the case may be, of the authority, undertakers or corporation, that the use

or occupation of the property or a part thereof shall be changed by a specified date.

(2) A certificate under the last foregoing subsection shall not be given unless the owner of the interest belonging or held as mentioned in the last foregoing subsection has given to the tenant a notice stating—

(*a*) that the question of the giving of such a certificate is under consideration by the Minister or Board specified in the notice, and

(*b*) that if within twenty-one days of the giving of the notice the tenant makes to that Minister or Board representations in writing with respect to that question, they will be considered before the question is determined,

and if the tenant makes any such representations within the said twenty-one days the Minister or Board shall consider them before determining whether to give the certificate.

(3) Where a certificate has been given under subsection (1) of this section in relation to any tenancy, then,—

(*a*) if a notice given under subsection (1) of section twenty-five of this Act specifies as the date of termination a date not earlier than the date specified in the certificate and contains a copy of the certificate subsections (5) and (6) of that section shall not apply to the notice and no application for a new tenancy shall be made by the tenant under section twenty-four of this Act;

(*b*) if such a notice specifies an earlier date as the date of termination and contains a copy of the certificate, then if the court makes an order under Part II of this Act for the grant of a new tenancy the new tenancy shall be for a term expiring not later than the date specified in the certificate and shall not be a tenancy to which Part II of this Act applies.

(4) Where a tenant makes a request for a new tenancy under section twenty-six of this Act, and the interest of the landlord or any superior landlord in the property comprised in the current tenancy belongs or is held as mentioned in subsection (1) of this section, the following provisions shall have effect:—

(*a*) if a certificate has been given under the said subsection (1) in relation to the current tenancy, and within two months after the making of the request the landlord gives notice to the tenant that the certificate has been given and the notice contains a copy of the certificate, then,—

(i) if the date specified in the certificate is not later than that specified in the tenant's request for a new tenancy, the tenant shall not make an application under section twenty-four of this Act for the grant of a new tenancy;

(ii) if, in any other case, the court makes an order under Part II of this Act for the grant of a new tenancy the new tenancy shall be for a term expiring not later than the date specified in the certificate and shall not be a tenancy to which Part II of this Act applies;

(*b*) if no such certificate has been given but notice under subsection (2) of this section has been given before the making of the request or within two months thereafter, the request shall not have effect, without prejudice however to the making of a new request when the Minister or Board has determined whether to give a certificate.

(5) Where application is made to the court under Part II of this Act for the

grant of a new tenancy and the landlord's interest in the property comprised in the tenancy belongs or is held as mentioned in subsection (1) of this section, the Minister or Board in charge of any Government department may certify that it is necessary in the public interest that if the landlord makes an application in that behalf the court shall determine as a term of the new tenancy that it shall be terminable by six months' notice to quit given by the landlord.

Subsection (2) of this section shall apply in relation to a certificate under this subsection, and if notice under the said subsection (2) has been given to the tenant—

(*a*) the court shall not determine the application for the grant of a new tenancy until the Minister or Board has determined whether to give a certificate,

(*b*) if a certificate is given, the court shall on the application of the landlord determine as a term of the new tenancy that it shall be terminable as aforesaid, and section twenty-five of this Act shall apply accordingly.

(6) The foregoing provisions of this section shall apply to an interest held by a [Regional Health Authority, Area Health Authority, [District Health Authority] [Family Practitioner Committee] or special health authority], as they apply to an interest held by a local authority but with the substitution, for the reference to the purposes of the authority, of a reference to the purposes of [the National Health Service Act 1977].

(7) Where the interest of the landlord or any superior landlord in the property comprised in any tenancy belongs to the National Trust the Minister of Works may certify that it is requisite for the purpose of securing that the property will as from a specified date be used or occupied in a manner better suited to the nature thereof that the use or occupation of the property should be changed; and subsections (2) to (4) of this section shall apply in relation to certificates under this subsection, and to cases where the interest of the landlord or any superior landlord belongs to the National Trust, as those subsections apply in relation to certificates under subsection (1) of this section and to cases where the interest of the landlord or any superior landlord belongs or is held as mentioned in that subsection.

(8) In this and the next following section the expression "Government department" does not include the Commissioners of Crown Lands and the expression "landlord" has the same meaning as in Part II of this Act; and in the last foregoing subsection the expression "National Trust" means the National Trust for Places of Historic Interest or Natural Beauty. **[156]**

NOTES

Sub-s (6): first amendment made by the National Health Service Reorganisation Act 1973, ss 57, 58, Sch 4, para 68; further amended by the Health Services Act 1980, ss 1, 2, Sch 1, Part I, and by SI 1985 No 39, art 3; final amendment made by the National Health Service Act 1977, s 129, Sch 15, para 13.

58. Termination on special grounds of tenancies to which Part II applies

(1) Where the landlord's interest in the property comprised in any tenancy belongs to or is held for the purposes of a Government department, and the Minister or Board in charge of any Government department certifies that for reasons of national security it is necessary that the use or occupation of the property should be discontinued or changed, then—

(*a*) if the landlord gives a notice under subsection (1) of section twenty-five of this Act containing a copy of the certificate, subsections (5) and (6) of that section shall not apply to the notice and no application for a new tenancy shall be made by the tenant under section twenty-four of this Act;

(*b*) if (whether before or after the giving of the certificate) the tenant makes a request for a new tenancy under section twenty-six of this Act, and within two months after the making of the request the landlord gives notice to the tenant that the certificate has been given and the notice contains a copy of the certificate,—

(i) the tenant shall not make an application under section twenty-four of this Act for the grant of a new tenancy, and

(ii) if the notice specifies as the date on which the tenancy is to terminate a date earlier than that specified in the tenant's request as the date on which the new tenancy is to begin but neither earlier than six months from the giving of the notice nor earlier than the earliest date at which apart from this Act the tenancy would come to an end or could be brought to an end, the tenancy shall terminate on the date specified in the notice instead of that specified in the request.

(2) Where the landlord's interest in the property comprised in any tenancy belongs to or is held for the purposes of a Government department, nothing in this Act shall invalidate an agreement to the effect—

(*a*) that on the giving of such a certificate as is mentioned in the last foregoing subsection the tenancy may be terminated by notice to quit given by the landlord of such length as may be specified in the agreement, if the notice contains a copy of the certificate; and

(*b*) that after the giving of such a notice containing such a copy the tenancy shall not be one to which Part II of this Act applies.

(3) Where the landlord's interest in the property comprised in any tenancy is held by statutory undertakers, nothing in this Act shall invalidate an agreement to the effect—

(*a*) that where the Minister or Board in charge of a Government department certifies that possession of the property comprised in the tenancy or a part thereof is urgently required for carrying out repairs (whether on that property or elsewhere) which are needed for the proper operation of the landlord's undertaking, the tenancy may be terminated by notice to quit given by the landlord of such length as may be specified in the agreement, if the notice contains a copy of the certificate; and

(*b*) that after the giving of such a notice containing such a copy, the tenancy shall not be one to which Part II of this Act applies.

(4) Where the court makes an order under Part II of this Act for the grant of a new tenancy and the Minister or Board in charge of any Government department certifies that the public interest requires the tenancy to be subject to such a term as is mentioned in paragraph (*a*) or (*b*) of this subsection, as the case may be, then—

(*a*) if the landlord's interest in the property comprised in the tenancy belongs to or is held for the purposes of a Government department, the court shall on the application of the landlord determine as a term of the new tenancy that such an agreement as is mentioned in subsection (2) of this section and specifying such length of notice as is mentioned in the certificate shall be embodied in the new tenancy;

(*b*) if the landlord's interest in that property is held by statutory undertakers, the court shall on the application of the landlord determine as a term of the new tenancy that such an agreement as is mentioned in subsection (3) of this section and specifying such length of notice as is mentioned in the certificate shall be embodied in the new tenancy. **[157]**

59. Compensation for exercise of powers under ss 57 and 58

(1) Where by virtue of any certificate given for the purposes of either of the two last foregoing sections [or, subject to subsections (1A) or (1B) below, sections 60A or 60B below] the tenant is precluded from obtaining an order for the grant of a new tenancy, or of a new tenancy for a term expiring later than a specified date, the tenant shall be entitled on quitting the premises to recover from the owner of the interest by virtue of which the certificate was given an amount by way of compensation, and subsections (2), (3) and (5) to (7) of section thirty-seven of this Act shall with the necessary modifications apply for the purposes of ascertaining the amount.

[(1A) No compensation shall be recoverable under subsection (1) above where the certificate was given under section 60A below and either—

(*a*) the premises vested in the Welsh Development Agency under section 7 (property of Welsh Industrial Estates Corporation) or 8 (land held under Local Employment Act 1972) of the Welsh Development Agency Act 1975, or

(*b*) the tenant was not tenant of the premises when the said Agency acquired the interest by virtue of which the certificate was given.]

[(1B) No compensation shall be recoverable under subsection (1) above where the certificate was given under section 60B below and either—

(*a*) the premises are premises which—

(i) were vested in the Welsh Development Agency by section 8 of the Welsh Development Agency Act 1975 or were acquired by the Agency when no tenancy subsisted in the premises; and

(ii) vested in the Development Board for Rural Wales under section 24 of the Development of Rural Wales Act 1976; or

(*b*) the tenant was not the tenant of the premises when the Board acquired the interest by virtue of which the certificate was given.]

(2) Subsections (2) and (3) of section thirty-eight of this Act shall apply to compensation under this section as they apply to compensation under section thirty-seven of this Act. **[158]**

NOTES

Commencement: Before 1 January 1970 (sub-ss (1), (2)); 1 January 1976 (sub-s (1A)); 1 April 1977 (sub-s (1B)).

Commencement order: SI 1977 No 116.

Sub-s (1): amended by the Development of Rural Wales Act 1976, s 27, Sch 7, para 1(2).

Sub-s (1A): added by the Welsh Development Agency Act 1975, s 11(2).

Sub-s (1B): added by the Development of Rural Wales Act 1976, s 27, Sch 7, para 1(2).

60. Special provisions as to premises provided under Distribution of Industry Acts 1945 and 1950, etc

(1) [Where the property comprised in a tenancy consists of premises of which the Minister of Technology or [the English Industrial Estates Corporation] is the landlord, being premises situated in a locality which is either—

(*a*) a development area . . . or
(*b*) an intermediate area . . .

and the Minister of Technology certifies that it is necessary or expedient for achieving [the purpose mentioned in section 2(1) of the said Act of 1972]] that the use or occupation of the property should be changed, paragraphs (*a*) and (*b*) of subsection (1) of section fifty-eight of this Act shall apply as they apply where such a certificate is given as is mentioned in that subsection.

(2) Where the court makes an order under Part II of this Act for the grant of a new tenancy of [any such premises] as aforesaid, and the [[Secretary of State] certifies] that it is necessary or expedient as aforesaid that the tenancy should be subject to a term, specified in the certificate, prohibiting or restricting the tenant from assigning the tenancy or sub-letting, charging or parting with possession of the premises or any part thereof or changing the use of premises or any part thereof, the court shall determine that the terms of the tenancy shall include the terms specified in the certificate.

[(3) In this section "development area" and "intermediate area" mean an area for the time being specified as a development area or, as the case may be, as an intermediate area by an order made, or having effect as if made, under section 1 of the Industrial Development Act 1982.] **[159]**

NOTES

Commencement: 28 January 1983 (sub-s (3)); before 1 January 1970 (sub-ss (1), (2)).

Sub-s (1): amendment in square brackets made by the Local Employment Act 1970, s 5, Schedule; further amended by the English Industrial Estates Corporation Act 1981, s 9(1), and the Local Employment Act 1972, s 22(1), Sch 3; words omitted repealed by the Industry Act 1972, s 19(3), Sch 4, Part I.

Sub-s (2): amended by the Local Employment Act 1970, s 5, Schedule; further amended by the Secretary of State for Trade and Industry Order 1970, SI 1970 No 1537, art 2(2).

Sub-s (3): substituted by the Industrial Development Act 1982, s 19, Sch 2, para 2.

Said Act of 1972: Local Employment Act 1972.

[60A. Welsh Development Agency premises

(1) Where the property comprised in a tenancy consists of premises of which the Welsh Development Agency is the landlord, and the Secretary of State certifies that it is necessary or expedient, for the purpose of providing employment appropriate to the needs of the area in which the premises are situated, that the use or occupation of the property should be changed, paragraphs (*a*) and (*b*) of section 58(1) above shall apply as they apply where such a certificate is given as is mentioned in that subsection.

(2) Where the court makes an order under Part II of this Act for the grant of a new tenancy of any such premises as aforesaid, and the Secretary of State certifies that it is necessary or expedient as aforesaid that the tenancy should be subject to a term, specified in the certificate, prohibiting or restricting the tenant from assigning the tenancy or sub-letting, charging or parting with possession of the premises or any part of the premises or changing the use of the premises or any part of the premises, the court shall determine that the terms of the tenancy shall include the terms specified in the certificate.] **[160]**

NOTES
Commencement: 1 January 1976.
Added by the Welsh Development Agency Act 1975, s 11(1).

[60B. Development Board for Rural Wales premises

(1) Where the property comprised in the tenancy consists of premises of which the Development Board for Rural Wales is the landlord, and the Secretary of State certifies that it is necessary or expedient, for the purpose of providing employment appropriate to the needs of the area in which the premises are situated, that the use or occupation of the property should be changed, paragraphs (*a*) and (*b*) of section 58(1) above shall apply as they apply where such a certificate is given as is mentioned in that subsection.

(2) Where the court makes an order under Part II of this Act for the grant of a new tenancy of any such premises as aforesaid, and the Secretary of State certifies that it is necessary or expedient as aforesaid that the tenancy should be subject to a term, specified in the certificate, prohibiting or restricting the tenant from assigning the tenancy or sub-letting, charging or parting with possession of the premises or any part of the premises or changing the use of the premises or any part of the premises, the court shall determine that the terms of the tenancy shall include the terms specified in the certificate.] **[161]**

NOTES
Commencement: 1 April 1977.
Commencement order: SI 1977 No 116.
Added by the Development of Rural Wales Act 1976, s 27, Sch 7, para 1(1).

63. Jurisdiction of court for purposes of Parts I and II and of Part I of Landlord and Tenant Act 1927

(1) Any jurisdiction conferred on the court by any provision of Part I of this Act shall be exercised by the county court.

(2) Any jurisdiction conferred on the court by any provision of Part II of this Act or conferred on the tribunal by Part I of the Landlord and Tenant Act 1927, shall, subject to the provisions of this section, be exercised,—

(*a*) where the rateable value of the holding [is not over the county court limit] by the county court;
(*b*) where it [is over the county court limit] by the High Court.

(3) Any jurisdiction exercisable under the last foregoing subsection may by agreement in writing between the parties be transferred from the county court to the High Court or from the High Court to a county court specified in the agreement.

(4) The following provisions shall have effect as respects transfer of proceedings from or to the High Court or the county court, that is to say—

(*a*) where an application is made to the one but by virtue of subsection (2) of this section cannot be entertained except by the other, the application shall not be treated as improperly made but any proceedings thereon shall be transferred to the other court;
(*b*) any proceedings under the provisions of Part II of this Act or of Part I of the Landlord and Tenant Act 1927, which are pending before one of those courts may by order of that court made on the application of any person interested be transferred to the other court, if it appears to the court making the order that it is desirable that the proceedings

and any proceedings before the other court should both be entertained by the other court.

(5) In any proceedings where in accordance with the foregoing provisions of this section the county court exercises jurisdiction the powers of the judge of summoning one or more assessors under subsection (1) of section eighty-eight of the County Courts Act 1934, may be exercised notwithstanding that no application is made in that behalf by any party to the proceedings.

(6) Where in any such proceedings an assessor is summoned by a judge under the said subsection (1),—

(*a*) he may, if so directed by the judge, inspect the land to which the proceedings relate without the judge and report to the judge in writing thereon;

(*b*) the judge may on consideration of the report and any observations of the parties thereon give such judgment or make such order in the proceedings as may be just;

(*c*) the remuneration of the assessor shall be at such rate as may be determined by the Lord Chancellor with the approval of the Treasury and shall be defrayed out of moneys provided by Parliament.

(7) In this section the expression "the holding"—

(*a*) in relation to proceedings under Part II of this Act, has the meaning assigned to it by subsection (3) of section twenty-three of this Act,

(*b*) in relation to proceedings under Part I of the Landlord and Tenant Act 1927, has the same meaning as in the said Part I.

(8) Subsections (5) to (7) of section thirty-seven of this Act shall apply for determining the rateable value of the holding for the purposes of this section as they apply for the purposes of subsection (2) of the said section thirty-seven, but with the substitution in paragraph (*a*) of the said subsection (5) of a reference to the time at which application is made to the court for the reference to the date mentioned in that subsection.

(9) Nothing in this section shall prejudice the operation of section one hundred and eleven of the County Courts Act 1934 (which relates to the removal into the High Court of proceedings commenced in a county court).

(10) . . . **[162]**

NOTES

Sub-s (2): amended by the Administration of Justice Act 1973, s 6, Sch 2, Part I.

Sub-s (10): amends the Landlord and Tenant Act 1927, s 21.

County Courts Act 1934, s 88(1): see now County Courts Act 1984, s 63(1).

County Courts Act 1934, s 111: replaced by the County Courts Act 1959, s 115, which was repealed by the Supreme Court Act 1981, s 152, Sch 7.

County court limit: see Administration of Justice Act 1973, Sch 2, Part I.

64. Interim continuation of tenancies pending determination by court

(1) In any case where—

(*a*) a notice to terminate a tenancy has been given under Part I or Part II of this Act or a request for a new tenancy has been made under Part II thereof, and

(*b*) an application to the court has been made under the said Part I or the said Part II, as the case may be, and

(*c*) apart from this section the effect of the notice or request would be to terminate the tenancy before the expiration of the period of three months beginning with the date on which the application is finally disposed of,

the effect of the notice or request shall be to terminate the tenancy at the expiration of the said period of three months and not at any other time.

(2) The reference in paragraph (*c*) of subsection (1) of this section to the date on which an application is finally disposed of shall be construed as a reference to the earliest date by which the proceedings on the application (including any proceedings on or in consequence of an appeal) have been determined and any time for appealing or further appealing has expired, except that if the application is withdrawn or any appeal is abandoned the reference shall be construed as a reference to the date of the withdrawal or abandonment. **[163]**

65. Provisions as to reversions

(1) Where by virtue of any provision of this Act a tenancy (in this subsection referred to as "the inferior tenancy") is continued for a period such as to extend to or beyond the end of the term of a superior tenancy, the superior tenancy shall, for the purposes of this Act and of any other enactment and of any rule of law, be deemed so long as it subsists to be an interest in reversion expectant upon the termination of the inferior tenancy and, if there is no intermediate tenancy, to be the interest in reversion immediately expectant upon the termination thereof.

(2) In the case of a tenancy continuing by virtue of any provision of this Act after the coming to an end of the interest in reversion immediately expectant upon the termination thereof, subsection (1) of section one hundred and thirty-nine of the Law of Property Act 1925 (which relates to the effect of the extinguishment of a reversion) shall apply as if references in the said subsection (1) to the surrender or merger of the reversion included references to the coming to an end of the reversion for any reason other than surrender or merger.

(3) Where by virtue of any provision of this Act a tenancy (in this subsection referred to as "the continuing tenancy") is continued beyond the beginning of a reversionary tenancy which was granted (whether before or after the commencement of this Act) so as to begin on or after the date on which apart from this Act the continuing tenancy would have come to an end, the reversionary tenancy shall have effect as if it had been granted subject to the continuing tenancy.

(4) Where by virtue of any provision of this Act a tenancy (in this subsection referred to as "the new tenancy") is granted for a period beginning on the same date as a reversionary tenancy or for a period such as to extend beyond the beginning of the term of a reversionary tenancy, whether the reversionary tenancy in question was granted before or after the commencement of this Act, the reversionary tenancy shall have effect as if it had been granted subject to the new tenancy. **[164]**

66. Provisions as to notices

(1) Any form of notice required by this Act to be prescribed shall be prescribed by regulations made by [the Secretary of State] by statutory instrument.

(2) Where the form of a notice to be served on persons of any description is to be prescribed for any of the purposes of this Act, the form to be prescribed shall include such an explanation of the relevant provisions of this Act as

appears to the Lord Chancellor requisite for informing persons of that description of their rights and obligations under those provisions.

(3) Different forms of notice may be prescribed for the purposes of the operation of any provision of this Act in relation to different cases.

(4) Section twenty-three of the Landlord and Tenant Act 1927 (which relates to the service of notices) shall apply for the purposes of this Act.

(5) Any statutory instrument under this section shall be subject to annulment in pursuance of a resolution of either House of Parliament. **[165]**

NOTES

Sub-s (1), (2): words in square brackets substituted by SI 1974 No 1896, arts 2, 3(2).

67. Provisions as to mortgagees in possession

Anything authorised or required by the provisions of this Act, other than subsection (2) or (3) of section forty, to be done at any time by, to or with the landlord, or a landlord of a specified description, shall, if at that time the interest of the landlord in question is subject to a mortgage and the mortgagee is in possession or a receiver appointed by the mortgagee or by the court is in receipt of the rents and profits, be deemed to be authorised or required to be done by, to or with the mortgagee instead of that landlord. **[166]**

68. Repeal of enactments and transitional provisions

(1) . . .

(2) The transitional provisions set out in the Ninth Schedule to this Act shall have effect. **[167]**

NOTES

Sub-s (1): repealed by the Statute Law (Repeals) Act 1974.

69. Interpretation

(1) In this Act the following expressions have the meanings hereby assigned to them respectively, that is to say:—

"agricultural holding" has the same meaning as in the *Agricultural Holdings Act 1948* [Agricultural Holdings Act 1986];

"development corporation" has the same meaning as in the New Towns Act 1946;

"local authority" has the same meaning as in the Town and Country Planning Act 1947 [except that it includes the Inner London Education Authority and a joint authority established by Part IV of the Local Government Act 1985];

"mortgage" includes a charge or lien and "mortgagor" and "mortgagee" shall be construed accordingly;

"notice to quit" means a notice to terminate a tenancy (whether a periodical tenancy or a tenancy for a term of years certain) given in accordance with the provisions (whether express or implied) of that tenancy;

"repairs" includes any work of maintenance, decoration or restoration, and references to repairing, to keeping or yielding up in repair and to state of repair shall be construed accordingly;

"statutory undertakers" has the same meaning as in the Town and Country Planning Act 1947, except that it includes the [British Coal Corporation];

"tenancy" means a tenancy created either immediately or derivatively out of the freehold, whether by a lease or underlease, by an agreement for a lease or underlease or by a tenancy agreement or in pursuance of any enactment (including this Act), but does not include a mortgage term or any interest arising in favour of a mortgagor by his attorning tenant to his mortgagee, and references to the granting of a tenancy and to demised property shall be construed accordingly;

"terms", in relation to a tenancy, includes conditions.

(2) References in this Act to an agreement between the landlord and the tenant (except in section seventeen and subsections (1) and (2) of section thirty-eight thereof) shall be construed as references to an agreement in writing between them.

(3) References in this Act to an action for any relief shall be construed as including references to a claim for that relief by way of counterclaim in any proceedings. **[168]**

NOTES

Sub-s (1): in definition "agricultural holding" words in italics repealed with savings and words in square brackets substituted with savings by the Agricultural Holdings Act 1986, ss 99, 100, Sch 13, para 3, Sch 14, para 22; definition "local authority" amended by the Local Government Act 1985, s 84, Sch 14, para 36; definition "statutory undertakers" amended by the Coal Industry Act 1987, s 1(2), Sch 1, para 4.

New Towns Act 1946: see now New Towns Act 1981, s 80.

Town and Country Planning Act 1947: see now Town and Country Planning Act 1971.

Modified by SI 1985 No 1884, art 10, Sch 3.

70. Short title and citation, commencement and extent

(1) This Act may be cited as the Landlord and Tenant Act 1954, and the Landlord and Tenant Act 1927, and this Act may be cited together as the Landlord and Tenant Acts 1927 and 1954.

(2) This Act shall come into operation on the first day of October, nineteen hundred and fifty-four.

(3) This Act shall not extend to Scotland or to Northern Ireland. **[169]**

SCHEDULES

SCHEDULE 1

Section 8

SUPPLEMENTARY PROVISIONS AS TO PAYMENTS FOR ACCRUED TENANT'S REPAIRS

PART I

PROVISIONS AS TO MAKING OF PAYMENT IN LUMP SUM

1. Subject to the provisions of this Part of this Schedule, a payment for accrued tenant's repairs which is to be payable otherwise than by instalments shall become payable when the relevant initial repairs have been completed unless the landlord and the tenant agree that it shall become payable wholly or in part at some other date.

2. Where it is determined by the court that a payment for accrued tenant's repairs is to be payable otherwise than by instalments, the court may determine that any specified part of the payment shall become payable when any specified part of the relevant initial repairs has been completed.

3. A payment for accrued tenant's repairs which is payable otherwise than by instalments, or any part of such a payment, shall be recoverable from the tenant.

4.—(1) Where it has been agreed or determined that a payment for accrued tenant's repairs should be paid otherwise than by instalments, and the period of the statutory tenancy ends before the relevant initial repairs have been begun, or at a time when they have been begun but not completed, the following provisions shall have effect.

(2) If the relevant initial repairs have not been begun and are no longer required, then notwithstanding anything in section eight of this Act no payment for accrued tenant's repairs shall be recoverable.

(3) In any other case, the time for recovery of the payment for accrued tenant's repairs shall be the same as if all the relevant initial repairs had been completed immediately before the end of the period of the statutory tenancy, and the amount of the payment shall be as hereinafter provided:—

(*a*) if the relevant initial repairs have not been begun, the amount of the payment shall be the estimated cost of the repairs or of so much thereof as is still required;
(*b*) if the relevant initial repairs have been begun but not completed, the amount of the payment shall be an amount equal to the expenses reasonably incurred by the landlord for the purposes of so much of the relevant initial repairs as has been carried out together (unless the remainder is no longer required) with the estimated cost of the remainder or of so much thereof as is still required:

Provided that there shall be disregarded so much (if any) of the said expenses or estimated cost as is recoverable by the landlord otherwise than from the tenant or his predecessor in title.

(4) Any question arising under this paragraph whether repairs are no longer required, whether any expenses were incurred, or reasonably incurred, by the landlord, or as to the amount of the estimated cost of any repairs shall be determined by agreement between the landlord and the tenant or by the court on the application of either of them.

(5) For the purposes of this paragraph initial repairs shall be deemed to be no longer required after the end of the period of the statutory tenancy if, and only if, it is shown that the dwelling-house, in whatever state of repair it may then be, is at or shortly after the end of that period to be pulled down, or that such structural alterations are to be made in the dwelling-house as would render those repairs valueless if they were completed.

(6) In a case falling within sub-paragraph (1) of this paragraph where a payment for accrued tenant's repairs would, apart from this paragraph, include an amount in respect of cost incurred by the landlord in ascertaining what initial repairs are required in consequence of failure by the tenant to fulfil his obligations under the former tenancy, the following provisions shall have effect—

(*a*) that amount shall be recoverable notwithstanding anything in sub-paragraph (2) of this paragraph;
(*b*) in a case falling within sub-paragraph (3) of this paragraph the said amount shall be recoverable in addition to the amount specified in that sub-paragraph;
(*c*) the time for recovery of the said amount shall, as well in a case falling within sub-paragraph (2) of this paragraph as in one falling within sub-paragraph (3) thereof, be that mentioned in the said sub-paragraph (3).

5. In relation to a case where the court exercises the power conferred by paragraph 2 of this Schedule references in the last foregoing paragraph to the relevant initial repairs shall be construed as references to any such part of those repairs as is referred to in the said paragraph 2, being a part which at the material time has not been begun or, as the case may be, has been begun but not completed, and references to the payment for accrued tenant's repairs shall be construed accordingly. **[170]**

PART II

PROVISIONS AS TO MAKING OF PAYMENT BY INSTALMENTS

6. Subject to the provisions of this Part of this Schedule, where under Part I of this Act it is agreed or determined that a payment for accrued tenant's repairs is to be payable by instalments, the instalments shall become payable at the times so agreed or determined.

7. Any such instalment becoming payable at a time falling before the end of the period of the statutory tenancy shall be payable by the tenant.

8.—(1) Where the landlord is not the immediate landlord of the dwelling-house, the landlord and the immediate landlord may serve on the tenant a notice in the prescribed form requiring him to pay the instalments of the payment for accrued tenant's repairs to the immediate landlord for transmission to the landlord.

(2) A notice under the last foregoing sub-paragraph may be revoked by a subsequent notice given to the tenant by the landlord, with or without the concurrence of the immediate landlord.

9. Any instalment becoming payable at a time when the landlord is the immediate landlord or when a notice under sub-paragraph (1) of the last foregoing paragraph is in force shall be recoverable by the immediate landlord in the like manner and subject to the like provisions as the rent.

10. If the period of the statutory tenancy comes to an end before all instalments of the payment for accrued tenant's repairs have been paid, the remaining instalments shall become payable immediately after the end of that period, shall be recoverable by the person who immediately before the end thereof was the landlord, and shall be so recoverable from the person who immediately before the end thereof was the tenant.

11. In the application of the last foregoing paragraph to a case where the period of the statutory tenancy comes to an end before the relevant initial repairs have been begun, or at a time when they have been begun but not completed, the provisions of paragraph 4 of this Schedule shall have effect (with the necessary modifications) for limiting the recovery of any remaining instalments under the last foregoing paragraph.

12. Where, during the period of the statutory tenancy and before all instalments of the payment for accrued tenant's repairs have become payable, the interest of the landlord comes to an end or ceases to be an interest falling within paragraphs (*a*) and (*b*) of the proviso to subsection (4) of section twenty-one of this Act, he shall thereupon be entitled to recover from the person who thereupon becomes the landlord such amount (if any) as is equal to so much of the expenses reasonably incurred by the landlord—

(*a*) in ascertaining what initial repairs are required in consequence of failure by the tenant to fulfil his obligations under the former tenancy; and
(*b*) for the purposes of the relevant initial repairs;

as is recoverable from the tenant and has not been recovered. **[171]**

PART III

VARIATION OF AGREEMENT OR DETERMINATION AS TO TIME FOR MAKING PAYMENT

13. The tenant may apply to the court for the variation, on the grounds and to the extent hereinafter specified, of any agreement or determination for the making of a payment for accrued tenant's repairs.

14. The grounds on which an agreement or determination may be varied on an application under the last foregoing paragraph are the following:—

(*a*) that the expenditure reasonably incurred by the landlord in carrying out the relevant initial repairs substantially exceeded the estimated cost thereof; or
(*b*) that the applicant is not the person who was the tenant at the time of the previous agreement or determination and that there are considerations arising out of the personal circumstances of the applicant which ought to be taken into account in determining the manner of making the payment.

15. The extent to which an agreement or determination may be so varied on an application under paragraph 13 of this Schedule is the following:—

(*a*) if the agreement or determination was for the making of the payment otherwise than by instalments, and the payment has not been fully made, by substituting therefor a determination that the payment or balance of the payment should be made by instalments;

(*b*) if the agreement or determination was for the making of a payment by instalments, by substituting for the instalments agreed or determined instalments of such smaller amounts, payable at such times, as may be determined by the court.

16. Where an agreement or determination is varied under this Part of this Schedule, the foregoing provisions of this Schedule shall thereafter apply with the necessary modifications. **[172]**

PART IV

SUPPLEMENTARY

17. Any failure by the tenant to make a payment for accrued tenant's repairs, or any part or instalment of such a payment, at the time when it becomes due shall be treated as a breach of the obligations of the tenancy for the purposes of [Case I in [Schedule 15] to the Rent Act] (which relates to recovery of possession where the rent has not been paid or any other obligation of the tenancy has not been performed).

18. Where any sum in respect of a payment for accrued tenant's repairs has been recovered in advance of the carrying out of the relevant initial repairs, then in any case where paragraph 4 or 11 of this Schedule applies such repayment shall be made as may be just.

19. In this Schedule the expression "immediate landlord" means the person who as respects the dwelling-house is the landlord of the tenant for the purposes of the [Rent Act] and the expression "relevant initial repairs" means the repairs in respect of which the payment for accrued tenant's repairs is payable. **[173]**

NOTES

Amended by the Rent Act 1968, s 117(2), Sch 15; further amended by the Rent Act 1977, s 155, Sch 23, para 19.

The Rent Act: Rent Act 1977.

SCHEDULE 2

Section 8

FURTHER PROVISIONS AS TO REPAIR WHERE TENANT RETAINS POSSESSION

Failure of landlord to carry out initial repairs

1.—(1) Where—

(*a*) the tenant retains possession of the dwelling-house by virtue of subsection (1) of section six of this Act, and

(*b*) by virtue of an agreement or of a determination of the court, the landlord is required to carry out initial repairs to the dwelling-house,

then if on an application made by the tenant during the period of the statutory tenancy the court is satisfied that the initial repairs have not been carried out within a reasonable time in accordance with the agreement or determination the court may by order direct that, until the discharge of the order as hereinafter provided or the end of the period of the statutory tenancy, whichever first occurs, the rent payable in respect of the dwelling-house shall be reduced to such amount specified in the order as the court may think just having regard to the extent to which the landlord has failed to comply with the agreement or determination.

(2) Where the court under the last foregoing sub-paragraph orders a reduction of rent, the court may further order that during the same period any instalments of a payment for accrued tenant's repairs shall be suspended.

(3) An order under this paragraph may include a provision that the reduction of rent shall take effect from a specified date before the making of the order, being such date as the court thinks just having regard to the landlord's delay in carrying out the initial repairs; and where an order contains such a provision then, in addition to the reduction ordered by virtue of sub-paragraph (1) of this paragraph, such number of payments of rent next falling due after the date of the order shall be reduced by such amount as may be specified in the order for the purpose of giving effect to the said provision.

2. Where an order under paragraph 1 of this Schedule is in force, and on an application by the landlord the court is satisfied that the initial repairs have been carried out in accordance with the agreement or with the determination of the court, as the case may be, the court shall discharge the order, but without prejudice to the operation thereof as respects any period before the date on which it is discharged or to any reduction ordered by virtue of sub-paragraph (3) of the last foregoing paragraph.

3. If, while an order under paragraph 1 of this Schedule is in force, it is agreed between the landlord and the tenant that the initial repairs in question have been carried out as mentioned in the last foregoing paragraph, the order shall be discharged by virtue of that agreement in the like manner as if it had been discharged by the court.

Failure of tenant to carry out initial repairs

4. Where, by virtue of an agreement or of a determination of the court, the tenant is required to carry out initial repairs to the dwelling-house, failure by the tenant to carry out the repairs within a reasonable time in accordance with the agreement or determination shall be treated as a breach of the obligations of the tenancy for the purposes of [Case 1 in [Schedule 15] to the Rent Act] (which relates to recovery of possession where the rent has not been paid or any other obligation of the tenancy has not been performed).

Expenses and receipts: mortgages, settlements, etc.

5. Any amount paid by a mortgagee in respect of expenses incurred in carrying out initial repairs in accordance with an agreement or determination under Part I of this Act, or in respect of any payment made in pursuance of a liability imposed by paragraph 12 of the First Schedule to this Act, shall be treated as if it were secured by the mortgage, with the like priority and with interest at the same rate as the mortgage money, so however that (without prejudice to the recovery of interest) any such amount shall not be recoverable from the mortgagor personally.

6. The purposes authorised for the application of capital money by section seventy-three of the Settled Land Act 1925, by that section as applied by section twenty-eight of the Law of Property Act 1925, in relation to trusts for sale, and by section twenty-six of the Universities and College Estates Act 1925, and the purposes authorised by section seventy-one of the Settled Land Act 1925, by that section as applied as aforesaid, and by section [thirty] of the Universities and College Estates Act 1925, as purposes for which moneys may be raised by mortgage, shall include the payment of any such expenses as are mentioned in the last foregoing paragraph and the making of any such payment as is mentioned in that paragraph:

Provided that the like provisions shall have effect as to the repayment of capital money applied by virtue of this paragraph as have effect in the case of improvements authorised by Part II of the Third Schedule to the Settled Land Act 1925 (which specifies improvements the cost of which may be required to be replaced out of income).

Record of state of repair of dwelling-house

7. A landlord's notice proposing a statutory tenancy may contain a requirement that if the tenant retains possession by virtue of subsection (1) of section six of this Act a record shall be made of the state of repair of the dwelling-house.

8. Where the landlord gives such a notice which does not contain such a requirement, then if the tenant elects to retain possession his notification in that behalf may include a requirement that a record shall be made of the state of repair of the dwelling-house.

9. Where the tenant retains possession of the dwelling-house by virtue of subsection (1) of section six of this Act and either the landlord or the tenant has made such a requirement as is mentioned in either of the two last foregoing paragraphs, the record of the state of repair of the dwelling-house shall be made as soon as may be after the completion of any initial repairs to be carried out or, in the absence of any agreement or determination requiring the carrying out of initial repairs, as soon as may be after the beginning of the period of the statutory tenancy.

10. Any record required to be made under the last foregoing paragraph shall be made by a person appointed, in default of agreement between the landlord and the tenant, by the President of the Royal Institution of Chartered Surveyors.

11. The cost of making any such record as aforesaid shall, in default of agreement between the landlord and the tenant, be borne by them in equal shares. **[174]**

NOTES

Para 4: amended by the Rent Act 1968, s 117(2), Sch 15; further amended by the Rent Act 1977, s 155, Sch 23, para 19.

Para 6: amended by the Universities and College Estates Act 1964, s 4(1), Sch 3, Part II.

The Rent Act: Rent Act 1977.

SCHEDULE 3

Sections 12, 13

Grounds for Possession on Termination of Tenancy

1. The grounds referred to in paragraph (*b*) of subsection (1) of section twelve of this Act are the following, that is to say:—

(*a*) that suitable alternative accommodation will be available for the tenant at the date of termination of the tenancy;

(*b*) that the tenant has failed to comply with any term of the tenancy as to payment of rent or rates or as to insuring or keeping insured any premises;

(*c*) that the tenant or a person residing or lodging with him or being his sub-tenant has been guilty of conduct which is a nuisance or annoyance to adjoining occupiers, or has been convicted of using any premises comprised in the tenancy or allowing such premises to be used for an immoral or illegal purpose and, where the person in question is a lodger or sub-tenant, that the tenant has not taken such steps as he ought reasonably to have taken for the removal of the lodger or sub-tenant;

(*d*) . . . ; and

(*e*) that premises comprised in the tenancy, and consisting of or including the relevant premises, are reasonably required by the landlord for occupation as a residence for himself or any son or daughter of his over eighteen years of age or his father or mother [or the father or mother of his spouse], and (if the landlord is not the immediate landlord) that he will be the immediate landlord at the date of termination:

Provided that the court shall not make an order under section thirteen of this Act on the grounds specified in sub-paragraph (*e*) of this paragraph—

(*a*) if the interest of the landlord, or an interest which has merged in that interest and but for the merger would be the interest of the landlord, was purchased or created after [the 18th February 1966]; or

(*b*) if the court is satisfied that having regard to all the circumstances of the case, including the question whether other accommodation is available for the landlord or the tenant, greater hardship would be caused by making the order than by refusing to make it.

[2. Part IV of [Schedule 15] to the Rent Act (which relates to the circumstances in which suitable accommodation is to be deemed to be available for the tenant) shall apply for the purposes of this Schedule as it applies for the purposes of [section 98(1)(*a*)] of that Act.]

[175]

NOTES
Para 1: words omitted repealed and amendments made by the Leasehold Reform Act 1967, ss 39(2), 41(2), Sch 5, para 1, Sch 7, Part I.
Para 2: substituted by the Rent Act 1968, s 117(2), Sch 15; amended by the Rent Act 1977, s 155, Sch 23, para 20.
The Rent Act: Rent Act 1977

SCHEDULE 4

Section 19

MODIFICATIONS OF PART I IN RELATION TO PERIODICAL TENANCIES

1. In relation to such a tenancy as is mentioned in subsection (2) of section nineteen of this Act, Part I of this Act shall have effect subject to the following provisions of this Schedule.

2. For subsection (6) of section two there shall be substituted the following:—

"(6)In this Part of this Act the expression "term date", in relation to any such tenancy as is mentioned in subsection (2) of section nineteen of this Act, means the first date after the commencement of this Act on which apart from this Act the tenancy could have been brought to an end by notice to quit given by the landlord."

3. For subsection (1) of section five there shall be substituted the following:—

"(1)A tenancy to which section one of this Act applies may be brought to an end at the term date thereof by notice in writing given by the tenant to the immediate landlord.

The length of any such notice shall be not less than one month nor less than the length of the notice by which the tenant could apart from this Act have brought the tenancy to an end at the term date thereof."

4. Notwithstanding anything in subsection (2) of section three, where by virtue of subsection (1) of that section the tenancy is continued after the term date thereof the provisions of Part I as to the termination of a tenancy by notice shall have effect in substitution for and not in addition to any such provisions included in the terms on which the tenancy had effect before the term date thereof.

5. Where the tenancy is not terminated under the provisions of Part I of this Act at the term date thereof, then, whether or not it would have continued after that date apart from this Act, it shall be treated for the purposes of this Act as being continued by virtue of subsection (1) of section three thereof. **[176]**

SCHEDULE 5

Section 21

PROVISIONS FOR PURPOSES OF PART I WHERE IMMEDIATE LANDLORD IS NOT THE FREEHOLDER

Definitions

1.—(1) In this Schedule the following expressions have the meanings hereby assigned to them in relation to a tenancy (in this Schedule referred to as "the relevant tenancy"), that is to say:—

"the competent landlord" means the person who in relation to the relevant tenancy is for the time being the landlord (as defined by section twenty-one of this Act) for the purposes of Part I of this Act;

"mesne landlord" means a tenant whose interest is intermediate between the relevant tenancy and the interest of the competent landlord; and

"superior landlord", except in paragraph 9 of this Schedule, means a person (whether the owner of the fee simple or a tenant) whose interest is superior to the interest of the competent landlord.

(2) References in this Schedule to "other landlords" are references to persons who are either mesne landlords or superior landlords.

Acts of competent landlord binding on other landlords

2. Any notice given by the competent landlord under subsection (1) of section four of this Act, any agreement made under Part I of this Act between that landlord and the tenant under the relevant tenancy, and any determination of the court under the said Part I in proceedings between that landlord and that tenant, shall bind the interest of every other landlord (if any).

Provisions as to consent of other landlords to acts of competent landlord

3.—(1) Where in the four next following paragraphs reference is made to other landlords or to mesne landlords, the reference shall be taken not to include a mesne landlord whose interest is due to expire within the period of two months beginning with the relevant date or is terminable within that period by notice to quit given by his landlord.

(2) In this paragraph the expression "the relevant date" means—

(*a*) if the term date of the relevant tenancy has not passed, that date;
(*b*) if that date has passed, and no notice has been given under subsection (1) of section four of this Act to terminate the relevant tenancy, the earliest date at which that tenancy could be brought to an end by such a notice;
(*c*) if such a notice has been given, the date of termination specified in the notice.

4.—(1) If a notice is given by the competent landlord under subsection (1) of section four of this Act, or an agreement under Part I of this Act is made with the tenant by that landlord, without the written consent of every other landlord (if any), any other landlord whose written consent has not been given thereto shall, subject to the next following paragraph, be entitled to compensation from the competent landlord for any loss arising in consequence of the giving of the notice or the making of the agreement.

(2) The amount of any compensation under this paragraph shall, in default of agreement, be determined by the court on the application of the person claiming it.

5. The competent landlord may serve on any other landlord a notice in the prescribed form requiring him to consent to the giving or making of any such notice or agreement as aforesaid; and if within one month after the service of a notice under this paragraph—

(*a*) the consent has not been given, or
(*b*) conditions have been imposed on the giving of the consent which are in the opinion of the court unreasonable in all the circumstances,

the court, on an application by the competent landlord, may if it thinks fit order that the other landlord shall be deemed to have consented, either without qualification or subject to such conditions (including conditions as to the modification of the proposed notice or agreement or as to the payment of compensation by the competent landlord) as may be specified in the order.

6.—(1) It may be made a condition either—

(*a*) of the giving of consent by a person whose consent is required under paragraph 4 of this Schedule, or
(*b*) of the making of an order under the last foregoing paragraph,

that the initial repairs which the competent landlord will agree to carry out, or which, as the case may be, he will specify in accordance with subsection (1) of section nine of this Act as repairs which he is willing to carry out, shall include such repairs as may be specified in the consent or order.

(2) In so far as any cost reasonably incurred by the competent landlord in carrying out repairs specified in accordance with the last foregoing sub-paragraph is not recovered by way of payment for accrued tenant's repairs and is not recoverable (apart from this sub-paragraph) otherwise than by way of such payment, it shall be recoverable by the competent landlord from the person whose consent was or is deemed to have been given subject to the condition or (if he is dead) from his personal representatives as a debt due from him at the time of his death.

7.—(1) Where under Part I of this Act the competent landlord is required by an agreement, or by a determination of the court, to carry out initial repairs to any premises, he may serve on any mesne landlord a notice requiring him to pay to the competent landlord a contribution towards the cost reasonably incurred by the competent landlord in carrying out those repairs, if and in so far as that cost is not recovered by way of payment for accrued tenant's repairs and is not recoverable (apart from this sub-paragraph) otherwise than by way of such payment.

(2) Where a notice has been served under the last foregoing sub-paragraph, then in default of agreement between the competent landlord and the mesne landlord on whom the notice was served the court may order the mesne landlord to pay such a contribution as aforesaid.

(3) A contribution ordered under this paragraph shall be such as the court determines to be reasonable having regard to the difference between the rent under the relevant tenancy and the rent which, if the tenant retains possession, will be recoverable . . . during the period of the statutory tenancy.

Failure of competent landlord to carry out initial repairs

8. Where, in consequence of the failure of the competent landlord to carry out initial repairs, the amount of any payment of rent is reduced under paragraph 1 of the Second Schedule to this Act, and the competent landlord is not the immediate landlord of the tenant, the person who is for the time being the immediate landlord shall be entitled to recover from the competent landlord the amount of the reduction.

Relief in proceedings by superior landlord

9.—(1) Where in the case of a tenancy to which section one of this Act applies—

(*a*) the interest of the immediate landlord is itself a tenancy (in this paragraph referred to as "the mesne tenancy"), and

(*b*) a superior landlord has brought proceedings to enforce a right of re-entry or forfeiture in respect of a failure to comply with any terms of the mesne tenancy or of a superior tenancy having effect subject to the mesne tenancy, and

(*c*) the court makes an order for the recovery by the superior landlord of possession of the property comprised in the tenancy,

the tenant shall not be required to give up possession of that property unless he has been a party to the proceedings or has been given notice of the order; and the provisions of the next following sub-paragraph shall have effect where he has been such a party or has been given such a notice:

Provided that where the tenant has been a party to the proceedings the said provisions shall not apply unless he has at any time before the making of the order made application in the proceedings for relief under this paragraph.

(2) If the tenant within fourteen days after the making of the order, or where he has not been a party to the proceedings, within fourteen days after the said notice, gives notice in writing to the superior landlord that he desires that the following provisions of this sub-paragraph shall have effect and lodges a copy of the notice in the court—

(*a*) the tenant shall not be required to give up possession of the said property but the tenancy mentioned in head (*b*) of the last foregoing sub-paragraph shall be deemed as between the tenant and the superior landlord to have been surrendered on the date of the order; and

(*b*) if the term date of the tenant's tenancy would otherwise fall later, it shall be deemed for the purposes of Part I of this Act to fall at the expiration of seven months from the making of the order.

(3) Nothing in the foregoing provisions of this paragraph shall prejudice the operation of any order for the recovery of possession from the tenant under the mesne tenancy, or from the tenant under any superior tenancy having effect subject to the mesne tenancy.

(4) Subsections (4), (6) and (7) of section sixteen of this Act shall with the necessary modifications apply for the purposes of this paragraph.

Relief for mesne landlord against damages for breach of covenant

10.—(1) The provisions of the next following sub-paragraph shall have effect where, in the case of a tenancy to which section one of this Act applies,—

(*a*) the competent landlord is not the immediate landlord, and

(*b*) the competent landlord has brought proceedings against a mesne landlord to enforce a right to damages in respect of a failure to comply with any terms of the mesne landlord's tenancy, and

(*c*) the mesne landlord has made application in the proceedings for relief under this paragraph, and

(*d*) the court makes an order for the payment by the mesne landlord of any such damages as aforesaid.

(2) The operation of the order shall be suspended for a period of fourteen days from the making thereof, and if before the end of that period the mesne landlord gives notice in writing to the competent landlord that he desires that the provisions of heads (*a*) and (*b*) of this sub-paragraph shall have effect, and lodges a copy of the notice in the court—

(*a*) the order shall not be enforceable except if and in so far as it provides for the payment of costs, and

(*b*) the interest of the mesne landlord (unless it has then come to an end) shall be deemed to be surrendered, and his rights and liabilities thereunder to be extinguished, as from the date of the giving of the notice.

(3) Subsections (4) to (7) of section sixteen of this Act shall with the necessary modifications apply for the purposes of this paragraph.

Provisions as to liabilities under tenants' covenants in superior leases

11.—(1) Where subsection (1) of section ten of this Act applies, any terms to which this paragraph applies shall cease to have effect in so far as they relate to the premises constituting the dwelling-house, and any liability of the competent landlord or any mesne landlord or of any predecessor in title of the competent landlord or of any mesne landlord, under any such terms, in so far as it related to those premises and was a liability subsisting at the termination of the relevant tenancy, shall be deemed to have been extinguished on the termination of that tenancy.

(2) This paragraph applies to any terms of any tenancy owned by the competent landlord or by any other landlord, whether to be performed during that tenancy or on or after the expiration or determination thereof, except any such terms as are mentioned in paragraph (*a*) or (*b*) of the proviso to subsection (1) of section ten of this Act:

Provided that where any term to which this paragraph applies relates both to the dwelling-house and to other premises, nothing in this paragraph shall affect its operation in relation to the other premises.

(3) Notwithstanding anything in sub-paragraph (1) of this paragraph, if the interest of the competent landlord, being a tenancy, or the interest of any mesne landlord, has not come to an end by the end of the period of the statutory tenancy, and the terms on which that interest was held included an obligation to repair or maintain the dwelling-house or the dwelling-house and other premises, then as from the end of the period of the statutory tenancy the instrument creating the interest of the competent landlord or mesne landlord shall be deemed to contain a covenant with the grantor of the interest that the grantee of the interest will at all times maintain the dwelling-house in a state of repair no less good than that in which it was after the completion of any initial repairs to be carried out thereon in accordance with the provisions of Part I of this Act, and will yield up possession of the dwelling-house in such a state on the coming to an end of the interest of the said landlord.

(4) Where, in a case falling within sub-paragraph (1) of this paragraph, the competent landlord satisfies the court—

(*a*) that the obligations under the tenancy which in relation to him is the immediate mesne tenancy differ from the obligations under the relevant tenancy, and (*b*) that if the obligations under the relevant tenancy had been the same as those under the first-mentioned tenancy he would have been entitled to recover any amount by way of payment for accrued tenant's repairs which he is not entitled to recover,

he shall be entitled to recover that amount from the tenant under the first-mentioned tenancy, or, if that tenancy has come to an end, from the person who was the tenant thereunder immediately before it came to an end.

(5) Where in accordance with the last foregoing sub-paragraph, or with that sub-paragraph as applied by the following provisions of this sub-paragraph, any sum is recoverable from a person, the last foregoing sub-paragraph shall with the necessary modifications apply as between him and the person entitled to the interest (if any) which in relation to him is the immediate mesne tenancy or, if such an interest formerly subsisted but has come to an end, as between him and the person last entitled to that interest.

(6) In this paragraph the expression "the immediate mesne tenancy", in relation to the competent landlord or to a mesne landlord, means the tenancy on which his interest in those premises is immediately expectant. **[177]**

NOTES

Para 7: words omitted repealed by the Leasehold Reform Act 1967, s 41(2), Sch 7.

SCHEDULE 6

Section 44

PROVISIONS FOR PURPOSES OF PART II WHERE IMMEDIATE LANDLORD IS NOT THE FREEHOLDER

Definitions

1. In this Schedule the following expressions have the meanings hereby assigned to them in relation to a tenancy (in this Schedule referred to as "the relevant tenancy"), that is to say:—

"the competent landlord" means the person who in relation to the tenancy is for the time being the landlord (as defined by section forty-four of this Act) for the purposes of Part II of this Act;

"mesne landlord" means a tenant whose interest is intermediate between the relevant tenancy and the interest of the competent landlord; and

"superior landlord" means a person (whether the owner of the fee simple or a tenant) whose interest is superior to the interest of the competent landlord.

Power of court to order reversionary tenancies

2. Where the period for which in accordance with the provisions of Part II of this Act it is agreed or determined by the court that a new tenancy should be granted thereunder will extend beyond the date on which the interest of the immediate landlord will come to an end, the power of the court under Part II of this Act to order such a grant shall include power to order the grant of a new tenancy until the expiration of that interest and also to order the grant of such a reversionary tenancy or reversionary tenancies as may be required to secure that the combined effects of those grants will be equivalent to the grant of a tenancy for that period; and the provisions of Part II of this Act shall, subject to the necessary modifications, apply in relation to the grant of a tenancy together with one or more reversionary tenancies as they apply in relation to the grant of one new tenancy.

Acts of competent landlord binding on other landlords

3.—(1) Any notice given by the competent landlord under Part II of this Act to terminate the relevant tenancy, and any agreement made between that landlord and the tenant as to the granting, duration, or terms of a future tenancy, being an agreement made for the purposes of the said Part II, shall bind the interest of any mesne landlord notwithstanding that he has not consented to the giving of the notice or was not a party to the agreement.

(2) The competent landlord shall have power for the purposes of Part II of this Act to give effect to any agreement with the tenant for the grant of a new tenancy beginning with the coming to an end of the relevant tenancy notwithstanding that the competent landlord will not be the immediate landlord at the commencement of the new tenancy, and any instrument made in the exercise of the power conferred by this sub-paragraph shall have effect as if the mesne landlord had been a party thereto.

(3) Nothing in the foregoing provisions of this paragraph shall prejudice the provisions of the next following paragraph.

Provisions as to consent of mesne landlord to acts of competent landlord

4.—(1) If the competent landlord, not being the immediate landlord, gives any such notice or makes any such agreement as is mentioned in sub-paragraph (1) of the last foregoing paragraph without the consent of every mesne landlord, any mesne landlord whose consent has not been given thereto shall be entitled to compensation from the competent landlord for any loss arising in consequence of the giving of the notice or the making of the agreement.

(2) If the competent landlord applies to any mesne landlord for his consent to such a notice or agreement, that consent shall not be unreasonably withheld, but may be given subject to any conditions which may be reasonable (including conditions as to the modification of the proposed notice or agreement or as to the payment of compensation by the competent landlord).

(3) Any question arising under this paragraph whether consent has been unreasonably withheld or whether any conditions imposed on the giving of consent are unreasonable shall be determined by the court.

Consent of superior landlord required for agreements affecting his interest

5. An agreement between the competent landlord and the tenant made for the purposes of Part II of this Act in a case where—

(*a*) the competent landlord is himself a tenant, and
(*b*) the agreement would apart from this paragraph operate as respects any period after the coming to an end of the interest of the competent landlord,

shall not have effect unless every superior landlord who will be the immediate landlord of the tenant during any part of that period is a party to the agreement.

[Withdrawal by competent landlord of notice given by mesne landlord

6. Where the competent landlord has given a notice under section 25 of this Act to terminate the relevant tenancy and, within two months after the giving of the notice, a superior landlord—

(*a*) becomes the competent landlord; and
(*b*) gives to the tenant notice in the prescribed form that he withdraws the notice previously given,

the notice under section 25 of this Act shall cease to have effect, but without prejudice to the giving of a further notice under that section by the competent landlord.

Duty to inform superior landlords

7. If the competent landlord's interest in the property comprised in the relevant tenancy is a tenancy which will come or can be brought to an end within sixteen months (or any further time by which it may be continued under section 36(2) or section 64 of this Act) and he gives to the tenant under the relevant tenancy a notice under section 25 of this Act to terminate the tenancy or is given by him a notice under section 26(3) of this Act:—

(*a*) the competent landlord shall forthwith send a copy of the notice to his immediate landlord; and (*b*) any superior landlord whose interest in the property is a tenancy shall forthwith send to his immediate landlord any copy which has been sent to him in pursuance of the preceding sub-paragraph or this sub-paragraph.] **[178]**

NOTES
Commencement: Before 1 January 1970 (pars 1-5); 1 January 1970 (paras 6, 7).
Paras 6, 7: added by the Law of Property Act 1969, s 14(2).

SCHEDULE 8

Section 56

APPLICATION OF PART II TO LAND BELONGING TO CROWN AND DUCHIES OF LANCASTER AND CORNWALL

1. Where an interest in any property comprised in a tenancy belongs to Her Majesty in right of the Duchy of Lancaster, then for the purposes of Part II of this Act the Chancellor of the Duchy shall represent Her Majesty and shall be deemed to be the owner of the interest.

2. Where an interest in any property comprised in a tenancy belongs to the Duchy of Cornwall, then for the purposes of Part II of this Act such person as the Duke of Cornwall, or other the possessor for the time being of the Duchy of Cornwall, appoints shall represent the Duke of Cornwall or other the possessor aforesaid, and shall be deemed to be the owner of the interest and may do any act or thing under the said Part II which the owner of that interest is authorised or required to do thereunder.

3 . . .

4. The amount of any compensation payable under section thirty-seven of this Act by the Chancellor of the Duchy of Lancaster shall be raised and paid as an expense incurred in improvement of land belonging to Her Majesty in right of the Duchy within section twenty-five of the Act of the fifty-seventh year of King George the Third, Chapter ninety-seven.

5. Any compensation payable under section thirty-seven of this Act by the person representing the Duke of Cornwall or other the possessor for the time being of the Duchy of Cornwall shall be paid, and advances therefor made, in the manner and subject to the provisions of section eight of the Duchy of Cornwall Management Act 1863 with respect to improvements of land mentioned in that section. **[179]**

NOTES
Para 3: repealed by the Crown Estate Act 1961, s 9(4), Sch 3, Part II.

SCHEDULE 9

Sections 41, 42, 56, 68

TRANSITIONAL PROVISIONS

1, 2 . . .

3. Where immediately before the commencement of this Act a person was protected by section seven of the Leasehold Property (Temporary Provisions) Act 1951, against the making of an order or giving of a judgment for possession or ejectment, the Rent Acts shall apply in relation to the dwelling-house to which that person's protection extended immediately before the commencement of this Act as if section fifteen of this Act had always had effect.

4. For the purposes of section twenty-six and subsection (2) of section forty of this Act a tenancy which is not such a tenancy as is mentioned in subsection (1) of the said section twenty-six but is a tenancy to which Part II of this Act applies and in respect of which the following conditions are satisfied, that is to say—

(*a*) that it took effect before the commencement of this Act at the coming to an end by effluxion of time or notice to quit of a tenancy which is such a tenancy as is mentioned in subsection (1) of the said section twenty-six or is by virtue of this paragraph deemed to be such a tenancy; and (*b*) that if this Act had then been in force the tenancy at the coming to an end of which it took effect would have been one to which Part II of this Act applies; and

(*c*) that the tenant is either the tenant under the tenancy at the coming to an end of which it took effect or a successor to his business,

shall be deemed to be such a tenancy as is mentioned in subsection (1) of the said section twenty-six.

5.—(1) A tenant under a tenancy which was current at the commencement of this Act shall not in any case be entitled to compensation under section thirty-seven or fifty-nine of this Act unless at the date on which he is to quit the holding the holding or part thereof has continuously been occupied for the purposes of the carrying on of the tenant's business (whether by him or by any other person) for at least five years.

(2) Where a tenant under a tenancy which was current at the commencement of this Act would but for this sub-paragraph be entitled both to—

(*a*) compensation under section thirty-seven or section fifty-nine of this Act; and

(*b*) compensation payable, under the provisions creating the tenancy, on the termination of the tenancy,

he shall be entitled, at his option, to the one or the other, but not to both.

6.—(1) Where the landlord's interest in the property comprised in a tenancy which, immediately before the commencement of this Act, was terminable by less than six months' notice to quit given by the landlord belongs to or is held for the purposes of a Government Department or is held by statutory undertakers, the tenancy shall have effect as if that shorter length of notice were specified in such an agreement as is mentioned in subsection (2) or (3) of section fifty-eight of this Act, as the case may be, and the agreement were embodied in the tenancy.

(2) The last foregoing sub-paragraph shall apply in relation to a tenancy where the landlord's interest belongs or is held as aforesaid and which, immediately before the commencement of this Act, was terminable by the landlord without notice as if the tenancy had then been terminable by one month's notice to quit given by the landlord.

7 . . .

8. Where at the commencement of this Act any proceedings are pending on an application made before the commencement of this Act to the tribunal under section five of the Landlord and Tenant Act 1927, no further step shall be taken in the proceedings except for the purposes of an order as to costs; and where the tribunal has made an interim order in the proceedings under subsection (13) of section five of that Act authorising the tenant to remain in possession of the property comprised in his tenancy for any period, the tenancy shall be deemed not to have come to an end before the expiration of that period, and section twenty-four of this Act shall have effect in relation to it accordingly.

9, 10 . . .

11. Notwithstanding the repeal of Part II of the Leasehold Property (Temporary Provisions) Act 1951, where immediately before the commencement of this Act a tenancy was being continued by subsection (3) of section eleven of that Act it shall not come to an end at the commencement of this Act, and section twenty-four of this Act shall have effect in relation to it accordingly. **[180]**

NOTES

Paras 1, 2, 7, 9, 10: repealed by the Statute Law (Repeals) Act 1976.

COSTS OF LEASES ACT 1958

(c 52)

An Act to make provision for the incidence of the costs of leases [23 July 1958]

1. Costs of leases

Notwithstanding any custom to the contrary, a party to a lease shall, unless the parties thereto agree otherwise in writing, be under no obligation to pay the whole or any part of any other party's solicitor's costs of the lease. **[181]**

2. Interpretation

In this Act—

(*a*) "lease" includes an underlease and an agreement for a lease or underlease or for a tenancy or sub-tenancy;

(*b*) "costs" includes fees, charges, disbursements (including stamp duty), expenses and remuneration. **[182]**

3. Short Title

This Act may be cited as the Costs of Leases Act 1958. **[183]**

LEASEHOLD REFORM ACT 1967

(c 88)

ARRANGEMENT OF SECTIONS

PART I

ENFRANCHISEMENT AND EXTENSION OF LONG LEASEHOLDS

Right to enfranchisement or extension

Section		Para
1	Tenants entitled to enfranchisement or extension	[184]
2	Meaning of "house" and "house and premises", and adjustment of boundary	[185]
3	Meaning of "long tenancy"	[186]
4	Meaning of "low rent"	[187]
5	General provisions as to claims to enfranchisement or extension	[188]
6	Rights of trustees	[189]
7	Rights of members of family succeeding to tenancy on death	[190]

Enfranchisement

8	Obligation to enfranchise	[191]
9	Purchase price and costs of enfranchisement, and tenant's right to withdraw	[192]
10	Rights to be conveyed to tenant on enfranchisement	[193]
11	Exoneration from, or redemption of, rentcharges etc	[194]
12	Discharge of mortgages etc on landlord's estate	[195]
13	Payment into court in respect of mortgages etc	[196]

Extension

14	Obligation to grant extended lease	[197]
15	Terms of tenancy to be granted on extension	[198]
16	Exclusion of further rights after extension	[199]

Section Para

Landlord's overriding rights

17 Redevelopment rights (exclusion or termination of extension) .. .. [200]
18 Residential rights (exclusion of enfranchisement or extension) .. .. [201]
19 Retention of management powers for general benefit of neighbourhood .. .. [202]

Determination of questions, procedure, etc

20 Jurisdiction and special powers of county court. .. .. [203]
21 Jurisdiction of Lands Tribunal .. .. [204]
22 Validity of tenants' notices, effect on Landlord and Tenant Act 1954 and on notices to quit, etc, and procedure generally .. .. [205]

Supplementary

23 Agreements excluding or modifying rights of tenant .. .. [206]
24 Application of price or compensation received by landlord, and charge of betterment levy on enfranchisement .. .. [207]
25 Mortgagee in possession of landlord's interest .. .. [208]
26 Person to act where landlord is custodian trustee or under disability .. .. .. [209]
27 Enfranchisement where landlord cannot be found .. .. [210]

Land held for public purposes, ecclesiastical land, etc

28 Retention or resumption of land required for public purposes .. .. [211]
29 Reservation of future right to develop .. .. [212]
30 Reservation of right of pre-emption in new town or overspill area .. .. .. [213]
31 Ecclesiastical property .. .. [214]
32 Saving for National Trust .. .. [215]
33 Crown land .. .. [216]
33A Exclusion of certain shared ownership leases .. .. [217]

ENFRANCHISEMENT AND EXTENSION OF LONG LEASEHOLDS

Transitional

34 Tenancies terminated since 8th December 1964, or subject to early termination .. [218]
35 Proceedings and orders under Landlord and Tenant Act 1954 .. .. [219]
36 Relief in respect of mortgages etc on landlord's estate .. .. [220]

Construction

37 Interpretation of Part I .. .. [221]

PART II

AMENDMENTS OF OTHER ACTS

38 Modification of right to possession under Landlord and Tenant Act 1954 .. .. [222]
39 Application of Rent Acts to long tenancies and adaptation of Landlord and Tenant Act 1954 .. .. [223]
40 Amendments of Places of Worship (Enfranchisement) Act 1920 .. .. .. [224]
41 Short title, repeals, extent and commencement .. .. [225]

SCHEDULES

Schedule 1—*Enfranchisement or Extension by Sub-Tenants* .. .. [226]
Schedule 2—*Provisions Supplementary to Sections 17 and 18 of this Act* .. .. [227]
Schedule 3—*Validity of Tenants' Notices, Effect on Landlord and Tenant Act 1954 etc and Procedure Generally* .. ..
Part I—Restrictions on claims by tenant, and effect of claims on other notices, forfeitures, etc .. .. [228]
Part II—Procedural Provisions .. .. [229]
Schedule 4—*Special Covenants with Local Authorities etc on Enfranchisement or Extension* .. ..
Part I—Operation and Enforcement of Covenants .. .. [230]
Part II—Re-acquisition for Development by New Towns Commission or University Body .. .. [231]

Section Para
Schedule 4A—*Exclusion of Certain Shared Ownership Leases* .. .. .. [232]
Schedule 5—*Landlord and Tenant Act 1954 Part I (Consequential Amendments, Effect of Rent Act 1965, etc)* .. .. [233]

An Act to enable tenants of houses held on long leases at low rents to acquire the freehold or an extended lease; to apply the Rent Acts to premises held on long leases at a rackrent, and to bring the operation of the Landlord and Tenant Act 1954 into conformity with the Rent Acts as so amended; to make other changes in the law in relation to premises held on long leases, including amendments of the Places of Worship (Enfranchisement) Act 1920; and for purposes connected therewith [27 October 1967]

PART I

ENFRANCHISEMENT AND EXTENSION OF LONG LEASEHOLDS

Right to enfranchisement or extension

1. Tenants entitled to enfranchisement or extension

(1) This Part of this Act shall have effect to confer on a tenant of a leasehold house, occupying the house as his residence, a right to acquire on fair terms the freehold or an extended lease of the house and premises where—

(*a*) his tenancy is a long tenancy at a low rent and [subject to subsections (5) and (6) below] the rateable value of the house and premises on the appropriate day is not (or was not) more than £200 or, if it is in Greater London, than £400; and

(*b*) at the relevant time (that is to say, at the time when he gives notice in accordance with this Act of his desire to have the freehold or to have an extended lease, as the case may be) he has been tenant of the house under a long tenancy at a low rent, and occupying it as his residence, for the last [three years] or for periods amounting to [three years] in the last ten years;

and to confer the like right in the other cases for which provision is made in this Part of this Act.

[(1A) The references in subsection (1)(*a*) and (*b*) to a long tenancy at a low rent do not include a tenancy excluded from the operation of this Part by section 33A of and Schedule 4A to this Act.]

(2) In this Part of this Act references, in relation to any tenancy, to the tenant occupying a house as his residence shall be construed as applying where, but only where, the tenant is, in right of the tenancy, occupying it as his only or main residence (whether or not he uses it also for other purposes); but—

(*a*) references to a person occupying a house shall apply where he occupies it in part only; and

(*b*) in determining in what right the tenant occupies, there shall be disregarded any mortgage term and any interest arising in favour of any person by his attorning tenant to a mortgagee or chargee.

(3) This Part of this Act shall not confer on the tenant of a house any right by reference to his occupation of it as his residence (but shall apply as if he were not so occupying it) at any time when—

(*a*) it is let to and occupied by him with other land or premises to which it is ancillary; or (*b*) it is comprised in an agricultural holding within the meaning of the *Agricultural Holdings Act 1948* [Agricultural Holdings Act 1986].

(4) In subsection (1)(*a*) above, "the appropriate day", in relation to any house and premises, means the 23rd March 1965 or such later day as by virtue of [section 25(3) of the Rent Act 1977] would be the appropriate day for purposes of that Act in relation to a dwelling house consisting of that house.

[(4A) Schedule 8 to the Housing Act 1974 shall have effect to enable a tenant to have the rateable value of the house and premises reduced for purposes of this section in consequence of tenant's improvements.]

[(5) If, in relation to any house and premises, the appropriate day for the purposes of subsection (1)(*a*) above falls on or after 1st April 1973 that subsection shall have effect in relation to the house and premises,—

(*a*) in a case where the tenancy was created on or before 18th February 1966, as if for the sums of £200 and £400 specified in that subsection there were substituted respectively the sums of £750 and £1,500; and
(*b*) in a case where the tenancy was created after 18th February 1966, as if for those sums of £200 and £400 there were substituted respectively the sums of £500 and £1,000.

(6) If, in relation to any house and premises,—

(*a*) the appropriate day for the purposes of subsection (1) (*a*) above falls before 1st April 1973, and
(*b*) the rateable value of the house and premises on the appropriate day was more than £200 or, if it was then in Greater London, £400, and
(*c*) the tenancy was created on or before 18th February 1966,

subsection (1) (*a*) above shall have effect in relation to the house and premises as if for the reference to the appropriate day there were substituted a reference to 1st April 1973 and as if for the sums of £200 and £400 specified in that subsection there were substituted respectively the sums of £750 and £1,500.]

[184]

NOTES

Commencement: 3 October 1980 (sub-s (4A)); 31 July 1974 (sub-ss (5), (6)); before 1 January 1970 (sub-ss (1), (2)-(4)); to be appointed (remainder).

Commencement order: SI 1980 No 1406.

Sub-s (1): first amendment made by the Housing Act 1974, s 118(1); other amendments made by the Housing Act 1980, s 141, Sch 21.

Sub-s (1A): prospectively added with savings by the Housing and Planning Act 1986, s 18, Sch 4, paras 3, 11, as from a day to be appointed.

Sub-s (3): words in italics repealed with savings and words in square brackets substituted with savings by the Agricultural Holdings Act 1986, ss 99, 100, Sch 13, para 3, Sch 14, para 43.

Sub-s (4): amended by the Rent Act 1977, s 155, Sch 23, para 42.

Sub-s (4A): substituted by the Housing Act 1980, s 141, Sch 21.

Sub-ss (5), (6): added by the Housing Act 1974, s 118(1), (3).

See further the Housing Act 1985, ss 172-175.

2. Meaning of "house" and "house and premises", and adjustment of boundary

(1) For purposes of this Part of this Act, "house" includes any building designed or adapted for living in and reasonably so called, notwithstanding that the building is not structurally detached, or was or is not solely designed or adapted for living in, or is divided horizontally into flats or maisonettes; and—

(*a*) where a building is divided horizontally, the flats or other units into which it is so divided are not separate "houses", though the building as a whole may be; and (*b*) where a building is divided vertically the building as a whole is not a "house" though any of the units into which it is divided may be.

(2) References in this Part of this Act to a house do not apply to a house which is not structurally detached and of which a material part lies above or below a part of the structure not comprised in the house.

(3) Subject to the following provisions of this section, where in relation to a house let to and occupied by a tenant reference is made in this Part of this Act to the house and premises, the reference to premises is to be taken as referring to any garage, outhouse, garden, yard and appurtenances which at the relevant time are let to him with the house and are occupied with and used for the purposes of the house or any part of it by him or by another occupant.

(4) In relation to the exercise by a tenant of any right conferred by this Part of this Act there shall be treated as included in the house and premises any other premises let with the house and premises but not at the relevant time occupied and used as mentioned in subsection (3) above (whether in consequence of an assignment of the term therein or a subletting or otherwise), if—

(*a*) the landlord at the relevant time has an interest in the other premises and, not later than two months after the relevant time, gives to the tenant written notice objecting to the further severance of them from the house and premises; and

(*b*) either the tenant agrees to their inclusion with the house and premises or the court is satisfied that it would be unreasonable to require the landlord to retain them without the house and premises.

(5) In relation to the exercise by a tenant of any right conferred by this Part of this Act there shall be treated as not included in the house and premises any part of them which lies above or below other premises (not consisting only of underlying mines or minerals), if—

(*a*) the landlord at the relevant time has an interest in the other premises and, not later than two months after the relevant time, gives to the tenant written notice objecting to the further severance from them of that part of the house and premises; and

(*b*) either the tenant agrees to the exclusion of that part of the house and premises or the court is satisfied that any hardship or incovenience likely to result to the tenant from the exclusion, when account is taken of anything that can be done to mitigate its effects and of any undertaking of the landlord to take steps to mitigate them, is outweighed by the difficulties involved in the further severance from the other premises and any hardship or inconvenience likely to result from that severance to persons interested in those premises.

(6) The rights conferred on a tenant by this Part of this Act in relation to any house and premises shall not extend to underlying minerals comprised in the tenancy if the landlord requires that the minerals be excepted, and if proper provision is made for the support of the house and premises as they have been enjoyed during the tenancy and in accordance with its terms.

(7) Where by virtue of subsection (4) above a tenant of a house acquiring the freehold or an extended lease is required to include premises of which the tenancy is not vested in him, this Part of this Act shall apply for the purpose as if in the case of those premises a tenancy on identical terms were vested in him and the holder of the actual tenancy were a sub-tenant; and where by virtue of subsection (5) or (6) above a tenant of a house acquiring the freehold or an extended lease is required to exclude property of which the tenancy is vested in

him, then unless the landlord and the tenant otherwise agree or the court for the protection of either of them from hardship or inconvenience otherwise orders, the grant to the tenant shall operate as a surrender of the tenancy in that property and the provision to be made by the grant shall be determined as if the surrender had taken place before the relevant time. **[185]**

NOTES

See further the Housing Act 1985, ss 172-175.

3. Meaning of "long tenancy"

(1) In this Part of this Act "long tenancy" means, subject to the provisions of this section, a tenancy granted for a term of years certain exceeding twenty-one years, whether or not the tenancy is (or may become) terminable before the end of that term by notice given by or to the tenant or by re-entry, forfeiture or otherwise, and includes a tenancy for a term fixed by law under a grant with a covenant or obligation for perpetual renewal unless it is a tenancy by sub-demise from one which is not a long tenancy:

Provided that a tenancy granted so as to become terminable by notice after a death or marriage is not to be treated as a long tenancy [if either—

(*a*) it was granted before 18th April 1980 or in pursuance of a contract entered into before that date; or

(*b*) the notice is capable of being given at any time after the death or marriage of the tenant, the length of the notice is not more than three months and the terms of the tenancy preclude both its assignment [otherwise than by virtue of section 92 of the Housing Act 1985 (assignments by way of exchange)] and the subletting of the whole of the premises comprised in it].

(2) Where the tenant of any property under a long tenancy at a low rent [(other than a lease excluded from the operation of this Part by s 33A of and Schedule 4A to this Act)], on the coming to an end of that tenancy, becomes or has become tenant of the property or part of it under another tenancy (whether by express grant or by implication of law), then the later tenancy shall be deemed for the purposes of this Part of this Act, including any further application of this subsection, to be a long tenancy irrespective of its terms.

(3) Where the tenant of any property under a long tenancy, on the coming to an end of that tenancy, becomes or has become tenant of the property or part of it under another long tenancy, then in relation to the property or that part of it this Part of this Act shall apply as if there had been a single tenancy granted for a term beginning at the same time as the term under the earlier tenancy and expiring at the same time as the term under the later tenancy.

(4) Where a tenancy is or has been granted for a term of years certain not exceeding twenty-one years, but with a covenant or obligation for renewal without payment of a premium (but not for perpetual renewal), and the tenancy is or has been once or more renewed so as to bring to more than twenty-one years the total of the terms granted (including any interval between the end of a tenancy and the grant of a renewal), then this Part of this Act shall apply as it would apply if the term originally granted had been one exceeding twenty-one years.

(5) References in this Part of this Act to a long tenancy include any period during which the tenancy is or was continued under Part I or II of the Landlord

and Tenant Act 1954 or under the Leasehold Property (Temporary Provisions) Act 1951.

(6) Where at any time there are separate tenancies, with the same landlord and the same tenant, of two or more parts of a house, or of a house or part of it and land or other premises occupied therewith, then in relation to the property comprised in such of those tenancies as are long tenancies this Part of this Act shall apply as it would if at that time there were a single tenancy of that property and the tenancy were a long tenancy, and for that purpose references in this Part of this Act to the commencement of the term or to the term date shall, if the separate tenancies commenced at different dates or have different term dates, have effect as references to the commencement or term date, as the case may be, of the tenancy comprising the house (or the earliest commencement or earliest term date of the tenancies comprising it):

Provided that this subsection shall have effect subject to the operation of subsections (2) to (5) above in relation to any of the separate tenancies. **[186]**

NOTES

Sub-s (1): first amendment in square brackets made by the Housing (Consequential Provisions) Act 1985, s 4, Sch 2, para 12; second amendment in square brackets made by the Housing and Building Control Act 1984, s 64, Sch 11, para 3.

Sub-s (2): words in square brackets prospectively added with savings by the Housing and Planning Act 1986, s 18, Sch 4, paras 4, 11, as from a day to be appointed.

See further the Housing Act 1985, ss 172-175.

4. Meaning of "low rent"

(1) For purposes of this Part of this Act a tenancy of any property is a tenancy at a low rent at any time when rent is not payable under the tenancy in respect of the property at a yearly rate equal to or more than two-thirds of the rateable value of the property on the appropriate day or, if later, the first day of the term:

Provided that a tenancy granted between the end of August 1939 and the beginning of April 1963 otherwise than by way of building lease (whether or not it is, by virtue of section 3(3) above, to be treated for other purposes as forming a single tenancy with a previous tenancy) shall not be regarded as a tenancy at a low rent if at the commencement of the tenancy the rent payable under the tenancy exceeded two-thirds of the letting value of the property (on the same terms).

For the purposes of this subsection—

(*a*) "appropriate day" means the 23rd March 1965 or such later day as by virtue of [section 25(3) of the Rent Act 1977] would be the appropriate day for purposes of that Act in relation to a dwelling-house consisting of the house in question; and

(*b*) "rent" means rent reserved as such, and there shall be disregarded any part of the rent expressed to be payable in consideration of services to be provided, or of repairs, maintenance or insurance to be effected by the landlord, or to be payable in respect of the cost thereof to the landlord or a superior landlord; and

(*c*) there shall be disregarded any term of the tenancy providing for suspension or reduction of rent in the event of damage to property demised, or for any penal addition to the rent in the event of a contravention of or non-compliance with the terms of the tenancy or an agreement collateral thereto; and

(*d*) "building lease" means a lease granted in pursuance or in consideration of an agreement for the erection or the substantial rebuilding or reconstruction of the whole or part of the house in question or a building comprising it.

(2) Where on a claim by the tenant of a house to exercise any right conferred by this Part of this Act a question arises under section 1(1) above whether his tenancy of the house is or was at any time a tenancy at a low rent, the question shall be determined by reference to the rent and rateable value of the house and premises as a whole, and in relation to a time before the relevant time shall be so determined whether or not the property then occupied with the house or any part of it was the same in all respects as that comprised in the house and premises for purposes of the claim; but, in a case where the tenancy derives (in accordance with section 3(6) above) from more than one separate tenancy, the proviso to subsection (1) above shall have effect if, but only if, it applies to one of the separate tenancies which comprises the house or part of it.

(3) Where on a claim by the tenant of a house to exercise any right conferred by this Part of this Act a question arises under section 3(2) above whether a tenancy is or was a long tenancy by reason of a previous tenancy having been a long tenancy at a low rent, the question whether the previous tenancy was one at a low rent shall be determined in accordance with subsection (2) above as if it were a question arising under section 1(1), and shall be so determined by reference to the rent and rateable value of the house and premises or the part included in the previous tenancy, exclusive of any other land or premises so included:

Provided that where an apportionment of rent or rateable value is required because the previous tenancy did not include the whole of the house and premises or included other property, the apportionment shall be made as at the end of the previous tenancy except in so far as, in the case of rent, an apportionment falls to be made at an earlier date under subsection (6) below.

(4) For purposes of subsection (2) or (3) above a house and premises shall be taken as not including any premises which are to be or may be included under section 2(4) above in giving effect to the tenant's claim, and as including any part which is to be or may be excluded under section 2(5) or (6).

(5) Where on a claim by the tenant of a house to exercise any right conferred by this Part of this Act a question arises whether a tenancy granted as mentioned in the proviso to subsection (1) above is or was at any time a tenancy at a low rent, it shall be presumed until the contrary is shown that the letting value referred to in that proviso was such that the proviso does not apply.

(6) Any entire rent payable at any time in respect of both a house and premises or part thereof and of property not included in the house and premises shall for purposes of this section be apportioned as may be just according to the circumstances existing at the date of the severance giving rise to the apportionment, and references in this section to the rent of a house and premises or of part thereof shall be construed accordingly. **[187]**

NOTES

Sub-s (1): amended by the Rent Act 1977, s 155, Sch 23, para 42.
See further the Housing Act 1985, ss 172-175.

5. General provisions as to claims to enfranchisement or extension

(1) Where under this Part of this Act a tenant of a house has the right to acquire the freehold or an extended lease and gives notice of his desire to have it, the rights and obligations of the landlord and the tenant arising from the notice

shall inure for the benefit of and be enforceable against them, their executors, administrators and assigns to the like extent (but no further) as rights and obligations arising under a contract for a sale or lease freely entered into between the landlord and tenant; and accordingly, in relation to matters arising out of any such notice, references in this Part of this Act to the tenant and the landlord shall, in so far as the context permits, include their respective executors, administrators and assigns.

(2) Notwithstanding anything in subsection (1) above, the rights and obligations there referred to of a tenant shall be assignable with, but not capable of subsisting apart from, the tenancy of the entire house and premises; and if the tenancy is assigned without the benefit of the notice, or if the tenancy of one part of the house and premises is assigned to or vests in any person without the tenancy of another part, the notice shall accordingly cease to have effect, and the tenant shall be liable to make such compensation as may be just to the landlord in respect of the interference (if any) by the notice with the exercise by the landlord of his power to dispose of or deal with the house and premises or any neighbouring property.

(3) In the event of any default by the landlord or the tenant in carrying out the obligations arising from any such notice, the other of them shall have the like rights and remedies as in the case of a contract freely entered into.

(4) The provisions of Schedule 1 to this Act shall have effect in relation to the operation of this Part of this Act where a person gives notice of his desire to have the freehold or an extended lease of a house and premises, and either he does so in respect of a sub-tenancy or there is a tenancy reversionary on his tenancy; but any such notice given in respect of a tenancy granted by sub-demise out of a superior tenancy other than a long tenancy at a low rent shall be of no effect if the grant was made in breach of the terms of the superior tenancy and there has been no waiver of the breach by the superior landlord.

(5) No lease shall be registrable under the Land Charges Act 1925 or be deemed to be an estate contract within the meaning of that Act by reason of the rights conferred on the tenant by this Part of this Act to acquire the freehold or an extended lease of property thereby demised, nor shall any right of a tenant arising from a notice under this Act of his desire to have the freehold or to have an extended lease be an overriding interest within the meaning of the Land Registration Act 1925; but any such notice shall be registrable under the Land Charges Act 1925 or may be the subject of a notice or caution under the Land Registration Act 1925, as if it were an estate contract.

(6) A notice of a person's desire to have the freehold or an extended lease of a house and premises under this Part of this Act—

(*a*) shall be of no effect if at the relevant time any person or body of persons who has or have been, or could be, authorised to acquire the whole or part of the house and premises compulsorily for any purpose has or have, with a view to its acquisition for that purpose, served notice to treat on the landlord or on the tenant, or entered into a contract for the purchase of the interest of either of them, and the notice to treat or contract remains in force; and

(*b*) shall cease to have effect if before the completion of the conveyance in pursuance of the tenant's notice any such person or body of persons serves notice to treat as aforesaid;

but where a tenant's notice ceases to have effect by reason of a notice to treat served on him or on the landlord, then on the occasion of the compulsory acquisition in question the compensation payable in respect of any interest in the house and premises (whether or not the one to which that notice to treat relates) shall be determined on the basis of the value of the interest subject to and with the benefit of the rights and obligations arising from the tenant's notice and affecting that interest.

(7) Where any such notice given by a tenant entitled to acquire the freehold or an extended lease has effect, then (without prejudice to the general law as to the frustration of contracts) the landlord and all other persons shall be discharged from the further performance, so far as relates to the disposal in any manner of the landlord's interest in the house and premises or any part thereof, of any contract previously entered into and not providing for the eventuality of such a notice (including any such contract made in pursuance of the order of any court):

Provided that, in the case of a notice of the tenant's desire to have an extended lease, this subsection shall not apply to discharge a person from performance of a contract unless the contract was entered into on the basis, common to both parties, that vacant possession of the house and premises or part thereof would or might be obtainable on the termination of the existing tenancy.

(8) A tenant's notice of his desire to have an extended lease under this Part of this Act shall cease to have effect if afterwards (being entitled to do so) he gives notice of his desire to have the freehold. **[188]**

NOTES

See further the Housing Act 1985, ss 172-175.

6. Rights of trustees

(1) Where a tenant of a house is occupying it as his residence, his occupation of it at any earlier time shall for purposes of this Part of this Act be treated as having been an occupation in right of the tenancy if at that time—

(*a*) the tenancy was settled land for purposes of the Settled Land Act 1925, and he was sole tenant for life within the meaning of that Act; or

(*b*) the tenancy was vested in trustees and he, as a person beneficially interested (whether directly or derivatively) under the trusts, was entitled or permitted to occupy the house by reason of that interest.

References in this section to trustees include persons holding on the statutory trusts arising by virtue of sections 34 to 36 of the Law of Property Act 1925 in cases of joint ownership or ownership in common.

(2) Where a tenancy of a house is settled land for purposes of the Settled Land Act 1925, a sole tenant for life within the meaning of that Act shall have the same rights under this Part of this Act in respect of his occupation of the house as if the tenancy of it belonged to him absolutely, but without prejudice to his position under the settlement as a trustee for all parties entitled under the settlement; and—

(*a*) the powers under that Act of a tenant for life shall include power to accept an extended lease under this Part of this Act; and

(*b*) an extended lease granted under this Part of this Act to a tenant for life or statutory owner shall be treated as a subsidiary vesting deed in accordance with section 53 (2) of that Act.

(3) Where a tenancy of a house is vested in trustees (other than a sole tenant for life within the meaning of the Settled Land Act 1925), and a person beneficially interested (whether directly or derivatively) under the trusts is entitled or permitted by reason of his interest to occupy the house, then the trustees shall have the like rights under this Part of this Act in respect of his occupation as he would have if he were the tenant occupying in right of the tenancy.

(4) Without prejudice to any powers exercisable under the Settled Land Act 1925 by tenants for life or statutory owners within the meaning of that Act, where a tenancy of a house is vested in trustees, then unless the instrument regulating the trusts (being made after the passing of this Act) contains an explicit direction to the contrary, the powers of the trustees under that instrument shall include power, with the like consent or on the like direction (if any) as may be required for the exercise of their powers (or ordinary powers) of investment, to acquire and retain the freehold or an extended lease under this Part of this Act.

(5) The purposes authorised for the application of capital money by section 73 of the Settled Land Act 1925, or by that section as applied by section 28 of the Law of Property Act 1925 in relation to trusts for sale, and the purposes authorised by section 71 of the Settled Land Act 1925 or by that section as applied as aforesaid as purposes for which moneys may be raised by mortgage, shall include the payment of any expenses incurred by a tenant for life or statutory owners or by trustees for sale, as the case may be, in or in connection with proceedings taken by him or them by virtue of subsection (2) or (3) above. **[189]**

NOTES
See further the Housing Act 1985, ss 172-175.

7. Rights of members of family succeeding to tenancy on death

(1) Where the tenant of a house dies while occupying it as his residence, and on his death a member of his family resident in the house becomes tenant of it under the same tenancy, then for the purposes of any claim by that member of the family to acquire the freehold or an extended lease under this Part of this Act he shall be treated as having been the tenant, and occupying the house as his residence, during any period when—

(*a*) he was resident in the house, and it was his only or main place of residence; and
(*b*) the deceased person was, as the tenant under that tenancy, occupying the house as his residence (or would for the purposes of a claim made by him at the time of his death have been treated as having been so occupying it).

(2) For purposes of this section—

(*a*) a member of a tenant's family on whom the tenancy devolves on the tenant's death by virtue of a testamentary disposition or the law of intestate succession shall, on the tenancy vesting in him, be treated as having become tenant on the death; and
(*b*) a member of a tenant's family who, on the tenant's death, acquires the tenancy by the appropriation of it in or towards satisfaction of any legacy, share in residue, debt or other share in or claim against the tenant's estate, or by the purchase of it on a sale made by the tenant's personal representatives in the administration of the estate,

shall be treated as a person on whom the tenancy devolved by direct bequest; and

(*c*) a person's interest in a tenancy as personal representative of a deceased tenant shall be disregarded, but references in paragraphs (*a*) and (*b*) above to a tenancy vesting in, or being acquired by, a member of a tenant's family shall apply also where, after the death of a member of the family, the tenancy vests in or is acquired by the personal representatives of that member.

(3) Where a tenancy for a house is settled land for purposes of the Settled Land Act 1925, and on the death of a tenant for life within the meaning of that Act a member of his family resident with him becomes entitled to the tenancy in accordance with the settlement or by any appropriation by or purchase from the personal representatives in respect of the settled land, this section shall apply as if the tenancy had belonged to the tenant for life absolutely and the trusts of the settlement taking effect after his death had been trusts of his will.

(4) Where in a case not falling within subsection (3) above a tenancy of a house is held on trust and—

(*a*) a person beneficially interested (whether directly or derivatively) under the trust is entitled or permitted by reason of his interest to occupy the house; and

(*b*) on his death a member of his family resident with him becomes tenant of the house in accordance with the terms of the trust or by any appropriation by or purchase from the trustees;

then this section shall apply as if the deceased person while so occupying the house had been tenant of it occupying in right of the tenancy, and as if after his death the trustees had held and dealt with the tenancy as his executors (the remaining trusts being trust of his will).

(5) Subsections (3) and (4) above shall apply, with any necessary adaptations, where a person becomes entitled to a tenancy on the termination of a settlement or trust as they would apply if he had become entitled in accordance with the settlement or trust.

(6) The reference in section 6(3) above to the rights which a beneficiary under a trust would have if he were the tenant occupying in right of the tenancy includes any rights which he would have by virtue of this section.

(7) For purposes of this section a person is a member of another's family if that person is—

(*a*) the other's wife or husband; or

(*b*) a son or daughter or a son-in-law or daughter-in-law of the other, or of the other's wife or husband; or

(*c*) the father or mother of the other, or of the other's wife or husband.

In paragraph (*b*) above any reference to a person's son or daughter includes a reference to any stepson or stepdaughter, any illegitimate son or daughter . . . of that person, and "son-in-law" and "daughter-in-law" shall be construed accordingly.

(8) In Schedule 2 to the Intestates' Estates Act 1952 (which gives a surviving spouse a right to require the deceased's interest in the matrimonial home to be appropriated to the survivor's interest in the deceased's estate, but by paragraph 1(2) excludes tenancies terminating or terminable by the landlord, within two years of the death), paragraph 1(2) shall not apply to a tenancy if—

(*a*) the surviving wife or husband would in consequence of an appropriation in accordance with that paragraph become entitled by virtue of this section to acquire the freehold or an extended lease under this Part of this Act, either immediately on the appropriation or before the tenancy can determine or be determined as mentioned in paragraph 1(2); or

(*b*) the deceased husband or wife, being entitled to acquire the freehold or an extended lease under this Part of this Act, had given notice of his or her desire to have it and the benefit of that notice is appropriated with the tenancy.

(9) This section shall have effect in relation to deaths occurring before this Act was passed as it has effect in relation to deaths occurring after. **[190]**

NOTES

Sub-s (7): words omitted repealed by the Children Act 1975, s 108(1)(*b*), Sch 4, Part I.
See further the Housing Act 1985, ss 172-175.

Enfranchisement

8. Obligation to enfranchise

(1) Where a tenant of a house has under this Part of this Act a right to acquire the freehold, and gives to the landlord written notice of his desire to have the freehold, then except as provided by this Part of this Act the landlord shall be bound to make to the tenant, and the tenant to accept, (at the price and on the conditions so provided) a grant of the house and premises for an estate in fee simple absolute, subject to the tenancy and to tenant's incumbrances, but otherwise free of incumbrances.

(2) For purposes of this Part of this Act "incumbrances" includes rentcharges and, subject to subsection (3) below, personal liabilities attaching in respect of the ownership of land or an interest in land though not charged on that land or interest; and "tenant's incumbrances" includes any interest directly or indirectly derived out of the tenancy, and any incumbrance on the tenancy or any such interest (whether or not the same matter is an incumbrance also on any interest reversionary on the tenancy).

(3) Burdens originating in tenure, and burdens in respect of the upkeep or regulation for the benefit of any locality of any land, building, structure, works, ways or watercourse shall not be treated as incumbrances for purposes of this Part of this Act, but any conveyance executed to give effect to this section shall be made subject thereto except as otherwise provided by section 11 below.

(4) A conveyance executed to give effect to this section—

(*a*) shall have effect under section 2(1) of the Law of Property Act 1925 to overreach any incumbrance capable of being overreached under that section as if, where the interest conveyed is settled land, the conveyance were made under the powers of the Settled Land Act 1925 and as if the requirements of section 2(1) as to payment of the capital money allowed any part of the purchase price paid or applied in accordance with sections 11 to 13 below to be so paid or applied;

(*b*) shall not be made subject to any incumbrance capable of being overreached by the conveyance, but shall be made subject (where they are not capable of being overreached) to rentcharges [redeemable under sections 8 to 10 of the Rentcharges Act 1977 and those falling within paragraphs (*c*) and (*d*) of section 2(3) of that Act (estate rentcharges and rentcharges imposed under certain enactments)], except as otherwise provided by section 11 below.

(5) Notwithstanding that on a grant to a tenant of a house and premises under this section no payment or a nominal payment only is required from the tenant for the price of the house and premises, the tenant shall nevertheless be deemed for all purposes to be a purchaser for a valuable consideration in money or money's worth. **[191]**

NOTES

Sub-s (4): amended by the Rentcharges Act 1977, s 17(1), Sch 1, para 4(1).
See further the Housing Act 1985, ss 172-175.

9. Purchase price and costs of enfranchisement, and tenant's right to withdraw

(1) Subject to subsection (2) below, the price payable for a house and premises on a conveyance under section 8 above shall be the amount which at the relevant time the house and premises, if sold in the open market by a willing seller [(with the tenant and members of his family who reside in the house not buying or seeking to buy)], might be expected to realise on the following assumptions:—

(*a*) on the assumption that the vendor was selling for an estate in fee simple, subject to the tenancy but on the assumption that this Part of this Act conferred no right to acquire the freehold; and if the tenancy has not been extended under this Part of this Act, on the assumption that (subject to the landlord's rights under section 17 below) it was to be so extended;

(*b*) on the assumption that (subject to paragraph (*a*) above) the vendor was selling subject, in respect of rentcharges . . . to which section 11 (2) below applies, to the same annual charge as the conveyance to the tenant is to be subject to, but the purchaser would otherwise be effectively exonerated until the termination of the tenancy from any liability or charge in respect of tenant's incumbrances; and

(*c*) on the assumption that (subject to paragraphs (*a*) and (*b*) above) the vendor was selling with and subject to the rights and burdens with and subject to which the conveyance to the tenant is to be made, and in particular with and subject to such permanent or extended rights and burdens as are to be created in order to give effect to section 10 below.

[The reference in this subsection to members of the tenant's family shall be construed in accordance with section 7 (7) of this Act.]

[(1A) Nothwithstanding, the foregoing subsection, the price payable for a house and premises, the rateable value of which is above £1,000 in Greater London and £500 elsewhere, on a conveyance under section 8 above, shall be the amount which at the relevant time the house and premises, if sold in the open market by a willing seller, might be expected to realise on the following assumptions:—

(*a*) on the assumption that the vendor was selling for an estate in fee simple, subject to the tenancy, but on the assumption that this Part of this Act conferred no right to acquire the freehold [or an extended lease and, where the tenancy has been extended under this Part of this Act, that the Tenancy will terminate on the original term date.];

(*b*) on the assumption that at the end of the tenancy the tenant has the right to remain in possession of the house and premises under the provisions of Part I of the Landlord and Tenant Act 1954;

(*c*) on the assumption that the tenant has no liability to carry out any repairs, maintenance or redecorations under the terms of the tenancy or Part I of the Landlord and Tenant Act 1954;

(*d*) on the assumption that the price be diminished by the extent to which the value of the house and premises has been increased by any improvement carried out by the tenant or his predecessors in title at their own expense;

(*e*) on the assumption that (subject to paragraph (*a*) above) the vendor was selling subject, in respect of rentcharges . . . to which section 11 (2) below applies, to the same annual charge as the conveyance to the tenant is to be subject to, but the purchaser would otherwise be effectively exonerated until the termination of the tenancy from any liability or charge in respect of tenant's incumbrances; and

(*f*) on the assumption that (subject to paragraphs (*a*) and (*b*) above) the vendor was selling with and subject to the rights and burdens with and subject to which the conveyance to the tenant is to be made, and in particular with and subject to such permanent or extended rights and burdens as are to be created in order to give effect to section 10 below.

(1B) For the purpose of determining whether the rateable value of the house and premises is above £1,000 in Greater London, or £500 elsewhere the rateable value shall be adjusted to take into account any tenant's improvements in accordance with Schedule 8 to the Housing Act 1974.]

(2) The price payable for the house and premises shall be subject to such deduction (if any) in respect of any defect in the title to be conveyed to the tenant as on a sale in the open market might be expected to be allowed between a willing seller and a willing buyer.

(3) On ascertaining the amount payable, or likely to be payable, as the price for a house and premises in accordance with this section (but not more than one month after the amount payable has been determined by agreement or otherwise), the tenant may give written notice to the landlord that he is unable or unwilling to acquire the house and premises at the price he must pay; and thereupon—

(*a*) the notice under section 8 above of his desire to have the freehold shall cease to have effect, and he shall be liable to make such compensation as may be just to the landlord in respect of the interference (if any) by the notice with the exercise by the landlord of his power to dispose of or deal with the house and premises or any neighbouring property; and

(*b*) any further notice given under that section with respect to the house or any part of it (with or without other property) shall be void if given within the following [three years].

(4) Where a person gives notice of his desire to have the freehold of a house and premises under this Part of this Act, then unless the notice lapses under any provision of this Act excluding his liability, there shall be borne by him (so far as they are incurred in pursuance of the notice) the reasonable costs of or incidental to any of the following matters:—

(*a*) any investigation by the landlord of that person's right to acquire the freehold;

(*b*) any conveyance or assurance of the house and premises or any part thereof or of any outstanding estate or interest therein;

(*c*) deducing, evidencing and verifying the title to the house and premises or any estate or interest therein;
(*d*) making out and furnishing such abstracts and copies as the person giving the notice may require;
(*e*) any valuation of the house and premises;

but so that this subsection shall not apply to any costs if on a sale made voluntarily a stipulation that they were to be borne by the purchaser would be void.

(5) The landlord's lien (as vendor) on the house and premises for the price payable shall extend—

(*a*) to any sums payable by way of rent or recoverable as rent in respect of the house and premises up to the date of the conveyance; and
(*b*) to any sums for which the tenant is liable under subsection (4) above; and
(*c*) to any other sums due and payable by him to the landlord under or in respect of the tenancy or any agreement collateral thereto. **[192]**

NOTES

Commencement: Before 1 January 1970 (sub-ss (1), (2)-(5)); 31 July 1974 (sub-ss (1A), (1B)).

Sub-s (1): amendments in square brackets made by the Housing Act 1969, s 82; words omitted repealed by the Rentcharges Act 1977, s 17(2), Sch 2.

Sub-s (1A): added by the Housing Act 1974, s 118(4); in para (*a*) words in square brackets added with savings by the Housing and Planning Act 1986, s 23(1), (3); in para (*e*) words omitted repealed by the Rentcharges Act 1977, s 17(2), Sch 2.

Sub-s (1B): added by the Housing Act 1974, s 118(4).

Sub-s (3): amended by the Housing Act 1980, s 141, Sch 21.

See further the Housing Act 1985, ss 172-175.

10. Rights to be conveyed to tenant on enfranchisement

(1) Except for the purpose of preserving or recognising any existing interest of the landlord in tenant's incumbrances or any existing right or interest of any other person, a conveyance executed to give effect to section 8 above shall not be framed so as to exclude or restrict the general words implied in conveyances under section 62 of the Law of Property Act 1925, or the all-estate clause implied under section 63, unless the tenant consents to the exclusion or restriction; but the landlord shall not be bound to convey to the tenant any better title than that which he has or could require to be vested in him, nor to enter into any covenant for title other than such covenant as under section 76(1)(F) of the Law of Property Act 1925 is implied in the case of a person conveying and expressed to convey as trustee or mortgagee.

(2) As regards rights of any of the following descriptions, that is to say,—

(*a*) rights of support for any building or part of a building;
(*b*) rights to the access of light and air to any building or part of a building;
(*c*) rights to the passage of water or of gas or other piped fuel, or to the drainage or disposal of water, sewage, smoke or fumes, or to the use or maintenance of pipes or other installations for such passage, drainage or disposal;
(*d*) rights to the use or maintenance of cables or other installations for the supply of electricity, for the telephone or for the receipt directly or by landline of visual or other wireless transmissions;

a conveyance executed to give effect to section 8 above shall by virtue of this subsection (but without prejudice to any larger operation it may have apart from this subsection) have effect—

(i) to grant with the house and premises all such easements and rights over other property, so far as the landlord is capable of granting them, as are necessary to secure to the tenant as nearly as may be the same rights as at the relevant time were available to him under or by virtue of the tenancy or any agreement collateral thereto, or under or by virtue of any grant, reservation or agreement made on the severance of the house and premises or any part thereof from other property then comprised in the same tenancy; and

(ii) to make the house and premises subject to all such easements and rights for the benefit of other property as are capable of existing in law and are necessary to secure the person interested in the other property as nearly as may be the same rights as at the relevant time were available against the tenant under or by virtue of the tenancy or any agreement collateral thereto, or under or by virtue of any grant, reservation or agreement made as is mentioned in paragraph (i) above.

(3) As regards rights of way, a conveyance executed to give effect to section 8 above shall include—

(*a*) such provisions (if any) as the tenant may require for the purpose of securing to him rights of way over property not conveyed, so far as the landlord is capable of granting them, being rights of way which are necessary for the reasonable enjoyment of the house and premises as they have been enjoyed during the tenancy and in accordance with its provisions; and

(*b*) such provisions (if any) as the landlord may require for the purpose of making the property conveyed subject to rights of way necessary for the reasonable enjoyment of other property, being property in which at the relevant time the landlord has an interest, or to rights of way granted or agreed to be granted before the relevant time by the landlord or by the person then entitled to the reversion on the tenancy.

(4) As regards restrictive covenants (that is to say, any covenant or agreement restrictive of the user of any land or premises), a conveyance executed to give effect to section 8 above shall include—

(*a*) such provisions (if any) as the landlord may require to secure that the tenant is bound by, or to indemnify the landlord against breaches of, restrictive covenants which affect the house and premises otherwise than by virtue of the tenancy or any agreement collateral thereto and are enforceable for the benefit of other property; and

(*b*) such provisions (if any) as the landlord or the tenant may require to secure the continuance (with suitable adaptations) of restrictions arising by virtue of the tenancy or any agreement collateral thereto, being either—

(i) restrictions affecting the house and premises which are capable of benefiting other property and (if enforceable only by the landlord) are such as materially to enhance the value of the other property; or

(ii) restrictions affecting other property which are such as materially to enhance the value of the house and premises;

(*c*) such further provisions (if any) as the landlord may require to restrict the use of the house and premises in any way which will not interfere with the reasonable enjoyment of the house and premises as they have been enjoyed during the tenancy but will materially enhance the value of other property in which the landlord has an interest.

(5) Neither the landlord nor the tenant shall be entitled under subsection (3) or (4) above to require the inclusion in a conveyance of any provision which is unreasonable in all the circumstances, in view—

(*a*) of the date at which the tenancy commenced, and changes since that date which affect the suitability at the relevant time of the provisions of the tenancy; and

(*b*) where the tenancy is or was one of a number of tenancies of neighbouring houses, of the interests of those affected in respect of other houses.

(6) The landlord may be required to give to the tenant an acknowledgment within the meaning of section 64 of the Law of Property Act 1925 as regards any documents of which the landlord retains possession, but not an undertaking for the safe custody of any such documents; and where the landlord is required to enter into any covenant under subsection (4) above, the person entering into the covenant as landlord shall be entitled to limit his personal liability to breaches of the covenant for which he is responsible. **[193]**

NOTES

See further the Housing Act 1985, ss 172-175.

11. Exoneration from, or redemption of, rentcharges etc

(1) Where a house and premises are to be conveyed to a tenant in pursuance of section 8 above, section (4)(*b*) shall not preclude the landlord from releasing, or procuring the release of, the house and premises from any rentcharge . . . ; and the conveyance may, with the tenant's agreement (which shall not be unreasonably withheld), provide in accordance with section 190(1) of the Law of Property Act 1925 that a rentcharge shall be charged exclusively on other land affected by it in exoneration of the house and premises, or be apportioned between other land affected by it and the house and premises.

(2) Where, but for this subsection, a conveyance of a house and premises to a tenant might in accordance with section 8 above be made subject, in respect of rents to which this subsection applies, to an annual charge exceeding the annual rent payable under the tenancy at the relevant time, then the landlord shall be bound on or before the execution of the conveyance to secure that the house and premises are discharged from the whole or part of any rents in question to the extent necessary to secure that the annual charge shall not exceed the annual rent so payable; and for this purpose the annual rent shall be calculated in accordance with section 4(1)(*b*) and (*c*) and (6) above.

(3) For purposes of subsection (2) above the house and premises shall be treated as discharged from a rent to the extent to which—

(*a*) the rent is charged on or apportioned to other land so as to confer on the tenant in respect of the house and premises the remedies against the other land provided for by section 190(2) of the Law of Property Act 1925; or

(*b*) the landlord is otherwise entitled to be exonerated from or indemnified against liability for the rent in respect of the house and premises and the tenant will (in so far as the landlord's right is not a right against the tenant himself or his land) become entitled on the conveyance to the like exoneration or indemnity.

(4) Where for the purpose of complying with subsection (2) above the house and premises are to be discharged from a rent by redemption of it (with or without prior apportionment), and for any reason mentioned in section [13(2) below] difficulty arises in paying the redemption price, the tenant may, and if so required by the landlord shall, before execution of the conveyance pay into court on account of the price for the house and premises an amount not exceeding the appropriate amount to secure redemption of the rent; and if the amount so paid by the tenant is less than that appropriate amount, the landlord shall pay into court the balance.

(5) Where payment is made into court in accordance with subsection (4) above, the house and premises shall on execution of the conveyance be discharged from the rent, and any claim to the redemption money shall lie against the fund in court and not otherwise.

(6) For purposes of subsection (4) above "the appropriate amount to secure redemption" of a rent is (subject to subsection (7) below) the amount of redemption money agreed to be paid or in default of agreement, the amount [specified as the redemption price in instructions for redemption under section 9(4) of the Rentcharges Act 1977].

(7) Where a rent affects other property as well as the house and premises, and the other property is not exonerated or indemnified by means of a charge on the house and premises, then—

(*a*) "the appropriate amount to secure redemption" of the rent for purposes of subsection (4) above shall, if no amount has been agreed or [specified] as mentioned in subsection (6), be such sum as, on an application under section [4 of the Rentcharges Act 1977] for the apportionment of the rent, may, pending the apportionment, be approved by the apportioning authority as suitable provision (with a reasonable margin) for the redemption money of the part likely to be apportioned to the house and premises; and

(*b*) the apportionment, when made, shall be deemed to have had effect from the date of the payment into court, and if in respect of any property affected by the rent there has been any overpayment or underpayment, the amount shall be made good by abatement of or addition to the next payment after the apportionment and (if necessary) later payments.

(8) Subsection (2) above applies to rentcharges [redeemable under sections 8 to 10 of the Rentcharges Act 1977] which during the continuance of the tenancy are, or but for the termination of the tenancy before their commencement would have been, recoverable from the landlord without his having a right to be indemnified by the tenant. **[194]**

NOTES

Words omitted repealed and amendments in square brackets made by the Rentcharges Act 1977, s 17(2), Sch 2.

See further the Housing Act 1985, ss 172-175.

12. Discharge of mortgages etc on landlord's estate

(1) Subject to the provisions of this section, a conveyance executed to give effect to section 8 above shall, as regards any charge on the landlord's estate (however created or arising) to secure the payment of money or the performance of any other obligation by the landlord or any other person, not being a charge subject to which the conveyance is required to be made or which would be

overreached apart from this section, be effective by virtue of this section to discharge the house and premises from the charge, and from the operation of any order made by a court for the enforcement of the charge, and to extinguish any term of years created for the purposes of the charge, and shall do so without the persons entitled to or interested in the charge or in any such order or term of years becoming parties to or executing the conveyance.

(2) Where in accordance with subsection (1) above the conveyance to a tenant will be effective to discharge the house and premises from a charge to secure the payment of money, then except as otherwise provided by this section it shall be the duty of the tenant to apply the price payable for the house and premises, in the first instance, in or towards the redemption of any such charge (and, if there are more than one, then according to their priorities); and if any amount payable in accordance with this subsection to the person entitled to the benefit of a charge is not so paid nor paid into court in accordance with section 13 below, then for the amount in question the house and premises shall remain subject to the charge, and to that extent subsection (1) above shall not apply.

(3) For the purpose of determining the amount payable in respect of any charge under subsection (2) above a person entitled to the benefit of a charge to which that subsection applies shall not be permitted to exercise any right to consolidate that charge with a separate charge on other property; and if the landlord or the tenant is himself entitled to the benefit of a charge to which that subsection applies, it shall rank for payment as it would if another person were entitled to it, and the tenant shall be entitled to retain the appropriate amount in respect of any such charge of his.

(4) For the purposes of discharging the house and premises from a charge to which subsection (2) above applies, a person may be required to accept three months or any longer notice of the intention to pay the whole or part of the principal secured by the charge, together with interest to the date of payment, notwithstanding that the terms of the security make other provision or no provision as to the time and manner of payment; but he shall be entitled, if he so requires, to receive such additional payment as is reasonable in the circumstances in respect of the costs of re-investment or other incidental costs and expenses and in respect of any reduction in the rate of interest obtainable on re-investment.

(5) Subsection (2) above shall not apply to any debenture-holders' charge, that is to say, any charge, whether a floating charge or not, in favour of the holders of a series of debentures issued by a company or other body of persons, or in favour of trustees for such debenture-holders; and any such charge shall be disregarded in determining priorities for purposes of subsection (2):

Provided that this subsection shall not have effect in relation to a charge in favour of trustees for debenture holders which at the date of the conveyance to the tenant is (as regards the house and premises) a specific and not a floating charge.

(6) Where the house and premises are discharged by this section from a charge (without the obligations secured by the charge being satisfied by the receipt of the whole or part of the price), the discharge of the house and premises shall not prejudice any right or remedy for the enforcement of those obligations against other property comprised in the same or any other security, nor prejudice any personal liability as principal or otherwise of the landlord or any other person.

(7) Subsections (1) and (2) above shall not be taken to prevent a person from

joining in the conveyance for the purpose of discharging the house and premises from any charge without payment or for a less payment than that to which he would otherwise be entitled; and, if he does so, the persons to whom the price ought to be paid shall be determined accordingly.

(8) A charge on the landlord's estate to secure the payment of money or the performance of any other obligation shall not be treated for the purposes of this Part of this Act as a tenant's incumbrance by reason only of the grant of the tenancy being subsequent to the creation of the charge and not authorised as against the persons interested in the charge; and this section shall apply as if the persons so interested at the time of the grant had duly concurred in the grant for the purpose (but only for the purpose) of validating it despite the charge on the grantor's estate:

Provided that, where the tenancy is granted after the commencement of this Part of this Act (whether or not it is, by virtue of section 3(3) above, to be treated for other purposes as forming a single tenancy with a previous tenancy) and the tenancy has not by the time of the conveyance of the house and premises to the tenant become binding on the persons interested in the charge, the conveyance shall not by virtue of this section discharge the house and premises from the charge except so far as it is satisfied by the application or payment into court of the price payable for the house and premises.

(9) Nothing in this section shall apply in relation to any charge falling within section 11 above, and for purposes of subsection (2) above the price payable for the house and premises shall be treated as reduced by any amount to be paid out of it before execution of the conveyance for the redemption of a rent in accordance with section 11(4). **[195]**

NOTES
See further the Housing Act 1985, ss 172-175.

13. Payment into court in respect of mortgages etc

(1) Where under section 12(1) above a house and premises are, on a conveyance to the tenant, to be discharged of any charge falling within that subsection, and in accordance with section 12(2) a person is or may be entitled in respect of the charge to receive the whole or part of the price payable for the house and premises, then if—

(*a*) for any reason difficulty arises in ascertaining how much is payable in respect of the charge; or
(*b*) for any reason mentioned in subsection (2) below difficulty arises in making a payment in respect of the charge;

the tenant may pay into court on account of the price for the house and premises the amount, if known, of the payment to be made in respect of the charge, or if that amount is not known, the whole of the price or such less amount as the tenant thinks right to order to provide for that payment.

(2) Payment may be made into court in accordance with subsection (1)(*b*) above where the difficulty arises for any of the following reasons:—

(*a*) because a person who is or may be entitled to receive payment cannot be found or ascertained;
(*b*) because any such person refuses or fails to make out a title, or to accept payment and give a proper discharge, or to take any steps reasonably required of him to enable the sum payable to be ascertained and paid; or

(*c*) because a tender of the sum payable cannot, by reason of complications in the title to it or the want of two or more trustees or for other reasons, be effected, or not without incurring or involving unreasonable cost or delay.

(3) Without prejudice to subsection (1)(*a*) above, the price payable for a house and premises on a conveyance under section 8 above shall be paid by the tenant into court if before execution of the conveyance written notice is given to him—

(*a*) that the landlord or a person entitled to the benefit of a charge on the house and premises so requires for the purpose of protecting the rights of persons so entitled, or for reasons related to any application made or to be made under section 36 below, or to the bankruptcy or winding up of the landlord; or

(*b*) that steps have been taken to enforce any charge on the landlord's interest in the house and premises by the bringing of proceedings in any court, or by the appointment of a receiver, or otherwise;

and where payment is to be made into court by reason only of a notice under this subsection, and the notice is given with reference to proceedings in a court specified in the notice other than the county court, payment shall be made into the court so specified.

(4) For the purpose of computing the amount payable into court under this section, the price payable for the house and premises shall be treated as reduced by any amount to be paid out of it before execution of the conveyance for the redemption of a rent in accordance with section 11(4) above. **[196]**

NOTES

See further the Housing Act 1985, ss 172-175.

Extension

14. Obligation to grant extended lease

(1) Where a tenant of a house has under this Part of this Act a right to an extended lease, and gives to the landlord written notice of his desire to have it, then except as provided by this Part of this Act the landlord shall be bound to grant to the tenant, and the tenant to accept, in substitution for the existing tenancy a new tenancy of the house and premises for a term expiring fifty years after the term date of the existing tenancy.

(2) Where a person gives notice of his desire to have an extended lease of a house and premises under this Part of this Act, then unless the notice lapses under any provision of this Act excluding his liability, there shall be borne by him (so far as they are incurred in pursuance of the notice) the reasonable costs of or incidental to any of the following matters:—

(*a*) any investigation by the landlord of that person's right to an extended lease;

(*b*) any lease granting the new tenancy;

(*c*) any valuation of the house and premises obtained by the landlord before the grant of the new tenancy for the purpose of fixing the rent payable under it in accordance with section 15 below.

(3) A tenant shall not be entitled to require the execution of a lease granting a new tenancy under this section otherwise than on tender of the amount, so far as ascertained,—

(*a*) of any sums payable by way of rent or recoverable as rent in respect of the house and premises up to the date of tender; and
(*b*) of any sums for which at that date the tenant is liable under subsection (2) above; and
(*c*) of any other sums due and payable by him to the landlord under or in respect of the existing tenancy or any agreement collateral thereto;

and, if the amount of any such sums is not or may not be fully ascertained, on offering reasonable security for the payment of such amount as may afterwards be found to be payable in respect of them.

(4) This section shall have effect notwithstanding that the grant of the existing tenancy was subsequent to the creation of a charge on the landlord's estate and not authorised as against the persons interested in the charge; and a lease executed to give effect to this section shall be deemed to be authorised as against the persons interested in any charge on the landlord's estate, however created or arising, and shall be binding on them:

Provided that, where the existing tenancy is granted after the commencement of this Part of this Act (whether or not it is, by virtue of section 3 (3) above, to be treated for other purposes as forming a single tenancy with a previous tenancy) and, the grant being subsequent to the creation of the charge on the landlord's estate, the existing tenancy is not binding on the persons interested in the charge, a lease executed to give effect to this section shall not by virtue of this subsection be binding on those persons.

(5) Where a lease is executed to give effect to this section, and any person having a charge on the landlord's estate is by reason thereof entitled to possession of the documents of title relating to that estate, the landlord shall within one month after execution of the lease deliver to that person a counterpart of it duly executed by the tenant, and the instrument creating or evidencing the charge shall apply in the event of his failing to deliver a counterpart in accordance with this subsection as if the obligation to do so were included in the terms of the charge as set out in that instrument.

(6) Where under a lease executed to give effect to this section the new tenancy takes effect subject to a subsisting charge on the existing tenancy, and at the time of its execution the person having the charge is by reason thereof entitled to possession of the documents of title relating to the existing tenancy, then he shall be similarly entitled to possession of the documents of title relating to the new tenancy and the tenant shall within one month of the execution of the lease deliver it to him, and the instrument creating or evidencing the charge shall apply in the event of the tenant failing to deliver the lease in accordance with this subsection as if the obligation to do so were included in the terms of the charge as set out in that instrument.

(7) A landlord granting a lease under this section shall be bound to take such steps as may be necessary to secure that it is not liable in accordance with the proviso to subsection (4) above to be defeated by persons interested in a charge on his estate; but a landlord is not obliged, in order to grant a lease under this section, to acquire a better title than he has or could require to be vested in him. **[197]**

NOTES
See further the Housing Act 1985, ss 172-175.

15. Terms of tenancy to be granted on extension

(1) Subject to the provisions of this Part of this Act, the new tenancy to be granted under section 14 above shall be a tenancy on the same terms as the existing tenancy as those terms apply at the relevant time, but with such modifications as may be required or appropriate to take account—

(*a*) of the omission from the new tenancy of property comprised in the existing tenancy; or

(*b*) of alterations made to the property demised since the grant of the existing tenancy; or

(*c*) in a case where the existing tenancy derives (in accordance with section 3(6) above) from more than one separate tenancies, of their combined effect and of the differences (if any) in their terms.

(2) The new tenancy shall provide that as from the original term date the rent payable for the house and premises shall be a rent ascertained or to be ascertained as follows:—

(*a*) the rent shall be a ground rent in the sense that it shall represent the letting value of the site (without including anything for the value of buildings on the site) for the uses to which the house and premises have been put since the commencement of the existing tenancy, other than uses which by the terms of the new tenancy are not permitted or are permitted only with the landlord's consent;

(*b*) the letting value for this purpose shall be in the first instance the letting value at the date from which the rent based on it is to commence, but as from the expiration of twenty-five years from the original term date the letting value at the expiration of those twenty-five years shall be substituted, if the landlord so requires, and a revised rent become payable accordingly;

(*c*) the letting value at either of the times mentioned shall be determined not earlier than twelve months before that time (the reasonable cost of obtaining a valuation for the purpose being borne by the tenant), and there shall be no revision of the rent as provided by paragraph (*b*) above unless in the last of the twenty-five years there mentioned the landlord gives the tenant written notice claiming a revision.

(3) Where during the continuance of the new tenancy the landlord will be under any obligation for the provision of services, or for repairs, maintenance or insurance, the rent payable in accordance with subsection (2) above shall be in addition to any sums payable (whether as rent or otherwise) in consideration of those matters or in respect of the cost thereof to the landlord; and if the terms of the existing tenancy include no provision for the making of any such payments by the tenant, or provision only for the payment of a fixed amount, the terms of the new tenancy shall make, as from the time when rent becomes payable in accordance with subsection (2) above, such provision as may be just for the making by the tenant of payments related to the cost from time to time to the landlord, and for the tenant's liability to make those payments to be enforceable by distress, re-entry or otherwise in like manner as the liability for the rent.

(4) Subject to subsection (5) below, provision shall be made by the terms of the new tenancy or by an instrument collateral thereto for the continuance with any suitable adaptations of any agreement collateral to the existing tenancy.

(5) For purposes of subsections (1) and (4) above, there shall be excluded any term of the existing tenancy or any agreement collateral thereto in so far as

that term provides for or relates to the renewal of the tenancy, or confers any option to purchase or right of pre-emption in relation to the house and premises, or provides for the termination of the tenancy before the term date otherwise than in the event of a breach of its terms; and there shall be made in the terms of the new tenancy or any instrument collateral thereto such modifications as may be required or appropriate to take account of the exclusion of any such term as aforesaid.

(6) Where the new tenancy is granted after the original term date, the first reference in subsection (2) above to that date shall have effect as a reference to the grant of the new tenancy; but on the grant of the new tenancy there shall be payable by the tenant to the landlord as an addition to the rent payable under the existing tenancy any amount by which for the period since the relevant time or the original term date (whichever is the later) the sums payable to the landlord in respect of the house and premises (after making any necessary apportionment) for rent and matters referred to in subsection (3) above fall short in total of the sums that would have been payable for rent and matters so referred to under the new tenancy, and section 14(3)(*a*) above shall apply accordingly.

(7) Subsections (1) to (6) above shall have effect subject to any agreement between the landlord and tenant as to the terms of the new tenancy or any agreement collateral thereto; and either of them may require that for purposes of the new tenancy there shall be excluded or modified any term of the existing tenancy or an agreement collateral thereto which it would be unreasonable in the circumstances to include unchanged in the new tenancy in view of the date at which the existing tenancy commenced and of changes since that date which affect the suitability at the relevant time of the provisions of that tenancy.

(8) The new tenancy shall make provision in accordance with section 16(4) below, and shall reserve to the landlord the right to resume possession in accordance with section 17.

(9) In granting the new tenancy, the landlord shall not be bound to enter into any covenant for title beyond that implied from the grant, and a person entering into any covenant required of him as landlord shall be entitled to limit his personal liability to breaches of the covenant for which he is responsible.

(10) Nothing in this section shall affect the rights or obligations of the landlord under section 35 of and Schedule 1 to the Sexual Offences Act 1956 (which apply where the tenant or occupier of any premises is convicted of permitting the whole or part of them to be used as a brothel). **[198]**

NOTES
See further the Housing Act 1985, ss 172-175.

16. Exclusion of further rights after extension

(1) Subject to subsections (2) and (3) below, where a tenancy of a house and premises has been extended under section 14 above, then as regards any property comprised in the extended tenancy—

(*a*) the right of a tenant under this Part of this Act to acquire the freehold by virtue of the tenancy shall not be exercisable unless notice of his desire to have the freehold is given not later than the original term date of the tenancy; and
(*b*) there shall be no further right to an extension of the tenancy under this Part of this Act; and

(*c*) neither section 1 of the Landlord and Tenant Act 1954 nor Part II of that Act shall apply to the tenancy; and

(*d*) after the extended term date neither section 1 of the Landlord and Tenant Act 1954 nor Part II of that Act shall apply to any sub-tenancy directly or indirectly derived out of the tenancy, nor shall a person be entitled by virtue of any such sub-tenancy to retain possession under [[Part VII of the Rent Act 1977 or any enactment applying or extending that Part of that Act] [or under the Rent (Agriculture) Act 1976].

[(1A) The Rent Act 1977 shall not apply to a tenancy extended under section 14 above; but if when this provision comes into force a rent is registered under Part IV of the 1977 Act for a dwelling-house which is the subject of an extended tenancy, the tenant shall not be obliged to pay more than the registered rent under the extended tenancy until the next rental period (within the meaning of the 1977 Act) after the landlord has served on him a notice in writing that the registered rent no longer applies.]

(2) Where—

(*a*) a tenancy of a house and premises has been extended under section 14 above; and

(*b*) any part other than the house of the property then comprised in that tenancy is afterwards (while so comprised) held or occupied with another house not so comprised;

subsection (1)(*a*) or (*b*) above shall not apply to exclude any right under this Part of this Act of a tenant of the other house to acquire the freehold or an extended lease of that part as being at the relevant time comprised in his house and premises, unless the landlord objects in accordance with subsection (3) below.

(3) If, in a case falling within subsection (2) above, a tenant of the other house gives notice of his desire to have the freehold or an extended lease under this Part of this Act, the landlord, not later than two months afterwards, may give him written notice objecting to the inclusion in his house and premises of the part in question; and, if the landlord does so, that part shall be treated as not so included and this Part of this Act shall apply as it applies where property is excluded from a house and premises under section 2(4):

Provided that if the tenant is seeking to acquire the freehold, this subsection shall apply only if his notice is given after the original term date of the tenancy under which the said part is held.

(4) Where a tenancy has been extended under section 14 above, no long tenancy created immediately or derivatively by way of sub-demise under the tenancy shall confer on the sub-tenant, as against the tenant's landlord, any right under this Part of this Act to acquire the freehold or an extended lease.

(5) Where a tenancy has been extended under section 14 above, and that tenancy and any subsequent tenancy at a low rent of property comprised in it (with or without intervening tenancies) are to be treated under section 3(3) above as a single tenancy of that property, the single tenancy shall be treated for purposes of this section as one which has been extended under section 14, and the instrument granting any such subsequent tenancy shall make provision in accordance with subsection (4) above.

(6) A person granting a sub-tenancy to which subsection (1)(*d*) above will apply, or negotiating with a view to the grant of such a sub-tenancy by him or by a person for whom he is acting as agent, shall inform the other party that the

sub-tenancy is to be derived out of a tenancy extended under section 14 of this Act (or one treated for purposes of this section as so extended), unless either he knows that the other party is aware of it or he himself is unaware of it.

(7) Where an instrument extending a tenancy at a low rent, or granting a further tenancy at a low rent in substitution for or in continuance of such a tenancy, contains a statement to the effect that the tenancy is being or has been previously extended under this Part of this Act, the statement shall be conclusive for purposes of this section in favour of any person not being a party to the instrument, unless the statement appears from the instrument to be untrue.

(8) Any person who—

(*a*) includes or causes to be included in an instrument a statement to the effect mentioned in subsection (7) above, knowing the statement to be untrue; or

(*b*) executes, or with intent to deceive makes use of, any instrument, knowing that it contains such a statement and that the statement is untrue;

shall be liable on conviction on indictment to imprisonment for a term not exceeding two years, or on summary conviction to imprisonment for a term not exceeding three months or to a fine not exceeding [the prescribed sum], or to both. **[199]**

NOTES

Commencement: 3 October 1980 (sub-s (1A)); before 1 January 1970 (remainder).

Commencement order: SI 1980 No 1406.

Sub-s (1): first amendment made by the Rent Act 1977, s 155, Sch 23, para 43; second amendment made by the Rent (Agriculture) Act 1976, s 40, Sch 8, para 17.

Sub-s (1A): added by the Housing Act 1980, s 141, Sch 21.

Sub-s (8): amended by the Magistrates' Courts Act 1980 s 32(2).

See further the Housing Act 1985, ss 172-175.

Landlord's overriding rights

17. Redevelopment rights (exclusion or termination of extension)

(1) Where a tenancy of a house and premises has been extended under section 14 above, the landlord may, at any time not earlier than twelve months before the original term date of the tenancy, apply to the court for an order that he may resume possession of the property on the ground that for purposes of redevelopment he proposes to demolish or reconstruct the whole or a substantial part of the house and premises.

(2) If on an application under subsection (1) above the court is satisfied that the landlord has established the ground mentioned in that subsection, then subject to the provisions of this section the court shall by order declare that the landlord is entitled as against the tenant to obtain possession of the house and premises and the tenant is entitled to be paid compensation by the landlord for the loss of the house and premises.

(3) Where an order is made under subsection (2) above, the tenancy shall determine and the compensation become payable in accordance with Schedule 2 to this Act; and the provisions of that Schedule shall have effect as regards the measure of compensation under any such order and the effects of the order where there are sub-tenancies, and as regards other matters relating to applications and orders under this section.

(4) Where the tenancy of a house and premises has not been extended under

section 14 above, but the tenant has a right to an extended lease and gives notice of his desire to have one, then this section shall apply as if the lease had been extended under section 14; and—

(*a*) on the making by the landlord of an application under this section, the notice shall be suspended until the time when an order under subsection (2) or an order dismissing the application becomes final or the application is withdrawn; and

(*b*) on an order under subsection (2) becoming final, the notice shall cease to have effect, but section 14(2) above shall not apply to require the tenant to make any payment to the landlord in respect of costs incurred by reason of the notice.

(5) For purposes of subsection (4) above, the reference in subsection (1) to the original term date shall have effect as a reference to the term date or, in a case where before the relevant time the landlord had given notice to quit terminating the tenancy at a date earlier than the term date, as a reference to the date specified in the notice to quit.

(6) Where a landlord makes an application under subsection (1) above, then—

(*a*) if the tenant afterwards gives notice of his desire to have the freehold of the house and premises under this Part of this Act, that notice shall be of no effect if it is not given before the date of the order fixing the date for the termination of the tenancy (in accordance with Schedule 2 to this Act), or if the tenant's notice of his desire to have an extended lease was given within twelve months before the making of the landlord's application; and

(*b*) if a notice given by the tenant (before or after the making of the landlord's application) of his desire to have the freehold has effect, no order or further order shall be made on the landlord's application except as regards costs, but without prejudice to the making of a further application by the landlord if the tenant's notice lapses without effect being given to it. **[200]**

NOTES

See further the Housing Act 1985, ss 172-175.

18. Residential rights (exclusion of enfranchisement or extension)

(1) Subject to subsection (2) below, where the tenancy of a house and premises has not been extended under section 14 above, but the tenant has a right to acquire the freehold or an extended lease and has given notice of his desire to have it, the landlord may, at any time before effect is given to the notice, apply to the court for an order that he may resume possession of the property on the ground that it or part of it is or will be reasonably required by him for occupation as the only or main residence of the landlord or of a person who is at the time of the application an adult member of the landlord's family.

(2) A landlord shall not be entitled to apply to the court under this section if his interest in the house and premises, or an interest which has merged in that interest but would otherwise have had a duration extending at least five years longer than that of the tenancy, was purchased or created after the 18th February 1966; and for purposes of this subsection the duration of any interest in the house and premises (including the tenancy) shall be taken to be the period until it is due to expire or, if capable of earlier determination by notice given by

a person as landlord the date or earliest date which has been or could be specified in such a notice.

(3) Where the landlord's interest is held on trust, subsection (1) above shall apply as if the reference to occupation as the residence of the landlord were a reference to the like occupation of a person having an interest under the trust (whether or not also a trustee), and the reference to a member of the landlord's family were a reference to the like member of such a person's family; and for purposes of subsection (1) a person is an adult member of another's family if that person is—

(*a*) the other's wife or husband; or

(*b*) a son or daughter or a son-in-law or daughter-in-law of the other, or of the other's wife or husband, who has attained the age of eighteen; or

(*c*) the father or mother of the other, or of the other's wife or husband.

In paragraph (*b*) above any reference to a person's son or daughter includes a reference to any stepson or stepdaughter, any illegitimate son or daughter, . . . of that person, and "son-in-law" and "daughter-in-law" shall be construed accordingly.

(4) If on an application under subsection (1) above the court is satisfied that the landlord has established the ground mentioned in that subsection and is not disentitled by subsection (2), the court shall by order declare that the landlord is entitled as against the tenant to obtain possession of the house and premises and the tenant is entitled to be paid compensation by the landlord for the loss of the house and premises:

Provided that the court shall not make an order under this subsection if the court is satisfied that having regard to all the circumstances of the case, including the question whether other accommodation is available for the landlord or the tenant, greater hardship would be caused by making the order than by refusing to make it.

(5) Where an order is made under subsection (4) above, the tenancy shall determine and the compensation become payable in accordance with Schedule 2 to this Act; and the provisions of that Schedule shall have effect as regards the measure of compensation under any such order and the effects of the order where there are sub-tenancies, and as regards other matters relating to applications and orders under this section.

(6) Where a landlord makes an application under this section,—

(*a*) any notice previously given by the tenant of his desire to have the freehold or an extended lease of the house and premises under this Part of this Act shall be suspended until the time when an order under subsection (4) or an order dismissing the application becomes final or the application is withdrawn; and

(*b*) on an order under subsection (4) becoming final, the notice shall cease to have effect, but section 9(4) or 14(2) above shall not apply to require the tenant to make any payment to the landlord in respect of costs incurred by reason of the notice;

and a notice of the tenant's desire to have the freehold shall be of no effect if given after the making of the application and before the time referred to in paragraph (*a*) above or after an order under subsection (4) above has become final. [201]

NOTES
Sub-s (3): words omitted repealed by the Children Act 1975, s 108(1)(*b*), Sch 4, Part I
See further the Housing Act 1985, ss 172-175.

19. Retention of management powers for general benefit of neighbourhood

(1) Where, in the case of any area which is occupied directly or indirectly under tenancies held from one landlord (apart from property occupied by him or his licensees or for the time being unoccupied), the Minister on an application made within the two years beginning with the commencement of this Part of this Act grants a certificate that, in order to maintain adequate standards of appearance and amenity and regulate redevelopment in the area in the event of tenants acquiring the landlord's interest in their house and premises under this Part of this Act, it is in the Minister's opinion likely to be in the general interest that the landlord should retain powers of management in respect of the house and premises or have rights against the house and premises in respect of the benefits arising from the exercise elsewhere of his powers of management, then the High Court may, on an application made within one year of the giving of the certificate, approve a scheme giving the landlord such powers and rights as are contemplated by this subsection.

For the purposes of this section "the Minister" means as regards areas within Wales and Monmouthshire the Secretary of State, and as regards other areas the Minister of Housing and Local Government.

(2) The Minister shall not give a certificate under this section unless he is satisfied that the applicant has, by advertisement or otherwise as may be required by the Minister, given adequate notice to persons interested, informing them of the application for a certificate and its purpose and inviting them to make representations to the Minister for or against the application within a time which appears to the Minister to be reasonable; and before giving a certificate the Minister shall consider any representations so made within that time, and if from those representations it appears to him that there is among the persons making them substantial opposition to the application, he shall afford to those opposing the application, and on the same occasion to the applicant and such (if any) as the Minister thinks fit of those in favour of the application, an opportunity to appear and be heard by a person appointed by the Minister for the purpose, and shall consider the report of that person.

(3) The Minister in considering whether to grant a certificate authorising a scheme for any area, and the High Court in considering whether to approve a scheme shall have regard primarily to the benefit likely to result from the scheme to the area as a whole (including houses likely to be acquired from the landlord under this Part of this Act), and the extent to which it is reasonable to impose, for the benefit of the area, obligations on tenants so acquiring their freeholds; but regard may also be had to the past development and present character of the area and to architectural or historical considerations, to neighbouring areas and to the circumstances generally.

(4) If, having regard to the matters mentioned in subsection (3) above, to the provision which it is practicable to make by a scheme, and to any change of circumstances since the giving of the certificate under subsection (1), the High Court think it proper so to do, then the High Court may by order—

(*a*) exclude from the scheme any part of the area certified under that subsection; or
(*b*) declare that no scheme can be approved for the area;

and before submitting for approval a scheme for an area so certified a person may, if he sees fit, apply to the High Court for general directions as to the matters proper to be included in the scheme and for a decision whether an order should be made under paragraph (*a*) or (*b*) above.

(5) Subject to subsections (3) and (4) above, on the submission of a scheme to the High Court, the High Court shall approve the scheme either as originally submitted or with any modifications proposed or agreed to by the applicant for the scheme, if the scheme (with those modifications, if any) appears to the court to be fair and practicable and not to give the landlord a degree of control out of proportion to that previously exercised by him or to that required for the purposes of the scheme; and the High Court shall not dismiss an application for the approval of a scheme, unless either—

(*a*) the Court makes an order under subsection (4)(*b*) above; or
(*b*) in the opinion of the Court the applicant is unwilling to agree to a suitable scheme or is not proceeding in the manner with due despatch.

(6) A scheme under this section may make different provision for different parts of the area, and shall include provision for terminating or varying all or any of the provisions of the scheme, or excluding part of the area, if a change of circumstances makes it appropriate, or for enabling it to be done by or with the approval of the High Court.

(7) Except as provided by the scheme, the operation of a scheme under this section shall not be affected by any disposition or devolution of the landlord's interest in the property within the area or part of that property; but the scheme—

(*a*) shall include provision for identifying the person who is for the purposes of the scheme to be treated as the landlord for the time being; and
(*b*) may include provision for transferring, or allowing the landlord for the time being to transfer, all or any of the powers and rights conferred by the scheme on the landlord for the time being to a local authority or other body, including a body constituted for the purpose.

In the following provisions of this section references to the landlord for the time being shall have effect, in relation to powers and rights transferred to a local authority or other body as contemplated by paragraph (*b*) above, as references to that authority or body.

(8) Without prejudice to any other provision of this section, a scheme under it may provide for all or any of the following matters:—

(*a*) for regulating the redevelopment, use or appearance of property of which tenants have acquired the landlord's interest under this Part of this Act; and
(*b*) for empowering the landlord for the time being to carry out work for the maintenance or repair of any such property or carry out work to remedy a failure in respect of any such property to comply with the scheme, or for making the operation of any provisions of the scheme conditional on his doing so or on the provision or maintenance by him of services, facilities or amenities of any description; and
(*c*) for imposing on persons from time to time occupying or interested in any such property obligations in respect of maintenance or repair of the property or of property used or enjoyed by them in common with others, or in respect of cost incurred by the landlord for the time being on any matter referred to in this paragraph or in paragraph (*b*) above;

(*d*) for the inspection from time to time of any such property on behalf of the landlord for the time being, and for the recovery by him of sums due to him under the scheme in respect of any such property by means of a charge on the property;

and the landlord for the time being shall have, for the enforcement of any charge imposed under the scheme, the same powers and remedies under the Law of Property Act 1925 and otherwise as if he were a mortgagee by deed having powers of sale and leasing and of appointing a receiver.

(9) A scheme under this section may extend to property in which the landlord's interest is disposed of otherwise than under this Part of this Act (whether residential property or not), so as to make that property, or allow it to be made, subject to any such provision as is or might be made by the scheme for property in which tenants acquire the landlord's interest under this Part of this Act.

(10) A certificate given or scheme approved under this section [shall (notwithstanding section 2(*a*) or (*b*) of the Local Land Charges Act 1975) be a local land charge and for the purposes of that Act the landlord for the area to which it relates shall be treated as the originating authority as respects such charge; and where a scheme is registered in the appropriate local land charges register;]

(*a*) the provisions of the scheme relating to property of any description shall, so far as they respectively affect the persons from time to time occupying or interested in that property, be enforceable by the landlord for the time being against them, as if each of them had covenanted with the landlord for the time being to be bound by the scheme; and

(*b*) in relation to a house and premises in the area section 10 above shall have effect subject to the provisions of the scheme, and the price payable under section 9 shall be adjusted accordingly.

[(10A) Section 10 of the Local Land Charges Act 1975 shall not apply in relation to schemes which, by virtue of this section, are local land charges.]

(11) Subject to subsections (12) and (13) below, a certificate shall not be given nor a scheme approved under this section for any area except on the application of the landlord.

(12) Where, on a joint application made by two or more persons as landlords of neighbouring areas, it appears to the Minister—

(*a*) that a certificate could in accordance with subsection (1) above be given as regards those areas, treated as a unit, if the interests of those persons were held by a single person; and

(*b*) that the applicants are willing to be bound by any scheme to co-operate in the management of their property in those areas and in the administration of the scheme;

the Minister may give a certificate under this section for those areas as a whole; and where a certificate is given by virtue of this subsection, this section shall apply accordingly, but so that any scheme made by virtue of the certificate shall be made subject to conditions (enforceable in such manner as may be provided by the scheme) for securing that the landlords and their successors co-operate as aforesaid.

(13) Where it appears to the Minister—

(*a*) that a certificate could be given under this section for any area or areas on the application of the landlord or landlords; and

(*b*) that any body of persons is so constituted as to be capable of representing for purposes of this section the persons occupying or interested in property in the area or areas (other than the landlord or landlords), or such of them as are or may become entitled to acquire their landlord's interest under this Part of this Act, and is otherwise suitable;

then on an application made by that body either alone or jointly with the landlord or landlords a certificate may be granted accordingly; and where a certificate is so granted, whether to a representative body alone or to a representative body jointly with the landlord or landlords,—

(i) an application for a scheme in pursuance of the certificate may be made by the representative body alone or by the landlord or landlords alone or by both jointly and, by leave of the High Court, may be proceeded with by the representative body or by the landlord or landlords though not the applicant or applicants; and

(ii) without prejudice to subsection (7)(*b*) above, the scheme may, with the consent of the landlord or landlords or on such terms as to compensation or otherwise as appear to the High Court to be just, confer on the representative body any such rights or powers under the scheme as might be conferred on the landlord or landlords for the time being, or enable the representative body to participate in the administration of the scheme or in the management by the landlord or landlords of his or their property in the area or areas.

(14) Where a certificate under this section has been given for an area, or an application for one is pending, then subject to subsection (15) below if (before or after the making of the application or the giving of the certificate) a tenant of a house in the area gives notice of his desire to have the freehold under this Part of this Act,—

(*a*) no further proceedings need be taken in relation to the notice beyond those which appear to the landlord to be reasonable in the circumstances; but

(*b*) the tenant may at any time withdraw the notice by a further notice in writing given to the landlord, and section 9(4) above shall not apply to require him to make any payment to the landlord in respect of costs incurred by reason of the notice withdrawn.

(15) Subsection (14) above shall cease to have effect by virtue of an application for a certificate if the application is withdrawn or the certificate refused, and shall cease to have effect as regards the whole or part of an area to which a certificate relates—

(*a*) on the approval of a scheme for the area or that part of it; or

(*b*) on the expiration of one year from the giving of the certificate without an application having been made to the High Court for the approval of a scheme for the area or that part of it, or on the withdrawal of an application so made without a scheme being approved; or

(*c*) on an order made under subsection (4) above with respect to the area or that part of it, or an order dismissing an application for the approval of a scheme for the area or that part of it, becoming final. **[202]**

NOTES
Commencement: Before 1 January 1970 (sub-ss (1)-(10), (11)-(15)); 1 August 1977 (sub-s (10A)).
Commencement order: SI 1977 No 984.
Amended by the Local Land Charges Act 1975, ss 17(2), Sch 1.
See further the Housing Act 1985, ss 172-175.

Determination of questions, procedure, etc

20. Jurisdiction and special powers of county court.

(1) Subject to section 115 of the County Courts Act 1959, any jurisdiction expressed to be conferred on the court by this Part of this Act shall, unless the contrary intention appears, be exercised by the county court.

(2) Except as provided by this section and section 21 below, there shall also be brought in the county court any proceedings under this Part of this Act of the following descriptions:—

(*a*) proceedings for determining whether a person is entitled to acquire the freehold or an extended lease of a house and premises, or to what property his right extends;
(*b*) proceedings for determining what provisions ought to be contained in a conveyance in accordance with section 10 or 29(1), or in a lease granting a new tenancy under section 14;
(*c*) any other proceedings relating to the performance or discharge of obligations arising out of a tenant's notice of his desire to have the freehold or an extended lease, including proceedings for the recovery of damages or compensation in the event of the obligations not being performed;
(*d*) any proceedings for determining the amount of a sub-tenant's share under Schedule 2 to this Act in compensation payable to a tenant under section 17 or 18, or for establishing or giving effect to his right to it.

(3) Where in connection with any acquisition by a tenant of the freehold or an extended lease under this Part of this Act it is necessary to apportion between the house and premises (or part of them) and other property the rent payable under his tenancy or any superior or reversionary tenancy, then, subject to section 115 of the County Courts Act 1959 and to section 21 below, the apportionment shall be made by the county court.

(4) Where it is made to appear to the court that the landlord or the tenant has been guilty of any unreasonable delay or default in the performance of obligations arising from a tenant's notice of his desire to have the freehold or an extended lease under this Part of this Act, then (without prejudice to any right to damages) the court may—

(*a*) by order revoke or vary, and direct repayment of sums paid under, any provision made by a previous order as to payment of the costs of proceedings in the court in relation to the matter, or, where costs have not been awarded, award costs;
(*b*) certify particulars of the delay or default to the Lands Tribunal with a view to enabling the Tribunal to exercise a like discretion in relation to costs of proceedings before the Tribunal.

(5) Where a person gives notice of his desire to have the freehold or to have an extended lease of a house and premises under this Part of this Act, and the notice either is set aside by the court or withdrawn, or ceases to have effect, or would, if valid, cease to have effect, then if it is made to appear to the court—

(*a*) that the notice was not given in good faith; or
(*b*) that the person giving the notice attempted in any material respect to support it by misrepresentation or the concealment of material facts;

the court may, on the application of the landlord, order that person to pay to the landlord such sum as appears sufficient as compensation for damage or loss sustained by the landlord as the result of the giving of the notice.

(6) In any case where under subsection (5) above the court has power, on the application of the landlord, to order a person to make a payment to the landlord, the court (whether or not it makes an order under that subsection) may, on the application of the landlord, order that any further notice given by that person under this Part of this Act of his desire to have the freehold or an extended lease of the same house or any part of it, with or without other property, shall be void if given within the five years beginning with the date of the order.

(7) Subsection (2)(*c*) above shall not prevent the bringing of proceedings in a court other than the county court where the claim is for damages or pecuniary compensation only. **[203]**

NOTES
See further the Housing Act 1985, ss 172-175.

21. Jurisdiction of Lands Tribunal

(1) The following matters shall, in default of agreement, be determined by [a leasehold valuation tribunal] namely,—

(*a*) the price payable for a house and premises under section 9 above;
(*b*) the amount of the rent to be payable (whether originally or on a revision) for a house and premises in accordance with section 15(2);
(*c*) the amount of any compensation payable to a tenant under section 17 or 18 for the loss of a house and premises.

[(1A) An application to a leasehold valuation tribunal under subsection (1) above must be in the prescribed form and contain the prescribed particulars.

(1B) No application may be made to a leasehold valuation tribunal under subsection (1) above to determine the price for a house and premises unless either—

(*a*) the landlord has informed the tenant of the price he is asking; or
(*b*) two months have elapsed without his doing so since the tenant gave notice of his desire to have the freehold under this Part of this Act.]

(2) Notwithstanding section 20(2) or (3) above, [a leasehold valuation tribunal] shall have jurisdiction, either by agreement or in a case where an application is made to [a tribunal] under subsection (1) above with reference to the same transaction,—

(*a*) to determine what provisions ought to be contained in a conveyance in accordance with section 10 or 29(1) of this Act, or in a lease granting a new tenancy under section 14; or
(*b*) to apportion between the house and premises (or part of them) and other property the rent payable under any tenancy; or
(*c*) to determine the amount of a sub-tenant's share under Schedule 2 to this Act in compensation payable to a tenant under section 17 or 18.

(3) Where, after an application has been made to the court with respect to any matter falling within the jurisdiction of [a leasehold valuation tribunal]

under subsection (2) above, an application is made to [a tribunal] under subsection (1) and it appears to the court convenient that the questions arising on the two applications should be disposed of together, the court may by order transfer to [a leasehold valuation tribunal] the proceedings on the application to the court.

[(4) Without prejudice to the generality of [section 75 of the County Courts Act 1984] or section 74 of the Rent Act 1977, the powers thereby conferred to make rules of procedure shall extend to prescribing the procedure consequent on any such transfer.]

[(4A) The Secretary of State may make regulations prescribing—

(*a*) the form of any application under subsection (1) above; and
(*b*) the particulars which it must contain;

and any such regulations shall be made by statutory instrument subject to annulment in pursuance of a resolution of either House of Parliament.]

(5) . . . **[204]**

NOTES

Commencement: Before 1 January 1970 (sub-ss (1), (2), (3)); 31 March 1981 (sub-ss (1A), (1B), (4A)).

Commencement order: SI 1981 No 119.

Sub-ss (1), (2), (3): amended by the Housing Act 1980, s 142, Sch 22.

Sub-ss (1A), (1B), (4A): added by the Housing Act 1980, s 142, Sch 22.

Sub-s (4): substituted by the Housing Act 1980, s 142, Sch 22; amended by the County Courts Act 1984, s 148(1), Sch 2, para 31.

Sub-s (5): repealed by the Housing Act 1980, ss 142, 152, Sch 22, Sch 26.

See further the Housing Act 1985, ss 172-175.

22. Validity of tenants' notices, effect on Landlord and Tenant Act 1954 and on notices to quit, etc, and procedure generally

(1) The provisions of Schedule 3 to this Act shall have effect—

(*a*) to exclude a tenant's right to acquire the freehold or an extended lease under this Part of this Act if a notice of his desire to have it is given too late; and
(*b*) to make a notice of a person's desire to have the freehold or an extended lease under this Part of this Act effectual where apart from the notice the tenancy would or might terminate by forfeiture or otherwise; and
(*c*) for adapting the procedure under Parts I and II of the Landlord and Tenant Act 1954, and for relating to one another proceedings under that Act and proceedings under this Part of this Act; and
(*d*) generally for regulating the procedure under this Part of this Act.

(2) Where a tenant having a right under this Part of this Act to acquire the freehold or an extended lease gives the landlord notice in accordance with this Part of this Act of his desire to have it, then except as otherwise provided by this Act the procedure for giving effect to the notice, and the rights and obligations of all parties in relation to the investigation of title and other matters arising in giving effect to the notice, shall be such as may be prescribed by regulations made by [the Secretary of State] by statutory instrument (which shall be subject to annulment in pursuance of a resolution of either House of Parliament), and subject to or in the absence of provision made by any such regulations as regards any matter shall be as nearly as may be the same as in the case of a contract of sale or leasing freely negotiated between the parties.

(3) In relation to a claim to acquire the freehold, regulations under subsection (2) above may include provision—

(*a*) for a sum on account of the price payable for the house and premises and landlord's costs to be deposited with the landlord or with some person as his agent or as stockholder, and for the return or forfeiture in any prescribed circumstances of the whole or part of the sum deposited;

(*b*) for enabling or requiring the tenant in any prescribed circumstances, instead of continuing to pay rent under the tenancy, to pay sums representing interest on the price payable or, at his option, either to pay such sums as aforesaid or to pay or deposit the price payable or the balance of it;

(*c*) for any matters incidental to or arising out of the matters mentioned above;

and in relation to any claim the regulations may provide for discharging the landlord or the tenant by reason of the other's default or delay from the obligations arising out of the claim.

(4) In the case of a claim to acquire the freehold, subsection (2) above shall not be taken in any case as applying forms prescribed under section 46 of the Law of Property Act 1925 for contracts entered into by correspondence; but, without prejudice to the generality of that subsection section 49 (which provides for the determination of questions arising between vendor and purchaser) shall apply.

(5) Section 66 of the Landlord and Tenant Act 1954 (which requires the prescribed form for a notice to be prescribed by regulations of [the Secretary of State], and makes provisions as to the contents of prescribed forms and as to the service of notices) shall have effect as if any reference therein to that Act were a reference also to this Part of this Act. **[205]**

NOTES

Sub-ss (2) and (5): amended by Transfer of Functions (Lord Chancellor and Secretary of State) Order 1974, SI 1974 No 1896.

See further the Housing Act 1985, ss 172-175.

Supplementary

23. Agreements excluding or modifying rights of tenant

(1) Except as provided by this section, any agreement relating to a tenancy (whether contained in the instrument creating the tenancy or not and whether made before the creation of the tenancy or not) shall be void in so far as it purports to exclude or modify any right to acquire the freehold or an extended lease or right to compensation under this Part of this Act, or provides for the termination or surrender of the tenancy in the event of a tenant acquiring or claiming any such right or for the imposition of any penalty or disability on the tenant in that event.

(2) Subsection (1) above shall not be taken to preclude a tenant from surrendering his tenancy, and shall not—

(*a*) invalidate any agreement for a tenant to acquire an interest superior to his tenancy or an extended lease on terms different from those provided for by this Part of this Act; or

(*b*) where a tenant has given notice of his desire to have the freehold or an extended lease under this Part of this Act, invalidate any agreement between the landlord and the tenant that that notice shall cease to be binding or any provision of such an agreement excluding or restricting for a period not exceeding [three years] the right to give a further notice of either kind with respect to the house or any part of it; or

(*c*) where a tenant's right to compensation has accrued, invalidate any agreement as to the amount of the compensation.

(3) Where—

(*a*) a person, being entitled as tenant of a house to acquire the freehold or an extended lease under this Part of this Act, enters into an agreement without the prior approval of the court for the surrender of his tenancy, or for the acquisition by him of an interest superior to his tenancy or of any extended lease; or

(*b*) a tenancy having been extended under this Part of this Act, the tenant, on the landlord claiming possession for purposes of redevelopment, enters into an agreement without prior approval of the court for the surrender of the tenancy;

then on the application of the tenant the county court or any court in which proceedings are brought against him on the agreement may, if in the opinion of the court he is not adequately recompensed under the agreement for his rights under this Part of this Act, set aside or vary the agreement and give such other relief as appears to the court to be just, having regard to the situation and conduct of the parties.

(4) Where a tenant of a house is under this Part of this Act entitled to acquire the freehold or an extended lease, or entitled to the benefit of a previous tenant's notice of his desire to have the freehold or an extended lease, there may with the approval of the court be granted to him in satisfaction of that right a new tenancy on such terms as may be approved by the court; and, subject to section 29 of the Charities Act 1960 and to section 31 below, a tenancy may be so granted by the landlord, and shall be binding on persons entitled to any interest in or charge on the landlord's estate, notwithstanding that it would not apart from this provision be authorised as against any such persons and notwithstanding any restriction imposed by statute or otherwise on the landlord's powers of leasing:

Provided that where the existing tenancy is granted after the commencement of this Part of this Act (whether or not it is, by virtue of section 3(3) above, to be treated for other purposes as forming a single tenancy with a previous tenancy) and, the grant being subsequent to the creation of a charge on the landlord's estate, the existing tenancy is not binding on the persons interested in the charge, a tenancy so granted shall not by virtue of this subsection be binding on those persons.

(5) Where a tenancy is granted by virtue of subsection (4) above,—

(*a*) the terms of the new tenancy may exclude any right to acquire the freehold under this Part of this Act; and

(*b*) [Section 9(1) and (1A) above,] section 14(5) and (6) above and, except in so far as provision is made to the contrary by the terms of the new tenancy, section 16(1) to (6) and section 17(1) to (3) (together with Schedule 2 to this Act and, so far as relevant, subsections (1) to (3) above) shall apply as if the new tenancy were granted by way of extension under this Part of this Act.

(6)Where an instrument extending a tenancy at a low rent, or granting a further tenancy at a low rent in substitution for or in continuance of such a tenancy, contains a statement to the effect that by virtue of subsection (4) above the tenancy is being or has previously been extended in satisfaction of the right to an extended lease under section 14 above, the statement shall be conclusive in favour of any person not being a party to the instrument, unless the statement appears from the instrument to be untrue.

(7) Any person who—

(*a*) includes or causes to be included in an instrument a statement to the effect mentioned in subsection (6) above, knowing the statement to be untrue; or

(*b*) executes, or with intent to deceive makes use of, any instrument, knowing that it contains such a statement and that the statement is untrue;

shall be liable on conviction on indictment to imprisonment for a term not exceeding two years, or on summary conviction to imprisonment for a term not exceeding three months or to a fine not exceeding [the prescribed sum], or to both. **[206]**

NOTES

Sub-s (2): amended by the Housing Act 1980, s 141, Sch 21.

Sub-s (5): in para (*b*) words in square brackets added with savings by the Housing and Planning Act 1986, s 23(2), (3).

Sub-s (7): amended by the Magistrates' Courts Act 1980, s 32(2).

See further the Housing Act 1985, ss 172-175.

24. Application of price or compensation received by landlord, and charge of betterment levy on enfranchisement

(1) Any sum received by the landlord by way of the price payable for a house and premises under section 9 above, or by way of compensation under any provision of this Part of this Act providing for compensation to be recovered by or awarded to a landlord,—

(*a*) where the interest of the landlord is held on trust for sale shall be dealt with as if it were proceeds of sale arising under the trust; and

(*b*) where the landlord is a university or college to which the Universities and College Estates Act 1925 applies, shall be dealt with as if it were an amount payable as consideration on a sale effected under that Act.

(2) For purposes of Part III of the Land Commission Act 1967 any conveyance executed to give effect to section 8 above shall be deemed to be a conveyance on sale of any interest transferred (or, as regards a tenancy, an assignment on sale of it), and the price payable for the interest under section 9 shall be deemed to be consideration payable in respect of the disposition of that interest. **[207]**

NOTES

See further the Housing Act 1985, ss 172-175.

25. Mortgagee in possession of landlord's interest

(1) Where a landlord's interest is subject to a mortgage and the mortgagee is in possession, then subject to the provisions of this section all such proceedings arising out of a person's notice of his desire to have the freehold or an extended lease under this Part of this Act as would apart from this provision be taken by or in relation to the landlord shall, as regards his interest, be conducted by and through the mortgagee as if he were the landlord, and any conveyance to be executed under section 8 of this Act or lease to be executed under section 14

shall, if it requires execution by the landlord, either be executed by the landlord by the direction of the mortgagee or be executed by the mortgagee in the name and on behalf of the landlord; but this subsection shall not affect the operation in relation to the mortgage of sections 12 and 13 above.

(2) Where a landlord's interest is subject to a mortgage and the mortgagee is in possession, then (without prejudice to subsection (1) above) any application under section 17 above shall be made by the mortgagee as if he were the landlord, and that section and Schedule 2 to this Act shall apply accordingly.

(3) Any compensation paid by a mortgagee in accordance with section 17 above (whether possession is obtained under that section or without an application thereunder) shall be treated as if it were secured by the mortgage, with the like priority and with interest at the same rate as the mortgage money, so however that (without prejudice to the recovery of interest) the amount shall not be recoverable from the mortgagor personally.

(4) Where a mortgagee is by virtue of this section acting as landlord and any case arises in which compensation may be recovered by or awarded to a landlord, compensation may be recovered by or awarded to the mortgagee accordingly, and shall be dealt with as if it were proceeds of sale of property subject to the mortgage.

(5) Where a landlord's interest is subject to a mortgage, and a receiver appointed by the mortgagee or by the court is in receipt of the rents and profits,—

(*a*) the landlord shall not make any application under section 17 or 18 above without the consent of the mortgagee; and

(*b*) the mortgagee may by written notice given to the landlord require that this section shall apply, either generally or so far as relates to section 17 above, as if he were a mortgagee in possession.

(6) In this section "mortgage" includes any charge or lien, and "mortgagor" and "mortgagee" shall be construed accordingly. **[208]**

NOTES

See further the Housing Act 1985, ss 172-175.

26. Person to act where landlord is custodian trustee or under disability

(1) Where the interest of a landlord in any property is vested in a person as custodian trustee, the managing trustees or committee of management shall be deemed to be the landlord for the purposes of this Part of this Act and the interest be deemed to be vested in them, except as regards the execution of any instrument disposing of or affecting that interest.

(2) Where a landlord is incapable by reason of mental disorder within the meaning of [the Mental Health Act 1983] of managing and administering his property and affairs, his receiver [appointed under Part VII of the said Act of 1983 or Part VIII of the Mental Health Act 1959] or (if no such receiver is acting for him) any person authorised in that behalf shall, under an order of the authority [having jurisdiction under Part VII of the said Act of 1983], take his place as landlord for purposes of this Part of this Act. **[209]**

NOTES

Sub-s (2): amended by the Mental Health Act 1983, s 148, Sch 4, para 22.
See further the Housing Act 1985, ss 172-175.

27. Enfranchisement where landlord cannot be found

(1) Where a tenant of a house having a right under this Part of this Act to acquire the freehold is prevented from giving notice of his desire to have the freehold because the person to be served with the notice cannot be found, or his identity cannot be ascertained, then on an application made by the tenant the High Court may, subject to and in accordance with the provisions of this section, make such order as the court thinks fit with a view to the house and premises being vested in him, his executors, administrators or assigns for the like estate and on the like terms (so far as the circumstances permit) as if he had at the date of his application to the High Court given notice of his desire to have the freehold.

(2) Before making any such order the High Court may require the applicant to take such further steps by way of advertisement or otherwise as the Court thinks proper for the purpose of tracing the landlord; and if after an application is made to the High Court and before the house and premises are vested in pursuance of the application the landlord is traced, then no further proceedings shall be taken with a view to the house and premises being so vested, but subject to subsection (7) below—

(*a*) the rights and obligations of all parties shall be determined as if the applicant had, at the date of the application, duly given notice of his desire to have the freehold; and

(*b*) the High Court may give such directions as the Court thinks fit as to the steps to be taken for giving effect to those rights and obligations, including directions modifying or dispensing with any of the requirements of this Act or of regulations made under this Act.

(3) Where a house and premises are to be vested in a person in pursuance of an application under this section, then on his paying into the Supreme Court the appropriate sum there shall be executed by such person as the High Court may designate a conveyance in a form approved by the High Court and containing such provisions as may be so approved for the purpose of giving effect so far as possible to the requirements of section 10 above; and that conveyance shall be effective to vest in the person to whom the conveyance is made the property expressed to be conveyed, subject as and in the manner in which it is expressed to be conveyed.

(4) For the purpose of any conveyance to be executed in accordance with subsection (3) above, any question as to the property to be conveyed and the rights with or subject to which it is to be conveyed shall be determined by the High Court, but it shall be assumed (unless the contrary is shown) that the landlord has no interest in property other than the property to be conveyed and, for the purpose of excepting them from the conveyance, any underlying minerals.

(5) The appropriate sum to be paid into the Supreme Court in accordance with subsection (3) above shall be such amount as a surveyor selected by the President of the Lands Tribunal may certify to be at a fair valuation the price payable in accordance with section 9 above, together with the amount or estimated amount remaining unpaid (as determined by the High Court) of any pecuniary rent payable for the house and premises up to the date of the conveyance.

(6) Where a house and premises are vested in a person in accordance with this section, the payment into the Supreme Court of the appropriate sum shall be taken to have satisfied any claims against the tenant, his executors,

administrators or assigns in respect of the price payable under this Part of this Act for the acquisition of the freehold in the house and premises.

(7) An application under this section may be withdrawn at any time before execution of a conveyance under subsection (3) above and, after it is withdrawn, subsection (2)(*a*) shall not apply; but where any step is taken (whether by the landlord or the tenant) for the purpose of giving effect to subsection (2)(*a*) in the case of any application, the application shall not afterwards be withdrawn except with the landlord's consent or by leave of the High Court, and the High Court shall not give leave unless it appears to the Court just to do so by reason of matters coming to the knowledge of the applicant in consequence of the landlord being traced.

(8) A conveyance executed under subsection (3) above shall have effect as provided by that subsection notwithstanding any interest of the Crown in the property expressed to be conveyed. **[210]**

Land held for public purposes, ecclesiastical land, etc

28. Retention or resumption of land required for public purposes

(1) Where the landlord of any property is a body to which this section applies, and a Minister of the Crown certifies that the property will in ten years or less be required for relevant development, then—

(*a*) a notice of a person's desire to have the freehold or an extended lease under this Part of this Act of a house comprised in the property shall be of no effect;

(*b*) if the tenancy of any such house has not been extended under this Part of this Act, but the tenant, being entitled to acquire the freehold or an extended lease thereunder, either—

(i) before a copy of the certificate has been served on him, has given notice of his desire to have the freehold or an extended lease; or

(ii) not later than two months after a copy of the certificate is served on him, gives the landlord written notice, in the prescribed form, claiming to be so entitled;

then section 17 above shall apply as if the tenancy had been so extended;

(*c*) for the purposes of any application by the landlord under section 17 above in relation to property comprised in the certificate (whether the application is made by virtue of paragraph (*b*) above or otherwise), the certificate shall be conclusive that the ground specified in section 17(1) is established.

(2) Where by virtue of subsection (1)(*b*) above a tenancy of any property is to be treated as having been extended, then as regards that property the tenancy shall not terminate either by effluxion of time or in pursuance of any notice given by the landlord or the tenant or by the termination of a superior tenancy.

(3) In the case of a tenancy to which Part II of the Landlord and Tenant Act 1954 applies, subsections (1) and (2) above shall have effect where a certificate is given under section 57 of that Act as they have effect where a certificate is given under this section; but where by virtue of subsection (1)(*b*) above a tenancy is to be treated as having been extended, no compensation shall be payable under section 59 of that Act in respect of the tenancy or any immediate or derivative sub-tenancy.

(4) A Minister shall not give a certificate under this section with respect to any house, unless the landlord has given to the tenant of the house written notice stating—

(*a*) that the question of giving such a certificate is under consideration by that Minister; and

(*b*) that if within twenty-one days of the giving of the notice the tenant makes to that Minister representations in writing with respect to that question, they will be considered before the question is determined;

and if the tenant makes any such representations within those twenty-one days the Minister shall consider them before determining whether to give the certificate.

(5) This section applies—

(*a*) to any local authority, that is to say, the Mayor and commonalty and citizens of the City of London, . . . any county council, borough council or district council, [the Inner London Education Authority, any joint authority established by Part IV of the Local Government Act 1985,] any joint board in which all the constituent authorities are local authorities within this paragraph and any combined police authority within the meaning of the Police Act 1964; and

(*b*) to the Commission for the New Towns and to any development corporation within the meaning of the New Towns Act 1965; and

[(*bb*) to the Development Board of Rural Wales]

(*c*) to any university body, that is to say, any university, university college or college of a university, and for this purpose "college of a university" includes, in the case of a university organised on a collegiate basis, a constituent college or other society recognised by the university and, in the case of a London University, a college incorporated in the university or a school of the university; and

[(*d*) to any Regional Health Authority, any Area Health Authority, [any District Health Authority] [any Family Practitioner Committee] and any special health authority; and]

(*e*) to any body corporate established by or under any enactment for the purpose of carrying on under national ownership any industry or part of an industry or undertaking; and

(*f*) to any body not included above which is a harbour authority within the meaning of the Harbours Act 1964 or a statutory water undertaker for purposes of the Water Act 1945, but in respect only of the body's functions as harbour authority or statutory water undertaker.

(6) In subsection (1) above "relevant development", in relation to any body to which this section applies, means development for purposes (other than investment purposes) of that body, but in relation to a local authority includes any development to be undertaken, whether or not by that authority, [in order to secure—

(*a*) the development or re-development of an area defined by a development plan under [the Town and Country Planning Act 1971] as an area of comprehensive development; or

(*b*) the treatment as a whole, by development, re-development, or improvement, or partly by one and partly by another method, of any area in which the property is situated].

However—

(*a*) the purposes of a county council or . . . council shall be taken to include the purposes of a police authority which is a committee of the council; and

(*b*) the purposes of a university body shall be taken to include the purposes of any related university body (a university and the colleges of that university within the meaning of subsection (5)(*c*) above being related to one another within the meaning of this paragraph); and

[(*c*) in the case of a Regional Health Authority, Area Health Authority, [District Health Authority][Family Practitioner Committee] or special health authority, the purposes of the [National Health Service Act 1977] shall be substituted for the purposes of the body.]

(7) If it appears to the Minister of Housing and Local Government or to the Secretary of State that this section should apply to any body or description of bodies having functions of a public nature but not included above, he may by order direct that this section shall apply to that body or description of bodies.

(8) The power to make orders under subsection (7) above shall include power to vary or revoke any order made for the purposes of that subsection, and shall be exercisable by statutory instrument of which a draft shall be laid before Parliament. **[211]**

NOTES

Sub-s (5): in para (*a*) words omitted repealed by the Local Government Act 1985, s 102, Sch 17, amendment in square brackets made by the Local Government Act 1985, s 84, Sch 14, para 43; para (*bb*) added by the Development of Rural Wales Act 1976, s 27, Sch 7, para 5(1), (2); para (*d*) substituted by the National Health Service Reorganisation Act 1973, ss 57, 58, Sch 4, para (111), amended by the Health Services Act 1980, ss 1, 2, Sch 1, Part I, and by SI 1985 No 39, art 5.

Sub-s (6): first amendment in square brackets made by the Town and Country Planning Act 1968, s 106, Sch 9, para 75, further amended by the Town and Country Planning Act 1971, s 291, Sch 23; words omitted repealed by the Local Government Act 1972, s 272(1), Sch 30; para (*c*) substituted by the National Health Service Reorganisation Act 1973, ss 57, 58, Sch 4, para (111), further amended by the Health Services Act 1980, ss 1, 2, Sch 1, Part I, the National Health Service Act 1977, s 129, Sch 15 para 42, and by SI 1985 No 39, art 5.

Modified by SI 1985 No 1884, art 10, Sch 3.

See further the Housing Act 1985, ss 172-175.

29. Reservation of future right to develop

(1) Where a tenant of a house and premises acquires the freehold under this Part of this Act, the landlord being a local authority, there shall, if so required by the local authority, be included in the conveyance under section 8 above such covenants on the part of the tenant restricting the carrying out of development or clearing of land as are necessary to reserve the land for possible development by the authority.

(2) Where a tenant of a house and premises acquires an extended lease under this Part of this Act, the landlord being a local authority, such covenants as are mentioned in subsection (1) above shall, if so required by the local authority, be included in the instrument extending the lease under section 14 above and, if so included, then in the terms of any subsequent tenancy at a low rent which is by virtue of section 3(3) above to be treated (with or without any intervening tenancies) as a single tenancy with that under the extended lease.

(3) Where a covenant is entered into to give effect to subsection (1) or (2) above, it shall be expressed to be so entered into, and Part I of Schedule 4 to this Act shall have effect with respect to the operation and enforcement of any covenant so entered into.

(4) Where a tenant of a house and premises acquires the freehold or an

extended lease under this Part of this Act, the landlord being a local authority, and afterwards the local authority or any other person acquires compulsorily any interest in the property, then for the purpose of assessing compensation in accordance with the Land Compensation Act 1961 no account shall be taken of any increase in the value of that interest which is attributable to the carrying out of development in contravention of a covenant entered into to give effect to subsection (1) or (2) above, or to any prospect of carrying out any such development; and any compensation payable to a tenant under section 17 above shall be assessed without regard to any increase in the value of his interest which under this subsection would be disregarded on a compulsory purchase of that interest.

(5) For purposes of this section "local authority" means a local authority as defined in section 28(5)(*a*) above.

(6) Subsections (1) to (4) above shall have effect in relation—

(*a*) to the Commission for the New Towns and to any development corporation within the meaning of the New Towns Act 1965; and

(*b*) to any university body as defined in section 28(5)(*c*) above;

as if any reference in those subsections or in Part I of Schedule 4 to this Act to a local authority were a reference to that Commission, corporation or university body; but a university body shall not require a covenant to be entered into under this section, unless they have first obtained the consent of the Secretary of State.

[(6A) Subsections (1) to (4) above shall have effect in relation to the Development Board for Rural Wales as if any reference in those subsections or in Part I of Schedule 4 to this Act to a local authority were a reference to the Board.]

[(6B) Where the landlord is a university body, the possible development for which land may be reserved by a covenant entered into to give effect to subsection (1) or (2) above includes development by a related university body (within the meaning of section 28(6)(*b*) above).]

(7) Part II of Schedule 4 to this Act shall have effect to enable property to be re-acquired compulsorily where it is subject to a covenant entered into to give effect to subsection (1) above with the Commission for the New Towns [the Development Board for Rural Wales] or a university body.

(8) This section shall apply, with the necessary adaptations, where a new tenancy is granted in satisfaction of the right to an extended lease under this Part of this Act, as it applies where a lease is extended in accordance with this Part of this Act. **[212]**

NOTES

Commencement: Before 1 January 1970 (sub-ss (1)-(6), (7), (8)); 1 April 1977 (sub-s (6A)); 3 October 1980 (sub-s (6B)).

Commencement orders: SI 1977 No 116, 1980 No 1406.

Sub-s (6A): added by the Development of Rural Wales Act 1976, s 27, Sch 7, para 5(1), (3).

Sub-s (6B): added by the Housing Act 1980, s 141, Sch 21.

Sub-s (7): amended by the Development of Rural Wales Act 1976, s 27, Sch 7, para 5(1), (3).

See further the Housing Act 1985, ss 172-175.

30. Reservation of right of pre-emption in new town or overspill area

(1) Where a tenant of a house and premises acquires the freehold under this Part of this Act, the landlord being a body to which this section applies, there shall, if so required by the landlord, be included in the conveyance under section 8 above the following covenants on the part of the tenant, that is to say,—

(*a*) a covenant that no tenancy of the property comprised in the conveyance or any part of that property shall be granted except with the consent in writing of the landlord; and

(*b*) such covenant as appears to the landlord to be requisite for securing that, in the event of any proposal to sell that property or any part of it, the landlord will have a right of pre-emption at the price mentioned in subsection (4) below.

(2) Where a tenant of a house and premises acquires an extended lease under this Part of this Act, the landlord being a body to which this section applies, such covenants as are mentioned in subsection (1) above shall, if so required by the landlord, be included in the instrument extending the lease under section 14 above and, if so included, then in the terms of any subsequent tenancy at a low rent which is by virtue of section 3(3) above to be treated (with or without intervening tenancies) as a single tenancy with that under the extended lease.

(3) Where a covenant is entered into to give effect to subsection (1) or (2) above, it shall be expressed to be so entered into, and Part I of Schedule 4 to this Act shall have effect, with respect to the operation and enforcement of any covenant so entered into as it applies in the case of a covenant entered into with the same body to give effect to section 29(1) or (2) above.

(4) The price referred to in subsection (1)(*b*) above, in relation to an interest in any property, is a sum equal to (and, in default of agreement, to be determined in the like manner as) the compensation which would be payable for that interest if acquired by the execution, on such date as may be determined in accordance with the covenant, of a vesting declaration under Schedule 4 to this Act.

(5) Section 19 of the Landlord and Tenant Act 1927 (covenants not to assign etc. without licence or consent) shall not have effect in relation to any covenant entered into to give effect to subsection (2) above.

(6) This section shall apply, with the necessary adaptations, where a new tenancy is granted in satisfaction of the right to an extended lease under this Part of this Act, as it applies where a lease is extended in accordance with this Part of this Act.

(7) This section applies—

(*a*) to the Commission for the New Towns [the Development Board for Rural Wales], and to a development corporation within the meaning of the New Towns Act 1965; and

(*b*) in respect of housing provided by them by virtue of section 5 of the Town Development Act 1952 (which authorises a council to exercise its powers for the purpose of relieving congestion or over-population outside their area), the council of any receiving district for purposes of that Act, ... **[213]**

NOTES

Sub-s (7): para (*a*) amended by the Development of Rural Wales Act 1976, s 27, Sch 7, para 5(1), (4); in para (*b*) words omitted repealed by the Housing (Consequential Provisions) Act 1985, s 3, Sch 1, Part I.

See further the Housing Act 1985, ss 172-175.

31. Ecclesiastical property

(1) The provisions of this section shall have effect as regards the operation of this Part of this Act on tenancies (including sub-tenancies) of ecclesiastical

property, that is to say, property belonging to a capitular body within the meaning of the Cathedrals Measure 1963 or belonging to an ecclesiastical benefice; and in this section "ecclesiastical landlord" means the capitular body or incumbent having an interest as landlord in ecclesiastical property.

(2) In relation to an interest of an ecclesiastical landlord, the consent of the Church Commissioners shall be required to sanction—

(*a*) the provisions to the contained in a conveyance in accordance with section 10 above, or in a lease granting a new tenancy under section 14, and the price or rent payable, except as regards matters determined by the court, [a leashold valuation tribunal] or the Lands Tribunal;

(*b*) any exercise of the ecclesiastical landlord's rights under section 17 above, except as aforesaid, and any agreement for the payment of compensation to a tenant in accordance with that section without an application thereunder;

(*c*) any grant of a tenancy in satisfaction of the right to an extended lease under this Part of this Act;

and the Church Commissioners shall be entitled to appear and be heard in any proceedings under this Part of this Act to which an ecclesiastical landlord is a party or in which he is entitled to appear and be heard.

(3) Where the ecclesiastical property forms part of the endowment of a cathedral church, any sum received by the capitular body by way of the price payable for the property under section 9 above, or by way of compensation under any provision of this Part of this Act providing for compensation to be recovered by or awarded to a landlord, shall be treated as part of that endowment; and the powers conferred by sections 21 and 23 of the Cathedrals Measure 1963 in relation to the investment in the acquisition of land of moneys forming part of the endowment of a cathedral church shall extend to the application of any such moneys in the payment of compensation in accordance with section 17 above (whether possession is obtained under that section or without an application thereunder).

(4) In the case of ecclesiastical property belonging to an ecclesiastical benefice—

(*a*) no consent or concurrence other than that of the Church Commissioners under subsection (2) above shall be required to a disposition under this Part of this Act of the incumbent's interest (including a grant of a tenancy in satisfaction of the right to an extended lease);

(*b*) during a vacancy in the benefice, the abeyance shall not affect the operation of this Part of this Act, but the place of the incumbent shall be taken by the person authorised to exercise in his place the powers conferred by the Ecclesiastical Leasing Acts, and the Ecclesiastical Commissioners (Powers) Measure 1963 (together with section 7 of the Vacancies in Sees Measure 1959) apply accordingly;

(*c*) any sum receivable by the incumbent by way of the price payable for the property under section 9 above, or of any such compensation as is mentioned in subsection (3) above, shall be paid to the Church Commissioners to be applied for purposes for which the proceeds of a sale by agreement of the property would be applicable under any enactment or Measure authorising such a sale or disposing of the proceeds of such a sale, and any sum required for the payment of compensation as mentioned in subsection (3) above may be paid by the Church Commissioners on behalf of the incumbent out of any moneys in their hands;

(*d*) the revenues and possessions of the benefice shall stand charged with the repayment of any sum expended by the Church Commissioners in pursuance of paragraph (*c*) above.

(5) This Part of this Act shall apply to land belonging to an ecclesiastical benefice, and this section shall have effect in relation thereto, notwithstanding that the patronage of the benefice belongs to Her Majesty in right of the Crown or the Duchy of Lancaster or to the Duchy of Cornwall. **[214]**

NOTES

Sub-s (2): amended by the Housing Act 1980, s 142, Sch 22.
See further the Housing Act 1985, ss 172-175.

32. Saving for National Trust

This Part of this Act shall not prejudice the operation of section 21 of the National Trust Act 1907, and accordingly a person shall not be entitled under this Part of this Act to acquire the freehold of property if an interest in the property is under that section vested inalienably in the National Trust for Places of Historic Interest or Natural Beauty. **[215]**

NOTES

See further the Housing Act 1985, ss 172-175.

33. Crown land

(1) In the case of a tenancy from the Crown this Part of this Act shall apply in favour of the tenant as in the case of any other tenancy if there has ceased to be a Crown interest in the land, and as against a landlord holding a tenancy from the Crown shall apply also if either—

(*a*) his sub-tenant is seeking an extended lease and the landlord, or a superior landlord holding a tenancy from the Crown, has a sufficient interest to grant it and is entitled to do so without the concurrence of the appropriate authority; or

(*b*) the appropriate authority notifies the landlord that as regards any Crown interest affected the authority will grant or concur in granting the freehold or extended lease.

(2) For purposes of this section "tenancy from the Crown" means a tenancy of land in which there is, or has during the subsistence of the tenancy been, a Crown interest superior to the tenancy, and "Crown interest" and "the appropriate authority" in relation to a Crown interest mean respectively—

(*a*) an interest comprised in the Crown Estate, and the Crown Estate Commissioners;

(*b*) an interest belonging to Her Majesty in right of the Duchy of Lancaster, and the Chancellor of the Duchy;

(*c*) an interest belonging to the Duchy of Cornwall, and such person as the Duke of Cornwall or the possessor for the time being of the Duchy appoints;

(*d*) any other interest belonging to a government department or held on behalf of Her Majesty for the purposes of a government department, and the Minister in charge of that department.

(3) The restriction imposed by section 3(2) of the Crown Estate Act 1961 on the term for which a lease may be granted by the Crown Estate Commissioners shall not apply where the lease is granted by way of extension of a long tenancy at a low rent and it appears to the Crown Estate Commissioners that, if the

tenancy were not a tenancy from the Crown, there would be a right to an extended lease under this Part of this Act.

(4) Where, in the case of land belonging to Her Majesty in right of the Duchy of Lancaster or to the Duchy of Cornwall, it appears to the appropriate authority that a tenant under a long lease at a low rent would, if the tenancy were not a tenancy from the Crown, be entitled to an extended lease under this Part of this Act, then a lease corresponding to that to which the tenant would be so entitled may be granted to take effect wholly or partly out of the Crown interest by the same person and with the same formalities as in the case of any other lease of such land.

(5) In the case of land belonging to the Duchy of Cornwall, the purposes authorised by section 8 of the Duchy of Cornwall Management Act 1863 for the advancement of parts of such gross sums as are therein mentioned shall include the payment to tenants of sums corresponding to those which, if the tenancies were not tenancies from the Crown, would be payable by way of compensation under section 17 above. **[216]**

NOTES

See further the Housing Act 1985, ss 172-175.

33A. Exclusion of certain shared ownership leases

[The provisions of Schedule 4A to this Act shall have effect to exclude certain shared ownership leases from the operation of this Part of this Act.] **[217]**

NOTES

Commencement: To be appointed.

Prospectively added with savings by the Housing and Planning Act 1986, s 18, Sch 4, paras 5, 11, as from a day to be appointed.

ENFRANCHISEMENT OF EXTENSION OF LONG LEASEHOLDS

Transitional

34. Tenancies terminated since 8th December 1964, or subject to early termination

(1) Where, before or after the passing of this Act, but after the 8th December 1964, a long tenancy at a low rent of a house ("the former long tenancy") has terminated at or after its term date, then subject to the provisions of this section there shall be treated for purposes of this Part of this Act as a long tenancy at a low rent—

(*a*) any tenancy which was granted by way of continuation of the former tenancy but is not or was not a tenancy at a low rent; and

(*b*) any statutory tenancy arising by virtue of Part I of the Landlord and Tenant Act 1954 or of the Rent Acts on the termination of the former tenancy or of any tenancy granted (or treated by implication of law as granted) by way of continuation of it.

For purposes of this subsection a tenancy granted to the tenant of the house under a tenancy granted by way of continuation of the former long tenancy, or to the person retaining possession of the house by virtue of any such statutory tenancy as aforesaid, shall be regarded as granted by way of continuation of the former long tenancy.

(2) A notice of a person's desire to have the freehold or an extended lease of a house and premises, if given by virtue of subsection (1) above, may be given

before the appointed day, but shall be of no effect if given more than three months after the day this Act is passed.

(3) A notice of a person's desire to have the freehold or an extended lease of a house and premises may also be given before the appointed day if it is given in respect of a tenancy of which the term date falls within twelve months after the day this Act is passed, or which is to be or can be terminated within those twelve months either by notice given by the landlord or by the operation of section 26 or 28 of the Landlord and Tenant Act 1954 in relation to a request or agreement for a new tenancy made before this Act is passed.

(4) Where by virtue of subsection (2) or (3) above a notice is given before the appointed day—

(*a*) it shall contain the particulars required by Schedule 3 to this Act, but need not be in the prescribed form;
(*b*) if it is given in respect of a sub-tenancy, copies of it shall be served on the same persons other than the recipient as in the case of a notice given after the appointed day;
(*c*) the landlord shall not be required to take any further proceedings before the appointed day and no notice in reply shall be required earlier than one month after the appointed day, but subject to that and to section 35 below, as from the appointed day, the notice shall have effect as if all the provisions of this Part of this Act had come into force on the day it is passed.

(5) In relation to a notice given by virtue of subsection (2) or (3) above, Part I of Schedule 3 to this Act shall have effect from the day it is passed; but in a case where (by virtue of those subsections or otherwise) a person gives notice, within three months after that day, of his desire to have the freehold or an extended lease and does so in respect of a tenancy falling within subsection (1) above or of any such tenancy as is mentioned in subsection (3), Part I of Schedule 3 shall not have effect to invalidate the notice by reason either—

(*a*) that it is given more than two months after a landlord's notice terminating the tenancy has been given under section 4 or 25 of the Landlord and Tenant Act 1954; or
(*b*) that it is given after a tenant has made a request for a new tenancy under section 26 of that Act, or is given during the subsistence of an agreement for a future tenancy to which section 28 of that Act applies, not being an agreement entered into after the passing of this Act.

(6) Where subsection (1) above applies to a tenancy, this Part of this Act shall have effect in relation to any claim by the tenant to acquire the freehold or an extended lease, and in relation to any new tenancy granted under section 14 above, subject to the following modifications:—

(*a*) the provisions to be contained in a conveyance in accordance with section 10 above, or in a lease granting a new tenancy under section 14, shall be determined by reference to the terms of the former long tenancy as they applied immediately before its termination and to the circumstances generally of that tenancy; and
(*b*) references to the term date of the existing tenancy, or to the original term date, shall have effect as references to the term date of the former long tenancy.

(7) Where a statutory tenancy of a house has arisen by virtue of Part I of the Landlord and Tenant Act 1954 and the terms of the tenancy include the carrying out of initial repairs, but (before or after it arose) a notice is by virtue of this

section given by the tenant of his desire to have the freehold or an extended lease, then the rights and obligations under the statutory tenancy in relation to initial repairs (together with any order of the court made with respect thereto before the relevant time) shall be suspended during the currency of the notice, except in so far as the court on the application of the landlord or of the tenant may otherwise order; and—

(*a*) if in pursuance of the notice the tenant acquires the freehold, the price payable for the house and premises shall be adjusted as may be proper (regard being had to the rent paid and to be paid under the statutory tenancy) so as to take account of any initial repairs carried out by the landlord before the relevant time, of any order or agreement for the further carrying out by him of any initial repairs thereafter and of any payments for tenant's accrued repairs received by the landlord; or

(*b*) if in pursuance of the notice the tenant acquires an extended lease, there shall be payable by the tenant to the landlord as if it were due under the statutory tenancy on its termination such sum, if any, as may be proper so as to take account of the matters aforesaid (regard being had to the rent paid under the statutory tenancy and to any terms of the new tenancy relating to repairs).

(8) Where a statutory tenancy of a house has arisen as mentioned in subsection (1)(*b*) above, and (before or after it arose) a notice is by virtue of this section given by the tenant of his desire to have the freehold or an extended lease, then so long as the notice has effect the tenancy shall continue, and on the tenant's death or bankruptcy shall devolve, as a contractual tenancy would, and the rights and obligations arising from the notice shall continue and devolve accordingly; but this shall not affect any right to retain possession by virtue of the Rent Acts which arises on a death. **[218]**

NOTES

See further the Housing Act 1985, ss 172-175.

Rent Acts: see now Rent Act 1977.

35. Proceedings and orders under Landlord and Tenant Act 1954

(1) Where a person's notice of his desire to have the freehold or an extended lease under this Part of this Act is given as mentioned in section 34(5)(*a*) or (*b*) above, but has effect by virtue of that subsection, then the following provisions of this section shall apply; and in those provisions "claim" and "claimant" mean that notice and the person giving it for the time being entitled to the rights under it of the person giving it.

(2) On the making of the claim and, if any application has been made to the court under the Landlord and Tenant Act 1954 in respect of a notice given by the landlord or a request by the claimant for a new tenancy, on the claimant lodging a copy of the claim in the court, any such notice or request under that Act and anything done in pursuance thereof (including any such application and any order resulting therefrom) shall cease to have effect, except as otherwise provided by this section:

Provided that this shall not affect any order as to costs (whether of proceedings in the court or of any appeal) or preclude the making of such an order.

(3) The making of the claim shall not affect the operation—

(*a*) of any landlord's notice containing proposals for a statutory tenancy where all the terms of the statutory tenancy have been agreed or determined in accordance with section 7 of the Landlord and Tenant Act 1954; or

(*b*) of any order of the court under section 29 of that Act for the grant of a new tenancy; or

(*c*) of any agreement for a future tenancy to which section 28 of that Act applies;

but subject to the provisions of that Act and of section 34 above, the notice, order or agreement, and any statutory tenancy or tenancy arising or granted under it, shall remain unaffected by the claim unless and until effect is given to the claim.

(4) Where either—

(*a*) the landlord has made an application to the court for, or has obtained, an order for the claimant to give up possession on the ground specified in section 12(1)(*a*) (redevelopment) of the Landlord and Tenant Act 1954, and the claim is for an extended lease; or

(*b*) the landlord has made an application to the court for, or has obtained, such an order on the ground specified in paragraph 1(*e*) (residence for landlord or his family) of Schedule 3 to that Act;

then if the landlord gives notice of his willingness to pay compensation and lodges a copy of it in the court, the application may be proceeded with or, as the case may be, the order shall have effect as if the claim had not been made.

(5) Where either—

(*a*) the court has refused an order for the grant of a new tenancy under Part II of the Landlord and Tenant Act 1954 on the ground specified in section 30(1)(*f*) (redevelopment), and the claim is for an extended lease; or

(*b*) the court has refused an order as aforesaid in accordance with section 30(1)(*g*) on the ground of the landlord's intention to occupy the holding as his residence;

then if the landlord gives notice of his willingness to pay compensation, the tenancy shall terminate in accordance with Part II of that Act as if the claim had not been made.

(6) Where the claimant's tenancy is terminated by virtue of subsection (4) or (5) above, and apart from those subsections (and sections 17 and 18 above) he would have been entitled to acquire the freehold or an extended lease in pursuance of the claim, he shall be entitled to recover from the landlord, in lieu of any compensation under the Landlord and Tenant Act 1927 or under section 37 of the Landlord and Tenant Act 1954, the like compensation as is payable where a claim to acquire the freehold or an extended lease is overridden under section 17 or 18 above.

(7) If the claimant's right to compensation under subsection (6) above is disputed, he may apply to the court for an order declaring that he is entitled to the compensation; and any compensation under that subsection shall in default of agreement be assessed, and may be recovered, in like manner as compensation under section 17 or 18 above.

(8) References in this section to the landlord giving notice of his willingness to pay compensation shall be construed as references to his giving to the claimant (whether before or after the making of the claim) written notice that he is willing to pay compensation in accordance with subsection (6) above if so required by that subsection; but a notice of a landlord's willingness to pay

compensation shall be of no effect if it is given after the tenancy in question would have terminated but for the claim, or if it is given more than one month after the day on which the claim is made.

(9) In this section references to the landlord shall be construed as references to the landlord proceeding under Part I or II, as the case may be, of the Landlord and Tenant Act 1954. **[219]**

NOTES

See further the Housing Act 1985, ss 172-175.

36. Relief in respect of mortgages etc on landlord's estate

(1) Where at the passing of this Act—

(*a*) a house is held on a long tenancy not having more than twenty years unexpired, or on a long tenancy capable of being determined within twenty years by notice given by the landlord; and

(*b*) the estate of the immediate or a superior landlord is charged to secure payment of any sum (otherwise than by way of rentcharge), whether or not the landlord is personally liable as principal or otherwise for the payment of that sum;

then on an application under subsection (2) or (3) below the court may make such order authorised by the subsection as the court thinks proper for the purpose of avoiding or mitigating any financial hardship that might otherwise be caused by the rights conferred on tenants by this Part of this Act.

(2) In any of the following cases, that is to say,—

(*a*) where the landlord proposes during the tenancy (including any extension thereof under this Act) to sell or realise any property which is subject to the charge, or a tenant of the house has given notice under this Part of this Act of his desire to have the freehold;

(*b*) where during the tenancy (including any such extension) the person entitled to the benefit of the charge has taken any steps to enforce the charge or demanded payment of the sum thereby secured or, if the house or any other property subject to the charge is subject also to another charge created or arising before the commencement of this Part of this Act, a person entitled to the benefit of the other charge has taken any steps to enforce the other charge or demanded payment of the sum thereby secured;

the court may on application of the landlord make an order providing for all or any of the following:—

(i) for discharging or modifying any liability in respect of the sum secured by the charge, whether of the landlord or of persons liable jointly with him or as surety for him;

(ii) for discharging or modifying the terms of the charge whether as respects the house or any other property subject to the charge, or the terms of any collateral charge;

(iii) for restricting the exercise of any right or remedy in respect of any such liability or charge.

(3) In any of the cases mentioned in subsection (2)(*a*) and (*b*) above the court may on the application of the person entitled to the benefit of the charge make an order providing for all or any of the following:—

(*a*) for discharging or modifying the terms of any prior charge, whether as respects the house or any other property subject to the charge;

(*b*) for restricting the exercise of any right or remedy in respect of any prior charge on the house or other property subject to the charge.

(4) Any order under this section may be made either unconditionally or subject to such terms and conditions, including conditions with respect to the payment of money, as the court may think just and equitable to impose.

(5) Where steps are taken in a court other than the county court to enforce a charge or recover any sum thereby secured, that other court shall have the like powers under this section in relation to that or any other charge as the county court would have in consequence of those steps being taken or, if an application under this section is pending in the county court, may on such terms as the other court thinks just suspend the proceedings for the enforcement of the charge or recovery of the said sum or direct that they be transferred to the county court.
[220]

NOTES
See further the Housing Act 1985, ss 172-175.

Construction

37. Interpretation of Part I

(1) For the purposes of this Part of this Act—

(*a*) "the appointed day" means the day appointed for the coming into force of the provisions of this Part of this Act other than sections 34 to 36, and references to the commencement of this Part of this Act shall be construed as referring to the commencement of those provisions;
(*b*) "incumbrance" and "tenant's incumbrance" have, subject to section 12(8) above, the meanings assigned to them by section 8;
(*c*) "notice to quit" means a notice to terminate a tenancy (whether a periodical tenancy or a tenancy for a term of years certain) given in accordance with the provisions (whether express or implied) of that tenancy;
(*d*) "relevant time" means, in relation to a person's claim to acquire the freehold or an extended lease under this Part of this Act, the time when he gives notice in accordance with this Act of his desire to have it;
(*e*) . . . ;
(*f*) "tenancy" means a tenancy at law or in equity, but does not include a tenancy at will, nor any interest created by way of security and liable to termination by the exercise of any right of redemption or otherwise, nor any interest created by way of trust under a settlement, and "demise" shall be construed accordingly;
(*g*) "term date", in relation to a tenancy granted for a term of years certain, means the date of expiry of that term, and "extended term date" and "original term date" mean respectively the term date of a tenancy with and without an extension under this Part of this Act.

(2) A tenancy to which section 19(2) of the Landlord and Tenant Act 1954 applies shall be treated for purposes of this Part of this Act as granted to expire at the date which is the term date for purposes of that Act (that is to say, the first date after the commencement of that Act on which, apart from that Act, the tenancy could have been brought to an end by notice to quit given by the landlord).

(3) Subject to subsection (2) above, where under section 3(2) of this Act a tenancy created or arising as a tenancy from year to year or other periodical tenancy is to be treated as a long tenancy, the term date of that tenancy shall be taken to be the date (if any) at which the tenancy is to terminate by virtue of a notice to quit given by the landlord before the relevant time, or else the earliest date at which it could at that time (in accordance with its terms and apart from any enactment) be brought to an end by a notice to quit given by the landlord.

(4) Subject to subsection (2) above, in the case of a tenancy granted to continue as a periodical tenancy after the expiration of a term of years certain, or to continue as a periodical tenancy if not terminated at the expiration of such a term, any question whether the tenancy is at any time to be treated for purposes of this Part of this Act as a long tenancy, and (if so) with what term date, shall be determined as it would be if there had been two tenancies, as follows—

(*a*) one granted to expire at the earliest time (at or after the expiry of the said term of years) at which the tenancy could (in accordance with its terms and apart from any enactment) be brought to an end by notice to quit given by the landlord; and

(*b*) the other granted to commence at the expiration of the first (and not being one to which subsection (2) above applies).

(5) References in this Part of this Act to a tenant occupying a house as his residence shall be construed in accordance with section 1(2) above; but no reference in this Part of this Act to a person occupying property as his residence shall be taken to extend to any occupation of a company or other artificial person nor, where the tenant is a corporation sole, shall the corporator, while in occupation, be treated as occupying as tenant.

(6) [Section 25(1), (2), (4) of the Rent Act 1977] shall apply to the ascertainment for purposes of this Part of this Act of the rateable value of a house and premises or any other property as they apply to the ascertainment of that of a dwelling-house for purposes of that Act.

(7) For purposes of this Part of this Act an order of a court is to be treated as becoming final—

(*a*) if not appealed against, on the expiration of the time for bringing an appeal; or

(*b*) if appealed against and not set aside in consequence of the appeal, at the time when the appeal and any further appeal is disposed of by the determination of it and the expiration of the time for bringing a further appeal (if any) or by its being abandoned or otherwise ceasing to have effect. **[221]**

NOTES

Sub-s (1): words omitted repealed by the Rent Act 1968, s 117(5), Sch 17.
Sub-s (6): amended by the Rent Act 1977, s 155, Sch 23, para 44.
See further the Housing Act 1985, ss 172-175.

PART II

AMENDMENTS OF OTHER ACTS

38. Modification of right to possession under Landlord and Tenant Act 1954

(1) The grounds on which under section 13 of the Landlord and Tenant Act 1954 a landlord may apply to the court for possession of property comprised in

a tenancy (and which may accordingly under section 4 be specified in a landlord's notice to resume possession), in the case of applications made after the commencement of this Part of this Act, shall not include the ground mentioned in section 12(1)(*a*) (redevelopment), except where the landlord seeking to obtain possession is a body to which section 28 above applies and the property is required for relevant development within the meaning of section 28; but on any application by such a body under section 13 of that Act for possession on that ground a certificate given by a Minister of the Crown as provided by section 28(1) above shall be conclusive that the property is so required.

(2) In section 57 of the Landlord and Tenant Act 1954 (under which a tenant's rights under Part II of that Act are curtailed if an authority within the section is the landlord or a superior landlord and obtains a certificate similar to that under section 28 above) references to a local authority shall apply to any body to which section 28 above applies and which is not otherwise within the said section 57.

(3) For purposes of this section, section 28(5) to (8) above shall have effect from the commencement of this Part of this Act. **[222]**

39. Application of Rent Acts to long tenancies and adaptation of Landlord and Tenant Act 1954

(1) Section 21(2) of the Rent Act 1957 (which applies Part I of the Landlord and Tenant Act 1954 to long tenancies not at a low rent) shall cease to have effect; and—

(*a–c*) . . .

(2) Subsection (1) above shall have effect subject to the adaptations of Part I of the Landlord and Tenant Act 1954, and of the [Rent Act 1968] as it applies to a statutory tenancy arising by virtue of the said Part I, which are made by Schedule 5 to this Act; and the transitional and supplementary provisions made by that Schedule shall have effect in relation to subsection (1) above and to statutory tenancies so arising.

(3) . . . **[223]**

NOTES

Sub-s (1): words omitted repealed by the Rent Act 1968, s 117(5), Sch 17, and the Counter-Inflation Act 1973, s 23(3), Sch 6.

Sub-s (2): amended by the Rent Act 1968, s 117(2), Sch 15.

Sub-s (3): repealed by the Statute Law (Repeals) Act 1976.

Rent Act 1968: see now Rent Act 1977.

40. Amendments of Places of Worship (Enfranchisement) Act 1920

(1)-(6) . . .

(7) In accordance with the provisions of this section the Places of Worship (Enfranchisement) Act 1920 shall, subject to subsection (8) below, have effect as set out in Schedule 6 to this Act.

(8) This section and the repeals made by Part II of Schedule 7 to this Act shall not affect the operation of the Places of Worship (Enfranchisement) Act 1920 where an interest has been acquired, or notice to treat for its acquisition has been served, under that Act before this section comes into force, except that section 4 of that Act shall cease to have effect for any purpose. **[224]**

NOTES

Sub-ss (1)-(6): amend the Places of Worship (Enfranchisement) Act 1920.

41. Short title, repeals, extent and commencement

(1) This Act may be cited as the Leasehold Reform Act 1967.

(2) The enactments mentioned in Schedule 7 to this Act are hereby repealed to the extent specified in the third column of that Schedule, but subject to the savings mentioned at the end of Parts I and II of the Schedule.

(3) This Act shall not extend to Scotland or Northern Ireland.

(4) Sections 34 to 36 of this Act shall come into force on the day it is passed; and, subject to section 34, the other provisions of Part I shall come into force on such day as the Minister of Housing and Local Government and the Secretary of State may appoint by order made by them jointly by statutory instrument, which shall be laid before Parliament after being made.

(5) Part II of this Act shall come into force at the end of one month following the day on which this Act is passed. **[225]**

SCHEDULES

SCHEDULE 1

Section 5

ENFRANCHISEMENT AND EXTENSION BY SUB-TENANTS

General

1.—(1) Where a person (in this Schedule referred to as "the claimant") gives notice of his desire to have the freehold or an extended lease of a house and premises under Part I of this Act, and does so in respect of a sub-tenancy (in this Schedule referred to as "the tenancy in possession"), then except as otherwise provided by this Schedule—

(*a*) the rights and obligations of the landlord under Part I of this Act shall, so far as their interests are affected, be rights and obligations respectively of the estate owner in respect of the fee simple and of each of the persons in whom is vested a concurrent tenancy superior to the tenancy in possession (and references to the landlord shall apply accordingly); and

(*b*) the proceedings arising out of the notice, whether for resisting or giving effect to the claim to acquire the freehold or extended lease, shall be conducted, on behalf of all the persons referred to in (*a*) above, by and through that one of them who is identified by this Schedule as "the reversioner".

(2) Where there is a tenancy reversionary on a tenancy in respect of which a person gives notice as aforesaid, then (except in so far as special provision is made for such a reversionary tenancy) this Schedule shall apply as if the reversionary tenancy were a concurrent tenancy intermediate between the tenancy in possession and any interest superior to it.

(3) In the following provisions of this Schedule the persons for whom the reversioner is by this paragraph authorised to act are referred to as "other landlords"; and in this Schedule references to superior interests mean the estate in fee simple and any tenancy superior (or treated by sub-paragraph (2) above as superior) to the inferior interest in question.

2. Subject to paragraph 3 below, "the reversioner" shall be—

(*a*) if any person has a tenancy of the house carrying an expectation of possession of thirty years or more, that person or, if there is more than one, that one of them to whose tenancy the other tenancies are superior;

(*b*) if there is no such tenancy, the estate owner in respect of the fee simple of the house.

3.—(1) If it appears to the court, on an application made by any of the persons having an interest superior to the tenancy in possession,—

(*a*) that the respective interests of those persons, the absence or incapacity of the person designated by paragraph 2 above or other special circumstances require that one of the other landlords should act as the reversioner instead of that person; or

(*b*) that the person so designated is unwilling to act as the reversioner, and that one of the other landlords could appropriately replace him and is willing to do so; or

(*c*) that by reason of complications in the title paragraph 2 above is inapplicable;

the court may, on such terms and conditions as it thinks fit, appoint such person as it thinks fit to be the reversioner.

(2) The court may also, on the application of any of the other landlords or of the claimant, remove the reversioner and appoint another person in his place, if it appears to the court proper to do so by reason of any delay or default, actual or apprehended, on the part of the reversioner.

4.—(1) Without prejudice to the generality of paragraph 1 above, the reversioner may on behalf and in the name of the other landlords—

(*a*) execute any conveyance to give effect to section 8 of this Act, or any lease to give effect to section 14; and

(*b*) take or defend any legal proceedings under Part I of this Act in respect of matters arising out of the claimant's notice.

(2) Subject to paragraphs 5 and 6 below, in relation to all matters within the authority given to him by this Schedule the reversioner's acts shall be binding on the other landlords and on their interests in the house and premises or any other property; but in the event of dispute either the reversioner or any of the other landlords may apply to the court for directions as to the manner in which he should act on the matter in dispute.

(3) If any of the other landlords cannot be found, or his identity cannot be ascertained, the reversioner shall apply to the court for directions, and the court may make such order in the matter as it thinks proper with a view to giving effect to the rights of the claimant and protecting the interests of other persons; but subject to the directions of the court—

(*a*) the reversioner shall proceed as in other cases;

(*b*) a conveyance or lease executed by the reversioner on behalf of that landlord by such description as will identify the interest intended to be conveyed or bound shall be of the same effect as if executed in his name;

(*c*) if the freehold is to be conveyed to the claimant, any sum paid as the price for that landlord's interest shall be paid into court.

(4) The reversioner, if he acts in good faith and with reasonable care and diligence, shall not be liable to any of the other landlords for any loss or damage caused by any act or omission in the exercise or intended exercise of the authority given to him by this Schedule.

5.—(1) Notwithstanding anything in paragraph 4(2) above, any of the other landlords shall be entitled, if he so desires, to be separately represented in any legal proceedings in which his title to any property comes in question, or in any legal proceedings relating to the price payable for the house and premises under section 9 of this Act.

(2) For the purpose of deducing, evidencing or verifying his title to any property, any of the other landlords, on giving written notice to the reversioner and to the claimant, may deal directly with the claimant, if he objects to disclosing his title to the reversioner; and he shall deal directly with the claimant if the claimant by written notice given to him and to the reversioner so requires.

(3) For the purpose of agreeing the price payable for his interest under section 9 of this Act, any of the other landlords, on giving written notice to the reversioner and to the claimant, may deal directly with the claimant; and whether he does that or not, he may require the reversioner to apply to [a leasehold valuation tribunal] for the price to be determined by [a leasehold valuation tribunal].

(4) Any of the other landlords shall be entitled to require that the price payable for his interest (or so much of it as it payable to him) shall be paid by the claimant to him or to a person authorised by him to receive it, instead of to the reversioner; but if, after being given proper notice of the time and place fixed for completion with the claimant, neither he nor a person so authorised attends to receive payment, and he has not made, and notified the reversioner of, other arrangements with the claimant to receive payment, the reversioner shall be authorised to receive it for him and the reversioner's written receipt for the amount payable shall be a complete discharge to the claimant.

(5) It shall be the duty of each of the other landlords—

(*a*) subject to sub-paragraphs (2) and (3) above, to give the reversioner all such information and assistance as he may reasonably require; and

(*b*) after being given proper notice of the time and place fixed for completion with the claimant (if the claimant is acquiring the freehold), to ensure that all deeds and other documents that ought on his part to be delivered to the claimant on completion are available for the purpose, including in the case of registered land the land certificate and any other documents necessary to perfect the claimant's title;

and, if any of the other landlords fails to do so, he shall indemnify the reversioner against any liability incurred by the reversioner in consequence of the failure.

(6) Each of the other landlords shall make such contribution as may be just to the costs and expenses incurred by the reversioner and not recoverable or not recovered from the claimant.

6.—(1) The authority given by this Schedule to the reversioner shall not extend to the bringing of proceedings under section 17 or 18 or this Act on behalf of any of the other landlords, or preclude any of the other landlords from bringing proceedings under that section on his own behalf; and (without prejudice to the operation of paragraph 1(2) above) a person entitled to a tenancy reversionary on the tenancy in possession may make an application under section 17 (by virtue of subsection (4)) or section 18 as a landlord.

(2) Sections 29 and 30 of this Act shall apply, and apply only, where the authority entitled to require the covenant under the section is the estate owner in respect of the fee simple and there is no tenancy carrying an expectation of possession of thirty years or more.

(3) For purposes of section 3(6) of this Act separate tenancies shall be deemed to be tenancies with the same landlord if the immediate landlord is the same.

Enfranchisement

7.—(1) Where a conveyance is executed to give effect to section 8 of this Act—

(*a*) section 10 shall have effect in relation to rights and restrictions arising by virtue of any tenancy superior to the tenancy in possession (or by virtue of an agreement collateral to such a tenancy), so far as they are directly or indirectly to the benefit of or enforceable against the claimant during the tenancy in possession, as if they arose by virtue of that tenancy; and

(*b*) [subject to paragraph 7A] a separate price shall be payable in accordance with section 9 for each of the interests superior to the tenancy in possession, and . . . section 9 shall apply to the computation of that price with such modifications as are appropriate to relate it to a sale of the interest in question subject to any tenancies intermediate between that interest and the tenancy in possession, together with tenant's incumbrances relative to those tenancies; and

(*c*) so much of section 11 as relates to the application of the purchase price for redemption of rentcharges . . . shall apply only to the price payable for the estate in fee simple; and

(*d*) so much of sections 12 and 13 as relates to the application of the price payable in or towards redemption of charges shall apply separately to the price payable for each interest together with the relative charges.

(2) Where by reason of section 11(2) of this Act it is necessary to make (otherwise than out of the price payable for the house and premises) any payment for the redemption of a rentcharge . . . the reversioner, if he is not the landlord liable or primarily liable in respect of the rentcharge . . ., shall not be required to make that payment otherwise than out of money made available for the purpose by that landlord, and it shall be the duty of that landlord to provide for the redemption; and similarly where by reason of section 12(8) proviso of this Act it is necessary to discharge the house and premises from a charge affecting the interest of any landlord.

[7A.—(1) The price payable for a minor superior tenancy shall be calculated (except where it has been determined by agreement or otherwise before this paragraph comes into force) by applying the formula set out in sub-paragraph (5) instead of in accordance with section 9.

(2) "A minor superior tenancy" means a superior tenancy having an expectation of possession of not more than one month and in respect of which the profit rent is not more than £5 per year.

(3) "Profit rent" means an amount equal to that of the rent payable under the tenancy on which the minor superior tenancy is in immediate reversion, less that of the rent payable under the minor superior tenancy.

(4) Where the minor superior tenancy or that on which it is in immediate reversion comprises property other than the house and premises, the reference in sub-paragraph (3) to the rent payable under it means so much of that rent as is apportioned to the house and premises.

(5) The formula is—

$$P = £\frac{R}{Y} - \frac{R}{Y(1+Y)^n}$$

where—

P = the price payable;

R = the profit rent;

Y = the yield (expressed as a decimal fraction) from 2½ per cent. Consolidated Stock;

n = the period, expressed in years (taking any part of a year as a whole year) which the minor superior tenancy would have to run if it were not extinguished by enfranchisement.

(6) In calculating the yield from 2½ per cent. Consolidated Stock, the price of that stock shall be taken to be the middle market price at the close of business on the last trading day in the week before the tenant gives notice in accordance with this Act of his desire to have the freehold.]

8 . . .

9. Nothing in this Schedule shall be taken to entitle the claimant to give notice under section 9(3) of this Act of his inability or unwillingness to acquire particular interests superior to the tenancy in possession, but any such notice shall extend to all those interests.

Extension

10.—(1) Where a lease is executed to give effect to section 14 of this Act, then except as provided by paragraph 11 below the new tenancy shall be granted by the landlord having an interest sufficient in point of duration which is not superior to another such interest.

(2) Subject to paragraph 11 below, the lease shall have effect for the creation of the new tenancy, and for the operation of the rights and obligations conferred and imposed by it, as if there had been a surrender and re-grant of any subsisting tenancy intermediate between the interest of the landlord granting the new tenancy and the tenancy in

possession, and the covenants and other provisions of the lease shall be framed and take effect accordingly.

(3) If there is no one landlord having such an interest in the whole of the house and premises as is referred to in sub-paragraph (1) above, then those having the appropriate interests in separate parts thereof shall instead grant the tenancy; and where it is necessary in accordance with this sub-paragraph for more than one landlord to join in granting the new tenancy, the lease shall have effect in accordance with sub-paragraph (2) above, but as if they had been jointly entitled to their interests and had become separately entitled by assignments taking effect immediately after the lease.

(4) The lease shall give effect to section 15(2) of this Act on the basis that the references there to the landlord include the landlord granting the new tenancy, the immediate landlord of whom the new tenancy will be held and any intermediate landlord, and shall give effect to section 15(3) on the basis that account is to be taken of obligations imposed on any of those landlords by virtue of the new tenancy or any superior tenancy; and section 16(4) of this Act shall apply on the basis that the reference there to the tenant's landlord includes the immediate landlord of whom the new tenancy will be held and all superior landlords, including any superior to the landlord granting the new tenancy.

11.—(1) Where a tenancy in the house and premises superior to the tenancy in possession is vested in the claimant or a trustee for him, the lease under section 14 of this Act shall include an actual surrender of that superior tenancy without a re-grant, and it shall accordingly be disregarded for purposes of paragraph 10 above.

(2) Where, apart from this provision, the effect of the lease under section 14 of this Act would be, as regards any tenancy superior to the new tenancy,—

(*a*) that the rent payable under that superior tenancy would be equal to or more than the rent payable under the tenancy on which it would be in immediate reversion (regard being had to the operation of this sub-paragraph in relation to any other tenancy); or

(*b*) that the difference between those rents would not be more than four pounds a year;

then the person entitled to that superior tenancy may by written notice given to his immediate landlord and, if neither of them is the reversioner, to the reversioner require that the lease shall include an actual surrender by him of his tenancy without a re-grant.

(3) Any person entitled to a tenancy superior to the new tenancy may by the like notice require that the lease shall confer on him the right to surrender his tenancy if by reason of any revision of the rent payable under the claimant's new tenancy (together with any consequent surrender under this provision of tenancies intermediate between the superior tenancy and that new tenancy) the rent payable under the superior tenancy will not thereafter be less by more than four pounds a year than the rent payable under the tenancy on which it will be in immediate reversion.

(4) Where a landlord required apart from this sub-paragraph (or by virtue of this sub-paragraph as it operates in relation to another landlord) to grant the new tenancy would do so by virtue of a tenancy in respect of which he claims, by the like notice, to have the benefit of sub-paragraph (2) or (3) above, he shall for purposes of paragraph 10 above be replaced, subject to any further operation of this sub-paragraph, by the next superior landlord.

(5) References in this paragraph to the rent payable under a tenancy mean, in relation to a tenancy comprising property other than the house and premises, so much of that rent as is apportionable to the house and premises, and any surrender or provision for the surrender of such a tenancy in accordance with this paragraph shall be limited to the house and premises.

12.—(1) No provision of any tenancy prohibiting, restricting or otherwise relating to a sub-demise by the tenant shall have effect with reference to any lease executed to give effect to section 14 of this Act.

(2) Where by reason of section 14(4) proviso of this Act it is necessary to make any

payment to discharge the house and premises from a charge affecting the interest of any landlord, the reversioner, if he is not the landlord liable or primarily liable in respect of the charge, shall not be required to make that payment otherwise than out of money made available for the purpose by that landlord, and it shall be the duty of that landlord to provide for the charge being discharged.

Supplementary

13.—(1) For purposes of this Schedule the expectation of possession carried by a tenancy is the expectation which it carries at the relevant time of possession after the tenancy in possession, on the basis that—

(*a*) subject to sub-paragraph (2) below, the tenancy in possession terminates at the relevant time if its term date fell before then, or else terminates at its term date or (in the case of a tenancy which has been extended) its original term date; and

(*b*) a tenancy other than the tenancy in possession terminates at its term date.

(2) In a case where before the relevant time the claimant's immediate landlord had given notice to quit terminating the tenancy in possession at a date earlier than the term date, the date specified in the notice to quit shall be substituted for the date in sub-paragraph (1)(*a*) above.

14.—(1) This Schedule shall apply notwithstanding that the tenancy in possession is a tenancy from the Crown within the meaning of section 33 of this Act; and, where under section 33(1)(*b*) the appropriate authority gives notice that as regards a Crown interest the authority will grant or concur in granting the freehold or an extended lease, then in relation to the Crown interest and the person to whom it belongs this Schedule shall have effect as it has effect in relation to other landlords and their interests, but with the appropriate authority having power to act as reversioner or otherwise for purposes of this Schedule on behalf of that person:

Provided that paragraph 4(1)(*a*) above shall not apply to the execution of a conveyance or lease on behalf of the person to whom a Crown interest belongs.

(2) A conveyance or lease executed in pursuance of paragraph 4(3) above shall be effective notwithstanding that the interest intended to be conveyed or bound is a Crown interest or a tenancy from the Crown. **[226]**

NOTES

Commencement: Before 1 January 1970 (paras 1-7, 8-14); 3 October 1980 (para 7A).

Commencement order: SI 1980 No 1406.

First words omitted repealed by the Housing Act 1980, s 152, Sch 26; other words omitted repealed by the Rentcharges Act 1977, s 17(2), (6), Sch 2; amendments in square brackets made by the Housing Act 1980, ss 141, 142, Schs 21, 22, Part II.

SCHEDULE 2

Sections 17, 18, 20, 21, 23, 25

Provisions Supplementary to Sections 17 and 18 of this Act

1.—(1) This Schedule has effect where a tenant of a house and premises is entitled to be paid compensation under section 17 or 18 of this Act, or would be so entitled on the landlord obtaining an order for possession, or where an application for such an order is dismissed or withdrawn; and for purposes of this Schedule—

(*a*) "application for possession" means a landlord's application under section 17(1) or 18(1); and

(*b*) "order for possession" means an order under section 17(2) or 18(4).

(2) Where the tenancy has not been extended under section 14 of this Act, references in this Schedule to the original term date shall be construed as references to the term date or, in a case where before the relevant time the landlord had given notice to quit terminating the tenancy at a date earlier than the term date, as references to the date specified in the notice to quit.

2.—(1) Where an order for possession is made, the tenancy shall determine, and the compensation payable to the tenant by virtue of the order shall become payable, on such date as may, when the amount of that compensation is known, be fixed by order of the court made on the application either of the landlord or of the tenant.

(2) An order of the court under this paragraph shall not fix a date earlier than the original term date of the tenancy, nor shall it fix a date less than four months or more than twelve months after the date of the order unless the court sees special reason for doing so; and in a case under section 18 of this Act an application to [a leasehold valuation tribunal] to determine the amount of the compensation payable to the tenant shall not be made more than twelve months before the original term date.

(3) In fixing the date the court shall have regard to the conduct of the parties and, in a case under section 17 of this Act, to the extent to which the landlord has made reasonable preparations for proceeding with the redevelopment (including the obtaining of or preparations relating to the obtaining of any requisite permission or consent, whether from any authority whose permission or consent is required under any enactment or from the owner of an interest in any property).

(4) The court may by order direct that the whole or part of the compensation payable to the tenant shall be paid into court, if the court thinks it expedient so to do for the purpose of ensuring that the sum paid is available for meeting charges on the tenant's interest in the house and premises, or for the purpose of division, or for any other purpose.

3.—(1) On the termination of a tenancy under an order for possession there shall terminate also any immediate or derivative sub-tenancy, and the tenant shall be bound to give up possession of the house and premises to the landlord except in so far as he is precluded from doing so by the rights of other persons to retain possession under or by virtue of any enactment.

(2) Where a sub-tenancy of property comprised in the tenancy has been created after the date of the application for possession (or any earlier date when, in the case of an application relying on section 28(1) of this Act, a copy of the Minister's certificate was served on the tenant), then no person shall in respect of that sub-tenancy be entitled under [[subsection (2) of section 137 of the Rent Act 1977] or any enactment (including [subsection (5)] of that section)] applying or extending it, [or under subsection (2) of section 9 of the Rent (Agriculture) Act 1976 as extended by subsection (5) of that section] to retain possession of that property after the termination of the tenancy under the order for possession.

(3) In exercising its jurisdiction under section 17 or 18 of this Act or this Schedule the court shall assume that the landlord, having obtained an order for possession, will not be precluded from obtaining possession by the right of any person to retain possession by virtue of [[Part VII of the Rent Act 1977] or any enactment applying or extending that Part of that Act] [or of the Rent (Agriculture) Act 1976] or otherwise.

(4) A person in occupation of the house and premises or part of them under a sub-tenancy liable to terminate under sub-paragraph (1) above may, with the leave of the court, appear and be heard on any application for possession or application under paragraph 2 above.

4. Where an order has been made under paragraph 2 above, the court making the order or another county court shall have jurisdiction to hear and determine any proceedings brought by virtue of the order to recover possession of the property or to recover the compensation, notwithstanding that by reason of the value of the property or the amount of the compensation the proceedings are not within the jurisdiction conferred on county courts apart from this provision.

5.—(1) The amount payable to a tenant, by virtue of an order for possession, by way of compensation for the loss of the house and premises shall be the amount which, if sections 17 and 18 of this Act had not been passed, the house and premises, if sold in the open market by a willing seller, might at the date when the order for possession becomes final be expected to realise, on the assumption that the vendor was selling the tenancy, and was selling—

(*a*) subject to the rights of any person who will on the termination of the tenancy be entitled to retain possession as against the landlord, but otherwise with vacant possession; and

(*b*) subject to any subsisting incumbrances which will not terminate with the tenancy and for which during the continuance of the tenancy the tenant is liable without having a right to be indemnified by the landlord, but otherwise free of incumbrances; and

(*c*) subject to any restriction which would be required (in addition to any imposed by the terms of the tenancy) to limit the uses of the house and premises to those to which they have been put since the commencement of the tenancy and to preclude the erection of any new dwelling-house or any other building not ancillary to the house as a dwelling-house;

but there shall be left out of account any value attaching to the right to acquire the freehold under Part I of this Act.

(2) The compensation payable in respect of a tenancy which has not been extended under section 14 of this Act shall be computed as if the tenancy was to be so extended.

6.—(1) Part I of the Landlord and Tenant Act 1927 (compensation for improvements on termination of business tenancies) shall not apply on the termination of the tenancy or any sub-tenancy in accordance with this Schedule; and a request for a new tenancy under section 26 of the Landlord and Tenant Act 1954 in respect of the tenancy or any sub-tenancy shall be of no effect if made after the application for possession, or shall cease to have effect on the making of that application.

(2) Where a sub-tenancy terminating with the tenancy in accordance with paragraph 3 above is one to which Part II of the Landlord and Tenant Act 1954 applies, the compensation payable to the tenant shall be divided between him and the sub-tenant in such proportions as may be just, regard being had to their respective interests in the house and premises and to any loss arising from the termination of those interests and not incurred by imprudence.

(3) Where the amount of the compensation payable to the tenant is agreed between him and the landlord without the consent of a sub-tenant entitled under sub-paragraph (2) above to a share in the compensation, and is shown by the sub-tenant to be less than might reasonably have been obtained by the tenant, the sub-tenant shall be entitled under sub-paragraph (2) above to recover from the tenant such increased share as may be just.

7.—(1) The landlord shall not be concerned with the application of the amount payable to the tenant by way of compensation under an order for possession, but (subject to any statutory requirements as to payment of capital money arising under a settlement or a disposition on trust for sale and to any order under paragraph 2(4) above for payment into court) the written receipt of the tenant shall be a complete discharge for the amount payable.

(2) The landlord shall be entitled to deduct from the amount so payable to the tenant—

(*a*) the amount of any sum payable by way of rent or recoverable as rent in respect of the house and premises up to the termination of the tenancy; and

(*b*) the amount of any other sums due and payable by the tenant to the landlord under or in respect of the tenancy or any agreement collateral thereto.

(3) Where the tenancy is held on trust for sale, and compensation is paid in respect of it in accordance with section 17 or 18 of this Act (whether possession is obtained under that section or without any application for possession), the sum received shall be dealt with as if it were proceeds of sale arising under the trust.

8.—(1) Where a landlord makes an application for possession, and it is made to appear to the court that in relation to matters arising out of that application (including the giving up of possession of the house and premises or the payment of compensation) the landlord or the tenant has been guilty of any unreasonable delay or default, the court may—

(*a*) by order revoke or vary, and direct repayment of sums paid under, any provision made by a previous order as to payment of the costs of proceedings taken in the court on or with reference to the application, or, where costs have not been awarded, award costs;

(*b*) certify particulars of the delay or default to the Lands Tribunal with a view to enabling the Tribunal to exercise a like discretion in relation to costs of proceedings before the Tribunal.

(2) . . .

(3) Where an application for possession is dismissed or withdrawn, and it is made to appear to the court—

(*a*) that the application was not made in good faith; or

(*b*) that the landlord had attempted in any material respect to support by misrepresentation or the concealment of material facts a request to the tenant to deliver up possession without an application for possession;

the court may order that no further application for possession of the house and premises made by the landlord shall be entertained if it is made within the five years beginning with the date of the order.

9.—(1) The purposes authorised for the application of capital money by section 73 of the Settled Land Act 1925, or by that section as applied by section 28 of the Law of Property Act 1925 in relation to trusts for sale, and the purposes authorised by section 71 of the Settled Land Act 1925 or by that section as applied as aforesaid as purposes for which moneys may be raised by mortgage, shall include the payment of compensation in accordance with section 17 or 18 of this Act (whether possession is obtained under that section or without any application for possession).

(2) The purposes authorised for the application of capital money by section 26 of the Universities and College Estates Act 1925, and the purposes authorised by section 31 of that Act as purposes for which moneys may be raised by mortgage, shall include the payment of compensation in accordance with section 17 of this Act (whether possession is obtained under that section or without any application for possession). **[227]**

NOTES

Para 2: amended by the Housing Act 1980, s 142, Sch 22.

Para 3: amended by the Rent Act 1968 s 117(2), Sch 15, the Rent (Agriculture) Act 1976, s 40, Sch 8, para 18, and the Rent Act 1977, s 155, Sch 23, para 45.

Para 8: words omitted repealed by the Housing Act 1980, ss 142, 152, Schs 22, 26.

SCHEDULE 3

Sections 22, 34

VALIDITY OF TENANTS' NOTICES, EFFECT ON LANDLORD AND TENANT ACT 1954 ETC AND PROCEDURE GENERALLY

PART I

RESTRICTIONS ON CLAIMS BY TENANT, AND EFFECT OF CLAIMS ON OTHER NOTICES, FORFEITURES, ETC

1.—(1) A claim to acquire the freehold or an extended lease of any property shall be of no effect if made after the tenant has given notice terminating the tenancy of that property (not being a notice that has been superseded by the grant, express or implied, of a new tenancy), or if made during the subsistence of an agreement for a future tenancy to which section 28 of the Landlord and Tenant Act 1954 applies.

(2) A tenant's notice terminating the tenancy of any property, shall be of no effect if given during the currency of a claim made in respect of the tenancy to acquire the freehold or an extended lease of that property.

(3) In sub-paragraphs (1) and (2) above references to a notice terminating a tenancy include a tenant's request for a new tenancy under section 26 of the Landlord and Tenant Act 1954, and a tenant's notice under section 27(1) of that Act that he does not desire the tenancy to be continued.

2.—(1) A claim to acquire the freehold or an extended lease of any property shall be of no effect if made more than two months after a landlord's notice terminating the tenancy of that property has been given under section 4 or 25 of the Landlord and Tenant Act 1954 (whether or not that notice has effect to terminate the tenancy):

Provided that—

(*a*) this sub-paragraph shall not apply where the landlord gives his written consent to a claim being made after the end of those two months; and

(*b*) where a tenant, having given notice of his desire to have the freehold, gives after the end of those two months a further notice under section 9(3) of this Act of his inability or unwillingness to acquire the house and premises at the price he must pay, he may with the notice under section 9(3) give a notice of his desire to have an extended lease (if he then has a right thereto).

(2) A landlord's notice terminating a tenancy of any property under section 4 or 25 of the Landlord and Tenant Act 1954 shall be of no effect if given during the currency of a claim made in respect of the tenancy to acquire the freehold or an extended lease of that property, and shall cease to have effect on the making of such a claim.

(3) Where any such landlord's notice ceases (by virtue of sub-paragraph (2) above or section 35 of this Act) to have effect on the making of a claim, but the claim is not effective, then if within one month after the period of currency of that claim (or any subsequent claim made by virtue of the proviso to sub-paragraph (1) above) a landlord's notice terminating the tenancy is given under section 4 or 25 of the Landlord and Tenant Act 1954, the earliest date which may be specified therein as the date of termination shall be the date of termination specified in the previous notice or the expiration of three months from the giving of the new notice, whichever is the later.

(4) Where by virtue of sub-paragraph (3) above a landlord's notice specifies as the date of termination of a tenancy a date earlier than six months after the giving of the notice, then—

(*a*) if it is a notice proposing a statutory tenancy, section 7(2) of the Landlord and Tenant Act 1954 shall apply in relation to the notice with the substitution, for references to the period of two months ending with the date of termination specified in the notice and the beginning of that period, of references to the period of three months beginning with the giving of the notice and the end of that period; and

(*b*) if it is a notice under section 25 of that Act, an application under section 24 for a new tenancy shall not be entertained unless it is made within three months after the giving of the notice.

3.—(1) Where a tenant makes a claim to acquire the freehold or an extended lease of any property, then during the currency of the claim and for three months thereafter the tenancy in that property shall not terminate either by effluxion of time or in pursuance of a notice to quit given by the landlord or by the termination of a superior tenancy; but if the claim is not effective, and but for this sub-paragraph the tenancy would have so terminated before the end of those three months, the tenancy shall so terminate at the end of the three months.

(2) Sub-paragraph (1) above shall not be taken to prevent an earlier termination of the tenancy in any manner not there mentioned, nor affect the power under section 146(4) of the Law of Property Act 1925 to grant a tenant relief against the termination of a superior tenancy, or any right to the tenant to relief under section 16(2) of the Landlord and Tenant Act 1954 or under paragraph 9 of Schedule 5 to that Act.

4.—(1) Where a tenant makes a claim to acquire the freehold or an extended lease of any property, then during the currency of the claim no proceedings to enforce any right of re-entry or forfeiture terminating the tenancy shall be brought in any court without the leave of that court, and leave shall not be granted unless the court is satisfied that the claim was not made in good faith; but where leave is granted, the claim shall cease to have effect.

(2) Where a claim is made to acquire the freehold or an extended lease of property comprised in a tenancy, the tenancy shall be deemed for purposes of the claim to be a

subsisting tenancy notwithstanding that the claim is made when proceedings are pending to enforce a right of re-entry or forfeiture terminating the tenancy and notwithstanding any order made afterwards in those proceedings, and if the claim is effective, the court in which the proceedings were brought may set aside or vary any such order to such extent and on such terms as appear to that court to be appropriate:

Provided that if it appears to that court that the claim is not made in good faith, or there has been unreasonable delay in making it, and that apart from the claim effect should be given to the right of re-entry or forfeiture, the court shall order that the tenancy shall not be treated as subsisting nor the claim as valid by virtue of this sub-paragraph.

(3) Where a court other than the county court—

(*a*) grants leave under sub-paragraph (1) above; or
(*b*) makes an order under the provisio to sub-paragraph (2) above on the ground that a claim was not made in good faith;

the court may make any such order as the county court is authorised to make by section 20(5) or (6) of this Act.

(4) A tenant who, in proceedings to enforce a right of re-entry or forfeiture or a right to damages in respect of a failure to comply with any terms of the tenancy, applies for relief under section 16 of the Landlord and Tenant Act 1954 is not thereby precluded from making a claim to acquire the freehold or an extended lease; but if he gives notice under section 16(2) (under which the tenant is relieved from any order for recovery of possession or for payment of damages, but the tenancy is cut short), any claim made by him to acquire the freehold or an extended lease of property comprised in the tenancy, with or without other property, shall be of no effect, or, if already made, shall cease to have effect.

(5) Sub-paragraph (4) above shall apply in relation to proceedings relating to a superior tenancy with the substitution for the references to section 16 and to section 16(2) of the Landlord and Tenant Act 1954 of references to paragraph 9 and to paragraph 9(2) of Schedule 5 to that Act.

5.—(1) For purposes of this Part of this Schedule—

(*a*) references to a claim to acquire the freehold or an extended lease shall be taken as references to a notice of a person's desire to acquire it under Part I of this Act and, except in so far as the contrary intention appears, as including a claim made by a tenant not entitled to acquire it and a claim made by a person who is not a tenant; and
(*b*) references to a claim being effective shall be taken as references to the freehold or an extended lease being acquired in pursuance of the claim; and
(*c*) references to the currency of a claim shall be taken as references to the period from the giving of a notice which has effect or would, if valid, have effect to the time when the notice is effective or ceases to have effect, or (not being a valid notice) is set aside by the court or withdrawn or would, if valid, cease to have effect, and those references shall include any period when the notice is suspended.

(2) For purposes of sub-paragraph (1)(*c*) above the date when a notice ceases to have effect or is set aside or would, if valid, cease to have effect in consequence of an order of a court shall be taken to be the date when the order becomes final. **[228]**

PART II

PROCEDURAL PROVISIONS

6.—(1) A tenant's notice under Part I of this Act of his desire to have the freehold or an extended lease of a house and premises shall be in the prescribed form, and shall contain the following particulars:—

(*a*) the address of the house, and sufficient particulars of the house and premises to identify the property to which the claim extends;
(*b*) such particulars of the tenancy and of the rateable value of the house and premises as serve to identify the instrument creating the tenancy and show that

[(i)] (apart from the operation, if any, of the proviso to section 4(1) of this Act) the tenancy is and has at the material times been a long tenancy at a low rent;
[(ii) at the material time the rateable value was within the limits specified for the purpose of section 1;]

(*c*) the date on which the tenant acquired the tenancy;
(*d*) the periods for which since the beginning of the preceding ten years and since acquiring the tenancy the tenant has and has not occupied the house as his residence, together with the following additional particulars about the periods for which during that time he has so occupied the house, that is to say,—
(i) what parts, if any, of the house have not been in his own occupation and for what periods; and
(ii) what other residence, if any, he has had for what periods, and which was his main residence.

(2) Where the tenant gives the notice by virtue of section 6 or 7 of this Act, sub-paragraph 1(*c*) and (*d*) above shall apply with the appropriate modifications of references to the tenant, so that the notice shall show the particulars bringing the case within section 6 or 7.

(3) The notice shall not be invalidated by any inaccuracy in the particulars required by this paragraph or any misdescription of the property to which the claim extends; and where the claim extends to property not properly included in the house and premises, or does not extend to property that ought to be so included, the notice may with the leave of the court, and on such terms as the court may see fit to impose, be amended so as to exclude or include that property.

7.—(1) Where a tenant of a house gives the landlord notice in accordance with Part I of this Act of the tenant's desire to have the freehold or an extended lease, the landlord shall within two months give the tenant a notice in reply in the prescribed form stating whether or not the landlord admits the tenant's right to have the freehold or extended lease (subject to any question as to the correctness of the particulars given in the tenant's notice of the house and premises); and if the landlord does not admit the tenant's right, the notice shall state the grounds on which it is not admitted.

(2) Subject to sub-paragraph (3) below, where under Part I of this Act the landlord may object to the inclusion of any part of the house and premises as described in the tenant's notice, or may object to the exclusion of other property, the notice of his objection shall be given with or before his notice in reply, unless the right to give it later is reserved by the notice in reply.

(3) If (on the assumption, where it is not admitted, that the tenant has the right claimed) it is intended to apply to the court for possession of the house and premises under section 17 or 18 of this Act, the notice in reply shall state that it is the intention to do so, and sub-paragraph (2) above shall not apply.

(4) Where a landlord's notice in reply admits the tenant's right to have the freehold or extended lease of a house and premises, the admission shall be binding on the landlord, so far as relates to the matters mentioned in section 1(1)(*a*) and (*b*) of this Act, unless the landlord shows that he was induced to make the admission by misrepresentation or the concealment of material facts; but the admission shall not conclude any question whether the particulars of the house and premises in the tenant's notice are correct.

(5) The tenant shall not institute proceedings in the court with a view to the enforcement of his right to have the freehold or an extended lease before the landlord has given his notice in reply or two months have elapsed without his doing so since the giving of the tenant's notice.

8.—(1) Where a person ("the claimant") gives notice as tenant of a house of his desire to have the freehold or an extended lease under Part I of this Act,—

(*a*) the notice shall be regarded as served on the landlord if it is served on any of the persons having an interest in the house and premises superior to the claimant's tenancy and references to the relevant time shall be construed accordingly;

(*b*) copies of the notice shall be served by the claimant on any other persons known or believed by him to have such an interest;

(*c*) the notice shall state whether copies are being served in accordance with paragraph (*b*) above on anyone other than the recipient and, if so, on whom;

(*d*) a recipient of the notice or a copy of it (including a person receiving a copy under this paragraph), unless he is a person having no such interest, shall forthwith serve a copy on any person who is known or believed by him to have such an interest and is not stated in the recipient's copy of the notice or known by him to have received a copy;

(*e*) a recipient of the notice or a copy of it shall, in any further copies served by him in accordance with paragraph (*d*) above, supplement the statement under paragraph (*c*) by adding any further persons on whom he is serving copies or who are known by him to have received one.

(2) Any recipient of any such notice or a copy of it—

(*a*) if he serves further copies of it on other persons in accordance with sub-paragraph (1)(*d*) above, shall notify the claimant of the persons added by him to the statement under sub-paragraph (1)(*c*); and

(*b*) if he knows who is, or believes himself to be, the person designated as the reversioner by paragraph 2 of Schedule 1 to this Act, shall give written notice to the claimant stating who is thought by him to be the reversioner, and shall serve copies of it on all persons known or believed by him to have an interest superior to the claimant's tenancy.

(3) Any person who fails without reasonable cause to comply with sub-paragraph (1) or (2) above, or is guilty of any unreasonable delay in doing so, shall be liable for any loss thereby occasioned to the claimant or to any person having an interest superior to the claimant's tenancy.

(4) In this paragraph references to an interest superior to the claimant's tenancy mean the estate in fee simple and any tenancy superior to the claimant's tenancy, but shall apply also to a tenancy reversionary on the claimant's tenancy.

9.—(1) Where the interest of a landlord is subject to a charge, and the person entitled to the benefit of the charge is in possession or a receiver appointed by him or by the court is in receipt of the rents and profits, a notice by a tenant of his desire to have the freehold or an extended lease under Part I of this Act shall be duly given if served either on the landlord or on that person or any such receiver; but the landlord or that person, if not the recipient of the notice, shall forthwith be sent the notice or a copy of it by the recipient:

Provided that in the case of a debenture-holders' charge within the meaning of section 12(5) of this Act this sub-paragraph shall not authorise the service of a notice on, or require a notice or copy to be sent to, the persons entitled to the benefit of the charge, other than trustees for the debenture-holders, but where the notice is served on the landlord and there is no trustee for the debenture-holders, he shall forthwith send it or a copy of it to any receiver appointed by virtue of the charge.

(2) Where a tenant of a house gives notice of his desire to have the freehold or an extended lease under Part I of this Act, and the interest of the person to whom the notice is given, or of any person receiving a copy of it under paragraph 8 above, is subject to a charge to secure the payment of money, then subject to sub-paragraph (3) below the recipient of the notice or copy shall forthwith inform the person entitled to the benefit of the charge (unless the notice was served on him or a receiver appointed by virtue of the charge) that the notice has been given, and shall give him such further information as may from time to time be reasonably required from the recipient by him.

(3) References in sub-paragraph (2) above to a charge shall not include a charge falling within section 11 of this Act or a debenture-holders' charge within the meaning of section 12(5) of this Act.

10.—(1) This paragraph shall have effect in relation to a landlord's notice terminating a tenancy of a house under section 4 or 25 of the Landlord and Tenant Act 1954 if—

(*a*) no previous notice terminating the tenancy has been given under either of those sections; and

(*b*) in the case of a notice under section 25, the tenancy is a long tenancy at a low rent, and the tenant is not a company or other artificial person.

(2) The landlord's notice shall not have effect unless it states—

(*a*) that, if the tenant has a right under Part I of this Act to acquire the freehold or an extended lease of property comprised in the tenancy, notice of his desire to have the freehold or an extended lease cannot be given more than two months after the service of the landlord's notice; and

(*b*) that, in the event of a tenant having that right and giving such a notice within those two months, the landlord's notice will not operate; and

(*c*) that, in the event of the tenant giving such a notice within those two months, the landlord will be entitled to apply to the court under section 17 or 18 of this Act and proposes to do so or, as the case may be, will not be entitled or does not propose to do so.

(3) The landlord shall also in the notice give the names and addresses of any other persons known or believed by him to have an interest superior to the tenancy terminated by the notice or to be the agent concerned with the property on behalf of a person having such an interest; and for this purpose "an interest superior to the tenancy terminated by the notice" means the estate in fee simple and any tenancy superior to that tenancy, but includes also a tenancy reversionary on that tenancy.

(4) Where a tenant's notice of his desire to have the freehold or an extended lease of a house and premises under Part I of this Act is given after the service of a landlord's notice terminating the tenancy under section 4 or section 25 of the Landlord and Tenant Act 1954, and the landlord's notice does not comply with sub-paragraph (2) above, no application made under section 17 or 18 of this Act with respect to the house and premises by the landlord giving the notice shall be entertained by the court (other than an application under section 17 after the grant of an extended lease).

(5) This paragraph shall not apply, or be treated by virtue of section 34(4)(*c*) as applying, to a landlord's notice given before the appointed day. **[229]**

NOTES

Prospectively amended by the Housing Act 1980, s 141, Sch 21, as from a day to be appointed.

SCHEDULE 4

Sections 29, 30

SPECIAL COVENANTS WITH LOCAL AUTHORITIES ETC ON ENFRANCHISEMENT OR EXTENSION

PART I

OPERATION AND ENFORCEMENT OF COVENANTS

1.—(1) A covenant entered into in accordance with section 29 or 30 of this Act (in this Part of this Schedule referred to as "a relevant covenant") shall not be enforceable by any means other than those provided by paragraphs 2 and 3 below.

(2) A relevant covenant affecting land other than registered land—

(*a*) may be registered under section 10 of the Land Charges Act 1925 as a restrictive covenant, if apart from this sub-paragraph it would not be registrable under that section as a restrictive covenant or as an estate contract; and

(*b*) subject to section 13 of that Act, shall be binding upon every successor of the covenantor, if apart from this sub-paragraph it would not be binding upon every such successor.

(3) Where a relevant covenant affects registered land,—

(*a*) notice of the covenant may be registered under section 59(2) of the Land Registration Act 1925 as a land charge (other than a local land charge) within the meaning of that Act, if apart from this subsection notice of the covenant would not be so registrable, and the provisions of that Act as to land charges shall apply accordingly; and

(*b*) where notice of the covenant has been so registered, the covenant shall be binding upon every successor of the covenantor, if apart from this subsection it would not be binding upon every such successor.

(4) In sub-paragraphs (2) and (3) above "successor of the covenantor", in relation to the covenants entered into on any disposition, means a person, other than the covenantor, who is for the time being entitled—

(*a*) to the interest disposed of, either in the whole or in part of the property comprised in the disposition; or

(*b*) to an interest consisting of a tenancy (whether of the whole or of part of that property) which has been created (directly or indirectly) out of the interest disposed of.

(5) Section 84 of the Law of Property Act 1925 (power to discharge or modify restrictive covenants affecting land) shall not have effect in relation to any relevant covenant.

(6) The rule against perpetuities and any enactment relating to that rule shall not apply to any right conferred by, or exercisable in relation to, a relevant covenant, if apart from this sub-paragraph it would apply to any such right.

(7) Where any such interest as is mentioned in sub-paragraph (4)(*a*) or (*b*) above is acquired (whether compulsorily or by agreement) by an authority possessing compulsory purchase powers within the meaning of the [Town and Country Planning Act 1971] (including any government department), nothing in the enactment which authorises that acquisition, or in any other enactment conferring powers on that authority, shall be construed as relieving that authority from the obligation to comply with any relevant covenant to which that interest remains subject; but the rights of the covenantee shall for purposes of any such acquisition be treated as an interest in the land affected, and as capable of being, and liable to be, extinguished by being compulsorily acquired in like manner and subject to the like conditions as other interests of the covenantee would be.

2.—(1) Where it appears to a local authority that a relevant covenant entered into on a disposition by that authority has been broken, the authority may serve written notice under this paragraph on any one or more of the following persons, that is to say—

(*a*) any person for the time being entitled to the interest disposed of either in the whole or in part of the land comprised in the disposition (in this paragraph referred to as "the land under covenant"); and

(*b*) any person entitled to an interest consisting of a tenancy (whether of the whole or of part of the land under covenant) which has been created (directly or indirectly) out of the interest disposed of.

(2) A notice served on any person under sub-paragraph (1) above shall—

(*a*) specify the covenant and the matters in respect of which it is alleged by the authority that the covenant has been broken; and

(*b*) state that, after the end of such period (not being less than six weeks from the date of service of the notice) as may be specified in the notice, the authority propose to execute a vesting declaration under paragraph 3 below in respect of that person's interest in the land under covenant unless before the end of that period he serves on the authority a counter-notice under sub-paragraph (3) below.

(3) Any person on whom a notice is served under sub-paragraph (1) above may, before the end of the period specified in the notice in accordance with sub-paragraph (2)(*b*) serve on the authority a counter-notice in writing objecting to the notice on such one or more of the following grounds as may be specified in the counter-notice, that is to say—

(*a*) that the relevant covenant specified in the notice under sub-paragraph (1) above has not been broken as alleged in the notice;

(*b*) that, if that covenant has been so broken, the breach does not relate to any part of the land under covenant in which the person serving the counter-notice has an interest;

(*c*) that in the circumstances he ought to be relieved against the execution of a vesting declaration under paragraph 3 below in respect of his interest.

(4) Where a person has served a counter-notice under sub-paragraph (3) above and that counter-notice has not been withdrawn, the authority shall not execute a vesting declaration under paragraph 3 below in respect of his interest except with the leave of the court; and on any application for such leave—

(*a*) where the grounds of objection specified in the counter-notice consist of or include that which is specified in sub-paragraph (3)(*a*) or (*b*) above, the court shall not grant leave unless satisfied that the objection on that ground is not well-founded; and

(*b*) without prejudice to paragraph (*a*) above, where the grounds of objection specified in the counter-notice consist of or include that which is specified in sub-paragraph (3)(*c*) above, the court, if having regard to the conduct of the parties and to all the other circumstances it appears to the court to be just and equitable to do so, may refuse to grant leave, either unconditionally or on such terms (as to costs, damages or otherwise) as the court think fit.

3.—(1) Where a local authority have served on any person a notice under paragraph 2 above in respect of such an interest as is mentioned in paragraph 2(1)(*a*) or (*b*), then subject to paragraph 2(4) above and to the provisions of any order made under it, the authority may execute a vesting declaration under this paragraph in respect of that interest—

(*a*) at any time within the six months following the end of the period specified in the notice in accordance with paragraph 2(2)(*b*), if no counter-notice under paragraph 2(3) is served before the end of that period; or

(*b*) if such a counter-notice is so served but is withdrawn, at any time within the six months following the withdrawal of the counter-notice; or

(*c*) if such a counter-notice is so served and is not withdrawn, at any time within the six months following the time when the order giving leave under paragraph 2(4) becomes final.

(2) A vesting declaration under this paragraph in respect of an interest in land shall be in such form as may be prescribed by regulations made by statutory instrument by the Minister of Housing and Local Government.

(3) Where a vesting declaration is executed under this paragraph the interest to which it relates shall vest in the authority on such date as is specified in that behalf in the declaration.

(4) Any reference in the Land Compensation Act 1961 to the compulsory acquisition of land, or of an interest in land, shall be construed as including a reference to the execution of a vesting declaration under this paragraph in respect of an interest in land; and that Act shall apply in relation to the execution of such a declaration as if the authority, having been duly authorised to acquire that interest compulsorily in accordance with the [Acquisition of Land Act 1981], had served notice to treat in respect of that interest on the date of execution of the declaration.

(5) In assessing compensation in accordance with the Land Compensation Act 1961 in respect of an interest in land vested in a local authority by a vesting declaration under this paragraph—

(*a*) nothing shall be included for damage sustained by reason that the land in which the interest subsists is severed from other land held therewith, or for disturbance or any other matter not directly based on the value of land or of an interest in land; and

(*b*) in a case where immediately before the execution of the declaration the interest is subject to a right of pre-emption under a covenant entered into in accordance with section 30(1)(*b*) of this Act, no account shall be taken of any diminution of the value of the interest which is attributable to that right. **[230]**

NOTES

Para 1: amended by the Town and Country Planning Act 1971, s 291, Sch 23.
Para 3: amended by the Acquisition of Land Act 1981, s 34, Sch 4, para 1.

PART II

RE-ACQUISITION FOR DEVELOPMENT BY NEW TOWNS COMMISSION OR UNIVERSITY BODY

4. Where a tenant of a house and premises acquires the freehold under Part I of this Act subject to a covenant entered into under section 29(1) with the Commission for the New Towns, and the property or any part of it is afterwards required for development for purposes (other than investment purposes) of the Commission, the Commission may be authorised by the Minister of Housing and Local Government to acquire the property or that part of it compulsorily; [and the Acquisition of Land Act 1981 shall apply to a compulsory purchase under this paragraph].

5.—(1) Where a tenant of a house and premises acquires the freehold under Part I of this Act subject to a covenant entered into under section 29(1) with a university body, and the property or any part of it is afterwards required for development for the purposes (other than investment purposes) of that or a related university body, the Secretary of State for Education and Science may at the cost and on behalf of the university body for which it is required acquire the property or that part of it by compulsory purchase.

[(2) The Acquisition of Land Act 1981 shall apply to a compulsory purchase under this paragraph.]

(3) For purposes of this paragraph a university and the colleges of that university (within the meaning of section 28(5)(*c*) of this Act) are university bodies related to one another.

[6.—(1) Where a tenant of a house and premises acquires the freehold under Part I of this Act subject to a covenant entered into under section 29(1) with the Development Board for Rural Wales, and the property or any part of it is afterwards acquired for development for purposes (other than investment purposes) of the Board the Board may be authorised by the Secretary of State to acquire the property or that part of it compulsorily.

[(2) The Acquisition of Land Act 1981 shall apply to a compulsory purchase under this paragraph.]] **[231]**

NOTES

Commencement: Before 1 January 1970 (paras 4, 5); 1 April 1977 (para 6).
Paras 4, 5: amended by the Acquisition of Land Act 1981, s 34, Sch 4, para 16.
Para 6: added by the Development of Rural Wales Act 1976, s 27, Sch 7, para 5(1), (5); amended by the Acquisition of Land Act 1981, s 34, Sch 4, para 16.

SCHEDULE 4A

EXCLUSION OF CERTAIN SHARED OWNERSHIP LEASES

[Leases granted in pursuance of right to be granted a shared ownership lease

1. A lease granted in pursuance of the right to be granted a shared ownership lease under Part V of the Housing Act 1985 is excluded from the operation of this Part of this Act.

Certain leases granted by certain public authorities

2.—(1) A lease which—

(*a*) was granted at a premium by a body mentioned in sub-paragraph (2), and
(*b*) complies with the conditions set out in sub-paragraph (3),

is excluded from the operation of this Part at any time when the interest of the landlord belongs to such a body.

(2) The bodies are—

(*a*) a county, district or London borough council, the Common Council of the City of London or the Council of the Isles of Scilly;
(*b*) the Inner London Education Authority or a joint authority established by Part IV of the Local Government Act 1985;
(*c*) the Commission for the New Towns or a development corporation established by an order made, or having effect as made, under the New Towns Act 1981;
(*d*) an urban development corporation within the meaning of Part XVI of the Local Government, Planning and Land Act 1980;
(*e*) the Development Board for Rural Wales;

(3) The conditions are that the lease—

(*a*) provides for the tenant to acquire the freehold for a consideration which is to be calculated in accordance with the lease and which is reasonable, having regard to the premium or premiums paid by the tenant under the lease, and
(*b*) states the landlord's opinion that by virtue of this paragraph the tenancy will be excluded from the operation of this Part of this Act at any time when the interest of the landlord belongs to a body mentioned in sub-paragraph (2) above.

(4) If, in proceedings in which it falls to be determined whether a lease complies with the condition in sub-paragraph (3)(*a*), the question arises whether the consideration payable by the tenant on acquiring the freehold is reasonable, it is for the landlord to show that it is.

Certain leases granted by housing associations

3.—(1) A lease granted by a housing association and which complies with the conditions set out in sub-paragraph (2) is excluded from the operation of this Part of this Act, whether or not the interest of the landlord still belongs to such an association.

(2) The conditions are that the lease—

(*a*) was granted for a term of 99 years or more and is not (and cannot become) terminable except in pursuance of a provision for re-entry or forfeiture;
(*b*) was granted at a premium, calculated by reference to the value of the house or the cost of providing it, of not less than 25 per cent., or such other percentage as may be prescribed, of the figure by reference to which it was calculated;
(*c*) provides for the tenant to acquire additional shares in the house on terms specified in the lease and complying with such requirements as may be prescribed;
(*d*) does not restrict the tenant's powers to assign, mortgage or charge his interest in the house;
(*e*) if it enables the landlord to require payment for outstanding shares in the house, does so only in such circumstances as may be prescribed;
(*f*) provides for the tenant to acquire the landlord's interest on terms specified in the lease and complying with such requirements as may be prescribed; and
(*g*) states the landlord's opinion that by virtue of this paragraph the lease is excluded from the operation of this Part of this Act.

(3) In any proceedings the court may, if of the opinion that it is just and equitable to do so, treat a lease as satisfying the conditions in sub-paragraph (2) notwithstanding that the condition specified in paragraph (*g*) of that sub-paragraph is not satisfied.

(4) In this paragraph "housing association" has the same meaning as in the Housing Associations Act 1985.

4.—(1) A lease for the elderly granted by a registered housing association and which complies with the conditions set out in sub-paragraph (2) is excluded from the operation of this Part of this Act at any time when the interest of the landlord belongs to such an association.

(2) The conditions are that the lease—

(*a*) is granted at a premium which is calculated by reference to a percentage of the value of the house or of the cost of providing it, (*b*) complies, at the time when it is granted, with such requirements as may be prescribed, and

(*c*) states the landlord's opinion that by virtue of this paragraph the lease will be excluded from the operation of this Part of this Act at any time when the interest of the landlord belongs to a registered housing association.

(3) In this paragraph—

"lease for the elderly" has such meaning as may be prescribed; and

"registered housing association" has the same meaning as in the Housing Associations Act 1985.

Power to prescribe matters by regulations

5.—(1) The Secretary of State may by regulations prescribe anything requiring to be prescribed for the purposes of this Schedule.

(2) The regulations may—

(*a*) make different provision for different cases or descriptions of case, including different provision for different areas, and

(*b*) contain such incidental, supplementary or transitional provisions as the Secretary of State considers appropriate,

and shall be made by statutory instrument which shall be subject to annulment in pursuance of a resolution of either House of Parliament.

Interpretation

6. In this Schedule "lease" means a lease at law or in equity, and references to the grant of a lease shall be construed accordingly.] **[232]**

NOTES

Commencement: To be appointed.

Prospectively added with savings by the Housing and Planning Act 1986, s 18, Sch 4, paras 6, 11, as from a day to be appointed.

SCHEDULE 5

Section 39

LANDLORD AND TENANT ACT 1954 PART I (CONSEQUENTIAL AMENDMENTS, EFFECT OF RENT ACT 1965, ETC)

Consequential amendments of Landlord and Tenant Act 1954

1 . . .

2. The following provisions of the Landlord and Tenant Act 1954 shall have effect as if the amendments and repeals made in them by the Rent Act 1957 in consequence of the passing of section 21 of that Act had not been made, that is to say,—

(*a*) section 2 (the words "at a low rent" being re-inserted in subsections (1), (2) and (3) after the words "long tenancy", and the words "if the tenancy had not been one at a low rent" being restored in place of the words "if the tenancy had not been a long tenancy and (in the case of a tenancy at a low rent) had not been a tenancy at a low rent");

(*b*) section 3(3) (the words "if the tenancy in question were not one at a low rent" being restored in place of the words "if the tenancy in question were not a long tenancy and (in the case of a tenancy at a low rent) were not a tenancy at a low rent");

(*c*) section 12(2)(*a*) and (*b*) (the words "if the tenancy were not one at a low rent" being in each case restored in place of the words "if the tenancy were not a long tenancy and (in the case of a tenancy at a low rent) were not a tenancy at a low rent");

(*d*) section 18(1) (the words "at a low rent" being re-inserted after the words "long tenancy" where first occurring);

(*e*) section 19(1) (the words "at a low rent" being re-inserted after the word "tenancy", where first occurring, and after the words "another tenancy", and there being omitted the words "and the second tenancy is a tenancy at a low rent").

Regulated tenancies

3.—(1) The amount of the rent payable under a regulated tenancy arising by virtue of Part I of the Landlord and Tenant Act 1954 shall, subject to the provisions of that Act as to initial repairs and subject to the operation (as regards the fixing of a fair rent and otherwise) of the [Rent Act 1977], be such amount as may be agreed between the landlord and the tenant or, in default of agreement, the same amount as the rent last payable under the long tenancy . . .

(2) Where the rent payable under a statutory tenancy is arrived at in accordance with sub-paragraph (1) above, then the [Rent Act 1977] shall apply with the following adaptations:—

(*a*) . . .
(*b*) [section 45(2)] (under which the rent payable for a statutory period of a tenancy is not to exceed that payable for the last contractual period) shall not apply;
(*c*) [[sections 46 to 48] (which provide] for variations of rent in respect of changes in the burden on the landlord for rates, provision of services etc.) shall apply only if the rent is one arrived at by agreement, and shall then apply as if references to the last contractual period were references to the first statutory period.

4.—(1) In relation to a rent registered or to be registered for a dwelling-house on an application made with reference to a regulated tenancy arising by virtue of Part I of the Landlord and Tenant Act 1954, the [Rent Act 1977] shall have effect subject to the provisions of this paragraph.

(2) An application for the registration of a rent may be made by the landlord or the tenant, or jointly by the landlord and the tenant, before the commencement of the statutory tenancy, but not before the terms of that tenancy other than the amount of the rent have been agreed or determined in accordance with section 7 of the Landlord and Tenant Act 1954; and the provisions of the [Rent Act 1977] (including the provisions of [section 72] as to the date from which the registration takes effect) shall apply accordingly.

(3) Where a rent is registered in pursuance of an application made by virtue of sub-paragraph (2) above, then a notice under [section 45(2)(*b*) of the Rent Act 1977] increasing the rent payable may, if the notice is given within four weeks after the date on which the rent is registered, specify as the date from which the increase is to take effect any date not earlier than the commencement of the tenancy nor earlier than the date from which the registration takes effect.

(4) Where initial repairs (within the meaning of Part I of the Landlord and Tenant Act 1954) remain to be carried out to the dwelling-house, then in determining what rent is or would be a fair rent regard shall be had under [section 70(1) of the Rent Act 1977] to the state of repair which may be expected to subsist after the completion of the initial repairs.

(5) The provisions of the [Rent Act 1977] as to the amount of the rent recoverable shall be taken as applying to the amount before account is taken of the provisions of the Landlord and Tenant Act 1954 as to initial repairs.

(6) Any entry in the register of a rent or of its confirmation by the rent assessment committee shall indicate that the rent is registered on an application made with reference to a statutory tenancy arising by virtue of Part I of the Landlord and Tenant Act 1954.

Transitional

5. In relation to a tenancy to which section 1 of the Landlord and Tenant Act 1954 applies immediately before the date of coming into operation of section 39 of this Act (in this and the following paragraphs referred to as "the operative date"), section 39 of this Act and paragraphs 1 to 4 above, together with the repeals made by Part I of Schedule 7

to this Act, shall not have effect if at the operative date there is in force a landlord's notice proposing a statutory tenancy and all the terms of the tenancy have been agreed or determined in accordance with section 7 of the Landlord and Tenant Act 1954 or an application for securing their determination by the court has been made.

6.—(1) Subject to paragraph 7(1) below, where at the operative date (within the meaning of paragraph 5 above) a tenancy is continuing by virtue of section 3 of the Landlord and Tenant Act 1954, section 39 of this Act and paragraphs 1 to 4 above, together with the repeals made by Part I of Schedule 7 to this Act, shall apply to the tenancy only to the extent provided for by this paragraph.

(2) Where at the operative date no notice under section 4 of the Landlord and Tenant Act 1954 terminating the tenancy is in force, Part I or, as the case may be, Part II of that Act shall apply as it would apply if the term date of the tenancy (within the meaning of Part I) had fallen on the operative date and if, in the case of a tenancy not at a low rent, it had been one at a low rent.

(3) Where at the operative date there is in force a landlord's notice proposing a statutory tenancy, sub-paragraph (2) above shall apply as it applies in a case where there is no such notice, unless either—

(*a*) all the terms of the tenancy have been agreed or determined in accordance with section 7 of the Landlord and Tenant Act 1954 or an application for securing their determination by the court has been made; or

(*b*) Part II of that Act would in accordance with sub-paragraph (2) above apply to the tenancy.

(4) Where a landlord's notice terminating the tenancy is in force at the operative date, and the notice ceases to have effect without the tenancy being terminated or a statutory tenancy arising, then sub-paragraph (2) above shall thereafter apply as it applies in a case where there is no such notice.

(5) Where a statutory tenancy arises by virtue of Part I of the Landlord and Tenant Act 1954 as it applies in accordance with sub-paragraph (2) above the [Rent Act 1977] shall have effect in relation to the statutory tenancy accordingly.

(6) Nothing in section 39 of this Act or in sub-paragraphs (2) to (5) above shall affect the operation of any notice given by a tenant under section 5 of the Landlord and Tenant Act 1954 to terminate the tenancy, if the notice is given while section 1 of the Act applies to the tenancy.

7.—(1) This paragraph shall have effect in relation to tenancies of the following description, except where paragraph 5 above applies, and paragraph 6 shall not have effect in relation to them, that is to say, tenancies—

(*a*) to which section 1 of the Landlord and Tenant Act 1954 applies immediately before the operative date (within the meaning of paragraph 5 above); but

(*b*) to which in accordance with section 39 of this Act section 1 of the Landlord and Tenant Act 1954 can no longer apply because the rateable value of the dwelling-house on the appropriate day for purposes of the [Rent Act 1977] exceeds the amount specified in section 1(1) of that Act.

(2) Where, on section 1 of the Landlord and Tenant Act 1954 ceasing by virtue of section 39 of this Act to apply to any such tenancy, Part II of that Act would not become applicable to it, then, if the term date falls or fell before the operative date or within the three months beginning with the operative date, the tenancy shall continue until the expiration of those three months unless sooner determined by a notice given by the tenant in accordance with section 5(1) or (2) of the Landlord and Tenant Act 1954 or by a landlord's notice to resume possession given before the operative date.

(3) Where, on section 1 of the Landlord and Tenant Act 1954 ceasing by virtue of section 39 of this Act to apply to any such tenancy, Part II of that Act would become applicable to it, section 39 of this Act and paragraphs 1 to 4 above, together with the repeals made by Part I of Schedule 7 to this Act, shall not have effect in relation to the tenancy if at the operative date there is in force a landlord's notice to resume possession, or there is in force a notice given by the tenant in accordance with section 5(1) or (2) of

the Landlord and Tenant Act 1954 to terminate the tenancy on a date within the three months beginning with the operative date:

Provided that this sub-paragraph shall cease to apply if the notice ceases to have effect without the tenancy being terminated.

8.—(1) Where a statutory tenancy has by virtue of Part I of the Landlord and Tenant Act 1954 arisen before the operative date (within the meaning of paragraph 5 above), the operation of Part I of that Act in relation to the tenancy shall not be affected by section 39 of this Act and paragraphs 2 to 4 above, or the repeals made by Part I of Schedule 7 to this Act, except as provided by sub-paragraph (2) below.

(2)–(4) . . .

9 . . .

Supplementary

[10.—(1) Section 74(2) of the Rent Act 1977 (which confers power by regulations to modify certain provisions of Part IV of that Act) shall apply also to this Schedule in so far as it affects section 67 or 72 of, or Schedule 11 to, that Act.

(2) In so far as they relate to the Rent Act 1977, section 39 of this Act and this Schedule shall have effect subject to section 153 of that Act (which confers power to adapt the Act in its application to the Isles of Scilly) as if those provisions of this Act were contained in that Act.] **[233]**

NOTES

Commencement: Before 1 January 1970 (paras 1-9); 29 August 1977 (para 10).

Para 1: amends the Landlord and Tenant Act 1954, Sch 3, para 1.

Paras 4, 6, 7: amendments in square brackets made by the Rent Act 1977, s 155, Sch 23, para 46.

Para 3: amendments in square brackets made by the Rent Act 1977, s 155, Sch 23, para 46; words omitted repealed by the Housing Finance Act 1972, s 108(4), Sch 11.

Para 8: sub-paras (2),(3) repealed by the Housing Finance Act 1972, s 108(4), Sch 11; sub-para (4) repealed by the Housing (Consequential Provisions) Act 1985, s 3, Sch 1, Part I.

Para 9: repealed by the Rent Act 1968, s 117(5), Sch 17.

Para 10: substituted by the Rent Act 1977, s 155, Sch 23, para 46.

DEFECTIVE PREMISES ACT 1972

(c 35)

An Act to impose duties in connection with the provision of dwellings and otherwise to amend the law of England and Wales as to liability for injury or damage caused to persons through defects in the state of premises [29 June 1972]

4. Landlord's duty of care in virtue of obligation or right to repair premises demised

(1) Where premises are let under a tenancy which puts on the landlord an obligation to the tenant for the maintenance or repair of the premises, the landlord owes to all persons who might reasonably be expected to be affected by defects in the state of the premises a duty to take such care as is reasonable in all the circumstances to see that they are reasonably safe from personal injury or from damage to their property caused by a relevant defect.

(2) The said duty is owed if the landlord knows (whether as the result of being notified by the tenant or otherwise) or if he ought in all the circumstances to have known of the relevant defect.

(3) In this section "relevant defect" means a defect in the state of the premises existing at or after the material time and arising from, or continuing

because of, an act or omission by the landlord which constitutes or would if he had had notice of the defect, have constituted a failure by him to carry out his obligation to the tenant for the maintenance or repair of the premises; and for the purposes of the foregoing provision "the material time" means—

(*a*) where the tenancy commenced before this Act, the commencement of this Act; and

(*b*) in all other cases, the earliest of the following times, that is to say—

(i) the time when the tenancy commences;

(ii) the time when the tenancy agreement is entered into;

(iii) the time when possession is taken of the premises in contemplation of the letting.

(4) Where premises are let under a tenancy which expressly or impliedly gives the landlord the right to enter the premises to carry out any description of maintenance or repair of the premises, then, as from the time when he first is, or by notice or otherwise can put himself, in a position to exercise the right and so long as he is or can put himself in that position, he shall be treated for the purposes of subsections (1) to (3) above (but for no other purpose) as if he were under an obligation to the tenant for that description of maintenance or repair of the premises; but the landlord shall not owe the tenant any duty by virtue of this subsection in respect of any defect in the state of the premises arising from, or continuing because of, a failure to carry out an obligation expressly imposed on the tenant by the tenancy.

(5) For the purposes of this section obligations imposed or rights given by any enactment in virtue of a tenancy shall be treated as imposed or given by the tenancy.

(6) This section applies to a right of occupation given by contract or any enactment and not amounting to a tenancy as if the right were a tenancy, and "tenancy" and cognate expressions shall be construed accordingly. **[234]**

NOTES

Commencement: 1 January 1974.

6. Supplemental

(1) In this Act—

"disposal", in relation to premises, includes a letting, and an assignment or surrender of a tenancy, of the premises and the creation by contract of any other right to occupy the premises, and "dispose" shall be construed accordingly;

"personal injury" includes any disease and any impairment of a person's physical or mental condition;

"tenancy" means—

(*a*) a tenancy created either immediately or derivatively out of the freehold, whether by a lease or underlease, by an agreement for a lease or underlease or by a tenancy agreement, but not including a mortgage term or any interest arising in favour of a mortgagor by his attorning tenant to his mortgagee; or

(*b*) a tenancy at will or a tenancy on sufferance; or

(*c*) a tenancy, whether or not constituting a tenancy at common law, created by or in pursuance of any enactment;

and cognate expressions shall be construed accordingly.

(2) Any duty imposed by or enforceable by virtue of any provision of this Act is in addition to any duty a person may owe apart from that provision.

(3) Any term of an agreement which purports to exclude or restrict, or has the effect of excluding or restricting, the operation of any of the provisions of this Act, or any liability arising by virtue of any such provision, shall be void.

(4) . . . **[235]**

NOTES
Commencement: 1 January 1974.
Words omitted repeal the Occupiers' Liability Act 1957, s 4

HOUSING ACT 1974
(c 44)

An Act to extend the functions of the Housing Corporation and provide for the registration of, and the giving of financial assistance to, certain housing associations; to make further provision in relation to clearance areas and other areas in which living conditions are unsatisfactory or otherwise in need of improvement; to provide for the making of grants towards the improvement, repair and provision of housing accommodation and for the compulsory improvement of such accommodation; to amend the law relating to assistance for house purchase and improvement and expenditure in connection with the provision and improvement of housing accommodation and of hostels; to raise the rateable value limits under the Leasehold Reform Act 1967; to amend the Housing Finance Act 1972; to amend the law relating to the rights and obligations of landlords and tenants and the enforceability of certain covenants relating to the development of land; and for purposes connected therewith

[31 July 1974]

PART IX
MISCELLANEOUS

118. Rateable value limits for enfranchisement or extension under Leasehold Reform Act 1967

(1) . . .

(2) In any case where, by virtue only of the amendments of section 1 of the Leasehold Reform Act 1967 effected by subsection (1) above, the right specified in subsection (1) of that section is conferred on a tenant, section 19 of that Act (retention of management powers for general benefit of neighbourhood) shall have effect in relation to the house and premises to which the tenant's right applies as if for the reference in subsection (1) of that section to an application made within two years beginning with the commencement of Part I of that Act there were substituted a reference to an application made within two years beginning with the date on which this Act is passed.

(3), (4) . . .

(5) This section shall come into force on the passing of this Act. **[236]**

NOTES
Commencement: 31 July 1974.
Sub-ss (1), (3), (4): amend Leasehold Reform Act 1967, ss 1, 9.

131. Short title, citation, commencement and extent

(1) This Act may be cited as the Housing Act 1974.

(2) . . .

(3) Except in so far as any provision of this Act otherwise provides, this Act shall come into operation on such day as the Secretary of State may by order appoint, and different days may be so appointed for different provisions and for different purposes.

(4) Without prejudice to any express saving contained in Schedule 14 to this Act, an order under subsection (3) above appointing a day for the coming into operation of any provision of Schedule 13 or Schedule 15 to this Act may contain such savings with respect to the operation of that provision as appear to the Secretary of State to be appropriate.

(5) . . ., in Part IX, sections . . . [116], 118, . . . of this Act extend to England and Wales only.

(6) . . .

(7) This Act does not extend to Northern Ireland. **[237]**

NOTES

Commencement: 20 August 1974.

Commencement order: SI 1974 No 1406.

Sub-s (2): repealed by the Housing (Consequential Provisions) Act 1985, s 3, Sch 1, Part I.

Sub-s (5): amendment in square brackets made by the Housing Rents and Subsidies (Scotland) Act 1975, s 15(1), Sch 3, para 17; words omitted repealed by the Housing (Consequential Provisions) Act 1985, s 3, Sch 1, Part I.

Sub-s (6): applies to Scotland only.

SCHEDULES

SCHEDULE 8

Section 118

Reduction of Rateable Value in Case of Certain Improvements

1.—(1) Where the tenant, or any previous tenant, has made or contributed to the cost of an improvement on the premises comprised in the tenancy and the improvement is one to which this Schedule applies, then, if the tenant serves on the landlord a notice in the prescribed form requiring him to agree to a reduction under this Schedule, their rateable value as ascertained for the purposes of [section 1 of the Leasehold Reform Act 1967] shall be reduced by such amount, if any, as may be agreed or determined in accordance with the following provisions of this Schedule.

(2) This Schedule applies to any improvement made by the execution of works amounting to structural alteration, extension or addition.

2.—(1) The amount of any such reduction may at any time be agreed in writing between the landlord and the tenant.

(2) Where, at the expiration of a period of six weeks from the service of a notice under paragraph 1 of this Schedule any of the following matters has not been agreed in writing between the landlord and the tenant, that is to say,—

(*a*) whether the improvement specified in the notice is an improvement to which this Schedule applies;
(*b*) what works were involved in it;
(*c*) whether the tenant or a previous tenant under the tenancy has made it or contributed to its cost; and

(*d*) what proportion his contribution, if any, bears to the whole cost;

the county court may on the application of the tenant determine that matter . . .

(3) An application under the last foregoing sub-paragraph must be made within six weeks from the expiration of the period mentioned therein or such longer time as the court may allow.

3.—(1) Where, after the service of a notice under paragraph 1 of this Schedule, it is agreed in writing between the landlord and tenant or determined by the county court—

(*a*) that the improvement specified in the notice is one to which this Schedule applies, and what works were involved in it, and

(*b*) that the tenant or a previous tenant under the tenancy has made it or contributed to its cost, and, in the latter case, what proportion his contribution bears to the whole cost, then if, at the expiration of a period of two weeks from the agreement or determination, it has not been agreed in writing between the landlord and the tenant whether any or what reduction is to be made under this Schedule, and the tenant, within four weeks from the expiration of that period, makes an application to the valuation officer for a certificate under the next following sub-paragraph, that question shall be determined in accordance with the certificate unless the landlord and the tenant otherwise agree in writing.

(2) On any such application the valuation officer shall certify—

(*a*) whether or not the improvement has affected the rateable value on the 1st April, 1973 (as ascertained for the purposes of [section 1 of the Leasehold Reform Act 1967], of the hereditament of which the premises consist or, as the case may be, in which they are wholly or partly comprised, and

(*b*) if it has, the amount by which the rateable value would have been less if the improvement had not been made.

(3) An application for such a certificate shall be in the prescribed form and shall state the name and address of the landlord, and the valuation officer shall send a copy of the certificate to the landlord.

(4) Where the amount of the reduction under this Schedule falls to be determined in accordance with such a certificate, it shall be equal to the amount specified in pursuance of head (*b*) of sub-paragraph (2) of this paragraph, but proportionately reduced in any case where a proportion only of the cost was contributed by the tenant or a previous tenant under the tenancy.

(5) Where at the time of an application for a certificate under this paragraph a proposal for an alteration in the valuation list relating to the hereditament is pending and the alteration would have effect from a date earlier than the 2nd April, 1973, the valuation officer shall not issue the certificate until the proposal is settled.

[4. Where a notice under paragraph 1 of this Schedule is served on or after 21st December 1979, the tenant shall bear the reasonable costs incurred by the landlord in investigating any matter specified in it.]

FORM

Leasehold Reform Act 1967

Notice by Tenant to Landlord of Tenant's Improvements affecting Rateable Value

Date...............

To...................landlord of...................

1. [I] [A previous tenant of the above mentioned premises under the tenancy] [made] [contributed to the cost of] the improvement[s] to the above mentioned premises particulars of which are set out in the First Schedule hereto [Note 1].

2. I hereby require you to agree to a reduction in the rateable value of the premises for the purposes of the Leasehold Reform Act 1967.

3. I propose that the rateable value shall be reduced to £ [Note 2].

4. If you do not agree to this reduction [Note 3], do you agree that—

(*a*) the improvement[s] [is] [are] [an] improvement[s] made by the execution of works amounting to the structural alteration or extension of the premises or a structural addition thereto;

(*b*) the works set out in the Second Schedule hereto were involved in the making of the improvement[s];

(*c*) [I] [A previous tenant under the tenancy] [made the improvement[s]] [contributed to the cost of the improvement[s]];

(*d*) the proportion of the cost borne by me or a previous tenant is] . . .

Signature of tenant ....

First Schedule

Description of Improvement(s)

Second Schedule

Description of Works

Strike out words in square brackets if inapplicable.

Note 1

The improvement must be one made by the execution of works amounting to the structural alteration or extension of the premises or a structural addition thereto, e.g. the erection of a garage in the grounds.

Note 2

If the amount of the reduction is agreed in writing between the landlord and the tenant, the amount of the reduced rateable value as so agreed will be substituted for the purposes of the Leasehold Reform Act 1967, for the rateable value on 1st April, 1973.

Note 3

If the amount of the reduction is not agreed in writing between the landlord and the tenant, the Valuation Officer will have to decide whether the improvement has affected the rateable value of the premises, and if so, what that value would have been had the improvement not been made. The name and address of the Valuation Officer can be obtained from the local authority. Before, however, an application is made to the Valuation Officer, the Landlord and the tenant must try to agree in writing on the items mentioned at (*a*) to (*d*) of this paragraph, or such of those items as are material. If at the end of a period of six weeks after the service of this notice any of these items have not been agreed, the tenant may, within a further six weeks or so much longer time as the court may allow, apply to the county court to settle the matter.

If it has either been agreed or determined by the county court that there has been an improvement of the kind described in Note 1 involving specified works, and that the improvement was carried out by the tenant or a previous tenant, or that the tenant or a previous tenant contributed to its cost, and in the latter case what proportion the contribution bears to the whole cost of the works, then, if within a period of two weeks after the agreement or determination of the county court the landlord and the tenant have still not agreed in writing whether any or what reduction is to be made, the tenant has a further four weeks in which to make an application in the statutory form to the Valuation Officer for a certificate as to whether or not the improvement has affected the rateable value, and if so, the amount by which that value would have been less if the improvement had not been made.

FORM

Leasehold Reform Act 1967

Application by Tenant to Valuation Officer for Certificate as to Reduction for the purposes of the Leasehold Reform Act 1967, in the Rateable Value of premises on account of Tenant's Improvements

Date................

To the Valuation Officer.

1 I am the tenant of , and my landlord is

of

2 It has been [agreed in writing between me and my landlord] [determined by the county court] that the improvement[s] specified in the First Schedule hereto [is an improvement] [are improvements] to which [Schedule 8 to the Housing Act 1974] applies, and that I or a previous tenant under the tenancy made the improvement[s] or contributed to [its] [their] cost, and that the works specified in the Second Schedule hereto were involved in the improvement[s].

3 It has not been agreed between me and my landlord whether any or what reduction is to be made under said Schedule [8] in the rateable value of the premises for the purposes of the Leasehold Reform Act 1967, and I hereby make application to you for a certificate under paragraph 3(2) of the said Schedule Seven [Note 4].

Signature of Tenant ....

First Schedule

Description of Improvement(s)

Second Schedule

Description of Works

Strike out words in brackets if inapplicable.

Note 4

If the Valuation Officer certifies that the rateable value would have been less but for the improvement by the amounts mentioned in the certificate, the rateable value will be reduced by those amounts for the purposes of the Leasehold Reform Act 1967 except in the case where a proportion only of the cost was contributed by the tenant, in which case the amounts of the reductions will be proportionately reduced accordingly. **[238]**

NOTES

Commencement: 31 July 1974.

Amended by the Housing Act 1980, s 141, Sch 21, para 8.

RENT (AGRICULTURE) ACT 1976

(c 80)

ARRANGEMENT OF SECTIONS

PART I

PRELIMINARY

Section Para

1 Interpretation and commencement .. .. [239]

Section Para

Protected occupancies

2 Protected occupiers in their own right .. .. [240]
3 Protected occupiers by succession .. .. [241]

Statutory tenancies

4 Statutory tenants and tenancies .. .. [242]
5 No statutory tenancy where landlord's interest belongs to Crown or to local authority, etc .. .. [243]

PART II

SECURITY OF TENURE

Protected occupancies and statutory tenancies

6 Grounds for possession .. .. [244]
7 Discretion of court in giving possession .. .. [245]
8 Restriction on levy of distress for rent .. .. [246]
9 Effect of determination of superior tenancy, etc .. .. [247]

Statutory tenancies

10 Terms and conditions .. .. [248]
11 Agreed rents .. .. [249]
12 Provisional rents .. .. [250]
13 Application for registration of rent .. .. [251]
14 Registered rents .. .. [252]
15 Phasing of rent increases .. .. [253]
16 Notices of increase .. .. [254]

General provisions

17 Adjustment for differences in lengths of rental periods .. .. [255]
18 Regulations .. .. [256]
19 Interpretation of Part II .. .. [257]

PART III

PROTECTED OCCUPANCIES AND STATUTORY TENANCIES: SUPPLEMENTAL

Recovery of rent

20 Avoidance of requirements for advance payment of rent .. .. [258]
21 Recovery from landlord of sums paid in excess of recoverable rent .. .. .. [259]
22 Rectification of rent books in light of determination of recoverable rent .. .. [260]

Miscellaneous

23 Tenant sharing accommodation with persons other than landlord .. .. .. [261]
24 Certain sub-lettings, not to exclude any part of sub-lessor's premises from protection .. [262]
25 Service of notices on landlord's agents .. .. [263]
26 Jurisdiction and procedure .. .. [264]

PART IV

REHOUSING

27 Applications to housing authority concerned .. .. [265]
28 Duty of housing authority concerned .. .. [266]
29 Agricultural dwelling-house advisory committees .. .. [267]

Section Para

PART V

POWER TO OBTAIN INFORMATION

30 Information about housing accommodation .. .. [268]
31 Kinds of information obtainable .. .. [269]

PART VI

MISCELLANEOUS AND SUPPLEMENTAL

33 Suspension of condition attached to planning permission .. .. [270]
34 Interpretation .. .. [271]
35 Isles of Scilly .. .. [272]
36 Application to Crown property .. .. [273]
37 Offences by bodies corporate .. .. [274]
38 Prosecution of offences .. .. [275]
39 Expenses .. .. [276]
40 Short title, etc .. .. [277]

SCHEDULES

Schedule 1—*Index of General Definitions* .. .. [278]
Schedule 2—*Meaning of "Relevant Licence" and "Relevant Tenancy"* .. .. [279]
Schedule 3—*Protected Occupiers in their own Right* .. ..
Part I—Definitions .. .. [280]
Part II—Temporary Provisions as Respects Certain Forestry Workers .. .. [281]
Part III—Supplemental .. .. [282]
Schedule 4—*Grounds for Possession of Dwelling-House Subject to Protected Occupancy or Statutory Tenancy* .. ..
Part I—Cases where Court has a Discretion .. .. [283]
Part II—Cases in which Court must Order Possession .. .. [284]
Schedule 5—*Terms of the Statutory Tenancy* .. .. [285]
Schedule 6—*Phasing of Rent Increases* .. .. [286]
Schedule 8—*Consequential and Minor Amendments* .. .. [287]
Schedule 9—*Transitional* .. .. [288]

An Act to afford security of tenure for agricultural workers housed by their employers, and their successors; to make further provision as to the rents and other conditions of tenure of such persons, including amendments of the Rent Act 1968; to impose duties on housing authorities as respects agricultural workers and their successors; and for purposes connected with those matters

[22 November 1976]

PART I

PRELIMINARY

1. Interpretation and commencement

(1) In this Act—

(*a*) "agriculture" includes—

(i) dairy-farming and livestock keeping and breeding (whether those activities involve the use of land or not);

(ii) the production of any consumable produce which is grown for sale or for consumption or other use for the purposes of a trade or business or of any other undertaking (whether carried on for profit or not);

(iii) the use of land as grazing, meadow or pasture land or orchard or osier land;

(iv) the use of land for market gardens or nursery grounds; and
(v) forestry;

(*b*) "forestry" includes—

(i) the use of land for nursery grounds for trees, and
(ii) the use of land for woodlands where that use is ancillary to the use of land for other agricultural purposes.

(2) For the purposes of the definition in subsection (1) (*a*) above—

"consumable produce" means produce grown for consumption or other use after severance or separation from the land or other growing medium on or in which it is grown;

"livestock" includes any animal which is kept for the production of food, wool, skins or fur, or for the purpose of its use in the carrying on of any agricultural activity, and for the purposes of this definition "animal" includes bird but does not include fish.

(3) The expressions listed in column I of Schedule I to this Act have for the purposes of this Act the meanings given by the provisions shown in column 2 of the Schedule.

(4) In this Act "relevant licence" and "relevant tenancy" have the meanings given by Schedule 2 to this Act.

(5) Schedule 3 to this Act, of which—

(*a*) Part I is for determining for the purposes of this Act—

(i) whether a person is a qualifying worker,
(ii) whether a person is incapable of whole-time work in agriculture, or work in agriculture as a permit worker, in consequence of a qualifying injury or disease, and
(iii) whether a dwelling-house is in qualifying ownership,

(*b*) Part II postpones the operation of this Act in relation to certain persons employed in forestry, and

(*c*) Part III contains supplementary provisions,

shall have effect.

(6) This Act shall, subject to subsection (7) below, come into force on such date as the Secretary of State and the Minister of Agriculture, Fisheries and Food acting jointly may by order contained in a statutory instrument appoint, and that date is in this Act called "the operative date".

(7) Subsection (6) above has effect subject to the said Part II of Schedule 3 to this Act. **[239]**

NOTES
Commencement: 1 October 1977 (certain purposes); 1 January 1977 (remainder).
Commencement orders: SI 1976 No 2124, 1977 No 1268.

Protected occupancies

2. Protected occupiers in their own right

(1) Where a person has, in relation to a dwelling-house, a relevant licence or tenancy and the dwelling-house is in qualifying ownership, or has been in qualifying ownership at any time during the subsistence of the licence or tenancy (whether it was at the time a relevant licence or tenancy or not), he shall be a protected occupier of the dwelling-house if—

(*a*) he is a qualifying worker, or
(*b*) he has been a qualifying worker at any time during the subsistence of the licence or tenancy (whether it was at the time a relevant licence or tenancy or not).

(2) Where a person has, in relation to a dwelling-house, a relevant licence or tenancy and the dwelling-house is in qualifying ownership, or has been in qualifying ownership at any time during the subsistence of the licence or tenancy (whether it was at the time a relevant licence or tenancy or not), he shall be a protected occupier of the dwelling-house if and so long as he is incapable of whole-time work in agriculture, or work in agriculture as a permit worker, in consequence of a qualifying injury or disease.

(3) A person who has in relation to a dwelling-house a relevant licence or tenancy shall be a protected occupier of the dwelling-house if—
(*a*) immediately before the licence or tenancy was granted, he was a protected occupier or statutory tenant of the dwelling-house in his own right, or
(*b*) the licence or tenancy was granted in consideration of his giving up possession of another dwelling-house of which he was such an occupier or such a tenant.

(4) In this Act—

"protected occupier in his own right" means a person who is a protected occupier by virtue of subsection (1), (2) or (3) above;
"statutory tenant in his own right" means a person who is a statutory tenant by virtue of section 4 (1) below and who, immediately before he became such a tenant, was a protected occupier in his own right. **[240]**

NOTES
Commencement: 1 October 1977 (certain purposes); 1 January 1977 (remainder).
Commencement orders: SI 1976 No 2124, 1977 No 1268.

3. Protected occupiers by succession

(1) Subsection (2) or, as the case may be, subsection (3) below shall have effect for determining what person (if any) is a protected occupier of a dwelling-house after the death of a person ("the original occupier") who, immediately before his death, was a protected occupier of the dwelling-house in his own right.

(2) Where the original occupier was a man who died leaving a widow who was residing [in the dwelling-house immediately before his death] then, after his death, if the widow has, in relation to the dwelling-house, a relevant licence or tenancy, she shall be a protected occupier of the dwelling-house.

This subsection is framed by reference to the case where the original occupier was a man, but is to be read as applying equally in the converse case where the original occupier was a woman.

(3) Where—
(*a*) the original occupier was not a person who died leaving a surviving spouse who was residing [in the dwelling-house immediately before his death], but
(*b*) one or more persons who were members of his family were residing with him at the time of and for the period of six months immediately before his death,

then, after his death, if that person or, as the case may be, any of those persons has, in relation to the dwelling-house, a relevant licence or tenancy, that person or, as the case may be, such one of the persons having such a licence or tenancy as may be decided by agreement, or in default of agreement by the county court, shall be a protected occupier of the dwelling-house.

(4) A person who has, in relation to a dwelling-house, a relevant licence or tenancy shall be a protected occupier of the dwelling-house if—

(*a*) immediately before the licence or tenancy was granted, he was a protected occupier or statutory tenant of the dwelling-house by succession, or

(*b*) the licence or tenancy was granted in consideration of his giving up possession of another dwelling-house of which he was such an occupier or such a tenant.

(5) In this Act—

"protected occupier by succession" means a person who is a protected occupier by virtue of subsection (2), (3) or (4) above;

"statutory tenant by succession" means a person who is a statutory tenant by virtue of section 4 (1) below and who, immediately before he became such a tenant, was a protected occupier by succession, or a person who is a statutory tenant by virtue of section 4 (3) or (4) below.

(6) A dwelling-house is, in this Act, referred to as subject to a protected occupancy where there is a protected occupier of it. **[241]**

NOTES

Commencement: 1 October 1977 (certain purposes); 1 January 1977 (remainder).
Commencement orders: SI 1976 No 2124, 1977 No 1268.
Sub-s (2), (3): amended by the Housing Act 1980, s 76(3).

Statutory tenancies

4. Statutory tenants and tenancies

(1) Subject to section 5 below, where a person ceases to be a protected occupier of a dwelling-house on the termination, whether by notice to quit or by virtue of section 16 (3) of this Act or otherwise, of his licence or tenancy he shall, if and so long as he occupies the dwelling-house as his residence, be the statutory tenant of it.

(2) Subject to section 5 below, subsection (3), or, as the case may be, subsection (4) below shall have effect for determining what person (if any) is the statutory tenant of a dwelling-house at any time after the death of a person ("the original occupier") who was, immediately before his death, a protected occupier or statutory tenant of the dwelling-house in his own right.

(3) If the original occupier was a man who died leaving a widow who was residing [in the dwelling-house immediately before his death] then, after his death, unless the widow is a protected occupier of the dwelling-house by virtue of section 3 (2) above, she shall be the statutory tenant if and so long as she occupies the dwelling-house as her residence.

This subsection is framed by reference to the case where the original occupier was a man, but is to be read as applying equally in the converse case where the original occupier was a woman.

(4) Where—

(*a*) the original occupier was not a person who died leaving a surviving spouse who was residing [in the dwelling-house immediately before his death], but

(*b*) one or more persons who were members of his family were residing with him at the time of and for the period of six months immediately before his death,

then, after his death, unless that person or, as the case may be, one of those persons is a protected occupier of the dwelling-house by virtue of section 3 (3) above, that person or, as the case may be, such one of those persons as may be decided by agreement, or in default of agreement by the county court, shall be the statutory tenant if and so long as he occupies the dwelling-house as his residence.

(5) In subsections (1), (3) and (4) above the phrase "if and so long as he occupies the dwelling-house as his residence" shall be construed in accordance with [section 2(3) of the Rent Act 1977] (construction of that phrase in the corresponding provisions of that Act).

(6) A dwelling-house is, in this Act, referred to as subject to a statutory tenancy where there is a statutory tenant of it. **[242]**

NOTES

Commencement: 1 October 1977 (certain purposes); 1 January 1977 (remainder).
Commencement orders: SI 1976 No 2124, 1977 No 1268.
Sub-ss (3), (4): amended by the Housing Act 1980, s 76(3).
Sub-s (5): amended by the Rent Act 1977, s 155, Sch 23, para 72.

5. No statutory tenancy where landlord's interest belongs to Crown or to local authority, etc

[(1) A person shall not at any time be a statutory tenant of a dwelling-house if the interest of his immediate landlord would, at that time—

(*a*) belong to Her Majesty in right of the Crown or to a government department, or

(*b*) be held in trust for Her Majesty for the purposes of a government department;

except that an interest belonging to Her Majesty in right of the Crown shall not prevent a person from being a statutory tenant if the interest is under the management of the Crown Estate Commissioners].

(2) A person shall not at any time be a statutory tenant of a dwelling-house if the interest of his immediate landlord, would, at that time, belong to any of the bodies specified in subsection (3) below.

(3) The bodies referred to in subsection (2) above are—

(*a*) the council of a county or district or, in the application of this Act to the Isles of Scilly, the Council of those Isles;

(*b*) . . . the council of a London borough or the Common Council of the City of London;

[(*ba*) the Inner London Education Authority;

(*bb*) a joint authority established by Part IV of the Local Government Act 1985;]

(*c*) the Commission for the New Towns;

(*d*) the Housing Corporation;

(*e*) a development corporation established by an order made, or having effect as if made, under the [New Towns Act 1981]; and (*f*) a housing trust (as defined in [section 15(5) of the Rent Act 1977]) which is a charity within the meaning of the Charities Act 1960.

(4) If any of the conditions for the time being specified in [section 15(4) of the Rent Act 1977] (conditions for the operation of the corresponding provision of that Act) is fulfilled, a person shall not be a statutory tenant of a dwelling-house at any time if the interest of his immediate landlord would, at that time,

[belong to a housing association which—

(*a*) is registered under the Housing Associations Act 1985, or
(*b*) is a co-operative housing association within the meaning of that Act.] **[243]**

NOTES

Commencement: 28 November 1980 (sub-s (1)); 1 October 1977 (remainder-certain purposes); 1 January 1977 (remainder).

Commencement orders: SI 1976 No 2124, 1977 No 1268, 1980 No 1706.

Sub-s (1): substituted by the Housing Act 1980, s 73(3).

Sub-s (3): in para (*b*) words omitted repealed by the Local Government Act 1985, s 102, Sch 17; paras (*ba*), (*bb*) added by the Local Government Act 1985, s 84, Sch 14, para 55; para (*e*) amended by the New Towns Act 1981, s 81, Sch 12; para (*f*) amended by the Rent Act 1977, s 155, Sch 23, para 73.

Sub-s (4): first amendment in square brackets made by the Rent Act 1977, s 155, Sch 23, para 73; second amendment in square brackets made by the Housing (Consequential Provisions) Act 1985, s 4, Sch 2, para 33.

Housing Finance Act 1972, s 80: repealed with savings by the Housing Rents and Subsidies Act 1975, s 17(3), (5), Sch 1, Part III, para 23(3)-(5), Sch 6, Part IV.

Modified by SI 1985 No 1884, art 10, Sch 3.

PART II

SECURITY OF TENURE

Protected occupancies and statutory tenancies

6. Grounds for possession

(1) A court shall not make an order for possession of a dwelling-house subject to a protected occupancy or statutory tenancy except in the Cases in Schedule 4 to this Act.

(2) A landlord who obtains an order for possession of a dwelling-house as against a statutory tenant shall not be required to give to the statutory tenant any notice to quit.

(3) Where in Case IX in the said Schedule a landlord obtains an order for possession of the dwelling-house, and it is subsequently made to appear to the court that the order was obtained by misrepresentation or concealment of material facts, the court may order the landlord to pay to the former tenant such sum as appears sufficient as compensation for damage or loss sustained by the tenant as a result of the order.

(4) In subsection (3) above and in Schedule 4 to this Act "tenant" means a protected occupier or a statutory tenant.

(5) Section 7 below has effect as regards the Cases in Part I of the said Schedule.

(6) If, apart from subsection (1) above, the landlord would be entitled to recover possession of a dwelling-house subject to a protected occupancy or

statutory tenancy, the court shall make an order for possession if the circumstances of the case are as specified in any of the Cases in Part II of the said Schedule. **[244]**

NOTES

Commencement: 1 October 1977 (certain purposes); 1 January 1977 (remainder).
Commencement orders: SI 1976 No 2124, 1977 No 1268.

7. Discretion of court in giving possession

(1) This section applies in the Cases in Part I of Schedule 4 to this Act.

(2) In those Cases the court shall not make an order unless it considers it reasonable to do so.

[(2A) In those cases the court may adjourn for such period or periods as it thinks fit.]

(3) On the making of the order for possession, or at any time before execution of the order, the court may—

(*a*) stay or suspend execution of the order, or
(*b*) postpone the date of possession,

for such period or periods as the court thinks fit.

[(4) On any such adjournment as is referred to in subsection (2A) above or any such stay, suspension or postponement as is referred to in subsection (3) above, the court shall, unless it considers that to do so would cause exceptional hardship to the tenant or would otherwise be unreasonable, impose conditions with regard to payment by the tenant of arrears of rent (if any) and rent or payments in respect of occupation after termination of the tenancy (mesne profits) and may impose such other conditions as it thinks fit.]

(5) If conditions so imposed are complied with, the court may if it thinks fit discharge or rescind the order for possession,

[(5A) Subsection (5B) below applies in any case where—

(*a*) proceedings are brought for possession of a dwelling-house which is subject to a protected occupancy or statutory tenancy;
(*b*) the tenant's spouse or former spouse, having rights of occupation under the Matrimonial Homes Act 1967, is then in occupation of the dwelling-house; and
(*c*) the tenancy is terminated as a result of those proceedings.

(5B) In any case to which this subsection applies, the spouse or former spouse shall, so long as he or she remains in occupation, have the same rights in relation to or in connection with any such adjournment as is referred to in subsection (2A) above or any such stay, suspension or postponement as is referred to in subsection (3) above as he or she would have if those rights of occupation were not affected by the termination of the tenancy.]

(6) In this section "tenant" means a protected occupier or a statutory tenant [and "tenancy" shall be construed accordingly]. **[245]**

NOTES

Commencement: 28 November 1980 (sub-ss (2A), (4), (5A), (5B)); 1 October 1977 (remainder-certain purposes); 1 January 1977 (remainder).
Commencement orders: SI 1976 No 2124, 1977 No 1268, 1980 No 1706.
Amended by the Housing Act 1980, ss 75, 152, Sch 25, para 23.

8. Restriction on levy of distress for rent

(1) Subject to subsection (2) below, no distress for the rent of any dwelling-house subject to a protected occupancy or statutory tenancy shall be levied except with the leave of the county court; and the court shall, with respect to any application for such leave, have the same or similar powers with respect to adjournment, stay, suspension, postponement and otherwise as are conferred by section 7 of this Act, in relation to proceedings for possession of such a dwelling-house.

(2) Nothing in subsection (1) above shall apply to distress levied under [section 102 of the County Courts Act 1984] (claims for rent where goods seized in execution). **[246]**

NOTES
Commencement: 1 October 1977 (certain purposes); 1 January 1977 (remainder).
Commencement orders: SI 1976 No 2124, 1977 No 1268.
Sub-s (2): amended by the County Courts Act 1984, s 148(1), Sch 2, para 62.

9. Effect of determination of superior tenancy, etc

(1) If a court makes an order for possession of a dwelling-house from a protected occupier or statutory tenant, or from a protected or statutory tenant for the purposes of the [Rent Act 1977], and the order is made by virtue of Part I of Schedule 4 to this Act or, as the case may be, [section 98 or 99(2)] of that Act, nothing in the order shall affect the right of any sub-tenant—

(*a*) to whom the dwelling-house or any part of it has been lawfully sublet before the commencement of the proceedings, and
(*b*) who is a protected occupier or statutory tenant thereof,

to retain possession by virtue of this Act, nor shall the order operate to give a right to possession against any such sub-tenant.

(2) Where a statutorily protected tenancy of a dwelling-house is determined, either as a result of an order for possession or for any other reason, any sub-tenant—

(*a*) to whom the dwelling-house or any part of it has been lawfully sublet, and
(*b*) who is a protected occupier or statutory tenant thereof,

shall, subject to the provisions of this Act, be deemed to become the tenant of the landlord on the same terms as if the tenant's statutorily protected tenancy had continued.

(3) Where a dwelling-house—

(*a*) forms part of premises which have been let as a whole on a superior tenancy but do not constitute a dwelling-house let on a statutorily protected tenancy; and
(*b*) is itself subject to a protected occupancy or statutory tenancy,

then, from the coming to an end of the superior tenancy, this Act shall apply in relation to the dwelling-house as if, in lieu of the superior tenancy, there had been separate tenancies of the dwelling-house and of the remainder of the premises, for the like purposes as under the superior tenancy, and at rents equal to the just proportion of the rent under the superior tenancy.

In this subsection "premises" includes an agricultural holding within the meaning of the *Agricultural Holdings Act 1948* [Agricultural Holdings Act 1986].

(4) In subsections (2) and (3) above "statutorily protected tenancy" means—

(*a*) a protected occupancy or statutory tenancy;
(*b*) a protected or statutory tenancy for the purposes of the [Rent Act 1977], or
(*c*) a tenancy of an agricultural holding within the meaning of the *Agricultural Holdings Act 1948* [Agricultural Holdings Act 1986].

(5) Subject to subsection (6) below, a long tenancy of a dwelling-house which is also a tenancy at a low rent but which, had it not been a tenancy at a low rent, would have been a protected tenancy for the purposes of the [Rent Act 1977], shall be treated for the purposes of subsection (2) above as a statutorily protected tenancy.

(6) Notwithstanding anything in subsection (5) above, subsection (2) above shall not have effect where the sub-tenancy in question was created (whether immediately or derivatively) out of a long tenancy falling within subsection (5) above and, at the time of the creation of the sub-tenancy—

(*a*) a notice to terminate the long tenancy had been given under section 4 (1) of the Landlord and Tenant Act 1954; or
(*b*) the long tenancy was being continued by section 3 (1) of that Act;

unless the sub-tenancy was created with the consent in writing of the person who at the time when it was created was the landlord, within the meaning of Part I of that Act.

(7) In subsections (5) and (6) above "long tenancy" means a tenancy granted for a term of years certain exceeding 21 years, whether or not subsequently extended by act of the parties or by any enactment; and in determining for the purposes of those subsections whether a long tenancy is a tenancy at a low rent, there shall be disregarded such part (if any) of the sums payable by the tenant as is expressed (in whatever terms) to be payable in respect of rates, service, repairs, maintenance or insurance, unless it would not have been regarded by the parties as so payable. **[247]**

NOTES

Commencement: 1 October 1977 (certain purposes); 1 January 1977 (remainder).
Commencement orders: SI 1976 No 2124, 1977 No 1268.
Sub-ss (1), (5): amended by the Rent Act 1977, s 155, Sch 23, para 74.
Sub-s (2) excluded by the Leasehold Reform Act 1967, Sch 2, para 3(2).
Sub-s (3): words in italics repealed with savings and words in square brackets substituted with savings by the Agricultural Holdings Act 1986, ss 99, 100, Sch 13, para 3, Sch 14, para 57.
Sub-s (4): first amendment in square brackets made by the Rent Act 1977, s 155, Sch 23, para 74; words in italics repealed with savings and subsequent words in square brackets substituted with savings by the Agricultural Holdings Act 1986, ss 99, 100, Sch 13, para 3, Sch 14, para 57.

Statutory tenancies

10. Terms and conditions

(1) Schedule 5 to this Act contains provisions about the terms of a statutory tenancy.

(2) Schedule 5 to this Act shall not impose any liability to pay rent under a statutory tenancy (whether the protected occupier was a tenant or a licensee), and accordingly no rent shall be payable under a statutory tenancy until rent becomes payable by virtue of an agreement under section 11 of this Act, or by virtue of a notice of increase under section 12 or 14 of this Act.

(3) Rent under a statutory tenancy which is a weekly tenancy shall be payable weekly in arrear, except that—

(*a*) if a rent or equivalent payment was payable under the protected occupancy, and was so payable otherwise than in arrear, rent under the statutory tenancy shall be payable in that other way, and
(*b*) this subsection has effect subject to any agreement between the landlord and the tenant.

(4) The day on which rent is payable weekly in arrear in accordance with subsection (3) above shall be—
(*a*) where rent or any equivalent payment was payable weekly in arrear under the protected occupancy, the day on which it was so payable,
(*b*) where paragraph (*a*) does not apply, and at the end of the protected occupancy the protected occupier was being paid weekly wages, the day on which the wages were paid,
(*c*) in any other case such day as the landlord and tenant may agree, or in default of agreement, Friday in each week.

(5) The covenants implied in the statutory tenancy shall include a covenant to pay rent in accordance with this Part of this Act. **[248]**

NOTES
Commencement: 1 October 1977 (certain purposes); 1 January 1977 (remainder).
Commencement orders: SI 1976 No 2124, 1977 No 1268.

11. Agreed rents

(1) The landlord and the statutory tenant may by agreement fix the rent payable under a statutory tenancy (or may agree that no rent shall be payable under the statutory tenancy).

(2) An agreement under this section may be made at any time, including a time before the beginning of the statutory tenancy, or a time when a rent is registered for the dwelling-house.

(3) The rent so fixed shall not exceed—
(*a*) where a rent is registered for the dwelling-house at the time when the agreement is made, the weekly or other periodical equivalent of the amount of the rent so registered,
(*b*) where a rent is not so registered, the amount of the rent based on rateable value defined in the next following section.

(4) Where a rent is registered for the dwelling-house at any time after the agreement is made, as from the date from which the registration takes effect the rent payable under the agreement shall not exceed the weekly or other periodical equivalent of the amount of the rent so registered.

(5) If the rent payable under the agreement exceeds the limit imposed by subsections (3) or (4) above, the amount of the excess shall be irrecoverable from the tenant.

(6) Unless the contrary intention appears from the agreement, it shall be terminable by the landlord or the tenant by notice in writing served on the other.

(7) The notice shall specify the date from which the agreement is terminated, which shall be not earlier than four weeks after service of the notice.

(8) Subject to subsection (3) above, an agreement made under this section may from time to time be varied by a further agreement so made, whether or not there has been a change in the persons who are landlord and tenant.

(9) If and so long as, in the period following the termination of an agreement under this section, no notice of increase under section 12 or section 14 of this Act takes effect (and no subsequent agreement is in force), the rent payable under the statutory tenancy shall be the same as the rent payable, or last payable, under the agreement, and it shall be payable for equivalent rental periods, and in other respects in the same way as, the rent was payable, or last payable, under the agreement.

(10) Where a rent is registered for the dwelling-house at any time after the termination of the agreement, as from the date from which the registration takes effect the rent payable under subsection (9) above shall not exceed the weekly or other periodical equivalent of the amount of the rent so registered; and if the rent so payable exceeds the limit imposed by the foregoing provision of this subsection, the amount of the excess shall be irrecoverable from the tenant.

(11) If the agreement mentioned in subsection (9) above provided that no rent was payable under the statutory tenancy, no rent shall be payable in the period for which that subsection applies. **[249]**

NOTES
Commencement: 1 October 1977 (certain purposes); 1 January 1977 (remainder).
Commencement orders: SI 1976 No 2124, 1977 No 1268.

12. Provisional rents

(1) This section applies where a rent is not registered for a dwelling-house which is subject to a statutory tenancy.

(2) If the rent payable for any period of the statutory tenancy would be less than the rent based on rateable value, it may be increased up to the amount of that rent by a notice of increase served by the landlord on the tenant.

(3) The notice shall specify the amount of the rent based on rateable value, and set out the landlord's calculation of that amount.

(4) The notice should also specify the date from which the notice is to take effect, which shall not be earlier than four weeks before service of the notice, and not at a time when an agreement under section 11 of this Act is in force.

(5) If the notice takes effect from the termination of an agreement under section 11 of this Act, it shall state that fact, and specify the rent payable, or last payable, under that agreement.

(6) If a notice is served under this section at a time when an agreement under section 11 of this Act is in force, and the date stated in the notice as that from which it is to take effect is—

(*a*) a date after service of the notice, and
(*b*) a date as at which the landlord could by notice served with the first-mentioned notice terminate the agreement,

the first-mentioned notice shall operate as a notice to terminate the agreement as at that date.

(7) Where a rent is registered for the dwelling-house at any time after notice is served, as from the date from which the registration takes effect the rent payable in accordance with the notice shall not exceed the weekly or other periodical equivalent of the amount of the rent so registered.

(8) If the rent payable in accordance with the notice exceeds the limit

imposed by subsection (7) above, the amount of the excess shall be irrecoverable from the tenant.

(9) In this section—

(*a*) "rent based on rateable value" means the weekly or other periodical equivalent of an annual amount equal to the prescribed multiple of the rateable value of the dwelling-house, and

(*b*) the "prescribed multiple" is 1.5, or such other number (whole or with a fraction) as the Secretary of State may by order prescribe.

(10) An order made under subsection (9) above—

(*a*) may contain such transitional and other supplemental and incidental provisions as appear to the Secretary of State expedient,

(*b*) may be varied or revoked by a subsequent order so made, and

(*c*) shall be contained in a statutory instrument subject to annulment in pursuance of a resolution of either House of Parliament.

(11) The date as at which the rateable value is to be determined for the purposes of this section, and for the purposes of any agreement made under section 11 of this Act, shall be the date on which the notice is served, or as the case may be the date when the agreement was made.

(12) If there is no separate rateable value for the dwelling-house the rateable value shall be ascertained by a proper apportionment or aggregation of the rateable value or values of the relevant hereditaments; and until the rateable value is so ascertained references in this section to the amount of the rent based on rateable value shall be construed as references to the amount of the rent based on the landlord's estimate of that value.

(13) Any question as to the proper apportionment or aggregation under subsection (12) above shall be determined by the county court, and the decision of the county court shall be final. **[250]**

NOTES

Commencement: 1 October 1977 (certain purposes); 1 January 1977 (remainder).
Commencement orders: SI 1976 No 2124, 1977 No 1268.

13. Application for registration of rent

(1) There shall be a part of the register under Part IV of the [Rent Act 1977] in which rents may be registered for dwelling-houses which are subject to statutory tenancies (as defined in this Act).

(2) In relation to that part of the register the following provision of the [Rent Act 1977], that is—

[(*a*) sections 67 and 70

(*b*) section 71, except subsection (3), and

(*c*) Part I of Schedule 11,]

shall have effect as if for any reference in those provisions to a regulated tenancy there were substituted a reference to a statutory tenancy (as defined in this Act).

(3) The preceding provisions of this section shall not be taken as applying [sections 68, 69, 71(3), 72 or 73 of the Rent Act 1977 or Part II of Schedule 11 or [Schedule 12] to that Act].

[(4) The registration of a rent in the said part of the register takes effect—

(*a*) if the rent is determined by the rent officer, from the date when it is registered, and

(*b*) if the rent is determined by a rent assessment committee, from the date when the committee make their decision.

(5) If the rent for the time being registered in the said part of the register is confirmed, the confirmation takes effect—

(*a*) if it is made by the rent officer, from the date when it is noted in the register, and

(*b*) if it is made by a rent assessment committee, from the date when the committee make their decision.

(6) If (by virtue of section 67(4) of the Rent Act 1977, as applied by subsection (2) above) an application for registration of a rent is made before the expiry of the period mentioned in section 67(3) and the resulting registration of a rent for the dwelling-house, or confirmation of the rent for the time being registered, would, but for this subsection, take effect before the expiry of that period it shall take effect on the expiry of that period.

(6A) The date from which the registration or confirmation of a rent takes effect shall be entered in the said part of the register.

(6B) As from the date on which the registration of a rent takes effect any previous registration of a rent for the dwelling-house ceases to have effect.]

(7) A rent registered in any part of the register for a dwelling-house which becomes, or ceases to be, one subject to a statutory tenancy shall be as effective as if it were registered in any other part of the register; but [section 67 (3) of the Rent Act 1977] (no application for registration of a different rent to be made within [two years] of the last registration) shall not apply to an application for the registration, as respects a dwelling-house which is subject to a statutory tenancy, of a rent different from one which is registered in a part of the register other than the part mentioned in subsection (1) above. **[251]**

NOTES

Commencement: 28 November 1980 (sub-ss (4)-(6B)); 1 October 1977 (remainder-certain purposes); 1 January 1977 (remainder).

Commencement orders: SI 1976 No 2124, 1977 No 1268, 1980 No 1706.

Sub-ss (1), (2): amended by the Rent Act 1977, s 155, Sch 23, para 75.

Sub-s (3): amended by the Rent Act 1977, s 155, Sch 23, para 75; further amended by the Housing Act 1980, s 152, Sch 25, para 33.

Sub-ss (4)–(6B): substituted by the Housing Act 1980, s 61(2).

Sub-s (7): first amendment made by the Rent Act 1977, s 155, Sch 23, para 75; second amendment made by the Housing Act 1980, s 152, Sch 25, para 33.

14. Registered rents

(1) This section applies where a rent is registered for a dwelling-house subject to a statutory tenancy.

(2) If the rent payable for any period of the statutory tenancy beginning on or after the date of registration would be less than the registered rent, it may be increased up to the amount of that rent by a notice of increase served by the landlord on the tenant.

(3) The notice shall specify the amount of the registered rent, and the date from which the notice is to take effect, which shall not be earlier than four weeks before service of the notice, and not at a time when an agreement under section 11 of this Act is in force.

(4) If the notice takes effect from the termination of an agreement under section 11 of this Act, it shall state that fact, and specify the rent payable, or last payable, under that agreement.

(5) If a notice is served under this section at a time when an agreement under section 11 of this Act is in force, and the date stated in the notice as that from which it is to take effect is—

(*a*) a date after service of the notice, and
(*b*) a date as at which the landlord could by notice served with the first-mentioned notice terminate the agreement,

the first-mentioned notice shall operate as a notice to terminate the agreement as at that date. **[252]**

NOTES
Commencement: 1 October 1977 (certain purposes); 1 January 1977 (remainder).
Commencement orders: SI 1976 No 2124, 1977 No 1268.

15. Phasing of rent increases

(1) The rent of a dwelling-house which is subject to a statutory tenancy qualifies for phasing under this section if—

(a) a rent is registered for that dwelling-house in the part of the register in which rents may be registered for dwelling-houses which are subject to statutory tenancies, and
(b) that rent is not the first rent to be registered for that dwelling-house in that part of that register during the subsistence of the statutory tenancy or, in the case of a statutory tenancy by succession, during the subsistence of any statutory tenancy which immediately preceded it.

(2) Where the rent of a dwelling-house qualifies for phasing under this section, and a provision of Schedule 6 to this Act imposes a rent limit for any period of the statutory tenancy falling within the period of delay imposed by that Schedule, sections 11 (3) and (4) and 14 (2) of this Act, shall have effect, in relation to that period of the statutory tenancy, as if for the references to the registered rent there were substituted references to the said rent limit.

(3) A notice of increase under section 14 of this Act which purports to increase a rent which qualifies for phasing under this section further than permitted by Schedule 6 to this Act shall have effect to increase it to the extent permitted by that Schedule and no further.

(4) Nothing in this section or in Schedule 6 to this Act shall prevent or limit any increase in rent by virtue of [section 71 (4) of the Rent Act 1977] (variable rents). **[253]**

NOTES
Commencement: 1 October 1977 (certain purposes); 1 January 1977 (remainder).
Commencement orders: SI 1976 No 2124, 1977 No 1268.
Repealed by SI 1987 No 264, art 2(2) except in relation to the circumstances and to the extent specified in Sch 2 to that Order; see para [1070] post.
Sub-s (4): amended by the Rent Act 1977, s 155, Sch 23, para 76.

16. Notices of increase

(1) Any reference in the following provisions of this section to a notice is a reference to a notice of increase under section 12 or section 14 of this Act.

(2) Notwithstanding that a notice relates to periods of a statutory tenancy it may be served before the statutory tenancy begins.

(3) Where a notice is served before the statutory tenancy begins, and the protected occupancy could, by a notice to quit served at the same time, be brought to an end before the date specified in the notice of increase, the notice shall operate to terminate the protected occupancy as from that date.

(4) If the county court is satisfied that any error or omission in a notice is due to a bona fide mistake on the part of the landlord, the court may by order amend the notice by correcting any errors or supplying any omission therein which, if not corrected or supplied, would render the notice invalid and if the court so directs, the notice as so amended shall have effect and be deemed to have had effect as a valid notice.

(5) If the county court is satisfied that—

(*a*) at the time when a notice under section 12 of this Act was served there was no separate rateable value for the dwelling-house, and

(*b*) the amount specified in the notice is the amount of the rent based on the landlord's estimate of the rateable value.

the court may by order amend the notice by substituting for the amount so specified the amount of the rent based on rateable value and, if the court so directs, the notice shall have effect and be deemed to have had effect and be deemed to have had effect as so amended.

(6) Any amendment of a notice under subsection (4) or (5) above may be made on such terms and conditions with respect to arrears of rent or otherwise as appear to the court to be just and reasonable.

(7) No increase of rent which becomes payable by reason of an amendment of a notice under subsection (4) or (5) above shall be recoverable in respect of any period of the statutory tenancy which ended more than six months before the date of the order making the amendment. **[254]**

NOTES

Commencement: 1 October 1977 (certain purposes); 1 January 1977 (remainder).
Commencement orders: SI 1976 No 2124, 1977 No 1268.

General provisions

17. Adjustment for differences in lengths of rental periods

In ascertaining for the purposes of this Part of this Act the weekly or other periodical equivalent of a registered rent, or of the annual amount mentioned in section 12(9) of this Act, a period of one month shall be treated as equivalent to one-twelfth of a year, and a period of a week as equivalent to one fifty-second of a year. **[255]**

NOTES

Commencement: 1 October 1977 (certain purposes); 1 January 1977 (remainder).
Commencement orders: SI 1976 No 2124, 1977 No 1268.

18. Regulations

(1) The Secretary of State may make regulations prescribing the form of any notice or other document to be given or used in pursuance of this Part of this Act.

(2) Any such regulations shall be made by statutory instrument which shall be subject to annulment in pursuance of a resolution of either House of Parliament. **[256]**

NOTES
Commencement: 1 October 1977 (certain purposes); 1 January 1977 (remainder).
Commencement orders: SI 1976 No 2124, 1977 No 1268.

19. Interpretation of Part II

In this Part of this Act, unless the context otherwise requires—

"registered" means registered in the register under Part IV of [the Rent Act 1977],

"rent based on rateable value" has the meaning given by section 12 (9) of this Act,

"rental period" means a period in respect of which a payment of rent, or in the case of a licence the equivalent of rent, falls to be made. **[257]**

NOTES
Commencement: 1 October 1977 (certain purposes); 1 January 1977 (remainder).
Commencement orders: SI 1976 No 2124, 1977 No 1268.
Amended by the Rent Act 1977, s 155, Sch 23, para 77.

PART III

PROTECTED OCCUPANCIES AND STATUTORY TENANCIES: SUPPLEMENTAL

Recovery of rent

20. Avoidance of requirements for advance payment of rent

(1) Any requirement that rent under a protected occupancy, or under a statutory tenancy, shall be payable—

(*a*) before the beginning of the rental period in respect of which it is payable, or

(*b*) earlier than 6 months before the end of the rental period in respect of which it is payable (if that period is more than 6 months),

shall be void, and any requirement avoided by this section is referred to in this section as a "prohibited requirement".

(2) Rent for any rental period to which a prohibited requirement relates shall be irrecoverable from the tenant.

(3) A person who purports to impose a prohibited requirement shall be liable on summary conviction to a fine not exceeding [level 3 on the standard scale] and the court by which he is convicted may order the amount of rent paid in compliance with the prohibited requirement to be repaid to the person by whom it was paid.

(4) In this section "rental period" means a period in respect of which a payment of rent falls to be made.

(5) For the avoidance of doubt it is hereby declared that this section does not render any amount recoverable more than once. **[258]**

NOTES
Commencement: 1 October 1977 (certain purposes); 1 January 1977 (remainder).
Commencement orders: SI 1976 No 2124, 1977 No 1268.
Sub-s (3): maximum fine increased and converted to a level on the standard scale by the Criminal Justice Act 1982, ss 37, 38, 46.

21. Recovery from landlord of sums paid in excess of recoverable rent

(1) Where a tenant has paid on account of rent any amount which, by virtue of Part II of this Act or this Part, is irrecoverable by the landlord, then, subject to subsection (3) below, the tenant who paid it shall be entitled to recover that amount from the landlord who received it or his personal representatives.

(2) Subject to subsection (3) below, any amount which a tenant is entitled to recover under subsection (1) above may, without prejudice to any other method of recovery, be deducted by the tenant from any rent payable by him to the landlord.

(3) No amount which a tenant is entitled to recover under subsection (1) above shall be recoverable at any time after the expiry of two years from the date of payment.

(4) Any person who, in any rent book or similar document, makes an entry showing or purporting to show any tenant as being in arrears in respect of any sum on account of rent which is irrecoverable by virtue of Part II of this Act or this Part shall be liable on summary conviction to a fine not exceeding [level 3 on the standard scale], unless he proves that, at the time of the making of the entry, the landlord had a bona fide claim that the sum was recoverable.

(5) If, where any such entry has been made by or on behalf of any landlord, the landlord on being requested by or on behalf of the tenant to do so, refuses or neglects to cause the entry to be deleted within seven days, the landlord shall be liable on summary conviction to a fine not exceeding [level 3 on the standard scale], unless he proves that, at the time of the neglect or refusal to cause the entry to be deleted, he had a bona fide claim that the sum was recoverable. **[259]**

NOTES

Commencement: 1 October 1977 (certain purposes); 1 January 1977 (remainder).
Commencement orders: SI 1976 No 2124, 1977 No 1268.
Sub-ss (4), (5): maximum fines increased and converted to levels on the standard scale by the Criminal Justice Act 1982, ss 37, 38, 46.

22. Rectification of rent books in light of determination of recoverable rent

Where, in any proceedings, the recoverable rent of a dwelling-house subject to a statutory tenancy is determined by a court, then, on the application of the tenant (whether in those or in any subsequent proceedings) the court may call for the production of the rent book or any similar document relating to the dwelling-house and may direct the registrar or clerk of the court to correct any entries showing, or purporting to show, the tenant as being in arrears in respect of any sum which the court has determined to be irrecoverable. **[260]**

NOTES

Commencement: 1 October 1977 (certain purposes); 1 January 1977 (remainder).
Commencement orders: SI 1976 No 2124, 1977 No 1268.

Miscellaneous

23. Tenant sharing accommodation with persons other than landlord

(1) Where a tenant has the exclusive occupation of any accommodation ("the separate accommodation"), and

(*a*) the terms as between the tenant and his landlord on which he holds the separate accommodation include the use of other accommodation (in this section referred to as "the shared accommodation") in common with another person or other persons, not being or including the landlord, and

(*b*) by reason only of the circumstances mentioned in paragraph (*a*) above, the separate accommodation would not, apart from this section, be a dwelling-house subject to a protected occupancy or statutory tenancy,

then, subject to subsection (2) below, the separate accommodation shall be deemed to be a dwelling-house subject to a protected occupancy or statutory tenancy as the case may be, and subsections (3) to (8) below shall have effect.

(2) Subsection (1) above shall not apply in relation to accommodation which would, apart from this subsection, be deemed to be a dwelling-house subject to a protected tenancy if—

(*a*) the accommodation consists of only one room, and

(*b*) at the time when the tenancy was granted, not less than three other rooms in the same building were let, or were available for letting, as residential accommodation to separate tenants on such terms as are mentioned in subsection (1) (*a*) above.

(3) For the avoidance of doubt it is hereby declared that where, for the purpose of determining the rateable value of the separate accommodation, it is necessary to make an apportionment under this Act, regard is to be had to the circumstances mentioned in subsection (1) (*a*) above.

(4) Subject to subsection (5) below, while the tenant is in possession of the separate accommodation (whether as a protected occupier or statutory tenant), any term or condition of the contract of tenancy terminating or modifying, or providing for the termination or modification of, his right to the use of any of the shared accommodation which is living accommodation shall be of no effect.

(5) Where the terms and conditions of the contract of tenancy are such that at any time during the tenancy the persons in common with whom the tenant is entitled to the use of the shared accommodation could be varied, or their number could be increased, nothing in subsection (4) above shall prevent those terms and conditions from having effect so far as they relate to any such variation or increase.

(6) Subject to subsection (7) below and without prejudice to the enforcement of any order made thereunder, while the tenant is in possession of the separate accommodation, no order shall be made for possession of any of the shared accommodation, whether on the application of the immediate landlord of the tenant or on the application of any person under whom that landlord derives title, unless a like order has been made, or is made at the same time, in respect of the separate accommodation; and the provisions of section 6 of this Act shall apply accordingly.

(7) On the application of the landlord, the county court may make such order, either terminating the right of the tenant to use the whole or any part of the shared accommodation other than living accommodation, or modifying his right to use the whole or any part of the shared accommodation, whether by varying the persons or increasing the number of persons entitled to the use of that accommodation, or otherwise, as the court thinks just:

Provided that no order shall be made under this subsection so as to effect any termination or modification of the rights of the tenant which, apart from subsection (4) above, could not be effected by or under the terms of the contract of tenancy.

(8) In this section the expression "living accommodation" means accommodation of such a nature that the fact that it constitutes or is included in the shared accommodation is (or, if the tenancy has ended, was) sufficient, apart from this section, to prevent the tenancy from constituting a protected occupancy of a dwelling-house. **[261]**

NOTES
Commencement: 1 October 1977 (certain purposes); 1 January 1977 (remainder).
Commencement orders: SI 1976 No 2124, 1977 No 1268.

24. Certain sub-lettings, not to exclude any part of sub-lessor's premises from protection

(1) Where the tenant of any premises, consisting of a house or part of a house, has sublet a part, but not the whole, of the premises, then, as against his landlord or any superior landlord, no part of the premises shall be treated as not being a dwelling-house subject to a protected occupancy or statutory tenancy by reason only that—

(*a*) the terms on which any person claiming under the tenant holds any part of the premises include the use of accommodation in common with other persons; or
(*b*) part of the premises is let to any such person at a rent which includes payments in respect of board or attendance.

(2) Nothing in this section affects the rights against, and liabilities to, each other of the tenant and any person claiming under him, or of any two such persons. **[262]**

NOTES
Commencement: 1 October 1977 (certain purposes); 1 January 1977 (remainder).
Commencement orders: SI 1976 No 2124, 1977 No 1268.

25. Service of notices on landlord's agents

(1) For the purposes of any proceedings arising out of Part I or II of this Act or this Part, a document shall be deemed to be duly served on the landlord of a dwelling-house if it is served—

(*a*) on any agent of the landlord named as such in the rent book or other similar document; or
(*b*) on the person who receives the rent of the dwelling-house.

(2) If for the purpose of any proceedings (whether civil or criminal) arising out of Part I or II of this Act, or this Part, any person serves upon any such agent or other person as is referred to in paragraph (*a*) or paragraph (*b*) of subsection (1) above a notice in writing requiring the agent or other person to disclose to him the full name and place of abode or place of business of the landlord, that agent or other person shall forthwith comply with the notice.

(3) If any such agent or other person as is referred to in subsection (2) above fails or refuses forthwith to comply with a notice served on him under that subsection, he shall be liable on summary conviction to a fine not exceeding [level 4 on the standard scale] unless he shows to the satisfaction of the court that he did not know, and could not with reasonable diligence have ascertained, such of the facts required by the notice to be disclosed as were not disclosed by him. **[263]**

NOTES

Commencement: 1 October 1977 (certain purposes); 1 January 1977 (remainder).

Commencement orders: SI 1976 No 2124, 1977 No 1268.

Sub-s (3): maximum fine increased and converted to a level on the standard scale by the Criminal Justice act 1982, ss 37, 39, 46, Sch 3.

26. Jurisdiction and procedure

(1) A county court shall have jurisdiction to determine—

(*a*) whether any person is or is not a protected occupier or a statutory tenant, or

(*b*) any question concerning the subject matter, terms or conditions of a statutory tenancy,

or any matter which is or may become material for determining a question under paragraph (*a*) or (*b*).

(2) A county court shall have jurisdiction to deal with any claim or other proceedings arising out of Part I of this Act, or Part II of this Act, except Part II of Schedule 4, or this Part, notwithstanding that the case would not, apart from this subsection, be within the jurisdiction of a county court.

(3) If, on a claim arising under Part I of this Act, or Part II of this Act except Part II of Schedule 4, or this Part, a person takes proceedings in the High Court which he could have taken in the county court, he shall not be entitled to any costs.

(4) The jurisdiction conferred by subsection (1) above is exercisable either in the course of any proceedings relating to the dwelling-house, or on an application made for the purpose by the landlord or tenant.

(5) The Lord Chancellor may make such rules and give such directions as he thinks fit for the purpose of giving effect to Part I or II of this Act, or this Part, and may, by those rules or directions, provide for the remission of any fees.

The power vested in the Lord Chancellor by this subsection may, when the Great Seal is in commission, be exercised by any Lord Commissioner. **[264]**

NOTES

Commencement: 1 October 1977 (certain purposes); 1 January 1977 (remainder).

Commencement orders: SI 1976 No 2124, 1977 No 1268.

PART IV

REHOUSING

27. Applications to housing authority concerned

(1) An application may be made by the occupier of land used for agriculture to the housing authority concerned ("the authority") on the ground that—

(*a*) vacant possession is or will be needed of a dwelling-house which is subject to a protected occupancy or statutory tenancy, or which is let on or subject to a tenancy to which subsection (2) below applies, in order to house a person who is or is to be employed in agriculture by the applicant, and that person's family,

(*b*) the applicant is unable to provide, by any reasonable means, suitable alternative accommodation for the occupier of the dwelling-house, and (*c*) the authority ought, in the interests of efficient agriculture, to provide the suitable alternative accommodation.

(2) This subsection applies to any tenancy which is a protected or statutory tenancy for the purposes of [the Rent Act 1977] and which—

(*a*) if it were a tenancy at a low rent, and
(*b*) if (where relevant) any earlier tenancy granted to the tenant, or to a member of his family, had been a tenancy at a low rent,

would be a protected occupancy or statutory tenancy.

[(3) In this Act the "housing authority concerned" is the local housing authority within the meaning of the Housing Act 1985.] **[265]**

NOTES

Commencement: 1 April 1986 (sub-s (3)); 1 October 1977 (certain purposes); 1 January 1977 (remainder).

Commencement orders: SI 1976 No 2124, 1977 No 1268.

Sub-s (2): amended by the Rent Act 1977, s 155, Sch 23, para 77.

Sub-s (3): substituted by the Housing (Consequential Provisions) Act 1985, s 4, Sch 2, para 33.

28. Duty of housing authority concerned

(1) An application to the authority shall be in writing and, if the authority so direct, shall be in such form as the authority direct; and there shall be a sufficient compliance with a direction under this subsection if the application is in a form substantially to that same effect as the form specified in the direction.

(2) The authority shall, within seven days of their receiving the application, notify the occupier of the dwelling-house of which possession is sought ("the dwelling-house") that the application has been made.

(3) The authority, or the applicant, or the occupier of the dwelling-house, may obtain advice on the case made by the applicant concerning the interests of efficient agriculture, and regarding the urgency of the application, by applying for the services of a committee under section 29 of this Act.

(4) The committee shall tender its advice in writing to the authority, and make copies of it available for the applicant and the occupier of the dwelling-house.

(5) In assessing the case made by the applicant and in particular the importance and degree of urgency of the applicant's need, the authority shall take full account of any advice tendered to them by the committee in accordance with section 29 of this Act, and in any legal proceedings relating to the duty imposed on the authority by this section, evidence shall be admissible of the advice so given.

[(6) The authority shall notify their decision on the application in writing to the applicant, and to the occupier of the dwelling-house, within three months of their receiving the application or, if an application is made for the services of a committee under section 29 of this Act, within two months of their receiving the committee's advice.

(6A) The notification shall state—

(*a*) if the authority are satisfied that the applicant's case is substantiated in accordance with section 27 above, what action they propose to take on the application;

(*b*) if they are not so satisfied, the reasons for their decision.]

(7) If the authority are satisfied that the applicant's case is substantiated in accordance with section 27 above, they shall use their best endeavours to provide the suitable alternative accommodation; and in assessing under this subsection the priority to be given to meet the applicant's case, the authority shall take into account the urgency of the case, the competing claims on the accommodation which they can provide and the resources at their disposal.

(8) Without prejudice to any other means of enforcing the duty imposed by subsection (7) above, that duty shall be enforceable, at the suit of the applicant, by an action against the authority for damages for breach of statutory duty.

(9) The authority shall not be obliged to provide suitable alternative accommodation if at the time when the accommodation becomes available the person for whom it is to be provided is employed by the applicant in the same capacity as that in which he was employed by the applicant at the time when the application was made, and he will continue to be so employed if provided with the alternative accommodation.

(10) The continuance of the obligation imposed on the authority by this section shall depend on compliance by the applicant with any reasonable request made by the authority for information about any change in circumstances which takes place after the making of the application, and which might affect the merits of the applicant's case.

(11) Any material change of facts which have been stated to the authority, or to the committee, by the applicant or, in relation to the application, by the occupier of the dwelling-house, shall be notified to the authority as soon as practicable by the person making the statement unless before the change accommodation has been provided in accordance with the application, or the authority have decided that the applicant's case is not substantiated.

A person who without reasonable excuse fails to comply with this subsection shall be liable on summary conviction to a fine not exceeding [level 5 on the standard scale].

(12) An application under this section shall lapse if the applicant ceases to be the occupier of the land used for agriculture, but without prejudice to the making of an application by any other person who is or becomes the occupier.

(13) In this section and section 27 of this Act references to the authority providing housing accommodation are references to its provision by any means open to the authority, whether direct or indirect.

(14) If in or in connection with an application under this section the applicant or any other person knowingly or recklessly makes a false statement for the purpose of inducing the authority to provide housing accommodation, he shall be liable on summary conviction to a fine not exceeding [level 5 on the standard scale]. **[266]**

NOTES

Commencement: 1 October 1977 (certain purposes); 1 January 1977 (remainder).

Commencement orders: SI 1976 No 2124, 1977 No 1268.

Sub-ss (6), (6A): substituted with a saving for existing sub-s (6) by the Rent (Agriculture) Amendment Act 1977, s 1.

Sub-ss (11), (14): maximum fines increased and converted to levels on the standard scale by the Criminal Justice Act 1982, ss 37, 38, 46.

29. Agricultural dwelling-house advisory committees

(1) In the area of each agricultural wages committee established under the Agricultural Wages Act 1948 there shall be one or more agricultural dwelling-house advisory committees (in this section called "committees") to perform the functions given them under section 28 of this Act.

(2) An application under section 28 of this Act for advice may be made to the chairman of the agricultural wages committee for the area in question for the appointment or designation of a committee to give the advice.

(3) Each committee shall be appointed by the chairman of the agricultural wages committee, and he may include persons who are not members of the agricultural wages committee.

(4) If there is no chairman, or if the chairman is unable to act, a vice-chairman of the agricultural wages committee may act in his place under this section.

(5) Each committee shall be composed of an independent member, who is the chairman, a member representing employers and a member representing workers in agriculture.

(6) The chairman of the committee shall be appointed from a panel of persons approved by the Minister.

(7) All three members of a committee must be present at any meeting of the committee, and no meeting shall be held during a vacancy in the membership.

(8) In carrying out their functions under section 28 of this Act committees shall act in accordance with any directions, whether general or specific, given to them by the Minister.

(9) The Minister may, if he thinks fit, make regulations contained in a statutory instrument regulating the procedure and meetings of committees, and may from time to time give directions, whether specific or general, regarding their procedure.

(10) Subject to regulations, or any direction, under subsection (9) above the procedure of any committee shall be such as the chairman of that committee may direct.

(11) The Minister may appoint a secretary for a committee, and there shall be paid to the members of a committee, and to the person who appoints or designates a committee, such fees and allowances by way of compensation for expenses incurred and time lost by them in the performance of their duties as the Minister may sanction with the consent of the Minister for the Civil Service.

(12) The Minister may with the consent of the Minister for the Civil Service make payments to persons other than members of a committee by way of fees or compensation for expenses incurred and time lost by them in or in connection with their giving, at the request of the committee, any advice or information.

(13) Payments made by the Minister under this section shall be defrayed out of money provided by Parliament.

(14) In this section "the Minister" means the Minister of Agriculture, Fisheries and Food. **[267]**

NOTES

Commencement: 1 October 1977 (certain purposes); 1 January 1977 (remainder).

Commencement orders: SI 1976 No 2124, 1977 No 1268.

The Minister: functions under this section, so far as they are exercisable in relation to Wales, are transferred to the Secretary of State for Wales, by SI 1978 No 272, art 2, Sch 1.

PART V

POWER TO OBTAIN INFORMATION

30. Information about housing accommodation

(1) The Minister may exercise the powers conferred on him by section 31 of this Act for the purpose of obtaining information about the housing accommodation which is on, or held in connection with, or used for, agricultural or forestry land.

(2) The Minister may give information so obtained—

(*a*) to the housing authority concerned for any part of the area to which the information relates, and

(*b*) where, since the giving of the information, other land has come into common ownership or occupation with the first-mentioned land, to the housing authority concerned for any part of the other land,

and information so given may be transmitted to any other authority to whom the Minister may give it under this subsection.

(3) The Minister may also give the information so obtained to any agricultural dwelling-house advisory committee which is to give advice under section 29 of this Act concerning any part of the area to which the information relates.

(4) No information relating to any particular land or business which has been obtained under section 31 of this Act shall be published or otherwise disclosed without the previous consent in writing—

(*a*) of the person giving the information, or

(*b*) (if different) of any person who at the time of the disclosure is the owner or occupier of the land, or as the case may be, the owner of the business.

(5) Subsection (4) does not apply—

(*a*) to disclosure under subsection (2) or (3) (but does apply to those to whom disclosure is so made),

(*b*) to disclosure for the purposes of any criminal proceedings, or of any report of those proceedings.

(6) A person who contravenes subsection (4) shall be liable on summary conviction to a fine not exceeding [level 5 on the standard scale].

(7) In this section and in section 31 of this Act—

"agricultural land" means land used for agriculture as defined in section 109 of the Agriculture Act 1947,

"forestry land" does not include agricultural land,

"occupier" includes a person responsible for the carrying on of any activity on agricultural or forestry land as servant or agent of the occupier,

"owner" includes a person exercising, as servant or agent of the owner, functions of estate management in relation to the land.

(8) In this section and in section 31 of this Act references to the Minister are references to the Minister of Agriculture, Fisheries and Food and, so far as the reference relates to forestry land, to the Forestry Commissioners. **[268]**

NOTES

Commencement: 1 October 1977 (certain purposes); 1 January 1977 (remainder).

Commencement orders: SI 1976 No 2124, 1977 No 1268.

Sub-s (6): maximum fine increased and converted to a level on the standard scale by the Criminal Justice Act 1982, ss 37, 38, 46.

The Minister: functions under this section, so far as they are exercisable in relation to Wales, are transferred to the Secretary of State for Wales, by SI 1978 No 272, art 2, Sch 1.

31. Kinds of information obtainable

(1) The Minister may serve on any owner or occupier of agricultural or forestry land a notice requiring him to give such information as is specified in the notice concerning housing accommodation on, or held in connection with, or used for, the land, being information within section 30 of this Act.

(2) The notice shall be complied with within such period, being not less than four weeks from service of the notice, as may be specified in the notice.

(3) The notice may in particular require information about—

(*a*) the extent and nature of the accommodation,
(*b*) the condition and location of the accommodation, including the state of repair of any dwelling-house, and the means of access to it,
(*c*) whether any accommodation is wholly or partly occupied by a person who is or has been employed in agriculture or by a person who has been married to such a person, or whether the accommodation is vacant, and any impending change in the state of occupation,
(*d*) so far as it lies within the knowledge of the person on whom the notice is served, facts about, or related to, housing accommodation on, or held in connection with, or used for, the land at some time or times prior to the service of the notice, or even prior to the operative date, but not at a time more than 5 years before the service of the notice.

(4) If the person served is not the owner or occupier of the land, the notice may require him to give any information in his possession which may identify the true owner or occupier and his address, or to state that he has no such information.

(5) The notice may be served either—

(*a*) by delivering it to the person on whom it is to be served, or
(*b*) by leaving it at the usual or last known place of abode of that person, or
(*c*) by sending it by the recorded delivery service or by registered post in a prepaid letter addressed to that person at his usual or last known place of abode, or
(*d*) in the case of an incorporated company or body, by delivering it to the secretary or clerk of the company or body at their registered or principal office or sending it, by the recorded delivery service or by registered post, in a prepaid letter addressed to the secretary or clerk of the company or body at that office, or
(*e*) if it is not practicable after reasonable inquiry to ascertain the name or address of an owner or occupier of the land, as being a person having any interest in the land or having particular functions or responsibilities, by addressing it to him by the description of the person having that interest in the land (naming it), or as the case may

be having that function or responsibility (naming it), and delivering the notice to some responsible person on the land, or by affixing it, or a copy of it, to some conspicuous object on the land.

(6) If any person—

(*a*) without reasonable excuse fails in any respect to comply with a notice under this section, or

(*b*) in purported compliance with a notice under this section knowingly or recklessly furnishes any information which is false in a material particular,

he shall be liable on summary conviction to a fine not exceeding [level 5 on the standard scale]. **[269]**

NOTES

Commencement: 1 October 1977 (certain purposes); 1 January 1977 (remainder).

Commencement orders: SI 1976 No 2124, 1977 No 1268.

Sub-s (6): maximum fine increased and converted to a level on the standard scale by the Criminal Justice Act 1982, ss 37, 38, 46.

The Minister: functions under this section, so far as they are exercisable in relation to Wales, are transferred to the Secretary of State for Wales, by SI 1978 No 272, art 2, Sch 1.

PART VI

MISCELLANEOUS AND SUPPLEMENTAL

33. Suspension of condition attached to planning permission

(1) This section applies where planning permission as respects a dwelling-house is or has been granted subject to a condition that the occupation of the dwelling-house is limited to a person employed in agriculture or forestry.

(2) If and so long as the dwelling-house is subject to a protected occupancy or statutory tenancy, or is let on or subject to a tenancy to which subsection (3) below applies, the condition shall be suspended.

(3) This subsection applies to any tenancy which is a protected or statutory tenancy for the purposes of [the Rent Act 1977] and which—

(*a*) if it were a tenancy at a low rent, and

(*b*) if (where relevant) any earlier tenancy granted to the tenant, or to a member of his family, had been a tenancy at a low rent,

would be a protected occupancy or statutory tenancy.

(4) Suspension of the condition shall not affect the operation of section 32 (1) (*b*) of the Town and Country Planning Act 1971 (application for continuance of planning permission without compliance with a condition subject to which permission was granted).

(5) Subsection (1) applies irrespective of the degree to which the condition circumscribes the employment in agriculture or forestry, irrespective of the other persons covered by the condition, and irrespective of the way in which agriculture or forestry is defined. **[270]**

NOTES

Commencement: 1 October 1977 (certain purposes); 1 January 1977 (remainder).

Commencement orders: SI 1976 No 2124, 1977 No 1268.

Sub-s (3): amended by the Rent Act 1977, s 155, Sch 23, para 77.

34. Interpretation

(1) In this Act, unless the context otherwise requires—

"landlord" includes any person from time to time deriving title under the original landlord and also includes, in relation to any dwelling-house, any person other than the tenant who is, or but for Part II of this Act would be, entitled to possession of the dwelling-house,

"licence" means any contract whereby (whether or not the contract contains other terms) one person grants to another, whether or not for any consideration, the right to occupy a dwelling-house as a residence, and references to the granting of a licence shall be construed accordingly,

"rates" includes water rates and charges and an occupier's drainage rate,

"tenancy" includes sub-tenancy,

"tenancy at a low rent" means a tenancy under which either no rent is payable or the rent payable is less than two-thirds of the rateable value which is or was the rateable value of the dwelling-house on the appropriate day for the purposes of [the Rent Act 1977],

"tenant" includes statutory tenant and also includes a sub-tenant and any person deriving title under the original tenant or sub-tenant.

(2) In this Act reference to tenancies include, unless the context otherwise requires, references to licences, and cognate expressions, including those in subsection (1) above, shall be construed accordingly.

(3) For the purposes of this Act a dwelling-house may be a house or part of a house.

(4) It is hereby declared that any power of giving directions conferred by this Act includes power to vary or revoke directions so given.

(5) Except in so far as the context otherwise requires, any reference in this Act to any other enactment shall be taken as referring to that enactment as amended by or under any other enactment, including this Act. **[271]**

NOTES

Commencement: 1 October 1977 (certain purposes); 1 January 1977 (remainder).
Commencement orders: SI 1976 No 2124, 1977 No 1268.
Sub-s (1): amended by the Rent Act 1977, s 155, Sch 23, para 77.

35. Isles of Scilly

(1) The Secretary of State and the Minister of Agriculture, Fisheries and Food acting jointly may by order direct that any of the provisions of this Act shall, in their application to the Isles of Scilly, have effect subject to such exceptions, adaptations and modifications as may be specified in the order.

(2) An order under this section shall be made by statutory instrument subject to annulment in pursuance of a resolution of either House of Parliament and may be varied or revoked by a subsequent order so made. **[272]**

NOTES

Commencement: 1 October 1977 (certain purposes); 1 January 1977 (remainder).
Commencement orders: SI 1976 No 2124, 1977 No 1268.

36. Application to Crown property

(1) Subject to section 5 (1) of this Act, this Act shall apply in relation to premises in which there subsists, or at any material time subsisted, a Crown interest as it

applies in relation to premises in which no such interest subsists or ever subsisted.

(2) In this section "Crown interest" means any interest which belongs to Her Majesty in right of the Crown or of the Duchy of Lancaster or to the Duchy of Cornwall or to a Government department, or which is held in trust for Her Majesty for the purposes of a Government department. **[273]**

NOTES

Commencement: 1 October 1977 (certain purposes); 1 January 1977 (remainder).
Commencement orders: SI 1976 No 2124, 1977 No 1268.

37. Offences by bodies corporate

(1) Where an offence under this Act which has been committed by a body corporate is proved to have been committed with the consent or connivance of, or to be attributable to any neglect on the part of, a director, manager, secretary or other similar officer of the body corporate, or any person who was purporting to act in any such capacity, he as well as the body corporate shall be guilty of that offence and be liable to be proceeded against and punished accordingly.

(2) Where the affairs of a body corporate are managed by its members, subsection (1) above shall apply in relation to the acts and defaults of a member in connection with his functions of management as if he were a director of the body corporate. **[274]**

NOTES

Commencement: 1 October 1977 (certain purposes); 1 January 1977 (remainder).
Commencement orders: SI 1976 No 2124, 1977 No 1268.

38. Prosecution of offences

Without prejudice to section 222 of the Local Government Act 1972 (power of local authorities to prosecute or defend legal proceedings), proceedings for an offence under any provision of this Act except section 31 (6) may be instituted by the housing authority concerned. **[275]**

NOTES

Commencement: 1 October 1977 (certain purposes); 1 January 1977 (remainder).
Commencement orders: SI 1976 No 2124, 1977 No 1268.

39. Expenses

There shall be paid out of moneys provided by Parliament—

(*a*) any expenses incurred by a Minister, or Government department, in consequence of the provisions of this Act, and

(*b*) any increase in sums so payable under any other Act which is attributable to the provisions of this Act. **[276]**

NOTES

Commencement: 1 October 1977 (certain purposes); 1 January 1977 (remainder).
Commencement orders: SI 1976 No 2124, 1977 No 1268.

40. Short title, etc

(1) This Act may be cited as the Rent (Agriculture) Act 1976.

(2) Schedule 8 to this Act contains consequential and minor amendments of other Acts.

(3) Schedule 9 to this Act contains transitional provisions.

(4) . . .

(5) This Act shall not extend to Scotland or Northern Ireland. [277]

NOTES

Commencement: 1 October 1977 (certain purposes); 1 January 1977 (remainder).
Commencement orders: SI 1976 No 2124, 1977 No 1268.
Sub-s (4): repealed by the Rent Act 1977, s 155, Sch 23.

SCHEDULES

SCHEDULE 1

Section 1

INDEX OF GENERAL DEFINITIONS

Expression defined	*Provisions in Act*
Agricultural dwelling-house advisory committee	Section 29(1).
Agriculture	Section 1(1).
Date of operation for forestry workers	Schedule 3, Part II.
Dwelling-house	Section 34(3).
Dwelling-house in qualifying ownership	Schedule 3, Part I.
Forestry	Section 1(1).
Housing authority concerned	Section 27(3).
Incapable of whole-time work in agriculture, or work in agriculture as a permit worker, in consequence of a qualifying injury or disease	Schedule 3, Part I.
Landlord	Section 34(1).
Licence	Section 34(1).
Operative date	Section 1(6).
Protected occupier	Sections 2 and 3.
Protected occupier by succession	Section 3(5).
Protected occupier in his own right	Section 2(4).
Rates	Section 34(1).
Relevant licence	Schedule 2.
Relevant tenancy	Schedule 2.
Qualifying worker	Schedule 3, Part I.
Statutory tenant	Sections 4 and 5.
Statutory tenant by succession	Section 3(5).
Statutory tenant in his own right	Section 2(4).
Subject to a protected occupancy	Section 3(6).
Subject to a statutory tenancy	Section 4(6).
Tenancy	Section 34(1).
Tenancy at a low rent	Section 34(1).
Tenant	Section 34(1). [278]

NOTES

Commencement: 1 October 1977 (certain purposes); 1 January 1977 (remainder).
Commencement orders: SI 1976 No 2124, 1977 No 1268.

SCHEDULE 2

Section 1

MEANING OF "RELEVANT LICENCE" AND "RELEVANT TENANCY"

Relevant licence

1. In this Act "relevant licence" means any licence under which a person has the exclusive occupation of a dwelling-house as a separate dwelling and which—

(*a*) if it were a tenancy, and

[(*b*) if the provisions of Part I of the Rent Act 1977 relating to exceptions to the definition of 'protected tenancy' were modified as mentioned in paragraph 3 below,]

would be a protected tenancy for the purposes of that Act.

Relevant tenancy

2. In this Act "relevant tenancy" means any tenancy under which a dwelling-house is let as a separate dwelling and which—

(*a*) is not a protected tenancy for the purposes of [the Rent Act 1977], but
(*b*) would be such a tenancy if [the provisions of the Act mentioned in paragraph 1 (*b*) above] were modified as mentioned in paragraph 3 below,

other than a tenancy to which Part I or Part II of the Landlord and Tenant Act 1954 applies and a tenancy of an agricultural holding within the meaning of the *Agricultural Holdings Act 1948* [Agricultural Holdings Act 1986].

[3.—(1) For the purposes of this Schedule the modifications of Part I of the Rent Act 1977 are as follows.

(2) Omit sections 5 (tenancies at low rents) and 10 (tenancy of a dwelling-house comprised in any agricultural holding etc.).

[(2A) In section 5A (exclusion of certain shared ownership leases), in subsection (2)(*g*) (condition that lease states landlord's opinion that 1977 Act does not apply) for the reference to the 1977 Act substitute a reference to this Act.]

(3) For section 7 (payments for board or attendance) substitute:—

'7.—(1) A tenancy is not a protected tenancy if it is a bona fide term of the tenancy that the landlord provides the tenant with board or attendance.

(2) For the avoidance of doubt it is hereby declared that meals provided in the course of a person's employment in agriculture do not constitute board for the purposes of this section; and a term that the landlord provides the tenant with attendance shall not be taken to be a bona fide term for those purposes unless, having regard to its value to the tenant, the attendance is substantial.']

4. The other provisions of [the Rent Act 1977] which are relevant for the purposes of the above definitions, and which are therefore also applied by this Schedule, include—

section 1 (definition of "protected tenancy");
[section 13] (no protected or statutory tenancy where landlord's interest belongs to Crown);
[sections 14 to 16] (no protected or statutory tenancy where landlord's interest belongs to local authority, etc.);
[section 12) (no protected tenancy in certain cases where landlord's interest belongs to resident landlord);
[section 25] (rateable value and appropriate day). **[279]**

NOTES

Commencement: 1 October 1977 (certain purposes); 1 January 1977 (remainder).
Commencement orders: SI 1976 No 2124, 1977 No 1268.
Words in italics repealed with savings and subsequent words in square brackets substituted with savings by the Agricultural Holdings Act 1986, ss 99, 100, Sch 13, para 3, Sch 14, para 58.
Para 3: substituted by the Rent Act 1977, s 155, Sch 23, para 80; sub-para (2A) added by the Housing and Planning Act 1986, s 18, Sch 4, para 2, as from a day to be appointed.
Other amendments made by the Rent Act 1977, s 155, Sch 23, paras 78–81.

SCHEDULE 3

Section 1

Protected Occupiers in their own Right

Part I

Definitions

Qualifying worker

1. A person is a qualifying worker for the purposes of this Act at any time if, at that time, he has worked whole-time in agriculture, or has worked in agriculture as a permit worker, for not less than 91 out of the last 104 weeks.

Incapable of whole-time work in agriculture, or work in agriculture as a permit worker, in consequence of a qualifying injury or disease

2.—(1) A person is, for the purposes of this Act, incapable of whole-time work in agriculture in consequence of a qualifying injury or disease if—

(*a*) he is incapable of such work in consequence of—

(i) an injury or disease prescribed in relation to him, by reason of his employment in agriculture, under section 76(2) of the Social Security Act 1975, or

(ii) an injury caused by an accident arising out of and in the course of his employment in agriculture, and

(*b*) at the time when he became so incapable, he was employed in agriculture as a whole-time worker.

(2) A person is, for the purposes of this Act, incapable of work in agriculture as a permit worker in consequence of a qualifying injury or disease if—

(*a*) he is incapable of such work in consequence of any such injury or disease as is mentioned in sub-paragraph (1) above, and

(*b*) at the time when he became so incapable, he was employed in agriculture as a permit worker.

(3) Where—

(*a*) a person has died in consequence of any such injury or disease as is mentioned in sub-paragraph (1) above, and

(*b*) immediately before his death, he was employed in agriculture as a whole-time worker, or as a permit worker,

he shall be regarded for the purposes of this Act as having been, immediately before his death, incapable of whole-time work in agriculture, or work in agriculture as a permit worker, in consequence of a qualifying injury or disease.

Dwelling-house in qualifying ownership

3.—(1) A dwelling-house in relation to which a person ("the occupier") has a licence or tenancy is in qualifying ownership for the purposes of this Act at any time if, at that time, the occupier is employed in agriculture and the occupier's employer either—

(*a*) is the owner of the dwelling-house, or

(*b*) has made arrangements with the owner of the dwelling-house for it to be used as housing accommodation for persons employed by him in agriculture.

(2) In this paragraph—

"employer", in relation to the occupier, means the person or, as the case may be, one of the persons by whom he is employed in agriculture;

"owner", in relation to the dwelling-house, means the occupier's immediate landlord or, where the occupier is a licensee, the person who would be the occupier's immediate landlord if the licence were a tenancy.

Supplemental

4.—(1) The provisions of this paragraph shall have effect for determining what is whole-time work in agriculture for the purposes of this Part of this Schedule.

(2) A person works whole-time in agriculture for any week in which—

(*a*) he is employed to work in agriculture, and
(*b*) the number of hours for which he works in agriculture, or in activities incidental to agriculture, for the person or persons by whom he is so employed is not less than the standard number of hours.

(3) Where a person is employed in agriculture as a whole-time worker, any week in which by agreement with his employer or, where he has two or more employers, by agreement with the employer or employers concerned he works less than the standard number of hours shall count as a week of whole-time work in agriculture.

(4) If in any week a person who is employed in agriculture as a whole-time worker is, for the whole or part of the week—

(*a*) absent from work in agriculture by reason of his taking a holiday to which he is entitled, or
(*b*) absent from work in agriculture with the consent of his employer or, where he has two or more employers, with the consent of the employer or employers concerned, or
(*c*) incapable of whole-time work in agriculture in consequence of an injury or disease (whether a qualifying injury or disease or not),

that week shall count as a week of whole-time work in agriculture.

(5) If in any week a person (whether employed in agriculture as a whole-time worker or not) is, for the whole or part of the week, incapable of whole-time work in agriculture in consequence of a qualifying injury or disease, that week shall count as a week of whole-time work in agriculture.

5.—(1) The provisions of this paragraph shall have effect for determining what is work in agriculture as a permit worker for the purposes of this Part of this Schedule.

(2) A person works in agriculture as a permit worker for any week in which he works in agriculture as an employee for the whole or part of the week and there is in force in relation to him a permit granted under section 5 of the Agricultural Wages Act 1948.

(3) If in any week a person who is employed in agriculture as a permit worker is, for the whole or part of the week—

(*a*) absent from work in agriculture by reason of his taking a holiday to which he is entitled, or
(*b*) absent from work in agriculture with the consent of his employer or, where he has two or more employers, with the consent of the employer or employers concerned, or
(*c*) incapable of work in agriculture as a permit worker in consequence of an injury or disease (whether a qualifying injury or disease or not),

that week shall count as a week of work in agriculture as a permit worker.

(4) If in any week a person (whether employed in agriculture as a permit worker or not) is, for the whole or part of the week, incapable of work in agriculture as a permit worker in consequence of a qualifying injury or disease, that week shall count as a week of work in agriculture as a permit worker.

6. For the purposes of this Part of this Schedule a person is employed in agriculture as a whole-time worker if he is employed to work in agriculture by the week, or by any period longer than a week, and the number of hours for which he is employed to work in agriculture, or in activities incidental to agriculture, in any week is not less than the standard number of hours.

7. For the purposes of this Part of this Schedule, a person is employed in agriculture as a permit worker if he is employed in agriculture and there is in force in relation to him a permit granted under section 5 of the Agricultural Wages Act 1948. **[280]**

NOTES
Commencement: 1 October 1977 (certain purposes); 1 January 1977 (remainder).
Commencement orders: SI 1976 No 2124, 1977 No 1268.

PART II

TEMPORARY PROVISIONS AS RESPECTS CERTAIN FORESTRY WORKERS

8. In this Act "the date of operation for forestry workers" means such date after the operative date as the Secretary of State and the Minister of Agriculture, Fisheries and Food acting jointly may appoint by order contained in a statutory instrument.

9.—(1) Whole-time work in forestry, and work in forestry as a permit worker, shall be left out of account in determining for the purposes of this Act whether, at a date before the date of operation for forestry workers, a person is a qualifying worker.

(2) Employment in forestry as a whole-time worker, or as a permit worker, shall be left out of account in determining for the purposes of this Act whether, at a date before the date of operation for forestry workers, a person is incapable of whole-time work in agriculture, or work in agriculture as a permit worker, in consequence of qualifying injury or disease.

10.—(1) The question of what is whole-time work in forestry, or work in forestry as a permit worker, for the purposes of this Part of this Schedule shall be determined in the same way as what is whole-time work in agriculture, or work in agriculture as a permit worker, is determined for the purposes of Part I of this Schedule, and for that purpose all work which is not work in forestry shall be disregarded.

(2) For the purposes of this Part of this Schedule a person is employed in forestry as a whole-time worker if he is employed to work in forestry by the week, or by any period longer than a week, and the number of hours for which he is employed to work in forestry, or in activities incidental to forestry, in any week is not less than the standard number of hours.

(3) For the purposes of this Part of this Schedule a person is employed in forestry as a permit worker if he is employed in forestry and there is in force in relation to him a permit granted under section 5 of the Agricultural Wages Act 1948. **[281]**

NOTES

Commencement: 1 October 1977 (certain purposes); 1 January 1977 (remainder).
Commencement orders: SI 1976 No 2124, 1977 No 1268.

PART III

SUPPLEMENTAL

11.—(1) In this Schedule "employment" means employment under one or more contracts of employment, and cognate expressions shall be construed accordingly.

(2) For the purposes of the definition in sub-paragraph (1) above "contract of employment" means a contract of employment or apprenticeship (whether express or implied and, if express, whether oral or in writing).

12.—(1) In this Schedule "the standard number of hours" means 35 hours or such other number of hours as may be specified in an order made by the Secretary of State and the Minister of Agriculture, Fisheries and Food acting jointly.

(2) An order under this paragraph shall be made by statutory instrument which shall be subject to annulment in pursuance of a resolution of either House of Parliament.

(3) An order made under this paragraph—

(*a*) may contain transitional and other supplemental and incidental provisions, and

(*b*) may be varied or revoked by a subsequent order so made.

13. Any reference in this Schedule, to work in agriculture or in forestry, or to employment in agriculture or in forestry, is a reference to such work or such employment, in the United Kingdom (including the Channel Islands and the Isle of Man) or in the territory of any other State which is a member of the European Economic Community. **[282]**

NOTES
Commencement: 1 October 1977 (certain purposes); 1 January 1977 (remainder).
Commencement orders: SI 1976 No 1224, 1977 No 1268.
The Minister of Agriculture etc: see further SI 1978 No 272, art 2, Sch 1.

SCHEDULE 4

Section 6

GROUNDS FOR POSSESSION OF DWELLING-HOUSE SUBJECT TO PROTECTED OCCUPANCY OR STATUTORY TENANCY

PART I

CASES WHERE COURT HAS A DISCRETION

Case 1

Alternative accommodation not provided or arranged by housing authority

1. The court is satisfied that suitable alternative accommodation is available for the tenant, or will be available for him when the order for possession takes effect.

2.—(1) Accommodation shall be deemed suitable in this Case if it consists of—

(*a*) premises which are to be let as a separate dwelling such that they will then be let on a protected tenancy within the meaning of [the Rent Act 1977], or

(*b*) premises which are to be let as a separate dwelling on terms which will, in the opinion of the court, afford to the tenant security of tenure reasonably equivalent to the security afforded by [Part VII of the Rent Act 1977] in the case of a protected tenancy,

and, in the opinion of the court, the accommodation fulfils the conditions in paragraph 3 below.

[(2) For the purposes of sub-paragraph (1)(*b*) the terms of a tenancy shall not be treated as affording the required security by reason only of the fact that the tenancy is an assured tenancy within the meaning of section 56 of the Housing Act 1980.]

3.—(1) The accommodation must be reasonably suitable to the needs of the tenant and his family as regards proximity to place of work and either—

(*a*) similar as regards rental and extent to the accommodation afforded by dwelling-houses provided in the neighbourhood by the housing authority concerned for persons whose needs as regards extent are similar to those of the tenant and his family, or

(*b*) reasonably suitable to the means of the tenant, and to the needs of the tenant and his family as regards extent and character.

(2) For the purposes of sub-paragraph (1)(*a*) above, a certificate of the housing authority concerned stating—

(*a*) the extent of the accommodation afforded by dwelling-houses provided by the authority to meet the needs of tenants with families of such number as may be specified in the certificate, and

(*b*) the amount of the rent charged by the housing authority concerned for dwelling-houses affording accommodation of that extent,

shall be conclusive evidence of the facts so stated.

(3) If any furniture was provided by the landlord for use under the tenancy, furniture must be provided for use in the alternative accommodation which is either similar, or is reasonably suitable to the needs of the tenant and his family.

4. Accommodation shall not be deemed to be suitable to the needs of the tenant and his family if the result of their occupation of the accommodation would be that it would be an overcrowded dwelling-house for the purposes of [Part X of the Housing Act 1985].

5. Any document purporting to be a certificate of the housing authority concerned

issued for the purposes of this Case and to be signed by the proper officer of the authority shall be received in evidence and, unless the contrary is shown, shall be deemed to be such a certificate without further proof.

6. In this Case no account shall be taken of accommodation as respects which an offer has been made, or notice has been given, as mentioned in paragraph 1 of Case II below.

Case II

Alternative accommodation provided or arranged by housing authority

1. The housing authority concerned have made an offer in writing to the tenant of alternative accommodation which appears to them to be suitable, specifying the date when the accommodation will be available and the date (not being less than 14 days from the date of offer) by which the offer must be accepted.

OR

The housing authority concerned have given notice in writing to the tenant that they have received from a person specified in the notice an offer in writing to rehouse the tenant in alternative accommodation which appears to the housing authority concerned to be suitable, and the notice specifies both the date when the accommodation will be available and the date (not being less than 14 days from the date when the notice was given to the tenant) by which the offer must be accepted.

2. The landlord shows that the tenant accepted the offer (by the housing authority or other person) within the time duly specified in the offer.

OR

The landlord shows that the tenant did not so accept the offer, and the tenant does not satisfy the court that he acted reasonably in failing to accept the offer

3.—(1) The accommodation offered must in the opinion of the court fulfil the conditions in this paragraph.

(2) The accommodation must be reasonably suitable to the needs of the tenant and his family as regards proximity to place of work.

(3) The accommodation must be reasonably suitable to the means of the tenant, and to the needs of the tenant and his family as regards extent.

4. If the accommodation offered is available for a limited period only, the housing authority's offer or notice under paragraph 1 above must contain an assurance that other accommodation—

(*a*) the availability of which is not so limited,
(*b*) which appears to them to be suitable, and
(*c*) which fulfils the conditions in paragraph 3 above, will be offered to the tenant as soon as practicable.

Case III

Rent lawfully due from the tenant has not been paid,

OR

Any other lawful obligation of the tenancy, whether or not it is an obligation created by this Act, has been broken or not performed.

Case IV

The tenant, or any person residing or lodging with him or sub-tenant of his, has been guilty of conduct which is a nuisance or annoyance to adjoining occupiers, or has been convicted of using the dwelling-house, or allowing the dwelling-house to be used, for immoral or illegal purposes.

Case V

1. The condition of the dwelling-house has, in the opinion of the court, deteriorated owing to acts of waste by, or the neglect or default of, the tenant or any person residing or lodging with him, or any sub-tenant of his.

2. If the person at fault is not the tenant, the court must be satisfied that the tenant has not, before the making of the order for possession, taken such steps as he ought reasonably to have taken for the removal of the person at fault.

Case VI

1. The condition of any furniture provided by the landlord for use under the tenancy has, in the opinion of the court, deteriorated owing to ill-treatment by the tenant or any person residing or lodging with him, or any sub-tenant of his.

2. If the person at fault is not the tenant, the court must be satisfied that the tenant has not, before the making of the order for possession, taken such steps as he ought reasonably to have taken for the removal of the person at fault.

Case VII

1. The tenant has given notice to quit and in consequence of that notice the landlord has contracted to sell or let the dwelling-house, or has taken any other steps as a result of which he would, in the opinion of the court, be seriously prejudiced if he could not obtain possession.

2. This Case does not apply where the tenant has given notice to terminate his employment and that notice has operated to terminate the tenancy.

Case VIII

1. The tenant has, without the consent of the landlord, assigned, sub-let or parted with possession of the dwelling-house, or any part of it.

2. This Case does not apply if the assignment, sub-letting or parting with possession was effected before the operative date.

Case IX

1. The dwelling-house is reasonably required by the landlord for occupation as a residence for—

(*a*) himself, or
(*b*) any son or daughter of his over 18 years of age, or
(*c*) his father or mother, or the father or mother of his wife, or husband, or
(*d*) his grandfather or grandmother, or the grandfather or grandmother of his wife, or husband,

and the landlord did not become landlord by purchasing the dwelling-house, or any interest in it, after 12th April 1976.

2. The court, having regard to all the circumstances of the case, including the question whether other accommodation is available for the landlord or tenant, is satisfied that no greater hardship would be caused by granting the order than by refusing to grant it.

Case X

1. Any part of the dwelling-house is sublet.

2. The court is satisfied that the rent charged by the tenant is or was in excess of the maximum rent recoverable for that part, having regard to the provisions of [. . . Part III or Part V of the Rent Act 1977] or Part II of this Act, as the case may require.

3. Paragraph 2 does not apply to a rental period beginning before the operative date. **[283]**

NOTES

Commencement: 1 October 1977 (certain purposes); 1 January 1977 (remainder).

Commencement orders: SI 1976 No 2124, 1977 No 1268.

Case I: para 2: sub-para (1) amended by the Rent Act 1977, s 155, Sch 23, para 82, sub-para (2) added by the Housing and Planning Act 1986, s 13(3); para 4 amended by the Housing (Consequential Provisions) Act 1985, s 4, Sch 2, para 33.

Case X: amendment in square brackets made by the Rent Act 1977, s 155, Sch 23, para 82; words omitted repealed by the Housing Act 1980, s 152, Sch 26.

PART II

CASES IN WHICH COURT MUST ORDER POSSESSION

Case XI

1. The person who granted the tenancy or, as the case may be, the original tenancy ("the original occupier") was, prior to granting it, occupying the dwelling house as his residence.

2 The court is satisfied that the dwelling-house is required as a residence for the original occupier or any member of his family who resided with the original occupier when he last occupied the dwelling-house as his residence.

3. Not later than the relevant date the original occupier gave notice in writing to the tenant that possession might be recovered under this Case.

4. The dwelling-house has not since the operative date been let by the original occupier to a tenant as respects whom the condition mentioned in paragraph 3 above was not satisfied.

5. The court may dispense with the requirements of either or both of paragraphs 3 and 4 if of opinion that it is just and equitable so to do.

6. In this Case and in Case XII below—

"original tenancy", in relation to a statutory tenancy, means the tenancy on the termination of which the statutory tenancy arose;

"the relevant date" means the date of the commencement of the tenancy, or as the case may be, the original tenancy, or the expiration of the period of six months beginning with the operative date, whichever is the later.

Case XII

1. The person who granted the tenancy, or, as the case may be, the original tenancy ("the owner") acquired the dwelling-house or any interest in it, with a view to occupying it as his residence at such time as he should retire from regular employment.

2. The court is satisfied—

(*a*) that the owner has retired from regular employment and requires the dwelling-house as his residence, or

(*b*) that the owner has died and the dwelling-house is required as a residence for a member of his family who was residing with him at the time of his death.

3. Not later than the relevant date the owner gave notice in writing to the tenant that possession might be recovered under this Case.

4. The dwelling-house has not since the operative date been let by the owner to a tenant as respects whom the condition mentioned in paragraph 3 above was not satisfied.

5. The court may dispense with the requirements of either or both of paragraphs 3 and 4 if of opinion that it is just and equitable so to do.

Case XIII

The dwelling-house is overcrowded, within the meaning of [Part X of the Housing Act 1985], in such circumstances as to render the occupier guilty of an offence. **[284]**

NOTES

Commencement: 1 October 1977 (certain purposes); 1 January 1977 (remainder).
Commencement orders: SI 1976 No 2124, 1977 No 1268.
Case XIII: amended by the Housing (Consequential Provisions) Act 1985, s 4, Sch 2, para 33.

SCHEDULE 5

Section 10

TERMS OF THE STATUTORY TENANCY

Preliminary

1.—(1) In this Schedule the "original contract", in relation to a statutory tenancy, means the licence or tenancy on the termination of which the statutory tenancy arose.

(2) No account shall be taken for the purposes of this Schedule of any term of the original contract under which the right of occupation depended, or which itself depended, on the occupier being employed in agriculture or in some other way.

(3) In this Schedule "term", in relation to the statutory tenancy, or in relation to the original contract, includes a condition of the tenancy or contract.

Terms derived from the original licence or tenancy

2.—(1) So long as he retains possession, the statutory tenant shall observe, and be entitled to the benefit of, all the terms of the original contract.

(2) Sub-paragraph (1) applies whether or not the terms are express or implied or statutory.

(3) Sub-paragraph (1) applies subject to the provisions of this Schedule, and of Part II of this Act.

Tenancy derived from licence

3. If the original contract was a licence, the statutory tenancy shall be a weekly tenancy.

Covenant for quiet enjoyment, etc.

4.—(1) If the original contract was a licence, the terms of the statutory tenancy shall include any term which would be implied if the contract had been a contract of tenancy.

(2) This applies in particular to the landlord's covenant for quiet enjoyment and the tenant's obligation to use the premises in a tenant-like manner, which are implied in any tenancy.

Non-contractual arrangements

5.—(1) It shall be a term of the statutory tenancy that the landlord provides the tenant with any services or facilities—

(*a*) which the landlord was providing for the occupier before the beginning of the statutory tenancy, though not under the original contract, or which he had provided for the occupier, but was not providing when the original contract terminated, and

(*b*) which are reasonably necessary for any person occupying the dwelling-house as a statutory tenant, but which such a tenant cannot reasonably be expected to provide for himself.

(2) This paragraph may apply, for example, where the only convenient electricity or water supplies, or the only convenient sewage disposal facilities, are those provided by the landlord from his own installations.

Landlord's obligation to repair

6.—(1) [section 11 of the Landlord and Tenant Act 1985] shall apply to the dwelling-house so long as it is subject to the statutory tenancy.

(2) This paragraph is without prejudice to the operation of paragraph 2 above where the original contract was a tenancy to which [the said section 11] applied.

Tenant's obligations

7.—(1) It shall be a condition of the statutory tenancy that the tenant will not use the dwelling-house, or any part of it, for purposes other than those of a private dwelling-house.

(2) It shall be a condition of the statutory tenancy that the tenant will not assign, sub-let, or part with possession of, the dwelling-house, or any part of it.

(3) Sub-paragraph (2) does not affect anything lawfully done before the beginning of the statutory tenancy.

Access by landlord

8. It shall be a condition of the statutory tenancy that the tenant will afford to the landlord access to the dwelling-house and all reasonable facilities for executing therein any repairs which the landlord is entitled to execute.

Access by tenant

9.—(1) The landlord shall afford any such right of access to the dwelling-house as is reasonable in the circumstances.

(2) In applying sub-paragraph (1) account shall be taken of any right of access to be afforded under paragraph 2 or 4 of this Schedule.

(3) Without prejudice to the definition of original contract in paragraph 1 of this Schedule, any right of access to be afforded under paragraph 2 of this Schedule shall be confined to such right of access to the dwelling-house as is reasonable in the circumstances, and without regard to any right of access afforded wholly or mainly because the occupier of the dwelling-house, or his predecessor, was employed on the land.

(4) Paragraph 5 of this Schedule shall not apply to facilities for access to the dwelling-house.

(5) If it is reasonably necessary in order to prevent the spread of disease which might otherwise affect livestock or crops, whether on the landlord's land or elsewhere, the landlord may temporarily restrict access to the dwelling-house made available in pursuance of this Schedule so long as suitable alternative access is available or is made available.

(6) If it is reasonably necessary in the interests of efficient agriculture, the landlord may permanently or temporarily deprive the dwelling-house of access made available in pursuance of this Schedule so long as suitable alternative access is available or is made available.

Notice to quit served on landlord

10.—(1) If the original contract—

(*a*) was not a tenancy, or
(*b*) was a tenancy the provisions of which did not require the tenant to give notice to quit before giving up possession,

the statutory tenant shall be entitled to give up possession of the dwelling-house if, and only if, he gives not less than four weeks' notice to quit.

(2) If the original contract required the tenant to give notice to quit before giving up possession, the statutory tenant shall be entitled to give up possession of the dwelling-

house, if, and only if, he gives that notice, or, if longer, the notice required by [section 5 of the Protection from Eviction Act 1977] (four weeks' notice).

Rates, water rates, etc.

11.—(1) Paragraph 2 of this Schedule shall not impose any liability on the tenant to make payments to the landlord in respect of rates borne by the landlord or a superior landlord.

(2) The following provisions of this paragraph shall apply as respects any rental period of the statutory tenancy, including one as respects which an agreement under section 11 of this Act either fixes the rent or provides that no rent is payable.

(3) Subject to sub-paragraph (4) below, where any rates in respect of the dwelling-house are borne by the landlord or a superior landlord, the amount of the rates for the rental period, as ascertained in accordance with [Schedule 5 to the Rent Act 1977], shall be recoverable from the statutory tenant as if it were rent payable under the statutory tenancy.

(4) The tenant's liability under sub-paragraph (3) above shall not arise unless notice in writing to that effect is served by the landlord on the tenant, and that notice shall take effect from such as may be specified in the notice, which shall not be earlier than four weeks before service of the notice.

(5) If the dwelling-house forms part only of a hereditament in respect of which any rates are charged, the proportion for which the statutory tenant is liable under this paragraph shall be such as may be agreed by him with the landlord, or as may be determined by the county court; and the decision of the county court shall be final.

(6) In this paragraph "rental period" means in relation to a statutory tenancy under which no rent is payable, any period of the statutory tenancy which would be a rental period if a rent were payable under that tenancy; and in [Schedule 5 to the Rent Act 1977] as applied by sub-paragraph (3) above any reference to a rental period, or to a rating period during which the rent for a rental period is payable, shall be construed accordingly.

Variation of statutory tenancy

12.—(1) Subject to the provisions of this paragraph, the landlord and the statutory tenant may by agreement in writing vary any of the provisions of the statutory tenancy.

(2) An agreement under this paragraph may be made at any time, including a time before the beginning of the statutory tenancy.

(3) So far as a variation of the provisions of the statutory tenancy concerns rent it shall be effected in accordance with section 11 of this Act, and no agreement under that section may conflict with any of the provisions of this Act.

(4) This paragraph shall not authorise an agreement which results in—

(*a*) a substantial addition to the land or premises which the statutory tenant is entitled to occupy, or
(*b*) the breach of any obligation implied by law, and in particular the breach of the obligation imposed by [section 11 of the Landlord and Tenant Act 1985] (landlord's obligation to repair), or
(*c*) the circumstances in which the statutory tenant can give notice to quit, or
(*d*) the inclusion of any term which relates to the employment by the landlord of the tenant, or of any other term unrelated to the occupation of the dwelling-house.

(5) The following bind any successor of the landlord or the tenant under a statutory tenancy to the same extent as they bind the landlord, or as the case may be the tenant—

(*a*) an agreement under this paragraph,
(*b*) an agreement under section 10(3)(*b*) of section 11 of this Act,
(*c*) section 11(9) (rent payable after termination of agreement),
(*d*) a notice of increase by the landlord under section 12 or section 14 of this Act,

(*e*) a notice under paragraph 11 of this Schedule (rates recoverable by landlord from statutory tenant). **[285]**

NOTES

Commencement: 1 October 1977 (certain purposes); 1 January 1977 (remainder).
Commencement orders: SI 1976 No 2124, 1977 No 1268.
Paras 6, 12: amended by the Housing (Consequential Provisions) Act 1985, s 4, Sch 2, para 33.
Para 10: amended by the Protection from Eviction Act 1977, s 12, Sch 1, para 4.
Para 11: amended by the Rent Act 1977, s 155, Sch 23, para 83.

SCHEDULE 6

Section 15

Phasing of Rent Increases

Interpretation

1.—(1) In this Schedule—

"noted amount" means an amount noted under paragraph 2(1) below;
"period of delay" [means—

(a) if the registered rent has been confirmed by a rent assessment committee, a period beginning with the date from which the registration of the rent took effect and ending one year after the date on which the committee took their decision; and
(b) in any other case, a period of one year beginning with the date from which the registration took effect.]

"permitted increase" means the amount by which the rent for any rental period may be increased;
"previous rent limit" means, subject to sub-paragraph (2) below, the amount which [immediately before the relevant date] was recoverable by way of rent or would have been so recoverable upon service of a notice or notices of increase under section 14 of this Act;
["relevant date" means, in relation to a registered rent—

[(a) if the rent was determined by the rent officer (and whether or not it was confirmed by a rent assessment committee), the date on which the rent was registered by the rent officer; and
(b) if the rent was determined by a rent assessment committee, the date on which the rent officer registered the rent determined by him or, as the case may be, noted in the register his confirmation of the rent for the time being registered];

"service element" means any amount calculated under paragraph 2 below;
"services" means services provided by the landlord or a superior landlord;
. . .

(2), (3) . . .

Service element

2—(1) Where—

(a) the registered rent includes a payment in respect of services, and
(b) the rent is not registered as a variable rent in accordance with [section 71 (4) of the Rent Act 1977] as applied by section 13 of this Act, but
(c) not less than 5 per cent. of the amount of the registered rent is in the opinion of the rent officer or rent assessment committee fairly attributable to the services,

the amount so attributable shall be noted in the register.

(2) In the cases mentioned in the first column of the Table below, the amount of the service element shall be calculated as specified in the second column.

Table

Calculation of service element

Case	*Service element*
Case A. A specified amount or proportion was in the previous rent limit attributable to the provision of services, and came to less than the noted amount.	*The service element is the difference between the amount or proportion and the noted amount.*
Case B. No amount or proportion attributable to the provision of services is specified, but an amount less than the noted amount appears to the rent officer or rent assessment committee to have been attributable to such provision.	*The service element is the difference between—* *(a) an amount bearing to the previous rent limit the same proportion as the noted amount bears to the registered rent, and* *(b) the noted amount.*
Case C. No amount appears to the rent officer or rent assessment committee to have been attributable in the previous rent limit to the provision of services.	*The service element is the noted amount.*

(3) The amount of the service element shall be recorded in the register, and in Case C above may be recorded by adding to the note under sub-paragraph (1) above a statement that the noted amount is the service element.

General formulae for calculating increases in rent

[3.—(1) Subject to sub-paragraph (2) below, the permitted increase for a period falling within the period of delay is an increase to an amount calculated by applying the formula—

$$\frac{1}{2}(P+S+R)$$

where—

P is the previous rent limit,
S is the service element, and
R is the registered rent.

(2) The maximum permitted increase by virtue of this Schedule is an increase to the registered rent.]

Subsequent registrations

[4. Where the registration of a rent takes effect in a period of delay which began by reference to an earlier registration, then—

(a) from the date on which the later registration takes effect the limitation under that period of delay shall cease to apply; and
(b) a fresh period of delay shall begin by reference to the later registration.]

General

5. The amount of any service element or of any amount sought to be noted in the register in pursuance of this Schedule shall be included among the matters with respect to which representations may be made or consultations are to be held or notices given under Part I of [Schedule 11 to the Rent Act 1977] as applied by section 13 of this Act.

6. In ascertaining for the purposes of this Schedule whether there is any difference between amounts, or what that difference is, such adjustments shall be made as may be necessary to take account of periods of different lengths; and for that purpose a month shall be treated as one-twelfth and a week as one-fifty-second of a year.

7. . . . **[286]**

NOTES

Commencement: 1 October 1977 (certain purposes); 1 January 1977 (remainder).

Commencement orders: SI 1976 No 2124, 1977 No 1268.

Repealed by SI 1987 No 264, art 2(3), Sch 1, except in relation to the circumstances and to the extent specified in Schedule 2 to that Order; see para [1070] post.

Para 1: amended by the Housing Act 1980, ss 61(6)(*a*) 152, Sch 26.

Paras 2, 5: amended by the Rent Act 1977, s 155, Sch 23, para 84.

Paras 3, 4: substituted by the Housing Act 1980, ss 60(3), 61(6)(*b*).

Para 7: repealed by the Housing Act 1980, ss 61(6)(*c*), 152, Sch 26.

SCHEDULE 8

Section 40

Consequential and Minor Amendments

. . . [287]

NOTES

Commencement: 1 October 1977 (certain purposes); 1 January 1977 (remainder).

This Schedule contains amendments only.

Repealed in part by the Acquisition of Land Act 1981, s 34, Sch 6, Part I, the New Towns Act 1981, s 81, Sch 13, the Protection from Eviction Act 1977, s 12, Sch 3, the Matrimonial Homes and Property Act 1981, s 10(2), Sch 3, the Rent Act 1977, s 155, Sch 25 and repealed in part by the Housing (Consequential Provisions) Act 1985, s 3, Sch 1, Part I.

SCHEDULE 9

Section 40

Transitional

Licence or tenancy granted before operative date: resident landlord on and after that date

1. A licence or tenancy which was granted before the operative date shall not be a relevant licence or tenancy if, on the assumption—

(*a*) that it was granted on the operative date, and
(*b*) that the condition in paragraph (*b*) of subsection (1) of section 5A of the Rent Act 1968 (no protected tenancy in certain cases where landlord's interest belongs to resident landlord) was fulfilled,

it would be precluded from being a relevant licence or tenancy by virtue of the said section 5A as applied by Schedule 2 to this Act.

Protected occupancy arising on or after operative date

2—(1) This paragraph applies as respects the question whether at any date which is on or after the operative date a person who has in relation to a dwelling-house a relevant licence or tenancy is a protected occupier of the dwelling-house.

(2) So far as the question depends on prior circumstances, they shall be taken into account even if occurring before the operative date.

(3) In applying this paragraph to section 2(3) or to section 3 of this Act (so that the question whether a person is a protected occupier depends on whether he or another person was, at a time before the material date, a protected occupier or statutory tenant) it shall be assumed that this Act and the provisions of the Rent Act 1968 which are applied by Schedule 2 to this Act, including (where relevant) any amendments to those provisions, were in force at all material times before the operative date.

Statutory tenancy arising on operative date

3. A person who is occupying a dwelling-house as his residence on the operative date shall become the statutory tenant of the dwelling-house if, on the assumption that this Act and the provisions of the Rent Act 1968 which are applied by Schedule 2 to this Act, including (where relevant) any amendments to those provisions, were in force at all material times before that date, he would be a statutory tenant of the dwelling-house on

that date, and this Act shall thereafter apply to him, and by reference to him, on that assumption.

Statutory tenancy: order for possession before operative date

4.—(1) Where before the operative date a court has made an order for possession of a dwelling-house which on the operative date is subject to a statutory tenancy and the order has not been executed, the court may, on the application of the person against whom the order was made, rescind or vary the order in such manner as the court thinks fit for the purpose of giving effect to this Act.

(2) If proceedings for possession of the dwelling-house are pending on the operative date, Part II of this Act shall apply as it would apply to proceedings commenced on the operative date.

Dwelling subject to Part VI contract: pending notice to quit

5.—(1) In any case where—

(*a*) before the operative date a notice to quit has been served in respect of a dwelling to which a Part VI contract then related, and
(*b*) the period at the end of which that notice to quit takes effect had, before the operative date, been extended under Part VI of the Rent Act 1968, and
(*c*) that period had not expired before the operative date, and
(*d*) on the operative date the Part VI contract becomes a protected occupancy,

the notice to quit shall take effect on the day following the operative date (whenever it would otherwise take effect) and, accordingly, on that day the protected occupancy shall become a statutory tenancy.

(2) In this paragraph "part VI contract" has the meaning given by section 70 (6) of the Rent Act 1968.

Section 10A tenancy: order for possession before operative date

6.—(1) This paragraph applies to a dwelling-house which is let on or subject to a tenancy which is a protected or statutory tenancy for the purposes of the Rent Act 1968 and which—

(*a*) if it were a tenancy at a low rent, and
(*b*) if (where relevant) any earlier tenancy granted to the tenant, or to a member of his family, had been a tenancy at a low rent,

would be a protected occupancy or statutory tenancy (that is to say a tenancy to which section 10A of that Act, inserted by this Act, applies).

(2) Where—

(*a*) before the operative date a court has made an order for possession of the dwelling-house, and
(*b*) the order has not been executed, and
(*c*) the order was made under Case 7, 12, 13 or 14 of Schedule 3 to the Rent Act 1968,

the court shall on the application of the person against whom the order was made rescind the order, or vary it in such manner as the court thinks fit for the purposes of giving effect to the said section 10A.

(3) If proceedings for an order for possession of a dwelling-house are pending on the operative date, the said section 10A shall apply to the proceedings as it would apply to proceedings commenced on the operative date.

Forestry workers

7.—(1) This paragraph applies to a person—

(*a*) who becomes a protected occupier or statutory tenant at a time on or after the date of operation for forestry workers, and (*b*) who, if the date of operation for forestry workers fell after that time, would not at that time (having regard to the provisions of paragraph 9 of Schedule 3 to this Act) have become a protected occupier or statutory tenant.

(2) In relation to such a person references to the operative date in—

(*a*) Classes VIII, X, XI and XII of Schedule 4, and
(*b*) paragraphs 4 and 5 of this Schedule,

shall be taken as references to the date of operation for forestry workers.

(3) In determining in accordance with paragraphs 1, 2 and 3 of this Schedule whether a person is a protected occupier or statutory tenant who would be a person to whom this paragraph applies, references in those paragraphs to the operative date shall be taken as references to the date of operation for forestry workers.

(4) If, on the assumptions in paragraphs (*a*) and (*b*) of paragraph 6(1) of this Schedule the tenant would be a person to whom this paragraph applies, references to the operative date in sub-paragraphs (2) and (3) of that paragraph shall be taken as references to the date of operation for forestry workers. **[288]**

NOTES
Commencement: 1 October 1977 (certain purposes); 1 January 1977 (remainder).
Commencement orders: SI 1976 No 2124, 1977 No 1268.
Rent Act 1968: repealed and replaced by the Rent Act 1977.

RENT ACT 1977

(c 42)

ARRANGEMENT OF SECTIONS

PART I

PRELIMINARY

Protected and statutory tenancies

Section		Para
1	Protected tenants and tenancies	[289]
2	Statutory tenants and tenancies	[290]
3	Terms and conditions of statutory tenancies	[291]

Exceptions

4	Dwelling-houses above certain rateable values	[292]
5	Tenancies at low rents	[293]
5A	Certain shared ownership leases	[294]
6	Dwelling-houses let with other land	[295]
7	Payments for board or attendance	[296]
8	Lettings to students	[297]
9	Holiday Lettings	[298]
10	Agricultural holdings	[299]
11	Licensed premises	[300]
12	Resident landlords	[301]
13	Landlord's interest belonging to Crown	[302]
14	Landlord's interest belonging to local authority, etc	[303]
15	Landlord's interest belonging to housing association, etc	[304]
16	Landlord's interest belonging to housing co-operative	[305]
16A	Assured tenancies	[306]

Controlled and regulated tenancies

18	Regulated tenancies	[307]
18A	Modification of Act for controlled tenancies converted into regulated tenancies	[308]

Section Para

Restricted contracts

19 Restricted contracts .. [309]
20 Certain unfurnished tenancies to be treated as restricted contracts .. [310]

Shared accommodation

21 Tenant sharing accommodation with landlord .. [311]
22 Tenant sharing accommodation with persons other than landlord .. [312]

Sublettings

23 Certain sublettings not to exclude any part of sub-lessor's premises from protection .. [313]

Business premises

24 Premises with a business use .. [314]

Miscellaneous

25 Rateable value and meaning of "appropriate day" .. [315]
26 Land and premises let with dwelling-house .. [316]

PART III

RENTS UNDER REGULATED TENANCIES

Regulation of rent

44 Limit of rent during contractual periods .. [317]
45 Limit of rent during statutory periods .. [318]
46 Adjustment, with respect to rates, of recoverable rent for statutory periods before registration .. [319]
47 Adjustment, with respect to services and furniture, of recoverable rent for statutory periods before registration .. [320]
49 Notices of increase .. [321]

Rent agreements with tenants having security of tenure

51 Protection of tenants with security of tenure .. [322]
52 Protection: special provisions following conversion .. [323]
54 Failure to comply with provisions for protection of tenants .. [324]

Phasing of rent increases

55 General provision for phasing of rent increases .. [325]

Enforcement provisions

57 Recovery from landlord of sums paid in excess of recoverable rent, etc .. [326]
58 Rectification of rent books in light of determination of recoverable rent .. [327]

General provisions

59 Adjustment for differences in lengths of rental periods .. [328]
60 Regulations .. [329]
61 Interpretation of Part III .. [330]

PART IV

REGISTRATION OF RENTS UNDER REGULATED TENANCIES

62 Registration areas .. [331]
63 Schemes for appointment of rent officers .. [332]
64 Default powers of Secretary of State .. [333]
65 Rent assessment committees .. [334]
66 Register of rents .. [335]
67 Application for registration of rent .. [336]
68 Application to rent officer by local authority .. [337]

Section		Para
69	Certificates of fair rent	[338]
70	Determination of fair rent	[339]
71	Amount to be registered as rent	[340]
72	Effect of registration of rent	[341]
73	Cancellation of registration of rent	[342]
74	Regulations	[343]
75	Interpretation of Part IV	[344]

PART V

RENTS UNDER RESTRICTED CONTRACTS

Control of rents

77	Reference of contracts to rent tribunals and obtaining by them of information	[345]
78	Powers of rent tribunals on reference of contracts	[346]
79	Register of rents under restricted contracts	[347]
80	Reconsideration of rent after registration	[348]
81	Effect of registration of rent	[349]
81A	Cancellation of registration of rent	[350]

Miscellaneous and General

82	Jurisdiction of rent tribunals	[351]
83	Local authorities for Part V	[352]
84	Regulations	[353]
85	Interpretation of Part V	[354]

PART VI

RENT LIMIT FOR DWELLINGS LET BY HOUSING ASSOCIATIONS, HOUSING TRUSTS AND THE HOUSING CORPORATION

Registration of rents

86	Tenancies to which Part VI applies	[355]
87	Rents to be registrable	[356]

Rent limit

88	Rent limit	[357]
89	Phasing of progression to registered rent	[358]

Conversion to regulated tenancies

92	Conversion of housing association tenancies into regulated tenancies	[359]

Miscellaneous

93	Increase of rent without notice to quit	[360]
94	Recovery from landlord of sums paid in excess of recoverable rent, etc	[361]
95	Duty of landlord to supply statement of rent under previous tenancy	[362]
96	Supplemental	[363]
97	Interpretation of Part VI	[364]

PART VII

SECURITY OF TENURE

Limitations on recovery of possession of dwelling-houses let on protected tenancies or subject to statutory tenancies

98	Grounds for possession of certain dwelling-houses	[365]
99	Grounds for possession of certain dwelling-houses let to agricultural workers, etc	[366]
100	Extended discretion of court in claims for possession of certain dwelling-houses	[367]
101	Overcrowded dwelling-houses	[368]
102	Compensation for misrepresentation or concealment in Cases 8 and 9	[369]
102A	Restricted application of sections 103 to 106	[370]

Section Para

Restricted contracts

103 Notice to quit served after reference of contract to rent tribunal .. .. .. [371]
104 Application to tribunal for security of tenure where notice to quit is served .. .. [372]
105 Notices to quit served by owner-occupiers .. .. [373]
106 Reduction of period of notice on account of lessee's default .. .. [374]
106A Discretion of court in certain proceedings for possession .. .. [375]

Miscellaneous

107 Interpretation of Part VII .. .. [376]

PART VIII

CONVERSION OF CONTROLLED TENANCIES INTO REGULATED TENANCIES

Miscellaneous

116 Consent of tenant .. .. [377]

PART IX

PREMIUMS, ETC

119 Prohibition of premiums and loans on grant of protected tenancies .. .. .. [378]
120 Prohibition of premiums and loans on assignment of protected tenancies .. .. [379]
121 Tenancies which became regulated by virtue of Counter-Inflation Act 1973 .. .. [380]
122 Prohibition of premiums on grant or assignment of rights under restricted contracts .. [381]
123 Excessive price for furniture to be treated as premium .. .. [382]
124 Punishment of attempts to obtain from prospective tenants excessive prices for furniture .. .. [383]
125 Recovery of premiums and loans unlawfully required or received .. .. .. [384]
126 Avoidance of requirements for advance payment of rent in certain cases .. .. [385]
127 Allowable premiums in relation to certain long tenancies .. .. [386]
128 Interpretation of Part IX .. .. [387]

PART X

MORTGAGES

129 Mortgages to which Part X applies .. .. [388]
131 Regulated mortgages .. .. [389]
132 Powers of court to mitigate hardship to mortgagors under regulated mortgages .. [390]
136 Interpretation of Part X .. .. [391]

PART XI

GENERAL

Sublettings

137 Effect on sub-tenancy of determination of superior tenancy .. .. [392]
138 Effect on furnished sub-tenancy of determination of superior unfurnished tenancy .. [393]
139 Obligation to notify sublettings of dwelling-houses let on or subject to protected or statutory tenancies .. .. [394]

Fire Precautions

140 Modification of Act in relation to fire precautions .. .. [395]

Jurisdiction and procedure

141 County court jurisdiction .. .. [396]
142 Rules as to procedure .. .. [397]

Section		Para
	Release from provisions of Act	
143	Release from rent regulation	[398]
144	Release from restricted contract provisions	[399]
	Miscellaneous	
146	Long tenancies at a low rent	[400]
147	Restriction on levy of distress for rent	[401]
148	Implied term in all protected tenancies	[402]
	Supplemental	
149	Powers of local authorities for the purposes of giving information	[403]
150	Prosecution of offences	[404]
151	Service of notices on landlord's agents	[405]
152	Interpretation	[406]
153	Application to Isles of Scilly	[407]
154	Application to Crown property	[408]
155	Modifications, amendments, transitional provisions, repeals etc	[409]
156	Short title, commencement and extent	[410]

SCHEDULES

Schedule 1—*Statutory Tenancies*
- Part I—Statutory Tenants by Succession .. [411]
- Part II—Relinquishing Tenancies and Changing Tenants .. [412]

Schedule 2—*Resident Landlords*
- Part I—Provisions for Determining Application of section 12 .. [413]
- Part II—Tenancies ceasing to fall within section 12 .. [414]

Schedule 5—*Calculation of Amount of Rates* .. [415]

Schedule 7—*Rent Limit for certain tenancies first regulated by virtue of the Counter-Inflation Act 1973* .. [416]

Schedule 8—*Phasing of Rent Increases: General Provisions* .. [417]

Schedule 10—*Rent Assessment Committees* .. [418]

Schedule 11—*Applications for Registration of Rent*
- Part I—Application Unsupported by Certificate of Fair Rent .. [419]
- Part II—Application Supported by Certificate of Fair Rent (Except where Certificate Issued by virtue of Part VIII) .. [420]

Schedule 12—*Certificates of Fair Rent* .. [421]

Schedule 14—*Conversion of Housing Association Tenancies into Regulated Tenancies* [422]

Schedule 15—*Grounds for Possession of Dwelling-Houses Let on or Subject to Protected or Statutory Tenancies*
- Part I—Cases in Which Court May Order Possession .. [423]
- Part II—Cases in Which Court Must Order Possession Where Dwelling-House Subject to Regulated Tenancy .. [424]
- Part III—Provisions Applicable to Case 9 and Part II of this Schedule .. [425]
- Part IV—Suitable Alternative Accommodation .. [426]
- Part V—Provisions applying to Cases 11, 12 and 20 .. [427]

Schedule 16—*Further Grounds for Possession of Dwelling-Houses let on or subject to Tenancies to which Section 99 applies* .. [428]

Schedule 17—*Converted Tenancies: Modification of Act* .. [429]

Schedule 18—*Allowable Premiums*
- Part I—Premium Allowed on Assignment of Tenancy where Premium Lawfully Paid on Grant .. [430]
- Part II—Premium Allowed under Sections 121 and 127 .. [431]

Schedule 20—*Modification of Act in Relation to Fire Precautions* .. [432]

Schedule 24—*Savings and Transitional Provisions* .. [433]

An Act to consolidate the Rent Act 1968, Parts III, IV and VIII of the Housing Finance Act 1972, the Rent Act 1974, sections 7 to 10 of the Housing Rents and Subsidies Act 1975, and certain related enactments, with amendments to give effect to recommendations of the Law Commission [28 July 1977]

PART I

PRELIMINARY

Protected and statutory tenancies

1. Protected tenants and tenancies

Subject to this Part of this Act, a tenancy under which a dwelling-house (which may be a house or part of a house) is let as a separate dwelling is a protected tenancy for the purposes of this Act.

Any reference in this Act to a protected tenant shall be construed accordingly. **[289]**

NOTES
Commencement: 29 August 1977.
This section derived from the Rent Act 1968, s 1(1).

2. Statutory tenants and tenancies

(1) Subject to this Part of this Act—

(*a*) after the termination of a protected tenancy of a dwelling-house the person who, immediately before that termination, was the protected tenant of the dwelling-house shall, if and so long as he occupies the dwelling-house as his residence, be the statutory tenant of it; and

(*b*) Part I of Schedule 1 to this Act shall have effect for determining what person (if any) is the statutory tenant of a dwelling-house at any time after the death of a person who, immediately before his death, was either a protected tenant of the dwelling-house or the statutory tenant of it by virtue of paragraph (*a*) above.

(2) In this Act a dwelling-house is referred to as subject to a statutory tenancy when there is a statutory tenant of it.

(3) In subsection (1)(*a*) above and in Part I of Schedule 1, the phrase "if and so long as he occupies the dwelling-house as his residence" shall be construed as it was immediately before the commencement of this Act (that is to say, in accordance with section 3(2) of the Rent Act 1968).

(4) A person who becomes a statutory tenant of a dwelling-house as mentioned in subsection (1)(*a*) above is, in this Act, referred to as a statutory tenant by virtue of his previous protected tenancy.

(5) A person who becomes a statutory tenant as mentioned in subsection 1(*b*) above is, in this Act, referred to as a statutory tenant by succession. **[290]**

NOTES
Commencement: 29 August 1977.
This section derived from the Rent Act 1968, s 3.

3. Terms and conditions of statutory tenancies

(1) So long as he retains possession, a statutory tenant shall observe and be entitled to the benefit of all the terms and conditions of the original contract of tenancy, so far as they are consistent with the provisions of this Act.

(2) It shall be a condition of a statutory tenancy of a dwelling-house that the statutory tenant shall afford to the landlord access to the dwelling-house and all

reasonable facilities for executing therein any repairs which the landlord is entitled to execute.

(3) Subject to section 5 of the Protection from Eviction Act 1977 (under which at least 4 weeks' notice to quit is required), a statutory tenant of a dwelling-house shall be entitled to give up possession of the dwelling-house if, and only if, he gives such notice as would have been required under the provisions of the original contract of tenancy, or, if no notice would have been so required, on giving not less than 3 months' notice.

(4) Notwithstanding anything in the contract of tenancy, a landlord who obtains an order for possession of a dwelling-house as against a statutory tenant shall not be required to give to the statutory tenant any notice to quit.

(5) Part II of Schedule 1 to this Act shall have effect in relation to the giving up of possession of statutory tenancies and the changing of statutory tenants by agreement. **[291]**

NOTES
Commencement: 29 August 1977.
Sub-ss (1)-(4) derived from the Rent Act 1968, s 12.

Exceptions

4. Dwelling-houses above certain rateable values

(1) A tenancy is not a protected tenancy if the dwelling-house falls within one of the Classes set out in subsection (2) below.

(2) Where alternative rateable values are mentioned in this subsection, the higher applies if the dwelling-house is in Greater London and the lower applies if it is elsewhere.

Class A

The appropriate day in relation to the dwelling-house falls or fell on or after 1st April 1973 and the dwelling-house on the appropriate day has or had a rateable value exceeding £1,500 or £750.

Class B

The appropriate day in relation to the dwelling-house fell on or after 22nd March 1973, but before 1st April 1973, and the dwelling-house—

(*a*) on the appropriate day had a rateable value exceeding £600 or £300, and
(*b*) on 1st April 1973 had a rateable value exceeding £1,500 or £750.

Class C

The appropriate day in relation to the dwelling-house fell before 22nd March 1973 and the dwelling-house—

(*a*) on the appropriate day had a rateable value exceeding £400 or £200, and
(*b*) on 22nd March 1973 had a rateable value exceeding £600 or £300, and
(*c*) on 1st April 1973 had a rateable value exceeding £1,500 or £750.

(3) If any question arises in any proceedings whether a dwelling-house falls

within a Class in subsection (2) above, by virtue of its rateable value at any time, it shall be deemed not to fall within that Class unless the contrary is shown. **[292]**

NOTES

Commencement: 29 August 1977.

This section derived from the Rent Act 1968, s 1.

5. Tenancies at low rents

(1) A tenancy is not a protected tenancy if under the tenancy either no rent is payable or, . . . the rent payable is less than two-thirds of the rateable value which is or was the rateable value of the dwelling-house on the appropriate day.

(2) Where—

(*a*) the appropriate day in relation to a dwelling-house fell before 22nd March 1973, and

(*b*) the dwelling-house had on the appropriate day a rateable value exceeding, if it is in Greater London, £400 or, if it is elsewhere, £200,

subsection (1) above shall apply in relation to the dwelling-house as if the reference to the appropriate day were a reference to 22nd March 1973.

(3) In this Act a tenancy falling within subsection (1) above, is referred to as a "tenancy at a low rent".

(4) In determining whether a long tenancy is a tenancy at a low rent, there shall be disregarded such part (if any) of the sums payable by the tenant as is expressed (in whatever terms) to be payable in respect of rates, services, repairs, maintenance, or insurance, unless it could not have been regarded by the parties as a part so payable.

(5) In subsection (4) above "long tenancy" means a tenancy granted for a term certain exceeding 21 years, other than a tenancy which is, or may become, terminable before the end of that term by notice given to the tenant. **[293]**

NOTES

Commencement: 29 August 1977.

Sub-ss (1)-(3) derived from the Rent Act 1968, s 2; sub-ss (4), (5) derived from the Housing Act 1968, s 80(1), (3).

Sub-s (1): words omitted repealed by the Housing Act 1980, s 152, Sch 26.

5A. Certain shared ownership leases

[(1) A tenancy is not a protected tenancy if it is a qualifying shared ownership lease, that is—

(*a*) a lease granted in pursuance of the right to be granted a shared ownership lease under Part V of the Housing Act 1985, or

(*b*) a lease granted by a housing association and which complies with the conditions set out in subsection (2) below.

(2) The conditions referred to in subsection (1)(*b*) above are that the lease—

(*a*) was granted for a term of 99 years or more and is not (and cannot become) terminable except in pursuance of a provision for re-entry or forfeiture;

(*b*) was granted at a premium, calculated by reference to the value of the dwelling-house or the cost of providing it, of not less than 25 per cent., or such other percentage as may be prescribed, of the figure by reference to which it was calculated;

(*c*) provides for the tenant to acquire additional shares in the dwelling-house on terms specified in the lease and complying with such requirements as may be prescribed;
(*d*) does not restrict the tenant's powers to assign, mortgage or charge his interest in the dwelling-house;
(*e*) if it enables the landlord to require payment for outstanding shares in the dwelling-house, does so only in such circumstances as may be prescribed;
(*f*) provides, in the case of a house, for the tenant to acquire the landlord's interest on terms specified in the lease and complying with such requirements as may be prescribed; and
(*g*) states the landlord's opinion that by virtue of this section the lease is excluded from the operation of this Act.

(3) The Secretary of State may by regulations prescribe anything requiring to be prescribed for the purposes of subsection (2) above.

(4) The regulations may—

(*a*) make different provision for different cases or descriptions of case, including different provision for different areas, and
(*b*) contain such incidental, supplementary or transitional provisions as the Secretary of State considers appropriate,

and shall be made by statutory instrument which shall be subject to annulment in pursuance of a resolution of either House of Parliament.

(5) In any proceedings the court may, if of opinion that it is just and equitable to do so, treat a lease as a qualifying shared ownership lease notwithstanding that the condition specified in subsection (2)(*g*) above is not satisfied.

(6) In this section—

"house" has the same meaning as in Part I of the Leasehold Reform Act 1967;
"housing association" has the same meaning as in the Housing Associations Act 1985; and
"lease" includes an agreement for a lease, and references to the grant of a lease shall be construed accordingly.] **[294]**

NOTES
Commencement: To be appointed.
Prospectively added with savings by the Housing and Planning Act 1986, s 18, Sch 4, paras 1, 11, as from a day to be appointed.

6. Dwelling-houses let with other land

Subject to section 26 of this Act, a tenancy is not a protected tenancy if the dwelling-house which is subject to the tenancy is let together with land other than the site of the dwelling-house. **[295]**

NOTES
Commencement: 29 August 1977.
This section derived from the Rent Act 1968, s 2(1)(*c*).

7. Payments for board or attendance

(1) A tenancy is not a protected tenancy if under the tenancy the dwelling-house is bona fide let at a rent which includes payments in respect of board or attendance.

(2) For the purposes of subsection (1) above, a dwelling-house shall not be taken to be bona fide let at a rent which includes payments in respect of attendance unless the amount of rent which is fairly attributable to attendance, having regard to the value of the attendance to the tenant, forms a substantial part of the whole rent. **[296]**

NOTES
Commencement: 29 August 1977.
This section derived from the Rent Act 1968, s 2.

8. Lettings to students

(1) A tenancy is not a protected tenancy if it is granted to a person who is pursuing, or intends to pursue, a course of study provided by a specified educational institution and is so granted either by that institution or by another specified institution or body of persons.

(2) In subsection (1) above "specified" means specified, or of a class specified, for the purposes of this section by regulations made by the Secretary of State by statutory instrument.

(3) A statutory instrument containing any such regulations shall be subject to annulment in pursuance of a resolution of either House of Parliament. **[297]**

NOTES
Commencement: 29 August 1977.
This section derived from the Rent Act 1968, s 2.

9. Holiday Lettings

A tenancy is not a protected tenancy if the purpose of the tenancy is to confer on the tenant the right to occupy the dwelling-house for a holiday. **[298]**

NOTES
Commencement: 29 August 1977.
This section derived from the Rent Act 1968, s 2(1)(*bbb*).

10. Agricultural holdings

A tenancy is not a protected tenancy if the dwelling-house is comprised in an agricultural holding (within the meaning of the *Agricultural Holdings Act 1948* [Agricultural Holdings Act 1986]) and is occupied by the person responsible for the control (whether as tenant or as servant or agent of the tenant) of the farming of the holding. **[299]**

NOTES
Commencement: 29 August 1977.
This section derived from the Rent Act 1968, s 2(1)(*d*).
Words in italics repealed with savings and words in square brackets substituted with savings by the Agricultural Holdings Act 1986, ss 99, 100, Sch 13, para 3, Sch 14, para 59.

11. Licensed premises

A tenancy of a dwelling-house which consists of or comprises premises licensed for the sale of intoxicating liquors for consumption on the premises shall not be a protected tenancy, nor shall such a dwelling-house be the subject of a statutory tenancy. **[300]**

NOTES
Commencement: 29 August 1977.
This section derived from the Rent Act 1968, s 9(2).

12. Resident landlords

(1) Subject to subsection (2) below, a tenancy of a dwelling-house granted on or after 14th August 1974 shall not be a protected tenancy at any time if—

[(*a*) the dwelling-house forms part only of a building and, except in a case where the dwelling-house also forms part of a flat, the building is not a purpose-built block of flats; and

(*b*) the tenancy was granted by a person who, at the time when he granted it, occupied as his residence another dwelling-house which—

(i) in the case mentioned in paragraph (*a*) above, also forms part of the flat; or

(ii) in any other case, also forms part of the building; and

(*c*) subject to paragraph 1 of Schedule 2 to this Act, at all times since the tenancy was granted the interest of the landlord under the tenancy has belonged to a person who, at the time he owned that interest, occupied as his residence another dwelling-house which—

(i) in the case mentioned in paragraph (*a*) above, also formed part of the flat; or

(ii) in any other case, also formed part of the building.]

[(2) This section does not apply to a tenancy of a dwelling-house which forms part of a building if the tenancy is granted to a person who, immediately before it was granted, was a protected or statutory tenant of that dwelling-house or of any other dwelling-house in that building.]

(3) . . .

(4) Schedule 2 to this Act shall have effect for the purpose of supplementing this section. **[301]**

NOTES

Commencement: 29 August 1977 (sub-ss (1), (4)); 28 November 1980 (sub-s (2)).
Commencement order: SI 1980 No 1706.
Amended by the Housing Act 1980, ss 65(1), 69(4).

13. Landlord's interest belonging to Crown

[(1) Except as provided by subsection (2) below—

(*a*) a tenancy shall not be a protected tenancy at any time when the interest of the landlord under the tenancy belongs to Her Majesty in right of the Crown or to a government department or is held in trust for Her Majesty for the purposes of a government department; and

(*b*) a person shall not at any time be a statutory tenant of a dwelling-house if the interest of his immediate landlord would at that time belong or be held as mentioned in paragraph (*a*) above.

(2) An interest belonging to Her Majesty in right of the Crown shall not prevent a tenancy from being a protected tenancy or a person from being a statutory tenant if the interest is under the management of the Crown Estate Commissioners.] **[302]**

NOTES

Commencement: 28 November 1980.
Commencement order: SI 1980 No 1706.
Substituted by the Housing Act 1980, s 73(1).

14. Landlord's interest belonging to local authority, etc

A tenancy shall not be a protected tenancy at any time when the interest of the landlord under that tenancy belongs to—

(*a*) the council of a county;
(*b*) the council of a district or, in the application of this Act to the Isles of Scilly, the Council of the Isles of Scilly;
(*c*) . . . the council of a London borough or the Common Council of the City of London;
[(*ca*) the Inner London Education Authority;
(*cb*) a joint authority established by Part IV of the Local Government Act 1985;]
(*d*) the Commission for the New Towns;
(*e*) a development corporation established by an order made, or having effect as if made, under the [New Towns Act 1981]; or
(*f*) the Development Board for Rural Wales; [or
(*g*) an urban development corporation within the meaning of Part XVI of the Local Government, Planning and Land Act 1980;]

nor shall a person at any time be a statutory tenant of a dwelling-house if the interest of his immediate landlord would belong at that time to any of those bodies. **[303]**

NOTES
Commencement: 29 August 1977.
This section derived from the Rent Act 1968, ss 1(1)(*c*), 5(1), (2)(*a*)-(*dd*), (*f*).
In para (*c*) words omitted repealed by the Local Government Act 1985, s 102, Sch 17; paras (*ca*), (*cb*) added by the Local Government Act 1985, s 84, Sch 14, para 56; para (*e*) amended by the New Towns Act 1981, s 81, Sch 12; para (*g*) added by the Local Government, Planning and Land Act 1980, s 155(1).
Modified by SI 1985 No 1884, art 10, Sch 3.

15. Landlord's interest belonging to housing association, etc

(1) A tenancy . . . shall not be a protected tenancy at any time when the interest of the landlord under that tenancy belongs to a housing association falling within subsection (3) below; nor shall a person at any time be a statutory tenant of a dwelling-house if the interest of his immediate landlord would belong at that time to such a housing association.

(2) A tenancy shall not be a protected tenancy at any time when the interest of the landlord under that tenancy belongs to—

(*a*) the Housing Corporation; or
(*b*) a housing trust which is a charity within the meaning of the Charities Act 1960;

nor shall a person at any time be a statutory tenant of a dwelling-house if the interest of his immediate landlord would belong at that time to any of those bodies.

[(3) A housing association falls within this subsection if—

(*a*) it is registered under the Housing Associations Act 1985, or
(*b*) it is a co-operative housing association within the meaning of that Act.]

(4) . . .

[(5) In subsection (2) above "housing trust" means a corporation or body of persons which—

(*a*) is required by the terms of its constituent instrument to use the whole of its funds, including any surplus which may arise from its operations, for the purpose of providing housing accommodation; or

(*b*) is required by the terms of its constituent instrument to devote the whole, or substantially the whole, of its funds to charitable purposes and in fact uses the whole, or substantially the whole, of its funds for the purpose of providing housing accommodation.]

(6) . . . **[304]**

NOTES

Commencement: 1 April 1986 (sub-s (3)); 29 August 1977 (sub-ss (1)-(4)); 28 November 1980 (sub-s (5)).

This section derived from the Rent Act 1968, ss 5, 15 and the Housing Act 1974, ss 18(1), 129(1).

Sub-s (3): substituted by the Housing (Consequential Provisions) Act 1985, s 4, Sch 2, para 35.

Other amendments made by the Housing Act 1980, ss 74, 152, Sch 26.

16. Landlord's interest belonging to housing co-operative

A tenancy shall not be a protected tenancy at any time when the interest of the landlord under that tenancy belongs to a housing co-operative, [within the meaning of section 27B of the Housing Act 1985 (agreements with housing co-operatives under certain superseded provisions) and the dwelling-house is comprised in a housing co-operative agreement within the meaning of that section]. **[305]**

NOTES

Commencement: 29 August 1977.

This section derived from the Rent Act 1968, s 5(7).

Amended by the Housing and Planning Act 1986, s 24(2), Sch 5, Part II, para 15.

[16A. Assured tenancies

A tenancy shall not be a protected tenancy at any time when it is an assured tenancy within the meaning of section 56 of the Housing Act 1980.] **[306]**

NOTES

Commencement: 6 October 1980.

Commencement order: SI 1980 No 1466.

Added by the Housing Act 1980, s 56(5).

Controlled and regulated tenancies

18. Regulated tenancies

(1) Subject to sections 24(3) and 143 of this Act, a "regulated tenancy" is, for the purposes of this Act, a protected or statutory tenancy . . .

(2) Where a regulated tenancy is followed by a statutory tenancy of the same dwelling-house, the two shall be treated for the purposes of this Act as together constituting one regulated tenancy.

(3), (4) . . . **[307]**

NOTES

Commencement: 27 August 1977.

Sub-ss (1), (2) derived from the Rent Act 1968, s 7.

Words omitted repealed by the Housing Act 1980, s 152, Schs 25, 26.

[18A. Modification of Act for controlled tenancies converted into regulated tenancies

Schedule 17 to this Act applies for the purpose of modifying the provisions of this Act in relation to a tenancy which, by virtue of any of the following enactments, was converted from a controlled tenancy into a regulated tenancy, that is to say—

(*a*) section 18(3) of this Act;
(*b*) paragraph 5 of Schedule 2 to the Rent Act 1968 (which was superseded by section 18(3));
(*c*) Part VIII of this Act;
(*d*) Part III of the Housing Finance Act 1972 (which was superseded by Part VIII);
(*e*) Part IV of the Act of 1972 (conversion by reference to rateable values);
(*f*) section 64 of the Housing Act 1980 (conversion of remaining controlled tenancies into regulated tenancies).] **[308]**

NOTES
Commencement: 28 November 1980.
Commencement order: SI 1980 No 1706.
Added by the Housing Act 1980, s 152, Sch 25.

Restricted contracts

19. Restricted contracts

(1) A contract to which this section applies is, in this Act, referred to as a "restricted contract".

(2) Subject to section 144 of this Act, this section applies to a contract, whether entered into before or after the commencement of this Act, whereby one person grants to another person, in consideration of a rent which includes payment for the use of furniture or for services, the right to occupy a dwelling as a residence.

(3) A contract is not a restricted contract if the dwelling falls within one of the Classes set out in subsection (4) below.

(4) Where alternative rateable values are mentioned in this subsection, the higher applies if the dwelling is in Greater London and the lower applies if it is elsewhere.

Class D

The appropriate day in relation to the dwelling falls or fell on or after 1st April 1973 and the dwelling on the appropriate day has or had a rateable value exceeding £1,500 or £750.

Class E

The appropriate day in relation to the dwelling fell before 1st April 1973 and the dwelling—

(*a*) on the appropriate day had a rateable value exceeding £400 or £200, and
(*b*) on 1st April 1973 had a rateable value exceeding £1,500 or £750.

(5) A contract is not a restricted contract if—

(*a*) it creates a regulated tenancy; or

[(*aa*) under the contract the interest of the lessor belongs to a body mentioned in section 14 of this Act;]

(*b*) under the contract the interest of the lessor belongs to Her Majesty in right of the Crown . . . or to a government department, or is held in trust for Her Majesty for the purposes of a government department; or

(*c*) it is a contract for the letting of any premises at a rent which includes payment in respect of board if the value of the board to the lessee forms a substantial proportion of the whole rent;

[(*cc*) it creates a qualifying shared ownership lease within the meaning of section 5A of this Act; or]

(*d*) it is a protected occupancy as defined in the Rent (Agriculture) Act 1976; or

(*e*) it creates a tenancy to which Part VI of this Act applies [except that an interest belonging to Her Majesty in right of the Crown does not prevent a contract from being a restricted contract if the interest is under the management of the Crown Estate Commissioners] [, or

(*f*) it creates an assured tenancy within the meaning of section 56 of the Housing Act 1980.]

(6) Subject to subsections (3) to (5) above, and to paragraph 17 of Schedule 24 of this Act, a contract falling within subsection (2) above and relating to a dwelling which consists of only part of a house is a restricted contract whether or not the lessee is entitled, in addition to exclusive occupation of that part, to the use in common with any other person of other rooms or accommodation in the house.

(7) No right to occupy a dwelling for a holiday shall be treated for the purposes of this section as a right to occupy it as a residence.

(8) In this section—

"dwelling" means a house or part of a house;

"lessee" means the person to whom is granted, under a restricted contract, the right to occupy the dwelling in question as a residence and any person directly or indirectly deriving title from the grantee; and

"lessor" means the person who, under a restricted contract, grants to another the right to occupy the dwelling in question as a residence and any person directly or indirectly deriving title from the grantor; and

"services" includes attendance, the provision of heating or lighting, the supply of hot water and any other privilege or facility connected with the occupancy of a dwelling, other than a privilege or facility requisite for the purposes of access, cold water supply or sanitary accommodation. **[309]**

NOTES

Commencement: 29 August 1977.

This section derived from the Rent Act 1968, ss 70, 71, 84(1).

Sub-s (5): paras (*aa*), (*b*), (*e*) amended by the Housing Act 1980, ss 73(2), 152, Schs 25, 26; para (*cc*), prospectively added with savings by the Housing and Planning Act 1986, s 18, Sch 4, para 1, as from a day to be appointed; para (*f*) added by the Housing and Planning Act 1986, s 13(1).

20. Certain unfurnished tenancies to be treated as restricted contracts

If and so long as a tenancy is, by virtue only of section 12 of this Act, precluded from being a protected tenancy it shall be treated as a restricted contract notwithstanding that the rent may not include payment for the use of furniture or for services. **[310]**

NOTES
Commencement: 29 August 1977.
This section derived from the Rent Act 1968, s 102A.

Shared accommodation

21. Tenant sharing accommodation with landlord

Where under any contract—

(*a*) a tenant has the exclusive occupation of any accommodation, and
(*b*) the terms on which he holds the accommodation include the use of other accommodation in common with his landlord or in common with his landlord and other persons, and
(*c*) by reason only of the circumstances mentioned in paragraph (*b*) above, or by reason of those circumstances and the operation of section 12 of this Act, the accommodation referred to in paragraph (*a*) above is not a dwelling-house let on a protected tenancy,

the contract is a restricted contract notwithstanding that the rent does not include payment for the use of furniture or for services. **[311]**

NOTES
Commencement: 29 August 1977.
This section derived from the Rent Act 1968, s 101.

22. Tenant sharing accommodation with persons other than landlord

(1) Where a tenant has the exclusive occupation of any accommodation ("the separate accommodation") and—

(*a*) the terms as between the tenant and his landlord on which he holds the separate accommodation include the use of other accommodation ("the shared accommodation") in common with another person or other persons, not being or including the landlord, and
(*b*) by reason only of the circumstances mentioned in paragraph (*a*) above, the separate accommodation would not, apart from this section, be a dwelling-house let on or subject to a protected or statutory tenancy,

the separate accommodation shall be deemed to be a dwelling-house let on a protected tenancy or, as the case may be, subject to a statutory tenancy and the following provisions of this section shall have effect.

(2) For the avoidance of doubt it is hereby declared that where, for the purpose of determining the rateable value of the separate accommodation, it is necessary to make an apportionment under this Act, regard is to be had to the circumstances mentioned in subsection (1)(*a*) above.

(3) While the tenant is in possession of the separate accommodation (whether as a protected or statutory tenant), any term or condition of the contract of tenancy terminating or modifying, or providing for the termination or modification of, his right to the use of any of the shared accommodation which is living accommodation shall be of no effect.

(4) Where the terms and conditions of the contract of tenancy are such that at any time during the tenancy the persons in common with whom the tenant is entitled to the use of the shared accommodation could be varied, or their number could be increased, nothing in subsection (3) above shall prevent those terms and conditions from having effect so far as they relate to any such variation or increase.

(5) Without prejudice to the enforcement of any order made under subsection (6) below, while the tenant is in possession of the separate accommodation, no order shall be made for possession of any of the shared accommodation, whether on the application of the immediate landlord of the tenant or on the application of any person under whom that landlord derives title, unless a like order has been made, or is made at the same time, in respect of the separate accommodation; and the provisions of section 98(1) of this Act shall apply accordingly.

(6) On the application of the landlord, the county court may make such order either—

(*a*) terminating the right of the tenant to use the whole or any part of the shared accommodation other than living accommodation, or

(*b*) modifying his right to use the whole or any part of the shared accommodation, whether by varying the persons or increasing the number of persons entitled to the use of that accommodation, or otherwise,

as the court thinks just.

(7) No order shall be made under subsection (6) above so as to effect any termination or modification of the rights of the tenant which, apart from subsection (3) above, could not be effected by or under the terms of the contract of tenancy.

(8) In this section "living accommodation" means accommodation of such a nature that the fact that it constitutes or is included in the shared accommodation is (or, if the tenancy has ended, was) sufficient, apart from this section, to prevent the tenancy from constituting a protected tenancy of a dwelling-house. **[312]**

NOTES
Commencement: 29 August 1977.
This section derived from the Rent Act 1968, s 102.

Sublettings

23. Certain sublettings not to exclude any part of sub-lessor's premises from protection

(1) Where the tenant of any premises, consisting of a house or part of a house, has sublet a part but not the whole of the premises, then, as against his landlord or any superior landlord, no part of the premises shall be treated as not being a dwelling-house let on or subject to a protected or statutory tenancy by reason only that—

(*a*) the terms on which any person claiming under the tenant holds any part of the premises include the use of accommodation in common with other persons; or

(*b*) part of the premises is let to any such person at a rent which includes payments in respect of board or attendance.

(2) Nothing in this section shall affect the rights against, and liabilities to, each other of the tenant and any person claiming under him, or of any 2 such persons. **[313]**

NOTES
Commencement: 29 August 1977.
This section derived from the Rent Act 1968, s 103.

Business premises

24. Premises with a business use

(1), (2) . . .

(3) A tenancy shall not be a regulated tenancy if it is a tenancy to which Part II of the Landlord and Tenant Act 1954 applies (but this provision is without prejudice to the application of any other provision of this Act to a sub-tenancy of any part of the premises comprised in such a tenancy). **[314]**

NOTES

Commencement: 29 August 1977.
This section derived from the Rent Act 1968, s 9(1), (3), (5).
Words omitted repealed by the Housing Act 1980, s 152, Sch 26.

Miscellaneous

25. Rateable value and meaning of "appropriate day"

(1) Except where this Act otherwise provides, the rateable value on any day of a dwelling-house shall be ascertained for the purposes of this Act as follows:—

(*a*) if the dwelling-house is a hereditament for which a rateable value is then shown in the valuation list, it shall be that rateable value;
(*b*) if the dwelling-house forms part only of such a hereditament or consists of or forms part of more than one such hereditament, its rateable value shall be taken to be such value as is found by a proper apportionment or aggregation of the rateable value or values so shown.

(2) Any question arising under this section as to the proper apportionment or aggregation of any value or values shall be determined by the county court, and the decision of the county court shall be final.

(3) In this Act "the appropriate day"—

(*a*) in relation to any dwelling-house which, on 23rd March 1965, was or formed part of a hereditament for which a rateable value was shown in the valuation list then in force, or consisted or formed part of more than one such hereditament, means that date, and
(*b*) in relation to any other dwelling-house, means the date on which such a value is or was first shown in the valuation list.

(4) Where, after the date which is the appropriate day in relation to any dwelling-house, the valuation list is altered so as to vary the rateable value of the hereditament of which the dwelling-house consists or forms part and the alteration has effect from a date not later than the appropriate day, the rateable value of the dwelling-house on the appropriate day shall be ascertained as if the value shown in the valuation list on the appropriate day had been the value shown in the list as altered.

(5) This section applies in relation to any other land as it applies in relation to a dwelling-house. **[315]**

NOTES

Commencement: 29 August 1977.
This section derived from the Rent Act 1968, s 6.

26. Land and premises let with dwelling-house

(1) For the purposes of this Act, any land or premises let together with a dwelling-house shall, unless it consists of agricultural land exceeding 2 acres in extent, be treated as part of the dwelling-house.

(2) For the purposes of subsection (1) above "agricultural land" has the meaning set out in section 26(3)(*a*) of the General Rate Act 1967 (exclusion of agricultural land and premises from liability for rating). **[316]**

NOTES

Commencement: 29 August 1977.
This section derived from the Rent Act 1968, s 1(2).

PART III

RENTS UNDER REGULATED TENANCIES

Regulation of rent

44. Limit of rent during contractual periods

(1) Where a rent for a dwelling-house is registered under Part IV of this Act, the rent recoverable for any contractual period of a regulated tenancy of the dwelling-house shall be limited to the rent so registered.

This subsection is subject to the following provisions of this Act: subsection (4) below, *sections 55 and 71(3)*, paragraph 1(3) of Schedule 7, ... and paragraph 3 of Schedule 20.

(2) Where a limit is imposed by subsection (1) above on the rent recoverable in relation to any contractual period of a regulated tenancy, the amount by which the rent payable under the tenancy exceeds that limit shall, notwithstanding anything in any agreement, be irrecoverable from the tenant.

(3) In this Part of this Act "contractual rent limit" means the limit specified in subsection (1) above.

(4) Schedule 7 to this Act shall have effect for the purpose of providing a special rent limit in relation to certain tenancies which became regulated tenancies by virtue of section 14 of the Counter-Inflation Act 1973. **[317]**

NOTES

Commencement: 29 August 1977.
Sub-ss (1)-(3) derived from the Rent Act 1968, s 20 (1), (2); sub-s (4) derived from the Counter-Inflation Act 1973, s 14(4).
Sub-s (1): words in italics repealed and words "section 71(3)" substituted by SI 1987 No 264, art 2(3), Sch 1, except in relation to the circumstances and to the extent specified in Sch 2 to that Order; see para [1070] post; words omitted repealed by the Housing Act 1980, s 152, Sch 26.

45. Limit of rent during statutory periods

(1) Except as otherwise provided by this Part of this Act, where the rent payable for any statutory period of a regulated tenancy of a dwelling-house would exceed the rent recoverable for the last contractual period thereof, the amount of the excess shall, notwithstanding anything in any agreement, be irrecoverable from the tenant.

(2) Where a rent for the dwelling-house is registered under Part IV of this Act, the following provisions shall apply with respect to the rent for any statutory period of a regulated tenancy of the dwelling-house:—

(*a*) if the rent payable for any statutory period would exceed the rent so registered, the amount of the excess shall, notwithstanding anything in any agreement, be irrecoverable from the tenant; and
(*b*) if the rent payable for any statutory period would be less than the rent so registered, it may be increased up to the amount of that rent by a notice of increase served by the landlord on the tenant and specifying the date from which the increase is to take effect.

This subsection is subject to the following provisions of this Act: *sections 55 and 71(3)*, paragraph 1(3) of Schedule 7, *paragraph 10 of Schedule 8*, . . . and paragraph 3 of Schedule 20.

(3) The date specified in a notice of increase under subsection (2)(*b*) above shall not be earlier than the date [from which the registration of the rent took effect] nor earlier than 4 weeks before the service of the notice.

(4) Where no rent for the dwelling-house is registered under Part IV of this Act, sections 46 [and 47] of this Act shall have effect with respect to the rent recoverable for any statutory period under a regulated tenancy of the dwelling-house. **[318]**

NOTES
Commencement: 29 August 1977.
This section derived from the Rent Act 1968, s 22.
Sub-s (2): words in italics repealed and words "section 71(3)" substituted for words "sections 55 and 71(3)" by SI 1987 No 264, art 2(3), Sch 1 except in relation to the circumstances and to the extent specified in Sch 2 to that Order; see para [1070] post; words omitted repealed by the Housing Act 1980, s 152, Sch 26.
Sub-s (3): amended by the Housing Act 1980, s 61(4).
Sub-s (4): amended by the Housing Act 1980, s 152, Sch 25.

46. Adjustment, with respect to rates, of recoverable rent for statutory periods before registration

(1) Where—

(*a*) section 45(4) of this Act applies, and
(*b*) any rates in respect of the dwelling-house are, or were during the last contractual period, borne by the landlord or a superior landlord,

then, for any statutory period for which the amount of the rates (ascertained in accordance with Schedule 5 to this Act) differs from the amount, so ascertained, of the rates for the last contractual period, the recoverable rent shall be increased or decreased by the amount of the difference.

(2) Where the amount of the recoverable rent is increased by virtue of this section, the increase shall not take effect except in pursuance of a notice of increase served by the landlord on the tenant and specifying the increase and the date from which it is to take effect.

(3) The date specified in a notice of increase under subsection (2) above shall be not earlier than 6 weeks before the service of the notice, and if it is earlier than the service of the notice any rent unpaid shall become due on the day after the service of the notice. **[319]**

NOTES
Commencement: 29 August 1977.
This section derived from the Rent Act 1968, s 23.

47. Adjustment, with respect to services and furniture, of recoverable rent for statutory periods before registration

(1) Where section 45(4) of this Act applies and for any statutory period there is with respect to—

(*a*) the provision of services for the tenant by the landlord or a superior landlord, or

(*b*) the use of furniture by the tenant,

or any circumstances relating thereto any difference, in comparison with the last contractual period, such as to affect the amount of the rent which it is reasonable to charge, the recoverable rent for the statutory period shall be increased or decreased by an appropriate amount.

(2) Any question whether, or by what amount, the recoverable rent for any period is increased or decreased by virtue of this section shall be determined by agreement in writing between the landlord and the tenant or by the county court; and any such determination—

(*a*) may be made so as to relate to past statutory periods; and

(*b*) shall have effect with respect to statutory periods subsequent to the periods to which it relates until revoked or varied by any such agreement as is referred to in this subsection or by the county court.

[320]

NOTES

Commencement: 29 August 1977.

This section derived from the Rent Act 1968, s 24.

49. Notices of increase

(1) Any reference in this section to a notice of increase is a reference to a notice of increase under section 45(2), [or 46] of this Act.

(2) A notice of increase must be in the prescribed form.

(3) Notwithstanding that a notice of increase relates to statutory periods, it may be served during a contractual period.

(4) Where a notice of increase is served during a contractual period and the protected tenancy could, by a notice to quit served by the landlord at the same time, be brought to an end before the date specified in the notice of increase, the notice of increase shall operate to convert the protected tenancy into a statutory tenancy as from that date.

(5) If the county court is satisfied that any error or omission in a notice of increase is due to a bona fide mistake on the part of the landlord, the court may by order amend the notice by correcting any errors or supplying any omission therein which, if not corrected or supplied, would render the notice invalid and, if the court so directs, the notice as so amended shall have effect and be deemed to have had effect as a valid notice.

(6) Any amendment of a notice of increase under subsection (5) above may be made on such terms and conditions with respect to arrears of rent or otherwise as appear to the court to be just and reasonable.

(7) No increase of rent which becomes payable by reason of an amendment

of a notice of increase under subsection (5) above shall be recoverable in respect of any statutory period which ended more than 6 months before the date of the order making the amendment. **[321]**

NOTES
Commencement: 29 August 1977.
This section derived from the Rent Act 1968, s 26.
Sub-s (1): amended by the Housing Act 1980, s 152, Sch 25.

Rent agreements with tenants having security of tenure

51. Protection of tenants with security of tenure

(1) In this Part of this Act a "rent agreement with a tenant having security of tenure" means—

(*a*) an agreement increasing the rent payable under a protected tenancy which is a regulated tenancy, or

(*b*) the grant to the tenant under a regulated tenancy, or to any person who might succeed him as a statutory tenant, of another regulated tenancy of the dwelling-house at a rent exceeding the rent under the previous tenancy.

(2) Where any rates in respect of the dwelling-house are borne by the landlord or a superior landlord, any increase of rent shall be disregarded for the purposes of the definition in subsection (1) above if the increase is no more than one corresponding to an increase in the rates borne by the landlord or a superior landlord in respect of the dwelling-house.

(3) If—

(*a*) a rent agreement with a tenant having security of tenure takes effect on or after the commencement of this Act, and was made at a time when no rent was registered for the dwelling-house under Part IV of this Act, . . .

(*b*) . . .

the requirements of subsection (4) below shall be observed as respects the agreement.

(4) The requirements are that—

(*a*) the agreement is in writing signed by the landlord and the tenant, and

(*b*) the document containing the agreement contains a statement, in characters not less conspicuous than those used in any other part of the agreement—

(i) that the tenant's security of tenure under this Act will not be affected if he refuses to enter into the agreement, and

[(*ia*) *that if the agreement were not made but instead a rent were registered under Part IV of this Act, then part only of any increase over the rent previously recoverable by the landlord would be payable by the tenant during the first year; and*]

(ii) that entry into the agreement will not deprive the tenant or landlord of the right to apply at any time to the rent officer for the registration of a fair rent under Part IV of this Act,

or words to that effect, and

(*c*) the statement mentioned in paragraph (*b*) above is set out at the head of the document containing the agreement. **[322]**

NOTES

Commencement: 29 August 1977.

This section derived from the Housing Finance Act 1972, s 43.

Sub-s (3): words omitted repealed by the Housing Act 1980, s 152, Sch 26.

Sub-s (4): sub-para (*b*)(ia) added by the Housing Act 1980, s 68(1); further repealed by SI 1987 No 264, art 2(3), Sch 1 except in relation to the circumstances and to the extent specified in Sch 2 to that Order; see para [1070] post.

52. Protection: special provisions following conversion

[(1) This section applies to an agreement with a tenant having security of tenure which is entered into after the commencement of section 68(2) of the Housing Act 1980 if the tenancy has become or, as the case may be, the previous tenancy became a regulated tenancy by conversion.

(2) Any such agreement which purports to increase the rent payable under a protected tenancy shall, if entered into at a time when no rent is registered for the dwelling-house under Part IV of this Act, be void.

(3) If any such agreement constitutes a grant of a regulated tenancy and is made at a time when no rent is so registered, any excess of the rent payable under the tenancy so granted (for any contractual or statutory period of the tenancy) over the rent limit applicable to the previous tenancy, shall be irrecoverable from the tenant; but this subsection ceases to apply if a rent is subsequently so registered.

(4) For the purposes of this section a tenancy is a regulated tenancy by conversion if it has become a regulated tenancy by virtue of—

(*a*) Part VIII of this Act, section 43 of the Housing Act 1969 or Part III or IV of the Housing Finance Act 1972 (conversion of controlled tenancies into regulated tenancies); or

(*b*) section 18(3) of this Act or paragraph 5 of Schedule 2 to the Rent Act 1968 (conversion on death of first successor); or

(*c*) section 64 of the Housing Act 1980 (conversion of all remaining controlled tenancies).

(5) This section does not apply to any agreement where the tenant is neither the person who, at the time of the conversion, was the tenant nor a person who might succeed the tenant at that time as a statutory tenant.

(6) Where a rent is registered for the dwelling-house and the registration is subsequently cancelled, this section shall not apply to the agreement submitted to the rent officer in connection with the cancellation nor to any agreement made so as to take effect after the cancellation.] **[323]**

NOTES

Commencement: 28 November 1980.

Commencement order: SI 1980 No 1706.

Substituted by the Housing Act 1980, s 68(2).

54. Failure to comply with provisions for protection of tenants

(1) If, in the case of a variation of the terms of a regulated tenancy, there is a failure to observe any of the requirements of section 51, . . . of this Act, any excess of the rent payable under the terms as varied over the terms without the variation shall be irrecoverable from the tenant.

(2) If, in the case of the grant of a tenancy, there is a failure to observe any of those requirements, any excess of the rent payable under the tenancy so

granted (for any contractual or any statutory period of the tenancy) over the previous limit shall be irrecoverable from the tenant.

(3) In subsection (2) above the "previous limit" shall be taken to be the amount which (taking account of any previous operation of this section or of section 46 of the Housing Finance Act 1972, which is superseded by this section) was recoverable by way of rent for the last period of the previous tenancy of the dwelling-house, or which would have been so recoverable if all notices of increase authorised by this Act, the Rent Act 1968 and section 37(3) of the Act of 1972 had been served.

(4), (5) . . . **[324]**

NOTES

Commencement: 29 August 1977.
This section derived from the Housing Finance Act 1972, s 46.
Words omitted repealed by the Housing Act 1980, s 152, Sch 26.

Phasing of rent increases

55. General provision for phasing of rent increases

(1) Where the rent of a dwelling-house qualifies for phasing under this section—

(a) a notice of increase of the rent for any statutory period, or part of a statutory period, falling within the period of delay imposed by Schedule 8 to this Act may increase it to the extent permitted by that Schedule;

(b) the rent for any contractual period, or part of a contractual period, falling within the period of delay shall not exceed the amount to which the rent could have been increased in accordance with Schedule 8 for a corresponding statutory period or part of a statutory period.

(2) A notice of increase which purports to increase rent which qualifies for phasing under this section further than permitted by Schedule 8 shall have effect to increase it to the extent so permitted but no further.

(3) The rent of a dwelling-house qualifies for phasing under this section if—

(a) a rent is registered for the dwelling-house under Part IV of this Act; and

[*(b)* the provisions of section 89 of this Act do not apply to it; and]

(c) the tenancy is a regulated tenancy which—

(i) was subsisting at 10th March 1975; or

(ii) was subsisting at the date of registration; or

(iii) was not subsisting at the date of registration but was granted after that date to a person to whom subsection (4) below applies.

(4) This subsection applies to a person who, at the date when the tenancy was granted, was either—

(a) the tenant under a previous regulated tenancy of the dwelling-house, or a person who might succeed the tenant as a statutory tenant, or

(b) a statutory tenant of a dwelling-house, within the meaning of the Rent (Agriculture) Act 1976, whose rent qualified for phasing under section 15 of that Act, or a person who might succeed such a tenant as a statutory tenant by succession, within the meaning of that Act.

(5) Nothing in this section or in Schedule 8 shall prevent or limit any increase in rent by virtue of section 71(4) of this Act (variable rents).

(6) In this section "notice of increase" means a notice under section 45(2) of this Act. **[325]**

NOTES

Commencement: 29 August 1977.

This section derived from the Housing Rents and Subsidies Act 1975, ss 7, 16(1).

Repealed by SI 1987 No 264, art 2(1)(*a*) except in relation to the circumstances and to the extent specified in Sch 2 to that Order; see para [1070] post.

Sub-s (3): amended by the Housing Act 1980, s 152, Sch 25.

Enforcement provisions

57. Recovery from landlord of sums paid in excess of recoverable rent, etc

(1) Where a tenant has paid on account of rent any amount which, by virtue of this Part of this Act, is irrecoverable by the landlord, the tenant who paid it shall be entitled to recover that amount from the landlord who received it or his personal representatives.

(2) Any amount which a tenant is entitled to recover under subsection (1) above may, without prejudice to any other method of recovery, be deducted by the tenant from any rent payable by him to the landlord.

[(3) No amount which a tenant is entitled to recover under subsection (1) above shall be recoverable at any time after the expiry of—

(*a*) one year, in the case of an amount which is irrecoverable by virtue of section 54 of this Act; or

(*b*) two years, in any other case.]

(4) Any person who, in any rent book or similar document, makes an entry showing or purporting to show any tenant as being in arrears in respect of any sum on account of rent which is irrecoverable by virtue of this Part of this Act shall be liable to a fine not exceeding [level 3 on the standard scale], unless he proves that, at the time of the making of the entry, the landlord had a bona fide claim that the sum was recoverable.

(5) If, where any such entry has been made by or on behalf of any landlord, the landlord on being requested by or on behalf of the tenant to do so, refuses or neglects to cause the entry to be deleted within 7 days, the landlord shall be liable to a fine not exceeding [level 3 on the standard scale], unless he proves that, at the time of the neglect or refusal to cause the entry to be deleted, he had a bona fide claim that the sum was recoverable. **[326]**

NOTES

Commencement: 28 November 1980 (sub-s (3)); 29 August 1977 (remainder).

Commencement order: SI 1980 No 1706.

This section derived from the Rent Act 1968, s 33.

Sub-s (3): substituted by the Housing Act 1980, s 68(3).

Sub-ss (4), (5): maximum fines increased and converted to levels on the standard scale by the Criminal Justice Act 1982, ss 37, 38, 46.

58. Rectification of rent books in light of determination of recoverable rent

Where, in any proceedings, the recoverable rent of a dwelling-house subject to a regulated tenancy is determined by a court, then, on the application of the tenant (whether in those or in any subsequent proceedings) the court may call for the production of the rent book or any similar document relating to the dwelling-house and may direct the registrar or clerk of the court to correct any entries showing, or purporting to show, the tenant as being in arrears in respect of any sum which the court has determined to be irrecoverable. **[327]**

NOTES
Commencement: 29 August 1977.
This section derived from the Rent Act 1968, s 34.

General provisions

59. Adjustment for differences in lengths of rental periods

In ascertaining for the purposes of this Part of this Act whether there is any difference with respect to rents or rates between one rental period and another (whether of the same tenancy or not) or the amount of any such difference, any necessary adjustment shall be made to take account of periods of different lengths; and for the purposes of such an adjustment a period of one month shall be treated as equivalent to one-twelfth of a year and a period of a week as equivalent to one-fifty-second of a year. **[328]**

NOTES
Commencement: 29 August 1977.
This section derived from the Rent Act 1968, s 36.

60. Regulations

(1) The Secretary of State may make regulations—

(*a*) prescribing the form of any notice or other document to be given or used in pursuance of this Part of this Act; and

(*b*) prescribing anything required or authorised to be prescribed by this Part of this Act.

(2) Any such regulations shall be made by statutory instrument which shall be subject to annulment in pursuance of a resolution of either House of Parliament. **[329]**

NOTES
Commencement: 29 August 1977.
This section derived from the Rent Act 1968, s 37.

61. Interpretation of Part III

(1) In this Part of this Act, except where the context otherwise requires—

"contractual period" means a rental period of a regulated tenancy which is a period beginning before the expiry or termination of the protected tenancy;

"contractual rent limit" has the meaning assigned to it by section 44(3) of this Act;

. . .

"prescribed" means prescribed by regulations under section 60 of this Act and references to a prescribed form include references to a form substantially to the same effect as the prescribed form;

"recoverable rent" means rent which, under a regulated tenancy, is or was for the time being recoverable, having regard to the provisions of this Part of this Act;

"rent agreement with a tenant having security of tenure" has the meaning assigned to it by section 51 of this Act;

"statutory period" means any rental period of a regulated tenancy which is not a contractual period.

(2) References in this Part of this Act to rates, in respect of a dwelling-house, include references to such proportion of any rates in respect of a hereditament of which the dwelling-house forms part as may be agreed in writing between the landlord and the tenant or determined by the county court.

[330]

NOTES

Commencement: 29 August 1977.

Sub-s (1) derived from the Rent Act 1968, s 38(1), the Housing Finance Act 1972, ss 44(9), 48 and the Housing Rents and Subsidies Act 1975, s 16(1); sub-s (2) derived from the Rent Act 1968, s 38(2).

Words omitted repealed by the Housing Act 1980, s 152, Sch 26.

PART IV

REGISTRATION OF RENTS UNDER REGULATED TENANCIES

62. Registration areas

(1) The registration areas for the purpose of this Part of this Act

[are—

(*a*) counties;
(*b*) London boroughs; and
(*c*) the City of London.]

(2) For the purposes of this Part of this Act—

(*a*) . . . the City of London shall be deemed to include the Inner Temple and the Middle Temple, and
(*b*) the Isles of Scilly shall be a registration area and the Council of the Isles of Scilly shall be the local authority for that registration area.

[331]

NOTES

Commencement: 29 August 1977.

This section derived from the Rent Act 1968, s 39.

Amendment in square brackets made and words omitted repealed by the Local Government Act 1985, s 16, Sch 8, para 13.

63. Schemes for appointment of rent officers

(1) The Secretary of State shall for every registration area make, after consultation with the local authority, a scheme providing for the appointment by the proper officer of the local authority—

(*a*) of such number of rent officers for the area as may be determined by or in accordance with the scheme, and
(*b*) of deputy rent officers to exercise the functions of rent officers when rent officers are absent or incapacitated.

(2) A scheme under this section—

(*a*) shall provide for the payment by the local authority to rent officers and deputy rent officers of remuneration and allowances in accordance with scales approved by the Secretary of State with the consent of the Treasury;

(*b*) shall prohibit the dismissal of a rent officer or deputy rent officer except by the proper officer of the local authority on the direction, or with the consent, of the Secretary of State;

(*c*) shall require the local authority to provide for the rent officers office accommodation and clerical and other assistance;

(*d*) shall allocate, or confer on the proper officer of the local authority the duty of allocating, work as between the rent officers and shall confer on the proper officer the duty of supervising the conduct of rent officers and deputy rent officers; [and

(*e*) may require the proper officer—

(i) to designate one of the rent officers as chief rent officer; and

(ii) to delegate to him such of the duties imposed on the proper officer by virtue of paragraph (*d*) above as may be specified in the scheme.]

(3) For the purposes of any local Act scheme, within the meaning of section 8 of the Superannuation Act 1972, rent officers and deputy rent officers appointed in pursuance of a scheme under this section shall be deemed to be officers in the employment of the local authority for whose area the scheme is made; and for the purposes of—

(*a*) Part III of the Social Security Pensions Act 1975, and

(*b*) the Social Security Act 1975,

they shall be deemed to be in that employment under a contract of service.

(4) References in this Part of this Act to the rent officer are references to any rent officer appointed for any area who is authorised to act in accordance with a scheme under this section.

(5) A scheme under this section may be varied or revoked by a subsequent scheme made thereunder.

(6) The Secretary of State shall, in respect of each financial year, make to any local authority incurring expenditure which is of a kind mentioned in subsection (7) below, a grant equal to that expenditure.

(7) The expenditure mentioned in subsection (6) above is any expenditure—

(*a*) attributable to this section, or

(*b*) incurred in respect of pensions, allowances or gratuities payable to or in respect of rent officers and deputy rent officers (appointed in pursuance of a scheme under this section) by virtue of regulations under section 7 of the Superannuation Act 1972 (superannuation of persons employed in local government service).

(8) Any expenditure incurred by the Secretary of State by virtue of subsection (6) above shall be paid out of money provided by Parliament.

[(9) In the case of a registration area which is a metropolitan county this section shall apply as if—

(*a*) the first reference to the local authority in subsection (1) were a reference to the council of each district in the county; and

(*b*) the second reference to the local authority in that subsection, the references to the local authority in subsection (2) and the reference to the local authority for whose area the scheme is made in subsection (3) were references to such one of the councils of the districts in that county as has been designated by the scheme.] **[332]**

NOTES
Commencement: 1 April 1986 (sub-s (9)); 29 August 1977 (remainder).
This section derived from the Rent Act 1968, s 40.
Sub-s (2): amended by the Housing Act 1980, s 59(1).
Sub-s (9): added by the Local Government Act 1985, s 16, Sch 8, para 13.

64. Default powers of Secretary of State

(1) If the Secretary of State is of opinion that a local authority have failed to carry out any function conferred on them by a scheme under section 63 of this Act he may, after such enquiry as he thinks fit, by order revoke the scheme and, without consulting the local authority, make another scheme under that section.

(2) A scheme made by virtue of subsection (1) above may confer functions otherwise exercisable by the local authority or the proper officer of the local authority on a person appointed by the Secretary of State and that person may, if another local authority consent, be that other local authority or, as the case may be, the proper officer of that other local authority.

(3) If the Secretary of State is of opinion that the proper officer of the local authority has failed to carry out any functions conferred on the proper officer by a scheme under section 63 he may (after consultation with the local authority) exercise his power under subsection (5) of that section by making a scheme providing for all or any of the functions otherwise exercisable by the proper officer to be exercised by some other person.

(4) A scheme made by virtue of this section may contain such incidental and transitional provisions as appear to the Secretary of State to be necessary or expedient. **[333]**

NOTES
Commencement: 29 August 1977.
This section derived from the Rent Act 1968, s 41.

65. Rent assessment committees

Rent assessment committees shall be constituted in accordance with Schedule 10 to this Act. **[334]**

NOTES
Commencement: 29 August 1977.
This section derived from the Rent Act 1968, s 42.

66. Register of rents

(1) The rent officer for any area shall prepare and keep up to date a register for the purposes of this Part of this Act and shall make the register available for inspection in such place or places and in such manner as may be provided by the scheme made for the area under section 63 of this Act.

(2) The register shall contain, in addition to the rent payable under a regulated tenancy of a dwelling-house—

(*a*) the prescribed particulars with regard to the tenancy; and
(*b*) a specification of the dwelling-house.

(3) A copy of an entry in the register certified under the hand of the rent

officer or any person duly authorised by him shall be receivable in evidence in any court and in any proceedings.

(4) A person requiring such a certified copy shall be entitled to obtain it on payment of the prescribed fee. **[335]**

NOTES

Commencement: 29 August 1977.

This section derived from the Rent Act 1968, s 43.

67. Application for registration of rent

(1) An application for the registration of a rent for a dwelling-house may be made to the rent officer by the landlord or the tenant, or jointly by the landlord and the tenant, under a regulated tenancy of the dwelling-house.

[(2) Any such application must be in the prescribed form and must—

(*a*) specify the rent which it is sought to register;

(*b*) where the rent includes any sum payable by the tenant to the landlord for services and the application is made by the landlord, specify that sum and be accompanied by details of the expenditure incurred by the landlord in providing those services; and

(*c*) contain such other particulars as may be prescribed.]

(3) Subject to subsection (4) below, where a rent for a dwelling-house has been registered under this Part of this Act, no application by the tenant alone or by the landlord alone for the registration of a different rent for that dwelling-house shall be entertained before the expiry of [2 years] from the relevant date (as defined in subsection (5) below) except on the ground that, since that date, there has been such a change in—

(*a*) the condition of the dwelling-house (including the making of any improvement therein),

(*b*) the terms of the tenancy,

(*c*) the quantity, quality or condition of any furniture provided for use under the tenancy (deterioration by fair wear and tear excluded), or

(*d*) any other circumstances taken into consideration when the rent was registered or confirmed,

as to make the registered rent no longer a fair rent.

(4) Notwithstanding anything in subsection (3) above, an application such as is mentioned in that subsection which is made by the landlord alone and is so made within the last 3 months of the period of [2 years] referred to in that subsection may be entertained notwithstanding that that period has not expired.

[(5) In this section and sections 68 and 69 of this Act "relevant date", in relation to a rent which has been registered under this Part of this Act, means the date from which the registration took effect or, in the case of a registered rent which has been confirmed, the date from which the confirmation (or, where there have been two or more successive confirmations, the last of them) took effect.]

(6) . . .

(7) Subject to section 69(4) of this Act, the provisions of Part I of Schedule 11 to this Act [as modified by the Regulated Tenancies (Procedure) Regulations 1980] shall have effect with respect to the procedure to be followed on applications for the registration of rents. **[336]**

NOTES

Commencement: 28 November 1980 (sub-ss (2), (5)); 29 August 1977 (remainder).
Commencement order: SI 1980 No 1706.
This section derived from the Rent Act 1968, s 44.
Sub-ss (2), (5): substituted by the Housing Act 1980, ss 59(2), 61(5).
Sub-ss (3), (4): amended by the Housing Act 1980, s 60(1).
Sub-s (6): repealed by the Housing Act 1980, s 152, Sch 26.
Sub-s (7): amended by SI 1980 No 1696, reg 2; further amended by SI 1981 No 1783, reg 2 by the insertion of the words "and by the Rent Assessment Committees (England and Wales) (Amendment) Regulations 1981" after the words "Regulations 1980".

68. Application to rent officer by local authority

(1) A local authority may apply to the rent officer for consideration of the fair rent for any dwelling-house within their area for which a rent may be or has been registered under this Part of this Act.

(2) If on the application the rent officer is satisfied that the rent, or the highest rent, payable for the dwelling-house under any lease or agreement exceeds what in his opinion is a fair rent, he shall register a rent for the dwelling-house.

(3) The rent officer may under subsection (2) above take account of the rent payable under any lease or agreement whether or not that exceeds the recoverable rent and whether or not the lease or agreement has taken effect.

(4) Where a rent for a dwelling-house has been registered under this Part of this Act, no application under this section shall be entertained before the expiry of [2 years] from the relevant date (as defined in section 67(5) of this Act) except on the ground that, since that date, there has been such a change in—

(*a*) the condition of the dwelling-house (including the making of any improvement therein);
(*b*) the terms of the tenancy;
(*c*) the quantity, quality or condition of any furniture provided for use under the tenancy (deterioration by fair wear and tear excluded), or
(*d*) any other circumstances taken into consideration when the rent was registered or confirmed,

as to make the registered rent no longer a fair rent.

(5) For the purposes of section 67(5)(*a*), a case where the rent officer does not register a rent on an application under this section shall not be treated as a confirmation of any rent already registered.

(6) . . .

(7) Regulations shall be made under section 74 of this Act prescribing the procedure on an application under this section, and the regulations shall prescribe the notices to be given to, and the rights to make representations of, the landlord and tenant.

(8) The regulations shall confer on the landlord and the tenant a right to object to the determination of a rent by the rent officer on an application under this section and, on receipt of such an objection in circumstances prescribed by the regulations, shall provide for the reference of the matter to a rent assessment committee.

(9) In this section "local authority" means a local authority to whom section 149 of this Act applies. **[337]**

NOTES
Commencement: 29 August 1977.
This section derived from the Rent Act 1968, s 44A.
Amended by the Housing Act 1980, s 152, Schs 25, 26.

69. Certificates of fair rent

(1) A person intending—

(*a*) to provide a dwelling-house by the erection or conversion of any premises or to make any improvements [or repairs] in a dwelling-house, or

(*b*) to let on a regulated tenancy a dwelling-house which is not for the time being subject to such a tenancy and which satisfies the condition either—

(i) that no rent for it is registered under this Part of this Act, or

(ii) that a rent is so registered but not less than [2 years] have elapsed since the relevant date (as defined in section 67(5) of this Act),

may apply to the rent officer for a certificate *(to be known as a certificate of fair rent)* specifying a rent which, in the opinion of the rent officer, would be a fair rent under a regulated tenancy of the dwelling-house or, as the case may be, of the dwelling-house after the erection or conversion or after the completion of the improvements [or repairs].

[No application shall be made under this subsection if an application could be made under subsection (1A) below.]

[(1A) A public sector body to which this subsection applies may, with a view to the disposal of an interest in a dwelling-house, apply to the rent officer for a certificate specifying a rent which in the opinion of the rent officer would be a fair rent under a regulated tenancy of the dwelling-house—

(*a*) in its present condition, or

(*b*) after the completion of works of improvement, conversion or repair.

(1B) In subsection (1A) "public sector body" means an authority or body within section 80(1) of the Housing Act 1985 (the landlord condition for secure tenancies) other than the Housing Corporation, a housing association or a housing trust which is a charity.

In this subsection "housing association", "housing trust" and "charity" have the same meaning as in Part IV of the Housing Act 1985.

(1C) A certificate under subsection (1) or (1A) shall be known as a certificate of fair rent.]

(2) The regulated tenancy to which the application for the certificate of fair rent relates shall be assumed to be a tenancy on such terms as may be specified in the application and, except in so far as other terms are so specified, on the terms that the tenant would be liable for internal decorative repairs, but no others, and that no services or furniture would be provided for him.

(3) Schedule 12 to this Act [as modified by the Regulated Tenancies (Procedure) Regulations 1980] shall have effect with respect to applications for certificates of fair rent.

(4) . . . where a certificate of fair rent has been issued in respect of a dwelling-house, an application for the registration of a rent for the dwelling-house in accordance with the certificate may be made within [2 years] of the date of the certificate either—

(*a*) by the landlord under such a regulated tenancy of the dwelling-house as is specified in the certificate; or

(*b*) . . .

and in lieu of the provisions of Part I of Schedule 11 to this Act, the provisions of Part II of that Schedule shall have effect with respect to an application so made.

(5) In this section "improvement", in addition to having the meaning given by section 75 of this Act, shall be construed in accordance with paragraph 2(2) of Schedule 20 to this Act. **[338]**

NOTES

Commencement: 29 August 1977 (sub-ss (1), (2)-(5)); to be appointed (remainder).

Sub-ss (1)-(4) derived from the Rent Act 1968, s 45; sub-s (5) derived from the Fire Precautions Act 1971, Schedule, para 2.

Sub-s (1): words "2 years" substituted by the Housing Act 1980, s 152, Sch 25; other words in square brackets prospectively added by the Housing and Planning Act 1986, s 7, as from a day to be appointed; words in italics prospectively repealed by the Housing and Planning Act 1986, s 24(3), Sch 12, Part I, as from a day to be appointed.

Sub-ss (1A)-(1C): prospectively added by the Housing and Planning Act 1986, s 7, as from a day to be appointed.

Sub-s (3): amended by SI 1980 No 1696, reg 3; further amended by SI 1981 No 1783, reg 2 by the insertion of the words "and by the Rent Assessment Committees (England and Wales) (Amendment) Regulations 1981" after the words "Regulations 1980".

Sub-s (4): amended by the Housing Act 1986, s 152, Schs 25, 26.

70. Determination of fair rent

(1) In determining, for the purposes of this Part of this Act, what rent is or would be a fair rent under a regulated tenancy of a dwelling-house, regard shall be had to all the circumstances (other than personal circumstances) and in particular to—

(*a*) the age, character, locality and state of repair of the dwelling-house, . . .

(*b*) if any furniture is provided for use under the tenancy, the quantity, quality and condition of the furniture [, and

(*c*) any premium, or sum in the nature of a premium, which has been or may be lawfully required or received on the grant, renewal, continuance or assignment of the tenancy.]

(2) For the purposes of the determination it shall be assumed that the number of persons seeking to become tenants of similar dwelling-houses in the locality on the terms (other than those relating to rent) of the regulated tenancy is not substantially greater than the number of such dwelling-houses in the locality which are available for letting on such terms.

(3) There shall be disregarded—

(*a*) any disrepair or other defect attributable to a failure by the tenant under the regulated tenancy or any predecessor in title of his to comply with any terms thereof;

(*b*) any improvement carried out, otherwise than in pursuance of the terms of the tenancy, by the tenant under the regulated tenancy or any predecessor in title of his;

(*c*), (*d*) . . .

(*e*) if any furniture is provided for use under the regulated tenancy, any improvement to the furniture by the tenant under the regulated tenancy or any predecessor in title of his or, as the case may be, any deterioration in the condition of the furniture due to any ill-treatment by the tenant, any person residing or lodging with him, or any sub-tenant of his.

(4) In this section "improvement" includes the replacement of any fixture or fitting.

[(4A) In this section "premium" has the same meaning as in Part IX of this Act, and "sum in the nature of a premium" means—

(*a*) any such loan as is mentioned in section 119 or 120 of this Act,
(*b*) any such excess over the reasonable price of furniture as is mentioned in section 123 of this Act, and
(*c*) any such advance payment of rent as is mentioned in section 126 of this Act.]

(5) . . . **[339]**

NOTES
Commencement: 7 January 1987 (sub-s (4A)); 29 August 1977 (remainder).
This section derived from the Rent Act 1968, s 46.
Sub-s (1): word omitted repealed and para (*c*) added by the Housing and Planning Act 1986, ss 17(2), 24(3), Sch 12, Part I: see further s 17(4).
Sub-s (3): paras (*c*), (*d*) repealed by the Housing and Planning Act 1980, s 152, Sch 25.
Sub-s (4A): added by the Housing and Planning Act 1986, s 17(3): see further s 17(4).
Sub-s (5): repealed by the Housing Act 1980, s 152, Sch 26.

71. Amount to be registered as rent

(1) The amount to be registered as the rent of any dwelling-house shall include any sums payable by the tenant to the landlord for the use of furniture or for services, whether or not those sums are separate from the sums payable for the occupation of the dwelling-house or are payable under separate agreements.

(2) Where any rates in respect of a dwelling-house are borne by the landlord or a superior landlord, the amount to be registered under this Part of this Act as the rent of the dwelling-house shall be the same as if the rates were not so borne; but the fact that they are so borne shall be noted on the register.

(3) Where subsection (2) above applies, the amount of the rates for any rental period, ascertained in accordance with Schedule 5 to this Act—

(*a*) shall, . . . be added to the limit imposed by section 44(1) of this Act . . . ; and
(*b*) if the rental period is a statutory period, as defined in section 61 of this Act, shall be recoverable, without service of any notice of increase, in addition to the sums recoverable from the tenant apart from this subsection.

(4) Where, under a regulated tenancy, the sums payable by the tenant to the landlord include any sums varying according to the cost from time to time of—

(*a*) any services provided by the landlord or a superior landlord, or
(*b*) any works of maintenance or repair carried out by the landlord or a superior landlord,

the amount to be registered under this Part of this Act as rent may, if the rent officer is satisfied or, as the case may be, the rent assessment committee are satisfied, that the terms as to the variation are reasonable, be entered as an amount variable in accordance with those terms. **[340]**

NOTES
Commencement: 29 August 1977.
This section derived from the Rent Act 1968, s 47.
Sub-s (3): First words omitted repealed by the Housing Act 1980, s 152, Sch 26; second words omitted repealed by SI 1987 No 264, art 2(3), Sch 1.

72. Effect of registration of rent

[(1) The registration of a rent for a dwelling-house takes effect—

(*a*) if the rent is determined by the rent officer, from the date when it is registered, and

(*b*) if the rent is determined by a rent assessment committee, from the date when the committee make their decision.

(2) If the rent for the time being registered is confirmed, the confirmation takes effect—

(*a*) if it is made by the rent officer, from the date when it is noted in the register, and

(*b*) if it is made by a rent assessment committee, from the date when the committee make their decision.

(3) If (by virtue of section 67(4) of this Act) an application for registration of a rent is made before the expiry of the period mentioned in section 67(3) and the resulting registration of a rent for the dwelling-house, or confirmation of the rent for the time being registered, would, but for this subsection, take effect before the expiry of that period it shall take effect on the expiry of that period.

(4) The date from which the registration or confirmation of a rent takes effect shall be entered in the register.

(5) As from the date on which the registration of a rent takes effect any previous registration of a rent for the dwelling-house ceases to have effect.

(6) Where a valid notice of increase under any provision of Part III of this Act has been served on a tenant and, in consequence of the registration of a rent, part but not the whole of the increase specified in the notice becomes irrecoverable from the tenant, the registration shall not invalidate the notice, but the notice shall, as from the date from which the registration takes effect, have effect as if it specified such part only of the increase as has not become irrecoverable.] **[341]**

NOTES
Commencement: 28 November 1980.
Commencement order: SI 1980 No 1706.
Substituted by the Housing Act 1980, s 61(1).

73. Cancellation of registration of rent

(1) An application may be made in accordance with this section for the cancellation of the registration of a rent for a dwelling-house where—

(*a*) a rent agreement as respects the dwelling-house takes effect, or is to take effect, after the expiration of a period of [2 years] beginning with the relevant date (as defined in section 67(5) of this Act), and

(*b*) the period for which the tenancy has effect cannot end, or be brought to an end by the landlord (except for non-payment of rent or a breach of the terms of the tenancy), earlier than 12 months after the date of the application, and (*c*) the application is made jointly by the landlord and the tenant under the agreement.

[(1A) Such an application may also be made where—

(*a*) not less than two years have elapsed since the relevant date (as defined in section 67(5) of this Act); and

(*b*) the dwelling-house is not for the time being subject to a regulated tenancy; and

(*c*) the application is made by the person who would be the landlord if the dwelling-house were let on such a tenancy.]

(2) The rent agreement may be one providing that the agreement does not take effect unless the application for cancellation of registration is granted.

[(3) An application under this section must—

(*a*) be in the form prescribed for the application concerned and contain the prescribed particulars; and

(*b*) be accompanied, in the case of an application under subsection (1) above, by a copy of the rent agreement.]

(4) If [the application is made under subsection (1) above and] the rent officer is satisfied that the rent, or the highest rent, payable under the rent agreement does not exceed a fair rent for the dwelling-house, he shall cancel the registration [and he shall also cancel the registration if the application is made under subsection (1A) above].

(5) Where [the application is made under subsection (1) above and] under the terms of the rent agreement the sums payable by the tenant to the landlord include any sums varying according to the cost from time to time of any services provided by the landlord or a superior landlord, or of any works of maintenance or repair carried out by the landlord or a superior landlord, the rent officer shall not cancel the registration unless he is satisfied that those terms are reasonable.

(6) [A cancellation made in pursuance of an application under subsection (1) above] shall not take effect until the date when the agreement takes effect; and if the cancellation is registered before that date, the date on which it is to take effect shall be noted on the register.

(7) The cancellation of the registration shall be without prejudice to a further registration of a rent at any time after cancellation.

(8) The rent officer shall notify the applicants of his decision to grant, or to refuse, any application under this section.

(9) In this section "rent agreement" means—

(*a*) an agreement increasing the rent payable under a protected tenancy which is a regulated tenancy, or

(*b*) where a regulated tenancy is terminated, and a new regulated tenancy is granted at a rent exceeding the rent under the previous tenancy, the grant of the new tenancy. **[342]**

NOTES

Commencement: 28 November 1980 (sub-ss (1A), (3)); 29 August 1977 (remainder).
Commencement order: SI 1980 No 1706.
This section derived from the Rent Act 1968, s 48A(1)-(3), (5)-(10).
Amended by the Housing Act 1980, ss 62, 152, Sch 25.

74. Regulations

(1) The Secretary of State may make regulations—

(*a*) prescribing the form of any notice, application, register or other document to be given, made or used in pursuance of this Part of this Act;

(*b*) regulating the procedure to be followed by rent officers and rent assessment committees; and

(*c*) prescribing anything required or authorised to be prescribed by this Part of this Act.

(2) Regulations under subsection (1)(*b*) above may contain provisions modifying the following provisions of this Act:—

(*a*) Section 67, 69 or 72;

(*b*) Part I or II of Schedule 11;

(*c*) Schedule 12;

but no regulations containing such provisions shall have effect unless approved by a resolution of each House of Parliament.

(3) Regulations made under this section shall be made by statutory instrument which, except in a case falling within subsection (2) above, shall be subject to annulment in pursuance of a resolution of either House of Parliament. **[343]**

NOTES

Commencement: 29 August 1977.

This section derived from the Rent Act 1968, s 50.

75. Interpretation of Part IV

(1) In this Part of this Act, except where the context otherwise requires—

"improvement" includes structural alteration, extension or addition and the provision of additional fixtures or fittings, but does not include anything done by way of decoration or repair;

"prescribed" means prescribed by regulations under section 74 of this Act, and references to a prescribed form include references to a form substantially to the same effect as the prescribed form.

(2) References in this Part of this Act to rates, in respect of a dwelling-house, include references to such proportion of any rates in respect of a hereditament of which the dwelling-house forms part as may be agreed in writing between the landlord and the tenant or determined by the county court. **[344]**

NOTES

Commencement: 29 August 1977.

This section derived from the Rent Act 1968, s 51.

PART V

RENTS UNDER RESTRICTED CONTRACTS

Control of rents

77. Reference of contracts to rent tribunals and obtaining by them of information

(1) Either the lessor or the lessee under a restricted contract or the local authority may refer the contract to the rent tribunal . . .

(2) Where a restricted contract is referred to a rent tribunal under subsection (1) above they may, by notice in writing served on the lessor, require him to give to them, within such period (not less than 7 days from the date of the service of the notice) as may be specified in the notice, such information as they may reasonably require regarding such of the prescribed particulars relating to the contract as are specified in the notice.

(3) If, within the period specified in a notice under subsection (2) above, the lessor fails without reasonable cause to comply with the provisions of the notice he shall be liable [to a fine not exceeding level 3 on the standard scale].

(4) Proceedings for an offence under this section shall not be instituted otherwise than by the local authority. **[345]**

NOTES

Commencement: 29 August 1977.

This section derived from the Rent Act 1968, s 72.

Sub-s (1): words omitted repealed by the Housing Act 1980, s 152, Sch 26.

Sub-s (3): enhanced penalty on a subsequent conviction now abolished, maximum fine on any conviction increased and converted to level 3 on the standard scale by the Criminal Justice Act 1982, ss 35, 37, 38, 46.

78. Powers of rent tribunals on reference of contracts

(1) Where a restricted contract is referred to a rent tribunal and the reference is not, before the tribunal have entered upon consideration of it, withdrawn by the party or authority who made it, the tribunal shall consider it.

(2) After making such inquiry as they think fit and giving to—

(*a*) each party to the contract, and
(*b*) if the general management of the dwelling is vested in and exercisable by a housing authority, that authority,

an opportunity of being heard or, at his or their option, of submitting representations in writing, the tribunal, subject to subsections (3) and (4) below,—

(i) shall approve the rent payable under the contract, or
(ii) shall reduce or increase the rent to such sum as they may, in all the circumstances, think reasonable, or
(iii) may, if they think fit in all the circumstances, dismiss the reference, and shall notify the parties . . . of their decision.

(3) On the reference of a restricted contract relating to a dwelling for which a rent is registered under Part IV of this Act, the rent tribunal may not reduce the rent payable under the contract below the amount which would be recoverable from the tenant under a regulated tenancy of the dwelling.

(4) An approval, reduction or increase under this section may be limited to rent payable in respect of a particular period.

(5) In [subsection (2)] above, "housing authority" [means a local housing authority within the meaning of the Housing Act 1985]. **[346]**

NOTES

Commencement: 29 August 1977.

This section derived from the Rent Act 1968, s 73.

Words omitted and first amendment in square brackets made by the Housing Act 1980, s 152, Schs 25, 26; amendment final in square brackets made by the Housing (Consequential Provisions) Act 1985, s 4, Sch 2, para 35.

79. Register of rents under restricted contracts

(1) The [president of every rent assessment panel] shall prepare and keep up to date a register for the purposes of this Part of this Act and shall make the register available for inspection in such place or places and in such manner as the Secretary of State may direct.

(2) The register shall be so prepared and kept up to date as to contain, with regard to any contract relating to a dwelling situated in the area of the [rent assessment panel] and under which a rent is payable which has been approved, reduced or increased under section 78 of this Act, entries of—

(*a*) the prescribed particulars with regard to the contract;
(*b*) a specification of the dwelling to which the contract relates; and
(*c*) the rent as approved, reduced or increased by the rent tribunal, and in a case in which the approval, reduction or increase is limited to rent payable in respect of a particular period, a specification of that period.

(3) Where any rates in respect of a dwelling are borne by the lessor or any person having any title superior to that of the lessor, the amount to be entered in the register under this section as the rent payable for the dwelling shall be the same as if the rates were not so borne; but the fact that they are so borne shall be noted in the register.

(4) . . .

(5) A copy of an entry in the register certified under the hand of an officer duly authorised in that behalf by the [president of the rent assessment panel concerned] shall be receivable in evidence in any court and in any proceedings.

(6) A person requiring such a certified copy shall be entitled to obtain it on payment of the prescribed fee.

[(6A) Every local authority shall, before the expiry of the period of three months beginning with the commencement of paragraph 44 of Schedule 25 to the Housing Act 1980, send to the president of the appropriate rent assessment panel the register previously kept by the authority under this section.] **[347]**

NOTES
Commencement: 28 November 1980 (sub-s (6A)); 29 August 1977 (remainder).
Commencement order: SI 1980 No 1706.
This section derived from the Rent Act 1968, s 74.
Amended by the Housing Act 1980, s 152, Schs 25, 26.

80. Reconsideration of rent after registration

(1) Where the rent payable for any dwelling has been entered in the register under section 79 of this Act the lessor or the lessee or the local authority may refer the case to the rent tribunal for reconsideration of the rent so entered.

(2) Where the rent under a restricted contract has been registered under section 79 of this Act, a rent tribunal shall not be required to entertain a reference, made otherwise than by the lessor and the lessee jointly, for the registration of a different rent for the dwelling concerned before the expiry of the period of [2 years] beginning on the date on which the rent was last considered by the tribunal, except on the ground that, since that date, there has been such a change in—

(*a*) the condition of the dwelling,
(*b*) the furniture or services provided,

(*c*) the terms of the contract, or

(*d*) any other circumstances taken into consideration when the rent was last considered,

as to make the registered rent no longer a reasonable rent. **[348]**

NOTES

Commencement: 29 August 1977.

This section derived from the Rent Act 1968, ss 73 (5), 75(1).

Amended by the Housing Act 1980, s 70.

81. Effect of registration of rent

(1) Where the rent payable for any dwelling is entered in the register under section 79 of this Act, it shall not be lawful to require or receive on account of rent for that dwelling under a restricted contract payment of any amount in excess of the rent so registered—

(*a*) in respect of any period subsequent to the date of the entry, or

(*b*) where a particular period is specified in the register, in respect of that period.

(2) Where subsection (3) of section 79 applies, the amount entered in the register under that section shall be treated for the purposes of this section as increased for any rental period by the amount of the rates for that period, ascertained in accordance with Schedule 5 to this Act.

(3) Where any payment has been made or received in contravention of this section, the amount of the excess shall be recoverable by the person by whom it was paid.

(4) Any person who requires or receives any payment in contravention of this section shall be liable to a fine not exceeding [level 3 on the standard scale] or to imprisonment for a term not exceeding 6 months or both, and, without prejudice to any other method of recovery, the court by which a person is found guilty of an offence under this subsection may order the amount paid in excess to be repaid to the person by whom the payment was made.

(5) Proceedings for an offence under this section shall not be instituted otherwise than by the local authority. **[349]**

NOTES

Commencement: 29 August 1977.

This section derived from the Rent Act 1968, s 76.

Sub-s (4): maximum fine increased and converted to a level on the standard scale by the Criminal Justice Act 1982, ss 37, 38, 46.

[81A. Cancellation of registration of rent

(1) Where the rent payable for any dwelling is entered in the register under section 79 of this Act, the rent tribunal shall cancel the entry, on an application made under this section, if—

(*a*) not less than two years have elapsed since the date of entry;

(*b*) the dwelling is not for the time being subject to a restricted contract; and

(*c*) the application is made by the person who would be the lessor if the dwelling were subject to a restricted contract.

(2) An application under this section must be in the prescribed form, and contain the prescribed particulars.

(3) Cancellation of the registration shall be without prejudice to a further registration of a rent at any time after the cancellation.

(4) The rent tribunal shall notify the applicant of their decision to grant, or to refuse, any application under this section.] **[350]**

NOTES
Commencement: 28 November 1980.
Commencement order: SI 1980 No 1706.
Added by the Housing Act 1980, s 71.

Miscellaneous and General

82. Jurisdiction of rent tribunals

Where a restricted contract is referred to a rent tribunal under this Part, or Part VII, of this Act and—

(*a*) the contract relates to a dwelling consisting of or comprising part only of a hereditament, and
(*b*) no apportionment of the rateable value of the hereditament has been made under section 25 of this Act,

then, unless the lessor in the course of the proceedings requires that such an apportionment shall be made and, within 2 weeks of making the requirement, brings proceedings in the county court for the making of the apportionment, the rent tribunal shall have jurisdiction to deal with the reference if it appears to them that, had the apportionment been made, they would have had jurisdiction. **[351]**

NOTES
Commencement: 29 August 1977.
This section derived from the Rent Act 1968, s 81.

83. Local authorities for Part V

(1) For the purposes of this Part of this Act, the local authority shall be—

(*a*) in a district or London borough, the council of the district or borough in question, and
(*b*) in the City of London, the Common Council.

(2) The local authority shall have power to publish information regarding the provisions of this Part, and sections 103 to 106, of this Act. **[352]**

NOTES
Commencement: 29 August 1977.
This section derived from the Rent Act 1968, s 82.

84. Regulations

The Secretary of State may by statutory instrument make regulations—

(*a*), (*b*) . . .
(*c*) for prescribing anything which is required by this Part of this Act to be prescribed; and
(*d*) generally for carrying into effect the provisions of this Part, and sections 103 to 106, of this Act. **[353]**

NOTES
Commencement: 29 August 1977.
This section derived from the Rent Act 1968, s 83.

Words omitted repealed by the Housing Act 1980, s 152, Sch 26.

85. Interpretation of Part V

(1) In this Part of this Act, except where the context otherwise requires,—

"dwelling" means a house or part of a house;

"lessee" means the person to whom is granted, under a restricted contract, the right to occupy the dwelling in question as a residence and any person directly or indirectly deriving title from the grantee;

"lessor" means the person who, under a restricted contract, grants to another the right to occupy the dwelling in question as a residence and any person directly or indirectly deriving title from the grantor;

"register" means the register kept by the [president of the rent assessment panel concerned] in pursuance of section 79 of this Act;

"rent tribunal" [shall be construed in accordance with section 72 of the Housing Act 1980];

"services" includes attendance, the provision of heating or lighting, the supply of hot water and any other privilege or facility connected with the occupancy of a dwelling, other than a privilege or facility requisite for the purposes of access, cold water supply or sanitary accommodation.

(2) References in this Part of this Act to a party to a contract include references to any person directly or indirectly deriving title from such a party.

(3) Where separate sums are payable by the lessee of any dwelling to the lessor for any two or more of the following:—

(*a*) occupation of the dwelling,
(*b*) use of furniture, and
(*c*) services,

any reference in this Part of this Act to "rent" in relation to that dwelling is a reference to the aggregate of those sums and, where those sums are payable under separate contracts, those contracts shall be deemed to be one contract.

(4) The references in sections 79(3) and 81(2) of this Act to rates, in respect of a dwelling, include references to such proportion of any rates in respect of a hereditament of which the dwelling forms part as may be agreed in writing between the lessor and the lessee or determined by the county court. **[354]**

NOTES
Commencement: 29 August 1977.
Sub-ss (1)-(3) derived from the Rent Act 1968, s 84.
Sub-s (1): amended by the Housing Act 1980, s 152, Sch 25.

PART VI

RENT LIMIT FOR DWELLINGS LET BY HOUSING ASSOCIATIONS, HOUSING TRUSTS AND THE HOUSING CORPORATION

Registration of rents

86. Tenancies to which Part VI applies

(1) In this Part of this Act "housing association tenancy" means a tenancy to which this Part of this Act applies.

(2) This Part of this Act applies to a tenancy [(other than a co-ownership tenancy)] where—

(*a*) the interest of the landlord under that tenancy belongs to a housing association or housing trust, or to the Housing Corporation, and
(*b*) the tenancy would be a protected tenancy but for section 15 or 16 of this Act, and is not a tenancy to which Part II of the Landlord and Tenant Act 1954 applies.

(3) In this Part of this Act "housing association" [has the same meaning as in the Housing Associations Act 1985].

[(3A) For the purposes of this section a tenancy is a 'co-ownership tenancy' if—

(*a*) it was granted by a housing association which [is a co-operative housing association within the meaning of the Housing Associations Act 1985]; and
(*b*) the tenant (or his personal representatives) will, under the terms of the tenancy agreement or of the agreement under which he became a member of the association, be entitled, on his ceasing to be a member and subject to any conditions stated in either agreement, to a sum calculated by reference directly or indirectly to the value of the dwelling-house.]

[(4) In this Part of this Act "housing trust" has the same meaning as in section 15 of this Act.]

(5) . . . **[355]**

NOTES
Commencement: 29 August 1977 (sub-ss (1)-(3)); 28 November 1980 (sub-ss (3A), (4)).
Commencement order: SI 1980 No 1706.
Sub-ss (1)-(3) derived from the Housing Finance Act 1972, ss 81(1), 104(1); sub-s (4) derived from the Rent Act 1968, s 5(3), (4).
Second and fourth amendments in square brackets made by the Housing (Consequential Provisions) Act 1985, s 4, Sch 2, para 35; other amendments made by the Housing Act 1980, ss 77, 152, Schs 10, 26.

87. Rents to be registrable

(1) There shall be a part of the register under Part IV of this Act in which rents may be registered for dwelling-houses which are let, or are, or are to be, available for letting under a housing association tenancy

(2) In relation to that part of the register the following (and no other) provisions of this Act:—

(*a*) sections 67, 69 [, 70 and 72],
(*b*) section 71, except subsection (3), and
(*c*) Schedules 11 and 12,

shall apply in relation to housing association tenancies, and in their application to such tenancies shall have effect as if for any reference in those provisions to a regulated tenancy there were substituted a reference to a housing association tenancy,

(3)-(5) . . .

(6) A rent registered in any part of the register for a dwelling-house which becomes, or ceases to be, one subject to a housing association tenancy, shall be as effective as if it were registered in any other part of the register. **[356]**

NOTES
Commencement: 29 August 1977.
Sub-ss (1), (2), (6) derived from the Housing Finance Act 1972, s 82.
Amended by the Housing Act 1980, ss 61(3), 152, Sch 26.

Rent limit

88. Rent limit

(1) Where the rent payable under a tenancy would exceed the rent limit determined in accordance with this Part of this Act, the amount of the excess shall be irrecoverable from the tenant.

(2) Where a rent for the dwelling-house is registered, then, subject to [section 89] of this Act, the rent limit is the rent so registered.

(3) Where any rates in respect of the dwelling-house are borne by the landlord, or a superior landlord, the amount of those rates for any rental period, ascertained in accordance with Schedule 5 to this Act, shall be added to the limit imposed by subsection (2) above, and in this Part of this Act references to the amount of the registered rent include any amount to be added under this subsection.

(4) Where no rent for the dwelling-house is registered, then, subject to subsection (5) below, the rent limit shall be determined as follows:—

(*a*) if the lease or agreement creating the tenancy was made before 1st January 1973, the rent limit is the rent recoverable under the tenancy, as varied by any agreement made before that date (but not as varied by any later agreement);

(*b*) if paragraph (*a*) above does not apply, and, not more than [2 years] before the tenancy began, the dwelling-house was subject to another tenancy (whether before 1973 or later) the rent limit is the rent recoverable under that other tenancy (or if there was more than one, the last of them) for the last rental period thereof;

(*c*) if paragraphs (*a*) and (*b*) above do not apply, the rent limit is the rent payable under the terms of the lease or agreement creating the tenancy (and not the rent so payable under those terms as varied by any subsequent agreement).

(5) The reference in subsection (4)(*b*) above to another tenancy includes, in addition to a housing association tenancy, a regulated tenancy—

(*a*) which subsisted at any time after 1st April 1975; and

(*b*) under which, immediately before it came to an end, the interest of the landlord belonged to a housing association.

(6) Where for any period there is a difference between the amount (if any) of the rates borne by the landlord or a superior landlord in respect of the dwelling-house and the amount (if any) so borne in the rental period on which the rent limit is based, the rent limit under this Part of this Act shall be increased or decreased by the amount of the difference.

(7) A tenancy commencing (whether before or after the coming into force of this Act) while there is in operation a condition imposed under any of the following enactments:—

(*a*) section 2 of the Housing (Financial Provisions) Act 1924;

[(*b*) paragraph 2 of Part II of Schedule 16 to the Housing Act 1985, or any corresponding earlier enactment] (*c*) section 23 of the Housing Act 1949; and

[(*d*) section 33 of the Housing Act 1985, or any corresponding earlier enactment;]

[which impose a rent limit in respect of the dwelling-house] shall be disregarded for the purposes of subsection (4)(*b*) above in determining the rent limit under any subsequent tenancy of the dwelling-house. **[357]**

NOTES

Commencement: 29 August 1977.
This section derived from the Housing Finance Act 1972, s 83.
Sub-ss (2), (4): amended by the Housing Act 1980, s 152, Sch 25.
Sub-s (7): amended by the Housing (Consequential Provisions) Act 1985, s 4, Sch 2, para 35.

89. Phasing of progression to registered rent

[(1) This section applies where a rent is registered for a dwelling-house (whether it is the first or any subsequent registration) unless at the date of registration there is no tenant and no person to whom a tenancy has been granted.

(2) The rent for any rental period, or part of a rental period, falling within the period of delay imposed by Schedule 8 to this Act may be increased in accordance with that Schedule.

(3) A notice of increase which purports to increase the rent further than permitted by Schedule 8 shall have effect to increase it to the extent permitted, but no further.

(4) Nothing in this section or in Schedule 8 prevents or limits any increase in rent by virtue of section 71(4) of this Act as applied by section 87(2) of this Act.] **[358]**

NOTES

Commencement: 28 November 1980.
Commencement order: SI 1980 No 1706.
This section derived from the Housing Finance Act 1972, s 84.
Substituted by the Housing Act 1980, s 77, Sch 10.

Conversion to regulated tenancies

92. Conversion of housing association tenancies into regulated tenancies

(1) If at any time, by virtue of subsections (1) and (3) of section 15 of this Act, a tenancy ceases to be one to which this Part of this Act applies and becomes a protected tenancy, that tenancy shall be a regulated tenancy and the housing association which is the landlord under that tenancy shall give notice in writing to the tenant, . . . , informing him that his tenancy is no longer excluded from protection under this Act.

(2) If, without reasonable excuse, a housing association fails to give notice to a tenant under subsection (1) above within the period of 21 days beginning on the day on which his tenancy becomes a protected tenancy, the association shall be liable to a fine not exceeding [level 3 on the standard scale].

(3) Where an offence under subsection (2) above committed by a body corporate is proved to have been committed with the consent or connivance of, or to be attributable to any neglect on the part of, any director, manager or secretary or other similar officer of the body corporate or any person who was purporting to act in any such capacity, he as well as the body corporate shall be

guilty of that offence and shall be liable to be proceeded against and punished accordingly.

(4) Schedule 14 to this Act shall have effect for supplementing this section.

(5) In this section—

"housing association" has the same meaning as in [the Housing Associations Act 1985]; . . .

(6), (7) . . . **[359]**

NOTES

Commencement: 29 August 1977.

This section derived from the Housing Act 1974, ss 18, 128, 129.

Sub-ss (1), (5) - (7): words omitted repealed by the Housing Act 1980, ss 77, 152, Schs 10, 26.

Sub-s (2): maximum fine increased and converted to a level on the standard scale by the Criminal Justice Act 1982, ss 37, 38, 46.

Sub-s (5): amended by the Housing (Consequential Provisions) Act 1985, s 4, Sch 2, para 35.

Miscellaneous

93. Increase of rent without notice to quit

(1) Subject to subsections (2) and (3) below, where a housing association tenancy is a weekly or other periodical tenancy, the rent payable to the housing association or, as the case may be, the housing trust or the Housing Corporation (in this section called "the landlord") may, without the tenancy being terminated, be increased with effect from the beginning of any rental period by a written notice of increase [specifying the date on which the increase is to take effect and given by the landlord to the tenant not later than four weeks before that date.]

[(2) Where a notice of increase is given under subsection (1) above and the tenant, before the date specified in the notice of increase, gives a valid notice to quit, the notice of increase does not take effect unless the tenant, with the written agreement of the landlord, withdraws his notice to quit before that date.]

(3) . . .

(4) This section shall apply to a tenancy notwithstanding that the letting took place before the coming into force of this Act.

(5) Nothing in this section shall authorise any rent to be increased above the rent limit, and any reference in section 88 of this Act to the variation by agreement of the rent recoverable under a tenancy shall include a reference to variation under this section. **[360]**

NOTES

Commencement: 29 August 1977 (sub-ss (1), (4), (5)); 28 November 1980 (sub-s (2)).

Commencement order: SI 1980 No 1706.

This section derived from the Housing Finance Act 1972, s 87.

Amended by the Housing Act 1980, ss 77, 152, Schs 10, 26.

94. Recovery from landlord of sums paid in excess of recoverable rent, etc

(1) Where a tenant has paid on account of rent any amount which, by virtue of this Part of this Act, is irrecoverable by the landlord, the tenant who paid it shall be entitled to recover that amount from the landlord who received it or his personal representatives.

(2) Any amount which a tenant is entitled to recover under subsection (1)

above may, without prejudice to any other method of recovery, be deducted by the tenant from any rent payable by him to the landlord.

(3) No amount which a tenant is entitled to recover under subsection (1) above shall be recoverable at any time after the expiry of 2 years from the date of payment.

(4) Any person who, in any rent book or similar document, makes an entry showing or purporting to show any tenant as being in arrears in respect of any sum on account of rent which is irrecoverable by virtue of this Part of this Act shall be liable to a fine not exceeding [level 3 on the standard scale], unless he proves that, at the time of the making of the entry, the landlord had a bona fide claim that the sum was recoverable.

(5) If, where any such entry has been made by or on behalf of any landlord, the landlord on being requested by or on behalf of the tenant to do so, refuses or neglects to cause the entry to be deleted within 7 days, the landlord shall be liable to a fine not exceeding [level 3 on the standard scale], unless he proves that, at the time of the neglect or refusal to cause the entry to be deleted, he had a bona fide claim that the sum was recoverable. **[361]**

NOTES

Commencement: 29 August 1977.

This section derived from the Rent Act 1968, s 33.

Sub-ss (4), (5): maximum fines increased and converted to levels on the standard scale by the Criminal Justice Act 1982, ss 37, 38, 46.

95. Duty of landlord to supply statement of rent under previous tenancy

(1) Where the rent payable under a tenancy is subject to the rent limit specified in section 88(4)(*b*) of this Act, the landlord shall, on being so requested in writing by the tenant, supply him with a statement in writing of the rent which was payable for the last rental period of the other tenancy referred to in that subsection.

(2) If, without reasonable excuse, a landlord who has received such a request—

(*a*) fails to supply the statement referred to in subsection (1) above within 21 days of receiving the request, or

(*b*) supplies a statement which is false in any material particular,

he shall be liable [to a fine not exceeding level 3 on the standard scale].

(3) Where an offence under this section committed by a body corporate is proved to have been committed with the consent or connivance of, or to be attributable to any neglect on the part of, any director, manager or secretary or other similar officer of the body corporate or any person who was purporting to act in any such capacity, he as well as the body corporate shall be guilty of that offence and shall be liable to be proceeded against and punished accordingly. **[362]**

NOTES

Commencement: 29 August 1977.

This section derived from the Rent Act 1968, s 35.

Sub-s (2): enhanced penalty on a subsequent conviction now abolished, maximum fine on any conviction increased and converted to level 3 on the standard scale by the Criminal Justice Act 1982, ss 35, 37, 38, 46.

96. Supplemental

(1), (2) . . .

(3) A county court shall have jurisdiction, either in the course of any proceedings relating to a dwelling-house or on an application made for the purpose by the landlord or the tenant, to determine any question as to the rent limit under this Part of this Act, or as to any matter which is or may become material for determining any such question.

(4) In ascertaining for the purposes of this Part of this Act whether there is any difference with respect to rents or rates between one rental period and another (whether of the same tenancy or not) or the amount of any such difference, any necessary adjustments shall be made to take account of periods of different lengths.

(5) For the purposes of such an adjustment a period of one month shall be treated as equivalent to one-twelfth of a year and a period of a week as equivalent to one-fifty-second of a year. **[363]**

NOTES

Commencement: 29 August 1977.

Sub-s (3) derived from the Housing Finance Act 1972, s 88; sub-ss (4), (5) derived from the Rent Act 1968, s 36.

Words omitted repealed by the Housing Act 1980, ss 61(3), 152, Sch 26.

97. Interpretation of Part VI

(1) In this Part of this Act, except where the context otherwise requires—

"housing association", "housing association tenancy" and "housing trust" have the meanings assigned to them by section 86 of this Act; and
"tenancy" means a housing association tenancy.

(2) In this Part of this Act references to registration are, subject to section 87(5) of this Act and unless the context otherwise requires, references to registration pursuant to section 87.

(3) It is hereby declared that any power of giving directions conferred on the Secretary of State by this Part of this Act includes power to vary or revoke directions so given. **[364]**

NOTES

Commencement: 29 August 1977.

This section derived from the Housing Finance Act 1972, ss 81(1), 82(6), 104(4).

PART VII

SECURITY OF TENURE

Limitations on recovery of possession of dwelling-houses let on protected tenancies or subject to statutory tenancies

98. Grounds for possession of certain dwelling-houses

(1) Subject to this Part of this Act, a court shall not make an order for possession of a dwelling-house which is for the time being let on a protected tenancy or subject to a statutory tenancy unless the court considers it reasonable to make such an order and either—

(*a*) the court is satisfied that suitable alternative accommodation is available for the tenant or will be available for him when the order in question takes effect, or
(*b*) the circumstances are as specified in any of the Cases in Part I of Schedule 15 to this Act.

(2) If, apart from subsection (1) above, the landlord would be entitled to recover possession of a dwelling-house which is for the time being let on or subject to a regulated tenancy, the court shall make an order for possession if the circumstances of the case are as specified in any of the Cases in Part II of Schedule 15.

(3) Part III of Schedule 15 shall have effect in relation to Case 9 in that Schedule and for determining the relevant date for the purposes of the Cases in Part II of that Schedule.

(4) Part IV of Schedule 15 shall have effect for determining whether, for the purposes of subsection (1)(*a*) above, suitable alternative accommodation is or will be available for a tenant.

[(5) Part V of Schedule 15 shall have effect for the purpose of setting out conditions which are relevant to Cases 11 and 12 of that Schedule.] **[365]**

NOTES
Commencement: 28 November 1980 (sub-s (5)); 29 August 1977 (remainder).
Commencement order: SI 1980 No 1706.
This section derived from the Rent Act 1968, s 10.
Sub-s (5): added by the Housing Act 1980, s 66(3).

99. Grounds for possession of certain dwelling-houses let to agricultural workers, etc

(1) This section applies to any protected or statutory tenancy which—

(*a*) if it were a tenancy at a low rent, and
(*b*) if (where relevant) any earlier tenancy granted to the tenant, or to a member of his family, had been a tenancy at a low rent,

would be a protected occupancy or statutory tenancy as defined in the Rent (Agriculture) Act 1976.

(2) Notwithstanding anything in section 98 of this Act, the court shall not make an order for possession of a dwelling-house which is for the time being let on or subject to a tenancy to which this section applies unless the court considers it reasonable to make such an order and the circumstances are as specified in any of the Cases (except Case 8) in Part I of Schedule 15 to this Act or in either of the Cases in Schedule 16 to this Act.

(3) If, apart from subsection (2) above, the landlord would be entitled to recover possession of a dwelling-house which is for the time being let on or subject to a tenancy to which this section applies, the court shall make an order for possession if the circumstances are as specified in any of the Cases (except Cases 16 to 18) in Part II of Schedule 15 to this Act. **[366]**

NOTES
Commencement: 29 August 1977.
This section derived from the Rent Act 1968, s 10A.

100. Extended discretion of court in claims for possession of certain dwelling-houses

(1) Subject to subsection (5) below, a court may adjourn, for such period or periods as it thinks fit, proceedings for possession of a dwelling-house which is let on a protected tenancy or subject to a statutory tenancy.

(2) On the making of an order for possession of such a dwelling-house, or at any time before the execution of such an order (whether made before or after the commencement of this Act), the court, subject to subsection (5) below, may—

(*a*) stay or suspend execution of the order, or
(*b*) postpone the date of possession,

for such period or periods as the court thinks fit.

[(3) On any such adjournment as is referred to in subsection (1) above or any such stay, suspension or postponement as is referred to in subsection (2) above, the court shall, unless it considers that to do so would cause exceptional hardship to the tenant or would otherwise be unreasonable, impose conditions with regard to payment by the tenant of arrears of rent (if any) and rent or payments in respect of occupation after termination of the tenancy (mesne profits) and may impose such other conditions as it thinks fit.]

(4) If any such conditions as are referred to in subsection (3) above are complied with, the court may, if it thinks fit, discharge or rescind any such order as is referred to in subsection (2) above.

[(4A) Subsection (4B) below applies in any case where—

(*a*) proceedings are brought for possession of a dwelling-house which is let on a protected tenancy or subject to a statutory tenancy;
(*b*) the tenant's spouse or former spouse, having rights of occupation under the Matrimonial Homes Act 1967, is then in occupation of the dwelling-house; and
(*c*) the tenancy is terminated as a result of those proceedings.

(4B) In any case to which this subsection applies, the spouse or former spouse shall, so long as he or she remains in occupation, have the same rights in relation to, or in connection with, any such adjournment as is referred to in subsection (1) above or any such stay, suspension or postponement as is referred to in subsection (2) above, as he or she would have if those rights of occupation were not affected by the termination of the tenancy.]

(5) This section shall not apply if the circumstances are as specified in any of the Cases in Part II of Schedule 15. **[367]**

NOTES

Commencement: 29 August 1977 (sub-ss (1), (2), (4), (5)); 28 November 1980 (remainder).
Commencement order: SI 1980 No 1706.
This section derived from the Rent Act 1968, s 11.
Amended by the Housing Act 1980, s 75(1)-(3).

[101. Overcrowded dwelling-houses

At any time when a dwelling-house is overcrowded within the meaning of Part X of the Housing Act 1985 in such circumstances as to render the occupier guilty of an offence, nothing in this Part of this Act shall prevent the immediate landlord of the occupier from obtaining possession of the dwelling-house.] **[368]**

NOTES

Commencement: 1 April 1986.

This section derived from the Rent Act 1968, s 17.

Substituted, in respect of a tenant (or statutory tenant) who occupies the dwelling-house under (or by virtue of) a tenancy granted on or after 1 April 1986, by the Housing (Consequential Provisions) Act 1985, ss 4, 5(1), Sch 2, para 35, Sch 3, para 3.

102. Compensation for misrepresentation or concealment in Cases 8 and 9

Where, in such circumstances as are specified in Case 8 or Case 9 in Schedule 15 to this Act, a landlord obtains an order for possession of a dwelling-house let on a protected tenancy or subject to a statutory tenancy and it is subsequently made to appear to the court that the order was obtained by misrepresentation or concealment of material facts, the court may order the landlord to pay to the former tenant such sum as appears sufficient as compensation for damage or loss sustained by that tenant as a result of the order. **[369]**

NOTES

Commencement: 29 August 1977.

This section derived from the Rent Act 1968, s 19.

Restricted contracts

[102A. Restricted application of sections 103 to 106

Sections 103 to 106 of this Act apply only to restricted contracts entered into before the commencement of section 69 of the Housing Act 1980.] **[370]**

NOTES

Commencement: 28 November 1980.

Commencement order: SI 1980 No 1706.

Added by the Housing Act 1980, s 69(3).

103. Notice to quit served after reference of contract to rent tribunal

(1) If, after a restricted contract has been referred to a rent tribunal by the lessee or the local authority under section 77 or 80 of this Act, a notice to quit the dwelling to which the contract relates is served by the lessor on the lessee at any time before the decision of the tribunal is given or within the period of 6 months thereafter, then, subject to sections 105 and 106 of this Act, the notice shall not take effect before the expiry of that period.

(2) In a case falling within subsection (1) above—,

(*a*) the rent tribunal may, if they think fit, direct that a shorter period shall be substituted for the period of 6 months specified in that subsection; and

(*b*) if the reference to the rent tribunal is withdrawn, the period during which the notice to quit is not to take effect shall end on the expiry of 7 days from the withdrawal of the reference. **[371]**

NOTES

Commencement: 29 August 1977.

This section derived from the Rent Act 1968, s 77.

104. Application to tribunal for security of tenure where notice to quit is served

(1) Subject to sections 105 and 106(3) of this Act, where—

(*a*) a notice to quit a dwelling the subject of a restricted contract has been served, and (*b*) the restricted contract has been referred to a rent tribunal under section 77 or 80 of this Act (whether before or after the service of the notice to quit) and the reference has not been withdrawn, and

(*c*) the period at the end of which the notice to quit takes effect (whether by virtue of the contract, of section 103 of this Act or of this section) has not expired,

the lessee may apply to the rent tribunal for the extension of that period.

(2) Where an application is made under this section, the notice to quit to which the application relates shall not have effect before the determination of the application unless the application is withdrawn.

(3) On an application under this section, the rent tribunal, after making such inquiry as they think fit and giving to each party an opportunity of being heard or, at his option, of submitting representations in writing, may direct that the notice to quit shall not have effect until the end of such period, not exceeding 6 months from the date on which the notice to quit would have effect apart from the direction, as may be specified in the direction.

(4) If the rent tribunal refuse to give a direction under this section,—

(*a*) the notice to quit shall not have effect before the expiry of 7 days from the determination of the application; and

(*b*) no subsequent application under this section shall be made in relation to the same notice to quit.

(5) On coming to a determination on an application under this section, the rent tribunal shall notify the parties of their determination. **[372]**

NOTES

Commencement: 29 August 1977.

This section derived from the Rent Act 1968, s 78.

105. Notices to quit served by owner-occupiers

Where a person who has occupied a dwelling as a residence (in this section referred to as "the owner-occupier") has, by virtue of a restricted contract, granted the right to occupy the dwelling to another person and—

(*a*) at or before the time when the right was granted (or, if it was granted before 8th December 1965, not later than 7th June 1966) the owner-occupier has given notice in writing to that other person that he is the owner-occupier within the meaning of this section, and

(*b*) if the dwelling is part of a house, the owner-occupier does not occupy any other part of the house as his residence,

neither section 103 nor 104 of this Act shall apply where a notice to quit the dwelling is served if, at the time the notice is to take effect, the dwelling is required as a residence for the owner-occupier or any member of his family who resided with him when he last occupied the dwelling as a residence. **[373]**

NOTES

Commencement: 29 August 1977.

This section derived from the Rent Act 1968, s 79.

106. Reduction of period of notice on account of lessee's default

(1) Subsections (2) and (3) below apply where a restricted contract has been referred to a rent tribunal and the period at the end of which a notice to quit

will take effect has been determined by virtue of section 103 of this Act or extended under section 104.

(2) If, in a case where this subsection applies, it appears to the rent tribunal, on an application made by the lessor for a direction under this section,—

(*a*) that the lessee has not complied with the terms of the contract, or
(*b*) that the lessee or any person residing or lodging with him has been guilty of conduct which is a nuisance or annoyance to adjoining occupiers or has been convicted of using the dwelling, or allowing the dwelling to be used, for an immoral or illegal purpose, or
(*c*) that the condition of the dwelling has deteriorated owing to any act or neglect of the lessee or any person residing or lodging with him, or
(*d*) that the condition of any furniture provided for the use of the lessee under the contract has deteriorated owing to any ill-treatment by the lessee or any person residing or lodging with him,

the rent tribunal may direct that the period referred to in subsection (1) above shall be reduced so as to end at a date specified in the direction.

(3) No application may be made under section 104 of this Act with respect to a notice to quit if a direction has been given under subsection (2) above reducing the period at the end of which the notice is to take effect.

(4) In any case where—

(*a*) a notice to quit a dwelling which is the subject of a restricted contract has been served, and
(*b*) the period at the end of which the notice to quit takes effect is for the time being extended by virtue of section 103 or 104 of this Act, and
(*c*) at some time during that period the lessor institutes proceedings in the county court for the recovery of possession of the dwelling, and
(*d*) in those proceedings the county court is satisfied that any of paragraphs (*a*) and (*d*) of subsection (2) above applies,

the court may direct that the period referred to in paragraph (*b*) above shall be reduced so as to end at a date specified in the direction. **[374]**

NOTES
Commencement: 29 August 1977.
This section derived from the Rent Act 1968, ss 80, 80A.

[106A. Discretion of court in certain proceedings for possession

(1) This section applies to any dwelling-house which is the subject of a restricted contract entered into after the commencement of section 69 of the Housing Act 1980.

(2) On the making of an order for possession of such a dwelling-house, or at any time before the execution of such an order, the court may—

(*a*) stay or suspend execution of the order, or
(*b*) postpone the date of possession,

for such period or periods as, subject to subsection (3) below, the court thinks fit.

(3) Where a court makes an order for possession of such a dwelling-house, the giving up of possession shall not be postponed (whether by the order or any variation, suspension or stay of execution) to a date later than 3 months after the making of the order.

(4) On any such stay, suspension or postponement as is referred to in subsection (2) above, the court shall, unless it considers that to do so would cause exceptional hardship to the lessee or would otherwise be unreasonable, impose conditions with regard to payment by the lessee of arrears of rent (if any) and rent or payments in respect of occupation after termination of the tenancy (mesne profits) and may impose such other conditions as it thinks fit.

(5) Subsection (6) below applies in any case where—

(*a*) proceedings are brought for possession of such a dwelling-house;

(*b*) the lessee's spouse or former spouse, having rights of occupation under the Matrimonial Homes Act 1967, is then in occupation of the dwelling-house; and

(*c*) the restricted contract is terminated as a result of those proceedings.

(6) In any case to which this subsection applies, the spouse or former spouse shall, so long as he or she remains in occupation, have the same rights in relation to, or in connection with, any such stay, suspension or postponement as is referred to in subsection (2) above, as he or she would have if those rights of occupation were not affected by the termination of the restricted contract.]

[375]

NOTES

Commencement: 28 November 1980.
Commencement order: SI 1980 No 1706.
Added by the Housing Act 1980, s 69(2).

Miscellaneous

107. Interpretation of Part VII

(1) In this Part of this Act, except where the context otherwise requires—

"dwelling" means a house or part of a house;

"lessee" means the person to whom is granted, under a restricted contract, the right to occupy the dwelling in question as a residence and any person directly or indirectly deriving title from the grantee; and

"lessor" means the person who, under a restricted contract, grants to another the right to occupy the dwelling in question as a residence and any person directly or indirectly deriving title from the grantor.

(2) References in this Part of this Act to a party to a contract include references to any person directly or indirectly deriving title from such a party.

[376]

NOTES

Commencement: 29 August 1977.
This section derived from the Rent Act 1968, s 84(1), (2).

PART VIII

CONVERSION OF CONTROLLED TENANCIES INTO REGULATED TENANCIES

Miscellaneous

116. Consent of tenant

[(1) This section applies where a dwelling-house is subject to a statutory tenancy and the landlord wishes to carry out works which cannot be carried out without the consent of the tenant.]

(2) If the tenant is unwilling to give his consent, then, if the condition specified in paragraph (*a*), or the condition specified in paragraph (*b*), of subsection (3) below is satisfied, the county court may, on the application of the landlord, make an order empowering him to enter and carry out the works.

[(3) The condition is—

(*a*) that the works were specified in an application for an *improvement, or intermediate, grant* [improvement grant, intermediate grant or common parts grant] under [Part XV of the Housing Act 1985] and the application has been approved, or

(*b*) that the works are specified in a certificate issued by [the local housing authority within the meaning of that Act] and stating that if an application were to be made by the landlord for such a grant in respect of the works, the application would be likely to be approved.]

(4) An order under subsection (2) above may be made subject to such conditions as to the time at which the works are to be carried out and as to any provision to be made for the accommodation of the tenant and his household while they are carried out as the court may think fit.

(5) Where such an order is made subject to any condition as to time, compliance with that condition shall be deemed to be also compliance with any condition imposed by the [local housing authority under section 512(2) of the Housing Act 1985].

(6) In determining whether to make such an order and, if it is made, what (if any) conditions it should be subject to, the court shall have regard to all the circumstances and in particular to—

(*a*) any disadvantage to the tenant that might be expected to result from the works, and

(*b*) the accommodation that might be available for him whilst the works are carried out, and

(*c*) the age and health of the tenant,

but the court shall not take into account the means or resources of the tenant.

[377]

NOTES

Commencement: 29 August 1977 (sub-ss (2), (4)-(6)); 28 November 1980 (remainder).

Commencement order: SI 1980 No 1706.

This section derived from the Housing Finance Act 1972, s 33.

Sub-s (1): substituted by the Housing Act 1980, s 152, Sch 25, para 47.

Sub-s (3): substituted by the Housing Act 1980, s 152, Sch 25, para 47; words in italics in para (*a*) prospectively repealed and first words in square brackets prospectively substituted by the Housing and Planning Act 1986, s 15, Sch 3, Part II, para 15, as from a day to be appointed; second words in square brackets in para (*a*) and amendment in para (*b*) made by the Housing (Consequential Provisons) Act 1985, s 4, Sch 2, para 35.

Sub-s (5): amended by the Housing (Consequential Provisions) Act 1985, s 4, Sch 2, para 35.

PART IX

PREMIUMS, ETC

119. Prohibition of premiums and loans on grant of protected tenancies

(1) Any person who, as a condition of the grant, renewal or continuance of a protected tenancy, requires, in addition to the rent, the payment of any premium or the making of any loan (whether secured or unsecured) shall be guilty of an offence.

(2) Any person who, in connection with the grant, renewal or continuance of a protected tenancy, receives any premium in addition to the rent shall be guilty of an offence.

(3) A person guilty of an offence under this section shall be liable to a fine not exceeding [level 3 on the standard scale].

(4) The court by which a person is convicted of an offence under this section relating to requiring or receiving any premium may order the amount of the premium to be repaid to the person by whom it was paid. **[378]**

NOTES

Commencement: 29 August 1977.

This section derived from the Rent Act 1968, s 85.

Sub-s (3): maximum fine increased and converted to a level on the standard scale by the Criminal Justice Act 1982, ss 37, 38, 46.

120. Prohibition of premiums and loans on assignment of protected tenancies

(1) Subject to section 121 of this Act, any person who, as a condition of the assignment of a protected tenancy, requires the payment of any premium or the making of any loan (whether secured or unsecured) shall be guilty of an offence.

(2) Subject to section 121 of this Act, any person who, in connection with the assignment of a protected tenancy, receives any premium shall be guilty of an offence.

(3) Notwithstanding anything in subsections (1) and (2) above, an assignor of a protected tenancy of a dwelling-house may, if apart from this section he would be entitled to do so, require the payment by the assignee or receive from the assignee a payment—

(*a*) of so much of any outgoings discharged by the assignor as is referable to any period after the assignment takes effect;

(*b*) of a sum not exceeding the amount of any expenditure reasonably incurred by the assignor in carrying out any structural alteration of the dwelling-house or in providing or improving fixtures therein, being fixtures which, as against the landlord, he is not entitled to remove;

(*c*) where the assignor became a tenant of the dwelling-house by virtue of an assignment of the protected tenancy, of a sum not exceeding any reasonable amount paid by him to his assignor in respect of expenditure incurred by that assignor, or by any previous assignor of the tenancy, in carrying out any such alteration or in providing or improving any such fixtures as are mentioned in paragraph (*b*) above; or

(*d*) where part of the dwelling-house is used as a shop or office, or for business, trade or professional purposes, of a reasonable amount in respect of any goodwill of the business, trade or profession, being goodwill transferred to the assignee in connection with the assignment or accruing to him in consequence thereof.

(4) Without prejudice to subsection (3) above, the assignor shall not be guilty of an offence under this section by reason only that—

(*a*) any payment of outgoings required or received by him on the assignment was a payment of outgoings referable to a period before the assignment took effect; or

(*b*) any expenditure which he incurred in carrying out structural alterations of the dwelling-house or in providing or improving fixtures therein and in respect of which he required or received the payment of any sum on the assignment was not reasonably incurred; or

(*c*) any amount paid by him as mentioned in subsection (3)(*c*) above was not a reasonable amount; or

(*d*) any amount which he required to be paid, or which he received, on the assignment in respect of goodwill was not a reasonable amount.

(5) Notwithstanding anything in subsections (1) and (2) above, Part I of Schedule 18 to this Act shall have effect in relation to the assignment of protected tenancies which are regulated tenancies in cases where a premium was lawfully required or received at the commencement of the tenancy.

(6) A person guilty of an offence under this section shall be liable to a fine not exceeding [level 3 on the standard scale].

(7) The court by which a person is convicted of an offence under this section relating to requiring or receiving any premium may order the amount of the premium, or so much of it as cannot lawfully be required or received under this section (including any amount which, by virtue of subsection (4) above, does not give rise to any offence) to be repaid to the person by whom it was paid. **[379]**

NOTES

Commencement: 29 August 1977.

This section derived from the Rent Act 1968, s 86.

Sub-s (6): maximum fine increased and converted to a level on the standard scale by the Criminal Justice Act 1982, ss 37, 38, 46.

121. Tenancies which became regulated by virtue of Counter-Inflation Act 1973

Part II of Schedule 18 to this Act shall have effect where a premium was lawfully required and paid on the grant, renewal or continuance of a regulated tenancy—

(*a*) which was granted before 8th March 1973, and

(*b*) which would not have been a regulated tenancy, but for section 14(1) of the Counter-Inflation Act 1973 (which brought certain tenancies of dwelling-houses with high rateable values within the protection of the Rent Act 1968). **[380]**

NOTES

Commencement: 29 August 1977.

This section derived from the Counter-Inflation Act 1973, s 14(4), Sch 5, para 5(1).

122. Prohibition of premiums on grant or assignment of rights under restricted contracts

(1) This section applies in relation to any premises if—

(*a*) under Part V of this Act, a rent is registered for those premises in the register kept in pursuance of section 79 of this Act; and

(*b*) in a case where the approval, reduction or increase of the rent by the rent tribunal is limited to rent payable in respect of a particular period, that period has not expired.

(2) Any person who, as a condition of the grant, renewal, continuance or assignment of rights under a restricted contract, requires the payment of any premium shall be guilty of an offence.

(3) Nothing in subsection (2) above shall prevent a person from requiring—

(*a*) that there shall be paid so much of any outgoings discharged by a grantor or assignor as is referable to any period after the grant or assignment takes effect; or

(*b*) that there shall be paid a reasonable amount in respect of goodwill of a business, trade, or profession, where the goodwill is transferred to a grantee or assignee in connection with the grant or assignment or accrues to him in consequence thereof.

(4) A person guilty of an offence under this section shall be liable to a fine not exceeding [level 3 on the standard scale].

(5) The court by which a person is convicted of an offence under this section may order the amount of the premium, or so much of it as cannot lawfully be required under this section, to be repaid to the person by whom it was paid. **[381]**

NOTES

Commencement: 29 August 1977.

This section derived from the Rent Act 1968, s 87.

Sub-s (4): maximum fine increased and converted to a level on the standard scale by the Criminal Justice Act 1982, ss 37, 38, 46.

123. Excessive price for furniture to be treated as premium

Where the purchase of any furniture has been required as a condition of the grant, renewal, continuance or assignment—

(*a*) of a protected tenancy, or

(*b*) of rights under a restricted contract which relates to premises falling within section 122(1) of this Act,

then, if the price exceeds the reasonable price of the furniture, the excess shall be treated, for the purposes of this Part of this Act, as if it were a premium required to be paid as a condition of the grant, renewal, continuance or assignment of the protected tenancy or, as the case may be, the rights under the restricted contract. **[382]**

NOTES

Commencement: 29 August 1977.

This section derived from the Rent Act 1968, s 88.

124. Punishment of attempts to obtain from prospective tenants excessive prices for furniture

(1) Any person who, in connection with the proposed grant, renewal, continuance or assignment, on terms which require the purchase of furniture, of a protected tenancy—

(*a*) offers the furniture at a price which he knows or ought to know is unreasonably high, or otherwise seeks to obtain such a price for the furniture, or

(*b*) fails to furnish, to any person seeking to obtain or retain accommodation whom he provides with particulars of the tenancy, a written inventory of the furniture, specifying the price sought for each item,

shall be liable to a fine not exceeding [level 3 on the standard scale].

(2) Where a local authority have reasonable grounds for suspecting that an offence under subsection (1)(*a*) above has been committed with respect to a protected tenancy or proposed protected tenancy of a dwelling-house, they may give notice to the person entitled to possession of the dwelling-house or his agent

that, on such date as may be specified in the notice, which shall not be earlier than—

(*a*) 24 hours after the giving of the notice, or

(*b*) if the dwelling-house is unoccupied, the expiry of such period after the giving of the notice as may be reasonable in the circumstances,

facilities will be required for entry to the dwelling-house and inspection of the furniture therein.

(3) A notice under this section may be given by post.

(4) Where a notice is given under this section, any person authorised by the local authority may avail himself of any facilities for such entry and inspection as are referred to in subsection (2) above which are provided on the specified date but shall, if so required, produce some duly authenticated document showing that he is authorised by the local authority.

(5) If it is shown to the satisfaction of a justice of the peace, on sworn information in writing, that a person required to give facilities under this section has failed to give them, the justice may, by warrant under his hand, empower the local authority, by any person authorised by them, to enter the dwelling-house in question, if need be by force, and inspect the furniture therein.

(6) A person empowered by or under the preceding provisions of this section to enter a dwelling-house may take with him such other persons as may be necessary and, if the dwelling-house is unoccupied, shall leave it as effectively secured against trespassers as he found it.

(7) Any person who wilfully obstructs a person acting in pursuance of a warrant issued under subsection (5) above shall be liable [to a fine not exceeding level 3 on the standard scale].

(8) In this section "local authority" means the council of a district or of a London borough or the Common Council of the City of London. **[383]**

NOTES

Commencement: 29 August 1977.

This section derived from the Rent Act 1968, s 89.

Sub-s (1): maximum fine increased and converted to a level on the standard scale by the Criminal Justice Act 1982, ss 37, 38, 46.

Sub-s (7): enhanced penalty on a subsequent conviction now abolished, maximum fine on any conviction increased and converted to level 3 on the standard scale by the standard scale by the Criminal Justice Act 1982, ss 35, 37, 38, 46.

125. Recovery of premiums and loans unlawfully required or received

(1) Where under any agreement (whether made before or after the commencement of this Act) any premium is paid after the commencement of this Act and the whole or any part of the premium could not lawfully be required or received under the preceding provisions of this Part of this Act, the amount of the premium, or, as the case may be, so much of it as could not lawfully be required or received, shall be recoverable by the person by whom it was paid.

(2) Nothing in section 119 or 120 of this Act shall invalidate any agreement for the making of a loan or any security issued in pursuance of such an agreement but, notwithstanding anything in the agreement for the loan, any sum lent in circumstances involving a contravention of either of those sections shall be repayable to the lender on demand. **[384]**

NOTES

Commencement: 29 August 1977.
This section derived from the Rent Act 1968, s 90.

126. Avoidance of requirements for advance payment of rent in certain cases

(1) Where a protected tenancy which is a regulated tenancy is granted, continued or renewed, any requirement that rent shall be payable—

(*a*) before the beginning of the rental period in respect of which it is payable, or
(*b*) earlier than 6 months before the end of the rental period in respect of which it is payable (if that period is more than 6 months),

shall be void, whether the requirement is imposed as a condition of the grant, renewal or continuance of the tenancy or under the terms thereof.

(2) Any requirement avoided by subsection (1) above is, in this section, referred to as a "prohibited requirement".

(3) Rent for any rental period to which a prohibited requirement relates shall be irrecoverable from the tenant.

(4) Any person who purports to impose any prohibited requirement shall be liable to a fine not exceeding [level 3 on the standard scale], and the court by which he is convicted may order any amount of rent paid in compliance with the prohibited requirement to be repaid to the person by whom it was paid.

(5) Where a tenant has paid on account of rent any amount which, by virtue of this section, is irrecoverable the tenant shall be entitled to recover that amount from the landlord who received it or his personal representatives.

(6) Any amount which a tenant is entitled to recover under subsection (5) above may, without prejudice to any other method of recovery, be deducted by the tenant from any rent payable by him to the landlord.

(7) No amount which a tenant is entitled to recover under subsection (5) above shall be recoverable at any time after the expiry of 2 years from the date of payment.

(8) Any person who, in any rent book or similar document makes an entry showing or purporting to show any tenant as being in arrears in respect of any sum on account of rent which is irrecoverable by virtue of this section shall be liable to a fine not exceeding [level 3 on the standard scale], unless he proves that, at the time of the making of the entry, the landlord had a bona fide claim that the sum was recoverable.

(9) If, where any such entry has been made by or on behalf of any landlord, the landlord on being requested by or on behalf of the tenant to do so, refuses or neglects to cause the entry to be deleted within 7 days, the landlord shall be liable to a fine not exceeding [level 3 on the standard scale], unless he proves that, at the time of the neglect or refusal to cause the entry to be deleted, he had a bona fide claim that the sum was recoverable. **[385]**

NOTES

Commencement: 29 August 1977.
This section derived from the Rent Act 1968, s 91.
Sub-ss (4), (8), (9): maximum fines increased and converted to levels on the standard scale by the Criminal Justice Act 1982, ss 37, 38, 46.

127. Allowable premiums in relation to certain long tenancies

(1) Where a tenancy is both a long tenancy within the meaning of Part I of the Landlord and Tenant Act 1954 and a protected tenancy, then—

(*a*) if the conditions specified in subsection (2) below are satisfied with respect to it, nothing in this Part of this Act or in Part VII of the Rent Act 1968 (provisions superseded by this Part) or the enactments replaced by the said Part VII shall apply or be deemed ever to have applied to the tenancy;

(*b*) if any of those conditions are not satisfied with respect to it, Part II of Schedule 18 to this Act shall apply and, if the tenancy was granted before the passing of this Act, be deemed always to have applied to it.

(2) The conditions mentioned in subsection (1)(*a*) above are—

(*a*) that the tenancy is not, and cannot become, terminable within 20 years of the date when it was granted by notice given to the tenant; and

(*b*) that, unless the tenancy was granted before 25th July 1969 or was granted in pursuance of Part I of the Leasehold Reform Act 1967, the sums payable by the tenant otherwise than in respect of rates, services, repairs, maintenance or insurance are not, under the terms of the tenancy, varied or liable to be varied within 20 years of the date when it was granted nor, thereafter, more than once in any 21 years; and

[(*c*) that the terms of the tenancy do not inhibit both the assignment and the underletting of the whole of the premises comprised in the tenancy.]

(3) Where the condition specified in subsection (2)(*b*) above would be satisfied with respect to a sub-tenancy but for a term providing for one variation, within 20 years of the date when the sub-tenancy was granted, of the sums payable by the sub-tenant, that condition shall be deemed to be satisfied notwithstanding that term, if it is satisfied with respect to a superior tenancy of the premises comprised in the sub-tenancy (or of those and other premises).

[(3A) If the conditions in subsection (3B) below are satisfied in respect of a tenancy, this Part of this Act shall not apply to that tenancy and, together with Part VII of the Rent Act 1968 and the enactments replaced by Part VII, shall be deemed never to have applied to it.

(3B) The conditions are that—

(*a*) the tenancy was granted before 16th July 1980;

(*b*) a premium was lawfully required and paid on the grant of the tenancy;

(*c*) the tenancy was, at the time when it was granted, a tenancy at a low rent; and

(*d*) the terms of the tenancy do not inhibit both the assignment and the underletting of the whole of the premises comprised in the tenancy.

(3C) If the conditions in subsection (3D) below are satisfied in respect of a tenancy, this section shall have effect, in relation to that tenancy, as if for the words "20 years" and "21 years", in subsections (2)(*b*) and (3) above there were substituted, respectively, the words "6 years" and "7 years".

(3D) The conditions are that—

(*a*) the tenancy is granted after 15th July 1980;

(*b*) at the time when it is granted it is a tenancy at a low rent; and (*c*) the terms of the tenancy ensure that any variation of the sums payable by the tenant otherwise than in respect of rates, services, repairs or maintenance, cannot lead to those sums exceeding an annual rate of two-thirds of the rateable value of the dwelling-house at the date when the variation is made.

For the purposes of this subsection the rateable value of a dwelling-house shall be ascertained in accordance with section 25 of this Act (disregarding subsection (4)) by reference to the value shown in the valuation list at the date when the variation is made.]

(4) Nothing in this section shall affect the recovery, in pursuance of any judgment given or order or agreement made before 20th May 1969, of any amount which it was not lawful to receive under the law in force at the time it was received.

(5) In this section "grant" includes continuance and renewal [and for the purposes of subsections (2)(*c*) and (3B)(*d*) above the terms of a tenancy inhibit an assignment or underletting if they—

(*a*) preclude it; or
(*b*) permit it subject to a consent but exclude section 144 of the Law of Property Act 1925 (no payment in nature of fine); or
(*c*) permit it subject to a consent but require in connection with a request for consent the making of an offer to surrender the tenancy.] **[386]**

NOTES
Commencement: 29 August 1977 (sub-ss (1)-(3), (4), (5)); 20 October 1980 (remainder).
Commencement order: SI 1980 No 1557.
This section derived from the Housing Act 1969, s 81.
Amended by the Housing Act 1980, s 78.

128. Interpretation of Part IX

(1) In this Part of this Act, unless the context otherwise requires,—
"furniture" includes fittings and other articles; and
["premium" includes—
(*a*) any fine or other like sum;
(*b*) any other pecuniary consideration in addition to rent; and
(*c*) any sum paid by way of a deposit, other than one which does not exceed one-sixth of the annual rent and is reasonable in relation to the potential liability in respect of which it is paid.]

(2) For the avoidance of doubt it is hereby declared that nothing in this Part of this Act shall render any amount recoverable more than once. **[387]**

NOTES
Commencement: 29 August 1977.
This section derived from the Rent Act 1968, s 92.
Amended by the Housing Act 1980, s 79.

PART X

MORTGAGES

129. Mortgages to which Part X applies

(1) This Part of this Act is concerned with mortgages which—
(*a*) were created before the relevant date, and

[(*b*) are regulated mortgages as defined in section 131 of this Act.]

(2) For the purposes of this Part of this Act, "relevant date"—

(*a*) in a case where, on 28th November 1967, land consisting of or including a dwelling-house was subject to a long tenancy which became a regulated tenancy on that date by virtue of section 39 of the Leasehold Reform Act 1967, means, in relation to that land, 28th November 1967;

(*b*) in a case where, on 22nd March 1973, land consisting of or including a dwelling-house was subject to a tenancy which became a regulated tenancy by virtue of section 14 of the Counter-Inflation Act 1973, means, in relation to that land, 22nd March 1973;

(*c*) in the case of land consisting of or including a dwelling-house subject to a regulated furnished tenancy, means, in relation to that land, 14th August 1974; and

(*d*) in any other case, means 8th December 1965. **[388]**

NOTES

Commencement: 29 August 1977.

Sub-s (1) derived from the Rent Act 1968, s 93(1); sub-s (2) derived from the Rent Act 1968, s 93, and the Rent Act 1974, Sch 1, Part II, para 10.

Amended by the Housing Act 1980, s 152, Sch 25.

131. Regulated mortgages

(1) Subject to subsection (2) below, a mortgage which falls within section 129(1)(*a*) of this Act . . . is a regulated mortgage if—

(*a*) it is a legal mortgage of land consisting of or including a dwelling-house which is let on or subject to a regulated tenancy; and

(*b*) the regulated tenancy is binding on the mortgagee.

(2) Notwithstanding that a mortgage falls within subsection (1) above, it is not a regulated mortgage if—

(*a*) the rateable value on the appropriate day of the dwelling-house which falls within subsection (1)(*a*) above, or if there is more than one such dwelling-house comprised in the mortgage, the aggregate of the rateable values of those dwelling-houses on the appropriate day is less than one-tenth of the rateable value on the appropriate day of the whole of the land comprised in the mortgage, or

(*b*) the mortgagor is in breach of covenant, but for this purpose a breach of the covenant for the repayment of the principal money otherwise than by instalments shall be disregarded.

(3) Subsection (2)(*a*) above shall have effect, in the case of land consisting of or including a dwelling-house which on 22nd March 1973, was subject to a tenancy which became a regulated tenancy by virtue of section 14 of the Counter-Inflation Act 1973, as if for the reference to the appropriate day there were substituted a reference to 7th March 1973.

(4) In this section "legal mortgage" includes a charge by way of legal mortgage.

(5) Any reference in this Part of this Act to a regulated mortgage shall be construed in accordance with this section. **[389]**

NOTES

Commencement: 29 August 1977.

This section derived from the Rent Act 1968, ss 93, 94.

Sub-s (1): words omitted repealed by the Housing Act 1980, s 152, Sch 26.

132. Powers of court to mitigate hardship to mortgagors under regulated mortgages

(1) The powers of the court under this section [become exercisable, in relation to a regulated mortgage] only on an application made by the mortgagor within 21 days, or such longer time as the court may allow, after the occurrence of one of the following events:—

(*a*) the rate of interest payable in respect of the mortgage is increased; or
(*b*) a rent for a dwelling-house comprised in the mortgage is registered under Part IV of this Act and the rent so registered is lower than the rent which was payable immediately before the registration; or
(*c*) the mortgagee, not being a mortgagee who was in possession on the relevant date demands payment of the principal money secured by the mortgage or takes any steps for exercising any right of foreclosure or sale or for otherwise enforcing his security.

Paragraph (*b*) above shall not apply to a case falling within section 129(2)(*b*) of this Act.

(2) If the court is satisfied on any such application that, by reason of the event in question and of the operation of this Act, the mortgagor would suffer severe financial hardship unless relief were given under this section, the court may by order make such provision—

(*a*) limiting the rate of interest,
(*b*) extending the time for the repayment of the principal money, or
(*c*) otherwise varying the terms of the mortgage or imposing any limitation or condition on the exercise of any right or remedy in respect thereof,

as it thinks appropriate.

(3) Where the court makes an order under subsection (2) above in relation to a mortgage which comprises other land as well as a dwelling-house or dwelling-houses subject to a regulated tenancy the order may, if the mortgagee so requests, make provision for apportioning the money secured by the mortgage between that other land and the dwelling-house or dwelling-houses.

(4) Where such an apportionment is made, the other provisions of the order made by the court shall not apply in relation to the other land referred to in that subsection and the money secured by the other land, and the mortgage shall have effect for all purposes as two separate mortgages of the apportioned parts.

(5) Where the court has made an order under this section it may vary or revoke it by a subsequent order.

(6) The court for the purposes of this section is a county court, except that where an application under subsection (1) above is made in pursuance of any step taken by the mortgagee in the High Court, it is the High Court. **[390]**

NOTES

Commencement: 29 August 1977.
This section derived from the Rent Act 1968, ss 93, 95.
Sub-s (1): amended by the Housing Act 1980, s 152, Sch 25.

136. Interpretation of Part X

In this Part of this Act, except where the context otherwise requires—

(*a*) "mortgagee" and "mortgagor" include any person from time to time deriving title under the original mortgagee or mortgagor; and

(*b*) "legal mortgage" in relation to regulated mortgages, [includes] any charge registered under the Land Registration Act 1925. **[391]**

NOTES

Commencement: 29 August 1977.

This section derived from the Rent Act 1968, s 99.

Amended by the Housing Act 1980, s 152, Sch 25.

PART XI

GENERAL

Sublettings

137. Effect on sub-tenancy of determination of superior tenancy

(1) If a court makes an order for possession of a dwelling-house from—

(*a*) a protected or statutory tenant, or

(*b*) a protected occupier or statutory tenant as defined in the Rent (Agriculture) Act 1976,

and the order is made by virtue of section 98(1) or 99(2) of this Act or, as the case may be, under Part I of Schedule 4 to that Act, nothing in the order shall affect the right of any sub-tenant to whom the dwelling-house or any part of it has been lawfully sublet before the commencement of the proceedings to retain possession by virtue of this Part of this Act, nor shall the order operate to give a right to possession against any such sub-tenant.

(2) Where a statutorily protected tenancy of a dwelling-house is determined, either as a result of an order for possession or for any other reason, any sub-tenant to whom the dwelling-house or any part of it has been lawfully sublet shall, subject to this Act, be deemed to become the tenant of the landlord on the same terms as if the tenant's statutorily protected tenancy has continued.

(3) Where a dwelling-house—

(*a*) forms part of premises which have been let as a whole on a superior tenancy but do not constitute a dwelling-house let on a statutorily protected tenancy; and

(*b*) is itself subject to a protected or statutory tenancy,

then, from the coming to an end of the superior tenancy, this Act shall apply in relation to the dwelling-house as if, in lieu of the superior tenancy, there had been separate tenancies of the dwelling-house and of the remainder of the premises, for the like purposes as under the superior tenancy, and at rents equal to the just proportion of the rent under the superior tenancy.

In this subsection "premises" includes, if the sub-tenancy in question is a protected or statutory tenancy to which section 99 of this Act applies, an agricultural holding within the meaning of the *Agricultural Holdings Act 1948* [Agricultural Holdings Act 1986].

(4) In subsections (2) and (3) above "statutorily protected tenancy" means—

(*a*) a protected or statutory tenancy;

(*b*) a protected occupancy or statutory tenancy as defined in the Rent (Agriculture) Act 1976; or

(*c*) if the sub-tenancy in question is a protected or statutory tenancy to which section 99 of this Act applies, a tenancy of an agricultural holding within the meaning of the *Agricultural Holdings Act 1948* [Agricultural Holdings Act 1986].

(5) Subject to subsection (6) below, a long tenancy of a dwelling-house which is also a tenancy at a low rent but which, had it not been a tenancy at a low rent, would have been a protected tenancy, shall be treated for the purposes of subsection (2) above as a statutorily protected tenancy.

(6) Notwithstanding anything in subsection (5) above, subsection (2) above shall not have effect where the sub-tenancy in question was created (whether immediately or derivatively) out of a long tenancy falling within subsection (5) above and, at the time of the creation of the sub-tenancy—

(*a*) a notice to terminate the long tenancy had been given under section 4(1) of the Landlord and Tenant Act 1954; or

(*b*) the long tenancy was being continued by section 3(1) of that Act;

unless the sub-tenancy was created with the consent in writing of the person who at the time when it was created was the landlord, within the meaning of Part I of that Act.

(7) This section shall apply equally where a protected occupier of a dwelling-house, or part of a dwelling-house, has a relevant licence as defined in the Rent (Agriculture) Act 1976, and in this section "tenancy" and all cognate expressions shall be construed accordingly. **[392]**

NOTES

Commencement: 29 August 1977.

This section derived from the Rent Act 1968, s 18.

Words in italics repealed with savings and words in square brackets substituted with savings by the Agricultural Holdings Act 1986, ss 99, 101, Sch 13, para 3, Sch 14, para 60.

138. Effect on furnished sub-tenancy of determination of superior unfurnished tenancy

(1) If, in a case where section 137(2) of this Act applies the conditions mentioned in subsection (2) below are fulfilled, the terms on which the sub-tenant is, by virtue of section 137(2), deemed to become the tenant of the landlord shall not include any terms as to the provision by the landlord of furniture or services.

(2) The conditions are:—

(*a*) that the statutorily protected tenancy which is determined as mentioned in section 137(2) was neither a protected furnished tenancy nor a statutory furnished tenancy; and

(*b*) that, immediately before the determination of that statutorily protected tenancy, the sub-tenant referred to in section 137(2) was the tenant under a protected furnished tenancy or a statutory furnished tenancy; and

(*c*) that the landlord, within the period of 6 weeks beginning with the day on which the statutorily protected tenancy referred to in section 137(2) is determined, serves notice on the sub-tenant that this section is to apply to his tenancy or statutory tenancy.

(3) In this section "statutorily protected tenancy" has the [same meaning as it has for the purposes of section 137(2) of this Act]. **[393]**

NOTES

Commencement: 29 August 1977.

This section derived from the Rent Act 1974, s 13.

Sub-s (3): amended by the Housing Act 1980, s 152, Sch 25.

139. Obligation to notify sublettings of dwelling-houses let on or subject to protected or statutory tenancies

(1) If the tenant of a dwelling-house let on or subject to a protected or statutory tenancy sublets any part of the dwelling-house on a protected tenancy, then, subject to subsection (2) below, he shall, within 14 days after the subletting, supply the landlord with a statement in writing of the subletting giving particulars of occupancy including the rent charged.

(2) Subsection (1) above shall not require the supply of a statement in relation to a subletting of any part of a dwelling-house if the particulars which would be required to be included in the statement as to the rent and other conditions of the sub-tenancy would be the same as in the last statement supplied in accordance with that subsection with respect to a previous subletting of that part.

(3) A tenant who is required to supply a statement in accordance with subsection (1) above and who, without reasonable excuse—

(*a*) fails to supply a statement, or
(*b*) supplies a statement which is false in any material particular,

shall be liable to a fine not exceeding [level 2 on the standard scale].

(4) In this section—

(*a*) "protected tenancy" includes a protected occupancy under the Rent (Agriculture) Act 1976;
(*b*) "statutory tenancy" includes a statutory tenancy under that Act. **[394]**

NOTES
Commencement: 29 August 1977.
This section derived from the Rent Act 1968, s 104.
Sub-s (3): maximum fine increased and converted to a level on the standard scale by the Criminal Justice Act 1982, ss 37, 38, 46.

Fire Precautions

140. Modification of Act in relation to fire precautions

Schedule 20 to this Act shall have effect for the purpose of modifying this Act in connection with certain provisions of the Fire Precautions Act 1971. **[395]**

NOTES
Commencement: 29 August 1977.
This section derived from the Fire Precautions Act 1971, s 34.

Jurisdiction and procedure

141. County court jurisdiction

(1) A county court shall have jurisdiction either in the course of any proceedings relating to a dwelling or on an application made for the purpose by the landlord or the tenant, to determine any question—

(*a*) as to whether a tenancy is a protected tenancy or whether any person is a statutory tenant of a dwelling-house, . . . ; or
(*b*) as to the rent limit; or
(*c*) . . .

(*d*) as to the application of Part V and sections 103 to 106 of this Act to a contract; or
(*e*) as to whether a protected, statutory or regulated tenancy is a protected, statutory or regulated furnished tenancy;

or as to any matter which is or may become material for determining any such question.

(2) . . .

(3) A county court shall have jurisdiction to deal with any claim or other proceedings arising out of any of the provisions of this Act specified in subsection (5) below, notwithstanding that by reason of the amount of the claim or otherwise the case would not, apart from this subsection, be within the jurisdiction of a county court.

(4) If, under any of the provisions of this Act specified in subsection (5) below, a person takes proceedings in the High Court which he could have taken in the county court, he shall not be entitled to recover any costs.

(5) The provisions referred to in subsections (3) and (4) above are—

(*a*) . . .
(*b*) in Part III, section 57;
(*c*) Part VII, except sections 98(2) and 101;
(*d*) in Part IX, sections 125 and 126;
(*e*) in Part X, sections 133(1), 134 and 135; and
(*f*) in this Part of this Act, sections 145 and 147. **[396]**

NOTES
Commencement: 29 August 1977.
This section derived from the Rent Act 1968, s 105.
Words omitted repealed by the Housing Act 1980, s 152, Sch 26.

142. Rules as to procedure

(1) The Lord Chancellor may make such rules and give such directions as he thinks fit for the purpose of giving effect to the provisions of this Act and may, by those rules or directions, provide for the conduct so far as desirable in private of any proceedings for the purposes of those provisions and for the remission of any fees.

(2) The power vested in the Lord Chancellor by subsection (1) above may, when the Great Seal is in commission, be exercised by any Lord Commissioner.

(3) The power conferred by subsection (1) above shall not be exercisable in relation to the following provisions of this Act:—

(*a*) Part IV, except section 75(2);
(*b*) Part V;
(*c*) Part VI;
(*d*) sections 103 to 106, except subsection (4).

(4) Any rules made under this section shall be contained in a statutory instrument. **[397]**

NOTES
Commencement: 29 August 1977.
This section derived from the Rent Act 1968, s 106.

Release from provisions of Act

143. Release from rent regulation

(1) Where the Secretary of State is satisfied with respect to every part of any area that the number of persons seeking to become tenants there—

(*a*) of dwelling-houses exceeding a specified rateable value, or

(*b*) of any class or description of dwelling-house or of dwelling-house exceeding a specified rateable value,

is not substantially greater than the number of such dwelling-houses in that part, he may by order provide that no such dwelling-house in the area shall be the subject of a regulated tenancy or the subject of a protected occupancy or statutory tenancy under the Rent (Agriculture) Act 1976.

(2) An order under this section may contain such transitional provisions, including provisions to avoid or mitigate hardship, as appear to the Secretary of State to be desirable.

(3) The power to make an order under this section shall be exercisable by statutory instrument and no such order shall have effect unless it is approved by a resolution of each House of Parliament. **[398]**

NOTES

Commencement: 29 August 1977.

This section derived from the Rent Act 1968, s 100.

144. Release from restricted contract provisions

(1) The Secretary of State may by order provide that, as from such date as may be specified in the order, section 19 of this Act shall not apply to a dwelling the rateable value of which on such day as may be specified in the order exceeds such amount as may be so specified.

(2) An order under this section—

(*a*) may be made so as to relate to the whole of England and Wales or to such area in England and Wales as may be specified in the order, and so as to apply generally or only to, or except to, such classes or descriptions of dwellings as may be specified in the order; and

(*b*) may contain such transitional provisions as appear to the Secretary of State to be desirable.

(3) The power to make an order under this section shall be exercisable by statutory instrument and no such order shall have effect unless it is approved by a resolution of each House of Parliament. **[399]**

NOTES

Commencement: 29 August 1977.

This section derived from the Rent Act 1968, s 71(2)-(4).

Miscellaneous

146. Long tenancies at a low rent

(1) In determining whether a long tenancy was, at any time,—

(*a*) a tenancy at a low rent within the meaning of the Rent Act 1968; or

(*b*) a tenancy to which, by virtue of section 12 (7) of the Act of 1920, the Rent Acts did not apply;

there shall be disregarded such part (if any) of the sums payable by the tenant as is expressed (in whatever terms) to be payable in respect of rates, services, repairs, maintenance, or insurance, unless it could not have been regarded by the parties as a part so payable.

(2) In subsection (1) above—

"long tenancy" means a tenancy granted for a term certain exceeding 21 years, other than a tenancy which is, or may become, terminable before the end of that term by notice given to the tenant;

"the Act of 1920" means the Increase of Rent and Mortgage Interest (Restrictions) Act 1920; and

"the Rent Acts" means the Rent and Mortgage Interest Restrictions Acts 1920 to 1939. **[400]**

NOTES

Commencement: 29 August 1977.
This section derived from the Housing Act 1969, s 80(1), (3).

147. Restriction on levy of distress for rent

(1) No distress for the rent of any dwelling-house let on a protected tenancy or subject to a statutory tenancy shall be levied except with the leave of the county court; and the court shall, with respect to any application for such leave, have the same or similar powers with respect to adjournment, stay, suspension, postponement and otherwise as are conferred by section 100 of this Act in relation to proceedings for possession of such a dwelling-house.

(2) Nothing in subsection (1) above shall apply to distress levied under [section 102 of the County Courts Act 1984]. **[401]**

NOTES

Commencement: 29 August 1977.
This section derived from the Rent Act 1968, s 111.
Sub-s (2): amended by the County Courts Act 1984, s 148(1), Sch 2, para 67.

148. Implied term in all protected tenancies

It shall be a condition of a protected tenancy of a dwelling-house that the tenant shall afford to the landlord access to the dwelling-house and all reasonable facilities for executing therein any repairs which the landlord is entitled to execute. **[402]**

NOTES

Commencement: 29 August 1977.
This section derived from the Rent Act 1968, s 112.

Supplemental

149. Powers of local authorities for the purposes of giving information

(1) Any local authority to which this section applies shall have power—

(*a*) to publish information, for the assistance of landlords and tenants and others, as to their rights and duties under—

[(i) sections 4 to 7 (provision of rent books) and sections 18 to 30 (service charges) of the Landlord and Tenant Act 1985,]

(ii) the Protection from Eviction Act 1977,

[(iii) Part II . . . , of the Housing Act 1980,]

(iv) this Act, and as to the procedure for enforcing those rights or securing the performance of those duties, and

(*b*) to publish information, for the assistance of owners and occupiers of dwelling-houses and others, as to their rights and duties under the Rent (Agriculture) Act 1976 and as to the procedure for enforcing those rights or securing the performance of those duties, and

(*c*) to make any such information as is mentioned in paragraph (*a*) or (*b*) above available in any other way, and

(*d*) to furnish particulars as to the availability, extent and character of alternative accommodation.

(2) This section applies to the following local authorities:—

(*a*) councils of districts and of London boroughs;

(*b*) the Common Council of the City of London; and

(*c*) the Council of the Isles of Scilly. **[403]**

NOTES

Commencement: 29 August 1977.

This section derived from the Rent Act 1968, s 107.

Sub-s (1): para (a), sub-para (i) substituted by the Housing (Consequential Provisions) Act 1985, s 4, Sch 2, para 35; sub-para (iii) amended by the Housing Act 1980, s 152, Sch 25, words omitted repealed by the Housing (Consequential Provisions) Act 1985, s 3, Sch 1, Part I.

150. Prosecution of offences

(1) Offences under this Act are punishable summarily.

(2) Proceedings for an offence under this Act . . . may be instituted by any local authority to which section 149 of this Act applies. **[404]**

NOTES

Commencement: 29 August 1977.

This section derived from the Rent Act 1968, s 108 and the Housing Act 1974, s 18(3).

Words omitted repealed by the Housing Act 1980, s 152, Sch 26.

151. Service of notices on landlord's agents

(1) Any document required or authorised by this Act to be served by the tenant of a dwelling-house on the landlord thereof shall be deemed to be duly served on him if it is served—

(*a*) on any agent of the landlord named as such in the rent book or other similar document; or

(*b*) on the person who receives the rent of the dwelling-house.

(2) Where a dwelling-house is subject to a regulated tenancy, subsection (1) above shall apply also in relation to any document required or authorised by this Act to be served on the landlord by a person other than the tenant.

(3) If for the purpose of any proceedings (whether civil or criminal) brought or intended to be brought under this Act, any person serves upon any such agent or other person as is referred to in paragraph (*a*) or paragraph (*b*) of subsection (1) above a notice in writing requiring the agent or other person to disclose to him the full name and place of abode or place of business of the landlord, that agent or other person shall forthwith comply with the notice.

(4) If any such agent or other person as is referred to in subsection (3) above fails or refuses forthwith to comply with a notice served on him under that subsection, he shall be liable to a fine not exceeding [level 4 on the standard scale], unless he shows to the satisfaction of the court that he did not know, and

could not with reasonable diligence have ascertained, such of the facts required by the notice to be disclosed as were not disclosed by him.

(5) So far as this section relates to Part V or IX or sections 103 to 107, of this Act, references to a landlord and to a tenant shall respectively include references to a lessor and to a lessee as defined by section 85 of this Act. **[405]**

NOTES

Commencement: 29 August 1977.

Sub-ss (1)-(4) derived from the Rent Act 1968, s 109; sub-s (5) derived from the Housing Finance Act 1977, Sch 9, para 12(3).

Sub-s (4): maximum fine increased and converted to a level on the standard scale by the Criminal Justice Act 1982, ss 37, 39, 46, Sch 3.

152. Interpretation

(1) In this Act, except where the context otherwise requires,—

"the appropriate day" has the meaning assigned to it by section 25(3) of this Act;

. . .

"landlord" includes any person from time to time deriving title under the original landlord and also includes, in relation to any dwelling-house, any person other than the tenant who is, or but for Part VII of this Act would be, entitled to possession of the dwelling-house;

"let" includes "sublet";

"long tenancy" means a tenancy granted for a term of years certain exceeding 21 years, whether or not subsequently extended by act of the parties or by any enactment;

"protected furnished tenancy", "regulated furnished tenancy" and "statutory furnished tenancy" mean a protected or, as the case may be, regulated or statutory tenancy—

(*a*) under which the dwelling-house concerned is bona fide let at a rent which includes payments in respect of furniture, and

(*b*) in respect of which the amount of rent which is fairly attributable to the use of furniture, having regard to the value of that use to the tenant, forms a substantial part of the whole rent;

"protected tenant" and "protected tenancy" shall be construed in accordance with section 1 of this Act;

"rates" includes water rates and charges but does not include an owner's drainage rate as defined in section 63(2)(*a*) of the Land Drainage Act 1976;

"rateable value" shall be construed in accordance with section 25 of this Act;

"regulated tenancy" shall be construed in accordance with section 18 of this Act;

"rent tribunal" has the meaning given by section 76(1) of this Act;

"rental period" means a period in respect of which a payment of rent falls to be made;

"restricted contract" shall be construed in accordance with section 19 of this Act;

"statutory tenant" and "statutory tenancy" shall be construed in accordance with section 2 of this Act;

"tenant" includes statutory tenant and also includes a sub-tenant and any person deriving title under the original tenant or sub-tenant;

"tenancy" includes "sub-tenancy";

"tenancy at a low rent" has the meaning assigned to it by section 5 of this Act.

(2) Except in so far as the context otherwise requires, any reference in this Act to any other enactment shall be taken as referring to that enactment as amended by or under any other enactment, including this Act. **[406]**

NOTES

Commencement: 29 August 1977.

This section derived from the Rent Act 1968, ss 38(1), 51(1), 67(1), 84(1), 92(1), 113(1), (2), the Housing Finance Act 1972, ss 48, 88(1), 104(1), the Counter-Inflation Act 1973, Sch 5, para 12, and the Rent Act 1974, ss 1(2), 15(1), (2).

Words omitted repealed by the Housing Act 1980.

153. Application to Isles of Scilly

(1) With the exception of Part V, and sections [102A to 106A], of this Act (which do not apply to the Isles of Scilly) this Act applies to the Isles subject to such exceptions, adaptations and modifications as the Secretary of State may by order direct.

(2) The power to make an order under this section shall be exercisable by statutory instrument which shall be subject to annulment in pursuance of a resolution of either House of Parliament.

(3) An order under this section may be varied or revoked by a subsequent order. **[407]**

NOTES

Commencement: 29 August 1977.

This section derived from the Rent Act 1968, ss 69(4), 115, the Housing Finance Act 1972, s 103 and the Housing Rents and Subsidies Act 1975, s 17(4), Sch 5, para 7.

Amended by the Housing Act 1980, s 152, Sch 25.

154. Application to Crown property

(1) Subject to sections 13 and 19(5)(*b*) of this Act this Act shall apply in relation to premises in which there subsists, or at any material time subsisted, a Crown interest as it applies in relation to premises in which no such interest subsists or ever subsisted.

(2) In this section "Crown interest" means an interest which belongs to Her Majesty in right of the Crown or of the Duchy of Lancaster or to the Duchy of Cornwall, or to a government department, or which is held in trust for Her Majesty for the purposes of a government department. **[408]**

NOTES

Commencement: 29 August 1977.

This section derived from the Rent Act 1968, s 116.

155. Modifications, amendments, transitional provisions, repeals etc

(1) . . .

(2) Subject to subsection (3) below, the enactments specified in Schedule 23 to this Act shall have effect subject to the amendments specified in that Schedule.

(3) The savings and transitional provisions in Schedule 24 to this Act shall have effect.

(4) The inclusion in this Act of any express saving, transitional provision or

amendment shall not be taken as prejudicing the operation of section 38 of the Interpretation Act 1889 (which relates to the effect of repeals).

(5) Subject to subsection (3) above, the enactments specified in Schedule 25 to this Act (which include enactments which were spent before the passing of this Act) are hereby repealed to the extent specified in the third column of that Schedule. **[409]**

NOTES
Commencement: 29 August 1977.
Sub-s (1): repealed by the Housing Act 1980, s 152, Schs 25, 26.

156. Short title, commencement and extent

(1) This Act may be cited as the Rent Act 1977.

(2) This Act shall come into force on the expiry of the period of one month beginning with the date on which it is passed.

(3) This Act does not extend to Scotland or Northern Ireland. **[410]**

NOTES
Commencement: 29 August 1977.

SCHEDULES

SCHEDULE 1

Sections 2, 3

STATUTORY TENANCIES

PART I

STATUTORY TENANTS BY SUCCESSION

1. Paragraph 2 or, as the case may be, paragraph 3 below shall have effect, subject to section 2(3) of this Act, for the purpose of determining who is the statutory tenant of a dwelling-house by succession after the death of the person (in this Part of this Schedule referred to as "the original tenant") who, immediately before his death, was a protected tenant of the dwelling-house or the statutory tenant of it by virtue of his previous protected tenancy.

[2. The surviving spouse (if any) of the original tenant, if residing in the dwelling-house immediately before the death of the original tenant, shall after the death be the statutory tenant if and so long as he or she occupies the dwelling-house as his or her residence.]

3. Where paragraph 2 above does not apply, but a person who was a member of the original tenant's family was residing with him at the time of and for the period of 6 months immediately before his death then, after his death, that person or if there is more than one such person such one of them as may be decided by agreement, or in default of agreement by the county court, shall be the statutory tenant if and so long as he occupies the dwelling-house as his residence.

4. A person who becomes the statutory tenant of a dwelling-house by virtue of paragraph 2 or 3 above is in this Part of this Schedule referred to as "the first successor".

5. If, immediately before his death, the first successor was still a statutory tenant, paragraph 6 or, as the case may be, paragraph 7 below shall have effect, subject to section 2(3) of this Act, for the purpose of determining who is the statutory tenant after the death of the first successor.

[6. The surviving spouse (if any) of the first successor, if residing in the dwelling-house immediately before the death of the first successor, shall after the death be the statutory tenant if and so long as he or she occupies the dwelling-house as his or her residence.]

7. Where paragraph 6 above does not apply but a person who was a member of the first successor's family was residing with him at the time of and for the period of 6 months immediately before his death then, after his death, that person or if there is more than one such person such one of them as may be decided by agreement, or in default of agreement by the county court, shall be the statutory tenant if and so long as he occupies the dwelling-house as his residence.

8. . . .

9. Paragraphs 5 to 8 above do not apply where the statutory tenancy of the original tenant arose by virtue of section 4 of the Requisitioned Houses and Housing (Amendment) Act 1955 or section 20 of the Rent Act 1965.

10.—(1) Where after a succession the successor becomes the tenant of the dwelling-house by the grant to him of another tenancy, "the original tenant" and "the first successor" in this Part of this Schedule shall, in relation to that other tenancy, mean the persons who were respectively the original tenant and the first successor at the time of the succession, and accordingly—

(*a*) if the successor was the first successor, and, immediately before his death he was still the tenant (whether protected or statutory), paragraphs 6 and 7 above shall apply on his death,

(*b*) if the successor was not the first successor, no person shall become a statutory tenant on his death by virtue of this Part of this Schedule.

(2) Sub-paragraph (1) above applies—

(*a*) even if a successor enters into more than one other tenancy of the dwelling-house, and

(*b*) even if both the first successor and the successor on his death enter into other tenancies of the dwelling-house.

(3) In this paragraph "succession" means the occasion on which a person becomes the statutory tenant of a dwelling-house by virtue of this Part of this Schedule and "successor" shall be construed accordingly.

(4) This paragraph shall apply as respects a succession which took place before 27th August 1972 if, and only if, the tenancy granted after the succession, or the first of those tenancies, was granted on or after that date, and where it does not apply as respects a succession, no account should be taken of that succession in applying this paragraph as respects any later succession.

11.—(1) Paragraphs 5 to 8 above do not apply where—

(*a*) the tenancy of the original tenant was granted on or after the operative date within the meaning of the Rent (Agriculture) Act 1976, and

(*b*) both that tenancy and the statutory tenancy of the first successor were tenancies to which section 99 of this Act applies.

(2) If the tenants under both of the tenancies falling within sub-paragraph (1)(*b*) above were persons to whom paragraph 7 of Schedule 9 to the Rent (Agriculture) Act 1976 applies, the reference in sub-paragraph (1)(*a*) above to the operative date shall be taken as a reference to the date of operation for forestry workers within the meaning of that Act. **[411]**

NOTES

Commencement: 28 November 1980 (paras 2, 6); 29 August 1977 (remainder).

Commencement order: SI 1980 No 1706.

This Part derived from the Rent Act 1968, Sch 1, paras 1-10 and the Housing Finance Act 1972, s 47(2).

Amended by the Housing Act 1980, ss 76, 152, Sch 26.

PART II

RELINQUISHING TENANCIES AND CHANGING TENANTS

Payments demanded by statutory tenants as a condition of giving up possession

12.—(1) A statutory tenant of a dwelling-house who, as a condition of giving up possession of the dwelling-house, asks for or receives the payment of any sum, or the giving of any other consideration, by any person other than the landlord, shall be guilty of an offence.

(2) Where a statutory tenant of a dwelling-house requires that furniture or other articles shall be purchased as a condition of his giving up possession of the dwelling-house, the price demanded shall, at the request of the person on whom the demand is made, be stated in writing, and if the price exceeds the reasonable price of the articles the excess shall be treated, for the purposes of sub-paragraph (1) above, as a sum asked to be paid as a condition of giving up possession.

(3) A person guilty of an offence under this paragraph shall be liable to a fine not exceeding [level 3 on the standard scale].

(4) The court by which a person is convicted of an offence under this paragraph may order the payment—

(*a*) to the person who made any such payment, or gave any such consideration, as is referred to in sub-paragraph (1) above, of the amount of that payment or the value of that consideration, or
(*b*) to the person who paid any such price as is referred to in sub-paragraph (2) above, of the amount by which the price paid exceeds the reasonable price.

Change of statutory tenant by agreement

13.—(1) Where it is so agreed in writing between a statutory tenant ("the outgoing tenant") and a person proposing to occupy the dwelling ("the incoming tenant"), the incoming tenant shall be deemed to be the statutory tenant of the dwelling as from such date as may be specified in the agreement ("the transfer date").

(2) Such an agreement shall not have effect unless the landlord is a party thereto, and, if the consent of any superior landlord would have been required to an assignment of the previous contractual tenancy, the agreement shall not have effect unless the superior landlord is a party thereto.

(3) If the outgoing tenant is the statutory tenant by virtue of his previous protected tenancy, then, subject to sub-paragraph (6) below, this Act shall have effect, on and after the transfer date, as if the incoming tenant had been a protected tenant and had become the statutory tenant by virtue of his previous protected tenancy.

(4) Subject to sub-paragraphs (5) and (6) below, if the outgoing tenant is a statutory tenant by succession, then, on and after the transfer date—

(*a*) this Act shall have effect as if the incoming tenant were a statutory tenant by succession, and
(*b*) the incoming tenant shall be deemed to have become a statutory tenant by virtue of that paragraph of Part 1 of this Schedule by virtue of which the outgoing tenant became (or is deemed to have become) a statutory tenant.

(5) If the outgoing tenant is a statutory tenant by succession, the agreement may provide that, notwithstanding anything in sub-paragraph (4) above, on and after the transfer date, this Act shall have effect, subject to sub-paragraph (6) below, as if the incoming tenant had been a protected tenant and had become the statutory tenant by virtue of his previous protected tenancy.

(6) Unless the incoming tenant is deemed, by virtue of sub-paragraph (4)(*b*) above, to have become a statutory tenant by virtue of paragraph 6 or 7 of Part I of this Schedule, paragraphs 5 to 7 of that Part shall not apply where a person has become a statutory tenant by virtue of this paragraph.

(7) In this paragraph "the dwelling" means the aggregate of the premises comprised in the statutory tenancy of the outgoing tenant.

No pecuniary consideration to be required on change of tenant under paragraph 13

14.—(1) Any person who requires the payment of any pecuniary consideration for entering into such an agreement as is referred to in paragraph 13 (1) above shall be liable to a fine not exceeding [level 3 on the standard scale].

(2) The court by which a person is convicted of an offence under sub-paragraph (1) above may order the amount of the payment to be repaid by the person to whom it was paid.

(3) Without prejudice to sub-paragraph (2) above, the amount of any such payment as is referred to in sub-paragraph (1) above shall be recoverable by the person by whom it was made either by proceedings for its recovery or, if it was made to the landlord by a person liable to pay rent to the landlord, by deduction from any rent so payable.

(4) Notwithstanding anything in sub-paragraph (1) above, if apart from this paragraph he would be entitled to do so, the outgoing tenant may require the payment by the incoming tenant—

(*a*) of so much of any outgoings discharged by the outgoing tenant as is referable to any period after the transfer date;

(*b*) of a sum not exceeding the amount of any expenditure reasonably incurred by the outgoing tenant in carrying out any structural alteration of the dwelling or in providing or improving fixtures therein, being fixtures which, as against the landlord, the outgoing tenant is not entitled to remove;

(*c*) where the outgoing tenant became a tenant of the dwelling by virtue of an assignment of the previous protected tenancy, of a sum not exceeding any reasonable amount paid by him to his assignor in respect of expenditure incurred by the assignor, or by any previous assignor of the tenancy, in carrying out any such alteration or in providing or improving any such fixtures as are mentioned in paragraph (*b*) above; or

(*d*) where part of the dwelling is used as a shop or office, or for business, trade or professional purposes, of a reasonable amount in respect of any goodwill of the business, trade or profession, being goodwill transferred to the incoming tenant in connection with his becoming a statutory tenant of the dwelling or accruing to him in consequence thereof.

(5) In this paragraph "outgoing tenant", "incoming tenant", "the transfer date" and "the dwelling" have the same meanings as in paragraph 13 above. **[412]**

NOTES

Commencement: 29 August 1977.

This Part derived from the Rent Act 1968, ss 13-15.

Maximum fines increased and converted to levels on the standard scale by the Criminal Justice Act 1982, ss 37, 38, 46.

SCHEDULE 2

Section 12 (4)

Resident Landlords

Part I

Provisions for Determining Application of Section 12

1. In determining whether the condition in section 12(1)(*c*) of this Act is at any time fulfilled with respect to a tenancy, there shall be disregarded—

(*a*) any period of not more than [28 days] beginning with the date on which the interest of the landlord under the tenancy becomes vested at law and in equity in an individual who, during that period, does not occupy as his residence another dwelling-house which forms part of the building [or, as the case may be, flat] concerned;

(*b*) if, within a period falling within paragraph (*a*) above, the individual concerned notifies the tenant in writing of his intention to occupy as his residence another [dwelling-house in the building or, as the case may be, flat concerned], the period beginning with the date on which the interest of the landlord under the tenancy becomes vested in that individual as mentioned in that paragraph and ending—

(i) at the expiry of the period of 6 months beginning on that date, or
(ii) on the date on which that interest ceases to be so vested, or
(iii) on the date on which the condition in section 12(1)(*c*) again applies, whichever is the earlier; and

(*c*) any period of not more than [2 years] beginning with the date on which the interest of the landlord under the tenancy becomes, and during which it remains, vested—

(i) . . .
(ii) in trustees as such; or
(iii) by virtue of section 9 of the Administration of Estates Act 1925, in the Probate Judge, within the meaning of that Act.

2. During any period when—

(*a*) the interest of the landlord under the tenancy referred to in section 12(1) is vested in trustees as such, and
(*b*) that interest is or, if it is held on trust for sale, the proceeds of its sale are held on trust for any person who occupies as his residence a dwelling-house which forms part of the building [or, as the case may be, flat] referred to in section 12(1)(*a*),

the condition in section 12(1)(*c*) shall be deemed to be fulfilled and, accordingly, no part of that period shall be disregarded by virtue of paragraph 1 above.

[2A.—(1) The tenancy referred to in section 12(1) falls within this paragraph if the interest of the landlord under the tenancy becomes vested in the personal representatives of a deceased person acting in that capacity.

(2) If the tenancy falls within this paragraph, the condition in section 12(1)(*c*) shall be deemed to be fulfilled for any period, beginning with the date on which the interest becomes vested in the personal representatives and not exceeding two years, during which the interest of the landlord remains so vested.]

3. Throughout any period which, by virtue of paragraph 1 above, falls to be disregarded for the purpose of determining whether the condition in section 12(1)(*c*) is fulfilled with respect to a tenancy, no order shall be made for possession of the dwelling-house subject to that tenancy, other than an order which might be made if that tenancy were or, as the case may be, had been a regulated tenancy.

4. For the purposes of section 12, a building is a purpose-built block of flats if as constructed it contained, and it contains, 2 or more flats; and for this purpose "flat" means dwelling-house which—

(*a*) forms part only of a building; and
(*b*) is separated horizontally from another dwelling-house which forms part of the same building.

5. For the purposes of section 12, a person shall be treated as occupying a dwelling-house as his residence if, so far as the nature of the case allows, he fulfils the same conditions as, by virtue of section 2(3) of this Act, are required to be fulfilled by a statutory tenant of a dwelling-house. **[413]**

NOTES

Commencement: 28 November 1980 (para 2A); 29 August 1977 (remainder).
Commencement order: SI 1980 No 1706.
This Part derived from the Rent Act 1968, ss 5A, 102A.
Amended by the Housing Act 1980, ss 65, 152, Sch 26.

PART II

TENANCIES CEASING TO FALL WITHIN SECTION 12

6.—(1) In any case where—

(*a*) a tenancy which, by virtue only of section 12, was precluded from being a protected tenancy ceases to be so precluded and accordingly becomes a protected tenancy and,

(*b*) before it became a protected tenancy a rent was registered for the dwelling concerned under Part V of this Act,

the amount which is so registered shall be deemed to be registered under Part IV of this Act as the rent for the dwelling-house which is let on that tenancy, and that registration shall be deemed to take effect on the day the tenancy becomes a protected tenancy.

(2) Section 67(3) of this Act shall not apply to an application for the registration under Part IV of a rent different from that which is deemed to be registered as mentioned in sub-paragraph (1) above.

(3) The reference in section 69(1)(*b*) of this Act to a rent being registered for a dwelling-house does not include a rent which is deemed to be registered as mentioned in sub-paragraph (1) above.

(4) If, immediately before a tenancy became a protected tenancy as mentioned in sub-paragraph (1)(*a*) above, the rates in respect of the dwelling-house concerned were borne as mentioned in subsection (3) of section 79 of this Act and the fact that they were so borne was noted as required by that subsection, then, in the application of Part IV in relation to the protected tenancy, section 71(2) of this Act shall be deemed to apply.

7. If, in a case where a tenancy becomes a protected tenancy as mentioned in sub-paragraph (1)(*a*) above—

(*a*) a notice to quit had been served in respect of the dwelling concerned before the date on which the tenancy became a protected tenancy, and

(*b*) the period at the end of which that notice to quit takes effect had, before that date, been extended under Part VII of this Act, and

(*c*) that period has not expired before that date,

the notice to quit shall take effect on the day following that date (whenever it would otherwise take effect) and, accordingly, on that day the protected tenancy shall become a statutory tenancy. **[414]**

NOTES

Commencement: 29 August 1977.
This Part derived from the Rent Act 1968, s 102A.

SCHEDULE 5

Section 27

CALCULATION OF AMOUNT OF RATES

1. For the purposes of this Act, the amount of rates for any rental period shall be taken, subject to this Schedule, to be an amount which bears to the total rates payable during the relevant rating period the same proportion as the length of the rental period bears to the length of the relevant rating period.

2. In this Schedule "the relevant rating period", in relation to a rental period, means the rating period during which the rent for that rental period is payable.

3. The amount of the rates for any rental period which precedes the making, by the authority levying the rates, of their first demand for, or for an instalment of, the rates for the relevant rating period shall be calculated on the basis that the rates for that rating period will be the same as for the last preceding rating period.

4.—(1) On the making, by the authority levying the rates, of their first such demand, and on the making by them of any subsequent such demand, the amount of the rates for any rental period shall if necessary be recalculated on the basis that the rates for the relevant rating period will be such as appears from the information given in the demand and any previous demands.

(2) Any such recalculation shall not affect the ascertainment of the rates for any rental period beginning more than 6 weeks before the date of the service of the demand giving rise to the recalculation.

5. If, as a result of the settlement of a proposal, the rates payable for the relevant rating period are decreased, the amount of the rates for a rental period shall be recalculated so as to give effect to the decrease; but any such recalculation shall not affect the ascertainment of the rates for any rental period beginning more than 6 weeks before the date of the settlement of the proposal.

6. In computing the rates for any rental period for the purposes of this Schedule, any discount, and any allowance made under any of the enactments relating to allowances given where rates are paid by the owner instead of by the occupier, shall be left out of account, and accordingly those rates shall be computed as if no such discount or allowance had fallen to be, or had been, allowed or made. **[415]**

NOTES

Commencement: 29 August 1977.
This Schedule derived from Rent Act 1968, Sch 4.

SCHEDULE 7

Section 44(4)

RENT LIMIT FOR CERTAIN TENANCIES FIRST REGULATED BY VIRTUE OF THE COUNTER-INFLATION ACT 1973

Special rent limit

1.—(1) This paragraph applies to a regulated tenancy—

(*a*) which was granted before 8th March 1973, and
(*b*) which would not have been a regulated tenancy but for section 14(1) of the Counter-Inflation Act 1973 (which brought certain tenancies of dwelling-houses with high rateable values within the protection of the Rent Act 1968).

(2) Subject to this Schedule, the recoverable rent for any contractual period of a tenancy to which this paragraph applies shall not exceed the limit specified in paragraph 2 below, and the amount of any excess shall, notwithstanding anything in any agreement, be irrecoverable from the tenant.

(3) Where a rent for the dwelling-house is registered under Part IV of this Act which is less than the limit specified in paragraph 2 below, neither section 44(1) nor section 45(2) of this Act shall apply to a tenancy to which this paragraph applies.

(4) Sub-paragraphs (2) and (3) above shall cease to apply if the landlord and the tenant so provide by an agreement conforming with the requirements of section 51(4) of this Act.

(5) Sub-paragraph (2) above shall not apply where a rent for the dwelling-house is registered under Part IV of this Act which is not less than the limit specified in paragraph 2 below.

2.—(1) Where, at 22nd March 1973, Article 10 of the Counter-Inflation (Rents) (England and Wales) Order 1972 applied to the rent under the tenancy (to which paragraph 1 above applies), the said limit is the rent payable under the tenancy as limited by the said Article 10 immediately before that date.

(2) In any other case the said limit is the rent payable under the terms of the tenancy (to which paragraph 1 above applies) at 22nd March 1973.

Adjustment for repairs, services or rates

3.—(1) This paragraph applies to a contractual period the rent for which is subject to paragraph 1 (2) above.

(2) In this paragraph "the previous terms" means the terms of the tenancy (to which paragraph 1 above applies) as at 22nd March 1973, and "the limit" means the limit in paragraph 2 above.

(3) Where under the terms of the tenancy there is with respect to—

(*a*) the responsibility for any repairs, or
(*b*) the provision of services by the landlord or any superior landlord, or
(*c*) the use of furniture by the tenant,

any difference compared with the previous terms, such as to affect the amount of the rent which it is reasonable to charge, the limit shall be increased by an appropriate amount.

(4) Where for the contractual period there is a difference between the amount (if any) of the rates borne by the landlord or a superior landlord in respect of the dwelling-house and the amount (if any) so borne during the first rental period for which the previous terms were agreed, the limit shall be increased or decreased by the difference.

(5) Where for the contractual period there is an increase in the cost of the provision of the services (if any) provided for the tenant by the landlord or a superior landlord compared with that cost at the time when the previous terms were agreed, such as to affect the amount of the rent which it is reasonable to charge, the limit shall be increased by an appropriate amount.

(6) Where the previous terms provide for a variation of the rent in any of the circumstances mentioned in this paragraph, the limit shall not be further varied under this paragraph by reason of the same circumstances.

(7) Any question whether, or by what amount, the limit is increased or decreased by sub-paragraph (3) or (5) above shall be determined by the county court, and any such determination—

(*a*) may be made so as to relate to past rental periods, and
(*b*) shall have effect with respect to rental periods subsequent to the periods to which it relates until revoked or varied by a subsequent determination.

4. . . . **[416]**

NOTES
Commencement: 29 August 1977.
This Schedule derived from the Counter-Inflation Act 1973, Sch 5, paras 1(1)-(5), 2-4.
Words omitted repealed by the Housing Act 1980, s 152, Sch 26.

SCHEDULE 8

Section 55

Phasing of Rent Increases: General Provisions

Interpretation

1.—(1) In this Schedule—

"noted amount" means an amount noted under paragraph 2(1) below;
"period of delay" [means—
(a) if the registered rent has been confirmed by a rent assessment committee, a period beginning with the date from which the registration of the rent took effect and ending one year after the date on which the committee took their decision; and
(b) in any other case, a period of one year beginning with the date from which the registration took effect];
"permitted increase" means the amount by which the rent for any period may be increased;
"previous rent limit" means, subject to sub-paragraphs (3) and (4) below, the amount which [immediately before the relevant date] was recoverable by way of rent or would have been so recoverable upon service of a notice or notices of increase;
"registered", in relation to a rent, means registered under Part IV of this Act and "registration" shall be construed accordingly;
["relevant date" means, in relation to a registered rent—

(a) if the rent was determined by the rent officer (and whether or not it was confirmed by a rent assessment committee), the date on which the rent was registered by the rent officer; and

(b) if the rent was determined by a rent assessment committee, the date on which the rent officer registered the rent determined by him or, as the case may be, noted in the register his confirmation of the rent for the time being registered];

"service element" means any amount calculated under paragraph 2 below;

"services" means services provided by the landlord or a superior landlord;

. . .

(2) In the case of a rent registered on or after 8th March 1974 but before 10th March 1975, the period of delay shall be taken to have begun on the later date.

(3) Where the rent includes an amount payable in respect of rates, the previous rent limit shall be decreased by the amount so payable, ascertained in accordance with Schedule 5 to this Act.

(4) Where the rent under a tenancy was rendered partly irrecoverable by an order under section 11 of the Counter-Inflation Act 1973, the previous rent limit is an amount equal to the part of the rent which was recoverable immediately before 10th March 1975.

(5), (6) . . .

Service element

2.—(1) Where—

(a) the registered rent includes a payment in respect of services, and

(b) the rent is not registered as a variable rent in accordance with section 71(4) of this Act, but

(c) not less than 5 per cent of the amount of the registered rent is in the opinion of the rent officer or rent assessment committee fairly attributable to the services,

the amount so attributable shall be noted in the register.

(2) In the Cases mentioned in the first column of the Table below, the amount of the service element shall be calculated as specified in the second column.

TABLE

CALCULATION OF SERVICE ELEMENT

Case	*Service element*
Case A. A specified amount or proportion was in the previous rent limit attributable to the provision of services, and came to less than the noted amount.	*The service element is the difference between the amount or proportion and the noted amount.*
Case B. No amount or proportion attributable to the provision of services is specified, but an amount less than the noted amount appears to the rent officer or rent assessment committee to have been attributable to such provision.	*The service element is the difference between—* *(a) an amount bearing to the previous rent limit the same proportion as the noted amount bears to the registered rent, and* *(b) the noted amount.*
Case C. No amount appears to the rent officer or rent assessment committee to have been attributable in the previous rent limit to the provision of services.	*The service element is the noted amount.*

(3) The amount of the service element shall be recorded in the register, and in Case C above may be recorded by adding to the note under sub-paragraph (1) above a statement that the noted amount is the service element.

General formulae for calculating increases in rent

[3.—(1) Subject to sub-paragraph (2) below, the permitted increase for a period falling within the period of delay is an increase to an amount calculated by applying the formula—

1/2 (P+S+R)

where—

P is the previous rent limit,
S is the service element, and
R is the registered rent.

(2) The maximum permitted increase by virtue of this Schedule is an increase to the registered rent.]

Subsequent registrations

[4. Where the registration of a rent takes effect in a period of delay which began by reference to an earlier registration, then—

(a) from the date on which the later registration takes effect the limitation under that period of delay shall cease to apply; and
(b) a fresh period of delay shall begin by reference to the later registration.]

Amounts to be noted on certificate of fair rent

5. Where the rent specified in a certificate of fair rent includes a payment in respect of services and the amount which in the opinion of the rent officer or rent assessment committee is fairly attributable to the provision of the services is not less than 5 per cent of the amount of the rent, then, if the applicant so requests, the amount so attributable shall be noted in the certificate of fair rent together with the amount of the service element.

General

6. The amount of any service element or of any amount sought to be noted in the register or in the certificate of fair rent in pursuance of this Schedule shall be included among the matters with respect to which representations may be made or consultations are to be held or notices given under Parts I and II of Schedule 11, and under Schedule 12 to this Act.

7. In ascertaining for the purposes of this Schedule whether there is any difference between amounts, or what that difference is, such adjustments shall be made as may be necessary to take account of periods of different lengths; and for that purpose a month shall be treated as one-twelfth and a week as one-fifty-second of a year.

8. . . .

9. This Schedule is subject to paragraph 3 of Schedule 20 to this Act.

10. Where any provision of this Schedule imposes a rent limit for a statutory period, or part of a statutory period, falling within the period of delay, section 45(2) of this Act shall have effect as if for references to the registered rent there were substituted references to that rent limit. **[417]**

NOTES

Commencement: 29 August 1977 (paras 1, 2, 5-10); 28 November 1980 (paras 3, 4).
Commencement order: SI 1980 No 1706.
Repealed in so far as it relates to s 55 by SI 1987 No 264, art 2 except in relation to the circumstances and to the extent specified in Sch 2 to that Order.
Paras 1-8, 10 derived from the Housing Rents and Subsidies Act 1975, s 16(1), Sch 2.
Amended by the Housing Act 1980, ss 60(3), 61(6), 152, Sch 26.

SCHEDULE 10

Section 65

RENT ASSESSMENT COMMITTEES

1. The Secretary of State shall draw up and from time to time revise panels of persons to act as chairmen and other members of rent assessment committees for such areas,

comprising together every registration area, as the Secretary of State may from time to time determine.

2. Each panel shall consist of a number of persons appointed by the Lord Chancellor and a number of persons appointed by the Secretary of State . . .

3. The Secretary of State shall nominate one of the persons appointed by the Lord Chancellor to act as president of the panel, and one or more such persons to act as vice-president or vice-presidents.

4. Subject to this Schedule, the number of rent assessment committees to act for an area and the constitution of those committees shall be determined by the president of the panel formed for that area or, in the case of the president's absence or incapacity, by the vice-president or, as the case may be, one of the vice-presidents.

5. Subject to [paragraphs 6 and 6A] below, each rent assessment committee shall consist of a chairman and one or two other members, and the chairman shall be either the president or vice-president (or, as the case may be one of the vice-presidents) of the panel or one of the other members appointed by the Lord Chancellor.

6. The president of the panel may, if he thinks fit, direct that when dealing with such cases or dealing with a case in such circumstances as may be specified in the direction, the chairman sitting alone may, with the consent of the parties, exercise the functions of a rent assessment committee.

[6A. When dealing with an application under section 81A of this Act a rent assessment committee carrying out the functions of a rent tribunal shall consist of the chairman of the committee sitting alone.]

7. There shall be paid to members of panels such remuneration and allowances as the Secretary of State, with the consent of the Minister for the Civil Service, may determine.

[7A. The Secretary of State may, with the consent of the Minister for the Civil Service, provide for the payment of pensions, allowances or gratuities to or in respect of any person nominated to act as president or vice-president of a panel.]

8. The president of the panel may appoint, with the approval of the Secretary of State as to numbers, such clerks and other officers and servants of rent assessment committees as he thinks fit, and there shall be paid to the clerks and other officers and servants such salaries and allowances as the Secretary of State, with the consent of the Minister for the Civil Service, may determine.

9. There shall be paid out of moneys provided by Parliament—

(*a*) the remuneration and allowances of members of panels;
(*b*) the salaries and allowances of clerks and other officers and servants appointed under this Schedule; and
(*c*) such other expenses of a panel as the Minister for the Civil Service may determine.

10. . . . **[418]**

NOTES
Commencement: 28 November 1980 (para 6A); 3 October 1980 (para 7A); 29 August 1977 (remainder).
Commencement orders: SI 1980 No 1406, 1980 No 1706.
This Schedule derived from the Rent Act 1968, Sch 5.
Amended by the Housing Act 1980, ss 71(2), 148, 152, Schs 25, 26.

SCHEDULE 11

Section 67

Applications for Registration of Rent

PART I

APPLICATION UNSUPPORTED BY CERTIFICATE OF FAIR RENT

Procedure on application to rent officer

1. On receiving any application for the registration of a rent, the rent officer may, by notice in writing served on the landlord or on the tenant (whether or not the applicant or one of the applicants) require him to give to the rent officer, within such period of not less than 7 days from the service of the notice as may be specified in the notice, such information as he may reasonably require regarding such of the particulars contained in the application as may be specified in the notice.

[2.—(1) Where the application is made jointly by the landlord and the tenant and it appears to the rent officer, after making such inquiry, if any, as he thinks fit and considering any information supplied to him in pursuance of paragraph 1 above, that the rent specified in the application is a fair rent, he may register that rent without further proceedings.

(2) Where the rent officer registers a rent under this paragraph he shall notify the landlord and tenant accordingly.

3.—(1) In the case of an application which does not fall within paragraph 2 above, the rent officer shall serve on the landlord and on the tenant a notice inviting the person on whom the notice is served to state in writing, within a period of not less than seven days after the service of the notice, whether he wishes the rent officer to consider, in consultation with the landlord and the tenant, what rent ought to be registered for the dwelling-house.

(2) A notice served under sub-paragraph (1) above on the person who did not make the application shall be accompanied—

(*a*) by a copy of the application; and
(*b*) where, in pursuance of section 67(2)(*b*), the application was accompanied by details of the landlord's expenditure in connection with the provisions of services, by a copy of those details.

3A. If, after service of a notice by the rent officer under paragraph 3 above, no request in writing is made within the period specified in the notice for the rent to be considered as mentioned in that paragraph, the rent officer after considering what rent ought to be registered or, as the case may be, whether a different rent ought to be registered, may—

(*a*) determine a fair rent and register it as the rent for the dwelling-house; or
(*b*) confirm the rent for the time being registered and note the confirmation in the register; or
(*c*) serve a notice under paragraph 4(2) below.]

4.—[(1) Where, in response to a notice served by the rent officer under paragraph 3(1) above, the landlord or the tenant states in writing that he wishes the rent to be considered as mentioned in that paragraph, the rent officer shall serve a notice under this paragraph.]

(2) A notice, under this paragraph shall be served on the landlord and on the tenant informing them that the rent officer proposes, at a time (which shall not be earlier than 7 days after the service of the [notice, or 14 days in a case falling within paragraph 3(2)(*b*) above)] and place specified in the notice, to consider in consultation with the landlord and the tenant, or such of them as may appear at that time and place, what rent ought to be registered for the dwelling-house or, as the case may be, whether a different rent ought to be so registered.

(3) At any such consultation the landlord and the tenant may each be represented by a person authorised by him in that behalf, whether or not that person is of counsel or a solicitor.

[(4) The rent officer may, where he considers it appropriate, arrange for consultations in respect of one dwelling-house to be held together with consultations in respect of one or more other dwelling-houses.

5. After considering, in accordance with paragraph 4 above, what rent ought to be registered or, as the case may be, whether a different rent ought to be registered, the rent officer shall, as the case may require,—

(*a*) determine a fair rent and register it as the rent for the dwelling-house; or

(*b*) confirm the rent for the time being registered and note the confirmation in the register;

. . .

[5A. Where a rent has been registered or confirmed by the rent officer under paragraph 3A or 5 above, he shall] notify the landlord and the tenant accordingly by a notice stating that if, within 28 days of the service of the notice or such longer period as he or a rent assessment committee may allow, an objection in writing is received by the rent officer from the landlord or the tenant the matter will be referred to a rent assessment committee.

6.—(1) If such an objection as is mentioned in paragraph [5A] above is received then—

(*a*) if it is received within the period of 28 days specified in that paragraph or a rent assessment committee so direct, the rent officer shall refer the matter to a rent assessment committee;

(*b*) if it is received after the expiry of that period the rent officer may either refer the matter to a rent assessment committee or seek the directions of a rent assessment committee whether so to refer it.

(2) The rent officer shall indicate in the register whether the matter has been referred to a rent assessment committee in pursuance of this paragraph.

Determination of fair rent by rent assessment committee

7.—(1) The rent assessment committee to whom a matter is referred under paragraph 6 above—

(*a*) may by notice in the prescribed form served on the landlord or the tenant require him to give to the committee, within such period of not less than [7 days] from the service of the notice as may be specified in the notice, such further information, in addition to any given to the rent officer in pursuance of paragraph 1 above, as they may reasonably require; and

(*b*) shall serve on the landlord and on the tenant a notice specifying a period of not less than 14 days from the service of the notice during which either representations in writing or a request to make oral representations may be made by him to the committee.

(2) If any person fails without reasonable cause to comply with any notice served on him under sub-paragraph (1)(*a*) above, he shall be liable [to a fine not exceeding level 3 on the standard scale].

(3) Where an offence under sub-paragraph (2) above committed by a body corporate is proved to have been committed with the consent or connivance of, or to be attributable to any neglect on the part of, any director, manager or secretary or other similar officer of the body corporate or any person who was purporting to act in any such capacity, he as well as the body corporate shall be guilty of that offence and shall be liable to be proceeded against and punished accordingly.

8. Where, within the period specified in paragraph 7(1)(*b*) above, or such further period as the committee may allow, the landlord or the tenant requests to make oral representations the committee shall give him an opportunity to be heard either in person or by a person authorised by him in that behalf, whether or not that person is of counsel or a solicitor.

9.—(1) The committee shall make such inquiry, if any, as they think fit and consider any information supplied or representation made to them in pursuance of paragraph 7 or paragraph 8 above and—

(*a*) if it appears to them that the rent registered or confirmed by the rent officer is a fair rent, they shall confirm that rent;
(*b*) if it does not appear to them that that rent is a fair rent, they shall determine a fair rent for the dwelling-house.

(2) Where the committee confirm or determine a rent under this paragraph they shall notify the landlord, the tenant and the rent officer [of their decision and of the date on which it was made].

(3) On receiving the notification, the rent officer shall, as the case may require, either indicate in the register that the rent has been confirmed or register the rent determined by the committee as the rent for the dwelling-house. **[419]**

NOTES
Commencement: 28 November 1980 (paras 2,3,3A,5A); 29 August 1977 (remainder).
This Part derived from the Rent Act 1968, Sch 6, paras 1-9.
Paras 2-6: amended by the Regulated Tenancies (Procedure) Regulations 1980, SI 1980 No 1696.
Para 7: sub-para (1) amended by the Rent Assessment Committees (England and Wales) (Amendment) Regulations 1981, SI 1981 No 1783 as respects matters referred after 1 January 1982; in sub-para (2) enhanced penalty on a subsequent conviction now abolished, maximum fine on any conviction increased and converted to level 3 on the standard scale by the Criminal Justice Act 1982, ss 35, 37, 38, 46.
Para 9: amended by the Housing Act 1980, s 61(7).

PART II

APPLICATION SUPPORTED BY CERTIFICATE OF FAIR RENT (EXCEPT WHERE CERTIFICATE ISSUED BY VIRTUE OF PART VIII)

Procedure on application to rent officer

10.—(1) On receiving an application for the registration of a rent which is made as mentioned in section 69(4) of this Act, the rent officer shall ascertain whether the works specified in the certificate have been carried out in accordance with the plans and specifications which accompanied the application for the certificate or, as the case may be, whether—

(*a*) the condition of the dwelling-house is the same as at the date of the certificate, and
(*b*) if any furniture is or is to be provided for use under a regulated tenancy of the dwelling-house, the quantity, quality and condition of the furniture in the dwelling-house accords with the prescribed particulars contained in the application for the certificate.

(2) If the rent officer is satisfied that the works have been so carried out or, as the case may be, that—

(*a*) the dwelling-house is in the same condition as at the date of the certificate, and
(*b*) if any furniture is or is to be provided for use under a regulated tenancy of the dwelling-house, the quantity, quality and condition of the furniture in the dwelling-house accords with the prescribed particulars contained in the application for the certificate,

he shall register the rent in accordance with the certificate,

(3) If the rent officer is not satisfied as mentioned in sub-paragraph (2) above, he shall serve on the applicant a notice stating the matters with respect to which he is not so satisfied and informing him that if, within 14 days from the service of the notice or such longer period as the rent officer or a rent assessment committee may allow, the applicant makes a request in writing to that effect, the rent officer will refer the matter to a rent assessment committee.

11. If such a request as is mentioned in paragraph 10(3) above is made, then—

(*a*) if it is made within the period of 14 days specified in that paragraph or a rent assessment committee so direct, the rent officer shall refer the matter to a rent assessment committee;

(*b*) if it is made after the expiry of that period, the rent officer may either refer the matter to a rent assessment committee or seek the directions of a rent assessment committee whether so to refer it.

Procedure on reference to rent assessment committee

12.—(1) The rent assessment committee to whom a matter is referred under paragraph 11 above shall give the applicant an opportunity to make representations in writing or to be heard either in person or by a person authorised by him in that behalf, whether or not that person is of counsel or a solicitor.

(2) After considering any representations made under sub-paragraph (1) above, the rent assessment committee shall notify the rent officer and the applicant whether they are satisfied as mentioned in paragraph 10(2) above and—

(*a*) if they are so satisfied they shall direct the rent officer to register the rent in accordance with the certificate;

(*b*) if they are not so satisfied they shall direct the rent officer to refuse the application for registration.

Provisional registration

13., 14. . . . **[420]**

NOTES

Commencement: 29 August 1977.
This Part derived from the Rent Act 1968, Sch 6, paras 10–14.
Words omitted repealed by the Housing Act 1980, s 152, Sch 26.

SCHEDULE 12

Section 69(3)

CERTIFICATES OF FAIR RENT

1. An application for a certificate of fair rent—

(*a*) must be in the prescribed form;

(*b*) must state the rent to be specified in the certificate;

(*c*) in the case mentioned in section 69(1)(*a*) [or (1A)(*b*)] of this Act . . . , must be accompanied by plans and specifications of the works to be carried out and, if the works to be carried out are works of improvement [or repair], must state whether the dwelling-house is for the time being subject to a regulated [or secure] tenancy; and

(*d*) if any furniture is to be provided for use under a regulated tenancy of the dwelling-house, must contain the prescribed particulars with regard to any such furniture.

[2. On receiving any application for a certificate of a fair rent, the rent officer may, by notice in writing served on the applicant or on the tenant, (if any), require him to give to the rent officer within such period of not less than seven days from the service of the notice as may be specified in the notice, such information as he may reasonably require regarding such of the particulars contained in the application as may be specified in the Notice.]

3. If [in the case of—

(*a*) an application under section 69(1) of this Act where the dwelling-house is not subject to a regulated tenancy, or

(*b*) an application under section 69(1A) of this Act where the dwelling-house is not subject to a secure tenancy,];

. . . it appears to the rent officer . . . that the rent stated in the application would be a fair rent he may, *unless the dwelling-house is subject to a regulated tenancy*, issue a certificate specifying that rent and the other terms referred to in section 69(2) of this Act.

[4. In the case of *an application which does not fall within paragraph 3 above and where the dwelling-house is not subject to a regulated tenancy*

[(*a*) an application under section 69(1) of this Act where the dwelling-house is not subject to a regulated tenancy and which does not fall within paragraph 3 above, or

(*b*) an application under section 69(1A) of this Act and which does not fall within paragraph 3 above and where the dwelling-house is not subject to a secure tenancy,], the rent officer shall, after consulting the applicant, consider what rent ought to be specified in the certificate, determine a fair rent, and serve notice under paragraph 7 below.

5.—(1) *Where the dwelling-house is subject to a regulated tenancy,* [In the case of—

(*a*) an application under section 69(1) of this Act where the dwelling-house is subject to a regulated tenancy, or

(*b*) an application under section 69(1A) of this Act where the dwelling-house is subject to a secure tenancy,] the rent officer shall serve on the applicant and on the tenant a notice inviting the person on whom it is served to state in writing, within a period of not less than seven days after the service of the notice, whether he wishes the rent officer in consultation with the applicant and the tenant to consider what rent ought to be specified in the certificate, and the notice served on the tenant shall be accompanied by a copy of the application for the certificate.

(2) If, after service of a notice by the rent officer under sub-paragraph (1) above, no request in writing is made within the period specified in the notice for the rent to be considered as mentioned in that sub-paragraph, the rent officer may—

(*a*) consider what rent ought to be specified in the certificate, determine a fair rent, and serve a notice under paragraph 7 below, or

(*b*) serve a notice under paragraph 6(2) below.

6.—(1) Where, in response to a notice served by a rent officer under paragraph 5(1) above the applicant or the tenant states in writing that he wishes the rent to be considered as mentioned in that paragraph, the rent officer shall serve a notice under this paragraph.

(2) A notice under this paragraph shall state that the rent officer proposes, at a time (which shall not be earlier than seven days after the service of the notice) and place specified in the notice, to consider in consultation with the applicant and with the tenant, or such of them as may appear at that time and place, what rent ought to be specified in the certificate.

(3) At any such consultation the applicant and the tenant may each be represented by a person authorised by him in that behalf, whether or not that person is of counsel or a solicitor.

(4) The rent officer may, where he considers it appropriate, arrange for consultations in respect of one dwelling-house to be held together with consultations in respect of one or more other dwelling-houses.

(5) After considering, in accordance with this paragraph, what rent ought to be specified in the certificate, the rent officer shall determine a fair rent and shall serve a notice under paragraph 7 below.

7. After determining a fair rent in accordance with paragraphs 4, 5(2) or 6(5) above, the rent officer shall serve on the applicant a notice stating that he proposes to issue a certificate specifying that rent, unless within 14 days from the service of the notice, or such longer period as the rent officer or a rent assessment committee may allow, the applicant requests in writing that the application should be referred to a rent assessment committee.

8.—(1) If such a request as is referred to in paragraph 7 above is made, then, subject to sub-paragraph (3) below—

(*a*) if it is made within the period of 14 days referred to in that paragraph or a rent assessment committee so direct, the rent officer shall refer the application to a rent assessment committee;

(*b*) if it is made after the expiry of those 14 days, the rent officer may either refer the application to a rent assessment committee or seek the directions of a rent assessment committee whether so to refer to it.

(2) The rent officer shall issue the certificate if—

(*a*) no such request is made, or
(*b*) such a request is made but the application is not referred to a rent assessment committee, or
(*c*) in a case where the dwelling-house is not subject to a regulated [or secure] tenancy, the applicant informs the rent officer in writing that he does not propose to make such a request.

(3) An application shall not be capable of being referred to a rent assessment commmittee at any time after the rent officer has issued the certificate in accordance with sub-paragraph (2) above.

9.—(1) Where an application is referred to a rent assessment committee, they shall serve on the applicant a notice specifying a period of not less than [7 days] from the service of the notice during which either representations in writing or a request to make oral representations may be made by him to the committee.

(2) Where, within the period specified under sub-paragraph (1) above or such further period as the committee may allow, the applicant requests to make oral representations, the committee shall give him an opportunity to be heard either in person or by a person authorised by him in that behalf, whether or not that person is of counsel or a solicitor.

10.—(1) After considering any representation made to them in pursuance of paragraph 9 above, the committee shall determine a fair rent for the dwelling-house and shall notify the applicant and the rent officer accordingly.

(2) On receiving the notification the rent officer shall issue to the applicant a certificate of fair rent specifying the rent determined by the committee.

11. Where an application under this Schedule is made with respect to a dwelling-house which is subject to a regulated [or secure] tenancy;

(*a*) a notice under paragraph 7, 9(1) or 10 above shall be served on the tenant as well as on the applicant and any notice served under paragraph 7 or 9(1) above shall refer to consultation with, or, as the case may be, a request or representations by, the tenant as well as the applicant;
(*b*) the tenant may make representations, request reference to a rent assessment committee and be present or represented in like manner as the applicant, and references in this Schedule to the applicant shall be construed accordingly; and
(*c*) a copy of any certificate of fair rent issued in pursuance of the application shall be sent to the tenant.]

[12. In this Schedule "secure tenancy" has the same meaning as in Part IV of the Housing Act 1985, but does not include such a tenancy where the landlord is the Housing Corporation, a housing association or a housing trust which is a charity.

In this paragraph "housing association", "housing trust" and "charity" have the same meaning as in Part IV of the Housing Act 1985.] **[421]**

NOTES

Commencement: 29 August 1977 (paras 1, 3); 28 November 1980 (paras 2, 4-11); to be appointed (remainder).

This Schedule derived from the Rent Act 1968, Sch 7.

Para 1: words omitted repealed by the Housing Act 1980, s 152, Sch 26; words in square brackets prospectively added by the Housing and Planning Act 1986, s 24(2), Sch 5, Part II, para 16, as from a day to be appointed.

Para 2: substituted by the Regulated Tenancies (Procedure) Regulations 1980, SI 1980 No 1696.

Para 3: words in square brackets prospectively added and words in italics prospectively repealed by the Housing and Planning Act 1986, s 24(2), (3), Sch 5, Part II, para 16, Sch 12, Part I, as from a day to be appointed; first words omitted repealed by the Housing Act 1980, s 152, Sch 26; second words omitted repealed by SI 1980 No 1696.

Paras 4, 5: substituted by SI 1980 No 1696, reg 3, Sch 2; words in italics prospectively repealed and words in square brackets prospectively substituted by the Housing and Planning Act 1986, s 24(2), Sch 5, Part II, para 16, as from a day to be appointed.

Paras 6, 7, 10: substituted by SI 1980 No 1696, reg 3, Sch 2.

Para 8: substituted by SI 1980 No 1696, reg 3, Sch 2; amendment in sub-para (2)(*c*) prospectively added by the Housing and Planning Act 1986, s 24(2), Sch 5, Part II, para 16, as from a day to be appointed.

Para 9: substituted by SI 1980 No 1696, reg 3, Sch 2; amended by the Rent Assessment Committees (England and Wales)(Amendment) Regulations 1981, SI 1981 No 1783.

Para 11: substituted by SI 1980 No 1696, reg 3, Sch 2; amendment in square brackets prospectively made by the Housing and Planning Act 1986, s 24(2), Sch 5, Part II, para 16, as from a day to be appointed.

Para 12: prospectively added by the Housing and Planning Act 1986, s 24(2), Sch 5, Part II, para 16, as from a day to be appointed.

SCHEDULE 14

Section 92

Conversion of Housing Association Tenancies into Regulated Tenancies

1.—(1) This paragraph applies in any case where—

(*a*) a tenancy of a dwelling-house under which the interest of the landlord belonged to a housing association came to an end at a time before 1st April 1975, and

(*b*) on the date when it came to an end, the tenancy was one to which Part VIII of the 1972 Act (which is superseded by Part VI of this Act) applied, and

(*c*) if the tenancy had come to an end on 1st April 1975 it would, by virtue of section 18(1) of the 1974 Act have then been a protected tenancy for the purposes of the Rent Act 1968.

(2) If on 1st April 1975 a person who was the tenant under the tenancy which came to an end duly retained possession of the dwelling-house, he shall be deemed to have done so as a statutory tenant under a regulated tenancy and as a person who became a statutory tenant on the termination of a protected tenancy under which he was the tenant.

(3) If on 1st April 1975 a person duly retained possession of the dwelling-house as being a person who, in the circumstances described in sub-paragraph (5) below, would have been the first successor, within the meaning of Schedule 1 to the Rent Act 1968, he shall be deemed to have done so as the statutory tenant under a regulated tenancy and as a person who became a statutory tenant by virtue of paragraph 2 or 3 of Schedule 1 to this Act.

(4) If on 1st April 1975 a person duly retained possession of the dwelling-house as being a person who, in the circumstances described in sub-paragraph (5) below, would have become the statutory tenant on the death of a first successor, he shall be deemed to have done so as a statutory tenant under a regulated tenancy and as a person who became a statutory tenant by virtue of paragraph 6 or 7 of Schedule 1 to this Act.

(5) The circumstances mentioned in sub-paragraphs (3) and (4) above are that—

(*a*) the tenant under the tenancy, or any person to whom the dwelling-house or any part thereof had been lawfully sublet has died; and

(*b*) if the deceased had been the original tenant within the meaning of Schedule 1 to the Rent Act 1968, the person duly retaining possession of the dwelling-house would have been the first successor within the meaning of that Schedule or would have become the statutory tenant on the death of that first successor.

(6) References in this paragraph to a person duly retaining possession of a dwelling-house are references to his retaining possession without any order for possession having been made or, where such an order has been made—

(*a*) during any period while its operation is postponed or its execution is suspended; or

(*b*) after it has been rescinded.

(7) Subject to sub-paragraph (8) below, the tenancy referred to in sub-paragraph (1) above shall be treated as the original contract of tenancy for the purposes of section 3 of

this Act in relation to a statutory tenancy imposed by any of sub-paragraphs (2) to (4) above.

(8) The High Court or the county court may by order vary all or any of the terms of a statutory tenancy imposed by any of sub-paragraphs (2) to (4) above in any way appearing to the court to be just and equitable (and whether or not in a way authorised by sections 46 and 47 of this Act).

2.—(1) If, in a case where either a tenancy has become a protected tenancy by virtue of section 18(1) of the 1974 Act or by virtue of subsections (1) and (3) of section 15 of this Act or a statutory tenancy has been imposed by virtue of paragraph 1 above—

(*a*) a rent (the "previous registered rent") was registered for the dwelling-house at a time when Part VIII of the 1972 Act or Part VI of this Act applied to that tenancy or, as the case may be, to the tenancy referred to in paragraph 1 (1) above; and

(*b*) a rent has subsequently been registered for the dwelling-house under Part IV of this Act but the rent so registered is less than the previous registered rent,

then subject to paragraph 4 below, until such time as a rent is registered under Part IV which is higher than the previous registered rent, the contractual rent limit or, as the case may be, the maximum rent recoverable during any statutory period of the regulated tenancy concerned shall be the previous registered rent.

(2) If in a case falling within sub-paragraph (1) above, the Secretary of State has, in a direction under section 90 of this Act, specified a rent limit for the dwelling-house higher than the previous registered rent, then, during the period for which that direction has effect as mentioned in that section, sub-paragraph (1) above shall have effect with the substitution for any reference to the previous registered rent of a reference to the rent limit so specified.

(3) Nothing in this paragraph shall affect the operation of section 73 of this Act and, accordingly, where the registration of a rent is cancelled in accordance with that section, sub-paragraph (1) above shall cease to apply in relation to the rent of the dwelling-house concerned.

3.—(1) This paragraph applies for the purposes of the application of Part III of this Act in relation to—

(*a*) a tenancy which has become a protected tenancy by virtue of section 18(1) of the 1974 Act or by virtue of subsections (1) and (3) of section 15 of this Act,

(*b*) a statutory tenancy arising on the termination of such a tenancy, and

(*c*) a statutory tenancy imposed by virtue of paragraph 1 above,

in any case where at the time when Part VIII of the 1972 Act or Part VI of this Act applied to the tenancy referred to in paragraph (*a*) above or, as the case may require, paragraph 1(1) above, section 83(3) of the 1972 Act or section 88(4) of this Act, applied.

(2) Where this paragraph applies, the rent limit applicable to the tenancy or statutory tenancy referred to in sub-paragraph (1) above shall be deemed to be (or, as the case may be, to have been) the contractual rent limit under the relevant tenancy, but without prejudice to the subsequent registration of a rent for the dwelling-house under Part IV of this Act or (during the currency of a protected tenancy) the making of an agreement under section 51 of this Act increasing the rent payable.

(3) Sub-paragraph (2) above shall have effect notwithstanding the repeal by the 1972 Act of section 20(3) of the Rent Act 1968 (contractual rent limit before registration), but nothing in this paragraph shall be taken as applying any provisions of section 88 of this Act to a tenancy at a time when it is a protected tenancy.

(4) In this paragraph "the relevant tenancy" means—

(*a*) in the case of a tenancy falling within sub-paragraph (1)(*a*) above, that tenancy;

(*b*) in the case of a statutory tenancy falling within sub-paragraph (1)(*b*) above, the tenancy referred to in sub-paragraph (1)(*a*) above; and

(*c*) in the case of a statutory tenancy falling within sub-paragraph (1)(*c*) above, the protected tenancy referred to in sub-paragraph (2) of paragraph 1 above or, in a case where sub-paragraph (3) or (4) of that paragraph applies, a notional protected tenancy which, when taken with that regulated tenancy would, by virtue of section 18(2) of this Act, be treated for the purposes of this Act as constituting one regulated tenancy when taken together with the statutory tenancy.

4.—(1) This paragraph applies where—

(*a*) a tenancy of a dwelling-house has become a protected tenancy by virtue of section 18(1) of the 1974 Act or by virtue of subsections (1) and (3) of section 15 of this Act, or a statutory tenancy is imposed by virtue of paragraph 1 above; and

(*b*) immediately before the tenancy became a protected tenancy or, as the case may require, immediately before the tenancy referred to in paragraph 1(1) above came to an end, section 84 of the 1972 Act or section 89 of this Act applied to the rent of the dwelling-house let on that tenancy.

(2) In this paragraph "the regulated tenancy" means the regulated tenancy consisting of the protected or statutory tenancy referred to in sub-paragraph (1)(*a*) above, together with any subsequent statutory tenancy which, when taken with that regulated tenancy is by virtue of section 18(2) of this Act treated for the purposes of this Act as constituting one regulated tenancy.

(3) Subject to the following provisions of this paragraph, section 89 of this Act shall apply to the rent of a dwelling-house subject to the regulated tenancy.

(4) Section 89 of this Act shall cease to apply by virtue of this paragraph to the rent of a dwelling-house—

(*a*) on the date on which a rent is registered for the dwelling-house under Part IV of this Act; or

(*b*) on the date on which a new regulated tenancy of the dwelling-house is granted to a person who is neither the tenant under the regulated tenancy nor a person who might succeed him as a statutory tenant.

(5) If and so long as, by virtue of this paragraph, subsection (2) of section 89 of this Act imposes for any rental period of a tenancy or statutory tenancy a rent limit below the rent registered for the dwelling-house as mentioned in subsection (1) of that section,—

(*a*) the contractual rent limit shall be the rent limit so imposed and not the registered rent (as provided by section 44(1) of this Act) and section 93 of this Act shall apply in relation to the tenancy as if it were one to which Part VI of this Act applied; and

(*b*) a notice of increase under section 45(2)(*b*) of this Act may not increase the rent for any statutory period above the rent limit so imposed, and any such notice which purports to increase it further shall have effect to increase it to that limit but no further.

5.—(1) This paragraph has effect with respect to the application of Schedule 9 to this Act in relation to a regulated tenancy consisting of—

(*a*) a tenancy which has become a protected tenancy by virtue of section 18(1) of the 1974 Act or by virtue of subsections (1) and (3) of section 15 of this Act, or

(*b*) a statutory tenancy imposed by virtue of paragraph 1 above,

together with any subsequent statutory tenancy which, when taken with that regulated tenancy, is by virtue of section 18(2) of this Act treated for the purposes of this Act as constituting one regulated tenancy.

(2) For the purposes of paragraph 1(1)(*b*) of Schedule 9, a tenancy falling within sub-paragraph (1)(*a*) above shall be deemed to have been a regulated tenancy throughout the period when Part VIII of the 1972 Act or Part VI of this Act applied to it.

(3) In the case of a regulated tenancy falling within sub-paragraph (1)(*b*) above, paragraph 1(1)(*b*) of Schedule 9 shall have effect as if the reference to the completion of works during the existence of the regulated tenancy included a reference to their completion during the period beginning on the day on which Part VIII of the 1972 Act or Part VI of this Act first applied to the tenancy referred to in paragraph 1(1) above and ending on the day on which the regulated tenancy came into existence.

(4) The reference in paragraph 3(1) of Schedule 9 to notices of increase authorised by this Act shall include a reference to notices of increase under section 87 of the 1972 Act.

6. . . .

7. In the application of section 70 of this Act in relation to a tenancy which has become a protected tenancy by virtue of section 18(1) of the 1974 Act or by virtue of subsections (1) and (3) of section 15 of this Act or a statutory tenancy which is imposed by virtue of paragraph 1 above, the reference in subsection (3) to a failure to comply with any terms of a regulated tenancy or to carrying out an improvement includes a reference to a failure occurring or an improvement carried out before the tenancy became a regulated tenancy or, as the case may be, before the statutory tenancy was imposed.

8. In this Schedule "the 1972 Act" means the Housing Finance Act 1972 and "the 1974 Act" means the Housing Act 1974. **[422]**

NOTES

Commencement: 29 August 1977.
This Schedule derived from the Housing Act 1974, Sch 3.
Para 6: repealed by the Housing Act 1980, s 152, Sch 26.

SCHEDULE 15

Section 98

GROUNDS FOR POSSESSION OF DWELLING-HOUSES LET ON OR SUBJECT TO PROTECTED OR STATUTORY TENANCIES

PART I

CASES IN WHICH COURT MAY ORDER POSSESSION

Case 1

Where any rent lawfully due from the tenant has not been paid, or any obligation of the protected or statutory tenancy which arises under this Act, or—

(*a*) in the case of a protected tenancy, any other obligation of the tenancy, in so far as is consistent with the provisions of Part VII of this Act, or
(*b*) in the case of a statutory tenancy, any other obligation of the previous protected tenancy which is applicable to the statutory tenancy,

has been broken or not performed.

Case 2

Where the tenant or any person residing or lodging with him or any sub-tenant of his has been guilty of conduct which is a nuisance or annoyance to adjoining occupiers, or has been convicted of using the dwelling-house or allowing the dwelling-house to be used for immoral or illegal purposes.

Case 3

Where the condition of the dwelling-house has, in the opinion of the court, deteriorated owing to acts of waste by, or the neglect or default of, the tenant or any person residing or lodging with him or any sub-tenant of his and, in the case of any act of waste by, or the neglect or default of, a person lodging with the tenant or a sub-tenant of his, where the court is satisfied that the tenant has not, before the making of the order in question, taken such steps as he ought reasonably to have taken for the removal of the lodger or sub-tenant, as the case may be.

Case 4

Where the condition of any furniture provided for use under the tenancy has, in the opinion of the court, deteriorated owing to ill-treatment by the tenant or any person residing or lodging with him or any sub-tenant of his and, in the case of any ill-treatment by a person lodging with the tenant or a sub-tenant of his, where the court is satisfied that the tenant has not, before the making of the order in question, taken such steps as he ought reasonably to have taken for the removal of the lodger or sub-tenant, as the case may be.

Case 5

Where the tenant has given notice to quit and, in consequence of that notice, the landlord has contracted to sell or let the dwelling-house or has taken any other steps as the result of which he would, in the opinion of the court, be seriously prejudiced if he could not obtain possession.

Case 6

Where, without the consent of the landlord, the tenant has, at any time after—

(*a*) . . .
(*b*) 22nd March 1973, in the case of a tenancy which became a regulated tenancy by virtue of section 14 of the Counter-Inflation Act 1973;
[(*bb*) the commencement of section 73 of the Housing Act 1980, in the case of a tenancy which became a regulated tenancy by virtue of that section;]
(*c*) 14th August 1974, in the case of a regulated furnished tenancy; or
(*d*) 8th December 1965, in the case of any other tenancy,

assigned or sublet the whole of the dwelling-house or sublet part of the dwelling-house, the remainder being already sublet.

. . .

Case 8

Where the dwelling-house is reasonably required by the landlord for occupation as a residence for some person engaged in his whole-time employment, or in the whole-time employment of some tenant from him or with whom, conditional on housing being provided, a contract for such employment has been entered into, and the tenant was in the employment of the landlord or a former landlord, and the dwelling-house was let to him in consequence of that employment and he has ceased to be in that employment.

Case 9

Where the dwelling-house is reasonably required by the landlord for occupation as a residence for—

(*a*) himself, or
(*b*) any son or daughter of his over 18 years of age, or
(*c*) his father or mother, or
(*d*) if the dwelling-house is let on or subject to a regulated tenancy, the father or mother of his wife or husband,

and the landlord did not become landlord by purchasing the dwelling-house or any interest therein after—

(i) 7th November 1956, in the case of a [tenancy which was then a controlled tenancy];
(ii) 8th March 1973, in the case of a tenancy which became a regulated tenancy by virtue of section 14 of the Counter-Inflation Act 1973;
(iii) 24th May 1974, in the case of a regulated furnished tenancy; or
(iv) 23rd March 1965, in the case of any other tenancy.

Case 10

Where the court is satisfied that the rent charged by the tenant—

(*a*) for any sublet part of the dwelling-house which is a dwelling-house let on a protected tenancy or subject to a statutory tenancy is or was in excess of the maximum rent for the time being recoverable for that part, having regard to . . . Part III of this Act, or (*b*) for any sublet part of the dwelling-house which is subject to a restricted contract is or was in excess of the maximum (if any) which it is lawful for the lessor, within the meaning of Part V of this Act to require or receive having regard to the provisions of that Part. **[423]**

NOTES

Commencement: 29 August 1977.
This Part derived from the Rent Act 1968, Sch 3, Part I.
Amended by the Housing Act 1980, ss 73, 152, Schs 8, 25, 26.

PART II

CASES IN WHICH COURT MUST ORDER POSSESSION WHERE DWELLING-HOUSE SUBJECT TO REGULATED TENANCY

Case 11

[Where a person (in this Case referred to as "the owner-occupier") who let the dwelling-house on a regulated tenancy had, at any time before the letting, occupied it as his residence] and—

(*a*) not later than the relevant date the landlord gave notice in writing to the tenant that possession might be recovered under this Case, and

(*b*) the dwelling-house has not, since—

(i) 22nd March 1973, in the case of a tenancy which became a regulated tenancy by virtue of section 14 of the Counter-Inflation Act 1973;

(ii) 14th August 1974, in the case of a regulated furnished tenancy; or

(iii) 8th December 1965, in the case of any other tenancy,

been let by the owner-occupier on a protected tenancy with respect to which the condition mentioned in paragraph (*a*) above was not satisfied, and

[(*c*) the court is of the opinion that of the conditions set out in Part V of this Schedule one of those in paragraphs (*a*) and (*c*) to (*f*) is satisfied.]

If the court is of the opinion that, notwithstanding that the condition in paragraph (*a*) or (*b*) above is not complied with, it is just and equitable to make an order for possession of the dwelling-house, the court may dispense with the requirements of either or both of those paragraphs, as the case may require.

The giving of a notice before 14th August 1974 under section 79 of the Rent Act 1968 shall be treated, in the case of a regulated furnished tenancy, as compliance with paragraph (*a*) of this Case.

[Where the dwelling-house has been let by the owner-occupier on a protected tenancy (in this paragraph referred to as "the earlier tenancy") granted on or after 16th November 1984 but not later than the end of the period of two months beginning with the commencement of the Rent (Amendment) Act 1985 and either—

(i) the earlier tenancy was granted for a term certain (whether or not to be followed by a further term or to continue thereafter from year to year or some other period) and was during that term a protected shorthold tenancy as defined in section 52 of the Housing Act 1980, or

(ii) the conditions mentioned in paragraphs (*a*) to (*c*) of Case 20 were satisfied with respect to the dwelling-house and the earlier tenancy,

then for the purposes of paragraph (*b*) above the condition in paragraph (*a*) above is to be treated as having been satisfied with respect to the earlier tenancy.]

Case 12

[Where the landlord (in this Case referred to as "the owner") intends to occupy the dwelling-house as his residence at such time as he might retire from regular employment and has let] it on a regulated tenancy before he has so retired and—

(*a*) not later than the relevant date the landlord gave notice in writing to the tenant that possession might be recovered under this Case; and (*b*) the dwelling-house has not, since 14th August 1974, been let by the owner on a protected tenancy with respect to which the condition mentioned in paragraph (*a*) above was not satisfied; and

[(*c*) the court is of the opinion that of the conditions set out in Part V of this Schedule one of those in paragraphs (*b*) to (*e*) is satisfied.]

If the court is of the opinion that, notwithstanding that the condition in paragraph (*a*) or (*b*) above is not complied with, it is just and equitable to make an order for possession of the dwelling-house, the court may dispense with the requirements of either or both of those paragraphs, as the case may require.

Case 13

Where the dwelling-house is let under a tenancy for a term of years certain not exceeding 8 months and—

(*a*) not later than the relevant date the landlord gave notice in writing to the tenant that possession might be recovered under this Case; and

(*b*) the dwelling-house was, at some time within the period of 12 months ending on the relevant date, occupied under a right to occupy it for a holiday.

For the purposes of this Case a tenancy shall be treated as being for a term of years certain notwithstanding that it is liable to determination by re-entry or on the happening of any event other than the giving of notice by the landlord to determine the term.

Case 14

Where the dwelling-house is let under a tenancy for a term of years certain not exceeding 12 months and—

(*a*) not later than the relevant date the landlord gave notice in writing to the tenant that possession might be recovered under this Case; and

(*b*) at some time within the period of 12 months ending on the relevant date, the dwelling-house was subject to such a tenancy as is referred to in section 8(1) of this Act.

For the purposes of this Case a tenancy shall be treated as being for a term of years certain notwithstanding that it is liable to determination by re-entry or on the happening of any event other than the giving of notice by the landlord to determine the term.

Case 15

Where the dwelling-house is held for the purpose of being available for occupation by a minister of religion as a residence from which to perform the duties of his office and—

(*a*) not later than the relevant date the tenant was given notice in writing that possession might be recovered under this Case, and

(*b*) the court is satisfied that the dwelling-house is required for occupation by a minister of religion as such a residence.

Case 16

Where the dwelling-house was at any time occupied by a person under the terms of his employment as a person employed in agriculture, and

(*a*) the tenant neither is nor at any time was so employed by the landlord and is not the widow of a person who was so employed, and

(*b*) not later than the relevant date, the tenant was given notice in writing that possession might be recovered under this Case, and

(*c*) the court is satisfied that the dwelling-house is required for occupation by a person employed, or to be employed, by the landlord in agriculture.

For the purposes of this Case "employed", "employment" and "agriculture" have the same meanings as in the Agricultural Wages Act 1948.

Case 17

Where proposals for amalgamation, approved for the purposes of a scheme under section 26 of the Agriculture Act 1967, have been carried out and, at the time when the proposals were submitted, the dwelling-house was occupied by a person responsible (whether as owner, tenant, or servant or agent of another) for the control of the farming of any part of the land comprised in the amalgamation and

(*a*) after the carrying out of the proposals, the dwelling-house was let on a regulated tenancy otherwise than to, or to the widow of, either a person ceasing to be so responsible as part of the amalgamation or a person who is, or at any time was, employed by the landlord in agriculture, and
(*b*) not later than the relevant date the tenant was given notice in writing that possession might be recovered under this Case, and
(*c*) the court is satisfied that the dwelling-house is required for occupation by a person employed, or to be employed, by the landlord in agriculture, and
(*d*) the proceedings for possession are commenced by the landlord at any time during the period of 5 years beginning with the date on which the proposals for the amalgamation were approved or, if occupation of the dwelling-house after the amalgamation continued in, or was first taken by, a person ceasing to be responsible as mentioned in paragraph (*a*) above or his widow, during a period expiring 3 years after the date on which the dwelling-house next became unoccupied.

For the purposes of this Case "employed" and "agriculture" have the same meanings as in the Agricultural Wages Act 1948 and "amalgamation" has the same meaning as in Part II of the Agriculture Act 1967.

Case 18

Where—

(*a*) the last occupier of the dwelling-house before the relevant date was a person, or the widow of a person, who was at some time during his occupation responsible (whether as owner, tenant, or servant or agent of another) for the control of the farming of land which formed, together with the dwelling-house, an agricultural unit within the meaning of the Agriculture Act 1947, and
(*b*) the tenant is neither—
    (i) a person, or the widow of a person, who is or has at any time been responsible for the control of the farming of any part of the said land, nor
    (ii) a person, or the widow of a person, who is or at any time was employed by the landlord in agriculture, and
(*c*) the creation of the tenancy was not preceded by the carrying out in connection with any of the said land of an amalgamation approved for the purposes of a scheme under section 26 of the Agriculture Act 1967, and
(*d*) not later than the relevant date the tenant was given notice in writing that possession might be recovered under this Case, and
(*e*) the court is satisfied that the dwelling-house is required for occupation either by a person responsible or to be responsible (whether as owner, tenant, or servant or agent of another) for the control of the farming of any part of the said land or by a person employed or to be employed by the landlord in agriculture, and
(*f*) in a case where the relevant date was before 9th August 1972, the proceedings for possession are commenced by the landlord before the expiry of 5 years from the date on which the occupier referred to in paragraph (*a*) above went out of occupation.

For the purposes of this Case "employed" and "agriculture" have the same meanings as in the Agricultural Wages Act 1948 and "amalgamation" has the same meaning as in Part II of the Agriculture Act 1967.

[Case 19

Where the dwelling-house was let under a protected shorthold tenancy (or is treated under section 55 of the Housing Act 1980 as having been so let) and—

(*a*) there either has been no grant of a further tenancy of the dwelling-house since the end of the protected shorthold tenancy or, if there was such a grant, it was to a person who immediately before the grant was in possession of the dwelling-house as a protected or statutory tenant; and

(*b*) the proceedings for possession were commenced after appropriate notice by the landlord to the tenant and not later than 3 months after the expiry of the notice.

A notice is appropriate for this Case if—

(i) it is in writing and states that proceedings for possession under this Case may be brought after its expiry; and

(ii) it expires not earlier than 3 months after it is served nor, if, when it is served, the tenancy is a periodic tenancy, before that periodic tenancy could be brought to an end by a notice to quit served by the landlord on the same day;

(iii) it is served—

(*a*) in the period of 3 months immediately preceding the date on which the protected shorthold tenancy comes to an end; or

(*b*) if that date has passed, in the period of 3 months immediately preceding any anniversary of that date; and

(iv) in a case where a previous notice has been served by the landlord on the tenant in respect of the dwelling-house, and that notice was an appropriate notice, it is served not earlier than 3 months after the expiry of the previous notice.]

[Case 20

Where the dwelling-house was let by a person (in this Case referred to as "the owner") at any time after the commencement of section 67 of the Housing Act 1980 and—

(*a*) at the time when the owner acquired the dwelling-house he was a member of the regular armed forces of the Crown;

(*b*) at the relevant date the owner was a member of the regular armed forces of the Crown;

(*c*) not later than the relevant date the owner gave notice in writing to the tenant that possession might be recovered under this Case;

(*d*) the dwelling-house has not, since the commencement of section 67 of the Act of 1980 been let by the owner on a protected tenancy with respect to which the condition mentioned in paragraph (*c*) above was not satisfied; and

(*e*) the court is of the opinion that—

(i) the dwelling-house is required as a residence for the owner; or

(ii) of the conditions set out in Part V of this Schedule one of those in paragraphs (*c*) to (*f*) is satisfied.

If the court is of the opinion that, notwithstanding that the condition in paragraph (*c*) or (*d*) above is not complied with, it is just and equitable to make an order for possession of the dwelling-house, the court may dispense with the requirements of either or both of these paragraphs, as the case may require.

For the purposes of this Case "regular armed forces of the Crown" has the same meaning as in section 1 of the House of Commons Disqualification Act 1975.] **[424]**

NOTES

Commencement: 29 August 1977.

This Part derived from the Rent Act 1968, Sch 3, Part II.

Case 11: first and final amendments made by the Rent (Amendment) Act 1985, s 2; second amendment made by the Housing Act 1980, s 66.

Case 12: amended by the Housing Act 1980, s 66.

Case 19: added by the Housing Act 1980, s 55.

Case 20: added by the Housing Act 1980, s 67.

PART III

PROVISIONS APPLICABLE TO CASE 9 AND PART II OF THIS SCHEDULE

Provision for Case 9

1. A court shall not make an order for possession of a dwelling-house by reason only that the circumstances of the case fall within Case 9 in Part I of this Schedule if the court is satisfied that, having regard to all the circumstances of the case, including the question whether other accommodation is available for the landlord or the tenant, greater hardship would be caused by granting the order than by refusing to grant it.

Provision for Part II

2. Any reference in Part II of this Schedule to the relevant date shall be construed as follows:—

(*a*) except in a case falling within paragraph (*b*) or (*c*) below, if the protected tenancy, or, in the case of a statutory tenancy, the previous contractual tenancy, was created before 8th December 1965, the relevant date means 7th June 1966; and

(*b*) except in a case falling within paragraph (*c*) below, if the tenancy became a regulated tenancy by virtue of section 14 of the Counter-Inflation Act 1973 and the tenancy or, in the case of a statutory tenancy, the previous contractual tenancy, was created before 22nd March 1973, the relevant date means 22nd September 1973; and

(*c*) in the case of a regulated furnished tenancy, if the tenancy or, in the case of a statutory furnished tenancy, the previous contractual tenancy was created before 14th August 1974, the relevant date means 13th February 1975; and

(*d*) in any other case, the relevant date means the date of the commencement of the regulated tenancy in question. **[425]**

NOTES

Commencement: 29 August 1977.

This Part derived from the Rent Act 1968, Sch 3, Part III.

PART IV

SUITABLE ALTERNATIVE ACCOMMODATION

3. For the purposes of section 98(1)(*a*) of this Act, a certificate of the [local housing authority] for the district in which the dwelling-house in question is situated, certifying that the authority will provide suitable alternative accommodation for the tenant by a date specified in the certificate, shall be conclusive evidence that suitable alternative accommodation will be available for him by that date.

4.—(1) Where no such certificate as is mentioned in [paragraph 3] above is produced to the court, accommodation shall be deemed to be suitable for the purposes of section 98(1)(*a*) of this Act if it consists of either—

(*a*) premises which are to be let as a separate dwelling such that they will then be let on a protected tenancy [(other than one under which the landlord might recover possession of the dwelling-house under one of the Cases in Part II of this Schedule)], or

(*b*) premises to be let as a separate dwelling on terms which will, in the opinion of the court, afford to the tenant security of tenure reasonably equivalent to the security afforded by Part VII of this Act in the case of a protected tenancy [of a kind mentioned in paragraph (*a*) above],

and, in the opinion of the court, the accommodation fulfils the relevant conditions as defined in paragraph 5 below.

[(2) For the purposes of sub-paragraph (1)(*b*) the terms of a tenancy shall not be treated as affording the required security by reason only of the fact that the tenancy is an assured tenancy within the meaning of section 56 of the Housing Act 1980.]

5.—(1) For the purposes of paragraph 4 above, the relevant conditions are that the accommodation is reasonably suitable to the needs of the tenant and his family as regards proximity to place of work, and either—

(*a*) similar as regards rental and extent to the accommodation afforded by dwelling-houses provided in the neighbourhood by any [local housing authority] for persons whose needs as regards extent are, in the opinion of the court, similar to those of the tenant and of his family; or

(*b*) reasonably suitable to the means of the tenant and to the needs of the tenant and his family as regards extent and character; and

that if any furniture was provided for use under the protected or statutory tenancy in question, furniture is provided for use in the accommodation which is either similar to that so provided or is reasonably suitable to the needs of the tenant and his family.

(2) For the purposes of sub-paragraph (1)(*a*) above, a certificate of a [local housing authority] stating—

(*a*) the extent of the accommodation afforded by dwelling-houses provided by the authority to meet the needs of tenants with families of such number as may be specified in the certificate, and

(*b*) the amount of the rent charged by the authority for dwelling-houses affording accommodation of that extent,

shall be conclusive evidence of the facts so stated.

6. Accommodation shall not be deemed to be suitable to the needs of the tenant and his family if the result of their occupation of the accommodation would be that it would be an overcrowded dwelling-house for the purposes of [Part X of the Housing Act 1985].

7. Any document purporting to be a certificate of a [local housing authority] named therein issued for the purposes of this Schedule and to be signed by the proper officer of that authority shall be received in evidence and, unless the contrary is shown, shall be deemed to be such a certificate without further proof.

[8. In this Part "local housing authority" and "district" in relation to such an authority have the same meaning as in the Housing Act 1985.] **[426]**

NOTES

Commencement: 1 April 1986 (para 8); 29 August 1977 (remainder).

This Part derived from the Rent Act 1968, Sch 3, Part IV.

Paras 3, 5, 6, 7: amended by the Housing (Consequential Provisions) Act 1985, s 4, Sch 2, para 35.

Para 4: sub-para (1) amended by the Housing Act 1980, s 152, Sch 25; sub-para (2) added by the Housing and Planning Act 1986, s 13(2).

Para 8: substituted by the Housing (Consequential Provisions) Act 1985, s 4, Sch 2, para 35.

[PART V

PROVISIONS APPLYING TO CASES 11, 12 AND 20

1. In this Part of this Schedule—

"mortgage" includes a charge and "mortgagee" shall be construed accordingly;

"owner" means, in relation to Case 11, the owner-occupier; and

"successor in title" means any person deriving title from the owner, other than a purchaser for value or a person deriving title from a purchaser for value.

2. The conditions referred to in paragraph (*c*) in each of Cases 11 and 12 and in paragraph (*e*)(ii) of Case 20 are that—

(*a*) the dwelling-house is required as a residence for the owner or any member of his family who resided with the owner when he last occupied the dwelling-house as a residence;

(*b*) the owner has retired from regular employment and requires the dwelling-house as a residence;

(*c*) the owner has died and the dwelling-house is required as a residence for a member of his family who was residing with him at the time of his death;

(*d*) the owner has died and the dwelling-house is required by a successor in title as his residence or for the purpose of disposing of it with vacant possession;

(*e*) the dwelling-house is subject to a mortgage, made by deed and granted before the tenancy, and the mortgagee—

(i) is entitled to exercise a power of sale conferred on him by the mortgage or by section 101 of the Law of Property Act 1925; and

(ii) requires the dwelling-house for the purpose of disposing of it with vacant possession in exercise of that power; and

(*f*) the dwelling-house is not reasonably suitable to the needs of the owner, having regard to his place of work, and he requires it for the purpose of disposing of it with vacant possession and of using the proceeds of that disposal in acquiring, as his residence, a dwelling-house which is more suitable to those needs.] **[427]**

NOTES
Commencement: 28 November 1980.
Commencement order: SI 1980 No 1706.
Added by the Housing Act 1980, s 66, Sch 7.

SCHEDULE 16

Section 99

FURTHER GROUNDS FOR POSSESSION OF DWELLING-HOUSES LET ON OR SUBJECT TO TENANCIES TO WHICH SECTION 99 APPLIES

Case I

Alternative accommodation not provided or arranged by housing authority

1. The court is satisfied that suitable alternative accommodation is available for the tenant, or will be available for him when the order for possession takes effect.

2. Accommodation shall be deemed suitable in this Case if it consists of—

(*a*) premises which are to be let as a separate dwelling such that they will then be let on a protected tenancy, or

(*b*) premises which are to be let as a separate dwelling on terms which will, in the opinion of the court, afford to the tenant security of tenure reasonably equivalent to the security afforded by Part VII of this Act in the case of a protected tenancy,

and, in the opinion of the court, the accommodation fulfils the conditions in paragraph 3 below.

3.—(1) The accommodation must be reasonably suitable to the needs of the tenant and his family as regards proximity to place of work and either—

(*a*) similar as regards rental and extent to the accommodation afforded by dwelling-houses provided in the neighbourhood by [the local housing authority] for persons whose needs as regards extent are similar to those of the tenant and his family, or

(*b*) reasonably suitable to the means of the tenant, and to the needs of the tenant and his family as regards extent and character.

(2) For the purposes of sub-paragraph (1) (*a*) above, a certificate of [the local housing authority] stating—

(*a*) the extent of the accommodation afforded by dwelling-houses provided by the authority to meet the needs of tenants with families of such number as may be specified in the certificate, and

(*b*) the amount of the rent charged by [the local housing authority] for dwelling-houses affording accommodation of that extent,

shall be conclusive evidence of the facts so stated.

(3) If any furniture was provided by the landlord for use under the tenancy, furniture must be provided for use in the alternative accommodation which is either similar, or is reasonably suitable to the needs of the tenant and his family.

4. Accommodation shall not be deemed to be suitable to the needs of the tenant and

his family if the result of their occupation of the accommodation would be that it would be an overcrowded dwelling-house for the purposes of [Part X of the Housing Act 1985].

5. Any document purporting to be a certificate of [the local housing authority] issued for the purposes of this Case and to be signed by the proper officer of the authority shall be received in evidence and, unless the contrary is shown, shall be deemed to be such a certificate without further proof.

6. In this Case no account shall be taken of accommodation as respects which an offer has been made, or notice has been given, as mentioned in paragraph 1 of Case II below.

[7. In this Case and in Case II below "the local housing authority" has the same meaning as in the Housing Act 1985.]

Case II

Alternative accommodation provided or arranged by housing authority

1. [The local housing authority] have made an offer in writing to the tenant of alternative accommodation which appears to them to be suitable, specifying the date when the accommodation will be available and the date (not being less than 14 days from the date of offer) by which the offer must be accepted.

OR

[The local housing authority] have given notice in writing to the tenant that they have received from a person specified in the notice an offer in writing to rehouse the tenant in alternative accommodation which appears to the [local housing authority] concerned to be suitable, and the notice specifies both the date when the accommodation will be available and the date (not being less than 14 days from the date when the notice was given to the tenant) by which the offer must be accepted.

2. The landlord shows that the tenant accepted the offer (by the housing authority or other person) within the time duly specified in the offer.

OR

The landlord shows that the tenant did not so accept the offer, and the tenant does not satisfy the court that he acted reasonably in failing to accept the offer.

3.—(1) The accommodation offered must in the opinion of the court fulfil the conditions of this paragraph.

(2) The accommodation must be reasonably suitable to the needs of the tenant and his family as regards proximity to place of work.

(3) The accommodation must be reasonably suitable to the means of the tenant, and to the needs of the tenant and his family as regards extent.

4. If the accommodation offered is available for a limited period only, the [local housing authority's offer] or notice under paragraph 1 of this Case must contain an assurance that other accommodation—

(*a*) the availability of which is not so limited,
(*b*) which appears to them to be suitable, and
(*c*) which fulfils the conditions in paragraph 3 above,

will be offered to the tenant as soon as practicable. **[428]**

NOTES

Commencement: 29 August 1977.

This Schedule derived from the Rent Act 1968, Sch 3A.

Case 1, para 7: substituted by the Housing (Consequential Provisions) Act 1985, s 4, Sch 2, para 35; other amendments made by the Housing (Consequential Provisions) Act 1985, s 4, Sch 2, para 35.

SCHEDULE 17

Sections 18A

CONVERTED TENANCIES: MODIFICATION OF ACT

1. In this Schedule—

"converted tenancy" means a tenancy which has become a regulated tenancy by virtue of [any of the enactments mentioned in section 18A of this Act.]

"the conversion" means the time when the tenancy became a regulated tenancy.

2. In relation to any rental period beginning after the conversion, sections 45 to 47 of this Act shall have effect as if references therein to the last contractual period were references to the last rental period beginning before the conversion.

3, 4 . . .

5. Section 5(1) of this Act shall not apply to the converted tenancy after the conversion.

6. Section 70 of this Act shall apply in relation to the converted tenancy as if the references in subsection (3) of that section to the tenant under the regulated tenancy included references to the tenant under the tenancy before the conversion.

7. [None of the enactments mentioned in section 18A of this Act shall] be taken as affecting any court proceedings, instituted under this Act (or, as the case may be, the Rent Act 1968) before the conversion, which may affect the recoverable rent before the conversion, or the rent under the regulated tenancy after the conversion so far as that depends on the previous rent.

8. Any court order in any proceedings to which paragraph 7 above applies which is made after the conversion may exclude from the effect of the order rent for any rental period beginning before the conversion, or for any later rental period beginning before the making of the order.

9. Any right conferred on a tenant by section 38 of, or paragraph 6(4) of Schedule 6 to, this Act to recover any amount by deducting it from rent shall be exercisable by deducting it from rent for any rental period beginning after the conversion to the same extent as the right would have been exercisable if the conversion had not taken place.

10, 11 . . . **[429]**

NOTES

Commencement: 29 August 1977.
This Schedule derived from the Housing Finance Act 1972, s 37.
Amended by the Housing Act 1980, s 152, Schs 25, 26.

SCHEDULE 18

Sections 120(5), 121, 127 (1)

ALLOWABLE PREMIUMS

PART I

PREMIUM ALLOWED ON ASSIGNMENT OF TENANCY WHERE PREMIUM LAWFULLY PAID ON GRANT

1.—(1) This Part of this Schedule applies where—

(*a*) a premium was lawfully required and paid, or lawfully received, in respect of the grant, renewal or continuance of a protected tenancy of a dwelling-house which is a regulated tenancy; and

(*b*) since that grant, renewal or continuance the landlord has not granted a tenancy of the dwelling-house under which, as against the landlord, a person became entitled to possession, other than the person who was so entitled to possession of the dwelling-house immediately before that tenancy began; and

(*c*) a rent for the dwelling-house is registered under Part IV of this Act and the rent so registered is higher than the rent payable under the tenancy.

(2) Any reference in this Part of this Schedule to a premium does not include a premium which consisted only of any such outgoings, sum or amount as fall within section 120(3) of this Act and, in the case of a premium which included any such outgoings, sum or amount, so much only of the premium as does not consist of those outgoings, sum or amount shall be treated as the premium for the purposes of this Part of this Schedule.

2. In a case where this Part of this Schedule applies, nothing in section 120 of this Act shall prevent any person from requiring or receiving, on an assignment of the protected tenancy referred to in paragraph 1(1)(*a*) above or any subsequent protected tenancy of the same dwelling-house, a premium which does not exceed an amount calculated (subject to paragraph 4 below) in accordance with the formula—

$$(P \times A)/G$$

where

P is the premium referred to in paragraph 1(1)(*a*) above;
A is the length of the period beginning on the date on which the assignment in question takes effect and ending on the relevant date; and
G is the length of the period beginning on the date of the grant, renewal or continuance in respect of which the premium was paid and ending on the relevant date.

3.—(1) If, although the registered rent is higher than the rent payable under the tenancy, the lump sum equivalent of the difference is less than the premium, paragraph 2 above shall have effect as if P were the lump sum equivalent.

(2) For the purposes of this Part of this Schedule, the lump sum equivalent of the difference between the two rents referred to in sub-paragraph (1) above shall be taken to be that difference multiplied by the number of complete rental periods falling within the period beginning with the grant, renewal or continuance in respect of which the premium was paid and ending on the relevant date.

4. Where any rates in respect of the dwelling-house are borne by the landlord or a superior landlord, the amount of the registered rent shall be taken, for the purposes of this Part of this Schedule, to be increased by the amount of the rates so borne in respect of the rental period comprising the date from which the registration took effect.

5.—(1) Any reference in this Part of this Schedule to the relevant date shall be construed in accordance with this paragraph.

(2) Where the tenancy referred to in paragraph 1(1)(*a*) above was granted, renewed or continued for a term of years certain exceeding 7 years and that term has not expired when the assignment takes effect, the relevant date is the date of the expiry of that term.

(3) In any other case, the relevant date is the date of the expiry of 7 years from the commencement of the term, or, as the case may be, the renewal or continuance of the term in respect of which the premium was paid.

(4) For the purposes of this paragraph—

(*a*) a term of years shall be treated as certain notwithstanding that it is liable to determination by re-entry or on the happening of any event other than the giving of notice by the landlord to determine the term; and
(*b*) a term of years determinable by the landlord giving notice to determine it shall be treated as a term of years certain expiring on the earliest date on which such a notice given after the date of the assignment would be capable of taking effect. **[430]**

NOTES
Commencement: 29 August 1977.
This Part derived from the Rent Act 1968, Sch 11.

PART II

PREMIUM ALLOWED UNDER SECTIONS 121 AND 127

6.—(1) Where this Part of this Schedule applies to any tenancy and a premium was lawfully required and paid on the grant or an assignment of the tenancy, nothing in section 120 of this Act shall prevent any person from requiring or receiving, on an assignment of the tenancy, the fraction of the premium specified below (without prejudice, however, to his requiring or receiving a greater sum in a case where he may lawfully do so under Part I of this Schedule).

(2) If there was more than one premium, sub-paragraph (1) above shall apply to the last of them.

7.—(1) The fraction is (X/Y) where—

X is the residue of the term of the tenancy at the date of the assignment, and
Y is the term for which the tenancy was granted.

(2) Sub-paragraph (1) above shall apply where a tenancy has been assigned as it applies where a tenancy has been granted and then Y in the fraction shall be the residue, at the date of that assignment, of the term for which the tenancy was granted.

8. Where the tenancy was granted on the surrender of a previous tenancy, and a premium had been lawfully required and paid on the grant or an assignment of the previous tenancy, the surrender value of the previous tenancy shall be treated, for the purposes of this Part of this Schedule, as a premium or, as the case may be, as part of the premium, paid on the grant of the tenancy.

9. For the purposes of paragraph 8 above, the surrender value of the previous tenancy shall be taken to be the amount which, had the previous tenancy been assigned instead of being surrendered and had this Part of this Schedule applied to it, would have been the amount that could have been required and received on the assignment in pursuance of this Part of this Schedule.

10. In determining for the purposes of this Part of this Schedule the amount which may or could have been required and received on the assignment of a tenancy terminable, before the end of the term for which it was granted, by notice to the tenant, that term shall be taken to be a term expiring at the earliest date on which such a notice given after the date of the assignment would have been capable of taking effect.

11. In this Part of this Schedule "grant" includes continuance and renewal. **[431]**

NOTES

Commencement: 29 August 1977.

This Part derived from the Housing Act 1969, s 81(5), Sch 7, and the Counter-Inflation Act 1973, Sch 5.

SCHEDULE 20

Section 140

MODIFICATION OF ACT IN RELATION TO FIRE PRECAUTIONS

Steps mentioned in certain notices under the Fire Precautions Act 1971 to count as improvements for certain purposes of this Act

1.—(1) This paragraph applies where a dwelling which is the subject of a regulated . . . tenancy consists of or is comprised in premises with respect to which there has been issued a fire certificate covering (in whatever terms) the use of the dwelling as a dwelling.

(2) The amount of any expenditure incurred by the landlord in taking, in relation to the relevant building, a step mentioned in a fire precaution notice served in connection with the premises, shall for the purposes of this Act be treated (whether or not apart from this paragraph it would be so treated) as expenditure incurred by the landlord on an improvement effected in the dwelling.

(3) If from the taking, in relation to the relevant building, of any such step as is referred to in sub-paragraph (2) above, there accrues benefit not only to the dwelling but

also to other premises of the landlord comprised in the relevant building, the amount to be treated as mentioned in that sub-paragraph shall be so much only of the expenditure as may be determined, by agreement in writing between the landlord and the tenant or by the county court, to be properly apportionable to the dwelling, having regard to the benefit accruing, from the taking of the step, to the dwelling and the other premises.

(4) Any apportionment made by the county court under sub-paragraph (3) above shall be final

(5) For the purposes of this paragraph, the amount of any expenditure shall be treated as diminished by the amount of any grant paid in respect of that expenditure under any enactment.

(6), (7) . . .

2.—(1) This paragraph applies in relation to a dwelling-house consisting of or comprised in premises—

- (*a*) with respect to which there has been issued a fire certificate covering (in whatever terms) the use of the dwelling-house as a dwelling; or
- (*b*) which are the subject of an application for a fire certificate specifying as a use of the premises which it is desired to have covered by the certificate a use such that, if a certificate covering that use were issued, it would cover (in whatever terms) the use of the dwelling-house as a dwelling.

(2) In a case to which this paragraph applies—

- (*a*) section 69 of, and Schedule 12 to, this Act shall have effect as if in subsection (1)(*a*) of that section the reference to making improvements in the dwelling-house included a reference to taking, in relation to the relevant building, any step mentioned in a fire precaution notice served in connection with the premises; and
- (*b*) any step mentioned in such a notice shall for the purposes of section 69 and Schedule 12, in their application to such a dwelling-house, be treated (whether or not apart from this paragraph it would be so treated) as an improvement.

Cases where rent is increased by virtue of section 28(3)(*b*) *of the Act of* 1971

3.—(1) This paragraph applies where, in the case of any premises consisting of a dwelling-house let on a protected tenancy which is a regulated tenancy, the rent payable in respect of the premises is increased by a section 28 order.

(2) If the increase takes effect while a rent for the dwelling-house is registered under Part IV of this Act, and was so registered before the completion of the relevant alterations—

- (*a*) the contractual rent limit for any contractual period beginning while the registration of that rent continues to have effect shall be what it would be for that period under section 44(1) of this Act if the rent so registered had been simultaneously increased by the same amount (and the reference in section 71(3)(*a*) of the Act to the limit imposed by section 44(1) shall be construed accordingly); [and]
- (*b*) if the regulated tenancy of the dwelling-house becomes a statutory tenancy, section 45(2) of this Act shall have effect, in relation to any statutory period of that tenancy beginning while the registration of that rent continues to have effect, as if the rent so registered had been simultaneously increased by the same amount; *and*
- *(c) Schedule 8 . . . to this Act shall have effect, in relation to any period of that tenancy (whether contractual or statutory) beginning while the registration of that rent continues to have effect, as if the amount to which the rent could be increased in accordance with that Schedule for a statutory period had been simultaneously increased by the same amount.*

(3) Where the rent payable under a tenancy to which Part VI of this Act applies is increased by a section 28 order, the rent limit for the dwelling-house under Part VI (including the rent limit specified in a direction of the Secretary of State) shall be

increased by an amount equal to the increase effected by the order in the rent payable for the rental period in question.

(4) If, at any time after the court order takes effect, a rent is registered for the dwelling-house (whether it is the first or any subsequent registration) sub-paragraph (2) above shall not apply to any period beginning after that time.

4. . . .

Interpretation

5. In this Schedule—

"contractual period" means a rental period of a regulated tenancy which is a period beginning before the expiry or termination of the protected tenancy;

"contractual rent limit" has the meaning assigned to it by section 44(3) of this Act;

. . .

"fire certificate" has the meaning given in section 1(1) of the Fire Precautions Act 1971;

"fire precautions notice" means a notice served under section 5(4), 8(4) or (5) or 12(8)(*b*) of the Act of 1971;

"landlord" includes a superior landlord;

. . .

"relevant alterations" means the alterations or other things falling within section 28(3) of the Act of 1971 the expense of which was taken into account by the court in making a section 28 order;

. . .

"section 28 order" means an order made by a court by virtue of section 28(3)(*b*) of the Act of 1971; and

"statutory period" means any rental period of a regulated tenancy which is not a contractual period. **[432]**

NOTES

Commencement: 29 August 1977.

This Schedule derived from the Fire Precautions Act 1971, Schedule.

Para 3: in sub-para (2) words in italics prospectively repealed and word in square brackets prospectively added by SI 1987 No 264, art 2(3), Sch 1, as from 4 May 1987.

Words omitted repealed by the Housing Act 1980, s 152, Sch 26.

SCHEDULE 24

Section 155(3)

Savings and Transitional Provisions

General transitional provisions

1.—(1) In so far as anything done, or having effect as if done, under an enactment repealed by this Act could have been done under a corresponding provision in this Act, it shall not be invalidated by the repeal but shall have effect as if done under that provision.

(2) Sub-paragraph (1) above applies, in particular, to any regulation, order, scheme, agreement, dissent, election, application, reference, representation, appointment or apportionment made, notice served, certificate issued, statement supplied, undertaking or direction given or rent registered.

(3) Subject to this Schedule, any document made, served or issued before the passing of this Act or at any time thereafter (whether before or after the commencement of this Act) and containing a reference to an enactment repealed by this Act, or having effect as if containing such a reference, shall, except in so far as a contrary intention appears, be construed as referring, or as the context requires, as including a reference, to the corresponding provision of this Act.

(4) Where a period of time specified in an enactment repealed by this Act is current

at the commencement of this Act, this Act shall have effect as if the corresponding provision thereof had been in force when that period began to run.

(5) Nothing in this Act shall affect the enactments repealed thereby in their operation in relation to offences committed before the commencement of this Act.

(6) A conviction for an offence under an enactment repealed by this Act shall be treated for the purposes of this Act as a conviction of an offence under the corresponding provision of this Act.

(7) Subject to the provisions of this Act, any reference in any document or enactment to a dwelling-house which is let on or subject to a protected or statutory tenancy (including any reference which, immediately before the commencement of this Act, was to be construed as such a reference by virtue of paragraph 5 of Schedule 16 to the Rent Act 1968) shall be construed, except in so far as the context otherwise requires, as a reference to a dwelling-house let on or subject to a protected or statutory tenancy within the meaning of this Act.

(8) Subject to the provisions of this Act, any reference in any document or enactment to a Part VI contract (within the meaning of Part VI of the Rent Act 1968) shall be construed, except in so far as the context otherwise requires, as a reference to a restricted contract.

Existing statutory tenants

2.—(1) If, immediately before the commencement of this Act, a person (the "existing statutory tenant") was a statutory tenant of a dwelling-house by virtue of any enactment repealed by this Act (a "repealed enactment") that person shall, on the commencement of this Act, be a statutory tenant of the dwelling-house for the purposes of this Act.

(2) If, immediately before the existing statutory tenant became a statutory tenant, he was a tenant of the dwelling-house under a tenancy then, for the purposes of this Act, he shall be the statutory tenant by virtue of his previous protected tenancy.

(3) If the existing statutory tenant became a statutory tenant on the death of a person who was himself a tenant or statutory tenant of the dwelling-house then, for the purposes of this Act, the existing statutory tenant shall be a statutory tenant by succession; and, unless he became a statutory tenant by virtue of section 13 of the Rent Act 1965, or paragraph 6 or 7 of Schedule 1 to the Rent Act 1968, he shall be deemed to be the first successor within the meaning of Schedule 1 to this Act.

(4) If the existing statutory tenant became a statutory tenant by virtue of an exchange under section 17 of the Rent Act 1957 or section 14 of the Rent Act 1968 then, for the purposes of this Act, he shall be deemed to be the statutory tenant by virtue of his previous protected tenancy or, as the case may be, a statutory tenant by succession, if immediately before the commencement of this Act he was so deemed for the purposes of the Rent Act 1968.

(5) If, by virtue of sub-paragraph (4) above, the existing statutory tenant is for the purposes of this Act a statutory tenant by succession, he shall be deemed to be the first successor, within the meaning of Schedule 1 to this Act if, and only if, the person who was a statutory tenant immediately before the date of exchange was not a statutory tenant by virtue of section 13 of the Rent Act 1965 or paragraph 6 or 7 of Schedule 1 to the Rent Act 1968.

(6) Without prejudice to the case where by virtue of sub-paragraph (4) or (5) above, the existing statutory tenant is deemed to be a statutory tenant by succession but is not deemed to be the first successor, within the meaning of Schedule 1 to this Act, paragraphs 5 to 7 of that Schedule shall not apply where the existing statutory tenant, or the person on whose death he became a statutory tenant, became a statutory tenant by virtue of an exchange under section 17 of the Rent Act 1957 or section 14 of the Rent Act 1968.

3.—(1) A person who, at any time before the commencement of this Act, became a statutory tenant of a dwelling-house by virtue of—

(*a*) section 12(10) of the Increase of Rent and Mortgage Interest (Restrictions) Act 1920 (under which workmen housed in certain dwelling-houses taken over by the Government during the 1914–18 war were to be treated as tenants of the landlords of those houses); and

(*b*) section 4 of the Requisitioned Houses and Housing (Amendment) Act 1955 (under which certain requisitioned dwelling-houses were returned to their owners on condition that the owners accepted the existing licensees as statutory tenants),

(and not by way of succession to a previous statutory tenancy) shall be treated for the purposes of this Act as having become the statutory tenant of that dwelling-house on the expiry of a protected tenancy thereof.

(2) A person who, on or after the commencement of the Rent Act 1965, retained possession of a dwelling-house by virtue of section 20 of that Act (which made transitional provisions in relation to tenancies which expired before the commencement of that Act) shall be deemed to have done so under a statutory tenancy arising on the termination of a tenancy which was a regulated tenancy, and the terms as to rent and otherwise of that tenancy shall be deemed to have been the same, subject to any variation specified by the court, as those of the tenancy mentioned in subsection (1) of that section (that is to say, the tenancy which ended before the commencement of the Rent Act 1965 but which would have been a regulated tenancy if that Act had then been in force).

4. A statutory tenancy subsisting at the commencement of this Act under section 4 of the Requisitioned Houses and Housing (Amendment) Act 1955 shall be treated, for the purposes of this Act—

(*a*) as a regulated tenancy if, by virtue of section 10 of the Rent Act 1965, it fell to be treated as a regulated tenancy after 31st March 1966; and

(*b*) in any other case, as a controlled tenancy.

Tenancies which ended before passing of Counter-Inflation Act 1973 (c. 9)

5.—(1) This paragraph applies where the tenancy of a dwelling-house came to an end at a time before 22nd March 1973 and the tenancy would have been a regulated tenancy, for the purposes of the Rent Act 1968, if section 14 of the Counter-Inflation Act 1973 had been in force at that time.

(2) If the tenant under the tenancy which came to an end duly retained possession of the dwelling-house after 22nd March 1973 without any order for possession having been made, or after the rescission of such an order, he shall be deemed to have done so under a statutory tenancy arising on the termination of the tenancy which came to an end and, subject to sub-paragraph (6) below, the terms of that tenancy (including the rent) shall be deemed to have been the same as those of the tenancy which came to an end.

(3) Any statutory tenancy arising by virtue of sub-paragraph (2) above, shall be treated as a statutory tenancy arising on the termination of a protected tenancy which was a regulated tenancy.

(4) Where Article 10 of the Counter-Inflation (Rents) (England and Wales) Order 1972 applied to the rent under the tenancy, the rent under the tenancy imposed by sub-paragraph (2) above shall be the rent as limited by Article 10.

(5) Schedule 7 to this Act shall not apply to a statutory tenancy arising under sub-paragraph (2) above.

(6) The High Court or the county court may by order vary all or any of the terms of the tenancy imposed by sub-paragraph (2) above in any way appearing to the court to be just and equitable (and whether or not in a way authorised by the provisions of sections 46 and 47 of this Act).

(7) If at 22nd March 1973 the dwelling-house was occupied by a person who would, if the tenancy had been a regulated tenancy, have been the "first successor" within the meaning of paragraph 4 of Schedule 1 to the Rent Act 1968 (which is re-enacted in Schedule 1 to this Act), sub-paragraphs (2), (4) and (5) above shall apply where that person retained possession as they apply where the tenant retained possession.

Protected furnished tenancies

6.—(1) In any case where—

(*a*) before 14th August 1974 a dwelling was subject to a tenancy which was a Part VI contract within the meaning of the Rent Act 1968, and

(*b*) the dwelling forms part only of a building, and that building is not a purpose-built block of flats within the meaning of section 12 of this Act, and

(*c*) on that date the interest of the lessor, within the meaning of Part VI of the Rent Act 1968, under the tenancy—

(i) belonged to a person who occupied as his residence another dwelling which also formed part of that building, or

(ii) was vested in trustees as such and was or, if it was held on trust for sale, the proceeds of its sale were held on trust for a person who occupied as his residence another dwelling which also formed part of that building, and

(*d*) apart from paragraph 1 of Schedule 3 to the Rent Act 1974 the tenancy would, on that date, have become a protected furnished tenancy,

this Act shall apply subject to sub-paragraph (2) below, as if the tenancy had been granted on that date and as if the condition in section 12(1)(*b*) of this Act were fulfilled in relation to the grant of the tenancy.

(2) In the application of this Act to a tenancy by virtue of this paragraph—

(*a*) subsection (2) of section 12 shall be omitted; and

(*b*) in section 20 and Part II of Schedule 2 any reference to section 12 of this Act shall be construed as including a reference to this paragraph.

(3) In any case where paragraphs (*a*), (*b*) and (*d*) of sub-paragraph (1) above apply but on 14th August 1974 the interest referred to in paragraph (*c*) of that sub-paragraph was vested—

(*a*) in the personal representatives of a deceased person acting in that capacity, or

(*b*) by virtue of section 9 of the Administration of Estates Act 1925, in the Probate Judge within the meaning of that Act, or

(*c*) in trustees as such,

then, if the deceased immediately before his death or, as the case may be, the settlor immediately before the creation of the trust occupied as his residence another dwelling which also formed part of the building referred to in paragraph (*b*) of sub-paragraph (1) above, that sub-paragraph shall apply as if the condition in paragraph (*c*) thereof were fulfilled.

(4) In the application of [paragraph 1(*c*)] of Schedule 2 to this Act in a case falling within sub-paragraph (3) above, any period before 14th August 1974 during which the interest of the landlord vested as mentioned in that subsection shall be disregarded in calculating the period of 12 months specified therein.

7.—(1) This paragraph applies where the tenancy of a dwelling-house came to an end before 14th August 1974 and, if it had come to an end immediately after that date it would then have been a protected furnished tenancy within the meaning of the Rent Act 1974.

(2) If the tenant under the tenancy which came to an end duly retained possession of the dwelling-house on 14th August 1974 without an order for possession having been made or after the rescission of such an order he shall be deemed to have done so as a statutory tenant under a regulated tenancy and, subject to sub-paragraph (5) below, as a person who became a statutory tenant on the termination of a protected tenancy under which he was the tenant; and, subject to sub-paragraphs (4) and (5) below, the tenancy referred to in sub-paragraph (1) above shall be treated, in relation to his statutory tenancy,—

(*a*) as the original contractual tenancy for the purposes of section 3 of this Act, and

(*b*) as the previous contractual tenancy for the purposes of paragraph 2 of Part III of Schedule 15 to this Act.

(3) In any case where—

(*a*) immediately before 14th August 1974 a rent was registered for a dwelling under Part VI of the Rent Act 1968, and

(*b*) on that date a person became a statutory tenant of that dwelling by virtue of paragraph 3(4) of Schedule 3 to the Rent Act 1974,

the amount which was so registered under Part VI shall be deemed to be registered under Part IV of this Act as the rent for that dwelling, and that registration shall be deemed to have taken effect on 14th August 1974.

(4) The High Court or the county court may by order vary all or any of the terms of the statutory tenancy imposed by sub-paragraph (2) above in any way appearing to the court to be just and equitable (and whether or not in a way authorised by the provisions of sections 46 and 47 of this Act).

(5) If on 14th August 1974 the dwelling-house was occupied by a person who would, if the tenancy had been a protected tenancy for the purposes of the Rent Act 1968, have been "the first successor" as defined in paragraph 4 of Schedule 1 to that Act, sub-paragraph (2) above shall apply where that person retained possession as it applies where the tenant retained possession, except that he shall be the first successor as so defined.

8.—(1) Where, immediately before the commencement of this Act, a rent was deemed (by virtue of section 5 of the Rent Act 1974) to have been registered under Part IV of the Rent Act 1968 with effect from 14th August 1974, it shall for the purposes of this Act be deemed to be registered under Part IV of this Act with effect from that date.

(2) Section 67(3) of this Act shall not apply to an application for the registration under Part IV of this Act of a rent different from that which is deemed to be registered as mentioned in sub-paragraph (1) above.

(3) The reference in section 69(1)(*b*) to a rent being registered for a dwelling-house shall not include a rent which is deemed to be so registered.

(4) A statutory furnished tenancy which arose on 15th August 1974, by virtue of section 5(4) of the Rent 1974, shall be treated as a statutory furnished tenancy for the purposes of this Act and as having arisen on that date.

Regulated tenancies of formerly requisitioned houses

9.—(1) This paragraph applies in relation to a regulated tenancy of a dwelling-house which is a statutory tenancy subsisting under section 4 of the Requisitioned Houses and Housing (Amendment) Act 1955 (under which licensees of previously requisitioned property became statutory tenants of the owners) and which, by virtue of section 10(1) of the Rent Act 1965, fell to be treated as a regulated tenancy after 31st March 1966.

(2) In relation to any rental period of a regulated tenancy to which this paragraph applies, sections 45 to 48 of this Act shall have effect as if—

(*a*) references therein to the last contractual period were references to the last rental period beginning before 31st March 1966, and

(*b*) the rent recoverable for that last rental period has included any sum payable for that period by the local authority to the landlord under section 4(4) of the said Act of 1955 (which provided for payments to make up the difference between the rent actually paid and the amount which would normally have been recoverable).

Miscellaneous

10. Any registration of a rent under Part IV of the Rent Act 1968 which, by virtue of paragraph 33(2) of Schedule 13 to the Housing Act 1974, fell to be treated as if it had been effected pursuant to an application under section 44 of the Rent Act 1968 shall continue to be so treated for the purposes of this Act.

11. In the case of a registration of a rent before 1st January 1973 which, by virtue of subsection (3) of section 82 of the Housing Finance Act 1972 (provision corresponding to section 87(3) of this Act), was provisional only, the date of registration for the purposes of this Act shall be 1st January 1973.

12. Where, by virtue of section 1(1)(*b*) of the Rent Act 1974, any reference in an enactment or instrument was, immediately before the coming into force of this Act, to be construed as having the same meaning as in the Rent Act 1968 as amended by section 1 of the Rent Act 1974, that reference shall be construed as having the same meaning as in this Act.

13. If, immediately before the commencement of this Act, a person's statutory tenancy was a regulated tenancy (and not a controlled tenancy), for the purposes of the Rent Act 1968, by virtue of paragraph 5 of Schedule 2 to that Act (second successors) it shall be a regulated tenancy for the purposes of this Act by virtue of that paragraph.

14. If, immediately before the commencement of this Act, a person's statutory tenancy was a regulated tenancy for the purposes of the Rent Act 1968, by virtue of paragraph 10 of Schedule 16 to that Act (statutory tenancies deemed to arise by virtue of section 20 of the Rent Act 1965) it shall be a regulated tenancy for the purposes of this Act.

15. In relation to any time before 1st January 1960, paragraph (*a*) of section 34(1) of this Act shall have effect as if it included a reference to section 150 of the Public Health Act 1875 and to the Private Street Works Act 1892.

16. [Sections 44(1), 45(2), 57 and 72(7)] of this Act shall have effect in relation to rent determined or confirmed in pursuance of Schedule 3 to the Housing Rents and Subsidies Act 1975.

17. If, immediately before the revocation of regulation 68CB of the Defence (General) Regulations 1939 accommodation was registered for the purposes of that regulation and was let in accordance with the terms and conditions so registered, any contract for the letting of the accommodation shall be treated, for the purposes of this Act, as not being a restricted contract, so long as any letting continues under which the accommodation was let in accordance with the terms and conditions on which it was let immediately before the revocation.

18. Section 54 of, and paragraph 5 of Schedule 9 to, this Act shall apply in relation to a failure to observe any of the requirements of section 43, 44(5) or 45 of the Housing Finance Act 1972 as they apply in relation to a failure to observe any of the corresponding requirements of section 51, 52(6) or 53 of this Act.

19. . . .

20. For the purposes of paragraph 3(3) of Schedule 9 to this Act a case where Schedule 2 to the Housing Rents and Subsidies Act 1975 had effect shall be treated as if it were a case where Schedule 8 to this Act had effect.

21. Subject to the provisions of this Act, any reference in any document or enactment to a Part VI letting (within the meaning of Part II of the Housing Finance Act 1972) shall be construed, except in so far as the context otherwise requires, as a reference to a restricted letting (within the meaning of Part II as amended by this Act).

Transitional provisions from Rent Act 1957

22. If the rent recoverable under a controlled tenancy for any rental period beginning immediately before the commencement of this Act was, by virtue of section 1(4) of the Rent Act 1957 and paragraph 15 of Schedule 16 to the Rent Act 1968, the same as the rent recoverable for the rental period comprising the commencement of the Act of 1957 then, after the commencement of this Act, that rent shall remain the rent recoverable under that tenancy for any rental period for which it is neither increased nor reduced under Part II of this Act (but without prejudice to paragraph 1 of this Schedule).

23. If, immediately before the commencement of this Act, an agreement or determination of a tribunal made or given for the purposes of paragraph (*b*) of section 24(3) of the Housing Repairs and Rents Act 1954 was deemed, by virtue of paragraph 1 of Schedule 7 to the Rent Act 1957 and paragraph 16 of Schedule 16 to the Rent Act 1968, to be an agreement or determination made under paragraph (*c*) of section 52(1) of the Act of 1968 then, after the commencement of this Act, that agreement or determination shall, until an agreement or determination is made as is mentioned in

paragraph (*c*) of section 27(1) of this Act, be deemed to be an agreement or determination made as mentioned in paragraph (*c*) of section 27(1).

24.—(1) If, immediately before the commencement of this Act, the rent limit under a controlled tenancy of a dwelling was increased, by virtue of paragraph 2 of Schedule 7 to the Rent Act 1957 and paragraph 17 of Schedule 16 to the Rent Act 1968, on account of an improvement, or a notice of increase relating to an improvement, completed before the commencement of the Act of 1957, the like increase shall apply after the commencement of this Act to the rent limit under that controlled tenancy.

(2) In sub-paragraph (1) above, "the rent limit", in relation to any time before the commencement of this Act, has the same meaning as in the Rent Act 1968, and in relation to any time after that commencement, has the same meaning as in Part II of this Act.

25.—(1) If, immediately before the commencement of this Act a certificate of a local authority under section 26(1) of the Housing Repairs and Rents Act 1954 or a certificate of a sanitary authority having effect as if it were a certificate under Part II of that Act had effect, by virtue of paragraph 3 of Schedule 7 to the Rent Act 1957 and paragraph 18 of Schedule 16 to the Rent Act 1968, as a certificate of disrepair under Schedule 9 to the Act of 1968, then after the commencement of this Act, the certificate shall have effect, to the like extent as before that commencement, as if it were a certificate of disrepair under Schedule 6 to this Act.

(2) Where any such certificate ceases to have effect (whether by virtue of an order of the court or in consequence of being cancelled by the local authority) sections 27 and 28 of this Act shall have effect, in relation to any rental period beginning after the date as from which the certificate ceases to have effect as if it had ceased to have effect immediately before the basic rental period (within the meaning of Part II of this Act).

26. Where any increase in the rent recoverable under a controlled tenancy current on 6th July 1957 took effect before that date but after the beginning of the basic rental period (within the meaning of Part II of this Act), section 27 of this Act shall have effect as if for references to the rent recoverable for the basic rental period there were substituted references to the rent which would have been recoverable for that period if the increase had taken effect before the beginning thereof.

Savings

27.—(1) Notwithstanding the repeal by this Act of the Rent Act 1968 and section 42 of the Housing Finance Act 1972:—

(*a*) sections 20(3) and 21 of the Rent Act 1968 (rent limit where no registered rent) shall continue to apply in relation to a regulated tenancy granted before 1st January 1973 if the rent under the tenancy, as varied by any agreement made before that date, exceeded the rent limit under section 20(3) with any adjustment under section 21);

(*b*) sections 30 (certain regulated tenancies to be disregarded in determining contractual rent limit) and 35 (duty of landlord to supply statement of rent under previous tenancy) of the Rent Act 1968 shall continue to apply in any case where section 20(3)(*a*) applies by virtue of this paragraph.

(2) In any case to which section 21 of the Rent Act 1968 applies by virtue of sub-paragraph (1) above, the reference in subsection (5) of that section to the amount expended on the improvement shall be construed as a reference to that amount diminished by the amount of any grant or repayment of the kind mentioned in section 48(2)(*a*) or (*b*) of this Act.

(3) This paragraph shall cease to apply if the landlord and the tenant enter into an agreement which is a rent agreement with a tenant having security of tenure (within the meaning of section 51 of this Act) which complies with the requirements of subsection (4) of that section, or if they provide that this paragraph is not to apply by an agreement conforming with those requirements.

28.—(1) Section 47 of the Housing Act 1969 (first registration of a rent after issue of qualification certificate) shall continue to have effect as respects an application for the first registration of a rent where the tenancy became a regulated tenancy before the date of the repeal of Part III of that Act by the Housing Finance Act 1972, but with the substitution, for the references to Part IV of the Rent Act 1968 and Schedule 6 to that Act, of references respectively to Part IV of, and Part II of Schedule 11 to, this Act.

(2) Paragraph 3 of Schedule 17 to this Act shall apply to a conversion under the said Part III as it applies to a conversion under Part VIII of this Act.

(3) Notwithstanding the said repeal, section 51(2)(*a*) of the Act of 1969 shall continue to have effect.

(4) Sections 45 to 47 of this Act shall have effect in relation to a tenancy which has become a regulated tenancy by virtue of the said Part III as if references therein to the last contractual period were references to the last rental period beginning before the tenancy became a regulated tenancy.

29. Subsections (2) and (5) of section 48 of this Act shall have effect, in relation to any grant paid under section 30 of the Housing (Financial Provisions) Act 1958 (improvement grants) or section 4 of the House Purchase and Housing Act 1959 (standard grants) in pursuance of an application made before 25th August 1969, as they have effect in relation to any of the grants mentioned in those subsections.

30. Notwithstanding the repeal by this Act of the Rent Act 1968, the amendments made in other enactments ("the amended enactments") by that Act shall, to the extent that they had effect immediately before the coming into force of this Act, continue to have effect subject to any amendment of any of the amended enactments by this Act.

31. Any registration of a rent made before the commencement of this Act—

(*a*) in the part of the register provided for by section 82 of the Housing Finance Act 1972, and

(*b*) in reliance on subsection (3A) of section 44 of the Rent Act 1968,

shall be as valid, and shall have effect, as if this Act had then been in force.

32. Notwithstanding the repeal by this Act of paragraphs 20 to 26 of Schedule 16 to the Rent Act 1968 (miscellaneous savings) any enactment which, immediately before the commencement of this Act, had effect by virtue of any of those paragraphs shall continue to have effect; and this Act shall have effect in relation to cases falling within any of those paragraphs as the Act of 1968 had effect immediately before the commencement of this Act. **[433]**

NOTES

Commencement: 29 August 1977.

This Schedule derived from the Rent Act 1968, ss 29, 70, 117, Sch 2, para 5, Schs 15, 16, the Housing Finance Act 1972, ss 42, 82, Sch 10, para 7, the Counter-Inflation Act 1973, Sch 5, para 7, the Rent Act 1974, ss 1, 5, Sch 3, paras 1, 3, the Housing Act 1974, Sch 13, para 33, and the Housing Rents and Subsidies Act 1975, Sch 3, para 10.

Paras 6, 16: amended by the Housing Act 1980, s 152, Sch 25, para 60.

Para 19: spent.

PROTECTION FROM EVICTION ACT 1977

(c 43)

ARRANGEMENT OF SECTIONS

PART I

UNLAWFUL EVICTION AND HARASSMENT

Section		Para
1	Unlawful eviction and harassment of occupier	[434]
2	Restriction on re-entry without due process of law	[435]

Section		Para
3	Prohibition of eviction without due process of law	[436]
4	Special provisions for agricultural employees	[437]

PART II

NOTICE TO QUIT

5	Validity of notices to quit	[438]

PART III

SUPPLEMENTAL PROVISIONS

6	Prosecution of offences	[439]
7	Service of notices	[440]
8	Interpretation	[441]
9	The court for purposes of Part I	[442]
10	Application to Crown	[443]
11	Application to Isles of Scilly	[444]
12	Consequential amendments, etc	[445]
13	Short title, etc	[446]

SCHEDULES

Schedule 2—*Transitional Provisions and Savings* .. [447]

An Act to consolidate section 16 of the Rent Act 1957 and Part III of the Rent Act 1965, and related enactments. [29 July 1977]

PART I

UNLAWFUL EVICTION AND HARASSMENT

1. Unlawful eviction and harassment of occupier

(1) In this section "residential occupier", in relation to any premises, means a person occupying the premises as a residence, whether under a contract or by virtue of any enactment or rule of law giving him the right to remain in occupation or restricting the right of any other person to recover possession of the premises.

(2) If any person unlawfully deprives the residential occupier of any premises of his occupation of the premises or any part thereof, or attempts to do so, he shall be guilty of an offence unless he proves that he believed, and had reasonable cause to believe, that the residential occupier had ceased to reside in the premises.

(3) If any person with intent to cause the residential occupier of any premises—

(*a*) to give up the occupation of the premises or any part thereof; or
(*b*) to refrain from exercising any right or pursuing any remedy in respect of the premises or part thereof;

does acts calculated to interfere with the peace or comfort of the residential occupier or members of his household, or persistently withdraws or withholds services reasonably required for the occupation of the premises as a residence, he shall be guilty of an offence.

(4) A person guilty of an offence under this section shall be liable—

(*a*) on summary conviction, to a fine not exceeding [the prescribed sum] or to imprisonment for a term not exceeding 6 months or to both;
(*b*) on conviction on indictment, to a fine or to imprisonment for a term not exceeding 2 years or to both.

(5) Nothing in this section shall be taken to prejudice any liability or remedy to which a person guilty of an offence thereunder may be subject in civil proceedings.

(6) Where an offence under this section committed by a body corporate is proved to have been committed with the consent or connivance of, or to be attributable to any neglect on the part of, any director, manager or secretary or other similar officer of the body corporate or any person who was purporting to act in any such capacity, he as well as the body corporate shall be guilty of that offence and shall be liable to be proceeded against and punished accordingly. **[434]**

NOTES
Commencement: 29 August 1977.
Sub-ss (1)-(5) derived from the Rent Act 1965, ss 30, 44.
Sub-s (4): amended by the Magistrates' Court Act 1980, s 32(2).

2. Restriction on re-entry without due process of law

Where any premises are let as a dwelling on a lease which is subject to a right of re-entry or forfeiture it shall not be lawful to enforce that right otherwise than by proceedings in the court while any person is lawfully residing in the premises or part of them. **[435]**

NOTES
Commencement: 29 August 1977.
This section derived from the Rent Act 1965, s 31.

3. Prohibition of eviction without due process of law

(1) Where any premises have been let as a dwelling under a tenancy which is not a statutorily protected tenancy and—

(*a*) the tenancy (in this section referred to as the former tenancy) has come to an end, but
(*b*) the occupier continues to reside in the premises or part of them,

it shall not be lawful for the owner to enforce against the occupier, otherwise than by proceedings in the court, his right to recover possession of the premises.

(2) In this section "the occupier", in relation to any premises, means any person lawfully residing in the premises or part of them at the termination of the former tenancy.

[(2A) Subsections (1) and (2) above apply in relation to any restricted contract (within the meaning of the Rent Act 1977) which—

(*a*) creates a licence; and
(*b*) is entered into after the commencement of section 69 of the Housing Act 1980;

as they apply in relation to a restricted contract which creates a tenancy.]

(3) This section shall, with the necessary modifications, apply where the

owner's right to recover possession arises on the death of the tenant under a statutory tenancy within the meaning of the Rent Act 1977 or the Rent (Agriculture) Act 1976. **[436]**

NOTES

Commencement: 29 August 1977 (sub-ss (1), (2), (3)); 28 November 1980 (sub-s (2A)).
Commencement order: SI 1980 No 1706.
This section derived from the Rent Act 1965, s 32.
Sub-s (2A): added by the Housing Act 1980, s 69(1).

4. Special provisions for agricultural employees

(1) This section shall apply where the tenant under the former tenancy (within the meaning of section 3 of this Act) occupied the premises under the terms of his employment as a person employed in agriculture, as defined in section 1 of the Rent (Agriculture) Act 1976, but is not a statutory tenant as defined in that Act.

(2) In this section "the occupier", in relation to any premises means—

(*a*) the tenant under the former tenancy; or

(*b*) the widow or widower of the tenant under the former tenancy residing with him at his death or, if the former tenant leaves no such widow or widower, any member of his family residing with him at his death.

(3) Without prejudice to any power of the court apart from this section to postpone the operation or suspend the execution of an order for possession, if in proceedings by the owner against the occupier the court makes an order for the possession of the premises the court may suspend the execution of the order on such terms and conditions, including conditions as to the payment by the occupier of arrears of rent, mesne profits and otherwise as the court thinks reasonable.

(4) Where the order for possession is made within the period of 6 months beginning with the date when the former tenancy came to an end, then, without prejudice to any powers of the court under the preceding provisions of this section or apart from this section to postpone the operation or suspend the execution of the order for a longer period, the court shall suspend the execution of the order for the remainder of the said period of 6 months unless the court—

(*a*) is satisfied either—

(i) that other suitable accommodation is, or will within that period be made, available to the occupier; or

(ii) that the efficient management of any agricultural land or the efficient carrying on of any agricultural operations would be seriously prejudiced unless the premises are available for occupation by a person employed or to be employed by the owner; or

(iii) that greater hardship (being hardship in respect of matters other than the carrying on of such a business as aforesaid) would be caused by the suspension of the order until the end of that period than by its execution within that period; or

(iv) that the occupier, or any person residing or lodging with the occupier, has been causing damage to the premises or has been guilty of conduct which is a nuisance or annoyance to persons occupying other premises; and

(*b*) considers that it would be reasonable not to suspend the execution of the order for the remainder of that period.

(5) Where the court suspends the execution of an order for possession under subsection (4) above it shall do so on such terms and conditions, including conditions as to the payment by the occupier of arrears of rent, mesne profits and otherwise as the court thinks reasonable.

(6) A decision of the court not to suspend the execution of the order under subsection (4) above shall not prejudice any other power of the court to postpone the operation or suspend the execution of the order for the whole or part of the period of 6 months mentioned in that subsection.

(7) Where the court has, under the preceding provisions of this section, suspended the execution of an order for possession, it may from time to time vary the period of suspension or terminate it and may vary any terms and conditions imposed by virtue of this section.

(8) In considering whether or how to exercise its powers under subsection (3) above, the court shall have regard to all the circumstances and, in particular, to—

(*a*) whether other suitable accommodation is or can be made available to the occupier;
(*b*) whether the efficient management of any agricultural land or the efficient carrying on of any agricultural operations would be seriously prejudiced unless the premises were available for occupation by a person employed or to be employed by the owner; and
(*c*) whether greater hardship would be caused by the suspension of the execution of the order than by its execution without suspension or further suspension.

(9) Where in proceedings for the recovery of possession of the premises the court makes an order for possession but suspends the execution of the order under this section, it shall make no order for costs, unless it appears to the court, having regard to the conduct of the owner or of the occupier, that there are special reasons for making such an order.

(10) Where, in the case of an order for possession of the premises to which subsection (4) above applies, the execution of the order is not suspended under that subsection or, the execution of the order having been so suspended, the suspension is terminated, then, if it is subsequently made to appear to the court that the failure to suspend the execution of the order or, as the case may be, the termination of the suspension was—

(*a*) attributable to the provisions of paragraph (*a*)(ii) of subsection (4), and
(*b*) due to misrepresentation or concealment of material facts by the owner of the premises,

the court may order the owner to pay to the occupier such sum as appears sufficient as compensation for damage or loss sustained by the occupier as a result of that failure or termination. **[437]**

NOTES
Commencement: 29 August 1977.
This section derived from the Rent Act 1965, s 33.

PART II

NOTICE TO QUIT

5. Validity of notices to quit

(1) No notice by a landlord or a tenant to quit any premises let (whether before or after the commencement of this Act) as a dwelling shall be valid unless—

(*a*) it is in writing and contains such information as may be prescribed, and

(*b*) it is given not less than 4 weeks before the date on which it is to take effect.

(2) In this section "prescribed" means prescribed by regulations made by the Secretary of State by statutory instrument, and a statutory instrument containing any such regulations shall be subject to annulment in pursuance of a resolution of either House of Parliament.

(3) Regulations under this section may make different provision in relation to different descriptions of lettings and different circumstances. **[438]**

NOTES

Commencement: 29 August 1977.

This section derived from the Rent Act 1957, s 16.

PART III

SUPPLEMENTAL PROVISIONS

6. Prosecution of offences

Proceedings for an offence under this Act may be instituted by any of the following authorities:—

(*a*) councils of districts and London boroughs;

(*b*) the Common Council of the City of London;

(*c*) the Council of the Isles of Scilly. **[439]**

NOTES

Commencement: 29 August 1977.

This section derived from the Rent Act 1968, ss 107(4), 108(2).

7. Service of notices

(1) If for the purpose of any proceedings (whether civil or criminal) brought or intended to be brought under this Act, any person serves upon—

(*a*) any agent of the landlord named as such in the rent book or other similar document, or

(*b*) the person who receives the rent of the dwelling,

a notice in writing requiring the agent or other person to disclose to him the full name and place of abode or place of business of the landlord, that agent or other person shall forthwith comply with the notice.

(2) If any such agent or other person as is referred to in subsection (1) above fails or refuses forthwith to comply with a notice served on him under that subsection, he shall be liable on summary conviction to a fine not exceeding [level 4 on the standard scale] unless he shows to the satisfaction of the court that he did not know, and could not with reasonable diligence have ascertained,

such of the facts required by the notice to be disclosed as were not disclosed by him.

(3) In this section "landlord" includes—

(*a*) any person from time to time deriving title under the original landlord,
(*b*) in relation to any dwelling-house, any person other than the tenant who is or, but for Part VII of the Rent Act 1977 would be, entitled to possession of the dwelling-house, and
(*c*) any person who, under a restricted contract (within the meaning of the Rent Act 1977) grants to another the right to occupy the dwelling in question as a residence and any person directly or indirectly deriving title from the grantor. **[440]**

NOTES
Commencement: 29 August 1977.
This section derived from the Rent Act 1968, ss 108(1), 109(3), (4), 113(1), and the Housing Finance Act 1972, Sch 9, para 12(3).
Sub-s (2): maximum fine increased and converted to a level on the standard scale by the Criminal Justice Act 1982, ss 37, 39, 46, Sch 3.

8. Interpretation

(1) In this Act "statutorily protected tenancy" means—

(*a*) a protected tenancy within the meaning of the Rent Act 1977 or a tenancy to which Part I of the Landlord and Tenant Act 1954 applies;
(*b*) a protected occupancy or statutory tenancy as defined in the Rent (Agriculture) Act 1976;
(*c*) a tenancy to which Part II of the Landlord and Tenant Act 1954 applies;
(*d*) a tenancy of an agricultural holding within the meaning of the *Agricultural Holdings Act 1948* [Agricultural Holdings Act 1986].

(2) For the purposes of Part I of this Act a person who, under the terms of his employment, had exclusive possession of any premises other than as a tenant shall be deemed to have been a tenant and the expressions "let" and "tenancy" shall be construed accordingly.

(3) In Part I of this Act "the owner", in relation to any premises, means the person who, as against the occupier, is entitled to possession thereof. **[441]**

NOTES
Commencement: 29 August 1977.
Sub-s (1) derived from the Rent Act 1965, ss 34, 47(1); sub-ss (2), (3) derived from the Rent Act 1965, s 32(2), (3).
Words in italics repealed with savings and words in square brackets substituted with savings by the Agricultural Holdings Act 1986, ss 99, 100, Sch 13, para 3, Sch 14, para 61.

9. The court for purposes of Part I

(1) The court for the purposes of Part I of this Act shall, subject to this section, be—

(*a*) the county court, in relation to premises with respect to which the county court has for the time being jurisdiction in actions for the recovery of land; and
(*b*) the High Court, in relation to other premises.

(2) Any powers of a county court in proceedings for the recovery of possession of any premises in the circumstances mentioned in section 3(1) of

this Act may be exercised with the leave of the judge by any registrar of the court, except in so far as rules of court otherwise provide.

(3) Nothing in this Act shall affect the jurisdiction of the High Court in proceedings to enforce a lessor's right of re-entry or forfeiture or to enforce a mortgagee's right of possession in a case where the former tenancy was not binding on the mortgagee.

(4) Nothing in this Act shall affect the operation of—

(*a*) section 59 of the Pluralities Act 1838;
(*b*) section 19 of the Defence Act 1842;
(*c*) section 6 of the Lecturers and Parish Clerks Act 1844;
(*d*) paragraph 3 of Schedule 1 to the Sexual Offences Act 1956; or
(*e*) section 13 of the Compulsory Purchase Act 1965. **[442]**

NOTES
Commencement: 29 August 1977.
This section derived from the Rent Act 1965, s 35(1)-(4).

10. Application to Crown

In so far as this Act requires the taking of proceedings in the court for the recovery of possession or confers any powers on the court it shall (except in the case of section 4(10)) be binding on the Crown. **[443]**

NOTES
Commencement: 29 August 1977.
This section derived from the Rent Act 1965, s 36.

11. Application to Isles of Scilly

(1) In its application to the Isles of Scilly, this Act (except in the case of section 5) shall have effect subject to such exceptions, adaptations and modifications as the Secretary of State may by order direct.

(2) The power to make an order under this section shall be exercisable by statutory instrument which shall be subject to annulment, in pursuance of a resolution of either House of Parliament.

(3) An order under this section may be varied or revoked by a subsequent order. **[444]**

NOTES
Commencement: 29 August 1977.
This section derived from the Rent Act 1965, s 49.

12. Consequental amendments, etc

(1) Schedule 1 to this Act contains amendments consequential on the provisions of this Act.

(2) Schedule 2 to this Act contains transitional provisions and savings.

(3) The enactments mentioned in Schedule 3 to this Act are hereby repealed to the extent specified in the third column of that Schedule.

(4) The inclusion in this Act of any express savings, transitional provisions

or amendment shall not be taken to affect the operation in relation to this Act of section 38 of the Interpretation Act 1889 (which relates to the effect of repeals). **[445]**

NOTES
Commencement: 29 August 1977.

13. Short title, etc

(1) This Act may be cited as the Protection from Eviction Act 1977.

(2) This Act shall come into force on the expiry of the period of one month beginning with the date on which it is passed.

(3) This Act does not extend to Scotland or Northern Ireland.

(4) References in this Act to any enactment are references to that enactment as amended, and include references thereto as applied by any other enactment including, except where the context otherwise requires, this Act. **[446]**

NOTES
Commencement: 29 August 1977.

SCHEDULES

SCHEDULE 2

Section 12

TRANSITIONAL PROVISIONS AND SAVINGS

1.—(1) In so far as anything done under an enactment repealed by this Act could have been done under a corresponding provision of this Act, it shall not be invalidated by the repeal but shall have effect as if done under that provision.

(2) Sub-paragraph (1) above applies, in particular, to any regulation, rule, notice or order.

2. The enactments mentioned in Schedule 6 to the Rent Act 1965 shall, notwithstanding the repeal of that Act by this Act, continue to have effect as they had effect immediately before the commencement of this Act. **[447]**

NOTES
Commencement: 29 August 1977.

LEASEHOLD REFORM ACT 1979

(c 44)

An Act to provide further protection, for a tenant in possession claiming to acquire the freehold under the Leasehold Reform Act 1967, against artificial inflation of the price he has to pay. [4 April 1979]

1. Price to tenant on enfranchisement

(1) As against a tenant in possession claiming under section 8 of the Leasehold Reform Act 1967, the price payable on a conveyance for giving effect to that section cannot be made less favourable by reference to a transaction since 15th February 1979 involving the creation or transfer of an interest superior to (whether or not preceding) his own, or an alteration since that date of the terms on which such an interest is held.

(2) References in this section to a tenant claiming are to his giving notice under section 8 of his desire to have the freehold.

(3) Subsection (1) applies to any claim made on or after the commencement date (which means the date of the passing of this Act), and also to a claim made before that date unless by then the price has been determined by agreement or otherwise. **[448]**

NOTES
Commencement: 4 April 1979.

2. Citation and extent

(1) This Act may be cited as the Leasehold Reform Act 1979; and the 1967 Act and this Act may be cited together as the Leasehold Reform Act 1967 and 1979.

(2) This Act extends to England and Wales only. **[449–479]**

NOTES
Commencement: 4 April 1979.

HOUSING ACT 1980

(c 51)

ARRANGEMENT OF SECTIONS

Section Para

PART II

PRIVATE SECTOR TENANTS

Protected shorthold tenancies

51 Preliminary .. [480]
52 Protected shorthold tenancies .. [481]
53 Right of tenant to terminate protected shorthold tenancy .. [482]
54 Subletting or assignment .. [483]
55 Orders for possession .. [484]

Assured tenancies

56 Assured tenancies .. [485]
56A Conditions for assured tenancy: newly erected buildings .. [486]
56B Conditions for assured tenancy: buildings to which works have been carried out .. [487]
56C Certification of fitness for purposes of s 56B .. [488]
56D Fitness for human habitation .. [489]
57 Effect of interest of landlord ceasing to belong to approved body .. [490]
58 Application of Landlord and Tenant Act 1954 .. [491]

Rents

59 Rent officers and applications for registration of rent .. [492]
60 Applications for new registered rents and phasing of increases .. [493]
61 Effect of registration of rent etc .. [494]

Conversion of controlled tenancies

64 Conversion of controlled tenancies into regulated tenancies .. [495]

Regulated tenancies

65 Resident landlords .. [496]
66 Amendment of Cases 11 and 12 of Schedule 15 to Rent Act 1977 .. [497]

Section Para

Restricted contracts

70 Reconsideration of registered rents under Part V of Rent Act 1977 .. .. .. [498]
72 Functions of rent tribunals .. .. [499]

Miscellaneous

73 Dwellings forming part of Crown Estate or belonging to Duchies .. .. .. [500]
74 Housing association and housing trust tenancies under Rent Act 1977 .. .. .. [501]
76 Statutory tenancies by succession .. .. [502]
77 Amendment of Part VI of Rent Act 1977 .. .. [503]

PART III

TENANT'S REPAIRS AND IMPROVEMENTS

81 Tenant's improvements .. .. [504]
82 Provisions as to consents required by section 81 .. .. [505]
83 Conditional consent to tenant's improvements .. .. [506]
84 Exclusion of certain housing associations from Part III .. .. [507]
85 Interpretation and application of Part III .. .. [508]

PART IV

JURISDICTION AND PROCEDURE

86 Jurisdiction of county court and rules of procedure .. .. [509]
88 Discretion of court in certain proceedings for possession .. .. [510]
89 Restriction on discretion of court in making orders for possession of land .. .. [511]

PART IX

GENERAL

Miscellaneous

140 Exclusion of shared ownership tenancies from Leasehold Reform Act 1967 .. .. [512]
142 Leasehold valuation tribunals .. .. [513]
143 Apportionment of rents .. .. [514]
147 Houses in multiple occupation: means of escape from fire .. .. [515]

Supplemental

150 Interpretation .. .. [516]
151 Regulations and orders .. .. [517]
152 Amendments, savings, transitional provisions and repeals .. .. [518]
153 Commencement .. .. [519]
154 Expenses and receipts .. .. [520]
155 Short title and extent .. .. [521]

SCHEDULES

Schedule 1A—*Qualification and Discount* .. ..
Part II—Reduction of Discount in Certain Circumstances .. .. .. [522]
Part III—Supplemental .. .. [523]
Schedule 2—*Conveyance of Freehold and Grant of Lease* .. ..
Part IV—[Charges and other matters] .. .. [524]
Schedule 5—*Application of Landlord and Tenant Act 1954 to Assured Tenancies* .. [525]
Schedule 8—*Crown Estate and Duchies—Consequential Provisions* .. ..
Part I—Rent Act 1977 .. .. [526]
Part II—Rent (Agriculture) Act 1976 .. .. [527]
Part III—General .. .. [528]
Schedule 9—*Provisions Supplementing Section 74* .. .. [529]
Schedule 10—*Amendment of Part VI of Rent Act 1977* .. ..
para 2 .. .. [530]
Schedule 22—*Leasehold Valuation Tribunals* .. ..
Part I—Supplementary Provisions .. .. [531]

Para
Schedule 25—*Minor and Consequential Amendments, Transitional Provisions and Savings* .. ..
Part I—Protection from Eviction Act 1977 (c 43), para 61 Minor and Consequential Amendments .. .. [532]
Part II—Transitional Provisions and Savings .. .. [533]

An Act to give security of tenure, and the right to buy their homes, to tenants of local authorities and other bodies; to make other provision with respect to those and other tenants; to amend the law about housing finance in the public sector; to make other provision with respect to housing; to restrict the discretion of the court in making orders for possession of land; and for connected purposes.

[8 August 1980]

PART II

PRIVATE SECTOR TENANTS

Protected shorthold tenancies

51. Preliminary

Sections 53 to 55 below modify the operation of the 1977 Act in relation to protected shorthold tenancies as defined in section 52 below. **[480]**

NOTES

Commencement: 28 November 1980.
Commencement order: SI 1980 No 1706.
1977 Act: Rent Act 1977.

52. Protected shorthold tenancies

(1) A protected shorthold tenancy is a protected tenancy granted after the commencement of this section which is granted for a term certain of not less than one year nor more than five years and satisfies the following conditions, that is to say,—

(*a*) it cannot be brought to an end by the landlord before the expiry of the term, except in pursuance of a provision for re-entry or forfeiture for non-payment of rent or breach of any other obligation of the tenancy; and

(*b*) before the grant the landlord has given the tenant a valid notice stating that the tenancy is to be a protected shorthold tenancy; and

(*c*) . . .

(2) A tenancy of a dwelling-house is not a protected shorthold tenancy if it is granted to a person who, immediately before it was granted, was a protected or statutory tenant of that dwelling-house.

(3) A notice is not valid for the purposes of subsection (1)(*b*) above unless it complies with the requirements of regulations made by the Secretary of State.

(4) The Secretary of State may by order direct that subsection (1) above shall have effect, either generally or in relation to any registration area specified in the order, as if paragraph (*c*) were omitted.

(5) If a protected tenancy is granted after the commencement of this section—

(*a*) for such a term certain as is mentioned in subsection (1) above, to be followed, at the option of the tenant, by a further term; or (*b*) for such a term certain and thereafter from year to year or some other period;

and satisfies the conditions stated in that subsection, the tenancy is a protected shorthold tenancy until the end of the term certain. **[481]**

NOTES

Commencement: 28 November 1980.
Commencement order: SI 1980 No 1706.
Sub-s (1): para (*c*) repealed by SI 1987 No 265, reg 2.
1977 Act: Rent Act 1977.

53. Right of tenant to terminate protected shorthold tenancy

(1) A protected shorthold tenancy may be brought to an end (by virtue of this section and notwithstanding anything in the terms of the tenancy) before the expiry of the term certain by notice in writing of the appropriate length given by the tenant to the landlord; and the appropriate length of the notice is—

(*a*) one month if the term certain is two years or less; and
(*b*) three months if it is more than two years.

(2) Any agreement relating to a protected shorthold tenancy (whether or not contained in the instrument creating the tenancy) shall be void in so far as it purports to impose any penalty or disability on the tenant in the event of his giving a notice under this section. **[482]**

NOTES

Commencement: 28 November 1980.
Commencement order: SI 1980 No 1706.

54. Subletting or assignment

(1) Where the whole or part of a dwelling-house let under a protected shorthold tenancy has been sublet at any time during the continuous period specified in subsection (3) below, and, during that period, the landlord becomes entitled, as against the tenant, to possession of the dwelling-house, he shall also be entitled to possession against the sub-tenant and section 137 of the 1977 Act shall not apply.

(2) A protected shorthold tenancy of a dwelling-house and any protected tenancy of the same dwelling-house granted during the continuous period specified in subsection (3) below shall not be capable of being assigned, except in pursuance of an order under section 24 of the Matrimonial Causes Act 1973.

(3) The continuous period mentioned in subsections (1) and (2) above is the period beginning with the grant of the protected shorthold tenancy and continuing until either—

(*a*) no person is in possession of the dwelling-house as a protected or statutory tenant; or
(*b*) a protected tenancy of the dwelling-house is granted to a person who is not, immediately before the grant, in possession of the dwelling-house as a protected or statutory tenant. **[483]**

NOTES

Commencement: 28 November 1980.
Commencement order: SI 1980 No 1706.
1977 Act: Rent Act 1977.

55. Orders for possession

(1) . . .

(2) If, in proceedings for possession under Case 19 set out above, the court is of opinion that, notwithstanding that the condition of paragraph (*b*) or (*c*) of section 52(1) above is not satisfied, it is just and equitable to make an order for possession, it may treat the tenancy under which the dwelling-house was let as a protected shorthold tenancy. **[484]**

NOTES
Commencement: 28 November 1980.
Commencement order: SI 1980 No 1706.
Sub-s (1): amends the Rent Act 1977, Sch 15, Part II.

Assured tenancies

56. Assured tenancies

(1) A tenancy under which a dwelling-house is let as a separate dwelling is an assured tenancy and not a housing association tenancy (within the meaning of section 86 of the 1977 Act) or a protected tenancy if—

[(*a*) the conditions described in section 56A or 56B are satisfied,
(*b*) the interest of the landlord has, since the creation of the tenancy, belonged to an approved body, and
(*c*) the tenancy would, when created, have been a protected tenancy or, as the case may be, a housing association tenancy but for this section.]

(2) In this Part of this Act "assured tenant" means the tenant under an assured tenancy.

(3) . . .

(4) In this Part of this Act "approved body" means a body, or one of a description of bodies, for the time being specified for the purposes of this Part of this Act in an order made by the Secretary of State.

(5) . . .

(6) The preceding provisions of this section do not apply to a tenancy if, before the grant of the tenancy, the landlord has given the tenant a valid notice stating that the tenancy is to be a protected tenancy or, as the case may be, a housing association tenancy and not an assured tenancy.

(7) A notice is not valid for the purposes of subsection (6) above unless it complies with the requirements of regulations made by the Secretary of State. **[485]**

NOTES
Commencement: 6 October 1980.
Commencement order: SI 1980 No 1466.
Sub-s (1): amended by the Housing and Planning Act 1986, s 12(1).
Sub-s (3): repealed by the Housing and Planning Act 1986, s 24(3), Sch 12, Part I.
Sub-s (5): adds the Rent Act 1977, s 16A.
1977 Act: Rent Act 1977.

[56A. Conditions for assured tenancy: newly erected buildings

The first set of conditions referred to in section 56(1)(*a*) above is that—

(*a*) the dwelling-house is, or forms part of, a building which was erected (and on which construction work first began) on or after 8th August 1980, and

(*b*) before the tenant first occupied the dwelling-house under the tenancy, no part of it had been occupied by any person as his residence except under an assured tenancy.] **[486]**

NOTES

Commencement: 7 January 1987.

Added by the Housing and Planning Act 1986, s 12(2).

[56B. Conditions for assured tenancy: buildings to which works have been carried out

(1) The second set of conditions referred to in section 56(1)(*a*) above is that—

(*a*) qualifying works have been carried out (whether before or after the commencement of this section),

(*b*) the dwelling-house is (or was) fit for human habitation at the relevant date, and

(*c*) since the qualifying works were carried out no part of the dwelling-house has been occupied by any person as his residence except under an assured tenancy,

and, in the case of the first relevant tenancy, that the person (or persons) to whom the tenancy is granted is not (or do not include) a person who was a secure occupier of the dwelling-house before the works were carried out.

(2) Qualifying works means works involving expenditure attributable to the dwelling-house of not less than the prescribed amount which are carried out within the period of two years preceding the relevant date at a time when the premises constituting the dwelling-house at the relevant date either were not a dwelling-house or no part of them was occupied by a person as his residence.

(3) Expenditure is attributable to a dwelling-house if it is incurred on works carried out to the premises constituting the dwelling-house at the relevant date or to other land or buildings let with the dwelling-house under the first relevant tenancy.

(4) Where the dwelling-house is a flat, there is also attributable to the dwelling-house a proportion of any expenditure incurred on works carried out to the structure, exterior or common parts of, or to common facilities in, the building of which the dwelling-house forms part.

(5) The proportion so attributable shall be taken to be the amount produced by dividing the total amount of such expenditure by the number of units of occupation in the building at the relevant date.

(6) In this section—

"flat" means a separate set of premises, whether or not on the same floor, which—

(*a*) forms part of a building, and

(*b*) is divided horizontally from some other part of the building;

"the first relevant tenancy" means the first tenancy after the carrying out of the qualifying works under which a person is entitled to occupy the dwelling-house as his residence;

"the prescribed amount" means the amount which at the relevant date is prescribed for the purposes of this section by order of the Secretary of State;

"the relevant date" means the date of grant of the first relevant tenancy;

"secure occupier" means a person who, whether alone or jointly with others, occupied or was entitled to occupy the dwelling-house as—

(*a*) a protected or statutory tenant within the meaning of the Rent Act 1977,

(*b*) a secure tenant within the meaning of Part IV of the Housing Act 1985, or

(*c*) a protected occupier or statutory tenant within the meaning of the Rent (Agriculture) Act 1976.] **[487]**

NOTES

Commencement: 7 January 1987.

Added by the Housing and Planning Act 1986, s 12(2).

[56C. Certification of fitness for purposes of s 56B

(1) An approved body having an interest in a dwelling-house which it proposes to let on an assured tenancy may—

(*a*) apply in writing to the local housing authority for a certificate that the dwelling-house is fit for human habitation, or

(*b*) submit to the local housing authority a list of works which it proposes to carry out to the dwelling-house with a request in writing for the authority's opinion whether the dwelling-house would, after the execution of the works, be fit for human habitation;

and the authority shall as soon as may be after receiving the application or request, and upon payment of such reasonable fee as they may determine, take the matter into consideration.

(2) If the authority are of opinion that the dwelling-house is fit for human habitation, they shall give the approved body a certificate to that effect.

(3) If the authority are of opinion that the dwelling-house will be fit for human habitation after the execution of the proposed works, they shall inform the approved body that they are of that opinion.

(4) In any other case, the authority shall give the approved body a list of the works which in their opinion are required to make the dwelling-house fit for human habitation.

(5) Where the authority have responded in accordance with subsection (3) or (4) and the works in question have been executed to their satisfaction, they shall, if the approved body applies in writing, and upon payment of such reasonable fee as the authority may determine, give the body a certificate that the dwelling-house is fit for human habitation.

(6) For the purpose of determining whether the condition in section 56B(1) was satisfied in any case (fitness of dwelling-house on relevant date), but not for any other purpose, a certificate given under this section is conclusive evidence that the dwelling-house was fit for human habitation on the date on which the certificate was given.

(7) In this section "the local housing authority" has the same meaning as in the Housing Act 1985.] **[488]**

NOTES
Commencement: 7 January 1987.
Added by the Housing and Planning Act 1986, s 12(2).

[56D. Fitness for human habitation

In determining for any of the purposes of section 56B or 56C whether a dwelling-house is, or would be, fit for human habitation, regard shall be had to its condition in respect of the following matters—

repair,
stability,
freedom from damp,
internal arrangement,
natural lighting,
ventilation,
water supply,
drainage and sanitary conveniences,
facilities for the preparation and cooking of food and the disposal of waste water;

and the dwelling-house shall be deemed to be unfit only if it is, or would be, so far defective in one or more of those matters as to be not reasonably suitable for occupation in that condition.] **[489]**

NOTES
Commencement: 7 January 1987.
Added by the Housing and Planning Act 1986, s 12(2).

57. Effect of interest of landlord ceasing to belong to approved body

(1) If the landlord under an assured tenancy ceases to be an approved body by reason only of a variation in the bodies or descriptions of bodies for the time specified in an order under section 56(4) of this Act, then in relation to—

(*a*) that tenancy; and
(*b*) any further tenancy granted by the landlord to the person who immediately before the grant was in possession of the dwelling-house as an assured tenant;

the landlord shall be treated, for the purposes of the condition in [section 56(1)(*b*)] above, as if it had remained an approved body.

(2) If, for any period—

(*a*) the interest of the landlord under an assured tenancy has ceased to belong to an approved body, for any reason other than that mentioned in subsection (1) above; and
(*b*) but for this subsection the tenancy would thereby have become a housing association tenancy (within the meaning of section 86 of the 1977 Act) or a protected tenancy;

then so much of that period as does not exceed 3 months shall be disregarded in determining whether the condition in [section 56(1)(*b*)] above is satisfied in relation to that tenancy. **[490]**

NOTES
Commencement: 6 October 1980.
Commencement order: SI 1980 No 1466.
Sub-ss (1), (2): amended by the Housing and Planning Act 1986, s 12(3).
1977 Act: Rent Act 1977.

58. Application of Landlord and Tenant Act 1954

(1) Part II of the Landlord and Tenant Act 1954 (renewal and continuation of tenancies) applies to assured tenancies as it applies to certain business and other tenancies by virtue of section 23 of that Act, but subject to the exceptions and modifications mentioned in Schedule 5 to this Act.

(2) Part IV of that Act (miscellaneous and supplementary provisions) applies to assured tenancies subject to the exceptions and modifications mentioned in Schedule 5.

[(3) In sections 56 to 58 of this Act "tenancy" has the same meaning as in the Landlord and Tenant Act 1954 and references to the granting of a tenancy shall be construed accordingly.] **[491]**

NOTES
Commencement: 7 January 1987 (sub-s (3)); 6 October 1980 (remainder).
Commencement order: SI 1980 No 1466.
Sub-s (3): added by the Housing and Planning Act 1986, s 13(5).

Rents

59. Rent officers and applications for registration of rent

(1), (2) . . .

(3) Schedule 6 to this Act has effect, in relation to applications made after the commencement of this subsection, for the purpose of amending the procedure provided for by the 1977 Act in relation to applications for the registration of rent. **[492]**

NOTES
Commencement: 28 November 1980 (sub-ss (1), (2)); to be appointed (sub-s (3)).
Commencement order: SI 1980 No 1706.
Sub-ss (1), (2): amend the Rent Act 1977, ss 63(2), 67(2).
1977 Act: Rent Act 1977.

60. Applications for new registered rents and phasing of increases

(1) . . .

(2) Subsection (1) above does not apply in any case where, on the determination or confirmation of a rent by the rent officer, the rent determined by him is registered, or his confirmation is noted in the register, before the commencement of this section.

(3) . . .

(4) . . . ; and the general rules relating to the phasing of rent increases contained in section 55 of, and Schedule 8 to, that Act shall apply in those cases.

(5) The Secretary of State may by order make provision—

(*a*) reducing or increasing the period for the time being mentioned in section 67(3) and (4) of the 1977 Act; or
(*b*) reducing or increasing the period of delay for the time being imposed by the Schedules mentioned in subsection (3) above; or
(*c*) repealing section 55 of the 1977 Act and section 15 of the 1976 Act (phasing of rent increases).

(6) An order under subsection (5)(*a*) above may make a corresponding reduction or increase in any of the periods for the time being mentioned in

section 13 of the 1976 Act (application for registration of rent) and sections 73(1)(*a*) and (1A)(*a*) (cancellation of registration of rent under Part IV), 80(2) (reconsideration of rent under restricted contract) and 81A (cancellation of registration of rent under Part V) of the 1977 Act.

(7) An order under subsection (5) above may make such supplemental, incidental and consequential provision as the Secretary of State considers necessary or expedient, including provision amending any enactment (including this Act). **[493]**

NOTES
Commencement: 28 November 1980.
Commencement order: SI 1980 No 1706.
Sub-s (1): amends the Rent Act 1977, s 67.
Sub-s (3): amends the Rent (Agriculture) Act 1976, Sch 6, and the Rent Act 1977, Sch 8.
Sub-s (4): words omitted repeal the Rent Act 1977, ss 56, 114, Sch 9.
1976 Act: Rent (Agriculture) Act 1976.
1977 Act: Rent Act 1977.

61. Effect of registration of rent etc

(1)-(7) . . .

(8) Subsections (1) to (5) above do not apply in any case where, on the determination or confirmation of a rent by the rent officer, the rent determined by him is registered, or his confirmation is noted in the register, before the commencement of this section. **[494]**

NOTES
Commencement: 28 November 1980.
Commencement order: SI 1980 No 1706.
Sub-s (1): substitutes the Rent Act 1977, s 72.
Sub-s (2): amends the Rent (Agriculture) Act 1976, s 13.
Sub-ss (3)-(5), (7): amend the Rent Act 1977, ss 45, 67, 87, 96, Sch 11.
Sub-s (6): amends the Rent (Agriculture) Act 1976, Sch 6, and the Rent Act 1977, Sch 8.

Conversion of controlled tenancies

64. Conversion of controlled tenancies into regulated tenancies

(1) At the commencement of this section every controlled tenancy shall cease to be a controlled tenancy and become a regulated tenancy, except in the case mentioned in subsection (2) below.

(2) If the controlled tenancy is one to which Part II of the Landlord and Tenant Act 1954 would apply, apart from section 24(2) of the 1977 Act, or would so apply if it were a tenancy within the meaning of the Act of 1954, it shall, when it ceases to be a controlled tenancy, be treated as a tenancy continuing by virtue of section 24 of the Act of 1954 after the expiry of a term of years certain. **[495]**

NOTES
Commencement: 28 November 1980.
Commencement order: SI 1980 No 1706.
1977 Act: Rent Act 1977.

Regulated tenancies

65. Resident landlords

(1)-(5) . . .

(6) Subject to subsection (7) below, this section, except subsection (1),

applies to tenancies granted before as well as those granted after the commencement of this section.

(7) In any case where the interest of the landlord under a tenancy vested in the personal representatives (acting in that capacity) of a person who died before the commencement of this section, Schedule 2 to the 1977 Act applies as if paragraph 2A had not been inserted and paragraph 1(*c*)(i) had not been repealed. **[496]**

NOTES
Commencement: 28 November 1980.
Commencement order: SI 1980 No 1706.
Sub-ss (1)-(5): amend the Rent Act 1977, s 12(1), Sch 2.

66. Amendment of Cases 11 and 12 of Schedule 15 to Rent Act 1977

(1)-(4) . . .

(5) Subject to subsection (6) below, Cases 11 and 12, as amended by this section, apply to tenancies granted before, as well as those granted after, the commencement of this section; and nothing in this section invalidates a notice that possession might be recovered under Case 11 or Case 12 which was duly given to a tenant before then.

(6) Paragraphs (*c*) and (*d*) of Part V of Schedule 15 do not apply to Case 11 if the tenancy was granted, and the owner died, before the commencement of this section; and paragraph (*d*) does not apply to Case 12 in any such case. **[497]**

NOTES
Commencement: 28 November 1980.
Commencement order: SI 1980 No 1706.
Sub-ss (1)-(4): amend the Rent Act 1977, s 98, Sch 15, Cases 11, 12.

Restricted contracts

70. Reconsideration of registered rents under Part V of Rent Act 1977

(1) . . .

(2) This section does not apply in any case where the date from which the period during which no application for registration can be made is to be calculated falls before the commencement of this section. **[498]**

NOTES
Commencement: 28 November 1980.
Commencement order: SI 1980 No 1706.
Sub-s (1): amends the Rent Act 1977, s 80(2).

72. Functions of rent tribunals

(1) Rent tribunals, as constituted for the purposes of the 1977 Act, are hereby abolished . . .

(2) As from the commencement of this section the functions which, under the 1977 Act, are conferred on rent tribunals shall be carried out by rent assessment committees.

(3) A rent assessment committee shall, when constituted to carry out functions so conferred, be known as a rent tribunal. **[499]**

NOTES
Commencement: 28 November 1980.
Commencement order: SI 1980 No 1706.
Words omitted repeal the Rent Act 1977, s 76.

Miscellaneous

73. Dwellings forming part of Crown Estate or belonging to Duchies

(1)-(4) . . .

(5) Schedule 8 to this Act has effect for making certain provisions consequential on this section. **[500]**

NOTES
Commencement: 28 November 1980.
Commencement order: SI 1980 No 1706.
Sub-ss (1), (2): amend the Rent Act 1977, ss 13, 19.
Sub-s (3): amends the Rent (Agriculture) Act 1976, s 5(1).
Sub-s (4): amends the Landlord and Tenant Act 1954, ss 56, 21(6).

74. Housing association and housing trust tenancies under Rent Act 1977

(1), (2) . . .

(3) Schedule 9 to this Act has effect for the purpose of supplementing this section. **[501]**

NOTES
Commencement: 28 November 1980.
Commencement order: SI 1980 No 1706.
Sub-ss (1), (2): amend the Rent Act 1977, s 15.

76. Statutory tenancies by succession

(1)–(3) . . .

(4) The amendments made by this section have effect only in relation to deaths occurring after the commencement of the subsection concerned. **[502]**

NOTES
Commencement: 28 November 1980.
Commencement order: SI 1980 No 1706.
Sub-ss (1), (2): amend the Rent Act 1977, Sch 1.
Sub-s (3): amends the Rent (Agriculture) Act 1976, ss 3, 4.

77. Amendment of Part VI of Rent Act 1977

Part VI of the 1977 Act (rent limit for dwellings let by housing associations, housing trusts and the Housing Corporation) is amended in accordance with the provisions of Schedule 10 to this Act. **[503]**

NOTES
Commencement: 28 November 1980.
Commencement order: SI 1980 No 1706.

PART III

TENANT'S REPAIRS AND IMPROVEMENTS

81. Tenant's improvements

(1) The following provisions of this section have effect with respect to . . . , protected tenancies and statutory tenancies in place of section 19(2) of the Landlord and Tenant Act 1927.

(2) It is by virtue of this section a term of every such tenancy that the tenant will not make any improvement without the written consent of the landlord.

(3) The consent required by virtue of subsection (2) above is not to be unreasonably withheld and, if unreasonably withheld, shall be treated as given.

(4) Subsections (1) to (3) above do not apply in any case where the tenant has been given a notice—

(*a*) of a kind mentioned in one of Cases 11 to 18 and 20 in Schedule 15 to the 1977 Act (notice that possession might be recovered under that Case); or

(*b*) under section 52(1)(*b*) of this Act (notice that a tenancy is to be a protected shorthold tenancy);

unless the tenant proves that, at the time when the landlord gave the notice, it was unreasonable for the landlord to expect to be able in due course to recover possession of the dwelling-house under that Case or, as the case may be, Case 19 of Schedule 15 (added by section 55 of this Act).

(5) In Part I, and in this Part, of this Act "improvement" means any alteration in, or addition to, a dwelling-house and includes—

(*a*) any addition to, or alteration in, landlord's fixtures and fittings and any addition or alteration connected with the provision of any services to a dwelling-house;

(*b*) the erection of any wireless or television aerial; and

(*c*) the carrying out of external decoration;

but paragraph (*c*) above does not apply in relation to a protected or statutory tenancy if the landlord is under an obligation to carry out external decoration or to keep the exterior of the dwelling-house in repair. **[504]**

NOTES

Commencement: 3 October 1980.

Commencement order: SI 1980 No 1406.

Sub-s (1): words omitted repealed by the Housing (Consequential Provisions) Act 1985, s 3, Sch 1, Part I.

1977 Act: Rent Act 1977.

82. Provisions as to consents required by section 81

(1) If any question arises whether the withholding of a consent required by virtue of section 81 above was unreasonable it is for the landlord to show that it was not; and in determining that question the court shall, in particular, have regard to the extent to which the improvement would be likely—

(*a*) to make the dwelling-house, or any other premises, less safe for occupiers;

(*b*) to cause the landlord to incur expenditure which it would be unlikely to incur if the improvement were not made; or (*c*) to reduce the price which the dwelling-house would fetch if sold on the open market or the rent which the landlord would be able to charge on letting the dwelling-house.

(2) A consent required by virtue of section 81 may be validly given notwithstanding that it follows, instead of preceding, the action requiring it and may be given subject to a condition.

(3) Where the tenant has applied in writing for a consent which is required by virtue of section 81 then—

(*a*) if the landlord refuses to give the consent it shall give to the tenant a written statement of the reasons why the consent was refused; and

(*b*) if the landlord neither gives nor refuses to give the consent within a reasonable time, the consent shall be taken to have been withheld, and if the landlord gives the consent but subject to an unreasonable condition, the consent shall be taken to have been unreasonably withheld.

(4) If any question arises whether a condition attached to a consent was reasonable, it is for the landlord to show that it was. **[505]**

NOTES
Commencement: 3 October 1980.
Commencement order: SI 1980 No 1406.

83. Conditional consent to tenant's improvements

Any failure by . . . , a protected tenant or a statutory tenant to satisfy any reasonable condition imposed by his landlord in giving consent to an improvement which the tenant proposes to make, or has made, shall be treated . . . , for the purposes of Chapter II of Part I of this Act or, as the case may be, of an obligation of the previous protected tenancy which is applicable to the statutory tenancy. **[506]**

NOTES
Commencement: 3 October 1980.
Commencement order: SI 1980 No 1406.
Words omitted repealed by the Housing (Consequential Provisions) Act 1985, s 3, Sch 1, Part I.
1977 Act: Rent Act 1977.

84. Exclusion of certain housing associations from Part III

This Part of this Act does not apply in relation to a housing association which falls within paragraph (*d*) of section 15(3) of the 1977 Act (certain societies registered under the Industrial and Provident Societies Act 1965). **[507]**

NOTES
Commencement: 3 October 1980.
Commencement order: SI 1980 No 1406.
1977 Act: Rent Act 1977.

85. Interpretation and application of Part III

(1) In this Part of this Act any expression used . . . in the 1977 Act has the same meaning as in . . . that Act.

(2) This Part of this Act applies to tenancies granted before as well as tenancies granted after the commencement of this Part of this Act. **[508]**

NOTES
Commencement: 3 October 1980.
Commencement order: SI 1980 No 1406.
Words omitted repealed by the Housing (Consequential Provisions) Act 1985, s 3, Sch 1, Part I.
1977 Act: Rent Act 1977.

PART IV
JURISDICTION AND PROCEDURE

86. Jurisdiction of county court and rules of procedure

[(1) A county court has jurisdiction to determine any question arising under Part III of this Act (tenant's improvements) and to entertain any proceedings brought thereunder.

(2) The juridiction conferred by this section includes jurisdiction to entertain proceedings on any question whether any consent required by section 81 was withheld or unreasonably withheld, notwithstanding that no other relief is sought than a declaration.]

(3) If a person takes proceedings in the High Court which, by virtue of this section, he could have taken in the county court he is not entitled to recover any costs.

(4) The Lord Chancellor may make such rules and give such directions as he thinks fit for the purpose of giving effect to this Part of this Act.

(5) The rules and directions may provide—

(*a*) for the exercise by any registrar of a county court of any jurisdiction exercisable under this section; and
(*b*) for the conduct of any proceedings in private.

(6) The power to make rules under this section is exercisable by statutory instrument and any such instrument is subject to annulment in pursuance of a resolution of either House of Parliament. **[509]**

NOTES
Commencement: 1 April 1986 (sub-ss (1), (2)); 3 October 1980 (remainder).
Commencement order: SI 1980 No 1406.
Sub-ss (1), (2): substituted by the Housing (Consequential Provisions) Act 1985, s 4, Sch 2, para 44.

88. Discretion of court in certain proceedings for possession

(1) Where, under the terms of a rental purchase agreement, a person has been let into possession of a dwelling-house and, on the termination of the agreement or of his right to possession under it, proceedings are brought for the possession of the dwelling-house, the court may—

(*a*) adjourn the proceedings; or
(*b*) on making an order for the possession of the dwelling-house, stay or suspend execution of the order or postpone the date of possession;

for such period or periods as the court thinks fit.

(2) On any such adjournment, stay, suspension or postponement the court may impose such conditions with regard to payments by the person in possession in respect of his continued occupation of the dwelling-house and such other conditions as the court thinks fit.

(3) The court may revoke or from time to time vary any condition imposed by virtue of this section.

(4) In this section "rental purchase agreement" means an agreement for the purchase of a dwelling-house (whether freehold or leashold property) under which the whole or part of the purchase price is to be paid in three or more instalments and the completion of the purchase is deferred until the whole or a specified part of the purchase price has been paid.

(5) This section extends to proceedings for the possession of a dwelling-house which were begun before the commencement of this section unless an order for the possession of the dwelling-house was made in the proceedings and executed before the commencement of this section. **[510]**

NOTES

Commencement: 3 October 1980.
Commencement order: SI 1980 No 1406.

89. Restriction on discretion of court in making orders for possession of land

(1) Where a court makes an order for the possession of any land in a case not falling within the exceptions mentioned in subsection (2) below, the giving up of possession shall not be postponed (whether by the order or any variation, suspension or stay of execution) to a date later than fourteen days after the making of the order, unless it appears to the court that exceptional hardship would be caused by requiring possession to be given up by that date; and shall not in any event be postponed to a date later than six weeks after the making of the order.

(2) The restrictions in subsection (1) above do not apply if—

(*a*) the order is made in an action by a mortgagee for possession; or
(*b*) the order is made in an action for forfeiture of a lease; or
(*c*) the court had power to make the order only if it considered it reasonable to make it; or
(*d*) the order relates to a dwelling-house which is the subject of a restricted contract (within the meaning of section 19 of the 1977 Act); or
(*e*) the order is made in proceedings brought as mentioned in section 88(1) above. **[511]**

NOTES

Commencement: 3 October 1980.
Commencement order: SI 1980 No 1406.
1977 Act: Rent Act 1977.

PART IX

GENERAL

Miscellaneous

140. Exclusion of shared ownership tenancies from Leasehold Reform Act 1967

(1) Where, after the commencement of this section, a tenancy of a house is created by the grant of a lease at a premium and either—

(a) the lease is granted by a body mentioned in subsection (2) below and complies with the conditions set out in subsection (3) below; or
(b) the lease is granted by a registered housing association and complies with the conditions set out in subsection (4) below;

the tenancy shall not be treated for the purposes of Part I of the Leasehold Reform Act 1967 (enfranchisement and extension of long leaseholds) as being a long tenancy at a low rent at any time when the interest of the landlord belongs to such a body or, as the case may be, to a registered association.

(2) The bodies referred to in subsection (1)(a) above are—

(a) the council of a district, the Greater London Council, the council of a London borough, the Common Council of the City of London or the Council of the Isles of Scilly;

[(*aa*) the Inner London Education Authority;

(*ab*) a joint authority established by Part IV of the Local Government Act 1985;]

(b) a development corporation established by an order made, or having effect as if made, under the [New Towns Act 1981];

(c) the Commission for the New Towns;

(d) the Development Board for Rural Wales.

(3) The conditions mentioned in subsection (1)(a) above are—

(a) that the lease provides for the tenant to acquire the freehold, whether under an option to purchase or otherwise, for a consideration which is to be calculated in accordance with the terms of the lease and which is reasonable, having regard to the premium or premiums paid by the tenant under the lease; and

(b) that it states the landlord's opinion that by virtue of this section the tenancy will not be a long tenancy at a low rent for the purposes of the Leasehold Reform Act 1967 at any time when the interest of the landlord belongs to a body mentioned in subsection (2) above.

(4) The conditions mentioned in subsection (1)(b) above are—

(a) that the lease is granted at a premium which is calculated by reference to a percentage of the value of the house or of the cost of providing it;

(b) that at the time when it is granted it complies with the requirements of regulations made by the Secretary of State for the purposes of this section; and

(c) that it states the landlord's opinion that by virtue of this section the tenancy will not be a long tenancy at a low rent for the purposes of the Leasehold Reform Act 1967 at any time when the interest of the landlord belongs to a registered housing association.

(5) If, in any proceedings in which it falls to be determined whether a lease complies with the condition in subsection (3)(a) above, the question arises whether the consideration payable by the tenant on acquiring the freehold is reasonable, it is for the landlord to show that it is.

(6) In this section "registered housing association" means an association registered under [the Housing Associations Act 1985]. **[512]**

NOTES

Commencement: 8 August 1980.

Prospectively repealed with savings by the Housing and Planning Act 1986, ss 18, 24(3), Sch 4, paras 7, 11, Sch 12, Part I, as from a day to be appointed.

Sub-s (2): paras (*aa*), (*ab*) added by the Local Government Act 1985, s 84, Sch 14, para 58; para (*b*) amended by the New Towns Act 1981, s 81, Sch 12, para 27.

Sub-s (6): amended by the Housing (Consequential Provisions) Act 1985, s 4, Sch 2, para 44.

1974 Act: Housing Act 1974.

142. Leasehold valuation tribunals

(1) Any matter which under section 21(1), (2) or (3) of the Leasehold Reform Act 1967 is to be determined by the Lands Tribunal shall instead be determined by a rent assessment committee constituted under Schedule 10 to the 1977 Act.

(2) A rent assessment committee shall, when constituted to make any such determination, be known as a leasehold valuation tribunal.

(3) Part I of Schedule 22 to this Act has effect with respect to leasehold valuation tribunals, and the 1967 Act is amended in accordance with Part II of that Schedule. **[513]**

NOTES
Commencement: 31 March 1981.
Commencement order: SI 1981 No 119.
1977 Act: Rent Act 1977.

143. Apportionment of rents

(1) . . .

(2) The Secretary of State may by order vary the amount there mentioned.

(3) . . . **[514–515]**

NOTES
Commencement: 3 October 1980.
Commencement order: SI 1980 No 1406.
Sub-s (1): amends the Landlord and Tenant Act 1927, s 20.
Sub-s (3): adds the Landlord and Tenant Act 1927, s 20(1A).

Supplemental

150. Interpretation

In this Act—

"protected tenant" and "statutory tenant" have the same meanings as in the 1977 Act;

"secure tenant" means the tenant under a secure tenancy and "secure tenancy" has the meaning given by section 28;

. . .

"the 1977 Act" means the Rent Act 1977

. . . **[516]**

NOTES
Commencement: 8 August 1980.
Words omitted repealed by the Housing (Consequential Provisions) Act 1985, s 3, Sch 1, Part I.

151. Regulations and orders

(1) Any power of the Secretary of State to make an order or regulations under this Act shall be exercisable by statutory instrument subject, except in the case of regulations under section . . . 52(3), 56(7) . . . or an order under section *[. . .]* 52(4), 60 or 153 to annulment in pursuance of a resolution of either House of Parliament.

(2) No order under section 52(4) or 60 shall be made unless a draft of it has been laid before Parliament and approved by a resolution of each House of Parliament.

(3) Any order or regulation under this Act may make different provision with respect to different cases or descriptions of cases, including different provision for different areas.

(4) . . . **[517]**

NOTES

Commencement: 8 August 1980.

Sub-s (1): words omitted (which, in the third place, had been inserted by the Housing and Building Control Act 1984, s 64, Sch 11, para 30) repealed by the Housing (Consequential Provisions) Act 1985, s 3, Sch 1, Part I.

Sub-s (4): repealed by the Housing (Consequential Provisions) Act 1985, s 3, Sch 1, Part I.

152. Amendments, savings, transitional provisions and repeals

(1) The enactments mentioned in Part I of Schedule 25 to this Act shall have effect subject to the amendments specified in that Schedule.

(2) The savings and transitional provisions in Part II of that Schedule shall have effect.

(3) The enactments specified in the first column of Schedule 26 to this Act are hereby repealed to the extent specified in column 3 of that Schedule. **[518]**

NOTES

Commencement: 8 August 1980 (sub-s (2)); 8 August 1980 - 1 April 1981 (sub-ss (1), (3) - in part); to be appointed (remainder).

Commencement orders: SI 1980 No 1406, 1980 No 1557, 1980 No 1706, 1980 No 1781, 1981 No 119, 1981 No 296.

153. Commencement

(1), (2) . . .

(3) Sections . . . 140, 150, 151, 152(2) and 153 to 155 shall come into operation on the passing of this Act.

(4) The remaining provisions of this Act shall come into operation on such day as the Secretary of State may by order appoint; and—

(*a*) different days may be appointed for different provisions; and
(*b*) any provision may be brought into force on different days for England, Wales and Scotland. **[519]**

NOTES

Commencement: 8 August 1980.

Words omitted repealed by the Housing (Consequential Provisions) Act 1985, s 3, Sch 1, Part I.

154. Expenses and receipts

(1) There shall be paid out of moneys provided by Parliament the administrative expenses of the Secretary of State under this Act and any increase attributable to this Act in the sums so payable under any other enactment.

(2) . . . **[520]**

NOTES

Commencement: 8 August 1980.

Sub-s (2): repealed by the Housing (Consequential Provisions) Act 1985, s 3, Sch 1, Part I.

155. Short title and extent

(1) This Act may be cited as the Housing Act 1980.

(2) Sections 114 to 116, 120 to 122(1), 123 to 133, 144, 151 to 153 of this Act, this section, Schedule 14, Part II of Schedule 16, paragraphs 1 to 3 of Schedule 17, Schedule 18, paragraphs 11 to 13, 24, 25 and 70 of Schedule 25 and the associated repeals in Schedule 26 extend to Scotland; but this Act does not otherwise so extend.

(3) Sections [111(8),] 152(1), 153, this section and paragraphs 11, 12, 18 and 19 of Part I of Schedule 25 extend to Northern Ireland; but this Act does not otherwise so extend. **[521–524]**

NOTES
Commencement: 8 August 1980.
Sub-s (3): amended by the Housing (Northern Ireland Consequential Amendments) Order 1983, SI 1983 No 1122.

SCHEDULES

SCHEDULE 5

Section 58

APPLICATION OF LANDLORD AND TENANT ACT 1954 TO ASSURED TENANCIES

1. The exceptions and modifications referred to in section 58(1) and (2) of this Act are as follows.

2. Sections 23, 43 and 56 to 60B do not apply.

3. In relation to an assured tenancy the expression "the holding" (which is defined for the purposes of Part II in section 23(3)) means the property comprised in the tenancy.

4.—(1) Section 30 applies as if—

(*a*) for paragraph (*d*) in subsection (1) there were substituted the following paragraph— "(*d*) that the landlord has offered and is willing to provide or secure the provision of suitable alternative accommodation for the tenant";
(*b*) in subsection (2) for the words from "a tenancy" to the end there were substituted the words "an assured tenancy or successive assured tenancies"; and
(*c*) at the end there were added the subsections set out in sub-paragraph (2) below.

(2) The following are the subsections added to section 30 in its application to assured tenancies—

"(4)Accommodation shall be deemed to be suitable if it consists of either—
(*a*) premises which are to be let as a separate dwelling such that they will then be let on an assured tenancy or on a protected or secure tenancy, or
(*b*) premises to be let as a separate dwelling on terms which will, in the opinion of the court, afford to the tenant security of tenure reasonably equivalent to that afforded by this Part of this Act in the case of an assured tenancy.

and, in the opinion of the court, the accommodation fulfils the conditions mentioned below.

(5) The conditions are that the accommodation is reasonably suitable to—

(*a*) the needs of the tenant and his family as regards proximity to place of work;
(*b*) the means of the tenant; and
(*c*) the needs of the tenant and his family as regards extent and character; and

that if any furniture was provided for use under the assured tenancy in question, furniture is provided for use in the accommodation which is either similar to that so provided, or is reasonably suitable to the needs of the tenant and his family.

(6) Accommodation shall not be deemed to be suitable to the needs of the tenant and

his family if the result of their occupation of the accommodation would be that it would be an overcrowded dwelling-house for the purposes of the Housing Act 1957.

(7) In this section—

"assured tenancy" has the same meaning as in section 56 of the Housing Act 1980;
"protected tenancy" means a protected tenancy within the meaning of the Rent Act 1977, other than one under which the landlord might recover possession of the dwelling-house under one of the Cases in Part II of Schedule 15 to that Act (cases where the court must order possession); and
"secure tenancy" has the same meaning as in section 28 of the Act of 1980.".

5. Section 31A applies as if in subsection (1)(*a*) for the words "for the purposes of the business carried on by the tenant" there were substituted "as a residence for the tenant and his family".

6. Section 34 applies as if in subsection (2)(*b*) for the words from "tenancies" to the end there were substituted the words "assured tenancies (within the meaning of section 56 of the Housing Act 1980); and".

7. Section 37 applies as if for subsections (2) and (3) there were substituted the following subsection—

"(2)The said amount shall be [the product of the appropriate multiplier and] the rateable value of the holding.".

[7A. The power to prescribe a multiplier conferred by subsection (8) of that section includes a power to prescribe a multiplier in relation to assured tenancies different from that prescribed in relation to other tenancies to which Part II of the Landlord and Tenant Act 1954 applies.]

8. Section 38 applies as if in subsection (2) the words from the beginning to the end of paragraph (b), and subsection (3), were omitted.

[8. Section 38 applies as if the following provisions were omitted—

(*a*) in subsection (1), the words "(except as provided by subsection (4) of this section)";
(*b*) in subsection (2), the words from the beginning to the end of paragraph (*b*);
(*c*) subsections (3) and (4).]

9. Section 63(7)(*a*) applies as if reference to section 23(3) of the Act of 1954 were a reference to paragraph 3 of this Schedule. **[525]**

NOTES

Commencement: 6 October 1980.
Commencement order: SI 1980 No 1466.
Para 7: amended by the Housing and Planning Act 1986, s 13(4).
Para 7A: added by the Local Government, Planning and Land Act 1980, s 193, Sch 33, para 14.
Para 8: substituted with savings by the Housing and Planning Act 1986, s 13(7).

SCHEDULE 8

Section 73

CROWN ESTATE AND DUCHIES—CONSEQUENTIAL PROVISIONS

PART I

RENT ACT 1977

1. Where a tenancy granted before the commencement of section 73 of this Act becomes, or would but for its low rent become, a protected tenancy by virtue of that section, section 5 of the 1977 Act applies as if in relation to the dwelling-house the appropriate day were the commencement of that section.

2. . . .

3. In Part II of Schedule 15 to the 1977 Act any reference to the relevant date shall (notwithstanding paragraph 2 of Part III of that Schedule) be construed, in the case of a

tenancy which becomes a regulated tenancy by virtue of section 73 of this Act as meaning the date falling six months after the passing of this Act.

4.—(1) Part II of Schedule 18 to the 1977 Act applies to a tenancy which becomes a regulated tenancy by virtue of section 73 of this Act (unless it is a tenancy falling within sub-paragraph (2) below).

(2) Nothing in Part IX of the 1977 Act applies to the assignment, before the end of the year 1990, of a tenancy which falls within this sub-paragraph; and a tenancy falls within this sub-paragraph if it was granted for a term certain and its terms do not inhibit both the assignment and the underletting of the whole of the premises comprised in the tenancy, and either—

(*a*) it was granted before the commencement of section 73 of this Act and became a regulated tenancy by virtue of that section; or
(*b*) it is a regulated tenancy by virtue of that section and was granted to a person who, at the time of the grant, was the tenant of the premises comprised in it under a regulated tenancy which also fell within this sub-paragraph.

(3) For the purposes of sub-paragraph (2) above the terms of a tenancy inhibit an assignment or underletting if they—

(*a*) preclude it; or
(*b*) permit it subject to a consent but exclude section 144 of the Law of Property Act 1925 (no payment in nature of fine); or
(*c*) permit it subject to a consent but require in connection with a request for consent the making of an offer to surrender the tenancy. **[526]**

NOTES
Commencement: 28 November 1980.
Commencement order: SI 1980 No 1706.
Para 2: amends the Rent Act 1977, Sch 15, Part I, Case 6.

Part II

Rent (Agriculture) Act 1976

5. Where the question whether a person is a qualifying worker for the purposes of the Rent (Agriculture) Act 1976 arises by virtue of section 73 of this Act, Part II of Schedule 3 to that Act applies as if the date of operation for forestry workers were the commencement of that section.

6. Where a protected occupancy or statutory tenancy within the meaning of the Rent (Agriculture) Act 1976 arises at the commencement of section 73 of this Act, Cases VIII and X in Schedule 4 to that Act apply in relation to it as if the operative date were that commencement.

7. For the purpose of determining whether, at the commencement of section 73 of this Act, a person becomes a statutory tenant for the purposes of the Rent (Agriculture) Act 1976 and of applying that Act to him if he does, paragraph 3 of Schedule 9 to that Act applies as if the operative date were that commencement.

8. Paragraphs 6 and 7 above apply in relation to forestry workers as they apply in relation to other persons and paragraph 7 of Schedule 9 to the Rent (Agriculture) Act 1976 does not apply. **[527]**

NOTES
Commencement: 28 November 1980.
Commencement order: SI 1980 No 1706.

Part III

General

9. Where an interest belongs to Her Majesty in right of the Duchy of Lancaster, then, for the purposes of Part I of the Landlord and Tenant Act 1954, the Rent (Agriculture)

Act 1976 or the 1977 Act, the Chancellor of the Duchy of Lancaster shall be deemed to be the owner of the interest.

10. Where an interest belongs to the Duchy of Cornwall, then, for the purposes of Part I of the Landlord and Tenant Act 1954, the Rent (Agriculture) Act 1976 or the 1977 Act, the Secretary of the Duchy of Cornwall shall be deemed to be the owner of the interest. **[528]**

NOTES
Commencement: 28 November 1980.
Commencement order: SI 1980 No 1706.
1977 Act: Rent Act 1977.

SCHEDULE 9

Section 74

Provisions Supplementing Section 74

1. Paragraphs 2 to 6 below apply to any tenancy which was a protected or statutory tenancy but which, by virtue of the landlord becoming a "housing trust" within the meaning of section 15 of the 1977 Act, has ceased to be such a tenancy.

2. If the tenancy—

(*a*) was a statutory tenancy; and
(*b*) would have become a secure tenancy had it previously been a protected tenancy;

it shall be treated for the purposes of . . . [Part IV of the Housing Act 1985 (secure tenancies)] as if it were a secure tenancy for a term certain which, at the time when it ceased to be a statutory tenancy, came to an end by effluxion of time.

3. Registration of a rent, or of a different rent, for the dwelling-house shall be effected in pursuance of section 87 of the 1977 Act; but until such time as a rent is so registered—

(*a*) the rent recoverable under the tenancy; and
(*b*) where a rent was registered for the dwelling-house under Part IV of the 1977 Act, the time at which an application for a different registered rent may be made;

shall be determined as if the tenancy had continued to be a regulated tenancy.

4. If the tenant was a successor within the meaning of Schedule 1 to the 1977 Act he shall not be treated as a successor for the purposes of [Part IV of the Housing Act 1985 (secure tenancies)].

5. [Section 83 of the Housing Act 1985 (notice of proceedings for possession)] does not apply in any case where proceedings for possession were begun before the tenancy ceased to be a protected or statutory tenancy; but in such a case the court shall allow the parties to take such steps in relation to the proceedings as it considers appropriate in consequence of the tenancy becoming a secure tenancy.

6.—(1) This paragraph applies in any case where—

(*a*) the tenant died before the date on which the tenancy ceased to be a protected or statutory tenancy; and
(*b*) there was then more than one member of his family entitled to succeed him as statutory tenant but no decision had, by that date, been reached as to which of them was to succeed.

(2) In a case to which this paragraph applies, the person who is to be the secure tenant of the dwelling-house on the tenancy becoming a secure tenancy shall be selected by the landlord from among those mentioned in sub-paragraph (1)(*b*) above notwithstanding that the question may have been referred to the county court in accordance with paragraph 1(7) of Schedule 1 to the 1977 Act. **[529]**

NOTES
Commencement: 28 November 1980.
Commencement order: SI 1980 No 1706.
Amended by the Housing (Consequential Provisions) Act 1985, s 4, Sch 2, para 44.
1977 Act: Rent Act 1977.

SCHEDULE 10

Section 77

AMENDMENT OF PART VI OF RENT ACT 1977

PARA 2

(1) . . .

(2) In relation to a rent registered before the commencement of sub-paragraph (1) above, that sub-paragraph and Schedule 8 to the 1977 Act as applied by that sub-paragraph are subject to the following modifications.

(3) The period of delay is a period ending one year after the end of the stage (within the meaning of section 89 of the 1977 Act as originally enacted) which last began before the commencement of sub-paragraph (1) above; and—

(*a*) for any period falling within that stage section 89 applies as originally enacted; and
(*b*) for any later period falling within the period of delay the permitted increase is whichever of the following is the greater—
  (i) the increase that would have been permitted if this Act had not been passed; and
  (ii) the increase that would be permitted under Schedule 8 to the 1977 Act if the formula set out in paragraph 3 (as substituted by section 60(3) of this Act) were P + 1/2(R - P) **[530]**

NOTES
Commencement: 28 November 1980.
Commencement order: SI 1980 No 1706.
Sub-para (1): amends the Rent Act 1977, s 89.

SCHEDULE 22

Section 142

LEASEHOLD VALUATION TRIBUNALS

PART I

SUPPLEMENTARY PROVISIONS

Constitution of tribunals

1. The president of a panel drawn up under Schedule 10 to the 1977 Act shall, when constituting a leasehold valuation tribunal, ensure that at least one of its members is a person who has experience in the valuation of land.

Appeals

2. No appeal shall lie from a decision of a leasehold valuation tribunal to the High Court by virtue of section 13(1) of the Tribunals and Inquiries Act 1971 and no case may be stated for the opinion of the High Court in respect of such a decision, but any person who—

(*a*) appeared before a tribunal in proceedings to which he was a party; and
(*b*) is dissatisfied with its decision,

may within such time as rules under section 3(6) of the Lands Tribunal Act 1949 may specify, appeal to the Lands Tribunal.

3. A leasehold valuation tribunal shall not be treated as a person aggrieved for the purposes of section 3(4) of the Lands Tribunal Act 1949 (which enables a person aggrieved by a decision of the Tribunal on a point of law to require the Tribunal to state a case for decision of the Court of Appeal).

4. For the purposes of Part I of the Leasehold Reform Act 1967 a matter is to be treated as determined by a leasehold valuation tribunal—

(*a*) if the tribunal's decision is not appealed against, on the expiration of the time for bringing an appeal; or

(*b*) if the decision is appealed against, and not set aside in consequence of the appeal, at the time when the appeal and any further appeal is disposed of by the determination of it and the expiration of the time for bringing a further appeal (if any) or by its being abandoned or otherwise ceasing to have effect.

Costs

5. The costs which a person may be required to bear under section 9(4) or 14(2) of the 1967 Act (matters the cost of which are to be borne by person giving notice of his desire to have the freehold or an extended lease) do not include costs incurred by a landlord in connection with a reference to a leasehold valuation tribunal.

6. Where the county court gives any such certificate as is authorised by section 20(4) of or paragraph 8(1) of Schedule 2 to the 1967 Act (certificate of unreasonable delay or default by landlord or tenant) the Lands Tribunal may make the like order as to costs of proceedings on an appeal before the Tribunal in relation to the matter in question as the county court is authorised to make by section 20(4) or paragraph 8(1).

Provision of information

7.—(1) Where a matter is referred to a leasehold valuation tribunal for determination, the tribunal may by notice in writing served on the tenant or landlord or on a superior landlord require him to give to the tribunal, within such period but not less than 14 days from the service of the notice as may be specified in the notice, such information as the tribunal may reasonably require.

(2) If any person fails without reasonable cause to comply with any notice served on him under this paragraph he shall be liable, on summary conviction, to a fine not exceeding [level 3 on the standard scale]. **[531]**

NOTES

Commencement: 31 March 1981.

Commencement order: SI 1981 No 119.

Para 7: maximum fine converted to a level on the standard scale by the Criminal Justice Act 1982, ss 37, 46.

1977 Act: Rent Act 1977.

SCHEDULE 25

Section 152

MINOR AND CONSEQUENTIAL AMENDMENTS, TRANSITIONAL PROVISIONS AND SAVINGS

PART I

PARA 61 MINOR AND CONSEQUENTIAL AMENDMENTS

The Protection from Eviction Act 1977 shall apply, where a person has been let into possession of a dwelling-house under the terms of a rental purchase agreement (within the meaning of section 88 of this Act) as if—

(*a*) the dwelling-house had been let to him as a dwelling under a tenancy which is not a statutorily protected tenancy (within the meaning of section 3 of that Act); and

(*b*) that tenancy had come to an end on the termination of the agreement or of his right to possession under it. **[532]**

NOTES
Commencement: 3 October 1980.
Commencement order: SI 1980 No 1406.

PART II

TRANSITIONAL PROVISIONS AND SAVINGS

62. . . .

63. Where, immediately before the commencement of section 60 of this Act, an increase in rent was subject to the provisions as to phasing of rent increases in Schedule 6 to the Rent (Agriculture) Act 1976 or in Schedule 8 or 9 to the 1977 Act that increase shall continue to be subject to those provisions as if this Act had not been passed.

64. Where the recoverable rent for any statutory period has been increased by a notice under section 48 of the 1977 Act, nothing in section 63 of this Act affects that increase or the operation of subsections (4) and (5) of section 48 in relation to the notice.

65. In a case where, by virtue of subsection (4) of section 52 of the 1977 Act, that section would not have applied to an agreement with a tenant having security of tenure had it not been replaced by the section substituted by section 68(2) of this Act, the substituted section 52 shall also not apply in relation to that agreement.

66. The repeal by this Act of subsections (4) and (5) of section 54 of the 1977 Act does not affect the operation of those subsections in relation to defaults occurring before the commencement of section 68 of this Act.

67. Where, immediately before the commencement of section 69(4) of this Act, a tenancy was, by virtue of section 12(2)(*b*) of the 1977 Act, a protected tenancy and not a restricted contract, the 1977 Act shall continue to apply in relation to that tenancy as if section 69(4) had not been enacted.

68. The repeals made by section 74 of this Act in section 15 of the 1977 Act shall not affect any tenancy which was, immediately before the commencement of section 74(1), a protected or statutory tenancy but which would, were it not for this paragraph, have ceased to be such a tenancy by virtue of the repeal of section 15(4)(*f*).

69. . . .

70. . . .

71. . . .

72.—(1) This paragraph applies in relation to the exceptions in paragraphs 6 and 11 of Schedule 3 to this Act.

(2) Notice given to a tenant at any time after 31st March 1980 but before the commencement of Schedule 3 shall be treated—

(*a*) as duly given in accordance with paragraph 6(*b*)(ii) if it would have been so treated had paragraph 6 then been in force; or
(*b*) as duly given in accordance with paragraph 11(*b*) if it would have been so treated had paragraph 11, and the regulations first made under that paragraph designating courses, then been in force.

73. In relation to a tenancy (or licence) granted before 8th May 1980 Schedule 3 to this Act has effect as if the following paragraph were added at the end of it:

"14. A tenancy is not a secure tenancy if—
(*a*) the landlord is a charity within the meaning of the Charities Act 1960; and
(*b*) before the tenancy was granted the tenant was informed in writing that the landlord intended to carry out works on the building or part of the building comprising the dwelling-house and could not reasonably do so without obtaining possession of the dwelling-house."

74. . . .

75. Section 5 of the 1977 Act (tenancies at low rents) shall continue not to apply to any tenancy which, immediately before the repeal by this Act of section 17 of the 1977 Act (categories of controlled tenancies) was a controlled tenancy by virtue of subsection (2) of section 17.

76. . . .

77. Section 90 of the 1977 Act continues to have effect, notwithstanding its repeal by this Act, in relation to any direction given by the Secretary of State under that section.

78. Paragraphs 3 and 4 of Schedule 17 to the 1977 Act continue to have effect, notwithstanding paragraph 59 of this Schedule, in relation to a notice of increase served under paragraph 4 before the commencement of paragraph 59. **[533]**

NOTES

Commencement: 8 August 1980.
1957 Act: Housing Act 1957.
1974 Act: Housing Act 1974.
1975 Act: Housing Rents and Subsidies Act 1975.
1977 Act: Rent Act 1977.
Paras 62, 69, 71, 74, 76: repealed by the Housing (Consequential Provisions) Act 1985, s 3, Sch 1, Part I.
Para 70: spent on repeal of s 114 of this Act by Finance Act 1982, s 157, Sch 22, Part V.

SUPREME COURT ACT 1981

(c 54)

An Act to consolidate with amendments the Supreme Court of Judicature (Consolidation) Act 1925 and other enactments relating to the Supreme Court in England and Wales and the administration of justice therein; to repeal certain obsolete or unnecessary enactments so relating; to amend Part VIII of the Mental Health Act 1959, the Courts-Martial (Appeals) Act 1968, the Arbitration Act 1979 and the law relating to county courts; and for connected purposes. [28 July 1981]

PART II

JURISDICTION: THE HIGH COURT

Powers

38. Relief against forfeiture for non-payment of rent

(1) In any action in the High Court for the forfeiture of a lease for non-payment of rent, the court shall have power to grant relief against forfeiture in a summary manner, and may do so subject to the same terms and conditions as to the payment of rent, costs or otherwise as could have been imposed by it in such an action immediately before the commencement of this Act.

(2) Where the lessee or a person deriving title under him is granted relief under this section, he shall hold the demised premises in accordance with the terms of the lease without the necessity for a new lease. **[534]**

NOTES

Commencement: 1 January 1982.
This section derived from the Supreme Court of Judicature (Consolidation) Act 1925, s 46.

COUNTY COURTS ACT 1984

(c 28)

An Act to consolidate certain enactments relating to county courts. [26 June 1984]

PART IX

MISCELLANEOUS AND GENERAL

Forfeiture for non-payment of rent

138. Provisions as to forfeiture for non-payment of rent

(1) This section has effect where a lessor is proceeding by action in a county court (being an action in which the county court has jurisdiction) to enforce against a lessee a right of re-entry or forfeiture in respect of any land for non-payment of rent.

(2) If the lessee pays into court not less than 5 clear days before the return day all the rent in arrear and the costs of the action, the action shall cease, and the lessee shall hold the land according to the lease without any new lease.

(3) If—

(*a*) the action does not cease under subsection (2); and
(*b*) the court at the trial is satisfied that the lessor is entitled to enforce the right of re-entry or forfeiture,

the court shall order possession of the land to be given to the lessor at the expiration of such period, not being less than 4 weeks from the date of the order, as the court thinks fit, unless within that period the lessee pays into court all the rent in arrear and the costs of the action.

(4) The court may extend the period specified under subsection (3) at any time before possession of the land is recovered in pursuance of the order under that subsection.

(5) . . . if—

(*a*) within the period specified in the order; or
(*b*) within that period as extended under subsection (4),

the lessee pays into court—

(i) all the rent in arrear; and
(ii) the costs of the action,

he shall hold the land according to the lease without any new lease.

(6) Subsection (2) shall not apply where the lessor is proceeding in the same action to enforce a right of re-entry or forfeiture on any other ground as well as for non-payment of rent, or to enforce any other claim as well as the right of re-entry or forfeiture and the claim for arrears of rent.

(7) If the lessee does not—

(*a*) within the period specified in the order; or
(*b*) within that period as extended under subsection (4), pay into court—

(i) all the rent in arrear; and
(ii) the costs of the action,

the order shall be [enforceable] in the prescribed manner and so long as the order remains unreversed the lessee shall [, subject to subsections (8) and (9A),] be barred from all relief.

(8) The extension under subsection (4) of a period fixed by a court shall not be treated as relief from which the lessee is barred by subsection (7) if he fails to

pay into court all the rent in arrear and the costs of the action within that period.

(9) Where the court extends a period under subsection (4) at a time when—

(*a*) that period has expired; and

(*b*) a warrant has been issued for the possession of the land, the court shall suspend the warrant for the extended period; and, if, before the expiration period, the lessee pays into court all the rent in arrear and all the costs of the action, the court shall cancel the warrant.

[(9A) Where the lessor recovers possession of the land at any time after the making of the order under subsection (3) (whether as a result of the enforcement of the order or otherwise) the lessee may, at any time within six months from the date on which the lessor recovers possession, apply to the court for relief; and on any such application the court may, if it thinks fit, grant to the lessee such relief, subject to such terms and conditions, as it thinks fit.

(9B) Where the lessee is granted relief on an application under subsection (9A) he shall hold the land according to the lease without any new lease.

(9C) An application under subsection (9A) may be made by a person with an interest under a lease of the land derived (whether immediately or otherwise) from the lessee's interest therein in like manner as if he were the lessee; and on any such application the court may make an order which (subject to such terms and conditions as the court thinks fit) vests the land in such a person, as lessee of the lessor, for the remainder of the term of the lease under which he has any such interest as aforesaid, or for any lesser term.

In this subsection any reference to the land includes a reference to a part of the land.]

(10) Nothing in this section or section 139 shall be taken to affect—

(*a*) the power of the court to make any order which it would otherwise have power to make as respects a right of re-entry or forfeiture on any ground other than non-payment of rent; or

(*b*) section 146(4) of the Law of Property Act 1925 (relief against forfeiture). **[535]**

NOTES

Commencement: 1 August 1984.

Sub-ss (1), (5) derived from the County Courts Act 1959, s 191(1), and the Administration of Justice Act 1965, s 23; sub-ss (2), (3), (6), (10) derived from the County Courts Act 1959, s 191(1), (4); sub-ss (4), (7)-(9) derived from the Administration of Justice Act 1965, s 23.

Sub-ss (5), (7): amended by the Administration of Justice Act 1985, ss 55(2), (3), 67(2), Sch 8, Part III.

Sub-ss (9A), (9B), (9C): added with savings by the Administration of Justice Act 1985, ss 55(4), 69(5), Sch 9, para 13.

139. Service of summons and re-entry

(1) In a case where section 138 has effect, if—

(*a*) one-half-year's rent is in arrear at the time of the commencement of the action; and

(*b*) the lessor has a right to re-enter for non-payment of that rent; and

(*c*) no sufficient distress is to be found on the premises countervailing the arrears then due,

the service of the summons in the action in the prescribed manner shall stand in lieu of a demand and re-entry.

(2) Where a lessor has enforced against a lessee, by re-entry without action, a right of re-entry or forfeiture as respects any land for non-payment of rent, the lessee may, if the net annual value for rating of the land does not exceed the

county court limit, at any time within six months from the date on which the lessor re-entered apply to the county court for relief, and on any such application the court may, if it thinks fit, grant to the lessee such relief as the High Court could have granted.

[(3) Subsections (9B) and (9C) of section 138 shall have effect in relation to an application under subsection (2) of this section as they have effect in relation to an application under subsection (9A) of that section.] **[536]**

NOTES

Commencement: 1 August 1984 (sub-ss (1)-(2)); 1 October 1986 (remainder).

Sub-s (1) derived from the County Courts Act 1959, s 191(2); sub-s (2) derived from the County Courts Act 1959, s 191(3), and the Administration of Justice Act 1973, Sch 2, Part I.

Sub-s (3): added with savings by the Administration of Justice Act 1985, ss 55, 69(5), Sch 9, para 13.

140. Interpretation of sections 138 and 139

For the purposes of sections 138 and 139—

"lease" includes—

(*a*) an original or derivative under-lease;
(*b*) an agreement for a lease where the lessee has become entitled to have his lease granted; and
(*c*) a grant at a fee farm rent, or under a grant securing a rent by condition;

"lessee" includes—

(*a*) an original or derivative under-lessee;
(*b*) the persons deriving title under a lessee;
(*c*) a grantee under a grant at a fee farm rent, or under a grant securing a rent by condition; and
(*d*) the persons deriving title under such a grantee;

"lessor" includes—

(*a*) an original or derivative under-lessor;
(*b*) the persons deriving title under a lessor;
(*c*) a person making a grant at a fee farm rent, or a grant securing a rent by condition; and
(*d*) the persons deriving title under such a grantor;

"under-lease" includes an agreement for an under-lease where the under-lessee has become entitled to have his underlease granted; and

"under-lessee" includes any person deriving title under an under-lessee. **[537]**

NOTES

Commencement: 1 August 1984.

This section derived from the County Courts Act 1959, s 191(5).

RENT (AMENDMENT) ACT 1985

(c 24)

An Act to make further provision as to the circumstances in which possession of a dwelling-house is recoverable under Case 11 in Schedule 15 to the Rent Act 1977 and Case 11 in Schedule 2 to the Rent (Scotland) Act 1984 and as to the parliamentary procedure applicable to an Order in Council under paragraph 1(1) of Schedule 1 to the Northern Ireland Act 1974 which states that it is made for corresponding purposes. [23 May 1985]

1. Recovery in possession under Case 11

(1)—(3) . . .

(4) Case 11 in Schedule 15 to the Rent Act 1977 and Case 11 in Schedule 2 to the Rent (Scotland) Act 1984, as those cases have effect by virtue of this section, apply to tenancies granted and notices given before, as well as after, the commencement of this Act. **[538]**

NOTES
Commencement: 23 May 1985.
Sub-ss (1)—(3): amend the Rent Act 1977, Sch 15, Case 11, and the Rent (Scotland) Act 1984, Sch 2, Case 11.

2. Northern Ireland

An Order in Council under paragraph 1(1)(*b*) of Schedule 1 to the Northern Ireland Act 1974 (legislation for Northern Ireland in the interim period) which states that it is made only for purposes corresponding to those of section 1 of this Act—

(*a*) shall not be subject to paragraph 1(4) and (5) of that Schedule (affirmative resolution of both Houses of Parliament); but
(*b*) shall be subject to annulment in pursuance of a resolution of either House. **[539]**

NOTES
Commencement: 23 May 1985.
This section extends to Northern Ireland.

3. Short title and extent

(1) This Act may be cited as the Rent (Amendment) Act 1985.

(2) Only section 2 of this Act extends to Northern Ireland. **[540]**

NOTES
Commencement: 23 May 1985.

HOUSING ACT 1985

(c 68)

ARRANGEMENT OF SECTIONS

PART IV

SECURE TENANCIES AND RIGHTS OF SECURE TENANTS

Security of tenure

Section		Para
79	Secure tenancies	[541]
80	The landlord condition	[542]
81	The tenant condition	[543]
82	Security of tenure	[544]
83	Notice of proceedings for possession or termination	[545]
84	Grounds and orders for possession	[546]

Section		Para
85	Extended discretion of court in certain proceedings for possession	[547]
86	Periodic tenancy arising on termination of fixed term	[548]

Succession on death of tenant

87	Persons qualified to succeed tenant	[549]
88	Cases where the tenant is a successor	[550]
89	Succession to periodic tenancy	[551]
90	Devolution of term certain	[552]

Assignment, lodgers and subletting

91	Assignment in general prohibited	[553]
92	Assignments by way of exchange	[554]
93	Lodgers and subletting	[555]
94	Consent to subletting	[556]
95	Assignment or subletting where tenant condition not satisfied	[557]

Repairs and improvements

96	Right to carry out repairs	[558]
97	Tenant's improvements require consent	[559]
98	Provisions as to consents required by s 97	[560]
99	Conditional consent to improvements	[561]
100	Power to reimburse cost of tenant's improvements	[562]
101	Rent not to be increased on account of tenant's improvements	[563]

Variation of terms of tenancy

102	Variation of terms of secure tenancy	[564]
103	Notice of variation of periodic tenancy	[565]

Provision of information and consultation

104	Provision of information about tenancies	[566]
105	Consultation on matters of housing management	[567]
106	Information about housing allocation	[568]
106A	Consultation before disposal to private sector landlord	[569]

Miscellaneous

107	Contributions towards costs of transfers and exchanges	[570]
108	Heating charges	[571]
109	Provisions not applying to tenancies of co-operative housing associations	[572]

Supplementary provisions

109A	Acquisition of dwelling-house subject to statutory tenancy	[573]
110	Jurisdiction of county court	[574]
111	County court rules and directions	[575]
112	Meaning of "dwelling-house"	[576]
113	Members of a person's family	[577]
114	Meaning of "landlord authority"	[578]
115	Meaning of "long tenancy"	[579]
116	Minor definitions	[580]
117	Index of defined expressions: Part IV	[581]

PART XVIII

MISCELLANEOUS AND GENERAL PROVISIONS

General provisions

612	Exclusion of Rent Act protection	[582]
613	Liability of directors, &c in case of offence by body corporate	[583]
614	Power to prescribe forms, &c	[584]
615	Dispensation with advertisements and notices	[585]
616	Local inquiries	[586]
617	Service of notices	[587]

Section		Para
618	The Common Council of the City of London	[588]
619	The Inner and Middle Temples	[589]
620	The Isles of Scilly	[590]
621	Meaning of "lease" and "tenancy" and related expressions	[591]
621A	Meaning of "service charge" and related expressions	[592]
622	Minor definitions: general	[593]
623	Minor definitions: Part XVIII	[594]
624	Index of defined expressions: Part XVIII	[595]

Final Provisions

625	Short title, commencement and extent	[596]

SCHEDULES

Schedule 1—*Tenancies which are not Secure Tenancies* .. [597]
Schedule 2—*Grounds for Possession of Dwelling-Houses Let under Secure Tenancies*
Part I—Grounds on which Court may order possession if it considers it reasonable .. [598]
Part II—Grounds on which the court may order possession if suitable alternative accommodation is available .. [599]
Part III—Grounds on which the court may order possession if it considers it reasonable and suitable alternative accommodation is available .. [600]
Part IV—Suitability of accommodation .. [601]
Part V—Approval of Redevelopment Schemes for purposes of Ground 10A .. [602]
Schedule 3—*Grounds for Withholding Consent to Assignment by Way of Exchange* .. [603]
Schedule 3A—*Consultation before Deposit to Private Sector Landlord* ..
Consultation before Deposit to Private Sector Landlord .. [604]

An Act to consolidate the Housing Acts (except those provisions consolidated in the Housing Associations Act 1985 and the Landlord and Tenant Act 1985), and certain related provisions, with amendments to give effect to recommendations of the Law Commission. [30 October 1985]

PART IV

SECURE TENANCIES AND RIGHTS OF SECURE TENANTS

Security of tenure

79. Secure tenancies

(1) A tenancy under which a dwelling-house is let as a separate dwelling is a secure tenancy at any time when the conditions described in sections 80 and 81 as the landlord condition and the tenant condition are satisfied.

(2) Subsection (1) has effect subject to—

(*a*) the exceptions in Schedule 1 (tenancies which are not secure tenancies),
(*b*) sections 89(3) and (4) and 90(3) and (4) (tenancies ceasing to be secure after death of tenant), and
(*c*) sections 91(2) and 93(2) (tenancies ceasing to be secure in consequence of assignment or subletting).

(3) The provisions of this Part apply in relation to a licence to occupy a dwelling-house (whether or not granted for a consideration) as they apply in relation to a tenancy.

(4) Subsection (3) does not apply to a licence granted as a temporary expedient to a person who entered the dwelling-house or any other land as a trespasser (whether or not, before the grant of that licence, another licence to occupy that or another dwelling-house had been granted to him). **[541]**

NOTES

Commencement: 1 April 1986.

Sub-ss (1), (2) derived from the Housing Act 1980, s 28(1); sub-ss (3), (4) derived from the Housing Act 1980, s 48(1), (2).

80. The landlord condition

(1) The landlord condition is that the interest of the landlord belongs to one of the following authorities or bodies—

a local authority,
a new town corporation,
an urban development corporation,
the Development Board for Rural Wales,
the Housing Corporation,
a housing trust which is a charity, or
a housing association or housing co-operative to which this section applies.

(2) This section applies to—

(*a*) a registered housing association other than a co-operative housing association, and
(*b*) an unregistered housing association which is a co-operative housing association.

(3) If a co-operative housing association ceases to be registered, it shall, within the period of 21 days beginning with the date on which it ceases to be registered, notify each of its tenants who thereby becomes a secure tenant, in writing, that he has become a secure tenant.

[(4) This section applies to a housing co-operative within the meaning of section 27B (agreements under certain superseded provisions) where the dwelling-house is comprised in a housing co-operative agreement within the meaning of that section.] **[542]**

NOTES

Commencement: 1 January 1987 (sub-s (4)); 1 April 1986 (remainder).

Sub-s (1) derived from the Housing Act 1980, s 28(2), (4), the Local Government, Planning and Land Act 1980, s 156(2)(*a*) and the Housing and Building Control Act 1984, s 36(1); sub-s (2) derived from the Housing (Homeless Persons) Act 1977, s 15(3) and the Housing Act 1980, ss 28(2), 49(1), (2); sub-ss (3), (4) derived from the Housing Act 1980,ss 28(2)(*c*), 49(4), (5), 50(1).

Sub-s (4): substituted by the Housing and Planning Act 1986, s 24(2), Sch 5, Part II, para 26.

81. The tenant condition

The tenant condition is that the tenant is an individual and occupies the dwelling-house as his only or principal home; or, where the tenancy is a joint tenancy, that each of the joint tenants is an individual and at least one of them occupies the dwelling-house as his only or principal home. **[543]**

NOTES

Commencement: 1 April 1986.

This section derived from the Housing Act 1980, s 28(3).

82. Security of tenure

(1) A secure tenancy which is either—

(*a*) a weekly or other periodic tenancy, or

(*b*) a tenancy for a term certain but subject to termination by the landlord,

cannot be brought to an end by the landlord except by obtaining an order of the court for the possession of the dwelling-house or an order under subsection (3).

(2) Where the landlord obtains an order for the possession of the dwelling-house, the tenancy ends on the date on which the tenant is to give up possession in pursuance of the order.

(3) Where a secure tenancy is a tenancy for a term certain but with a provision for re-entry or forfeiture, the court shall not order possession of the dwelling-house in pursuance of that provision, but in a case where the court would have made such an order it shall instead make an order terminating the tenancy on a date specified in the order and section 86 (periodic tenancy arising on termination of fixed terms) shall apply.

(4) Section 146 of the Law of Property Act 1925 (restriction on and relief against forfeiture), except subsection (4) (vesting in under-lessee), and any other enactment or rule of law relating to forfeiture, shall apply in relation to proceedings for an order under subsection (3) of this section as if they were proceedings to enforce a right of re-entry or forfeiture. **[544]**

NOTES

Commencement: 1 April 1986.

Sub-ss (1), (2), (4) derived from the Housing Act 1980, s 32(1), (3); sub-s (3) derived from the Housing Act 1980, ss 29(1), 32(3).

83. Notice of proceedings for possession or termination

(1) The court shall not entertain—

(*a*) proceedings for the possession of a dwelling-house let under a secure tenancy, or
(*b*) proceedings for the termination of a secure tenancy,

unless the landlord has served on the tenant a notice complying with the provisions of this section.

(2) The notice shall—

(*a*) be in a form prescribed by regulations made by the Secretary of State,
(*b*) specify the ground on which the court will be asked to make an order for the possession of the dwelling-house or for the termination of the tenancy, and
(*c*) give particulars of that ground.

(3) Where the tenancy is a periodic tenancy the notice—

(*a*) shall also specify a date after which proceedings for the possession of the dwelling-house may be begun, and
(*b*) ceases to be in force twelve months after the date so specified;

and the date so specified must not be earlier than the date on which the tenancy could, apart from this Part, be brought to an end by notice to quit given by the landlord on the same date as the notice under this section.

(4) Where the tenancy is a periodic tenancy, the court shall not entertain any such proceedings unless they are begun after the date specified in the notice and at a time when the notice is still in force.

(5) Where a notice under this section is served with respect to a secure tenancy for a term certain, it has effect also with respect to any periodic tenancy

arising on the termination of that tenancy by virtue of section 86; and subsections (3) and (4) of this section do not apply to the notice.

(6) Regulations under this section shall be made by statutory instrument and may make different provision with respect to different cases or descriptions of case, including different provision for different areas. **[545]**

NOTES

Commencement: 1 April 1986.

Sub-ss (1)-(5) derived from the Housing Act 1980, s 33(1)-(4); sub-s (6) derived from the Housing Act 1980, s 151(1), (3).

84. Grounds and orders for possession

(1) The court shall not make an order for the possession of a dwelling-house let under a secure tenancy except on one or more of the grounds set out in Schedule 2.

(2) The court shall not make an order for possession—

(*a*) on the grounds set out in Part I of that Schedule (grounds 1 to 8), unless it considers it reasonable to make the order,

(*b*) on the grounds set out in Part II of that Schedule (grounds 9 to 11), unless it is satisfied that suitable accommodation will be available for the tenant when the order takes effect,

(*c*) on the grounds set out in Part III of that Schedule (grounds 12 to 16), unless it both considers it reasonable to make the order and is satisfied that suitable accommodation will be available for the tenant when the order takes effect;

and Part IV of that Schedule has effect for determining whether suitable accommodation will be available for a tenant.

(3) The court shall not make such an order on any of those grounds unless the ground is specified in the notice in pursuance of which proceedings for possession are begun; but the grounds so specified may be altered or added to with the leave of the court. **[546]**

NOTES

Commencement: 1 April 1986.

Sub-ss (1), (3) derived from the Housing Act 1980, s 34(1); sub-s (2) derived from the Housing Act 1980, s 34(2)-(4) and the Housing and Building Control Act 1984, s 25(2).

85. Extended discretion of court in certain proceedings for possession

(1) Where proceedings are brought for possession of a dwelling-house let under a secure tenancy on any of the grounds set out in Part I or Part III of Schedule 2 (grounds 1 to 8 and 12 to 16: cases in which the court must be satisfied that it is reasonable to make a possession order), the court may adjourn the proceedings for such period or periods as it thinks fit.

(2) On the making of an order for possession of such a dwelling-house on any of those grounds, or at any time before the execution of the order, the court may—

(*a*) stay or suspend the execution of the order, or

(*b*) postpone the date of possession,

for such period or periods as the court thinks fit.

(3) On such an adjournment, stay, suspension or postponement the court—

(*a*) shall impose conditions with respect to the payment by the tenant of arrears of rent (if any) and rent or payments in respect of occupation after the termination of the tenancy (mesne profits), unless it considers that to do so would cause exceptional hardship to the tenant or would otherwise be unreasonable, and

(*b*) may impose such other conditions as it thinks fit.

(4) If the conditions are complied with, the court may, if it thinks fit, discharge or rescind the order for possession.

(5) Where proceedings are brought for possession of a dwelling-house which is let under a secure tenancy and—

(*a*) the tenant's spouse or former spouse, having rights of occupation under the Matrimonial Homes Act 1983, is then in occupation of the dwelling-house, and

(*b*) the tenancy is terminated as a result of those proceedings,

the spouse or former spouse shall, so long as he or she remains in occupation, have the same rights in relation to, or in connection with, any adjournment, stay, suspension or postponement in pursuance of this section as he or she would have if those rights of occupation were not affected by the termination of the tenancy. **[547]**

NOTES

Commencement: 1 April 1986.

This section derived from the Housing Act 1980, s 87(1)-(6); sub-s (1) gives effect to the Law Commission Recommendation No 6, Cmnd 9515.

86. Periodic tenancy arising on termination of fixed terms

(1) Where a secure tenancy ("the first tenancy") is a tenancy for a term certain and comes to an end—

(*a*) by effluxion of time, or

(*b*) by an order of the court under section 82(3) (termination in pursuance of provision for re-entry or forfeiture),

a periodic tenancy of the same dwelling-house arises by virtue of this section, unless the tenant is granted another secure tenancy of the same dwelling-house (whether a tenancy for a term certain or a periodic tenancy) to begin on the coming to an end of the first tenancy.

(2) Where a periodic tenancy arises by virtue of this section—

(*a*) the periods of the tenancy are the same as those for which rent was last payable under the first tenancy, and

(*b*) the parties and the terms of the tenancy are the same as those of the first tenancy at the end of it;

except that the terms are confined to those which are compatible with a periodic tenancy and do not include any provision for re-entry or forfeiture. **[548]**

NOTES

Commencement: 1 April 1986.

This section derived from the Housing Act 1980, s 29(1), (2).

Succession on death of tenant

87. Persons qualified to succeed tenant

A person is qualified to succeed the tenant under a secure tenancy if he occupies the dwelling-house as his only or principal home at the time of the tenant's death and either—

(*a*) he is the tenant's spouse, or
(*b*) he is another member of the tenant's family and has resided with the tenant throughout the period of twelve months ending with the tenant's death;

unless, in either case, the tenant was himself a successor, as defined in section 88. **[549]**

NOTES
Commencement: 1 April 1986.
This section derived from the Housing Act 1980, ss 30(1), (2), 37B(2)(*b*) and the Housing and Building Control Act 1984, s 26(1).

88. Cases where the tenant is a successor

(1) The tenant is himself a successor if—

(*a*) the tenancy vested in him by virtue of section 89 (succession to a periodic tenancy), or
(*b*) he was a joint tenant and has become the sole tenant, or
(*c*) the tenancy arose by virtue of section 86 (periodic tenancy arising on ending of term certain) and the first tenancy there mentioned was granted to another person or jointly to him and another person, or
(*d*) he became the tenant on the tenancy being assigned to him (but subject to subsections (2) and (3)), or
(*e*) he became the tenant on the tenancy being vested in him on the death of the previous tenant.

(2) A tenant to whom the tenancy was assigned in pursuance of an order under section 24 of the Matrimonial Causes Act 1973 (property adjustment orders in connection with matrimonial proceedings) is a successor only if the other party to the marriage was a successor.

(3) A tenant to whom the tenancy was assigned by virtue of section 92 (assignments by way of exchange) is a successor only if he was a successor in relation to the tenancy which he himself assigned by virtue of that section.

(4) Where within six months of the coming to an end of a secure tenancy which is a periodic tenancy ("the former tenancy") the tenant becomes a tenant under another secure tenancy which is a periodic tenancy, and—

(*a*) the tenant was a successor in relation to the former tenancy, and
(*b*) under the other tenancy either the dwelling-house or the landlord, or both, are the same as under the former tenancy,

the tenant is also a successor in relation to the other tenancy unless the agreement creating that tenancy otherwise provides. **[550]**

NOTES
Commencement: 1 April 1986.
Sub-ss (1), (4) derived from the Housing Act 1980, s 31(1), (2); sub-ss (2), (3) derived from the Housing Act 1980, s 31(1A) and the Housing and Building Control Act 1984, Sch 11, para 23.

89. Succession to periodic tenancy

(1) This section applies where a secure tenant dies and the tenancy is a periodic tenancy.

(2) Where there is a person qualified to succeed the tenant, the tenancy vests by virtue of this section in that person, or if there is more than one such person in the one to be preferred in accordance with the following rules—

(*a*) the tenant's spouse is to be preferred to another member of the tenant's family;
(*b*) of two or more other members of the tenant's family such of them is to be preferred as may be agreed between them or as may, where there is no such agreement, be selected by the landlord.

(3) Where there is no person qualified to succeed the tenant and the tenancy is vested or otherwise disposed of in the course of the administration of the tenant's estate, the tenancy ceases to be a secure tenancy unless the vesting or other disposal is in pursuance of an order made under section 24 of the Matrimonial Causes Act 1973 (property adjustment orders in connection with matrimonial proceedings).

(4) A tenancy which ceases to be a secure tenancy by virtue of this section cannot subsequently become a secure tenancy. **[551]**

NOTES
Commencement: 1 April 1986.
Sub-ss (1), (2) derived from the Housing Act 1980, s 30(1), (3); sub-ss (3), (4) derived from the Housing Act 1980, s 37B(2), (3)(*a*) and the Housing and Building Control Act 1984, s 26(1).

90. Devolution of term certain

(1) This section applies where a secure tenant dies and the tenancy is a tenancy for a term certain.

(2) The tenancy remains a secure tenancy until—
(*a*) it is vested or otherwise disposed of in the course of the administration of the tenant's estate, as mentioned in subsection (3), or
(*b*) it is known that when it is so vested or disposed of it will not be a secure tenancy.

(3) The tenancy ceases to be a secure tenancy on being vested or otherwise disposed of in the course of administration of the tenant's estate, unless—
(*a*) the vesting or other disposal is in pursuance of an order made under section 24 of the Matrimonial Causes Act 1973 (property adjustment orders in connection with matrimonial proceedings), or
(*b*) the vesting or other disposal is to a person qualified to succeed the tenant.

(4) A tenancy which ceases to be a secure tenancy by virtue of this section cannot subsequently become a secure tenancy. **[552]**

NOTES
Commencement: 1 April 1986.
Sub-s (2) derived from the Housing Act 1980, s 28(5); sub-ss (3), (4) derived from the Housing Act 1980, s 37B(2), (3)(*a*) and the Housing and Building Control Act 1984, s 26(1).

Assignment, lodgers and subletting

91. Assignment in general prohibited

(1) A secure tenancy which is—
(*a*) a periodic tenancy, or
(*b*) a tenancy for a term certain granted on or after 5th November 1982,
is not capable of being assigned except in the cases mentioned in subsection (3).

(2) If a secure tenancy for a term certain granted before 5th November 1982

is assigned, then, except in the cases mentioned in subsection (3), it ceases to be a secure tenancy and cannot subsequently become a secure tenancy.

(3) The exceptions are—

(*a*) an assignment in accordance with section 92 (assignment by way of exchange);

(*b*) an assignment in pursuance of an order made under section 24 of the Matrimonial Causes Act 1973 (property adjustment orders in connection with matrimonial proceedings);

(*c*) an assignment to a person who would be qualified to succeed the tenant if the tenant died immediately before the assignment. **[553]**

NOTES

Commencement: 1 April 1986.

This section derived from the Housing Act 1980, s 37(1), (2)(*a*), (3), (4)(*a*) and the Housing and Building Control Act 1984, s 26(1).

92. Assignments by way of exchange

(1) It is a term of every secure tenancy that the tenant may, with the written consent of the landlord, assign the tenancy to another secure tenant who satisfies the condition in subsection (2).

(2) The condition is that the other secure tenant has the written consent of his landlord to an assignment of his tenancy either to the first-mentioned tenant or to another secure tenant who satisfies the condition in this subsection.

(3) The consent required by virtue of this section shall not be withheld except on one or more of the grounds set out in Schedule 3, and if withheld otherwise than on one of those grounds shall be treated as given.

(4) The landlord may not rely on any of the grounds set out in Schedule 3 unless he has, within 42 days of the tenant's application for the consent, served on the tenant a notice specifying the ground and giving particulars of it.

(5) Where rent lawfully due from the tenant has not been paid or an obligation of the tenancy has been broken or not performed, the consent required by virtue of this section may be given subject to a condition requiring the tenant to pay the oustanding rent, remedy the breach or perform the obligation.

(6) Except as provided by subsection (5), a consent required by virtue of this section cannot be given subject to a condition, and a condition imposed otherwise than as so provided shall be disregarded. **[554]**

NOTES

Commencement: 1 April 1986.

This section derived from the Housing Act 1980, s 37A(1)-(5) and the Housing and Building Control Act 1984, s 26(1).

93. Lodgers and subletting

(1) It is a term of every secure tenancy that the tenant—

(*a*) may allow any persons to reside as lodgers in the dwelling-house, but

(*b*) will not, without the written consent of the landlord, sublet or part with possession of part of the dwelling-house.

(2) If the tenant under a secure tenancy parts with the possession of the

dwelling-house or sublets the whole of it (or sublets first part of it and then the remainder), the tenancy ceases to be a secure tenancy and cannot subsequently become a secure tenancy. **[555]**

NOTES

Commencement: 1 April 1986.

Sub-s (1) derived from the Housing Act 1980, s 35(1), (2); sub-s (2) derived from the Housing Act 1980, s 37B(1), (3)(*a*) and the Housing and Building Control Act 1984, s 26(1).

94. Consent to subletting

(1) This section applies to the consent required by virtue of section 93(1)(*b*) (landlord's consent to subletting of part of dwelling-house).

(2) Consent shall not be unreasonably withheld (and if unreasonably withheld shall be treated as given), and if a question arises whether the withholding of consent was unreasonable it is for the landlord to show that it was not.

(3) In determining that question the following matters, if shown by the landlord, are among those to be taken into account—

(*a*) that the consent would lead to overcrowding of the dwelling-house within the meaning of Part X (overcrowding);

(*b*) that the landlord proposes to carry out works on the dwelling-house, or on the building of which it forms part, and that the proposed works will affect the accommodation likely to be used by the sub-tenant who would reside in the dwelling-house as a result of the consent.

(4) Consent may be validly given notwithstanding that it follows, instead of preceding, the action requiring it.

(5) Consent cannot be given subject to a condition (and if purporting to be given subject to a condition shall be treated as given unconditionally).

(6) Where the tenant has applied in writing for consent, then—

(*a*) if the landlord refuses to give consent, it shall give the tenant a written statement of the reasons why consent was refused, and

(*b*) if the landlord neither gives nor refuses to give consent within a reasonable time, consent shall be taken to have been withheld. **[556]**

NOTES

Commencement: 1 April 1986.

Sub-ss (1), (4)-(6) derived from the Housing Act 1980, s 36(2)-(5); sub-ss (2), (3) derived from the Housing Act 1980, ss 35(3), 36(1).

95. Assignment or subletting where tenant condition not satisfied

(1) This section applies to a tenancy which is not a secure tenancy but would be if the tenant condition referred to in section 81 (occupation by the tenant) were satisfied.

(2) Sections 91 and 93(2) (restrictions on assignment or subletting of whole dwelling-house) apply to such a tenancy as they apply to a secure tenancy, except that—

(*a*) section 91(3)(*b*) and (*c*) (assignments excepted from restrictions) do not apply to such a tenancy for a term certain granted before 5th November 1982, and (*b*) references to the tenancy ceasing to be secure shall be disregarded, without prejudice to the application of the remainder of the provisions in which those references occur. **[557]**

NOTES

Commencement: 1 April 1986.

This section derived from the Housing Act 1980, ss 37(1), (2)(*b*), (3), (4)(*b*), 37B(3)(*b*) and the Housing and Building Control Act 1984, s 26(1).

Repairs and improvements

96. Right to carry out repairs

(1) The Secretary of State may by regulations make a scheme for entitling secure tenants, subject to and in accordance with the provisions of the scheme—

(*a*) to carry out to the dwelling-houses of which they are secure tenants repairs which their landlords are obliged by repairing covenants to carry out, and

(*b*) after carrying out the repairs, to recover from their landlords such sums as may be determined by or under the scheme.

(2) The regulations may make such procedural, incidental, supplementary and transitional provision as may appear to the Secretary of State to be necessary or expedient, and may in particular—

(*a*) provide for questions arising under the scheme to be referred to and determined by the county court;

(*b*) provide that where a secure tenant makes application under the scheme his landlord's obligation under the repairing covenants shall cease to apply for such period and to such extent as may be determined by or under the scheme.

(3) The regulations may make different provision with respect to different cases or descriptions of case, including different provision for different areas.

(4) Regulations under this section shall be made by statutory instrument which shall be subject to annulment in pursuance of a resolution of either House of Parliament.

(5) In this section "repairing covenant", in relation to a dwelling-house, means a covenant, whether express or implied, obliging the landlord to keep in repair the dwelling-house or any part of the dwelling-house. **[558]**

NOTES

Commencement: 1 April 1986.

Sub-ss (1), (2), (5) derived from the Housing Act 1980, s 41A(1)-(4) and the Housing and Building Control Act 1984, s 28; sub-ss (3), (4) derived from the Housing Act 1980, s 151(1), (3).

97. Tenant's improvements require consent

(1) It is a term of every secure tenancy that the tenant will not make any improvement without the written consent of the landlord.

(2) In this Part "improvement" means any alteration in, or addition to, a dwelling-house, and includes—

(*a*) any addition to or alteration in landlord's fixtures and fittings,

(*b*) any addition or alteration connected with the provision of services to the dwelling-house,

(*c*) the erection of a wireless or television aerial, and

(*d*) the carrying out of external decoration.

(3) The consent required by virtue of subsection (1) shall not be unreasonably withheld, and if unreasonably withheld shall be treated as given.

(4) The provisions of this section have effect, in relation to secure tenancies, in place of section 19(2) of the Landlord and Tenant Act 1927 (general provisions as to covenants, &c. not to make improvements without consent). **[559]**

NOTES
Commencement: 1 April 1986.
This section derives from the Housing Act 1980, s 81(1), (2), (5).

98. Provisions as to consents required by s 97

(1) If a question arises whether the withholding of a consent required by virtue of section 97 (landlord's consent to improvements) was unreasonable, it is for the landlord to show that it was not.

(2) In determining that question the court shall, in particular, have regard to the extent to which the improvement would be likely—

(*a*) to make the dwelling-house, or any other premises, less safe for occupiers,
(*b*) to cause the landlord to incur expenditure which it would be unlikely to incur if the improvement were not made, or
(*c*) to reduce the price which the dwelling-house would fetch if sold on the open market or the rent which the landlord would be able to charge on letting the dwelling-house.

(3) A consent required by virtue of section 97 may be validly given notwithstanding that it follows, instead of preceding, the action requiring it.

(4) Where a tenant has applied in writing for a consent which is required by virtue of section 97—

(*a*) the landlord shall if it refuses consent give the tenant a written statement of the reason why consent was refused, and
(*b*) if the landlord neither gives nor refuses to give consent within a reasonable time, consent shall be taken to have been withheld. **[560]**

NOTES
Commencement: 1 April 1986.
Sub-ss (1), (2) derived from the Housing Act 1980, ss 81(3), 82(1); sub-ss (3), (4) derived from the Housing Act 1980, s 82(2), (3).

99. Conditional consent to improvements

(1) Consent required by virtue of section 97 (landlord's consent to improvements) may be given subject to conditions.

(2) If the tenant has applied in writing for consent and the landlord gives consent subject to an unreasonable condition, consent shall be taken to have been unreasonably withheld.

(3) If a question arises whether a condition was reasonable, it is for the landlord to show that it was.

(4) A failure by a secure tenant to satisfy a reasonable condition imposed by

his landlord in giving consent to an improvement which the tenant proposes to make, or has made, shall be treated for the purposes of this Part as a breach by the tenant of an obligation of his tenancy. **[561]**

NOTES

Commencement: 1 April 1986.

This section derived from the Housing Act 1980, ss 82(2), (3)(*b*), (4), 83.

100. Power to reimburse cost of tenant's improvements

(1) Where a secure tenant has made an improvement and—

(*a*) the work on the improvement was begun on or after 3rd October 1980,

(*b*) the landlord, or a predecessor in title of the landlord, has given its written consent to the improvement or is treated as having given its consent, and

(*c*) the improvement has materially added to the price which the dwelling-house may be expected to fetch if sold on the open market, or the rent which the landlord may be expected to be able to charge on letting the dwelling-house,

the landlord may, at or after the end of the tenancy, make to the tenant (or his personal representatives) such payment in respect of the improvement as the landlord considers to be appropriate.

(2) The amount which a landlord may pay under this section in respect of an improvement shall not exceed the cost, or likely cost, of the improvement after deducting the amount of any improvement grant, intermediate grant, special grant *or repairs grant* [, repairs grant or common parts grant] under Part XV in respect of the improvement.

(3) The power conferred by this section to make such payments as are mentioned in subsection (1) is in addition to any other power of the landlord to make such payments. **[562]**

NOTES

Commencement: 1 April 1986.

This section derived from the Housing Act 1980, s 38(1)-(3).

Sub-s (2): words in italics prospectively repealed and words in square brackets prospectively substituted by the Housing and Planning Act 1986, s 15, Sch 3, Part II, para 16(2), as from a day to be appointed.

101. Rent not to be increased on account of tenant's improvements

(1) This section applies where a person (the "improving tenant") who is or was the secure tenant of a dwelling-house has lawfully made an improvement and has borne the whole or part of its cost; and for the purposes of this section a person shall be treated as having borne any cost which he would have borne but for an improvement grant, intermediate grant, special grant *or repairs grant* [, repairs grant or common parts grant] under Part XV.

(2) In determining, at any time whilst the improving tenant or his qualifying successor is a secure tenant of the dwelling-house, whether or to what extent to increase the rent, the landlord shall treat the improvement as justifying only such part of an increase which would otherwise be attributable to the improvement as corresponds to the part of the cost which was not borne by the tenant (and accordingly as not justifying an increase if he bore the whole cost).

(3) The following are qualifying successors of an improving tenant—

(*a*) a person in whom the tenancy vested under section 89 (succession to periodic tenancy) on the death of the tenant;

(*b*) a person to whom the tenancy was assigned by the tenant and who would have been qualified to succeed him if he had died immediately before the assignment;

(*c*) a person to whom the tenancy was assigned by the tenant in pursuance of an order made under section 24 of the Matrimonial Causes Act 1973 (property adjustment orders in connection with matrimonial proceedings);

(*d*) a spouse or former spouse of the tenant to whom the tenancy has been transferred by an order under paragraph 2 of Schedule 1 to the Matrimonial Homes Act 1983.

(4) This section does not apply to an increase of rent attributable to rates. **[563]**

NOTES

Commencement: 1 April 1986.

This section derived from the Housing Act 1980, s 39 and the Housing and Building Control Act 1984, s 27.

Sub-s (1): words in italics prospectively repealed and words in square brackets prospectively substituted by the Housing and Planning Act 1986, s 15, Sch 3, Part II, para 16(3), as from a day to be appointed.

Variation of terms of tenancy

102. Variation of terms of secure tenancy

(1) The terms of a secure tenancy may be varied in the following ways, and not otherwise—

(*a*) by agreement between the landlord and the tenant;

(*b*) to the extent that the variation relates to rent or to payments in respect of rates or services, by the landlord or the tenant in accordance with a provision in the lease or agreement creating the tenancy, or in an agreement varying it;

(*c*) in accordance with section 103 (notice of variation of periodic tenancy).

(2) References in this section and section 103 to variation include addition and deletion; and for the purposes of this section the conversion of a monthly tenancy into a weekly tenancy, or a weekly tenancy into a monthly tenancy, is a variation of a term of the tenancy, but a variation of the premises let under a tenancy is not.

(3) This section and section 103 do not apply to a term of a tenancy which—

(*a*) is implied by an enactment, or

(*b*) may be varied under section 93 of the Rent Act 1977 (housing association and other tenancies: increase of rent without notice to quit).

(4) This section and section 103 apply in relation to the terms of a periodic tenancy arising by virtue of section 86 (periodic tenancy arising on termination of a fixed term) as they would have applied to the terms of the first tenancy mentioned in that section had that tenancy been a periodic tenancy. **[564]**

NOTES

Commencement: 1 April 1986.

This section derived from the Housing Act 1980, s 40(1)-(4), (9), (10).

103. Notice of variation of periodic tenancy

(1) The terms of a secure tenancy which is a periodic tenancy may be varied by the landlord by a notice of variation served on the tenant.

(2) Before serving a notice of variation on the tenant the landlord shall serve on him a preliminary notice—

(*a*) informing the tenant of the landlord's intention to serve a notice of variation,
(*b*) specifying the proposed variation and its effect, and
(*c*) inviting the tenant to comment on the proposed variation within such time, specified in the notice, as the landlord considers reasonable;

and the landlord shall consider any comments made by the tenant within the specified time.

(3) Subsection (2) does not apply to a variation of the rent, or of payments in respect of services or facilities provided by the landlord or of payments in respect of rates.

(4) The notice of variation shall specify—

(*a*) the variation effected by it, and
(*b*) the date on which it takes effect;

and the period between the date on which it is served and the date on which it takes effect must be at least four weeks or the rental period, whichever is the longer.

(5) The notice of variation, when served, shall be accompanied by such information as the landlord considers necessary to inform the tenant of the nature and effect of the variation.

(6) If after the service of a notice of variation the tenant, before the date on which the variation is to take effect, gives a valid notice to quit, the notice of variation shall not take effect unless the tenant, with the written agreement of the landlord, withdraws his notice to quit before that date. **[565]**

NOTES
Commencement: 1 April 1986.
This section derived from the Housing Act 1980, s 40(4)-(8).

Provision of information and consultation

104. Provision of information about tenancies

(1) Every body which lets dwelling-houses under secure tenancies shall from time to time publish information about its secure tenancies, in such form as it considers best suited to explain in simple terms, and so far as it considers it appropriate, the effect of—

(*a*) the express terms of its secure tenancies,
(*b*) the provisions of this Part and Part V (the right to buy), and
(*c*) the provisions of sections 11 to 16 of the Landlord and Tenant Act 1985 (landlord's repairing obligations),

and shall ensure that so far as is reasonably practicable the information so published is kept up to date.

(2) The landlord under a secure tenancy shall supply the tenant with—

(*a*) a copy of the information for secure tenants published by it under subsection (1), and (*b*) a written statement of the terms of the tenancy, so far as they are neither expressed in the lease or written tenancy agreement (if any) nor implied by law;

and the statement required by paragraph (*b*) shall be supplied on the grant of the tenancy or as soon as practicable afterwards. **[566]**

NOTES

Commencement: 1 April 1986.

This section derived from the Housing Act 1980, s 41(1)-(4).

105. Consultation on matters of housing management

(1) A landlord authority shall maintain such arrangements as it considers appropriate to enable those of its secure tenants who are likely to be substantially affected by a matter of housing management to which this section applies—

(*a*) to be informed of the authority's proposals in respect of the matter, and

(*b*) to make their views known to the authority within a specified period;

and the authority shall, before making any decision on the matter, consider any representations made to it in accordance with those arrangements.

(2) For the purposes of this section, a matter is one of housing management if, in the opinion of the landlord authority, it relates to—

(*a*) the management, maintenance, improvement or demolition of dwelling-houses let by the authority under secure tenancies, or

(*b*) the provision of services or amenities in connection with such dwelling-houses;

but not so far as it relates to the rent payable under a secure tenancy or to charges for services or facilities provided by the authority.

(3) This section applies to matters of housing management which, in the opinion of the landlord authority, represent—

(*a*) a new programme of maintenance, improvement or demolition, or

(*b*) a change in the practice or policy of the authority,

and are likely substantially to affect either its secure tenants as a whole or a group of them who form a distinct social group or occupy dwelling-houses which constitute a distinct class (whether by reference to the kind of dwelling-house, or the housing estate or other larger area in which they are situated).

(4) In the case of a landlord authority which is a local housing authority, the reference in subsection (2) to the provision of services or amenities is a reference only to the provision of services or amenities by the authority acting in its capacity as landlord of the dwelling-houses concerned.

(5) A landlord authority shall publish details of the arrangements which it makes under this section, and a copy of the documents published under this subsection shall—

(*a*) be made available at the authority's principal office for inspection at all reasonable hours, without charge, by members of the public, and

(*b*) be given, on payment of a reasonable fee, to any member of the public who asks for one.

(6) A landlord authority which is a registered housing association shall, instead of complying with paragraph (*a*) of subsection (5), send a copy of any document published under that subsection—

(*a*) to the Housing Corporation, and
(*b*) to the council of any district or London borough in which there are dwelling-houses let by the association under secure tenancies;

and a council to whom a copy is sent under this subsection shall make it available at its principal office for inspection at all reasonable hours, without charge, by members of the public. **[567]**

NOTES
Commencement: 1 April 1986.
Sub-ss (1), (5) derived from the Housing Act 1980, s 43(1)-(3); sub-ss (2)-(4) derived from the Housing Act 1980, s 42(2)(*a*)-(*c*), (3)-(5); sub-s (6) derived from the Rent Act 1977, s 15(3)(*a*) and the Housing Act 1980, s 43(4), (5).

106. Information about housing allocation

(1) A landlord authority shall publish a summary of its rules—

(*a*) for determining priority as between applicants in the allocation of its housing accommodation, and
(*b*) governing cases where secure tenants wish to move (whether or not by way of exchange of dwelling-houses) to other dwelling-houses let under secure tenancies by that authority or another body.

(2) A landlord authority shall—

(*a*) maintain a set of the rules referred to in subsection (1) and of the rules which it has laid down governing the procedure to be followed in allocating its housing accommodation, and
(*b*) make them available at is principal office for inspection at all reasonable hours, without charge, by members of the public.

(3) A landlord authority which is a registered housing association shall, instead of complying with paragraph (*b*) of subsection (2), send a set of the rules referred to in paragraph (*a*) of that subsection—

(*a*) to the Housing Corporation, and
(*b*) to the council of any district or London borough in which there are dwelling-houses let or to be let by the association under secure tenancies;

and a council to whom a set of rules is sent under this subsection shall make it available at its principal office for inspection at all reasonable hours, without charge, by members of the public.

(4) A copy of the summary published under subsection (1) shall be given without charge, and a copy of the set of rules maintained under subsection (2) shall be given on payment of a reasonable fee, to any member of the public who asks for one.

(5) At the request of a person who has applied to it for housing accommodation, a landlord authority shall make available to him, at all reasonable times and without charge, details of the particulars which he has given to the authority about himself and his family and which the authority has recorded as being relevant to his application for accommodation. **[568]**

NOTES
Commencement: 1 April 1986.
This section derived from the Housing Act 1980, s 44(1)-(6).

[106A. Consultation before disposal to private sector landlord

(1) The provisions of Schedule 3A have effect with respect to the duties of—

(*a*) a local authority proposing to dispose of dwelling-houses subject to secure tenancies, and

(*b*) the Secretary of State in considering whether to give his consent to such a disposal,

to have regard to the views of tenants liable as a result of the disposal to cease to be secure tenants.

(2) In relation to a disposal to which that Schedule applies, the provisions of that Schedule apply in place of the provisions of section 105 (consultation on matters of housing management).] **[569]**

NOTES

Commencement: To be appointed.

Prospectively added with respect to disposals after the commencement of this section by the Housing and Planning Act 1986, s 6(1), (3), as from a day to be appointed.

Miscellaneous

107. Contributions towards costs of transfers and exchanges

(1) The Secretary of State may with the consent of the Treasury make grants or loans towards the cost of arrangements for facilitating moves to and from homes by which—

(*a*) a secure tenant becomes, at his request, the secure tenant of a different landlord, or

(*b*) each of two or more tenants of dwelling-houses, one at least of which is let under a secure tenancy, becomes the tenant of the other or one of the others.

(2) The grants or loans may be made subject to such conditions as the Secretary of State may determine, and may be made so as to be repayable, or as the case may be repayable earlier, if there is a breach of such a condition. **[570]**

NOTES

Commencement: 1 April 1986.

This section derived from the Housing Act 1980, s 46(1), (2).

108. Heating charges

(1) This section applies to secure tenants of dwelling-houses to which a heating authority supply heat produced at a heating installation.

(2) The Secretary of State may by regulations require heating authorities to adopt such methods for determining heating charges payable by such tenants as will secure that the proportion of heating costs borne by each of those tenants is no greater than is reasonable.

(3) The Secretary of State may by regulations make provision for entitling such tenants, subject to and in accordance with the regulations, to require the heating authority—

(*a*) to give them, in such form as may be prescribed by the regulations, such information as to heating charges and heating costs as may be so prescribed, and

(*b*) where such information has been given, to afford them reasonable facilities for inspecting the accounts, receipts and other documents supporting the information and for taking copies or extracts from them.

(4) Regulations under this section—

(*a*) may make different provision with respect to different cases or descriptions of case, including different provision for different areas;

(*b*) may make such procedural, incidental, supplementary and transitional provision as appears to the Secretary of State to be necessary or expedient, and may in particular provide for any question arising under the regulations to be referred to and determined by the county court; and

(*c*) shall be made by statutory instrument which shall be subject to annulment in pursuance of a resolution of either House of Parliament.

(5) In this section—

(*a*) "heating authority" means a housing authority who operate a heating installation and supply to premises heat produced at the installation;

(*b*) "heating installation" means a generating station or other installation for producing heat;

(*c*) references to heat produced at an installation include steam produced from, and air and water heated by, heat so produced;

(*d*) "heating charge" means an amount payable to a heating authority in respect of heat produced at a heating installation and supplied to premises, including in the case of heat supplied to premises let by the authority such an amount payable as part of the rent;

(*e*) "heating costs" means expenses incurred by a heating authority in operating a heating installation. **[571]**

NOTES

Commencement: 1 April 1986.

Sub-ss (1)-(3), (5) derived from the Housing Act 1980, s 41B(1)-(3), (6); sub-s (4) derived from the Housing Act 1980, ss 41B(4), (5), 151(1), (3) and the Housing and Building Control Act 1984, s 29.

109. Provisions not applying to tenancies of co-operative housing associations

Sections 91 to 108 (assignment and subletting, repairs and improvements, variation of terms, provision of information and consultation, contributions to costs of transfers and heating charges) do not apply to a tenancy when the interest of the landlord belongs to a co-operative housing association. **[572]**

NOTES

Commencement: 1 April 1986.

This section derived from the Housing Act 1980, ss 49(3), 84.

Supplementary provisions

[109A. Acquisition of dwelling-house subject to statutory tenancy

(1) Where an authority or body within section 80 (the landlord condition for secure tenancies) becomes the landlord of a dwelling-house subject to a statutory tenancy, the tenancy shall be treated for all purposes as if it were a contractual tenancy on the same terms, and the provisions of this Part apply accordingly.] **[573]**

NOTES

Commencement: 7 January 1987.

Added by the Housing and Planning Act 1986, s 24(1), Sch 5, Part I, para 2.

110. Jurisdiction of county court

(1) A county court has jurisdiction to determine questions arising under this Part and to entertain proceedings brought under this Part and claims, for whatever amount, in connection with a secure tenancy.

(2) That jurisdiction includes jurisdiction to entertain proceedings on the following questions—

(*a*) whether a consent required by section 92 (assignment by way of exchange) was withheld otherwise than on one or more of the grounds set out in Schedule 3,

(*b*) whether a consent required by section 93(1)(*b*) or 97(1) (landlord's consent to subletting of part of dwelling-house or to carrying out of improvements) was withheld or unreasonably withheld, or

(*c*) whether a statement supplied in pursuance of section 104(2)(*b*) (written statement of certain terms of tenancy) is accurate,

notwithstanding that no other relief is sought than a declaration.

(3) If a person takes proceedings in the High Court which, by virtue of this section, he could have taken in the county court, he is not entitled to recover any costs. **[574]**

NOTES

Commencement: 1 April 1986.

Sub-ss (1), (3) derived from the Housing Act 1980, s 86(1), (3); sub-s (2) derived from the Housing Act 1980, s 86(2) and the Housing and Building Control Act 1984, Sch 11, para 25(1).

111. County court rules and directions

(1) The Lord Chancellor may make such rules and give such directions as he thinks fit for the purpose of giving effect to—

(*a*) section 85 (extended discretion of court in certain proceedings for possession), and

(*b*) section 110 (jurisdiction of county court to determine questions arising under this Part).

(2) The rules and directions may provide—

(*a*) for the exercise by a registrar of a county court of any jurisdiction exercisable under the provisions mentioned in subsection (1), and

(*b*) for the conduct of proceedings in private.

(3) The power to make rules is exercisable by statutory instrument which shall be subject to annulment in pursuance of a resolution of either House of Parliament. **[575]**

NOTES

Commencement: 1 April 1986.

This section derived from the Housing Act 1980, s 86(4)-(6).

112. Meaning of "dwelling-house"

(1) For the purposes of this Part a dwelling-house may be a house or a part of a house.

(2) Land let together with a dwelling-house shall be treated for the purposes of this Part as part of the dwelling-house unless the land is agricultural land (as

defined in section 26(3)(*a*) of the General Rate Act 1967) exceeding two acres. **[576]**

NOTES
Commencement: 1 April 1986.
This section derived from the Housing Act 1980, s 50(2).

113. Members of a person's family

(1) A person is a member of another's family within the meaning of this Part if—

(*a*) he is the spouse of that person, or he and that person live together as husband and wife, or
(*b*) he is that person's parent, grandparent, child, grandchild, brother, sister, uncle, aunt, nephew or niece.

(2) For the purpose of subsection (1)(*b*)—

(*a*) a relationship by marriage shall be treated as a relationship by blood,
(*b*) a relationship of the half-blood shall be treated as a relationship of the whole blood,
(*c*) the stepchild of a person shall be treated as his child, and
(*d*) an illegitimate child shall be treated as the legitimate child of his mother and reputed father. **[577]**

NOTES
Commencement: 1 April 1986.
This section derived from the Housing Act 1980, s 50(3).

114. Meaning of "landlord authority"

(1) In this Part "landlord authority" means—

a local housing authority,
a registered housing association other than a co-operative housing association,
a housing trust which is a charity,
a development corporation,
an urban development corporation, or
the Development Board for Rural Wales,

other than an authority in respect of which an exemption certificate has been issued.

(2) The Secretary of State may, on an application duly made by the authority concerned, issue an exemption certificate to—

a development corporation,
an urban development corporation, or
the Development Board for Rural Wales,

if he is satisfied that it has transferred, or otherwise disposed of, at least three-quarters of the dwellings which have at any time before the making of the application been vested in it.

(3) The application shall be in such form and shall be accompanied by such information as the Secretary of State may, either generally or in relation to a particular case, direct. **[578]**

NOTES

Commencement: 1 April 1986.

Sub-s (1) derived from the Rent Act 1977, s 15(3), the Housing Act 1980, ss 42(1), 49(3) and the Local Government, Planning and Land Act 1980, s 156(2)(*b*); sub-ss (2), (3) derived from the Housing Act 1980, s 45(1), (2).

115. Meaning of "long tenancy"

(1) The following are long tenancies for the purposes of this Part, subject to subsection (2)—

(*a*) a tenancy granted for a term certain exceeding 21 years, whether or not it is (or may become) terminable before the end of that term by notice given by the tenant or by re-entry or forfeiture;

(*b*) a tenancy for a term fixed by law under a grant with a covenant or obligation for perpetual renewal, other than a tenancy by sub-demise from one which is not a long tenancy;

(*c*) any tenancy granted in pursuance of Part V (the right to buy).

(2) A tenancy granted so as to become terminable by notice after a death is not a long tenancy for the purposes of this Part, unless—

(*a*) it is granted by a housing association which at the time of the grant is registered.

(*b*) it is granted at a premium calculated by reference to a percentage of the value of the dwelling-house or of the cost of providing it, and

(*c*) at the time it is granted it complies with the requirements of the regulations then in force under section 140(4)(*b*) of the Housing Act 1980 (conditions for exclusion of shared ownership leases from Part I of the Leasehold Reform Act 1967) or, in the case of a tenancy granted before any such regulations were brought into force, with the first such regulations to be in force. **[579]**

NOTES

Commencement: 1 April 1986.

Sub-s (1) derived from the Housing Act 1980, Sch 3, para 1(2), (2A) and the Housing and Building Control Act 1984, Sch 1, para 12, Sch 11, para 33(1); sub-s (2) derived from the Housing Act 1980, Sch 3, para 1(2), (3).

116. Minor definitions

In this Part—

"common parts", in relation to a dwelling-house let under a tenancy, means any part of a building comprising the dwelling-house and any other premises which the tenant is entitled under the terms of the tenancy to use in common with the occupiers of other dwelling-houses let by the landlord;

"housing purposes" means the purposes for which dwelling-houses are held by local housing authorities under Part II (provision of housing) or purposes corresponding to those purposes;

"rental period" means a period in respect of which a payment of rent falls to be made;

"term", in relation to a secure tenancy, includes a condition of the tenancy. **[580]**

NOTES

Commencement: 1 April 1986.

This section derived from the Housing Act 1980, s 50(1), Sch 1, para 1(2), Sch 4, Part I, grounds 3, 4 and the Housing and Building Control Act 1984, s 2(1).

117. Index of defined expressions: Part IV

The following Table shows provisions defining or otherwise explaining expressions used in this Part (other than provisions defining or explaining an expression in the same section or paragraph):—

cemetery	section 622
charity	section 622
common parts (in relation to a dwelling-house let under a tenancy)	section 116
co-operative housing association	section 5(2)
development corporation	section 4(*c*)
dwelling-house	section 112
family (member of)	section 113
housing association	section 5(1)
housing authority	section 4(*a*)
housing purposes	section 116
housing trust	section 6
improvement	section 97(2)
landlord authority	section 114
local authority	section 4(*e*)
local housing authority	sections 1, 2(2)
long tenancy	section 115
new town corporation	section 4(*b*)
qualified to succeed (on the death of a secure tenant)	section 87
registered and unregistered (in relation to a housing association)	section 5(4)
rental period	section 116
secure tenancy	section 79
term (in relation to a secure tenancy)	section 116
urban development corporation	section 4(*d*)
variation (of the terms of a secure tenancy)	section 102(2)

[581]

NOTES

Commencement: 1 April 1986.

Items in square brackets prospectively added by the Housing and Planning Act 1986, s 24(2), Sch 5, Part II, para 27, as from a day to be appointed.

PART XVIII

MISCELLANEOUS AND GENERAL PROVISIONS

General provisions

612. Exclusion of Rent Act protection

Nothing in the Rent Acts prevents possession being obtained of a house of which possession is required for the purpose of enabling a local housing authority to exercise their powers under any enactment relating to housing.

[582]

NOTES
Commencement: 1 April 1986.
This section derived from the Housing Act 1957, s 158(1), the Rent (Agriculture) Act 1976, Sch 8, para 4 and the Rent Act 1977, Sch 23, para 26.

613. Liability of directors, &c in case of offence by body corporate

(1) Where an offence under this Act committed by a body corporate is proved to have been committed with the consent or connivance of, or to be attributable to any neglect on the part of, a director, manager, secretary or other similar officer of the body corporate, or a person purporting to act in any such capacity, he, as well as the body corporate, is guilty of an offence and liable to be proceeded against and punished accordingly.

(2) Where the affairs of a body corporate are managed by its members, subsection (1) applies in relation to the acts and defaults of a member in connection with his functions of management as if he were a director of the body corporate. **[583]**

NOTES
Commencement: 1 April 1986.
This section derived from the Housing Act 1961, s 23(4), (5), the Housing Act 1964, s 65(6), the Housing Act 1969, s 61(3), the Housing Act 1974, s 47(8), (9) and the Housing and Building Control Act 1984, Sch 4, para 9(2), (3) and the Law Commission Recommendation No 28, Cmnd 9515.

614. Power to prescribe forms, &c

(1) The Secretary of State may by regulations prescribe—

(*a*) anything which by this Act is to be prescribed; or
(*b*) the form of any notice, advertisement, statement or other document which is required or authorised to be used under or for the purposes of this Act.

(2) The regulations shall be made by statutory instrument which shall be subject to annulment in pursuance of a resolution of either House of Parliament.

(3) The power conferred by this section is not exercisable where specific provision for prescribing a thing, or the form of a document, is made elsewhere. **[584]**

NOTES
Commencement: 1 April 1986.
Sub-ss (1), (2) derived from the Public Health Act 1936, s 283(2), the Housing Act 1957, s 178, the Housing Act 1974, s 104(4)(*c*), Sch 10, para 1(2) and the Housing Rents and Subsidies Act 1975, Sch 25, para 25 and gives effect to the Law Commission Recommendation No 27, Cmnd 9515.

615. Dispensation with advertisements and notices

(1) The Secretary of State may dispense with the publication of advertisements or the service of notices required to be published or served by a local authority under this Act if he is satisfied that there is reasonable cause for dispensing with the publication or service.

(2) A dispensation may be given by the Secretary of State—

(*a*) either before or after the time at which the advertisement is required to be published or the notice is required to be served, and (*b*) either unconditionally or upon such conditions, as to the publication of other advertisements or the service of other notices or otherwise, as the Secretary of State thinks fit,

due care being taken by him to prevent the interests of any persons being prejudiced by the dispensation. **[585]**

NOTES

Commencement: 1 April 1986.

This section derived from the Housing Act 1957, s 179, the Housing Act 1969, Sch 8, para 13 and the Housing Act 1974, s 104(4)(*d*) and the Law Commission Recommendation No 27, Cmnd 9515.

616. Local inquiries

For the purposes of the execution of his powers and duties under this Act, the Secretary of State may cause such local inquiries to be held as he may think fit. **[586]**

NOTES

Commencement: 1 April 1986.

This section derived from the Public Health Act 1936, s 318, the Housing Act 1957, s 181 and the Housing Act 1969, Sch 8, para 14 and the Law Commission Recommendation No 27, Cmnd 9515.

617. Service of notices

(1) Where under any provision of this Act it is the duty of a local housing authority to serve a document on a person who is to the knowledge of the authority—

(*a*) a person having control of premises, however defined, or
(*b*) a person managing premises, however defined, or
(*c*) a person having an estate or interest in premises, whether or not restricted to persons who are owners or lessees or mortgagees or to any other class of those having an estate or interest in premises,

the authority shall take reasonable steps to identify the person or persons coming within the description in that provision.

(2) A person having an estate or interest in premises may for the purposes of any provision to which subsection (1) applies give notice to the local housing authority of his interest in the premises and they shall enter the notice in their records.

(3) A document required or authorised by this Act to be served on a person as being a person having control of premises (however defined) may, if it is not practicable after reasonable enquiry to ascertain the name or address of that person, be served by—

(*a*) addressing it to him by the description of "person having control of" the premises (naming them) to which it relates, and
(*b*) delivering it to some person on the premises or, if there is no person on the premises to whom it can be delivered, by affixing it, or a copy of it, to some conspicuous part of the premises.

(4) Where under any provision of this Act a document is to be served on—

(*a*) the person having control of premises, however defined, or
(*b*) the person managing premises, however defined, or

(*c*) the owner of premises, however defined,

and more than one person comes within the description in the enactment, the document may be served on more than one of those persons. **[587]**

NOTES

Commencement: 1 April 1986.

Sub-s (1) derived from the Housing Act 1964, s 102(1), and the Housing Act 1974, s 103(1); sub-s (2) derived from the Housing Act 1964, s 102(2); sub-ss (3), (4) derived from the Housing Act 1964, s 103(1), (2) and the Housing Act 1974, s 103(2), (3).

618. The Common Council of the City of London

(1) The Common Council of the City of London may appoint a committee, consisting of so many persons as they think fit, for any purposes of this Act or the Housing Associations Act 1985 which in their opinion may be better regulated and managed by means of a committee.

(2) A committee so appointed—

(*a*) shall consist as to a majority of its members of the Common Council, and

(*b*) shall not be authorised to borrow money or to make a rate,

and shall be subject to any regulations and restrictions which may be imposed by the Common Council.

(3) A person is not, by reason only of the fact that he occupies a house at a rental from the Common Council, disqualified from being elected or being a member of that Council or any committee of that Council; but no person shall vote as a member of that Council, or any such committee, on a resolution or question which is proposed or arises in pursuance of this Act or the Housing Associations Act 1985 and relates to land in which he is beneficially interested.

(4) A person who votes in contravention of subsection (3) commits a summary offence and is liable on conviction to a fine not exceeding *level 2 on the standard scale* [level 4 on the standard scale]; but the fact of his giving the vote does not invalidate any resolution or proceeding of the authority. **[588]**

NOTES

Commencement: 1 April 1986.

Sub-ss (1)-(3) derived from the Housing Act 1957, s 187(1), (2) and give effect to the Law Commission Recommendation No 27, Cmnd 9515; sub-s (4) derived from the Housing Act 1957, s 187(3), and the Criminal Justice Act 1982, ss 37, 46(1).

Sub-s (4): words in italics repealed with savings and words in square brackets substituted with savings by the Housing and Planning Act 1986, s 24(1), Sch 5, Part I, para 6.

619. The Inner and Middle Temples

(1) For the purposes of Part XII (common lodging houses) the local housing authority—

(*a*) for the Inner Temple is the Sub-Treasurer of the Inner Temple, and

(*b*) for the Middle Temple is the Under-Treasurer of the Middle Temple.

(2) The other provisions of this Act are among those for which provision may be made by Order in Council under section 94 of the Local Government Act 1985 (general power to provide for exercise of local authority functions as respects the Temples). **[589]**

NOTES
Commencement: 1 April 1986.
Sub-s (1) derived from the Local Government Act 1972, s 180(1)(*d*); sub-s (2) derived from the Local Government Act 1985, s 94(1).

620. The Isles of Scilly

(1) This Act applies to the Isles of Scilly subject to such exceptions, adaptations and modifications as the Secretary of State may by order direct.

(2) An order shall be made by statutory instrument which shall be subject to annulment in pursuance of a resolution of either House of Parliament. **[590]**

NOTES
Commencement: 1 April 1986.
This section derived from the Housing Finance Act 1972, s 103, the Housing Rents and Subsidies Act 1975, Sch 5, para 7(1), SI 1972 No 1204, SI 1973 No 886, SI 1975 No 512 and gives effect to the Law Commission Recommendation No 29, Cmnd 9515.

621. Meaning of "lease" and "tenancy" and related expressions

(1) In this Act "lease" and "tenancy" have the same meaning.

(2) Both expressions include—

(*a*) a sub-lease or sub-tenancy, and
(*b*) an agreement for a lease or tenancy (or sub-lease or sub-tenancy).

(3) The expressions "lessor" and "lessee" and "landlord" and "tenant", and references to letting, to the grant of a lease or to covenants or terms, shall be construed accordingly. **[591]**

NOTES
Commencement: 1 April 1986.

[621A. Meaning of "service charge" and related expressions

(1) In this Act "service charge" means an amount payable by a purchaser or lessee of premises—

(*a*) which is payable, directly or indirectly, for services, repairs, maintenance or insurance or the vendor's or lessor's costs of management, and
(*b*) the whole or part of which varies or may vary according to the relevant costs.

(2) The relevant costs are the costs or estimated costs incurred or to be incurred by or on behalf of the payee, or (in the case of a lease) a superior landlord, in connection with the matters for which the service charge is payable.

(3) For this purpose—

(*a*) "costs" includes overheads, and
(*b*) costs are relevant costs in relation to a service charge whether they are incurred, or to be incurred, in the period for which the service charge is payable or in an earlier or later period.

(4) In relation to a service charge—

(*a*) the "payee" means the person entitled to enforce payment of the charge, and (*b*) the "payer" means the person liable to pay it.] **[592]**

NOTES
Commencement: 1 January 1987.
Added by the Housing and Planning Act 1986, s 24(2), Sch 5, Part II, para 39.

622. Minor definitions: general

In this Act—

"bank" means—

(a) a recognised bank within the meaning of the Banking Act 1979, or
[(*a*) an institution authorised under the Banking Act 1987, or]
(*b*) a company as to which the Secretary of State was satisfied immediately before the repeal of the Protection of Depositors Act 1963 that it ought to be treated as a banking company or discount company for the purposes of that Act;

"building regulations" means—

(*a*) building regulations made under Part I of the Building Act 1984,
(*b*) new street byelaws made under Part X of the Highways Act 1980, or
(*c*) any provision of a local Act, or of a byelaw made under a local Act, dealing with the construction and drainage of new buildings and the laying out and construction of new streets;

"building society" means a building society within the meaning of the Building Societies Act 1962 or the Building Societies Act (Northern Ireland) 1967;

["building society" means a building society within the meaning of the Building Societies Act 1986];

"cemetery" has the same meaning as in section 214 of the Local Government Act 1972;

"charity" has the same meaning as in the Charities Act 1960;

"district valuer" means an officer of the Commissioners of Inland Revenue appointed to be, in relation to the valuation list for the area in which the land in question is situated, the valuation or deputy valuation officer or one of the valuation officers or deputy valuation officers;

"friendly society" means a friendly society, or a branch of a friendly society, registered under the Friendly Societies Act 1974 or earlier legislation;

"general rate fund" means—

(*a*) in relation to the Council of the Isles of Scilly, the general fund of that council;
(*b*) in relation to the Common Council of the City of London, that council's general rate;

"hostel" means a building in which is provided, for persons generally or for a class or classes of persons—

(*a*) residential accommodation otherwise than in separate and self-contained sets of premises, and
(*b*) either board or facilities for the preparation of food adequate to the needs of those persons, or both;

"insurance company" means an insurance company to which Part II of the Insurance Companies Act 1982 applies;

"protected occupancy" and "protected occupier" have the same meaning as in the Rent (Agriculture) Act 1976;

"protected tenancy" has the same meaning as in the Rent Act 1977;

"regular armed forces of the Crown" means the Royal Navy, the regular forces as defined by section 225 of the Army Act 1955, the regular air force as defined by section 223 of the Air Force Act 1955, Queen Alexandra's Royal Naval Nursing Service and the Women's Royal Naval Service;

"the Rent Acts" means the Rent Act 1977 and the Rent (Agriculture) Act 1976;

"restricted contract" has the same meaning as in the Rent Act 1977;

"shared ownership lease" means a lease—

(*a*) granted on payment of a premium calculated by reference to a percentage of the value of the dwelling or of the cost of providing it, or

(*b*) under which the tenant (or his personal representatives) will or may be entitled to a sum calculated by reference, directly or indirectly, to the value of the dwelling;

"standard scale", in reference to the maximum fine on conviction of a summary offence, has the meaning given by section 75 of the Criminal Justice Act 1982;

"statutory maximum", in reference to the maximum fine on summary conviction of an offence triable either summarily or on indictment, has the meaning given by section 74 of the Criminal Justice Act 1982;

"statutory tenancy" and "statutory tenant" mean a statutory tenancy or statutory tenant within the meaning of the Rent Act 1977 or the Rent (Agriculture) Act 1976;

"street" includes any court, alley, passage, square or row of houses, whether a thoroughfare or not;

"subsidiary" has the same meaning as in the Companies Act 1985;

"trustee savings bank" means a trustee savings bank registered under the Trustee Savings Banks Act 1981 or earlier legislation. **[593]**

NOTES

Commencement: 1 April 1986.

This section derived from the Housing Act 1957, ss 12(4), 29(2), 59(2), 189(1), Sch 2, para 3(2), the Public Health Act 1961, Sch 1, Part III, the General Rate Act 1967, s 115(1), the Housing Finance Act 1972, s 104(1), the Housing Act 1974, s 129(1), the Housing Rents and Subsidies Act 1975, s 16(1), the House of Commons Disqualification Act 1975, s 1(3), the Armed Forces Act 1976, s 20(6), the Housing (Homeless Persons) Act 1977, s 18(4), the Home Purchase Assistance and Housing Corporation Guarantee Act 1978, Sch 1, paras 6-9, the Interpretation Act 1978, s 17(2)(*a*), the Banking Act 1979, Sch 6, para 11, the Housing Act 1980, ss 2(1), (2)(*a*), 27(1), (2), 28(4)(*e*), 50(1), Sch 1A, para 10(1), the Criminal Justice Act 1982, ss 74(1), 75(*a*), the Housing and Building Control Act 1984, s 3(5), Sch 2, Sch 11, para 24, the Building Act 1984, s 89(2), Sch 5, para 2 and the Housing Defects Act 1984, s 9(11), Sch 2, para 3(7), and gives effect to the Law Commission Recommendation No 14(i), Cmnd 9515.

In definition "bank" para (*a*) prospectively substituted by the Banking Act 1987, s 108(1), Sch 6, para 21, as from a day to be appointed; definition "building society" prospectively substituted by the Building Societies Act 1986, s 120, Sch 19, Part I, as from 1 January 1987.

623. Minor definitions: Part XVIII

In this Part—

"house" includes any yard, garden, outhouses and appurtenances belonging to the house or usually enjoyed with it;

"owner", in relation to premises—

(*a*) means a person (other than a mortgagee not in possession) who is for the time being entitled to dispose of the fee simple absolute in the premises, whether in possession or in reversion, and (*b*) includes also a person holding or entitled to the rents and profits of the premises under a lease of which the unexpired term exceeds three years. **[594]**

NOTES
Commencement: 1 April 1986.
This section derived from the Housing Act 1957, s 189(1).

624. Index of defined expressions: Part XVIII

The following Table shows provisions defining or otherwise explaining expressions used in this Part (other than provisions defining or explaining an expression used in the same section):—

clearance area	section 289
district (of a local housing authority)	section 2(1)
house	section 623
lease and let	section 621
local housing authority	section 1, 2(2)
owner	section 623
Rent Acts	section 622
standard scale (in reference to the maximum fine on summary conviction)	section 622
street	section 622
unfit for human habitation	section 604

[595]

NOTES
Commencement: 1 April 1986.

Final Provisions

625. Short title, commencement and extent

(1) This Act may be cited as the Housing Act 1985.

(2) This Act comes into force on 1st April 1986.

(3) This Act extends to England and Wales only. **[596]**

NOTES
Commencement: 1 April 1986.

SCHEDULES

SCHEDULE 1

Section 79

TENANCIES WHICH ARE NOT SECURE TENANCIES

Long leases

1. A tenancy is not a secure tenancy if it is a long tenancy.

Premises occupied in connection with employment

2.—(1) A tenancy is not a secure tenancy if the tenant is an employee of the landlord or of—

a local authority,

a new town corporation,
an urban development corporation,
the Development Board for Rural Wales, or
the governors of an aided school,

and his contract of employment requires him to occupy the dwelling-house for the better performance of his duties.

(2) A tenancy is not a secure tenancy if the tenant is a member of a police force and the dwelling-house is provided for him free of rent and rates in pursuance of regulations made under section 33 of the Police Act 1964 (general regulations as to government, administration and conditions of service of police forces).

(3) A tenancy is not a secure tenancy if the tenant is an employee of a fire authority (within the meaning of the Fire Services Acts 1947 to 1959) and—

(*a*) his contract of employment requires him to live in close proximity to a particular fire station, and
(*b*) the dwelling-house was let to him by the authority in consequence of that requirement.

(4) A tenancy is not a secure tenancy if—

(*a*) within the period of three years immediately preceding the grant the conditions mentioned in sub-paragraph (1), (2) or (3) have been satisfied with respect to a tenancy of the dwelling-house, and
(*b*) before the grant the landlord notified the tenant in writing of the circumstances in which this exception applies and that in its opinion the proposed tenancy would fall within this exception,

until the periods during which those conditions are not satisfied with respect to the tenancy amount in aggregate to more than three years.

(5) In this paragraph "contract of employment" means a contract of service or apprenticeship, whether express or implied and (if express) whether oral or in writing.

Land acquired for development

3.—(1) A tenancy is not a secure tenancy if the dwelling-house is on land which has been acquired for development and the dwelling-house is used by the landlord, pending development of the land, as temporary housing accommodation.

(2) In this paragraph "development" has the meaning given by section 22 of the Town and Country Planning Act 1971 (general definition of development for purposes of that Act).

Accommodation for homeless persons

4.—(1) A tenancy granted in pursuance of—

(*a*) section 63 (duty to house pending inquiries in case of apparent priority need),
(*b*) section 65(3) (duty to house temporarily person found to have priority need but to have become homeless intentionally), or
(*c*) section 68(1) (duty to house pending determination whether conditions for referral of application are satisfied),

is not a secure tenancy before the expiry of the period of twelve months beginning with the date specified in sub-paragraph (2), unless before the expiry of that period the tenant is notified by the landlord that the tenancy is to be regarded as a secure tenancy.

(2) The date referred to in sub-paragraph (1) is the date on which the tenant received the notification required by section 64(1) (notification of decision on question of homelessness or threatened homelessness) or, if he received a notification under section 68(3) (notification of which authority has duty to house), the date on which he received that notification.

Temporary accommodation for persons taking up employment

5.—(1) A tenancy is not a secure tenancy before the expiry of one year from the grant if—

(*a*) the person to whom the tenancy was granted was not, immediately before the grant, resident in the district in which the dwelling-house is situated,

(*b*) before the grant of the tenancy, he obtained employment, or an offer of employment, in the district or its surrounding area,

(*c*) the tenancy was granted to him for the purpose of meeting his need for temporary accommodation in the district or its surrounding area in order to work there, and of enabling him to fine permanent accommodation there, and

(*d*) the landlord notified him in writing of the circumstances in which this exception applies and that in its opinion the proposed tenancy would fall within this exception;

unless before the expiry of that year the tenant has been notified by the landlord that the tenancy is to be regarded as a secure tenancy.

(2) In this paragraph—

"district" means district of a local housing authority; and

"surrounding area", in relation to a district, means the area consisting of each district that adjoins it.

Short-term arrangements

6. A tenancy is not a secure tenancy if—

(*a*) the dwelling-house has been leased to the landlord with vacant possession for use as temporary housing accommodation,

(*b*) the terms on which it has been leased include provision for the lessor to obtain vacant possession from the landlord on the expiry of a specified period or when required by the lessor,

(*c*) the lessor is not a body which is capable of granting secure tenancies, and

(*d*) the landlord has no interest in the dwelling-house other than under the lease in question or as a mortgagee.

Temporary accommodation during works

7. A tenancy is not a secure tenancy if—

(*a*) the dwelling-house has been made available for occupation by the tenant (or a predecessor in title of his) while works are carried out on the dwelling-house which he previously occupied as his home, and

(*b*) the tenant or predecessor was not a secure tenant of that other dwelling-house at the time when he ceased to occupy it as his home.

Agricultural holdings

8. A tenancy is not a secure tenancy if the dwelling-house is comprised in an agricultural holding (within the meaning of the *Agricultural Holdings Act 1948* [Agricultural Holdings Act 1986]) and is occupied by the person responsible for the control (whether as tenant or as servant or agent of the tenant) of the farming of the holding.

Licensed premises

9. A tenancy is not a secure tenancy if the dwelling-house consists of or includes premises licensed for the sale of intoxicating liquor for consumption on the premises.

Student lettings

10.—(1) A tenancy of a dwelling-house is not a secure tenancy before the expiry of the period specified in sub-paragraph (3) if—

(*a*) it is granted for the purpose of enabling the tenant to attend a designated course at an educational establishment, and (*b*) before the grant of the tenancy the landlord notified him in writing of the circumstances in which this exception applies and that in its opinion the proposed tenancy would fall within this exception;

unless the tenant has before the expiry of that period been notified by the landlord that the tenancy is to be regarded as a secure tenancy.

(2) A landlord's notice under sub-paragraph (1)(*b*) shall specify the educational establishment which the person concerned proposes to attend.

(3) The period referred to in sub-paragraph (1) is—

(*a*) in a case where the tenant attends a designated course at the educational establishment specified in the landlord's notice, the period ending six months after the tenant ceases to attend that (or any other) designated course at that establishment;

(*b*) in any other case, the period ending six months after the grant of the tenancy.

(4) In this paragraph—

"designated course" means a course of any kind designated by regulations made by the Secretary of State for the purposes of this paragraph;

"educational establishment" means a university or establishment of further education.

(5) Regulations under sub-paragraph (4) shall be made by statutory instrument and may make different provision with respect to different cases or descriptions of case, including different provision for different areas.

1954 Act tenancies

11. A tenancy is not a secure tenancy if it is one to which Part II of the Landlord and Tenant Act 1954 applies (tenancies of premises occupied for business purposes).

Almshouses

12.—(1) A licence to occupy a dwelling-house is not a secure tenancy if—

(*a*) the licence was granted by an almshouse charity, and

(*b*) any sum payable by the licensee under the licence does not exceed the maximum contribution that the Charity Commissioners have from time to time authorised or approved for the almshouse charity as a contribution towards the cost of maintaining its almshouses and essential services in them.

(2) In this paragraph "almshouse charity" means a corporation or body of persons which is a charity and is prevented by its rules or constituent instrument from granting a tenancy of the dwelling-house. **[597]**

NOTES

Commencement: 1 April 1986.

Paras 1, 3, 4, 6, 7, 9, 11, 12 derived from the Housing Act 1980, Sch 3, paras 1(1), 4, 5, 7, 9, 10, 12, 13; para 2, sub-para (1) derived from the Housing Act 1980, Sch 1, para 1(3), Sch 3, para 2(1) and the Housing and Building Control Act 1984, s 2(2), Sch 11, para 33(2), sub-paras (2)-(5) derived from the Housing Act 1980, Sch 3, paras 2(2), 2A, 2B(1), (2), 2C and the Housing and Building Control Act 1984, s 36(2); para 5 derived from the Housing Act 1980, Sch 3, para 6 and the Housing and Building Control Act 1984, s 36(3); para 8 derived from the Housing Act 1980, Sch 3, para 8 and the Housing and Building Control Act 1984, Sch 11, para 33(3); para 10, sub-paras (1)-(4) derived from the Housing Act 1980, Sch 3, para 11, sub-para 5 derived from the Housing Act 1980, s 151(1), (3).

Words in italics repealed with savings and words in square brackets substituted with savings by the Agricultural Holdings Act 1986, ss 99, 100, Sch 13, para 3, Sch 14, para 63.

SCHEDULE 2

Section 84

GROUNDS FOR POSSESSION OF DWELLING-HOUSES LET UNDER SECURE TENANCIES

PART I

GROUNDS ON WHICH COURT MAY ORDER POSSESSION IF IT CONSIDERS IT REASONABLE

Ground 1

Rent lawfully due from the tenant has not been paid or an obligation of the tenancy has been broken or not performed.

Ground 2

The tenant or a person residing in the dwelling-house has been guilty of conduct which is a nuisance or annoyance to neighbours, or has been convicted of using the dwelling-house or allowing it to be used for immoral or illegal purposes.

Ground 3

The condition of the dwelling-house or of any of the common parts has deteriorated owing to acts of waste by, or the neglect or default of, the tenant or a person residing in the dwelling-house and, in the case of an act of waste by, or the neglect or default of, a person lodging with the tenant or a sub-tenant of his, the tenant has not taken such steps as he ought reasonably to have taken for the removal of the lodger or sub-tenant.

Ground 4

The condition of furniture provided by the landlord for use under the tenancy, or for use in the common parts, has deteriorated owing to ill-treatment by the tenant or a person residing in the dwelling-house and, in the case of ill-treatment by a person lodging with the tenant or a sub-tenant of his, the tenant has not taken such steps as he ought reasonably to have taken for the removal of the lodger or sub-tenant.

Ground 5

The tenant is the person, or one of the persons, to whom the tenancy was granted and the landlord was induced to grant the tenancy by a false statement made knowingly or recklessly by the tenant.

Ground 6

The tenancy was assigned to the tenant, or to a predecessor in title of his who is a member of his family and is residing in the dwelling-house, by an assignment made by virtue of section 92 (assignments by way of exchange) and a premium was paid either in connection with that assignment or the assignment which the tenant or predecessor himself made by virtue of that section.

In this paragraph "premium" means any fine or other like sum and any other pecuniary consideration in addition to rent.

Ground 7

The dwelling-house forms part of, or is within the curtilage of, a building which, or so much of it as is held by the landlord, is held mainly for purposes other than housing purposes and consists mainly of accommodation other than housing accommodation, and—

(*a*) the dwelling-house was let to the tenant or a predecessor in title of his in consequence of the tenant or predecessor being in the employment of the landlord, or of—

a local authority,
a new town corporation,
an urban development corporation,
the Development Board for Rural Wales, or
the governors of an aided school,

and

(*b*) the tenant or a person residing in the dwelling-house has been guilty of conduct such that, having regard to the purpose for which the building is used, it would not be right for him to continue in occupation of the dwelling-house.

Ground 8

The dwelling-house was made available for occupation by the tenant (or a predecessor in title of his) while works were carried out on the dwelling-house which he previously occupied as his only or principal home and—

(*a*) the tenant (or predecessor) was a secure tenant of the other dwelling-house at the time when he ceased to occupy it as his home,
(*b*) the tenant (or predecessor) accepted the tenancy of the dwelling-house of which possession is sought on the understanding that he would give up occupation when, on completion of the works, the other dwelling-house was again available for occupation by him under a secure tenancy, and
(*c*) the works have been completed and the other dwelling-house is so available.

[598]

NOTES

Commencement: 1 April 1986.

Grounds 1-5 derived from the Housing Act 1980, Sch 4, Part I, grounds 1-5; ground 6 derived from the Housing Act 1980, Sch 4, Part I, ground 5A and the Housing and Building Control Act 1984, s 25(1); ground 7 derived from the Housing Act 1980, Sch 1, para 1(2), (3), Sch 4, Part I, ground 5B and the Housing and Building Control Act 1984, ss 2(1), 25(1); ground 8 derived from the Housing Act 1980, Sch 4, Part I, ground 6 and the Housing and Building Control Act 1984, Sch 11, para 34.

PART II

GROUNDS ON WHICH THE COURT MAY ORDER POSSESSION IF SUITABLE ALTERNATIVE ACCOMMODATION IS AVAILABLE

Ground 9

The dwelling-house is overcrowded, within the meaning of Part X, in such circumstances as to render the occupier guilty of an offence.

Ground 10

The landlord intends, within a reasonable time of obtaining possession of the dwelling-house—

(*a*) to demolish or reconstruct the building or part of the building comprising the dwelling-house, or
(*b*) to carry out work on that building or on land let together with, and thus treated as part of, the dwelling-house,

and cannot reasonably do so without obtaining possession of the dwelling-house.

[Ground 10A

The dwelling-house is in an area which is the subject of a redevelopment scheme approved by the Secretary of State or the Housing Corporation in accordance with Part V of this Schedule and the landlord intends within a reasonable time of obtaining possession to dispose of the dwelling-house in accordance with the scheme.

or

Part of the dwelling-house is in such an area and the landlord intends within a reasonable time of obtaining possession to dispose of that part in accordance with the scheme and for that purpose reasonably requires possession of the dwelling-house.]

Ground 11

The landlord is a charity and the tenant's continued occupation of the dwelling-house would conflict with the objects of the charity. **[599]**

NOTES

Commencement: 13 May 1987 (Ground 10A); 1 April 1986 (remainder).
This Part derived from the Housing Act 1980, Sch 4, Part I, grounds 7-9.
Ground 10A: added by the Housing and Planning Act 1986, s 9(1).

PART III

GROUNDS ON WHICH THE COURT MAY ORDER POSSESSION IF IT CONSIDERS IT REASONABLE AND SUITABLE ALTERNATIVE ACCOMMODATION IS AVAILABLE

Ground 12

The dwelling-house forms part of, or is within the curtilage of, a building which, or so much of it as is held by the landlord, is held mainly for purposes other than housing purposes and consists mainly of accommodation other than housing accommodation, or is situated in a cemetery, and—

(*a*) the dwelling-house was let to the tenant or a predecessor in title of his in consequence of the tenant or predecessor being in the employment of the landlord or of—

a local authority,
a new town corporation,
an urban development corporation,
the Development Board for Rural Wales, or
the governors of an aided school,

and that employment has ceased, and

(*b*) the landlord reasonably requires the dwelling-house for occupation as a residence for some person either engaged in the employment of the landlord, or of such a body, or with whom a contract for such employment has been entered into conditional on housing being provided.

Ground 13

The dwelling-house has features which are substantially different from those of ordinary dwelling-houses and which are designed to make it suitable for occupation by a physically disabled person who requires accommodation of a kind provided by the dwelling-house and—

(*a*) there is no longer such a person residing in the dwelling-house, and
(*b*) the landlord requires it for occupation (whether alone or with members of his family) by such a person.

Ground 14

The landlord is a housing association or housing trust which lets dwelling-houses only for occupation (whether alone or with others) by persons whose circumstances (other than merely financial circumstances) make it especially difficult for them to satisfy their need for housing, and—

(*a*) either there is no longer such a person residing in the dwelling-house or the tenant has received from a local housing authority an offer of accommodation in premises which are to be let as a separate dwelling under a secure tenancy, and
(*b*) the landlord requires the dwelling-house for occupation (whether alone or with members of his family) by such a person.

Ground 15

The dwelling-house is one of a group of dwelling-houses which it is the practice of the landlord to let for occupation by persons with special needs and—

(*a*) a social service or special facility is provided in close proximity to the group of dwelling-houses in order to assist persons with those special needs,
(*b*) there is no longer a person with those special needs residing in the dwelling-house, and
(*c*) the landlord requires the dwelling-house for occupation (whether alone or with members of his family) by a person who has those special needs.

Ground 16

The accommodation afforded by the dwelling-house is more extensive than is reasonably required by the tenant and—

(*a*) the tenancy vested in the tenant by virtue of section 89 (succession to periodic tenancy), the tenant being qualified to succeed by virtue of section 87(*b*) (members of family other than spouse), and
(*b*) notice of the proceedings for possession was served under section 83 more than six months but less than twelve months after the date of the previous tenant's death.

The matters to be taken into account by the court in determining whether it is reasonable to make an order on this ground include—

(*a*) the age of the tenant,
(*b*) the period during which the tenant has occupied the dwelling-house as his only or principal home, and
(*c*) any financial or other support given by the tenant to the previous tenant. **[600]**

NOTES

Commencement: 1 April 1986.

Ground 12 derived from the Housing Act 1980, Sch 1, para 1(2), (3), Sch 4, Part I, ground 9A and the Housing and Building Control Act 1984, ss 2(1), 25(2); grounds 13-15 derived from the Housing Act 1980, Sch 4, Part I, grounds 10-12; ground 16 derived from the Housing Act 1980, s 34(3A), Sch 4, Part I, ground 13 and the Housing and Building Control Act 1984, s 25(3).

PART IV

SUITABILITY OF ACCOMMODATION

1. For the purposes of section 84(2)(*b*) and (*c*) (case in which court is not to make an order for possession unless satisfied that suitable accommodation will be available) accommodation is suitable if it consists of premises—

(*a*) which are to be let as a separate dwelling under a secure tenancy, or
(*b*) which are to be let as a separate dwelling under a protected tenancy, not being a tenancy under which the landlord might recover possession under one of the Cases in Part II of Schedule 15 to the Rent Act 1977 (cases where court must order possession),

and, in the opinion of the court, the accommodation is reasonably suitable to the needs of the tenant and his family.

2. In determining whether the accommodation is reasonably suitable to the needs of the tenant and his family, regard shall be had to—

(*a*) the nature of the accommodation which it is the practice of the landlord to allocate to persons with similar needs;
(*b*) the distance of the accommodation available from the place of work or education of the tenant and of any members of his family;
(*c*) its distance from the home of any member of the tenant's family if proximity to it is essential to that member's or the tenant's well-being;
(*d*) the needs (as regards extent of accommodation) and means of the tenant and his family;
(*e*) the terms on which the accommodation is available and the terms of the secure tenancy;
(*f*) if furniture was provided by the landlord for use under the secure tenancy, whether furniture is to be provided for use in the other accommodation, and if so the nature of the furniture to be provided.

3. Where possession of a dwelling-house is sought on ground 9 (overcrowding such as to render occupier guilty of offence), other accommodation may be reasonably suitable to the needs of the tenant and his family notwithstanding that the permitted number of persons for that accommodation, as defined in section 326(3) (overcrowding: the space standard), is less than the number of persons living in the dwelling-house of which possession is sought.

4.—(1) A certificate of the appropriate local housing authority that they will provide suitable accommodation for the tenant by a date specified in the certificate is conclusive evidence that suitable accommodation will be available for him by that date.

(2) The appropriate local housing authority is the authority for the district in which the dwelling-house of which possession is sought is situated.

(3) This paragraph does not apply where the landlord is a local housing authority. **[601]**

NOTES

Commencement: 1 April 1986.
This Part derived from the Housing Act 1980, Sch 4, Part II, paras 1(1), (2), 2, 3.

PART V

APPROVAL OF REDEVELOPMENT SCHEMES FOR PURPOSES OF GROUND 10A

[1.—(1) The Secretary of State may, on the application of the landlord, approve for the purposes of ground 10A in Part II of this Schedule a scheme for the disposal and redevelopment of an area of land consisting of or including the whole or part of one or more dwelling-houses.

(2) For this purpose—

(*a*) "disposal" means a disposal of any interest in the land (including the grant of an option), and
(*b*) "redevelopment" means the demolition or reconstruction of buildings or the carrying out of other works to buildings or land;

and it is immaterial whether the disposal is to precede or follow the redevelopment.

(3) The Secretary of State may on the application of the landlord approve a variation of a scheme previously approved by him and may, in particular, approve a variation adding land to the area subject to the scheme.

2.—(1) Where a landlord proposes to apply to the Secretary of State for the approval of a scheme or variation it shall serve a notice in writing on any secure tenant of a dwelling-house affected by the proposal stating—

(*a*) the main features of the proposed scheme or, as the case may be, the scheme as proposed to be varied,
(*b*) that the landlord proposes to apply to the Secretary of State for approval of the scheme or variation, and
(*c*) the effect of such approval, by virtue of section 84 and ground 10A in Part II of this Schedule, in relation to proceedings for possession of the dwelling-house,

and informing the tenant that he may, within such period as the landlord may allow (which shall be at least 28 days from service of the notice), make representations to the landlord about the proposal.

(2) The landlord shall not apply to the Secretary of State until it has considered any representations made to it within that period.

(3) In the case of a landlord to which section 105 applies (consultation on matters of housing management) the provisions of this paragraph apply in place of the provisions of that section in relation to the approval or variation of a redevelopment scheme.

3.—(1) In considering whether to give his approval to a scheme or variation the Secretary of State shall take into account, in particular—

(*a*) the effect of the scheme on the extent and character of housing accommodation in the neighbourhood,
(*b*) over what period of time it is proposed that the disposal and redevelopment will take place in accordance with the scheme, and
(*c*) to what extent the scheme includes provision for housing provided under the scheme to be sold or let to existing tenants or persons nominated by the landlord;

and he shall take into account any representations made to him and, so far as they are brought to his notice, any representations made to the landlord.

(2) The landlord shall give to the Secretary of State such information as to the representations made to it, and other relevant matters, as the Secretary of State may require.

4. The Secretary of State shall not approve a scheme or variation so as to include in the area subject to the scheme—

(*a*) part only of one or more dwelling-houses, or
(*b*) one or more dwelling-houses not themselves affected by the works involved in redevelopment but which are proposed to be disposed of along with other land which is so affected,

unless he is satisfied that the inclusion is justified in the circumstances.

5.—(1) Approval may be given subject to conditions and may be expressed to expire after a specified period.

(2) The Secretary of State, on the application of the landlord or otherwise, may vary an approval so as to—

(*a*) add, remove or vary conditions to which the approval is subject; or
(*b*) extend or restrict the period after which the approval is to expire.

(3) Where approval is given subject to conditions, the landlord may serve a notice under section 83 (notice of proceedings for possession) specifying ground 10A notwithstanding that the conditions are not yet fulfilled but the court shall not make an order for possession on that ground unless satisfied that they are or will be fulfilled.

6. Where the landlord is a registered housing association, the Housing Corporation, and not the Secretary of State, has the functions conferred by this Part of this Schedule.

7. In this Part of this Schedule references to the landlord of a dwelling-house include any authority or body within section 80 (the landlord condition for secure tenancies) having an interest of any description in the dwelling-house.] **[602]**

NOTES
Commencement: 13 May 1987.
Added by the Housing and Planning Act 1986, s 9(2).

SCHEDULE 3

Section 92

Grounds for Withholding Consent to Assignment by Way of Exchange

Ground 1

The tenant or the proposed assignee is obliged to give up possession of the dwelling-house of which he is the secure tenant in pursuance of an order of the court, or will be so obliged at a date specified in such an order.

Ground 2

Proceedings have been begun for possession of the dwelling-house of which the tenant or the proposed assignee is the secure tenant on one or more of grounds 1 to 6 in Part I of Schedule 2 (grounds on which possession may be ordered despite absence of suitable alternative accommodation), or there has been served on the tenant or the proposed assignee a notice under section 83 (notice of proceedings for possession) which specifies one or more of those grounds and is still in force.

Ground 3

The accommodation afforded by the dwelling-house is substantially more extensive than is reasonably required by the proposed assignee.

Ground 4

The extent of the accommodation afforded by the dwelling-house is not reasonably suitable to the needs of the proposed assignee and his family.

Ground 5

The dwelling-house—

(*a*) forms part of or is within the curtilage of a building which, or so much of it as is held by the landlord, is held mainly for purposes other than housing purposes and consists mainly of accommodation other than housing accommodation, or is situated in a cemetery, and

(*b*) was let to the tenant or a predecessor in title of his in consequence of the tenant or predecessor being in the employment of—

the landlord,
a local authority,
a new town corporation,
the Development Board for Rural Wales,
an urban development corporation, or
the governors of an aided school.

Ground 6

The landlord is a charity and the proposed assignee's occupation of the dwelling-house would conflict with the objects of the charity.

Ground 7

The dwelling-house has features which are substantially different from those of ordinary dwelling-houses and which are designed to make it suitable for occupation by a physically disabled person who requires accommodation of the kind provided by the dwelling-house and if the assignment were made there would no longer be such a person residing in the dwelling-house.

Ground 8

The landlord is a housing association or housing trust which lets dwelling-houses only for occupation (alone or with others) by persons whose circumstances (other than merely financial circumstances) make it especially difficult for them to satisfy their need for housing and if the assignment were made there would no longer be such a person residing in the dwelling-house.

Ground 9

The dwelling-house is one of a group of dwelling-houses which it is the practice of the landlord to let for occupation by persons with special needs and a social service or special facility is provided in close proximity to the group of dwelling-houses in order to assist persons with those special needs and if the assignment were made there would no longer be a person with those special needs residing in the dwelling-house.

[Ground 10

The dwelling-house is the subject of a management agreement under which the manager is a housing association of which at least half the members are tenants of dwelling-houses subject to the agreement, at least half the tenants of the dwelling-houses are members of the association and the proposed assignee is not, and is not willing to become, a member of the association.] **[603]**

NOTES

Commencement: 7 January 1987 (Ground 10); 1 April 1986 (remainder).

This Schedule derived from the Housing Act 1980, Sch 1, para 1, Sch 4A and the Housing and Building Control Act 1984, s 26(2), Sch 7.

Ground 10: added by the Housing and Planning Act 1986, s 24(1), Sch 5, Part I, para 7.

SCHEDULE 3A

CONSULTATION BEFORE DEPOSIT TO PRIVATE SECTOR LANDLORD

[Disposals to which this Schedule applies

1.—(1) This Schedule applies to the disposal by a local authority of an interest in land as a result of which a secure tenant of the authority will become the tenant of a private sector landlord.

(2) For the purposes of this Schedule the grant of an option which if exercised would result in a secure tenant of a local authority becoming the tenant of a private sector landlord shall be treated as a disposal of the interest which is the subject of the option.

(3) Where a disposal of land by a local authority is in part a disposal to which this Schedule applies, the provisions of this Schedule apply to that part as to a separate disposal.

(4) In this paragraph "private sector landlord" means a person other than an authority or body within section 80 (the landlord condition for secure tenancies).

Application for Secretary of State's consent

2.—(1) The Secretary of State shall not entertain an application for his consent to a disposal to which this Schedule applies unless the authority certify either—

(*a*) that the requirements of paragraph 3 as to consultation have been complied with, or

(*b*) that the requirements of that paragraph as to consultation have been complied with except in relation to tenants expected to have vacated the dwelling-house in question before the disposal;

and the certificate shall be accompanied by a copy of the notices given by the authority in accordance with that paragraph.

(2) Where the certificate is in the latter form, the Secretary of State shall not determine the application until the authority certify as regards the tenants not originally consulted—

(*a*) that they have vacated the dwelling-house in question, or

(*b*) that the requirements of paragraph 3 as to consultation have been complied with;

and a certificate under sub-paragraph (*b*) shall be accompanied by a copy of the notices given by the authority in accordance with paragraph 3.

(3) References in this Schedule to the Secretary of State's consent to a disposal are to the consent required by section 32 or 43 (general requirement of consent for disposal of houses or land held for housing purposes).

Requirements as to consultation

3.—(1) The requirements as to consultation referred to above are as follows.

(2) The authority shall serve notice in writing on the tenant informing him of—

(*a*) such details of their proposal as the authority consider appropriate, but including the identity of the person to whom the disposal is to be made,

(*b*) the likely consequences of the disposal for the tenant, and (*c*) the effect of the provisions of this Schedule and of sections 171A to 171H (preservation of right to buy on disposal to private sector landlord),

and informing him that he may, within such reasonable period as may be specified in the notice, make representations to the authority.

(3) the authority shall consider any representations made to them within that period and shall serve a further written notice on the tenant informing him—

(*a*) of any significant changes in their proposal, and

(*b*) that he may within such period as is specified (which must be at least 28 days after the service of the notice) communicate to the Secretary of State his objection to the proposal,

and informing him of the effect of paragraph 5 (consent to be withheld if majority of tenants are opposed).

Power to require further consultation

4. The Secretary of State may require the authority to carry out such further consultation with their tenants, and to give him such information as to the results of that consultation, as he may direct.

Consent to be withheld if majority of tenants are opposed

5.—(1) The Secretary of State shall not give his consent if it appears to him that a majority of the tenants of the dwelling-houses to which the application relates do not wish the disposal to proceed; but this does not affect his general discretion to refuse consent on grounds relating to whether a disposal has the support of the tenants or on any other ground.

(2) In making his decision the Secretary of State may have regard to any information available to him; and the local authority shall give him such information as to the representations made to them by tenants and others, and other relevant matters, as he may require.

Protection of purchasers

6. The Secretary of State's consent to a disposal is not invalidated by a failure on his part or that of the local authority to comply with the requirements of this Schedule.]

[604]

NOTES

Commencement: To be appointed.

Prospectively added with respect to disposals made after the commencement of this Schedule by the Housing and Planning Act 1986, s 6(2), (3), Sch 1, as from a day to be appointed.

LANDLORD AND TENANT ACT 1985

(c 70)

ARRANGEMENT OF SECTIONS

INFORMATION TO BE GIVEN TO TENANT

Section		Para
1	Disclosure of landlord's identity	[605]
2	Disclosure of directors, &c of corporate landlord	[606]
3	Duty to inform tenant of assignment of landlord's interest	[607]

PROVISION OF RENT BOOKS

4	Provision of rent books	[608]
5	Information to be contained in rent books	[609]

Section		Para
6	Information to be supplied by companies	[610]
7	Offences	[611]

IMPLIED TERMS AS TO FITNESS FOR HUMAN HABITATION

8	Implied terms as to fitness for human habitation	[612]
9	Application of s 8 to certain houses occupied by agricultural workers	[613]
10	Fitness for human habitation	[614]

REPAIRING OBLIGATIONS

11	Repairing obligations in short leases	[615]
12	Restriction on contracting out of s 11	[616]
13	Leases to which s 11 applies: general rule	[617]
14	Leases to which s 11 applies: exceptions	[618]
15	Jurisdiction of county court	[619]
16	Meaning of "lease" and related expressions	[620]
17	Specific performance of landlord's repairing obligations	[621]

SERVICE CHARGES

18	Meaning of "service charge" and "relevant costs"	[622]
19	Limitation of service charges: reasonableness	[623]
20	Limitation of service charges: estimates and consultation	[624]
20A	Limitation of service charges: grant-aided works	[625]
20B	Limitation of service charges: time limit on making demands	[626]
20C	Limitation of service charges: costs of court proceedings	[627]
21	Request for summary of relevant costs	[628]
22	Request to inspect supporting accounts &c	[629]
23	Request relating to information held by superior landlord	[630]
24	Effect of assignment on request	[631]
25	Failure to comply with ss 21, 22, or 23 an offence	[632]
26	Exception: tenants of certain public authorities	[633]
27	Exception: rent registered and not entered as variable	[634]
28	Meaning of "qualified accountant"	[635]
29	Meaning of "recognised tenants' association"	[636]
30	Meaning of "flat", "landlord" and "tenant"	[637]

INSURANCE

30A	Rights of tenants with respect to insurance	[638]

MANAGING AGENTS

30B	Recognised tenants' associations to be consulted about managing agents	[639]

MISCELLANEOUS

31	Reserve power to limit rents	[640]

SUPPLEMENTARY PROVISIONS

32	Provisions not applying to tenancies within Part II of the Landlord and Tenant Act 1954	[641]
33	Liability of directors, &c for offences by body corporate	[642]
34	Power of local housing authority to prosecute	[643]
35	Application to Isles of Scilly	[644]
36	Meaning of "lease" and "tenancy" and related expressions	[645]
37	Meaning of "statutory tenant" and related expessions	[646]
38	Minor definitions	[647]
39	Index of defined expressions	[648]

Section Para

FINAL PROVISIONS

40 Short title, commencement and extent .. .. [649]
Schedule—*Rights of Tenants with Respect to Insurance* .. .. [650]

An Act to consolidate certain provisions of the law of landlord and tenant formerly found in the Housing Acts, together with the Landlord and Tenant Act 1962, with amendments to give effect to recommendations of the Law Commission.
[30 October 1985]

INFORMATION TO BE GIVEN TO TENANT

1. Disclosure of landlord's identity

(1) If the tenant of premises occupied as a dwelling makes a written request for the landlord's name and address to—

(*a*) any person who demands, or the last person who received, rent payable under the tenancy, or
(*b*) any other person for the time being acting as agent for the landlord, in relation to the tenancy,

that person shall supply the tenant with a written statement of the landlord's name and address within the period of 21 days beginning with the day on which he receives the request.

(2) A person who, without reasonable excuse, fails to comply with subsection (1) commits a summary offence and is liable on conviction to a fine not exceeding level 4 on the standard scale.

(3) In this section and section 2—

(*a*) "tenant" includes a statutory tenant; and
(*b*) "landlord" means the immediate landlord. **[605]**

NOTES
Commencement: 1 April 1986.
Sub-ss (1), (3) derived from the Housing Act 1974, s 121(1), (9); sub-s (2) derived from the Housing Act 1974, s 121(1), the Housing Act 1980, s 144 and the Criminal Justice Act 1982, ss 37, 46(1).

2. Disclosure of directors, &c of corporate landlord

(1) Where a tenant is supplied under section 1 with the name and address of his landlord and the landlord is a body corporate, he may make a further written request to the landlord for the name and address of every director and of the secretary of the landlord.

(2) The landlord shall supply the tenant with a written statement of the information requested within the period of 21 days beginning with the day on which he receives the request.

(3) A request under this section is duly made to the landlord if it is made to—

(*a*) an agent of the landlord, or
(*b*) a person who demands the rent of the premises concerned;

and any such agent or person to whom such a request is made shall forward it to the landlord as soon as may be.

(4) A landlord who, without reasonable excuse, fails to comply with a request under this section, and a person who, without reasonable excuse, fails to comply with a requirement imposed on him by subsection (3), commits a summary offence and is liable on conviction to a fine not exceeding level 4 on the standard scale. **[606]**

NOTES

Commencement: 1 April 1986.

Sub-ss (1)-(3) derived from the Housing Act 1974, s 121(2), (4); sub-s (4) derived from the Housing Act 1974, s 121(5), the Housing Act 1980, s 144 and the Criminal Justice Act 1982, ss 37, 46(1).

3. Duty to inform tenant of assignment of landlord's interest

(1) If the interest of the landlord under a tenancy of premises which consist of or include a dwelling is assigned, the new landlord shall give notice in writing of the assignment, and of his name and address, to the tenant not later than the next day on which rent is payable under the tenancy or, if that is within two months of the assignment, the end of that period of two months.

(2) If trustees constitute the new landlord, a collective description of the trustees as the trustees of the trust in question may be given as the name of the landlord, and where such a collective description is given—

(*a*) the address of the new landlord may be given as the address from which the affairs of the trust are conducted, and

(*b*) a change in the persons who are for the time being the trustees of the trust shall not be treated as an assignment of the interest of the landlord.

(3) A person who is the new landlord under a tenancy falling within subsection (1) and who fails, without reasonable excuse, to give the notice required by that subsection, commits a summary offence and is liable on conviction to a fine not exceeding level 4 on the standard scale.

[(3A) The person who was the landlord under the tenancy immediately before the assignment ("the old landlord") shall be liable to the tenant in respect of any breach of any covenant, condition or agreement under the tenancy occurring before the end of the relevant period in like manner as if the interest assigned were still vested in him; and where the new landlord is also liable to the tenant in respect of any such breach occurring within that period, he and the old landlord shall be jointly and severally liable in respect of it.

(3B) In subsection (3A) "the relevant period" means the period beginning with the date of the assignment and ending with the date when—

(*a*) notice in writing of the assignment, and of the new landlord's name and address, is given to the tenant by the new landlord (whether in accordance with subsection (1) or not), or

(*b*) notice in writing of the assignment, and of the new landlord's name and last-known address, is given to the tenant by the old landlord,

whichever happens first.]

(4) In this section—

(*a*) "tenancy" includes a statutory tenancy, and

(*b*) references to the assignment of the landlord's interest include any conveyance other than a mortgage or charge. **[607]**

NOTES

Commencement: 1 April 1986 (sub-ss (1)-(3), (4)); to be appointed (remainder).

Sub-ss (1), (2), (4) derived from the Housing Act 1974, s 122(1), (2), (4), (8), (9)(*a*); sub-s (3) derived from the Housing Act 1974, s 122(5), the Housing Act 1980, s 144 and the Criminal Justice Act 1982, ss 37, 46(1).

Sub-ss (3A), (3B): prospectively added by the Landlord and Tenant Act 1987, s 50, as from a day to be appointed.

PROVISION OF RENT BOOKS

4. Provision of rent books

(1) Where a tenant has a right to occupy premises as a residence in consideration of a rent payable weekly, the landlord shall provide a rent book or other similar document for use in respect of the premises.

(2) Subsection (1) does not apply to premises if the rent includes a payment in respect of board and the value of that board to the tenant forms a substantial proportion of the whole rent.

(3) In this section and sections 5 to 7—

(*a*) "tenant" includes a statutory tenant and a person having a contractual right to occupy the premises; and

(*b*) "landlord", in relation to a person having such a contractual right, means the person who granted the right or any successor in title of his, as the case may require. **[608]**

NOTES

Commencement: 1 April 1986.

Sub-ss (1), (2) derived from the Landlord and Tenant Act 1962, s 1(1), (2); sub-s (3) derived from the Landlord and Tenant Act 1962, ss 1(1), 6(1)(*a*).

5. Information to be contained in rent books

(1) A rent book or other similar document provided in pursuance of section 4 shall contain notice of the name and address of the landlord of the premises and—

(*a*) if the premises are occupied by virtue of a restricted contract, particulars of the rent and of the other terms and conditions of the contract and notice of such other matters as may be prescribed;

(*b*) if the premises are let on or subject to a protected or statutory tenancy, notice of such matters as may be prescribed.

(2) If the premises are occupied by virtue of a restricted contract or let on or subject to a protected or statutory tenancy, the notice and particulars required by this section shall be in the prescribed form.

(3) In this section "prescribed" means prescribed by regulations made by the Secretary of State, which—

(*a*) may make different provision for different cases, and

(*b*) shall be made by statutory instrument which shall be subject to annulment in pursuance of a resolution of either House of Parliament. **[609]**

NOTES

Commencement: 1 April 1986.

Sub-s (1) derived from the Landlord and Tenant Act 1962, s 2(1), the Rent (Agriculture) Act

1976, Sch 8, para 9 and the Rent Act 1977, Sch 23, para 31(*a*), (*b*); sub-s (2) derived from the Landlord and Tenant Act 1962, s 2(1) and the Rent Act 1968, Sch 15; sub-s (3) derived from the Landlord and Tenant Act 1962, s 6(1)(*b*).

6. Information to be supplied by companies

(1) Where the landlord of premises to which section 4(1) applies (premises occupied as a residence at a weekly rent) is a company, and the tenant serves on the landlord a request in writing to that effect, the landlord shall give the tenant in writing particulars of the name and address of every director and of the secretary of the company.

(2) A request under this section is duly served on the landlord if it is served—

(*a*) on an agent of the landlord named as such in the rent book or other similar document, or

(*b*) on the person who receives the rent of the premises;

and a person on whom a request is so served shall forward it to the landlord as soon as may be. **[610]**

NOTES

Commencement: 1 April 1986.

This section derived from the Landlord and Tenant Act 1962, s 3(1), (2).

7. Offences

(1) If the landlord of premises to which section 4(1) applies (premises occupied as a residence at a weekly rent) fails to comply with any relevant requirement of—

section 4 (provision of rent book),
section 5 (information to be contained in rent book), or
section 6 (information to be supplied by companies),

he commits a summary offence and is liable on conviction to a fine not exceeding level 4 on the standard scale.

(2) If a person demands or receives rent on behalf of the landlord of such premises while any relevant requirement of—

section 4 (provision of rent book), or
section 5 (information to be contained in rent book),

is not complied with, then, unless he shows that he neither knew nor had reasonable cause to suspect that any such requirement had not been complied with, he commits a summary offence and is liable to a fine not exceeding level 4 on the standard scale.

(3) If a person fails to comply with a requirement imposed on him by section 6(2) (duty to forward request to landlord), he commits a summary offence and is liable on conviction to a fine not exceeding level 4 on the standard scale.

(4) If a default in respect of which—

(*a*) a landlord is convicted of an offence under subsection (1), or

(*b*) another person is convicted of an offence under subsection (3),

continues for more than 14 days after the conviction, the landlord or other person commits a further offence under that subsection in respect of the default. **[611]**

NOTES

Commencement: 1 April 1986.

Sub-ss (1)-(3) derived from the Landlord and Tenant Act 1962, s 4(1)-(3) and the Criminal Justice Act 1982, ss 37, 46(1), Sch 3; sub-s (4) derived from the Landlord and Tenant Act 1962, s 4(4).

IMPLIED TERMS AS TO FITNESS FOR HUMAN HABITATION

8. Implied terms as to fitness for human habitation

(1) In a contract to which this section applies for the letting of a house for human habitation there is implied, notwithstanding any stipulation to the contrary—

(*a*) a condition that the house is fit for human habitation at the commencement of the tenancy, and

(*b*) an undertaking that the house will be kept by the landlord fit for human habitation during the tenancy.

(2) The landlord, or a person authorised by him in writing, may at reasonable times of the day, on giving 24 hours' notice in writing, to the tenant or occupier, enter premises to which this section applies for the purpose of viewing their state and condition.

(3) This section applies to a contract if—

(*a*) the rent does not exceed the figure applicable in accordance with subsection (4), and

(*b*) the letting is not on such terms as to the tenant's responsibility as are mentioned in subsection (5).

(4) The rent limit for the application of this section is shown by the following Table, by reference to the date of making of the contract and the situation of the premises:

TABLE

Date of making of contract	*Rent limit*
Before 31st July 1923.	In London: £40. Elsewhere: £26 or £16 (see Note 1).
On or after 31st July 1923 and before 6th July 1957.	In London: £40. Elsewhere: £26.
On or after 6th July 1957.	In London: £80. Elsewhere: £52.

NOTES

1. The applicable figure for contracts made before 31st July 1923 is £26 in the case of premises situated in a borough or urban district which at the date of the contract had according to the last published census a population of 50,000 or more. In the case of a house situated elsewhere, the figure is £16.

2. The references to "London" are, in relation to contracts made before 1st April 1965, to the administrative county of London and, in relation to contracts made on or after that date, to Greater London exclusive of the outer London boroughs.

(5) This section does not apply where a house is let for a term of three years or more (the lease not being determinable at the option of either party before the expiration of three years) upon terms that the tenant puts the premises into a condition reasonably fit for human habitation.

(6) In this section "house" includes—

(*a*) a part of a house, and
(*b*) any yard, garden, outhouses and appurtenances belonging to the house or usually enjoyed with it. **[612]**

NOTES
Commencement: 1 April 1986.
Sub-ss (1)-(3), (5) derived from the Housing Act 1957, s 6(1)-(3); sub-s (4) derived from the Housing Act 1957, s 6(1), the London Government Act 1963, Sch 8, para 2; sub-s (6) derived from the Housing Act 1957, s 189(1)(*a*).

9. Application of s 8 to certain houses occupied by agricultural workers

(1) Where under the contract of employment of a worker employed in agriculture the provision of a house for his occupation forms part of his remuneration and the provisions of section 8 (implied terms as to fitness for human habitation) are inapplicable by reason only of the house not being let to him—

(*a*) there are implied as part of the contract of employment, notwithstanding any stipulation to the contrary, the like condition and undertaking as would be implied under that section if the house were so let, and
(*b*) the provisions of that section apply accordingly, with the substitution of "employer" for "landlord" and such other modifications as may be necessary.

(2) This section does not affect any obligation of a person other than the employer to repair a house to which this section applies, or any remedy for enforcing such an obligation.

(3) In this section "house" includes—

(*a*) a part of a house, and
(*b*) any yard, garden, outhouses and appurtenances belonging to the house or usually enjoyed with it. **[613]**

NOTES
Commencement: 1 April 1986.
Sub-ss (1), (2) derived from the Housing Act 1957, s 7; sub-s (3) derived from the Housing Act 1957, ss 7, 189(1)(*a*).

10. Fitness for human habitation

In determining for the purposes of this Act whether a house is unfit for human habitation, regard shall be had to its condition in respect of the following matters—

repair,
stability,
freedom from damp,
internal arrangement,
natural lighting,
ventilation,
water supply,
drainage and sanitary conveniences,
facilities for preparation and cooking of food and for the disposal of waste water;

and the house shall be regarded as unfit for human habitation if, and only if, it is so far defective in one or more of those matters that it is not reasonably suitable for occupation in that condition. **[614]**

NOTES
Commencement: 1 April 1986.
This section derived from the Housing Act 1957, s 4(1) and the Housing Act 1969 s 71.

REPAIRING OBLIGATIONS

11. Repairing obligations in short leases

(1) In a lease to which this section applies (as to which, see sections 13 and 14) there is implied a covenant by the lessor—

(*a*) to keep in repair the structure and exterior of the dwelling-house (including drains, gutters and external pipes),
(*b*) to keep in repair and proper working order the installations in the dwelling-house for the supply of water, gas and electricity and for sanitation (including basins, sinks, baths and sanitary conveniences, but not other fixtures, fittings and appliances for making use of the supply of water, gas or electricity), and
(*c*) to keep in repair and proper working order the installations in the dwelling-house for space heating and heating water.

(2) The covenant implied by subsection (1) ("the lessor's repairing covenant") shall not be construed as requiring the lessor—

(*a*) to carry out works or repairs for which the lessee is liable by virtue of his duty to use the premises in a tenant-like manner, or would be so liable but for an express covenant on his part,
(*b*) to rebuild or reinstate the premises in the case of destruction or damage by fire, or by tempest, flood or other inevitable accident, or
(*c*) to keep in repair or maintain anything which the lessee is entitled to remove from the dwelling-house.

(3) In determining the standard of repair required by the lessor's repairing covenant, regard shall be had to the age, character and prospective life of the dwelling-house and the locality in which it is situated.

(4) A covenant by the lessee for the repair of the premises is of no effect so far as it relates to the matters mentioned in subsection (1)(*a*) to (*c*), except so far as it imposes on the lessee any of the requirements mentioned in subsection (2)(*a*) or (*c*).

(5) The reference in subsection (4) to a covenant by the lessee for the repair of the premises includes a covenant—

(*a*) to put in repair or deliver up in repair,
(*b*) to paint, point or render,
(*c*) to pay money in lieu of repairs by the lessee, or
(*d*) to pay money on account of repairs by the lessor.

(6) In a lease in which the lessor's repairing covenant is implied there is also implied a covenant by the lessee that the lessor, or any person authorised by him in writing, may at reasonable times of the day and on giving 24 hours' notice in writing to the occupier, enter the premises comprised in the lease for the purpose of viewing their condition and state of repair. **[615]**

NOTES
Commencement: 1 April 1986.
This section derived from the Housing Act 1961, s 32(1)-(4).
See further ss 12-15.

12. Restriction on contracting out of s 11

(1) A covenant or agreement, whether contained in a lease to which section 11 applies or in an agreement collateral to such a lease, is void in so far as it purports—

(*a*) to exclude or limit the obligations of the lessor or the immunities of the lessee under that section, or

(*b*) to authorise any forfeiture or impose on the lessee any penalty, disability or obligation in the event of his enforcing or relying upon those obligations or immunities,

unless the inclusion of the provision was authorised by the county court.

(2) The county court may, by order made with the consent of the parties, authorise the inclusion in a lease, or in an agreement collateral to a lease, of provisions excluding or modifying in relation to the lease, the provisions of section 11 with respect to the repairing obligations of the parties if it appears to the court that it is reasonable to do so, having regard to all the circumstances of the case, including the other terms and conditions of the lease. **[616]**

NOTES

Commencement: 1 April 1986.

This section derived from the Housing Act 1961, s 33(6), (7).

13. Leases to which s 11 applies: general rule

(1) Section 11 (repairing obligations) applies to a lease of a dwelling-house granted on or after 24th October 1961 for a term of less than seven years.

(2) In determining whether a lease is one to which section 11 applies—

(*a*) any part of the term which falls before the grant shall be left out of account and the lease shall be treated as a lease for a term commencing with the grant,

(*b*) a lease which is determinable at the option of the lessor before the expiration of seven years from the commencement of the term shall be treated as a lease for a term of less than seven years, and

(*c*) a lease (other than a lease to which paragraph (*b*) applies) shall not be treated as a lease for a term of less than seven years if it confers on the lessee an option for renewal for a term which, together with the original term, amounts to seven years or more.

(3) This section has effect subject to—

section 14 (leases to which section 11 applies: exceptions), and

section 32(2) (provisions not applying to tenancies within Part II of the Landlord and Tenant Act 1954). **[617]**

NOTES

Commencement: 1 April 1986.

This section derived from the Housing Act 1961, s 33(1), (2), (5).

14. Leases to which s 11 applies: exceptions

(1) Section 11 (repairing obligations) does not apply to a new lease granted to an existing tenant, or to a former tenant still in possession, if the previous lease was not a lease to which section 11 applied (and, in the case of a lease granted before 24th October 1961, would not have been if it had been granted on or after that date).

(2) In subsection (1)—

"existing tenant" means a person who is when, or immediately before, the new lease is granted, the lessee under another lease of the dwelling-house;

"former tenant still in possession" means a person who—

(*a*) was the lessee under another lease of the dwelling-house which terminated at some time before the new lease was granted, and

(*b*) between the termination of that other lease and the grant of the new lease was continuously in possession of the dwelling-house or of the rents and profits of the dwelling-house; and

"the previous lease" means the other lease referred to in the above definitions.

(3) Section 11 does not apply to a lease of a dwelling-house which is a tenancy of an agricultural holding within the meaning of the *Agricultural Holdings Act 1948* [Agricultural Holdings Act 1986].

(4) Section 11 does not apply to a lease granted on or after 3rd October 1980 to—

a local authority,
a new town corporation,
an urban development corporation,
the Development Board for Rural Wales,
a registered housing association,
a co-operative housing association, or
an educational institution or other body specified, or of a class specified, by regulations under section 8 of the Rent Act 1977 (bodies making student lettings).

(5) Section 11 does not apply to a lease granted on or after 3rd October 1980 to—

(*a*) Her Majesty in right of the Crown (unless the lease is under the management of the Crown Estate Commissioners), or

(*b*) a government department or a person holding in trust for Her Majesty for the purposes of a government department. **[618]**

NOTES

Commencement: 1 April 1986.

Sub-ss (1)-(3) derived from the Housing Act 1961, s 33(3), (4); sub-s (4) derived from the Rent Act 1977, ss 14, 15(3), the Housing Act 1980, s 80(1)(*a*)-(*c*), (2), (3), the Local Government, Planning and Land Act 1980, s 155(1) and the New Towns Act 1981, Sch 12, para 24; sub-s (5) derived from the Housing Act 1980, s 80(1)(*d*), (*e*).

Words in italics repealed with savings and words in square brackets substituted with savings by the Agricultural Holdings Act 1986, ss 99, 100, Sch 13, para 3, Sch 14, para 64.

15. Jurisdiction of county court

The county court has jurisdiction to make a declaration that section 11 (repairing obligations) applies, or does not apply, to a lease—

(*a*) whatever the net annual value of the property in question, and

(*b*) notwithstanding that no other relief is sought than a declaration. **[619]**

NOTES

Commencement: 1 April 1986.

This section derived from the Housing Act 1961, s 33(8).

16. Meaning of "lease" and related expressions

In sections 11 to 15 (repairing obligations in short leases)—

(*a*) "lease" does not include a mortgage term;
(*b*) "lease of a dwelling-house" means a lease by which a building or part of a building is let wholly or mainly as a private residence, and "dwelling-house" means that building or part of a building;
(*c*) "lessee" and "lessor" mean, respectively, the person for the time being entitled to the term of a lease and to the reversion expectant on it.

[620]

NOTES

Commencement: 1 April 1986.
This section derived from the Housing Act 1961, s 32(5).

17. Specific performance of landlord's repairing obligations

(1) In proceedings in which a tenant of a dwelling alleges a breach on the part of his landlord of a repairing covenant relating to any part of the premises in which the dwelling is comprised, the court may order specific performance of the covenant whether or not the breach relates to a part of the premises let to the tenant and notwithstanding any equitable rule restricting the scope of the remedy, whether on the basis of a lack of mutuality or otherwise.

(2) In this section—

(*a*) "tenant" includes a statutory tenant,
(*b*) in relation to a statutory tenant the reference to the premises let to him is to the premises of which he is a statutory tenant,
(*c*) "landlord", in relation to a tenant, includes any person against whom the tenant has a right to enforce a repairing covenant, and
(*d*) "repairing covenant" means a covenant to repair, maintain, renew, construct or replace any property. **[621]**

NOTES

Commencement: 1 April 1986.
This section derived from the Housing Act 1974, s 125(1), (2) and sub-s (2) gives effect to the Law Commission Recommendation 14(i), Cmnd 9515.

SERVICE CHARGES

18. Meaning of "service charge" and "relevant costs"

(1) In the following provisions of this Act "service charge" means an amount payable by a tenant of a *flat* [dwelling] as part of or in addition to the rent—

(*a*) which is payable, directly or indirectly, for services, repairs, maintenance or insurance or the landlord's costs of management, and
(*b*) the whole or part of which varies or may vary according to the relevant costs.

(2) The relevant costs are the costs or estimated costs incurred or to be incurred by or on behalf of the landlord, or a superior landlord, in connection with the matters for which the service charge is payable.

(3) For this purpose—

(*a*) "costs" includes overheads, and

(*b*) costs are relevant costs in relation to a service charge whether they are incurred, or to be incurred, in the period for which the service charge is payable or in an earlier or later period. **[622]**

NOTES

Commencement: 1 April 1986.

Sub-s (1): word underlined prospectively repealed and subsequent word in square brackets prospectively substituted by the Landlord and Tenant Act 1987, s 41, Sch 2, para 1, as from a day to be appointed.

This section derived from the Housing Act 1980, Sch 19, para 1(1).

See further s 27.

19. Limitation of service charges: reasonableness

(1) Relevant costs shall be taken into account in determining the amount of a service charge payable for a period—

(*a*) only to the extent that they are reasonably incurred, and

(*b*) where they are incurred on the provision of services or the carrying out of works, only if the services or works are of a reasonable standard;

and the amount payable shall be limited accordingly.

(2) Where a service charge is payable before the relevant costs are incurred, no greater amount than is reasonable is so payable, and after the relevant costs have been incurred any necessary adjustment shall be made by repayment, reduction or subsequent charges or otherwise.

(3) An agreement by the tenant of a *flat* [dwelling] (other than an arbitration agreement with the meaning of section 32 of the Arbitration Act 1950) is void in so far as it purports to provide for a determination in a particular manner, or on particular evidence, of any question—

(*a*) whether costs incurred for services, repairs, maintenance, insurance or management were reasonably incurred,

(*b*) whether services or works for which costs were incurred are of a reasonable standard, or

(*c*) whether an amount payable before costs are incurred is reasonable.

(4) A county court may make a declaration—

(*a*) that any such costs were or were not reasonably incurred,

(*b*) that any such services or works are or are not of a reasonable standard, or

(*c*) that any such amount is or is not reasonable,

notwithstanding that no other relief is sought in the proceedings.

[(5) If a person takes any proceedings in the High Court in pursuance of any of the provisions of this Act relating to service charges and he could have taken those proceedings in the county court, he shall not be entitled to recover any costs.] **[623]**

NOTES

Commencement: 1 April 1986, (sub-ss (1)-(4)); to be appointed (remainder).

Sub-s (3): word underlined prospectively repealed and subsequent word in square brackets prospectively substituted by the Landlord and Tenant Act 1987, s 41, Sch 2, para 2, as from a day to be appointed.

Sub-s (5): prospectively added by the Landlord and Tenant Act 1987, s 41, Sch 2, para 2, as from a day to be appointed.

This section derived from the Housing Act 1980, Sch 19, paras 2, 3, 11, 12.

See further s 27.

20. Limitation of service charges: estimates and consultation

(1) Where relevant costs incurred on the carrying out of works on a building exceed the limit specified in subsection (2), the excess shall not be taken into account in determining the amount of a service charge unless—

(a) the requirements of subsection (3) as to estimates and consultation have been complied with, or
(b) those requirements have been dispensed with by the court in accordance with subsection (5);

and the amount payable shall be limited accordingly.

(2) The limit is whichever is the greater of—

(a) £25, or such other amount as may be prescribed by order of the Secretary of State, multiplied by the number of flats in the building, or
(b) £500, or such other amount as may be so prescribed.

(3) The requirements are:—

(a) At least two estimates for the works shall be obtained, one of them from a person wholly unconnected with the landlord.
(b) A notice accompanied by a copy of the estimates shall be given to each of the tenants concerned or shall be displayed in the buildings so as to be likely to come to the notice of all those tenants; and, if there is a recognised tenants' association for the building, the notice and copy of the estimates shall also be given to the secretary of the association.
(c) The notice shall describe the works to be carried out and invite observations on them and on the estimates and shall state the name and the address in the United Kingdom of the person to whom the observations may be sent and the date by which they are to be received.
(d) The date stated in the notice shall not be earlier than one month after the date on which the notice is given or displayed as required by paragraph (b).
(e) The landlord shall have regard to any observations received in pursuance of the notice; and unless the works are urgently required they shall not be begun earlier than the date specified in the notice.

(4) For the purposes of subsection (3) the tenants concerned are all the landlord's tenants of flats in the building by whom a service charge is payable to which the costs of the proposed works are relevant.

(5) In proceedings relating to a service charge the court may, if satisfied that the landlord acted reasonably, dispense with all or any of the requirements of subsection (3).

(6) An order under this section—

(a) may make different provision with respect to different cases or descriptions of case, including different provision for diffrent areas, and
(b) shall be made by statutory instrument which shall be subject to annulment in pursuance of a resolution of either House of Parliament.

[(1) Where relevant costs incurred on the carrying out of any qualifying works exceed the limit specified in subsection (3), the excess shall not be taken into account in determining the amount of a service charge unless the relevant requirements have been either—

(*a*) complied with, or
(*b*) dispensed with by the court in accordance with subsection (9);

and the amount payable shall be limited accordingly.

(2) In subsection (1) "qualifying works", in relation to a service charge, means works (whether on a building or on any other premises) to the costs of which the tenant by whom the service charge is payable may be required under the terms of his lease to contribute by the payment of such a charge.

(3) The limit is whichever is the greater of—

(*a*) £25, or such other amount as may be prescribed by order of the Secretary of State, multiplied by the number of dwellings let to the tenants concerned; or

(*b*) £500, or such other amount as may be so prescribed.

(4) The relevant requirements in relation to such of the tenants concerned as are not represented by a recognised tenants' association are—

(*a*) At least two estimates for the works shall be obtained, one of them from a person wholly unconnected with the landlord.

(*b*) A notice accompanied by a copy of the estimates shall be given to each of those tenants or shall be displayed in or more places where it is likely to come to the notice of all those tenants.

(*c*) The notice shall describe the works to be carried out and invite observations on them and on the estimates and shall state the name and the address in the United Kingdom of the person to whom the observations may be sent and the date by which they are to be received.

(*d*) The date stated in the notice shall not be earlier than one month after the date on which the notice is given or displayed as required by paragraph (*b*).

(*e*) The landlord shall have regard to any observations received in pursuance of the notice; and unless the works are urgently required they shall not be begun earlier than the date specified in the notice.

(5) The relevant requirements in relation to such of the tenants concerned as are represented by a recognised tenants' association are—

(*a*) The landlord shall give to the secretary of the association a notice containing a detailed specification of the works in question and specifying a reasonable period within which the association may propose to the landlord the names of one or more persons from whom estimates for the works should in its view be obtained by the landlord.

(*b*) At least two estimates for the works shall be obtained, one of them from a person wholly unconnected with the landlord.

(*c*) A copy of each of the estimates shall be given to the secretary of the association.

(*d*) A notice shall be given to each of the tenants concerned represented by the association, which shall—

(i) describe briefly the works to be carried out,

(ii) summarise the estimates,

(iii) inform the tenant that he has a right to inspect and take copies of a detailed specification of the works to be carried out and of the estimates,

(iv) invite observations on those works and on the estimates, and

(v) specify the name and the address in the United Kingdom of the person to whom the observations may be sent and the date by which they are to be received.

(*e*) The date stated in the notice shall not be earlier than one month after the date on which the notice is given as required by paragraph (*d*).

(*f*) If any tenant to whom the notice is given so requests, the landlord shall afford him reasonable facilities for inspecting a detailed specification of the works to be carried out and the estimates, free of charge, and for taking copies of them on payment of such reasonable charge as the landlord may determine.

(*g*) The landlord shall have regard to any observations received in pursuance of the notice and, unless the works are urgently required, they shall not be begun earlier than the date specified in the notice.

(6) Paragraphs (*d*)(ii) and (iii) and (*f*) of subsection (5) shall not apply to any estimate of which a copy is enclosed with the notice given in pursuance of paragraph (*d*).

(7) The requirement imposed on the landlord by subsection (5)(*f*) to make any facilities available to a person free of charge shall not be construed as precluding the landlord from treating as part of his costs of management any costs incurred by him in connection with making those facilities so available.

(8) In this section "the tenants concerned" means all the landlord's tenants who may be required under the terms of their leases to contribute to the costs of the works in question by the payment of service charges.

(9) In proceedings relating to a service charge the court may, if satisfied that the landlord acted reasonably, dispense with all or any of the relevant requirements.

(10) An order under this section—

(*a*) may make different provision with respect to different cases or descriptions of case, including different provision for different areas, and

(*b*) shall be made by statutory instrument which shall be subject to annulment in pursuance of a resolution of either House of Parliament.] **[624]**

NOTES

Commencement: 1 April 1986.

Sub-ss (1)-(5) derived from the Housing Act 1980, Sch 19, paras 2, 4(1), (2), 5(1)-(7), 6; sub-s (6) derived from the Housing Act 1980, s 151(1), (3).

Prospectively substituted by the Landlord and Tenant Act 1987, s 41, Sch 2, para 3, as from a day to be appointed.

See further s 27.

[20A. Limitation of service charges: grant-aided works

Where relevant costs are incurred or to be incurred on the carrying out of works in respect of which a grant has been or is to be paid under Part XV of the Housing Act 1985 (grants for works of improvement, repair or conversion), the amount of the grant shall be deducted from the costs and the amount of the service charge payable shall be reduced accordingly.] **[625]**

NOTES

Commencement: To be appointed.

Prospectively added by the Housing and Planning Act 1986, s 24(1), Sch 5, Part I, para 9(1), as from a day to be appointed.

[20B. Limitation of service charges: time limit on making demands

(1) If any of the relevant costs taken into account in determining the amount of any service charge were incurred more than 18 months before a demand for

payment of the service charge is served on the tenant, then (subject to subsection (2)), the tenant shall not be liable to pay so much of the service charge as reflects the costs so incurred.

(2) Subsection (1) shall not apply if, within the period of 18 months beginning with the date when the relevant costs in question were incurred, the tenant was notified in writing that those costs had been incurred and that he would subsequently be required under the terms of his lease to contribute to them by the payment of a service charge.] **[626]**

NOTES

Commencement: To be appointed.

Prospectively added by the Landlord and Tenant Act 1987, s 41, Sch 2, para 4, as from a day to be appointed.

[20C. Limitation of service charges: costs of court proceedings

(1) A tenant may make an application to the appropriate court for an order that all or any of the costs incurred, or to be incurred, by the landlord in connection with any proceedings are not to be regarded as relevant costs to be taken into account in determining the amount of any service charge payable by the tenant or any other person or persons specified in the application; and the court may make such order on the application as it considers just and equitable in the circumstances.

(2) In subsection (1) "the appropriate court" means—

(*a*) if the application is made in the course of the proceedings in question, the court before which the proceedings are taking place; and

(*b*) if the application is made after those proceedings are concluded, a county court.] **[627]**

NOTES

Commencement: To be appointed.

Prospectively added by the Landlord and Tenant Act 1987, s 41, Sch 2, para 4, as from a day to be appointed.

21. Request for summary of relevant costs

(1) A tenant may require the landlord in writing to supply him with a written summary of the costs incurred—

(*a*) if the relevant accounts are made up for periods of twelve months, in the last such period ending not later than the date of the request, or

(*b*) if the accounts are not so made up, in the period of twelve months ending with the date of the request,

and which are relevant costs in relation to the service charges payable or demanded as payable in that or any other period.

(2) If *there is a recognised tenants' association for the building and the tenant* [the tenant is represented by a recognised tenants' association and he] consents, the request may be made by the secretary of the association instead of by the tenant and may then be for the supply of the summary to the secretary.

(3) A request is duly served on the landlord if it is served on—

(*a*) an agent of the landlord named as such in the rent book or similar document, or

(*b*) the person who receives the rent on behalf of the landlord;

and a person on whom a request is so served shall forward it as soon as may be to the landlord.

(4) The landlord shall comply with the request within one month of the request or within six months of the end of the period referred to in subsection (1)(*a*) or (*b*) whichever is the later.

(5) The summary shall [state whether any of the costs relate to works in respect of which a grant has been or is to be paid under Part XV of the Housing Act 1985 (grants for works of improvement, repair or conversion) and] set out the costs in a way showing *how they are or will be reflected in demands for services charges* [how they have been or will be reflected in demands for service charges and, in addition, shall summarise each of the following items, namely—

(*a*) any of the costs in respect of which no demand for payment was received by the landlord within the period referred to in subsection (1)(*a*) or (*b*),

(*b*) any of the costs in respect of which—

(i) a demand for payment was so received, but

(ii) no payment was made by the landlord within that period, and

(*c*) any of the costs in respect of which—

(i) a demand for payment was so received, and

(ii) payment was made by the landlord within that period,

and specify the aggregate of any amounts received by the landlord down to the end of that period on account of service charges in respect of relevant dwellings and still standing to the credit of the tenants of those dwellings at the end of that period.

(5A) In subsection (5) "relevant dwelling" means a dwelling whose tenant is either—

(*a*) the person by or with the consent of whom the request was made, or

(*b*) a person whose obligations under the terms of his lease as regards contributing to relevant costs relate to the same costs as the corresponding obligations of the person mentioned in paragraph (*a*) above relate to.]

(6) *If there are more than four flats in the building or the costs also relate to another building* [If the service charges in relation to which the costs are relevant costs as mentioned in subsection (1) are payable by the tenants of more than four dwellings], the summary shall be certified by a qualified accountant as—

(*a*) in his opinion a fair summary complying with the *requirement* [requirements] of subsection (5), and

(*b*) being sufficiently supported by accounts, receipts and other documents which have been produced to him. **[628]**

NOTES

Commencement: 1 April 1986 (sub-ss (1)-(5), (6)); to be appointed (remainder).

Sub-ss (1), (2), (4)-(6) derived from the Housing Act 1980, Sch 19, para 7(1)-(3), (5); sub-s (3) derived from the Housing Act 1980, Sch 19, para 9.

Sub-ss (2), (6): words in italics prospectively repealed and words in square brackets prospectively substituted by the Landlord and Tenant Act 1987, s 41, Sch 2, para 5, as from a day to be appointed.

Sub-s (5): first words in square brackets prospectively added by the Housing and Planning Act 1986, s 24(1), Sch 5, Part I, para 9(2), as from a day to be appointed; second words in italics prospectively repealed and subsequent words in square brackets prospectively substituted by the Landlord and Tenant Act 1987, s 41, Sch 2, para 5, as from a day to be appointed.

Sub-s (5A): prospectively added by the Landlord and Tenant Act 1987, s 41, Sch 2, para 5, as from a day to be appointed.

See further s 27.

22. Request to inspect supporting accounts &c

(1) This section applies where a tenant, or the secretary of a recognised tenants' association, has obtained such a summary as is referred to in section 21(1) (summary of relevant costs), whether in pursuance of that section or otherwise.

(2) The tenant, or the secretary with the consent of the tenant, may within six months of obtaining the summary require the landlord in writing to afford him reasonable facilities—

(*a*) for inspecting the accounts, receipts and other documents supporting the summary, and

(*b*) for taking copies or extracts from them.

(3) A request under this section is duly served on the landord if it is served on—

(*a*) an agent of the landlord named as such in the rent book or similar document, or

(*b*) the person who receives the rent on behalf of the landlord;

and a person on whom a request is so served shall forward it as soon as may be to the landlord.

(4) The landlord shall make such facilities available to the tenant or secretary for a period of two months beginning not later than one month after the request is made.

[(5) The landlord shall—

(*a*) where such facilities are for the inspection of any documents, make them so available free of charge;

(*b*) where such facilities are for the taking of copies or extracts, be entitled to make them so available on payment of such reasonable charge as he may determine.

(6) The requirement imposed on the landlord by subsection (5)(*a*) to make any facilities available to a person free of charge shall not be construed as precluding the landlord from treating as part of his costs of management any costs incurred by him in connection with making those facilities so available.]

[629]

NOTES

Commencement: 1 April 1986 (sub-ss (1)-(4)); to be appointed (remainder).

Sub-ss (1), (2), (4) derived from the Housing Act 1980, Sch 19, para 7(4); sub-s (3) derived from the Housing Act 1980, Sch 19, para 9.

Sub-ss (5), (6): prospectively added by the Landlord and Tenant Act 1987, s 41, Sch 2, para 6, as from a day to be appointed.

See further s 27.

23. Request relating to information held by superior landlord

(1) If a request under section 21 (request for summary of relevant costs) relates in whole or in part to relevant costs incurred by or on behalf of a superior landlord, and the landlord to whom the request is made is not in possession of the relevant information—

(*a*) he shall in turn make a written request for the relevant information to the person who is his landlord (and so on, if that person is not himself the superior landlord), (*b*) the superior landlord shall comply with that request within a reasonable time, and

(*c*) the immediate landlord shall then comply with the tenant's or secretary's request, or that part of it which relates to the relevant costs incurred by or on behalf of the superior landlord, within the time allowed by section 21 or such further time, if any, as is reasonable in the circumstances.

(2) If a request under section 22 (request for facilities to inspect supporting accounts, &c.) relates to a summary of costs incurred by or on behalf of a superior landlord—

(*a*) the landlord to whom the request is made shall forthwith inform the tenant or secretary of that fact and of the name and address of the superior landlord, and

(*b*) section 22 shall then apply to the superior landlord as it applies to the immediate landlord. **[630]**

NOTES

Commencement: 1 April 1986.

This section derived from the Housing Act 1980, Sch 19, para 8(1), (2).

See further s 27.

24. Effect of assignment on request

(1) The assignment of a tenancy does not affect the validity of a request made under section 21, 22 or 23 before the assignment; but a person is not obliged to provide a summary or make facilities available more than once for the same *flat* [dwelling] and for the same period. **[631]**

NOTES

Commencement: 1 April 1986.

This section derived from the Housing Act 1980, Sch 19, para 10.

Word in italics prospectively repealed and subsequent word in square brackets prospectively substituted by the Landlord and Tenant Act 1987, s 41, Sch 2, para 7, as from a day to be appointed.

See further s 27.

25. Failure to comply with ss 21, 22, or 23 an offence

(1) It is a summary offence for a person to fail, without reasonable excuse, to perform a duty imposed on him by section 21, 22 or 23.

(2) A person committing such an offence is liable on conviction to a fine not exceeding level 4 on the standard scale. **[632]**

NOTES

Commencement: 1 April 1986.

This section derived from the Housing Act 1980, Sch 19, para 13(1) and the Criminal Justice Act 1982, ss 37, 46(1).

See further s 27.

26. Exception: tenants of certain public authorities

(1) Sections 18 to 25 (limitation on service charges and requests for information about costs) do not apply to a service charge payable by a tenent of—

a local authority,
a new town corporation, or
the Development Board for Rural Wales,

unless the tenancy is a long tenancy, in which case sections 18 to 24 apply but section 25 (offence of failure to comply) does not.

(2) The following are long tenancies for the purposes of subsection (1), subject to subsection (3)—

(*a*) a tenancy granted for a term certain exceeding 21 years, whether or not it is (or may become) terminable before the end of that term by notice given by the tenant or by re-entry or forfeiture;
(*b*) a tenancy for a term fixed by law under a grant with a covenant or obligation for perpetual renewal, other than a tenancy by sub-demise from one which is not a long tenancy;
(*c*) any tenancy granted in pursuance of Part V of the Housing Act 1985 (the right to buy).

(3) A tenancy granted so as to become terminable by notice after a death is not a long tenancy for the purposes of subsection (1), unless—

(*a*) it is granted by a housing association which at the time of the grant is registered,
(*b*) it is granted at a premium calculated by reference to a percentage of the value of the dwelling-house or the cost of providing it, and
(*c*) at the time it is granted it complied with the requirements of the regulations then in force under section 140(4)(*b*) of the Housing Act 1980 (conditions for exclusion of shared ownership leases from Part I of Leasehold Reform Act 1967) or, in the case of a tenancy granted before any such regulations were brought into force, with the first such regulations to be in force. **[633]**

NOTES
Commencement: 1 April 1986.
Sub-s (1): derived from the Housing Act 1980, s 50(1), Sch 19, para 14(1), (2)(*a*); sub-ss (2), (3) derived from the Housing Act 1980, Sch 3, para 1(2), (2A), (3), Sch 19, para 14(1).

27. Exception: rent registered and not entered as variable

Sections 18 and 25 (limitation on service charges and requests for information about costs) do not apply to a service charge payable by the tenant of a *flat* [dwelling] the rent of which is registered under Part IV of the Rent Act 1977, unless the amount registered is, in pursuance of section 71(4) of that Act, entered as a variable amount. **[634]**

NOTES
Commencement: 1 April 1986.
This section derived from the Housing Act 1980, Sch 19, para 15.
Word in italics prospectively repealed and word in square brackets prospectively substituted by the Landlord and Tenant Act 1987, s 41, Sch 2, para 8, as from a day to be appointed.

28. Meaning of "qualified accountant"

(1) The reference to a "qualified accountant" in section 21(6) (certification of summary of information about relevant costs) is to a person who, in accordance with the following provisions, has the necessary qualification and is not disqualified from acting.

(2) A person has the necessary qualification if he is a member of one of the following bodies—

the Institute of Chartered Accountants in England and Wales,
the Institute of Chartered Accountants in Scotland,
the Association of Certified Accountants,
the Institute of Chartered Accountants in Ireland, or

any other body of accountants established in the United Kingdom and recognised by the Secretary of State for the purposes of section 389(1)(*a*) of the Companies Act 1985,

or if he is a person who is for the time being authorised by the Secretary of State under section 389(1)(*b*) of that Act (or the corresponding provision of the Companies Act 1948) as being a person with similar qualifications obtained outside the United Kingdom.

(3) A Scottish firm has the necessary qualification if each of the partners in it has the necessary qualification.

(4) The following are disqualified from acting—

(*a*) a body corporate, except a Scottish firm;
(*b*) an officer *or employee* [, employee or partner] of the landlord or, where the landlord is a company, of an associated company;
(*c*) a person who is a partner or employee of any such officer or employee.
[(*d*) an agent of the landlord who is a managing agent for any premises to which any of the costs covered by the summary in question relate;
(*e*) an employee or partner of any such agent.]

(5) For the purposes of subsection (4)(*b*) a company is associated with a landlord company if it is (within the meaning of section 736 of the Companies Act 1985) the landlord's holding company, a subsidiary of the landlord or another subsidiary of the landlord's holding company.

[(5A) For the purposes of subsection (4)(*d*) a person is a managing agent for any premises to which any costs relate if he has been appointed to discharge any of the landlord's obligations relating to the management by him of the premises and owed to the tenants who may be required under the terms of their leases to contribute to those costs by the payment of service charges.]

(6) Where the landlord is a local authority, a new town corporation or the Development Board for Rural Wales—

(*a*) the persons who have the necessary qualification include members of the Chartered Institute of Public Finance and Accountancy, and
(*b*) subsection (4)(*b*) (disqualification of officers and employees of landlord) does not apply. **[635]**

NOTES

Commencement: 1 April 1986 (sub-ss (1)-(5), (6)); to be appointed (remainder).

Sub-s (2) derived from the Housing Act 1980, Sch 16, para 3(2), Sch 19, para 17(1) and the Companies Consolidation (Consequential Provisions) Act 1985, Sch 2; sub-s (3) derived from the Housing Act 1980, Sch 16, para 3(4), Sch 19, para 17(1); sub-ss (4), (6) derived from the Housing Act 1980, Sch 19, paras 14(1), (2)(*b*), 17(2); sub-s (5) derived from the Housing Act 1980, Sch 19, para 17(2)(*b*) and the Companies Consolidation (Consequential Provisions) Act 1985, Sch 2.

Sub-s (4): words in italics prospectively repealed and words in square brackets prospectively substituted or added by the Landlord and Tenant Act 1987, s 41, Sch 2, para 9, as from a day to be appointed.

Sub-s (5A): prospectively added by the Landlord and Tenant Act 1987, s 41, Sch 2, para 9, as from a day to be appointed.

29. Meaning of "recognised tenants' association"

(1) A recognised tenants' association is an association of *tenants of flats in a building* [qualifying tenants (whether with or without other tenants)] which is recognised for the purposes of the provisions of this Act relating to service charges either—

(*a*) by notice in writing given by the landlord to the secretary of the association, or
(*b*) by a certificate of a member of the local rent assessment committee panel.

(2) A notice given under subsection (1)(*a*) may be withdrawn by the landlord by notice in writing given to the secretary of the association not less than six months before the date on which it is to be withdrawn.

(3) A certificate given under subsection (1)(*b*) may be cancelled by any member of the local rent assessment committee panel.

(4) In this section the "local rent assessment committee panel" means the persons appointed by the Lord Chancellor under the Rent Act 1977 to the panel of persons to act as members of a rent assessment committee for the registration area in which *the building is situated* [the dwellings let to the qualifying tenants are situated, and for the purposes of this section a number of tenants are qualifying tenants if each of them may be required under the terms of his lease to contribute to the same costs by the payment of a service charge].

(5) The Secretary of State may by regulations specify the matters to which regard is to be had in giving or cancelling a certificate under subsection (1)(b).

[(5) The Secretary of State may by regulations specify—
(*a*) the procedure which is to be followed in connection with an application for, or for the cancellation of, a certificate under subsection (1)(*b*);
(*b*) the matters to which regard is to be had in giving or cancelling such a certificate;
(*c*) the duration of such a certificate; and
(*d*) any circumstances in which a certificate is not to be given under subsection (1)(*b*).]

(6) Regulations under subsection (5)—
(*a*) may make different provisions with respect to different cases or descriptions of case, including different provision for different areas, and
(*b*) shall be made by statutory instrument which shall be subject to annulment in pursuance of a resolution of either House of Parliament. **[636]**

NOTES
Commencement: 1 April 1986.
Sub-ss (1)-(5) derived from the Housing Act 1980, Sch 19, paras 20, 21; sub-s (6) derived from the Housing Act 1980, s 151(1), (3).
Sub-s (4): words in italics prospectively repealed and subsequent words in square brackets prospectively substituted by the Landlord and Tenant Act 1987, s 41, Sch 2, para 10, as from a day to be appointed.
Sub-s (5): prospectively substituted by the Landlord and Tenant Act 1987, s 41, Sch 2, para 10, as from a day to be appointed.

30. Meaning of "flat", "landlord" and "tenant"

In the provisions of this Act relating to service charges—

"flat" means a separate set of premises, whether or not on the same floor, which—
(a) forms part of a building,
(b) is divided horizontally from some other part of the building, and

(c) is constructed or adapted for use for the purposes of a dwelling and is occupied wholly or mainly as a private dwelling;

"landlord" includes any person who has a right to enforce payment of a service charge;

"tenant" includes

(*a*) a statutory tenant, and
(*b*) where the *flat* [dwelling] or part of it is sub-let, the sub-tenant. **[637]**

NOTES
Commencement: 1 April 1986.
This section derived from the Housing Act 1980, Sch 19, paras 16, 18, 19.
Definition "flat" prospectively repealed by the Landlord and Tenant Act 1987, ss 41, 61(2), Sch 2, para 11, Sch 5, as from a day to be appointed; in definition "tenant", word in italics prospectively repealed and subsequent word in square brackets prospectively substituted by the Landlord and Tenant Act 1987, s 41, Sch 2, para 11, as from a day to be appointed.

INSURANCE

[30A. Rights of tenants with respect to insurance

The Schedule to this Act (which confers on tenants certain rights with respect to the insurance of their dwellings) shall have effect.] **[638]**

NOTES
Commencement: To be appointed.
Prospectively added by the Landlord and Tenant Act 1987, s 43(1), as from a day to be appointed.

MANAGING AGENTS

[30B. Recognised tenants' associations to be consulted about managing agents

(1) A recognised tenants' association may at any time serve a notice on the landlord requesting him to consult the association in accordance with this section on matters relating to the appointment or employment by him of a managing agent for any relevant premises.

(2) Where, at the time when any such notice is served by a recognised tenants' association, the landlord does not employ any managing agent for any relevant premises, the landlord shall, before appointing such a managing agent, serve on the association a notice specifying—

(*a*) the name of the proposed managing agent;
(*b*) the landlord's obligations to the tenants represented by the association which it is proposed that the managing agent should be required to discharge on his behalf; and
(*c*) a period of not less than one month beginning with the date of service of the notice within which the association may make observations on the proposed appointment.

(3) Where, at the time when a notice is served under subsection (1) by a recognised tenants' association, the landlord employs a managing agent for any relevant premises, the landlord shall, within the period of one month beginning with the date of service of that notice serve on the association a notice specifying—

(*a*) the landlord's obligations to the tenants represented by the association which the managing agent is required to discharge on his behalf; and
(*b*) a reasonable period within which the association may make observations on the manner in which the managing agent has been discharging those obligations, and on the desirability of his continuing to discharge them.

(4) Subject to subsection (5), a landlord who has been served with a notice by an association under subsection (1) shall, so long as he employs a managing agent for any relevant premises—

(*a*) serve on that association at least once in every five years a notice specifying—
  (i) any change occurring since the date of the last notice served by him on the association under this section in the obligations which the managing agent has been required to discharge on his behalf; and
  (ii) a reasonable period within which the association may make observations on the manner in which the managing agent has discharged those obligations since that date, and on the desirability of his continuing to discharge them;
(*b*) serve on that association, whenever he proposes to appoint any new managing agent for any relevant premises, a notice specifying the matters mentioned in paragraphs (*a*) to (*c*) of subsection (2).

(5) A landlord shall not, by virtue of a notice served by an association under subsection (1), be required to serve on the association a notice under subsection (4)(*a*) or (*b*) if the association subsequently serves on the landlord a notice withdrawing its request under subsection (1) to be consulted by him.

(6) Where—

(*a*) a recognised tenants' association has served a notice under subsection (1) with respect to any relevant premises, and
(*b*) the interest of the landlord in those premises becomes vested in a new landlord,

that notice shall cease to have effect with respect to those premises (without prejudice to the service by the association on the new landlord of a fresh notice under that subsection with respect to those premises).

(7) Any notice served by a landlord under this section shall specify the name and the address in the United Kingdom of the person to whom any observations made in pursuance of the notice are to be sent; and the landlord shall have regard to any such observations that are received by that person within the period specified in the notice.

(8) In this section—

"landlord", in relation to a recognised tenants' association, means the immediate landlord of the tenants represented by the association or a person who has a right to enforce payment of service charges payable by any of those tenants;
"managing agent", in relation to any relevant premises, means an agent of the landlord appointed to discharge any of the landlord's obligations to the tenants represented by the recognised tenants' association in question which relate to the management by him of those premises; and
"tenant" includes a statutory tenant;

and for the purposes of this section any premises (whether a building or not) are relevant premises in relation to a recognised tenants' association if any of the tenants represented by the association may be required under the terms of their leases to contribute by the payment of service charges to costs relating to those premises.] **[639]**

NOTES

Commencement: To be appointed.

Prospectively added by the Landlord and Tenant Act 1987, s 44, as from a day to be appointed.

MISCELLANEOUS

31. Reserve power to limit rents

(1) The Secretary of State may by order provide for—

(*a*) restricting or preventing increases of rent for dwellings which would otherwise take place, or

(*b*) restricting the amount of rent which would otherwise be payable on new lettings of dwellings;

and may so provide either generally or in relation to any specified description of dwelling.

(2) An order may contain supplementary or incidental provisions, including provisions excluding, adapting or modifying any provision made by or under an enactment (whenever passed) relating to rent or the recovery of overpaid rent.

(3) In this section—

"new letting" includes any grant of a tenancy, whether or not the premises were previously let, and any grant of a licence;

"rent" includes a sum payable under a licence, but does not include a sum attributable to rates or, in the case of dwellings of local authorities or new town corporations, to the use of furniture, or the provision of services;

and for the purposes of this section an increase in rent takes place at the beginning of the rental period for which the increased rent is payable.

(4) An order under this section shall be made by statutory instrument which shall be subject to annulment in pursuance of a resolution of either House of Parliament. **[640]**

NOTES

Commencement: 1 April 1986.

Sub-ss (1), (2), (4): derived from the Housing Rents and Subsidies Act 1975, ss 11(1)-(3), 15(1), (5); sub-s (3) derived from the Housing Rents and Subsidies Act 1975, s 11(10), (11).

SUPPLEMENTARY PROVISIONS

32. Provisions not applying to tenancies within Part II of the Landlord and Tenant Act 1954

(1) The following provisions do not apply to a tenancy to which Part II of the Landlord and Tenant Act 1954 (business tenancies) applies—

sections 1 to 3 (information to be given to tenant),
section 17 (specific performance of landlord's repairing obligations).

(2) Section 11 (repairing obligations) does not apply to a new lease granted

to an existing tenant, or to a former tenant still in possession, if the new lease is a tenancy to which Part II of the Landlord and Tenant Act 1954 applies and the previous lease either is such a tenancy or would be but for section 28 of that Act (tenancy not within Part II if renewal agreed between the parties).

In this subsection "existing tenant", "former tenant still in possession" and "previous lease" have the same meaning as in section 14(2).

(3) Section 31 (reserve power to limit rents) does not apply to a dwelling forming part of a property subject to a tenancy to which Part II of the Landlord and Tenant Act 1954 applies; but without prejudice to the application of that section in relation to a sub-tenancy of a part of the premises comprised in such a tenancy. **[641]**

NOTES

Commencement: 1 April 1986.

Sub-s (1) derived from the Housing Act 1974, ss 121(9), 122(8), 125(2); sub-s (2) derived from the Housing Act 1961, s 33(3); sub-s (3) derived from the Housing Rents and Subsidies Act 1975, s 11(11).

33. Liability of directors, &c for offences by body corporate

(1) Where an offence under this Act which has been committed by a body corporate is proved—

(*a*) to have been committed with the consent or connivance of a director, manager, secretary or other similar officer of the body corporate, or a person purporting to act in any such capacity, or

(*b*) to be attributable to any neglect on the part of such an officer or person,

he, as well as the body corporate, is guilty of an offence and liable to be proceeded against and punished accordingly.

(2) Where the affairs of a body corporate are managed by its members, subsection (1) applies in relation to the acts and defaults of a member in connection with his functions of management as if he were a director of the body corporate. **[642]**

NOTES

Commencement: 1 April 1986.

Sub-s (1) derived from the Landlord and Tenant Act 1962, s 4(6), the Housing Act 1974, ss 121(6), 122(6) and the Housing Act 1980, Sch 19, para 13(2); sub-s (2) derived from the Housing Act 1974, ss 121(7), 122(7), the Housing Act 1980, Sch 19, para 13(3) and gives effect to the Law Commission Recommendation No 28, Cmnd 9515.

34. Power of local housing authority to prosecute

Proceedings for an offence under any provision of this Act may be brought by a local housing authority. **[643]**

NOTES

Commencement: 1 April 1986.

This section derived from the Landlord and Tenant Act 1962, s 5(2), the Rent Act 1968, Sch 15, the Local Government Act 1972, s 222(1), the Housing Act 1974, s 121(8), the Rent Act 1977, s 149(2), Sch 23, para 32, Sch 24, para 30.

35. Application to Isles of Scilly

(1) This Act applies to the Isles of Scilly subject to such exceptions, adaptations and modifications as the Secretary of State may by order direct.

(2) An order shall be made by statutory instrument which shall be subject to annulment in pursuance of a resolution of either House of Parliament. **[644]**

NOTES
Commencement: 1 April 1986.
This section derived from the Local Government Act 1972, s 103, the Housing Rent and Subsidies Act 1975, s 17(11), Sch 5, para 7(1), SI 1972 No 1204, SI 1975 No 512 and gives effect to the Law Commission Recommendation No 29, Cmnd 9515.

36. Meaning of "lease" and "tenancy" and related expressions

(1) In this Act "lease" and "tenancy" have the same meaning.

(2) Both expressions include—

(*a*) a sub-lease or sub-tenancy, and
(*b*) an agreement for a lease or tenancy (or sub-lease or sub-tenancy).

(3) The expressions "lessor" and "lessee" and "landlord" and "tenant", and references to letting, to the grant of a lease or to covenants or terms, shall be construed accordingly. **[645]**

NOTES
Commencement: 1 April 1986.
This section derived from the Housing Act 1961, s 32(5), the Housing Act 1974, ss 121(9), 125(2) and the Housing Rent and Subsidies Act 1975, s 11(11).

37. Meaning of "statutory tenant" and related expessions

In this Act—

(*a*) "statutory tenancy" and "statutory tenant" mean a statutory tenancy or statutory tenant within the meaning of the Rent Act 1977 or the Rent (Agriculture) Act 1976; and
(*b*) "landlord", in relation to a statutory tenant, means the person who, apart from the statutory tenancy, would be entitled to possession of the premises. **[646]**

NOTES
Commencement: 1 April 1986.
This section derived from the Landlord and Tenant Act 1962, s 6(1)(*a*), the Housing Act 1974, s 121(9), 122(8), 125(2), the Rent (Agriculture) Act 1976, Sch 8 para 31, the Rent Act 1977, Sch 23, para 66 and the Housing Act 1980, Sch 19, para 18 and gives effect to the Law Commission Recommendation No 14(i), Cmnd 9515.

38. Minor definitions

In this Act—

"address" means a person's place of abode or place of business or, in the case of a company, its registered office;

"co-operative housing association" has the same meaning as in the Housing Associations Act 1985;

"dwelling" means a building or part of a building occupied or intended to be occupied as a separate dwelling, together with any yard, garden, outhouses and appurtenances belonging to it or usually enjoyed with it;

"housing association" has the same meaning as in the Housing Associations Act 1985;

"local authority" means a district, county or London borough council, the Common Council of the City of London or the Council of the Isles of Scilly and in sections 14(4), 26(1) and 28(6) includes the Inner London Education Authority and a joint authority established by Part IV of the Local Government Act 1985;

"local housing authority" has the meaning given by section 1 of the Housing Act 1985;

"new town corporation" means—

(*a*) a development corporation established by an order made, or treated as made, under the New Towns Act 1981, or
(*b*) the Commission for the New Towns;

"protected tenancy" has the same meaning as in the Rent Act 1977;

"registered", in relation to a housing association, means registered under the Housing Associations Act 1985;

"restricted contract" has the same meaning as in the Rent Act 1977;

"urban development corporation" has the same meaning as in Part XVI of the Local Government, Planning and Land Act 1980. **[647]**

NOTES
Commencement: 1 April 1986.
Modified by SI 1985 No 1884, art 10, Sch 3.
This section derived from the Landlord and Tenant Act 1962, ss 2(1), 5(2), 6(2), the Rent Act 1968, Sch 15, the Housing Act 1974, ss 121(3), (8), 122(3), 129(1), Sch 13, para 9, the Housing Rent and Subsidies Act 1975, ss 11(11), 16(1), SI 1975 No 512, the Rent Act 1977, ss 14(*a*)-(*e*), (*g*), 15(3)(*a*), (*d*), 149(2), Sch 23, paras 31(*a*), (*b*), 32, Sch 24, para 30, the Housing Act 1980, ss 50(1), 80(1)(*b*), (*c*), Sch 19, para 14(1)(*a*), (*c*), the Local Government, Planning and Land Act 1980, s 155(1), the New Towns Act 1981, Sch 12, para 24 and the Local Government Act 1985, Sch 13, para 21, Sch 14, paras 56, 58(*h*).

39. Index of defined expressions

The following Table shows provisions defining or otherwise explaining expressions used in this Act (other than provisions defining or explaining an expression in the same section):

address	section 38
co-operative housing association	section 38
dwelling	section 38
dwelling-house (in the provisions relating to repairing obligations)	section 16
fit for human habitation	section 10
flat (in the provisions relating to service charges)	section 30
housing association	section 38
landlord—	section 36(3)
(generally)	
(in sections 1 and 2)	section 1(3)
(in the provisions relating to rent books)	section 4(3)
(in the provisions relating to service charges)	section 30
(in relation to a statutory tenancy)	section 37(*b*)
lease, lessee and lessor—	section 36
(generally)	
(in the provisions relating to repairing obligations)	section 16

local authority	section 38
local housing authority	section 38
new town corporation	section 38
protected tenancy	section 38
qualified accountant (for the purposes of section 21(6))	section 28
registered (in relation to a housing association)	section 38
recognised tenants' association	section 29
relevant costs (in relation to a service charge)	section 18(2)
restricted contract	section 38
service charge	section 18(1)
statutory tenant	section 37(*a*)
tenancy and tenant—	section 36
(generally)	
(in sections 1 and 2)	section 1(3)
(in the provisions relating to rent books)	section 4(3)
(in the provisions relating to service charges)	section 30
urban development corporation	section 38

[648]

NOTES
Commencement: 1 April 1986.

Final Provisions

40. Short title, commencement and extent

(1) This Act may be cited as the Landlord and Tenant Act 1985.

(2) This Act comes into force on 1st April 1986.

(3) This Act extends to England and Wales. **[649]**

NOTES
Commencement: 1 April 1986.

SCHEDULE
Rights of Tenants with Respect to Insurance

[Construction

1. In this Schedule—

"landlord", in relation to a tenant by whom a service charge is payable which includes an amount payable directly or indirectly for insurance, includes any person who has a right to enforce payment of that service charge;
"relevant policy", in relation to a dwelling, means any policy of insurance under which the dwelling is insured (being, in the case of a flat, a policy covering the building containing it); and
"tenant" includes a statutory tenant.

Request for summary of insurance cover

2.—(1) Where a service charge is payable by the tenant of a dwelling which consists of or includes an amount payable directly or indirectly for insurance, the tenant may require the landlord in writing to supply him with a written summary of the insurance for the time being effected in relation to the dwelling.

(2) If the tenant is represented by a recognised tenants' association and he consents, the request may be made by the secretary of the association instead of by the tenant and may then be for the supply of the summary to the secretary.

(3) A request is duly served on the landlord if it is served on—

(*a*) an agent of the landlord named as such in the rent book or similar document, or
(*b*) the person who receives the rent on behalf of the landlord;

and a person on whom a request is so served shall forward it as soon as may be to the landlord.

(4) The landlord shall, within one month of the request, comply with it by supplying to the tenant or the secretary of the recognised tenants' association (as the case may require) such a summary as is mentioned in sub-paragraph (1), which shall include—

(*a*) the insured amount or amounts under any relevant policy, and
(*b*) the name of the insurer under any such policy, and
(*c*) the risks in respect of which the dwelling or (as the case may be) the building containing it is insured under any such policy.

(5) In sub-paragraph (4)(*a*) "the insured amount or amounts", in relation to a relevant policy, means—

(*a*) in the case of a dwelling other than a flat, the amount for which the dwelling is insured under the policy; and
(*b*) in the case of a flat, the amount for which the building containing it is insured under the policy and, if specified in the policy, the amount for which the flat is insured under it.

(6) The landlord shall be taken to have complied with the request if, within the period mentioned in sub-paragraph (4), he instead supplies to the tenant or the secretary (as the case may require) a copy of every relevant policy.

(7) In a case where two or more buildings are insured under any relevant policy, the summary or copy supplied under sub-paragraph (4) or (6) so far as relating to that policy need only be of such parts of the policy as relate—

(*a*) to the dwelling, and
(*b*) if the dwelling is a flat, to the building containing it.

Request to inspect insurance policy etc.

3.—(1) This paragraph applies where a tenant, or the secretary of a recognised tenants' association, has obtained either—

(*a*) such a summary as is referred to in paragraph 2(1), or
(*b*) a copy of any relevant policy or of any such parts of any relevant policy as relate to the premises referred to in paragraph 2(7)(*a*) or (*b*),

whether in pursuance of paragraph 2 or otherwise.

(2) The tenant, or the secretary with the consent of the tenant, may within six months of obtaining any such summary or copy as is mentioned in sub-paragraph (1)(*a*) or (*b*) require the landlord in writing to afford him reasonable facilities—

(*a*) for inspecting any relevant policy,
(*b*) for inspecting any accounts, receipts or other documents which provide evidence of payment of any premiums due under any such policy in respect of the period of insurance which is current when the request is made and the period of insurance immediately preceding that period, and
(*c*) for taking copies of or extracts from any of the documents referred to in paragraphs (*a*) and (*b*).

(3) Any reference in this paragraph to a relevant policy includes a reference to a policy of insurance under which the dwelling in question was insured for the period of insurance immediately preceding that current when the request is made under this paragraph (being, in the case of a flat, a policy covering the building containing it).

(4) Subsections (3) to (6) of section 22 shall have effect in relation to a request made under this paragraph as they have effect in relation to a request made under that section.

Request relating to insurance effected by superior landlord

4.—(1) If a request is made under paragraph 2 in a case where a superior landlord has effected, in whole or in part, the insurance of the dwelling in question and the landlord to whom the request is made is not in possession of the relevant information—

(*a*) he shall in turn make a written request for the relevant information to the person who is his landlord (and so on, if that person is not himself the superior landlord),

(*b*) the superior landlord shall comply with that request within a reasonable time, and

(*c*) the immediate landlord shall then comply with the tenant's or secretary's request in the manner provided by sub-paragraphs (4) to (7) of paragraph 2 within the time allowed by that paragraph or such further time, if any, as is reasonable in the circumstances.

(2) If, in a case where a superior landlord has effected, in whole or in part, the insurance of the dwelling in question, a request under paragraph 3 relates to any policy of insurance effected by the superior landlord—

(*a*) the landlord to whom the request is made shall forthwith inform the tenant or secretary of that fact and of the name and address of the superior landlord, and

(*b*) that paragraph shall then apply to the superior landlord in relation to that policy as it applies to the immediate landlord.

Effect of assignment on request

5. The assignment of a tenancy does not affect the validity of a request made under paragraph 2, 3 or 4 before the assignment; but a person is not obliged to provide a summary or make facilities available more than once for the same dwelling and for the same period.

Failure to comply with paragraph 2, 3 or 4 an offence

6.—(1) It is a summary offence for a person to fail, without reasonable excuse, to perform a duty imposed on him by or by virtue of paragraph 2, 3 or 4.

(2) A person committing such an offence is liable on conviction to a fine not exceeding level 4 on the standard scale.

Tenant's right to notify insurers of possible claim

7.—(1) This paragraph applies to any dwelling in respect of which the tenant pays to the landlord a service charge consisting of or including an amount payable directly or indirectly for insurance.

(2) Where—

(*a*) it appears to the tenant of any such dwelling that damage has been caused—

(i) to the dwelling, or

(ii) if the dwelling is a flat, to the dwelling or to any other part of the building containing it,

in respect of which a claim could be made under the terms of a policy of insurance, and

(*b*) it is a term of that policy that the person insured under the policy should give notice of any claim under it to the insurer within a specified period,

the tenant may, within that specified period, serve on the insurer a notice in writing stating that it appears to him that damage has been caused as mentioned in paragraph (*a*) and describing briefly the nature of the damage.

(3) Where—

(*a*) any such notice is served on an insurer by a tenant in relation to any such damage, and

(*b*) the specified period referred to in sub-paragraph (2)(*b*) would expire earlier than the period of six months beginning with the date on which the notice is served, the policy in question shall have effect as regards any claim subsequently made in respect of that damage by the person insured under the policy as if for the specified period there were substituted that period of six months.

(4) Where the tenancy of a dwelling to which this paragraph applies is held by joint tenants, a single notice under this paragraph may be given by any one or more of those tenants.

(5) The Secretary of State may by regulations prescribe the form of notices under this paragraph and the particulars which such notices must contain.

(6) Any such regulations—

(*a*) may make different provision with respect to different cases or descriptions of case, including different provision for different areas, and

(*b*) shall be made by statutory instrument.

Right to challenge landlord's choice of insurers

8.—(1) This paragraph applies to a tenancy of a dwelling which requires the tenant to insure the dwelling with an insurer nominated by the landlord.

(2) Where, on an application made by the tenant under any such tenancy, the court is satisfied—

(*a*) that the insurance which is available from the nominated insurer for insuring the tenant's dwelling is unsatisfactory in any respect, or

(*b*) that the premiums payable in respect of any such insurance are excessive,

the court may make either an order requiring the landlord to nominate such other insurer as is specified in the order or an order requiring him to nominate another insurer who satisfies such requirements in relation to the insurance of the dwelling as are specified in the order.

(3) A county court shall have jurisdiction to hear and determine any application under this paragraph.

Exception for tenants of certain public authorities

9.—(1) Paragraphs 2 to 8 do not apply to a tenant of—

a local authority,
a new town corporation, or
the Development Board for Rural Wales,

unless the tenancy is a long tenancy, in which case paragraphs 2 to 5 and 7 and 8 apply but paragraph 6 does not.

(2) Subsections (2) and (3) of section 26 shall apply for the purposes of sub-paragraph (1) as they apply for the purposes of subsection (1) of that section.] **[650]**

NOTES

Commencement: To be appointed.

Prospectively added by the Landlord and Tenant Act 1987, s 43(2), Sch 3, as from a day to be appointed.

LANDLORD AND TENANT ACT 1987

(c 31)

ARRANGEMENT OF SECTIONS

PART I

TENANTS' RIGHTS OF FIRST REFUSAL

Preliminary

Section		Para
1	Qualifying tenants to have rights of first refusal on diposals by landlord	[651]

Section Para
2 Landlords for the purposes of Part I .. .. [652]
3 Qualifying tenants .. .. [653]
4 Relevant disposals .. .. [654]

Notices conferring rights of first refusal

5 Requirement to serve notice conferring rights of first refusal .. .. [655]
6 Acceptance of landlord's offer .. .. [656]
7 Rejection of landlord's offer: counter-offer by tenants .. .. [657]
8 Fresh offer by landlord: further negotiations between parties .. .. .. [658]
9 Withdrawal of either party from transaction .. .. [659]
10 Lapse of landlord's offer .. .. [660]

Enforcement by tenants of rights against new landlords

11 Duty of new landlord to furnish particulars of disposal made in contravention of Part I [661]
12 Rights of qualifying tenants to compel sale etc by new landlord .. .. [662]
13 Determination by rent assessment committees of questions relating to purchase notices .. .. [663]
14 Withdrawal of nominated person from transaction .. .. [664]
15 Right of qualifying tenants to compel grant of new tenancy by superior landlord .. [665]

Enforcement by tenants of rights against subsequent purchasers

16 Right of qualifying tenants to compel sale etc. by subsequent purchaser .. .. [666]

Termination of rights against new landlords etc

17 Termination of rights against new landlord or subsequent purchaser .. .. .. [667]

Notices served by prospective purchasers

18 Notices served by prospective purchasers to ensure that rights of first refusal do not arise .. .. [668]

Supplementary

19 Enforcement of obligations under Part I .. .. [669]
20 Construction of Part I and power of Secretary of State to prescribe modifications .. [670]

PART II

APPOINTMENT OF MANAGERS BY THE COURT

21 Tenant's right to apply to court for appointment of manager .. .. [671]
22 Preliminary notice by tenant .. .. [672]
23 Application to court for appointment of manager .. .. [673]
24 Appointment of manager by the court .. .. [674]

PART III

COMPULSORY ACQUISITION BY TENANTS OF THEIR LANDLORD'S INTEREST

25 Compulsory acquisition of landlord's interest by qualifying tenants .. .. .. [675]
26 Qualifying tenants .. .. [676]
27 Preliminary notice by tenants .. .. [677]
28 Applications for acquisition orders .. .. [678]
29 Conditions for making acquisition orders .. .. [679]
30 Content of acquisition orders .. .. [680]
31 Determination of terms by rent assessment committees .. .. [681]
32 Discharge of existing mortgages .. .. [682]
33 Acquisition order where landlord cannot be found .. .. [683]
34 Discharge of acquisition order and withdrawal by tenants .. .. [684]

Section Para

PART IV

VARIATION OF LEASES

Applications relating to flats

35 Application by party to lease for variation of lease .. .. [685]
36 Application by respondent for variation of other leases .. .. [686]
37 Application by majority of parties for variation of leases .. .. [687]

Orders varying leases

38 Orders by the court varying leases .. .. [688]
39 Effect of orders varying leases: applications by third parties .. .. [689]

Applications relating to dwellings other than flats

40 Application for variation of insurance provisions of lease of dwelling other than a flat [690]

PART V

MANAGEMENT OF LEASEHOLD PROPERTY

Service charges

41 Amendments relating to service charges .. .. [691]
42 Service charge contributions to be held in trust .. .. [692]

Insurance

43 Rights of tenants with respect to insurance .. .. [693]

Managing agents

44 Recognised tenants' associations to be consulted about managing agents .. .. [694]

Management by registered housing associations

45 Extension of permissible objects of registered housing associations as regards the management of leasehold property .. .. [695]

PART VI

INFORMATION TO BE FURNISHED TO TENANTS

46 Application of Part VI, etc .. .. [696]
47 Landlord's name and address to be contained in demands for rent etc .. .. .. [697]
48 Notification by landlord of address for service of notices .. .. [698]
49 Extension of circumstances in which notices are sufficiently served .. .. .. [699]
50 Continuation of former landlord's liability to tenant where no notice of assignment .. [700]
51 Right of tenant to search proprietorship register for landlord's name and address .. [701]

PART VII

GENERAL

52 Jurisdiction of county courts .. .. [702]
53 Regulations and orders .. .. [703]
54 Notices .. .. [704]
55 Application to Isles of Scilly .. .. [705]
56 Crown land .. .. [706]
57 Financial provision .. .. [707]
58 Exempt landlords and resident landlords .. .. [708]
59 Meaning of "lease", "long lease" and related expressions .. .. [709]
60 General interpretation .. .. [710]

Section		Para
61	Consequential amendments and repeals	[711]
62	Short title, commencement and extent	[712]

SCHEDULES

Schedule 1—*Discharge of Mortgages Etc: Supplementary Provisions*	
Part I—Discharge in Pursuance of Purchase Notices	[713]
Part II—Discharge in Pursuance of Acquisition Orders	[714]
Schedule 2—*Amendments relating to Service Charges*	[715]
Schedule 3—*Rights of Tenants with Respect to Insurance*	[716]
Schedule 4—*Consequential Amendments*	[717]
Schedule 5—*Repeals*	[718]

An Act to confer on tenants of flats rights with respect to the acquisition by them of their landlord's reversion; to make provision for the appointment of a manager at the instance of such tenants and for the variation of long leases held by such tenants; to make further provision with respect to service charges payable by tenants of flats and other dwellings; to make other provision with respect to such tenants; to make further provision with respect to permissible purposes and objects of registered housing associations as regards the management of leasehold property; and for connected purposes. [15 May 1987]

PART I

TENANTS' RIGHTS OF FIRST REFUSAL

Preliminary

1. Qualifying tenants to have rights of first refusal on diposals by landlord

(1) A landlord shall not make a relevant disposal affecting any premises to which at the time of the disposal this Part applies unless—

(*a*) he has in accordance with section 5 previously served a notice under that section with respect to the disposal on the qualifying tenants of the flats contained in those premises (being a notice by virtue of which rights of first refusal are conferred on those tenants); and
(*b*) the disposal is made in accordance with the requirements of sections 6 to 10.

(2) Subject to subsections (3) and (4), this part applies to premises if—

(*a*) they consist of the whole or part of a building; and
(*b*) they contain two or more faults held by qualifying tenants; and
(*c*) the number of flats held by such tenants exceeds 50 per cent. of the total number of flats contained in the premises.

(3) This Part does not apply to premises falling within subsection (2) if—

(*a*) any part or parts of the premises is or are occupied or intended to be occupied otherwise than for residential purposes; and
(*b*) the internal floor area of that part or those parts (taken together) exceeds 50 per cent. of the internal floor area of the premises (taken as a whole);

and for the purposes of this subsection the internal floor area of any common parts shall be disregarded.

(4) This Part also does not apply to any such premises at a time when the interest of the landlord in the premises is held by an exempt landlord or a residential landlord.

(5) The Secretary of State may by order substitute for the percentage for the time being specified in subsection (3)(*b*) such other percentage as is specified in the order. **[651]**

NOTES
Commencement: To be appointed.

2. Landlords for the purposes of Part I

(1) Subject to subsection (2), a person is for the purposes of this Part the landlord in relation to any premises consisting of the whole or part of a building if he is—

(*a*) the immediate landlord of the qualifying tenants of the flats contained in those premises, or
(*b*) where any of those tenants is a statutory tenant, the person who, apart from the statutory tenancy, would be entitled to possession of the flat in question.

(2) Where the person who is, in accordance with subsection (1), the landlord in relation to any such premises for the purposes of this Part ("the immediate landlord") is himself a tenant of those premises under a tenancy which is either—

(*a*) a tenancy for a term of less than seven years, or
(*b*) a tenancy for a longer term but terminable within the first seven years at the option of the person who is the landlord under that tenancy ("the superior landlord"),

the superior landlord shall also be regarded as the landlord in relation to those premises for the purposes of this Part and, if the superior landlord is himself a tenant of those premises under a tenancy falling within paragraph (*a*) or (*b*) above, the person who is the landlord under that tenancy shall also be so regarded (and so on). **[652]**

NOTES
Commencement: To be appointed.

3. Qualifying tenants

(1) Subject to the following provisions of this section, a person is for the purposes of this Part a qualifying tenant of a flat if he is the tenant of the flat under a tenancy other than—

(*a*) a protected shorthold tenancy as defined in section 52 of the Housing Act 1980;
(*b*) a tenancy to which Part II of the Landlord and Tenant Act 1954 (business tenancies) applies; or
(*c*) a tenancy terminable on the cessation of his employment.

(2) A person is not to be regarded as being a qualifying tenant of any flat contained in any particular premises consisting of the whole or part of a building if—

(*a*) he is the tenant of any such flat solely by reason of a tenancy under which the demised premises consist of or include—
  (i) the flat and one or more other flats, or
  (ii) the flat and any common parts of the building; or
(*b*) he is the tenant of more than 50 per cent. of the total number of flats contained in those premises.

(3) For the purposes of subsection (2)(*b*) any tenant of a flat contained in the premises in question who is a body corporate shall be treated as the tenant of any other flat so contained and let to an associated company.

(4) A tenant of a flat whose landlord is a qualifying tenant of that flat is not to be regarded as being a qualifying tenant of that flat. **[653]**

NOTES
Commencement: To be appointed.

4. Relevant disposals

(1) In this Part references to a relevant disposal affecting any premises to which this Part applies are references to the disposal by the landlord of any estate or interest (whether legal or equitable) in any such premises, including the disposal of any such estate or interest in any common parts of any such premises but excluding—

(*a*) the grant of any tenancy under which the demised premises consist of a single flat (whether with or without any appurtenant premises); and
(*b*) any of the disposals falling within subsection (2).

(2) The disposals referred to in subsection (1)(*b*) are—

(*a*) a disposal of—

(i) any interest of a beneficiary in settled land within the meaning of the Settled Land Act 1925,
(ii) any interest under a mortgage, or
(iii) any incorporeal hereditament;

(*b*) a disposal to a trustee in bankruptcy or to the liquidator of a company;
(*c*) a disposal in pursuance of an order made under section 24 or 24A of the Matrimonial Causes Act 1973 or section 2 of the Inheritance (Provision for Family and Dependants) Act 1975;
(*d*) a disposal in pursuance of a compulsory purchase order or in pursuance of an agreement entered into in circumstances where, but for the agreement, such an order would have been made or (as the case may be) carried into effect;
(*e*) a disposal by way of gift to a member of the landlord's family or to a charity;
(*f*) a disposal by one charity to another of an estate or interest in land which prior to the disposal is functional land of the first-mentioned charity and which is intended to be functional land of the other charity once the disposal is made;
(*g*) a disposal consisting of the transfer of an estate or interest held on trust for any person where the disposal is made in connection with the appointment of a new trustee or in connection with the discharge of any trustee;
(*h*) a disposal consisting of a transfer by two or more persons who are members of the same family either—

(i) to fewer of their number, or
(ii) to a different combination of members of the family (but one that includes at least one of the transferors);

(*i*) a disposal in pursuance of—

(i) any option or right of pre-emption binding on the landlord (whether granted before or after the commencement of this section), or

(ii) any other obligation binding on him and created before that commencement;

(*j*) a disposal consisting of the surrender of a tenancy in pursuance of any covenant, condition or agreement contained in it;

(*k*) a disposal to the Crown; and

(*l*) where the landlord is a body corporate, a disposal to an associated company.

(3) In this Part "disposal" means a disposal whether by the creation or the transfer of an estate or interest and—

(*a*) includes the surrender of a tenancy and the grant of an option or right of pre-emption, but

(*b*) excludes a disposal under the terms of a will or under the law relating to intestacy;

and references in this Part to the transferee in connection with a disposal shall be construed accordingly.

(4) In this section "appurtenant premises", in relation to any flat, means any yard, garden, outhouse or appurtenance (not being a common part of the building containing the flat) which belongs to, or is usually enjoyed with, the flat.

(5) A person is a member of another's family for the purposes of this section if—

(*a*) that person is the spouse of that other person, or the two of them live together as husband and wife, or

(*b*) that person is that other person's parent, grandparent, child, grandchild, brother, sister, uncle, aunt, nephew or niece.

(6) For the purposes of subsection (5)(*b*)—

(*a*) a relationship by marriage shall be treated as a relationship by blood,

(*b*) a relationship of the half-blood shall be treated as a relationship of the whole blood,

(*c*) the stepchild of a person shall be treated as his child, and

(*d*) the illegitimate child shall be treated as the legitimate child of his mother and reputed father. **[654]**

NOTES

Commencement: To be appointed.

Notices conferring rights of first refusal

5. Requirement to serve notice conferring rights of first refusal

(1) Where, in the case of any premises to which this Part applies, the landlord proposes to make a relevant disposal affecting the premises, he shall serve a notice under this section on the qualifying tenants of the flats contained in the premises.

(2) A notice under this section must—

(*a*) contain particulars of the principal terms of the disposal proposed by the landlord, including in particular—

(i) the property to which it relates and the estate or interest in that property proposed to be disposed of, and

(ii) the consideration required by the landlord for making the disposal;

(*b*) state that the notice constitutes an offer by the landlord to dispose of the property on those terms which may be accepted by the requisite majority of qualifying tenants of the constituent flats;

(*c*) specify a period within which that offer may be so accepted, being a period of not less than two months which is to begin with the date of service of the notice; and

(*d*) specify a further period within which a person or persons may be nominated for the purposes of section 6, being a period of not less than two months which is to begin with the end of the period specified under paragraph (*c*).

(3) Where, as the result of a notice under this section being served on different tenants on different dates, the period specified in the notice under subsection (2)(*c*) would, apart from this subsection, end on different dates—

(*a*) the notice shall have effect in relation to all the qualifying tenants on whom it is served as if it provided for that period to end with the latest of those dates, and for the period specified in the notice under subsection (2)(*d*) to begin with the end of that period; and

(*b*) references in this Part to the period specified in the notice under subsection (2)(*c*) or (as the case may be) subsection (2)(*d*) shall be construed accordingly.

(4) Where a landlord has not served a notice under this section on all of the qualifying tenants on whom it was required to be served by virtue of subsection (1), he shall nevertheless be treated as having complied with that subsection if—

(*a*) he has served such a notice on not less than 90 per cent. of the qualifying tenants on whom it was so required to be served, or

(*b*) where the qualifying tenants on whom it was so required to be served number less than ten, he has served such a notice on all but one of them.

(5) Where a landlord proposes to effect a transaction that would involve both—

(*a*) a disposal of an estate or interest in the whole or part of a building constituting a relevant disposal affecting any premises to which this Part applies, and

(*b*) a disposal of an estate or interest in the whole or part of another building (whether or not constituting a relevant disposal affecting any premises to which this Part applies) or more than one such disposal,

the landlord shall, for the purpose of complying with this section in relation to any relevant disposal falling within paragraph (*a*) or (*b*) above, sever the transaction in such a way as to secure that, in the notice served by him under this section with respect to that disposal, the terms specified in pursuance of subsection (2)(*a*) are the terms on which he is willing to make that disposal.

(6) References in this Part to the requisite majority of qualifying tenants of the constituent flats are references to qualifying tenants of those flats with more than 50 per cent. of the available votes; and for the purposes of this subsection—

(*a*) the total number of available votes shall be determined as follows, namely—

(i) in a case where a notice has been served under this section, that number shall correspond to the total number of constituent flats let to qualifying tenants on the date when the period specified in that notice under subsection (2)(*c*) expires,

(ii) in a case where a notice is served under section 11 without a notice having been previously served under this section, that number shall correspond to the total number of constituent flats let to qualifying tenants on the date of service of the notice under section 11, and

(iii) in a case where a notice is served under section 12 or 15 without a notice having been previously served under this section or under section 11, that number shall correspond to the total number of constituent flats let to qualifying tenants on the date of service of the notice under section 12 or 15; and

(*b*) there shall be one available vote in respect of each of the flats so let on the date referred to in the relevant provision of paragraph (*a*) which shall be attributed to the qualifying tenant to whom it is let.

(7) Nothing in this Part shall be construed as requiring the persons constituting the requisite majority of qualifying tenants in any one context to be the same as the persons constituting any such majority in any other context.

(8) For the purposes of—

(*a*) subsection (2) above and sections 6 to 10, and
(*b*) subsection (6) above so far as it has effect for the purposes of those provisions,

a flat is a constituent flat if it is contained in the premises affected by the relevant disposal with respect to which the notice was served under this section; and for the purposes of sections 11 to 17, and subsection (6) above so far as it has effect for the purposes of those sections, a flat is a constituent flat if it is contained in the premises affected by the relevant disposal referred to in section 11(1)(*a*). **[655]**

NOTES
Commencement: To be appointed.

6. Acceptance of landlord's offer

(1) Where—

(*a*) the landlord has, in accordance with the provisions of section 5, served an offer notice on the qualifying tenants of the constituent flats, and
(*b*) within the period specified in that notice under section 5(2)(*c*), a notice is served on him by the requisite majority of qualifying tenants of the constituent flats informing him that the persons by whom it is served accept the offer contained in his notice,

the landlord shall not during the relevant period dispose of the protected interest except to a person or persons nominated for the purposes of this section by the requisite majority of qualifying tenants of the constituent flats.

(2) In subsection (1) "the relevant period" means—

(*a*) in every case, the period beginning with the date of service of the acceptance notice and ending with the end of the period specified in the offer notice under section 5(2)(*d*), and (*b*) if any person is nominated for the purposes of this section within that period, an additional period of three months beginning with the end of the period so specified.

(3) If no person has been nominated for the purposes of this section during the period so specified, the landlord may, during the period of 12 months beginning with the end of that period, dispose of the protected interest to such person as he thinks fit, but subject to the following restrictions, namely—

(*a*) that the consideration required by him for the disposal must not be less than that specified in the offer notice, and

(*b*) that the other terms on which the disposal is made must, so far as relating to any matters covered by the terms specified in the offer notice, correspond to those terms.

(4) It is hereby declared that the entitlement of a landlord, by virtue of subsection (3) or any other corresponding provision of this Part, to dispose of a particular estate or interest in any property during a specified period of 12 months extends only to a disposal of that estate or interest in the property, and accordingly the requirements of section 1(1) must be satisfied with respect to any other disposal by him affecting that property and made during that period of 12 months (unless the disposal is not a relevant disposal affecting any premises to which at the time of the disposal this Part applies).

(5) A person nominated for the purposes of this section by the requisite majority of qualifying tenants of the constituent flats may only be replaced by another person so nominated if he has (for any reason) ceased to be able to act as a person so nominated.

(6) Where two or more persons have been so nominated and any of them ceases to act as such a person without being replaced in accordance with subsection (5), any remaining person or persons so nominated shall be entitled to continue to act in his or their capacity as such.

(7) Where subsection (1) above applies to the landlord, and he is precluded by virtue of any covenant, condition or other obligation from disposing of the protected interest to the nominated person unless the consent of some other person is obtained, then, subject to subsection (8)—

(*a*) he shall use his best endeavours to secure that the consent of that person to that disposal is given, and

(*b*) if it appears to him that that person is obliged not to withhold his consent unreasonably but has nevertheless so withheld it, he shall institute proceedings for a declaration to that effect.

(8) Subsection (7) shall not apply once a notice is served by or on the landlord in accordance with any provision of section 9 or 10.

(9) In this Part—

"acceptance notice" means a notice served on the landlord in pursuance of subsection (1)(*b*);

"offer notice" means a notice served under section 5; and

"the protected interest" means (subject to section 9(9)) any such estate or interest in any property as is specified in an offer notice in pursuance of section 5(2)(*a*). **[656]**

NOTES

Commencement: To be appointed.

7. Rejection of landlord's offer: counter-offer by tenants

(1) Where—

(*a*) a landlord has, in accordance with section 5, served an offer notice on the qualifying tenants of the constituent flats, and

(*b*) an acceptance notice is not served on the landlord by the requisite majority of qualifying tenants of the constituent flats within the period specified in the offer notice under section 5(2)(*c*), and

(*c*) paragraph (*b*) of subsection (2) below does not apply,

the landlord may, during the period of 12 months beginning with the end of that period, dispose of the protected interest to such person as he thinks fit, but subject to the restrictions mentioned in section 6(3)(*a*) and (*b*).

(2) Where—

(*a*) a landlord has served an offer notice as mentioned in subsection (1)(*a*), and

(*b*) within the period specified in the offer notice under section 5(2)(*c*), a notice is served on the landlord by the requisite majority of qualifying tenants of the constituent flats stating that the persons by whom it is served are making him a counter-offer for the acquisition by them of such estate or interest in the property specified in the offer notice under section 5(2)(*a*) as is specified in their notice,

the landlord shall serve on such person as is specified in that notice in pursuance of subsection (3)(*b*) a notice which either accepts the counter-offer or rejects it.

(3) Any notice making a counter-offer in accordance with subsection (2)(*b*) must specify—

(*a*) the terms (including those relating to the consideration payable) on which the counter-offer is made; and

(*b*) the name and address of a person on whom any notice by the landlord under subsection (2) is to be served.

(4) If the landlord serves a notice under subsection (2) above accepting the counter-offer, section 6(1) and the other provisions of section 6 shall apply to him as if an acceptance notice had been served on him as mentioned in section 6(1)(*b*), except that—

(*a*) any reference to the protected interest shall be read as a reference to any such estate or interest as is specified in the notice making the counter-offer in accordance with subsection (2)(*b*) above;

(*b*) any reference in section 6(3) to the offer notice shall be read as a reference to the notice making the counter-offer; and

(*c*) where the landlord's notice is served under subsection (2) above after the end of the period specified under section 5(2)(*c*), section 6(2) and (3) shall have effect as if the period specified under section 5(2)(*d*) began with the date of service of the landlord's notice.

(5) If the landlord serves a notice under subsection (2) above rejecting the counter-offer notice, then, unless it is a notice falling within section 8(1), subsection (1) above shall apply to him as if no such notice as is mentioned in subsection (2)(*b*) above had been served on him (except that where he serves his notice under subsection (2) above after the end of the period specified under section 5(2)(*c*), subsection (1) above shall have effect as if the period of 12 months there mentioned began with the date of service of that notice). **[657]**

NOTES

Commencement: To be appointed.

8. Fresh offer by landlord: further negotiations between parties

(1) This section applies where the landlord serves a notice under subsection (2) of section 7 rejecting a counter-offer but the notice—

(*a*) states that it constitutes a fresh offer by the landlord to dispose of an estate or interest in the property specified in the offer notice under section 5(2)(*a*) which may be accepted by the requisite majority of qualifying tenants of the constituent flats;

(*b*) contains particulars of the estate or interest in that property which he proposes to dispose of, the consideration required by him for the disposal and the other principal terms of the disposal; and

(*c*) specifies a period within which the offer may be accepted as mentioned in paragraph (*a*) above.

(2) If, within the period specified in the landlord's notice under subsection (1)(*c*) above, a notice is served on the landlord by the requisite majority of qualifying tenants of the constituent flats informing him tht the persons by whom it is served accept the offer contained in the landlord's notice, section 6(1) and the other provisions of section 6 shall apply to the landlord as if an acceptance notice had been served on him as mentioned in section 6(1)(*b*), except that—

(*a*) any reference to the protected interest shall be read as a reference to any such estate or interest as is specified in the landlord's notice in pursuance of subsection (1)(*b*) above; and

(*b*) any reference in section 6(3) to the offer notice shall be read as a reference to the landlord's notice under subsection (1) above; and

(*c*) where the notice served on the landlord in pursuance of this subsection is served after the end of the period specified under section 5(2)(*c*), section 6(2) and (3) shall have effect as if the period specified under section 5(2)(*d*) began with the date of service of that notice.

(3) If, within the period specified in the landlord's notice under subsection (1)(*c*) above, no notice is served on the landlord as mentioned in subsection (2) above and subsection (4) below does not apply, the landlord may, during the period of 12 months beginning with the end of that period dispose of any such estate or interest as is specified in the landlord's notice under subsection (1)(*b*) above to such person as he thinks fit, but subject to the following restrictions, namely—

(*a*) that the consideration required by him for the disposal must not be less than that specified in his notice under subsection (1), and

(*b*) that the other terms on which the disposal is made must, so far as relating to any matters covered by the terms specified in that notice, correspond to those terms.

(4) If, within the period so specified in the landlord's notice, a notice is served on him by the requisite majority of qualifying tenants of the constituent flats stating that the perosns by whom it is served are making him a further counter-offer for the acquisition by them of such estate or interest in the property specified in the offer notice under section 5(2)(*a*) as is specified in their notice, the provisions of subsections (2) to (5) of section 7 and the provisions of this

section (including this subsection) shall apply, with any necessary modifications, in relation to any such notice as they apply in relation to a notice served as mentioned in subsection (2)(*b*) of section 7. **[658]**

NOTES

Commencement: To be appointed.

9. Withdrawal of either party from transaction

(1) Where—

(*a*) section 6(1) applies to a landlord by virtue of any provision of sections 6 to 8, and

(*b*) any person has been nominated for the purposes of section 6 by the requisite majority of qualifying tenants of the constituent flats within the period specified by the landlord in his offer notice under section 5(2)(*d*) (taking into account any postponement of the commencement of that period effected by any of the preceding provisions of this Part), and

(*c*) the nominated person serves a notice on the landlord indicating an intention no longer to proceed with the acquisition of the protected interest,

the landlord may, during the period of 12 months beginning with the date of service of the nominated person's notice, dispose of the protected interest to such person as he thinks fit, but subject to the restrictions mentioned in subsection (2).

(2) The restrictions referred to in subsection (1) are—

(*a*) that the consideration required by him for the disposal must not be less than the amount which has been agreed to by the parties (subject to contract) for the disposal of the protected interest, and

(*b*) that the other terms on which the disposal is made must correspond to those so agreed to by the parties in relation to the disposal.

(3) If at any time the nominated person becomes aware that the number of the qualifying tenants of the constituent flats desiring to proceed with the acquisition of the protected interest is less than the requisite majority of qualifying tenants of those flats, he shall forthwith serve on the landlord such a notice as is mentioned in subsection (1)(*c*).

(4) Where—

(*a*) paragraphs (*a*) and (*b*) of subsection (1) apply, and

(*b*) the landlord serves a notice on the nominated person indicating an intention no longer to proceed with the disposal of the protected interest,

the landlord shall not be entitled to dispose of that interest in accordance with that subsection but the notice shall have the consequences set out in subsection (5) or (6) (as the case may be).

(5) If any notice served in pursuance of subsection (1), (3) or (4) above is served not later than the end of the first four weeks of the period referred to in subsection (1)(*b*) above, the party serving it shall not be liable for any costs incurred by the other party in connection with the disposal.

(6) If any such notice is served after the end of those four weeks, the party on whom it is served may recover from the other party any costs reasonably

incurred by the first-mentioned party in connection with the disposal between the end of those four weeks and the time when that notice is served on him.

(7) For the purposes of this section the parties are—

(*a*) the landlord, and
(*b*) the qualifying tenants who served the acceptance notice or other notice accepting an offer by the landlord, or (as the case may be) the notice making the counter-offer which was accepted by the landlord, together with the nominated person,

and any liability of those tenants and the nominated person which arises under this section shall be a joint and several liability.

(8) Nothing in this section applies where a binding contract for the disposal of the protected interest has been entered into by the landlord and the nominated person.

(9) In this section and section 10—

"the nominated person" means the person or persons for the time being nominated for the purposes of section 6 by the requisite majority of qualifying tenants of the constituent flats; and
"the protected interest" means—
(*a*) except where section 6(1) applies to the landlord by virtue of section 7(4) or 8(2), the protected interest as defined by section 6(9); and
(*b*) where section 6(1) applies to the landlord by virtue of section 7(4) or 8(2), any such estate or interest as is mentioned in section 7(4)(*a*) or (as the case may be) in section 8(2)(*a*). **[659]**

NOTES
Commencement: To be appointed.

10. Lapse of landlord's offer

(1) If, at any time after a landlord has served an offer notice with respect to any relevant disposal affecting any premises to which this Part applies, those premises cease to be premises to which this Part applies, the landlord may serve a notice on the qualifying tenants of the constituent flats stating—

(*a*) that the premises have ceased to be premises to which this Part applies, and
(*b*) that the offer notice, and anything done in pursuance of it, is to be treated as not having been served or done;

and, on the service of any such notice, the provisions of this Part shall cease to have effect in relation to that disposal.

(2) Subsection (4) of section 5 shall apply to a notice under subsection (1) above as it applies to a notice under that section, but as if the references to the qualifying tenants on whom such a notice is required to be served by virtue of subsection (1) of that section were references to the qualifying tenants mentioned in subsection (1) above.

(3) In a case where a landlord is entitled to serve a notice under subsection (1) above but does not do so, this Part shall continue to have effect in relation to the disposal in question as if the premises in question were still premises to which this Part applies.

(4) Where—

(*a*) in the case of a landlord to whom section 6(7) applies—

(i) the landlord has discharged any duty imposed on him by that provision, and
(ii) any such consent as is there mentioned has been withheld, and
(iii) no such declaration as is there mentioned has been made, or

(*b*) the period specified in section 6(2)(*b*) has expired without any binding contract having been entered into between the landlord and the nominated person,

and the landlord serves a notice on the nominated person stating that paragraph (*a*) or (*b*) above applies, the landlord may, during the period of 12 months beginning with the end of the period specified in section 6(2)(*b*), dispose of the protected interest to such person as he thinks fit, but subject to the restrictions mentioned in section 9(2).

References in this subsection to section 6(2)(*b*) include references to that provision as it has effect by virtue of section 7(4)(*c*) or 8(2)(*c*).

(5) Where any such notice is served in a case to which paragraph (*b*) of subsection (4) applies, the landlord may recover from the other party any costs reasonably incurred by him in connection with the disposal to the nominated person between the end of the first four weeks of the period referred to in section 9(1)(*b*) and the time when that notice is served by him; and section 9(7) shall apply for the purposes of this section as it applies for the purposes of section 9.

(6) Where any binding contract with respect to the disposal of the protected interest has been entered into between the landlord and the nominated person but it has been lawfully rescinded by the landlord, the landlord may, during the period of 12 months beginning with the date of the rescission of the contract, dispose of that interest to such person (and on such terms) as he thinks fit.

(7) Section 9(9) applies for the purposes of this section. **[660]**

NOTES
Commencement: To be appointed.

Enforcement by tenants of rights against new landlords

11. Duty of new landlord to furnish particulars of disposal made in contravention of Part I

(1) Where—

(*a*) a landlord has made a relevant disposal affecting any premises to which at the time of the disposal this Part applied ("the original disposal"), and
(*b*) either no notice was served by the landlord under section 5 with respect to that disposal or it was made in contravention of any provision of sections 6 to 10, and
(*c*) those premises are still premises to which this Part applies,

the requisite majority of qualifying tenants of the constituent flats may, before the end of the period specified in subsection (2) below, serve a notice on the transferee under the original disposal requiring him to furnish a person (whose name and address are specified for the purpose in the notice) with particulars of the terms on which the original disposal was made (including those relating to the consideration payable) and the date on which it was made; and in the following provisions of this Part the transferee under that disposal is referred to as "the new landlord".

(2) The period referred to in subsection (1) is the period of two months beginning with the date by which—

(*a*) notices under section 3 of the Landlord and Tenant Act 1985 (in this Act referred to as "the 1985 Act") relating to the original disposal, or

(*b*) documents of any other description indicating that the original disposal has taken place,

have been served on the requisite majority of qualifying tenants of the constituent flats.

(3) Any person served with a notice in accordance with subsection (1) shall comply with the notice within the period of one month beginning with the date on which it is served on him. **[661]**

NOTES

Commencement: To be appointed.

12. Rights of qualifying tenants to compel sale etc by new landlord

(1) Where—

(*a*) paragraphs (*a*) and (*b*) of section 11(1) apply to a relevant disposal affecting any premises to which at the time of the disposal this Part applied (other than a disposal consisting of such a surrender as is mentioned in section 15(1)(*b*)), and

(*b*) those premises are still premises to which this Part applies,

the requisite majority of qualifying tenants of the constituent flats may, before the end of the period specified in subsection (2), serve a notice ("a purchase notice") on the new landlord requiring him (except as provided by the following provisions of this Part) to dispose of the estate or interest that was the subject-matter of the original disposal, on the terms on which it was made (including those relating to the consideration payable), to a person or persons nominated for the purposes of this section by any such majority of qualifying tenants of those flats.

(2) The period referred to in subsection (1) is—

(*a*) in a case where a notice has been served on the new landlord under section 11(1), the period of three months beginning with the date on which a notice is served by him under section 11(3); and

(*b*) in any other case, the period of three months beginning with the date mentioned in section 11(2).

(3) A purchase notice—

(*a*) shall, where the estate or interest that was the subject-matter of the original disposal related to any property in addition to the premises to which this Part applied at the time of the disposal—

(i) require the new landlord to dispose of that estate or interest only so far as relating to those premises, and

(ii) require him to do so on the terms referred to in subsection (1) subject to such modifications as are necessary or expedient in the circumstances;

(*b*) may, instead of specifying the estate or interest to be disposed of or any particular terms on which the disposal is to be made by the new landlord (whether doing so expressly or by reference to the original disposal), provide for that estate or interest, or (as the case may be) for any such terms, to be determined by a rent assessment committee in accordance with section 13.

(4) Where the property which the new landlord is required to dispose of in pursuance of the purchase notice has at any time since the original disposal become subject to any charge or other incumbrance, then, unless the court by order directs otherwise—

(*a*) in the case of a charge to secure the payment of money or the performance of any other obligation by the new landlord or any other person, the instrument by virtue of which the property is disposed of by the new landlord to the person or persons nominated for the purposes of this section shall (subject to the provisions of Part I of Schedule 1) operate to discharge the property from that charge; and

(*b*) in the case of any other incumbrance, the property shall be so disposed of subject to the incumbrance but with a reduction in the consideration payable to the new landlord corresponding to the amount by which the existence of the incumbrance reduces the value of the property.

(5) Subsection (4)(*a*) and Part I of Schedule 1 shall apply, with any necessary modifications, to mortgages and liens as they apply to charges; but nothing in those provisions shall apply to a rentcharge.

(6) Where the property referred to in subsection (4) has at any time since the original disposal increased in monetary value owing to any change in circumstances (other than a change in the value of money), the amount of the consideration payable to the new landlord for the disposal by him of the property in pursuance of the purchase notice shall be the amount that might reasonably have been obtained on a corresponding disposal made on the open market at the time of the original disposal if the change in circumstances had already taken place.

(7) The person or persons initially nominated for the purposes of this section shall be so nominated in the purchase notice; and any such person may only be replaced by another person so nominated by the requisite majority of qualifying tenants of the constituent flats if he has (for any reason) ceased to be able to act as a person so nominated.

(8) Where two or more persons have been so nominated and any of them ceases to act as such a person without being replaced in accordance with subsection (7), any remaining person or persons so nominated shall be entitled to continue to act in his or their capacity as such.

(9) Where, in the exercise of its power to award costs, the court or the Lands Tribunal makes, in connection with any proceedings arising under or by virtue of this Part, an award of costs against the person or persons so nominated, the liability for those costs shall be the joint and several liability of that person or those persons together with the qualifying tenants by whom the relevant purchase notice was served. **[662]**

NOTES

Commencement: To be appointed.

13. Determination by rent assessment committees of questions relating to purchase notices

(1) A rent assessment committee shall have jurisdiction to hear and determine—

(*a*) any question arising in relation to any matters specified in a purchase notice (whether relating to the nature of the estate or interest, or the identity of the property, to be disposed of or relating to any other terms on which the disposal by the new landlord is to be made); and

(*b*) any question arising for determination in consequence of a provision in a purchase notice such as is mentioned in section 12(3)(*b*).

(2) An application to a rent assessment committee under this section must be in such form, and contain such particulars, as the Secretary of State may by regulations prescribe.

(3) On any application under this section the interests of the persons by whom a purchase notice has been served shall be represented by the nominated person, and accordingly the parties to any such application shall not include those persons.

(4) Any costs incurred by a party to an application under this section in connection with the application shall be borne by that party.

(5) A rent assessment committee shall, when constituted for the purpose of hearing and determining any question falling within subsection (1) above, be known as a leasehold valuation tribunal, and paragraphs 1 to 3 and 7 of Schedule 22 to the Housing Act 1980 (provisions relating to leasehold valuation tribunals) shall accordingly apply to any such committee when so constituted.

(6) In this section and sections 14, 16 and 17 "the nominated person" means (subject to section 15(5)) the person or persons for the time being nominated for the purposes of section 12 by the requisite majority of qualifying tenants of the constituent flats. **[663]**

NOTES

Commencement: To be appointed.

14. Withdrawal of nominated person from transaction

(1) Where, at any time before a binding contract is entered into in pursuance of a purchase notice, the nominated person serves a notice on the new landlord indicating an intention no longer to proceed with the disposal required by the purchase notice, the new landlord may recover from that person any costs reasonably incurred by him in connection with that disposal down to the time when the notice is served on him under this subsection.

(2) If, at any such time as is mentioned in subsection (1) above, the nominated person becomes aware that the number of qualifying tenants of the constituent flats desiring to proceed with the disposal required by the purchase notice is less than the requisite majority of those tenants, he shall forthwith serve on the new landlord a notice indicating such an intention as is mentioned in subsection (1), and that subsection shall apply accordingly.

(3) If a notice is served under this section at a time when any proceedings arising under or by virtue of this Part are pending before the court or the Lands Tribunal, the liability of the nominated person for any costs incurred by the new landlord as mentioned in subsection (1) above shall be such as may be determined by the court or (as the case may be) by the Tribunal.

(4) By virtue of section 13(4) the costs that may be recovered by the new landlord under the preceding provisions of this section do not include any costs incurred by him in connection with an application to a rent assessment committee.

(5) Any liability for costs to which a nominated person becomes subject by virtue of this section shall be such a joint and several liability as is mentioned in section 12(9).

(6) Section 13(6) applies for the purposes of this section. **[664]**

NOTES

Commencement: To be appointed.

15. Right of qualifying tenants to compel grant of new tenancy by superior landlord

(1) Where—

(*a*) paragraphs (*a*) and (*b*) of section 11(1) apply to a relevant disposal affecting any premises to which at the time of the disposal this Part applied, and

(*b*) the disposal consisted of the surrender by the landlord of a tenancy held by him ("the relevant tenancy"), and

(*c*) those premises are still premises to which this Part applies,

the requisite majority of qualifying tenants of the constituent flats may, before the end of the period specified in section 12(2), serve a notice on the new landlord requiring him (except as provided by the following provisions of this Part) to grant a new tenancy of the premises subject to the relevant tenancy, on the terms referred to in subsection (2) below and expiring on the date on which that tenancy would have expired, to a person or persons nominated for the purposes of this section by any such majority of qualifying tenants of those flats.

(2) Those terms are—

(*a*) the terms of the relevant tenancy; and

(*b*) if the new landlord paid any amount to the landlord as consideration for the surrender by him of that tenancy, that any such amount is paid to the new landlord by the person or persons so nominated.

(3) A notice under this section—

(*a*) shall, where the premises subject to the relevant tenancy included premises other than those to which this Part applied at the time of the original disposal—

(i) require the new landlord to grant a new tenancy only of the premises to which this Part so applied, and

(ii) require him to do so on the terms referred to in subsection (2) subject to such modifications as are necessary or expedient in the circumstances;

(*b*) may, instead of specifying the premises to be demised under the new tenancy or any particular terms on which that tenancy is to be granted by the new landlord (whether doing so expressly or by reference to the relevant tenancy), provide for those premises, or (as the case may be) for any such terms, to be determined by a rent assessment committee in accordance with section 13 (as applied by subsection (4) below).

(4) The following provisions, namely—

section 12(7) to (9),
sections 13 and 14, and
sections 16 and 17,

shall apply in relation to a notice under this section as they apply in relation to a purchase notice (whether referred to as such or as a notice served under section 12(1)) but subject to the modifications specified in subsection (5) below.

(5) Those modifications are as follows—

(*a*) any reference to the purposes of section 12 shall be read as a reference to the purposes of this section;

(*b*) the reference in section 13(1)(*b*) to section 12(3)(*b*) shall be read as a reference to subsection (3)(*b*) above;

(*c*) the references in section 16 to the estate or interest that was the subject-matter of the original disposal shall be read as a reference to the estate or interest which, prior to the surrender of the relevant tenancy, constituted the reversion immediately expectant on it; and

(*d*) the references in sections 16 and 17 to sections 12 to 14 shall be read as references to sections 12(7) to (9), 13 and 14 (as applied by subsection (4) above) and this section. **[665]**

NOTES

Commencement: To be appointed.

Enforcement by tenants of rights against subsequent purchasers

16. Right of qualifying tenants to compel sale etc. by subsequent purchaser

(1) Where, at the time when a notice is served under section 11(1) or 12(1) on the new landlord, he no longer holds the estate or interest that was the subject-matter of the original disposal, then—

(*a*) in the case of a notice served under section 11(1), the new landlord shall, within the period specified in section 11(3)—

(i) furnish such person as is specified in the notice with the information that he is required to furnish by virtue of it, and

(ii) serve on that person a notice informing him of the name and address of the person to whom the new landlord disposed of that estate or interest ("the subsequent purchaser"), and

(iii) serve on the subsequent purchaser a copy of the notice under section 11(1) and of the information furnished by him under sub-paragraph (i) above;

(*b*) in the case of a notice served under section 12(1), the new landlord shall forthwith—

(i) forward the notice to the subsequent purchaser, and

(ii) serve on the nominated person such a notice as is mentioned in paragraph (*a*)(ii) above.

(2) If the new landlord serves a notice in accordance with subsection (1)(*a*)(ii) or (*b*)(ii) above, sections 12 to 14 shall, instead of applying to the new landlord, apply to the subsequent purchaser as if he were the transferee under the original disposal.

(3) Subsections (1) and (2) above shall have effect, with any necessary modifications, in a case where, instead of disposing of the whole of the estate or interest referred to in subsection (1) to another person, the new landlord has disposed of it in part or in parts to one or more other persons and accordingly sections 12 to 14 shall—

(*a*) in relation to any part of that estate or interest retained by the new landlord, apply to the new landlord, and (*b*) in relation to any part of that estate or interest disposed of to any other person, apply to that other person instead as if he were (as respects that part) the transferee under the original disposal.

(4) Subsection (1) shall not apply in a case where the premises affected by the original disposal have ceased to be premises to which this Part applies.

(5) Section 13(6) applies for the purposes of this section. **[666]**

NOTES
Commencement: To be appointed.

Termination of rights against new landlords etc

17. Termination of rights against new landlord or subsequent purchaser

(1) If, at any time after a notice has been served under section 11(1) or 12(1), the premises affected by the original disposal cease to be premises to which this Part applies, the new landlord may serve a notice on the qualifying tenants of the constituent flats stating—

(*a*) that the premises have ceased to be premises to which this Part applies, and
(*b*) that any notice served on him under section 11(1) or 12(1), and anything done in pursuance of it, is to be treated as not having been served or done.

(2) Subsection (4) of section 5 shall apply to a notice under subsection (1) above as it applies to a notice under that section, but as if the references to the qualifying tenants on whom such a notice is required to be served by virtue of subsection (1) of that section were references to the qualifying tenants mentioned in subsection (1) above.

(3) Where a period of three months beginning with the date of service of a purchase notice on the new landlord has expired—

(*a*) without any binding contract having been entered into between the new landlord and the nominated person, and
(*b*) without there having been made any application in connection with the purchase notice to the court or to a rent assessment committee under section 13,

the new landlord may serve on the nominated person a notice containing such a statement as is mentioned in subsection (1)(*b*) above.

(4) Where—

(*a*) any such application as is mentioned in paragraph (*b*) of subsection (3) was made within the period of three months referred to in that subsection, but
(*b*) a period of two months beginning with the date of the determination of that application has expired, and
(*c*) no binding contract has been entered into between the new landlord and the nominated person, and
(*d*) no other such application as is mentioned in subsection (3)(*b*) is pending,

the new landlord may serve on the nominated person a notice containing such a statement as is mentioned in subsection (1)(*b*).

(5) Where the new landlord serves a notice in accordance with subsection

(1), (3) or (4), this Part shall cease to have effect in relation to him in connection with the original disposal.

(6) In a case where a new landlord is entitled to serve a notice under subsection (1) above but does not do so, this Part shall continue to have effect in relation to him in connection with the original disposal as if the premises in question were still premises to which this Part applies.

(7) References in this section to the new landlord shall be read as including references to any other person to whom sections 12 to 14 apply by virtue of section 16(2) or (3).

(8) Section 13(6) applies for the purposes of this section. **[667]**

NOTES

Commencement: To be appointed.

Notices served by prospective purchasers

18. Notices served by prospective purchasers to ensure that rights of first refusal do not arise

(1) Where—

(*a*) any disposal of an estate or interest in any premises consisting of the whole or part of a building is proposed to be made by a landlord, and

(*b*) it appears to the person who would be the transferee under that disposal ("the purchaser") that any such disposal would, or might, be a relevant disposal affecting premises to which this Part applies,

the purchaser may serve notices under this subsection on the tenants of the flats contained in the premises referred to in paragraph (*a*) ("the flats affected").

(2) Any notice under subsection (1) shall—

(*a*) inform the person on whom it is served of the general nature of the principal terms of the proposed disposal, including in particular—

(i) the property to which it would relate and the estate or interest in that property proposed to be disposed of by the landlord, and

(ii) the consideration required by him for making the disposal;

(*b*) invite that person to serve a notice on the purchaser stating—

(i) whether the landlord has served on him, or on any predecessor in title of his, a notice under section 5 with respect to the disposal, and

(ii) if the landlord has not so served any such notice, whether he is aware of any reason why he is not entitled to be served with any such notice by the landlord, and

(iii) if he is not so aware, whether he would wish to avail himself of the right of first refusal conferred by any such notice if it were served; and

(*c*) inform that person of the effect of the following provisions of this section.

(3) Where the purchaser has served notices under subsection (1) on at least 80 per cent. of the tenants of the flats affected and—

(*a*) not more than 50 per cent. of the tenants on whom those notices have been served by the purchaser have served notices on him in pursuance of subsection (2)(*b*) by the end of the period of 28 days beginning with the date on which the last of them was served by him with a notice under this section, or

(*b*) more than 50 per cent. of the tenants on whom those notices have been served by the purchaser have served notices on him in pursuance of subsection (2)(*b*) but the notices in each case indicate that the tenant serving it either—

(i) does not regard himself as being entitled to be served by the landlord with a notice under section 5 with respect to the disposal, or

(ii) would not wish to avail himself of the right of first refusal conferred by such a notice if it were served,

the premises affected by the disposal shall, in relation to the disposal, be treated for the purposes of this Part as premises to which this Part does not apply.

(4) For the purposes of subsection (3) each of the flats affected shall be regarded as having one tenant, who shall count towards any of the percentages specified in that subsection whether he is a qualifying tenant of the flat or not. **[668]**

NOTES
Commencement: To be appointed.

Supplementary

19. Enforcement of obligations under Part I

(1) The court may, on the application of any person interested, make an order requiring any person who has made default in complying with any duty imposed on him by any provision of this Part to make good the default within such time as is specified in the order.

(2) An application shall not be made under subsection (1) unless—

(*a*) a notice has been previously served on the person in question requiring him to make good the default, and

(*b*) more than 14 days have elapsed since the date of service of that notice without his having done so.

(3) The restriction imposed by section 1(1) may be enforced by an injunction granted by the court. **[669]**

NOTES
Commencement: To be appointed.

20. Construction of Part I and power of Secretary of State to prescribe modifications

(1) In this Part—

"acceptance notice" means a notice served on a landlord in pursuance of section 6(1)(*b*);

"associated company", in relation to a body corporate, means another body corporate which is (within the meaning of section 736 of the Companies Act 1985) that body's holding company, a subsidiary of that body or another subsidiary of that body's holding company;

"constituent flat" shall be construed in accordance with section 5(8);

"disposal" has the meaning given by section 4(3), and references to the acquisition of an estate or interest shall be construed accordingly;

"landlord", in relation to any premises, shall be construed in accordance with section 2;

"the new landlord" means any such transferee under a relevant disposal as is mentioned in section 11(1);

"offer notice" means a notice served by a landlord under section 5;

"the original disposal" means the relevant disposal referred to in section 11(1);

"the protected interest" means (subject to section 9(9)) any such estate or interest in any property as is specified in an offer notice in pursuance of section 5(2)(*a*);

"purchase notice" means a notice served on a new landlord in pursuance of section 12(1);

"qualifying tenant", in relation to a flat, shall be construed in accordance with section 3;

"relevant disposal" shall be construed in accordance with section 4;

"the requisite majority", in relation to qualifying tenants, shall be construed in accordance with section 5(6) and (7);

"transferee", in relation to a disposal, shall be construed in accordance with section 4(3).

(2) In this Part—

(*a*) any reference to an offer or counter-offer is a reference to an offer or counter-offer made subject to contract, and

(*b*) any reference to the acceptance of an offer or counter-offer is a reference to its acceptance subject to contract.

(3) Any reference in this Part to a tenant of a particular description shall be construed, in relation to any time when the interest under his tenancy has ceased to be vested in him, as a reference to the person who is for the time being the successor in title to that interest.

(4) The Secretary of State may by regulations make such modifications of any of the provisions of sections 5 to 18 as he considers appropriate, and any such regulations may contain such incidental, supplemental or transitional provisions as he considers appropriate in connection with the regulations.

(5) In subsection (4) "modifications" includes additions, omissions and alterations. **[670]**

NOTES

Commencement: To be appointed.

PART II

APPOINTMENT OF MANAGERS BY THE COURT

21. Tenant's right to apply to court for appointment of manager

(1) The tenant of a flat contained in any premises to which this Part applies may, subject to the following provisions of this Part, apply to the court for an order under section 24 appointing a manager to act in relation to those premises.

(2) Subject to subsection (3), this Part applies to premises consisting of the whole or part of a building if the building or part contains two or more flats.

(3) This Part does not apply to any such premises at a time when—

(*a*) the interest of the landlord in the premises is held by an exempt landlord or a resident landlord, or
(*b*) the premises are included within the functional land of any charity.

(4) An application for an order under section 24 may be made—

(*a*) jointly by tenants of two or more flats if they are each entitled to make such an application by virtue of this section, and
(*b*) in respect of two or more premises to which this Part applies;

and, in relation to any such joint application as is mentioned in paragraph (*a*), references in this Part to a single tenant shall be construed accordingly.

(5) Where the tenancy of a flat contained in any such premises is held by joint tenants, an application for an order under section 24 in respect of those premises may be made by any one or more of those tenants.

(6) An application to the court for it to exercise in relation to any premises any jurisdiction existing apart from this Act to appoint a receiver or manager shall not be made by a tenant (in his capacity as such) in any circumstances in which an application could be made by him for an order under section 24 appointing a manager to act in relation to those premises.

(7) References in this Part to a tenant do not include references to a tenant under a tenancy to which Part II of the Landlord and Tenant Act 1954 applies. **[671]**

NOTES
Commencement: To be appointed.

22. Preliminary notice by tenant

(1) Before an application for an order under section 24 is made in respect of any premises to which this Part applies by a tenant of a flat contained in those premises, a notice under this section must (subject to subsection (3)) be served on the landlord by the tenant.

(2) A notice under this section must—

(*a*) specify the tenant's name, the address of his flat and an address in England and Wales (which may be the address of his flat) at which the landlord may serve notices, including notices in proceedings, on him in connection with this Part;
(*b*) state that the tenant intends to make an application for an order under section 24 to be made by the court in respect of such premises to which this Part applies as are specified in the notice, but (if paragraph (*d*) is applicable) that he will not do so if the landlord complies with the requirement specified in pursuance of that paragraph;
(*c*) specify the grounds on which the court would be asked to make such an order and the matters that would be relied on by the tenant for the purpose of establishing those grounds;
(*d*) where those matters are capable of being remedied by the landlord, require the landlord, within such reasonable period as is specified in the notice, to take steps for the purpose of remedying them as are so specified; and
(*e*) contain such information (if any) as the Secretary of State may by regulations prescribe.

(3) The court may (whether on the hearing of an application for an order under section 24 or not) by order dispense with the requirement to serve a notice

under this section in a case where it is satisfied that it would not be reasonably practicable to serve such a notice on the landlord, but the court may, when doing so, direct that such other notices are served, or such other steps are taken, as it thinks fit.

(4) In a case where—

(*a*) a notice under this section has been served on the landlord, and
(*b*) his interest in the premises specified in pursuance of subsection (2)(*b*) is subject to a mortgage,

the landlord shall, as soon as is reasonably practicable after receiving the notice, serve on the mortgagee a copy of the notice. **[672]**

NOTES
Commencement: To be appointed.

23. Application to court for appointment of manager

(1) No application for an order under section 24 shall be made to the court unless—

(*a*) in a case where a notice has been served under section 22, either—
  (i) the period specified in pursuance of paragraph (*d*) of subsection (2) of that section has expired without the landlord having taken the steps that he was required to take in pursuance of that provision, or
  (ii) that paragraph was not applicable in the circumstances of the case; or
(*b*) in a case where the requirement to serve such a notice has been dispensed with by an order under subsection (3) of that section, either—
  (i) any notices required to be served, and any other steps required to be taken, by virtue of the order have been served or (as the case may be) taken, or
  (ii) no direction was given by the court when making the order.

(2) Rules of court shall make provision—

(*a*) for requiring notice of an application for an order under section 24 in respect of any premises to be served on such descriptions of persons as may be specified in the rules; and
(*b*) for enabling persons served with any such notice to be joined as parties to the proceedings. **[673]**

NOTES
Commencement: To be appointed.

24. Appointment of manager by the court

(1) The court may, on an application for an order under this section, by order (whether interlocutory or final) appoint a manager to carry out in relation to any premises to which this Part applies—

(*a*) such functions in connection with the management of the premises, or
(*b*) such functions of a receiver,

or both, as the court thinks fit.

(2) The court may only make an order under this section in the following circumstances, namely—

(*a*) where the court is satisfied—

(i) that the landlord either is in breach of any obligation owed by him to the tenant under his tenancy and relating to the management of the premises in question or any part of them or (in the case of an obligation dependent on notice) would be in breach of any such obligation but for the fact that it has not been reasonably practicable for the tenant to give him the appropriate notice, and

(ii) that the circumstances by virtue of which he is (or would be) in breach of any such obligation are likely to continue, and

(iii) that it is just and convenient to make the order in all the circumstances of the case; or

(*b*) where the court is satisfied that other circumstances exist which make it just and convenient for the order to be made.

(3) The premises in respect of which an order is made under this section may, if the court thinks fit, be either more or less extensive than the premises specified in the application on which the order is made.

(4) An order under this section may make provision with respect to—

(*a*) such matters relating to the exercise by the manager of his functions under the order, and

(*b*) such incidental or ancillary matters,

as the court thinks fit; and, on any subsequent application made for the purpose by the manager, the court may give him directions with respect to any such matters.

(5) Without prejudice to the generality of subsection (4), an order under this section may provide—

(*a*) for rights and liabilities arising under contracts to which the manager is not a party to become rights and liabilities of the manager;

(*b*) for the manager to be entitled to prosecute claims in respect of causes of action (whether contractual or tortious) accruing before or after the date of his appointment;

(*c*) for remuneration to be paid to the manager by the landlord, or by the tenants of the premises in respect of which the order is made or by all or any of those persons;

(*d*) for the manager's functions to be exercisable by him (subject to subsection (9)) either during a specified period or without limit of time.

(6) Any such order may be granted subject to such conditions as the court thinks fit, and in particular its operation may be suspended on terms fixed by the court.

(7) In a case where an application for an order under this section was preceded by the service of a notice under section 22, the court may, if it thinks fit, make such an order notwithstanding—

(*a*) that any period specified in the notice in pursuance of subsection (2)(*d*) of that section was not a reasonable period, or

(*b*) that the notice failed in any other respect to comply with any requirement contained in subsection (2) of that section or in any regulations applying to the notice under section 54(3).

(8) The Land Charges Act 1972 and the Land Registration Act 1925 shall apply in relation to an order made under this section as they apply in relation to an order appointing a receiver or sequestrator of land.

(9) The court may, on the application of any person interested, vary or discharge (whether conditionally or unconditionally) an order made under this section; and if the order has been protected by an entry registered under the Land Charges Act 1972 or the Land Registration Act 1925, the court may by order direct that the entry shall be cancelled.

(10) An order made under this section shall not be discharged by the court by reason only that, by virtue of section 21(3), the premises in respect of which the order was made have ceased to be premises to which this Part applies.

(11) References in this section to the management of any premises include references to the repair, maintenance or insurance of those premises. **[674]**

NOTES

Commencement: To be appointed.

PART III

COMPULSORY ACQUISITION BY TENANTS OF THEIR LANDLORD'S INTEREST

25. Compulsory acquisition of landlord's interest by qualifying tenants

(1) This Part has effect for the purpose of enabling qualifying tenants of flats contained in any premises to which this Part applies to make an application to the court for an order providing for a person nominated by them to acquire their landlord's interest in the premises without his consent; and any such order is referred to in this Part as "an acquisition order".

(2) Subject to subsections (4) and (5), this Part applies to premises if—

(*a*) they consist of the whole or part of a building; and
(*b*) they contain two or more flats held by tenants of the landlord who are qualifying tenants; and
(*c*) the appropriate requirement specified in subsection (3) is satisfied with respect to them.

(3) For the purposes of subsection (2)(*c*) the appropriate requirement is—

(*a*) where the premises contain less than four flats, that all of the flats are let by the landlord on long leases;
(*b*) where the premises contain more than three but less than ten flats, that all, or all but one, of the flats are so let; and
(*c*) where the premises contain ten or more flats, that at least 90 per cent. of the flats are so let.

(4) This Part does not apply to premises falling within subsection (2) if—

(*a*) any part or parts of the premises is or are occupied or intended to be occupied otherwise than for residential purposes; and
(*b*) the internal floor area of that part or those parts (taken together) exceeds 50 per cent. of the internal floor area of the premises (taken as a whole);

and for the purposes of this subsection the internal floor area of any common parts shall be disregarded.

(5) This Part also does not apply to any such premises at a time when—

(*a*) the interest of the landlord in the premises is held by an exempt landlord or a resident landlord, or
(*b*) the premises are included within the functional land of any charity.

(6) The Secretary of State may by order substitute for the percentage for the time being specified in subsection (4)(*b*) such other percentage as is specified in the order. **[675]**

NOTES
Commencement: To be appointed.

26. Qualifying tenants

(1) Subject to subsections (2) and (3), a person is a qualifying tenant of a flat for the purposes of this Part if he is the tenant of the flat under a long lease other than one constituting a tenancy to which Part II of the Landlord and Tenant Act 1954 applies.

(2) A person is not to be regarded as being a qualifying tenant of a flat contained in any particular premises consisting of the whole or part of a building if he is the tenant of the flat solely by reason of a long lease under which the demised premises consist of or include—

(*a*) the flat and one or more other flats, or
(*b*) the flat and any common parts of the building.

(3) A tenant of a flat under a long lease whose landlord is a qualifying tenant of that flat is not to be regarded as being a qualifying tenant of that flat. **[676]**

NOTES
Commencement: To be appointed.

27. Preliminary notice by tenants

(1) Before an application for an acquisition order is made in respect of any premises to which this Part applies, a notice under this section must (subject to subsection (3)) be served on the landlord by qualifying tenants of the flats contained in the premises who, at the date when it is served, constitute the requisite majority of such tenants.

(2) A notice under this section must—

(*a*) specify the names of the qualifying tenants by whom it is served, the addresses of their flats and the name and the address in England and Wales of a person on whom the landlord may serve notices (including notices in proceedings) in connection with this Part instead of serving them on those tenants;
(*b*) state that those tenants intend to make an application for an acquisition order to be made by the court in respect of such premises to which this Part applies as are specified in the notice, but (if paragraph (*d*) is applicable) that they will not do so if the landlord complies with the requirement specified in pursuance of that paragraph;
(*c*) specify the grounds on which the court would be asked to make such an order and the matters that would be relied on by the tenants for the purpose of establishing those grounds;
(*d*) where those matters are capable of being remedied by the landlord, require the landlord, within such reasonable period as is specified in

the notice, to take such steps for the purpose of remedying them as are so specified; and

(*e*) contain such information (if any) as the Secretary of State may by regulations prescribe.

(3) The court may by order dispense with the requirement to serve a notice under this section in a case where it is satisfied that it would not be reasonably practicable to serve such a notice on the landlord, but the court may, when doing so, direct that such other notices are served, or such other steps are taken, as it thinks fit.

(4) Any reference in this Part to the requisite majority of qualifying tenants of the flats contained in any premises is a reference to qualifying tenants of the flats so contained with more than 50 per cent. of the available votes; and for the purposes of this subsection—

(*a*) the total number of available votes shall correspond to the total number of those flats for the time being let to qualifying tenants; and

(*b*) there shall be one available vote in respect of each of the flats so let which shall be attributed to the qualifying tenant to whom it is let.

(5) Nothing in this Part shall be construed as requiring the persons constituting any such majority in any one context to be the same as the persons constituting any such majority in any other context. **[677]**

NOTES

Commencement: To be appointed.

28. Applications for acquisition orders

(1) An application for an acquisition order in respect of any premises to which this Part applies must be made by qualifying tenants of the flats contained in the premises who, at the date when it is made, constitute the requisite majority of such tenants.

(2) No such application shall be made to the court unless—

(*a*) in a case where a notice has been served under section 27, either—

(i) the period specified in pursuance of paragraph (*d*) of subsection (2) of that section has expired without the landlord having taken the steps that he was required to take in pursuance of that provision, or

(ii) that paragraph was not applicable in the circumstances of the case; or

(*b*) in a case where the requirement to serve such a notice has been dispensed with by an order under subsection (3) of that section, either—

(i) any notices required to be served, and any other steps required to be taken, by virtue of the order have been served or (as the case may be) taken, or

(ii) no direction was given by the court when making the order.

(3) An application for an acquisition order may, subject to the preceding provisions of this Part, be made in respect of two or more premises to which this Part applies.

(4) Rules of court shall make provision—

(*a*) for requiring notice of an application for an acquisition order in respect of any premises to be served on such descriptions of persons as may be specified in the rules; and

(*b*) for enabling persons served with any such notice to be joined as parties to the proceedings.

(5) The Land Charges Act 1972 and the Land Registration Act 1925 shall apply in relation to an application for an acquisition order as they apply in relation to other pending land actions.

(6) The persons applying for an acquisition order in respect of any premises to which this Part applies shall be treated for the purposes of section 57 of the Land Registration Act 1925 (inhibitions) as persons interested in relation to any registered land containing the whole or part of those premises. **[678]**

NOTES
Commencement: To be appointed.

29. Conditions for making acquisition orders

(1) The court may, on an application for an acquisition order, make such an order in respect of any premises if—

(*a*) the court is satisfied—

(i) that those premises were, at the date of service on the landlord of the notice (if any) under section 27 and on the date when the application was made, premises to which this Part applies, and

(ii) that they have not ceased to be such premises since the date when the application was made, and

(*b*) either of the conditions specified in subsections (2) and (3) is fulfilled with respect to those premises, and

(*c*) the court considers it appropriate to make the order in the circumstances of the case.

(2) The first of the conditions referred to in subsection (1)(*b*) is that the court is satisfied—

(*a*) that the landlord either is in breach of any obligation owed by him to the applicants under their leases and relating to the repair, maintenance, insurance or management of the premises in question, or any part of them, or (in the case of an obligation dependent on notice) would be in breach of any such obligation but for the fact that it has not been reasonably practicable for the tenant to give him the appropriate notice, and

(*b*) that the circumstances by virtue of which he is (or would be) in breach of any such obligation are likely to continue, and

(*c*) that the appointment of a manager under Part II to act in relation to those premises would not be an adequate remedy.

(3) The second of those conditions is that, both at the date when the application was made and throughout the period of three years immediately preceding that date, there was in force an appointment under Part II of a person to act as manager in relation to the premises in question.

(4) An acquisition order may, if the court thinks fit—

(*a*) include any yard, garden, outhouse or appurtenance belonging to, or usually enjoyed with, the premises specified in the application on which the order is made;

(*b*) exclude any part of the premises so specified.

(5) Where—

(*a*) the premises in respect of which an application for an acquisition order is made consist of part only of more extensive premises in which the landlord has an interest, and

(*b*) it appears to the court that the landlord's interest in the latter premises is not reasonably capable of being severed, either in the manner contemplated by the application or in any manner authorised by virtue of subsection (4)(*b*),

then, notwithstanding that paragraphs (*a*) and (*b*) of subsection (1) apply, the court shall not make an acquisition order on the application.

(6) In a case where an application for an acquisition order was preceded by the service of a notice under section 27, the court may, if it thinks fit, make such an order notwithstanding—

(*a*) that any period specified in the notice in pursuance of subsection (2)(*d*) of that section was not a reasonable period, or

(*b*) that the notice failed in any other respect to comply with any requirement contained in subsection (2) of that section or in any regulations applying to the notice under section 54(3).

(7) Where any premises are premises to which this Part applies at the time when an application for an acquisition order is made in respect of them, then, for the purposes of this section and the following provisions of this Part, they shall not cease to be such premises by reason only that—

(*a*) the interest of the landlord in them subsequently becomes held by an exempt landlord or a resident landlord, or

(*b*) they subsequently become included within the functional land of any charity. **[679]**

NOTES

Commencement: To be appointed.

30. Content of acquisition orders

(1) Where an acquisition order is made by the court, the order shall (except in a case falling within section 33(1)) provide for the nominated person to be entitled to acquire the landlord's interest in the premises specified in the order on such terms as may be determined—

(*a*) by agreement between the landlord and the qualifying tenants in whose favour the order is made, or

(*b*) in default of agreement, by a rent assessment committee under section 31.

(2) An acquisition order may be granted subject to such conditions as the court thinks fit, and in particular its operation may be suspended on terms fixed by the court.

(3) References in this Part, in relation to an acquisition order, to the nominated person are references to such person or persons as may be nominated for the purposes of this Part by the persons applying for the order.

(4) Those persons must secure that the nominated person is joined as a party to the application, and no further nomination of a person for the purposes of this Part shall be made by them after the order is made (whether in addition to,

or in substitution for, the existing nominated person) except with the approval of the court.

(5) Where the landlord is, by virtue of any covenant, condition or other obligation, precluded from disposing of his interest in the premises in respect of which an acquisition order has been made unless the consent of some other person is obtained—

(*a*) he shall use his best endeavours to secure that the consent of that person to that disposal is obtained and, if it appears to him that that person is obliged not to withhold his consent unreasonably but has nevertheless so withheld it, shall institute proceedings for a declaration to that effect; but

(*b*) if—

(i) the landlord has discharged any duty imposed on him by paragraph (*a*), and

(ii) the consent of that person has been withheld, and

(iii) no such declaration has been made,

the order shall cease to have effect.

(6) The Land Charges Act 1972 and the Land Registration Act 1925 shall apply in relation to an acquisition order as they apply in relation to an order affecting land made by the court for the purpose of enforcing a judgment or recognisance. **[680]**

NOTES
Commencement: To be appointed.

31. Determination of terms by rent assessment committees

(1) A rent assessment committee shall have jurisdiction to determine the terms on which the landlord's interest in the premises specified in an acquisition order may be acquired by the nominated person to the extent that those terms have not been determined by agreement between the landlord and either—

(*a*) the qualifying tenants in whose favour the order was made, or

(*b*) the nominated person;

and (subject to subsection (2)) such a committee shall determine any such terms on the basis of what appears to them to be fair and reasonable.

(2) Where an application is made under this section for such a committee to determine the consideration payable for the acquisition of a landlord's interest in any premises, the committee shall do so by determining an amount equal to the amount which, in their opinion, that interest might be expected to realise if sold on the open market by a willing seller on the appropriate terms and on the assumption that none of the tenants of the landlord of any premises comprised in those premises was buying or seeking to buy that interest.

(3) In subsection (2) "the appropriate terms" means all the terms to which the acquisition of the landlord's interest in pursuance of the order is to be subject (whether determined by agreement as mentioned in subsection (1) or on an application under this section) apart from those relating to the consideration payable.

(4) On any application under this section the interests of the qualifying tenants in whose favour the acquisition order was made shall be represented by the nominated person, and accordingly the parties to any such application shall not include those tenants.

(5) Subsections (2), (4) and (5) of section 13 shall apply for the purposes of this section as they apply for the purposes of that section, but as if the reference in subsection (5) to subsection (1) of that section were a reference to subsection (1) of this section.

(6) Nothing in this section shall be construed as authorising a rent assessment committee to determine any terms dealing with matters in relation to which provision is made by section 32 or 33. **[681]**

NOTES
Commencement: To be appointed.

32. Discharge of existing mortgages

(1) Where the landlord's interest in any premises is acquired in pursuance of an acquisition order, the instrument by virtue of which it is so acquired shall (subject to subsection (2) and Part II of Schedule 1) operate to discharge the premises from any charge on that interest to secure the payment of money or the performance of any other obligation by the landlord or any other person.

(2) Subsection (1) does not apply to any such charge if—

(*a*) it has been agreed between the landlord and either—

(i) the qualifying tenants in whose favour the order was made, or
(ii) the nominated person,

that the landlord's interest should be acquired subject to the charge, or

(*b*) the court is satisfied, whether on the application for the order or on an application made by the person entitled to the benefit of the charge, that in the exceptional circumstances of the case it would be fair and reasonable that the landlord's interest should be so acquired, and orders accordingly.

(3) This section and Part II of Schedule 1 shall apply, with any necessary modifications, to mortgages and liens as they apply to charges; but nothing in those provisions shall apply to a rentcharge. **[682]**

NOTES
Commencement: To be appointed.

33. Acquisition order where landlord cannot be found

(1) Where an acquisition order is made by the court in a case where the landlord cannot be found, or his identity cannot be ascertained, the order shall provide for the landlord's interest in the premises specified in the order to vest in the nominated person on the following terms, namely—

(*a*) such terms as to payment as are specified in subsection (2), and
(*b*) such other terms as the court thinks fit, being terms which, in the opinion of the court, correspond so far as possible to those on which the interest might be expected to be transferred if it were being transferred by the landlord.

(2) The terms as to payment referred to in subsection (1)(*a*) are terms requiring the payment into court of—

(*a*) such amount as a surveyor selected by the President of the Lands Tribunal may certify to be in his opinion the amount which the landlord's interest might be expected to realise if sold as mentioned in section 31(2); and

(*b*) any amounts or estimated amounts remaining due to the landlord from any tenants of his of any premises comprised in the premises in respect of which the order is made, being amounts or estimated amounts determined by the court as being due from those persons under the terms of their leases.

(3) Where any amount or amounts required by virtue of subsection (2) to be paid into court are so paid, the landlord's interest shall, by virtue of this section, vest in the nominated person in accordance with the order. **[683]**

NOTES
Commencement: To be appointed.

34. Discharge of acquisition order and withdrawal by tenants

(1) If, on an application by a landlord in respect of whose interest an acquisition order has been made, the court is satisfied—

(*a*) that the nominated person has had a reasonable time within which to effect the acquisition of that interest in pursuance of the order but has not done so, or

(*b*) that the number of qualifying tenants of flats contained in the premises in question who desire to proceed with the acquisition of the landlord's interest is less than the requisite majority of qualifying tenants of the flats contained in those premises, or

(*c*) that the premises in question have ceased to be premises to which this Part applies,

the court may discharge the order.

(2) Where—

(*a*) a notice is served on the landlord by the qualifying tenants by whom a notice has been served under section 27 or (as the case may be) by whom an application has been made for an acquisition order, or by the person nominated for the purposes of this Part by any such tenants, and

(*b*) the notice indicates an intention no longer to proceed with the acquisition of the landlord's interest in the premises in question,

the landlord may (except in a case where subsection (4) applies) recover under this subsection any costs reasonably incurred by him in connection with the disposal by him of that interest down to the time when the notice is served; and, if the notice is served after the making of an acquisition order, that order shall cease to have effect.

(3) If (whether before or after the making of an acquisition order) the nominated person becomes aware—

(*a*) that the number of qualifying tenants of flats contained in the premises in question who desire to proceed with the acquisition of the landlord's interest is less than the requisite majority of qualifying tenants of the flats contained in those premises, or

(*b*) that those premises have ceased to be premises to which this Part applies,

he shall forthwith serve on the landlord a notice indicating an intention no longer to proceed with the acquisition of that interest, and subsection (2) shall apply accordingly.

(4) If, at any time when any proceedings taken under or by virtue of this Part are pending before the court or the Lands Tribunal—

(*a*) such a notice as is mentioned in subsection (2) or (3) is served on the landlord, or
(*b*) the nominated person indicates that he is no longer willing to act in the matter and nobody is nominated for the purposes of this Part in his place, or
(*c*) the number of qualifying tenants of flats contained in the premises in question who desire to proceed with the acquisition of the landlord's interest falls below the requisite majority of qualifying tenants of the flats contained in those premises, or
(*d*) those premises cease to be premises to which this Part applies,

or if the court discharges an acquisition order under subsection (1), the landlord may recover such costs incurred by him in connection with the disposal by him of his interest in those premises as the court or (as the case may be) the Tribunal may determine.

(5) The costs that may be recovered by the landlord under subsection (2) or (4) include costs incurred by him in connection with any proceedings under this Part (other than proceedings before a rent assessment committee).

(6) Any liability for costs arising under this section shall be the joint and several liability of the following persons, namely—

(*a*) where the liability arises before the making of an application for an acquisition order, the tenants by whom a notice was served under section 27, or
(*b*) where the liability arises after the making of such an application, the tenants by whom the application was made,

together with (in either case) any person nominated by those tenants for the purposes of this Part.

(7) In relation to any time when a tenant falling within paragraph (*a*) or (*b*) of subsection (6) has ceased to have vested in him the interest under his lease, that paragraph shall be construed as applying instead to the person who is for the time being the successor in title to that interest.

(8) Nothing in this section shall be construed as authorising the court to discharge an acquisition order where the landlord's interest has already been acquired in pursuance of the order.

(9) If—

(*a*) an acquisition order is discharged, or ceases to have effect, by virtue of any provision of this Part, and
(*b*) the order has been protected by an entry registered under the Land Charges Act 1972 or the Land Registration Act 1925,

the court may by order direct that that entry shall be cancelled. **[684]**

NOTES
Commencement: To be appointed.

Part IV

Variation of Leases

Applications relating to flats

35. Application by party to lease for variation of lease

(1) Any party to a long lease of a flat may make an application to the court for an order varying the lease in such manner as is specified in the application.

(2) The grounds on which any such application may be made are that the lease fails to make satisfactory provision with respect to one or more of the following matters, namely—

(*a*) the repair or maintenance of—

(i) the flat in question, or

(ii) the building containing the flat, or

(iii) any land or building which is let to the tenant under the lease or in respect of which rights are conferred on him under it;

(*b*) the insurance of the flat or of any such building or land as is mentioned in paragraph (*a*)(ii) or (iii);

(*c*) the repair or maintenance of any installations (whether they are in the same building as the flat or not) which are reasonably necessary to ensure that occupiers of the flat enjoy a reasonable standard of accommodation;

(*d*) the provision or maintenance of any services which are reasonably necessary to ensure that occupiers of the flat enjoy a reasonable standard of accommodation (whether they are services connected with any such installations or not, and whether they are services provided for the benefit of those occupiers or services provided for the benefit of the occupiers of a number of flats including that flat);

(*e*) the recovery by one party to the lease from another party to it of expenditure incurred or to be incurred by him, or on his behalf, for the benefit of that other party or of a number of persons who include that other party;

(*f*) the computation of a service charge payable under the lease.

(3) For the purposes of subsection (2)(*c*) and (*d*) the factors for determining, in relation to the occupiers of a flat, what is a reasonable standard of accommodation may include—

(*a*) factors relating to the safety and security of the flat and its occupiers and of any common parts of the building containing the flat; and

(*b*) other factors relating to the condition of any such common parts.

(4) For the purposes of subsection (2)(*f*) a lease fails to make satisfactory provision with respect to the computation of a service charge payable under it if—

(*a*) it provides for any such charge to be a proportion of expenditure incurred, or to be incurred, by or on behalf of the landlord or a superior landlord; and

(*b*) other tenants of the landlord are also liable under their leases to pay by way of service charges proportions of any such expenditure; and

(*c*) the aggregate of the amounts that would, in any particular case, be payable by reference to the proportions referred to in paragraphs (*a*) and (*b*) would exceed the whole of any such expenditure.

(5) Rules of court shall make provision—

(*a*) for requiring notice of any application under this Part to be served by the person making the application, and by any respondent to the application, on any person who the applicant, or (as the case may be) the respondent, knows or has reason to believe is likely to be affected by any variation specified in the application, and

(*b*) for enabling persons served with any such notice to be joined as parties to the proceedings.

(6) For the purposes of this Part a long lease shall not be regarded as a long lease of a flat if the demised premises consist of or include—

(*a*) the flat and one or more other flats, or

(*b*) the flat and any common parts of the building containing the flat.

(7) This Part does not apply to a long lease of a flat if it constitutes a tenancy to which Part II of the Landlord and Tenant Act 1954 applies (other than an assured tenancy as defined in section 56(1) of the Housing Act 1980).

(8) In this section "service charge" has the meaning given by section 18(1) of the 1985 Act. **[685]**

NOTES

Commencement: To be appointed.

36. Application by respondent for variation of other leases

(1) Where an application ("the original application") is made under section 35 by any party to a lease, any other party to the lease may make an application to the court asking it, in the event of its deciding to make an order effecting any variation of the lease in pursuance of the original application, to make an order which effects a corresponding variation of each of such one or more other leases as are specified in the application.

(2) Any lease so specified—

(*a*) must be a long lease of a flat under which the landlord is the same person as the landlord under the lease specified in the original application; but

(*b*) need not be a lease of a flat which is in the same building as the flat let under that lease, nor a lease drafted in terms identical to those of that lease.

(3) The grounds on which an application may be made under this section are—

(*a*) that each of the leases specified in the application fails to make satisfactory provision with respect to the matter or matters specified in the original application; and

(*b*) that, if any variation is effected in pursuance of the original application, it would be in the interests of the person making the application under this section, or in the interests of the other persons who are parties to the leases specified in that application, to have all of the leases in question (that is to say, the ones specified in that application together with the one specified in the original application) varied to the same effect. **[686]**

NOTES

Commencement: To be appointed.

37. Application by majority of parties for variation of leases

(1) Subject to the following provisions of this section, an application may be made to the court in respect of two or more leases for an order varying each of those leases in such manner as is specified in the application.

(2) Those leases must be long leases of flats under which the landlord is the same person, but they need not be leases of flats which are in the same building, nor leases which are drafted in identical terms.

(3) The grounds on which an application may be made under this section are that the object to be achieved by the variation cannot be satisfactorily achieved unless all the leases are varied to the same effect.

(4) An application under this section in respect of any leases may be made by the landlord or any of the tenants under the leases.

(5) Any such application shall only be made if—

(*a*) in a case where the application is in respect of less than nine leases, all, or all but one, of the parties concerned consent to it; or

(*b*) in a case where the application is in respect of more than eight leases, it is not opposed for any reason by more than 10 per cent. of the total number of the parties concerned and at least 75 per cent. of that number consent to it.

(6) For the purposes of subsection (5)—

(*a*) in the case of each lease in respect of which the application is made, the tenant under the lease shall constitute one of the parties concerned (so that in determining the total number of the parties concerned a person who is the tenant under a number of such leases shall be regarded as constituting a corresponding number of the parties concerned); and

(*b*) the landlord shall also constitute one of the parties concerned. **[687]**

NOTES
Commencement: To be appointed.

Orders varying leases

38. Orders by the court varying leases

(1) If, on an application under section 35, the grounds on which the application was made are established to the satisfaction of the court, the court may (subject to subsection (6) and (7)) make an order varying the lease specified in the application in such manner as is specified in the order.

(2) If—

(*a*) an application under section 36 was made in connection with that application, and

(*b*) the grounds set out in subsection (3) of that section are established to the satisfaction of the court with respect to the leases specified in the application under section 36,

the court may (subject to subsection (6) and (7)) also make an order varying each of those leases in such manner as is specified in the order.

(3) If, on an application under section 37, the grounds set out in subsection (3) of that section are established to the satisfaction of the court with respect to the leases specified in the application, the court may (subject to subsections (6)

and (7)) make an order varying each of those leases in such manner as is specified in the order.

(4) The variation specified in an order under subsection (1) or (2) may be either the variation specified in the relevant application under section 35 or 36 or such other variation as the court thinks fit.

(5) If the grounds referred to in subsection (2) or (3) (as the case may be) are established to the satisfaction of the court with respect to some but not all of the leases specified in the application, the power to make an order under that subsection shall extend to those leases only.

(6) The court shall not make an order under this section effecting any variation of a lease if it appears to the court—

(*a*) that the variation would be likely substantially to prejudice—

(i) any respondent to the application, or
(ii) any person who is not a party to the application,

and that an award under subsection (10) would not afford him adequate compensation, or

(*b*) that for any other reason it would not be reasonable in the circumstances for the variation to be effected.

(7) The court shall not, on an application relating to the provision to be made by a lease with respect to insurance, make an order under this section effecting any variation of the lease—

(*a*) which terminates any existing right of the landlord under its terms to nominate an insurer for insurance purposes; or
(*b*) which requires the landlord to nominate a number of insurers from which the tenant would be entitled to select an insurer for those purposes; or
(*c*) which, in a case where the lease requires the tenant to effect insurance with a specified insurer, requires the tenant to effect insurance otherwise than with another specified insurer.

(8) The court may, instead of making an order varying a lease in such manner as is specified in the order, make an order directing the parties to the lease to vary it in such manner as is so specified; and accordingly any reference in this Part (however expressed) to an order which effects any variation of a lease or to any variation effected by an order shall include a reference to an order which directs the parties to a lease to effect a variation of it or (as the case may be) a reference to any variation effected in pursuance of such an order.

(9) The court may by order direct that a memorandum of any variation of a lease effected by an order under this section shall be endorsed on such documents as are specified in the order.

(10) Where the court makes an order under this section varying a lease the court may, if it thinks fit, make an order providing for any party to the lease to pay, to any other party to the lease or to any other person, compensation in respect of any loss or disadvantage that the court considers he is likely to suffer as a result of the variation. **[688]**

NOTES
Commencement: To be appointed.

39. Effect of orders varying leases: applications by third parties

(1) Any variation effected by an order under section 38 shall be binding not only on the parties to the lease for the time being but also on other persons (including any predecessors in title of those parties), whether or not they were parties to the proceedings in which the order was made or were served with a notice by virtue of section 35(5).

(2) Without prejudice to the generality of subsection (1), any variation effected by any such order shall be binding on any surety who has guaranteed the performance of any obligation varied by the order; and the surety shall accordingly be taken to have guaranteed the performance of that obligation as so varied.

(3) Where any such order has been made and a person was, by virtue of section 35(5), required to be served with a notice relating to the proceedings in which it was made, but he was not so served, he may—

(*a*) bring an action for damages for breach of statutory duty against the person by whom any such notice was so required to be served in respect of that person's failure to serve it;
(*b*) apply to the court for the cancellation or modification of the variation in question.

(4) The court may, on an application under subsection (3)(*b*) with respect to any variation of a lease—

(*a*) by order cancel that variation or modify it in such manner as is specified in the order, or
(*b*) make such an order as is mentioned in section 38(10) in favour of the person making the application,

as it thinks fit.

(5) Where a variation is cancelled or modified under paragraph (*a*) of subsection (4)—

(*a*) the cancellation or modification shall take effect as from the date of the making of the order under that paragraph or as from such later date as may be specified in the order, and
(*b*) the court may by order direct that a memorandum of the cancellation or modification shall be endorsed on such documents as are specified in the order;

and, in a case where a variation is so modified, subsections (1) and (2) above shall, as from the date when the modification takes effect, apply to the variation as modified. **[689]**

NOTES
Commencement: To be appointed.

Applications relating to dwellings other than flats

40. Application for variation of insurance provisions of lease of dwelling other than a flat

(1) Any party to a long lease of a dwelling may make an application to the court for an order varying the lease, in such manner as is specified in the application, on the grounds that the lease fails to make satisfactory provision with respect to any matter relating to the insurance of the dwelling, including the recovery of the costs of such insurance.

(2) Sections 36 and 38 shall apply to an application under subsection (1) subject to the modifications specified in subsection (3).

(3) Those modifications are as follows—

(*a*) in section 36—

(i) in subsection (1), the reference to section 35 shall be read as a reference to subsection (1) above, and

(ii) in subsection (2), any reference to a flat shall be read as a reference to a dwelling; and

(*b*) in section 38—

(i) any reference to an application under section 35 shall be read as a reference to an application under subsection (1) above, and

(ii) any reference to an application under section 36 shall be read as a reference to an application under section 36 as applied by subsection (2) above.

(4) For the purposes of this section a long lease shall not be regarded as a long lease of a dwelling if the demised premises consist of or include the dwelling and one or more other dwellings; and this section does not apply to a long lease of a dwelling if it constitutes a tenancy to which Part II of the Landlord and Tenant Act 1954 applies (other than an assured tenancy as defined in section 56(1) of the Housing Act 1980).

(5) In this section "dwelling" means a dwelling other than a flat. **[690]**

NOTES
Commencement: To be appointed.

PART V

MANAGEMENT OF LEASEHOLD PROPERTY

Service charges

41. Amendments relating to service charges

(1) Sections 18 to 30 of the 1985 Act (regulation of service charges payable by tenants) shall have effect subject to the amendments specified in Schedule 2 (which include amendments—

(*a*) extending the provisions of those sections to dwellings other than flats, and

(*b*) introducing certain additional limitations on service charges).

(2) Sections 45 to 51 of the Housing Act 1985 (which are, so far as relating to dwellings let on long leases, superseded by sections 18 to 30 of the 1985 Act as amended by Schedule 2) shall cease to have effect in relation to dwellings so let. **[691]**

NOTES
Commencement: To be appointed.

42. Service charge contributions to be held in trust

(1) This section applies where the tenants of two or more dwellings may be required under the terms of their leases to contribute to the same costs by the payment of service charges; and in this section—

"the contributing tenants" means those tenants;

"the payee" means the landlord or other person to whom any such charges are payable by those tenants under the terms of their leases;
"relevant service charges" means any such charges;
"service charge" has the meaning given by section 18(1) of the 1985 Act, except that it does not include a service charge payable by the tenant of a dwelling the rent of which is registered under Part IV of the Rent Act 1977, unless the amount registered is, in pursuance of section 71(4) of that Act, entered as a variable amount;
"tenant" does not include a tenant of an exempt landlord; and
"trust fund" means the fund, or (as the case may be) any of the funds, mentioned in subsection (2) below.

(2) Any sums paid to the payee by the contributing tenants by way of relevant service charges, and any investments representing those sums, shall (together with any income accruing thereon) be held by the payee either as a single fund or, if he thinks fit, in two or more separate funds.

(3) The payee shall hold any trust fund—

(*a*) on trust to defray costs incurred in connection with the matters for which the relevant service charges were payable (whether incurred by himself or by any other person), and
(*b*) subject to that, on trust for the persons who are the contributing tenants for the time being.

(4) Subject to subsections (6) to (8), the contributing tenants shall be treated as entitled by virtue of subsection (3)(*b*) to such shares in the residue of any such fund as are proportionate to their respective liabilities to pay relevant service charges.

(5) If the Secretary of State by order so provides, any sums standing to the credit of any trust fund may, instead of being invested in any other manner authorised by law, be invested in such manner as may be specified in the order; and any such order may contain such incidental, supplemental or transitional provisions as the Secretary of State considers appropriate in connection with the order.

(6) On the termination of the lease of a contributing tenant the tenant shall not be entitled to any part of any trust fund, and (except where subsection (7) applies) any part of any such fund which is attributable to relevant service charges paid under the lease shall accordingly continue to be held on the trusts referred to in subsection (3).

(7) If after the termination of any such lease there are no longer any contributing tenants, any trust fund shall be dissolved as at the date of the termination of the lease, and any assets comprised in the fund immediately before its dissolution shall—

(*a*) if the payee is the landlord, be retained by him for his own use and benefit, and
(*b*) in any other case, be transferred to the landlord by the payee.

(8) Subsections (4), (6) and (7) shall have effect in relation to a contributing tenant subject to any express terms of his lease which relate to the distribution, either before or (as the case may be) at the termination of the lease, of amounts attributable to relevant service charges paid under its terms (whether the lease was granted before or after the commencement of this section).

(9) Subject to subsection (8), the provisions of this section shall prevail over

the terms of any express or implied trust created by a lease so far as inconsistent with those provisions, other than an express trust so created before the commencement of this section. **[692]**

NOTES
Commencement: To be appointed.

Insurance

43. Rights of tenants with respect to insurance

(1) . . .

(2) Schedule 3 to this Act shall be added to the 1985 Act as the Schedule to that Act. **[693]**

NOTES
Commencement: To be appointed.
Sub-s (1): adds the Landlord and Tenant Act 1985, s 30A.
1985 Act: Landlord and Tenant Act 1985.

Managing agents

44. Recognised tenants' associations to be consulted about managing agents

. . . **[694]**

NOTES
Commencement: To be appointed.
This section adds the Landlord and Tenant Act 1985, s 30B.

Management by registered housing associations

45. Extension of permissible objects of registered housing associations as regards the management of leasehold property

(1)-(3) . . .

(4) The amendments made by this section shall not extend to Scotland. **[695]**

NOTES
Commencement: To be appointed.
Sub-ss (1)-(3): amend the Housing Associations Act 1985, s 4.

PART VI

INFORMATION TO BE FURNISHED TO TENANTS

46. Application of Part VI, etc

(1) This Part applies to premises which consist of or include a dwelling and are not held under a tenancy to which Part II of the Landlord and Tenant Act 1954 applies.

(2) In this Part "service charge" has the meaning given by section 18(1) of the 1985 Act. **[696]**

NOTES
Commencement: To be appointed.
1985 Act: Landlord and Tenant Act 1985.

47. Landlord's name and address to be contained in demands for rent etc

(1) Where any written demand is given to a tenant of premises to which this Part applies, the demand must contain the following information, namely—

(*a*) the name and address of the landlord, and
(*b*) if that address is not in England and Wales, an address in England and Wales at which notices (including notices in proceedings) may be served on the landlord by the tenant.

(2) Where—

(*a*) a tenant of any such premises is given such a demand, but
(*b*) it does not contain any information required to be contained in it by virtue of subsection (1),

then (subject to subsection (3)) any part of the amount demanded which consists of a service charge ("the relevant amount") shall be treated for all purposes as not being due from the tenant to the landlord at any time before that information is furnished by the landlord by notice given to the tenant.

(3) The relevant amount shall not be so treated in relation to any time when, by virtue of an order of any court, there is in force an appointment of a receiver or manager whose functions include the receiving of service charges from the tenant.

(4) In this section "demand" means a demand for rent or other sums payable to the landlord under the terms of the tenancy. **[697]**

NOTES
Commencement: To be appointed.

48. Notification by landlord of address for service of notices

(1) A landlord of premises to which this Part applies shall by notice furnish the tenant with an address in England and Wales at which notices (including notices in proceedings) may be served on him by the tenant.

(2) Where a landlord of any such premises fails to comply with subsection (1), any rent or service charge otherwise due from the tenant to the landlord shall (subject to subsection (3)) be treated for all purposes as not being due from the tenant to the landlord at any time before the landlord does comply with that subsection.

(3) Any such rent or service charge shall not be so treated in relation to any time when, by virtue of an order of any court, there is in force an appointment of a receiver or manager whose functions include the receiving of rent or (as the case may be) service charges from the tenant. **[698]**

NOTES
Commencement: To be appointed.

49. Extension of circumstances in which notices are sufficiently served

In section 196 of the Law of Property Act 1925 (regulations respecting notices), any reference in subsection (3) or (4) to the last known place of abode or business of the person to be served shall have effect, in its application to a notice to be served by a tenant on a landlord of premises to which this Part applies, as if that reference included a reference to—

(*a*) the address last furnished to the tenant by the landlord in accordance with section 48, or

(*b*) if no address has been so furnished in accordance with section 48, the address last furnished to the tenant by the landlord in accordance with section 47. **[699]**

NOTES

Commencement: To be appointed.

50. Continuation of former landlord's liability to tenant where no notice of assignment

. . . **[700]**

NOTES

Commencement: To be appointed.

This section amends the Landlord and Tenant Act 1985, s 3.

51. Right of tenant to search proprietorship register for landlord's name and address

. . . **[701]**

NOTES

Commencement: To be appointed.

This section amends the Land Registration Act 1925, s 112 and adds s 112C.

PART VII

GENERAL

52. Jurisdiction of county courts

(1) A county court shall have jurisdiction to hear and determine any question arising under any provision to which this section applies (other than a question falling within the jurisdiction of a rent assessment committee by virtue of section 13(1) or 31(1)).

(2) This section applies to—

(*a*) any provision of Parts I to IV;

(*b*) any provision of section 42; and

(*c*) any provision of sections 46 to 48.

(3) Where any proceedings under any provision to which this section applies are being taken in a county court, the county court shall have jurisdiction to hear and determine any other proceedings joined with those proceedings, notwithstanding that the other proceedings would, apart from this subsection, be outside the court's jurisdiction.

(4) If a person takes any proceedings under any such provision in the High Court he shall not be entitled to recover any more costs of those proceedings than those to which he would have been entitled if the proceedings had been taken in a county court; and in any such case the taxing master shall have the same power of directing on what county court scale costs are to be allowed, and of allowing any item of costs, as the judge would have had if the proceedings had been taken in a county court.

(5) Subsection (4) shall not apply where the purpose of taking the proceedings

in the High Court was to enable them to be joined with any proceedings already pending before that court (not being proceedings taken under any provision to which this section applies). **[702]**

NOTES
Commencement: To be appointed.

53. Regulations and orders

(1) Any power of the Secretary of State to make an order or regulations under this Act shall be exercisable by statutory instrument and may be exercised so as to make different provision for different cases, including different provision for different areas.

(2) A statutory instrument containing—

(*a*) an order made under section 1(5), 25(6), 42(5) or 55, or
(*b*) any regulations made under section 13(2) (including any made under that provision as it applies for the purposes of section 31) or under section 20(4),

shall be subject to annulment in pursuance of a resolution of either House of Parliament. **[703]**

NOTES
Commencement: To be appointed.

54. Notices

(1) Any notice required or authorised to be served under this Act—

(*a*) shall be in writing; and
(*b*) may be sent by post.

(2) Any notice purporting to be a notice served under any provision of Part I or III by the requisite majority of any qualifying tenants (as defined for the purposes of that provision) shall specify the names of all of the persons by whom it is served and the addresses of the flats of which they are qualifying tenants.

(3) The Secretary of State may by regulations prescribe—

(*a*) the form of any notices required or authorised to be served under or in pursuance of any provision of Parts I to III, and
(*b*) the particulars which any such notices must contain (whether in addition to, or in substitution for, any particulars required by virtue of the provision in question).

(4) Subsection (3)(*b*) shall not be construed as authorising the Secretary of State to make regulations under subsection (3) varying either of the periods specified in section 5(2) (which accordingly can only be varied by regulations under section 20(4)). **[704]**

NOTES
Commencement: To be appointed.

55. Application to Isles of Scilly

This Act shall apply to the Isles of Scilly subject to such exceptions, adaptations and modifications as the Secretary of State may by order direct. **[705]**

NOTES
Commencement: To be appointed.

56. Crown land

(1) This Act shall apply to a tenancy from the Crown if there has ceased to be a Crown interest in the land subject to it.

(2) A variation of any such tenancy effected by or in pursuance of an order under section 38 shall not, however, be treated as binding on the Crown, as a predecessor in title under the tenancy, by virtue of section 39(1).

(3) Where there exists a Crown interest in any land subject to a tenancy from the Crown and the person holding that tenancy is himself the landlord under any other tenancy whose subject-matter comprises the whole or part of that land, this Act shall apply to that other tenancy, and to any derivative sub-tenancy, notwithstanding the existence of that interest.

(4) For the purposes of this section "tenancy from the Crown" means a tenancy of land in which there is, or has during the subsistence of the tenancy been, a Crown interest superior to the tenancy, and "Crown interest" means—

(*a*) an interest comprised in the Crown Estate;
(*b*) an interest belonging to Her Majesty in right of the Duchy of Lancaster;
(*c*) an interest belonging to the Duchy of Cornwall;
(*d*) any other interest belonging to a government department or held on behalf of Her Majesty for the purposes of a government department.
[706]

NOTES
Commencement: To be appointed.

57. Financial provision

There shall be paid out of money provided by Parliament any increase attributable to this Act in the sums payable out of money so provided under any other Act. **[707]**

NOTES
Commencement: To be appointed.

58. Exempt landlords and resident landlords

(1) In this Act "exempt landlord" means a landlord who is one of the following bodies, namely—

(*a*) a district, county or London borough council, the Common Council of the City of London, the Council of the Isles of Scilly, the Inner London Education Authority, or a joint authority established by Part IV of the Local Government Act 1985;
(*b*) the Commission for the New Towns or a development corporation established by an order made (or having effect as if made) under the New Towns Act 1981;
(*c*) an urban development corporation within the meaning of Part XVI of the Local Government, Planning and Land Act 1980;
(*d*) the Development Board for Rural Wales;
(*e*) the Housing Corporation;
(*f*) a housing trust (as defined in section 6 of the Housing Act 1985) which is a charity;

(*g*) a registered housing association, or an unregistered housing association which is a fully mutual housing association, within the meaning of the Housing Associations Act 1985; or

(*h*) an authority established under section 10 of the Local Government Act 1985 (joint arrangements for waste disposal functions).

(2) For the purposes of this Act the landlord of any premises consisting of the whole or part of a building is a resident landlord of those premises at any time if—

(*a*) the premises are not, and do not form part of, a purpose-built block of flats; and

(*b*) at that time the landlord occupies a flat contained in the premises as his only or principal residence; and

(*c*) he has so occupied such a flat throughout a period of not less than 12 months ending with that time.

(3) In subsection (2) "purpose-built block of flats" means a building which contained as constructed, and contains, two or more flats. **[708]**

NOTES

Commencement: To be appointed.

59. Meaning of "lease", "long lease" and related expressions

(1) In this Act "lease" and tenancy" have the same meaning; and both expressions include—

(*a*) a sub-lease or sub-tenancy, and

(*b*) an agreement for a lease or tenancy (or for a sub-lease or sub-tenancy).

(2) The expressions "landlord" and "tenant", and references to letting, to the grant of a lease or to covenants or the terms of a lease shall be construed accordingly.

(3) In this Act "long lease" means—

(*a*) a lease granted for a term certain exceeding 21 years, whether or not it is (or may become) terminable before the end of that term by notice given by the tenant or by re-entry or forfeiture;

(*b*) a lease for a term fixed by law under a grant with a covenant or obligation for perpetual renewal, other than a lease by sub-demise from one which is not a long lease; or

(*c*) a lease granted in pursuance of Part V of the Housing Act 1985 (the right to buy). **[709]**

NOTES

Commencement: To be appointed.

60. General interpretation

(1) In this Act—

"the 1985 Act" means the Landlord and Tenant Act 1985;

"charity" means a charity within the meaning of the Charities Act 1960, and "charitable purposes", in relation to a charity, means charitable purposes whether of that charity or of that charity and other charities;

"common parts", in relation to any building or part of a building, includes the structure and exterior of that building or part and any common facilities within it;

"the court" means the High Court or a county court;

"dwelling" means a building or part of a building occupied or intended to be occupied as a separate dwelling, together with any yard, garden, outhouses and appurtenances belonging to it or usually enjoyed with it;

"exempt landlord" has the meaning given by section 58(1);

"flat" means a separate set of premises, whether or not on the same floor, which—

(*a*) forms part of a building, and

(*b*) is divided horizontally from some other part of that building, and

(*c*) is constructed or adapted for use for the purposes of a dwelling;

"functional land", in relation to a charity, means land occupied by the charity, or by trustees for it, and wholly or mainly used for charitable purposes;

"landlord" (except for the purposes of Part I) means the immediate landlord or, in relation to a statutory tenant, the person who, apart from the statutory tenancy, would be entitled to possession of the premises subject to the tenancy;

"lease" and related expressions shall be construed in accordance with section 59(1) and (2);

"long lease" has the meaning given by section 59(3);

"mortgage" includes any charge or lien, and references to a mortgagee shall be construed accordingly;

"notices in proceedings" means notices or other documents served in, or in connection with, any legal proceedings;

"rent assessment committee" means a rent assessment committee constituted under Schedule 10 to the Rent Act 1977;

"resident landlord" shall be construed in accordance with section 58(2);

"statutory tenancy" and "statutory tenant" mean a statutory tenancy or statutory tenant within the meaning of the Rent Act 1977 or the Rent (Agriculture) Act 1976;

"tenancy" includes a statutory tenancy.

(2) In this Act (except in Part IV) any reference to a tenancy to which Part II of the Landlord and Tenant Act 1954 applies includes a reference to an assured tenancy (as defined in section 56(1) of the Housing Act 1980). **[710]**

NOTES

Commencement: To be appointed.

61. Consequential amendments and repeals

(1) The enactments mentioned in Schedule 4 shall have effect subject to the amendments there specified (being amendments consequential on the preceding provisions of this Act).

(2) The enactments mentioned in Schedule 5 are hereby repealed to the extent specified in the third column of that Schedule. **[711]**

NOTES

Commencement: To be appointed.

62. Short title, commencement and extent

(1) This Act may be cited as the Landlord and Tenant Act 1987.

(2) This Act shall come into force on such day as the Secretary of State may by order appoint.

(3) An order under subsection (2)—

(*a*) may appoint different days for different provisions or for different purposes; and

(*b*) may make such transitional, incidental, supplemental or consequential provision or saving as the Secretary of State considers necessary or expedient in connection with the coming into force of any provision of this Act or the operation of any enactment which is repealed or amended by a provision of this Act during any period when the repeal or amendment is not wholly in force.

(4) This Act extends to England and Wales only. **[712]**

NOTES

Commencement: To be appointed.

SCHEDULES

SCHEDULE 1

Sections 12, 32

DISCHARGE OF MORTGAGES ETC: SUPPLEMENTARY PROVISIONS

PART I

DISCHARGE IN PURSUANCE OF PURCHASE NOTICES

Construction

1. In this Part of this Schedule—

"the consideration payable" means the consideration payable to the new landlord for the disposal by him of the property referred to in section 12(4);

"the new landlord" has the same meaning as in secton 12, and accordingly includes any person to whom that section applies by virtue of section 16(2) or (3); and

"the nominated person" means the person or persons nominated as mentioned in section 12(1).

Duty of nominated person to redeem mortgages

2.—(1) Where in accordance with section 12(4)(*a*) an instrument will operate to discharge any property from a charge to secure the payment of money, it shall be the duty of the nominated person to apply the consideration payable, in the first instance, in or towards the redemption of any such charge (and, if there are more than one, then according to their priorities).

(2) Where sub-paragraph (1) applies to any charge or charges, then if (and only if) the consideration payable is applied by the nominated person in accordance with that sub-paragraph or paid into court by him in accordance with paragraph 4, the instrument in question shall operate as mentioned in sub-paragraph (1) notwithstanding that the consideration payable is insufficient to enable the charge or charges to be redeemed in its or their entirety.

(3) Subject to sub-paragraph (4), sub-paragraph (1) shall not apply to a charge which is a debenture holders' charge, that is to say, a charge (whether a floating charge or not) in favour of the holders of a series of debentures issued by a company or other body of persons, or in favour of trustees for such debenture holders; and any such charge shall be disregarded in determining priorities for the purposes of sub-paragraph (1).

(4) Sub-paragraph (3) above shall not have effect in relation to a charge in favour of trustees for debenture holders which at the date of the instrument by virtue of which the property is disposed of by the new landlord is (as regards that property) a specific and not a floating charge.

Determination of amounts due in respect of mortgages

3.—(1) For the purpose of determining the amount payable in respect of any charge under paragraph 2(1), a person entitled to the benefit of a charge to which that provision applies shall not be permitted to exercise any right to consolidate that charge with a separate charge on other property.

(2) For the purpose of discharging any property from a charge to which paragraph 2(1) applies, a person may be required to accept three months or any longer notice of the intention to pay the whole or part of the principal secured by the charge, together with interest to the date of payment, notwithstanding that the terms of the security make other provision or no provision as to the time and manner of payment; but he shall be entitled, if he so requires, to receive such additional payment as is reasonable in the circumstances in respect of the costs of re-investment or other incidental costs and expenses and in respect of any reduction in the rate of interest obtainable on re-investment.

Payments into court

4.—(1) Where under section 12(4)(*a*) any property is to be discharged from a charge and, in accordance with paragraph 2(1), a person is or may be entitled in respect of the charge to receive the whole or part of the consideration payable, then if—

(*a*) for any reason difficulty arises in ascertaining how much is payable in respect of the charge, or
(*b*) for any reason mentioned in sub-paragraph (2) below difficulty arises in making a payment in respect of the charge,

the nominated person may pay into court on account of the consideration payable the amount, if known, of the payment to be made in respect of the charge or, if that amount is not known, the whole of that consideration or such lesser amount as the nominated person thinks right in order to provide for that payment.

(2) Payment may be made into court in accordance with sub-paragraph (1)(*b*) where the difficulty arises for any of the following reasons, namely—

(*a*) because a person who is or may be entitled to receive payment cannot be found or ascertained;
(*b*) because any such person refuses or fails to make out a title, or to accept payment and give a proper discharge, or to take any steps reasonably required of him to enable the sum payable to be ascertained and paid;
(*c*) because a tender of the sum payable cannot, by reason of complications in the title to it or the want of two or more trustees or for other reasons, be effected, or not without incurring or involving unreasonable cost or delay.

(3) Without prejudice to sub-paragraph (1)(*a*), the whole or part of the consideration payable shall be paid into court by the nominated person if, before execution of the instrument referred to in paragraph 2(1), notice is given to him—

(*a*) that the new landlord or a person entitled to the benefit of a charge on the property in question requires him to do so for the purpose of protecting the rights of persons so entitled, or for reasons related to the bankruptcy or winding up of the new landlord, or
(*b*) that steps have been taken to enforce any charge on the new landlord's interest in that property by the bringing of proceedings in any court, or by the appointment of a receiver or otherwise;

and where payment into court is to be made by reason only of a notice under this sub-paragraph, and the notice is given with reference to proceedings in a court specified in the notice other than a county court, payment shall be made into the court so specified.

Savings

5.—(1) Where any property is discharged by section 12(4)(*a*) from a charge (without the obligations secured by the charge being satisfied by the receipt of the whole or part of the consideration payable), the discharge of that property from the charge shall not prejudice any right or remedy for the enforcement of those obligations against other property comprised in the same or any other security, nor prejudice any personal liability as principal or otherwise of the new landlord or any other person.

(2) Nothing in this Schedule shall be construed as preventing a person from joining in the instrument referred to in paragraph 2(1) for the purpose of discharging the property in question from any charge without payment or for a lesser payment than that to which he would otherwise be entitled; and, if he does so, the persons to whom the consideration payable ought to be paid shall be determined accordingly. **[713]**

NOTES
Commencement: To be appointed.

PART II

DISCHARGE IN PURSUANCE OF ACQUISITION ORDERS

Construction

6. In this Part of this Schedule—

"the consideration payable" means the consideration payable for the acquisition of the landlord's interest referred to in section 32(1); and

"the nominated person" means the person or persons nominated for the purposes of Part III by the persons who applied for the acquisition order in question.

Duty of nominated person to redeem mortgages

7.—(1) Where in accordance with section 32(1) an instrument will operate to discharge any premises from a charge to secure the payment of money, it shall be the duty of the nominated person to apply the consideration payable, in the first instance, in or towards the redemption of any such charge (and, if there are more than one, then according to their priorities).

(2) Where sub-paragraph (1) applies to any charge or charges, then if (and only if) the consideration payable is applied by the nominated person in accordance with that sub-paragraph or paid into court by him in accordance with paragraph 9, the instrument in question shall operate as mentioned in sub-paragraph (1) notwithstanding that the consideration payable is insufficient to enable the charge or charges to be redeemed in its or their entirety.

(3) Subject to sub-paragraph (4), sub-paragraph (1) shall not apply to a charge which is a debenture holders' charge within the meaning of paragraph 2(3) in Part I of this Schedule; and any such charge shall be disregarded in determining priorities for the purposes of sub-paragraph (1).

(4) Sub-paragraph (3) above shall not have effect in relation to a charge in favour of trustees for debenture holders which at the date of the instrument by virtue of which the landlord's interest in the premises in question is acquired is (as regards those premises) a specific and not a floating charge.

Determination of amounts due in respect of mortgages

8.—(1) For the purpose of determining the amount payable in respect of any charge under paragraph 7(1), a person entitled to the benefit of a charge to which that provision applies shall not be permitted to exercise any right to consolidate that charge with a separate charge on other property.

(2) For the purpose of discharging any premises from a charge to which paragraph 7(1) applies, a person may be required to accept three months or any longer notice of the intention to pay the whole or part of the principal secured by the charge, together with interest to the date of payment, notwithstanding that the terms of the security make other provision or no provision as to the time and manner of payment; but he shall be entitled, if he so requires, to receive such additional payment as is reasonable in the circumstances in respect of the costs of re-investment or other incidental costs and

expenses and in respect of any reduction in the rate of interest obtainable on re-investment.

Payments into court

9.—(1) Where under section 32 any premises are to be discharged from a charge and, in accordance with paragraph 7(1), a person is or may be entitled in respect of the charge to receive the whole or part of the consideration payable, then if—

(*a*) for any reason difficulty arises in ascertaining how much is payable in respect of the charge, or

(*b*) for any reason mentioned in sub-paragraph (2) below difficulty arises in making a payment in respect of the charge,

the nominated person may pay into court on account of the consideration payable the amount, if known, of the payment to be made in respect of the charge or, if that amount is not known, the whole of that consideration or such lesser amount as the nominated person thinks right in order to provide for that payment.

(2) Payment may be made into court in accordance with sub-paragraph (1)(*b*) where the difficulty arises for any of the following reasons, namely—

(*a*) because a person who is or may be entitled to receive payment cannot be found or ascertained;

(*b*) because any such person refuses or fails to make out a title, or to accept payment and give a proper discharge, or to take any steps reasonably required of him to enable the sum payable to be ascertained and paid; or

(*c*) because a tender of the sum payable cannot, by reason of complications in the title to it or the want of two or more trustees or for other reasons, be effected, or not without incurring or involving unreasonable cost or delay.

(3) Without prejudice to sub-paragraph (1)(*a*), the whole or part of the consideration payable shall be paid into court by the nominated person if, before execution of the instrument referred to in paragraph 7(1), notice is given to him—

(*a*) that the landlord or a person entitled to the benefit of a charge on the premises in question requires him to do so for the purpose of protecting the rights of persons so entitled, or for reasons related to the bankruptcy or winding up of the landlord, or

(*b*) that steps have been taken to enforce any charge on the landlord's interest in those premises by the bringing of proceedings in any court, or by the appointment of a receiver or otherwise;

and where payment into court is to be made by reason only of a notice under this sub-paragraph, and the notice is given with reference to proceedings in a court specified in the notice other than a county court, payment shall be made into the court so specified.

Savings

10.—(1) Where any premises are discharged by section 32 from a charge (without the obligations secured by the charge being satisfied by the receipt of the whole or part of the consideration payable), the discharge of those premises from the charge shall not prejudice any right or remedy for the enforcement of those obligations against other property comprised in the same or any other security, nor prejudice any personal liability as principal or otherwise of the landlord or any other person.

(2) Nothing in this Schedule shall be construed as preventing a person from joining in the instrument referred to in paragraph 7(1) for the purpose of discharging the premises in question from any charge without payment or for a lesser payment than that to which he would otherwise be entitled; and, if he does so, the persons to whom the consideration payable ought to be paid shall be determined accordingly. **[714]**

NOTES

Commencement: To be appointed.

SCHEDULE 2

Section 41

AMENDMENTS RELATING TO SERVICE CHARGES

. . . **[715]**

NOTES

Commencement: To be appointed.

This Schedule contains amendments only.

SCHEDULE 3

Section 43(2)

RIGHTS OF TENANTS WITH RESPECT TO INSURANCE

. . . **[716]**

NOTES

Commencement: To be appointed.

This Schedule is added as the Landlord and Tenant Act 1985, Schedule.

SCHEDULE 4

Section 61(1)

CONSEQUENTIAL AMENDMENTS

. . . **[717]**

NOTES

Commencement: To be appointed.

This Schedule contains amendments only.

SCHEDULE 5

Section 61(2)

REPEALS

Chapter	Short title	Extent of repeal
1985 c 51	Local Government Act 1985	In paragraph 24 of Schedule 13, the word "and" in the second place where it occurs.
1985 c 68	Housing Act 1985	In section 45(2), the words from "(a) the" to "; and (b)". Section 49. In section 50(1), the words "or 49".
1985 c 70	Landlord and Tenant Act 1985	In section 30, the definition of "flat".

[718]

NOTES

Commencement: To be appointed.

PART II
STATUTORY INSTRUMENTS

RENEWABLE LEASEHOLDS REGULATIONS 1925
(SR & O 1925 NO 857)

NOTES
Made: 24 August 1925
Authority: Law of Property Act 1922, Sch 15

1. For the purposes of paragraph 12(6) of the Fifteenth Schedule to the Law of Property Act 1922, as amended by the Law of Property (Amendment) Act 1924, five per cent. shall be the prescribed percentage applicable generally except where the Minister in any particular instance with a view to maintaining any existing practice prescribed any other percentage. **[719]**

2. (1) Where any question or dispute is under paragraph 16 of the Fifteenth Schedule to the Law of Property Act 1922, submitted to the Minister of Agriculture and Fisheries for determination, the matter shall be determined under and in accordance with the provisions of the Arbitration Act 1889, and—

(*a*) unless either party to the arbitration shall, within seven days after receipt of a written notice by the Minister that he proposes that a person to be appointed by him shall act as arbitrator, give notice in writing to the Minister that he objects to such proposal, the Minister may appoint an officer of the Ministry of Agriculture and Fisheries or other person to act as the arbitrator, in which case the award made by the person so appointed shall be deemed to be an award by the Minister; or

(*b*) the Minister may appoint any officer of the Ministry or other person to hear on his behalf the parties or their solicitors or counsel and the witnesses in the arbitration and to report thereon to the Minister to enable him to make an award, and for the purposes of or in connection with such hearing the person appointed shall have all the powers of an arbitrator.

(2) If any person appointed to act under this Regulation shall die or in the judgment of the Minister become incapable or unfit the Minister may appoint another person to act in his place.

(3) The remuneration of any person, other than an officer of the Ministry, who is appointed to act under this Regulation shall be fixed by the Minister.

(4) The submission of any question or dispute to the Minister for determination shall be in writing signed by or on behalf of the party submitting the same and shall set out the question or dispute to be determined. Provided that the submission may, with the sanction of the Minister or any person appointed by him to act under this Regulation, be amended or varied on such terms as to payment of costs or otherwise as the Minister or such person as aforesaid may determine.

(5) These Regulations shall come into operation on the first day of January, nineteen hundred and twenty-six, and may be cited as the Renewable Leaseholds Reglations 1925.

(6) These Regulations do not extend to Scotland or Ireland. **[720]**

NOTES
Arbitration Act 1889: see now Arbitration Act 1950.

FILING OF LEASES RULES 1925
(SR & O 1925 NO 1128)

NOTES
Made: 11 November 1925
Authority: Law of Property Act 1922, Sch 15

ARRANGEMENT OF RULES

Rule		Para
1	Deposit and index of instruments	[721]
2	Requisition for search	[722]
3	Form and contents of requisition	[723]
4	Acceptance or refusal of requisition	[724]
5	Office copies	[725]
6	Conversion of copies into office copies	[726]
7	Notes authorised on a search	[727]
8	Application forms	[728]
9	Short title, commencement	[729]
	Schedule—	
	Form 1	[730]
	Form 2	[731]
	Form 3	[732]
	Form 4	[733]

1. Deposit and index of instruments

(1) Any person may, subject to the payment of the prescribed fee, deposit at the Central Office of the Supreme Court the original or counterpart of any instrument to which these Rules apply.

(2) There shall be deposited, together with any such instrument, a short description of the instrument in Form No. 1 in the Schedule to these Rules.

(3) An alphabetical index of the name of each lessee, lessor, or underlessee under any deposited instrument, and of the names of the assignors or assignees under any such instrument shall be kept in the Filing Department of the Central Office.

(4) The instruments to which these Rules apply are leases, underleases, and assignments of leases and underleases, and office copies of any such lease, underlease, or assignment. **[721]**

2. Requisition for search

Any person who desires—

(*a*) to search the alphabetical index or the file of instruments; or
(*b*) to inspect any deposited instrument

shall deliver at the Filing Department a requisition for that purpose signed by himself or by his solicitor, together with the prescribed fee. **[722]**

3. Form and contents of requisition

(1) The requisition shall be in Form No. 2 in the Schedule to these Rules and shall state—

(*a*) the name, address and description of the applicant and, where a solicitor is acting on behalf of the applicant, the name and address of that solicitor, and
(*b*) the purpose for which the search and inspection are required, and
(*c*) the interest which the applicant has or claims to have under the instrument or in any reversion expectant upon the term implied therein by operation of law,

and shall contain a declaration that the statements made in the requisition are true.

(2) Where the requisition is signed by a solicitor, it shall state that he is duly authorised to act on behalf of the applicant.

(3) The requisition shall be filed in the Central Office. **[723]**

4. Acceptance or refusal of requisition

If the requisition complies with these Rules and the applicant appears to have an interest (whether or not being a charge) either beneficial or in a fiduciary capacity under the instrument or any reversion expectant upon the term implied therein by operation of law, the applicant shall be allowed to search for and inspect the instrument. Any doubt arising under this rule shall be referred to the Senior Master of the Supreme Court who shall decide whether the search and inspection shall be allowed. **[724]**

5. Office copies

(1) When a search has been authorised, the applicant may require an office copy of the deposited instrument or any part thereof to be issued to him with or without any endorsements thereon or with or without any plan.

(2) The request for the issue of an office copy shall be in Form No. 3 in the Schedule to these Rules and shall contain an undertaking to pay the prescribed fee when ascertained.

(3) When the office copy is ready for issue, notification thereof shall be sent by post to the applicant or his solicitor, with a memorandum of the amount of the fee payable.

(4) The applicant or his solicitor shall, after the payment of the prescribed fee, apply for the office copy to be delivered to the bearer of the request or to be sent by post, at the risk of the applicant, to the applicant or his solicitor. Any such application shall be in the Form No. 4 in the Schedule to these Rules and, where it includes a request that the office copy shall be sent by post, shall be accompanied by a stamped envelope (draft size) addressed to the person to whom the copy is to be sent. **[725]**

6. Conversion of copies into office copies

(1) On presentation at the Filing Department of a copy of any deposited instrument for the purpose of having it stamped as an office copy, the copy shall be examined and, if found correct, shall, subject to the payment of the prescribed fee, be stampted as an office copy.

(2) Where the instrument to which any copy so presented has annexed to it or endorsed upon it any plan or endorsements, the copy presented shall be accompanied by a tracing of the plan and a copy of the endorsements. **[726]**

7. Notes authorised on a search

No copies of or extracts from any deposited instrument shall be made except as provided in the foregoing provisions of these Rules, and no person authorised to inspect an instrument under these Rules shall be allowed to use any ink when inspecting a deposited instrument, but any person so authorised shall be entitled in the course of inspection to take a note in pencil of—

(*a*) the date of the instrument,
(*b*) the parties to the instrument,
(*c*) the parcels, plan and rent,
(*d*) the nature of the covenants, and
(*e*) the endorsements, if any, upon the instrument. **[727]**

8. Application forms

(1) Copies of the Forms prescribed under these Rules will be supplied free of cost on application at the Central Office Filing Department.

(2) The forms shall be adhered to with such modifications only as the circumstances of each case may render necessary. **[728]**

9. Short title, commencement

(1) These Rules may be cited as the Filing of Leases Rules 1925.

(2) These Rules shall come into operation on the first day of January, nineteen hundred and twenty-six. **[729]**

SCHEDULE

FORM 1

Application under the Fifteenth Schedule to the Law of Property Act 1922 for deposit of an Instrument.

In the Supreme Court of Judicature.

To the Registrar,

Filing Department, Central Office,

Royal Courts of Justice, London.

IN THE MATTER OF a Lease [an Underlease] dated .... and made between.. .... of property at.. ....

[We.. .... of.. .... Solicitors on behalf of].. .... of.. .... (the Applicant) herewith deposit the original [counterpart] of the above mentioned Lease [Underlease] [*or* an Assignment dated.. ... . and made between .... being an Assignment of the above mentioned Lease [Underlease]] [*or* an Office Copy of a Lease [an Underlease] [an Assignment] dated.. .... and made between.. .... which was formerly deposited in this Office and has perished or become undecipherable] and apply for the same to be filed.

Dated this.. ....day of.. .... 19.. .....

Signed [by the applicant or his solicitor].. ....

Address.. ....

Description.. ....

Note.—This application must be stamped with the prescribed fee. **[730]**

FORM 2

REQUISITION under the Fifteenth Schedule to the Law of Property Act 1922 for a Search.

In the Supreme Court of Judicature.

To the Registrar,

Filing Department, Central Office,

Royal Courts of Justice, London.

IN THE MATTER OF a Lease [an Underlease] [an Assignment] dated.. .. .. and made between.. .. .. affecting property at .. ..

WE.. .. .. of.. .. .. Solicitors duly authorised to act on behalf of].. .. .. of.. .. .. in the County of.. .. ..(hereinafter called "the Applicant") require[s] to search the alphabetical index and file of instruments deposited in the Central Office pursuant to paragraph twenty of the Fifteenth Schedule to the said Act for the purpose of finding and inspecting the above mentioned instrument.

The Applicant requires to make the search and inspection for the purpose of.. .. .. .. [state shortly the purpose for which the search and inspection are required to be made].. .. ..

The Applicant has or claims to be entitled to the following interest in the property comprised in the above mentioned instrument, namely— .. ..[state the interest or charge].. .. ..

The claim to the said interest is made by virtue of.. .. .. [state the facts or instrument under which the claim is made].. .. ..

THE above statements are to the best of my [our] knowledge and belief true in all respects.

Dated this.. .. .. day of.. .. .. 19.. ..

Signed [by the applicant or his solicitor].. .. .. ..

Address.. .. ..

Description.. .. ..

Note.—This application must be stamped with the prescribed fee. **[731]**

FORM 3

REQUEST for Office Copy to be prepared.

In the Supreme Court of Judicature.

To the Registrar,

Filing Department, Central Office,

Royal Courts of Justice, London.

IN THE MATTER of a Lease [an Underlease] [an Assignment] dated.. .. .. and made between.. .. .. affecting property at.. .. ..

I [We] request an Office Copy of the above mentioned instrument [the following parts of the above mentioned instrument namely.. .. ..] being an instrument filed in this Office pursuant to paragraph twenty of the Fifteenth Schedule to the Law of Property Act 1922, to be prepared and I [we] undertake to pay the prescribed fees for the same when ascertained.

Dated this.. .. .. day of.. .. ..19.. ..

Signed [by the applicant or his solicitor]... ..

Address.. .. ..

Description.. .. .. **[732]**

FORM 4

REQUEST for Office Copy to be delivered or sent by post.

In the Supreme Court of Judicature.

To the Registrar,

Filing Department, Central Office,

Royal Courts of Justice, London.

IN THE MATTER of a Lease [an Underlease] [an Assignment] dated.. .. .. and made between.. .. .. affecting property at .. ..

I [We] direct that the Office Copy of the above mentioned instrument [or parts thereof] prepared at my [our] request be delivered at my [our] risk to bearer [be sent by post at my [our] risk to the address shown on the accompanying stampted envelope].

Dated this.. .. .. day of.. .. ..19.. .. ..

Signed [by the applicant or his solicitor].. .. .. ..

Address.. .. ..

Description.. .. ..

Note.—This description must be stamped with the prescribed fee. **[733]**

LANDLORD AND TENANT (DETERMINATION OF RATEABLE VALUE PROCEDURE) RULES 1954
(SI 1954 NO 1255)

NOTES

Made: 24 September 1954

Authority: Landlord and Tenant Act 1954, s 37(6)

ARRANGEMENT OF RULES

Rule	Para
1	[734]
2	[735]
3	[736]
4	[737]
5	[738]
6	[739]
7	[740]
8	[741]
Schedule—Forms "A", "B"	[742]

1. These Rules may be cited as the Landlord and Tenant (Determination of Rateable Value Procedure) Rules 1954, and shall come into operation on the first day of October, 1954. **[734]**

2. (1) In these Rules—

"Commissioners" means the Commissioners of Inland Revenue;

"The Act" means the Landlord and Tenant Act 1954, and other expressions have the same meaning as in that Act.

(2) The Interpretation Act 1889 shall apply to these Rules as it applies to an Act of Parliament. **[735]**

3. (1) Any reference to the Commissioners of a dispute arising as to the determination of the rateable value of any holding for the purposes of Sections 37(2) and 63(2) of the Act, shall be in the form "A" in the Schedule hereto, or in a form substantially to the like effect. A separate form shall be completed in respect of each holding.

(2) The said reference may be made either:—

(*a*) by one of the parties, or
(*b*) jointly by two or more of the parties to the dispute:

Provided that, where the said reference is not made by all the parties jointly, the party or parties making the reference shall, on the same day as the reference is made, send a copy thereof to the other party, or parties, to the dispute. **[736]**

NOTES
The Act: Landlord and Tenant Act 1954.

4. The Commissioners shall, so soon as may be after the receipt of a reference, send a copy thereof to the Valuation Officer. **[737]**

5. The Valuation Officer shall, upon receipt of the copy of the reference, inform the parties that the dispute has been referred to him for determination and that they may make representations to him on the matter in writing within twenty-eight days, or such longer time as he may in a particular case allow. **[738]**

6. The Valuation Officer may require the parties to furnish him with such information as he may reasonably require for the proper determination of the rateable value of the holding. **[739]**

7. The Valuation Officer may, before making his determination, invite all the parties to a meeting at his office or at such other place as he may think convenient. **[740]**

8. The Valuation Officer shall so soon as may be determine the rateable value of the holding and shall send a notification of his determination to the Commissioners and to each of the parties together with a statement of their right of appeal to the Lands Tribunal under Section 37(5) of the Act. The notification of such determination shall be in the form "B" in the Schedule hereto, and a separate notification shall be sent in respect of each holding. **[741]**

NOTES
The Act: Landlord and Tenant Act 1954.

SCHEDULE

Regulations 3, 8

FORMS "A", "B"

FORM "A"

Landlord and Tenant Act 1954

Reference of a dispute arising as to the determination of the Rateable Value of any holding for the purposes of Section 37(2) *or of Section* 63(2).

To:— The Commissioners of Inland Revenue,

Somerset House,

London, W.C.2.

PART I (*Applicable to all references*).

I/We* being a party/parties* to a dispute which has arisen as to the determination for the purposes of Section [37(2)/63(2)]* of the rateable value of a holding known as (*Insert here address or situation, and such further particulars as may be necessary for the identification of the holding.*) .. .. hereby refer the dispute for decision by a Valuation Officer.

*(Delete as appropriate)

Signed	‡(1)	‡(2)	‡(3)
Capacity in which reference made (eg Tenant, Landlord, etc)	....	....	....
	....	....	....
	....	....	....
Address	....	....	....
	....	....	....
	....	....	....
Date	....	....	....

(* See headnote to Part II of form.)

Part II (*Applicable where the reference is not made by all the parties to the dispute*).

Note.—Where the reference is not made by all the parties, the party or parties making the reference should sign and complete the form in Part 1 above, and should give below the name or names of the other party or parties to the dispute, and should send a copy of this form, as completed, to the other party or parties.

Name(s) and address(es) of other party(ies)

	(A)	(B)
Name	....	....
Address	....	....
	....	....
	....	....

FORM "B"

Landlord and Tenant Act 1954

Determination of Rateable Value

Whereas a dispute has arisen as to the determination for the purposes of Section [37(2)/63(2)]* of the rateable value of the holding described in the first column of the Schedule hereto.

*(*Delete as appropriate*)

Now I the undersigned being the Valuation Officer to whom the Commissioners of Inland Revenue have pursuant to Section 37(5) referred the dispute for determination hereby determine that for the said purposes the rateable value of the said holding shall be the amount set out in the second column of the said Schedule.

THE SCHEDULE above referred to

†Description of Holding	Rateable Value as Determined

† The description will follow that in "A".

Dated this . . . . day of . . . . ., 19 . . .
Signed . . . .
Valuation Officer
for . . . .
Official Address . . . .
. . . .
To:—The Commissioners of Inland Revenue and to:—[The Parties to the Dispute]

Any party who is dissatisfied with the foregoing determination may appeal to the Lands Tribunal by giving written notice of such appeal to the Registrar of the Lands Tribunal within 21 days from the date hereof. **[742]**

LANDLORD AND TENANT (NOTICES) REGULATIONS 1957
(SI 1957 NO 1157)

NOTES
Made: 3 July 1957
Authority: Landlord and Tenant Act 1954, s 66

ARRANGEMENT OF REGULATIONS

Regulation	Para
1	[743]
2	[744]
3	[745]
4	[746]

APPENDIX LANDLORD AND TENANT ACT 1954 (REG 4)

1	Form 1 Landlord's Notice proposing a Statutory Tenancy	[747]
2	Form 2 Landlord's Notice to resume Possession	[748]
3	Form 3 Notice Requiring Information about Sub-tenancies of Residential Property	[749]
4	Form 4 Notice Requiring Instalments to be paid to immediate Landlord	[750]
5	Form 5 Notice by Competent Landlord Requiring Consent of other Landlord to Notice under section 4(1)	[751]
6	Form 6 Notice by Competent Landlord Requiring Consent of other Landlord to Agreement under Part I	[752]
7	Form 7 Landlord's Notice to Terminate Business Tenancy	[753]
8	Form 8 Landlord's Notice to Terminate Business Tenancy on Grounds of Public Interest	[754]
9	Form 9 Landlord's Notice to Terminate' Business Tenancy where Change Required at Future Date on Grounds of Public Interest	[755]
10	Form 10 Landlord's Notice to Terminate Business Tenancy on Grounds of National Security	[756]
11	Form 11 Landlord's Notice to Terminate Business Tenancy by reason of the Objects of the Local Employment Act 1972	[757]

Regulation		Para
12	Form 12 Tenant's Request for New Tenancy of Business Premises	[758]
13	Form 13 Notice Requiring Information about Occupation and Sub-tenancies of Business Premises	[759]
14	Form 14 Notice by Tenant of Business Premises Requiring Information from Landlord about Landlord's Interest	[760]
15	Form 15 Notice by Tenant of Business Premises Requiring Information from Mortgagee about Landlord's Interest	[761]
16	Form 16 Superior Landlord's Notice Withdrawing Notice to Terminate Business Tenancy	[762]

1. These Regulations may be cited as the Landlord and Tenant (Notices) Regulations 1957, and shall come into operation on the 9th day of July, 1957. **[743]**

2. The Interpretation Act 1889 applies to the interpretation of these Regulations as it applies to the interpretation of an Act of Parliament. **[744]**

3. In these Regulations, unless the context otherwise requires,—

(*a*) "The Act" means the Landlord and Tenant Act 1954.
(*b*) A form referred to by number means the form so numbered in the Appendix to these Regulations. **[745]**

4. The forms in the Appendix to these Regulations, or forms substantially to the like effect, shall be used for the following purposes, that is to say:—

(i) A landlord's notice proposing a statutory tenancy given under the provisions of section 4 of the Act shall be in Form 1;
(ii) A landlord's notice to resume possession given under the provisions of section 4 of the Act shall be in Form 2;
(iii) A notice under the provisions of section 18 of the Act, being a notice requiring a tenant or sub-tenant of residential property to give information about sub-tenancies, shall be in Form 3;
(iv) A notice under the provisions of paragraph 8 of the First Schedule to the Act, being a notice requiring a tenant to pay instalments of his payment for accrued tenant's repairs to his immediate landlord for transmission to the person who is the landlord for the purpose of the Act, shall be in Form 4;
(v) A notice served by a landlord under the provisions of paragraph 5 of the Fifth Schedule to the Act on another landlord, being a notice requiring that other landlord to consent to the giving of a landlord's notice proposing a statutory tenancy or of a landlord's notice to resume possession, shall be in Form 5;
(vi) A notice served by a landlord under the provisions of paragraph 5 of the Fifth Schedule to the Act on another landlord, being a notice requiring that other landlord to consent to the making of an agreement under Part I of the Act between the landlord serving the notice and the tenant, shall be in Form 6;
(vii) A notice under the provisions of section 25 of the Act, being a notice terminating a tenancy to which Part II of the Act applies, shall, unless it contains a copy of a certificate given under the provisions of section 57, 58 or 60 of the Act, be in Form 7;

(viii) A notice under the provisions of section 25 of the Act, being a notice terminating a tenancy to which Part II of the Act applies and containing a copy of a certificate given under subsection (1) of section 57 of the Act (whereby the Minister or Board in charge of any Government department certifies that the use or occupation of property or part of it should be changed by a specified date), shall be—

(*a*) in Form 8, where the date of termination of the tenancy specified in the notice is not earlier than the date specified in the certificate; or

(*b*) in Form 9, where the date of termination of the tenancy specified in the notice is earlier than the date specified in the certificate;

(ix) A notice under the provisions of section 25 of the Act, being a notice terminating a tenancy to which Part II of the Act applies and containing a copy of a certificate given under subsection (1) of section 58 of the Act (whereby the Minister or Board in charge of any Government department certifies that for reasons of national security it is necessary that the use or occupation of property should be discontinued or changed), shall be in Form 10;

(x) A notice under the provisions of section 25 of the Act, being a notice terminating a tenancy to which Part II of the Act applies and containing a copy of a certificate given under section 60 of the Act (whereby the Board of Trade certify that it is necessary or expedient for achieving the objects of the Distribution of Industry Acts 1945 and 1950, that the use or occupation of property should be changed), shall be in Form 11;

(xi) A notice under the provisions of section 26 of the Act, being a tenant's request for a new tenancy of premises to which Part II of the Act applies, shall be in Form 12;

(xii) A notice under the provisions of subsection (1) of section 40 of the Act, being a notice requiring a tenant of business premises to give information as to his occupation of the premises and as to any sub-tenancies, shall be in Form 13;

(xiii) A notice served under the provisions of subsection (2) of section 40 of the Act on a landlord of business premises, being a notice requiring that landlord to give information about his interest in the premises, shall be in Form 14;

(xiv) A notice served under the provisions of subsection (2) of section 40 of the Act on a mortgagee to give information about his mortgagor's interest in the premises, shall be in Form 15. **[746]**

NOTES

Words in italics revoked with savings by the Landlord and Tenant Act 1954, Part II (Notices) Regulations 1983, SI 1983 No 133, reg 4, Sch 3.

Distribution of Industry Acts 1945, 1950: see now Local Employment Act 1972.

The Act: Landlord and Tenant Act 1954.

APPENDIX LANDLORD AND TENANT ACT 1954 (REG 4)

1. Form 1 Landlord's Notice proposing a Statutory Tenancy

[To .. .., tenant of premises known as .. ..
.. ..

1. I, ... of.. .. .. , landlord of the above-mentioned premises, hereby give you notice terminating your tenancy of the premises on the .. .. day of .. .. , 19 .. ..

(See Notes 4 & 12)

2. You are requested within 2 months after the giving of this Notice to notify me in writing whether you are willing to give up possession of the premises on the said date.

(See Notes 6 & 7)

Consequences of this Notice if tenant claims the freehold or an extended lease.

3. If you have a right under Part I of the Leasehold Reform Act 1967 to acquire the freehold or an extended lease of property comprised in the tenancy, you must give me notice of your desire to have the freehold or an extended lease not later than 2 months after the service of this Notice: in that event, this Notice will not operate, and I will [or will not, *as the case may be*] be entitled to apply to the county court for possession of the premises under section 17 [*or* 18, *as the case may be*] of that Act and propose (*or* do not propose, *as the case may be*] to do so.

(See Note 3)

4. The following are the names and addresses of other persons known or believed by me to have an interest superior to your tenancy or to be the agent concerned with the premises on behalf of a person having such an interest— [*The names and addresses of any such persons should be stated here*]

Consequences of this Notice if tenant does not claim the freehold or an extended lease.

5. I believe that you are entitled to the protection of Part I of the Landlord and Tenant Act 1954 in respect of the whole of the premises [*or, if part only of the premises qualifies for protection*, in respect of the following part of the premises, namely .. ..], and the proposals contained in the next following paragraph are made on the assumption that the statutory tenancy would be a tenancy of the whole of the premises [*or* the said part of the premises].

(See Note 2)

6. If you are not willing to give up possession of the premises on the.. .. .. day of .. .., 19 .. .. , I propose that you should continue as a statutory tenant of the premises [*or* of the said part of the premises] on the following terms—

(See Note 5)

[*Here should be stated—*

(i) rent, intervals at which rent is to be paid and whether payable in advance or in arrear;
(ii) whether any, and if so what, initial repairs are to be carried out;
(iii) which, if any, of the initial repairs are to be carried out by the landlord and which, if any, by the tenant;
(iv) which, if any, of the initial repairs are to be carried out by the landlord are required in consequence of failure by the tenant to fulfil his obligations under the current tenancy, and the estimated cost of such repairs (excluding any part recoverable otherwise than from the tenant or his predecessors in title);

(v) what amount the landlord proposes that the tenant should pay in respect of the cost incurred by the landlord in ascertaining the initial repairs set out in item (iv);
(vi) whether payment for the amounts mentioned in items (iv) and (v) above is to be made by instalments or otherwise, and if by instalments, the amount of each instalment, the time at which the first is to be payable and the frequency of the instalments;
(vii) obligations as to repairs other than the initial repairs mentioned above;
(viii) any other terms.]

(See Notes 8, 9 & 10)

If the amount of the rent cannot be settled by agreement between us, I propose to apply to the rent officer for the registration of a fair rent.

If any of the other terms cannot be settled by agreement between us, I propose to apply to the county court for a determination.

[*Paragraph 7 should be struck out, if not required*

7. If you continue in possession of the premises I require a record to be made of the state of repair of the premises as soon as may be after the completion of the initial repairs or, if the carrying out of the initial repairs is not agreed between us or determined by the county court, as soon as may be after the beginning of the statutory tenancy.]

(See Note 11)

8. This Notice is given under the provisions of section 4 of the Landlord and Tenant Act 1954.

Your attention is called to the Notes below.

Dated this .. .. day of .. .. .., 19 .. ..

Signed .. .. (Landlord)

.. .. (Address)

Form 1

Notes

1. Part I of the Landlord and Tenant Act 1954, as amended by the Leasehold Reform Act 1967, provides that a tenant of residential premises under a tenancy granted for more than 21 years at a rent which is less than two-thirds of the rateable value of the premises shall, at the end of the period of the original tenancy, be entitled to continue as a tenant on the same terms as before unless he terminates the tenancy himself or it is terminated by the landlord in accordance with the provisions of the Act. For the purposes of the Act the reateable value is normally that shown in the valuation list on 23rd March 1965. The rateable value of the premises must not, however, have exceeded £400 in Greater London or £200 elsewhere.

2. The tenant's right to remain in occupation is confined to parts of the premises which he occupies at the end of the original tenancy.

3. Your rights under Part I of the Landlord and Tenant Act 1954 are in addition to, and distinct from, any right you may have under the Leasehold Reform Act 1967 to acquire the freehold or an extended lease of the premises. Any such right must, however, be exercised by service of the appropriate notice

(in the form prescribed by the Leasehold Reform (Notices) Regulations 1967) within 2 months of the giving of this Notice. As a general rule, a person has such a right if:—

(*a*) he has his only or main residence in a house which he occupies under a tenancy granted for more than 21 years at a rent which is less than two-thirds of its rateable value;
(*b*) he has so occupied the house for at least the previous 5 years or a total of 5 out of the previous 10 years; and
(*c*) the house has a rateable value not exceeding £400 in Greater London, or £200 elsewhere.

4. The landlord may terminate the tenancy by notice which, as a general rule, must be given not more than 12 nor less than 6 months before the date of termination specified in the notice. That date must not normally be earlier than the date on which the original tenancy expires. When the landlord terminates the tenancy, he may (*a*) propose in its place a statutory tenancy under the Rent Act 1965, or (*b*) give notice of his intention to apply to the court for possession of the premises.

5. This is a notice proposing a statutory tenancy. It sets out the landlord's proposals for the terms of your future tenancy should you decide that you wish to remain in possession of the premises, and do not have the right to acquire the freehold or an extended lease of the premises under the Leasehold Reform Act 1967, or have that right but do not wish to exercise it.

6. If you wish to give up possession of the premises comprised in the tenancy, you should notify the landlord to that effect within 2 months of the giving of this Notice and vacate the premises on the date of termination specified in it. Failure to notify the landlord may lead to an unnecessary application to the county court and consequent expense, which you may have to bear.

7. If you do not wish to give up possession of the premises comprised in the tenancy, you should within 2 months after the giving of this Notice notify the landlord to that effect. This will ensure that you do not lose the right conferred by the Landlord and Tenant Act 1954 to remain in possession as a statutory tenant on terms to be agreed between you and the landlord, or settled by the county court or the rent officer, as appropriate. If you fail to notify the landlord and are not in occupation of the premises 2 months after the giving of this Notice, you may lose the protection of the Act. If you fail to notify the landlord, but are in occupation 2 months after the giving of this Notice, you will not lose that protection.

8. After this Notice has been given, it will be open to you and the landlord to settle the terms of the statutory tenancy by agreement. If you cannot agree, the landlord may apply to the county court for a decision on any of the terms except the rent, which will be fixed as set out in Note 10 below.

9. The terms of the statutory tenancy may provide for the carrying out of certain repairs at the start of the tenancy. These are known as "initial repairs". You cannot be required to carry out any initial repairs yourself unless you are willing to do so. If the landlord carries out initial repairs he will be entitled to recover from you (*a*) the reasonable cost of the repairs, in so far as they are required in consequence of your failure to fulfil your obligations under your current tenancy; and (*b*) the reasonable cost of ascertaining what repairs are required for this reason. Whatever the obligations under your current tenancy, the Act provides that you will not be obliged to pay for more initial repairs than

are needed to bring the premises into good repair, having regard to their age, character and locality.

If it is proposed that the terms of the statutory tenancy should include provisions for initial repairs, several matters relating to the repairs and payment for them will have to be agreed between you and the landlord, or determined by the court. These are—

(i) what, if any, initial repairs are required;
(ii) which, if any, of them are to be carried out by you, and which by the landlord;
(iii) which of the repairs to be carried out by the landlord are to be paid for by you;
(iv) whether any such payment is to be made by lump sum or by instalments and, if by instalments, the amount of each and the tems for payment.

10. If you and the landlord cannot agree the amount of the rent (or if you or the landlord wish to have a fair rent registered), an application for the registration of a fair rent may be made to the rent officer by the landlord, or by you, or by the landlord and you jointly. In determining a fair rent regard will be had to all the circumstances (other than personal circumstances and excluding scarcity value) and in particular to the state in which the dwelling house will be when the initial repairs, if any, have been completed. An objection may be made to the rent officer's determination by either party, in which case the matter is referred to a rent assessment committee.

11. The Act enables the landlord to require that, if you retain possession of the premises, a record shall be made of their state of repair as soon as may be after the completion of the initial repairs or, in the absence of any agreement or determination requiring the carrying out of initial repairs, as soon as may be after the beginning of the statutory tenancy. If this Notice does not require a record to be made and you do not wish to give up possession, you may include such a requirement in your notificatin to the landlord that you are unwilling to give up possession. Any record required to be made will have to be made by a person appointed by the landlord and yourself, of, if you and the landlord cannot agree, by the President of the Royal Institution of Chartered Surveyors; and the cost of making the record will, in default of agreement, have to be met by the landlord and yourself in equal shares.

12. The term "landlord" for the purposes of this Notice does not necessarily mean the landlord to whom you pay the rent; it means the person who is your landlord for the purposes of Part I of the Act.] **[747]**

NOTES
Substituted by SI 1967 No 1831.

2. Form 2 Landlord's Notice to resume Possession

[To .. .., tenant of premises known as .. ..

1. I, ... of .. .., landlord of the above-mentioned premises, hereby give you notice terminating your tenancy of the said premises on the .. .. day of.. .. .. .. 19.. ..

(See Notes 4 & 10)

2. You are requested within 2 months after the giving of this Notice to

notify me in writing whether you are willing to give up possession of the premises on the said date.

(See Notes 5 & 6)

Consequences of this Notice if tenant claims the freehold or an extended lease

3. If you have a right under Part I of the Leasehold Reform Act 1967 to acquire the freehold or an extended lease of property comprised in the tenancy, you must give me notice of your desire to have the freehold or an extended lease not later than 2 months after the service of this Notice: in that event, this Notice will not operate, and I will [*or* will not, *as the case may be*] be entitled to apply to the county court for possession of the premises under section 17 [*or* 18, *as the case may be*] of that Act and propose [*or* do not propose, *as the case may be*] to do so.

(See Note 3)

4. The following are the names and addresses of other persons known or believed by me to have an interest superior to your tenancy or to be the agent concerned with the premises on behalf of a person having such an interest—[*The names and addresses of any such persons should be stated here*]

Consequences of this Notice if tenant does not claim the freehold or an extended lease

5. I believe that you are entitled to the protection of Part I of the Landlord and Tenant Act 1954 in respect of the whole of the premises [*or, if part only of the premises qualifies for protection*, in respect of the following part of the premises, namely .. ..].

(See Note 2)

6. If you are not willing to give up possession of the premises on the .. .. day of .. .., 19 .. .., I propose to apply to the county court for possession of the premises on the ground that [*here state ground or grounds*]

(See Notes 7 & 8)

7. This Notice is given under the provisions of section 4 of the Landlord and Tenant Act 1954.

Your attention is called to the Notes below.

Dated this .. .. day of.. .. .. .., 19.. .. ..

Signed.. .. ..(Landlord)

.. ..(Address)

Form 2

Notes

1. Part I of the Landlord and Tenant Act 1954, as amended by the Leasehold Reform Act 1967, provides that a tenant of residential premises under a tenancy granted for more than 21 years at a rent which is less than two-thirds of the rateable value of the premises shall, at the end of the period of the original tenancy, be entitled to continue as a tenant on the same terms as before unless he terminates the tenancy himself or it is terminated by the landlord in accordance with the provisions of the Act. For the purposes of the Act the reateable value is normally that shown in the valuation list on 23rd March 1965:

the rateable value of the premises must not, however, have exceeded £400 in Greater London or £200 elsewhere.

2. The tenant's right to remain in occupation is confined to parts of the premises which he occupies at the end of the original tenancy.

3. Your rights under Part I of the Landlord and Tenant Act 1954 are in addition to, and distinct from, any right you may have under the Leasehold Reform Act 1967 to acquire the freehold or an extended lease of the premises. Any such right must, however, be exercised by service of the appropriate notice (in the form prescribed by the Leasehold Reform (Notices) Regulations 1967) within two months of the giving of this Notice. As a general rule, a person has such a right if:—

(*a*) he has his only or main residence in a house which he occupies under a tenancy granted for more than 21 years at a rent which is less than two-thirds of its rateable value;
(*b*) he has so occupied the house for at least the previous 5 years or a total of 5 out of the previous 10 years; and
(*c*) the house has a rateable value not exceeding £400 in Greater London, or £200 elsewhere.

4. The landlord may terminate the tenancy by notice given not more than 12 nor less than 6 months before the date of termination specified in the notice. That date must not normally be earlier than the date on which the original tenancy expires.

5. If you are willing to give up possession of the premises comprised in the tenancy, you should notify the landlord to that effect within 2 months of the giving of this Notice and vacate the premises on the date of termination specified in it. Failure to notify the landlord may lead to an unnecessary application to the county court and consequent expense, which you may have to bear.

6. If you are not willing to give up possession of the premises comprised in the tenancy you should within 2 months after the giving of this Notice notify the landlord to that effect. This will ensure that you do not lose the right conferred by the Landlord and Tenant Act 1954 to remain in possession unless the landlord obtains an order for possession of the premises from the county court. If you fail to notify the landlord and are not in occupation of the premises 2 months after the giving of this notice, you may lose the protection of the Act. If you fail to notify the landlord, but are in occupation 2 months after the giving of this notice, you will not lose that protection.

7. The grounds on which a landlord may apply for possession are—

(i) that suitable alternative accommodation will be available for the tenant at the date of termination of the tenancy;
(ii) that the tenant has failed to comply with any term of the tenancy as to payment of rent or rates or as to insuring or keeping insured any premises;
(iii) that the tenant or a person residing or lodging with him or being his sub-tenant has been guilty of conduct which is a nuisance or annoyance to adjoing occupiers, or has been convicted of using any premises comprised in the tenancy or allowing such premises to be used for an immoral or illegal purpose and, where the person in question is a lodger or sub-tenant, that the tenant has not taken such steps as he ought reasonably to have taken for the removal of the lodger or sub-tenant;

(iv) that the premises, or any part of them which is entitled to protection under the Act, are reasonably required by the landlord for occupation as a residence for himself or any son or daughter of his over 18 years of age or his father, mother, father-in-law or mother-in-law. But the court is precluded from making an order for possession on this ground where the landlord's interest was purchased or created after 18th February 1966, or where it is satisfied that having regard to all the circumstances of the case, including the question whether other accommodation is available for the landlord or the tenant, greater hardship would be caused by making the order than by refusing to make it;

(v) in certain cases where the landlord is a public body, that for the purposes of redevelopment relevant to its functions the landlord proposes after the termination of the tenancy to demolish or reconstruct the whole or a substantial part of the premises.

The landlord must state in this Notice on which of these grounds he proposes to apply for possession.

8. The landlord may apply to the county court for an order for possession on any of the grounds listed above which he has stated in this Notice. In order to succeed in his application he must establish that ground and also, except where he is applying on ground (v) above, satisfy the court that it is reasonable that he should be granted possession. You will be given the opportunity to state your case before the court if you wish to resist the landlord's application.

9. Should the landlord fail in his application for possession this Notice will lapse, but he will then be at liberty to serve a fresh notice on you proposing the new terms on which your tenancy is to continue, and it will be open to you and the landlord either to agree the terms or to have them determined by the court or the rent officer, as appropriate.

10. The term "landlord" for the purposes of this Notice does not necessarily mean the landlord to whom you pay the rent; it means the person who is your landlord for the purposes of Part I of the Act.] **[748]**

NOTES

Substituted by SI 1967 No 1831.

3. Form 3 Notice Requiring Information about Sub-tenancies of Residential Property

To .. .., tenant of premises known as .. ..

1. I, ... of .. .., landlord of the above-mentioned premises hereby require you within one month after receiving this Notice to notify me whether you have a sub-tenant of the whole or any part of the above-named premises.

2. If you have a sub-tenant, I hereby require you to state—

(i) what premises are comprised in the sub-tenancy;

(ii) if the sub-tenancy is for a fixed term, what is the term, or, if the sub-tenancy is terminable by notice, by what notice it can be terminated;

(iii) the rent payable under the sub-tenancy;

(iv) the full name of the sub-tenant; and

(v) whether to the best of your knowledge and belief the sub-tenant is in occupation of the premises sublet to him or any part of them, and, if not, what is the sub-tenant's address.

. This Notice is given under the provisions of section 18 of the Landlord and Tenant Act 1954.

Your attention is called to the Notes below.

Dated this .. ..day of .. .. .. 19.. ..

Signed.. .. ..(Landlord)

.. ..(Address)

Form 3

NOTES

1. Section 18 of the Landlord and Tenant Act 1954 provides that a tenant or sub-tenant of any premises comprised in a tenancy to which the section applies may be required to give information about sublettings at the instance of his immediate landlord or any superior landlord.

2. You are a tenant or sub-tenant for the purposes of section 18 if you hold a tenancy of residential premises granted for a term exceeding 21 years [at a rent which is less than two-thirds of the rateable value of the premises,] or if you are a sub-tenant of a person holding such a tenancy.

3. Accordingly, if you are a tenant or sub-tenant of the premises to which this Notice relates, you should within one month of receipt of this Notice supply the information asked for. If you have sublet to more than one sub-tenant, you should give the required information in respect of each subletting. Failure to give the information asked for or the giving of incorrect information could involve the landlord in loss for which you might in certain circumstances be held liable.

4. The information asked for is required to enable the landlord giving this Notice to ascertain who will be in occupation when the current tenancy comes to an end. The Landlord is entitled to seek this information at any time not earlier than two years before the tenancy is due to expire. **[749]**

NOTES
Amended by SI 1967 No 1831.

4. Form 4 Notice Requiring Instalments to be paid to immediate Landlord

To .. .., tenant of premises known as .. ..

1. I, ... of .. .., your immediate landlord of the above-mentioned premises, and I, ... of .. .., the superior landlord of the said premises entitled to your payment for accrued tenant's repairs under section 8 of the Act, hereby require you to pay future instalments of that payment to the said .. .., your immediate landlord.

2. Under the terms of your statutory tenancy, instalments of £ .. .. are payable by you at intervals of .. .. weeks/months, the next instalment being due on the .. .. day of .. .., 19 .. ..

3. This Notice is given under the provisions of paragraph 8 of the First Schedule to the Landlord and Tenant Act 1954.

Your attention is called to the Notes below.

Dated this .. .. day of .. .. , 19 .. ..

Signed .. .. (Immediate landlord)

.. .. (Address)

.. ..(Superior landlord)

.. .. (Address)

Form 4

NOTES

1. Under the terms of your statutory tenancy you are under an obligation to pay by instalments for accrued tenant's repairs.

2. The Landlord and Tenant Act 1954 provides that, where the immediate landlord's interest in the premises has less than 5 years to run, the person entitled to receive payment for the accrued tenant's repairs is a superior landlord. Accordingly, the person entitled to receive payment of the instalments due from you is not your immediate landlord.

3. Under the provisions of paragraph 8 of the First Schedule to the Act, the superior landlord entitled to receive payment and your immediate landlord may require you to pay the instalments to your immediate landlord for transmission to the superior landlord. After receipt of this Notice you should, therefore, pay the instalments to the person named in this Notice as your immediate landlord.

[750]

5. Form 5 Notice by Competent Landlord Requiring Consent of other Landlord to Notice under section 4(1)

To .. .. , of .. ..

1. Take notice that I propose to give to .. .. , the tenant of premises known as .. .., of which I am the landlord for the purposes of Part I of the Act and you are another landlord, a landlord's notice proposing a statutory tenancy [*or* a landlord's notice to resume possession], a copy of which is attached hereto;

2. And further take notice that I require you within one month after service of this Notice to inform me in writing whether you consent to the giving of the said notice.

3. This Notice is given under the provisions of paragraph 5 of the Fifth Schedule to the Landlord and Tenant Act 1954.

Your attention is called to the Notes below.

Dated this .. .. day of .. .. , 19 .. .. ..

Signed .. .. (Landlord)

.. ..(Address)

[*Attach copy of Landlord's Notice proposing a Statutory Tenancy or, as the case may be, Landlord's Notice to Resume Possession.*]

Form 5

NOTES

1. This Notice requires you to give your consent to a landlord's notice proposing a statutory tenancy or a landlord's notice to resume possession in respect of premises of which you are a superior or intermediate landlord.

2. Under the provisions of the Landlord and Tenant Act 1954, a notice proposing a statutory tenancy or a notice to resume possession can be given to the tenant only by the person who is his landlord for the purposes of Part I of the Act. Under the Fifth Schedule to the Act such a notice is binding on every other landlord, but any such landlord (except one whose interest has two months or less to run after the termination of the tenant's interest) who suffers loss in consequence of the giving of such a notice is entitled to compensation unless his written consent to it has been obtained.

3. If you do not give your consent within one month after service of this Notice, or give it subject to conditions which the county court considers unreasonable, that court may, on the application of the landlord giving this Notice, order that you shall be deemed to have consented either without qualification or subject to such conditions (including conditions as to the modification of the proposed notice or as to payment to you of compensation) as it may specify.

4. You may make it a condition of your consent that such repairs as you may specify shall be included in the initial repairs which the landlord giving this Notice will specify as repairs which he is willing to carry out, when he applies to the court for a determination of the terms on which the tenant is to continue in occupation. **[751]**

6. Form 6 Notice by Competent Landlord Requiring Consent of other Landlord to Agreement under Part I

To .. .., of .. ..

1. Take notice that I propose to make an agreement with .. .. , the tenant of premises known as .. .. , of which I am the landlord for the purposes of Part I of the Act and you are another landlord, concerning the terms of a statutory tenancy under Part I of the Act [*or as the case may be*] and that the terms of the proposed agreement are those set out in the Schedule to this Notice;

2. And further take notice that I require you within one month after service of this Notice to inform me in writing whether you consent to the making of the agreement.

3. This Notice is given under the provisions of paragraph 5 of the Fifth Schedule to the Landlord and Tenant Act 1954.

Your attention is called to the Notes below.

Dated this .. .. day of .. .. .., 19.. .. ..

Signed .. .. (Landlord)

.. ..(Address)

THE SCHEDULE

[*Here set out the terms of the proposed agreement*]

Form 6

NOTES

1. This Notice requires you to give your consent to an agreement under Part I of the Landlord and Tenant Act 1954 in respect of premises of which you are a superior or intermediate landlord.

2. Under the provisions of the Act such an agreement can be made only between the tenant and the person who is the landlord for the purposes of Part I of the Act. Under the Fifth Schedule to the Act such an agreement is binding on every other landlord, but any such landlord (except one whose interest has two months or less to run after the termination of the tenant's interest) who suffers loss in consequence of the making of such an agreement is entitled to compensation unless his written consent to it has been obtained.

3. If you do not give your consent within one month after service of this Notice, or give it subject to conditions which the county court considers unreasonable, that court may, on the application of the landlord giving this Notice, order that you shall be deemed to have consented either without qualification or subject to such conditions (including conditions as to the modification of the proposed agreement or as to payment to you of compensation) as it may specify.

4. You may make it a condition of your consent that such repairs as you may specify shall be included in the initial repairs which the landlord giving this Notice will agree to carry out under the terms of the proposed agreement.

[752]

7. Form 7 Landlord's Notice to Terminate Business Tenancy

[To .. .. , of .. .. , tenant of premises known as .. ..

1. I, ... of .. .. , landlord of the above-mentioned premises, hereby give you notice terminating your tenancy on the .. .. day of.. .. .. , 19.. .. .. ..

(See Note 1.)

2. You are required within two months after the giving of this Notice to notify me in writing whether or not you will be willing to give up possession of the premises on that date.

(See Note 2.)

3. I would not oppose an application to the Court under Part II of the Act for a grant of a new tenancy, or

(See Note 6.)

I would oppose an application to the Court under Part II of the Act for the grant of a new tenancy on the ground that [state ground or grounds].

(See Note 4.)

4. This Notice is given under the provisions of section 25 of the Landlord and Tenant Act 1954.

Your attention is called to the Notes below.

Dated this . . . . day of . . . . , 19 . . . .

Signed . . . . (Landlord)

. . . . .(Address)

Form 7

NOTES

1. Under the Landlord and Tenant Act 1954, a tenancy of premises to which Part II of the Act applies continues until it is brought to an end in accordance with the Act. One of the ways in which it can be brought to an end is by a landlord's notice to terminate the tenancy. As a general rule, that notice must be given not more than 12 nor less than 6 months before the date specified in it for the termination of the current tenancy of the premises. This date must not be earlier than the date on which apart from Part II of the Act the current tenancy would expire or could be terminated by notice to quit given by the landlord on the date of the notice.

2. Part II of the Act enables the tenant, on being served with a notice in this form, to apply to the court for an order for the grant of a new tenancy. Such an application, however, will not be entertained unless the tenant has within 2 months after the giving of the notice terminating the tenancy notified the landlord in writing that he will not be willing to give up possession of the premises on the date specified in the notice. The application must be made not less than 2 or more than 4 months after the giving of the notice.

3. Where the rateable value of the premises (excluding any part which is not occupied by the tenant or by an employee in his business) does not exceed [£5,000], an application for an order for the grant of a new tenancy must be made to the County Court and in any other case it must be made to the High Court.

4. The court has no power to make an order for the grant of a new tenancy if the landlord, having stated in his notice that he will oppose an application to the court on one of the grounds specified in the Act, establishes that ground to the satisfaction of the court. The grounds specified in the Act are—

(a) where under the current tenancy the tenant has any obligations as respects the repair and maintenance of the premises, that the tenant ought not to be granted a new tenancy in view of the state of repair of the premises which has resulted from the tenant's failure to comply with these obligations;

(b) that the tenant ought not to be granted a new tenancy in view of his persistent delay in paying rent which has become due;

(c) that the tenant ought not to be granted a new tenancy in view of other substantial breaches by him of his obligations under the current tenancy, or for any other reason connected with the tenant's use or management of the premises;

(d) that the landlord has offered and is willing to provide or secure the provision of alternative accommodation for the tenant, that the terms on which the alternative accommodation is available are reasonable having regard to the terms of the current tenancy and to all other relevant circumstances, and that the accommodation and the time at which it will be available are suitable for the tenant's requirements (including the

requirement to preserve goodwill) having regard to the nature and class of his business and to the situation and extent of, and facilities afforded by, the premises which he occupies;

(*e*) *where the current tenancy was created by the subletting of part only of the property comprised in a superior tenancy, that the aggregate of the rents reasonably obtainable on separate lettings of the tenant's premises and the remainder of that property would be substantially less than the rent reasonably obtainable on a letting of that property as a whole, and that on the termination of the current tenancy the landlord requires possession of the tenant's premises for the purpose of letting or otherwise disposing of the said property as a whole and therefore the tenant ought not to be granted a new tenancy;*

(*f*) *that on the termination of the current tenancy the landlord intends to demolish or reconstruct the whole or a substantial part of the premises or to carry out substantial work of construction on the whole or part of them and that he could not reasonably do so without obtaining possession of the premises; but where the landlord opposes the application on this ground, the court can still order the grant of a new tenancy, if*

(*i*) *the tenant agrees to the inclusion in the new tenancy of terms giving the landlord facilities for carrying out the work intended and, given those facilities, the landlord could reasonably carry out the work without obtaining possession of the tenant's premises and without interfering to a substantial extent or for a substantial time with the use of the premises for the tenant's business; or*

(*ii*) *the tenant is willing to accept a tenancy of a part of the premises, which can be let separately without substantially reducing the rental income obtainable from the entire premises, and either the tenant agrees to give the landlord facilities for carrying out work as under paragraph (i) above, or possession of the remainder of the premises would be reasonably sufficient to enable the landlord to carry out the intended work;*

(*g*) *that on the termination of the current tenancy the landlord intends to occupy the premises for the purposes, or partly for the purposes, of a business to be carried on by him in them or as his residence; but the landlord cannot rely on this ground if his interest was purchased or created less than 5 years before the termination of the current tenancy and at all times since the purchase or creation of the landlord's interest the premises have been let to a tenant occupying them for the purposes of his business.*

5. *If the only grounds for opposing an application for the grant of a new tenancy stated in paragraph 3 of this notice are grounds set out in (e),* (*f*) and (*g*) above, the tenant is entitled on leaving the premises to recover compensation from the landlord at the rate specified in the Act. If other grounds are also stated, the tenant is entitled to the compensation if the court on an application for a new tenancy finds that it is precluded from making an order by reason only of any of the grounds set out in (*e*), (*f*) and (*g*).

6. *If the landlord states in this notice that he will not oppose an application to the court for the grant of a new tenancy, it will be open to the tenant and the landlord to negotiate on the terms of the tenancy. If all the terms are agreed between them, an application to the court will not be necessary; if some but not all of the terms are agreed, the agreed terms will be incorporated in any tenancy granted by the court and the other terms will be such as the court may determine. A new tenancy, if granted by the court, will not include any part of the property comprised in the*

current tenancy which is occupied neither by the tenant, nor by a person employed by him for the purposes of his business, unless the landlord requires the new tenancy to include the whole of the property.

7. The term "landlord" in this notice does not necessarily mean the landlord to whom the rent is paid; it means the person who is the landlord for the purposes of Part II of the Act. The term "business" includes a trade, profession or employment and any activity carried on by a body of persons, whether corporate or unincorporate. **[753]**

NOTES

Commencement: 1 January 1970.

Revoked with savings by the Landlord and Tenant Act 1954, Part II (Notices) Regulations 1983, SI 1983 No 133, reg 4, Sch 3.

Substituted by SI 1969 No 1771; amended by SI 1973 No 792.

8. Form 8 Landlord's Notice to Terminate Business Tenancy on Grounds of Public Interest

To . . . ., tenant of premises known as . . . .

1. I, ..., landlord of the above-mentioned premises, hereby give you notice terminating your tenancy on the . . . . day of . . . ., 19 . . . .

(See Note 1.)

2. A certificate has been given by . . . . that it is requisite for the purposes of the [here insert name of Government department or local authority, statutory undertakers, development corporation, or as the case may be] that the use or occupation of the property or of a part thereof shall be changed by the . . . . . . day of . . . . , 19 . . . . , and a copy of the certificate is set out in the schedule to this Notice.

(See Note 2.)

3. This Notice is given under the provisions of section 25 and section 57 of the Landlord and Tenant Act 1954.

Your attention is called to the Notes below.

Dated this . . . . . . day of . . . . , 19 . . . .

Signed . . . .

for . . . . (Landlord)

. . . . (Address)

THE SCHEDULE

[Here insert a copy of the relevant certificate]

Form 8

NOTES

1. Under the Landlord and Tenant Act 1954, a tenancy of premises to which Part II of the Act applies continues until it is brought to an end in accordance with the Act. One of the ways in which it can be brought to an end is by a landlord's notice to terminate the tenancy. As a general rule, that notice must be given not more than 12 nor less than 6 months before the date specified in it for the termination of the current tenancy. This date must not be earlier than the date on which apart from Part II of the Act the current tenancy would expire or could be terminated by notice to quit given by the landlord on the date of the notice.

2. The Notice you are now given contains a copy of the certificate stating that a change in the use or occupation of the premises or part of them is required for the purposes of a Government department or public body. Where such a certificate has been given in accordance with the provisions of the Act, and the date on which the change is stated to be required is not later than the date of termination of your tenancy specified in paragraph 1 of this Notice, no application for the grant of a new tenancy can be made to the court.

3. On quitting the premises, a tenant who is precluded from applying to the court for a new tenancy by reason of a Ministerial certificate is generally entitled to recover compensation from the landlord at the rate specified in section 37 of the Act.

4. The term "landlord" in this Notice does not necessarily mean the landlord to whom the rent is paid; it means the person, Government department or public body who is the landlord for the purposes of Part II of the Act. **[754]**

NOTES

Revoked with savings by the Landlord and Tenant Act 1954, Part II (Notices) Regulations 1983, SI 1983 No 133, reg 4, Sch 3.

9. Form 9 Landlord's Notice to Terminate' Business Tenancy where Change Required at Future Date on Grounds of Public Interest

[To ...., tenant of premises known as ....

1. I, ..., landlord of the above-mentioned premises, hereby give you notice terminating your tenancy on the .... day of..........., 19 ......

(See Note 1.)

2. You are required within two months after the giving of this Notice to notify me in writing whether or not you will be willing to give up possession of the premises on that date.

(See Note 2.)

3. A certificate has been given by .... that it is requisite for the purposes of the .... [insert name of Government department, local authority, statutory undertakers, development corporation, or as the case may be] that the use or occupation of the property or of a part of the property shall be changed by the .... day of..........., 19 ...... and a copy of the certificate is set out in the schedule to this Notice.

(See Note 2.)

4. I would not oppose an application to the court under Part II of the Act for the grant of a new tenancy terminating on or before the .....day of ......, 19 ......, or

(See Note 6.)

I would oppose an application to the court under Part II of the Act for the grant of a new tenancy on the ground that .... [state ground or grounds].

(See Note 4.)

5. This Notice is given under the provisions of section 25 and section 57 of the Landlord and Tenant Act 1954.

Your attention is called to the Notes below.

Dated this .... day of ...., 19 .....
Signed ....
for ....(Landlord)
..................(Address)

THE SCHEDULE

[Insert a copy of the relevant certificate]

Form 9

NOTES

1. Under the Landlord and Tenant Act 1954 a tenancy of premises to which Part II of the Act applies continues until it is brought to an end in accordance with the Act. One of the ways in which it can be brought to an end is by a landlord's notice to terminate the tenancy. As a general rule, that notice must be given not more than 12 nor less than 6 months before the date specified in it for the termination of the current tenancy. This date must not be earlier than the date on which apart from Part II of the Act the current tenancy would expire, or could be terminated by notice to quit given by the landlord on the date of the notice.

2. Part II of the Act enables the tenant, on being served with a notice in this form, to apply to the court for an order for the grant of a new tenancy. Such an application, however, will not be entertained unless the tenant has within 2 months after the giving of the notice terminating the tenancy notified the landlord in writing that he will not be willing to give up possession of the premises on the date specified in the notice. The application must be made not less than 2 nor more than 4 months after the giving of the notice.

The notice you are now given contains a copy of a certificate stating that a change in the use or occupation of the premises or part of them is required for the purposes of a Government department or public body. The date on which the change is stated to be required is later than the date of termination of your tenancy specified in paragraph 1 of this notice. Where such a certificate has been given in accordance with the provisions of the Act, any new tenancy granted by the court must expire on or before the date stated in the certificate.

3. Where the rateable value of the premises (exluding any part which is not occupied by the tenant or by an employee in his business) does not exceed [£5,000], an application for an order for the grant of a new tenancy must be made to the County Court and in any other case it must be made to the High Court.

4. The court has no power to make an order for the grant of a new tenancy if the landlord has stated in this notice that he will oppose an application to the court on one of the grounds specified in the Act, and establishes that ground to the court's satisfaction. The grounds specified in the Act are—

- *(a) where under the current tenancy the tenant has any obligations as respects the repair and maintenance of the premises, that the tenant ought not to be granted a new tenancy in view of the state of repair of the premises which has resulted from the tenant's failure to comply with these obligations;*
- *(b) that the tenant ought not to be granted a new tenancy in view of his persistent delay in paying rent which has become due;*

(c) that the tenant ought not to be granted a new tenancy in view of other substantial breaches by him of his obligations under the current tenancy, or for any other reason connected with the tenant's use or management of the premises;

(d) that the landlord has offered and is willing to provide or secure the provision of alternative accommodation for the tenant, that the terms on which the alternative accommodation is available are reasonable having regard to the terms of the current tenancy and to all other relevant circumstances, and that the accommodation and the time at which it will be available are suitable for the tenant's requirements (including the requirement to preserve goodwill) having regard to the nature and class of his business and to the situation and extent of, and facilities afforded by, the premises which he occupies;

(e) where the current tenancy was created by the subletting of part only of the property comprised in a superior tenancy, that the aggregate of the rents reasonably obtainable on separate lettings of the tenant's premises and the remainder of that property would be substantially less than the rent reasonably obtainable on a letting of that property as a whole, and that on the termination of the current tenancy the landlord requires possession of the tenant's premises for the purpose of letting or otherwise disposing of the said property as a whole and therefore the tenant ought not to be granted a new tenancy;

(f) that on the termination of the current tenancy the landlord intends to demolish or reconstruct the whole or a substantial part of the premises or to carry out substantial work of construction on the whole or part of them and that he could not reasonably do so without obtaining possession of the premises; but where the landlord opposes the application on this ground the court can still order the grant of a new tenancy, if

(i) the tenant agrees to the inclusion in the new tenancy of terms giving the landlord facilities for carrying out the work intended and, given those facilities, the landlord could reasonably carry out the work without obtaining possession of the tenant's premises and without interfering to a substantial extent or for a substantial time with the use of the premises for the tenant's business; or

(ii) the tenant is willing to accept a tenancy of a part of the premises, which can be let separately without substantially reducing the rental income obtainable from the entire premises, and either the tenant agrees to give the landlord facilities for carrying out work as under paragraph (i) above, or possession of the remainder of the premises would be reasonably sufficient to enable the landlord to carry out the intended work;

(g) that on the termination of the current tenancy the landlord intends to occupy the premises for the purposes, or partly for the purposes, of a business to be carried on by him in them or as his residence; but the landlord cannot rely on this ground if his interest was purchased or created less than 5 years before the termination of the current tenancy and at all times since the purchase or creation of the landlord's interest the premises have been let to a tenant occupying them for the purposes of his business.

5. If no grounds for opposing an application for the grant of a new tenancy are stated in paragraph 4 of this notice or if the only grounds there stated are those set out in (*e*), (*f*) and (*g*) above, the tenant is entitled on leaving the premises to recover compensation from the landlord at the rate specified in the Act. If other grounds are also stated, the tenant is entitled to the compensation if the court on an application for a new tenancy finds that it is precluded from making an order by reason only of any of the grounds set out in (*e*), (*f*) and (*g*). If the court makes an order for a new tenancy but is precluded from ordering a new tenancy expiring later than the date specified in the Ministerial certificate, the tenant may similarly be entitled to compensation.

6. If the landlord states in this notice that he will not oppose an application to the court for the grant of a new tenancy, it will be open to the tenant and the landlord to negotiate on the terms of the tenancy. If all the terms are agreed between them, an application to the court will not be necessary; if some but not all of the terms are agreed, the agreed terms will be incorporated in any tenancy granted by the court and the other terms will be such as the court may determine. If the court grants a new tenancy it will not include any part of the property comprised in the current tenancy which is occupied neither by the tenant nor by a person employed by him for the purposes of his business, unless the landlord requires the new tenancy to include the whole of the property.

7. The term "landlord" in this notice does not necessarily mean the landlord to whom the rent is paid; it means the person or body who is the landlord for the purposes of Part II of the Act. The term "business" includes a trade, profession or employment and any activity carried on by a body of persons, whether corporate or unincorporate.] **[755]**

NOTES
Commencement: 1 January 1970.
Revoked with savings by the Landlord and Tenant Act 1954, Part II (Notices) Regulations 1983, SI 1983 No 133, reg 4, Sch 3.
Substituted by SI 1969 No 1771; amended by SI 1973 No 792.

10. Form 10 Landlord's Notice to Terminate Business Tenancy on Grounds of National Security

[To ...., tenant of premises known as ....

1. I, ... , landlord of the above-mentioned premises, hereby give you notice terminating your tenancy on the .... day of ...... , 19 ....

(See Note 1.)

2. A certificate has been given by .... that it is necessary for reasons of national security that the use or occupation of the property should be discontinued or changed, and a copy of the certificate is set out in the schedule to this Notice.

(See Note 2.)

3. This Notice is given under the provisions of section 25 and section 58 of the Landlord and Tenant Act 1954.

Your attention is called to the Notes below.

Dated this .... day of ...., 19 .....

Signed ....

for .... (Landlord)

.... (Address)

The Schedule

[Here insert a copy of the relevant certificate]

Form 10

Notes

1. Under the Landlord and Tenant Act 1954, a tenancy of premises to which Part II of the Act applies continues until it is brought to an end in accordance with the Act. One of the ways in which it can be brought to an end is by a landlord's notice to terminate the tenancy. As a general rule, that notice must be given not more than 12 nor less than 6 months before the date specified in it for the termination of the current tenancy. This date must not be earlier than the date on which apart from Part II of the Act the current tenancy would expire or could be terminated by notice to quit given by the landlord on the date of the notice.

2. The Notice you are now given contains a copy of a certificate stating that it is necessary for reasons of national security that the use or occupation of the premises should be discontinued or changed. Where such a certificate has been given in accordance with the provisions of the Act, no application for the grant of a new tenancy can be made to the court.

3. On quitting the premises a tenant who is precluded from applying to the court for a new tenancy by reason of a Ministerial certificate is generally entitled to recover compensation from the landlord at the rate specified in section 37 of the Act.

4. The term "landlord" in this Notice does not necessarily mean the landlord to whom the rent is paid; it means the person or Government department who is the landlord for the purposes of Part II of the Act. **[756]**

NOTES

Revoked with savings by the Landlord and Tenant Act 1954, Part II (Notices) Regulations 1983, SI 1983 No 133, reg 4, Sch 3.

11. Form 11 Landlord's Notice to Terminate Business Tenancy by reason of the Objects of the Local Employment Act 1972

[To ...., tenant of premises known as ....

1. I, ... , landlord of the above-mentioned premises, hereby give you notice terminating your tenancy on the .... day of ......, 19 ....

2. A certificate has been given by .... that it is necessary or expedient for achieving the objects of the Local Employment Act 1972, that the use or occupation of the property should be changed, and a copy of the certificate is set out in the Schedule to this Notice.

3. This Notice is given under the provisions of sections 25, 58 and 60 of the Landlord and Tenant Act 1954.

Your attention is called to the Notes below.

Dated this .... day of ...., 19 .....

Signed ....

for .... (Landlord)

.... (Address)

THE SCHEDULE

[Here insert a copy of the relevant certificate]

Form 11

NOTES

1. Under the Landlord and Tenant Act 1954, a tenancy of premises to which Part II of the Act applies continues until it is brought to an end in accordance with the Act. One of the ways in which it can be brought to an end is by a landlord's notice to terminate the tenancy. As a general rule, that notice must be given not more than 12 nor less than 6 months before the date specified in it for the termination of the current tenancy. This date must not be earlier than the date on which apart from Part II of the Act the current tenancy would expire or could be terminated by notice to quit given by the landlord on the date of the notice.

2. The Notice you are now given contains a copy of a certificate issued by the Secretary of State for Trade and Industry stating that it is necessary or expedient for achieving the objects of the Local Employment Act 1972, that the use or occupation of the premises should be changed. Where the property comprised in a tenancy consists of premises of which the Secretary of State for Trade and Industry or an Industrial Estates Corporation is the landlord and such a certificate has been given in accordance with the provisions of the Landlord and Tenant Act 1954, no application for the grant of a new tenancy can be made to the court.

3. The term "landlord" in this Notice does not necessarily mean the landlord to whom the rent is paid; it means the person or Government department who is the landlord for the purposes of Part II of the Act.] **[757]**

NOTES

Commencement: 29 May 1973.

Revoked with savings by the Landlord and Tenant Act 1954, Part II (Notices) Regulations 1983, SI 1983 No 133, reg 4, Sch 3.

Substituted by SI 1973 No 792.

12. Form 12 Tenant's Request for New Tenancy of Business Premises

To . . . ., of . . . ., landlord of premises known as . . . .

1. I, ... of . . . ., tenant of the above-mentioned premises, hereby request you to grant me a new tenancy commencing on the . . . . day of . . . ., 19 . . . . . .

2. I propose that the property to be comprised in the new tenancy should be [here state the property.].

(See Note 1.)

3. My proposals as to the rent to be payable under the new tenancy and as to the other tems of the new tenancy are [here state the rent and terms proposed].

(See Note 2.)

4. This Request is made under the provisions of section 26 of the Landlord and Tenant Act 1954.

Your attention is called to the Notes below.

Dated this . . . . . day of . . . . ., 19 . . . . .

Signed . . . . (Tenant)

. . . . . (Address)

Form 12

NOTES

1. Under the Landlord and Tenant Act 1954, a tenant of business premises under a tenancy granted from more than one year may make a Request for a new tenancy commencing on such date as may be specified in the Request. This date must not be more than 12 nor less than 6 months after the making of the Request and it must not be earlier than the date on which apart from the Act the current tenancy would expire or could be terminated by a notice to quit given by the tenant. If a Request is made, the current tenancy will terminate immediately before the date specified in the Request for the beginning of the new tenancy.

2. The Request must set out the tenant's proposals as to the property to be comprised in the new tenancy. This may be either the whole or part of the property comprised in the current tenancy. The Request must also set out the tenant's proposals as to the rent to be payable under the new tenancy and as to the other terms of the new tenancy.

3. If a Request for a new tenancy is not granted by the landlord, the tenant may, not less than 2 nor more than 4 months after the making of the Request, apply to the court for a new tenancy. Where the rateable value of the premises (excluding any part which is not occupied by the tenant or by an employee in his business) does not exceed [£5,000], an application for an order for the grant of a new tenancy must be made to the County Court and in any other case it must be made to the High Court.

4. If you intend to oppose an application to the court for the grant of a new tenancy, you must within 2 months of the making of this Request give notice to the tenant to that effect. In the notice you must state on which of the grounds specified in the Act you will oppose the application. The grounds specified in the Act are—

(a) where under the current tenancy the tenant has any obligation as respects the repair and maintenance of the premises, that the tenant ought not to be granted a new tenancy in view of the state of repair of the premises which has resulted from the tenant's failure to comply with these obligations;

(b) that the tenant ought not to be granted a new tenancy in view of his persistent delay in paying rent which has become due;

(c) that the tenant ought not to be granted a new tenancy in view of other substantial breaches by him of his obligations under the current tenancy, or for any other reason connected with the tenant's use or management of the premises;

(d) that the landlord has offered and is willing to provide or secure the provision of alternative accommodation for the tenant, that the terms on which the alternative accommodation is available are reasonable having regard to the terms of the current tenancy and to all other relevant circumstances, and that the accommodation and the time at which it will be available are suitable for the tenant's requirements (including the requirement to preserve goodwill) having regard to the nature and class of his business and to the situation and extent of, and facilities afforded by, the premises which he occupies;

(e) where the current tenancy was created by the subletting of part only of the property comprised in a superior tenancy, that the aggregate of the rents reasonably obtainable on separate lettings of the tenant's premises

and the remainder of that property would be substantially less than the rent reasonably obtainable on a letting of that property as a whole, and that on the termination of the current tenancy the landlord requires possession of the tenant's premises for the purpose of letting or otherwise disposing of the said property as a whole and therefore the tenant ought not to be granted a new tenancy;

(f) that on the termination of the current tenancy the landlord intends to demolish or reconstruct the whole or a substantial part of the premises or to carry out substantial work of construction on the whole or part of them and that he could not reasonably do so without obtaining possession of the premises;

[but where the landlord opposes the application on this ground, the court can still order the grant of a new tenancy, if

(i) the tenant agrees to the inclusion in the new tenancy of terms giving the landlord facilities for carrying out the work intended and, given those facilities, the landlord could reasonably carry out the work without obtaining possession of the tenant's premises and without interfering to a substantial extent or for a substantial time with the use of the premises for the tenant's business; or

(ii) the tenant is willing to accept a tenancy of a part of the premises, which can be let separately without substantially reducing the rental income obtainable from the entire premises, and either the tenant agrees to give the landlord facilities for carrying out work as under paragraph (i) above, or possession of the remainder of the premises would be reasonably sufficient to enable the landlord to carry out the intended work;]

(g) that on the termination of the current tenancy the landlord intends to occupy the premises for the purposes, or partly for the purposes, of a business to be carried on by him in them or as his residence; but the landlord cannot rely on this ground if his interest was purchased or created less than 5 years before the termination of the current tenancy and at all times since the purchase or creation of the landlord's interest the premises have been let to a tenant occupying them for the purposes of his business.

5. If you do not intend to oppose an application to the court for the grant of a new tenancy, it will be open to you and the tenant to negotiate on the terms of the tenancy. If all the terms are agreed between you, an application the court will not be necessary; if some but not all of the terms are agreed, they will be incorporated in any tenancy granted by the court and the other terms will be such as the court may determine.

6. The term "landlord" in this Request does not necessarily mean the landlord to whom the tenant pays his rent; it means the person who is the tenant's landlord for the purposes of Part II of the Act. The term "business" includes a trade, profession or employment and any activity carried on by a body of persons whether corporate or unincorporate. **[758]**

NOTES

Revoked with savings by the Landlord and Tenant Act 1954, Part II (Notices) Regulations 1983, SI 1983 No 133, reg 4, Sch 3.

Amended by SI 1969 No 1771, 1973 No 792.

13. Form 13 Notice Requiring Information about Occupation and Sub-tenancies of Business Premises

To .. .., of .. .., tenant of premises known as .. ..

I, ... of .. .. , landlord of the above-mentioned premises, hereby require you, within one month of the service of this Notice upon you, to notify me in writing—

(a) whether you occupy the premises or any part of them wholly or partly for the purposes of a business carried on by you, and
(b) whether you have a sub-tenant of the whole or any part of the premises.

If you have a sub-tenant I hereby require you to state—

(i) what premises are comprised in the sub-tenancy;
(ii) if the sub-tenancy is for a fixed term, what is the term, or, if the sub-tenancy is terminable by notice, by what notice it can be terminated;
(iii) the rent payable under the sub-tenancy;
(iv) the full name of the sub-tenant;
(v) whether, to the best of your knowledge and belief, the sub-tenant is in occupation of the premises sublet to him or any part of them, and, if not, what is the sub-tenant's address.

This Notice is given under the provisions of section 40(1) of the Landlord and Tenant Act 1954.

Your attention is called to the Notes below.

Dated this .. ..day of .. .. .. 19.. ..

Signed.. .. ..(Landlord)

.. ..(Address)

Form 13

NOTES

1. Section 40(1) of the Landlord and Tenant Act 1954 provides that a tenant of premises used wholly or partly for a business may be required by his immediate landlord or any superior landlord to state whether he occupies the premises for his business and whether he has sublet. A "business" includes a trade, profession or employment and includes any activity carried on by a body of persons, whether corporate or unincorporate.

2. Accordingly, if you are a tenant of the premises to which this Notice relates, you must give the information asked for within one month of the service of this Notice. If you have sublet to more than one sub-tenant, you should give the required information in respect of each subletting. Failure to give the information asked for or the giving of incorrect information could involve the landlord in loss for which you might in certain circumstances be held liable.

3. The information asked for is required to enable the landlord to ascertain his position under Part II of the Landlord and Tenant Act 1954. A landlord may seek this information at any time not earlier than two years before the current tenancy is due to expire or could be brought to an end by notice to quit served by the landlord.

[759]

NOTES
Revoked with savings by the Landlord and Tenant Act 1954, Part II (Notices) Regulations 1983, SI 1983 No 133, reg 4, Sch 3.

14. Form 14 Notice by Tenant of Business Premises Requiring Information from Landlord about Landlord's Interest

To . . . ., of . . . ., landlord of premises known as . . . .

1. I, ... of . . . ., tenant of the above-mentioned premises, hereby require you, within one month of the service of this Notice upon you, to notify me in writing whether you are the freeholder of the whole or any part of the premises. If you are not the freeholder, I hereby require you to state to the best of your knowledge and belief—

(a) the name and address of the person who is your immediate landlord in respect of the premises or of the part of which you are not the freeholder;
(b) what is the term of your tenancy; and
(c) what is the earliest date (if any) at which your tenancy is terminable by notice to quit given by your immediate landlord.

2. I also require you to notify me whether there is a mortgagee in possession of your interest in the premises and, if so, what is the name and address of the mortgagee and, if there is a receiver appointed by the mortgagee or by the court, of the receiver.

3. This Notice is given under the provisions of section 40(2) of the Landlord and Tenant Act 1954.

Your attention is called to the Notes below.

Dated this . . . . day of . . . ., 19 . . . .

Signed . . . . (Tenant)

. . . . . (Address)

Form 14

NOTES

1. Section 40(2) of the Landlord and Tenant Act 1954 provides that a tenant of premises used wholly or partly for a business may, if his tenancy is for more than one year, require his immediate landlord or any superior landlord to give information about his interests in the property. If the landlord has mortgaged his interest and the mortgagee is in possession; the mortgagee can be required to give this information. A "business" includes a trade, profession or employment and includes any activity carried on by a body of persons, whether corporate or unincorporate.

2. Accordingly, if you are a tenant of the premises to which this Notice relates you must give the information asked for within one month of the service of this Notice. Failure to give this information asked for or the giving of incorrect information could involve the tenant in loss for which you might in certain circumstances be held liable.

3. The information asked for is required to enable the tenant to ascertain who is his landlord for the purposes of Part II of the Landlord and Tenant Act 1954, which in certain circumstances enables a tenant of business premises to obtain a new lease from that landlord. A notice requiring this information cannot be served more than two years before the tenant's current tenancy is due to expire or could be brought to an end by notice to quit served by the landlord. **[760]**

NOTES

Revoked with savings by the Landlord and Tenant Act 1954, Part II (Notices) Regulations 1983, SI 1983 No 133, reg 4, Sch 3.

15. Form 15 Notice by Tenant of Business Premises Requiring Information from Mortgagee about Landlord's Interest

To .. .., of .. .., mortgagee in possession of premises known as .. ..

1. I, ... of .. .., tenant of the above-mentioned premises, hereby require you, within one month of the service of this Notice upon you, to notify me whether your mortgagor is the freeholder of the whole or any part of the premises.

2. If your mortgagor is not the freeholder of the whole of the premises, I hereby require you to state to the best of your knowledge and belief—

(a) the name and address of the person who is your mortgagor's immediate landlord in respect of the premises or of the part of which your mortgagor is not the freeholder;
(b) what is the term of your motgagor's tenancy; and
(c) what is the earliest date (if any) at which the tenancy is terminable by notice to quit given by him immediate landlord.

3. This Notice is given under the provisions of section 40(2) of the Landlord and Tenant Act 1954.

Your attention is called to the Notes below.

Dated this .. .. day of .. .., 19 .. .. ..

Signed .. .. (Tenant)

.. .. (Address)

Form 15

NOTES

1. Section 40(2) of the Landlord and Tenant Act 1954 provides that a tenant of any premises used wholly or partly for a business may, if his tenancy is for more than one year, require his immediate landlord or any superior landlord to give information about his interest in the property. If the landlord has mortgaged his interest and the mortgagee is in possession, the mortgagee can be required to give this information. A "business" includes a trade, profession or employment and includes any activity carried on by a body of persons, whether corporate or unincorporate.

2. Accordingly, if your mortgagor is a landlord of premises to which this Notice relates and you are in possession, you must give the information asked for within one month of the service of this Notice upon you. Failure to give this information or the giving of incorrect information could involve the tenant in loss for which you might in certain circumstances be held liable.

3. The information asked for is required to enable the tenant to ascertain who is his landlord for the purposes of Part II of the Landlord and Tenant Act 1954, which in certain circumstances enables a tenant of business premises to obtain a new lease from that landlord. A notice requiring this information cannot be served more than two years before the tenant's current tenancy is due to expire or could be brought to an end by notice to quit served by the landlord.

4. The term "mortgagee in possession" in this Notice includes a receiver appointed by the mortgagee or by the court. Accordingly, where there is such a receiver, information may be required of him instead of being required of the mortgagee. **[761]**

NOTES

Revoked with savings by the Landlord and Tenant Act 1954, Part II (Notices) Regulations 1983, SI 1983 No 133, reg 4, Sch 3.

16. Form 16 Superior Landlord's Notice Withdrawing Notice to Terminate Business Tenancy

[To .. .., of .. .. tenant of premises known as .. ..

1. Notice terminating your tenancy of the premises has been given you by a Landlord's Notice to Terminate Business Tenancy dated the .. .. given by our landlord, [state name and address]

2. I, ... of .. .., have now become the landlord for the purposes of Part II of the Landlord and Tenant Act 1954, because—

(See Note 1.)

**your landlord's tenancy will expire by effluxion of time on the .. .. day of .. .. 19 .. .. ..,*

or

I have served a notice on your landlord terminating his tenancy on the day of .. .. 19 .. .. ..

[or state for what reason intermediate landlord's interest is coming to an end]

*(*Delete whichever is not appropriate.)*

3. I hereby give you notice that I withdraw the Landlord's Notice referred to in paragraph 1 above, which shall cease to have effect from the date of this Notice.

(See Note 2.)

4. This Notice is given under the provisions of section 44 of and paragraph 6 of the Sixth Schedule to the Landlord and Tenant Act 1954, as amended by section 14 of the Law of Property Act 1969.

Your attention is called to the Notes below.

Dated this .. .. day of .. .. 19 .. .. ..

Signed .. ..

.. .. (Address)

NOTES

1. The "landlord" who can terminate a business tenancy is not necessarily the landlord to whom the rent is paid; it is, broadly, the person who qualifies as landlord for the purposes of Part II of the Landlord and Tenant Act 1954 because he has an interest in the property which is superior to that of the tenant and has at least 14 months to run.

2. This notice can be given by a superior landlord who becomes the landlord for the purposes of the Act and wishes to withdraw a notice to terminate a business tenancy given by the person who previously qualified as the landlord. When this notice is given the earlier notice ceases to have effect, but the tenant may be given a fresh notice terminating the tenancy by the newly qualified landlord. [762]

NOTES

Commencement: 1 January 1970.

Revoked with savings by the Landlord and Tenant Act 1954, Part II (Notices) Regulations 1983, SI 1983 No 133, reg 4, Sch 3.

Added by SI 1969 No 1771.

LEASEHOLD REFORM (NOTICES) REGULATIONS 1967
(SI 1967 NO 1768)

NOTES

Made: 27 November 1967

Authority: Landlord and Tenant Act 1954, s 66; Leasehold Reform Act 1967, s 22(5)

ARRANGEMENT OF REGULATIONS

Regulation	Para
1	[763]
2	[764]
3	[765]
4	[766]

APPENDIX: LEASEHOLD REFORM ACT 1967

Notice of Leaseholder's Claim (reg 4)

1 Form 1 .. .. [767]

Notice in Reply to Leaseholder's Claim (reg 4)

2 Form 2 .. .. [768]

Notice of Leaseholder's Claim under section 28(1)(b)(ii) (reg 4)

3 Form 3 .. .. [769]

1. These Regulations may be cited as the Leasehold Reform (Notices) Regulations 1967 and shall come into operation on 1st January 1968. **[763]**

2. The Interpretation Act 1889 shall apply to the interpretation of these Regulations as it applies to the interpretation of an Act of Parliament. **[764]**

3. In these Regulations, unless the context otherwise requires—

"the Act" means the Leasehold Reform Act 1967;

a Form referred to by number means the Form so numbered in the Appendix to these Regulations. **[765]**

4. The Forms in the Appendix to these Regulations or Forms substantially to the like effect shall be used for the following purposes:—

(i) a tenant's notice of his desire to have the freehold or an extended lease of a house and premises given under Part I of the Act shall be in Form 1;

(ii) a landlord's notice in reply to a tenant's notice of his desire to have the freehold or an extended lease of a house and premises, or in reply to a tenant's notice claiming to be entitled to acquire the freehold or an extended lease, given under Part I of the Act shall be in Form 2;

(iii) a tenant's notice claiming to be entitled to acquire the freehold or an extended lease given under section 28(1) of the Act to a landlord who is a body to which that section applies shall be in Form 3. **[766]**

NOTES

The Act: Leasehold Reform Act 1967.

APPENDIX: LEASEHOLD REFORM ACT 1967

Notice of Leaseholder's Claim (reg 4)

1. Form 1

To [*Name and address of landlord* .. ..] and all others on whom a copy of this notice may be served. (Notes 1, 2 & 3.)

1. Take notice that I, as tenant of the house and premises described in the Schedule hereto, desire to have *[the freehold *or* an extended lease] of the said house and premises. I am making this claim in the exercise of my rights under the Leasehold Reform Act 1967. The particulars on which I rely are set out in the Schedule to this notice.

(*Delete whichever is inapplicable)

2. You are required, if you are both my immediate landlord and the freeholder, to give me, within two months of the service of this notice, a notice in reply in the prescribed form stating whether or not you admit my right to have *[the freehold *or* an extended lease] (subject to any question as to the correctness of the particulars of the house and premises given in this notice) and, if you do not admit my right, stating the grounds upon which you do not admit it.

(*Delete whichever is inapplicable)

(Note 4.)

(*The remaining paragraphs of this form should be deleted where the claimant's immediate landlord is known to be the freeholder of the house and premises.*)

3. If you are not my immediate landlord, or if you are my immediate landlord but not the freeholder, you must comply with the requirements of paragraphs 5 and 6 below, but you need only give me the notice in reply mentioned above if you are the person designated as "the reversioner" in accordance with paragraph 2 of Schedule 1 to the Act. If you are the reversioner, you must give the notice in reply within 2 months of the first service of this notice on any landlord.

(Note 5.)

4. I have served a copy of this notice on the following other person[s] known or believed by me to have an interest in the house and premises superior to my tenancy, namely—

(*The names and addresses of the persons on whom copies of this notice have been served should be stated here.*)

5. You are required to serve a copy of this notice forthwith on any person who is known or believed by you to have such an interest, but is not stated in this notice to have been served with a copy or known by you to have received a copy. If you serve a copy on any person you are required to add his name to the

list of persons receiving copies as set out in paragraph 4 of this notice, and to notify me.

6. If you know who is, or you believe yourself to be, the person designated as the reversioner in accordance with paragraph 2 of Schedule 1 to the Act, you are required to give written notice to me stating whom you know or believe to be the reversioner, and to serve copies of it on all persons known or believed by you to have an interest superior to my tenancy.

(Note 5.)

7. Anyone who receives a copy of this notice is required forthwith to serve a copy on any person who is known or believed by him to have such an interest but is not stated in the copy to have received a copy. If he serves such a further copy on any person he is required to add that person's name to the list of persons receiving copies set out in paragraph 4 of this notice and to notify me.

8. If anyone who receives a copy of this notice knows who is or believes himself to be the person designated as the reversioner he is required to give written notice to me stating whom he knows or believes to be the reversioner and to serve copies of it on all persons known or believed by him to have an interest superior to my tenancy.

(Note 5.)

Dated this .. .. day of .. .. 19 .. .. ..

Signed .. .. (Tenant)

.. .. (Address)

[The name and address of my solicitor or agent, to whom further communications may be sent is .. ..]

THE SCHEDULE

1. *The address of the house.*

2. *Particulars of the house and premises sufficient to identify the property to which the claim extends.*

(Note 6.)

3. *The rateable value of the house and premises on 23rd March 1965 (or on the date such a value was first shown in the valuation list, if this date is after 23rd March 1965).*

4. *Particulars of the tenancy of the house and premises sufficient to identify the instrument creating the tenancy and to show that the tenancy is and has at the material times been a long tenancy at a low rent.*

(Note 7.)

5. *The date on which the claimant acquired the tenancy.*

6. *The periods for which in the last ten years and since acquiring the tenancy, the claimant has and has not occupied the house as his residence; and the following particulars about any such periods during which the claimant has occupied the house as his residence—*

(i) *what parts (if any) of the house have not been in his own occupation and for what periods;*

(ii) *what other residence (if any) he has had and for what periods, and which was his main residence.*

7. *Additional particulars where claimant relies on section 6 or 7 of the Act.* (Note 8.)

Notes

1. Where the tenant's immediate landlord is not the freeholder, the claim may in accordance with the provisions of the Leasehold Reform Act 1967 be served on him or any superior landlord, and copies of the notice must be served by the tenant on anyone else known or believed by him to have an interest superior to his own. (Schedule 3, paragraph 8(1))

2. Where the landlord's interest is subject to a mortgage or other charge and the mortgagee or person entitled to the benefit of the charge is in possession of that interest, or a receiver appointed by him or by the court is in receipt of the rents and profits, the notice may be served either on the landlord or on the person in possession or the receiver. (Schedule 3, paragraph 9(1))

3. Any landlord whose interest is subject to a mortgage or other charge (not being a rent-charge) to secure the payment of money must (subject to special provisions applicable to debenture-holders' charges) on receipt of the claim inform the mortgagee or person entitled to the benefit of the charge. (Schedule 3, paragraph 9(2))

4. The landlord must (unless note 5 applies) serve a notice in reply in Form 2 prescribed in the Leasehold Reform (Notices) Regulations 1967 within two months of service on him of this notice. If he does not admit the tenant's right to have the freehold or an extended lease the notice in reply must state the grounds on which it is not admitted. If the landlord intends to apply to the court for possession of the house and premises in order to redevelop it (section 17) or to occupy it (section 18), his notice must say so. If he does not so intend, but he objects under subsections (4) or (5) of section 2 of the Act to the inclusion in the claim of a part of the house and premises which projects into other property, or to the exclusion from the claim of property let with the house and premises but not occupied with and used for the purposes of the house by any occupant thereof, he must give notice of his objection with or before his notice in reply; unless in his notice in reply he reserves the right to give it later, in which case it must still be given within two months of the service on him of the tenant's notice. If the landlord admits the claim, the admission is binding on him, unless he shows that he was misled by misrepresentation or concealment of material facts, but it does not conclude any question of the correctness of the particulars of the house and premises as set out in the claim. (Schedule 3, paragraph 7)

5. Where the tenant's immediate landlord is not the freeholder any proceedings arising out of the tenant's notice, whether for resisting or for giving effect to the claim, must be conducted by the person who is designated "the reversioner" in accordance with paragraph 2 of Schedule 1 to the Act and he must give the notice in reply. The reversioner means the landlord whose tenancy carries an expectation of possession of the house and premises of 30 years or more after the expiration of all inferior tenancies, and if there is more than one such landlord, it means the landlord whose tenancy is nearest to that of the tenant; if there is no such landlord, it means the owner of the freehold.

The tenant will be informed in the notice in reply if it is given by a landlord acting as the reversioner.

6. "Premises" to be included with the house in the claim are any garage, outhouse, garden, yard and appurtenances which at the time of the notice are let to the tenant with the house and are occupied with and used for the purposes of the house or any part of it by him or by another occupant.

7. Where there have been successive tenancies particulars should be given of each tenancy. In the case of a lease already extended under the Act, the date of the extension and the original term date should be given.

8. Where the claimant is giving the notice by virtue of section 6 (rights of trustees and beneficiaries under trusts) or section 7 (rights of members of family succeeding to tenancy on death) he is required (by paragraph 6(2) of Schedule 3) to adapt the notice and show under paragraph 7 of the Schedule to this notice the additional particulars bringing the claim within section 6 or 7. Where the tenancy is or was vested in trustees the claimant should, for the purposes of a claim made in reliance on section 6 of the Act, state the date when the tenancy was acquired by the trustees, the date when the beneficiary occupied the house by virtue of his interest under the trust, and particulars of any periods of occupation by the beneficiary which are relied upon as bringing the case within section 6 of the Act. Where the claimant was a member of the previous tenant's family and became tenant on the latter's death, then, for the purposes of a claim made in reliance on section 7 of the Act, the claimant should state the date on which the previous tenant acquired the tenancy, particulars of his relationship to the previous tenant and his succession to the tenancy, and particulars in respect of any period of occupation by the previous tenant and by himself on which the claimant relies as bringing the case within section 7 of the Act. **[767]**

Notice in Reply to Leaseholder's Claim (reg 4)

2. Form 2

To [*Name and address of the claimant* .. ..]

(Note 1.)

1. I have received *[a copy of] your notice dated .. .. claiming the right to have *[the freehold *or* an extended lease] of the house and premises described in your notice in accordance with the provisions of the Leasehold Reform Act 1967.

2. *[I admit your right (subject to any question as to the correctness of the particulars given in your notice of the house and premises), *or* I do not admit your right, on the following grounds—

(*State grounds on which the tenant's right is not admitted*) .. ..
.. ..
.. ..]

(Note 2.)

*[3. I intend *[*or* .. .. intends] to apply to the court for possession of the house and premises under *[section 17 *or* section 18] of the Act.]

(Note 3.)

*[4. I reserve the right to give notice under section 2 of the Act of my objection to the exclusion from the house and premises claimed by you of premises let to you with the house and premises but not at present occupied by

you, or to the continued inclusion in the house and premises of parts lying above or below premises in which I have an interest.]

(Note 4.)

†[5. This notice is given by me as the person designated by paragraph 2 of Schedule 1 to the Act as the reversioner of the house and premises.]

(Note 5.)

(† Delete if you are the claimant's immediate landlord and also the freeholder.)

Signed . . . .

Date . . . .

[The name and address of my solicitor or agent to whom all further communications may be sent is . . . .]

(* Delete any words or paragraphs in square brackets which are inapplicable.)

Notes

1. This notice must be given within two months of the service of Notice of Leaseholder's Claim. Where there is a chain of landlords the time limit will run from the date of the first service of the claimant's notice on any landlord. (Schedule 3, paragraph 7(1))

2. If the landlord admits the claim he will not thereafter be able to dispute the claimant's right to have the freehold or an extended lease, unless he shows that he was misled by misrepresentation or concealment of material facts, but the admission does not conclude any question as to the correctness of the particulars of the house and premises as set out in the claim. (Schedule 3, paragraph 7(4))

3. If the landlord (on the assumption, where this is not admitted, that the claimant has the right claimed) intends to apply to the court for an order for possession of the premises for use as a residence under section 18 or for redevelopment under section 17 of the Act, the notice must say so. (Schedule 3, paragraph 7(3)). (Where the claim is to have the freehold, only certain public authorities or bodies can resist it on the ground of an intention to redevelop the property.)

4. If the landlord intends to object (under subsections (4) or (5) of section 2 of the Act) to the exclusion from the claim of property let with the house and premises but not occupied and used for the purposes of the house by any occupant thereof, or to the inclusion of part of the house and premises which projects into other property of the landlord's, notice of his objection must be given before or with this notice, unless the right to give it later is reserved by this notice. (Schedule 3, paragraph 7(2)). In any case notice of the objection must be given within two months of the service of the claimant's notice.

5. Where there is a chain of landlords this notice must be given by the landlord who is designated "the reversioner" in accordance with paragraph 2 of Schedule 1 to the Act. The reversioner means the landlord whose tenancy carries an expectation of possession of the house and premises of 30 years or

more after the expiration of all inferior tenancies, and if there is more than one such landlord it means the landlord whose tenancy is nearest to that of the tenant; if there is no such landlord, it means the owner of the freehold. **[768]**

Notice of Leaseholder's Claim under section 28(1)(b)(ii) (reg 4)

3. Form 3

To [*Name and address of landlord* .. ..]

1. Take notice that I, as tenant of the house and premises described in the Schedule hereto, claim to be entitled to acquire the freehold or an extended lease of the said house and premises. The particulars on which I rely are set out in the Schedule to this notice.

2. On .. .. you served on me a copy of a certificate given under *[section 28 of the Leasehold Reform Act 1967, certifying that the house and premises will in ten years or less be required for relevant development, *or* section 57 of the Landlord and Tenant Act 1954, certifying that it is requisite that the use or occupation of the house and premises or a part thereof should be changed,] and I am making this claim in the exercise of my rights under section 28 of the Leasehold Reform Act 1967.

(Note 1.)

(**Delete whichever alternative is inapplicable*)

3. You are required to give me, within two months of the service of this notice, a notice in reply in the prescribed form stating whether or not you admit my claim (subject to any question as to the correctness of the particulars of the house and premises given in this notice) and, if you do not admit my claim, stating the grounds upon which you do not admit it.

(Notes 2 & 3.)

Dated this .. .. day of .. .. 19 .. .. ..

Signed .. ..(Tenant)

.. .. (Address)

[The name and address of my solicitor or agent, to whom all further communications may be sent is .. ..]

THE SCHEDULE

1. *The address of the house.*

2. *Particulars of the house and premises sufficient to identify the property to which the claim extends.*

(Note 4.)

3. *The rateable value of the house and premises on 23rd March 1965 (or on the date such a value was first shown in the valuation list, if this date is after 23rd March 1965).*

4. *Particulars of the tenancy of the house and premises sufficient to identify the instrument creating the tenancy and to show that the tenancy is and has at the material times been a long tenancy at a low rent.*

(Note 5.)

5. *The date on which the claimant acquired the tenancy.*

6. *The periods for which in the last ten years and since acquiring the tenancy, the claimant has and has not occupied the house as his residence; and the following particulars about any such periods during which the claimant has occupied the house as his residence—*

(i) *what parts (if any) of the house have not been in his own occupation and for what periods;*

(ii) *what other residence (if any) he has had and for what periods, and which was his main residence.*

7. *Additional particulars where the claimant relies on section 6 or 7 of the Act.* (Note 6.)

Notes

1. In accordance with the provisions of the Leasehold Reform Act 1967 this notice may not be served later than two months after a copy of the certificate has been served on the tenant.

2. The landlord must serve a notice in reply in Form 2 prescribed in the Leasehold Reform (Notices) Regulations 1967 within two months of service on him of this notice. If he does not admit the tenant's claim to be entitled to acquire the freehold or an extended lease the notice in reply must state the grounds on which it is not admitted. If the landlord admits the claim, the admission is binding on him, unless he shows that he was misled by misrepresentation or concealment of material facts, but it does not conclude any question of the correctness of the particulars of the house and premises as set out in the claim. (Schedule 3, paragraph 7)

3. If the landlord admits the claim the tenant will not be entitled to a grant of the freehold or a new tenancy of the house and premises, but, if the landlord obtains an order of the court under section 17 of the Act for possession of the house and premises in order to redevelop it, the tenant will become entitled to be paid compensation for the loss of the house and premises in accordance with Schedule 2 to the Act.

4. "Premises" to be included with the house in the claim are any garage, outhouse, garden, yard and appurtenances which at the time of the notice are let to the tenant with the house and are occupied with and used for the purposes of the house or any part of it by him or by another occupant.

5. Where there have been successive tenancies particulars should be given of each tenancy. In the case of a lease already extended under the Act, the date of the extension and the original term date should be given.

6. Where the claimant is giving the notice by virtue of section 6 (rights of trustees and beneficiaries under trusts) or section 7 (rights of members of family succeeding to tenancy on death) he is required (by paragraph 6(2) of Schedule 3) to adapt the notice and show under paragraph 7 of the Schedule to this Notice the additional particulars bringing the claim within section 6 or 7. Where the tenancy is or was vested in trustees the claimant should, for the purposes of a claim made in reliance on section 6 of the Act, state the date when the tenancy was acquired by the trustees, the date when the beneficiary occupied the house by virtue of his interest under the trust, and particulars of any periods of occupation by the beneficiary which are relied upon as bringing the case within section 6 of the Act. Where the claimant was a member of the previous tenant's

family and became tenant on the latter's death, then, for the purposes of a claim made in reliance on section 7 of the Act, the claimant should state the date on which the previous tenant acquired the tenancy, particulars of his relationship to the previous tenant and his succession to the tenancy, and particulars in respect of any period of occupation by the previous tenant and by himself on which the claimant relies as bringing the case within section 7 of the Act.
[769]–[774]

LEASEHOLD REFORM (ENFRANCHISEMENT AND EXTENSION) REGULATIONS 1967
(SI 1967 NO 1879)

NOTES
Made: 15 December 1967
Authority: Leasehold Reform Act 1967, s 22(2)

ARRANGEMENT OF REGULATIONS

Regulation	Para
1	[775]
2	[776]
3	[777]
4	[778]
Schedule—	
Part 1—Enfranchisement	[779]
Part 2—Extension	[780]

1. (1) These Regulations may be cited as the Leasehold Reform (Enfranchisement and Extension) Regulations 1967 and shall come into operation on 1st January 1968.

(2) In these Regulations and the conditions set out in the Schedule to them, unless the context otherwise requires:—

"the Act" means the Leasehold Reform Act 1967;

"conveyance" includes any conveyance, assignment, transfer or other assurance for giving effect to section 8 of the Act;

"landlord" means the estate owner in respect of the fee simple of the property to which the tenant's notice relates, or the reversioner within the meaning of Schedule 1 to the Act, or any other person who is conducting the proceedings arising out of the notice in accordance with the provisions of the Act or an order of the court;

"lease" means a lease to be granted to give effect to a tenant's notice;

"property" means the house and premises which are required to be granted to the tenant for an estate in fee simple, pursuant to section 8, or for a term of years pursuant to section 14 of the Act;

"tenant" means a tenant of a house who has given notice under Part I of the Act of his desire to have the freehold or an extended lease and includes his executors, administrators and assigns;

"tenant's notice" means in relation to Part I of the Schedule a notice given by a tenant under Part I of the Act of his desire to have a freehold, and in relation to Part 2 of the Schedule a notice given by a tenant under Part I of the Act of his desire to have an extended lease.

(3) The Interpretation Act 1889 shall apply to the interpretation of these Regulations as it applies to the interpretation of an Act of Parliament. **[775]**

2. In any transactions undertaken to give effect to a tenant's notice of his desire to have a freehold the landlord and the tenant shall, unless they otherwise agree, be bound by the conditions laid down in Part I of the Schedule to these Regulations as if the conditions formed part of a contract between them. **[776]**

3. In any transactions undertaken to give effect to a tenant's notice of his desire to have an extended lease the landlord and the tenant shall, unless they otherwise agree, be bound by the conditions laid down in Part 2 of the Schedule to these Regulations as if the conditions formed part of a contract between them. **[777]**

4. Where as a result of non-compliance with the conditions laid down in the Schedule to these Regulations, the landlord and the tenant are discharged from the performance of the obligations arising in giving effect to the tenant's notice, such obligations arising between the tenant and persons other than the landlord having an interest superior to the tenancy shall likewise be discharged. **[778]**

SCHEDULE

PART 1
ENFRANCHISEMENT

Payment of deposit

1.—At any time after receipt of the tenant's notice the landlord may, by notice in writing given to the tenant, require a sum equal to three times the annual rent for the property payable under his tenancy (or, in the case of a notice given under section 34 of the Act, the former long tenancy) or £25, whichever is the greater, to be deposited with the landlord, or a person nominated by him in the notice as his agent or as stakeholder, on account of the price payable for the property and any other sums payable by a tenant in accordance with the provisions of the Act; and the tenant shall, within 14 days of the giving of the notice, pay the sum demanded to the landlord or person nominated by him.

Evidence of tenant's right to enfranchise

2.—At any time after receipt of the tenant's notice the landlord may, by notice in writing given to the tenant, require him to deduce his title to the tenancy and to furnish a statutory declaration as to the particulars of occupation of the property on which the tenant relies in the tenant's notice; and the tenant shall within 21 days of the giving of the landlord's notice comply with the requirement.

Delivery of proof of landlord's title

3.—(1) Where—

(i) a tenant has received no notice in reply to his tenant's notice within 2 months of giving it, or

(ii) a tenant has

(*a*) received a notice in reply stating that his right to have the freehold is admitted, or

(*b*) has received a notice in reply that his right is disputed but has established that right by agreement or an order of the court,

and, in either case, the property to be conveyed has been established by agreement or an order of the court,

the tenant may by notice in writing given to the landlord require him to deduce his title by delivering:—

(*a*) in the case of land registered in the register of title kept at Her Majesty's Land Registry an authority to inspect the register together with all the particulars and information which pursuant to section 110 of the Land Registration Act 1925 have been or may be required to be furnished on a sale of registered land,

(b) in the case of any other land, an abstract of his title to the property,

and the landlord shall not later than 4 weeks after receipt of the notice, comply with the requirement contained therein.

(2) Where any landlord or the tenant has served notice under paragraph 5(2) of Schedule 1 to the Act, "landlord" in this condition includes a landlord who served the notice or upon whom such a notice has been served.

Requisitions

4.—(1) The tenant shall within 14 days after delivery of the abstract or of the authority to inspect the register together with particulars and information (whether or not delivered within the time required) send to the landlord a statement in writing of all objections and requisitions (if any) to or on the title or the evidence of the title, and the abstract or the particulars and information.

(2) All objections and requisitions, other than those going to the root of the title, not included in any statement sent within the aforesaid period shall be deemed waived, and any matters which could have been raised in such objections or requisitions, other than matters going to the root of the title, shall be deemed not to form a defect in the title for the purposes of section 9(2) of the Act.

(3) The landlord shall give a written answer to any objections or requisitions within 14 days of their receipt, and any observations on the answer shall be made within 7 days of the receipt of the answer, and if they are not so made, the answer shall be considered satisfactory.

(4) Any objections not included in any observations so made shall be deemed waived and any matter which could have been raised in any observations so made shall be deemed not to form a defect in the title for the purposes of section 9(2) of the Act.

Particulars of rights of way and restrictions

5.—(1) When or at any time after giving his notice in reply to the tenant's notice the landlord may by notice in writing given to the tenant require him within 4 weeks to state what rights of way and provisions concerning restrictive covenants he requires to be included in the conveyance in accordance with section 10 of the Act.

(2) At any time when under condition 3 the tenant would be entitled to require the landlord to deduce his title he may by notice in writing given to the landlord require him within 4 weeks to state what rights of way over the property and provisions concerning restrictive covenants he requires to be included in the conveyance in accordance with the provisions of the Act.

(3) A notice given under this condition shall contain a statement as to the rights of way and provisions concerning restrictive covenants required by the person giving the notice to be included in the conveyance.

(4) If the tenant does not comply with a notice given under this condition within the time specified or, where no such notice has been given, does not communicate to the landlord a statement of the rights and provisions he requires to be included in the conveyance when or before serving a notice on the landlord under condition 3, the tenant shall be deemed to require no rights of way or provisions concerning restrictive covenants to be included in the conveyance.

(5) If the landlord does not comply with a notice given under this condition within the time specified, or, where no such notice is given, does not communicate to the tenant a statement of the rights and provisions he requires to be included in the conveyance at or before the time fixed for compliance with a notice served on him under condition 3, the landlord shall be deemed to require no rights of way or provisions concerning restrictive covenants to be included in the conveyance.

Completion

6.—(1) After the expiration of one month after the price payable for the property under section 9 of the Act has been determined by agreement or otherwise, either the tenant or the landlord may give the other notice in writing requiring him to complete the conveyance of the property to the tenant, and thereupon the completion date shall be the first working day after the expiration of 4 weeks from giving of the notice.

(2) Completion shall take place at the office of the landlord's solicitor or, if he so requires, at the office of the solicitor of his mortgagee.

Apportionment of rent and outgoings

7. The tenant shall (subject to the next following condition) pay rent up to the date when the conveyance is completed (whether on the completion date or subsequently) and shall as from that date pay all outgoings; and any current rent and all rates and other outgoings shall, if necessary, be apportioned as on that date (the date itself being apportioned to the landlord) and the balance be paid by or allowed to the tenant.

Election for interest in lieu of rent

8.—(1) If from any cause whatsoever (save as hereinafter mentioned) completion is delayed beyond the completion date, the rent shall continue to be payable under the tenancy until actual completion unless the landlord by notice in writing given to the tenant elects to receive interest on the price payable for the property in lieu of rent, in which event in lieu of the rent payable under the tenancy, the price payable (or if a deposit has been paid the balance thereof) shall bear interest at a rate per annum of 2 per cent above the bank rate from time to time in force as from the giving of the notice to the tenant until actual completion.

Provided that, unless the delay in completion is attributable solely to the tenant's own act or default, the tenant may—

(*a*) at his own risk, deposit the price payable or, where a deposit has been paid, the balance thereof, at any bank in England or Wales, and
(*b*) forthwith give to the landlord or his solicitor notice in writing of the deposit,

and in that case the landlord shall (unless and until there is further delay in completion which is attributable solely to the tenant's own act or default) be bound to accept the interest, if any, allowed thereon, as from the date of such deposit, instead of the interest accruing after such date which would otherwise be payable to him under the foregoing provisions of this condition.

(2) No interest under paragraph (1) of this condition shall become payable by a tenant if, and so long as, delay in completion is attributable to any act or default of the landlord or his mortgagee or Settled Land Act trustees.

Preparation of conveyance

9.—(1) The conveyance shall be prepared by the tenant.

(2) A draft of the conveyance shall be delivered at the office of the landlord's solicitor at least 14 days before the date fixed for completion in accordance with condition 6 and the engrossment of the conveyance for execution by the landlord and other parties, if any, shall be delivered at that office a reasonable time before the date for completion.

(3) Where the conveyance is to contain restrictive covenants and the tenant intends contemporaneously with the conveyance to execute a mortgage or convey any interest in the property to a third party, he shall inform the landlord of his intention and, if necessary, allow the landlord time to give a priority notice for the registration of the intended covenants at least 14 days before the conveyance is completed.

(4) Where a conveyance is to contain any covenant by the tenant or any grant or reservation of rights affecting other property of the landlord, the tenant shall, if the landlord so requires, execute and hand over to the landlord on completion as many duplicates of the conveyance as the landlord may reasonably require and the duplicates shall be prepared and engrossed by the tenant, and where any duplicate is executed the tenant shall, if so required by the landlord, produce the original duly stamped so as to enable the stamp on the duplicate to be denoted.

Failure to comply with obligations

10.—(1) If either the landlord or the tenant shall neglect or fail to perform any of his obligations arising from the tenant's notice or arising out of any of these conditions, then the other party may give to the party in default at least 2 months' notice in writing referring to this condition, specifying the default and requiring him to make it good before the expiration of the notice.

(2) If the tenant does not comply with such a notice given by the landlord then, without prejudice to any other rights or remedies available to the landlord under the Act or otherwise,

(*a*) the landlord and tenant shall thereupon be discharged from the further performance of their obligations, other than the tenant's obligation to pay the landlord's costs, and

(*b*) the deposit money, if any, shall be forfeited to the landlord,

but if the landlord recovers any sums in the exercise of any remedy he shall give credit for the deposit against any sums so recovered.

(3) If the landlord does not comply with such a notice given by the tenant, then the tenant may require the deposit money, if any, to be returned to him forthwith and shall be discharged from the obligation to pay the landlord's reasonable costs imposed by section 9 of the Act, and thereupon the landlord and the tenant shall be discharged from the further performance of their obligations, but without prejudice to any other rights or remedies available to the tenant under the Act or otherwise.

Cancellation of land charges etc.

11. Where under section 5(5) of the Act a tenant's notice has been registered as a land charge or a notice or caution in respect thereof has been registered and either the tenant gives notice of withdrawal under section 9(3) or section 19(14) of the Act or the landlord is otherwise discharged from the obligations arising out of the notice, the tenant shall at the request of the landlord forthwith at his own cost procure the cancellation of the registration.

Notices

12. Any notice to be given to any person in accordance with these conditions shall be deemed to be effectively given if served personally on that person, or left at his last known place of residence, or sent by post to him or his solicitor or other duly authorised agent at his last known address.

Extension of time limits

13.—(1) These conditions shall have effect as if any period of time for the performance of any act or compliance with any notice (except a notice given under condition 10) by the landlord were twice the length of the period thereby laid down, where a person acting as reversioner under the provisions of Schedule 1 to the Act so requires by notice in writing given to the tenant at any time before the expiration of that period.

(2) Any period when proceedings are pending in any court or tribunal with reference to any matter arising in giving effect to a tenant's notice shall be disregarded in computing any period of time laid down by these conditions or any notice served thereunder.

(3) Any period of time laid down by these conditions or any notice served thereunder shall be extended for such further period as may be reasonable in all the circumstances if any party required to do any act within that period dies or becomes incapable of managing his affairs before the expiration of that period. **[779]**

PART 2

EXTENSION

Evidence of tenant's right to have an extended lease

1. At any time after receipt of the tenant's notice the landlord may, by notice in writing given to the tenant, require him to deduce his title to the tenancy and to furnish a statutory declaration as to the particulars of occupation of the property on which the tenant relies in the tenant's notice; and the tenant shall within 21 days of the giving of the landlord's notice comply with the requirement.

Terms of new tenancy

2.—(1) Where—

(*a*) a tenant has received no notice in reply to his tenant's notice within 2 months of giving it, or

(*b*) a tenant has

(i) received a notice in reply stating that his right to have an extended lease is admitted, or

(ii) has received a notice in reply that his right is disputed but has established that right by agreement or an order of the court,

and, in either case, the property to be leased has been established by agreement or an order of the court,

then the tenant may, by notice in writing given to the landlord, require him within 4 weeks to state what modifications in the terms of the existing tenancy, and what further provisions, other than as to payment of rent, are to be made by the terms of the new tenancy in accordance with section 15 of the Act.

(2) Where the requirements of paragraph (1)(*b*) of this condition are satisfied the landlord may, by notice in writing given to the tenant, require him within four weeks to state what modifications in the terms of the existing tenancy and what further provisions other than as to payment of rent are to be made by the terms of the new tenancy, in accordance with section 15 of the Act.

(3) A notice given under this condition shall contain a statement as to the modifications in the terms of the existing tenancy and the further provisions to be made by the terms of the new tenancy, required by the person giving the notice.

(4) If either party does not comply with a notice given under this condition within the time specified or, where no such notice has been given, does not communicate to the other a statement of the modifications and provisions he requires to be made when or before serving a notice under this condition, he shall be deemed to require the new tenancy to be on the same terms as the existing tenancy and not to require any further provisions (other than as to payment of rent) to be made by the terms of the new tenancy in accordance with section 15 of the Act.

Preparation of lease

3.—(1) Within eight weeks after the giving of a notice by either party under condition 2, a draft of the lease shall be submitted by the landlord to the tenant for approval, and the tenant shall approve the draft in writing with or without amendments within 21 days thereafter.

(2) If the tenant does not approve the draft with any amendment required by him within the time laid down by this condition, he shall be deemed to have approved it in the form submitted by the landlord.

(3) The lease and as many counterparts as the landlord may reasonably require shall be prepared by the landlord and the counterpart or counterparts shall be delivered to the tenant for execution a reasonable time before the completion date, and on completion (whether on the completion date or subsequently) the tenant shall deliver the counterpart or counterparts of the lease, duly executed, to the landlord and the landlord shall deliver the lease, duly executed, to the tenant.

Completion

4.—(1) After the expiration of the time for approval of the draft lease by the tenant either the landlord or the tenant may give the other notice in writing requiring him to complete the grant of the lease, and thereupon the completion date shall be the first working day after the expiration of 4 weeks from the giving of the notice.

(2) Completion shall take place at the office of the landlord's solicitor.

Failure to comply with obligations

5.—(1) If either the landlord or the tenant shall neglect or fail to perform any of his obligations arising from the tenant's notice or arising out of any of these conditions, then the other party may give to the party in default at least 2 months' notice in writing referring to this condition, specifying the default and requiring him to make it good before the expiration of the notice.

(2) If the tenant does not comply with such a notice given by the landlord, the landlord and the tenant shall be discharged from the further performance of their obligations, other than the tenant's obligation to pay the landlord's costs, but without prejudice to any other rights or remedies available to the landlord under the Act or otherwise.

(3) If the landlord does not comply with such a notice given by the tenant, the tenant shall be discharged from the obligation to pay the landlord's reasonable costs imposed by section 14 of the Act, and thereupon the landlord and the tenant shall be discharged from the further performance of their obligations, but without prejudice to any other rights or remedies available to the tenant under the Act or otherwise.

Cancellation of land charges etc.

6. Where under section 5(5) of the Act a tenant's notice has been registered as a land charge or a notice or caution in respect thereof has been registered and the landlord is discharged from the obligations arising out of the notice, the tenant shall at the request of the landlord forthwith at his own cost procure the cancellation of the registration.

Notices

7. Any notice to be given to any person in accordance with these conditions shall be deemed to be effectively given if served personally on that person, or left at his last known place of residence, or sent by post to him or his solicitor or other duly authorised agent at his last known address.

Extension of time limits

8.—(1) These conditions shall have effect as if any period of time for the performance of any act or compliance with any notice (except a notice given under condition 5) by the landlord were twice the length of the period thereby laid down, where a person acting as reversioner under the provisions of Schedule 1 to the Act so requires by notice in writing given to the tenant at any time before the expiration of that period.

(2) Any period when proceedings are pending in any court or tribunal with reference to any matter arising in giving effect to a tenant's notice shall be disregarded in computing any period of time laid down by these conditions or any notice served thereunder.

(3) Any period of time laid down by these conditions or any notice served thereunder shall be extended for such further period as may be reasonable in all the circumstances if any party required to do any act within that period dies or becomes incapable of managing his affairs before the expiration of that period. **[780]**

RENT (COUNTY COURT PROCEEDINGS) RULES 1970
(SI 1970 NO 1851)

NOTES
Made: 8 December 1970
Authority: Rent Act 1977, ss 142, 155(3), Sch 24, para 1

ARRANGEMENT OF RULES

Rule		Para
1	Citation, commencement, interpretation and application	[781]
2	Application of county court rules	[782]
3	Applications to the county court	[783]
4	Proceedings for compensation under s 19 of the Act of 1968	[784]

Appendix Forms

Form		Para
1	Form 1 General Form of Title of Proceedings	[785]
2	Form 2 General Form of Conclusion of Originating Application	[786]
3	Form 3 General Form of Conclusion of Order on Originating Application	[787]
4	Form 4 Application for Apportionment of Rateable Value or Rates or 1956 Gross Value (Rent Act 1968, ss 6(2), 7(1), Sch 2, Part I; s 7(3), Sch 2, Part II; ss 38(2), 51(2), 52, Sch 8; s 67(4))	[788]
5	Form 5 Order on Application for Apportionment of Rateable Value or Rates or 1956 Gross Value (Rent Act 1968, ss 6(2), 7(1), Sch 2, Part I; s 7(3), Sch 2, Part II; ss 38(2), 51(2), 52, Sch 8; s 67(4))	[789]
6	Form 6 Application for Leave to Distrain (Rent Act 1968, s 111)	[790]
7	Form 7 Order on Application for Leave to Distrain (Rent Act 1968, s 111)	[791]
8	Form 8 Application to Determine an Adjustment of Recoverable Rent or Rent Limit with Respect to Repairs, Services or Furniture (Rent Act 1968, ss 21(7), 24(2), 55(3), 60(4))	[792]
9	Form 9 Order on Application to Determine an Adjustment of Recoverable Rent or Rent Limit with Respect to Services or Furniture (Rent Act 1968, ss 21(7), 24(2), 55(3), 60(4))	[793]
10	Form 10 Tenant's Application to Cancel or Reduce Increases of Rent for Improvement (Rent Act 1968, ss 25(3), 59(1))	[794]
11	Form 11 Order on Tenant's Application to Cancel or Reduce Increase of Rent for Improvement (Rent Act 1968, ss 25(3), 59(1))	[795]
12	Form 12 Application to Determine a Reasonable Charge for Services or the Use of Furniture (Rent Act 1968, s 52(1)(*c*))	[796]
13	Form 13 Order on Application to Determine a Reasonable Charge for Services or the Use of Furniture (Rent Act 1968, s 52(1)(*c*))	[797]
14	Form 14 Application to Determine the Appropriate Factor by which Gross Value is to be Multiplied on Account of the Tenant's Responsibility for Repairs (Rent Act 1968, s 52(2), Sch 9, para 1(3))	[798]
15	Form 15 Order on Application to Determine the Appropriate Factor by which Gross Value is to be Multiplied on Account of the Tenant's Responsiblity for Repairs (Rent Act 1968, s 52(2), Sch 9, para 1(3))	[799]
16	Form 16 Tenant's Application for Direction that Certificate of Disrepair should have been Issued or have Specified Further Defects, or for Reversal of Cancellation of Certificate (Rent Act 1968, s 52(3), Sch 9, paras 4(5), 6(4))	[800]
17	Form 17 Order on Tenant's Application for Direction that Certificate of Disrepair should have been Issued or have Specified Further Defects, or for Reversal of Cancellation of Certificate (Rent Act 1968, s 52(3), Sch 9, paras 4(5), 6(4))	[801]
18	Form 18 Application by Landlord for Cancellation, in Whole or in Part, of a Certificate of Disrepair (Rent Act 1968, s 52(3), Sch 9, paras 4(6), (7), 6(3))	[802]
19	Form 19 Order on Application by Landlord for Cancellation, in Whole or in Part of a Certificate of Disrepair (Rent Act 1968, s 52(3), Sch 9, paras 4(6), (7), 6(3))	[803]
20	Form 20 Application by Mortgagor to Vary the Terms of a Regulated Mortgage or Limit the Exercise of a Right or Remedy in respect thereof on Grounds of Financial Hardship (Rent Act 1968, s 95(2), (3))	[804]
21	Form 21 Order on Application by Mortgagor to Vary the Terms of a Regulated Mortgage or Limit the Exercise of a Right or Remedy in respect thereof on Grounds of Financial Hardship (Rent Act 1968, s 95(2), (3))	[805]
22	Form 22 Application to Vary or Revoke an Order under Section 95(2) Rent Act 1968 (Rent Act 1968, s 95(5))	[806]
23	Form 23 Order on Application to Vary or Revoke an Order under section 95(2) Rent Act 1968 (Rent Act 1968, s 95(5))	[807]
24	Form 24 Application to Determine a Question Relating to a Tenancy or Mortgage or any Matter material thereto (Rent Act 1968, s 105)	[808]
25	Form 25 Order on an Application to Determine a Question Relating to a Tenancy or Mortgage or any Matter material thereto (Rent Act 1968, s 105)	[809]
26	Form 26 Application for Order to Local Authority to Issue Qualificaction Certificate, or for Cancellation of Qualification Certificate (Housing Act 1969, s 49(1), (2))	[810]
27	Form 27 Order on Application for Order to Local Authority to Issue Qualification Certificate, or for Cancellation of Qualification Certificate (Housing Act 1969, s 49(1), (2))	[811]
28	Form 28 Application for Order Empowering Landlord to Enter Premises and Carry out Works (Housing Act 1969, s 54)	[812]
29	Form 29 Order Empowering Landlord to Enter Premises and Carry out Works (Housing Act 1969, s 54)	[813]

1. Citation, commencement, interpretation and application

(1) These Rules may be cited as the Rent (County Court Proceedings) Rules 1970 and shall come into operation on 1st February 1971.

(2) The Interpretation Act 1889 shall apply to the interpretation of these Rules as it applies to the interpretation of an Act of Parliament.

(3) In these Rules—

"the Act of 1968" means the Rent Act 1968;
"the Act of 1969" means Part III of the Housing Act 1969;

an Order and Rule referred to by number means the Order and Rule so numbered in the County Court Rules 1936, as amended. **[781]**

NOTES

Commencement: 1 February 1971.
Rent Act 1968: see now Rent Act 1977.
Housing Act 1969, Part III: see now Housing Finance Act 1972, Part III.

2. Application of county court rules

Proceedings in a county court under the Act of 1968 or the Act of 1969 shall, subject to the provisions of these Rules, be instituted and prosecuted in accordance with the County Court Rules and any powers exercisable by the court in relation to proceedings to which those Rules apply shall be exercisable in relation to proceedings to which these Rules apply. **[782]**

NOTES

Commencement: 1 February 1971.
Act of 1968: Rent Act 1968: see now Rent Act 1977.
Act of 1969: Housing Act 1969: see now Housing Finance Act 1972.

3. Applications to the county court

(1) An application to the county court under the Act of 1968 and an appeal or application to the county court under the Act of 1969 shall be made by way of originating application to the court for the district in which the premises concerned are situate:

Provided that, where in proceedings in any county court a question arises which might be made the subject of an originating application under this Rule, that court may determine the question in the course of those proceedings and without a separate application being made.

(2) . . .

(3) The documents required by Order 6, Rule 4(2)(*c*)(ii), to be served on each respondent shall be served not less than 10 or, in the case of an application for leave to distrain, not less than 4 clear days before the day fixed for hearing.

(4) Service may be effected in accordance with the provision of Order 8, Rule 39, by any person authorised by Order 8, Rule 2, to effect personal service of a document and by any officer of the court where service is to be effected by post. Service of an application for leave to distrain may also be effected by any person regularly authorised by or on behalf of the applicant to collect the rent of the premises in question.

(5)(a) Except where the application is for leave to distrain, a respondent who wishes to oppose the application or to dispute any allegation contained therein shall, within 8 days of the service upon him of a copy thereof inclusive of the day of service, deliver at the court office an answer, together with as many copies thereof as there are applicants, stating the grounds of his opposition and specifying the allegations which he disputes.

(*b*) On receipt of the answer and copies the registrar shall send a copy to each applicant.

(*c*) If the respondent fails to deliver an answer within the time limited by sub-paragraph (*a*) of this paragraph, he may nevertheless deliver an answer at any time before the day fixed for hearing, and if time permits the procedure prescribed by sub-paragraph (*b*) of this paragraph shall be followed, or the respondent may, without delivering an answer, appear on the day fixed for hearing and oppose the application or dispute any allegation made therein, but the court may order him to pay any costs properly incurred in consequence of his delay or failure.

(6) The application may be heard by the registrar who may, and shall if so required by any party at any time before he has given his decision, refer it to the judge:

Provided that an application under paragraph 3 or paragraph 7 of Schedule 1 to the Act of 1968 shall be heard in the first place by the judge, who may dispose of it himself or refer it to the registrar.

(7) The judge or registrar may hear the application or any part thereof in private or in open court as he may think desirable.

(8) Where the court makes an order for the payment of any costs of the application, such costs shall be taxed on Scale 1 in Appendix B to the County Court Rules unless the court otherwise directs:

Provided that the court may, in lieu of ordering the costs to be taxed, fix the amount to be paid.

(9) Unless the court otherwise directs, the local authority concerned shall not be made a respondent to an application under sub-paragraph (5), (6) or (7) of paragraph 4, or sub-paragraph (4) of paragraph 6, or paragraph 18 of Schedule 9 to the Act of 1968.

(10) . . .

(11) The registrar shall serve a copy of the order made on the application on every party thereto and, where the order relates to a certificate of repair or disrepair, on the local authority concerned.

(12) The forms in the Appendix to these Rules or forms substantially to the same effect shall be used where appropriate with such modifications as the circumstances may require. **[783]**

NOTES

Commencement: 1 February 1971.
Words omitted spent.
Act of 1968: Rent Act 1968: see now Rent Act 1977.
Act of 1969: Housing Act 1969: see now Housing Finance Act 1972.

4. Proceedings for compensation under s 19 of the Act of 1968

Proceedings in a county court for compensation under section 19 of the Act of 1968 shall be commenced by plaint and, if the judgment complained of was obtained in a county court, the action shall be brought in that court. **[784]**

NOTES
Commencement: 1 February 1971.
Act of 1968, s 19: see now Rent Act 1977, s 102.

APPENDIX FORMS

1. Form 1 General Form of Title of Proceedings

In the .. .. County Court

No. of Application .. ..

In the Matter of the Rent Act 1968 [*or* the Housing Act 1969]

Between .. .. .. A.B. .. .. .. Applicant,

and

.. .. C.D .. .. .. Respondent. [785]

NOTES
Commencement: 1 February 1971.

2. Form 2 General Form of Conclusion of Originating Application

The names and addresses of the persons on whom it is intended to serve this application are: (*state names and addresses of persons intended to be served*).

My address for service is (*state applicant's address for service*).

Dated this .. .. day of .. ..

(*Signed*) .. ..

.. .. Applicant.

(*Add, except in the case of an application for leave to distrain*)

To the Respondent

If you wish to oppose this application or to dispute any allegation contained in it, you must, within 8 days of its being served on you inclusive of the day of service, deliver at the court office an answer, together with as many copies as there are applicants. The documents may be sent by post so as to arrive at the court office within the time allowed.

In your answer you must state the grounds on which you oppose the application and specify any allegation which you dispute.

If you do not deliver an answer, or if you deliver your answer out of time, you may be ordered to pay costs incurred in consequence of your failure or delay.

You should attend the hearing even if you have delivered an answer. [786]

NOTES
Commencement: 1 February 1971.

3. Form 3 General Form of Conclusion of Order on Originating Application

[*Add, if so ordered*]

And it is ordered that the applicant [respondent] do recover against the respondent [applicant] his costs of the application, which are hereby allowed at £ .. .. [*or* to be taxed on Scale .. ..].

And it is ordered that the respondent [applicant] do pay the said sum of £ .. .. [*or* the amount of the said costs when taxed] to the Registrar of this Court on or before the .. .. day of .. .. , or (*where the costs are to be taxed*), if the costs have not been taxed before the expiration of that day, within 3 days after taxation [*or* by instalments of £ .. .. for every calendar month, the first instalment to be paid on the .. .. day of .. ..].

Dated this .. .. day of .. ..

.. ..Registrar. **[787]**

NOTES

Commencement: 1 February 1971.

4. Form 4 Application for Apportionment of Rateable Value or Rates or 1956 Gross Value

(*Rent Act 1968, ss 6(2), 7(1), Sch 2, Part I; s 7(3), Sch 2, Part II; ss 38(2), 51(2), 52, Sch 8; s 67(4)*)

(*General Title—Form 1*)

I, ... (*name of applicant*)

of .. .. (*address and occupation of applicant*) hereby apply to the Court for the apportionment of .. .. [the rateable value on the .. .. day of .. ..][*or* the gross value on the 7th day of November 1956] [*or* the rates payable in respect].. .. .. of certain property known as.. .. .., and comprising certain premises known as.. .. .., for the purpose of determing the rateable value [*or* the 1956 gross value][*or* the rates payable in respect] of the said premises for the purposes of the above mentioned Act:

And for an order providing for the costs of this application.

(*General Conclusion—Form 2*) **[788]**

NOTES

Commencement: 1 February 1971.

5. Form 5 Order on Application for Apportionment of Rateable Value or Rates or 1956 Gross Value

(*Rent Act 1968, ss 6(2), 7(1), Sch 2, Part I; s 7(3), Sch 2, Part II; ss 38(2), 51(2), 52, Sch 8; s 67(4)*)

(*General Title—Form 1*)

.. .. (Seal)

Upon hearing

It is hereby determined that .. .. [the rateable value on the .. ..

.. .. day of .. ..] [*or* the gross value on the 7th day of November 1956] (*or as the case may be*).. .. .. [*or* the rates payable in respect] of certain property known as .. .., and comprising certain premises known as .. .., shall be apportioned between the said premises and the rest of the said property as follows:—

£.. .. .. to the said premises
and
£.. .. .. to the remainder of the said property.

(*General Conclusion—Form* 3) [789]

NOTES
Commencement: 1 February 1971.

6. Form 6 Application for Leave to Distrain

(*Rent Act 1968, s 111*)

(*General Title—Form 1*)

I, ... (*name of applicant*)

of .. .. (*address and occupation of applicant*) hereby apply to the Court for an order under section 111 of the Rent Act 1968 giving me leave to levy a distress for rent amounting to £ .. .. on premises known as .. .. ; And for an order providing for the costs of this application.

The grounds of my application are that the said premises are let by me to the respondent on a [weekly] tenancy at £ .. .. per [week] and that rent amounting to £ .. .. was, by the .. .. day of.. .. .. , and is still in arrear.

(*General Conclusion—Form* 2) [790]

NOTES
Commencement: 1 February 1971.

7. Form 7 Order on Application for Leave to Distrain

(*Rent Act 1968, s 111*)

(*General Title—Form 1*)

.. .. (Seal)

Upon hearing

It is hereby ordered, under section 111 of the Rent Act 1968, that the applicant be at liberty to levy a distress for rent amounting to £.. .. .. due to him from the respondent in respect of premises known as.. .. ..

(*Add, if so ordered—in lieu of General Conclusion*)

And it is ordered that the applicant [respondent] do recover against the respondent [applicant] his costs of the application, which are hereby allowed at £.. .. .. [*or* to be taxed on Scale .. ..].

And it is ordered that the respondent [applicant] do pay the said sum of £.. .. .. [*or* the amount of the said costs when taxed] to the Registrar of this

Court on or before the .. .. day of.. .. .., or (*where the costs are to be taxed*), if the costs have not been taxed before the expiration of that day, within 3 days after taxation [*or* by instalments of £.. .. .. for every calendar month, the first instalment to be paid on the .. .. day of .. ..].

[*Or (where the order giving leave to distrain and for costs is suspended on payment of the current rent and instalments of the arrears and costs*)

And it is further ordered that the operation of this order shall be suspended so long as the respondent punctually pays to the applicant or his agent the said arrears and costs by instalments of £.. .. .. per week in addition to the current rent.]

Dated this .. .. day of .. ..,

.. .. Registrar. **[791]**

NOTES
Commencement: 1 February 1971.

8. Form 8 Application to Determine an Adjustment of Recoverable Rent or Rent Limit with Respect to Repairs, Services or Furniture

(*Rent Act 1968, ss 21(7), 24(2), 55(3), 60(4)*)

(*General Title—Form 1*)

I, ... (*name of applicant*)

of .. .. (*address and occupation of applicant*) hereby apply to the Court for an order determining that the recoverable rent [*or* the rent limit][*or* the contractual rent limit] of the premises known as.. .. .., of which I am the landlord [tenant] and the respondent is the tenant [landlord], shall be increased [decreased] by the amount of £.. .. .. per .. .., or such other sum as the Court may determine, by reason of a difference with respect to the responsibility for any repairs [*or* the provision of services] [*or* the use of furniture] or any circumstances relating thereto in comparison with the terms of the previous tenancy [*or* the previous terms][*or* the last contractual period] [*or* the basic rental period],

And for an order that the determination of the Court shall relate to the following statutory periods [*or* rental periods]:

.. .. (*state the periods*)

And for an order providing for the costs of this application.

The grounds of this application are: (*state the grounds of application, specifying the terms of the tenancy, the nature and extent of the premises, particulars of the services provided, or the furniture in question, and the difference which is alleged*).

(*General Conclusion—Form 2*) **[792]**

NOTES
Commencement: 1 February 1971.

9. Form 9 Order on Application to Determine an Adjustment of Recoverable Rent or Rent Limit with Respect to Services or Furniture

(*Rent Act 1968, ss 21(7), 24(2), 55(3), 60(4)*)

(*General Title—Form 1*)

.. .. (Seal)

Upon hearing

It is hereby ordered that by reason of a difference with respect to the responsibility for repairs of [*or* the services provided for][*or* the use of furniture by] the respondent [applicant] or the circumstances relating thereto in comparison with the terms of the previous tenancy [*or* the previous terms] [*or* the last contractual period][*or* the basic rental period] in respect of premises known as.. .. .. the recoverable rent [*or* the rent limit][*or* the contractual rent limit] of the said premises be increased [decreased] by £.. .. .. per .. ..

And it is ordered that the determination do relate to the following statutory periods [*or* rental periods]:

.. .. (*state the periods*)

(*General Conclusion—Form 3*) **[793]**

NOTES
Commencement: 1 February 1971.

10. Form 10 Tenant's Application to Cancel or Reduce Increase of Rent for Improvement

(*Rent Act 1968, ss 25(3), 59(1)*)

(*General Title—Form 1*)

I, ... (*name of applicant*)

of .. .. (*address and occupation of applicant*) hereby apply to the Court for an order cancelling [*or* reducing by £.. .. .. per .. .. or such other sum as the court may determine] an increase of rent specified in a notice dated the .. .. day of.. .. .. and served on me by the respondent in respect of an improvement in certain premises known as.. .. .. of which I am the tenant and the respondent is the landlord;

And for an order providing for the costs of this application

The grounds of this application are:—

The said improvement was unnecessary [and [*or*] a greater amount was spent on the said improvement than was reasonable] because (*here state why the improvement was unnecessary or the amount spent on it was unreasonable, as the case may be*).

(*General Conclusion—Form 2*) **[794]**

NOTES
Commencement: 1 February 1971.

11. Form 11 Order on Tenant's Application to Cancel or Reduce Increase of Rent for Improvement

(*Rent Act 1968, ss 25(3), 59(1)*)

(*General Title—Form 1*)

.. .. (Seal)

Upon hearing

It is ordered that the increase of rent specified in a notice dated the .. .. day of .. .. , and served on the applicant by the respondent in respect of an improvement in premises known as .. .. be cancelled [*or* reduced to £.. .. .. per .. ..] as from the .. .. day of.. .. .. 19.. .. ..

(*General Conclusion—Form 3*) **[795]**

NOTES

Commencement: 1 February 1971.

12. Form 12 Application to Determine a Reasonable Charge for Services or the Use of Furniture

(*Rent Act 1968, s 52(1)(c)*)

(*General Title—Form 1*)

I, ... (*name of applicant*)

of .. .. (*address and occupation of applicant*) hereby apply to the Court for an order determining that a reasonable charge for services provided by me [the respondent (*or as the case may be*) [for] *or* for the use of furniture by] the respondent [me] during the basic rental period in respect of premises known as .. .. (of which I am the landlord [tenant] and the respondent is the tenant [landlord]), is £.. .. .. per annum, or such other sum as the Court may determine;

And for an order providing for the costs of this application.

The grounds of this application are: (*state grounds of application, specifying the terms of the tenancy, the nature and extent of the premises and particulars of the services provided (or, as the case may be, the furniture in question)*).

(*General Conclusion—Form 2*) **[796]**

NOTES

Commencement: 1 February 1971.

13. Form 13 Order on Application to Determine a Reasonable Charge for Services or the Use of Furniture

(*Rent Act 1968, s 52(1)(c)*)

(*General Title—Form 1*)

.. .. (Seal)

Upon hearing

It is hereby determined that a reasonable charge for the undermentioned services provided for [*or* the use of the undermentioned furniture by] the respondent [applicant] during the basic rental period in respect of premises known as . . . . is £. . . . . per . . . . :

(*Particulars of the services or furniture in question, described by reference to the application or otherwise*).

(*General Conclusion—Form 3*) [797]

NOTES
Commencement: 1 February 1971.

14. Form 14 Application to Determine the Appropriate Factor by which Gross Value is to be Multiplied on Account of the Tenant's Responsibility for Repairs

(*Rent Act 1968, s 52(2), Sch 9, para 1(3)*)

(*General Title—Form 1*)

I, ... (*name of applicant*)

of . . . . (*address and occupation of applicant*) hereby apply to the Court for an order determining the appropriate factor by which the gross value of premises known as . . . . of which I am the landlord [tenant] and the respondent is the tenant [landlord], is to be multiplied for the purpose of ascertaining the rent limit applicable thereto:

And for an order providing for the costs of this application.

The grounds of this application are: (*state grounds of application, specifying the terms of the tenancy, the nature and extent of the premises and the repairs for which the landlord and tenant are respectively responsible*).

(*General Conclusion—Form 2*) [798]

NOTES
Commencement: 1 February 1971.

15. Form 15 Order on Application to Determine the Appropriate Factor by which Gross Value is to be Multiplied on Account of the Tenant's Responsiblity for Repairs

(*Rent Act 1968, s 52(2), Sch 9, para 1(3)*)

(*General Title—Form 1*)

. . . . (Seal)

Upon hearing

It is hereby ordered and declared that the appropriate factor by which the gross value of certain premises known as . . . . of which the applicant is the landlord [tenant] and the respondent is the tenant [landlord], is to be multiplied for the purpose of ascertaining the rent limit applicable thereto is

(*General Conclusion—Form 3*) [799]

NOTES
Commencement: 1 February 1971.

16. Form 16 Tenant's Application for Direction that Certificate of Disrepair should have been Issued or have Specified Further Defects, or for Reversal of Cancellation of Certificate

(*Rent Act 1968, s 52(3), Sch 9, paras 4(5), 6(4)*)

(*General Title—Form 1*)

I, ... (*name of applicant*)

of .. .. (*address and occupation of applicant*) hereby apply to the Court for an order directing .. .. the.. .. .. Council to proceed on the footing that they are satisfied that premises known as .. .., of which I am the tenant and the respondent is the landlord, are in disrepair by reason of the undermentioned defects and that, having regard to the age, character and locality of the said premises, those defect [*or* such of those defects as are specified herein] ought reasonably to be remedied: [*or* that the undermentioned defects shall be deemed to be specified in a certificate of disrepair issued by the .. .. Council on the .. .. day of.. .. .. and relating to premises known as .. .., of which I am the tenant and the respondent is the landlord:]

(*give particulars of defects in question*)

[*or* that a certificate of disrepair relating to premises known as.. .. .. (of which I am the tenant and the respondent is the landlord), issued by the .. .. Council on the .. .. day of.. .. .. and cancelled by the said Council, shall be deemed not to have been cancelled;]

And for an order providing for the costs of this application.

The grounds of this application are: (*state the grounds of the application*).

(*General Conclusion—Form 2*) **[800]**

NOTES

Commencement: 1 February 1971.

17. Form 17 Order on Tenant's Application for Direction that Certificate of Disrepair should have been Issued or have Specified Further Defects, or for Reversal of Cancellation of Certificate

(*Rent Act 1968, s 52(3), Sch 9, paras 4(5), 6(4)*)

(*General Title—Form 1*)

.. ..(Seal)

Upon hearing

It is hereby ordered and directed that .. .. the .. .. Council do proceed on the footing that they are satisfied that premises known as .. .. are in disrepair by reason of the undermentioned defects and that, having regard to the age, character and locality of the said premises, those defects [*or* such of those defects as are specified herein] ought reasonably to be remedied: [*or* the undermentioned defects shall be deemed to be specified in the certificate of disrepair issued by the .. .. Council on the .. .. day of.. .. .. and relating to premises known as .. .. :]

(*particulars of defects in question*).

[*or* the certificate of disrepair relating to premises known as .. .. issued by the .. .. Council on the .. .. day of.. .. .. and cancelled by the said Council, shall be deemed not to have been cancelled].

(*General Conclusion—Form 3*) **[801]**

NOTES
Commencement: 1 February 1971.

18. Form 18 Application by Landlord for Cancellation, in Whole or in Part, of a Certificate of Disrepair

(*Rent Act 1968, s 52(3), Sch 9, paras 4(6), (7), 6(3)*)

(*General Title—Form 1*)

I, ... (*name of applicant*)
of .. .. (*address and occupation of applicant*) hereby apply to the Court for an order cancelling [in respect of the following defects, namely .. .. ,] a certificate of disrepair dated the .. .. day of.. .. .. and issued by the .. .. Council in respect of premises known as .. .. , of which I am the landlord and the respondent is the tenant;

[And for an order that the said certificate shall cease to have effect as from the .. .. day of.. .. .. ;]

And for an order providing for the costs of this application.

The grounds of this application are: (*state grounds of application, e.g. that the defects specified in the certificate are the responsibility of the tenant, or ought not, for some other reason, to have been specified; or that the local authority should have cancelled the certificate on the ground that the defects have been remedied*).

(*General Conclusion—Form 2*) **[802]**

NOTES
Commencement: 1 February 1971.

19. Form 19 Order on Application by Landlord for Cancellation, in Whole or in Part of a Certificate of Disrepair

(*Rent Act 1968, s 52(3), Sch 9, paras 4(6), (7), 6(3)*)

(*General Title—Form 1*)

.. .. (Seal)

Upon hearing

It is ordered that the certificate of disrepair, dated the .. .. day of .. .. and issued by the .. .. Council in respect of premises known as .. .. of which the applicant is the landlord and the respondent is the tenant, shall be cancelled [in respect of the following defects: .. ..].

[And it is ordered that the said certificate shall cease to have effect as from the .. .. day of.. .. .. [*or* the date of this order]].

(*General Conclusion—Form 3*) **[803]**

NOTES
Commencement: 1 February 1971.

20. Form 20 Application by Mortgagor to Vary the Terms of a Regulated Mortgage or Limit the Exercise of a Right or Remedy in respect thereof on Grounds of Financial Hardship

(*Rent Act 1968, s 95(2), (3)*)

(*General Title—Form 1*)

I, ... (*name of applicant*)
of .. .. (*address and occupation of applicant*) hereby apply to the Court for an order varying the terms of, or imposing a limitation or condition on the exercise of a right or remedy in respect of, a regulated mortgage dated the .. .. day of.. .. .. 19 .. .., in respect of which I am the mortgagor and the respondent is the mortgagee relating to the property known as

And for an order providing for the costs of this application.

The grounds of this application are that by reason of (*state which of the events referred to in section* 95(1) *of the Rent Act* 1968 *has occurred*).

I would suffer severe financial hardship unless the relief applied for were given.

The relief applied for is (*state what relief is applied for*) or such other relief as the Court thinks appropriate.

(*General Conclusion—Form 2*) **[804]**

NOTES
Commencement: 1 February 1971.

21. Form 21 Order on Application by Mortgagor to Vary the Terms of a Regulated Mortgage or Limit the Exercise of a Right or Remedy in respect thereof on Grounds of Financial Hardship

(*Rent Act 1968, s 95(2), (3)*)

(*General Title—Form 1*)

.. .. (Seal)

Upon hearing

and the Court being satisfied that the applicant would suffer severe financial hardship unless relief were given in the terms of this order

It is hereby ordered that the rate of interest payable in respect of the undermentioned mortgage be limited to £.. .. .. per centum per annum (*or as the case may be according to the relief awarded*):

(*Particulars of mortgage to which the relief applies, including, where appropriate, an apportionment of the money secured by the mortgage between the dwelling-house[s] subject to a regulated tenancy and other land comprised in the mortgage*)

(*General Conclusion—Form 3*) **[805]**

NOTES
Commencement: 1 February 1971.

22. Form 22 Application to Vary or Revoke an Order under Section 95(2) Rent Act 1968

(*Rent Act 1968, s 95(5)*)

(*General Title—Form 1*)

I, ... (*name of applicant*)

of .. .. (*address and occupation of applicant*) being the mortgagor [mortgagee] in relation to the undermentioned mortgage in respect of which the Court made an order under section 95(2) of the Rent Act 1968 on the .. .. day of .. .. 19 .. .. hereby apply to te Court for an order varying the said order in the manner set out below [*or* revoking the said order].

And for an order providing for the costs of this application.

The particulars of the said mortgage are as follows: .. .. (*state particulars of mortgage*)

The variation applied for is that .. .. (*state the variation*) or such other variation as the Court thinks appropriate.

The grounds of this application are: (*state the grounds*).

(*General Conclusion—Form 2*) **[806]**

NOTES
Commencement: 1 February 1971.

23. Form 23 Order on Application to Vary or Revoke an Order under section 95(2) Rent Act 1968

(*Rent Act 1968, s 95(5)*)

(*General Title—Form 1*)

.. .. (Seal)

Upon hearing

It is hereby ordered that the order made by this Court on the .. .. day of.. .. .. 19.. .. .. in respect of the undermentioned mortgage be varied by substituting £.. .. .. per centum per annum as the rate of interest payable under the said mortgage (*or as the case may be*) [*or* be revoked].

(*Particulars of the mortgage referred to in the order*)

(*General Conclusion—Form 3*) **[807]**

NOTES
Commencement: 1 February 1971.

24. Form 24 Application to Determine a Question Relating to a Tenancy or Mortgage or any Matter material thereto

(*Rent Act 1968, s 105*)

(*General Title—Form 1*)

I, ... (*name of applicant*)

of .. .. (*address and occupation of applicant*) hereby apply to the Court for an order determining whether the tenancy of the premises known as .. .. under which I am the tenant [landlord] and the respondent is the landlord [tenant] is a protected tenancy [*or* whether .. .. is a statutory tenant of the dwelling house known as .. ..] [*or* whether the mortgage made between .. .. and .. .. .. relating the premises known as .. .. is a controlled mortgage within the meaning of Part VIII of the Rent Act 1968][*or* what is the rent limit [*or* the rent actually recoverable from the tenant] in respect of the premises known as .. .. of which I am the landlord [tenant] and the respondent is the tenant [landlord]] [*or* whether Part VI of the Rent Act 1968 applies to a contract made on the .. .. day of.. .. .. between .. .. and .. .. relating to the occupation of the dwelling known as .. ..] (*or as the case may be*).

And for an order providing for the costs of this application.

The grounds of this application are: (*state the grounds*).

(*General Conclusion—Form 3*) **[808]**

NOTES

Commencement: 1 February 1971.

25. Form 25 Order on an Application to Determine a Question Relating to a Tenancy or Mortgage or any Matter material thereto

(*Rent Act 1968, s 105*)

(*General Title—Form 1*)

.. .. (Seal)

Upon hearing

It is hereby ordered and declared that the tenancy of the premises known as .. .. under which the applicant is the tenant [landlord] and the respondent is the landlord [tenant] is [is not] a protected tenancy [*or* that .. .. is [is not] a statutory tenant of the dwelling house known as .. ..] [*or* that the mortgage made between .. .. and .. .. on the .. .. .. day of.. .. .. in respect of premises known as .. .. is [is not] a controlled mortgage within the meaning of Part VIII of the Rent Act 1968] [*or* that the rent limit [*or* the rent actually recoverable from the tenant] in respect of the premises known as .. .. is £ .. .. per .. ..] [*or* that Part VI of the Rent Act 1968 applies [does not apply] to a contract made on the .. .. .. day of .. .. .. 19 .. .. .. between .. .. .. and .. .. .. relating to the occupation of premises known as .. .. (*or as the case may be*) .. ..

(*General Conclusion—Form 3*) **[809]**

NOTES
Commencement: 1 February 1971.

26. Form 26 Application for Order to Local Authority to Issue Qualification Certificate, or for Cancellation of Qualification Certificate

(*Housing Act 1969, s 49(1), (2)*)

(*General Title—Form 1*)

I, ... (*name of applicant*)
of .. .. (*address and occupation of applicant*) hereby apply to the Court for an order [directing the Council [*name of local authority*] to issue a qualification certificate in respect of the premises known as .. .. of which I am the landlord and .. .. [*name of tenant*] is the tenant. Notice of refusal of my application for a certificate was served on me by the .. .. Council on the day .. .. .. day of .. ..]

[*or* quashing a qualification certificate issued by the .. .. Council [*name of local authority*] on the .. .. .. day of.. .. .., in respect of the premises known as .. .. of which I am the tenant and .. .. [*name and address of landlord]* is the landlord.

A copy of the certificate was served on me on the .. .. day of .. ..

The grounds for this application are: (*state the grounds of the application*).

(*General Conclusion—Form 2*) **[810]**

NOTES
Commencement: 1 February 1971.

27. Form 27 Order on Application for Order to Local Authority to Issue Qualification Certificate, or for Cancellation of Qualification Certificate

(*Housing Act 1969, s 49(1), (2)*)

(*General Title—Form 1*)

.. .. (Seal)
Upon hearing

It is hereby ordered [that the .. .. Council do issue a certificate in respect of the premises known as .. .., of which the applicant is the landlord certifying that the premises satisfy the qualifying conditions under section 43(1) of the Housing Act 1969].

[*or* that the qualification certificate dated the .. .. day of .. .. and issued by the .. .. Council under section 45 of the Housing Act 1969 in respect of the premises known as .. .., of which the applicant is the tenant shall be quashed and deemed never to have had effect.]

(*General Conclusion—Form 3*) **[811]**

NOTES
Commencement: 1 February 1971.

28. Form 28 Application for Order Empowering Landlord to Enter Premises and Carry out Works

(*Housing Act 1969, s 54*)

(*General Title—Form 1*)

I, ... (*name of applicant*)

of .. .. (*address and occupation of applicant*) hereby apply to the Court for an order authorising me to enter the premises known as .. .., of which I am the landlord and [*name of tenant*], is the tenant, in order to carry out works covered by a certificate of fair rent relating to those premises dated .. .., being works required to satisfy the conditions laid down in section 43 of the Housing Act 1969.

And for an order for the costs of this application.

The grounds for this application are: (*state the grounds of the application*).

(*General Conclusion—Form 2*) **[812]**

NOTES
Commencement: 1 February 1971.

29. Form 29 Order Empowering Landlord to Enter Premises and Carry out Works

(*Housing Act 1969, s 54*)

(*General Title—Form 1*)

.. .. (Seal)

Upon hearing

It is hereby ordered that the applicant, being the landlord of the premises known as .. .. of which the respondent is the tenant, or the applicant's duly authorised agent, be entitled to enter the said premises in order to carry out [the works] [*or* the following works, namely .. ..] which are covered by the certificate of fair rent relating to the said premises dated .. .., being works required to satisfy the conditions laid down in section 43 of the Housing Act 1969.

(*General Conclusion—Form 3*) **[813]**

NOTES
Commencement: 1 February 1971.

RENT ASSESSMENT COMMITTEES (ENGLAND AND WALES) REGULATIONS 1971
(SI 1971 NO 1065)

NOTES
Made: 29 June 1971
Authority: Rent Act 1977, ss 74, 155(3), Sch 24, para 1

ARRANGEMENT OF REGULATIONS

Citation and commencement

Regulation	Para
1	[814]

Interpretation

2	[815]

Hearings

3	[816]
4	[817]

Documents, etc

5	[818]
6	[819]

Inspection of dwelling-house

7	[820]

Adjournment

8	[821]

Non-appearance

9	[822]

Decisions

10	[823]
10A	[824]

Giving of notices, etc

11	[825]

CITATION AND COMMENCEMENT

1. These regulations may be cited as the Rent Assessment Committees (England and Wales) Regulations 1971 and shall come into operation on 2nd August 1971. **[814]**

NOTES

Commencement: 2 August 1971.

INTERPRETATION

2. (1) The Interpretation Act 1889 shall apply for the interpretation of these regulations as it applies for the interpretation of an Act of Parliament.

(2) In these regulations, unless the context otherwise requires—

"chairman" means the chairman of a committee;

["committee" means a rent assessment committee constituted under Schedule 10 to the Rent Act 1977, to which a reference is made, but does not include a rent assessment committee carrying out the functions conferred on it by section 72 (Functions of Rent Tribunals) or section 142 (Leasehold Valuation Tribunals) of the Housing Act 1980.]

"hearing" means the meeting or meetings of a committee to hear oral representations made in relation to a reference;

"party" means, in the case where a reference is subject to a hearing, any person who is entitled under regulation 3(3) of these regulations to receive notice of the hearing and, in the case where a reference is not to be subject to a hearing, any person who is entitled to make representations in writing to the committee;

"reference" means a matter or an application, as the case may be, which is referred by a rent officer to a rent assessment committee under Schedule 6 or Schedule 7 to the Rent Act 1968, or Part II of Schedule 2 to the Housing Act 1969.

(3) For the purpose of any of these regulations relating to procedure at a hearing, any reference to a party shall be construed as including a reference to a person authorised by a party to make oral representations on his behalf pursuant to paragraph 8, or paragraph 12(1), of Schedule 6, or paragraph 7(3) of Schedule 7, to the Rent Act 1968, or paragraph 13 of Schedule 2 to the Housing Act 1969, as the case may be. **[815]**

NOTES

Commencement: 2 August 1971.

Amended by SI 1980 No 1699.

Rent Act 1968, Schs 5, 6, 7: see now Rent Act 1977, Schs 10, 11, 12.

Housing Act 1969, Sch 2: see now Rent Act 1977, Sch 11.

HEARINGS

3. (1) A hearing by a committee shall be in public unless, for special reasons, the committee decide otherwise; but nothing in these regulations shall prevent a member of the Council on Tribunals in that capacity from attending any hearing.

(2) Such hearing shall be on such date and at such time and place as the committee shall appoint.

[(3) Notices of such date, time and place shall be given by the committee, not less than [10 days (subject to paragraph (4) below)] before the said date—

(*a*) Where the reference is an application for a certificate of fair rent referred pursuant to paragraph 7 of Schedule 12 to the Rent Act 1977, to the applicant and, in a case to which paragraph 11 of the said Schedule applies, to the tenant;

(*b*) where the reference is an application supported by a certificate of fair rent referred pursuant to paragraph 11 of Schedule 11 to the Rent Act 1977, to the applicant; and

(*c*) in every other case, to the landlord and tenant.]

[(4) The notice referred to in paragraph (3) above may be given not less than 7 days before the date of the hearing if that date has been referred to in the notice given under paragraph 7(1)(*b*) of Schedule 11 or under paragraph 9(1) of Schedule 12 to the Rent Act 1977 as the date when the hearing would be held if a request to make oral representations were to be made.] **[816]**

NOTES

Commencement: 2 August 1971 (paras (1), (2)); 28 November 1980 (para (3)); 1 January 1982 (para (4)).

Para (3): substituted by SI 1980 No 1699; amended by SI 1981 No 1783, reg 4.

Para (4): added by SI 1981 No 1783, reg 4.

Rent Act 1968, Schs 6, 7: see now Rent Act 1977, Schs 11, 12.

4. At the hearing—

(*a*) the parties shall be heard in such order, and, subject to the provisions of these regulations, the procedure shall be such as the committee shall determine;

(*b*) a party may call witnesses, give evidence on his own behalf and cross-examine any witnesses called by the other party. **[817]**

NOTES

Commencement: 2 August 1971.

DOCUMENTS, ETC

5. (1) The committee shall, where the reference is to be subject to a hearing, take all reasonable steps to ensure that there is supplied to each of the parties before the date of the hearing—

(*a*) a copy of, or sufficient extracts from or particulars of, any document relevant to the reference which has been received from the rent officer or from a party (other than a document which is in the possession of such party, or of which he has previously been supplied with a copy by the rent officer); and

(*b*) a copy of any document which embodies the results of any enquiries made by or for the committee for the purposes of that reference, or which contains relevant information in relation to fair rents previously determined for other dwelling-houses and which has been prepared for the committee for the purposes of that reference.

(2) Where at any hearing—

(i) any document relevant to the reference is not in the possession of a party present at that hearing; and

(ii) that party has not been supplied with a copy of, or sufficient extracts from or particulars of, that document by the rent officer or by the committee in accordance with the provisions of paragraph (1) of this regulation,

then unless—

(*a*) that party consents to the continuation of the hearing; or

(*b*) the committee consider that that party has a sufficient opportunity of dealing with that document without an adjournment of the hearing,

the committee shall adjourn the hearing for a period which they consider will afford that party a sufficient opportunity of dealing with that document. **[818]**

NOTES

Commencement: 2 August 1971.

6. Where a reference is not to be subject to a hearing, the committee shall supply to each of the parties a copy of, or sufficient extracts from or particulars of, any such document as is mentioned in paragraph (1)(*a*) of regulation 5 of these regulations (other than a document excepted from that paragraph) and a copy of any such document as is mentioned in paragraph (1)(*b*) of that regulation, and they shall not reach their decision until they are satisfied that each party has been given a sufficient opportunity of commenting upon any document of which a copy, or from which extracts or of which particulars, has or have been so supplied, and upon the other's case. **[819]**

NOTES
Commencement: 2 August 1971.

INSPECTION OF DWELLING-HOUSE

7. (1) The committee may of their own motion, and shall at the request of one of the parties (subject in either case to any necessary consent being obtained) inspect the dwelling-house which is the subject of the reference.

(2) An inspection may be made before, during or after the close of the hearing, or at such stage in relation to the consideration of the representations in writing, as the committee shall decide, and the committee shall give to the parties and their representatives an opportunity to attend.

(3) Notice of an inspection shall be given as though it were notice of a hearing, save that the requirements for such notice may be dispensed with or relaxed in so far as the committee are satisfied that the parties have received sufficient notice.

(4) Where an inspection is made after the close of a hearing, the committee shall, if they consider that it is expedient to do so on account of any matter arising from the inspection, reopen the hearing; and if the hearing is to be reopened paragraph (3) of regulation 3 of these regulations shall apply as it applied to the original hearing, save in so far as its requirements may be dispensed with or relaxed with the consent of the parties. **[820]**

NOTES
Commencement: 2 August 1971.

ADJOURNMENT

8. The committee at their discretion may of their own motion, or at the request of the parties, or one of them, at any time and from time to time postpone or adjourn a hearing; but they shall not do so at the request of one party only unless, having regard to the grounds on which and the time at which such request is made and to the convenience of the parties, they deem it reasonable to do so. Such notice of any postponed or adjourned hearing as is reasonable in the circumstances shall be given to the parties by the committee. **[821]**

NOTES
Commencement: 2 August 1971.

NON-APPEARANCE

9. If a party does not appear at a hearing the committee, on being satisfied that the requirements of these regulations regarding the giving of notice of hearings have been duly complied with, may proceed to deal with the reference upon the representations of any party present and upon the documents and information which they may properly consider. **[822]**

NOTES
Commencement: 2 August 1971.

DECISIONS

10. (1) The decision of the committee upon a reference shall be recorded in a document signed by the chairman (or in the event of his absence or incapacity, by another member of the committee) which . . . shall contain no reference to the decision being by a majority (if that be the case) or to any opinion of a minority.

(2) The chairman (or in the event of his absence or incapacity, either of the other members of the committee) shall have power, by certificate under his hand, to correct any clerical or accidental error or omission in the said document.

(3) A copy of the said document and of any such correction shall be sent by the committee to the parties and to the rent officer. **[823]**

NOTES
Commencement: 2 August 1971.

10A. [(1) Where the committee are requested, on or before the giving or notification of the decision, to state the reasons for the decision, those reasons shall be recorded in a document.

(2) Regulation 10 above shall apply to the document recording the reasons as it applies to the document recording the decision.] **[824]**

NOTES
Commencement: 1 January 1982.
Added by SI 1981 No 1783, reg 4(4).

GIVING OF NOTICES, ETC

11. Where any notice or other written matter is required under the provisions of these regulations to be given or supplied by the committee (including any such matter to be supplied to a party for the purposes of a reference to which regulation 6 of these regulations applies) it shall be sufficient compliance with the regulations if such notice or matter is sent by post in a prepaid letter and addressed to the party for whom it is intended at his usual or last known address, or if that party has appointed an agent to act on his behalf in relation to the reference, to that agent at the address of the agent supplied to the committee. **[825]**

NOTES
Commencement: 2 August 1971.

SECURE TENANCIES (DESIGNATED COURSES) REGULATIONS 1980
(SI 1980 NO 1407)

NOTES
Made: 17 September 1980
Authority: Housing Act 1980, s 151, Sch 3, para 11

1. Citation and Commencement

These Regulations may be cited as the Secure Tenancies (Designated Courses) Regulations 1980 and shall come into operation on 3rd October 1980. **[826]**

NOTES
Commencement: 3 October 1980.

2. Designated Courses

There are hereby designated for the purposes of paragraph 11 of Schedule 3 to the Housing Act 1980—

(*a*) any full-time course to which section 1 of the Education Act 1962 from time to time applies;
(*b*) any full-time post-graduate course, that is to say, a course to which only students who hold a first degree of a university or an equivalent qualification are admitted; and
(*c*) any other full-time course provided by an establishment of further education which is maintained or assisted by a local education authority or in respect of the maintenance of which grants are for the time being paid in pursuance of Regulations made under section 100(1)(*b*) of the Education Act 1944. **[827]**

NOTES
Commencement: 3 October 1980.

NOTICES TO QUIT (PRESCRIBED INFORMATION) REGULATIONS 1980
(SI 1980 NO 1624)

NOTES
Made: 28 October 1980
Authority: Protection from Eviction Act 1977, s 5

1. These regulations may be cited as the Notices to Quit (Prescribed Information) Regulations 1980 and shall come into operation on 28th November 1980. **[828]**

NOTES
Commencement: 28 November 1980.

2. Where a notice to quit is given by a landlord on or after the coming into operation of these regulations to determine a tenancy of any premises let as a dwelling the information prescribed for the purposes of section 5 of the Protection from Eviction Act 1977 (which deals with the minimum length of, and other matters relating to, a notice to quit any premises let as a dwelling) shall be that in the Schedule to these regulations. **[829]**

NOTES

Commencement: 28 November 1980.

SCHEDULE

PRESCRIBED INFORMATION

1. If the tenant does not leave the dwelling, the landlord must get an order for possession from the court before the tenant can lawfully be evicted. The landlord cannot apply for such an order before the notice to quit has run out.

2. A tenant who does not know if he has any right to remain in possession after a notice to quit runs out or is otherwise unsure of his rights, can obtain advice from a solicitor. Help with all or part of the cost of legal advice and assistance may be available under the Legal Aid Scheme. He should also be able to obtain information from a Citizens' Advice Bureau, a Housing Aid Centre, a Rent Officer or a Rent Tribunal Office. **[830]**

NOTES

Commencement: 28 November 1980.

ASSURED TENANCIES (APPROVED BODY) (NO 1) ORDER 1980

(SI 1980 NO 1694)

NOTES

Made: 5 November 1980

Authority: Housing Act 1980, ss 56(4), 151

1. This order may be cited as the Assured Tenancies (Approved Body) (No. 1) Order 1980 and shall come into operation on 4th December 1980. **[831]**

NOTES

Commencement: 4 December 1980.

2. The Abbey Housing Association Limited is hereby specified for the purposes of Part II of the Housing Act 1980. **[832]**

NOTES

Commencement: 4 December 1980.

RENT ACT 1977 (FORMS ETC) REGULATIONS 1980

(SI 1980 NO 1697)

NOTES

Made: 30 October 1980

Authority: Rent Act 1977, ss 49, 60, 66, 67, 73, 74, 77, 79, 81A, 84, Sch 12, para 1; Rent (Agriculture) Act 1976, s 13

ARRANGEMENT OF REGULATIONS

Regulation	Para
1	[833]
2	[834]
3	[835]
4	[836]
5	[837]
6	[838]
7	[839]
8	[840]
9	[841]

SCHEDULES

Schedule 1—

Form 1 Notice of increase of rent under regulated tenancy where a rent determined by the Rent Officer has been registered on or after 28th November 1980 [*Notice of increase of rent under regulated tenancy where a fair rent has been registered and the increase is not subject to the phasing provisions of Schedule 8 to the Rent Act 1977*] .. .. [842]

Form 2 Notice of increase of rent under regulated tenancy where the rent determined by the Rent Officer was registered before 28th November 1980 and the increase is not subject to the phasing provisions of Schedule 9 to the Act [*Notice of increase of rent under regulated tenancy where a fair rent has been registered and the increase is subject to the phasing provisions of Schedule 8 to the Rent Act 1977*] .. .. [843]

Form 4 Notice of increase of unregistered rent under regulated Tenancy on account of increased rates .. .. [845]

Form 5 Application for registration of fair rent .. .. [846]

Form 6 Application for registration of fair rent in the case of a statutory tenancy arising at the end of a long tenancy under Part I of the Landlord and Tenant Act 1954 .. .. [847]

Form 7 Application for registration of fair rent where dwelling-house subject to a statutory tenancy under the Rent (Agriculture) Act 1976 .. .. [848]

Form 8 Application for certificate of fair rent .. .. [849]

Form 9 Application for registration of fair rent supported by certificate of fair rent .. .. [850]

Form 10 Joint application for cancellation of a registered rent .. .. .. [851]

Form 11 Application for cancellation of registration of rent where there is no regulated tenancy .. .. [852]

Form 12 Notice by Rent Officer of application for registration of fair rent .. [853]

Form 13 Notice by Rent Officer of application for registration of fair rent where landlord includes an amount for services .. .. [854]

Form 14 Notice by Rent Assessment Committee requiring further information [855]

Form 15 Application for cancellation of a rent registered by a rent tribunal where the dwelling is not subject to a restricted contract .. .. [856]

Schedule 2—*Particulars with regard to the tenancy to be registered in the register of rents kept by the rent officer* .. .. [857]

Schedule 3—*Particulars relating to a restricted contract regarding which lessors may by notice be required to give information* .. .. [858]

Schedule 4—*Particulars with regard to the contract to be entered in the register* .. [859]

1. These regulations may be cited as the Rent Act 1977 (Forms etc.) Regulations 1980 and shall come into operation on 28th November 1980. **[833]**

NOTES

Commencement: 28 November 1980.

2. (1) In these regulations the "1976 Act" means the Rent (Agriculture) Act 1976 and the "1977 Act" means the Rent Act 1977.

(2) In these regulations any reference to a numbered form shall be construed as a reference to the form bearing that number in Schedule 1 hereto, or to a form substantially to the like effect. **[834]**

NOTES
Commencement: 28 November 1980.

3. (1) The forms prescribed for the purposes of notices of increase of rent under Part III of the 1977 Act shall be as follows:—

[(*a*) in the case of a notice under section 45(2) of the 1977 Act where the rent is not subject to the phasing provisions of Schedule 8 to the Act, form No. 1;

(*b*) in the case of a notice under section 45(2) of the 1977 Act where a rent is subject to the phasing provisions of Schedule 8 to the Act, form No. 2; and]

(*c*) in the case of a notice under section 46(2) of the 1977 Act, form No. 4.

(2) The forms prescribed for the purpose of Part IV of the 1977 Act, where an application is made to the rent officer, shall be as follows:—

(*a*) in the case of an application under section 67 of the Act—

(i) where a statutory tenancy arises at the end of a long tenancy under Part I of the Landlord and Tenant Act 1954, form No. 6;

(ii) where the dwelling house is subject to a statutory tenancy as defined in the 1976 Act, form No. 7; and

(iii) in any other case, form No. 5;

(*b*) in the case of an application under section 69(1) of the 1977 Act for a certificate of fair rent, form No. 8, and in the case of an application under section 69(4) for the registration of a rent in accordance with such a certificate, form No. 9;

(*c*) in the case of an application under section 73 of the 1977 Act where the application is made by the landlord and the tenant jointly, form No. 10, and in any other case, form No. 11.

(3) The form of notice to be served by a rent officer under paragraph 3(1) of Schedule 11 to the 1977 Act, as modified by the Regulated Tenancies (Procedure) Regulations 1980, shall be form No. 13 if, in pursuance of section 67(2)(*b*) of the 1977 Act the application was accompanied by details of the landlord's expenditure in connection with the provision of services, and shall be form No. 12 in any other case.

(4) The form of notice to be served by a rent assessment committee under paragraph 7 of Schedule 11 to the 1977 Act, shall be form No. 14.

(5) The form of an application under section 81A of the 1977 Act shall be form No. 15. **[835]**

NOTES
Commencement: 28 November 1980.
Para (1): sub-paras (*a*), (*b*) substituted by SI 1987 No 266, reg 2(i).
The 1977 Act: Rent Act 1977.
The 1976 Act: Rent (Agriculture) Act 1976.

4. An application made under section 67, 69, 73 or 81A of the 1977 Act, as the case may be, shall contain the particulars specified in the relevant prescribed form. **[836]**

NOTES

Commencement: 28 November 1980.
The 1977 Act: Rent Act 1977.

5. The register kept for the purposes of Part IV of the 1977 Act under section 66(1) thereof shall contain the particulars with regard to a regulated tenancy or, as the case may be, housing association tenancy, specified in Schedule 2 hereto. **[837]**

NOTES

Commencement: 28 November 1980.
The 1977 Act: Rent Act 1977.

6. The fee to be paid under section 66(4) of the 1977 Act for a copy of an entry in the register certified under the hand of the rent officer or person duly authorised by him shall be [£1.00]. **[838]**

NOTES

Commencement: 28 November 1980.
Amended by SI 1984 No 1391, reg 3.
The 1977 Act: Rent Act 1977.

7. The particulars relating to a restricted contract, referred to a rent tribunal, regarding which the lessor may be required by notice to give information reasonably required by the tribunal, are those specified in Schedule 3 hereto. **[839]**

NOTES

Commencement: 28 November 1980.

8. The register kept for the purposes of Part V of the 1977 Act under section 79(1) thereof shall contain the particulars with regard to a restricted contract specified in Schedule 4 hereto. **[840]**

NOTES

Commencement: 28 November 1980.
The 1977 Act: Rent Act 1977.

9. The fee to be paid under section 79(6) of the 1977 Act for a copy of an entry in the register certified under the hand of an officer duly authorised in that behalf by the president of the rent assessment panel concerned shall be [£1.00]. **[841]**

NOTES

Commencement: 28 November 1980.
Amended by SI 1984 No 1391, reg 3.
The 1977 Act: Rent Act 1977.

SCHEDULES

SCHEDULE 1

FORM 1 *NOTICE OF INCREASE OF RENT UNDER REGULATED TENANCY WHERE A RENT DETERMINED BY THE RENT OFFICER HAS BEEN REGISTERED ON OR AFTER 28TH NOVEMBER 1980* [NOTICE OF INCREASE OF RENT UNDER REGULATED TENANCY WHERE A FAIR RENT HAS BEEN REGISTERED AND THE INCREASE IS NOT SUBJECT TO THE PHASING PROVISIONS OF SCHEDULE 8 TO THE RENT ACT 1977]

[RENT ACT 1977, SECTION 45(2), AS AMENDED BY HOUSING ACT 1980 AND RENT (RELIEF FROM PHASING) ORDER 1987

NOTICE OF INCREASE OF RENT UNDER REGULATED TENANCY WHERE A FAIR RENT HAS BEEN REGISTERED AND THE INCREASE IS *NOT* SUBJECT TO THE PHASING PROVISIONS OF SCHEDULE 8 TO THE RENT ACT 1977 (See Notes 1 to 3)

PLEASE READ THE NOTES CAREFULLY AND KEEP THIS FORM (See Note 4)

To .. .., tenant of .. ..

1. A rent of £ .. .. .. per .. .. (exclusive of rates) has been [registered by the Rent Officer] [determined by a Rent Assessment Committee] for the above premises and takes effect from .. .. (Cross out words which do not apply)

2. Unless—

(*a*) a different rent is registered by the Rent Officer or determined by a Rent Assessment Committee, or (See Note 5)
(*b*) the Rent Officer agrees to cancel the registration, or (See Note 6)
(*c*) the rent is registered as variable (See Note 7)—

the maximum rent (exclusive of rates) you can be charged from the date in paragraph 1 is the full registered rent as shown in that paragraph.

3. I hereby give you notice that your rent (exclusive of rates) will be increased as follows—

Present rent £
per

New rent from
.. .. *£
per

The date at * must not be earlier than the date in paragraph 1 above nor 4 weeks before the date of service of this Notice.

[It is noted in the rent register that rates in respect of the above premises are borne by me or a superior landlord. I am entitled to add the amount for rates to the rent and to pass on to you future increases in rates without serving a Notice of Increase.] (Cross out this paragraph if tenant pays rates)

Signed .. ..

[On behalf of .. ..]

Address of Landlord .. ..

[Name and Address of Agent .. ..]

Date .. .. (Cross out words in square brackets if they do not apply)

Notes

Use of Notice

1. This notice is for use for rent increases which are not subject to phasing. Except in the circumstances described in paragraph 2 below, phasing does not apply to increases which result from a determination by the rent officer or rent assessment committee if the registration (or confirmation of the existing registration) resulting from the rent officer's determination of the fair rent takes effect *on or after 4th May 1987*.

2. Phasing does apply in the circumstances described above if the registration of rent is the first such registration for a tenancy which has been converted from a controlled tenancy to a regulated tenancy. Form No. 2 should be used for these cases.

3. This Notice can only be used for increases which are to take effect when the tenancy is a statutory tenancy. A statutory tenancy comes into being when a tenancy agreed between the landlord and tenant (known as a contractual tenancy) has come to an end and the tenant has security of tenure under the Rent Act 1977. The Notice can be served while there is still a contractual tenancy. If the contractual tenancy can be terminated before the date in paragraph 3, this notice can be used instead of a notice to quit to turn the contractual tenancy into a statutory tenancy from that date.

Explanatory booklet

4. The Department of the Environment and Welsh Office booklet "Regulated Tenancies" explains in more detail than these Notes how the fair rent system works and the rights and duties of landlords and tenants under the Rent Act. It is available free from Rent Officers, and Citizens' Advice Bureaux, and you are advised to obtain a copy.

Re-registration

5. No application for a new registration may be made during the two years from the date in paragraph 1 of the Notice unless either—

(*a*) it is made by the landlord and the tenant acting together, or
(*b*) there has been such a change in the circumstances taken into account when the rent was registered (e.g. the making of an improvement to the premises) as to make the registered rent no longer a fair rent.

But the landlord may apply three months in advance for a new registration to take effect after the end of the two year period.

Cancellation

6. As long as there is a regulated tenancy an application to the Rent Officer to cancel the registration can only be made jointly by landlord and tenant.

Limitation of rent increases

7. The rent shown in paragraph 1 of the Notice may not be exceeded unless the rent is registered as variable. It will only be registered as variable if the terms of the tenancy provide for the rent to be varied according to the cost of services or works of maintenance and repair carried out by the landlord or superior landlord and the Rent Officer considers the terms reasonable.

Help with rent and rates

8. If the tenant has difficulty in paying his rent or rates he should apply to the local council offices for details of the rent allowance and rate rebate schemes. The council will also advise if he may be better off receiving supplementary benefit from the Department of Health and Social Security.] **[842]**

NOTES

Commencement: 28 November 1980.
Substituted by SI 1987 No 266, reg 2(iii), Schedule.

FORM 2 *NOTICE OF INCREASE OF RENT UNDER REGULATED TENANCY WHERE THE RENT DETERMINED BY THE RENT OFFICER WAS REGISTERED BEFORE 28TH NOVEMBER 1980 AND THE INCREASE IS NOT SUBJECT TO THE PHASING PROVISIONS OF SCHEDULE 9 TO THE ACT*
[NOTICE OF INCREASE OF RENT UNDER REGULATED TENANCY WHERE A FAIR RENT HAS BEEN REGISTERED AND THE INCREASE IS SUBJECT TO THE PHASING PROVISIONS OF SCHEDULE 8 TO THE RENT ACT 1977]

[RENT ACT 1977, SECTION 45(2), AS AMENDED BY HOUSING ACT 1980

NOTICE OF INCREASE OF RENT UNDER REGULATED TENANCY WHERE A FAIR RENT HAS BEEN REGISTERED AND THE INCREASE IS SUBJECT TO THE PHASING PROVISIONS OF SCHEDULE 8 TO THE RENT ACT 1977
(See Notes 1 and 2)

PLEASE READ THE NOTES CAREFULLY AND KEEP THIS FORM (See Note 3)

To .. .., tenant of .. ..

1. A rent of £ .. .. .. per .. .. (exclusive of rates) has been [registered by the Rent Officer] [determined by a Rent Assessment Committee] for the above premises and takes effect from .. .. (Cross out words which do not apply) (See Note 4)

2. Unless—

(*a*) a different rent is registered by the Rent Officer or determined by a Rent Assessment Committee, or (See Note 5)
(*b*) the Rent Officer agrees to cancel the registration, or (See Note 6)—
(*c*) the rent is registered as variable—

the maximum rent (exclusive of rates) you can be charged during the first year from the date in paragraph 1 is (See Note 7)

£ per

This is calculated as follows:—

New registered rent
£ per +
Previous rent limit
(See Note 8) £
per +
Service element (if
any) (See Note 9) £
per –
divided by 2
=£ per

3. After the end of the first year from the date in paragraph 1 the maximum rent (unless 2(*a*), (*b*) or (*c*) applies) is the full registered rent as shown in 1 above of

£ per

4. I hereby give notice that your rent (exclusive of rates) will be increased as follows:—

Present rent £
per
New rent from .. ..
.. * £ per
New rent from .. ..
.. £ per

If two increases are shown above I am not obliged to remind you when the second increase becomes payable. The date at * must not be earlier than the date in paragraph 1 above nor 4 weeks before the date of service of this Notice.

[It is noted in the rent register that rates in respect of the above premises are borne by me or a superior landlord. I am entitled to add the amount for rates to the rent and to pass on to you future increases in rates without serving a Notice of Increase.] (Cross out this paragraph if tenant pays rates)

Signed .. ..

[On behalf of .. ..]

Address of Landlord .. ..

[Name and Address of Agent .. ..]

Date .. .. (Cross out words in square brackets if they do not apply)

Notes

Use of Notice

1. This Notice is only for use for rent increases which are subject to phasing. Phasing applies in the following circumstances—

(*a*) if the registration of rent is the first such registration for a tenancy which has been converted from a controlled tenancy to a regulated tenancy, or
(*b*) if the rent was determined by a rent officer or rent assessment committee and the registration (or confirmation of the existing registration) resulting from the rent officer's determination of the fair rent took effect *before 4th May 1987*.

2. The Notice can only be used for increases which are to take effect when the tenancy is a statutory tenancy. A statutory tenancy comes into being when a tenancy agreed between the landlord and tenant (known as a contractual tenancy) has come to an end and the tenant has security of tenure under the Rent Act 1977. The Notice can be served while there is still a contractual tenancy. If the contractual tenancy can be terminated before the (earliest) date in paragraph 4, this Notice can be used instead of a notice to quit to turn the contractual tenancy into a statutory tenancy from that date.

Explanatory booklet

3. The Department of the Environment and Welsh Office booklet "Regulated Tenancies" explains in more detail than these Notes how the fair rent system works and the rights and duties of landlords and tenants under the Rent Act. It is available free from Rent Officers, and Citizens' Advice Bureaux, and you are advised to obtain a copy.

Limitation of rent increase

4. The rent shown in paragraph 1 of the Notice may not be exceeded unless the rent is registered as variable. It will only be registered as variable if the terms of the tenancy provide for the rent to be varied according to the cost of services or works of maintenance and repair carried out by the landlord or superior landlord and the Rent Officer considers the terms reasonable. Secondly, the landlord may only increase the rent during the first year from the date in paragraph 1 of the notice to the extent allowed under the provisions for the phasing of increases.

Re-registration

5. No application for a new registration may be made during the two years from the date in paragraph 1 of the Notice unless either—

(*a*) it is made by the landlord and the tenant acting together, or
(*b*) there has been such a change in the circumstances taken into account when the rent was registered (e.g. the making of an improvement to the premises) as to make the registered rent no longer a fair rent.

But the landlord may apply three months in advance for a new registration to take effect after the end of the two year period.

Cancellation

6. As long as there is a regulated tenancy an application to the Rent Officer to cancel the registration can only be made jointly by landlord and tenant.

How phasing works

7. During the first year from the date in paragraph 1 of the Notice the landlord is permitted to charge half of the increase, except that where there is a service element he may charge this in full at once. After the end of the first year he can charge the full registered rent shown in paragraph 1.

Previous rent limit

8. The amount of increase permitted has to be worked out by taking as a starting point the previous rent limit. The previous rent limit is the amount the landlord was permitted by the Rent Act to charge immediately before the Rent Officer registered the rent (whether or not there has been an appeal to a Rent Assessment Committee). (Rates are disregarded for this purpose.) The landlord may not actually have been charging this amount.

Service element

9. The service element is the increase in the rent permitted on account of services provided by the landlord or a superior landlord. If there is a service element it has to be recorded in the Rent Officer's register.

Help with rent and rates

10. If the tenant has difficulty in paying his rent or rates he should apply to the local

council offices for details of the rent allowance and rate rebate schemes. The council will also advise if he may be better off receiving supplementary benefit from the Department of Health and Social Security.] **[843–844]**

NOTES

Commencement: 28 November 1980.
Substituted by SI 1987 No 266, reg 2(iii), Schedule.

FORM 4 NOTICE OF INCREASE OF UNREGISTERED RENT UNDER REGULATED TENANCY ON ACCOUNT OF INCREASED RATES

RENT ACT 1977, SECTION 46

NOTICE OF INCREASE OF UNREGISTERED RENT UNDER REGULATED TENANCY ON ACCOUNT OF INCREASED RATES. (See Notes 1-3)

Please read all the notes carefully

To .. .. tenant of .. ..

1. The rates in respect of the above premises have been increased as follows:—

Previous rates .. .. New rates .. .. Date of new rates

per [half year][year] per [half year][year] as from .. .. ..

2. From .. .. .. * your rent will be increased accordingly as follows:—

Present rent £ .. .. per .. ..

Increase in rent £ .. .. per .. ..

New rent £ .. .. per .. ..

*The date must not be earlier than 6 weeks before the service of this Notice.

[3. On the day after the service of this Notice you will owe the sum of £ .. .., for arrears of the above increase] (See Note 4).

Signature .. ..

[On behalf of .. ..]

Address of landlord .. ..

[Name and address of agent .. ..]

Date .. ..

NOTES

Use of Notice

1. This notice is for use to increase the rent on account of an increase in rates where—
   (*a*) the rent is inclusive of rates borne by the landlord or a superior landlord; and
   (*b*) the tenancy is a regulated tenancy under the Rent Act 1977; and
   (*c*) a fair rent has *not* been registered for the premises under the Act; and
   (*d*) the increase is to take effect when the tenancy is a statutory tenancy. A statutory tenancy comes into being when a tenancy agreed between the landlord and the tenant (known as a contractual tenancy) has come to an end and the tenant has security of tenure under the Rent Act 1977.

2. The notice can be served while there is still a contractual tenancy. If the contractual tenancy can be terminated before the date in paragraph 2, this notice can be used instead of a notice to quit to turn the contractual tenancy into a statutory tenancy from that date.

Rate demands

3. Until the local authority's demand for rates in a new rating period is made, the tenant's liability on account of rates continues to be based on the rates for the previous rating period. When the demand for the new period is received, the tenant's liability must be recalculated. If the rates have gone up, the landlord is entitled on serving this notice to an increase of rent on account of the increased rates. If there is a further

demand for rates during the rating period, for example, because the rateable value has been increased, the tenant's liability must similarly be recalculated in order to ascertain what increase of rent the landlord is entitled to on account of the increased rates.

Arrears

4. This paragraph will only be needed where the date for the increase is a date earlier than the service of this Notice, and there have been rent days between the earlier date and the date of service of this Notice.

Help with rent and rates

5. If the tenant has difficulty in paying his rent or rates, he should apply to the local Council Offices for details of the rent allowance and rate rebate schemes. The Council will also advise if he may be better off receiving Supplementary Benefit from the Department of Health and Social Security. **[845]**

NOTES
Commencement: 28 November 1980.

FORM 5 APPLICATION FOR REGISTRATION OF FAIR RENT

RENT ACT 1977 Section 67 as amended by the Housing Act 1980

APPLICATION FOR REGISTRATION OF FAIR RENT

Use this form except in the special cases set out in the Note at the end of the form

To the Rent Officer

1. Address of Premises

"Premises" means the property, for example the house, flat or room(s) for which you want a rent registered

2. Name of Tenant

Also give the tenant's address if it is different from the above

3. Name and Address of Landlord

If a registered housing association or housing trust, or the Housing Corporation, tick here .. ..

4. Details of Premises

Say what type of property it is, for example, a house, flat or room(s). If it is a flat or room(s), say what floor or floors it is on

Give number and type of rooms .. ..

5. Does the tenancy include any other property?

Such as garage, or other separate building or land

Yes .. .. No .. .. Tick one box

If 'Yes', give details .. ..

6. Does the tenant share any accommodation

— with the landlord?

Yes .. .. No .. .. Tick one box

If 'Yes', give details .. ..

— with another tenant?

Yes .. .. No .. .. Tick one box

If 'Yes', give details .. ..

7. What rent do you want the rent officer to register as a fair rent?

£ .. .. .. per .. .. .. (eg per week, month, quarter etc)

Include any amount for services and/or furniture provided by the landlord or superior landlord.

Do not include anything for rates

The rent officer cannot deal with your application unless you answer this question

8. Are any services provided under the tenancy?

Such as cleaning, lighting, heating, hot water or gardening

Yes .. .. No .. .. Tick one box

If 'Yes', give details .. ..

9. If you are the landlord (and this is not a joint application) how much of the proposed rent do you think is due to these services?

£ .. .. .. per .. .. .. (eg per week, month, quarter etc)

If this is a landlord's application, he must attach details of the expenditure incurred in providing any services, otherwise the rent officer cannot deal with the application

10. Is any furniture provided under the tenancy?

Yes .. .. No .. .. Tick one box

If 'Yes', give details or attach a list to the form .. ..

11. When did the tenancy begin? .. ..

If for a fixed term, say how long .. ..

What repairs are the responsibility of

— the landlord?
— the tenant?

Give details of the other terms of the tenancy (except the rent) .. ..

If you have a tenancy agreement attach it or a copy to this form. It will be sent back to you without delay

12. What is the rent now?

£ .. .. .. per .. .. .. (eg per week, month, quarter etc)

Does this include any rates?

Yes .. .. No .. .. Tick one box

If 'Yes', give details .. ..

State which rates are included

13. Has the rent officer previously registered or confirmed a fair rent for the premises?

Yes .... No .... Tick
one box

If 'Yes', did it come into effect less than 1 year 9 months ago?

Yes .... No .... Tick
one box

If you answer 'Yes' to the second question give reasons for your application, unless it is a joint application by landlord and tenant

14. During the present tenancy

— has the tenant* carried out improvements or replaced fixtures, fittings or furniture for which he is not responsible under the terms of his tenancy?

Yes .... No .... Tick
one box

If 'Yes', give details ....

— is any disrepair or other defect to the property or to any fixtures, fittings or furniture due to the tenant* failing to comply with the terms of the tenancy?

Yes .... No .... Tick
one box

If 'Yes', give details ....

**including a former tenant under the present tenancy*

15. If the rent officer has registered a fair rent for the premises before, has the landlord carried out any major works or improvements since then?

Yes .... No .... Tick
one box

If 'Yes', give details ....

16. I/We apply for registration of a rent

Signed ....
Say whether you are the landlord or the landlord's agent

Date ....
Signed ....
Say whether you are the tenant or the tenant's agent

Date ....
If signed by agent, name ....
and address of agent ....

If the application is being made jointly by landlord and tenant, both should sign. If this is a joint application, the rent officer may register the rent asked for at question 7 without further consultation. If he does so, there is no right of objection to a rent assessment committee. In an application by joint tenants or joint landlords, they should each sign, unless one signs as agent for the rest with their agreement. In such a case he should state that he is acting as agent.

Note

This form should not be used for:

— a statutory tenancy arising at the end of a long tenancy under Part I of the Landlord and Tenant Act 1954 (use Form No. 6)
— a statutory tenancy under the Rent (Agriculture) Act 1976 (use Form No. 7)
— an application supported by a certificate of fair rent (use Form No. 9) **[846]**

NOTES
Commencement: 29 October 1984.
Substituted by SI 1984 No 1391, reg 4, Schedule.

FORM 6 APPLICATION FOR REGISTRATION OF FAIR RENT IN THE CASE OF A STATUTORY TENANCY ARISING AT THE END OF A LONG TENANCY UNDER PART I OF THE LANDLORD AND TENANT ACT 1954

RENT ACT 1977 Section 67 as amended by the Housing Act 1980

APPLICATION FOR REGISTRATION OF FAIR RENT IN THE CASE OF A STATUTORY TENANCY ARISING AT THE END OF A LONG TENANCY UNDER PART I OF THE LANDLORD AND TENANT ACT 1954

Use this form in the case of a statutory tenancy arising at the end of a long tenancy under Part I of the Landlord and Tenant Act 1954

To the Rent Officer

1. Address of Premises

"Premises" means the property, for example the house, flat or room(s) for which you want a rent registered

2. Name of Tenant

Also give the tenant's address if it is different from the above

3. Name and Address of Landlord

If a registered housing association or housing trust, or the Housing Corporation, tick here .. ..

4. Details of Premises

Say what type of property it is, for example, a house, flat or room(s). If it is a flat or room(s), say what floor or floors it is on

Give number and type of rooms .. ..

5. Does the tenancy include any other property?

Such as garage, or other separate building or land

Yes .. .. No .. .. Tick one box

If 'Yes', give details .. ..

6. Does the tenant share any accommodation

— with the landlord?

Yes .. .. No .. .. Tick one box

If 'Yes', give details .. ..

— with another tenant?

Yes .. .. No .. .. Tick one box

If 'Yes', give details .. ..

7. What rent do you want the rent officer to register as a fair rent?

£ .. .. .. per .. .. .. (eg per week, month, quarter etc)

Include any amount for services and/or furniture provided by the landlord or superior landlord.

Do not include anything for rates

The rent officer cannot deal with your application unless you answer this question

8. Are any services provided under the tenancy?

Such as cleaning, lighting, heating, hot water or gardening

Yes .. .. No .. .. Tick one box

If 'Yes', give details .. ..

9. If you are the landlord (and this is not a joint application) how much of the proposed rent do you think is due to these services?

£ .. .. .. per .. .. .. (eg per week, month, quarter etc)

If this is a landlord's application he must attach details of the expenditure incurred in providing any services, otherwise the rent officer cannot deal with the application

10. Is any furniture provided under the tenancy?

Yes .. .. No .. .. Tick one box

If 'Yes', give details or attach a list to the form .. ..

11. The tenancy

On what date did, or will, the statutory tenancy begin? .. ..

What are the terms of the tenancy agreed between the landlord and tenant, or determined by the Court? .. ..

Were any initial repairs to be carried out?

Yes .. .. No .. .. Tick one box

If 'Yes', have they been completed?

Yes .. .. No .. .. Tick one box

If 'No', give details of repairs still to be completed

If you have a tenancy agreement or court order attach it or a copy to this form. It will be sent back to you without delay

12. During the present tenancy

— has the tenant* carried out improvements or replaced fixtures, fittings or furniture for which he is not responsible under the terms of his tenancy?

Yes .. .. No .. .. Tick one box

If 'Yes', give details .. ..

— is any disrepair or other defect to the property or to any fixtures, fittings or furniture due to the tenant* failing to comply with the terms of the tenancy?

Yes .. .. No .. .. Tick one box

If 'Yes', give details .. ..

**including a former tenant under the present tenancy*

13. I/We apply for registration of a rent

Signed .. ..
Say whether you are the landlord or the landlord's agent

Date .. ..
Signed .. ..
Say whether you are the tenant or the tenant's agent

Date .. ..
If signed by agent, name .. ..
and address of agent .. ..

If the application is being made jointly by landlord and tenant, both should sign. If this is a joint application, the rent officer may register the rent asked for at question 7 without further consultation. If he does so, there is no right of objection to a rent assessment committee. In an application by joint tenants or joint landlords, they should each sign, unless one signs as agent for the rest with their agreement. In such a case he should state that he is acting as agent.] **[847]**

NOTES

Commencement: 29 October 1984.

Substituted by SI 1984 No 1391, reg 4, Schedule.

FORM 7 APPLICATION FOR REGISTRATION OF FAIR RENT WHERE DWELLING-HOUSE SUBJECT TO A STATUTORY TENANCY UNDER THE RENT (AGRICULTURE) ACT 1976

RENT ACT 1977 Section 67 and RENT (AGRICULTURE) ACT 1976 as amended by the Housing Act 1980

APPLICATION FOR REGISTRATION OF FAIR RENT WHERE DWELLING-HOUSE SUBJECT TO A STATUTORY TENANCY UNDER THE RENT (AGRICULTURE) ACT 1976

Use this form in the case of a statutory tenancy under the Rent (Agriculture) Act 1976 (see the Note at the end of the form)

To the Rent Officer

1. Address of Premises

"Premises" means the property, for example the house, flat or room(s) for which you want a rent registered

2. Name of Statutory Tenant

Also give the tenant's address if it is different from the above

3. Name and Address of Landlord

4. Details of Premises

Say what type of property it is, for example, a house, flat or room(s). If it is a flat or room(s), say what floor or floors it is on

Give number and type of rooms .. ..

5. Does the tenancy include any other property?

Such as garage, or other separate building or land

Yes .. .. No .. .. Tick
one box

If 'Yes', give details .. ..

6. Does the tenant share any accommodation

— with the landlord?

Yes .. .. No .. .. Tick
one box

If 'Yes', give details .. ..

— with another tenant?

Yes .. .. No .. .. Tick
one box

If 'Yes', give details .. ..

7. What rent do you want the rent officer to register as a fair rent?

£ .. .. .. per .. .. .. (eg
per week, month,
quarter etc)

Include any amount for services and/or furniture provided by the landlord or superior landlord. Do not include anything for rates

The rent officer cannot deal with your application unless you answer this question

8. Are any services provided under the tenancy?

Such as cleaning, lighting, heating, hot water or gardening

Yes .. .. No .. .. Tick
one box

If 'Yes', give details .. ..

9. If you are the landlord (and this is not a joint application) how much of the proposed rent do you think is due to these services?

£ .. .. .. per .. .. .. (eg
per week, month,
quarter etc)

If this is a landlord's application, he must attach details of the expenditure incurred in providing any services, otherwise the rent officer cannot deal with the application

10. Is any furniture provided under the tenancy?

Yes .. .. No .. .. Tick
one box

If 'Yes', give details or attach a list to the form .. ..

11. The tenancy

Is there an agreement (whether or not in writing) that no rent shall be paid under the statutory tenancy?

Yes .. .. No .. .. Tick
one box

If 'No', is any rent presently payable under an agreement (whether or not in writing)?

Yes .. .. No .. .. Tick
one box

If 'Yes', what is the rent?

£ .. .. .. per .. .. .. (eg
per week, month,
quarter etc)

How long is the agreement for? .. ..

Is there an agreement in writing varying the terms of the statutory tenancy?

Yes .. .. No .. .. Tick
one box

If 'Yes', give details of the agreement

If you have an agreement attach it or a copy to this form. It will be sent back to you without delay

12. Has the rent officer previously registered or confirmed a fair rent for the premises?

Yes .. .. No .. .. Tick
one box

If 'Yes', did it come into effect less than 1 year 9 months ago?

Yes .. .. No .. .. Tick
one box

If you answer 'Yes' to the second question give reasons for your application, unless it is a joint application by landlord and tenant

13. During the present tenancy

— has the tenant* carried out improvements or replaced fixtures, fittings or furniture for which he is not responsible under the terms of his tenancy?

Yes .. .. No .. .. Tick
one box

If 'Yes', give details .. ..

— is any disrepair or other defect to the property or to any fixtures, fittings or furniture due to the tenant* failing to comply with the terms of the tenancy?

Yes .... No .... Tick
one box

If 'Yes', give details ....

**including a former tenant under the present tenancy*

14. If the rent officer has registered a fair rent for the premises before, has the landlord carried out any major works or improvements since then?

Yes .... No .... Tick
one box

If 'Yes', give details ....

15. I/We apply for registration of a rent

Signed ....
Say whether you are the landlord or the landlord's agent

Date ....
Signed ....
Say whether you are the tenant or the tenant's agent

Date ....
If signed by agent, name ....
and address of agent ....

If the application is being made jointly by landlord and tenant, both should sign. If this is a joint application, the rent officer may register the rent asked for at question 7 without further consultation. If he does so, there is no right of objection to a rent assessment committee. In an application by joint tenants or joint landlords, they should each sign, unless one signs as agent for the rest with their agreement. In such a case he should state that he is acting as agent.

Note

The tenancy will **not** be a statutory tenancy under the Rent (Agriculture) Act 1976 where the tenant:

— shares essential living accommodation such as a kitchen with other tenants (not the landlord), and
— has exclusive occupation of only one room, and at the time the tenancy or licence was granted at least three other rooms in the same building were let (or available for letting) on similar terms as separate residential accommodation.

[848]

NOTES
Commencement: 29 October 1984.
Substituted by SI 1984 No 1391, reg 4, Schedule.

FORM 8 APPLICATION FOR CERTIFICATE OF FAIR RENT

RENT ACT 1977 Section 69 as amended by the Housing Act 1980

APPLICATION FOR CERTIFICATE OF FAIR RENT

Use this form to apply for a Certificate of Fair Rent

To the Rent Officer

1. Address of Premises

"Premises" means the property, for example the house, flat or room(s) for which you want a certificate of fair rent

2. Grounds of application

— the applicant intends to provide a dwelling-house by the erection or conversion of the premises ....
— the applicant intends to make improvements in the dwelling-house ....

—the applicant intends to let the premises on a regulated tenancy (or if the applicant is a registered housing association or housing trust or the Housing Corporation, a Part VI tenancy) .. ..

Tick one box

A Certificate of Fair Rent cannot be issued unless one of these grounds applies

3. Is there an existing tenancy of the premises?

Yes .. .. No .. .. Tick one box

If NO, go to question 10.

4. Name of Tenant

Also give the tenant's address if it is different from the above

5. When did the tenancy begin? .. ..

If for a fixed term, say how long .. ..

What repairs are the responsibility of

— the landlord?
— the tenant?

Give details of the other terms of the tenancy (except the rent) .. ..

Attach the tenancy agreement or a copy to this form. It will be sent back to you without delay

6. What is the rent now?

£ .. .. .. per .. .. .. (eg per week, month, quarter etc)

Do not include anything for rates

7. During the present tenancy

— has the tenant* carried out improvements or replaced fixtures, fittings or furniture for which he is not responsible under the terms of his tenancy?

Yes .. .. No .. .. Tick one box

If 'Yes', give details .. ..

— is any disrepair or other defect to the property or to any fixtures, fittings or furniture due to the tenant* failing to comply with the terms of the tenancy?

Yes .. .. No .. .. Tick one box

If 'Yes', give details .. ..

**including a former tenant under the present tenancy*

8. Are any services provided under the tenancy?

Such as cleaning, lighting, heating, hot water or gardening

Yes .. .. No .. .. Tick one box

If 'Yes', give details .. ..

9. Is any furniture provided under the tenancy?

Yes .. .. No .. .. Tick one box

If 'Yes', give details or attach a list to the form .. ..

10. What rent do you want the rent officer to specify as a fair rent?

£ .. .. .. per .. .. .. (eg per week, month, quarter etc)

Include any amount for services and/or furniture provided by the landlord or superior landlord. Do not include anything for rates

The rent officer cannot deal with your application unless you answer this question

11. Has the rent officer previously registered or confirmed a fair rent for the premises?

Yes .... No .... Tick one box

12. Details of Premises

Say what type of property it is, for example, a house, flat or room(s). If it is a flat or room(s), say what floor or floors it is on

Give number and type of rooms .. ..

13. Does the tenancy include any other property?

Such as garage, or other separate building or land

Yes .... No .... Tick one box

If 'Yes', give details .. ..

14. Does or will the tenant share any part of the premises

— with the landlord?

Yes .... No .... Tick one box

If 'Yes', give details .. ..

— with another tenant?

Yes .... No .... Tick one box

If 'Yes', give details .. ..

15. Give a brief description of the works (if any) proposed to be carried out to the premises and the improvements that will result from them

You must enclose plans and specifications of the works

16. Where there is no existing tenancy give details of the tenancy it is proposed to grant

If for a fixed term, say how long .. ..

What repairs are the responsibility of

— the landlord?
— the tenant?

How often will the rent be payable? .. ..

Give details of the other terms of the tenancy. Include details of any services and furniture that are to be provided

Attach the proposed tenancy agreement if there is one or a copy to this form. It will be sent back to you without delay

17. State how much of the rent you think is or will be due to these services

£ ...... per ...... (eg per week, month, quarter etc)

18. I/We apply for a Certificate of Fair Rent for the premises named in paragragh 1 above

Signed .. ..
Date.. .. ..
(On behalf of .. ..)
Address of applicant .. ..
.. ..

If signed by an agent, name and address of agent ....

....

If a registered housing association or a housing trust, or the Housing Corporation, tick here ....

In an application by joint landlords, they should each sign, unless one signs as an agent for the rest with their agreement. In such a case he should state that he is acting as agent. **[849]**

NOTES

Commencement: 29 October 1984.
Substituted by SI 1984 No 1391, reg 4, Schedule.

FORM 9 APPLICATION FOR REGISTRATION OF FAIR RENT SUPPORTED BY CERTIFICATE OF FAIR RENT

RENT ACT 1977 Section 69(4) as amended by the Housing Act 1980

APPLICATION FOR REGISTRATION OF FAIR RENT SUPPORTED BY CERTIFICATE OF FAIR RENT

Use this form where the application is supported by a Certificate of Fair Rent and where there is a regulated tenancy of the premises or a tenancy to which Part VI of the Act applies. Part VI of the Act applies to tenancies where the landlord is a registered housing association or a housing trust or the Housing Corporation, which would otherwise be protected tenancies and which are not business tenancies.

To the Rent Officer

1. Address of Premises to which Certificate of Fair Rent relates
2. Name and Address of Landlord (the applicant)
3. Name of tenant

Also give the tenant's address if it is different from the above

4. Date of Certificate of Fair Rent
5. When did the tenancy begin?
6. Are the premises separately rated?

Yes .... No .... Tick one box

Are the rates paid by the landlord?

Yes .... No .... Tick one box

If 'Yes', give details ....

State which rates are paid by the landlord

7. Have the works (if any) specified in the Certificate of Fair Rent been carried out?

Yes .... No .... Tick one box

The rent officer cannot deal with the application if any works specified have not been carried out

8. Are services provided?

Yes .... No .... Tick one box

If 'Yes', are they as specified in the Certificate of Fair Rent?

Yes .... No .... Tick one box

If you answer 'No' to the second question, give details of the differences

9. Is furniture provided?

Yes .... No .... Tick
one box

If 'Yes', is this as specified in the Certificate of Fair Rent?

Yes .... No .... Tick
one box

If you answer 'No' to the second question, give details of the differences

10. I/We apply for the registration of a rent in accordance with the Certificate of Fair Rent

Signed ....
Date ....
If signed by agent, give ....
name and address of agent ....

....
......

The landlord or his agent should sign. In an application by joint landlords, they should each sign, unless one signs as an agent for the rest with their agreement. In such a case he should state that he is acting as agent. **[850]**

NOTES
Commencement: 29 October 1984.
Substituted by SI 1984 No 1391, reg 4, Schedule.

Form 10 Joint application for cancellation of a registered rent

Rent Act 1977 Section 73 as amended by the Housing Act 1980

Joint Application for Cancellation of a Registered Rent

This form should be used for a joint application by both landlord and tenant to cancel the rent registered for the premises named in question 1 below where a new rent agreement is attached—

(i) increases the rent under the existing regulated tenancy; or
(ii) grants a new regulated tenancy at a rent exceeding the rent under the previous tenancy; and

the tenancy runs for a minimum period of 12 months from the date of application. A copy of the rent agreement must be enclosed with the application.

IMPORTANT: A registered rent cannot be cancelled until at least two years have passed since the effective date of the last registration or confirmation of the rent.

To the Rent Officer

1. Address of Premises

"Premises" means the property, for example the house, flat or room(s) for which the rent is registered

2. Name of Tenant

Also give the tenant's address if it is different from the above

3. Name and Address of Landlord

4. Details of Premises

Say what type of property it is, for example, a house, flat or room(s). If it is a flat or room(s), say what floor or floors it is on

Give number and type of rooms ....

5. Does the tenancy include any other property?

Such as garage, or other separate building or land

Yes .... No .... Tick
one box

If 'Yes', give details . . . .

6. Does the tenant share any accommodation

— with the landlord?

Yes .... No .... Tick
one box

If 'Yes', give details . . . .

— with another tenant?

Yes .... No .... Tick
one box

If 'Yes', give details . . . .

7. Are any services provided under the tenancy?

Such as cleaning, lighting, heating, hot water or gardening

Yes .... No .... Tick
one box

If 'Yes', give details . . . .

8. Is any furniture provided under the tenancy?

Yes .... No .... Tick
one box

If 'Yes', give details or attach a list to the form . . . .

9. When did the tenancy begin? . . . .

If for a fixed term, say how long . . . .

What repairs are the responsibility of

— the landlord?
— the tenant?

Give details of the other terms of the tenancy (except the rent) . . . .

If you have a tenancy agreement attach it or a copy to this form. It will be sent back to you without delay

10. During the present tenancy

— has the tenant* carried out improvements or replaced fixtures, fittings or furniture for which he is not responsible under the terms of his tenancy?

Yes .... No .... Tick
one box

If 'Yes', give details . . . .

— is any disrepair or other defect to the property or to any fixtures, fittings or furniture due to the tenant* failing to comply with the terms of the tenancy?

Yes .... No .... Tick
one box

If 'Yes', give details . . . .

**including a former tenant under the present tenancy*

11. Has the landlord carried out any major works or improvements since the rent was last registered?

Yes .... No .... Tick
one box

If 'Yes', give details . . . .

12. We apply for the cancellation of the rent registered for the premises named in paragraph 1 above

Signed . . . .
Say whether you are the landlord or the landlord's agent

Date .. ..
Signed .. ..
Say whether you are the tenant or the tenant's agent

Date .. ..
If signed by agent, name .. ..
and address of agent .. ..

The form should be signed by both the landlord (or his agent) and the tenant (or his agent).

In an application by joint landlords or joint tenants, they should each sign, unless one signs as an agent for the rest with their agreement. In such a case he should state that he is acting as agent. **[851]**

NOTES
Commencement: 29 October 1984.
Substituted by SI 1984 No 1391, reg 4, Schedule.

FORM 11 APPLICATION FOR CANCELLATION OF REGISTRATION OF RENT WHERE THERE IS NO REGULATED TENANCY

RENT ACT 1977, SECTION 73, as amended by the Housing Act 1980

APPLICATION FOR CANCELLATION OF REGISTRATION OF RENT WHERE THERE IS NO REGULATED TENANCY

To the Rent Officer

I/We apply for the cancellation of the registered rent of the premises named below. At least 2 years have elapsed since the effective date of the registration or confirmation.

The premises are not for the time being subject to a regulated tenancy. If they were let on a regulated tenancy I/we would be the landlord.

Address of the premises:

Signed .. ..

[On behalf of .. ..]

Address of applicant .. ..

[If signed by an agent, name and address of agent .. ..

Date .. .. **[852]**

NOTES
Commencement: 28 November 1980.

FORM 12 NOTICE BY RENT OFFICER OF APPLICATION FOR REGISTRATION OF FAIR RENT

RENT ACT 1977 as amended by the Housing Act 1980

Dear Sir/Madam

NOTIFICATION OF APPLICATION FOR REGISTRATION OF A FAIR RENT

1. I have been asked to register a fair rent for:

.. ..
..
.. ..
..
.. ..
..

2. If you are not the applicant, I enclose a copy of the application. **Please keep it.** The rent the applicant has asked for is shown at question 7 on the form. **I do not have to register this amount as the fair rent; I may register a higher or lower figure.**

3. You have the right to a meeting with me to discuss what rent I should register. This is known as a consultation. If you wish to have a consultation, or if you have any

other comments, you must write to me within 14 days of the date of this letter. I would ask both parties to the consultation.

4. A consultation will be held if either you or the other party asks for one, or if I decide that there should be one. I shall tell you if a consultation is to be held. If there is no consultation, I will go ahead and register a rent.

5. You have the right to object to a Rent Assessment Committee if you disagree with the rent I register.

6. I may decide to inspect the premises. If a rent officer has inspected the premises before, and there have been major changes since then, you should let me know in writing within 14 days of the date of this letter (unless these changes are already noted on the application form).

7. If you would like more information please contact my office.

Yours faithfully

for Rent Officer **[853]**

NOTES

Commencement: 29 October 1984.
Substituted by SI 1984 No 1391, reg 4, Schedule.

FORM 13 NOTICE BY RENT OFFICER OF APPLICATION FOR REGISTRATION OF FAIR RENT WHERE LANDLORD INCLUDES AN AMOUNT FOR SERVICES

[RENT ACT 1977 as amended by the Housing Act 1980

Dear Sir/Madam

NOTIFICATION OF APPLICATION FOR REGISTRATION OF A FAIR RENT

1. I have been asked to register a fair rent for:

.. ..
..
.. ..
..
.. ..
..

2. If you are not the applicant, I enclose a copy of the application. **Please keep it.** The rent the applicant has asked for is shown at question 7 on the form and includes an amount for services provided by the landlord. If you are the tenant and the application was made by the landlord I also enclose a copy of a statement from the landlord about his expenditure in providing the services.

3. I do not have to register the rent asked for by the applicant as the fair rent; I may register a higher or lower figure.

4. You have the right to a meeting with me to discuss what rent I should register. This is known as a consultation. If you wish to have a consultation, or if you have any other comments, you must write to me within 14 days of the date of this letter. I would ask both parties to the consultation.

5. A consultation will be held if either you or the other party asks for one, or if I decide that there should be one. I shall tell you if a consultation is to be held. If there is no consultation, I will go ahead and register a fair rent.

6. You have the right to object to a Rent Assessment Committee if you disagree with the rent I register.

7. I may decide to inspect the premises. If a rent officer has inspected the premises before, and there have been major changes since then, you should let me know in writing within 14 days of the date of this letter (unless these changes are already noted on the application form).

8. If you would like more information please contact my office.

Yours faithfully

for Rent Officer **[854]**

NOTES

Commencement: 29 October 1984.

Substituted by SI 1984 No 1391, reg 4, Schedule.

FORM 14 NOTICE BY RENT ASSESSMENT COMMITTEE REQUIRING FURTHER INFORMATION

RENT ACT 1977, Schedule 11, paragraph 7

NOTICE BY RENT ASSESSMENT COMMITTEE REQUIRING FURTHER INFORMATION

Date .. ..

To .. .. [landlord][tenant] of .. ..

.. ..(address of premises)

(1) The application for registration of a fair rent for the above-named premises, made by .. ..has been referred by the Rent Officer for .. .. to a Rent Assessment Committee. To enable them to consider this application the Committee require you to give them the further information indicated below. You should send this information by not later than .. .. to:

(2) The further information required is:

(3) If you fail without reasonable cause to comply with this notice you will be liable on first conviction to a fine not exceeding £50 and on a second or subsequent conviction to a fine not exceeding £100.

Signed .. ..

for the Rent Assessment Committee **[855]**

NOTES

Commencement: 28 November 1980.

FORM 15 APPLICATION FOR CANCELLATION OF A RENT REGISTERED BY A RENT TRIBUNAL WHERE THE DWELLING IS NOT SUBJECT TO A RESTRICTED CONTRACT

RENT ACT 1977, SECTION 81A, as amended by Housing Act 1980

APPLICATION FOR CANCELLATION OF RENT REGISTERED BY RENT TRIBUNAL

To the Rent Tribunal

I/We apply for the cancellation of the rent registered by the Rent Tribunal for the premises named below. At least 2 years have elapsed since the rent was entered on the register.

The dwelling is not for the time being subject to a restricted contract. If it were subject to a restricted contract, I/We would be the lessor.

Address of the premises:

Signed .. ..

[On behalf of .. ..

Address of applicant .. ..

[If signed by an agent, name and address of agent .. ..]

Date .. .. **[856]**

NOTES

Commencement: 28 November 1980.

SCHEDULE 2

PARTICULARS WITH REGARD TO THE TENANCY TO BE REGISTERED IN THE REGISTER OF RENTS KEPT BY THE RENT OFFICER

1. Address of premises.

2. Names and addresses of landlord and tenant.

3. If granted for a term, date of commencement of the tenancy and length of term.

4. The rental period.

5. Allocation between landlord and tenant of liabilities for repairs.

6. Details of services provided by the landlord or a superior landlord.

7. Details of furniture provided by the landlord or a superior landlord.

8. In the case of a statutory tenancy which has arisen by virtue of Part I of the Landlord and Tenant Act 1954, particulars of the initial repairs.

9. Any other terms of the tenancy taken into consideration in determining the fair rent. **[857]**

NOTES
Commencement: 28 November 1980.

SCHEDULE 3

PARTICULARS RELATING TO A RESTRICTED CONTRACT REGARDING WHICH LESSORS MAY BY NOTICE BE REQUIRED TO GIVE INFORMATION

1. The name of the lessee.

2. A specification of the dwelling to which the contract relates.

3. Accommodation occupied or used by the lessee (*a*) exclusively, (*b*) in common with the lessor (*c*) in common with persons other than the lessor.

4. Furniture provided by the lessor for the use of the lessee.

5. Services provided by the lessor for the use of the lessee.

6. The rateable value of the accommodation occupied by the lessee, where this has been separately assessed, or, where it has not, the rateable value of the dwelling of which the accommodation forms part.

7. Responsibility for payment of the rates for the accommodation occupied by the lessee.

8. Payments contracted to be made by the lessee to the lessor, and if separate payments are made in respect of occupation, furniture and services the separate payments in respect of each.

9. Whether board is supplied, and if so the nature and amount of the board.

10. The date the occupation of the accommodation began. **[858]**

NOTES
Commencement: 28 November 1980.

SCHEDULE 4

PARTICULARS WITH REGARD TO THE CONTRACT TO BE ENTERED IN THE REGISTER

1. Names and addresses of parties to the restricted contract referred to the rent tribunal.

2. (*a*) The accommodation of which the lessee is entitled to exclusive occupation;

(*b*) the accommodation of which the lessee is entitled to the use in common with—

(i) the lessor

(ii) persons other than the lessor.

3. Details of any furniture provided by the lessor for the use of the lessee.

4. Details of any services provided by the lessor.

5. Whether board is supplied, and if so the nature and amount of the board,

6. Any other terms of the contract taken into consideration in determining the rent. **[859]**

NOTES
Commencement: 28 November 1980.

RENT REGULATION (CANCELLATION OF REGISTRATION OF RENT) REGULATIONS 1980
(SI 1980 NO 1698)

NOTES
Made: 30 October 1980
Authority: Rent Act 1977, s 74

ARRANGEMENT OF REGULATIONS

Regulation		Para
1	Citation and commencement	[860]
2	Interpretation	[861]
	PROCEDURES ON JOINT APPLICATION TO RENT OFFICER	
3		[862]
4		[863]
5	Notices	[864]

1. Citation and commencement

These regulations may be cited as the Rent Regulation (Cancellation of Registration of Rent) Regulations 1980 and shall come into operation on 28th November 1980. **[860]**

NOTES
Commencement: 28 November 1980.

2. Interpretation

In these regulations—

"the 1977 Act" means the Rent Act 1977;

"a joint application" means an application for the cancellation of a fair rent under section 73(1) of the Rent Act 1977; and

"relevant rent agreement" means the rent agreement, within the meaning of section 73(1)(*a*) of the 1977 Act, as the result of which a joint application is made. **[861]**

NOTES
Commencement: 28 November 1980.

PROCEDURES ON JOINT APPLICATION TO RENT OFFICER

3. If, in the case of a joint application, after making such inquiry, if any, as he thinks fit and considering any information supplied to him, the rent officer is not satisfied that the rent, or the highest rent, payable under the relevant rent agreement does not exceed a fair rent for the dwelling-house, he shall serve a notice under regulation 4 below. **[862]**

NOTES
Commencement: 28 November 1980.

4. (1) A notice under this regulation shall be served on the landlord and on the tenant informing them that the rent officer proposes, at a time (which shall not be earlier than seven days after the service of the notice) and place specified in the notice to consider in consultation with the landlord and the tenant, or such of them as may appear at that time and place, whether the registration of the rent for the dwelling-house should be cancelled pursuant to section 73(4) of the 1977 Act.

(2) At any such consultation the landlord and the tenant may each be represented by a person authorised by him in that behalf, whether or not that person is of counsel or a solicitor.

(3) Where the rent officer is to consider, in accordance with paragraph (1) above, whether the registration of the rent for the dwelling-house should be cancelled, he shall not reach his decision until after such consideration.

(4) The rent officer may, where he considers it appropriate, arrange for consultation in respect of more than one joint application to be held together with consultations in respect of one or more other joint applications. **[863]**

NOTES
Commencement: 28 November 1980.
The 1977 Act: Rent Act 1977.

5. Notices

(1) In the case of a joint application, any notices required to be served under regulation 4 above, and any notifications to be given under section 73(8) of the 1977 Act (notification of rent officer's decision) shall be sent by post in a prepaid letter or delivered—

(*a*) to the landlord and to the tenant at their respective addresses given in the application; or
(*b*) where the application is made on behalf of the landlord or of the tenant by an agent acting on his behalf, to that agent at the address of the agent given in the application.

(2) In the case of an application under section 73(1A) of the 1977 Act, any notification to be given under section 73(8) of the 1977 Act shall be sent by post in a prepaid letter or delivered—

(*a*) to the applicant at the address given in the application; or
(*b*) where the application is made by an agent acting on behalf of the applicant, to that agent at the address of the agent given in the application. **[864]**

NOTES
Commencement: 28 November 1980.
1977 Act: Rent Act 1977.

RENT ASSESSMENT COMMITTEES (ENGLAND AND WALES) (RENT TRIBUNAL) REGULATIONS 1980

(SI 1980 NO 1700)

NOTES
Made: 30 October 1980
Authority: Rent Act 1977, s 74

ARRANGEMENT OF REGULATIONS

Regulation		Para
1	Citation and Commencement	[865]
2	Interpretation	[866]
	PROCEEDINGS BEFORE RENT TRIBUNALS	
3		[867]
4		[868]
5		[869]
6		[870]
7		[871]
8		[872]
9		[873]

1. Citation and Commencement

These regulations may be cited as the Rent Assessment Committees (England and Wales) (Rent Tribunal) Regulations 1980 and shall come into operation on 28th November 1980. **[865]**

NOTES
Commencement: 28 November 1980.

2. Interpretation

In these regulations, unless the context otherwise requires, "the Act" means the Rent Act 1977 and "Chairman" means the person acting as chairman of the rent tribunal. **[866]**

NOTES
Commencement: 28 November 1980.

PROCEEDINGS BEFORE RENT TRIBUNALS

3. Reference to a rent tribunal shall be by written notice. The notice shall specify the address of the house or part of a house to which the restricted contract relates, the names of the lessor and lessee, and the address of the lessor. The notice may be delivered at an office of the rent assessment panel, in which case it shall be deemed to have reached the rent tribunal on the day when it is so delivered, or may be posted to the rent assessment panel, in which case it shall be deemed to have reached the rent tribunal on the day when it would be delivered in the ordinary course of post. **[867]**

NOTES
Commencement: 28 November 1980.

4. Where any reference is made to a rent tribunal, the rent tribunal shall give notice in writing to each party to the restricted contract informing him that he may within such time as the rent tribunal may allow (not being less than [7 days] from the date of the notice) give notice to the rent tribunal that he desires to be heard by them, or may send to the rent tribunal representations in writing:

Provided that the rent tribunal may extend the time stated in the notice. **[868]**

NOTES
Commencement: 28 November 1980.
Amended by SI 1981 No 1493, reg 2.

5. (1) If any party to the restricted contract informs the rent tribunal that he desires to be heard, the rent tribunal shall give to each party not less than [7 clear days'] notice in writing of the time and place at which the parties will be heard.

(2) If the house to which the reference relates is one the general management whereof is vested in and exercisable by the local authority as housing authority, the said local authority shall be given an opportunity of being heard, or if they so desire, of submitting representations in writing. **[869]**

NOTES
Commencement: 28 November 1980.
Para (1): amended by SI 1981 No 1493, reg 2.

6. At any hearing before a rent tribunal a party to the restricted contract may appear in person or by counsel or a solicitor or by any other representative or may be accompanied by any person whom he may wish to assist him thereat. **[870]**

NOTES
Commencement: 28 November 1980.

7. (1) Subject to the provisions of these regulations the procedure at a hearing shall be such as the rent tribunal may determine, and the rent tribunal may if they think fit, and at the request of either party shall, unless for some special reason they consider it undesirable, allow the hearing to be held in public; but nothing in these regulations shall prevent a member of the Council on Tribunals in that capacity from attending any hearing.

(2) The rent tribunal may postpone or adjourn the hearing from time to time as they think fit. **[871]**

NOTES
Commencement: 28 November 1980.

8. (1) The decision of the majority of a rent tribunal shall be the decision of the tribunal. The decision shall be in writing, signed by the chairman, and shall be sent as soon as may be to the parties to the restricted contract, and to the local authority in cases where the restricted contract was referred to the rent tribunal by the authority.

(2) The chairman shall have power, by certificate under his hand, to correct any clerical or accidental error or omission in the said decision. **[872]**

NOTES
Commencement: 28 November 1980.

9. Where any notice is required or authorised by the Act or by these regulations to be given by the rent tribunal it shall be sufficient compliance with the Act or the regulations if the notice is sent by post in a pre-paid letter addressed to the party for whom it is intended at his usual or last known address. **[873]**

NOTES
Commencement: 28 November 1980.
The Act: Rent Act 1977.

RENT ACT (COUNTY COURT PROCEEDINGS FOR POSSESSION) RULES 1981
(SI 1981 NO 139)

NOTES
Made: 4 February 1981
Authority: Rent Act 1977, s 142

ARRANGEMENT OF RULES

Rule	Para
1	[874]
2	[875]
3	[876]
4	[877]
5	[878]
6	[879]

APPENDIX A FORM OF ORIGINATING APPLICATION FOR POSSESSION UNDER CASE 11, 12 OR 20 (SCHEDULE 15 TO THE RENT ACT 1977)

7 Appendix A .. .. [880]

APPENDIX B FORM OF ORIGINATING APPLICATION FOR POSSESSION UNDER CASES 13 TO 18 INCLUSIVE (SCHEDULE 15 TO THE RENT ACT 1977)

8 Appendix B .. .. [881]

APPENDIX C FORM OF ORIGINATING APPLICATION FOR POSSESSION UNDER CASE 19 (SCHEDULE 15 TO THE RENT ACT 1977)

10 Appendix C .. .. [882]

1. (1) These Rules may be cited as the Rent Act (County Court Proceedings for Possession) Rules 1981 and shall come into operation on 6th April 1981.

(2) In these Rules an Order and Rule referred to by number means the Order and Rule so numbered in the County Court Rules 1936, and a Case referred to by number means the Case so numbered in Schedule 15 to the Rent Act 1977. **[874]**

NOTES
Commencement: 6 April 1981.

2. (1) These Rules apply to proceedings for recovery of possession of a dwelling-house—

(*a*) under Cases 11, 12 or 20, provided that

(i) the dwelling-house is required as a residence for the owner or for any member of the owner's family who resided with him at his death or, where the proceedings are brought under Case 11, for any member of the owner's family who resided with him when he last occupied the dwelling-house as a residence and

(ii) the tenant was given the requisite notice, not later than the relevant date, that possession might be recovered under the Case relied on;

(*b*) under Cases 13 to 18 inclusive;

(*c*) under Case 19 provided that the dwelling-house was let on a protected shorthold tenancy.

(2) Where these Rules apply, the person with a claim for possession may, instead of bringing an action for possession, make his claim pursuant to these Rules by an originating application in the county court for the district in which the dwelling-house is situated.

(3) Subject to the provisions of these Rules, the County Court Rules 1936 shall apply, with the necessary modifications, to proceedings begun by an originating application pursuant to these Rules; and any provision of these Rules authorising or requiring anything to be done in such proceedings shall be treated as if it were a provision of the County Court Rules 1936. **[875]**

NOTES

Commencement: 6 April 1981.

Cases 11 to 20: Rent Act 1977, Sch 15.

3. The originating application shall be in the form prescribed—

(*a*) for any of Cases 11, 12 or 20, by Appendix A;

(*b*) for any of Cases 13 to 18 inclusive, by Appendix B;

(*c*) for Case 19, by Appendix C. **[876]**

NOTES

Commencement: 6 April 1981.

Cases 11 to 20: Rent Act 1977, Sch 15.

4. An affidavit shall be filed in support of the originating application which shall verify the statements in the application, depose to any other material matters and exhibit any material documents; and a copy of the affidavit and copies of any exhibits shall be served on the respondent with the documents mentioned in Order 6, Rule 4(2)(*c*). **[877]**

NOTES

Commencement: 6 April 1981.

Order 6, Rule 4(2)(*c*): SR & O 1936 No 626, Order 6, r 4(2)(*c*).

5. (1) Where possession is claimed under Case 11, 12 or 20, each respondent must be served at least seven clear days before the return day and in any other Case at least 14 clear days before the return day.

(2) Order 8, Rule 24 shall apply to the originating application, with such modifications as may be necessary, as if it were a summons in an action for the recovery of land. **[878]**

NOTES
Commencement: 6 April 1981.
Cases 11, 12, 20: Rent Act 1977, Sch 15.
Order 8, Rule 24: SR & O 1936 No 626, Order 8, r 24.

6. (1) The originating application may be heard by the registrar or may be referred by him to the judge.

(2) The judge or registrar may hear the application or any part of it in private or in open court as he may think desirable. **[879]**

NOTES
Commencement: 6 April 1981.

APPENDIX A FORM OF ORIGINATING APPLICATION FOR POSSESSION UNDER CASE 11, 12 OR 20 (SCHEDULE 15 TO THE RENT ACT 1977)

7. Appendix A

In the County Court

No. of Application

In the Matter of the Rent Act 1977

Between

A.B. Applicant,

and

C.D. Respondent.

1. I, [*state name*] of [*state address and occupation of the applicant*] apply to the Court for an order for recovery of possession of [*here describe the premises*] under Case [11][1], [12][2], [20][3] of Schedule 15 to the Rent Act 1977.

2. The premises were let to the respondent on [*here give the date*] on a protected tenancy having the following terms [*here set out the terms material to the proceedings*].

3. Notice in writing was given to the respondent on [*here give the date*] that possession might be recovered under Case [11][1], [12][2], [20][3] of Schedule 15 to the Rent Act 1977.

4. As regards previous lettings of the premises [since they became protected by the Rent Acts][1] [since 14th August 1974][2] [since 28th November 1980][3],

(*a*) There has been no such letting; or
(*b*) There has been such a letting, but a notice, such as is mentioned in paragraph 3, was given on each occasion, namely [*state, in respect of each notice, the date when it was given and the person to whom it was given]*; or
(*c*) There has been such a letting, or lettings, for which no notice, such as is mentioned in paragraph 3, was given and I ask the Court to make an order for possession notwithstanding on the grounds set out below. [*Here identify the letting, or lettings, referred to and set out the grounds for dispensing with the requirements as to notice*].

[*Delete whichever two are not applicable*]

[5. I[4] previously occupied the premises as a residence.][1]

[5. I[4] intended, at all material times, to occupy the premises as a residence on retirement and retired on [*state the date*].][2]

[5. I[4] was a member of the regular armed forces of the Crown when the premises were acquired and when the tenancy was granted.][3]

6. The premises are required as a residence

(*a*) for myself; *or*
(*b*) for [*here identify the person concerned*], who is a member of the family of the original owner by whom the tenancy was granted and who was residing with the original owner at the time of his (*or* her) death; *or*
(*c*) for [*here identify the person concerned*], who was residing with me when I last occupied the premises as a residence.[5]

[*Delete whichever two are not applicable*]

7. The protected tenancy has come to an end as follows:—

(*a*) by expiring on [*here give date of expiry*], *or*
(*b*) by a notice to quit being served on [*here give the date*] which expired on [*here give the date*],

[*Delete whichever is not applicable*]
but the respondent remains in occupation.

8. There are rent arrears in the sum of £ , calculated at the rate of [*here give the weekly or other rent*] and I apply to the Court for an order for payment.

[*Delete if inapplicable*]

The names and addresses of the persons on whom it is intended to serve this application are: [*state names and addresses of persons intended to be served*].

My address for service is [*state applicant's address for service*].

Dated this day of

[*Signed*]

Applicant.

[1] Include this and delete the others where the claim is under Case 11.

[2] Include this and delete the others where the claim is under Case 12.

[3] Include this and delete the others where the claim is under Case 20.

[4] Where the original owner by whom the tenancy was granted has died substitute, for "I", the words "The original owner by whom the tenancy was granted"; and where Case 12 is relied on delete from paragraph 5 the words "and retired" to the end.

[5] Sub-paragraph (*c*) applies to claims under Case 11 only. **[880]**

NOTES
Commencement: 6 April 1981.

Appendix B Form of Originating Application for Possession under Cases 13 to 18 inclusive (Schedule 15 to the Rent Act 1977)

8. Appendix B

[*Title: as in Appendix A*]

1. I, [*state name*] of [*state address and occupation of the applicant*] apply to the Court for an order for recovery of possession of [*here describe the premises*] under Case [*here identify the Case relied on*] of Schedule 15 to the Rent Act 1977.

2. [*As in Appendix A*.]

3. [*As in Appendix A except that the Case referred to in the notice must correspond with the Case cited in paragraph 1, above.*]

4, 5 and 6. [*Here set out the matters of substance on which the applicant relies as bringing the claim within the Case cited in paragraph 1, above, and state, where relevant, the purpose for which possession is required.*]

7 and 8. [*As in Appendix A*.]

The names and addresses of the persons on whom it is intended to serve this application are: [*state names and addresses of persons intended to be served*].

My address for service is [*state applicant's address for service*].

Dated this .. .. day of

.. .. [*Signed*]

.. .. Applicant. **[881]**

NOTES

Commencement: 6 April 1981.

Appendix C Form of Originating Application for Possession under Case 19 (Schedule 15 to the Rent Act 1977)

10. Appendix C

[*Title: as in Appendix A*]

1. I, [*state name*] of [*state address and occupation of applicant*] apply to the Court for an order for recovery of possession of [*here describe the premises*] under Case 19 of Schedule 15 to the Rent Act 1977.

2. On [*insert the date of the grant*] the respondent was granted a protected shorthold tenancy of the premises for a fixed term beginning on [*insert the date when the tenancy began*] and ending on [*insert the expiry date*]; the respondent did not at the time have a protected or statutory tenancy of the premises.

3. The respondent was given notice in writing, before the tenancy was granted, that it was to be a protected shorthold tenancy.

4. Before the grant, a rent for the premises was registered on [*insert the date*]

or Before the grant, a certificate of fair rent for the premises was issued on [*insert the date*]; and the rent payable under the tenancy did not exceed the rent specified in the certificate for any period before the registration of a rent; and an application for the registration of a rent was made on [*insert the date*] and not subsequently withdrawn.

[*Complete or delete as may be appropriate in the circumstances*]

5. The respondent's protected shorthold tenancy has ended and there is no subsisting protected tenancy in its place; but the respondent remains in occupation.

6. Notice in writing was given to the respondent on [*state the date when notice was served*] that proceedings for possession under Case 19 might be brought after the expiry of the notice on [*insert the date*].

7. There are rent arrears in the sum of £ , calculated at the rate of [*here give the weekly or other rent*] and I apply to the Court for an order for payment.

The names and addresses of the persons on whom it is intended to serve this application are [*state names and addresses of persons intended to be served*].

My address for service is [*state applicant's address for service*].

Dated this .. .. day of

.. .. [*Signed*]

.. .. Applicant. **[882]**

NOTES

Commencement: 6 April 1981.

RENT ASSESSMENT COMMITTEE (ENGLAND AND WALES) (LEASEHOLD VALUATION TRIBUNAL) REGULATIONS 1981

(SI 1981 NO 271)

NOTES

Made: 24 February 1981

Authority: Rent Act 1977, s 74; Leasehold Reform Act 1967, s 21(4A)

ARRANGEMENT OF REGULATIONS

Regulation		Para
1	Citation and commencement	[883]
2	Interpretation	[884]
	APPLICATIONS	
3		[885]
4		[886]
	HEARINGS	
5		[887]
6		[888]
7	Non-appearance	[889]
8	Adjournment	[890]
9	Documents	[891]

Regulation		Para
10	Inspections	[892]
11	Decisions	[893]
12	Provision of information	[894]
13	Giving of Notice	[895]
	Schedule	[896]

1. Citation and commencement

These regulations may be cited as the Rent Assessment Committee (England ad Wales) (Leasehold Valuation Tribunal) Regulations 1981 and shall come into operation on 31st March 1981. **[883]**

NOTES

Commencement: 31 March 1981.

2. Interpretation

In these regulations, unless the context otherwise requires—

"application" means an application to a leasehold valuation tribunal under section 21(1) of the Leasehold Reform Act 1967, and

"tribunal" means a leasehold valuation tribunal. **[884]**

NOTES

Commencement: 31 March 1981.

APPLICATIONS

3. The form of application prescribed under section 21(4A) of the Leasehold Reform Act 1967 is as follows:—

(*a*) in the case of an application under section 21(1)(*a*) of the 1967 Act, form number 1 in the Schedule hereto,

(*b*) in the case of an application under section 21(1)(*b*) of the 1967 Act, form number 2 in the Schedule hereto, and

(*c*) in the case of an application under section 21(1)(*c*) of the 1967 Act, form number 3 in the Schedule hereto,

or, in each case, a form substantially to the like effect. **[885]**

NOTES

Commencement: 31 March 1981.

4. On receipt of an application, the tribunal shall send a copy of the application and of each of the documents which accompanied it to each person named in it as a respondent. **[886]**

NOTES

Commencement: 31 March 1981.

Hearings

5. (1) A hearing shall be on such date, and at such time and place as the tribunal shall appoint.

(2) Notice of such date, time and place shall be given by the tribunal to the parties to the proceedings not less than 14 days before the said date, and a copy of the notice shall be sent to any other person who is not already a party to the proceedings and gives notice to the tribunal of his intention to appear at the hearing.

(3) The notice referred to in paragraph (2) above shall contain a statement to the effect that an appeal to the Lands Tribunal from a decision of a tribunal may only be made by a person who appeared before the tribunal in proceedings to which he was a party.

(4) The tribunal may, where they consider it appropriate, arrange that a hearing in respect of one application shall be held together with the hearings in respect of one or more other applications.

(5) A hearing shall be in public unless, for special reasons, the tribunal decide otherwise, but nothing in these regulations shall prevent a member of the Council on Tribunals in that capacity from attending any hearing. **[887]**

NOTES
Commencement: 31 March 1981.

6. At a hearing—
(*a*) the parties shall be heard in such order and, subject to the provisions of these regulations, the procedure shall be such as the tribunal shall determine;
(*b*) a party may call witnesses, give evidence on his own behalf and cross-examine any witnesses called by any other party; and
(*c*) a party may appear either in person or by a person authorised by him in that behalf whether or not that person is of counsel or a solicitor.
[888]

NOTES
Commencement: 31 March 1981.

7. Non-appearance

If a party does not appear at a hearing, the tribunal, on being satisfied that the requirements of these regulations regarding the giving of notice of a hearing have been duly complied with, may proceed to deal with the application. **[889]**

NOTES
Commencement: 31 March 1981.

8. Adjournment

(1) The tribunal at their discretion may of their own motion, or at the request of the parties, or one of them, at any time and from time to time, postpone or adjourn a hearing, but they shall not do so at the request of one party only unless, having regard to the grounds on which and the time at which such

request is made and to the convenience of the parties, they deem it reasonable to do so.

(2) The tribunal shall give to the parties such notice of any postponed or adjourned hearing as is reasonable in the circumstances. **[890]**

NOTES

Commencement: 31 March 1981.

9. Documents

(1) Before the date of a hearing, the tribunal shall take all reasonable steps to ensure that there is supplied to each of the parties—

(*a*) a copy of, or sufficient extracts from or particulars of, any document relevant to the application which has been received from a party (other than a document which is in the possession of such a party or of which he has previously been supplied with a copy); and

(*b*) a copy of any document which embodies the results of any enquiries made by or for the tribunal for the purposes of the application.

(2) Where at a hearing—

(i) any document relevant to the application is not in the possession of a party present at that hearing; and

(ii) that party has not been supplied with a copy of, or sufficient extracts from or particulars of, that document;

then unless—

(*a*) that party consents to the continuation of the hearing; or

(*b*) the tribunal consider that that party has a sufficient opportunity to deal with that document without an adjournment of the hearing;

the tribunal shall adjourn the hearing for a period which they consider will afford that party a sufficient opportunity for dealing with that document. **[891]**

NOTES

Commencement: 31 March 1981.

10. Inspections

(1) The tribunal may, and shall at the request of any of the parties (subject in either case to any necessary consent being obtained), inspect the house and premises which are the subject of the application.

(2) An inspection may be made before, during or after the close of a hearing, as the tribunal may decide, and the tribunal shall give to the parties and their representatives an opportunity to attend.

(3) Notice of an inspection shall be given as though it were notice of a hearing, but the requirements for such notice may be dispensed with or relaxed in so far as the tribunal are satisfied that the parties have received sufficient notice.

(4) The provisions of this regulation shall apply, so far as is reasonable and practicable, to any comparable house or premises to which the attention of the tribunal is directed as they apply to the house and premises which are the subject of the application.

(5) Where an inspection is made after the close of a hearing, the tribunal shall, if they consider it expedient to do so on account of any matter arising

from the inspection, reopen the hearing; and if the hearing is to be reopened paragraph (2) of regulation 5 of these regulations shall apply as it applied to the original hearing, save in so far as its requirements may be dispensed with or relaxed with the consent of the parties. **[892]**

NOTES
Commencement: 31 March 1981.

11. Decisions

(1) The decision of a tribunal shall be recorded in a document signed by the chairman of the tribunal (or in the event of his absence or incapacity, by another member of the tribunal) which shall contain the reasons for the decision but shall contain no reference to the decision being by a majority (if that be the case) or to any opinion of a minority.

(2) The chairman (or in the event of his absence or incapacity, another member of the tribunal) shall have power, by certificate under his hand, to correct any clerical mistakes in the said document or any errors arising in it from an accidental slip or omission.

(3) A copy of the said document and of any such correction shall be sent by the tribunal to each party. **[893]**

NOTES
Commencement: 31 March 1981.

12. Provision of information

Where, under paragraph 7 of Schedule 22 to the Housing Act 1980 a tribunal by notice in writing require the giving of such information as the tribunal may reasonably require, the notice shall contain a statement to the effect that any person who fails without reasonable cause to comply with the notice is liable on summary conviction to a fine not exceeding £200. **[894]**

NOTES
Commencement: 31 March 1981.

13. Giving of Notice

Where any notice or other written matter is required under the provisions of these regulations to be given or supplied by the tribunal it shall be sufficient compliance with these regulations if such notice or other matter is sent by post in pre-paid letter and addressed to the party for whom it is intended at his usual or last known address, or if that party has appointed an agent to act on his behalf, to that agent at the address of the agent supplied to the tribunal. **[895]**

NOTES
Commencement: 31 March 1981.

SCHEDULE

FORM NO 1

LEASEHOLD REFORM ACT 1967

APPLICATION FOR DETERMINATION BY LEASEHOLD VALUATION TRIBUNAL ON ACQUISITION OF FREEHOLD

I/We apply for the determination by a Leasehold Valuation Tribunal of the price payable under section 9 of the Leasehold Reform Act 1967 for the house and premises named in paragraph 1 below and submit the following particulars. The respondents to this application are the persons (other than myself/ourselves) named in paragraphs 2 to 5 of those particulars.

*[I/We also apply to the Leasehold Valuation Tribunal for the determination under section 21(2) of the 1967 Act of the matters described in paragraph 12 below relating to the house and premises.]

* Cross out this paragraph if it does not apply.

THE PARTICULARS

1. Address of house and premises . . . .

2. Name and address of landlord to whom rent is payable by the tenant . . . .

3. Name of tenant (and address if different from 1 above) . . . .

4. Is the landlord mentioned in (2) above the freehold owner of the premises? Yes ☐ No ☐
   If NO, give the names and addresses of
   (*a*) the freeholder . . . .
   (*b*) any additional, intermediate landlords standing between the landlord mentioned in paragraph 2 and the freeholder . . . .

5. Is anyone, to the applicant's knowledge, entitled to the benefit of a charge on the freeholder's, or any other landlord's interest in the house and premises, such as a mortgagee (eg a building society)? Yes ☐ No ☐
   If YES, give names and addresses, if known . . . .

6. State the date on which notice was given by the tenant of his desire to acquire the freehold . . . .
   and enclose a copy of the notice.

7. Has the landlord given notice stating whether or not he admits the tenant's right to have the freehold? Yes ☐ No ☐
   If YES, give the date of the notice . . . . and enclose a copy of it.

8. Has the landlord informed the tenant of the price he is asking? Yes ☐ No ☐
   If YES, enclose a copy of the letter or notice from the landlord giving details of it.

9. Have any other formal notices been given following the notice by the tenant of his desire to have the freehold? Yes ☐ No ☐
   If YES, enclose copies of all the notices.

10. State the price which the applicant considers to be appropriate £. . . . .

11. Have the terms of the conveyance (other than the price) been agreed? Yes ☐ No ☐
   If YES, enclose details or a copy of a draft conveyance.

12. Is this also an application under section 21(2) of the Leasehold Reform Act 1967:—
   (*a*) to determine what provisions ought to be contained in the conveyance? Yes ☐ No ☐
   If YES, give details on a separate sheet and enclose a copy of the existing lease.
   (*b*) to apportion between the house and premises (or part of them) and other property, the rent payable under any tenancy? Yes ☐ No ☐
   If YES, give details on a separate sheet.

13. (*a*) Has any application been made to a Court to determine any question relating to this matter? Yes ☐ No ☐
   (*b*) if YES, has the Court made an Order? Yes ☐ No ☐
   If YES, enclose a copy of the Order.

14. Is the applicant
   (*a*) the owner of the freehold? Yes ☐ No ☐
   (*b*) a landlord? Yes ☐ No ☐
   (*c*) the tenant? Yes ☐ No ☐

Signed . . . .
[On behalf of . . . .]
If signed by an agent, give name and address of agent . . . .
. . . .
Date . . . .

Form No 2

Leasehold Reform Act 1967

Application for determination by Leasehold Valuation Tribunal of the rent to be payable

I/We apply for the determination by a Leasehold Valuation Tribunal of the amount of the rent to be payable under section 15(2) of the Leasehold Reform Act 1967 for the house and premises named in paragraph 1 below and submit the following particulars. The respondents to this application are the persons (other than myself/ourselves) named in paragraphs 2 to 5 of those particulars.

*[I/We also apply to the Leasehold Valuation Tribunal for the determination under section 21(2) of the 1967 Act of the matters described in paragraph 11 below relating to the house and premises.]

* Cross out this paragraph if it does not apply.

THE PARTICULARS

1. Address of house and premises ....

2. Name and address of landlord to whom rent is payable by the tenant ....

3. Name of tenant (and address if different from 1 above) ....

4. Has a new tenancy, expiring 50 years after the original tenancy, already been granted for the house and premises? Yes ☐ No ☐
If YES, give the names and addresses of—
(*a*) the landlord named in the new lease ....
(*b*) any additional, intermediate landlords standing between the landlord named in the new lease and the tenant ....
Enclose a copy of the new lease and then GO TO QUESTION 10.

5. If a new tenancy has *not* yet been granted give the name and address of—
(*a*) the person who will grant the new lease ....
(*b*) any additional, intermediate landlords standing between that person and the tenant ....
and enclose a copy of the existing lease.

6. Have the terms (other than rent) for the new tenancy been agreed? Yes ☐ No ☐
If YES, enclose a copy.

7. Give the date of the notice by the tenant of his desire to have an extended lease....
and enclose a copy of the notice.

8. Has the landlord given notice stating whether or not he admits the tenant's right to have an extended lease? Yes ☐ No ☐
If YES, give the date of the notice .... and enclose a copy of it.

9. Have any other formal notices been given following the notice by the tenant of his desire to have an extended lease? Yes ☐ No ☐
If YES, enclose copies of all the notices.

10. State the amount of rent the applicant considers appropriate—£ ....

11. Is this also an application under section 21(2) of the Leasehold Reform Act 1967:—
(*a*) to determine what provisions ought to be contained in the lease granting the new tenancy? Yes ☐ No ☐
If YES, give details on a separate sheet.
(*b*) to apportion between the house and premises (or part of them) and other property, the rent payable under any tenancy? Yes ☐ No ☐
If YES, give details on a separate sheet.

12. (*a*) Has any application been made to a Court to determine any question relating to this matter? Yes ☐ No ☐
(*b*) If YES, has the Court made an Order? Yes ☐ No ☐
If YES, enclose a copy of the Order.

13. Is the applicant—
(*a*) the owner of the freehold? Yes ☐ No ☐
(*b*) a landlord? Yes ☐ No ☐
(*c*) the tenant? Yes ☐ No ☐

Signed . . . .
[On behalf of . . . .]
If signed by an agent, give name and address of agent . . . .
. . . .
Date . . . .

FORM NO 3

LEASEHOLD REFORM ACT 1967

APPLICATION FOR DETERMINATION BY LEASEHOLD VALUATION TRIBUNAL OF COMPENSATION PAYABLE TO A TENANT

I/We apply for the determination by a Leasehold Valuation Tribunal of the amount of the compensation payable under section 17 or 18 of the Leasehold Reform Act 1967 for the loss of the house and premises named in paragraph 1 below and submit the following particulars. The respondents to this application are the persons (other than myself/ourselves) named in paragraphs 2 to 4 of those particulars.

*[I/We also apply to the Leasehold Valuation Tribunal for the determination under section 21(2) of the 1967 Act of the amount of a sub-tenant's share under Schedule 2 to the Act of the compensation payable to the tenant.]
* Cross out this paragraph if it does not apply.

THE PARTICULARS

1. Address of house and premises . . . .
2. Name and address of landlord by whom compensation is payable . . . .
3. Name of tenant (and address if different from 1 above) . . . .
4. Is this also an application under section 21(2) of the Leasehold Reform Act 1967 to determine the amount of a sub-tenant's share under Schedule 2 to the Act of the compensation payable to the tenant. Yes ☐ No ☐
If YES, give the name and address of the sub-tenant . . . .
5. Give full details on a separate sheet of the circumstances under which the claim for compensation arises and enclose copies of—
(*a*) the lease and of any agreements for sub-tenancies, and
(*b*) all other relevant documents, applications to the Court and Court Orders, or notices.
6. State the amount of compensation which the applicant considers appropriate £. . . .
7. Is the applicant—
(*a*) the landlord? Yes ☐ No ☐
(*b*) the tenant? Yes ☐ No ☐

Signed . . . .
[On behalf of . . . .]
If signed by an agent, give name and address of agent . . . .
. . . .
Date . . . .

[896]

NOTES
Commencement: 31 March 1981.

ASSURED TENANCIES (APPROVED BODY) (NO 1) ORDER 1981

(SI 1981 NO 590)

NOTES
Made: 7 April 1981
Authority: Housing Act 1980, ss 56(4), 151

1. This order may be cited as the Assured Tenancies (Approved Body) (No. 1) Order 1981 and shall come into operation on 14th May 1981. **[897]**

NOTES
Commencement: 14 May 1981.

2. Wates Limited is hereby specified for the purposes of Part II of the Housing Act 1980. **[898]**

NOTES
Commencement: 14 May 1981.

ASSURED TENANCIES (NOTICE TO TENANT) REGULATIONS 1981
(SI 1981 NO 591)

NOTES
Made: 7 April 1981
Authority: Housing Act 1980, ss 56(7), 151

1. These regulations may be cited as the Assured Tenancies (Notice to Tenant) Regulations 1981 and shall come into operation on 14th May 1981. **[899]**

NOTES
Commencement: 14 May 1981.

2. The requirements with which a notice is to comply in order to be valid for the purposes of section 56(6) of the Housing Act 1980 are that it shall be in the form set out in the Schedule to these regulations or in a form substantially to the like effect. **[900]**

NOTES
Commencement: 14 May 1981.

SCHEDULE
NOTICE OF THE GRANT OF A PROTECTED OR HOUSING ASSOCIATION TENANCY BY A BODY APPROVED UNDER SECTION 56(4) OF THE HOUSING ACT 1980

The landlord must give this to the tenant *before* the grant of the tenancy if a dwelling house which could be let on an assured tenancy is instead to be let on a protected or housing association tenancy.

To .. ..

(Name of proposed tenant)

PLEASE READ THIS NOTICE CAREFULLY AND KEEP IT

1. You are proposing to take a tenancy of the dwelling known as .. .. from .. .. (day) .. .. (month) 19 .. .. .. (year).

*2. This notice is to tell you that your tenancy is to be a protected tenancy and *not* an assured tenancy. Full details about protected tenancies are given in the Department of the Environment and Welsh Office booklet "Regulated Tenancies" obtainable free from Rent Officers, council offices and housing aid centres.

*2. This notice is to tell you that your tenancy is to be a housing association tenancy and *not* an assured tenancy. Full details about housing association tenancies are given in the Department of the Environment and Welsh Office booklets "Housing Association Rents" and "The Tenants' Charter—New Rights for council, new town and housing association tenants". Both are obtainable free from Rent Officers, council offices and housing aid centres.

(* The Landlord must delete whichever does not apply.)

3. This notice is given to you on .... (date).

Signed

(on behalf of) ....

(name and address of landlord)

a body approved by the Secretary of State under

....

(Title and number of Order granting approval) [901]

NOTES

Commencement: 14 May 1981.

ASSURED TENANCIES (APPROVED BODY) (NO 2) ORDER 1981

(SI 1981 NO 1009)

NOTES

Made: 9 July 1981

Authority: Housing Act 1980, ss 56(4), 151

1. This order may be cited as the Assured Tenancies (Approved Body) (No 2) Order 1981 and shall come into operation on 13th August 1981. [902]

NOTES

Commencement: 13 August 1981.

2. Rushey Development Company Limited is hereby specified for the purposes of Part II of the Housing Act 1980. [903]

NOTES

Commencement: 13 August 1981.

RENT ASSESSMENT COMMITTEES (ENGLAND AND WALES) (AMENDMENT) REGULATIONS 1981

(SI 1981 NO 1783)

NOTES

Made: 20 October 1981

Authority: Rent Act 1977, s 74

1. (1) These regulations may be cited as the Rent Assessment Committees (England and Wales) (Amendment) Regulations 1981 and shall come into operation on 1st January 1982.

(2) In these regulations "the principal regulations" means the Rent Assessment Committees (England and Wales) Regulations 1971. [904]

NOTES
Commencement: 1 January 1982.

2. (1) The procedures to be followed by rent assessment committees on—

(*a*) matters referred to them under paragraph 6 of Part I of Schedule 11 to the Rent Act 1977, or

(*b*) applications referred to them under paragraph 8 of Schedule 12 to the 1977 Act

where the reference is made after the coming into operation of these regulations, shall be that set out in the said Part I of Schedule 11 or in the said Schedule 12 (as the case may be) and in the principal regulations as modified or amended by these regulations.

(2) Accordingly, as respects such applications, section 67(7) and section 69(3) of the Rent Act 1977 shall each be modified by the insertion of the words "and by the Rent Assessment Committees (England and Wales) (Amendment) Regulations 1981" after the words "Regulations 1980". **[905]**

NOTES
Commencement: 1 January 1982.

3. Paragraph 7(1)(*b*) of Schedule 11 and paragraph 9(1) of Schedule 12 to the Rent Act 1977 are each modified by the substitution of the words "7 days" for the words "14 days". **[906]**

NOTES
Commencement: 1 January 1982.

HOUSING (EXCLUSION OF SHARED OWNERSHIP TENANCIES FROM THE LEASEHOLD REFORM ACT 1967) REGULATIONS 1982

(SI 1982 NO 62)

NOTES
Made: 20 January 1982
Authority: Housing Act 1980, s 140

1. Citation and commencement

These regulations may be cited as the Housing (Exclusion of Shared Ownership Tenancies from the Leasehold Reform Act 1967) Regulations 1982, and shall come into operation on 22nd February 1982. **[907]**

NOTES
Commencement: 22 February 1982.

2. Requirement for exclusion of tenancies from Leasehold Reform Act 1967

A lease granted by a registered housing association complies with these regulations for the purposes of section 140(4)(*b*) of the Housing Act 1980 if—

(i) it provides for the tenant to acquire the landlord's interest in the property, whether under an option to purchase or otherwise, for a consideration which is to be calculated in accordance with the terms of the lease and which is reasonable, having regard to the premium or premiums paid by the tenant under the lease; or

(ii) it is a lease for the elderly, as defined in regulation 3 below. **[908]**

NOTES

Commencement: 22 February 1982.

3. Interpretation

In regulation 2 above, "lease for the elderly" means a lease which—

(i) is a lease of one of a group of dwellinghouses which it is the practice of a registered housing association to let for occupation by persons of pensionable age, where a social service or special facilities are provided in close proximity to the group of dwellinghouses for the only or main purpose of assisting those persons;

(ii) does not provide for the tenant to acquire the interest of the landlord under an option to purchase;

(iii) provides for an absolute covenant by the tenant not to underlet or part with possession of the property or any part thereof, nor to assign the same except—

(*a*) to the tenant's spouse if he is residing at the property at the date of the tenant's death, or

(*b*) to a member of the tenant's family or household, who was residing with him at the time of his death, where the grant of a tenancy in the property to that person would not infringe the objects of the lanlord;

(iv) provides that, if during the term the tenant's affairs are made subject to the jurisdiction of the Court of Protection or if the tenant shall die, then the landlord shall be entitled to determine the term by giving to the tenant not less than six months notice in writing; and

(v) provides that the tenant shall at any time be entitled to surrender the term by giving to the landlord not less than six months notice in writing. **[909]**

NOTES

Commencement: 22 February 1982.

ASSURED TENANCIES (APPROVED BODIES) (NO 1) ORDER 1982

(SI 1982 NO 582)

NOTES

Made: 19 April 1982

Authority: Housing Act 1980, ss 56(4), 151

1. This order may be cited as the Assured Tenancies (Approved Bodies) (No. 1) Order 1982 and shall come into operation on 27th May 1982. **[910]**

NOTES

Commencement: 27 May 1982.

2. The bodies set out in the Schedule to these Regulations are hereby specified for the purposes of Part II of the Housing Act 1980. **[911]**

NOTES
Commencement: 27 May 1982.

SCHEDULE

BODIES SPECIFIED FOR THE PURPOSES OF PART II OF THE HOUSING ACT 1980

1. Prudential Assurance Company Limited.
2. Prudential Pensions Limited.
3. Prudential Nominees Limited.
4. Vanbrugh Life Assurance Limited.
5. Edger Investments Limited. **[912]**

NOTES
Commencement: 27 May 1982.

ASSURED TENANCIES (APPROVED BODY) (NO 2) ORDER 1982
(SI 1982 NO 850)

NOTES
Made: 22 June 1982
Authority: Housing Act 1980, ss 56(4), 151

1. This order may be cited as the Assured Tenancies (Approved Body) (No. 2) Order 1982 and shall come into operation on 22nd July 1982. **[913]**

NOTES
Commencement: 22 July 1982.

2. J & D Davies Investments Ltd. is hereby specified for the purposes of Part II of the Housing Act 1980. **[914]**

NOTES
Commencement: 22 July 1982.

RENT REGULATION (LOCAL AUTHORITY APPLICATIONS) REGULATIONS 1982
(SI 1982 NO 1015)

NOTES
Made: 21 July 1982
Authority: Rent Act 1977, ss 68(7), (8), 74

ARRANGEMENT OF REGULATIONS

CITATION AND COMMENCEMENT

Regulation	Para
1	[915]

INTERPRETATION

Regulation	Para
2	[916]

PROCEDURE ON APPLICATION TO RENT OFFICER

3	[917]
4	[918]
5	[919]

DECISION OF A RENT OFFICER

6	[920]

REFERENCES TO A COMMITTEE

7	[921]

PROCEDURE ON A REFERENCE

8	[922]

THE HEARING AND REPRESENTATIONS

9	[923]

DOCUMENTS

10	[924]

TIME AND PLACE OF HEARING

11	[925]

PROCEDURE AT A HEARING

12	[926]

INSPECTION OF A DWELLING HOUSE

13	[927]

ADJOURNMENT

14	[928]

DECISION OF A COMMITTEE

15	[929]
16	[930]
17	[931]

GIVING OF NOTICES, ETC

18	[932]
19	[933]

CITATION AND COMMENCEMENT

1. These regulations may be cited as the Rent Regulation (Local Authority Applications) Regulations 1982 and shall come into operation on 23rd August 1982. **[915]**

NOTES
Commencement: 23 August 1982.

INTERPRETATION

2. In these regulations, unless the context otherwise requires:—

"the Act" means the Rent Act 1977;

"committee" means a rent assessment committee;

"parties" means the landlord and the tenant under the regulated tenancy of the dwelling house to which an application under section 68 of the Act relates. **[916]**

NOTES
Commencement: 23 August 1982.

PROCEDURE ON APPLICATION TO RENT OFFICER

3. (1) On receiving an application made by a local authority for consideration of a fair rent under section 68 of the Act, a rent officer—

(*a*) may by notice in writing served on a party, require him to give to the rent officer, within such period of not less than 7 days from the service of the notice as may be specified in the notice, such information as he may reasonably require regarding the rent and the other terms of the tenancy and the dwelling house; and
(*b*) shall serve on each of the parties a notice inviting him to state in writing, within a period of not less than 7 days after the service of the notice, whether he wishes the rent officer to consider, in consultation with the parties, whether a rent should be registered in pursuance of section 68(2) of the Act and, if so, what the amount of that rent should be.

(2) A notice served under paragraph (1)(*b*) above shall be accompanied by a copy of the application. **[917]**

NOTES
Commencement: 23 August 1982.

4. If, after service of a notice by the rent officer under regulation 3(1)(*b*) above, no request in writing is made within the period specified in the notice for the matter to be considered as mentioned in that regulation, the rent officer may either:—

(*a*) consider whether a rent should be registered in pursuance of section 68(2) of the Act and, if so, determine what the amount of that rent should be; or (*b*) serve a notice under regulation 5(2) below. **[918]**

NOTES
Commencement: 23 August 1982.

5. (1) Where, in response to a notice served by the rent officer under regulation 3(1)(*b*) above, a party states in writing that he wishes the rent officer to consider the matter as mentioned in that regulation, the rent officer shall serve a notice under this regulation.

(2) A notice under this regulation shall be served on the parties, informing them that the rent officer proposes, at a time (which shall not be earlier than 7 days after the service of the notice) and place specified in the notice, to consider in consultation with the parties, or such of them as may appear at that time and place, whether a rent should be registered in pursuance of section 68(2) of the Act and, if so, what the amount of that rent should be.

(3) At any such consultation the parties may each be represented by a person authorised by him in that behalf, whether or not that person is of counsel or a solicitor.

(4) The rent officer may, where he considers it appropriate, arrange for consultations in respect of one dwelling house to be held together with consultations in respect of one or more other dwelling houses. **[919]**

NOTES
Commencement: 23 August 1982.

Decision of a rent officer

6. (1) When, after such consideration as is mentioned in regulations 4(*a*) or 5 above, the rent officer has reached his decision, he shall notify each of the parties and the local authority whether or not he is satisfied that the rent, or the highest rent, payable for the dwelling house exceeds what in his opinion is a fair rent, and, if he is so satisfied, the amount of the rent he has registered pursuant to section 68(2) of the Act.

(2) When the rent officer registers a rent pursuant to section 68(2) of the Act, the notification of that registration to be given to the parties pursuant to paragraph (1) above shall be given by a notice stating that if, within twenty-eight days of the service of the notice or such longer period as he or a committee may allow, an objection in writing is received by the rent officer from either of the parties the matter will be referred to a committee. **[920]**

NOTES
Commencement: 23 August 1982.

References to a committee

7. (1) If such an objection as is mentioned in regulation 6(2) above is received, then—

(*a*) if it is received within the period of 28 days specified in that regulation or a committee so direct, the rent officer shall refer the matter to a committee;

(*b*) if it is received after the expiry of that period, the rent officer may either refer the matter to a committee or seek the directions of a committee whether so to refer it.

(2) The rent officer shall indicate in the register whether the matter has been referred to a committee in pursuance of this regulation. **[921]**

NOTES
Commencement: 23 August 1982.

PROCEDURE ON A REFERENCE

8. The committee to whom a reference is made under regulation 7 above—

(*a*) may by notice in writing served on a party require him to give to the committee, within such period of not less than 14 days from the service of the notice as may be specified in the notice, such further information, in addition to any given to the rent officer in pursuance of regulation 3(1)(*a*) above, as they may reasonably require;
(*b*) shall serve on each of the parties a notice specifying a period of not less than 7 days from the service of the notice during which either representation in writing or a request to make oral representations may be made by him to the committee; and
(*c*) shall make such further inquiry, if any, as they think fit. **[922]**

NOTES
Commencement: 23 August 1982.

THE HEARING AND REPRESENTATIONS

9. (1) Where, within the period specified in regulation 8 above or such further period as the committee may allow, either of the parties requests to make oral representations the committee shall give the parties an opportunity to be heard at a hearing.

(2) At a hearing each party may be heard either in person or by a person authorised by him in that behalf, whether or not that person is of counsel or a solicitor. **[923]**

NOTES
Commencement: 23 August 1982.

DOCUMENTS

10. (1) The committee shall, where the reference is to be subject to a hearing, take all reasonable steps to ensure that there is supplied to each of the parties before the date of the hearing—

(*a*) a copy of, or sufficient extracts from or particulars of, any document relevant to the reference which has been received from the rent officer or from a party (other than a document which is in the possession of such party, or of which he has previously been supplied with a copy by the rent officer); and (*b*) a copy of any document which embodies the results of any enquiries made by or for the committee for the purposes of that reference, or which contains relevant information in relation to fair rents previously determined for other dwelling houses and which has been prepared for the committee for the purposes of that reference.

(2) Where a reference is not to be subject to a hearing, the committee shall supply to each of the parties a copy of, or sufficient extracts from or particulars of, any such document as is mentioned in paragraph 1(*a*) above (other than a document excepted from that paragraph) and a copy of any such document as is mentioned in paragraph 1(*b*) above, and they shall not reach their decision until they are satisfied that each party has been given a sufficient opportunity of commenting upon any document of which a copy, or from which extracts or of which particulars, has or have been so supplied, and upon the other's case. **[924]**

NOTES
Commencement: 23 August 1982.

Time and place of hearing

11. (1) A hearing shall be on such date and at such time and place as the committee shall appoint.

(2) Notices of such date, time and place shall be given by the committee, subject to paragraph (3) below, not less than 10 days before the said date to each of the parties.

(3) The notice referred to in paragraph (2) above may be given not less than 7 days before the date of the hearing if that date has been referred to in the notice given under regulation 8(*b*) above, as the date when the hearing would be held if a request to make oral representations were to be made. **[925]**

NOTES
Commencement: 23 August 1982.

Procedure at a hearing

12. (1) A hearing shall be in public unless, for special reasons, the committee decide otherwise; but nothing in these regulations shall prevent a member of the Council on Tribunals in that capacity from attending any hearing.

(2) At the hearing—

(*a*) the parties shall be heard in such order, and, subject to the provisions of these regulations, the procedure shall be such as the committee shall determine;

(*b*) a party may call witnesses, give evidence on his own behalf and cross-examine any witnesses called by the other party.

(3) If a party does not appear at a hearing the committee, on being satisfied that the requirements of these regulations regarding the giving of notice of hearings have been duly complied with, may proceed to deal with the reference upon the representations of any party present and upon the documents and information which they may properly consider. **[926]**

NOTES
Commencement: 23 August 1982.

INSPECTION OF A DWELLING HOUSE

13. (1) The committee may, and shall at the request of one of the parties (subject in either case to any necessary consent being obtained), inspect the dwelling house which is the subject of the reference.

(2) An inspection may be made before, during or after the close of the hearing, or at such stage in relation to the consideration of the representations in writing, as the committee shall decide, and the committee shall give to the parties and their representatives an opportunity to attend.

(3) Notice of an inspection shall be given as though it were notice of a hearing, save that the requirements for such notice may be dispensed with or relaxed in so far as the committee are satisfied that the parties have received sufficient notice.

(4) Where an inspection is made after the close of a hearing, the committee shall, if they consider that it is expedient to do so on account of any matter arising from the inspection, re-open the hearing; and if the hearing is to be re-opened, regulation 11(2) above shall apply as it applied to the original hearing, save in so far as its requirements may be dispensed with or relaxed with the consent of the parties. **[927]**

NOTES
Commencement: 23 August 1982.

ADJOURNMENT

14. (1) The committee at their discretion may of their own motion, or at the request of the parties, or one of them, at any time and from time to time postpone or adjourn a hearing.

(2) Where at any hearing—

(*a*) any document relevant to the reference is not in the possession of a party present at that hearing; and
(*b*) that party has not been supplied with a copy of, or sufficient extracts from or particulars of, that document by the rent officer or by the committee in accordance with the provisions of regulation 10(1) above,

then unless—

(i) that party consents to the continuation of the hearing; or
(ii) the committee consider that that party has a sufficient opportunity of dealing with that document without an adjournment of the hearing,

the committee shall adjourn the hearing for a period which they consider will afford that party a sufficient opportunity of dealing with that document.

(3) Such notice of any postponed or adjourned hearing as is reasonable in the circumstances shall be given to each of the parties by the committee. **[928]**

NOTES
Commencement: 23 August 1982.

Decision of a committee

15. (1) The committee shall consider any information supplied or representations made to them in pursuance of regulation 8 or regulation 9 above and, where there is a hearing, any evidence adduced at that hearing, and—

(*a*) if it appears to them that the rent registered by the rent officer is a fair rent, they shall confirm that rent;

(*b*) if it does not appear to them that that rent is a fair rent, they shall determine a fair rent for the dwelling house.

(2) Where the committee confirm or determine a rent under this regulation they shall notify each of the parties, the local authority and the rent officer of their decision and of the date on which it was made.

(3) On receiving the notification, the rent officer shall, as the case may require, either indicate in the register that the rent has been confirmed or register the rent determined by the committee as the rent for the dwelling house. **[929]**

NOTES
Commencement: 23 August 1982.

16. (1) The decision of the committee upon a reference shall be recorded in a document signed by the chairman (or in the event of his absence or incapacity, by another member of the committee) which shall contain no reference to the decision being by a majority (if that be the case) or to any opinion of a minority.

(2) The chairman (or in the event of his absence or incapacity, either of the other members of the committee) shall have power, by certificate under his hand, to correct any clerical mistakes in the said document, or any errors arising in it from an accidental slip or omission.

(3) A copy of the said document and of any such correction shall be sent by the committee to each of the parties and to the rent officer. **[930]**

NOTES
Commencement: 23 August 1982.

17. (1) Where the committee are requested, on or before the giving or notification of the decision, to state the reasons for the decision, those reasons shall be recorded in a document.

(2) Regulation 16 above shall apply to the document recording the reasons as it applies to the document recording the decision. **[931]**

NOTES
Commencement: 23 August 1982.

Giving of notices, etc

18. Where any notice or other written matter is required under the provisions of these regulations to be given or supplied by the committee it shall be sufficient compliance with the regulations if such notice or matter is sent by post in a prepaid letter and addressed to the party for whom it is intended at his usual or last known address, or if that party has appointed an agent to act on his behalf in relation to the reference, to that agent at the address of the agent supplied to the committee. **[932]**

NOTES
Commencement: 23 August 1982.

19. . . . **[933]**

NOTES
Commencement: 23 August 1982.
This regulation revokes SI 1972 No 1307.

ASSURED TENANCIES (APPROVED BODIES) (NO 3) ORDER 1982
(SI 1982 NO 1016)

NOTES
Made: 21 July 1982
Authority: Housing Act 1980, ss 56(4), 151

1. This order may be cited as the Assured Tenancies (Approved Bodies) (No. 3) Order 1982 and shall come into operation on 23rd August 1982. **[934]**

NOTES
Commencement: 23 August 1982.

2. The bodies set out in the Schedule to this Order are hereby specified for the purposes of Part II of the Housing Act 1980. **[935]**

NOTES
Commencement: 23 August 1982.

SCHEDULE
BODIES SPECIFIED FOR THE PURPOSES OF PART II OF THE HOUSING ACT 1980

1. Barratt Developments p.l.c.
2. Eaton Square Properties Limited.
3. L.J. Developments Limited.
4. Oakmead Estates Limited.
5. Pattinson Estates Limited.
6. Pattinsons (Windermere) Limited.
7. Pearce Homes Limited.
8. Pullwoods Estates Company.
9. . . .
10. Snowmountain Investments Limited.
11. Sorrec Limited.
12. Tay Developments (Airedale) Limited. **[936]**

NOTES
Commencement: 23 August 1982.
Words omitted revoked by SI 1984 No 1443, art 3.

ASSURED TENANCIES (APPROVED BODIES) (NO 4) ORDER 1982
(SI 1982 NO 1229)

NOTES
Made: 18 August 1982
Authority: Housing Act 1980, ss 56(4), 151

1. This order may be cited as the Assured Tenancies (Approved Bodies)(No.4) Order 1982 and shall come into operation on 30th September 1982. **[937]**

NOTES
Commencement: 30 September 1982.

2. The bodies set out in the Schedule to this order are hereby specified for the purposes of Part II of the Housing Act 1980. **[938]**

NOTES
Commencement: 30 September 1982.

SCHEDULE
BODIES SPECIFIED FOR THE PURPOSES OF PART II OF THE HOUSING ACT 1980

1. Glynbridge Developments Limited.
2. C. A. Goymour & Son Limited.
3. Lancaster Court (Hove) Limited.
4. Thos. Swift Holdings Limited.
5. . . .

[939]

NOTES
Commencement: 30 September 1982.
Words omitted revoked by SI 1986 No 1208, art 2.

RENT BOOK (FORMS OF NOTICE) REGULATIONS 1982
(SI 1982 NO 1474)

NOTES
Made: 15 October 1982
Authority: Landlord and Tenant Act 1962, ss 2(1), 6(1)(*b*)

ARRANGEMENT OF REGULATIONS

Regulation	Para
1	[940]
2	[941]
3	[942]
4	[943]
Schedule—	
Part I—(Form for Rent Book for Restricted Contract)	[944]
Part II—(Form for Rent Book for Protected or Statutory Tenancy)	[945]
Part III—(Form for Rent Book for Tenancy under the Rent (Agriculture) Act 1976)	[946]

1. These regulations may be cited as the Rent Book (Forms of Notice) Regulations 1982 and shall come into operation on 1st January 1983. **[940]**

NOTES
Commencement: 1 January 1983.

2. In these regulations:—

"the 1962 Act" means the Landlord and Tenant Act 1962;

"the 1976 Act" means the Rent (Agriculture) Act 1976; and

"the 1977 Act" means the Rent Act 1977. **[941]**

NOTES
Commencement: 1 January 1983.

3. (1) The prescribed form in which, under section 2(1) of the 1962 Act, notice or particulars are required to be contained in a rent book or other similar document provided in pursuance of section 1 of the 1962 Act shall be as follows:—

(*a*) if the premises are occupied by virtue of a restricted contract within the meaning of the 1977 Act, the form set out in Part I of the Schedule to these regulations;
(*b*) if the premises are a dwelling house let on or subject to a protected or statutory tenancy within the meaning of the 1977 Act, the form set out in Part II of the Schedule to these regulations; and
(*c*) if the premises are a dwelling house subject to a statutory tenancy as defined in the 1976 Act, the form set out in Part III of the Schedule to these regulations

or, in each case, a form substantially to the same effect.

(2) In the cases referred to in paragraphs (*a*), (*b*) and (*c*) above, such rent book or similar document shall contain notice of the matters set out in the appropriate prescribed form, in addition to the name and address of the landlord and the particulars required by section 2(1) of the 1962 Act. **[942]**

NOTES
Commencement: 1 January 1983.
1962 Act: Landlord and Tenant Act 1962.
1976 Act: Rent (Agriculture) Act 1976.
1977 Act: Rent Act 1977.

4. . . . **[943]**

NOTES
Commencement: 1 January 1983.
This regulation revokes SI 1976 No 378.

SCHEDULE

PART I

(FORM FOR RENT BOOK FOR RESTRICTED CONTRACT)

INFORMATION FOR TENANT

IMPORTANT—PLEASE READ THIS

If the rent for the premises you occupy as your residence is payable weekly, the landlord must provide you with a rent book or similar document. If you have a "restricted contract" (see paragraph 9 below), the rent book or similar document must contain this notice, properly filled in.

1. Address of premises .. ..

*2. Name and address of landlord .. ..

*3. Name and address of agent (if any) .. ..

*4. The rent payable including/excluding**rates is £ .. .. .. per week.

If a reasonable rent is registered by the Rent Tribunal, paragraph 5 and, where it applies, paragraph 6 must be filled in, otherwise they should be crossed out.

*5. The registered rent (which excludes rates) is £ .. .. per week,

registered on .. .. (date).

*6. In addition to the registered rent, £ .. .. per week is payable to cover rates paid by the landlord or a superior landlord.

7. Details of accommodation (if any) which the occupier has the right to share with other persons .. ..

8. The other terms and conditions of the contract are .. ..

9. *Restricted contracts* are usually lettings by landlords who live in the same house. There are rules about your rights to stay in the accommodation and the rent you pay for restricted contracts. Full details are given in the Department of the Environment and Welsh Office booklets "Letting Rooms in Your Home" and "Notice to Quit", nos. 4 and 11 in the series of housing booklets. These booklets are obtainable free from rent officers, council offices and housing aid centres, some of which also give advice.

10. If your letting began on or after 28th November 1980, you cannot be evicted unless the landlord gets a possession order from the courts. The rules for lettings which began before 28th November 1980 are different. You may have the right to apply to the Rent Tribunal to postpone any notice to quit and the landlord often also needs a court order. Whether your letting began before or after 28th November 1980, either you or the landlord can apply to the Rent Tribunal to fix a reasonable rent. It is unwise to apply without first getting advice.

11. You may be entitled to get help to pay your rent. Apply to your local council for details of the rent allowance and rate rebate schemes.

12. It is a criminal offence for your landlord to harass you or interfere with your possessions or use of facilities in order to force you to leave.

13. If you are in any doubt about your legal rights or obligations, particularly if your landlord has asked you to leave, you should go to a Citizens Advice Bureau, housing aid centre, law centre or solicitor. Help with all or part of the cost of legal advice from a solicitor may be available under the Legal Aid Scheme.

(* These entries must be kept up to date.)

(** Cross out whichever does not apply.) [944]

NOTES

Commencement: 1 January 1983.

PART II

(FORM FOR RENT BOOK FOR PROTECTED OR STATUTORY TENANCY)

INFORMATION FOR TENANT

IMPORTANT—PLEASE READ THIS

If the rent for the premises you occupy as your residence is payable weekly, the landlord must provide you with a rent book or similar document. If you have a protected or statutory tenancy (see paragraph 9 below), the rent book or similar document must contain this notice, properly filled in.

1. Address of premises .. ..

*2. Name and address of landlord .. ..

*3. Name and address of agent (if any) . . ..

*4. The rent payable including/excluding**rates is £ .. .. .. per week.

If a fair rent is registered paragraph 5 and, where it applies, paragraph 6 must be filled in, otherwise they should be crossed out.

*5. The registered rent (which excludes rates) is £ .. .. per week,

effective from .. .. (date).

If the rent is registered as variable (because it includes service charges which vary), this should be indicated by placing a tick in the box. ☐

*6. In addition to the registered rent, £ .. .. per week is payable to cover rates paid by the landlord or a superior landlord.

7. Details of accommodation (if any) which the occupier has the right to share with other persons .. ..

8. The other terms and conditions of the tenancy are .. ..

9. You are protected by the Rent Act 1977 and known as a "regulated tenant". The Rent Act contains important rules concerning the amount of rent you have to pay and your rights to stay in your home. Details of these rules are set out in the Department of the Environment and Welsh Office booklets "Regulated Tenancies" and "Notice to Quit", nos. 7 and 11 in the series of housing booklets. These booklets are available from rent officers, council offices and housing aid centres, some of which also give advice.

10. Either you or your landlord may apply to the rent officer for a fair rent to be registered. It is wise to get advice before doing so. Whether or not your rent is registered by the rent officer there are rules about how and when it can be increased. You cannot be evicted from your home unless your landlord gets a possession order from the courts, and the courts can grant an order only in special circumstances.

11. If you have a protected *shorthold* tenancy, special rules apply. You should read housing booklet no. 8 "Shorthold Tenancies—First Revision" which sets out these rules.

12. The Housing Act 1980 converted most *controlled* tenancies into regulated tenancies. If your tenancy was formerly a controlled one, you should read housing booklet no. 6 "Controlled Tenancies" which explains your position.

13. You may be entitled to get help to pay your rent. Apply to your local council for details of the rent allowance and rate rebate schemes.

14. It is a criminal offence for your landlord to evict you without an order from the court or to harass you or interfere with your possessions or use of facilities in order to force you to leave.

15. If you are in any doubt about your legal rights or obligations, particularly if your landlord has asked you to leave, you should go to a Citizens Advice Bureau, housing aid centre, law centre or solicitor. Help with all or part of the cost of legal advice from a solicitor may be available under the Legal Aid Scheme.

(*These entries must be kept up to date.)

(**Cross out whichever does not apply.) **[945]**

NOTES

Commencement: 1 January 1983.

PART III

(FORM FOR RENT BOOK FOR TENANCY UNDER THE RENT (AGRICULTURE) ACT 1976)

INFORMATION FOR TENANT

IMPORTANT—PLEASE READ THIS

If the rent for the premises you occupy as your residence is payable weekly, the landlord must provide you with a rent book or similar document. If you have a statutory tenancy under the Rent (Agriculture) Act 1976 (see paragraph 9 below), the rent book or similar document must contain this notice, properly filled in.

*1. Address of premises .. ..

*2. Name and address of landlord . .. .

*3. Name and address of agent (if any) . .. .

*4. The rent payable (or to be deducted from pay) including/excluding**rates is £ .. .. .. per week.

If a fair rent is registered paragraph 5 and, where it applies, paragraph 6 must be filled in, otherwise they should be crossed out.

*5. The registered rent (which excludes rates) is £ .. .. per week,

effective from .. .. (date).

If the rent is registered as variable (because it includes service charges which vary), this should be indicated by placing a tick in the box. ☐

*6. In addition to the registered rent, £ .. .. per week is payable to cover rates paid by the landlord or a superior landlord.

7. Details of accommodation (if any) which the occupier has the right to share with other persons .. ..

8. The other terms and conditions of the tenancy are .. ..

9. You are protected by the Rent (Agriculture) Act 1976 and known as a "statutory tenant" under that Act. The Act contains important rules concerning the amount of rent you have to pay and your rights to stay in your home. Details of these rules are set out in the booklet "Some Questions and Answers about the Rent (Agriculture) Act 1976". This booklet is available free from rent officers, council offices and housing aid centres, some of which also give advice.

10. The rules about the amount of rent you can be charged depend on whether a fair rent has been registered by the rent oficer. If a fair rent has been registered, that is the most that your landlord can charge. If no fair rent is registered, the landlord can charge a provisional rent at a yearly level currently fixed at 1 1/2 times the rateable value of your cottage. There is nothing to prevent you and your landlord agreeing upon a lower figure. You cannot be evicted from your home unless your landlord gets a possession order from the courts. The courts can grant an order only if suitable alternative accommodation is made available to you or in certain other special cases.

11. You may be entitled to get help to pay your rent. Apply to your local council for details of the rent allowance and rate rebate schemes.

12. It is a criminal offence for your landlord to evict you without an order from the court or to harass you or interfere with your possessions or use of facilities in order to force you to leave.

13. If you are in doubt about your legal rights or obligations, particularly if your landlord has asked you to leave, you should go to a Citizens Advice Bureau, housing aid centre, law centre or solicitor. Help with all or part of the cost of legal advice from a solicitor may be available under the Legal Aid Scheme.

(*These entries must be kept up to date.)

(**Cross out whichever does not apply.) [946]

NOTES

Commencement: 1 January 1983.

ASSURED TENANCIES (APPROVED BODIES) (NO 5) ORDER 1982
(SI 1982 NO 1481)

NOTES
Made: 15 October 1982
Authority: Housing Act 1980, ss 56(4), 151

1. This order may be cited as the Assured Tenancies (Approved Bodies) (No. 5) Order 1982 and shall come into operation on 22nd November 1982. **[947]**

NOTES
Commencement: 22 November 1982.

2. The bodies set out in the Schedule to this order are hereby specified for the purposes of Part II of the Housing Act 1980. **[948]**

NOTES
Commencement: 22 November 1982.

SCHEDULE
BODIES SPECIFIED FOR THE PURPOSES OF PART II OF THE HOUSING ACT 1980

Albert Brothers Limited.
J.S. Bloor Limited.
Poco Properties Limited.
A.H. Wilson Group Limited. **[949]**

NOTES
Commencement: 22 November 1982.

ASSURED TENANCIES (APPROVED BODIES) (NO 6) ORDER 1982
(SI 1982 NO 1551)

NOTES
Made: 28 October 1982
Authority: Housing Act 1980, ss 56(4), 151

1. This order may be cited as the Assured Tenancies (Approved Bodies)(No.6) Order 1982 and shall come into operation on 1st December 1982. **[950]**

NOTES
Commencement: 1 December 1982.

2. The bodies set out in the Schedule to this order are hereby specified for the purposes of Part II of the Housing Act 1980. **[951]**

NOTES
Commencement: 1 December 1982.

SCHEDULE
BODIES SPECIFIED FOR THE PURPOSES OF PART II OF THE HOUSING ACT 1980

1. . . .
2. Greenwood Homes Limited.
3. Longfeld Investment Company Limited.

4. The Tilt Estate Company.
5. Yelcon Limited. [952]

NOTES
Commencement: 1 December 1982.
Words omitted revoked by SI 1985 No 1311, art 2.

ASSURED TENANCIES (APPROVED BODIES) (NO 7) ORDER 1982
(SI 1982 NO 1638)

NOTES
Made: 18 November 1982
Authority: Housing Act 1980, ss 56(4), 151

1. This order may be cited as the Assured Tenancies (Approved Bodies) (No. 7) Order 1982 and shall come into operation on 23rd December 1982. [953]

NOTES
Commencement: 23 December 1982.

2. The bodies set out in the Schedule to this order are hereby specified for the purpose of Part II of the Housing Act 1980. [954]

NOTES
Commencement: 23 December 1982.

SCHEDULE
BODIES SPECIFIED FOR THE PURPOSES OF PART II OF THE HOUSING ACT 1980

1. The Bradford Property Trust p.l.c.
2. I.B.C. (Civil Engineering, Wakefield) Limited.
3. V. Wykes (Builders) Limited. [955]

NOTES
Commencement: 23 December 1982.

ASSURED TENANCIES (APPROVED BODIES) (NO 8) ORDER 1982
(SI 1982 NO 1815)

NOTES
Made: 15 December 1982
Authority: Housing Act 1980, ss 56(4), 151

1. This order may be cited as the Assured Tenancies (Approved Bodies) (No. 8) Order 1982 and shall come into operation on 31st January 1983. [956]

NOTES
Commencement: 31 January 1983.

2. The bodies set out in the Schedule to this order are hereby specified for the purposes of Part II of the Housing Act 1980. **[957]**

NOTES
Commencement: 31 January 1983.

SCHEDULE

BODIES SPECIFIED FOR THE PURPOSES OF PART II OF THE HOUSING ACT 1980

1. F. Goulden and Sons Limited.
2. Norwich Union Life Insurance Society.
3. Ryefield Properties Limited. **[958]**

NOTES
Commencement: 31 January 1983.

ASSURED TENANCIES (APPROVED BODIES) (NO 1) ORDER 1983

(SI 1983 NO 19)

NOTES
Made: 13 January 1983
Authority: Housing Act 1980, ss 56(4), 151

1. This order may be cited as the Assured Tenancies (Approved Bodies) (No. 1) Order 1983 and shall come into operation on 17th February 1983. **[959]**

NOTES
Commencement: 17 February 1983.

2. The bodies set out in the Schedule to this order are hereby specified for the purposes of Part II of the Housing Act 1980. **[960]**

NOTES
Commencement: 17 February 1983.

SCHEDULE

BODIES SPECIFIED FOR THE PURPOSES OF PART II OF THE HOUSING ACT 1980

1. J. S. Bloor (Investments) Limited.
2. S. Byron Limited.
3. Grimwood Properties Limited.
4. Jamon Construction Limited.
5. New Ideal Holdings p.l.c.
6. New Ideal Homes Limited.
7. Northern Ideal Homes Limited.
8. P.B. Property Company (Romford) Limited.
9. Scruton & Co., (Builders) Limited.
10. Sherwood Property Company Limited.
11. Simons Construction Group Limited.
12. Southern Ideal Homes Limited. **[961]**

NOTES
Commencement: 17 February 1983.

ASSURED TENANCIES (APPROVED BODIES) (NO 2) ORDER 1983
(SI 1983 NO 88)

NOTES
Made: 28 January 1983
Authority: Housing Act 1980, ss 56(4), 151

1. This order may be cited as the Assured Tenancies (Approved Bodies) (No. 2) Order 1983 and shall come into operation on 4th March 1983. **[962]**

NOTES
Commencement: 4 March 1983.

2. The bodies set out in the Schedule to this order are hereby specified for the purposes of Part II of the Housing Act 1980. **[963]**

NOTES
Commencement: 4 March 1983.

SCHEDULE
BODIES SPECIFIED FOR THE PURPOSES OF PART II OF THE HOUSING ACT 1980

1. Michael John Cozens and John Haydon Jackson trading as C J Housing.
2. Ellis Campbell Housing Limited
3. Inner Town Homes Limited.
4. John Street & Company (Surrey) Limited. **[964]**

NOTES
Commencement: 4 March 1983.

LANDLORD AND TENANT ACT 1954, PART II (NOTICES) REGULATIONS 1983
(SI 1983 NO 133)

NOTES
Made: 8 February 1983
Authority: Landlord and Tenant Act 1954, s 66

ARRANGEMENT OF REGULATIONS

Regulation	Para
	Para
1	[965]
2	[966]
3	[967]
4	[968]

SCHEDULES

Schedule 1—	*[969]*
Schedule 2—	
Form 1	[970]
Form 2	[971]
Form 3	[972]
Form 4	[973]
Form 5	[974]
Form 6	[975]

	Para
Form 7	[976]
Form 8	[977]
Form 9	[978]
Form 10	[979]
Form 11	[980]
Form 12	[981]
Form 13	[982]
Form 14	[983]
Form 15	[984]
Form 16	[985]
Form 17	[986]
Form 18	[987]
Schedule 3—	*[988]*

1. These regulations may be cited as the Landlord and Tenant Act 1954, Part II (Notices) Regulations 1983 and shall come into operation on 1st April 1983. **[965]**

NOTES
Commencement: 1 April 1983.

2. (1) In these regulations "the Act" means the Landlord and Tenant Act 1954.

(2) Any reference in these regulations to a numbered form shall be construed as a reference to the form bearing that number in Schedule 2 hereto, or to a form substantially to the like effect.

(3) Regulation 3 below does not apply to notices given under Part II of the Act as applied by section 58 of the Housing Act 1980 to assured tenancies under that Act. **[966]**

NOTES
Commencement: 1 April 1983.

3. (1) Subject to paragraph (2), the form with the number shown in column 1 of Schedule 1 to these regulations shall be used for the purpose shown in column 2 of that Schedule.

(2) Where a number is shown in brackets in column 1 of Schedule 1 to these regulations, the form with that number shall be used for the purpose shown in column 2 of that Schedule (instead of the form with the number not in brackets) if—

(*a*) no previous notice terminating the tenancy has been given under section 25 of the Act, and
(*b*) the tenancy is the tenancy of a house (as defined for the purposes of Part I of the Leasehold Reform Act 1967), and
(*c*) the tenancy is a long tenancy at a low rent (within the meaning of that Act of 1967), and
(*d*) the tenant is not a company or other artificial person. **[967]**

NOTES
Commencement: 1 April 1983.
The Act: Landlord and Tenant Act 1954.

4. Nothing in these regulations shall invalidate any notice served before 1st August 1983 which complies with the requirements of the Landlord and Tenant (Notices) Regulations 1957, but save as aforesaid those Regulations and the other statutory instruments shown in column 1 of Schedule 3 to these regulations are revoked to the extent specified in column 2 of that Schedule. **[968]**

NOTES
Commencement: 1 April 1983.

SCHEDULES

SCHEDULE 1

Form number	Purpose for which to be used
1(13)*	A notice under section 25 of the Act, being a notice terminating a tenancy to which Part II of the Act applies which does not contain a certificate given under the provisions of section 57, 58, 60, 60A or 60B of the Act.
2(14)*	A notice under section 25 of the Act, being a notice terminating a tenancy to which Part II of the Act applies, which contains a copy of a certificate given under section 57 of the Act (whereby the Minister or Board in charge of any Government department certifies that the use or occupation of the property or part of it shall be changed by a specified date) where the date of termination of the tenancy specified in the notice is not earlier than the date specified in the certificate.
3(15)*	A notice under section 25 of the Act, being a notice terminating a tenancy to which Part II of the Act applies, which contains a copy of a certificate given under section 57 of the Act (whereby the Minister or Board in charge of any Government department certifies that the use or occupation of the property or part of it shall be changed by a specified date) where the date of termination of the tenancy is earlier than the date specified in the certificate.
4	A notice under section 25 of the Act, being a notice terminating a tenancy to which Part II of the Act applies, which contains a copy of a certificate given under section 58 of the Act (whereby the Minister or Board in charge of any Government department certifies that for reasons of national security it is necessary that the use or occupation of the property should be discontinued or changed).
5(16)*	A notice under section 25 of the Act, being a notice terminating a tenancy to which Part II of the Act applies, which contains a certificate under section 60 of the Act (whereby the Secretary of State certifies that it is necessary or expedient for achieving the purpose mentioned in section 2(1) of the Local Employment Act 1972 that the use or occupation of the property should be changed).
6(17)*	A notice under section 25 of the Act, being a notice terminating a tenancy to which Part II of the Act applies, which contains a copy of a certificate given under section 60A (Welsh Development Agency premises) of the Act (whereby the Secretary of State certifies that it is necessary or expedient for the purpose of providing employment appropriate to the needs of the area in which the premises are situated, that the use or occupation of the property should be changed.)

Form number	Purpose for which to be used
7(18)*	A notice under section 25 of the Act, being a notice terminating a tenancy to which Part II of the Act applies, which contains a copy of a certificate given under section 60B (Development Board for Rural Wales premises) of the Act (whereby the Secretary of State certifies that it is necessary or expedient for the purpose of providing employment appropriate to the needs of the area in which the premises are situated, that the use or occupation of the property should be changed).
8	A notice under section 26 of the Act, being a tenant's request for a new tenancy of premises to which Part II of the Act applies.
9	A notice under section 40(1) of the Act, being a notice requiring a tenant of business premises to give information as to his occupation of the premises and as to any sub-tenancies.
10	A notice served under section 40(2) of the Act on a landlord of business premises, being a notice requiring that landlord to give information about his interest in the premises.
11	A notice served under section 40(2) of the Act on a mortgagee in possession of business premises, being a notice requiring that mortgagee to give information about his mortgagor's interest in the premises.
12	A notice under section 44 of and paragraph 6 of Schedule 6 to the Act, being a notice withdrawing a previous notice given under section 25 of the Act to terminate a tenancy to which Part II of the Act applies.

*Where a form number is shown in brackets the form with that number must be used if—

(*a*) no previous notice terminating the tenancy has been given under section 25 of the Act, and
(*b*) the tenancy is the tenancy of a house (as defined for the purposes of Part I of the Leasehold Reform Act 1967), and
(*c*) the tenancy is a long tenancy at a low rent (within the meaning of that Act of 1967), and
(*d*) the tenancy is not a company or other artificial person. **[969]**

NOTES
Commencement: 1 April 1983.
The Act: Landlord and Tenant Act 1954.

SCHEDULE 2

FORM 1

LANDLORD'S NOTICE TO TERMINATE BUSINESS TENANCY*

*This form must *not* be used if—

(*a*) no previous notice terminating the tenancy has been given under section 25 of the Act, and
(*b*) the tenancy is the tenancy of a house (as defined for the purposes of Part I of the Leasehold Reform Act 1967), and
(*c*) the tenancy is a long tenancy at a low rent (within the meaning of that Act of 1967), and
(*d*) the tenant is not a company or other artificial person.

(LANDLORD AND TENANT ACT 1954, SECTION 25)

To: *(name of tenant)*
of *(address of tenant)*

IMPORTANT—THIS NOTICE IS INTENDED TO BRING YOUR TENANCY TO AN END. IF YOU WANT TO CONTINUE TO OCCUPY YOUR PROPERTY YOU MUST ACT QUICKLY. READ THE NOTICE AND ALL THE NOTES CAREFULLY. IF YOU ARE IN ANY DOUBT ABOUT THE ACTION YOU SHOULD TAKE, GET ADVICE IMMEDIATELY e.g. FROM A SOLICITOR OR SURVEYOR OR A CITIZENS ADVICE BUREAU.

1. This notice is given under section 25 of the Landlord and Tenant Act 1954.

2. It relates to . . . . *(description of property)* of which you are the tenant.

3. I/we give you notice terminating your tenancy on . . . .
(See notes 1 and 8.)

4. If you are not willing to give up possession of the property comprised in the tenancy on the date stated in paragraph 3, you must notify me/us in writing within two months after the giving of this notice.
(See notes 2 and 3.)

5.* If you apply to the court under Part II of the Landlord and Tenant Act 1954 for the grant of a new tenancy, I/we will not oppose your application.
(*The landlords must cross out one version of paragraph 5. If the second version is used the paragraph letter(s) must be filled in.)

OR

5.* If you apply to the court under Part II of the Landlord and Tenant Act 1954 for the grant of a new tenancy, I/we will oppose it on the grounds mentioned in paragraph(s). . . . . .of section 30(1) of the Act.
(See notes 4 and 5.)

6. All correspondence about this notice should be sent to †[the landlord] [the landlord's agent] at the address given below.

Date . . . .

Signature of †[landlord] [landlord's agent]

. . . .

Name of landlord . . . .

Address of landlord . . . .

. . . .

. . . .

†[Address of agent . . . .

. . . .

. . . .]

†Cross out words in square brackets if they do not apply.

NOTES

Termination of tenancy

1. This notice is intended to bring your tenancy to an end. You can apply to the court for a new tenancy under the Landlord and Tenant Act 1954 by following the procedure outlined in notes 2 and 3 below. If you do your tenancy will continue after the date shown in paragraph 3 of this notice while your claim is being considered. The landlord can ask the court to fix the rent which you will have to pay while the tenancy continues. The terms of any *new* tenancy not agreed between you and the landlord will be settled by the court.

Claiming a new tenancy

2. If you want to apply to the court for a new tenancy you must:—

(1) notify the landlord in writing not later than 2 months after the giving of this notice that you are not willing to give up possession of the property;

AND

(2) apply to the court, not earlier than 2 months nor later than 4 months after the giving of this notice, for a new tenancy. You should apply to the County Court

unless the rateable value of the business part of your premises is above the current County Court limit. In that case you should apply to the High Court.

3. The time limits in note 2 run from the giving of the notice. The date of the giving of the notice may not be the date written on the notice or the date on which you actually saw it. It may, for instance, be the date on which the notice was delivered through the post to your last address known to the person giving the notice. If there has been any delay in your seeing this notice you may need to act very quickly. If you are in any doubt get advice immediately.

WARNING TO TENANT

IF YOU DO NOT KEEP TO THE TIME LIMITS IN NOTE 2, YOU WILL *LOSE* YOUR RIGHT TO APPLY TO THE COURT FOR A NEW TENANCY.

Landlord's opposition to claim for a new tenancy

4. If you apply to the court for a new tenancy, the landlord can only oppose your application on one or more of the grounds set out in section 30(1) of the 1954 Act. These grounds are set out below. The paragraph letters are those given in the Act. The landlord can only use a ground if its paragraph letter is shown in paragraph 5 of the notice.

Grounds

(*a*) where under the current tenancy the tenant has any obligations as respects the repair and maintenance of the holding, that the tenant ought not to be granted a new tenancy in view of the state of repair of the holding, being a state resulting from the tenant's failure to comply with the said obligations;

(*b*) that the tenant ought not to be granted a new tenancy in view of his persistent delay in paying rent which has become due;

(*c*) that the tenant ought not to be granted a new tenancy in view of other substantial breaches by him of his obligations under the current tenancy, or for any other reason connected with the tenant's use or management of the holding;

(*d*) that the landlord has offered and is willing to provide or secure the provision of alternative accommodation for the tenant, that the terms on which the alternative accommodation is available are reasonable having regard to the terms of the current tenancy and to all other relevant circumstances, and that the accommodation and the time at which it will be available are suitable for the tenant's requirements (including the requirement to preserve goodwill) having regard to the nature and class of his business and to the situation and extent of, and facilities afforded by, the holding;

(*e*) where the current tenancy was created by the sub-letting of part only of the property comprised in a superior tenancy and the landlord is the owner of an interest in reversion expectant on the termination of that superior tenancy, that the aggregate of the rents reasonably obtainable on separate lettings of the holding and the remainder of that property would be substantially less than the rent reasonably obtainable on a letting of that property as a whole, that on the termination of the current tenancy the landlord requires possession of the holding for the purposes of letting or otherwise disposing of the said property as a whole, and that in view thereof the tenant ought not to be granted a new tenancy;

(*f*) that on the termination of the current tenancy the landlord intends to demolish or reconstruct the premises comprised in the holding or a substantial work of construction on the holding or part thereof and that he could not reasonably do so without obtaining possession of the holding;
(If the landlord uses this ground, the court can sometimes still grant a new tenancy if certain conditions set out in section 31A of the Act can be met.)

(*g*) that on the termination of the current tenancy the landlord intends to occupy the holding for the purposes, or partly for the purposes, of a business to be carried on by him therein, or as his residence.
(The landlord must normally have been the landlord for at least five years to use this ground.)

Compensation

5. If you cannot get a new tenancy solely because grounds (*e*), (*f*) or (*g*) apply, you are entitled to compensation under the 1954 Act. If your landlord has opposed your application on any of the other grounds as well as (*e*), (*f*) or (*g*) you can only get compensation if the Court's refusal to grant a new tenancy is based solely on grounds (*e*), (*f*) or (*g*). In other words you cannot get compensation under the 1954 Act if the Court has refused your tenancy on *other* grounds even if (*e*), (*f*) or (*g*) also apply.

6. If your landlord is an authority possessing compulsory purchase powers (such as a local authority) you may be entitled to a disturbance payment under Part III of the Land Compensation Act 1973.

Negotiating a new tenancy

7. Most leases are renewed by negotiation. If you do try to agree a new tenancy with your landlord, remember—

(1) that your present tenancy will not be extended after the date in paragraph 3 of this notice unless you *both*
 (*a*) give written notice that you will not vacate (note 2(1) above); *and*
 (*b*) apply to the court for a new tenancy (note 2(2) above);

(2) that you will lose your right to apply to the court if you do not keep to the time limits in note 2.

Validity of this notice

8. The landlord who has given this notice may not be the landlord to whom you pay your rent. "Business" is given a wide meaning in the 1954 Act and is used in the same sense in this notice. The 1954 Act also has rules about the date which the landlord can put in paragraph 3. This depends on the terms of your tenancy. If you have any doubts about whether this notice is valid, get immediate advice.

Explanatory booklet

9. The Department of the Environment booklet "Business Tenancies" explains the provisions of Part II of the 1954 Act in more detail than these notes. It is available from Her Majesty's Stationery Office or through booksellers. **[970]**

NOTES

Commencement: 1 April 1983.

FORM 2

LANDLORD'S NOTICE TO TERMINATE BUSINESS TENANCY ON GROUNDS OF PUBLIC INTEREST*

*This form must *not* be used if

(*a*) no previous notice terminating the tenancy has been given under section 25 of the Act, and

(*b*) the tenancy is the tenancy of a house (as defined for the purposes of Part I of the Leasehold Reform Act 1967), and

(*c*) the tenancy is a long tenancy at a low rent (within the meaning of that Act of 1967), and

(*d*) the tenant is not a company or other artificial person.

If the above apply, use form number 14 instead of this form.

(LANDLORD AND TENANT ACT 1954, SECTIONS 25 AND 57)

To *(name of tenant)*

of *(address of tenant)*

IMPORTANT—THIS NOTICE IS INTENDED TO BRING YOUR TENANCY TO AN END. READ THE NOTICE AND ALL THE NOTES CAREFULLY. IF YOU ARE IN ANY DOUBT ABOUT THE ACTION

YOU SHOULD TAKE, GET ADVICE IMMEDIATELY e.g. FROM A SOLICITOR OR SURVEYOR OR A CITIZENS ADVICE BUREAU.

1. This notice is given under sections 25 and 57 of the Landlord and Tenant Act 1954.

2. It relates to .. .. *(description of property)* of which you are the tenant.

3. We give you notice terminating your tenancy on .. ..

4. A certificate has been given by .. .. that it is requisite for **[our purposes] [the purposes of .. ..] that the use or occupation of all or part of the property shall be changed by .. .. A copy of the certificate is contained in the Schedule to this notice.

5. All correspondence about this notice should be sent to **[the landlord] [the landlord's agent] at the address given below.

Date .. ..

Signature of **[landlord] [landlord's agent]

.. ..

Name of landlord .. ..

Address of landlord .. ..

**[Address of agent .. ..]

(**Cross out words in square brackets if they do not apply.)

SCHEDULE

[Insert a copy of the certificate]

Notes

Termination of tenancy

1. This notice is intended to bring your tenancy to an end. Usually tenants under tenancies to which Part II of the Landlord and Tenant Act 1954 applies can apply to the court for a new tenancy. You cannot do so because a certificate has been given under section 57 of the Act and the date in paragraph 3 of the notice is not earlier than the date specified in the certificate (set out in the Schedule to this notice) as the date by which the use or occupation of all or part of the property shall be changed.

Compensation

2. Because the court cannot order the grant of a new tenancy in your case, you are entitled to compensation under the 1954 Act when you leave the property. Also if your landlord is an authority possessing compulsory purchase powers (such as a local authority) you may be entitled to a disturbance payment under Part III of the Land Compensation Act 1973.

Validity of notice

3. The landlord who has given this notice may not be the landlord to whom you pay your rent. "Business" is given a wide meaning in the 1954 Act and is used in the same sense in this notice. The 1954 Act also has rules about the date which the landlord can put in paragraph 3. This depends on the terms of your tenancy. If you have any doubts about whether this notice is valid, get immediate advice.

Explanatory booklet

4. The Department of the Environment booklet "Business Tenancies" explains the provisions of Part II of the 1954 Act in more detail than these notes. It is available from Her Majesty's Stationery Office or through booksellers. **[971]**

NOTES
Commencement: 1 April 1983.

FORM 3

LANDLORD'S NOTICE TO TERMINATE BUSINESS TENANCY WHERE CHANGE REQUIRED AT FUTURE DATE ON GROUNDS OF PUBLIC INTEREST*

*This form must *not* be used if—

(*a*) no previous notice terminating the tenancy has been given under section 25 of the Act, and

(*b*) the tenancy is the tenancy of a house (as defined for the purpose of Part I of the Leasehold Reform Act 1967), and

(*c*) the tenancy is a long tenancy at a low rent (within the meaning of that Act of 1967), and

(*d*) the tenant is not a company or other artificial person.

If the above apply, use form number 15 instead of this form.

(LANDLORD AND TENANT ACT 1954, SECTIONS 25 AND 57)

To *(name of tenant)*

of *(address of tenant)*

IMPORTANT—THIS NOTICE IS INTENDED TO BRING YOUR TENANCY TO AN END. IF YOU WANT TO CONTINUE TO OCCUPY YOUR PROPERTY YOU MUST ACT QUICKLY. READ THE NOTICE AND ALL THE NOTES CAREFULLY. IF YOU ARE IN ANY DOUBT ABOUT THE ACTION YOU SHOULD TAKE, GET ADVICE IMMEDIATELY e.g. FROM A SOLICITOR OR SURVEYOR OR A CITIZENS ADVICE BUREAU.

1. This notice is given under sections 25 and 57 of the Landlord and Tenant Act 1954.

2. It relates to .... *(description of property)* of which you are the tenant.

3. We give you notice terminating your tenancy on ....
(See notes 1 and 8.)

4. If you are not willing to give up possession of the property comprised in the tenancy on the date stated in paragraph 3, you must notify us in writing within two months after the giving of this notice.
(See notes 2 and 3.)

5.* If you apply to the court under Part II of the Landlord and Tenant Act 1954 for the grant of a new tenancy, we will not oppose your application.
(*The landlord must cross out one version of paragraph 5. If the second version is used the paragraph letter(s) must be filled in.)

OR

5.* If you apply to the court under Part II of the Landlord and Tenant Act 1954 for the grant of a new tenancy, we will oppose it on the grounds mentioned in paragraph(s)..........of section 30(1) of that Act.
(See notes 4 and 5.)

6. A certificate has been given by ....
that it is requisite for †[our purposes] [the purposes of............] that the use or occupation of all or part of the property shall be changed by......................
A copy of the certificate is contained in the Schedule to this notice.
(See notes 1 and 6.)

7. All correspondence about this notice should be sent to †[the landlord] [the landlord's agent] at the address given below.

Date ....

Signature of †[landlord] [landlord's agent]

....

Name of landlord

....

Address of landlord . . . .

. . . .

. . . .

†[Address of agent . . . .

. . . .

. . . .]

†Cross out words in square brackets if they do not apply.

SCHEDULE

[Insert a copy of the certificate]

Notes

Termination of tenancy

1. This notice is intended to bring your tenancy to an end. You can apply to the court for a new tenancy under the Landlord and Tenant Act 1954 by following the procedure outlined in notes 2 and 3 below. If you do your tenancy will continue after the date shown in paragraph 3 of this notice while your claim is being considered. The landlord can ask the court to fix the rent which you will have to pay while the tenancy continues. The terms of any *new* tenancy not agreed between you and the landlord will be settled by the court. However, a certificate has been given under section 57 of the 1954 Act and a copy is contained in the Schedule to this notice. This means that if the court orders the grant of a new tenancy the new tenancy must end not later than the date specified in the certificate. Any new tenancy ordered to be granted will not be a tenancy to which Part II of the 1954 Act applies.

Claiming a new tenancy

2. If you want to apply to the court for a new tenancy you must:—

(1) notify the landlord in writing not later than two months after the giving of this notice that you are not willing to give up possession of the property;

AND

(2) apply to the court, not earlier than two months nor later than four months after the giving of this notice, for a new tenancy. You should apply to the County Court unless the rateable value of the business part of your premises is above the current County Court limit. In that case you should apply to the High Court.

3. The time limits in note 2 run from the giving of the notice. The date of the giving of the notice may not be the date written on the notice or the date on which you actually saw it. It may, for instance, be the date on which the notice was delivered through the post to your last address known to the person giving the notice. If there has been any delay in your seeing this notice you may need to act very quickly. If you are in any doubt get advice immediately.

WARNING TO TENANT

IF YOU DO NOT KEEP TO THE TIME LIMITS IN NOTE 2, YOU WILL *LOSE* YOUR RIGHT TO APPLY TO THE COURT FOR A NEW TENANCY.

Landlord's opposition to claim for a new tenancy

4. If you apply to the court for a new tenancy, the landlord can only oppose your application on one or more of the grounds set out in section 30(1) of the 1954 Act. These grounds are set out below. The paragraph letters are those given in the Act. The landlord can only use a ground if its paragraph letter is shown in paragraph 5 of the notice.

Grounds

(*a*) where under the current tenancy the tenant has any obligations as respects the repair and maintenance of the holding, that the tenant ought not to be granted a new tenancy in view of the state of repair of the holding, being a state resulting from the tenant's failure to comply with the said obligations;

(*b*) that the tenant ought not to be granted a new tenancy in view of his persistent delay in paying rent which has become due;

(*c*) that the tenant ought not to be granted a new tenancy in view of other substantial breaches by him of his obligations under the current tenancy, or for any other reason connected with the tenant's use or management of the holding;

(*d*) that the landlord has offered and is willing to provide or secure the provision of alternative accommodation for the tenant, that the terms on which the alternative accommodation is available are reasonable having regard to the terms of the current tenancy and to all other relevant circumstances, and that the accommodation and the time at which it will be available are suitable for the tenant's requirements (including the requirement to preserve goodwill) having regard to the nature and class of his business and to the situation and extent of, and facilities afforded by, the holding;

(*e*) where the current tenancy was created by the sub-letting of part only of the property comprised in a superior tenancy and the landlord is the owner of an interest in reversion expectant on the termination of that superior tenancy, that the aggregate of the rents reasonably obtainable on separate lettings of the holding and the remainder of that property would be substantially less than the rent reasonably obtainable on a letting of that property as a whole, that on the termination of the current tenancy the landlord requires possession of the holding for the purposes of letting or otherwise disposing of the said property as a whole, and that in view thereof the tenant ought not to be granted a new tenancy;

(*f*) that on the termination of the current tenancy the landlord intends to demolish or reconstruct the premises comprised in the holding or a substantial part of those premises or to carry out substantial work of construction on the holding or part thereof and that he could not reasonably do so without obtaining possession of the holding;
(If the landlord uses this ground, the court can sometimes still grant a new tenancy if certain conditions set out in section 31A of the Act can be met).

(*g*) that on the termination of the current tenancy the landlord intends to occupy the holding for the purposes, or partly for the purposes, of a business to be carried on by him therein, or as his residence.
(The landlord must normally have been the landlord for at least five years to use this ground.)

Compensation

5. If you cannot get a new tenancy solely because grounds (*e*), (*f*) or (*g*) apply, you are entitled to compensation under the 1954 Act. If your landlord has opposed your application on any of the other grounds as well as (*e*), (*f*) or (*g*) you can only get compensation if the Court's refusal to grant a new tenancy is based solely on grounds (*e*), (*f*) or (*g*). In other words, you cannot get compensation under the 1954 Act if the court has refused your tenancy on *other* grounds even if (*e*), (*f*) or (*g*) also apply. If the court *does* order the grant of a new tenancy you will be entitled to compensation under the 1954 Act because the new tenancy cannot expire later than the date specified in the certificate in the Schedule.

6. If your landlord is an authority possessing compulsory purchase powers (such as a local authority) you may be entitled to a disturbance payment under Part III of the Land Compensation Act 1973.

Negotiating a new tenancy

7. Most leases are renewed by negotiation. If you do try to agree a new tenancy with your landlord, remember—

(1) that your present tenancy will not be extended after the date in paragraph 3 of this notice unless you *both*

(*a*) give written notice that you will not vacate (note 2(1) above); *and* (*b*) apply to the court for a new tenancy (note 2(2) above);

(2) that you will lose your right to apply to the court if you do not keep to the time limits in note 2.

Validity of this notice

8. The landlord who has given this notice may not be the landlord to whom you pay your rent. "Business" is given a wide meaning in the 1954 Act and is used in the same sense in this notice. The 1954 Act also has rules about the date which the landlord can put in paragraph 3. This depends on the terms of your tenancy. If you have any doubts about whether this notice is valid, get immediate advice.

Explanatory booklet

9. The Department of the Environment booklet "Business Tenancies" explains the provisions of Part II of the 1954 Act in more detail than these notes. It is available from Her Majesty's Stationery Office or through booksellers. **[972]**

NOTES
Commencement: 1 April 1983.

FORM 4

LANDLORD'S NOTICE TO TERMINATE BUSINESS TENANCY ON GROUNDS OF NATIONAL SECURITY

(LANDLORD AND TENANT ACT 1954, SECTIONS 25 AND 58)

To: *(name of tenant)*

of *(address of tenant)*

IMPORTANT—THIS NOTICE IS INTENDED TO BRING YOUR TENANCY TO AN END. READ THE NOTICE AND ALL THE NOTES CAREFULLY. IF YOU ARE IN ANY DOUBT ABOUT THE ACTION YOU SHOULD TAKE, GET ADVICE IMMEDIATELY e.g. FROM A SOLICITOR OR SURVEYOR OR A CITIZENS ADVICE BUREAU.

1. This notice is given under sections 25 and 58 of the Landlord and Tenant Act 1954.

2. It relates to .... *(description of property)* of which you are the tenant.

3. We give you notice terminating your tenancy on ....

4. A certificate has been given by .... that it is necessary for reasons of national security that the use or occupation of the property should be discontinued or changed. A copy of the certificate is contained in the Schedule to this notice.

5. All correspondence about this notice should be sent to **[the landlord] [the landlord's agent] at the address given below.

*Cross out words in square brackets if they do not apply.

Date ....

Signature of **[landlord][landlord's agent]

....

Name of landlord ....

Address of landlord ....

**[Address of agent ....]

SCHEDULE

[Insert a copy of the certificate]

Notes

Termination of tenancy

1. This notice is intended to bring your tenancy to an end. Usually tenants under tenancies to which Part II of the Landlord and Tenant Act 1954 applies can apply to the court for a new tenancy. You cannot do so because a certificate has been given under section 58 of the Act that it is necessary for reasons of national security that the use or occupation of the property should be discontinued or changed.

Compensation

2. Because the court cannot order the grant of a new tenancy in your case, you are entitled to compensation under the 1954 Act when you leave the property. Also you may be entitled to a disturbance payment under Part II of the Land Compensation Act 1973.

Validity of notice

3. The landlord who has given this notice may not be the landlord to whom you pay your rent. "Business" is given a wide meaning in the 1954 Act and is used in the same sense in this notice. The 1954 Act also has rules about the date which the landlord can put in paragraph 3. This depends on the terms of your tenancy. If you have any doubts about whether this notice is valid, get immediate advice.

Explanatory booklet

4. The Department of the Environment booklet "Business Tenancies" explains the provisions of Part II of the 1954 Act in more detail than these notes. It is available from Her Majesty's Stationery Office through booksellers. **[973]**

NOTES
Commencement: 1 April 1983.

FORM 5

LANDLORD'S NOTICE TO TERMINATE BUSINESS TENANCY BY REASON OF THE LOCAL EMPLOYMENT ACT 1972*

*This form must *not* be used if—

(*a*) no previous notice terminating the tenancy has been given under section 25 of the Act, and
(*b*) the tenancy is the tenancy of a house (as defined for the purposes of Part I of the Leasehold Reform Act 1967), and
(*c*) the tenancy is a long tenancy at a low rent (within the meaning of that Act of 1967), and
(*d*) the tenant is not a company or other artificial person.

If the above apply, use form number 16 instead of this form.

(LANDLORD AND TENANT ACT 1954, SECTIONS 25, 58 AND 60)

To: *(name of tenant)*

of *(address of tenant)*

IMPORTANT—THIS NOTICE IS INTENDED TO BRING YOUR TENANCY TO AN END. READ THE NOTICE AND ALL THE NOTES CAREFULLY. IF YOU ARE IN ANY DOUBT ABOUT THE ACTION YOU SHOULD TAKE, GET ADVICE IMMEDIATELY e.g. FROM A SOLICITOR OR SURVERYOR OR A CITIZENS ADVICE BUREAU.

1. This notice is given under sections 25, 58 and 60 of the Landlord and Tenant Act 1954.

2. You are the tenant of . . . . *(description of property)* which is situated in a locality which is either—

(*a*) a development area, or
(*b*) an intermediate area.

3. We give you notice terminating your tenancy on . . . .

4. A certificate has been given by the Secretary of State that it is necessary or expedient for the purposes mentioned in section 2(1) of the Local Employment Act 1972 that the use or occupation of the property should be changed. A copy of the certificate is contained in the Schedule to this notice.

5. All correspondence about this notice should be sent to **[the landlord] [the landlord's agent] at the address given below.

**Cross out words in square brackets if they do no apply.

Date . . . .

Signature of **[landlord] [landlord's agent]

. . . .

Name of landlord . . . .

Address of landlord . . . .

**[Address of agent . . . .]

SCHEDULE

[Insert a copy of the certificate]

Notes

Termination of tenancy

1. This notice is intended to bring your tenancy to an end. Usually tenants under tenancies to which Part II of the Landlord and Tenant Act 1954 applies can apply to the court for a new tenancy. You cannot do so because the Secretary of State has certified that it is necessary or expedient for achieving the purposes mentioned in section 2(1) of the Local Employment Act 1972 that the use or occupation of the property should be changed.

Validity of this notice

2. The landlord who has given this notice may not be the landlord to whom you pay your rent. "Business" is given a wide meaning in the 1954 Act and is used in the same sense in this notice. The 1954 Act also has rules about the date which the landlord can put in paragraph 3. This depends on the terms of your tenancy. If you have any doubts about whether this notice is valid, get immediate advice.

Explanatory booklet

3. The Department of the Environment booklet "Business Tenancies" explains the provisions of Part II of the 1954 Act in more detail than these notes. It is available from Her Majesty's Stationery Office or through booksellers. **[974]**

NOTES
Commencement: 1 April 1983.

FORM 6

LANDLORD'S NOTICE TO TERMINATE BUSINESS TENANCY OF WELSH DEVELOPMENT AGENCY PREMISES*

*This form must *not* be used if—

(*a*) no previous notice terminating the tenancy has been given under section 25 of the Act; and (*b*) the tenancy is the tenancy of a house (as defined for the purposes of Part I of the Leasehold Reform Act 1967); and

(*c*) the tenancy is a long tenancy at a low rent (within the meaning of the Act of 1967); and

(*d*) the tenant is not a company or other artificial person.

If the above apply, use form number 17 instead of this form.

(LANDLORD AND TENANT ACT 1954, SECTIONS 25, 58 AND 60A)

To: *(name of tenant)*

of *(address of tenant)*

IMPORTANT—THIS NOTICE IS INTENDED TO BRING YOUR TENANCY TO AN END. READ THE NOTICE AND ALL THE NOTES CAREFULLY. IF YOU ARE IN ANY DOUBT ABOUT THE ACTION YOU SHOULD TAKE, GET ADVICE IMMEDIATELY e.g. FROM A SOLICITOR OR SURVEYOR OR A CITIZENS ADVICE BUREAU.

1. This notice is given under sections 25, 58 and 60A of the Landlord and Tenant Act 1954.

2. It relates to .. .. *(description of property)* of which you are the tenant.

3. We give you notice terminating your tenancy on .. .. ..

4. A certificate has been given by the Secretary of State that it is necessary or expedient, for the purposes of providing employment appropriate to the needs of the area in which the premises are situated, that the use or occupation of the premises should be changed. A copy of the certificate is contained in the Schedule to this notice.

5. All correspondence about this notice should be sent to **[the landlord] [the landlord's agent] at the address given below.

**[Cross out words in square brackets if they do not apply.

Date .. ..

Signature of **[landlord] [landlord's agent]

.. ..

Name of landlord .. ..

Address of landlord .. .. ..

**[Address of agent .. .. ..]

SCHEDULE

[Insert a copy of the certificate]

Notes

Termination of tenancy

1. This notice is intended to bring your tenancy to an end. Usually tenants under tenancies to which Part II of the Landlord and Tenant Act 1954 applies can apply to the court for a new tenancy. You cannot do so because the Secretary of State has given a certificate under section 60A of the Act that it is necessary or expedient, for the purpose of providing employment appropriate to the needs of the area in which the premises are situated, that the use or occupation of the property should be changed.

Compensation

2. Because the court cannot order the grant of a new tenancy in your case, you may be entitled to compensation under the 1954 Act when you leave the property. You will *not* be entitled to compensation if either:

(*a*) the premises were vested in the Welsh Development Agency under section 7 or 8 of the Welsh Development Agency Act 1975; or (*b*) you were not the tenant of the premises when the Agency acquired the interest by virtue of which the certificate contained in the Schedule was given.

3. You may be entitled to a disturbance payment under Part III of the Land Compensation Act 1973.

Validity of this notice

4. The landlord who has given this notice may not be the landlord to whom you pay your rent. "Business" is given a wide meaning in the 1954 Act and is used in the same sense in this notice. The 1954 Act also has rules about the date which the landlord can put in paragraph 3. This depends on the terms of your tenancy. If you have any doubts about whether this notice is valid, get immediate advice.

Explanatory booklet

5. The Department of the Environment booklet "Business Tenancies" explains the provisions of Part II of the 1954 Act in more detail than these notes. It is available from Her Majesty's Stationery Office or through booksellers. **[975]**

NOTES
Commencement: 1 April 1983.

FORM 7

LANDLORD'S NOTICE TO TERMINATE BUSINESS TENANCY OF PREMISES OF THE DEVELOPMENT BOARD FOR RURAL WALES*

*This form must *not* be used if—

(*a*) no previous notice terminating the tenancy has been given under section 25 of the Act, and
(*b*) the tenancy is the tenancy of a house (as defined for the purposes of Part I of the Leasehold Reform Act 1967); and
(*c*) the tenancy is a long tenancy at a low rent (within the meaning of that Act of 1967), and
(*d*) the tenant is not a company or other artificial person.

If the above apply, use form number 18 instead.

LANDLORD AND TENANT ACT 1954, SECTIONS 25, 58 AND 60B)

To: *(name of tenant)*

of *(address of tenant)*

IMPORTANT—THIS NOTICE IS INTENDED TO BRING YOUR TENANCY TO AN END. READ THE NOTICE AND ALL THE NOTES CAREFULLY. IF YOU ARE IN ANY DOUBT ABOUT THE ACTION YOU SHOUD TAKE, GET ADVICE IMMEDIATELY e.g. FROM A SOLICITOR OR SURVEYOR OR A CITIZENS ADVICE BUREAU.

1. This notice is given under sections 25, 58 and 60B of the Landlord and Tenant Act 1954.

2. It relates to .. .. *(description of property)* of which you are the tenant.

3. We give you notice terminating your tenancy on .. .. ..

4. A certificate has been given by the Secretary of State that it is necessary or expedient, for the purposes of providing employment appropriate to the needs of the area in which the premises are situated, that the use or occupation of the premises should be changed. A copy of the certificate is contained in the Schedule to this notice.

5. All correspondence about this notice should be sent to **[the landlord] [the landlord's agent] at the address given below.

**Cross out words in square brackets if they do not apply.

Date .. ..

Signature of **[landlord] [landlord's agent]

.. ..

Name of landlord .. .. ..

Address of landlord .. .. ..

**[Address of agent .. .. ..]

SCHEDULE

[Insert a copy of the certificate]

Notes

Termination of tenancy

1. This notice is intended to bring your tenancy to an end. Usually tenants under tenancies to which Part II of the Landlord and Tenant Act 1954 applies can apply to the court for a new tenancy. You cannot do so because the Secretary of State has given a certificate under section 60B of the Act that it is necessary or expedient, for the purpose of providing employment appropriate to the needs of the area in which the premises are situated, that the use or occupation of the property should be changed.

Compensation

2. Because the court cannot order the grant of a new tenancy in your case, you may be entitled to compensation under the 1954 Act when you leave the property. You will not be entitled to compensation if either:

(*a*) the premises are premises which—

(i) were vested in the Welsh Development Agency by section 8 of the Welsh Development Agency Act 1975 or were acquired by the Agency when no tenancy subsisted in the premises; and

(ii) subsequently vested in the Development Board under section 24 of the Development of Rural Wales Act 1976; or

(*b*) you were not a tenant of the premises when the Board acquired the interest by virtue of which the certificate contained in the Schedule was given.

3. You may be entitled to a disturbance payment under Part III of the Land Compensation Act 1973.

Validity of this notice

4. The landlord who has given this notice may not be the landlord to whom you pay your rent. "Business" is given a wide meaning in the 1954 Act and is used in the same sense in this notice. The 1954 Act also has rules about the date which the landlord can put in paragraph 3. This depends on the terms of your tenancy. If you have any doutbs about whether this notice is valid, get immediate advice.

Explanatory booklet

5. The Department of the Environment booklet "Business Tenancies" explains the provisions of Part II of the 1954 Act in more detail than these notes. It is available from Her Majesty's Stationery Office or through booksellers. **[976]**

NOTES

Commencement: 1 April 1983.

FORM 8

TENANT'S REQUEST FOR NEW TENANCY OF BUSINESS PREMISES

(LANDLORD AND TENANT ACT 1954, SECTION 26)

To: *(name of landlord)*

of *(address of landlord)*

IMPORTANT—THIS IS A REQUEST FOR A NEW TENANCY OF YOUR PROPERTY OR PART OF IT. IF YOU WANT TO OPPOSE THIS

REQUEST YOU MUST ACT QUICKLY. READ THE REQUEST AND ALL THE NOTES CAREFULLY. IF YOU ARE IN ANY DOUBT ABOUT THE ACTION YOU SHOULD TAKE, GET ADVICE IMMEDIATELY e.g. FROM A SOLICITOR OR SURVEYOR OR A CITIZENS ADVICE BUREAU.

1. This request is made under section 26 of the Landlord and Tenant Act 1954.

2. You are the landlord of .. ..

(description of property)

3. I/we request you to grant a new tenancy beginning on .. .. ..

4. I/we propose that:

(*a*) the property comprised in the new tenancy should be .. ..
(*b*) the rent payable under the new tenancy should be .. .. ..
(*c*) the other terms of the new tenancy should be .. ..

5. All correspondence about this request should be sent to **[the tenant] [the tenant's agent] at the address given below.

**Cross out words in square brackets if they do not apply.

Date .. .. ..
Signature of **[tenant] [tenant's agent]
.. ..
Name of tenant .. .. ..
Address of tenant .. .. ..
**[Address of agent .. ..]

Notes

Request for a new tenancy

1. This request by your tenant for a new tenancy brings his current tenancy to an end on the day before the date mentioned in paragraph 3 above. He can apply to the court under the Landlord and Tenant Act 1954 for a new tenancy. If he does, his current tenancy will continue after the date mentioned in paragraph 3 of this request while his application is being considered by the court. You can ask the court to fix the rent which your tenant will have to pay whilst his tenancy continues. The terms of any *new* tenancy not agreed between you and your tenant will be settled by the court.

Opposing a request for a new tenancy

2. If you do not want to grant a new tenancy, you *must* within two months of the making of this request, give your tenant notice saying that you will oppose any application he makes to the court for a new tenancy. You do not need a special form to do this, but you must state on which of the grounds set out in the 1954 Act you will oppose the application—see note 4.

3. The time limit in note 2 runs from the making of this request. The date of the making of the request may not be the date written on the request or the date on which you actually saw it. It may, for instance, be the date on which the request was delivered through the post to your last address known to the person giving the request. If there has been any delay in your seeing this request you may need to act very quickly. If you are in any doubt get advice immediately.

WARNING TO LANDLORD
IF YOU DO NOT KEEP TO THE TIME LIMIT IN NOTE 2, YOU WILL *LOSE* YOUR RIGHT TO OPPOSE YOUR TENANT'S APPLICATION TO THE COURT FOR A NEW TENANCY IF HE MAKES ONE.

Grounds for opposing an application

4. If your tenant applies to the court for a new tenancy, you can only oppose the

application on one or more of the grounds set out in section 30(1) of the 1954 Act. These grounds are set out below. The paragraph letters are those given in the Act.

Grounds

(*a*) where under the current tenancy the tenant has any obligations as respects the repair and maintenance of the holding, that the tenant ought not to be granted a new tenancy in view of the state or repair of the holding, being a state resulting from the tenant's failure to comply with the said obligations;

(*b*) that the tenant ought not to be granted a new tenancy in view of his persistent delay in paying rent which has become due;

(*c*) that the tenant ought not to be granted a new tenancy in view of other substantial breaches by him of his obligations under the current tenancy, or for any other reason connected with the tenant's use or management of the holding;

(*d*) that you have offered and are willing to provide or secure the provision of alternative accommodation for the tenant, that the terms on which the alternative accommodation is available are reasonable having regard to the terms of the current tenancy and to all other relevant circumstances, and that the accommodation and the time at which it will be available are suitable for the tenant's requirements (including the requirement to preserve goodwill) having regard to the nature and class of his business and to the situation and to the situation and extent of, and facilities afforded by, the holding;

(*e*) where the current tenancy was created by the sub-letting of part only of the property comprised in a superior tenancy and you are the owner of an interest in reversion expectant on the termination of that superior tenancy, that the aggregate of the rents reasonably obtainable on separate lettings of the holding and the remainder of that property would be substantially less than the rent reasonably obtainable on a letting of that property as a whole, that on the termination of the current tenancy you require possession of the holding for the purpose of letting or otherwise disposing of the said poroperty as a whole, and that in view thereof the tenant ought not to be granted a new tenancy;

(*f*) that on the termination of the current tenancy you intend to demolish or reconstruct the premises comprised in the holding or a substantial part of those premises or to carry out substantial work of construction on the holding or part thereof and that you could not reasonably do so without obtaining possession of the holding;
(If you use this ground, the court can sometimes still grant a new tenancy if certain conditions set out in section 31A of the Act can be met.)

(*g*) that on the termination of the current tenancy you intend to occupy the holding for the purposes, or partly for the puroses, of a business to be carried on by you therein, or as your residence.
(You must normally have been the landlord for at least five years to use this ground.)

You can only use one or more of the above grounds if you have stated them in the notice referred to in note 2 above.

Compensation

5. If your tenant cannot get a new tenancy solely because grounds (*e*), (*f*) or (*g*) apply, he is entitled to compensation from you under the 1954 Act. If you have opposed his application on any of the other grounds as well as (*e*), (*f*) or (*g*) he can only get compensation if the court's refusal to grant a new tenancy is based solely on grounds (*e*), (*f*) or (*g*). In other words he cannot get compensation under the 1954 Act if the court has refused his tenancy on *other* grounds even if (*e*), (*f*) or (*g*) also apply.

6. If you are an authority possessing compulsory purchase powers (such as a local authority) you will be aware that your tenant may be entitled to a disturbance payment under Part III of the Land Compensation Act 1973.

Negotiating a new tenancy

7. Most leases are renewed by negotiation. If you do try to agree a new tenancy with your tenant—

(1) YOU should remember you will not be able to oppose an application to the court for a new tenancy unless you give the notice mentioned in note 2 above within the time limit in that note;

(2) YOUR TENANT should remember that he will lose his right to apply to the court for a new tenancy unless he makes the application not less than two nor more than four months after the making of this request.

Validity of this notice

8. The landlord to whom this request is made may not be the landlord to whom the tenant pays the rent. "Business" is given a wide meaning in the 1954 Act and is used in the same sense in this request. The 1954 Act also has rules about the date which the tenant can put in paragraph 3. This depends on the terms of the tenancy. If you have any doubts about whether this request is valid, get immediate advice.

Explanatory booklet

9. The Department of the Environment booklet "Business Tenancies" explains the provisions of Part II of the 1954 Act in more detail than these notes. It is available from Her Majesty's Stationery Office or through booksellers. **[977]**

NOTES

Commencement: 1 April 1983.

FORM 9

NOTICE BY LANDLORD REQUIRING INFORMATION ABOUT OCCUPATION AND SUB-TENANCIES OF BUSINESS PREMISES

(LANDLORD AND TENANT ACT 1954, SECTION 40(1))

To: *(name of tenant)*

of *(address of tenant)*

IMPORTANT—THIS NOTICE REQUIRES YOU TO GIVE YOUR LANDLORD CERTAIN INFORMATION. YOU MUST ACT QUICKLY. READ THE NOTICE AND ALL THE NOTES CAREFULLY. IF YOU ARE IN ANY DOUBT ABOUT THE ACTION YOU SHOULD TAKE, GET ADVICE IMMEDIATELY e.g. FROM A SOLICITOR OR SURVEYOR OR A CITIZENS ADVICE BUREAU.

1. This notice is given under section 40(1) of the Landlord and Tenant Act 1954.

2. It relates to .. .. *(description of business premises)* of which you are the tenant.

3. I/we require you to notify me/us in writing, within one month of the service of this notice on you—

(*a*) whether you occupy the premises or any part of them wholly or partly for business purposes; and
(*b*) whether you have a sub-tenant.

4. If you have a sub-tenant, I/we also require you to state—

(*a*) what premises are comprised in the sub-tenancy;
(*b*) if the sub-tenancy is for a fixed term, what the term is, or, if the sub-tenancy is terminable by notice, by what notice it can be terminated;
(*c*) what rent the sub-tenant pays;
(*d*) the sub-tenant's full name;
(*e*) whether, to the best of your knowledge and belief, the sub-tenant occupies either the whole or part of the premises sub-let to him and, if not, what is his address.

5. All correspondence about this notice should be sent to **[the landlord] [the landlord's agent] at the address given below.

**Cross out words in square brackets if they do not apply.

Date .. .. ..

Signature of **[landlord] [landlord's agent]

Name of landlord .. .. ..

Address of landlord .. .. ..

**[Address of agent .. ..]

Notes

Purpose of this notice

1. Your landlord (or if he is a tenant himself, possibly his landlord) has served this notice on you to obtain the information he needs in order to find out his position under Part II of the Landlord and Tenant Act 1954 in relation to your tenancy. He will then know, for example, whether, when your tenancy expires, you will be entitled to apply to the court for a new tenancy of the whole of the premises comprised in your present tenancy; you may not be entitled to a new tenancy of any part of the premises which you have sub-let. (In certain circumstances, a sub-tenant may become a direct tenant of the landlord.)

Replying to this notice

2. Section 40 of the 1954 Act says that you *must* answer the questions asked in the notice and you *must* let the landlord have your answers in writing within one month of the service of the notice. You do not need a special form for this. If you don't answer these questions or give the landlord incorrect information he might suffer a loss for which, in certain circumstances, you could be held liable.

3. If you have let to more than one sub-tenant you should give the information required in respect of each sub-letting.

Validity of this notice

4. The landlord who has given this notice may not be the landlord to whom you pay rent. "Business" is given a wide meaning in the 1954 Act and is used in the same sense in this notice. The landlord cannot ask for this information earlier than two years before your tenancy is due to expire or could be brought to an end by notice given by him. If you have any doubts about whether this notice is valid get immediate advice.

Explanatory booklet

5. The Department of the Environment booklet "Business Tenancies" explains the provisions of Part II of the 1954 Act in more detail than these notes. It is available from Her Majesty's Stationery Office or through booksellers. **[978]**

NOTES

Commencement: 1 April 1983.

FORM 10

NOTICE BY TENANT OF BUSINESS PREMISES REQUIRING INFORMATION FROM LANDLORD ABOUT LANDLORD'S INTEREST

(LANDLORD AND TENANT ACT 1954, SECTION 40(2))

To: *(name of landlord)*

of *(address of landlord)*

IMPORTANT—THIS NOTICE REQUIRES YOU TO GIVE YOUR TENANT CERTAIN INFORMATION. YOU MUST ACT QUICKLY. READ THE NOTICE AND ALL THE NOTES CAREFULLY. IF YOU ARE IN ANY DOUBT ABOUT THE ACTION YOU SHOULD TAKE, GET ADVICE IMMEDIATELY e.g. FROM A SOLICITOR OR SURVEYOR OR A CITIZENS ADVICE BUREAU.

1. This notice is given under section 40(2) of the Landlord and Tenant Act 1954.

2. It relates to ...... *(description of business premises)* of which you are the landlord.

3. I/we give you notice requiring you to notify me/us in writing, within one month of the service of this notice on you—

(*a*) whether you are the freeholder of the whole or part of the premises.
If you are *not* the freeholder:
(*b*) I/we also require you to state, to the best of your knowledge and belief—

(i) the name and address of the person who is your immediate landlord in respect of the premises or the part of which you are not the freeholder;
(ii) the length of your tenancy; and
(iii) the earliest date (if any) at which your tenancy can be terminated by notice to quit given by your immediate landlord.

4. I/we also require you to notify me/us—

(*a*) whether there is a mortgagee in possession of your interest in the property and, if so, his name and address; and
(*b*) if there is a receiver appointed by the mortgagee or by the court, his name and address also.

5. All correspondence about this notice should be sent to **[the tenant] [the tenant's agent] at the address given below.

**Cross out words in square brackets if they do not apply.

Date ......

Signature of **[tenant] [tenant's agent]

Name of tenant ......

Address of tenant ......

**[Address of agent ......]

Notes

Purpose of this notice

1. Your tenant has served this notice on you to obtain the information he needs in order to find out who is his landlord for the purposes of Part II of the Landlord and Tenant Act 1954. The Act in certain circumstances enables a tenant of business premises to obtain a new tenancy from that landlord.

Replying to this notice

2. Section 40 of the 1954 Act says that you *must* answer the questions asked in the notice and you *must* let your tenant have your answers in writing within one month of the service of this notice. You do not need a special form for this. If you do not answer these questions or give your tenant incorrect information he might suffer a loss for which, in certain circumstances, you could be held liable.

Validity of this notice

3. "Business" is given a wide meaning in the 1954 Act and is used in the same sense in this notice. Your tenant cannot ask for this information earlier than two years before his current tenancy is due to expire or could be brought to an end by notice to quit given by you. If you have any doubts about whether this notice is valid, get immediate advice.

Explanatory booklet

4. The Department of the Environment booklet "Business Tenancies" explains the provisions of Part II of the 1954 Act in more detail than these notes. It is available from Her Majesty's Stationery Office or through booksellers. **[979]**

NOTES
Commencement: 1 April 1983.

FORM 11

NOTICE BY TENANT OF BUSINESS PREMISES REQUIRING INFORMATION FROM MORTGAGEE ABOUT LANDLORD'S INTEREST

(LANDLORD AND TENANT ACT 1954, SECTION 40(2))

To: *(name of mortgagee)*

of *(address of mortgagee)*

IMPORTANT—THIS NOTICE REQUIRES YOU TO GIVE THE TENANT OF PREMISES OF WHICH YOU ARE THE MORTGAGEE IN POSSESSION, CERTAIN INFORMATION. YOU MUST ACT QUICKLY. READ THE NOTICE AND ALL THE NOTES CAREFULLY. IF YOU ARE IN ANY DOUBT ABOUT THE ACTION YOU SHOULD TAKE, GET ADVICE IMMEDIATELY e.g. FROM A SOLICITOR OR SURVEYOR OR A CITIZENS ADVICE BUREAU.

1. This notice is given under section 40(2) of the Landlord and Tenant Act 1954.

2. It relates to .. .. .. *(description of business premises)* which I/we believe to be in mortgage to you.

3. I/we give you notice requiring you to notify me/us in writing, within one month of the service of this notice on you—

(*a*) whether the mortgagor is the freeholder of the whole or part of the premises;
If he is *not* the freeholder:
(*b*) I/we also require you to state, to the best of your knowledge and belief,—

(i) the name and address of the person who is your mortgagor's immediate landlord in respect of the premises or part of which he is not the freeholder;
(ii) the length of your mortgagor's tenancy; and
(iii) the earliest date (if any) at which his tenancy can be terminated by notice to quit given by his immediate landlord.

4. All correspondence about this notice should be sent to **[the tenant] [the tenant's agent] at the address given below.

**Cross out words in square brackets if they do not apply.

Date .. .. ..

Signature of **[tenant] [tenant's agent]

Name of tenant .. .. ..

Address of tenant .. .. ..

**[Address of agent .. .. ..

Notes

Purpose of this notice

1. You are either the mortgagee in possession of business premises or a receiver appointed by the mortgagee or by the court. A tenant of the whole or part of the premises has served this notice on you to obtain the information he needs in order to find out who is his landlord for the purposes of Part II of the Landlord and Tenant Act 1954. The Act in certain circumstances enables a tenant of business premises to obtain a new tenancy from that landlord.

Replying to this notice

2. Section 40 of the 1954 Act says that you *must* answer the questions asked in the notice and you *must* let the tenant have your answers in writing within one month of the service of this notice. You do not need a special form for this. If you don't answer these questions or give the tenant incorrect information he might suffer a loss for which, in certain circumstances, you could be held liable.

Validity of this notice

3. "Business" is given a wide meaning in the 1954 Act and is used in same sense in this notice. The tenant cannot ask for this information earlier than two years before his current tenancy is due to expire or could be brought to an end by notice to quit given by his landlord. If you have any doubts about whether this notice is valid, get immediate advice.

Explanatory booklet

4. The Department of the Environment booklet "Business Tenancies" explains the provisions of Part II of the 1954 Act in more detail than these notes. It is available from Her Majesty's Stationery Office or through booksellers. **[980]**

NOTES

Commencement: 1 April 1983.

FORM 12

WITHDRAWAL OF LANDLORD'S NOTICE TO TERMINATE BUSINESS TENANCY

(LANDLORD AND TENANT ACT 1954, SECTION 44 AND PARAGRAPH 6 OF SCHEDULE 6)

To: *(name of tenant)*

of *(address of tenant)*

IMPORTANT—THIS NOTICE IS INTENDED TO WITHDRAW A PREVIOUS NOTICE TO TERMINATE YOUR TENANCY. READ THIS NOTICE AND ALL THE NOTES CAREFULLY. IF YOU ARE IN ANY DOUBT ABOUT YOUR POSITION, GET ADVICE IMMEDIATELY e.g. FROM A SOLICITOR OR SURVEYOR OR A CITIZENS ADVICE BUREAU.

1. This notice is given under section 44 of, and paragraph 6 of Schedule 6 to, the Landlord and Tenant Act 1954.

2. It relates to .. .. .. *(description of property)* of which you are the tenant.

3. I/we have become your landlord for the purposes of the Act.

4. I/we withdraw the notice given to you by .. .. *(name of former landlord)*

of .. ..

(address of former landlord) terminating your tenancy on .. ..

5. Any correspondence about this notice should be sent to **[the landlord] [the landlord's agent] at the address given below.

**Cross out words in square brackets if they do not apply.

Date .. .. ..

Signature of **[landlord] [landlord's agent]

Name of landlord .. .. ..

Address of landlord .. ..

**[Address of agent .. ..]

Notes

Purpose of this notice

1. You were earlier given a notice bringing your tenancy to an end, but there has now been a change of landlord for the purposes of the 1954 Act. This new notice has been given to you by your new landlord and withdraws the earlier notice, which now has no effect. However, the new landlord can, if he wishes, give you a fresh notice with the intention of bringing your tenancy to an end.

Validity of this notice

2. The landlord who has given this notice may not be the landlord to whom you pay your rent. "Business" is given a wide meaning in the 1954 Act and is used in the same sense in this notice. This notice can only be given within two months after giving of the earlier notice. If you have any doubts about whether this notice is valid, get immediate advice. If it is *not* valid you may have to act quickly to preserve your position under the earlier notice.

Explanatory booklet

3. The Department of the Environment booklet "Business Tenancies" explains the provisions of Part II of the 1954 Act in more detail than these notes. It is available from Her Majesty's Stationery Office or through booksellers. **[981]**

NOTES

Commencement: 1 April 1983.

FORM 13

LANDLORD'S NOTICE TO TERMINATE BUSINESS TENANCY WHERE LEASEHOLD REFORM ACT 1967 MAY APPLY*

*This form *must* be used (instead of form number 1) if—

(*a*) no previous notice terminating the tenancy has been given under section 25 of the Act, and

(*b*) the tenancy is the tenancy of a house (as defined for the purposes of Part I of the Leasehold Reform Act 1967), and

(*c*) the tenancy is a long tenancy at a low rent (within the meaning of that Act of 1967), and

(*d*) the tenant is not a company or other artificial person.

(LANDLORD AND TENANT ACT 1954, SECTION 25 AND LEASEHOLD REFORM ACT 1967, SCHEDULE 3, PARAGRAPH 10)

To: . . . . (*name of tenant*)

of . . . . (*address of tenant*)

IMPORTANT - THIS NOTICE IS INTENDED TO BRING YOUR TENANCY TO AN END. IF YOU WANT TO CONTINUE TO OCCUPY YOUR PROPERTY YOU MUST ACT QUICKLY. READ THE NOTICE AND ALL THE NOTES CAREFULLY. IF YOU ARE IN ANY DOUBT ABOUT THE ACTION YOU SHOULD TAKE, GET ADVICE IMMEDIATELY e.g. FROM A SOLICITOR OR SURVEYOR OR A CITIZENS ADVICE BUREAU.

1. This notice is given under section 25 of the Landlord and Tenant Act 1954.

2. It relates to . . . . (*description of property*)

of which you are the tenant.

3. I/we give you notice terminating your tenancy on . . . .
(See notes 1 and 13.)

4. If you are not willing to give up possession of the property comprised in the tenancy on the date specified in paragraph 3, you must notify me/us in writing within two months after the giving of this notice.
(See notes 2 to 4.)

5.* If you apply to the court under Part II of the Landlord and Tenant Act 1954 for the grant of a new tenancy, I/we will not oppose your application.

OR

5.* If you apply to the court under Part II of the Landlord and Tenant Act 1954 for

the grant of a new tenancy, I/we will oppose it on the grounds mentioned in paragraph(s)............of section 30(1) of that Act.
(*The landlord must cross out one version of paragraph 5. If the second version is used the paragraph letter(s) must be filled in.)

6. (*a*) If you have a right under the Leasehold Reform Act 1967 to acquire the freehold or an extended lease of the property comprised in the tenancy, notice of your desire to have the freehold or an extended lease cannot be given more than two months after the service of this notice on you.
(See notes 6 and 7.)

(*b*) If you have that right and give such a notice within those two months, *this* notice will not operate.

(*c*) If you give such a notice within those two months—

†[(i) I/we shall be entitled to apply to the court under section †[17] [18] of the Leasehold Reform Act 1967 and I/we †[propose] [do not propose] to do so.]

†[(ii) I/we shall not be entitled to apply to the court under section †[17] [18] of the Leasehold Reform Act 1967.]
(See notes 8 and 11.)

†[7. The following persons are known or believed by me/us to have an interest superior to your tenancy or to be the agents concerned with the property on behalf of someone who has such an interest ....
....
....
....]

8. All correspondence about this notice should be sent to **[the landlord] [the landlord's agent] at the address given below.

Date ....

Signature of **[landlord] [landlord's agent] ....

Name of landlord ....

Address of landlord ....

**[Address of agent ....]

**Cross out words in square brackets if they do not apply.

Notes

Termination of tenancy

1. This notice is intended to bring your tenancy to an end. Because your tenancy is one to which Part II of the Landlord and Tenant Act 1954 applies, you can apply to the court under that Act for a new tenancy—see notes 2 to 5 below. However, the Leasehold Reform Act 1967 may also apply in your case. If it does you may be able to buy the freehold of the property or get an extended lease under *that* Act—see notes 6 to 8 below. In some circumstances your landlord may still be able to get possession of the property. If he does, you may be able to get compensation. The amount of any compensation (see notes 9 to 11) will depend on the steps you have taken and under which Act (it is likely to be greater under the 1967 Act.) If you have any doubt about what you should do, get advice immediately.

Claiming a new tenancy under the 1954 Act

2. If you apply to the court for a new tenancy under the 1954 Act, your present tenancy will be continued by that Act after the date shown in paragraph 3 of this notice whilst your claim is being considered. The landlord can ask the court to fix the rent which you will have to pay whilst the tenancy is continued. The terms of any *new* tenancy not agreed between you and the landlord will be determined by the court.

3. If you want to apply to the court for a new tenancy you must:—

(1) notify the landlord in writing not later than two months after the giving of this notice that you are not willing to give up possession of the property;

AND

(2) apply to the court, not earlier than two months nor later than four months after the giving of this notice, for a new tenancy. You should apply to the County Court unless the rateable value of the business part of your premises is above the current County Court limit. In that case you should apply to the High Court.

4. The time limits in note 3 run from the giving of the notice. The date of the giving of the notice may not be the date written on the notice or the date on which you actually saw it. It may, for instance, be the date on which the notice was delivered through the post to your last address known to the person giving the notice. If there has been any delay in your seeing this notice you may need to act very quickly. If you are in any doubt get advice immediately.

Landlord's opposition to claim for a new tenancy

5. If you apply to the court for a new tenancy, the landlord can only oppose your application on one or more of the grounds set out in section 30(1) of the 1954 Act. These grounds are set out below. The paragraph letters are those given in the Act. The landlord can only use a ground if its paragraph letter is shown in paragraph 5 of this notice.

Grounds

(*a*) where under the current tenancy the tenant has any obligations as respects the repair and maintenance of the holding, that the tenant ought not to be granted a new tenancy in view of the state of repair of the holding, being a state resulting from the tenant's failure to comply with the said obligations;

(*b*) that the tenant ought not to be granted a new tenancy in view of his persistent delay in paying rent which has become due;

(*c*) that the tenant ought not to be granted a new tenancy in view of other substantial breaches by him of his obligations under the current tenancy, or for any other reason connected with the tenant's use or management of the holding;

(*d*) that the landlord has offered and is willing to provide or secure the provision of alternative accommodation for the tenant, that the terms on which the alternative accommodation is available are reasonable having regard to the terms of the current tenancy and to all other relevant circumstances, and that the accommodation and the time at which it will be available are suitable for the tenant's requirements (including the requirement to preserve goodwill) having regard to the nature and class of his business and to the situation and extent of, and facilities afforded by, the holding;

(*e*) where the current tenancy was created by the sub-letting of part only of the property comprised in a superior tenancy and the landlord is the owner of an interest in reversion expectant on the termination of that superior tenancy, that the aggregate of the rents reasonably obtainable on separate lettings of the holding and the remainder of that property would be substantially less than the rent reasonably obtainable on a letting of that property as a whole, that on the termination of the current tenancy the landlord requires possession for the purposes of letting or otherwise disposing of the said property as a whole, and that in view thereof the tenant ought not to be granted a new tenancy;

(*f*) that on the termination of the current tenancy the landlord intends to demolish or reconstruct the premises comprised in the holding or a substantial part of those premises or to carry out substantial work of construction on the holding or part thereof and that he could not reasonably do so without obtaining possession of the holding.
(If the landlord uses this ground, the court can sometimes still grant a new tenancy if certain conditions set out in section 31A of the Act can be met.)

(*g*) that on the termination of the current tenancy the landlord intends to occupy the holding for the purposes, or partly for the purposes, of a business to be carried on by him therein, or as his residence.
(The landlord must normally have been the landlord for at least five years to use this ground.)

Rights under the Leasehold Reform Act 1967

6. If the property comprised in your tenancy is a house, as defined in the 1967 Act, you may have the right to buy the freehold of the property or to extend your lease for fifty years. You can do so if *all* the following conditions are met:—

(i) your lease was originally granted for a term of more than 21 years, or it was preceded by such a lease which was granted or assigned to you; *and*
(ii) your lease is of the whole house; *and*
(iii) your lease is at a low rent. That is, your present annual rent is less than two-thirds of the rateable value of your house as assessed either on 23rd March 1965, or on the first day of the term in the case of a lease granted to commence after 23rd March 1965; *and*
(iv) you are occupying the house as your only or main residence and you have been doing so either for the whole of the last three years, or for a total of three years during the last ten years under this lease; *and*
(v) the rateable value of your house was at one time within certain limits.

Claiming your rights under the 1967 Act

7. If you do have the right to buy the freehold or to extend the lease and wish to exercise it you must serve the appropriate notice (on a special form prescribed under the 1967 Act) on the landlord. You must do so within two months after the date this notice was served on you. The date of service of the notice may not be the date written on the notice or the date on which you actually saw it. It may, for instance, be the date on which the notice was delivered through the post to your last address known to the person serving the notice. If there has been any delay in your seeing this notice you may need to act very quickly. If you are in any doubt get advice immediately.

WARNING TO TENANT

IF YOU DO NOT KEEP TO THE TIME LIMITS IN NOTES 3 AND 7 YOU WILL *LOSE* YOUR RIGHT TO APPLY TO THE COURT FOR A NEW TENANCY UNDER THE 1954 ACT OR TO CLAIM THE FREEHOLD OR AN EXTENDED LEASE UNDER THE 1967 ACT.

Landlord's opposition to claims under the 1967 Act

8. If your landlord acquired his interest in the house not later than 18th February 1966 he can object to your claim to buy the freehold or to extend the lease on the grounds that he needs the house for occupation by himself or a member of his family. This objection will be under section 18 of the 1967 Act. If you claim a fifty year extension of your lease, your landlord can object under section 17 of the 1967 Act on the grounds that he wishes to redevelop the property. Paragraph (6)(*c*) of the notice will tell you whether the landlord believes he has the right to apply to the court under sections 17 and 18 and whether or not he proposes to do so.

Compensation

9. If you cannot get a new tenancy solely because grounds (*e*), (*f*) or (*g*) in note 5 apply, you are entitled to compensation under the 1954 Act. If your landlord has opposed your application on any of the other grounds as well as (*e*), (*f*) or (*g*) you can only get compensation if the court's refusal to grant a new tenancy is based solely on grounds (*e*), *(f) or (g)*. In other words you cannot get compensation under the 1954 Act if the court has refused your tenancy on *other* grounds even if (*e*), (*f*) or (*g*) also apply.

10. If your landlord is an authority possessing compulsory purchase powers (such as a local authority) you may be entitled to a disturbance payment under Part III of the Land Compensation Act 1973.

11. If you have a right under the 1967 Act to buy the freehold or get an extended lease of your premises but the landlord, as mentioned in note 8, is able to obtain possession of the premises, compensation under the 1967 Act is payable. This is normally higher than the compensation mentioned in note 9 above. Your solicitor or surveyor will be able to advise you on this.

Negotiations with your landlord

12. Many tenants buy their houses or renew their leases by negotiation. If you do try to buy the property by agreement or to negotiate a new lease with your landlord, remember—

(1) that your present tenancy will not be extended under the 1954 Act after the date in paragraph 3 of this notice unless you *both*—

(*a*) give written notice that you will not vacate (note 3(1) above); *and*
(*b*) apply to the court for a new tenancy (note 3(2) above);

(2) that you will lose your right to apply to the court for a new tenancy under the 1954 Act if you do not keep to the time limits in note 3; and

(3) that you will lose your right to serve a notice claiming to buy the freehold or to have an extended lease under the 1967 Act if you do not keep to the time limit in note 7.

Validity of this notice

13. The landlord who has given this notice may not be the landlord to whom you pay your rent. "Business" is given a wide meaning in the 1954 Act and it is used in the same sense in this notice. The 1954 Act also has rules about the date which the landlord can put in paragraph 3. This depends on the terms of your tenancy. If you have any doubts about whether this notice is valid, get immediate advice.

Explanatory booklets

14. The Department of the Environment booklet "Business Tenancies" explains the provisions of Part II of the 1954 Act in more detail than these notes. The Department of the Environment and Welsh Office booklet "Leasehold Reform" gives details of the rights of leaseholders to claim to buy the freehold or to have an extension to the lease of their house.

"Business Tenancies" is available from Her Majesty's Stationery Office or through booksellers. "Leasehold Reform" is available from Council Offices and housing aid centres. **[982]**

NOTES
Commencement: 1 April 1983.

Form 14

LANDLORD'S NOTICE TO TERMINATE BUSINESS TENANCY ON GROUNDS OF PUBLIC INTEREST WHERE LEASEHOLD REFORM ACT 1967 MAY APPLY*

*This form *must* be used (instead of form number 2) if—

(*a*) no previous notice terminating the tenancy has been given under section 25 of the Act; and
(*b*) the tenancy is the tenancy of a house (as defined for the purposes of Part I of the Leasehold Reform Act 1967); and
(*c*) the tenancy is a long tenancy at a low rent (within the meaning of that Act of 1967); and
(*d*) the tenant is not a company or other artificial person.

(Landlord and Tenant Act 1954, sections 25 and 57 and leasehold reform Act 1967, Schedule 3, paragraph 10)

To: *(name of tenant)*

of *(address of tenant)*

IMPORTANT— THIS NOTICE IS INTENDED TO BRING YOUR TENANCY TO AN END. READ THE NOTICE AND ALL THE NOTES CAREFULLY. IF YOU ARE IN ANY DOUBT ABOUT THE ACTION YOU SHOULD TAKE, GET ADVICE IMMEDIATELY e.g. FROM A SOLICITOR OR SURVEYOR OR A CITIZENS ADVICE BUREAU.

1. This notice is given under sections 25 and 57 of the Landlord and Tenant Act 1954.

2. It relates to . . . . *(description of property)*
of which you are the tenant.

3. We give you notice terminating your tenancy on . . . .
(See notes 1 and 5.)

4. A certificate has been given under section 57 of the 1954 Act by . . . . that it is requisite for †[our purposes] [the purposes of. . . . .] that the use or occupation of all or part of the property shall be changed by. . . . . A copy of the certificate is contained in the Schedule to this notice.

5. (*a*) If you have a right under the Leasehold Reform Act 1967 to acquire the freehold or an extended lease of the property comprised in the tenancy, notice of your desire to have the freehold or an extended lease cannot be given more than two months after the service of this notice on you.
(See note 2.)

(*b*) If you have that right and give such a notice within those two months, *this* notice will not operate.
(See note 4.)

(*c*) If within those two months you give written notice claiming to be entitled to acquire the freehold or an extended lease we will be entitled to apply to the court under section 17 of the Leasehold Reform Act 1967 and we propose to do so.

*[6. The following persons are known or believed by us to have an interest superior to your tenancy or to be the agents concerned with the property on behalf of someone who has such an interest . . . .
. . . .
. . . .
. . . .]

7. All correspondence about this notice should be sent to †[the landlord] [the landlord's agent] at the address given below.

Date . . . .

Signature of †[landlord] [landlord's agent]
. . . .

Name of landlord . . . .

Address of landlord . . . .
. . . .
. . . .

†[Address of agent. . . . .
. . . .
. . . .]

*Cross out words in square brackets if they do not apply.

SCHEDULE

[Insert a copy of the certificate]

Notes

Termination of tenancy

1. This notice is intended to bring your tenancy to an end. Usually tenants under tenancies to which Part II of the Landlord and Tenant Act 1954 applies can apply to the court for a new tenancy. You cannot do so because a certificate has been given under setion 57 of the Act and the date in paragraph 3 of this notice is not earlier than the date in the certificate (set out in the Schedule to this notice) as the date by which the use or occupation of all or part of the property shall be changed. Because of this you will be entitled to compensation-see note 3.

Rights under the Leasehold Reform Act 1967

2. If the property comprised in your tenancy is a house, as defined in the 1967 Act, and if *all* the following conditions are met—

(i) your lease was originally granted for a term of more than 21 years, or it was preceded by such a lease which was granted or assigned to you; *and*
(ii) your lease is of the whole house; *and*
(iii) your lease is at a low rent. That is, your present annual rent is less than two-thirds of the rateable value of your house as assessed either on 23 March 1965, or on the first day of the term in the case of a lease granted to commence after 23 March 1965; *and*
(iv) you are occupying the house as your only or main residence and you have been doing so either for the whole of the last three years, or for a total of three years during the last ten years under this lease; *and*
(v) the rateable value of your house was at one time within certain limits

you would usually have the right to buy the freehold of the property or to extend your lease for fifty years under the 1967 Act. You cannot do so when a certificate has been given under section 57 of the 1954 Act, because section 28 of the 1967 Act says that any notice you give to exercise such a right shall be of no effect. However, you may be entitled to compensation—see note 4.

Compensation

3. Because the court cannot order the grant of a new tenancy under the 1954 Act you are entitled to compensation under that Act when you leave the property. Also if your landlord is an authority possessing compulsory purchase powers (such as a local authority) you may be entitled to a disturbance payment under Part III of the Land Compensation Act 1973.

4. Because in your case you cannot buy the freehold of the property or extend your lease for 50 years under the 1967 Act, you may also be entitled to compensation under that Act. You cannot, however, get compensation under both the 1954 Act and under the 1967 Act. The compensation payable under the 1967 Act is likely to be greater than that payable under the 1954 Act. In order to be able to claim compensation under the 1967 Act you must, *within two months* serve a written notice on your landlord claiming to be entitled to acquire the freehold or an extended lease (i.e. to say, in effect, that you would have been able to acquire the freehold or an extended lease were it not for the certificate under section 57 of the 1954 Act). The notice must be on a special form prescribed under the 1967 Act. The two months time limit runs from the service of the notice. The date of service of the notice may not be the date written on the notice or the date on which you actually saw it. It may, for instance, be the date on which the notice was delivered through the post to your last address known to the person serving the notice. If there has been any delay in your seeing this notice you may need to act very quickly. If you are in any doubt about what you should do get advice immediately.

WARNING TO TENANT

IF YOU DO NOT KEEP TO THE TIME LIMIT IN NOTE 4 YOU WILL *LOSE* YOUR RIGHT TO COMPENSATION UNDER THE 1967 ACT.

Validity of this notice

5. The landlord who has given this notice may not be the landlord to whom you pay your rent. "Business" is given a wide meaning in the 1954 Act and is used in the same sense in this notice. The 1954 Act also has rules about the date which the landlord can put in paragraph 3. This depends on the terms of your tenancy. If you have any doubts about whether this notice is valid, get immediate advice.

Explanatory booklets

6. The Department of the Environment booklet "Business Tenancies" explains the provisions of Part II of the 1954 Act in more detail than these notes. The Department of the Environment and Welsh Office booklet "Leasehold Reform" gives details of the rights of leaseholders to claim to buy the freehold or to have an extension to the lease of their house. "Business Tenancies" is available from Her Majesty's Stationery Office or through booksellers. "Leasehold Reform" is available from Council Offices and housing aid centres. **[983]**

NOTES
Commencement: 1 April 1983.

FORM 15

LANDLORD'S NOTICE TO TERMINATE BUSINESS TENANCY WHERE CHANGE REQUIRED AT FUTURE DATE ON GROUNDS OF PUBLIC INTEREST AND WHERE LEASEHOLD REFORM ACT 1967 MAY APPLY*

*This form *must* be used (instead of form number 3) if—

(*a*) no previous notice terminating the tenancy has been given under section 25 of the Act; and

(*b*) the tenancy is the tenancy of a house (as defined for the purpose of Part I of the Leasehold Reform Act 1967); and

(*c*) the tenancy is a long tenancy at a low rent (within the meaning of that Act of 1967); and

(*d*) the tenant is not a company or other artificial person.

(LANDLORD AND TENANT ACT 1954, SECTIONS 25 AND 57 AND LEASEHOLD REFORM ACT 1967, SCHEDULE 3, PARAGRAPH 10)

To: . . . .(*name of tenant*)

of . . . . (*address of tenant*)

IMPORTANT—THIS NOTICE IS INTENDED TO BRING YOUR TENANCY TO AN END. IF YOU WANT TO CONTINUE TO OCCUPY YOUR PROPERTY YOU MUST ACT QUICKLY. READ THE NOTICE AND ALL THE NOTES CAREFULLY. IF YOU ARE IN ANY DOUBT ABOUT THE ACTION YOU SHOULD TAKE, GET ADVICE IMMEDIATELY e.g. FROM A SOLICITOR OR SURVEYOR OR A CITIZENS ADVICE BUREAU.

1. This notice is given under sections 25 and 57 of the Landlord and Tenant Act 1954.

2. It relates to . . . .(*description of property*)

of which you are the tenant.

3. We give you notice terminating your tenancy on . . . .
(See notes 1 and 9.)

4. If you are not willing to give up possession of the property comprised in the tenancy on the date stated in paragraph 3, you must notify us in writing within two months after the giving of this notice.
(See notes 2 to 4.)

5.* If you apply to the court under Part II of the Landlord and Tenant Act 1954 for the grant of a new tenancy, we will not oppose your application.

OR

5.* If you apply to the court under Part II of the Landlord and Tenant Act 1954 for the grant of a new tenancy, we will oppose it on the grounds mentioned in paragraph(s). . . . . .of section 30(1) of that Act.
(See notes 5 to 7.)

(*The landlord must cross out one version of paragraph 5. If the second version is used the paragraph letter(s) must be filled in.)

6. A certificate has been given under section 57 of the 1954 Act by. . . . . .that it is requisite for †[our purposes] [the purposes of. . . . .] that the use or occupation of all or part of the property shall be changed by . . . . A copy of the certificate is contained in the Schedule to this notice.

7. (*a*) If you have a right under the Leasehold Reform Act 1967 to acquire the freehold or an extended lease of the property comprised in the tenancy, notice of your desire to have the freehold or an extended lease cannot be given more than two months after the service of this notice on you.

(*b*) If you have the right and give such a notice within those two months, *this* notice will not operate.

(*c*) If within those two months you give written notice claiming to be entitled to acquire the freehold or an extended lease we will be entitled to apply to the court under section 17 of the Leasehold Reform Act 1967 and we propose to do so.

(See notes 1 and 8.)

†[8. The following persons are known or believed by us to have an interest superior to your tenancy or to be the agents concerned with the property on behalf of someone who has such an interest ....

....

....

....]

9. All correspondence about this notice should be sent to †[the landlord] [the landlord's agent] at the address given below.

Date ....

Signature of †[landlord] [landlord's agent]

....

Name of landlord ....

Address of landlord ....

....

....

†[Address of agent..

....

....]

†Cross out words in square brackets if they do not apply.

SCHEDULE

[Insert a copy of the certificate]

Notes

Termination of tenancy

1. This notice is intended to bring your tenancy to an end. Because your tenancy is one to which Part II of the Landlord and Tenant Act 1954 applies, you can apply to the court under that Act for a new tenancy. However a certificate has been given under section 57 of the 1954 Act and a copy is contained in the Schedule to this notice. This means that if the court orders the grant of a new tenancy, the new tenancy must end not later than the date specified in the certificate. Any new tenancy ordered to be granted will *not* be a tenancy to which Part II of the 1954 Act applies. However the Leasehold Reform Act 1967 may also apply in your case. If it does, you would usually have the right to buy the freehold of the property or to extend the lease for 50 years under the 1967 Act. You cannot do so when a certificate has been given under section 57 of the 1954 Act, because section 28 of the 1967 Act says that any notice you give to exercise such a right shall be of no effect. However you may be entitled to compensation. If you want to apply to the court under the 1954 Act, see notes 2 to 5 below. If you want to know about compensation, see notes 6 to 8 below. The amount of any compensation will depend on the steps you have taken and under which Act (it is likely to be greater under the 1967 Act). If you have any doubt about what you should do, get advice immediately.

Claiming a new tenancy under the 1954 Act

2. If you apply to the court for a new tenancy under the 1954 Act, your present tenancy will be continued by that Act after the date shown in paragraph 3 of this notice whilst your claim is being considered. The landlord can ask the court to fix the rent which you will have to pay whilst the tenancy is continued. The terms of any *new* tenancy not agreed between you and the landlord will be determined by the court.

3. If you want to apply to the court for a new tenancy you must:—

(1) notify the landlord in writing not later than two months after the giving of this notice that you are not willing to give up possession of the property;

AND

(2) apply to the court, not earlier than two months nor later than four months after the giving of this notice, for a new tenancy. You should apply to the County Court unless the rateable value of the business part of your premises is above the current County Court limit. In that case you should apply to the High Court.

4. The time limits in note 3 run from the giving of the notice. The date of the giving of the notice may not be the date written on the notice or the date on which you actually saw it. It may, for instance, be the date on which the notice was delivered through the post to your last address known to the person giving the notice. If there has been any delay in your seeing this notice you may need to act very quickly. If you are in any doubt get advice immediately.

Landlord's opposition to claim for a new tenancy

5. If you apply to the court for a new tenancy, the landlord can only oppose your application on one or more of the gounds set out in section 30(1) of the 1954 Act. These grounds are set out below. The paragraph letters are those given in the Act. The landlord can only use a ground if its paragraph letter is shown in paragraph 5 of the notice.

Grounds

(*a*) where under the current tenancy the tenant has any obligations as respects the repair and maintenance of the holding, that the tenant ought not to be granted a new tenancy in view of the state of repair of the holding, being a state resulting from the tenant's failure to comply with the said obligations;

(*b*) that the tenant ought not to be granted a new tenancy in view of his persistent delay in paying rent which has become due;

(*c*) that the tenant ought not to be granted a new tenancy in view of other substantial breaches by him of his obligations under the current tenancy, or for any other reason connected with the tenant's use or management of the holding;

(*d*) that the landlord has offered and is willing to provide or secure the provision of alternative accommodation for the tenant, that the terms on which the alternative accommodation is available are reasonable having regard to the terms of the current tenancy and to all other relevant circumstances, and that the accommodation and the time at which it will be available are suitable for the tenant's requirements (including the requirement to preserve goodwill) having regard to the nature and class of his business and to the situation and extent, and facilities afforded by, the holding;

(*e*) where the current tenancy was created by the sub-letting of part only of the property comprised in a superior tenancy and the landlord is the owner of an interest in reversion expectant on the termination of that superior tenancy, that the aggregate of the rent reasonably obtainable on separate lettings of the holding and the remainder of that property would be substantially less than the rent reasonably obtainable on a letting of that property as a whole, that on the termination of the current tenancy the landlord requires possession for the purposes of letting or otherwise disposing of the said property as a whole, and that in view thereof the tenant ought not to be granted a new tenancy;

(*f*) that on the termination of the current tenancy the landlord intends to demolish or reconstruct the premises comprised in the holding or a substantial part of those premises or to carry out substantial work of construction on the holding or part thereof and that he could not reasonably do so without obtaining possession of the holding;

(If the landlord uses this ground, the court can sometimes still grant a new tenancy if certain conditions set out in section 31A of the Act can be met.)

(*g*) that on the termination of the current tenancy the landlord intends to occupy the holding for the purposes, or partly for the purposes, of a business to be carried on by him therein, or as his residence.
(The landlord must normally have been the landlord for at least five years to use this ground.)

Compensation under the 1954 Act

6. If you cannot get a new tenancy solely because grounds (*e*), (*f*) or (*g*) in note 5 apply, you are entitled to compensation under the 1954 Act. If your landlord has opposed your application on any of the other grounds as well as (*e*), (*f*) or (*g*) you can only get compensation if the court's refusal to grant a new tenancy is based solely on grounds (*e*), (*f*) or (*g*). In other words you cannot get compensation under the 1954 Act if the court has refused your tenancy on *other* grounds even if (*e*), (*f*) or (*g*) also apply. If the court *does* order the grant of a new tenancy, you will be entitled to compensation under the 1954 Act because the new tenancy cannot expire later than the date specified in the certificate in the Schedule.

7. If your landlord is an authority possessing compulsory purchase powers (such as a local authority) you may be entitled to a disturbance payment under Part III of the Land Compensation Act 1973.

Compensation under the 1967 Act

8. If the property comprised in your tenancy is a house, as defined in the 1967 Act, and *all* the following conditions are met—

(i) your lease was originally granted for a term of more than 21 years, or it was preceded by such a lease which was granted or assigned to you; *and*

(ii) your lease is of the whole house; *and*

(iii) your lease is at a low rent. That is, your present annual rent is less than two-thirds of the rateable value of your house as assessed either on 23 March 1965, or on the first day of the term in the case of a lease granted to commence after 23 March 1965; *and*

(iv) you are occupying the house as your only or main residence and you have been doing so for the whole of the last three years, or for a total of three years during the last ten years under this lease; *and*

(v) the rateable value of your house was at one time within certain limits

you may be entitled to compensation under the 1967 Act. You cannot, however, get compensation under both the 1954 Act and the 1967 Act. The compensation payable under the 1967 Act is likely to be greater than that payable under the 1954 Act. In order to claim compensation under the 1967 Act you must, *within two months,* serve a written notice on your landlord claiming to be entitled to acquire the freehold or an extended lease (i.e. to say, in effect, that you would have been able to acquire the freehold or an extended lease were it not for the certificate under section 57 of the 1954 Act). The notice must be on a special form prescribed under the 1967 Act. The two month time limit runs from the service of the notice. The date of service of the notice may not be the date written on the notice or the date on which you actually saw it. It may, for instance, be the date on which the notice was delivered through the post to your last address known to the person serving the notice. If there has been any delay in your seeing this notice you may need to act very quickly. If you are in any doubt about what you should do, get advice immediately.

WARNING TO TENANT

IF YOU DO NOT KEEP TO THE TIME LIMITS IN NOTES 3 AND 8 YOU WILL *LOSE* YOUR RIGHT TO APPLY TO THE COURT FOR A NEW TENANCY UNDER THE 1954 ACT OR YOUR RIGHT TO COMPENSATION UNDER THE 1967 ACT.

Validity of this notice

9. The landlord who has given this notice may not be the landlord to whom you pay your rent. "Business" is given a wide meaning in the 1954 Act and is used in the same sense in this notice. The 1954 Act also has rules about the date which the landlord can put in paragraph 3. This depends on the terms of your tenancy. If you have any doubts about whether this notice is valid, get immediate advice.

Explanatory booklets

10. The Department of the Environment booklet "Business Tenancies" explains the provisions of Part II of the 1954 Act in more detail than these notes. The Department of the Environment and Welsh Office booklet "Leasehold Reform" gives details of the rights of leaseholders to claim to buy the freehold or to have an extension to the lease of their house. "Business Tenancies" is available from Her Majesty's Stationery Office or through booksellers. "Leashold Reform" is available from Council Offices and housing aid centres. **[984]**

NOTES

Commencement: 1 April 1983.

FORM 16

LANDLORD'S NOTICE TO TERMINATE BUSINESS TENANCY BY REASON OF THE LOCAL EMPLOYMENT ACT 1972 WHERE LEASEHOLD REFORM ACT 1967 MAY APPLY*

*This form *must* be used (instead of form number 5) if—

(*a*) no previous notice terminating the tenancy has been given under section 25 of the Act; and
(*b*) the tenancy is the tenancy of a house (as defined for the purposes of Part I of the Leashold Reform Act 1967); and
(*c*) the tenancy is a long tenancy at a low rent (within the meaning of that Act of 1967); and
(*d*) the tenant is not a company or other artificial person.

(LANDLORD AND TENANT ACT 1954, SECTIONS 25, 58 AND 60 AND LEASEHOLD REFORM ACT 1967, SCHEDULE 3, PARAGRAPH 10)

To: *(name of tenant)*

of *(address of tenant)*

IMPORTANT—THIS NOTICE IS INTENDED TO BRING YOUR TENANCY TO AN END. READ THE NOTICE AND ALL THE NOTES CAREFULLY. IF YOU ARE IN ANY DOUBT ABOUT THE ACTION YOU SHOULD TAKE, GET ADVICE IMMEDIATELY e.g. FROM A SOLICITOR OR SURVEYOR OR A CITIZENS ADVICE BUREAU.

1. This notice is given under sections 25, 58 and 60 of the Landlord and Tenant Act 1954.

2. You are the tenant of .. ..*(description of property)*

which is situated in a locality which is either—

(*a*) a development area, or
(*b*) an intermediate area.

3. We give you notice terminating your tenancy on .. ..

4. A certificate has been given by the Secretary of State that it is necessary or expedient for the purposes mentioned in section 2(1) of the Local Employment Act 1972 that the use or occupation of the property should be changed. A copy of the certificate is contained in the Schedule to this notice.
(See note 1.)

5. (*a*) If you have a right under the Leasehold Reform Act 1967 to acquire the freehold or an extended lease of the property comprised in the tenancy, notice of your desire to have the freehold or an extended lease cannot be given more than two months after the service of this notice on you.
(See notes 2 to 4.)

(*b*) If you have that right and give such a notice within those two months, *this* notice will not operate.

(*c*) If you give such a notice within those two months—

*[(i) We shall be entitled to apply to the court under section 17 of the Leasehold Reform Act 1967 and we *[propose] [do not propose] to do so.]

*[(ii) We shall not be entitled to apply to the court under section 17 of the Leasehold Reform Act 1967.]

(See notes 4 and 5.)

*[6. The following persons are known or believed by us to have an interest superior to your tenancy or to be the agents concerned with the property on behalf of someone who has such an interest . . . .

. . . .

. . . .]

7. All correspondence about this notice should be sent to *[the landlord] [the landlord's agent] at the address given below.

Date . . . .

Signature of *[landlord] [landlord's agent]

. . . .

Name of landlord . . . .

Address of landlord . . . .

. . . .

. . . .

*[Address of agent . . . .

. . . .

. . . .]

* Cross out words in square brackets if they do not apply.

SCHEDULE

[Insert a copy of the certificate]

NOTES

Termination of tenancy

1. This notice is intended to bring your tenancy to an end. Usually tenants under tenancies to which Part II of the Landlord and Tenant Act 1954 applies can apply to the court for a new tenancy. You cannot do so because the Secretary of State has certified that it is necessary or expedient for achieving the purposes mentioned in section 2(1) of the Local Employment Act 1972 that the use or occupation of the property should be changed. However, the Leasehold Reform Act 1967 may also apply in your case. If it does you may be able to buy the freehold of the property or get an extended lease under *that* Act—see notes 2 and 3 below. If you claim an extended lease your landlord may still be able to get possession of the property—see note 4. If he does, and you have served notice under the 1967 Act, you may be able to get compensation— see note 5 below. If you have any doubt about what you should do, get advice immediately.

Rights under the Leasehold Reform Act 1967

2. If the property comprised in your tenancy is a house, as defined in the 1967 Act, you may have the right to buy the freehold of the property or to extend your lease for fifty years. You can do so if *all* the following conditions are met:—

(i) your lease was originally granted for a term of more than 21 years, or it was preceded by such a lease which was granted or assigned to you; *and*

(ii) your lease is of the whole house; *and*

(iii) your lease is at a low rent. That is, your present annual rent is less than two-thirds of the rateable value of your house as assessed either on 23 March 1965, or on the first day of the term in the case of a lease granted to commence after 23 March 1965; *and*

(iv) you are occupying the house as your only or main residence and you have been doing so either for the whole of the last three years, or for a total of three years during the last ten years under this lease; *and*

(v) the rateable value of your house was at one time within certain limits.

Claiming your rights under the 1967 Act

3. If you do have the right to buy the freehold or to extend the lease and wish to exercise it you must serve the appropriate notice (on a special form prescribed under the Act) on the landlord. You must do so within two months after the date this notice was served to you. The date of service of the notice may not be the date written on the notice or the date on which you actually saw it. It may, for instance, be the date on which the notice was delivered through the post to your last address known to the person serving the notice. If there has been any delay in your seeing this notice you may need to act very quickly. If you are in any doubt get advice immediately.

WARNING TO TENANT

IF YOU DO NOT KEEP TO THE TIME LIMIT IN NOTE 3 YOU WILL *LOSE* YOUR RIGHT TO CLAIM THE FREEHOLD OR AN EXTENDED LEASE UNDER THE 1967 ACT.

Landlord's opposition to claims under the 1967 Act

4. If you claim a fifty year extension of your lease, your landlord can object under section 17 of the 1967 Act on the grounds that he wishes to redevelop the property. Paragraph 5(*c*) of the notice will tell you whether the landlord believes he has the right to apply to the court under section 17 and whether or not he proposes to do so.

Compensation

5. If you have a right under the 1967 Act to buy the freehold or get an extended lease of your premises but the landlord, as mentioned in note 4, is able to obtain possession of the premises, compensation is payable under the 1967 Act. Your solicitor or surveyor will be able to advise you on this.

Negotiations with your landlord

6. Many tenants buy their houses or renew their leases by negotiation. If you do try to buy the property by agreement or to negotiate a new lease with your landlord, remember that you will lose your right to serve a notice claiming to buy the freehold or to have an extended lease under the 1967 Act if you do not keep to the time limit in note 3.

Validity of this notice

7. The landlord who has given this notice may not be the landlord to whom you pay your rent. "Business" is given a wide meaning in the 1954 Act and is used in the same sense in this notice. The 1954 Act also has rules about the date which the landlord can put in paragraph 3. This depends on the terms of your tenancy. If you have any doubts about whether this notice is valid, get immediate advice.

Explanatory booklets

8. The Department of the Environment booklet "Business Tenancies" explains the provisions of Part II of the 1954 Act in more detail than these notes. The Department of the Environment and Welsh Office booklet "Leasehold Reform" gives details of the rights of leaseholders to claim to buy the freehold or to have an extension to the lease of their house. "Business Tenancies" is available from Her Majesty's Stationery Office or through booksellers. "Leasehold Reform" is available from Council Offices and housing aid centres. **[985]**

NOTES

Commencement: 1 April 1983.

FORM 17

LANDLORD'S NOTICE TO TERMINATE BUSINESS TENANCY OF WELSH DEVELOPMENT AGENCY PREMISES WHERE LEASEHOLD REFORM ACT 1967 MAY APPLY*

*This form *must* be used (instead of form number 6) if

(*a*) no previous notice terminating the tenancy has been given under section 25 of the Act; and

(*b*) the tenancy is the tenancy of a house (as defined for the purposes of Part I of the Leasehold Reform Act 1967); and

(*c*) the tenancy is a long tenancy at a low rent (within the meaning of that Act of 1967); and

(*d*) the tenant is not a company or other artificial person.

(LANDLORD AND TENANT ACT 1954, SECTIONS 25, 58 AND 60A AND LEASEHOLD REFORM ACT 1967, SCHEDULE 3, PARAGRAPH 10)

To: *(name of tenant)*

of *(address of tenant)*

IMPORTANT-THIS NOTICE IS INTENDED TO BRING YOUR TENANCY TO AN END. READ THE NOTICE AND ALL THE NOTES CAREFULLY. IF YOU ARE IN ANY DOUBT ABOUT THE ACTION YOU SHOULD TAKE, GET ADVICE IMMEDIATELY e.g. FROM A SOLICITOR OR SURVEYOR OR A CITIZENS ADVICE BUREAU.

1. This notice is given under sections 25, 58 and 60A of the Landlord and Tenant Act 1954.

2. It relates to .. ..*(description of property)*

of which you are the tenant.

3. We give you notice terminating your tenancy on .. ..

4. A certificate has been given by the Secretary of State that it is necessary or expedient, for the purposes of providing employment appropriate to the needs of the area in which the premises are situated, that the use or occupation of the premises should be changed.

(See note 1.)

A copy of the certificate is contained in the Schedule to this notice.

5. (*a*) If you have a right under the Leasehold Reform Act 1967 to acquire the freehold or an extended lease of the property comprised in the tenancy, notice of your desire to have the freehold or an extended lease cannot be given more than two months after the service of this notice on you.

(See notes 2 and 3.)

(*b*) If you have that right and give such a notice within those two months, *this* notice will not operate.

(*c*) If you give such a notice within those two months—

*[(i) We shall be entitled to apply to the court under section 17 of the Leasehold Reform Act 1967 and we *[propose] [do not propose] to do so.]

*[(ii) We shall not be entitled to apply to the court under section 17 of the Leasehold Reform Act 1967.]

(See notes 4 to 7.)

*[6. The following persons are known or believed by us to have an interest superior to your tenancy or to be the agents concerned with the property on behalf of someone who has such an interest . . . .

. . . .

. . . .]

7. All correspondence about this notice should be sent to *[the landlord] [the landlord's agent] at the address given below.

Date . . . .

Signature of *[landlord] [landlord's agent]

. . . .

Name of landlord . . . .

Address of landlord . . . .

. . . .

. . . .

*[Address of agent . . . .

. . . .

. . . .]

* Cross out words in square brackets if they do not apply.

SCHEDULE

[Insert a copy of the certificate]

NOTES

Termination of tenancy

1. This notice is intended to bring your tenancy to an end. Usually tenants under tenancies to which Part II of the Landlord and Tenant Act 1954 applies can apply to the court for a new tenancy. You cannot do so because the Secretary of State has given a certificate under section 60A of the Act that it is necessary or expedient, for the purpose of providing employment appropriate to the needs of the area in which the premises are situated, that the use or occupation of the property should be changed. However, the Leasehold Reform Act 1967 may also apply in your case. If it does, you may be able to buy the freehold of the property or get an extended lease under *that* Act—see notes 2 and 3 below. If you claim an extended lease your landlord may still be able to get possession of the property—see note 4. If he does, you may be able to get compensation. The amount of any compensation (see notes 5 to 7) will depend on the steps you have taken and under which Act (it is likely to be greater under the 1967 Act). If you have any doubt about what you should do, get advice immediately.

Rights under the Leasehold Reform Act 1967

2. If the property comprised in your tenancy is a house, as defined in the 1967 Act, you may have the right to buy the freehold of the property or to extend your lease for fifty years. You can do so if *all* the following conditions are met:—

(i) your lease was originally granted for a term of more than 21 years, or it was preceded by such a lease which was granted or assigned to you; *and*

(ii) your lease is of the whole house; *and*

(iii) your lease is at a low rent. That is, your present annual rent is less than two-thirds of the rateable value of your house as assessed either on 23 March 1965 or on the first day of the term if the case of a lease granted to commence after 23 March 1965; *and*

(iv) you are occupying the house as your only or main residence and you have been doing so either for the whole of the last three years, or for a total of three years during the last ten years under this lease; *and*

(v) the rateable value of your house was at one time within certain limits.

Claiming your rights under the 1967 Act

3. If you do have the right to buy the freehold or to extend the lease and wish to exercise it, you must serve the appropriate notice (on a special form prescribed under the Act) on the landlord. You must do so within two months after the date this notice was served on you. The date of service of the notice may not be the date written on the notice or the date on which you actually saw it. It may, for instance, be the date on which the notice was delivered through the post to your last address known to the person serving the notice. If there has been any delay in your seeing this notice you may need to act very quickly. If you are in any doubt get advice immediately.

WARNING TO TENANT
IF YOU DO NOT KEEP TO THE TIME LIMIT IN NOTE 3 YOU WILL *LOSE* YOUR RIGHT TO CLAIM THE FREEHOLD OR AN EXTENDED LEASE UNDER THE 1967 ACT.

Landlord's opposition to claims under the 1967 Act

4. If you claim a fifty year extension of your lease, your landlord can object under section 17 of the 1967 Act on the grounds that he wishes to redevelop the property. Paragraph 5(*c*) of the notice will tell you whether the landlord believes he has the right to apply to the court under section 17 and whether or not he proposes to do so.

Compensation

5. Because the court cannot order the grant of a new tenancy in your case, you may be entitled to compensation under the 1954 Act when you leave the property. You will *not* be entitled to such compensation if either:

(*a*) the premises were vested in the Welsh Development Agency under section 7 or 8 of the Welsh Development Agency Act 1975; or
(*b*) you were not the tenant of the premises when the Agency acquired the interest by virtue of which the certificate contained in the Schedule was given.

6. You may be entitled to a disturbance payment under Part III of the Land Compensation Act 1973.

7. If you have a right under the 1967 Act to buy the freehold or get an extended lease of your premises but the landlord, as mentioned in note 4 is able to obtain possession of the premises, compensation under the 1967 Act is payable. This is normally higher than the compensation mentioned in note 5 above. Your solicitor or surveyor will be able to advise you on this.

Negotiations with your landlord

8. Many tenants buy their houses or renew their leases by negotiation. If you do try to buy the property by agreement or to negotiate a new lease with your landlord, remember that you will lose your right to serve a notice claiming to buy the freehold or to have an extended lease under the 1967 Act if you do not keep to the time limit in note 3.

Validity of this notice

9. The landlord who has given this notice may not be the landlord to whom you pay your rent. "Business" is given a wide meaning in the 1954 Act and is used in the same sense in this notice. The 1954 Act also has rules about the date which the landlord can put in paragraph 3. This depends on the terms of your tenancy. If you have any doubts about whether this notice is valid, get immediate advice.

Explanatory booklets

10. The Department of the Environment booklet "Business Tenancies" explains the provisions of Part II of the 1954 Act in more detail than these notes. The Department of the Environment and Welsh Office booklet "Leasehold Reform" gives details of the rights of leaseholders to claim to buy freehold or to have an extension to the lease of their house. "Business Tenancies" is available from Her Majesty's Stationery Office or through booksellers. "Leasehold Reform" is available from Council Offices and housing aid centres. **[986]**

NOTES
Commencement: 1 April 1983.

FORM 18

LANDLORD'S NOTICE TO TERMINATE BUSINESS TENANCY OF PREMISES OF THE DEVELOPMENT BOARD FROM RURAL WALES WHERE LEASEHOLD REFORM ACT 1967 MAY APPLY*

*This form *must* be used (instead of form number 7) if—

(*a*) no previous notice terminating the tenancy has been given under section 25 of the Act, and
(*b*) the tenancy is the tenancy of a house (as defined for the purposes of Part I of the Leasehold Reform Act 1967), and
(*c*) the tenancy is a long tenancy at a low rent (within the meaning of that Act of 1967), and
(*d*) the tenant is not a company or other artificial person.

(LANDLORD AND TENANT ACT 1954, SECTIONS 25, 58 AND 60B AND LEASEHOLD REFORM ACT 1967, SCHEDULE 3, PARAGRAPH 10)

To: *(name of tenant)*
of *(address of tenant)*

IMPORTANT—THIS NOTICE IS INTENDED TO BRING YOUR TENANCY TO AN END. READ THE NOTICE AND ALL THE NOTES CAREFULLY. IF YOU ARE IN ANY DOUBT ABOUT THE ACTION YOU SHOULD TAKE, GET ADVICE IMMEDIATELY e.g. FROM A SOLICITOR OR SURVEYOR OR A CITIZENS ADVICE BUREAU.

1. This notice is given under sections 25, 58 and 60B of the Landlord and Tenant Act 1954.

2. It relates to ....*(description of property)*
of which you are the tenant.

3. We give you notice terminating your tenancy on ....

4. A certificate has been given by the Secretary of State that it is necessary or expedient, for the purposes of providing employment appropriate to the needs of the area in which the premises are situated, that the use or occupation of the premises should be changed. A copy of the certificate is contained in the Schedule to this notice.
(See note 1.)

5. (*a*) If you have a right under the Leasehold Reform Act 1967 to acquire the freehold or an extended lease of the property comprised in the tenancy, notice of your desire to have the freehold or an extended lease cannot be given more than two months after the service of this notice on you.
(See notes 2 and 3.)
(*b*) If you have that right and give such a notice within those two months, *this* notice will not operate.
(*c*) If you give such a notice within those two months—
*[(i) We shall be entitled to apply to the court under section 17 of the Leasehold Reform Act 1967 and we *[propose] [do not propose] to do so.]
*[(ii) We shall not be entitled to apply to the court under section 17 of the Leasehold Reform Act 1967.]
(See notes 4 to 7.)

*[6. The following persons are known or believed by us to have an interest superior to your tenancy or to be the agents concerned with the property on behalf of someone who has such an interest ....
....
....]

7. All correspondence about this notice should be sent to *[the landlord] [the landlord's agent] at the address given below.

Date ....

Signature of *[landlord] [landlord's agent]
....

Name of landlord ....

Address of landlord ....
....
....

*[Address of agent ....

....

....]

* Cross out words in square brackets if they do not apply.

SCHEDULE

[Insert a copy of the certificate]

NOTES

Termination of tenancy

1. This notice is intended to bring your tenancy to an end. Usually tenants under tenancies to which Part II of the Landlord and Tenant Act 1954 applies can apply to the court for a new tenancy. You cannot do so because the Secretary of State has given a certificate under section 60B of the Act that it is necessary or expedient, for the purposes of providing employment appropriate to the needs of the area in which the premises are situated, that the use or occupation of the property should be changed. However, the Leasehold Reform Act 1967 may also apply in your case. If it does, you may be able to buy freehold of the property or get an extended lease under *that* Act-see notes 2 and 3 below. If you claim an extended lease your landlord may still be able to get possession of the property—see note 4. If he does, you may be able to get compensation. The amount of any compensation (see notes 5 to 7) will depend on the steps you have taken and under which Act (it is likely to be greater under the 1967 Act). If you have any doubt about what you should do, get advice immediately.

Rights under the Leasehold Reform Act 1967

2. If the property comprised in your tenancy is a house, as defined in the 1967 Act, you may have the right to buy the freehold of the property or to extend your lease for fifty years. You can do so if *all* the following conditions are met:—

(i) your lease was originally granted for a term of more than 21 years, or it was preceded by such a lease which was granted or assigned to you; and
(ii) your lease is of the whole house; and
(iii) your lease is at a low rent. That is, your present annual rent is less two-thirds of the rateable value of your house as assessed either on 23 March 1965 or on the first day of the term in the case of a lease granted to commence after 23 March 1965; and
(iv) you are occupying the house as your only or main residence and you have been doing so either for the whole of the last three years, or for a total of three years during the last ten years under this lease; and
(v) the rateable value of your house was at one time within certain limits.

Claiming your rights under the 1967 Act

3. If you do have the right to buy the freehold or to extend the lease and wish to exercise it you must serve the appropriate notice (on a special form prescribed under the Act) on the landlord. You must do so within two months after the date this notice was served on you. The date of service of the notice may not be the date written on the notice or the date on which you actually saw it. It may, for instance, be the date on which the notice was delivered through the post to your last address known to the person serving the notice. If there has been any delay in your seeing this notice you may need to act very quickly. If you are in any doubt get advice immediately.

WARNING TO TENANT

IF YOU DO NOT KEEP TO THE TIME LIMIT IN NOTE 3 YOU WILL *LOSE* YOUR RIGHT TO CLAIM THE FREEHOLD OR AN EXTENDED LEASE UNDER THE 1967 ACT.

Landlord's opposition to claims under the 1967 Act

4. If you claim a fifty year extension of your lease, your landlord can object under section 17 of the 1967 Act on the grounds that he wishes to redevelop the property. Paragraph 5(*c*) of the notice will tell you whether the landlord believes he has the right to apply to the court under section 17 and whether or not he proposes to do so.

Compensation

5. Because the court cannot order the grant of a new tenancy in your case you may be entitled to compensation under the 1954 Act when you leave the property. You will *not* be entitled to such compensation if either:—

(*a*) the premises are premises which—

(i) were vested in the Welsh Developmet Agency by section 8 of the Welsh Development Agency Act 1975 or were acquired by the Agency when no tenancy subsisted in the premises; and

(ii) subsequently vested in the Development Board for Rural Wales under section 24 of the Development of Rural Wales Act 1976; or

(*b*) you were not a tenant of the premises when the Board acquired the interest by virtue of which the certificate contained in the Schedule was given.

6. You may be entitled to a disturbance payment under Part III of the Land Compensation Act 1973.

7. If you have a right under the 1967 Act to buy the freehold or get an extended lease of your premises but the landlord, as mentioned in note 4, is able to obtain possession of the premises, compensation under the 1967 Act is payable. This is normally higher than the compensation mentioned in note 5 above. Your solicitor or surveyor will be able to advise you on this.

Negotiations with your landlord

8. Many tenants buy their houses or renew their leases by negotiation. If you do try to buy the property by agreement or to negotiate a new lease with your landlord, remember that you will lose your right to serve a notice claiming to buy the freehold or to have an extended lease under the 1967 Act if you do not keep to the time limit in note 3.

Validity of this notice

9. The landlord who has given this notice may not be the landlord to whom you pay your rent. "Business" is given a wide meaning in the 1954 Act and is used in the same sense in this notice. The 1954 Act also has rules about the date which the landlord can put in paragraph 3. This depends on the terms of your tenancy. If you have any doubts about whether this notice is valid, get immediate advice.

Explanatory booklets

10. The Department of the Environment booklet "Business Tenancies" explains the provisions of Part II of the 1954 Act in more detail than these notes. The Department of the Environment and Welsh Office booklet "Leasehold Reform" gives details of the rights of leaseholders to claim to buy the freehold or to have an extension to the lease of their house. "Business Tenancies" is available from Her Majesty's Stationery Office or through booksellers. "Leasehold Reform" is available from Council Offices and housing aid centres. **[987]**

NOTES

Commencement: 1 April 1983.

SCHEDULE 3

Name of Statutory Instrument	Extent of revocation
The Landlord and Tenant (Notices) Regulations 1957 (SI 1957/1157)	Paragraphs (vii) to (xiv) of Regulation 4. Forms 7 to 16 in the Appendix.
The Landlord and Tenant (Notices) Regulations 1963 (SI 1963/795)	The whole Instrument.
The Landlord and Tenant (Notices) Regulations 1967 (SI 1967/1831)	Regulations 6 and 7. Appendix 2.
The Landlord and Tenant (Notices) Regulations 1969 (SI 1969/1771)	The whole Instrument.
The Landlord and Tenant (Notices) Regulations 1973 (SI 1973/792)	The whole Instrument.

[988]

NOTES
Commencement: 1 April 1983.

ASSURED TENANCIES (APPROVED BODIES) (NO 3) ORDER 1983
(SI 1983 NO 364)

NOTES
Made: 8 March 1983
Authority: Housing Act 1980, ss 56(4), 151

1. This order may be cited as the Assured Tenancies (Approved Bodies) (No. 3) Order 1983 and shall come into operation on 12th April 1983. **[989]**

NOTES
Commencement: 12 April 1983.

2. The bodies set out in the Schedule to this order are hereby specified for the purposes of Part II of the Housing Act 1980. **[990]**

NOTES
Commencement: 12 April 1983.

SCHEDULE
BODIES SPECIFIED FOR THE PURPOSES OF PART II OF THE HOUSING ACT 1980

1. Carlton (Hull) Limited.
2. Henry Ibbotson & Son Limited.
3. Long Acre Securities Limited.
4. Stepnell Properties Limited.
5. Terment Limited. **[991]**

NOTES
Commencement: 12 April 1983.

ASSURED TENANCIES (APPROVED BODIES) (NO 4) ORDER 1983
(SI 1983 NO 511)

NOTES
Made: 30 March 1983
Authority: Housing Act 1980, ss 56(4), 151

1. This order may be cited as the Assured Tenancies (Approved Bodies) (No. 4) Order 1983 and shall come into operation on 5th May 1983. **[992]**

NOTES
Commencement: 5 May 1983.

2. The bodies set out in the Schedule to this order are hereby specified or the purposes of Part II of the Housing Act 1980. **[993]**

NOTES
Commencement: 5 May 1983.

SCHEDULE

BODIES SPECIFIED FOR THE PURPOSES OF PART II OF THE HOUSING ACT 1980

1. Leslie M. Barwood & Co. Limited.
2. Clifford Bown & Son Limited.
3. Escadale Properties Limited.
4. Park Road Properties Company Limited.
5. Trimscale Limited. **[994]**

NOTES
Commencement: 5 May 1983.

ASSURED TENANCIES (APPROVED BODIES) (NO 5) ORDER 1983
(SI 1983 NO 840)

NOTES
Made: 9 May 1983
Authority: Housing Act 1980, ss 56(4), 151

1. This order may be cited as the Assured Tenancies (Approved Bodies) (No. 5) Order 1983 and shall come into operation on 15th July 1983. **[995]**

NOTES
Commencement: 15 July 1983.

2. The bodies set out in the Schedule to this order are hereby specified for the purposes of Part II of the Housing Act 1980. **[996]**

NOTES
Commencement: 15 July 1983.

SCHEDULE

BODIES SPECIFIED FOR THE PURPOSES OF PART II OF THE HOUSING ACT 1980

1. Belton Estates Limited.
2. Green Shutters Farm and Estates Limited.
3. London and Mayfair Properties Limited.
4. Mayflower Manhattan Limited. **[997]**

NOTES
Commencement: 15 July 1983.

ASSURED TENANCIES (APPROVED BODIES) (NO 6) ORDER 1983
(SI 1983 NO 1079)

NOTES
Made: 21 July 1983
Authority: Housing Act 1980, ss 56(4), 151

1. This order may be cited as the Assured Tenancies (Approved Bodies) (No.6) Order 1983 and shall come into operation on 24th August 1983. **[998]**

NOTES
Commencement: 24 August 1983.

2. The bodies set out in the Schedule to this order are hereby specified for the purposes of Part II of the Housing Act 1980. **[999]**

NOTES
Commencement: 24 August 1983.

SCHEDULE

BODIES SPECIFIED FOR THE PURPOSES OF PART II OF THE HOUSING ACT 1980

1. Geneens (Properties) Limited.
2. Hawkestone Park Homes Limited.
3. MEPC p.l.c.
4. Zonnia Investments Limited. **[1000]**

NOTES
Commencement: 24 August 1983.

ASSURED TENANCIES (APPROVED BODIES) (NO 7) ORDER 1983

(SI 1983 NO 1375)

NOTES
Made: 6 September 1983
Authority: Housing Act 1980, ss 56(4), 151

1. This order may be cited as the Assured Tenancies (Approved Bodies) (No. 7) Order 1983 and shall come into operation on 11th October 1983. **[1001]**

NOTES
Commencement: 11 October 1983.

2. The bodies set out in the Schedule to this order are hereby specified for the purposes of Part II of the Housing Act 1980. **[1002]**

NOTES
Commencement: 11 October 1983.

SCHEDULE

BODIES SPECIFIED FOR THE PURPOSES OF PART II OF THE HOUSING ACT 1980

1. Alvic Construction (Northern) Limited.
2. Brunswick Manor Limited.
3. Construction (UK) Limited.

4. Stephen Stuart Conway and Phillip George Davies trading as Conway-Davies Investments.

5. . . .

6. Jeffrey Charles Greeves and Susan Elizabeth Greeves trading as Greeves Property Company.

7. Griffon Land and Estates Limited.

8. Ingrow Properties Limited.

9. Leech Homes (Humberside) Limited.

10. Leech Homes (Midlands) Limited.

11. Leech Homes (North East) Limited.

12. Leech Homes (North West) Limited.

13. Leech (Northumbria) Limited.

14. Leech Homes (Scotland) Limited.

15. Leech Homes (Wales) Limited.

16. Leech Homes (Yorkshire) Limited.

17. Nationwide Housing Trust Limited.

18. Pelham Homes Limited.

19. St. James Properties (Newcastle) Limited.

20. . . .

21. Starhomes Builders Limited.

22. Trencherwood Investments Limited.

23. Trident Construction Limited.

24. William Leech Buildings (North West) Limited.

25. William Leech p.l.c. **[1003]**

NOTES

Commencement: 11 October 1983.

First words omitted revoked by SI 1985 No 1311, art 3; amendment in square brackets made by SI 1983 No 1675; second words omitted revoked by SI 1986 No 864, art 2.

ASSURED TENANCIES (APPROVED BODIES) (NO 8) ORDER 1983

(SI 1983 NO 1537)

NOTES

Made: 19 October 1983

Authority: Housing Act 1980, ss 56(4), 151

1. This order may be cited as the Assured Tenancies (Approved Bodies) (No 8) Order 1983 and shall come into operation on 22nd November 1983. **[1004]**

NOTES

Commencement: 22 November 1983.

2. The bodies set out in the Schedule to this order are hereby specified for the purposes of Part II of the Housing Act 1980. **[1005]**

NOTES

Commencement: 22 November 1983.

SCHEDULE

BODIES SPECIFIED FOR THE PURPOSES OF PART II OF THE HOUSING ACT 1980

1. Arkley Investments Limited.

2. Alfred Samuel Bolwell, Peter Alfred David Bolwell and Richard Leighton Hayward trading as Bolwell, Bolwell and Hayward.

3. Alfred Samuel Bolwell, Peter Alfred David Bolwell, Donald Hayward and Richard Leighton Hayward trading as Bolwell and Hayward - County Hall.

4. Peter Alfred David Bolwell and Richard Leighton Hayward trading as Bolwell and Hayward.

5. Brighouse Estate Co. (Contractors) Limited.

6. Broseley Investment Co. Limited.

7. Donald Hayward, Richard Leighton Hayward and Peter Alfred David Bolwell trading as Hayward, Hayward and Bolwell.

8. Kingdomwide Limited.

9. Malthouse Investments Limited.

10. Mid-Cornwall Builders & Contractors Limited.

11. Seddon Estates Limited.

12. Seddon Group Limited.

13. The United Women's Homes Association Limited. **[1006]**

NOTES

Commencement: 22 November 1983.

ASSURED TENANCIES (APPROVED BODIES) (NO 9) ORDER 1983

(SI 1983 NO 1856)

NOTES

Made: 13 December 1983

Authority: Housing Act 1980, ss 56(4), 151

1. This order may be cited as the Assured Tenancies (Approved Bodies) (No. 9) Order 1983 and shall come into operation on 13th January 1984. **[1007]**

NOTES

Commencement: 13 January 1984.

2. The bodies set out in the Schedule to this order are hereby specified for the purposes of Part II of the Housing Act 1980. **[1008]**

NOTES

Commencement: 13 January 1984.

SCHEDULE

BODIES SPECIFIED FOR THE PURPOSES OF PART II OF THE HOUSING ACT 1980

1. Bailey Holdings Limited.

2. Broadgate Builders (Spalding) Limited.

3. Colegrave Group Limited.

4. Costain Homes Limited.

5. Hampton Housing Association Limited.

6. Joseph John Kennedy and Bernard Land trading as Kennedy Land Properties.

7. McCarthy and Stone (Developments) Limited.

8. Strathurst Limited. **[1009]**

NOTES
Commencement: 13 January 1984.

ASSURED TENANCIES (APPROVED BODIES) (NO 1) ORDER 1984
(SI 1984 NO 276)

NOTES
Made: 5 March 1984
Authority: Housing Act 1980, s 56(4)

1. This order may be cited as the Assured Tenancies (Approved Bodies) (No. 1) Order 1984 and shall come into operation on 5th April 1984. **[1010]**

NOTES
Commencement: 5 April 1984.

2. The bodies set out in the Schedule to this order are hereby specified for the purposes of Part II of the Housing Act 1980. **[1011]**

NOTES
Commencement: 5 April 1984.

SCHEDULE
BODIES SPECIFIED FOR THE PURPOSES OF PART II OF THE HOUSING ACT 1980

1. Assured Housing Limited and Richard Jeffrey Smith trading as Assured Housing.

2. Baylight Limited.

3. CCHA/Davis Limited.

4. Coffers Limited.

5. Coventry Churches (Third) Housing Association Limited.

6. Davies General Builders (Estates) Limited.

7. Dringeen (Holdings) Limited.

8. John Martyn Construction Limited.

9. Management Services Limited.

10. Sherbourne (Developments) Limited.

11. St Phillips Garden Properties Ltd.

12. Stanley Robert Williamson, Patricia Ann Williamson and Terence Michael Williamson trading as A C Williamson & Son. **[1012]**

NOTES
Commencement: 5 April 1984.

ASSURED TENANCIES (APPROVED BODIES) (NO 2) ORDER 1984
(SI 1984 NO 638)

NOTES
Made: 1 May 1984
Authority: Housing Act 1980, s 56(4)

1. This order may be cited as the Assured Tenancies (Approved Bodies) (No. 2) Order 1984 and shall come into operation on 2nd June 1984. **[1013]**

NOTES
Commencement: 2 June 1984.

2. The bodies set out in the Schedule to this order are hereby specified for the purposes of Part II of the Housing Act 1980. **[1014]**

NOTES
Commencement: 2 June 1984.

SCHEDULE
BODIES SPECIFIED FOR THE PURPOSES OF PART II OF THE HOUSING ACT 1980

1. Bellway p.l.c.
2. Coniston Real Estates Limited.
3. Kenold (Canterbury).
4. Kenold (Shepperton).
5. Mooney Investments Limited.
6. Northern Estates (Manchester) Limited.
7. North Housing Limited.
8. Orion Developments Limited.
9. J. Properties (Oldham) Limited.
10. Rhodaus Property Company.
11. Rugby Manor Limited.
12. Sloggetts (Properties).
13. Somerlee Homes Limited.
14. South Heath Developments Limited.
15. The Airways Housing Trust Limited.
16. Violet Sills and Alfred John Sills trading as Wellowgate Properties.
17. Wimborne Estates Limited. **[1015]**

NOTES
Commencement: 2 June 1984.

ASSURED TENANCIES (APPROVED BODIES) (NO 3) ORDER 1984
(SI 1984 NO 1312)

NOTES
Made: 14 August 1984
Authority: Housing Act 1980, s 56(4)

1. This order may be cited as the Assured Tenancies (Approved Bodies) (No. 3) Order 1984 and shall come into operation on 15th September 1984. **[1016]**

NOTES
Commencement: 15 September 1984.

2. The bodies set out in the Schedule to this order are hereby specified for the purposes of Part II of the Housing Act 1980. **[1017]**

NOTES
Commencement: 15 September 1984.

SCHEDULE

BODIES SPECIFIED FOR THE PURPOSES OF PART II OF THE HOUSING ACT 1980

1. Abbey Commercial Investments Limited.
2. E. W. Ballard Limited.
3. Buckingham & Sparrow Limited.
4. Forebury Estates Limited.
5. Jephson (Third) Housing Association Limited. **[1018]**

NOTES
Commencement: 15 September 1984.

ASSURED TENANCIES (APPROVED BODIES) (NO 4) ORDER 1984

(SI 1984 NO 1827)

NOTES
Made: 21 November 1984
Authority: Housing Act 1980, s 56(4)

1. This order may be cited as the Assured Tenancies (Approved Bodies) (No. 4) Order 1984 and shall come into operation on 25th December 1984. **[1019]**

NOTES
Commencement: 25 December 1984.

2. The bodies set out in the Schedule to this order are hereby specified for the purposes of Part II of the Housing Act 1980. **[1020]**

NOTES
Commencement: 25 December 1984.

SCHEDULE

BODIES SPECIFIED FOR THE PURPOSES OF PART II OF THE HOUSING ACT 1980

1. Brian Mager Limited.
2. Jack Lunn & Company Limited.
3. Mager Homes Limited.
4. Marchwood Construction (Investment) Company Limited.

5. New Ebor Homes Limited.

6. R. H. Settlement Limited.

7. Robert Hitchins Builders Limited. **[1021]**

NOTES
Commencement: 25 December 1984.

LANDLORD AND TENANT ACT 1954 (APPROPRIATE MULTIPLIER) ORDER 1984
(SI 1984 NO 1932)

NOTES
Made: 11 December 1984
Authority: Landlord and Tenant Act 1954, s 37(8)

1. This Order may be cited as the Landlord and Tenant Act 1954 (Appropriate Multiplier) Order 1984 and shall come into operation on 7th May 1985. **[1022]**

NOTES
Commencement: 7 May 1985.

2. The appropriate multiplier for the purposes of paragraphs (*a*) and (*b*) of section 37(2) of the Landlord and Tenant Act 1954 shall be 3. **[1023]**

NOTES
Commencement: 7 May 1985.

3. The previous instrument made in the exercise of the above-mentioned powers and known as the Landlord and Tenant Act 1954 (Appropriate Multiplier) Regulations 1981 is hereby revoked. **[1024]**

NOTES
Commencement: 7 May 1985.

ASSURED TENANCIES (APPROVED BODIES) (NO 1) ORDER 1985
(SI 1985 NO 812)

NOTES
Made: 21 May 1985
Authority: Housing Act 1980, s 56(4)

1. This order may be cited as the Assured Tenancies (Approved Bodies) (No. 1) Order 1985 and shall come into operation on 2nd July 1985. **[1025]**

NOTES
Commencement: 2 July 1985.

2. The bodies set out in the Schedule to this order are hereby specified for the purposes of Part II of the Housing Act 1980. **[1026]**

NOTES
Commencement: 2 July 1985.

SCHEDULE

BODIES SPECIFIED FOR THE PURPOSES OF PART II OF THE HOUSING ACT 1980

1. Asda Properties Limited.
2. Brightside Securities Limited.
3. Brookhouse Estates Limited.
4. Corlan Retirement Housing Limited.
5. Durkan Bros Limited.
6. M. F. West Properties (Tonbridge) Limited. **[1027]**

NOTES
Commencement: 2 July 1985.

ASSURED TENANCIES (APPROVED BODIES) (NO 2) ORDER 1985
(SI 1985 NO 1312)

NOTES
Made: 9 August 1985
Authority: Housing Act 1980, s 56(4)

1. This order may be cited as the Assured Tenancies (Approved Bodies) (No. 2) Order 1985 and shall come into operation on 19th September 1985. **[1028]**

NOTES
Commencement: 19 September 1985.

2. The bodies set out in the Schedule to this order are hereby specified for the purposes of Part II of the Housing Act 1980. **[1029]**

NOTES
Commencement: 19 September 1985.

SCHEDULE

BODIES SPECIFIED FOR THE PURPOSES OF PART II OF THE HOUSING ACT 1980

1. Acoustic Enclosures Limited.
2. Asset Funding Limited.
3. N. Blake Limited.
4. Business Support Unit Limited.
5. Coastal Counties Home Ownership Limited.
6. Frogmore Estates PLC.
7. Idris Davies Limited.
8. Investment Properties (Luton) Limited.
9. Northern Rock Housing Trust Limited.
10. Park Housing Association Limited.
11. Wates Built Homes (Blakes) Limited.
12. Wates Built Homes Limited.
13. Wates Built Retirement Homes Limited.

14. Wates (Crawley) Limited.
15. Wates Second Land Estates Limited.
16. Wates Second Land Limited.
17. Woodside Lands Estates Limited.
18. Woodside Lands Limited.
19. W.W.R. Housing Company Limited. **[1030]**

NOTES
Commencement: 19 September 1985.

SECURE TENANCIES (RIGHT TO REPAIR SCHEME) REGULATIONS 1985
(SI 1985 NO 1493)

NOTES
Made: 26 September 1985
Authority: Housing Act 1980, s 41A

1. These regulations may be cited as the Secure Tenancies (Right to Repair Scheme) Regulations 1985 and shall come into operation on 1st January 1986. **[1031]**

NOTES
Commencement: 1 January 1986.

2. The scheme for entitling secure tenant to carry out repairs to their dwelling-houses which their landlords are obliged by repairing covenants to carry out and, after carrying out the repairs, to recover sums from their landlords, shall be the scheme set out in the Schedule to these regulations. **[1032]**

NOTES
Commencement: 1 January 1986.

SCHEDULE
HOUSING ACT 1980: SECTION 41A SECURE TENANCIES (RIGHT TO REPAIR) SCHEME 1985

Citation and interpretation

1.—(1) This scheme may be cited as the Secure Tenancies (Right to Repair) Scheme 1985.

(2) In this scheme, unless the context otherwise requires—

"the additional further repair works" has the meaning given by paragraph 20(3), and includes those works as varied by any agreement under paragraph 24;

"the authorised materials" means—

(*a*) in a default case, the materials specified in the tenant's repair claim; and
(*b*) in any other case, the materials authorised by the landlord in accordance with paragraph 7,

as varied by any agreement under paragraph 24;

"default case" means a case to which paragraph 11(2) applies;

"flat" means a separate set of premises, whether or not on the same floor, which—

(*a*) forms part of a building; and
(*b*) is divided horizontally from some other part of that building; and
(*c*) is constructed or adapted for use for the purposes of a dwelling-house;

"the further repair works" has the meaning given by paragraph 14(2), and includes those works as varied by any agreement under paragraph 24;

"the landlord's costs" means the costs (including administrative costs) which, in the landlord's opinion, it would incur, if it were to carry out the landlord's works;

"the landlord's repairing obligation" means the landlord's obligation to its secure tenant under its repairing covenant, in respect of the lack of repair to which the works specified in the tenant's repair claim relate;

"the landlord's works" means the works which, in the landlord's opinion, it would be necessary to carry out in order to fulfil the landlord's repairing obligation using such materials as it considers appropriate;

"qualifying repair" means any repair which the landlord of a secure tenant is obliged by a repairing covenant to carry out, other than a repair to the structure or exterior of a flat;

"the repair works" means—

(*a*) in a default case, the works specified in the tenant's repair claim; and

(*b*) in any other case, those works as approved by the landlord with or without modifications in accordance with paragraph 7,

as varied by any agreement under paragraph 24; and

"the tenant's repair claim" has the meaning given by paragraph 3(1).

(3) Any reference in this scheme to a numbered form shall be construed as a reference to the form bearing that number in Annex A to this scheme, or to a form substantially to the like effect.

(4) Any reference in this scheme to a numbered or lettered ground shall be construed as a reference to the ground bearing that number or that letter in Annex B or, as the case may be, Annex C to this scheme.

(5) Any reference in this scheme to a numbered paragraph shall be construed as a reference to the paragraph bearing that number in this scheme.

(6) Any notice in writing to be served under this scheme may be served by sending it by post.

Entitlement

2. A secure tenant is entitled to carry out a qualifying repair to his dwelling-house and, after carrying out such a repair, to recover a sum from his landlord, subject to and in accordance with the following provisions of this scheme.

Tenant's notice claiming the right to repair

3.—(1) A secure tenant who wishes to carry out a qualifying repair to the dwelling-house of which he is the secure tenant shall serve on his landlord a notice in Form 1 claiming the right to repair ("the tenant's repair claim").

(2) A notice in Form 1 shall contain the following particulars—

(*a*) a description of the works proposed to be carried out and the reasons why they are needed; and

(*b*) a description of the materials proposed to be used.

(3) A notice in Form 1 shall state whether the tenant wishes to carry out all or any of the repair works himself or, as the case may be, to have them carried out by a person named by him.

Landlord's notice in reply to tenant's repair claim

4. Within 21 days of the service on the landlord of the tenant's repair claim, the landlord shall (unless the notice is withdrawn) serve on the tenant either a notice in Form 2 refusing the tenant's repair claim in accordance with paragraphs 5 and 6 or, as the case may be, a notice in Form 3 accepting the tenant's repair claim in accordance with paragraphs 7 and 8.

Grounds for refusal

5.—(1) The landlord shall refuse the tenant's repair claim in any case where any of the grounds set out in Part I of Annex B to this scheme applies.

(2) The landlord may refuse the tenant's repair claim on any one or more of the grounds set out in Part II of Annex B to this scheme.

Landlord's notice refusing tenant's repair claim

6. A landlord's notice in Form 2 refusing the tenant's repair claim shall contain the following particulars—

(*a*) every ground for refusal of the tenant's repair claim, together with an explanation of the landlord's reasons for relying on that ground;
(*b*) where one or more of grounds 1, 4, 5 or 6 is relied on, the amount of the landlord's costs; and
(*c*) where ground 3 is relied on, the landlord's works and the amount of the landlord's costs.

Landlord's acceptance of tenant's repair claim etc.

7.—(1) Where none of the grounds set out in Annex B is relied on by the landlord, the landlord shall—

(*a*) accept the tenant's repair claim;
(*b*) approve the works specified in the tenant's repair claim with or without modifications; and
(*c*) authorise the materials to be used in carrying out the works specified in the tenant's repair claim.

(2) In any of the circumstances described in sub-paragraph (3) below (but not otherwise), the landlord may, in accepting the tenant's repair claim, impose a condition that all or any of the repair works shall be carried out by a person approved by the landlord.

(3) The circumstances referred to in sub-paragraph (2) above are that—

(i) the tenant does not wish to carry out the repair works himself; or
(ii) in the landlord's opinion, the tenant is not likely to carry out the repair works without risk to his safety or that of any other person.

(4) The landlord may impose no condition of acceptance of the tenant's repair claim other than that specified in sub-paragraph (2) above.

Landlord's notice accepting tenant's repair claim

8.—(1) A landlord's notice in Form 3 shall contain the following particulars—

(i) the date before which a claim for payment following the completion of the repair works must be made by the tenant, being a date not less than 3 months after the date of service of such notice;
(ii) the amount of the landlord's costs;
(iii) the amount, which shall be at least 75 per cent. but not more than 100 per cent. of the landlord's costs, which the landlord will pay in the circumstances provided for in paragraph 22; and
(iv) any modifications of the works made, and the materials authorised, under paragraph 7.

(2) Where, in accepting the tenant's repair claim, the landlord imposes the condition specified in paragraph 7(2), the landlord's notice in Form 3 shall specify that condition and the names and addresses of no less than 3 persons approved by the landlord for the purposes of that condition.

Default notice

9.—(1) Where—

(*a*) the landlord has failed to serve on the tenant a notice in Form 2 or Form 3 as required by paragraph 4; or
(*b*) the landlord has served on the tenant a notice in Form 2 as required by paragraph 4, specifying ground 5 or ground 6, but has not carried out the landlord's works within the period specified in that ground,

the tenant may, in any case where the tenant's estimate of the cost to him of carrying out the works specified in the tenant's repair claim, using the materials specified therein, is not more than £200, serve a default notice on the landlord in Form 4.

(2) A default notice in Form 4 shall contain the following particulars—

(*a*) the circumstances in which the tenant is entitled, under sub-paragraph (1) above, to serve the default notice; and
(*b*) the tenant's estimate of the cost to him of carrying out the repair works.

Landlord's response to tenant's default notice

10.—(1) Within 7 days of the service of a default notice in Form 4, the landlord shall (unless the notice is withdrawn) either accept the tenant's repair claim in accordance with paragraph 7 and serve on the tenant a notice in Form 3 or, as the case may be, serve on the tenant a notice in Form 5 refusing the tenant's repair claim and the default notice.

(2) The landlord shall refuse the tenant's repair claim and the default notice where either—

(i) the conditions for serving a default notice have not been fulfilled; or
(ii) any of the grounds in Part I of Annex B to this scheme applies.

(3) The landlord may refuse the tenant's repair claim and the default notice—

(*a*) on any one or more of grounds 4, 7 and 8;
(*b*) on the ground that the landlord intends to carry out the landlord's works within 7 days of service on the tenant of a notice in Form 5; or
(*c*) on the ground that the landlord has served on the tenant a notice in Form 2, specifying ground 5 or ground 6, and the landlord reasonably requires access to the dwelling-house in order to carry out the landlord's works, but the tenant has failed to provide such access, although he has been given a reasonable opportunity to do so.

(4) A notice in Form 5 shall contain the following particulars—

(*a*) every ground for refusal of the tenant's repair claim and the default notice, together with an explanation of the landlord's reasons for relying on that ground;
(*b*) where ground 1, ground 4 or the ground in sub-paragraph (3)(*b*) above is relied on, the amount of the landlord's costs; and
(*c*) where ground 3 is relied on, the landlord's works and the amount of the landlord's costs.

Carrying out of the works by the tenant

11.—(1) Following the service on the tenant of the landlord's notice in Form 3, the tenant may carry out the repair works using the authorised materials and claim payment as provided for in paragraph 12.

(2) Where a tenant has served a default notice on the landlord in Form 4 in accordance with paragraph 9 and either—

(*a*) the landlord has failed to serve a notice on him as provided for in paragraph 10; or
(*b*) the landlord has served on him a notice in Form 5 specifying the ground in paragraph 10(3)(*b*) as a ground for refusal, but has not carried out the landlord's works within the period specified in that ground,

the tenant may carry out the works specified in the tenant's repair claim using the materials specified therein and claim payment as provided for in paragraph 12.

Tenant's claim for payment

12.—(1) Except where sub-paragraph (2) below applies, the tenant's claim for payment shall only be made where, in the tenant's opinion, the repair works have been completed.

(2) This sub-paragraph applies where, after the repair works have been started, it is discovered that the condition of the dwelling-house is such that it is not reasonable for the tenant to proceed further with those works.

(3) The tenant's claim for payment shall be made by serving notice in writing on the landlord—

(*a*) in a case to which paragraph 11(1) applies, before the date specified in the landlord's notice in Form 3, as the date before which the tenant's claim for payment must be made;

(*b*) in a default case, not later than the end of the period of four months beginning with the date of service on the landlord of the tenant's default notice,

or before such later date as the landlord may in any case allow.

(4) The tenant's claim for payment shall contain the following particulars—

(*a*) the costs the tenant has incurred in carrying out the repair works;

(*b*) whether, in the tenant's opinion, the repair works have been completed;

(*c*) where, in the tenant's opinion, the repair works have not been completed, the reason for their not being completed; and

(*d*) whether all or any of the repair works have been carried out by a person other than the tenant and, if so, the name of that person.

(5) For the purposes of sub-paragraph (4) above, any reference to the repair works includes, in a case to which sub-paragraph (2) above applies, a reference to such part of such works as has been completed.

Landlord's notice in reply to tenant's claim for payment

13. Within 21 days of the service on the landlord of the tenant's claim for payment under paragraph 12, the landlord shall serve on the tenant a notice in writing either refusing the tenant's claim for payment in accordance with paragraphs 14 and 15 or, as the case may be, accepting it in accordance with paragraph 22.

Refusal of tenant's claim for payment

14.—(1) The landlord shall refuse the tenant's claim for payment under paragraph 12 where any of the grounds set out in Part I of Annex C to this scheme applies.

(2) Where ground A is relied on, the landlord—

(*a*) shall specify such further works using such materials as the landlord considers reasonably necessary to remedy the inadequacy or the incompleteness of the works that have been carried out ("the further repair works"); and

(*b*) may impose a condition that all or any of the further repair works must be carried out by a person approved by the landlord.

(3) The landlord may refuse the tenant's claim for payment on any one or more of the grounds set out in Part II of Annex C to this scheme.

(4) Where ground D is relied on, the landlord shall specify a date and time at which an inspection of the repair works will take place.

Landlord's notice of refusal of tenant's claim for payment

15. The landlord's notice under paragraph 13 refusing the tenant's claim for payment shall contain the following particulars—

(*a*) every ground for refusal, together with an explanation of the landlord's reasons for relying on that ground;

(*b*) where ground A is relied on, the further repair works and the materials specified under paragraph 14(2)(*a*);

(*c*) where ground D is relied on, the date and time specified under paragraph 14(4);

(*d*) where ground A or D is relied on, the date before which a further claim for payment must be made, being a date not less than 2 months after service of such notice; and

(*e*) where the landlord imposes the condition specified in paragraph 14(2)(*b*), that condition and the names and addresses of no less than 3 persons approved by the landord for the purposes of that condition.

Further repair works

16. Where the landlord's notice in accordance with paragraphs 14 and 15 refusing

the tenant's claim for payment has been served on the tenant specifying ground A as a ground for refusal, the tenant may carry out the further repair works specified in that notice using the materials specified therein.

Tenant's further claim for payment

17.—(1) The tenant's further claim for payment shall only be made where—

(*a*) in a case to which paragraph 16 applies, the tenant has, in his opinion, completed the further repair works or sub-paragraph (2) below applies;

(*b*) in a case where the landlord's notice under paragraph 15 refusing the tenant's claim for payment relied on ground D, an inspection of the repair works has been made.

(2) This sub-paragraph applies where, after the further repair works have been started, it is discovered that the condition of the dwelling-house is such that it is not reasonable for the tenant to proceed further with those works.

(3) The tenant's further claim for payment shall be made by serving notice in writing on the landlord before the date specified in the landlord's notice of refusal of payment in accordance with paragraph 15 or before such later date as the landlord may in any case allow.

(4) The tenant's further claim for payment shall state—

(*a*) in a case to which paragraph 16 applies,

(i) whether, in the tenant's opinion, the further repair works have been completed and, if they have not, the reason for their not being completed;

(ii) whether all or any of the further repair works have been carried out by a person other than the tenant and, if so, the name of that person;

(*b*) in a case where the landlord's notice under paragraph 15 refusing the tenant's claim for payment specified ground D as a reason for refusal, the date on which the inspection of the repair works was made; and

(*b*) the costs the tenant has incurred in carrying out the further repair works.

Landlord's notice in reply to tenant's further claim for payment

18.—(1) Within 21 days of the service on the landlord of the tenant's further claim for payment in accordance with paragraph 17, the landlord shall serve on the tenant a notice in writing either refusing the tenant's further claim for payment in accordance with paragraph 19 or, as the case may be, accepting it in accordance with paragraph 22.

(2) The grounds set out in Annex C to this scheme shall apply to the further repair works as they apply in relation to repair works and accordingly—

(*a*) ground A shall apply as if the reference to paragraph 12(2) were a reference to paragraph 17(2);

(*b*) ground B shall apply as if the reference to paragraph 11 were a reference to paragraph 16;

(*c*) ground C shall apply in relation to the materials specified under paragraph 14(2)(*a*), as it applies to the authorised materials;

(*d*) ground E shall apply in relation to any condition imposed under paragraph 14(2)(*b*), as it applies to a condition imposed under paragraph 7(2); and

(*e*) ground F shall apply in relation to the period specified under paragraph 17(3), as it applies to the period specified in paragraph 12(3).

Landlord's refusal of tenant's further claim for payment

19.—(1) The landlord shall refuse the tenant's further claim for payment under paragraph 17 where ground A or ground B applies in relation to the further repair works.

(2) The landlord may refuse the tenant's further claim for payment—

(*a*) on any one or more of grounds set out in Part II of Annex C to this scheme; or

(*b*) on the ground that no inspection of the repair works has taken place as provided for in paragraph 17(1)(*b*).

Further opportunity for tenant to carry out works and claim for payment

20.—(1) Where the landlord refuses the tenant's further claim for payment under paragraph 19 on ground A, it may, if it thinks fit, give the tenant a further opportunity to complete or, as the case may be, to remedy the inadequacy of the further repair works, using such materials, subject to such conditions and before such date as the landlord may specify.

(2) Where the landlord refuses the tenant's further claim for payment under paragraph 19 on ground D or on the ground specified in sub-paragraph (2)(*b*) of that paragraph, it may, if it thinks fit, give the tenant a further opportunity to provide access for an inspection, at such date and time as the landlord may specify.

(3) Where the landlord gives the tenant a further opportunity to carry out works as provided for in sub-paragraph (1) above, paragraphs 16 to 19 shall apply as if—

(*a*) for the references to the landlord's notice in accordance with paragraphs 14 and 15, there were substituted references to the landlord's notice in accordance with paragraph 21;
(*b*) for the references to further repair works, there were substituted references to the works specified in that notice ("the additional further repair works");
(*c*) for the references to the date specified under paragraph 15(*d*), there were substituted references to the date specified under paragraph 21(*d*); and
(*d*) for the references in paragraph 18(2) to paragraph 14(2)(*a*) and paragraph 14(2)(*b*), there were substituted references to paragraph 20(1).

(4) Where the landlord gives the tenant a further opportunity to provide access for an inspection as provided for in sub-paragraph (2) above, paragraphs 16 to 19 shall apply as if—

(*a*) for the references to the landlord's notice in accordance with paragraphs 14 and 15, there were substituted references to the landlord's notice in accordance with paragraph 21;
(*b*) for the references to the date and time specified under paragraph 15(*c*) there were substituted references to the date and time specified in that notice; and
(*c*) for the references to the date specified under paragraph 15(*d*) were substituted references to the date specified under paragraph 21(*d*).

Landlord's notice of refusal of tenant's further claim for payment

21. The landlord's notice refusing the tenant's further claim for payment under paragraph 19 shall contain the following particulars—

(*a*) every ground for refusal, together with an explanation of the landlord's reasons for relying on that ground;
(*b*) the specification of any works which the tenant is to have an opportunity to carry out under paragraph 20(1) and of any materials, any conditions, and the date specified under that paragraph;
(*c*) the specification of a date and time for any further opportunity for inspection in a case to which paragraph 20(2) applies; and
(*d*) in any case to which sub-paragraph (*b*) or (*c*) above applies, the specification of a date before which any further claim for payment must be made.

Landord's acceptance of tenant's claim for payment or further claim for payment

22.—(1) Where none of the grounds set out in Annex C is relied on by the landlord and paragraph 19(2)(*b*) does not apply, the landlord shall accept the tenant's claim for payment under paragraph 12 or, as the case may be, the tenant's further claim for payment under paragraph 17 (or that paragraph as applied by paragraph 20).

(2) Where the landlord accepts the tenant's claim for payment or, as the case may be, the tenant's further claim for payment and the repair works or, as the case may be, the further repair works or the additional further repair works have been completed, the amount to be paid by the landlord shall be—

(*a*) except where sub-paragraph (2)(*b*) below applies, the amount specified in the landlord's notice in Form 3 as the amount the landlord would pay to the tenant, as modified by any notification in accordance with paragraph 24(3); or
(*b*) in a default case the amount of the costs incurred by the tenant in carrying out the repair works and, as the case may be, the further repair works and the additional further repair works, if any, or £200, whichever is the less.

(3) Where the landlord accepts the tenant's claim for payment or, as the case may be, the tenant's further claim for payment, in a case to which paragraph 12(2) or paragraph 17(2) (or pararaph 17(2) as applied by paragraph 20) applies, the amount to be paid by the landlord shall be—

(*a*) in a case where the landlord accepted the tenant's repair claim by serving a notice in Form 3, whichever is the lesser of the following—

(i) the amount specified in that notice as the amount the landlord would pay, as modified by any notification in accordance with paragraph 24(3); and

(ii) an amount equal to the costs which, in the landlord's opinion, the tenant has reasonably incurred in carrying out those works which he has carried out; and

(*b*) in a default case, an amount equal to the cost which, in the landlord's opinion, the tenant has reasonably incurred in carrying out those works which he has carried out, or £200, whichever is the less.

Payment by the landlord

23.—(1) The landlord may make payment to the tenant in any manner that it thinks fit, except that the landlord may only credit the tenant's rent account in any case where the tenant is in arrears with the rent for his dwelling-house at the date of the payment, and to the extent of the arrears.

(2) The landlord's notice accepting the tenant's claim for payment under paragraph 12 or, as the case may be, the tenant's further claim for payment under paragraph 17 (or that paragraph as applied by paragraph 20) shall contain the following particulars—

(*a*) the amount to be paid;
(*b*) the manner by which payment is to be made; and
(*c*) a date, no later than 14 days after service of such notice, by which payment is to be made, where such payment is not concurrent with the notice.

Variations etc. by agreement

24.—(1) The landlord may at any time agree with the tenant a variation to any of the following—

(*a*) the repair works, the further repair works, or the additional further repair works;
(*b*) the authorised materials, the materials specified under paragraph 14(2) or the materials specified under paragraph 20(1),

and may make its agreement conditional upon the requirement that any such works are carried out by a person approved by the landlord.

(2) The landlord may at any time agree with the tenant—

(*a*) to remove any condition of acceptance of the tenant's repair claim imposed under paragraph 7(2), paragraph 14(2), paragraph 20(1) or under sub-paragraph (1) above;
(*b*) to approve additional persons for the purposes of any condition referred to in sub-paragraph (2)(*a*) above.

(3) Where the landlord agrees any variation under sub-paragraph (1) or (2) above, it shall notify the tenant in writing within 7 days, where appropriate, of any consequent modification to the amount of the landlord's costs or to the amount specified in the landlord's notice in Form 3 as the amount the landlord will pay the tenant.

Suspension of repairing obligation

25.—(1) Where the repair works may be carried out by the tenant in accordance with paragraph 11, the landlord's obligation to its secure tenant under its repairing covenant, in respect of the lack of repair to which the repair works relate, shall cease to apply—

(*a*) from the service of the landlord's notice in Form 3 accepting the tenant's claim; or
(*b*) in a default case, from the date on which the tenant may carry out the repair works as provided for in paragraph 11(2),

until whichever is the earliest of the following—

(i) the service on the landlord of the tenant's claim for payment in accordance with paragraph 12;
(ii) the service on the landlord of notice in writing by the tenant that he does not intend to carry out or to proceed further with the repair works; or
(iii) the expiry of the period during which the tenant's claim for payment must be made in accordance with paragraph 12.

(2) Where the further repair works or the additional further repair works may be carried out in accordance with paragraph 16 (or that paragraph as applied by paragraph 20), the landlord's obligation to its secure tenant under its repairing covenant, in respect of the lack of repair to which the repair works relate, shall cease to apply from the service of the landlord's notice in accordance with paragraphs 14 and 15 or paragraph 21, until whichever is the earliest of the following—

(*a*) the service on the landlord of the tenant's further claim for payment in accordance with paragraph 17 (or that paragraph as applied by paragraph 20);
(*b*) the service on the landlord of notice in writing by the tenant that he does not intend to carry out or to proceed further with the further repair works or, as the case may be, the additional further repair works; or
(*c*) the expiry of the period during which the tenant's further claim for payment must be made in accordance with paragraph 17 (or that paragraph as applied by paragraph 20).

Disputes

26. Any question arising under this scheme may be referred by the landlord or the tenant to and determined by the county court. **[1033]**

NOTES
Commencement: 1 January 1986.

HOUSING

ACT 1980: SECTION 41A SECURE TENANCIES (RIGHT TO REPAIR) SCHEME 1985: ANNEX A

ANNEX A, FORM 1 TENANT'S REPAIR CLAIM, HOUSING ACT 1980, SECTION 41A, ADDED BY THE HOUSING AND BUILDING CONTROL ACT 1984, SECTION 28

Important—you should use this form if you intend to claim the right to repair under the Right to Repair Scheme.

You will not receive any payment under the scheme unless you follow the correct procedure. You can only claim this right if you are a secure tenant of a council or of certain other public bodies (e.g. housing associations and new town corporations).

You will find a full explanation of the scheme in the booklet Right to Repair produced jointly by the Department of the Environment and the Welsh Office. If there is is anything you do not understand you should get advice (for example, from your landlord, a solicitor or a Citizens' Advice Bureau).

To (give landlord's name)

1. Give your name and address.

Name(s) of tenant(s)
Address of property

2. What repair works do you intend to carry out under the scheme? Give details.

What materials do you intend to use? Give details.

NOTE—The landlord may require alterations to the works and materials.

3. Why are the works needed? Give details. (Explain what is wrong with the property).

Tick one box.

4. Do you intend to do all of the works yourself?

Yes If yes, go to section 5.
No

If you do not intend to do all of the works yourself, give the name and address of the person who is to do the works.

Address

Give details of the works which this person is to do.

5. I/We claim the right to repair under the scheme.

Signature(s)

NOTE—To be signed by each tenant or each tenant's agent (someone acting for him). If there are joint tenants then each should sign unless one signs on behalf of the rest with their agreement.

Date

If signed by an agent, give name and address of the agent.

Name
Address

NOTE:—The landlord must serve on the tenant within 21 days of service of this repair claim either a notice (Form 2) refusing this claim or a notice (Form 3) accepting it. **[1034]**

NOTES
Commencement: 1 January 1986.

ANNEX A, FORM 2 NOTICE REFUSING TENANT'S REPAIR CLAIM, HOUSING ACT 1980, SECTION 41A, ADDED BY THE HOUSING AND BUILDING CONTROL ACT 1984, SECTION 28

Important note to tenant—a landlord can only refuse a secure tenant's repair claim for a limited number of reasons. You will find a full explanation in the booklet Right to Repair produced jointly by the Department of the Environment and the Welsh Office. If there is anything you do not understand you should get advice (for example, from your landlord, a solicitor or a Citizens' Advice Bureau).

To (give tenant's name)

1. Give address of property.

Address

Give date written on the tenant's repair claim.

Date

2. On what ground(s) is the claim being refused? Tick appropriate box(es).

1. The landlord's costs would be less than £20.

2. The works specified in the tenant's repair claim do not constitute a qualifying repair.

3. The works specified in the tenant's repair claim, if carried out using the materials specified therein, would not in the landlord's opinion satisfactorily remedy the lack of repair to which they relate.

4. The landlord's costs would be more than £200.

5. The landlord intends to carry out the landlord's works within 28 days of the service on it of the tenant's repair claim. This means the landlord will do the works by/(give date).

6. The works specified in the tenant's repair claim are not, in the landlord's opinion, reasonably necessary for the personal comfort or safety of the tenant or any other person living in the dwelling-house and the landlord intends to carry out the landlord's works within one year of the service on it of the tenant's repair claim, as part of a planned programme of repair or maintenance. This means the landlord will do the works by/(give date).

7. Carrying out the works specified in the tenant's repair claim would infringe the terms of any guarantee of which the landlord has the benefit in respect of any work already done or materials supplied.

8. The landlord reasonably requires access to the dwelling-house in order to inspect the site of the works specified in the tenant's repair claim but the tenant has failed to provide such access, although he has been given a reasonable opportunity to do so by the landlord.

3. Explain why each ground is used.

4. If ground(s) 1, 3, 4, 5 or 6 is used, how much will it cost the landlord to put right what is wrong with the property (including administrative costs)? Give estimate of costs. £

If ground 3 is used, what works and materials does the landlord consider would be necessary to put right what is wrong with the property? Give details.

5. The landlord refuses the tenant's repair claim.

Signed on behalf of the landlord

Office held

Landlord's name

Date

NOTE TO TENANT—If the landlord has refused your claim on ground 5 or ground 6, but the work is not then carried out in the time stated, you may be entitled to serve a default notice—see the Right to Repair booklet for a fuller explanation.

If you disagree with the landlord's reasons for refusal, seek advice (e.g. from a solicitor or a Citizens' Advice Bureau). **[1035]**

NOTES

Commencement: 1 January 1986.

ANNEX A, FORM 3 NOTICE ACCEPTING TENANT'S REPAIR CLAIM, HOUSING ACT 1980, SECTION 41A, ADDED BY THE HOUSING AND BUILDING CONTROL ACT 1984, SECTION 28

Important note to tenant—you will find a full explanation of the Right to Repair Scheme in the booklet produced jointly by the Department of the Environment and the Welsh Office. If there is anything you do not understand you should get advice (for example, from your landlord, a solicitor or a Citizens' Advice Bureau).

To (give tenant's name)

1. Give address of property.

Address

Give date written on the tenant's repair claim.

Date

2. Must the tenant use an approved person for any part of the works?

Tick one box.

No If no, go to section 3

Yes

If yes, you must specify three approved persons. Give names and addresses.

Name of approved person

Address

Name of approved person

Address

Name of an approved person

Address

NOTE TO TENANT—If you do not intend to do the works yourself or if the landlord thinks you are not likely to carry out the works safely, the landlord may accept your repair claim on condition that the works are done by a person approved by the landlord. In such a case, if you still intend to do the works under the Right to Repair Scheme you must use one of these persons.

Name of approved person

Address

For which part of the works must the approved person be used? Give details.

3. Do you approve the works specified in the tenant's repair claim without modification?

Tick one box.

Yes

No

If not, what changes are required? Give details.

4. Do you authorise the materials specified in the tenant's repair claim?

Tick one box.

Yes

No

If not, what materials do you authorise? Give details

NOTE TO TENANT—If you still intend to do the works under the Right to Repair Scheme you must do the works as modified by the landlord and use the materials authorised by the landlord.

5. How much would it cost you to put right what is wrong with the property (including administrative costs)?

£

6. How much will you pay the tenant if he carries out the repair works under the Right to Repair Scheme?

£

NOTE—This amount must be between 75% and 100% of the amount given in section 5 above.

7. What is the latest date before which the tenant should claim payment?

Date

NOTE—The tenant must have at least three months after service of the notice to do the work and to claim payment. The date of service of the notice might not be the date written on it. For a fuller explanation see the Right to Repair booklet.

NOTE TO TENANT—If you do not claim payment before this date, the landlord need not pay you under the Right to Repair Scheme, unless the landlord has agreed to an extension of time.

8. The landlord accepts the tenant's repair claim.

Signed on behalf of the landlord

Office held

Landlord's name

Date

IMPORTANT NOTE TO TENANT

The landlord is not responsible to you under its repairing obligations in respect of the lack of repair to which the works relate from the date this notice is served until

(*a*) *you notify the landlord that you do not intend to proceed with the works, or*
(*b*) *you serve on the landlord a notice claiming payment for the works, or*

(*c*) *the time for claiming payment runs out-see section 7 of this notice.*

This means that you may be liable for any damage that may be caused meanwhile, even if the damage only becomes apparent later.

You should check your insurance position carefully.

If you decide not to carry out the works under the Right to Repair Scheme, you should write to your landlord at once saying so. **[1036]**

NOTES

Commencement: 1 January 1986.

ANNEX A, FORM 4 RIGHT TO REPAIR DEFAULT NOTICE, HOUSING ACT 1980, SECTION 41A, ADDED BY THE HOUSING AND BUILDING CONTROL ACT 1984, SECTION 28

Important—you should use this form if you have claimed a right to repair under the Right to Repair Scheme and:

(*a*) *your landlord has not replied to your repair claim within 21 days of its service; or*
(*b*) *your landlord has not carried out the repair works by the date set out in its notice refusing your repair claim*

and you intend to do the works yourself or arrange for them to be done.

The estimated cost to you of the works must not be more than £200. You must not start the works until you have allowed the landlord 7 days after the service of this notice to reply. The date of service might not be the date on which you send the notice. For further information see the Right to Repair booklet.

To (give landlord's name)

1. Give your name and address.

Name(s) of tenant(s)

Address of property

2. Give date written on your repair claim.

Date

If you have a copy of your repair claim (Form 1) attach it to this form.

3. Why are you serving this notice? Tick one box.

Your landlord has not replied to your repair claim within 21 days.

Your landlord said it would carry out the landlord's works within 28 days or within 1 year but has not done so.

4 How much do you estimate the works will cost you? (The estimate must not be more than £200). Give estimate.

£

IMPORTANT NOTE

After 7 days from service of this notice you may start the works (provided your landlord has not replied in the meantime).

From that date the landlord will not be responsible to you under the landlord's repairing obligations in respect of the lack of repair to which the works specified in your repair claim relate. This will last until you claim payment or you run out of time for claiming payment (see note at foot of page) or until you tell the landlord that you withdraw your repair claim.

This means that you may be liable for any damage that may be caused in the meanwhile, even if the damage only becomes apparent later.

You should check your insurance position carefully.

5. I/We serve this right to repair default notice.

Signature(s)

NOTE—To be signed by each tenant or each tenant's agent (someone acting for him). If there are joint tenants then each must sign unless one signs on behalf of the rest with their agreement.

Date

If signed by an agent, give name and address of the agent.

Address

NOTE—If you do not claim payment within 4 months of the service of this notice, or within such later period which may be agreed by the landlord, the landlord need not pay you under the Right to Repair Scheme. Different rules may apply if the landlord replies to this notice—see the Right to Repair booklet for a fuller explanation. If you decide not to carry out the works under the Right to Repair Scheme, you should write to your landlord at once saying so.
[1037]

NOTES

Commencement: 1 January 1986.

ANNEX A, FORM 5 REFUSAL OF RIGHT TO REPAIR DEFAULT NOTICE, HOUSING ACT 1980, SECTION 41A, ADDED BY THE HOUSING AND BUILDING CONTROL ACT 1984, SECTION 28

Important note to tenant—a landlord can only refuse a secure tenant's default notice for a limited number of reasons. You will find a full explanation in the booklet Right to Repair.

To/(give tenant's name)

1. Give address of the property.

Address

Give date written in section 5 of the default notice.

Date

2. On what ground(s) is the default notice being refused? Tick appropriate box(es).

Grounds in Annex B of the Right to Repair Scheme

1. The landlord's costs would be less than £20.

2. The works specified in the tenant's repair claim do not constitute a qualifying repair.

3. The works specified in the tenant's repair claim, if carried out using the materials specified therein, would not in the landlord's opinion satisfactorily remedy the lack of repair to which they relate.

4. The landlord's costs would be more than £200.

(Grounds 5 and 6 may not be used to refuse a default notice.)

7. Carrying out the works specified in the tenant's repair claim would infringe the terms of any guarantee of which the landlord has the benefit in respect of any work already done or materials supplied.

8. The landlord reasonably requires access to the dwelling-house in order to inspect the site of the works specified in the tenant's repair claim, but the tenant has failed to provide such access, although he has been given a reasonable opportunity to do so by the landlord.

Additional grounds for refusal

9. The landlord intends to carry out the landlord's works within 7 days of the service of this notice.

10. The landlord has served on the tenant a notice in Form 2, specifying ground 5 or ground 6, and the landlord reasonably requires access to the dwelling-house in order to carry out the landlord's works, but the tenant has failed to give such access, although he has been given a reasonable opportunity to do so.

11. The conditions for serving a default notice have not been fulfilled.

3. Explain why each ground is used. Give details.

4. If ground(s) 1, 3, 4 or 9 is used how much would it cost the landlord to put right what is wrong with the property (including administrative costs)? Give estimate.

£

If ground 3 is used, what works and materials does the landlord consider would be necessary to put right what is wrong with the property? Give details.

5. The landlord refuses the tenant's right to repair default notice and repair claim.

Signed on behalf of the landlord

Office held

Landlord's name

Date

IMPORTANT NOTE TO TENANT

If the landlord has refused your default notice on ground 9 but has not carried out the works within 7 days of the service of this notice, you may carry out the works and claim payment from the landlord within 4 months of the service of the default notice on the landlords. You cannot normally claim more than £200 and you should check your insurance position carefully.

From the date you may start the works the landlord will not be responsible to you under the landlord's repairing obligations in respect of the lack of repair to which the works specified in your repair claim relate. This will last until you claim payment or you run out of time for claiming payment or until you tell the landlord that you withdraw your repair claim. This means that you may be liable for any damage that may be caused in the meanwhile, even if the damage only becomes apparent later. If you decide not to carry out the works under the Right to Repair Scheme, you should write to your landlord at once saying so.

If you disagree with the landlord's reasons for refusing your default claim, you should seek advice (e.g. from a solicitor or a Citizens' Advice Bureau). **[1038]**

NOTES

Commencement: 1 January 1986.

HOUSING ACT 1980: SECTION 41A SECURE TENANCIES (RIGHT TO REPAIR) SCHEME 1985: ANNEX B

ANNEX B, PART I MANDATORY GROUNDS OF REFUSAL OF TENANT'S CLAIM

Ground 1

The landlord's costs would be less than £20.

Ground 2

The works specified in the tenant's repair claim do not constitute a qualifying repair.

Ground 3

The works specified in the tenant's repair claim, if carried out using the materials specified therein, would not in the landlord's opinion satisfactorily remedy the lack of repair to which they relate. **[1039]**

NOTES

Commencement: 1 January 1986.

ANNEX B, PART II DISCRETIONARY GROUNDS FOR REFUSAL OF TENANT'S CLAIM

Ground 4

The landlord's costs would be more than £200.

Ground 5

The landlord intends to carry out the landlord's works within 28 days of the service on it of the tenant's repair claim.

Ground 6

The works specified in the tenant's repair claim are not, in the landlord's opinion, reasonably necessary for the personal comfort or safety of the tenant or any other person living in the dwelling-house and the landlord intends to carry out the landlord's works, within one year of the service on it of the tenant's repair claim, as part of a planned programme of repair or maintenance.

Ground 7

Carrying out the works specified in the tenant's repair claim would infringe the terms of any guarantee of which the landlord has the benefit in respect of any work already done or materials supplied.

Ground 8

The landlord reasonably requires access to the dwelling-house in order to inspect the site of the works specified in the tenant's repair claim but the tenant has failed to provide such access, although he has been given a reasonable opportunity to do so by the landlord. **[1040]**

NOTES
Commencement: 1 January 1986.

HOUSING

ACT 1980: SECTION 41A SECURE TENANCIES (RIGHT TO REPAIR) SCHEME 1985: ANNEX C

ANNEX C, PART I MANDATORY GROUNDS FOR REFUSAL OF TENANT'S CLAIM FOR PAYMENT

Ground A

The repair works have not been properly carried out or (except in a case to which paragraph 12(2) applies) the repair works have not been completed.

Ground B

The tenant was not entitled to carry out the repair works under the provisions of paragraph 11. **[1041]**

NOTES
Commencement: 1 January 1986.

ANNEX C, PART II DISCRETIONARY GROUNDS FOR REFUSAL OF TENANT'S CLAIM FOR PAYMENT

Ground C

The authorised materials have not been used.

Ground D

The landlord reasonably requires access to the dwelling-house in order to inspect the site of the repair works, but the tenant has failed to provide such access, although he has been given a reasonable opportunity to do so by the landlord.

Ground E

A condition of acceptance of the tenant's repair claim was imposed under paragraph 7 and the repair works have not been carried out by a person approved by the landlord.

Ground F

The tenant's claim for payment was not served on the landlord within the period specified in paragraph 12(3). **[1042]**

NOTES
Commencement: 1 January 1986.

PROTECTED TENANCIES (EXCEPTIONS) REGULATIONS 1986
(SI 1986 NO 541)

NOTES
Made: 4 March 1986
Authority: Rent Act 1977, s 8

ARRANGEMENT OF REGULATIONS

Regulation		Para
1	Citation and operation	[1043]
2	Revocations	[1044]
3	Specified educational institutions	[1045]
4	Specified bodies	[1046]
	Schedule—*Specified Bodies under Regulation 4(c)*	[1047]

1. Citation and operation

These Regulations may be cited as the Protected Tenancies (Exceptions) Regulations 1986 and shall come into operation on 1st May 1986. **[1043]**

NOTES
Commencement: 1 May 1986.

2. Revocations

. . . **[1044]**

NOTES
Commencement: 1 May 1986.
This regulation revokes the Protected Tenancies (Exceptions) Regulations 1974, SI 1974 No 1366, the Protected Tenancies (Further Exceptions) Regulations 1976, SI 1976 No 905 and the Further Education Regulations 1975, SI 1975 No 1054.

3. Specified educational institutions

The following institutions are hereby specified as educational institutions for the purposes of section 8 of the Rent Act 1977 (lettings to students), that is to say—

(*a*) any university or university college and any constituent college, school or hall or other institution of a university;

(*b*) any establishment of further education which is provided or assisted by a local education authority or in respect of the maintenance of which grants are for the time being paid in pursuance of regulations made under section 100(1)(*b*) of the Education Act 1944;

(*c*) the David Game Tutorial College, London. **[1045]**

NOTES

Commencement: 1 May 1986.

4. Specified bodies

The following bodies of persons (whether unincorporated or bodies corporate) are hereby specified as bodies for the purposes of section 8 of the Rent Act 1977 that is to say—

(*a*) the governing body of any educational institution specified in Regulation 3 above;

(*b*) the body, other than a local education authority, providing any such educational institution, and

(*c*) a body listed in the Schedule to these Regulations. **[1046]**

NOTES

Commencement: 1 May 1986.

SCHEDULE

SPECIFIED BODIES UNDER REGULATION 4(*c*)

Birmingham Friendship Housing Association

Bishop Creighton House, London

Carrs Lane Church Centre, Birmingham

Hamtun Housing Association Limited, Southampton

Hull Students Welfare Association

International Students Housing Society, Woolwich

International Students Trust, London

Leicester University Students Union

London House for Overseas Graduates, London

Oxford Overseas Student Housing Association Limited

Oxford Polytechnic Housing Association Limited

St Thomas More Housing Society Limited, Oxford

Student Homes Limited, London

Victoria League for Commonwealth Friendship, London

Wandsworth Students Housing Association Limited

York Housing Association Limited **[1047]**

NOTES

Commencement: 1 May 1986.

ASSURED TENANCIES (APPROVED BODIES) (NO 1) ORDER 1986
(SI 1986 NO 866)

NOTES
Made: 15 May 1986
Authority: Housing Act 1980, s 56(4)

1. This order may be cited as the Assured Tenancies (Approved Bodies) (No. 1) Order 1986 and shall come into operation on 21st June 1986. **[1048]**

NOTES
Commencement: 21 June 1986.

2. The bodies mentioned in the Schedule to this order are hereby specified for the purposes of Part II of the Housing Act 1980. **[1049]**

NOTES
Commencement: 21 June 1986.

SCHEDULE
BODIES SPECIFIED FOR THE PURPOSES OF PART II OF THE HOUSING ACT 1980

1. Corlan Co-operative Housing Association Limited.
2. North British Urban Renewal Limited.
3. The Elim Trust Corporation. **[1050]**

NOTES
Commencement: 21 June 1986.

ASSURED TENANCIES (APPROVED BODIES) (NO 2) ORDER 1986
(SI 1986 NO 1209)

NOTES
Made: 10 July 1986
Authority: Housing Act 1980, s 56(4)

1. This order may be cited as the Assured Tenancies (Approved Bodies) (No. 2) Order 1986 and shall come into operation on 11th August 1986. **[1051]**

NOTES
Commencement: 11 August 1986.

2. The bodies named in the Schedule to this order are hereby specified for the purposes of Part II of the Housing Act 1980. **[1052]**

NOTES
Commencement: 11 August 1986.

SCHEDULE
BODIES SPECIFIED FOR THE PURPOSES OF PART II OF THE HOUSING ACT 1980

1. Domus Services Limited.

2. Fairlake Housing Association Limited.
3. Idris Davies Holdings Limited.
4. Milton Keynes Housing Association Limited.
5. North Housing Association Limited.
6. Orbit Housing Society Limited.
7. S. B. & C. Developments Limited.
8. WSJ (Holdings) Limited. **[1053]**

NOTES
Commencement: 11 August 1986.

ASSURED TENANCIES (APPROVED BODIES) (NO 3) ORDER 1986
(SI 1986 NO 1729)

NOTES
Made: 2 October 1986
Authority: Housing Act 1980, s 56(4)

1. This order may be cited as the Assured Tenancies (Approved Bodies) (No 3) Order 1986 and shall come into operation on 4th November 1986. **[1054]**

NOTES
Commencement: 4 November 1986.

2. The bodies named in the Schedule to this order are hereby specified for the purposes of Part II of the Housing Act 1980. **[1055]**

NOTES
Commencement: 4 November 1986.

SCHEDULE
BODIES SPECIFIED FOR THE PURPOSES OF PART II OF THE HOUSING ACT 1980

1. Battlebridge Basing Housing Association Limited.
2. C.S.M. Properties Limited.
3. Great Linford Housing Association Limited.
4. Kensington Housing Association Limited.
5. Local Housing Services Limited.
6. Mersea Housing Association Limited.
7. Nimbus Limited.
8. Unihab Limited. **[1056]**

NOTES
Commencement: 4 November 1986.

LANDLORD AND TENANT ACT 1954, PART II (ASSURED TENANCIES) (NOTICES) REGULATIONS 1986
(SI 1986 NO 2181)

NOTES
Made: 10 December 1986
Authority: Landlord and Tenant Act 1954, s 66; Housing Act 1980, s 58(2)

ARRANGEMENT OF REGULATIONS

Regulation	Para
1	[1057]
2	[1058]
3	[1059]
4	[1060]
Schedule—	
Form A Landlord's Notice to Terminate Assured Tenancy	[1061]
Form B Tenant's Request for New Assured Tenancy	[1062]
Form C Withdrawal of Landlord's Notice to Terminate Assured Tenancy ..	[1063]

1. These regulations may be cited as the Landlord and Tenant Act 1954, Part II (Assured Tenancies) (Notices) Regulations 1986 and shall come into operation on 7th January 1987. **[1057]**

NOTES
Commencement: 7 January 1987.

2. In these regulations "the Act" means the Landlord and Tenant Act 1954. **[1058]**

NOTES
Commencement: 7 January 1987.

3. The forms prescribed for the purposes of the Act in respect of assured tenancies shall be as follows:—

(i) for a notice by a landlord terminating a tenancy under section 25 of the Act, the form set out as Form A in the Schedule to these regulations;

(ii) for a notice by a tenant to request a new tenancy under section 26 of the Act, the form set out as Form B in the Schedule to these regulations; and

(iii) for a notice under section 44 of and paragraph 6 of Schedule 6 to the Act, being a notice withdrawing a previous notice terminating a tenancy given under section 25 of the Act, the form set out as Form C in the Schedule to these regulations;

or in each case a form substantially to the like effect. **[1059]**

NOTES
Commencement: 7 January 1987.
The Act: Landlord and Tenant Act 1954.

4. (1) . . .

(2) Nothing in these regulations shall affect the validity of any notice served before 7th May 1987 if the notice was in the form prescribed by the regulations mentioned in paragraph (1) above or in a form substantially to the like effect. **[1060]**

NOTES
Commencement: 7 January 1987.
Para (1): revokes SI 1983 No 132.

SCHEDULE

FORM A LANDLORD'S NOTICE TO TERMINATE ASSURED TENANCY

(Landlord and Tenant Act 1954, section 25; Housing Act 1980, sections 56-58 and Schedule 5, as amended by the Housing and Planning Act 1986, sections 12-13)

To: (name of tenant) of (address of tenant)

IMPORTANT—THIS NOTICE IS INTENDED TO BRING YOUR TENANCY TO AN END. IF YOU WANT TO STAY IN YOUR HOME YOU MUST ACT QUICKLY. READ THE NOTICE AND ALL THE NOTES CAREFULLY. IF YOU ARE IN ANY DOUBT ABOUT THE ACTION YOU SHOULD TAKE, GET ADVICE IMMEDIATELY e.g. FROM A SOLICITOR OR A CITIZENS ADVICE BUREAU.

1. This notice is given under section 25 of the Landlord and Tenant Act 1954.

2. It relates to .. .. (description of property) of which you are the tenant.

3. I/we give you notice terminating your tenancy on .. ..

See notes 1 and 7.

4. If you are not willing to give up possession of the property comprised in the tenancy on the date stated in paragraph 3, you must notify me/us in writing within two months after the giving of this notice.

See notes 2 and 3.

5.* If you apply to the court under Part II of the Landlord and Tenant Act 1954 for the grant of a new tenancy, I/we will not oppose your application.

*The landlord must cross out one version of paragraph 5. If the second version is used the paragraph letter(s) must be filled in. See notes 4 and 5.

OR

5.* If you apply to the court under Part II of the Landlord and Tenant Act 1954 for the grant of a new tenancy, I/we will oppose it on the grounds mentioned in paragraph(s) .. .. of section 30(1) of that Act.

6. All correspondence about this notice should be sent to** [the landlord] [the landlord's agent] at the address given below.

**Cross out words in square brackets if they do not apply.

Date .. ..
Signature of*[landlord] [landlord's agent] .. ..
Name of landlord .. ..
Address of landlord .. ..
*[Address of agent .. ..
.. ..]

NOTES

Termination of tenancy

1. This notice is intended to bring your tenancy to an end. You can apply to the court for a new tenancy under the Landlord and Tenant Act 1954 by following the procedure outlined in notes 2 and 3 below. If you do, your tenancy will continue after the date shown in paragraph 3 of this notice while your claim is being considered. The landlord can ask the court to fix the rent which you will have to pay while the tenancy continues. The terms of any *new* tenancy not agreed between you and the landlord will be settled by the court.

Claiming a new tenancy

2. If you want to apply to the court for a new tenancy you must:—

(1) notify the landlord in writing not later than 2 months after the giving of this notice that you are not willing to leave your home;

AND

(2) apply to the County Court, not earlier than 2 months nor later than 4 months after the giving of this notice, for a new tenancy.

3. The time limits in note 2 run from the giving of the notice. The date of the giving of the notice may not be the date written on the notice or the date on which you actually saw it. It may, for instance, be the date on which the notice was delivered through the post to your last address known to the person giving the notice. If there has been any delay in your seeing this notice you may need to act very quickly. If you are in any doubt get advice immediately.

WARNING TO TENANT
IF YOU DO NOT KEEP TO THE TIME LIMITS IN NOTE 2. YOU WILL *LOSE* YOUR RIGHT TO APPLY TO THE COURT FOR A NEW TENANCY.

Landlord's opposition to claim for a new tenancy

4. If you apply to the court for a new tenancy, the landlord can only oppose your application on one or more of the grounds set out in section 30(1) of the 1954 Act. These grounds are set out below. The paragraph letters are those given in the Act. The landlord can only use a ground if its paragraph letter is shown in paragraph 5 of the notice.

Grounds

(*a*) where under the current tenancy the tenant has any obligations as respects the repair and maintenance of the holding, that the tenant ought not to be granted a new tenancy in view of the state of repair of the holding, being a state resulting from the tenant's failure to comply with the said obligations;

(*b*) that the tenant ought not to be granted a new tenancy in view of his persistent delay in paying rent which has become due;

(*c*) that the tenant ought not to be granted a new tenancy in view of other substantial breaches by him of his obligations under the current tenancy, or for any other reason connected with the tenant's use or management of the holding;

(*d*) that the landlord has offered and is willing to provide or secure the provision of suitable alternative accommodation for the tenant;
(The 1954 Act as applied by the 1980 Act lays down detailed rules about what accommodation is "suitable". In brief it must give comparable security of tenure and be reasonably suited to the means and needs of the tenant and his family.)

(*e*) where the current tenancy was created by the sub-letting of part only of the property comprised in a superior tenancy and the landlord is the owner of an interest in reversion expectant on the termination of that superior tenancy, that the aggregate of the rents reasonably obtainable on separate lettings of the holding and the remainder of that property would be substantially less than the rent reasonably obtainable on a letting of that property as a whole, that on the termination of the current tenancy the landlord requires possession of the holding for the purposes of letting or otherwise disposing of the said property as a whole, and that in view thereof the tenant ought not to be granted a new tenancy;

(*f*) that on the termination of the current tenancy the landlord intends to demolish or reconstruct the premises comprised in the holding or a substantial part of those premises or to carry out substantial work of construction on the holding or part thereof and that he could not reasonably do so without obtaining possession of the holding;
(If the landlord uses this ground, the court can sometimes still grant a new tenancy if certain conditions set out in section 31A of the Act can be met.)

(*g*) that on termination of the current tenancy the landlord intends to occupy the holding for the purposes, or partly for the purposes, of a business to be carried on by him therein, or as his residence.
(The landlord must normally have been the landlord for at least five years to use this ground.)

Compensation

5. If you cannot get a new tenancy solely because grounds (*e*), (*f*), or (*g*) apply, you are entitled to compensation under the 1954 Act. If your landlord has opposed your application on any of the other grounds as well as (*e*), (*f*), or (*g*) you can only get

compensation if the Court's refusal to grant a new tenancy is based solely on grounds (*e*), (*f*) or (*g*). In other words you cannot get compensation under the 1954 Act if the court has refused your tenancy on *other* grounds even if (*e*), (*f*) or (*g*) also apply.

Negotiating a new tenancy

6. Most leases are renewed by negotiation. If you do try to agree a new tenancy with your landlord, remember—

(1) that your present tenancy will not be extended after the date in paragraph 3 of this notice unless you *both*

(*a*) give written notice that you will not leave your home (see note 2(1) above); *and*
(*b*) apply to the court for a new tenancy (note 2(2) above);

(2) that your will lose your right to apply to the court if you do not keep to the time limits in note 2.

Validity of this notice

7. The landlord who has given this notice may not be the landlord to whom you pay your rent. The 1954 Act has rules about who can serve this notice and also about the date which the landlord can put in paragraph 3. This depends on the terms of your tenancy. If you have any doubts about whether this notice is valid, get immediate advice.

Assured tenancies

8. Assured tenancies are residential tenancies under the Housing Act 1980 as amended by the Housing and Planning Act 1986. Assured tenancies can be granted only by landlords approved by the Secretary of State. The property must either—

(1) be newly built (building work must have started on or after 8th August 1980) and must not have been occupied as a residence at any time except under an assured tenancy, or

(2) have been subject to "qualifying works". These are works which: were carried out while the property was empty or in non-residential use; were carried out within 2 years preceding the first letting on an assured tenancy; and which did not cost less than a minimum amount, prescribed by order. The property must also be fit for human habitation when first let on an assured tenancy.

There are certain other conditions which must also be fulfilled.

9. The rules that apply to assured tenancies are a modified version of those applying to business tenancies under Part II of the Landlord and Tenant Act 1954. (Further information about assured tenancies is given in the Department of the Environment and Welsh Office booklet "Assured Tenancies", obtainable free from rent offices, council offices and housing aid centres). **[1061]**

NOTES
Commencement: 7 January 1987.

FORM B TENANT'S REQUEST FOR NEW ASSURED TENANCY

(Landlord and Tenant Act 1954, section 26; Housing Act 1980, sections 56-58 and Schedule 5, as amended by the Housing and Planning Act 1986, sections 12-13)

To: (name of landlord) of (address of landlord)

IMPORTANT—THIS IS A REQUEST FOR A NEW TENANCY OF YOUR PROPERTY OR PART OF IT. IF YOU WANT TO OPPOSE THIS REQUEST YOU MUST ACT QUICKLY. READ THE REQUEST AND ALL THE NOTES CAREFULLY. IF YOU ARE IN ANY DOUBT ABOUT THE ACTION YOU SHOULD TAKE, GET ADVICE IMMEDIATELY e.g. FROM A SOLICITOR OR A CITIZENS ADVICE BUREAU.

1. This request is made under section 26 of the Landlord and Tenant Act 1954.

2. You are the landlord of .. .. (description of property)

3. I/we request you to grant a new tenancy beginning on .. .. ..

4. I/we propose that:

(*a*) the property comprised in the new tenancy should be .. ..
(*b*) the rent payable under the new tenancy should be .. ..
(*c*) the other terms of the new tenancy should be .. ..

5. All correspondence about this request should be sent to*[the tenant] [the tenant's agent] at the address given below.

*Cross out words in square brackets if they do not apply.

Date .. ..
Signature of*[tenant] [tenant's agent]
.. ..
Name of tenant .. ..
Address of tenant .. ..
*[Address of agent .. ..
.. ..]

NOTES

Request for a new tenancy

1. This request by your tenant for a new tenancy brings his current tenancy to an end on the day before the date mentioned in paragraph 3 above. He can apply to the court under the Landlord and Tenant Act 1954 for a new tenancy. If he does, his current tenancy will continue after the date mentioned in paragraph 3 of this request while his application is being considered by the court. You can ask the court to fix the rent which your tenant will have to pay while his tenancy continues. The terms of any *new* tenancy not agreed between you and your tenant will be settled by the court.

Opposing a request for a new tenancy

2. If you do not want to grant a new tenancy, you *must*, not later than 2 months after the making of this request, give your tenant notice saying that you will oppose any application he makes to the court for a new tenancy. You do not need a special form to do this, but you must state on which of the grounds set out in the 1954 Act you will oppose the application - see note 4.

3. The time limit in note 2 runs from the making of this request. The date of the making of the request may not be the date written on the request or the date on which you actually saw it. It may, for instance, be the date on which the request was delivered through the post to your last address known to the person making the request. If there has been any delay in your seeing this request you may need to act very quickly. If you are in any doubt get advice immediately.

WARNING TO LANDLORD
IF YOU DO NOT KEEP TO THE TIME LIMIT IN NOTE 2, YOU WILL *LOSE* YOUR RIGHT TO OPPOSE YOUR TENANT'S APPLICATION TO THE COURT FOR A NEW TENANCY IF HE MAKES ONE.

Grounds for opposing an application

4. If your tenant applies to the court for a new tenancy, you can only oppose the application on one or more of the grounds set out in section 30(1) of the 1954 Act. These grounds are set out below. The paragraph letters are those given in the Act.

Grounds

(*a*) where under the current tenancy the tenant has any obligations as respects the repair and maintenance of the holding, that the tenant ought not to be granted a new tenancy in view of the state of repair of the holding, being a state resulting from the tenant's failure to comply with the said obligations;
(*b*) that the tenant ought not to be granted a new tenancy in view of his persistent delay in paying rent which has become due;
(*c*) that the tenant ought not to be granted a new tenancy in view of other substantial breaches by him of his obligations under the current tenancy, or for any other reason connected with the tenant's use or management of the holding;

(*d*) that you have offered and are willing to provide or secure the provision of suitable alternative accommodation for the tenant;
(The 1954 Act as applied by the 1980 Act lays down detailed rules about what accommodation is "suitable". In brief, it must give comparable security of tenure and be reasonably suited to the means and needs of the tenant and his family.)

(*e*) where the current tenancy was created by the sub-letting of part only of the property comprised in a superior tenancy and you are the owner of an interest in reversion expectant on the termination of that superior tenancy, that the aggregate of the rents reasonably obtainable on separate lettings of the holding and the remainder of that property would be substantially less than the rent reasonably obtainable on a letting of that property as a whole, that on the termination of the current tenancy you require possession of the holding for the purpose of letting or otherwise disposing of the said property as a whole, and that in view thereof the tenant ought not to be granted a new tenancy;

(*f*) that on the termination of the current tenancy you intend to demolish or reconstruct the premises comprised in the holding or a substantial part of those premises or to carry out substantial work of construction on the holding or part thereof and that you could not reasonably do so without obtaining possession of the holding;
(If you use this ground, the court can sometimes still grant a new tenancy if certain conditions set out in section 31A of the Act can be met).

(*g*) that on the termination of the current tenancy, you intend to occupy the holding for the purposes, or partly for the purposes, of a business to be carried on by you therein, or as your residence.
(You must normally have been the landlord for at least five years to use this ground.)

You can only use one or more of the above grounds if you have stated them in the notice referred to in note 2 above.

Compensation

5. If your tenant cannot get a new tenancy solely because grounds (*e*), (*f*) or (*g*) apply, he is entitled to compensation from you under the 1954 Act. If you have opposed his application on any of the other grounds as well as (*e*), (*f*) or (*g*) he can only get compensation if the court's refusal to grant a new tenancy is based solely on grounds (*e*), (*f*) or (*g*). In other words, he cannot get compensation under the 1954 Act if the court has refused his tenancy on *other* grounds even if (*e*), (*f*), or (*g*) also apply.

Negotiating a new tenancy

6. Most leases are renewed by negotiation. If you do try to agree a new tenancy with your tenant—

(1) YOU should remember that you will not be able to oppose an application to the court for a new tenancy unless you give the notice mentioned in note 2 above within the time limit in that note;

(2) YOUR TENANT should remember that he will lose his right to apply to the court for a new tenancy unless he makes the application not less than 2 nor more than 4 months after the making of this request.

Validity of this notice

7. The landlord to whom this request is made may not be the landlord to whom the tenant pays the rent. The 1954 Act has rules about who the request should be made to and also about the date which the tenant can put in paragraph 3. This depends on the terms of the tenancy. If you have any doubts about whether this request is valid, get immediate advice.

Assured tenancies

8. Assured tenancies are residential tenancies under the Housing Act 1980 as amended by the Housing and Planning Act 1986. Assured tenancies can be granted only by landlords approved by the Secretary of State. The property must either—

(1) be newly built (building work must have started on or after 8th August 1980) and must not have been occupied as a residence at any time except under an assured tenancy, or

(2) have been subject to "qualifying works". These are works which: were carried out while the property was empty or in non-residential use; were carried out within 2 years preceding the first letting on an assured tenancy; and which did not cost less than a minimum amount, prescribed by order. The property must also be fit for human habitation when first let on an assured tenancy.

There are certain other conditions which must also be fulfilled.

9. The rules that apply to assured tenancies are a modified version of those applying to business tenancies under Part II of the Landlord and Tenant Act 1954. (Further information about assured tenancies is given in the Department of the Environment and Welsh Office booklet "Assured Tenancies", obtainable free from rent offices, council offices and housing aid centres.) **[1062]**

NOTES

Commencement: 7 January 1987.

FORM C WITHDRAWAL OF LANDLORD'S NOTICE TO TERMINATE ASSURED TENANCY

(Landlord and Tenant Act 1954, section 44 and paragraph 6 of Schedule 6, Housing Act 1980, sections 56-58 and Schedule 5, as amended by the Housing and Planning Act 1986, sections 12-13)

To: (name of tenant) of (address of tenant)

IMPORTANT—THIS NOTICE IS INTENDED TO WITHDRAW A PREVIOUS NOTICE TO TERMINATE YOUR TENANCY. READ THIS NOTICE AND ALL THE NOTES CAREFULLY. IF YOU ARE IN ANY DOUBT ABOUT YOUR POSITION, GET ADVICE IMMEDIATELY e.g. FROM A SOLICITOR OR A CITIZENS ADVICE BUREAU.

1. This notice is given under section 44 of, and paragraph 6 of Schedule 6 to, the Landlord and Tenant Act 1954.

2. It relates to .. .. (description of property) of which you are the tenant.

3. I/we have become your landlord for the purposes of the Act.

4. I/we withdraw the notice given to you by .. .. .. (name of former landlord) of .. .. (address of former landlord) terminating your tenancy on .. ..

5. Any correspondence about this notice should be sent to *[the landlord] [the landlord's agent] at the address given below.

*Cross out words in square brackets if they do not apply.

Date .. ..
Signature of*[landlord] [landlord's agent]
.. ..
Address of landlord .. ..
.. ..
*[Address of agent .. ..
.. ..]

NOTES

Purpose of this notice

1. You were earlier given a notice bringing your tenancy to an end, but there has now been a change of landlord for the purposes of the 1954 Act. This new notice has been given to you by your new landlord and withdraws the earlier notice, which now has no effect. However, the new landlord can, if he wishes, give you a fresh notice with the intention of bringing your tenancy to an end.

Validity of this notice

2. The landlord who has given this notice may not be the landlord to whom you pay your rent. The 1954 Act has rules about who can serve this notice and also provides that this notice can only be given within 2 months after the giving of the earlier notice. If you have any doubts about whether this notice is valid, get immediate advice. If it is *not* valid you may have to act quickly to preserve your position under the earlier notice.

Assured tenancies

3. Assured tenancies are residential tenancies under the Housing Act 1980 as amended by the Housing and Planning Act 1986. Assured tenancies can be granted only by landlords approved by the Secretary of State. The property must either—

(1) be newly built (building work must have started on or after 8th August 1980) and must not have been occupied as a residence at any time except under an assured tenancy, or

(2) have been subject to "qualifying works". These are works which: were carried out while the property was empty or in non-residential use; were carried out within 2 years preceding the first letting on an assured tenancy; and which did not cost less than a minimum amount, prescribed by order. The property must also be fit for human habitation when first let on an assured tenancy.

There are certain other conditions which must also be fulfilled.

4. The rules that apply to assured tenancies are a modified version of those applying to business tenancies under Part II of the Landlord and Tenant Act 1954. (Further information about assured tenancies is given in the Department of the Environment and Welsh Office booklet "Assured Tenancies", obtainable free from rent offices, council offices and housing aid centres). **[1063]**

NOTES
Commencement: 7 January 1987.

ASSURED TENANCIES (APPROVED BODIES) (NO 4) ORDER 1986

(SI 1986 NO 2240)

NOTES
Made: 16 December 1986
Authority: Housing Act 1980, s 56(4)

1. This order may be cited as the Assured Tenancies (Approved Bodies) (No. 4) Order 1986 and shall come into operation on 28th January 1987. **[1064]**

NOTES
Commencement: 28 January 1987.

2. The bodies named in the Schedule to this order are hereby specified for the purposes of Part II of the Housing Act 1980. **[1065]**

NOTES
Commencement: 28 January 1987.

SCHEDULE

Order 2

BODIES SPECIFIED FOR THE PURPOSES OF PART II OF THE HOUSING ACT 1980

1. CCHA (Midland House) Limited.

2. CCHA (Waterloo Court) Limited.
3. Hemingford Properties Limited.
4. Jemima's Housing Limited.
5. Knumzi Securities Limited.
6. Midlands Provident Housing Association Limited.
7. Nomad Housing Group Limited.
8. Tenderness Limited.
9. The Letchworth Garden City Corporation.
10. Timewell Investments Limited.
11. Woodgavil Properties Limited.
12. Yorkshire Retirement Homes Limited. **[1066]**

NOTES
Commencement: 28 January 1987.

ASSURED TENANCIES (PRESCRIBED AMOUNT) ORDER 1987

(SI 1987 NO 122)

NOTES
Made: 2 February 1987
Authority: Housing Act 1980, s 56B(6)

1. This Order may be cited as the Assured Tenancies (Prescribed Amount) Order 1987 and shall come into force on 25th February 1987. **[1067]**

NOTES
Commencement: 25 February 1987.

2. The prescribed amount for the purposes of section 56B of the Housing Act 1980 is—

(*a*) in the case of a dwelling-house in Greater London, £7,000; and
(*b*) in the case of a dwelling-house elsewhere in England or Wales, £5,000. **[1068]**

NOTES
Commencement: 25 February 1987.

3. . . . **[1069]**

NOTES
Commencement: 25 February 1987.
This article revokes SI 1986 No 2180.

RENT (RELIEF FROM PHASING) ORDER 1987
(SI 1987 NO 264)

NOTES
Made: 23 February 1987
Authority: Housing Act 1980, ss 60(5), (7), 151(3)

ARRANGEMENT OF ARTICLES

Article	Para
1	[1070]
2	[1071]
3	[1072]

SCHEDULES

Schedule 1—*Consequential Amendments* .. .. [1073]
Schedule 2—*Circumstances where Phasing is to Continue* .. .. [1074]

1. This Order may be cited as the Rent (Relief from Phasing) Order 1987 and shall come into force on the expiry of the period of ten weeks beginning with the day on which this Order is made. **[1070]**

NOTES
Commencement: 4 May 1987.

2. (1) The following provisions of the Rent Act 1977 are repealed—

(*a*) section 55;
(*b*) Schedule 8, in so far as it relates to section 55.

(2) The following provisions of the Rent (Agriculture) Act 1976 are repealed—

(*a*) section 15;
(*b*) Schedule 6.

(3) The consequential amendments to the Rent Act 1977 specified in Schedule 1 to this Order are made. **[1071]**

NOTES
Commencement: 4 May 1987.

3. The repeals and amendments made by this Order do not have effect in the circumstances and to the extent specified in Schedule 2 to this Order. **[1072]**

NOTES
Commencement: 4 May 1987.

SCHEDULES

SCHEDULE 1

Article 2(3)

CONSEQUENTIAL AMENDMENTS

. . . **[1073]**

NOTES

Commencement: 4 May 1987.

This Schedule contains amendments to the Rent Act 1977, ss 44(1), 45(2), 51(4), 71(3), Sch 20, para 3(2).

SCHEDULE 2

Article 3

CIRCUMSTANCES WHERE PHASING IS TO CONTINUE

1.—(1) Subject to sub-paragraph (2), where a relevant application has been made, in relation to any increase in rent pursuant to that application following a determination by the rent officer or a determination, whether before or after this Order comes into force, by a rent assessment committee.

(2) Sub-paragraph (1) does not apply to a case to which section 72(3) of the Rent Act 1977 or section 13(6) of the Rent (Agriculture) Act 1976 applies if the resulting registration takes effect after this Order comes into force.

(3) In this paragraph "a relevant application" means an application under section 67 or section 68 of the Rent Act 1977 pursuant to which, before this Order comes into force, a rent has been registered or confirmation noted on the register following a determination by a rent officer.

2. Where a controlled tenancy has been converted into a regulated tenancy and no rent for it has been registered under Part IV of the Rent Act 1977 before this Order comes into force, in relation to any increase in rent pursuant to the first application under section 67 or section 68 of that Act. **[1074]**

NOTES

Commencement: 4 May 1987.

PROTECTED SHORTHOLD TENANCIES (RENT REGISTRATION) ORDER 1987
(SI 1987 NO 265)

NOTES

Made: 23 February 1987

Authority: Housing Act 1980, s 52(4)

1. This Order may be cited as the Protected Shorthold Tenancies (Rent Registration) Order 1987 and shall come into force on the expiry of the period of ten weeks beginning with the day on which this Order is made. **[1075]**

NOTES

Commencement: 4 May 1987.

2. . . . **[1076]**

NOTES

Commencement: 4 May 1987.

This article repeals the Housing Act 1980, s 52(1)(*c*).

3. . . . **[1077]**

NOTES

Commencement: 4 May 1987.

This article revokes SI 1981 No 1578.

RENT ACT 1977 (FORMS ETC) (AMENDMENT) REGULATIONS 1987
(SI 1987 NO 266)

NOTES
Made: 23 February 1987
Authority: Rent Act 1977, ss 49, 60, 61

1. These Regulations may be cited as the Rent Act 1977 (Forms etc.) (Amendment) Regulations 1987 and shall come into force on 4th May 1987. **[1078]**

NOTES
Commencement: 4 May 1987.

2. The Rent Act 1977 (Forms etc.) Regulations 1980 are amended as follows—

(i), (ii) . . .
(iii) In Schedule 1, for forms Nos. 1 and 2 substitute the forms bearing those numbers in the Schedule to these Regulations and omit form No. 3. **[1079]**

NOTES
Commencement: 4 May 1987.
Words omitted amend SI 1980 No 1697, reg 3(1), Sch 1.

SCHEDULE

Regulation 2(iii)

. . . **[1080]**

NOTES
Commencement: 4 May 1987.
This Schedule sets out forms to be substituted for SI 1980 No 1697, Sch 1, forms 1, 2.

PROTECTED SHORTHOLD TENANCIES (NOTICE TO TENANT) REGULATIONS 1987
(SI 1987 NO 267)

NOTES
Made: 23 February 1987
Authority: Housing Act 1980, s 52(3)

ARRANGEMENT OF REGULATIONS

Regulation	Para
1	[1081]
2	[1082]
3	[1083]
Schedule—*Notice of a Protected Shorthold Tenancy - Second Revision*	[1084]

1. These Regulations may be cited as the Protected Shorthold Tenancies (Notice to Tenant) Regulations 1987 and shall come into force on 4th May 1987. **[1081]**

NOTES
Commencement: 4 May 1987.

2. The requirement with which a notice has to comply in order to be valid for the purposes of section 52(1)(b) of the Housing Act 1980 is that it shall be in the form set out in the Schedule to these Regulations or in a form substantially to the like effect. **[1082]**

NOTES
Commencement: 4 May 1987.

3. . . . **[1083]**

NOTES
Commencement: 4 May 1987.
This regulation revokes SI 1981 No 1579.

SCHEDULE

NOTICE OF A PROTECTED SHORTHOLD TENANCY—SECOND REVISION

(The landlord must give this to the tenant *before* a protected shorthold tenancy is granted. It does not commit the tenant to take the tenancy.)

To . . . .

(Name of proposed tenant)

IMPORTANT—PLEASE READ THIS NOTICE CAREFULLY. IF THERE IS ANYTHING YOU DO NOT UNDERSTAND YOU SHOULD GET ADVICE (FOR EXAMPLE, FROM A SOLICITOR OR A CITIZENS' ADVICE BUREAU) BEFORE YOU AGREE TO TAKE A SHORTHOLD TENANCY.

NB: This document is important; keep it in a safe place.

1. You are proposing to take a tenancy of the dwelling known as . . . .

from . . . . 19 . . .

(day) (month) (year)

to . . . . 19 . . .

(day) (month) (year)

2. This notice is to tell you that your tenancy is to be a *protected shorthold tenancy*. Under shorthold, provided you keep the terms of the tenancy, you are entitled to remain in the dwelling for the fixed period agreed at the start of the tenancy. At the end of this period the landlord has the right to repossession if he wants. Full details about shorthold are given in the Department of the Environment and Welsh Office booklet "Shorthold Tenancies. Second Revision" obtainable free from Rent Officers, council offices and housing aid centres. You are advised to read this booklet before you agree to take a shorthold tenancy.

*The landlord must cross out the version of paragraph 3 below which does not apply.

*3. A fair rent of per is already registered for the dwelling under the Rent Act 1977.

This is the most you can be required to pay as rent until such time as a higher rent is registered. If I apply for a higher rent to be registered you will be told about my application and you will have the opportunity of a consultation with the Rent Officer.

*3. The rent for this tenancy is the rent that we have agreed, and has not been registered by the Rent Officer. But this does not affect your right as tenant or my right as landlord to apply at any time to the Rent Officer for the registration of a fair rent. This is fully explained in the booklet "Shorthold Tenancies. Second Revision.".

4. This notice is given to you on .. .. 19 .. ..

Signed .. .. (on behalf of) .. ..

(Name and address of landlord) .. ..

SPECIAL NOTE FOR EXISTING TENANTS

IF YOU ARE ALREADY A PROTECTED OR STATUTORY TENANT UNDER THE RENT ACT 1977 YOUR PRESENT TENANCY CANNOT LAWFULLY BE CONVERTED INTO A SHORTHOLD. BUT SHOULD YOU GIVE IT UP AND TAKE A SHORTHOLD TENANCY IN SOME OTHER ACCOMMODATION, INCLUDING ANOTHER FLAT IN THE SAME BUILDING, YOU WILL ALMOST CERTAINLY HAVE *LESS* SECURITY UNDER SHORTHOLD THAN UNDER YOUR EXISTING TENANCY. **[1084]**

NOTES
Commencement: 4 May 1987.

ASSURED TENANCIES (APPROVED BODIES) (NO 1) ORDER 1987

(SI 1987 NO 737)

NOTES
Made: 15 April 1987
Authority: Housing Act 1980, s 56(4)

1. This Order may be cited as the Assured Tenancies (Approved Bodies) (No. 1) Order 1987 and shall come into force on 21st May 1987. **[1085]**

NOTES
Commencement: 21 May 1987.

2. The bodies named in the Schedule to this Order are hereby specified for the purposes of Part II of the Housing Act 1980. **[1086]**

NOTES
Commencement: 21 May 1987.

SCHEDULE

Order 2

BODIES SPECIFIED FOR THE PURPOSE OF PART II OF THE HOUSING ACT 1980

1. Bradford & Northern Housing Association Limited.
2. BTE Limited.
3. CCHA (Coventry) Limited.
4. Cheviot Housing Limited.
5. Hyde Housing Association Limited.
6. Kingdomwide Housing Association Limited.
7. Metropolitan Home Ownership Limited.
8. Orbit Housing Association.
9. Paddington Churches Housing Association Limited.

10. Thames Valley Housing Society Limited.
11. The North British Housing Association Limited.
12. Wealden Housing Association Limited.
13. Woolwich Homes Limited. **[1087]**

NOTES
Commencement: 21 May 1987.

SECURE TENANCIES (NOTICES) REGULATIONS 1987
(SI 1987 NO 755)

NOTES
Made: 22 April 1987
Authority: Housing Act 1985, s 83(2), (6)

1. These Regulations may be cited as the Secure Tenancies (Notices) Regulations 1987 and shall come into force on 13th May 1987. **[1088]**

NOTES
Commencement: 13 May 1987.

2. (1) The notice to be served on a secure tenant under section 83 of the Housing Act 1985 before the court can entertain proceedings for possession of a dwelling-house let under a secure tenancy which is a periodic tenancy, shall be in the form specified in Part I of the Schedule to these Regulations, or in a form substantially to the same effect.

(2) The notice to be served on a secure tenant under section 83 of the Housing Act 1985 before the court can entertain proceedings for the termination of a secure tenancy which is a tenancy for a term certain, and for possession of the dwelling-house let under that tenancy, shall be in the form specified in Part II of the Schedule to these Regulations, or in a form substantially to the same effect.

(3) . . . **[1089]**

NOTES
Commencement: 13 May 1987.
Para (3): revokes SI 1980 No 1339 and SI 1984 No 1224.

SCHEDULE

Regulation 2

PART I

NOTICE OF SEEKING POSSESSION—HOUSING ACT 1985, S 83

This Notice is the first step towards requiring you to give up possession of your dwelling. You should read it very carefully.

1. To . . . . (name(s) of secure tenant(s))

If you need advice about this Notice, and what you should do about it, take it as quickly as possible to a Citizens' Advice Bureau, a Housing Aid Centre, or a Law Centre, or to a Solicitor. You may be able to receive Legal Aid but this will depend on your personal circumstances.

2. The [name of landlord] intends to apply to the Court for an order requiring you to give up possession of:

…………………… (address of property)

……………………

……………………

If you are a secure tenant under the Housing Act 1985, you can only be required to leave your dwelling if your landlord obtains an order for possession from the Court. The order must be based on one of the Grounds which are set out in the 1985 Act (see paragraph 3 and 4 below).

If you are willing to give up possession without a Court order, you should notify the person who signed this Notice as soon as possible and say when you would leave.

3. Possession will be sought on Ground(s) …… of Schedule 2 to the Housing Act 1985, which reads:—

[*give the text in full of each Ground which is being relied on*]

Whatever Grounds for possession are set out in paragraph 3 of this Notice, the Court may allow any of the other Grounds to be added at a later stage. If this is done, you will be told about it so you can argue at the hearing in Court about the new Ground, as well as the Grounds set out in paragraph 3, if you want to.

4. Particulars of each Ground are as follows:—

[give a full explanation of why each Ground is being relied upon]

Before the Court will grant an order on any of the Grounds 1 to 8 or 12 to 16, it must be satisfied that it is reasonable to require you to leave. This means that, if one of these Grounds is set out in paragraph 3 of this Notice, you will be able to argue at the hearing in Court that it is not reasonable that you should have to leave, even if you accept that the Ground applies.

Before the Court grants an order on any of the Grounds 9 to 16, it must be satisfied that there will be suitable alternative accommodation for you when you have to leave. This means that the Court will have to decide that, in its opinion, there will be other accommodation which is reasonably suitable for the needs of you and your family, taking into particular account various factors such as the nearness of your place of work, and the sort of housing that other people with similar needs are offered. Your new home will have to be let to you on another secure tenancy or a private tenancy under the Rent Act of a kind that will give you similar security. There is no requirement for suitable alternative accommodation where Grounds 1 to 8 apply.

If your landlord is not a local authority, and the local authority gives a certificate that it will provide you with suitable accommodation, the Court has to accept the certificate.

One of the requirements of Ground 10A is that the landlord must have approval for the redevelopment scheme from the Secretary of State (or, in the case of a housing association landlord, the Housing Corporation). The landlord must have consulted all secure tenants affected by the proposed redevelopment scheme.

5. The Court proceedings will not be begun until after

………………………

[give the date after which Court proceedings can be brought]

Court proceedings cannot be begun until after this date, which cannot be earlier than the date when your tenancy or licence could have been brought to an end. This means that if you have a weekly or fortnightly tenancy, there should be at least 4 weeks between the date this Notice is given and the date in this paragraph.

After this date, court proceedings may be begun at once or at any time during the following twelve months. Once the twelve months are up this Notice will lapse and a new Notice must be served before possession can be sought.

Signed …………

……

On behalf of ……

………

Address …………

………

………………

……

....
....
Tel. No ....
....
Date ....
....

[1090]

NOTES

Commencement: 13 May 1987.

PART II

NOTICE OF SEEKING TERMINATION OF TENANCY AND RECOVERY OF POSSESSION - HOUSING ACT 1985, S 83

This Notice may lead to your being required to leave your dwelling. You should read it very carefully.

1. To .... (name(s) of secure tenant(s))

If you need advice about this Notice, and what you should do about it, take it as quickly as possible to a Citizen's Advice Bureau, a Housing Aid Centre, or a Law Centre, or to a Solicitor. You may be able to receive Legal Aid but this will depend on your personal circumstances.

2. The [name of landlord] intends to apply to the Court for an order terminating your tenancy and requiring you to give up possession of:

.... (address of property)
....
....

This Notice applies to you if you are a secure tenant under the Housing Act 1985 and if your tenancy is for a fixed term, containing a provision which allows your landlord to bring it to an end before the fixed term expires. This may be because you have got into arrears with your rent or have broken some other condition of the tenancy. This is known as a provision for re-entry or forfeiture. The Act does not remove the need for your landlord to bring an action under such a provision, nor does it affect your right to seek relief against re-entry or forfeiture, in other words to ask the Court not to bring the tenancy to an end. The Act gives additional rights to tenants, as described below.

If you are a secure tenant and have a fixed term tenancy, it can only be terminated and you can only be evicted if your landlord obtains an order for possession from the Court. The order must be based an one of the Grounds which are set out in the 1985 Act (see paragraphs 3 and 4 below).

If you are willing to give up possession without a Court order, you should notify the person who signed this Notice as soon as possible and say when you would leave.

3. Termination of your tenancy and possession will be sought on Ground(s) .... of Schedule 2 to the Housing Act 1985, which reads:—

[give the text in full of each Ground which is being relied on]

Whatever Grounds for possession are set out in paragraph 3 of this Notice, the Court may allow any of the other Grounds to be added at a later stage. If this is done, you will be told about it so you can argue at the hearing in Court about the new Ground, as well as the Grounds set out in paragraph 3, if you want to.

4. Particulars of each Ground are as follows:—

Before the Court will grant an order on any of the Grounds 1 to 8 or 12 to 16, it must be satisfied that it is reasonable to require you to leave. This means that, if one of these Grounds is set out in paragraph 3 of this Notice, you will be able to argue at the hearing in Court that it is not reasonable that you should have to leave, even if you accept that the Ground applies.

Before the Court grants an order on any of the Grounds 9 to 16, it must be satisfied that there will be suitable alternative accommodation for you when you have to leave. This means that the Court will have to decide that, in its opinion, there will be other accommodation which is reasonably suitable for the needs of you and your family, taking into particular account various factors such as the nearness of your place of work, and the sort of housing that other people with similar needs are offered. Your new home will have to be let to you on another secure tenancy or a private tenancy under the Rent Act of a kind that will give you similar security. There is no requirement for suitable alternative accommodation where Grounds 1 to 8 apply.

If your landlord is not a local authority, and the local authority gives a certificate that it will provide you with suitable accommodation, the Court has to accept the certificate.

One of the requirements of Ground 10A is that the landlord must have approval for the redevelopment scheme from the Secretary of State (or, in the case of a housing association landlord, the Housing Corporation). The landlord must have consulted all secure tenants affected by the proposed redevelopment scheme.

Signed .. ..

On behalf of .. ..
.. .. ..

Address .. ..
.. ..
.. ..
.. ..

Tel. No .. ..
.. ..

Date .. ..
.. [1091]

NOTES
Commencement: 13 May 1987.

ASSURED TENANCIES (APPROVED BODIES) (NO 2) ORDER 1987
(SI 1987 NO 822)

NOTES
Made: 6 May 1987
Authority: Housing Act 1980, s 56(4)

1. This Order may be cited as the Assured Tenancies (Approved Bodies) (No. 2) Order 1987 and shall come into force on 1st June 1987. **[1092]**

NOTES
Commencement: 1 June 1987.

2. The bodies named in the Schedule to this Order are hereby specified for the purposes of Part II of the Housing Act 1980. **[1093]**

NOTES
Commencement: 1 June 1987.

SCHEDULE

BODIES SPECIFIED FOR THE PURPOSES OF PART II OF THE HOUSING ACT 1980

1. Abbey National Building Society.
2. Addison Housing Association Limited.
3. Airways Housing Society Limited.
4. Aldwyck Housing Association Limited.
5. Boleyn and Forest Housing Society Limited.

6. Bridge Housing Society Limited.
7. Brook Street Housing Association Limited.
8. Cheltenham and District Housing Association Limited.
9. Cherwell Homes Limited.
10. Cherwell Housing Trust.
11. Clwyd Alyn Housing Association Limited.
12. Coastal Counties Housing Association Limited.
13. Colombo Estates Limited.
14. Copec Housing Trust.
15. Copec Three Housing Association Limited.
16. Copec Two Housing Association Limited.
17. Corlan Housing Association Limited.
18. Fairlake Second Housing Association Limited.
19. Family Care Housing Association Limited.
20. Harewood Housing Society Limited.
21. Harry Arthur Bookbinder, Margaret Bookbinder, Nicholas Bookbinder, and Penelope Luiten trading as Abco Homes.
22. Headrow Housing Group Limited.
23. Jephson Second Housing Association Limited.
24. Metropolitan Housing Trust Limited.
25. MHT Services Limited.
26. MIH Special Projects Housing Association Limited.
27. Muir Group Housing Association Limited.
28. Nene Housing Society Limited.
29. Notting Hill Housing Trust.
30. Secondary Housing Association for Wales Limited.
31. Secondary Housing Association for Wales (Co-operative) Limited.
32. South East Lancashire Housing Association Limited.
33. South West Housing Society Limited.
34. S.R.J. Properties Limited.
35. The St. Pancras Housing Association in Camden.
36. Third Caldmore Housing Association Limited.
37. United Kingdom Housing Trust Limited.
38. Wales & West Housing Association Limited.
39. Western Permanent Housing Society Limited.
40. R W Willan (Estates) Limited.
41. Yorkshire Metropolitan Housing Association Limited. **[1094]**

NOTES

Commencement: 1 June 1987.

ASSURED TENANCIES (APPROVED BODIES) (NO 3) ORDER 1987
(SI 1987 NO 1164)

NOTES
Made: 6 July 1987
Authority: Housing Act 1980, s 56(4)

1. This Order may be cited as the Assured Tenancies (Approved Bodies) (No. 3) Order 1987 and shall come into force on 6th August 1987. **[1095]**

NOTES
Commencement: 6 August 1987.

2. The bodies named in the Schedule to this Order are hereby specified for the purposes of Part II of the Housing Act 1980. **[1096]**

NOTES
Commencement: 6 August 1987.

SCHEDULE
BODIES SPECIFIED FOR THE PURPOSES OF PART II OF THE HOUSING ACT 1980

1. Assured Developments Limited.
2. Brian Pickard, Barbara Pickard, Simon Winston Pickard and Miles Brian Pickard trading as Pickard Partners Properties.
3. Devon and Cornwall Housing Association Limited.
4. Durham Mineworkers' Housing Association Limited.
5. First Rung Housing Association Limited.
6. Gordon Hoyland Spencer and Jacqueline Elsie Spencer trading as G H and J E Spencer Properties.
7. Harden Housing Association (Midlands) Limited.
8. Inner City Housing Limited.
9. Knightstone Housing Association Limited.
10. Longhurst Housing Association Limited.
11. MPC Properties Limited.
12. Nationwide Housing Trust (1987) Limited.
13. Norman Goodfriend and Hava Goodfriend trading as The Latin Property Company.
14. Northern Counties Housing Association Limited.
15. Paul Henry Reik and Patricia Lynn Reik trading as The Rainbow Property Investment Group.
16. Perseus Housing Limited.
17. Prowting Holdings Limited.

18. Staffordshire Housing Association Limited.
19. The Buckinghamshire Housing Association Limited.
20. Trident Housing Society Limited.
21. Two Castles Housing Association Limited. **[1097]**

NOTES
Commencement: 6 August 1987.

ASSURED TENANCIES (APPROVED BODIES) (NO 4) ORDER 1987

(SI 1987 NO 1525)

NOTES
Made: 26 August 1987
Authority: Housing Act 1980, s 56(4)

1. This Order may be cited as the Assured Tenancies (Approved Bodies) (No 4) Order 1987 and shall come into force on 1 October 1987. **[1098]**

NOTES
Commencement: 1 October 1987.

2. The bodies named in the Schedule to this Order are hereby specified for the purposes of Part II of the Housing Act 1980. **[1099]**

NOTES
Commencement: 1 October 1987.

SCHEDULE

BODIES SPECIFIED FOR THE PURPOSES OF PART II OF THE HOUSING ACT 1980

1. Albion Mills Housing Co-operative Limited.
2. Anglia Housing Association Limited.
3. Belmont Housing Association Limited.
4. Broadcasting Employees Housing Development Association Limited.
5. CCHA (Sunbourne Court) Limited.
6. Collingwood Housing Association.
7. Croydon Churches Housing Association Limited.
8. Derwent Housing Society Limited.
9. Donald Halliday and Joyce Mary Halliday trading as Homefinders.
10. Equity Housing Association Limited.
11. Fairlake Third Housing Association Limited.
12. Four Rivers Housing Limited.
13. G. H. Ball Limited.
14. Grosvenor Housing Association Limited.
15. "Johnnie" Johnson Housing Association Limited.
16. Liver Housing Association Limited.

17. Martha Mockford Limited.
18. Merseyside Housing Association Limited.
19. Mid-Wales Housing Association Limited.
20. Monmouth & Llandaff Housing Association Limited.
21. Nationwide Anglia Building Society.
22. North Wales Housing Association Limited.
23. Orbit Housing Developments Limited.
24. Parklands Housing Society Limited.
25. Richmond-upon-Thames Leasehold Housing Association Limited.
26. Stepnell Developments Limited.
27. Stepnell Estates Limited.
28. Swansea Hillside Housing Association Limited.
29. Swansea Housing Association Limited.
30. The Cambridge Housing Society Limited.
31. The Corporation of the Dean and Chapter of the Cathedral Church of Christ in Liverpool.
32. The Railway Housing Association and Benefit Fund.
33. The Sutton (Hastoe) Housing Association Limited.
34. Wessex Housing Society Limited.
35. Westland Homes Housing Society Limited. **[1100]**

NOTES
Commencement: 1 October 1987.

INDEX

References are to paragraph numbers

A

ACCOMMODATION AGENCIES ACT 1953
illegal commissions and advertisements, [99]
short title, extent and commencement, [100]

ACQUISITION ORDERS. *See* Compulsory acquisition of landlord's interest

ADVERTISEMENTS
dispensation with, [585]
illegal, [99]

AGRICULTURAL HOLDINGS. *See also* Agricultural rents and housing
not protected tenancy, where, [299]

AGRICULTURAL HOLDINGS ACT 1923
application of s 20 to Landlord and Tenant Act 1927, [75], [89]

AGRICULTURAL HOLDINGS ACT 1986
application of provisions of, to Leasehold Property (Repairs) Act 1938, [97]

AGRICULTURAL RENTS AND HOUSING. *See also* Agricultural holdings
adjustment for differences in lengths of rental periods, [255]
Crown Estate, dwellings forming part of, [500], [527], [528]
Duchies, dwellings forming part of, [500] [527], [528]
eviction, special provisions as to, [437]
fitness for human habitation, [613], [614]
information, [268], [269]
jurisdiction and procedure as to, [264]
notices of increases, [254]
planning permission, suspension of condition attached to, [270]
protected occupancies,
forestry workers, [281]
own right, in their, [240], [280]–[282]
recovery of rent. *See* recovery of rent, *below*
succession, by, [241], [502]
recovery of rent,
avoidance of requirements for advance payment of, [258]
rectification of rent books, [260]
sub-lettings, [262]
sums paid in excess of recoverable rent, of, [259]
rehousing. *See* Rehousing
rent book for, [946]
security of tenure,
court must order possession, where, [284]
discretion of court in giving possession, [245], [283]
grounds for possession, [244], [283], [284], [366], [428]
restriction on levy of distress for rent, [246]
superior tenancy, effect of determination of, [247]
service of notices on landlord's agents, [263]
sharing accommodation with persons other than landlord, [261]

AGRICULTURAL RENTS AND HOUSING—*cont*.
statutory tenancies,
agreed rents, [249]
application for registration of rent, [251]
form, [848]
conditions of, [248]
general provisions, [242]
landlord's interest belongs to Crown, etc, where, [243]
phasing of increases, [253], [286]
provisional rents, [250]
recovery of rent. *See* recovery of rent, *above*
registered rents, [252]
terms of, [248], [285]

ASSIGNMENT
landlord's interest, of, duty to inform tenant of, [607]
protected shorthold tenancy, [483]
requests for summary of relevant costs, effect on, [631]
secure tenancy, of, [553], [554], [557], [603]

ASSURED TENANCIES
application of Landlord and Tenant Act 1954, [491], [525]
Approved Bodies,
(No 1) Order 1980, [831], [832]
(No 1) Order 1981, [897], [898]
(No 2) Order 1981, [902], [903]
(No 1) Order 1982, [910]–[912]
(No 2) Order 1982, [913], [914]
(No 3) Order 1982, [934]–[936]
(No 4) Order 1982, [937]–[939]
(No 5) Order 1982, [947]–[949]
(No 6) Order 1982, [950]–[952]
(No 7) Order 1982, [953]–[955]
(No 8) Order 1982, [956]–[958]
(No 1) Order 1983, [959]–[961]
(No 2) Order 1983, [962]–[964]
(No 3) Order 1983, [989]–[991]
(No 4) Order 1983, [992]–[994]
(No 5) Order 1983, [995]–[997]
(No 6) Order 1983, [998]–[1000]
(No 7) Order 1983, [1001]–[1003]
(No 8) Order 1983, [1004]–[1006]
(No 9) Order 1983, [1007]–[1009]
(No 1) Order 1984, [1010]–[1012]
(No 2) Order 1984, [1013]–[1015]
(No 3) Order 1984, [1016]–[1018]
(No 4) Order 1984, [1019]–[1021]
(No 1) Order 1985, [1025]–[1027]
(No 2) Order 1985, [1028]–[1030]
(No 1) Order 1986, [1048]–[1050]
(No 2) Order 1986, [1051]–[1053]
(No 3) Order 1986, [1054]–[1056]
(No 4) Order 1986, [1064]–[1066]
(No 1) Order 1987, [1085]–[1087]
(No 2) Order 1987, [1092]–[1094]
(No 3) Order 1987, [1095]–[1097]
(No 4) Order 1987, [1098]–[1100]

ASSURED TENANCIES—*cont.*
conditions for,
buildings to which works have been carried out, [487], [1068]
certification of fitness following carrying out of works, [488]
fitness for human habitation, [489]
newly erected buildings, [486]
generally, under Housing Act 1980, [485]
landlord's interest ceasing to belong to approved body, [490]
new, tenant's request for, form, [1062]
notice to tenant regulations 1981, [899]–[901]
notices, regulations 1986, [1057]–[1063]
prescribed amount order 1987, [1067]–[1069]
protected tenancy, not, [306]
termination of, landlord's notice as to,
form, [1061]
withdrawal of, form, [1063]

B

BETTERMENT LEVY
enfranchisement, charge on, of, [207]

BOARD OF ATTENDANCE
payments for, not protected tenancy, [296]

BUILDING LEASES. *See* Tenant for life

BUSINESS AND PROFESSIONAL TENANCIES
application of statutory provisions to, [121]
compensation for improvements to. *See* Compensation for improvements to business premises
compulsory acquisitions, [139]
continuation of, [122], [123]
Development Board for Rural Wales premises, [161]
Distribution of Industry Acts, special provisions as to premises provided under, [159]
exclusions, [144]
groups of companies, [143]
information,
duty of tenants and landlords to give, to each other, [140]
notices requiring, forms, [759]–[761], [978]–[980]
jurisdiction of county court to make declaration, [145]
modification on grounds of public interest of rights, [156], [158]
new,
application to court for, [128]–[138]
compensation for possession obtained by misrepresentation, [154]
dismissal of application for, [130]
duration of, [133]
grant of, [122], [128], [131]
opposition by landlord to, [129]
order by court for grant of, [128]
property to be comprised in, [132]
rent under, [134]
tenant's request for, [125]
forms, [758], [977]
occupation, information about, forms, [759], [978]
partnerships, [142]
regulated tenancy, business premises as, [314]
renewal by agreement, [127]

BUSINESS AND PROFESSIONAL TENANCIES—*cont.*
rent while tenancy continues, [123]
restriction on agreements excluding provisions relating to, [138]
sub-tenancy, information about, forms, [759], [978]
termination of,
landlord, by, [124]
landlord's notices, forms, [753]–[757], [774], [970]–[976], [982]–[987]
special grounds, on, [157], [158]
superior landlord's withdrawal, form, [762]
tenant, by, of tenancy for fixed term, [126]
withdrawal of landlord's notice, [981]
trust held on, [141]
Welsh Development Agency premises, [160]

C

CHARGES
compensation, in relation to, [75], [89]

CHARITY LANDS
Landlord and Tenant Act 1927, application of, to, [86], [91]

COMMISSIONS
illegal, [99]

COMMON COUNCIL OF THE CITY OF LONDON
Housing Act 1985 and, [588]

COMMON LAW PROCEDURE ACT 1852
ejectment, provisions relating to, [1]–[6]
exemption for Ireland and Scotland, [9]
interpretation of terms, [7]
short title of Act, [8]

COMPANIES
groups of, and tenancies, [143]

COMPENSATION. *See also* Compensation for improvements to business premises
modification on grounds of public interest of rights, for, [158]
new tenancy precluded on certain grounds, where, [137]
possession of property obtained by misrepresentation, by, [154]
termination of business tenancy on special grounds, for, [158]

COMPENSATION FOR IMPROVEMENTS TO BUSINESS PREMISES. *See also* Improvements to business premises
charges, provisions as to, [75], [89]
deductions from, landlord's right to make, [74]
landlord's power to apply and raise capital for, [76]
limitation on right to, [69], [149]
tenant's right to, [68]
time for making claims, [148]

COMPULSORY ACQUISITION OF LANDLORD'S INTEREST
acquisition orders,
applications for, [678]
conditions for making, [679]
content of, [680]

COMPULSORY ACQUISITION OF LANDLORD'S INTEREST—*cont*.
acquisition orders—*cont*.
determination of terms by rent assessment committees, [681]
discharge of, [684]
existing mortgages, discharge of, [682], [714]
landlord cannot be found, where, [683]
withdrawal by tenants, [684]
preliminary notice by tenants, [677]
qualifying tenants, by, [675], [676]

CONTRACT
fitness for human habitation, implied terms as to, [612]–[614]
restricted. *See* Restricted contracts
sale, etc, of land, for, to be in writing, [20]

CONTROLLED TENANCIES
regulated tenancies, converted into, [308], [377], [495]

CONVEYANCE
deed, by, [23], [25]
definition of, [49]
persons taking who are not parties, [26]
subject to rents, implied covenants in, [28]

CO-OPERATIVE HOUSING ASSOCIATION. *See also* Housing associations
landlord's interest belongs to, [305], [572]

COSTS OF LEASES ACT 1958
interpretation, [182]
provision for incidence of, [181]
short title, [183]

COUNTER-INFLATION ACT 1973
tenancies regulated by virtue of, [380]
rent limit for, [416]

COUNTY COURT
applications to, [783]
forfeiture for non-payment of rent, powers in relation to, [535]–[537]
forms, [785]–[813]
jurisdiction of,
declaration in relation to business tenancies, to make, [145]
determination of questions, procedure, etc, [203]
Landlord and Tenant Act 1987, in relation to, [702]
lessor refuses licence or consent, where, [152]
Rent Act 1977, in relation to, [396]
repairing obligations, as to, [619]
secure tenancies, as to, [574]
tenant's improvements, as to, [509]
proceedings for possession, rules 1981, [874]–[879]
forms, [880]–[882]
rules and directions in relation to secure tenancies, [575]

COUNTY COURT RULES
application of, [782]

COUNTY COURTS ACT 1984
forfeiture for non payment of rent, [535], [536]
interpretation, [537]

COVENANTS
assign, etc, without licence or consent, not to, [82]
benefit of, [29]
burden of, [30]
implied, [28], [50]–[59]
landlord proceeding to enforce, relief for tenant where, [114]
lessee's,
rent and benefit of, to run with reversion, [34]
saving of, [18]
lessor's,
obligation of, to run with reversion, [35]
saving of, [18]
local authorities, etc, with, on enfranchisement or extension of long leaseholds, [230], [231]
repair, to, [81], [92]
restrictive, power to discharge or modify, [31]
title, for, [27]
waiver of, in lease, [41]

CROWN
dwellings forming part of Crown Estate, [500], [526]–[528]
Landlord and Tenant Act 1927, application of, to, [86], [90]
Landlord and Tenant Act 1954, application of, to, [155], [179]
Landlord and Tenant Act 1987, application of, to, [706]
landlord's interest belongs to,
no statutory tenancy where, [243]
protected tenancy where, [302]
lands, [216]
property,
Rent Act 1977, application of, [408]
Rent (Agriculture) Act 1976, application of, [273]

D

DEATH
succession,
family, to tenancy on death, [190]
secure tenancy, of. *See* Secure tenancy

DECORATIVE REPAIRS
relief against notice to effect, [40]

DEFECTIVE PREMISES ACT 1972
landlord's duty of care in relation to, [234]
supplemental provisions, [235]

DEVELOPMENT BOARD FOR RURAL WALES
landlord's notice to terminate business tenancy, form, [976], [987]
premises of, [161]

DISREPAIR. *See also* Repairs
certificate of, forms, [800]–[803]

DISTRAINT
application for leave, [790], [791]

DISTRESS
restriction on levy of, [246], [401]

DISTRIBUTION OF INDUSTRY ACTS
premises provided under, special provisions as to, [159]

DUCHIES OF LANCASTER AND CORNWALL
dwellings belong to, [500], [526]–[528]
Landlord and Tenant Act 1927, application of, to, [86], [90]
Landlord and Tenant Act 1954, application of, to, [179]

DWELLING-HOUSE. *See also* Housing
agricultural worker, let to, grounds for possession of, [366]. *See also* Agricultural rents and housing
"house", meaning of, [185]
"house and premises", meaning of, [185]
inspection of, [820], [927]
land and premises let with, [316]
let with other land, [295]
meaning of, [576]
multiple occupation, in, means of escape from fire, [515]
overcrowded, [368]
possession of,
extended discretion of court as to, [367]
grounds for, [365], [366], [423]
See also Possession

E

ECCLESIASTICAL LAND
amendments of Places of Worship (Enfranchisement) Act 1920, [224]
Landlord and Tenant Act 1927, application of, to, [86], [91]
long leaseholds, [214]

EDUCATIONAL INSTITUTIONS
specified, exception in relation to protected tenancies, [1045]
university, re-acquisition for development by, [1045]

EJECTMENT
damages for mesne profits on trial of any, [4]
lessee proceeding in equity, [2]
non-payment of rent, proceedings in ejectment by landlord for, [1]
notice of, [38]
tenant paying all rent, [3]

ENFRANCHISEMENT. *See* Long leasehold

ENTRY
landlord, by,
carry out works, to, forms, [812], [813]
rights of, [73]

EVICTION. *See also* Notice to quit; Protection from Eviction Act 1977
agricultural employees, special provisions for, [437]
prohibition of, without due process of law, [436]
prosecution of offences, [439]
restriction on re-entry without due process of law, [435]
service of notices, [440]
unlawful, [434]–[437]

EXTENSIONS
leases, of. *See* Long leaseholds

F

FAIR RENT. *See* Rent

FAMILY
meaning of "members of a person's family", [577]
succession to tenancy on death, [190]

FEE SIMPLE ESTATES
enlargement of residue of long terms into, [46]

FILING OF LEASES RULES 1925
application forms, [728], [730]–[733]
conversion of copies into office copies, [726]
deposit and index of instruments, [721]
form, [730]
notes authorised on a search, [727]
office copies, [725]
form, [732]
requisition for search,
acceptance or refusal of, [724]
form and contents of, [723], [731]
procedure as to, [722]

FIRE PRECAUTIONS
houses in multiple occupations, means of escape from fire, [515]
modification of Rent Act 1977 in relation to, [395], [432]

FITNESS FOR HUMAN HABITATION
application to agricultural workers' houses, [613]
implied terms as to, [612]
nature of, [614]

FLAT
meaning of, [637]
variation of lease. *See* Variation of lease

FORESTRY
leases. *See* Tenant for life
workers, protected occupier, as, [281]

FURNITURE
adjustment of rent and, [320]
excessive price for, [382], [383]
furnished sub-tenancy, effect on, of determination of unfurnished tenancy, [393]
reasonable charge for use of,
application to determine, [796]
order on, [797]

H

HARASSMENT
occupier, of, [434]–[437]

HEATING CHARGES
secure tenancies, in relation to, [571]

HIGH COURT
jurisdiction of, regarding relief against forfeiture for non-payment of rent, [534]

HOLIDAY LETTINGS
not protected tenancy, [298]

HOUSE. *See also* Dwelling-house; Housing
"house and premises", meaning of, [185]
meaning of, [185]

HOUSING. *See also* Dwelling-house
allocation, information about, [568]
management, consultation on matters of, [567]
rehousing. *See* Rehousing

HOUSING ACT 1974
commencement, [237]
extent, [237]
short title, [237]

HOUSING ACT 1980
amendments, [518], [532]
Rent Act 1977, Part VI, to, [503], [530]
application of Part III, [508]
commencement, [519]
expenses and receipts, [520]
extent, [521]
interpretation, [508], [516]
jurisdiction of county court, [509]
orders, [517]
regulations, [517]
repeals, [518]
rules of procedure, [509]
savings, [518], [533]
short title, [521]
transitional provisions, [518], [533]

HOUSING ACT 1985
advertisements, dispensation with, [585]
commencement, [596]
Common Council of the City of London, [588]
county court,
jurisdiction, [574]
rules and directions, [575]
definitions, [576]–[580], [591]–[594]
index of, [581], [595]
extent, [596]
Inner and Middle Temples, [589]
Isles of Scilly, application to, [590]
liability of directors, [583]
local inquiries, [586]
notices,
dispensation with, [585]
service of, [587]
power to prescribed forms, etc, [584]
Rent Act protection, exclusion of, [582]
short title, [596]

HOUSING ASSOCIATIONS
conversion of tenancies into regulated tenancies, [359], [422]
exclusion from provisions relating to tenant's improvements, [507]
extension of permissible objects of, [695]
landlord's interest belongs to, [304], [501], [529], [572]
rent limit for dwellings let by, [355]–[364]. *See also* Rent limit

HOUSING CO-OPERATIVE
landlord's interest belongs to, [305], [572]

HOUSING CORPORATION
landlord's interest belongs to, [304]
rent limit for dwellings let by, [355]–[364]. *See also* Rent limit

HOUSING TRUST
landlord's interest belongs to, [304], [501], [529]
rent limit for dwellings let by, [355]–[364]. *See also* Rent limit

I

IMPROVEMENTS
exclusion of certain housing associations, [507]
reduction of rateable value in case of certain, [238]
secure tenant, by,
conditional consent to, [561]
consent required, [559]
power to reimburse cost of, [562]
provisions as to requirements, [560]
rent not to be increased, [563]
tenant, by,
conditional consent to, [506]
consents required for, [505]
generally, under Housing Act 1980, [504]
See also secure tenant, by, *above*

IMPROVEMENTS TO BUSINESS PREMISES. *See also* Compensation for improvements to business premises
landlord,
capital money, power to apply and raise in connection with, [76]
right of entry of, in connection with, [73]
right to object of, [70]

INDENTURE
deed between parties as, [26]

INFORMATION
companies, to be supplied by, [610]
housing accommodation, about,
kinds obtainable, [269]
power to obtain, [268]
leasehold valuation tribunal, provision by, of, [894]
notice requiring, about sub-tenancies of residential property, form, [749]
powers of local authorities as to, under Rent Act 1977, [403]
rent books, in, [609]
secure tenancies, about, [566]
tenant, to be furnished to,
address for service of notices to landlord, [698], [699]
assignment of landlord's interest, as to, [607], [700]
directors, etc, of corporate landlord, as to, [606]
identity of landlord, [605]
name and address of landlord in rent demands, [697]
proprietorship register, tenant's right to search, [701]

INNER TEMPLE
Housing Act 1985 in relation to, [589]

INSURANCE
landlord's right to reimbursement of increased premiums, [79]
tenants' rights as to, [638], [650], [693], [716]
variation of insurance provisions of lease, application for, [690]

INTERESSE TERMINI
abolition of, [42]

ISLES OF SCILLY
application to,
Housing Act 1985, of, [590]
Landlord and Tenant Act 1985, of, [644]
Landlord and Tenant Act 1987, of, [705]
Protection from Eviction Act 1977, of, [444]
Rent Act 1977, of, [407]
Rent (Agriculture) Act 1976, of, [272]

L

LAND
creation of interests in, by parol, [24], [25]
definition of, [49]
derelict, determination of tenancies on, [153]
ecclesiastical. *See* Ecclesiastical land
public purposes, held for. *See* Public purposes

LANDLORD
application of price or compensation received by, [207]
condition in relation to secure tenancies, [542]
corporate, disclosure of directors, etc, of, [606]
custodian trustee, person to act where, [209]
disclosure of identity of, [605]
disposals by, tenants' rights of first refusal. *See* Tenants' rights of first refusal
enfranchisement where cannot be found, [210]
entry by,
carry out works, to, forms, [812], [813]
rights of, [73]
exempt from provisions of Landlord and Tenant Act 1987, [708]
information, duty to give to tenants of business premises, [140]
interest of,
compulsory acquisition by tenants of, [675]–[684]. *See also* Compulsory acquisition of landlord's interest
Crown, belongs to, [243], [302]
duty to inform tenant of assignment of, [607]
housing association, belongs to, [304]
housing co-operative, belongs to, [305]
information about, forms, [760], [761], [979], [980]
local authority, belongs to [243], [303]
"landlord authority", meaning of, [578]
meaning of, [119], [146], [177], [178], [637]
powers of,
apply and raise capital money in connection with improvements, [76]
sell or grant leases notwithstanding restrictions, [77]
reimbursement of increased taxes, rates or insurance premiums, right to, [79]
requiring consent of other landlord to notice, forms, [751], [752]
resident, [301], [413], [414], [496], [708]
rights of,
deductions from compensation to tenant, to make, [74]
entry, as to, [73]. *See also* entry by, *above*
mesne landlord, of, [71]
object to improvements, to, [70]
redevelopment, as to, [200]
residential rights, [201]
retention of management powers for benefit of neighbourhood, [202]
supplementary provisions, [227]

LANDLORD—*cont*.
shared accommodation with, [311]
termination of tenancy by, [104], [124]
under disability, person to act where, [209]

LANDLORD AND TENANT ACT 1927
Agricultural Holdings Act 1923, s 20, application of, to, [75], [89]
contracting out, restriction on, [72]
Crown, Duchy, ecclesiastical and charity land, application to, [86], [90], [91]
extent of, [88]
holdings to which Part I applies, [80]
interpretation of, [87]
jurisdiction of court, [162]
short title of, [88]
tribunal for, [84]

LANDLORD AND TENANT ACT 1954
adaptation of, [223]
agreements excluding Part I, prohibition of, [115]
application of,
assured tenancies, to, [491], [525]
Part I to continuation of long tenancies, [117]
assumptions on which court to determine future questions, [118]
consequential amendments of, [233]
Crown, application to, [155]
interpretation of,
generally, [168]
Part I, [120]
Part II, [147]
Part III, [150]
jurisdiction of court, [162]
Landlord and Tenant Act 1985 not applying to tenancies within Part II, [641]
modification of right to possession under, [222]
proceedings and orders under, [219]
public interest of rights under Part II, [156], [158]
transitional provisions, [167], [180]

LANDLORD AND TENANT ACT 1954, PART II (ASSURED TENANCIES) (NOTICES) REGULATIONS 1986, [1057]–[1063]

LANDLORD AND TENANT ACT 1985
commencement, [649]
definitions, [645]–[647]
index of, [648]
extent, [649]
Isles of Scilly, application to, [644]
liability of directors, [642]
Landlord and Tenant Act 1954, Part II, provisions not applying to tenancies within, [641]
local housing authority's power to prosecute, [643]
short title, [649]

LANDLORD AND TENANT ACT 1987
amendments, [711], [717]
commencement, [712]
Crown land, application to, [706]
definitions in relation to, [709], [710]
exempt landlords and resident landlords, [708]
extent, [712]
financial provision, [707]

LANDLORD AND TENANT ACT 1987—*cont.*
general interpretation, [710]
Isles of Scilly, application to, [705]
jurisdiction of county courts, [702]
notices under, [704]
Part VI, application of, [696]
regulations and orders, [703]
repeals, [711], [718]
short title, [712]
LANDLORD AND TENANT (APPROPRIATE MULTIPLIER) ORDER 1984, [1022]–[1024]
LANDLORD AND TENANT (DETERMINATION OF RATEABLE VALUE PROCEDURE) RULES 1954, [734]–[742]
LANDLORD AND TENANT (NOTICES) REGULATIONS 1957, [743]–[762]
LANDLORD AND TENANT (NOTICES) REGULATIONS 1967, [770]–[774]
LANDLORD AND TENANT PART II (NOTICES) REGULATIONS 1983, [965]–[988]
LANDS TRIBUNAL
jurisdiction of, [204]
LAW OF PROPERTY ACT 1922
perpetually renewable leaseholds, conversion of, [14], [15]
LAW OF PROPERTY ACT 1925
contracts, conveyances and other instruments, [20]–[31]
definitions, [49]
general principles, [16]–[19]
leases and tenancies, [32]–[47]
notices, [48]
schedules, [50]–[59]
LEASE. *See also* Leasehold; Lessee; Lessor
assign, covenants not to, [82]
building. *See* Tenant for life
costs of, [181]
decorative repairs, relief against notice to effect, [40]
effect of extinguishment of reversion, [32]
existing before Law of Property Act 1925, application to, [47]
fee simple estates, [46]
filing of. *See* Filing of Leases Rules 1925
forestry. *See* Tenant for life
forfeiture of, [39]
grant, landlord's power to, [77]
invalidation of, [45]
licence to assign, no fine to be exacted for, [37]
lives, for, [42]
long lease,
meaning of, [709]
See also Long leaseholds; Long tenancies
meaning of, [591], [620], [645], [709]
mining. *See* Tenant for life
notice of ejectment, lessee to give to lessor, [38]
repairs to leasehold property. *See* Repairs
reversionary, [42], [78]
saving of certain legal powers, [19]
sell, landlord's power to, [77]
LEASE—*cont.*
severance, apportionment of conditions on, [33]
surrender of, [43]
variation of. *See* Variation of lease
waiver of covenant in, [41]
LEASEHOLD. *See also* Lease
long. *See* Long leasehold
perpetually renewable, conversion of, [14], [15]
renewable, [719], [720]
valuation tribunals. *See* Leasehold valuation tribunal
LEASEHOLD PROPERTY (REPAIRS) ACT 1938
Agricultural Holdings Act, application of provisions of, [97]
application to past breaches of, [95]
court having jurisdiction under, [96]
extension of, [151]
extent of, [98]
short title of, [98]
LEASEHOLD REFORM ACT 1967
amendments of other Acts, [222]–[224], [233]
commencement, [225]
exclusion, shared ownership leases from, [217], [232]
extent, [225]
interpretation of Part I, [221]
short title, [225]
transitional provisions, [218]–[220]
LEASEHOLD REFORM ACT 1979
citation, [449]
extent, [449]
price to tenant on enfranchisement, [448]
LEASEHOLD REFORM (ENFRANCHISEMENT AND EXTENSION) REGULATIONS 1967, [775]–[780]
LEASEHOLD REFORM (NOTICES) REGULATIONS 1967, [763]–[769]
LEASEHOLD VALUATION TRIBUNAL
adjournment, [890]
applications to, [885]
forms, [896]
constitution of, [513], [531]
decisions, [893]
documents, [891]
giving of notice, [895]
hearings, [887], [888]
information, provision of, [894]
inspections, [892]
non-appearance, [889]
regulations 1981, [883]–[896]
LEGAL ESTATES
definition of, [49]
equitable interests and, [16]
LESSEE. *See also* Lease
covenants of,
rent and benefit of, to run with reversion, [34]
saving of, [18]
licences granted to, effect of, [36]
proceeding in equity, in relation to ejectment, [2]

LESSOR. *See also* Lease
covenants of,
obligation of, to run with reversion, [35]
saving of, [18]
licence or consent, jurisdiction of county court where refused, [152]

LICENCE
assign, to, no fine to be exacted for, [37]
jurisdiction of county court where refused, [152]
lessee, granted to, effect of, [36]

LICENSED PREMISES
not protected tenancy, where, [300]

LOANS
prohibition of, [378], [379]
unlawfully required or received, recovery of, [384]

LOCAL AUTHORITY
landlord's interest belongs to,
no statutory tenancy where, [243]
protected tenancy where, [302]
powers of, as to information under Rent Act 1977, [403]
Rent Act 1977, Part V, for, [352]
rent officer, application to, [337]
rent regulation applications, regulations 1982, [915]–[933]
special covenants with, on enfranchisement or extension of long leaseholds, [230], [231]

LODGERS
secure tenancies, [555]

LONG LEASEHOLD. *See also* Long tenancy
agreements excluding or modifying rights of tenant, [206]
application of price or compensation received by landlord, [207]
county court, jurisdiction and special powers of, [203]
Crown land, [216]
ecclesiastical lands, [214]
enfranchisement,
betterment levy on, [207]
claims to, [188], [766]
forms, [767]–[769]
definitions in relation to, [185]–[187]
interpretation, [221]
landlord cannot be found, where, [210]
mortgages and, [195], [196]
obligation as to, [191]
purchase price and costs of, [192]
rateable value limits, [236]
regulations, [775]–[779]
rent charges, exoneration from, or redemption of, [194]
right to, [184]–[190]
rights to be conveyed to tenant on, [193]
special covenants with local authorities, etc, on, [230], [231]
sub-tenants, by, [226]
tenants entitled to, [184]
transitional provisions, [218]–[220]
withdraw, tenant's right to, [192]
extensions of,
claims to, [188], [766]
forms, [767]–[769]

LONG LEASEHOLD—*cont.*
extensions of—*cont.*
definitions in relation to, [185]–[187]
exclusion of further rights after, [199]
interpretation, [221]
obligations to grant, [197]
rateable value limits, [236]
regulations, [775]–[778], [780]
right to, [184]–[190]
sub-tenants, by, [226]
tenants entitled to, [184]
terms of tenancy to be granted on, [198]
transitional provisions, [218]–[220]
family succession to tenancy on death, [190]
landlord custodian trustee or under disability, person to act where, [209]
landlord's overriding rights,
redevelopment rights, [200]
residential rights, [201]
retention of management powers for benefit of neighbourhood, [202]
supplementary provisions, [227]
Lands Tribunal, jurisdiction of, [204]
mortgagee in possession of landlord's interest, [208]
National Trust, saving for, [215]
procedure generally, [205], [228], [229]
public purposes, etc, land held for, [211]–[216]
tenants' notices, [205], [228], [229]
trustees, rights of, [189]

LONG TENANCY. *See also* Long leaseholds
allowable premiums, [386]
continuation of, [117], [176]
low rent, at,
Rent Act 1977, under, [400]
termination of, [101], [102]
meaning of, [186], [579]
possession on termination of,
application by landlord, [112]
grounds for, [111], [175]
tenant not ordered to give up possession where, [113]

M

MANAGER
appointment by court,
application for, [673]
preliminary notice by tenant, [672]
procedure as to, [674]
tenant's right to apply for, [671]

MANAGING AGENTS
recognised tenants' associations to be consulted about, [639], [694]

MESNE LANDLORD
provisions as to, [119], [146], [177], [178]
rights of, [71]

MIDDLE TEMPLE
Housing Act 1985 in relation to, [589]

MINING LEASES. *See* Tenant for life

MORTGAGE
determine question relating to,
application, form, [808]
order on application to, form, [809]
discharge of, on landlord's estate, [195]
payment into court in respect of, [196]

MORTGAGE—*cont.*
regulated. *See* Regulated mortgage
relief in respect of, [220]
Rent Act 1977, application of, [388]
vary or revoke,
application to, form, [806]
order on application to, form, [807]

MORTGAGEE
possession, in,
landlord's interest, of, [208]
provisions as to, under Landlord and Tenant Act 1954, [166]

MULTIPLE OCCUPATION
houses in, means of escape from fire, [515]

N

NATIONAL TRUST
saving for, [215]

NEW TOWNS
Re-acquisition for development by New Towns Commission, [231]
reservation of right of pre-emption in, [213]

NORTHERN IRELAND
application to, of Rent (Amendment) Act 1985, [539]

NOTICE TO QUIT
increase of rent without, [360]
prescribed information regulations, [828]–[830]
reduction of period of, [374]
service of,
after reference of contract to rent tribunal, [371]
application to tribunal for security of tenure after, [372]
owner-occupiers, by, [373]
validity of, [438]

NOTICES. *See also* Notice to quit
dispensation with, [585]
Landlord and Tenant Act 1987, under, [704]
Landlord and Tenant Act 1954, Part II (Assured Tenancies) (Notices) Regulations 1986, under, [1057]–[1063]
Landlord and Tenant (Notice) Regulations 1957, under, [743]–[746]
forms, [747]–[762], [774]
Landlord and Tenant (Notices) Regulations 1967, under, [770]–[774]
Landlord and Tenant, Part II (Notices) Regulations 1983, under, [978]–[987]
Law of Property Act 1925, under, [48]
Leasehold Reform (Notices) Regulations 1967, under, [763]–[766]
forms, [767]–[769]
proceedings for possession or termination of secure tenancy, of, [545]
Protected Shorthold Tenancies (Notice to Tenant) Regulations 1987, under, [1081]–[1084]
provisions as to, under Landlord and Tenant Act 1954, [165]
rent assessment committees, giving of, by, [825]
rent increases, of, [254], [321]
Secure Tenancies (Notices) Regulations 1987, under, [1088]–[1091]

NOTICES—*cont.*
service of,
eviction, in relation to, [440]
Housing Act 1985, under, [587]
Landlord and Tenant Act 1927, under, [85]
landlord's agents, on, [263], [405]
notification by landlord of address for, [698]
sufficiently served, extension of circumstances in which, [699]
tenants', [205], [228], [229]
tenants' rights of first refusal, in relation to, [655], [668]
variation of term of periodic secure tenancy, [565]

O

ORIGINATING APPLICATION
form of, [786], [787]

OVERSPILL AREA
reservation of right of pre-emption in, [213]

P

PARTNERSHIPS
tenancies and, [142]

PLACES OF WORSHIP (ENFRANCHISEMENT) ACT 1920
amendments of, [224]

PLANNING PERMISSION
suspension of condition attached to, [270]

POSSESSION. *See also* Notice to quit
compensation for misrepresentation concealment, [369]
county court proceedings for, [874]–[882]
court may order, where, [423], [425]
court must order, where, [284], [424], [425], [497]
discretion of court,
certain proceedings, in, [375], [510], [547]
extended,
claims for possession, in, [367]
giving, in, [245], [283]
restriction on, in making orders for possession of land, [511]
forms of originating application for, [880]–[882]
grounds for,
agricultural workers, dwelling-houses let to, [244], [283], [284], [366], [428]
overcrowded dwelling-houses, [368]
protected occupancies, [244], [283]
protected tenancies, [365], [423], [425]
regulated tenancies, [424]–[428]
secure tenancies, [546], [598]–[600]
statutory tenancies, [244], [283], [365]
landlord's notice to resume, form, [748]
orders for, in relation to protected shorthold tenancy, [484]
recovery in, [538]
restricted application of provisions, [370]
secure tenancies,
extended discretion of court in certain proceedings, [547]
grounds and orders for, [546], [598]–[600]
notice of proceedings for, [545]
notice of seeking, [1089]
redevelopment schemes, [602]
suitability of accommodation, [601]

PREMISES
defective, landlord's duty of care in relation to, [234], [235]
meaning of "house and premises", [185]

PREMIUMS
allowable, [386], [430], [431]
furniture, excessive price for, treated as, [382]
prohibition of, [378], [379], [381]
tenancies regulated by Counter-Inflation Act, [380]
unlawfully required or received, recovery of, [384]

PRIVATE SECTOR
landlord, disposal of secure tenancies to, [569], [604]
tenants in. *See* Tenant

PROFESSIONAL TENANCIES. *See* Business and professional tenancies

PROTECTED OCCUPIERS
agricultural property, of. *See* Agricultural rents and housing

PROTECTED SHORTHOLD TENANCIES
assignment, [483]
generally, under Housing Act 1980, [481]
notice to tenant, regulations 1987, [1081]–[1084]
orders for possession, [484]
preliminary, [480]
rent registration order, 1987, [1075]–[1077]
subletting, [483]
terminate, right of tenant to, [482]

PROTECTED TENANCIES. *See also* Protected shorthold tenancies
assignment of, prohibition of premiums and loans on, [379]
educational institutions, specified, [1045]
exceptions, [292]–[306]
regulations, [1043]–[1047]
grant of, prohibition of premiums and loans on, [378]
implied term in, [402]
possession, grounds for, [365], [423], [425]
Rent Act 1977, under, [289]
rent book for, [945]
specified bodies, [1046], [1047]
suitable alternative accommodation, [426]

PROTECTION FROM EVICTION ACT 1977. *See also* Eviction
amendments, [445]
court for purposes of Part I, [442]
interpretation, [441]
Isles of Scilly, application to, [444]
savings, [447]
short title, [446]
transitional provisions, [447]

PUBLIC PURPOSES
land held for,
future right to develop, reservation of, [212]
new town or overspill area, reservation of right of pre-emption, [213]
retention or resumption of land required for, [211]

Q

QUALIFICATION CERTIFICATE
forms, [810], [811]

QUALIFIED ACCOUNTANT
meaning of, [635]

R

RATEABLE VALUE
above certain, not protected tenancy, [292]
apportionment, application for, forms, [788], [789]
ascertainment of, [315]
limits for enfranchisement or extension under Leasehold Reform Act 1967, [236]
procedure, determination of, [734]–[741]
forms, [742]
reduction of, in case of certain improvements, [238]

RATES
apportionment, application for, forms, [788], [789]
calculation of amount of, [415]
landlord's right to reimbursement of increased, [79]
rent, included in, demands and receipts where, [10]–[12]
Statement of Rates Act 1919, [10]–[13]

RECOGNISED TENANTS' ASSOCIATIONS
consulted about managing agents, to be, [639], [694]
meaning of, [636]

RE-ENTRY
non-payment of rent, right in relation to, [536]

REGULATED MORTGAGE
application to vary terms, form, [804]
order on application to vary terms, form, [805]
powers of court to mitigate hardship, [390]
Rent Act 1977, under, generally, [389]

REGULATED TENANCIES. *See also* Rent
controlled tenancies converted into, [308], [377], [495]
housing association tenancies converted into, [359], [422]
meaning of "regulated tenancy", [307]
possession,
forms of originating application for, [880]–[882]
grounds for, [424]–[428]
recovery in, [538]
registration of rents under, [331]–[344]
rents under,
enforcement provisions, [326], [327]
general provisions, [328]–[330]
increase of, forms, [842]–[845]
phasing of rent increases, [325]
regulation of, [317]–[321]
rent agreements with tenants having security of tenure, [322]–[324]
See also Rent
resident landlords, [496]

REHOUSING
agricultural dwelling-house advisory committees, [267]
applications to housing authority concerned, [265]
duty of housing authority, [266]
RENEWABLE LEASEHOLDS
regulations, [719], [720]
RENEWABLE LEASEHOLDS REGULATIONS 1925, [719], [720]
RENT
adjustment for differences in lengths of rental periods, [328]
advance payment, avoidance of requirements for, [385]
agreed, [249]
agreements with tenants having security of tenure. *See* Security of Tenure
agricultural. *See* Agricultural rents and housing: Rent (Agriculture) Act 1976
amount to be registered as, [340]
application for registration of, [336], [419]
apportionment of, [83], [514]
assessment committees. *See* Rent assessment committees
books. *See* Rent book
business and professional tenancies, while tenancy continues, [123]
conveyance subject to, implied covenant in, [28]
default powers of Secretary of State, [333]
definition of, [49]
"demand for rent", definition of, [11]
demands, landlord's name and address to be contained in, [697]
fair,
applications for registration of, [419], [420]
forms, [846]–[848], [853], [854]
certificate of,
application for, and issue of, [338], [421]
form for application for, [849]
registration of fair rent and, [419], [420], [850]
determination of, [339]
increases,
forms, [842]–[845]
improvements by tenant, no increase for, [563]
notice to quit, without, [360]
notices of, [254], [321]
phasing of, [253], [286], [325], [417], [493]
tenant's application to cancel or reduce, forms, [794], [795]
leave to distrain, application for, [790], [791]
levy of distress for, restriction on, [246], [401]
limit. *See* Rent limit
low rent,
meaning of, [187]
where not protected tenancy, [293]
new business tenancy, under, [134]
new registered, applications for, [493]
nonpayment of,
forfeiture for,
provisions as to, [535]
relief against, [534]
service of summons and re-entry, [536]
proceedings in ejectment for, [1]
tenant paying all rent, cessation of proceedings where, [3]

RENT—*cont.*
officer. *See* Rent officer
previous tenancy, statement of rent under, [362]
provisional, [250]
rates included in, demands and receipts where, [10]–[12]
"receipt for rent", definition of, [11]
recoverable,
adjustment of, [319], [320]
application to determine, forms, [792], [793]
recovery of sums paid in excess of, [326], [361]
rectification of rent books, [327]
recovery of, agricultural tenancies. *See* Agricultural rents and housing
register of,
regulated tenancies, as to, [335]
restricted contracts, under, [347]
registration areas, [331]
registration of,
applications for, [251], [419], [420], [492]
cancellation of, [342], [350]
forms, [851], [852]
regulations 1980, [860]–[864]
effect of, [341], [349], [494]
reconsideration of rent after, [348], [498]
Rent Tribunal, by, application for cancellation of, [856]
subject to a statutory tenancy, [252]
regulation. *See* Rent regulation
relief from phasing, order 1987, [1070]–[1074]
reserve power to limit, [640]
statutory tenancy, [109]
tribunals. *See* Rent Tribunals
RENT ACT 1977
amendment to Part VI of, [503], [530]
amendments, [409]
commencement, [410]
county court jurisdiction, [396]
Crown property, application to, [408]
extent, [410]
forms,
amendment regulations 1987, [1078]–[1080]
regulations 1980, [833]–[859]
interpretation of,
generally, [406]
Part III, [330]
Part IV, [344]
Part V, [354]
Part VI, [364]
Part VII, [376]
Part IX, [387]
Part X, [391]
Isles of Scilly, application to, [407]
local authorities,
Part V, for, [352]
powers of, as to information, [403]
prosecution of offences, [404]
regulations under, [329], [343], [353]
repeals, [409]
rules as to procedure, [397]
savings, [433]
short title, [410]
transitional provisions, [409], [433]
RENT ACTS
application of,
long tenancies, to, [223], [233]
tenant retains possession, where, [106]

RENT (AGRICULTURE) ACT 1976. *See also* Agricultural rents and housing
amendments, [287]
commencement, [239]
Crown property, application to, [273]
expenses, [276]
extent, [277]
index of general definitions, [278]
interpretation, [239], [257], [279], [280]–[282]
Isles of Scilly, application to, [272]
offences by bodies corporate, [274]
prosecution of offences, [275]
regulations under, [256]
short title, [277]
transitional provisions, [288]

RENT (AMENDMENT) ACT 1985
extent, [540]
Northern Ireland, application to, [539]
short title, [540]

RENT ASSESSMENT COMMITTEES
adjournment, [821]
amendment regulations 1981, [904]–[906]
constitution of, [334], [418]
decisions, [823], [824]
documents, [818], [819]
further information, notice requiring, [855]
giving of notices, [825]
hearings, [816], [817]
inspection of dwelling-house, [820]
interpretation of regulations, [815]
Leasehold Valuation Tribunal regulations 1981, [883]–[896]
non-appearance, [822]
regulations 1971, [814]–[825]
regulations 1980, [865]–[873]

RENT BOOK
forms of notice, regulations 1982, [940]–[946]
information,
companies, to be supplied by, [610]
contained in, to be, [609]
offences, [611]
protected tenancy, for, [945]
provision of, [608]
rectification of, [260], [327]
restricted contract, for, [944]
statutory tenancy, for, [945]

RENT (COUNTY COURT PROCEEDINGS) RULES 1970, [781]–[813]

RENT LIMIT
amendments, [503], [530]
contractual periods, during, [317]
conversion of housing association tenancies into regulated tenancies, [359], [422]
generally, [357]
housing associations, for dwellings let by, [355]–[364]
housing corporation, for dwellings let by, [355]–[364]
housing trusts, for dwellings let by, [355]–[364]
increase of rent without notice to quit, [360]
phasing of progression to registered rent, [358]
recovery of sums paid in excess of recoverable rent, [361]
registrable, rents to be, [356]
statement of rent under previous tenancy, [362]

RENT LIMIT—*cont.*
statutory periods, during, [318]
tenancies first regulated by virtue of Counter-Inflation Act 1973, for, [416]
tenancies to which applies, [355]

RENT OFFICER
application to, by local authority, [337]
committee hearing,
adjournment of, [928]
decision of, [929]–[931]
procedure at, [926]
representations at, [923]
time and place of, [925]
giving of notices, [932]
joint application to,
notices, [864]
procedures on, [862]
particulars of tenancy to be registered by, [857]
procedure on application to, [917]–[919]
reference to a committee by,
documents, [924]
hearing. *See* committee hearing, *above*
inspection of dwelling-house, [927]
procedure on, [922]
requirement for, [921]
registration of fair rent, application for, [853], [854]
schemes for appointment of, [332]

RENT REGULATION
cancellation of registration regulations 1980, [860]–[864]
local authority applications, regulations 1982, [915]–[933]
release from, [398]

RENT TRIBUNALS
application to, for security of tenure after notice to quit, [372]
functions of, [499]
jurisdiction of, [351]
notice to quit served after reference of contract to, [371]
powers of, on reference of contracts, [346]
proceedings before, [867]–[873]
reference of restricted contracts to, [345]

RENTCHARGES
exoneration from, or redemption of, [194]

REPAIRS. *See also* Leasehold Property (Repairs) Act 1938
covenants to, [81]
decorative, relief against notice to effect, [40]
disrepair, certificate of, forms, [800]–[803]
leasehold property, to,
enforcement of repairing covenants, restriction on, [92]
obligation to repair on taking possession, saving for, [94]
right to recover expenses of survey, etc, restriction on, [93]
obligations as to,
exceptions, [618]
general rule as to application, [617]
jurisdiction of county court, [619]
meaning of "lease" in relation to, [620]
restriction on contracting out, [616]
short leases, [615]–[618]

REPAIRS—*cont.*
obligations as to—*cont.*
specific performance, [621]
secure tenancy, right to repair scheme, regulations 1985, [1031]–[1042]
secure tenants, by, right to carry out, [558]
statutory tenancy,
during period of, [108], [170]–[174]
instalments, payment by, [180]
form, [750]
lump sum, payment in, [170]
tenant retains possession, where, [174]
terms of, as to, [109]
variation of agreement or determination as to time for making payment, [172]
tenant's responsibility for, gross value and, forms, [798], [799]

RESIDENTIAL TENANTS
security of tenure for, [101]–[120]. *See also* Security of tenure

RESTRICTED CONTRACTS. *See also* Rent
discretion of court in certain proceedings for possession, [375]
generally, under Rent Act 1977, [309]
lessors required to give information, [858]
notice to quit,
reduction of period of, [374]
service of, [371]–[373]
particulars to be entered in the register, [859]
prohibition of premiums on grant or assignment under, [381]
release from provisions, [399]
rent book for, [944]
rents under, [345]–[350], [498], [499]
unfurnished tenancies treated as, [310]

REVERSIONARY LEASES
provisions as to, [78]

REVERSIONS
extinguishment of, effect of, [32]
obligation of lessor's covenants to run with, [35]
provisions as to, under Landlord and Tenant Act 1954, [164]
rent and benefit of lessee's covenants to run with, [34]

S

SALE
contracts for, to be in writing, [20]
definition of, [49]

SATISFIED TERMS
cessation of, [17]

SCILLY ISLES. *See* Isles of Scilly

SECURE TENANCY
acquisition of dwelling-house subject to statutory tenancy, [573]
assignment,
general prohibition, [553]
tenant condition not satisfied, where, [557]
way of exchange, by, [554], [603]
consultation,
before disposal to private sector landlord, [569], [604]
housing management, on, [567]

SECURE TENANCY—*cont.*
county court,
jurisdiction of, [574]
rules and directions, [575]
definitions in relation to,
"dwelling-house", [576]
index of, [581]
"landlord authority", [578]
"long tenancy", [579]
"members of a person's family", [577]
minor, [580]
designated courses regulations, [826], [827]
exchanges, contribution towards costs of, [570]
exemption as to co-operative housing associations, [572]
generally, under Housing Act 1985, [541]
heating charges, [571]
improvements. *See* Improvements
information,
housing allocation, about, [568]
provision of, [566]
landlord condition, [542]
notices, regulations 1987, [1088]–[1091]
periodic tenancy,
arising on termination of fixed terms, [548]
succession to, [551]
variation of, notice of, [565]
possession,
extended discretion of court in certain proceedings for, [547]
grounds and orders for, [546], [598]–[600]
notice of proceedings for, [545]
notice of seeking, [1089]
recovery of, notice, [1091]
redevelopment schemes, [602]
suitability of accommodation, [601]
repairs,
right to repair scheme, regulations 1985, [1031]–[1042]
tenant's right to carry out, [558]
security of tenure, [544]
subletting,
consent to, [556]
generally, [555]
tenant condition not satisfied, where, [557]
succession on death of tenant,
cases where tenant is a successor, [550]
devolution of term certain, [552]
periodic tenancy, to, [551]
persons qualified to succeed, [549]
tenancies which are not, [597]
tenant condition, [543], [557]
termination of,
notice of seeking, [1091]
See also possession, *above*
transfers, contribution towards costs of, [570]
variation of terms of, [564], [565]

SECURITY OF TENURE
business, professional and other tenants, for, [121]–[147]. *See also* Business and professional tenancies
compensation for possession obtained by misrepresentation, [154]
continuation of tenancies, [103]
court must order possession, where, [284]
discretion of court in giving possession, [245], [283]

SECURITY OF TENURE—*cont.*
grounds for possession, [244], [283], [284]
information to landlords, duty of tenants to give, [116]
interim continuation of tenancies pending determination by court, [163]
landlord, termination by, [104]
long tenancies. *See* Long tenancy
overcrowded dwelling-houses, [368]
periodical tenancies, [176]
possession,
compensation for misrepresentation or concealment, [369]
extended discretion of court, [367]
grounds for, of certain dwelling houses, [365], [366], [423]–[428]
See also Possession
relief for tenant where landlord proceeding to enforce covenants, [114]
rent agreements with tenants having,
failure to comply with provisions, [324]
protection of tenants, [322]
special provisions following conversion, [323]
residential tenants, for, [101]–[120]
restriction on levy of distress for rent, [246]
secure tenancies, [544]
statutory tenancies. *See* Statutory tenancies
superior tenancy, effect of determination of, [247]
tenant, termination by, [105]

SERVICE CHARGE
amendments relating to, [691], [715]
consultation, [624]
contributions to be held in trust, [692]
costs of court proceedings, [627]
estimates, [624]
"flat", meaning of, [637]
grant-aided works, [625]
"landlord", meaning of, [637]
limitation of, [623]–[627]
exceptions, [633], [634]
meaning of, [592], [622]
"qualified accountant", meaning of, [635]
reasonableness of, [623]
"recognised tenants' association", meaning of, [636]
relevant costs,
effect of assignment on request, [631]
exceptions, [633], [634]
failure to comply with provisions an offence, [632]
information held by superior landlord, request relating to, [630], [632]
meaning of, [622]
request for summary of, [628], [632]
supporting accounts, request for, [629], [632]
rent registered but not variable, exception as to, [634]
"tenant", meaning of, [637]
tenants of certain public authorities, exception in relation to, [633]
time limit on making demands, [626]

SETTLED LAND ACT 1925
powers of a tenant for life under, [60]–[67]

SHARED ACCOMMODATION
landlord, with, [311]
persons other than landlord, with, [312]

SHARED OWNERSHIP
leases,
certain not protected tenancy, [294]
exclusion of, from Leasehold Reform Act 1967, [217], [232]
tenancy,
exclusion of, from Leasehold Reform Act 1967, [512]
regulations 1982, [907]–[909]

SOLICITOR
employment of, void stipulations as to, [22]

STATEMENT OF RATES ACT 1919
provisions of, [10]–[13]

STATUTORY TENANCIES
acquisition of dwelling-house subject to, [573]
application of Rent Acts where tenant retains possession, [106]
changing tenants, [412]
conditions, [248], [291]
fair rent, application for registration of, forms, [847], [848]
generally, under Rent Act 1977, [290]
landlord's interest belongs to Crown, etc, [243]
landlord's notice proposing, form, [747]
liabilities under tenant's covenants in former lease, [110]
meaning of, [646]
possession, grounds for, [365], [423], [425]
reliquishing tenancies, [412]
Rent (Agriculture) Act 1976, under, [242], [243], [248]–[254]. *See also* Agricultural rents and housing
rent book for, [945]
rent, determination of terms as to, [109]
repairs,
during period of, [108], [170]–[174]
instalments, payment by, [180]
form, [750]
lump sum, payment in, [170]
tenant retains possession, where, [174]
terms as to, determination of, [109]
variation of agreement or determination as to time for making payment, [172]
settlement of terms of, [107]
succession, [411], [502]
suitable alternative accommodation, [426]
terms, [248], [285], [291]

STUDENTS
lettings to, [297], [1045]–[1047]

SUB-LETTINGS. *See also* Sub-tenancy
exclude any part of sub-lessor's premises from protection, certain not to, [313]
obligation to notify, [394]
protected shorthold tenancy, [483]
recovery of rent, protection in relation to, [262]
secure tenancies, [555]–[557]

SUB-TENANCY. *See also* Sub-lettings
business premises, of, information about, forms, [759], [978]
effect on, determination of superior tenancy, [392]
enfranchisement and extension by sub-tenants, [226]
furnished, effect on, of determination of superior unfurnished tenancy, [393]

SUCCESSION
death, on,
family succession, [190]
secure tenancy, to. *See* Secure tenancy
statutory tenants by, [411], [502]
SUMMONS
service of, in relation to non-payment of rent, [536]
SUPREME COURT ACT 1981, [538]

T

TAXES
landlord's right to reimbursement of increased, [79]
TENANCIES
assured. *See* Assured tenancies
business. *See* Business and professional tenancies
continuation of, [103]
controlled, converted into regulated tenancies, [308], [377], [495]
converted, modification of Rent Act 1977, [429]
derelict land, on, [153]
determine questions relating to,
application, form, [808]
order on application to, form, [809]
family succession to, on death, [190]
long. *See* Long tenancy
meaning of "tenancy", [235], [591], [645]
new,
business and professional. *See* Business and professional tenancies
carrying out of order for, [136]
compensation where order precluded on certain grounds, [137]
other terms of, [135]
professional. *See* Business and professional tenancies
protected. *See* Protected tenancies
regulated. *See* Regulated tenancies
secure. *See* Secure tenancy
statutory. *See* Statutory tenancies
termination of,
assured, forms, [1061], [1063]
business and professional tenancies, of. *See* Business and professional tenancies
fixed term business tenancy, of, by tenant, [126]
landlord, by, [104], [124]
long tenancies at low rents, [101], [102]
periodic tenancy arising on termination of fixed terms, [548]
protected shorthold tenancy, [482]
secure tenancy, notice of proceedings for, [545]
tenant, by, [105], [126]
unfurnished, [310]
TENANT. *See also* Recognised tenants' associations; Tenant for life
agreements excluding or modifying rights of, [206]
attornments by, [44]
compensation for improvements. *See* Compensation for improvements to business premises
TENANT—*cont*.
compulsory acquisition by. *See* Compulsory acquisition of landlord's interest
first refusal, rights of. *See* Tenants' rights of first refusal
improvements. *See* Improvements
information,
duty to give to landlords, [116], [140]
to be given to tenant. *See* Information
insurance, rights as to, [638], [650]
manager, application to court for appointment of, [671]–[674]. *See also* Manager
meaning of, [637]
private sector,
assured tenancies, [485]–[491]. *See also* Assured tenancies
protected shorthold tenancies. *See* Protected shorthold tenancies
rents, [492]–[494]
repairs and improvements by. *See* Improvements
statutory,
meaning of, [646]
See also Statutory tenancies
termination of tenancy by, [105]
TENANT FOR LIFE
building leases,
power as to, [60]
regulations respecting, [63]
variation of, [65]
capitalisation of mining rent, [66]
forestry leases,
power as to, [60]
regulations respecting, [67]
leasing powers,
ordinary, building, mining or forestry purposes, for, [60]
regulations respecting leases generally, [61]
special objects, for, [62]
mining leases,
power as to, [60]
regulations respecting, [64]
variation of, [65]
TENANT'S RIGHTS OF FIRST REFUSAL
acceptance of landlord's offer, [656]
construction, [670]
counter-offer by tenants, [657]
enforcement of obligations, [669]
fresh offer by landlord, [658]
further negotiations between parties, [658]
landlords for purposes of, [652]
lapse of landlord's offer, [660]
modifications, power of Secretary of State to prescribe, [670]
new landlords, enforcement of rights against,
duty to furnish particulars where disposal contravened provisions, [661]
grant of new tenancy, right to compel, [665]
rent assessment committees' jurisdiction in relation to purchase notices, [663]
sale, right to compel, [662], [713]
termination of rights, [667]
withdrawal of nominated person from transaction, [664]
notices conferring, requirement to serve, [655]
prospective purchasers, notices served by, [668]
qualifying tenants to have, [651], [653]

TENANT'S RIGHTS OF FIRST REFUSAL—*cont.*
rejection of landlord's offer, [657]
relevant disposals, [654]
subsequent purchaser,
right to compel sale by, [666]
termination of rights against, [667]
withdrawal of either party from transaction, [659]

TENURE
security of. *See* Security of tenure

TERMINATION OF TENANCY. *See* Tenancies

TITLE
covenants for, [27]
statutory commencement of, [21]

TRIBUNAL
Landlord and Tenant Act 1927, for purposes of, [84]
leasehold valuation. *See* Leasehold valuation tribunal
rent. *See* Rent tribunals

TRUST
tenancy held on, [141]

TRUSTEE
custodian, person to act where landlord is, [209]
long leaseholds, rights as to, of, [189]

U

UNDERLEASES
forfeiture of, [39]

UNFURNISHED TENANCIES
restricted contracts, certain treated as, [310]

UNIVERSITY
re-acquisition for development by, [231]

V

VARIATION OF LEASE
dwellings other than flats, [690]
flats, relating to,
application,
majority of parties, by, [687]
party to lease, by, [685]
respondent, by, [686]
third parties, by, [689]
effect of orders, [689]
orders by court, [688]

W

WALES
Development Board for Rural Wales. *See* Development Board for Rural Wales

WELSH DEVELOPMENT AGENCY
landlord's notice to terminate business tenancy, form, [975], [986]
premises of, [160]